"God, there is no god but He, the Living, the Eternal. He sent down to you the Book with the Truth, confirming what came before it; and He sent down the Torah and the Gospel."

Verses 3:2-3

THE

Quran

Translated to English by
TALAL ITANI

QURAN IN ENGLISH
Modern English Translation
Clear and Easy to Read

Translated from Arabic by **Talal Itani**

Published by ClearQuran
Dallas, Beirut

To Contact the Author:
Phone: 1 (214) 718-1424
Email: talal@ClearQuran.com

www.ClearQuran.com

"When you read the Quran, seek refuge with God from Satan the outcast. He has no authority over those who believe and trust in their Lord. His authority is only over those who follow him, and those who associate others with Him."

Verses 16:98-100

TABLE OF CONTENTS

1. THE OPENING
(al-Fatihah)

1. In the name of God, the Gracious, the Merciful.

2. Praise be to God, Lord of the Worlds.

3. The Most Gracious, the Most Merciful.

4. Master of the Day of Judgment.

5. It is You we worship, and upon You we call for help.

6. Guide us to the straight path.

7. The path of those You have blessed, not of those against whom there is anger, nor of those who are misguided.

2. THE HEIFER
(al-Baqarah)

In the name of God,
the Gracious, the Merciful.

1. Alif, Lam, Meem.

2. This is the Book in which there is no doubt, a guide for the righteous.

3. Those who believe in the unseen, and perform the prayers, and give from what We have provided for them.

4. And those who believe in what was revealed to you, and in what was revealed before you, and are certain of the Hereafter.

5. These are upon guidance from their Lord. These are the successful.

6. As for those who disbelieve—it is the same for them, whether you have warned them, or have not warned them—they do not believe.

7. God has set a seal on their hearts and on their hearing, and over their vision is a veil. They will have a severe torment.

8. Among the people are those who say, "We believe in God and in the Last Day," but they are not believers.

9. They seek to deceive God and those who believe, but they deceive none but themselves, though they are not aware.

10. In their hearts is sickness, and God has increased their sickness. They will have a painful punishment because of their denial.

11. And when it is said to them, "Do not make trouble on earth," they say, "We are only reformers."

12. In fact, they are the troublemakers, but they are not aware.

13. And when it is said to them, "Believe as the people have believed," they say, "Shall we believe as the fools have believed?" In fact, it is they who are the fools, but they do not know.

14. And when they come across those who believe, they say, "We believe"; but when they are alone with their devils, they say, "We are with you; we were only ridiculing."

15. It is God who ridicules them, and leaves them bewildered in their transgression.

16. Those are they who have bartered error for guidance; but their trade does not profit them, and they are not guided.

17. Their likeness is that of a person who kindled a fire; when it illuminated all around him, God took away their light, and left them in darkness, unable to see.

18. Deaf, dumb, blind. They will not return.

19. Or like a cloudburst from the sky, in which is darkness, and thunder, and lightning. They press their fingers into their

ears from the thunderbolts, in fear of death. But God surrounds the disbelievers.

20. The lightning almost snatches their sight away. Whenever it illuminates for them, they walk in it; but when it grows dark over them, they stand still. Had God willed, He could have taken away their hearing and their sight. God is capable of everything.

21. O people! Worship your Lord who created you and those before you, that you may attain piety.

22. He who made the earth a habitat for you, and the sky a structure, and sends water down from the sky, and brings out fruits thereby, as a sustenance for you. Therefore, do not assign rivals to God while you know.

23. And if you are in doubt about what We have revealed to Our servant, then produce a chapter like these, and call your witnesses apart from God, if you are truthful.

24. But if you do not—and you will not—then beware the Fire whose fuel is people and stones, prepared for the disbelievers.

25. And give good news to those who believe and do righteous deeds; that they will have gardens beneath which rivers flow. Whenever they are provided with fruit therefrom as sustenance, they will say, "This is what we were provided with before," and they will be given the like of it. And they will have pure spouses therein, and they will abide therein forever.

26. God does not shy away from making an example of a gnat, or something above it. As for those who believe, they know that it is the Truth from their Lord. But as for those who disbelieve, they say, "What did God intend by this example?" He leads astray many thereby, and He guides many thereby; but He misleads thereby only the evildoers.

27. Those who violate God's covenant after its confirmation, and sever what God has commanded to be joined, and commit evil on earth. These are the losers.

28. How can you deny God, when you were dead and He gave you life, then He will put you to death, then He will bring you to life, then to Him you will be returned?

29. It is He who created for you everything on earth, then turned to the heaven, and made them seven heavens. And He is aware of all things.

30. When your Lord said to the angels, "I am placing a successor on earth." They said, "Will You place in it someone who will cause corruption in it and shed blood, while we declare Your praises and sanctify You?" He said, "I know what you do not know."

31. And He taught Adam the names, all of them; then he presented them to the angels, and said, "Tell Me the names of these, if you are sincere."

32. They said, "Glory be to You! We have no knowledge except what You have taught us. It is you who are the Knowledgeable, the Wise."

33. He said, "O Adam, tell them their names." And when he told them their names, He said, "Did I not tell you that I know the secrets of the heavens and the earth, and that I know what you reveal and what you conceal?"

34. And We said to the angels, "Bow down to Adam." They bowed down, except for Satan. He refused, was arrogant, and was one of the disbelievers.

35. We said, "O Adam, inhabit the Garden, you and your spouse, and eat from it freely as you please, but do not approach this tree, lest you become wrongdoers."

36. But Satan caused them to slip from it, and caused them to depart the state they were in. We said, "Go down, some of you enemies of one another. And you will have residence on earth, and enjoyment for a while."

37. Then Adam received words from his Lord, so He relented towards him. He is the Relenting, the Merciful.

38. We said, "Go down from it, all of you. Yet whenever guidance comes to you from Me, then whoever follows My guidance—they have nothing to fear, nor shall they grieve.

39. But as for those who disbelieve and reject Our signs—these are the inmates of the Fire—wherein they will remain forever."

40. O Children of Israel! Remember My blessings which I bestowed upon you, and fulfill your pledge to Me, and I will fulfill My pledge to you, and fear Me.

41. And believe in what I revealed, confirming what is with you; and do not be the first to deny it; and do not exchange My revelations for a small price; and be conscious of Me.

42. And do not mix truth with falsehood, and do not conceal the truth while you know.

43. And attend to your prayers, and practice regular charity, and kneel with those who kneel.

44. Do you command people to virtuous conduct, and forget yourselves, even though you read the Scripture? Do you not understand?

45. And seek help through patience and prayer. But it is difficult, except for the devout.

46. Those who know that they will meet their Lord, and that to Him they will return.

47. O Children of Israel! Remember My favor which I bestowed upon you, and I that favored you over all nations.

48. And beware of a Day when no soul will avail another in the least, nor will any intercession be accepted on its behalf, nor will any ransom be taken from it, nor will they be helped.

49. And recall that We delivered you from the people of Pharaoh. They inflicted on you terrible persecution, killing your sons and sparing your women. Therein was a tremendous trial from your Lord.

50. And recall that We parted the sea for you, so We saved you, and We drowned the people of Pharaoh as you looked on.

51. And recall that We appointed for Moses forty nights. Then you took to worshiping the calf after him, and you turned wicked.

52. Then We pardoned you after that, so that you might be grateful.

53. And recall that We gave Moses the Scripture and the Criterion, so that you may be guided.

54. And recall that Moses said to his people, "O my people, you have done wrong to yourselves by worshiping the calf. So repent to your Maker, and kill your egos. That would be better for you with your Maker." So He turned to you in repent-

ance. He is the Accepter of Repentance, the Merciful.

55. And recall that you said, "O Moses, we will not believe in you unless we see God plainly." Thereupon the thunderbolt struck you, as you looked on.

56. Then We revived you after your death, so that you may be appreciative.

57. And We shaded you with clouds, and We sent down to you manna and quails: "Eat of the good things We have provided for you." They did not wrong Us, but they used to wrong their own souls.

58. And recall that We said, "Enter this town, and eat plentifully from it whatever you wish; but enter the gate humbly, and say, 'Pardon.' We will forgive your sins, and give increase to the virtuous."

59. But the wrongdoers among them substituted words other than those given to them, so We sent down on the wrongdoers a plague from heaven, because of their wicked behavior.

60. And recall when Moses prayed for water for his people. We said, "Strike the rock with your staff." Thereupon twelve springs gushed out from it, and each tribe recognized its drinking-place. "Eat and drink from God's provision, and do not corrupt the earth with disobedience."

61. And recall when you said, "O Moses, we cannot endure one kind of food, so call to your Lord to produce for us of what the earth grows: of its herbs, and its cucumbers, and its garlic, and its lentils, and its onions." He said, "Would you substitute worse for better? Go down to Egypt, where you will have what you asked for." They were struck with humiliation and poverty, and incurred wrath from God. That was because they rejected God's revelations and wrongfully killed the prophets. That was because they disobeyed and transgressed.

62. Those who believe, and those who are Jewish, and the Christians, and the Sabeans—any who believe in God and the Last Day, and act righteously—will have their reward with their Lord—they have nothing to fear, nor will they grieve.

63. And recall when We received a pledge from you, and raised the Mount above you: "Take what We have given you earnestly, and remember what is in it, that you may attain righteousness."

64. But after that you turned away. Were it not for God's grace and mercy towards you, you would have been among the losers.

65. And you surely knew those of you who violated the Sabbath. We said to them, "Be despicable apes!"

66. Thus We made it a deterrent for their generation, and for subsequent generations, and a lesson for the righteous.

67. And recall when Moses said to his people, "God commands you to sacrifice a heifer." They said, "Do you make a mockery of us?" He said, "God forbid that I should be so ignorant."

68. They said, "Call upon your Lord to show us which one." He said, "He says she is a heifer, neither too old, nor too young, but in between. So do what you are commanded."

69. They said, "Call upon your Lord to show us what her color is." He said, "He says she is a yellow heifer, bright in color, pleasing to the beholders."

70. They said, "Call upon your Lord to show us which one; the heifers look alike to us, and God willing, we will be guided."

71. He said, "He says she is a heifer, neither yoked to plow the earth, nor to irrigate the field—sound without blemish." They said, "Now you have brought the truth." So they slew her—though they almost did not.

72. And recall when you killed a person, and disputed in the matter—but God was to expose what you were hiding.

73. We said, "Strike him with part of it." Thus God brings the dead to life; and He shows you His signs, that you may understand.

74. Then after that your hearts hardened. They were as rocks, or even harder. For there are some rocks from which rivers gush out, and others that splinter and water comes out from them, and others that sink in awe of God. God is not unaware of what you do.

75. Do you hope that they will believe in you, when some of them used to hear the Word of God, and then deliberately distort it, even after understanding it?

76. And when they come across those who believe, they say, "We believe," but when they come together privately, they say, "Will you inform them of what God has disclosed to you, so that they might dispute with you concerning it before your Lord?" Do you not understand?

77. Do they not know that God knows what they conceal and what they reveal?

78. And among them are uneducated who know the Scripture only through hearsay, and they only speculate.

79. So woe to those who write the Scripture with their own hands, and then say, "This is from God," that they may exchange it for a little price. Woe to them for what their hands have written, and woe to them for what they earn.

80. And they say, "The Fire will not touch us except for a number of days." Say, "Have you received a promise from God—God never breaks His promise—or are you saying about God what you do not know?"

81. Indeed, whoever commits misdeeds, and becomes besieged by his iniquities—these are the inmates of the Fire, wherein they will dwell forever.

82. As for those who believe and do righteous deeds—these are the inhabitants of Paradise, wherein they will dwell forever.

83. We made a covenant with the Children of Israel: "Worship none but God; and be good to parents, and relatives, and orphans, and the needy; and speak nicely to people; and pray regularly, and give alms." Then you turned away, except for a few of you, recanting.

84. And We made a covenant with you: "You shall not shed the blood of your own, nor shall you evict your own from your homes." You agreed, and were all witnesses.

85. But here you are, killing your own, and expelling a group of your own from their homes—conspiring against them in wrongdoing and hostility. And if they come to you as captives, you ransom them, although it was forbidden to you. Is it that you believe in part of the Scripture, and disbelieve in part? What is the reward for those among you who do that but humiliation in this life? And on the Day of Resurrection, they will be assigned to the most severe torment. God is not unaware of what you do.

86. Those are they who bought the present life for the Hereafter, so the punishment will not be lightened for them, nor will they be helped.

87. We gave Moses the Scripture, and sent a succession of messengers after him. And We gave Jesus son of Mary the clear proofs, and We supported him with the Holy Spirit. Is it that whenever a messenger comes to you with anything your souls do not desire, you grew arrogant, calling some impostors, and killing others?

88. And they said, "Our hearts are sealed." Rather, God has cursed them for their ingratitude. They have little faith.

89. And when a Scripture came to them from God, confirming what they have—although previously they were seeking victory against those who disbelieved—but when there came to them what they recognized, they disbelieved in it. So God's curse is upon the disbelievers.

90. Miserable is what they sold their souls for—rejecting what God has revealed, out of resentment that God would send down His grace upon whomever He chooses from among His servants. Thus they incurred wrath upon wrath. And there is a demeaning punishment for the disbelievers.

91. And when it is said to them, "Believe in what God has revealed," they say, "We believe in what was revealed to us," and they reject anything beyond that, although it is the truth which confirms what they have. Say, "Why did you kill God's prophets before, if you were believers?"

92. Moses came to you with clear proofs, yet you adopted the calf in his absence, and you were in the wrong.

93. And We made a covenant with you, and raised the Mount above you: "Take what We have given you firmly, and listen." They said, "We hear and disobey." And their hearts became filled with the love of the calf because of their disbelief. Say, "Wretched is what your faith commands you to do, if you are believers."

94. Say, "If the Final Home with God is yours alone, to the exclusion of all other people, then wish for death if you are sincere."

95. But they will never wish for it, because of what their hands have forwarded. God is aware of the evildoers.

96. You will find them, of all mankind, the most eager for life, even more than the polytheists. Every one of them wishes he could live a thousand years; but to be granted a long life will not nudge him from the punishment. God is Seeing of what they do.

97. Say, "Whoever is hostile to Gabriel—it is he who revealed it to your heart by God's leave, confirming what preceded it, and guidance and good news for the believers."

98. Whoever is hostile to God, and His angels, and His messengers, and Gabriel, and Michael—God is hostile to the faithless.

99. We have revealed to you clear signs, and none rejects them except the sinners.

100. Is it not that whenever they make a covenant, some of them toss it aside? In fact, most of them do not believe.

101. And when there came to them a messenger from God, confirming what they had, a faction of those who were given the Book threw the Book of God behind their backs, as if they do not know.

102. And they followed what the devils taught during the reign of Salomon. It was not Solomon who disbelieved, but it was the devils who disbelieved. They taught the people witchcraft and what was revealed in Babylon to the two angels Harut and Marut. They did not teach anybody until they had said, "We are a test, so do not lose faith." But they learned from them the means to cause separation between man and his wife. But they cannot harm anyone except with God's permission. And they learned what would harm them and not benefit them. Yet they knew that whoever deals in it will have no share in the Hereafter. Miserable is what they sold their souls for, if they only knew.

103. Had they believed and been righteous, the reward from God would have been better, if they only knew.

104. O you who believe! Do not say ambiguous words, but say words of respect, and listen. The disbelievers will have a painful torment.

105. It is never the wish of the disbelievers from among the People of the Book, nor of the polytheists, that any good should be sent down to you from your Lord. But God chooses for His mercy whomever He wills. God is Possessor of Sublime Grace.

106. We never nullify a verse, nor cause it to be forgotten, unless We bring one better than it, or similar to it. Do you not know that God is capable of all things?

107. Do you not know that to God belongs the sovereignty of the heavens and the earth, and that apart from God you have no guardian or helper?

108. Or do you want to question your Messenger as Moses was questioned before? Whoever exchanges faith for disbelief has strayed from the right path.

109. Many of the People of the Book wish, out of envy on their part, to turn you back into disbelievers, after the Truth has become clear to them. But pardon and overlook, until God brings His command. God has power over all things.

110. And perform the prayer, and give alms. Whatever good you forward for yourselves, you will find it with God. God is Seeing of everything you do.

111. And they say, "None will enter Heaven unless he is a Jew or a Christian." These are their wishes. Say, "Produce your proof, if you are truthful."

112. In fact, whoever submits himself to God, and is a doer of good, will have his reward with his Lord—they have nothing to fear, nor shall they grieve.

113. The Jews say, "The Christians are not based on anything," and the Christians say, "The Jews are not based on anything." Yet they both read the Scripture. Similarly, the ignorant said the same thing. God will judge between them on the Day of Resurrection regarding their differences.

114. Who is more unjust than one who forbids the remembrance of God's name in places of worship, and contributes to their ruin? These ought not to enter them except in fear. For them is disgrace in this world, and for them is a terrible punishment in the Hereafter.

115. To God belongs the East and the West. Whichever way you turn, there is God's presence. God is Omnipresent and Omniscient.

116. And they say, "God has begotten a son." Be He glorified. Rather, His is everything in the heavens and the earth; all are obedient to Him.

117. Originator of the heavens and the earth. Whenever He decrees a thing, He says to it, "Be," and it becomes.

118. Those who do not know say, "If only God would speak to us, or a sign would come to us." Thus said those who were before them. Their hearts are alike. We have made the signs clear for people who are certain.

119. We have sent you with the truth—bringing good news, and giving warnings. You will not be questioned about the inmates of Hell.

120. The Jews and the Christians will not approve of you, unless you follow their creed. Say, "God's guidance is the guidance." Should you follow their desires, after the knowledge that has come to you, you will have in God neither guardian nor helper.

121. Those to whom We have given the Scripture follow it, as it ought to be followed—these believe in it. But as for those who reject it—these are the losers.

122. O Children of Israel! Remember My blessing which I bestowed upon you, and that I have favored you over all people.

123. And beware of a Day when no soul will avail another soul in any way, and no ransom will be accepted from it, and no intercession will benefit it, and they will not be helped.

124. And when his Lord tested Abraham with certain words, and he fulfilled them. He said, "I am making you a leader of humanity." He said, "And my descendants?" He said, "My pledge does not include the wrongdoers."

125. And We made the House a focal point for the people, and a sanctuary. Use the shrine of Abraham as a place of prayer. And We commissioned Abraham and Ishmael, "Sanctify My House for those who circle around it, and those who seclude themselves in it, and those who kneel and prostrate."

126. When Abraham said, "O My Lord, make this a peaceful land, and provide its people with fruits—whoever of them believes in God and the Last Day." He said, "And whoever disbelieves, I will give him a little enjoyment, then I will consign him to the punishment of the Fire; how miserable the destiny!"

127. As Abraham raises the foundations of the House, together with Ishmael, "Our Lord, accept it from us, You are the Hearer, the Knower.

128. Our Lord, and make us submissive to You, and from our descendants a community submissive to You. And show us our rites, and accept our repentance. You are the Acceptor of Repentance, the Merciful.

129. Our Lord, and raise up among them a messenger, of themselves, who will recite to them Your revelations, and teach them the Book and wisdom, and purify them. You are the Almighty, the Wise."

130. Who would forsake the religion of Abraham, except he who fools himself? We chose him in this world, and in the Hereafter he will be among the righteous.

131. When his Lord said to him, "Submit!" He said, "I have submitted to the Lord of the Worlds."

132. And Abraham exhorted his sons, and Jacob, "O my sons, God has chosen this religion for you, so do not die unless you have submitted."

133. Or were you witnesses when death approached Jacob, and he said to his sons, "What will you worship after Me?" They

said, "We will worship your God, and the God of your fathers, Abraham, Ishmael, and Isaac; One God; and to Him we submit."

134. That was a community that has passed; for them is what they have earned, and for you is what you have earned; and you will not be questioned about what they used to do.

135. And they say, "Be Jews or Christians, and you will be guided." Say, "Rather, the religion of Abraham, the monotheist; he was not an idolater."

136. Say, "We believe in God, and in what was revealed to us, and in what was revealed to Abraham, and Ishmael, and Isaac, and Jacob, and the Patriarchs; and in what was given to Moses, and Jesus, and the prophets from their Lord. We make no distinction between any of them, and to Him we surrender."

137. If they believe in the same as you have believed in, then they have been guided. But if they turn away, then they are in schism. God will protect you against them; for He is the Hearer, the Knower.

138. God's coloring. And who gives better coloring than God? "And we are devoted to Him."

139. Say, "Do you argue with us about God, when He is our Lord and your Lord, and We have our works, and you have your works, and we are sincere to Him?"

140. Or do you say that Abraham, Ishmael, Isaac, Jacob, and the Patriarchs were Jews or Christians? Say, "Do you know better, or God?" And who does greater wrong than he who conceals a testimony he has from God? God is not unaware of what you do.

141. That was a community that has passed. To them is what they have earned, and to you is what you have earned. And you will not be questioned about what they used to do.

142. The ignorant among the people will say, "What has turned them away from the direction of prayer they once followed?" Say, "To God belongs the East and the West. He guides whom He wills to a straight path."

143. Thus We have made you a moderate community, that you may be witnesses to humanity, and that the Messenger may be a witness to you. We only established the direction of prayer, which you once followed, that We may distinguish those who follow the Messenger from those who turn on their heels. It is indeed difficult, except for those whom God has guided. But God would never let your faith go to waste. God is Kind towards the people, Merciful.

144. We have seen your face turned towards the heaven. So We will turn you towards a direction that will satisfy you. So turn your face towards the Sacred Mosque. And wherever you may be, turn your faces towards it. Those who were given the Book know that it is the Truth from their Lord; and God is not unaware of what they do.

145. Even if you were to bring to those who were given the Book every proof, they would not follow your direction, nor are you to follow their direction, nor do they follow the direction of one another. And if you were to follow their desires, after the knowledge that has come to you, you would be in that case one of the wrongdoers.

146. Those to whom We have given the Book recognize it as they recognize their

own children. But some of them conceal the truth while they know.

147. The truth is from your Lord, so do not be a skeptic.

148. To every community is a direction towards which it turns. Therefore, race towards goodness. Wherever you may be, God will bring you all together. God is capable of everything.

149. And wherever you come from, turn your face towards the Sacred Mosque. This is the truth from your Lord, and God is not heedless of what you do.

150. And wherever you come from, turn your face towards the Sacred Mosque. And wherever you may be, turn your faces towards it. So that the people may not have any argument against you—except those who do wrong among them. So do not fear them, but fear Me, that I may complete My blessings upon you, and that you may be guided.

151. Just as We sent to you a messenger from among you, who recites Our revelations to you, and purifies you, and teaches you the Book and wisdom, and teaches you what you did not know.

152. So remember Me, and I will remember you. And thank Me, and do not be ungrateful.

153. O you who believe! Seek help through patience and prayers. God is with the steadfast.

154. And do not say of those who are killed in the cause of God, "Dead." Rather, they are alive, but you do not perceive.

155. We will certainly test you with some fear and hunger, and some loss of possessions and lives and crops. But give good news to the steadfast.

156. Those who, when a calamity afflicts them, say, "To God we belong, and to Him we will return."

157. Upon these are blessings and mercy from their Lord. These are the guided ones.

158. Safa and Marwa are among the rites of God. Whoever makes the Pilgrimage to the House, or performs the Umrah, commits no error by circulating between them. Whoever volunteers good—God is Appreciative and Cognizant.

159. Those who suppress the proofs and the guidance We have revealed, after We have clarified them to humanity in the Scripture—those—God curses them, and the cursers curse them.

160. Except those who repent, and reform, and proclaim. Those—I will accept their repentance. I am the Acceptor of Repentance, the Merciful.

161. But as for those who reject faith, and die rejecting—those—upon them is the curse of God, and of the angels, and of all humanity.

162. They will remain under it forever, and the torment will not be lightened for them, and they will not be reprieved.

163. Your God is one God. There is no god but He, the Benevolent, the Compassionate.

164. In the creation of the heavens and the earth; in the alternation of night and day; in the ships that sail the oceans for the benefit of mankind; in the water that God sends down from the sky, and revives the earth with it after it had died, and scatters in it all kinds of creatures; in the changing of the winds, and the clouds disposed between the sky and the earth; are signs for people who understand.

165. Yet among the people are those who take other than God as equals to Him. They love them as the love of God. But those who believe have greater love for God. If only the wrongdoers would realize, when they see the torment; that all power is God's, and that God is severe in punishment.

166. Those who were followed will then disown those who followed them, and they will see the retribution, and ties between them will be severed.

167. Those who followed will say, "If only we can have another chance, we will disown them, as they disowned us." Thus God will show them their deeds, as regrets to them, and they will not come out of the Fire.

168 O people! Eat of what is lawful and good on earth, and do not follow the footsteps of Satan. He is to you an open enemy.

169. He commands you to do evil and vice, and to say about God what you do not know.

170. And when it is said to them, "Follow what God has revealed," they say, "We will follow what we found our ancestors following." Even if their ancestors understood nothing, and were not guided?

171. The parable of those who disbelieve is that of someone who calls upon someone who hears nothing except screaming and yelling. Deaf, dumb, and blind—they do not understand.

172. O you who believe! Eat of the good things We have provided for you, and give thanks to God, if it is Him that you serve.

173. He has forbidden you carrion, and blood, and the flesh of swine, and what was dedicated to other than God. But if anyone is compelled, without desiring or exceeding, he commits no sin. God is Forgiving and Merciful.

174. Those who conceal what God revealed in the Book, and exchange it for a small price—those swallow nothing but fire into their bellies. And God will not speak to them on the Day of Resurrection, nor will He purify them, and they will have a painful punishment.

175. It is they who exchange guidance for error, and forgiveness for punishment. But why do they insist on the Fire?

176. That is because God has revealed the Book in truth; and those who differ about the Book are in deep discord.

177. Righteousness does not consist of turning your faces towards the East and the West. But righteous is he who believes in God, and the Last Day, and the angels, and the Scripture, and the prophets. Who gives money, though dear, to near relatives, and orphans, and the needy, and the homeless, and the beggars, and for the freeing of slaves; those who perform the prayers, and pay the obligatory charity, and fulfill their promise when they promise, and patiently persevere in the face of persecution, hardship, and in the time of conflict. These are the sincere; these are the pious.

178. O you who believe! Retaliation for the murdered is ordained upon you: the free for the free, the slave for the slave, the female for the female. But if he is forgiven by his kin, then grant any reasonable demand, and pay with good will. This is a concession from your Lord, and a mercy. But whoever commits aggression after that, a painful torment awaits him.

179. There is life for you in retaliation, O people of understanding, so that you may refrain.

180. It is decreed for you: when death approaches one of you, and he leaves wealth, to make a testament in favor of the parents and the relatives, fairly and correctly—a duty upon the righteous.

181. But whoever changes it after he has heard it, the guilt is upon those who change it. God is All-Hearing, All-Knowing.

182. Should someone suspect bias or injustice on the part of a testator, and then reconciles between them, he commits no sin. God is Forgiving and Merciful.

183. O you who believe! Fasting is prescribed for you, as it was prescribed for those before you, that you may become righteous.

184. For a specified number of days. But whoever among you is sick, or on a journey, then a number of other days. For those who are able: a ransom of feeding a needy person. But whoever volunteers goodness, it is better for him. But to fast is best for you, if you only knew.

185. Ramadan is the month in which the Quran was revealed. Guidance for humanity, and clear portents of guidance, and the Criterion. Whoever of you witnesses it, shall fast it. But whoever is sick, or on a journey, then a number of other days. God desires ease for you, and does not desire hardship for you, that you may complete the number, and celebrate God for having guided you, so that you may be thankful.

186. And when My servants ask you about Me, I Am near; I answer the call of the caller when he calls on Me. So let them answer Me, and have faith in Me, that they may be rightly guided.

187. Permitted for you is intercourse with your wives on the night of the fast. They are a garment for you, and you are a garment for them. God knows that you used to betray yourselves, but He turned to you and pardoned you. So approach them now, and seek what God has ordained for you, and eat and drink until the white streak of dawn can be distinguished from the black streak. Then complete the fast until nightfall. But do not approach them while you are in retreat at the mosques. These are the limits of God, so do not come near them. God thus clarifies His revelations to the people, that they may attain piety.

188. And do not consume one another's wealth by unjust means, nor offer it as bribes to the officials in order to consume part of other people's wealth illicitly, while you know.

189. They ask you about the crescents. Say, "They are timetables for people, and for the Hajj." It is not virtuous that you approach homes from their backs, but virtue is to be pious. So approach homes from their doors, and observe God, that you may succeed.

190. And fight in the cause of God those who fight you, but do not commit aggression; God does not love the aggressors.

191. And kill them wherever you overtake them, and expel them from where they had expelled you. Oppression is more serious than murder. But do not fight them at the Sacred Mosque, unless they fight you there. If they fight you, then kill them. Such is the retribution of the disbelievers.

192. But if they cease, then God is Forgiving and Merciful.

193. And fight them until there is no oppression, and worship becomes devoted to God alone. But if they cease, then let there be no hostility except against the oppressors.

194. The sacred month for the sacred month; and sacrilege calls for retaliation. Whoever commits aggression against you, retaliate against him in the same measure as he has committed against you. And be conscious of God, and know that God is with the righteous.

195. And spend in the cause of God, and do not throw yourselves with your own hands into ruin, and be charitable. God loves the charitable.

196. And carry out the Hajj and the Umrah for God. But if you are prevented, then whatever is feasible of offerings. And do not shave your heads until the offering has reached its destination. Whoever of you is sick, or has an injury of the head, then redemption of fasting, or charity, or worship. When you are secure: whoever continues the Umrah until the Hajj, then whatever is feasible of offering. But if he lacks the means, then fasting for three days during the Hajj and seven when you have returned, making ten in all. This is for he whose household is not present at the Sacred Mosque. And remain conscious of God, and know that God is stern in retribution.

197. The Hajj is during specific months. Whoever decides to perform the Hajj—there shall be no sexual relations, nor misconduct, nor quarrelling during the Hajj. And whatever good you do, God knows it. And take provisions, but the best provision is righteousness. And be mindful of Me, O people of understanding.

198. You commit no error by seeking bounty from your Lord. When you disperse from Arafat, remember God at the Sacred Landmark. And remember Him as He has guided you. Although, before that, you were of those astray.

199. Then disperse from where the people disperse, and ask God for forgiveness. God is Most Forgiving, Most Merciful.

200. When you have completed your rites, remember God as you remember your parents, or even more. Among the people is he who says, "Our Lord, give us in this world," yet he has no share in the Hereafter.

201. And among them is he who says, "Our Lord, give us goodness in this world, and goodness in the Hereafter, and protect us from the torment of the Fire."

202. These will have a share of what they have earned. God is swift in reckoning.

203. And remember God during the designated days. But whoever hurries on in two days commits no wrong, and whoever stays on commits no wrong—provided he maintains righteousness. And obey God, and know that to Him you will be gathered.

204. Among the people is he whose speech about the worldly life impresses you, and he calls God to witness what is in his heart, while he is the most hostile of adversaries.

205. When he gains power, he strives to spread corruption on earth, destroying properties and lives. God does not like corruption.

206. When he is told, "Beware of God," his pride leads him to more sin. Hell is enough for him—a dreadful abode.

207. And among the people is he who sells himself seeking God's approval. God is kind towards the servants.

208. O you who believe! Enter into submission, wholeheartedly, and do not follow the footsteps of Satan; he is to you an outright enemy.

209. But if you slip after the proofs have come to you, know that God is Powerful and Wise.

210. Are they waiting for God Himself to come to them in the shadows of the clouds, together with the angels, and thus the matter is settled? All things are returned to God.

211. Ask the Children of Israel how many clear signs We have given them. Whoever alters the blessing of God after it has come to him—God is severe in retribution.

212. Beautified is the life of this world for those who disbelieve, and they ridicule those who believe. But the righteous will be above them on the Day of Resurrection. God provides to whomever He wills without measure.

213. Humanity used to be one community; then God sent the prophets, bringing good news and giving warnings. And He sent down with them the Scripture, with the truth, to judge between people regarding their differences. But none differed over it except those who were given it—after the proofs had come to them—out of mutual envy between them. Then God guided those who believed to the truth they had disputed, in accordance with His will. God guides whom He wills to a straight path.

214. Or do you expect to enter Paradise before the example of those who came before you had reached you? Adversity and hardship had afflicted them, and they were so shaken up, that the Messenger and those who believed with him said, "When is God's victory?" Indeed, God's victory is near.

215. They ask you what they should give. Say, "Whatever charity you give is for the parents, and the relatives, and the orphans, and the poor, and the wayfarer. Whatever good you do, God is aware of it.

216. Fighting is ordained for you, even though you dislike it. But it may be that you dislike something while it is good for you, and it may be that you like something while it is bad for you. God knows, and you do not know.

217. They ask you about fighting during the Holy Month. Say, "Fighting during it is deplorable; but to bar others from God's path, and to disbelieve in Him, and to prevent access to the Holy Mosque, and to expel its people from it, are more deplorable with God. And persecution is more serious than killing. They will not cease to fight you until they turn you back from your religion, if they can. Whoever among you turns back from his religion, and dies a disbeliever, his deeds will come to nothing, in this life, and in the Hereafter. These are the inmates of the Fire, abiding in it forever.

218. Those who believed, and those who migrated and fought for the sake of God—those look forward to God's mercy. God is Forgiving and Merciful.

219. They ask you about intoxicants and gambling: say, "There is gross sin in both, and some benefits for people, but their sinfulness outweighs their benefit." And they ask you about what they should give: say, "The surplus." Thus God explains the revelations to you, so that you may think.

220. About this world and the next. And they ask you about orphans. Say, "Improvement for them is best. And if you intermix with them, then they are your brethren." God knows the dishonest from the honest. Had God willed, He could have overburdened you. God is Mighty and Wise.

221. Do not marry idolatresses, unless they have believed. A believing maid is better than an idolatress, even if you like her. And do not marry idolaters, unless they have believed. A believing servant is better than an idolater, even if you like him. These call to the Fire, but God calls to the Garden and to forgiveness, by His leave. He makes clear His communications to the people, that they may be mindful.

222. And they ask you about menstruation: say, "It is harmful, so keep away from women during menstruation. And do not approach them until they have become pure. Once they have become pure, approach them in the way God has directed you." God loves the repentant, and He loves those who keep clean."

223. Your women are cultivation for you; so approach your cultivation whenever you like, and send ahead for yourselves. And fear God, and know that you will meet Him. And give good news to the believers.

224. And do not allow your oaths in God's name to hinder you from virtue, and righteousness, and making peace between people. God is Listener and Knower.

225. God does not hold you responsible for your unintentional oaths, but He holds you responsible for your intentions. God is Forgiving and Forbearing.

226. Those who vow abstinence from their wives must wait for four months. But if they reconcile—God is Forgiving and Merciful.

227. And if they resolve to divorce—God is Hearing and Knowing.

228. Divorced women shall wait by themselves for three periods. And it is not lawful for them to conceal what God has created in their wombs, if they believe in God and the Last Day. Meanwhile, their husbands have the better right to take them back, if they desire reconciliation. And women have rights similar to their obligations, according to what is fair. But men have a degree over them. God is Mighty and Wise.

229. Divorce is allowed twice. Then, either honorable retention, or setting free kindly. It is not lawful for you to take back anything you have given them, unless they fear that they cannot maintain God's limits. If you fear that they cannot maintain God's limits, then there is no blame on them if she sacrifices something for her freedom. These are God's limits, so do not transgress them. Those who transgress God's limits are the unjust.

230. If he divorces her, she shall not be lawful for him again until she has married another husband. If the latter divorces her, then there is no blame on them for reuniting, provided they think they can maintain God's limits. These are God's limits; He makes them clear to people who know.

231. When you divorce women, and they have reached their term, either retain them amicably, or release them amicably. But do not retain them to hurt them and commit aggression. Whoever does that has wronged himself. And do not take God's revelations for a joke. And remember God's favor to you, and that He revealed to you the Scripture and Wisdom to teach

you. And fear God, and know that God is aware of everything.

232. When you divorce women, and they have reached their term, do not prevent them from marrying their husbands, provided they agree on fair terms. Thereby is advised whoever among you believes in God and the Last Day. That is better and more decent for you. God knows, and you do not know.

233. Mothers may nurse their infants for two whole years, for those who desire to complete the nursing-period. It is the duty of the father to provide for them and clothe them in a proper manner. No soul shall be burdened beyond its capacity. No mother shall be harmed on account of her child, and no father shall be harmed on account of his child. The same duty rests upon the heir. If the couple desire weaning, by mutual consent and consultation, they commit no error by doing so. You commit no error by hiring nursing-mothers, as long as you pay them fairly. And be wary of God, and know that God is Seeing of what you do.

234. As for those among you who die and leave widows behind, their widows shall wait by themselves for four months and ten days. When they have reached their term, there is no blame on you regarding what they might honorably do with themselves. God is fully acquainted with what you do.

235. You commit no error by announcing your engagement to women, or by keeping it to yourselves. God knows that you will be thinking about them. But do not meet them secretly, unless you have something proper to say. And do not confirm the marriage tie until the writing is fulfilled. And know that God knows what is in your

souls, so beware of Him. And know that God is Forgiving and Forbearing.

236. You commit no error by divorcing women before having touched them, or before having set the dowry for them. And compensate them—the wealthy according to his means, and the poor according to his means—with a fair compensation, a duty upon the doers of good.

237. If you divorce them before you have touched them, but after you had set the dowry for them, give them half of what you specified—unless they forego the right, or the one in whose hand is the marriage contract foregoes it. But to forego is nearer to piety. And do not forget generosity between one another. God is seeing of everything you do.

238. Guard your prayers, and the middle prayer, and stand before God in devotion.

239. But if you are in fear, then on foot, or riding. And when you are safe, remember God, as He taught you what you did not know.

240. Those of you who die and leave wives behind—a will shall provide their wives with support for a year, provided they do not leave. If they leave, you are not to blame for what they do with themselves, provided it is reasonable. God is Mighty and Wise.

241. And divorced women shall be provided for, equitably—a duty upon the righteous.

242. God thus explains His revelations to you, so that you may understand.

243. Have you not considered those who fled their homes, by the thousands, fearful of death? God said to them, "Die. Then He revived them. God is Gracious towards the

people, but most people are not appreciative.

244. Fight in the cause of God, and know that God is Hearing and Knowing.

245. Who is the he who will offer God a generous loan, so He will multiply it for him manifold? God receives and amplifies, and to Him you will be returned.

246. Have you not considered the notables of the Children of Israel after Moses? When they said to a prophet of theirs, "Appoint a king for us, and we will fight in the cause of God." He said, "Is it possible that, if fighting was ordained for you, you would not fight?" They said, "Why would we not fight in the cause of God, when we were driven out of our homes, along with our children?" But when fighting was ordained for them, they turned away, except for a few of them. But God is aware of the wrongdoers.

247. Their prophet said to them, "God has appointed Saul to be your king." They said, "How can he have authority over us, when we are more worthy of authority than he, and he was not given plenty of wealth?" He said, "God has chosen him over you, and has increased him in knowledge and stature." God bestows His sovereignty upon whomever He wills. God is Embracing and Knowing.

248. And their prophet said to them, "The proof of his kingship is that the Ark will be restored to you, bringing tranquility from your Lord, and relics left by the family of Moses and the family of Aaron. It will be carried by the angels. In that is a sign for you, if you are believers."

249. When Saul set out with the troops, he said, "God will be testing you with a river. Whoever drinks from it does not belong with me. But whoever does not drink from

it, does belong with me, except for whoever scoops up a little with his hand." But they drank from it, except for a few of them. Then, when he crossed it, he and those who believed with him, they said, "We have no strength to face Goliath and his troops today." But those who knew that they would meet God said, "How many a small group has defeated a large group by God's will. God is with the steadfast."

250. And when they confronted Goliath and his troops, they said, "Our Lord, pour down patience on us, and strengthen our foothold, and support us against the faithless people."

251. And they defeated them by God's leave, and David killed Goliath, and God gave him sovereignty and wisdom, and taught him as He willed. Were it not for God restraining the people, some by means of others, the earth would have gone to ruin. But God is gracious towards mankind.

252. These are God's revelations, which We recite to you in truth. You are one of the messengers.

253. These messengers: We gave some advantage over others. To some of them God spoke directly, and some He raised in rank. We gave Jesus son of Mary the clear miracles, and We strengthened him with the Holy Spirit. Had God willed, those who succeeded them would not have fought one another, after the clear signs had come to them; but they disputed; some of them believed, and some of them disbelieved. Had God willed, they would not have fought one another, but God does whatever He desires.

254. O you who believe! Spend from what We have given you, before a Day comes in which there is neither trading, nor friend-

ship, nor intercession. The disbelievers are the wrongdoers.

255. God! There is no god except He, the Living, the Everlasting. Neither slumber overtakes Him, nor sleep. To Him belongs everything in the heavens and everything on earth. Who is he that can intercede with Him except with His permission? He knows what is before them, and what is behind them; and they cannot grasp any of His knowledge, except as He wills. His Throne extends over the heavens and the earth, and their preservation does not burden Him. He is the Most High, the Great.

256. There shall be no compulsion in religion: the right way has become distinct from the wrong way. Whoever renounces evil and believes in God has grasped the most trustworthy handle, which does not break. God is Hearing and Knowing.

257. God is the Lord of those who believe; He brings them out of darkness and into light. As for those who disbelieve, their lords are the evil ones; they bring them out of light and into darkness—these are the inmates of the Fire, in which they will abide forever.

258. Have you not considered him who argued with Abraham about his Lord, because God had given him sovereignty? Abraham said, "My Lord is He who gives life and causes death." He said, "I give life and cause death." Abraham said, "God brings the sun from the East, so bring it from the West," so the blasphemer was confounded. God does not guide the wrongdoing people.

259. Or like the one who passed by a town collapsed on its foundations. He said, "How can God revive this after its demise?" Thereupon God caused him to die for a hundred years, and then resurrected

him. He said, "For how long have you tarried?" He said, "I have tarried for a day, or part of a day." He said, "No. You have tarried for a hundred years. Now look at your food and your drink—it has not spoiled—and look at your donkey. We will make you a wonder for mankind. And look at the bones, how We arrange them, and then clothe them with flesh." So when it became clear to him, he said, "I know that God has power over all things."

260. And when Abraham said, "My Lord, show me how You give life to the dead." He said, "Have you not believed?" He said, "Yes, but to put my heart at ease." He said, "Take four birds, and incline them to yourself, then place a part on each hill, then call to them, and they will come rushing to you. And know that God is Powerful and Wise."

261. The parable of those who spend their wealth in God's way is that of a grain that produces seven spikes; in each spike is a hundred grains. God multiplies for whom He wills. God is Bounteous and Knowing.

262. Those who spend their wealth in the way of God—and then do not follow up what they spent with reminders of their generosity or with insults—they will have their reward with their Lord; they have nothing to fear, nor shall they grieve.

263. Kind words and forgiveness are better than charity followed by insults. God is Rich and Clement.

264. O you who believe! Do not nullify your charitable deeds with reminders and hurtful words, like him who spends his wealth to be seen by the people, and does not believe in God and the Last Day. His likeness is that of a smooth rock covered with soil: a downpour strikes it, and leaves it bare—

they gain nothing from their efforts. God does not guide the disbelieving people.

265. And the parable of those who spend their wealth seeking God's approval, and to strengthen their souls, is that of a garden on a hillside. If heavy rain falls on it, its produce is doubled; and if no heavy rain falls, dew is enough. God is seeing of everything you do.

266. Would anyone of you like to have a garden of palms and vines, under which rivers flow—with all kinds of fruit in it for him, and old age has stricken him, and he has weak children—then a tornado with fire batters it, and it burns down? Thus God makes clear the signs for you, so that you may reflect.

267. O you who believe! Give of the good things you have earned, and from what We have produced for you from the earth. And do not pick the inferior things to give away, when you yourselves would not accept it except with eyes closed. And know that God is Sufficient and Praiseworthy.

268. Satan promises you poverty, and urges you to immorality; but God promises you forgiveness from Himself, and grace. God is Embracing and Knowing.

269. He gives wisdom to whomever He wills. Whoever is given wisdom has been given much good. But none pays heed except those with insight.

270. Whatever charity you give, or a pledge you fulfill, God knows it. The wrongdoers have no helpers.

271. If you give charity openly, that is good. But if you keep it secret, and give it to the needy in private, that is better for you. It will atone for some of your misdeeds. God is cognizant of what you do.

272. Their guidance is not your responsibility, but God guides whom He wills. Any charity you give is for your own good. Any charity you give shall be for the sake of God. Any charity you give will be repaid to you in full, and you will not be wronged.

273. It is for the poor, those who are restrained in the way of God, and unable to travel in the land. The unaware would think them rich, due to their dignity. You will recognize them by their features. They do not ask from people insistently. Whatever charity you give, God is aware of it.

274. Those who spend their wealth by night and day, privately and publicly, will receive their reward from their Lord. They have nothing to fear, nor shall they grieve.

275. Those who swallow usury will not rise, except as someone driven mad by Satan's touch. That is because they say, "Commerce is like usury." But God has permitted commerce, and has forbidden usury. Whoever, on receiving advice from his Lord, refrains, may keep his past earnings, and his case rests with God. But whoever resumes—these are the dwellers of the Fire, wherein they will abide forever.

276. God condemns usury, and He blesses charities. God does not love any sinful ingrate.

277. Those who believe, and do good deeds, and pray regularly, and give charity—they will have their reward with their Lord; they will have no fear, nor shall they grieve.

278. O you who believe! Fear God, and forgo what remains of usury, if you are believers.

279. If you do not, then take notice of a war by God and His Messenger. But if you repent, you may keep your capital, neither wronging, nor being wronged.

280. But if he is in hardship, then deferment until a time of ease. But to remit it as charity is better for you, if you only knew.

281. And guard yourselves against a Day when you will be returned to God; then each soul will be rewarded fully for what it has earned, and they will not be wronged.

282. O you who believe! When you incur debt among yourselves for a certain period of time, write it down. And have a scribe write in your presence, in all fairness. And let no scribe refuse to write, as God has taught him. So let him write, and let the debtor dictate. And let him fear God, his Lord, and diminish nothing from it. But if the debtor is mentally deficient, or weak, or unable to dictate, then let his guardian dictate with honesty. And call to witness two men from among you. If two men are not available, then one man and two women whose testimony is acceptable to all—if one of them fails to remember, the other would remind her. Witnesses must not refuse when called upon. And do not think it too trivial to write down, whether small or large, including the time of repayment. That is more equitable with God, and stronger as evidence, and more likely to prevent doubt—except in the case of a spot transaction between you—then there is no blame on you if you do not write it down. And let there be witnesses whenever you conclude a contract, and let no harm be done to either scribe or witness. If you do that, it is corruption on your part. And fear God. God teaches you. God is aware of everything.

283. If you are on a journey, and cannot find a scribe, then a security deposit should be handed over. But if you trust one another, let the trustee fulfill his trust, and let him fear God, his Lord. And do not conceal testimony. Whoever conceals it is sinner at heart. God is aware of what you do.

284. To God belongs everything in the heavens and the earth. Whether you reveal what is within your selves, or conceal it, God will call you to account for it. He forgives whom He wills, and He punishes whom He wills. God is Able to do all things.

285. The Messenger has believed in what was revealed to him from his Lord, as did the believers. They all have believed in God, and His angels, and His Scriptures, and His messengers: "We make no distinction between any of His messengers." And they say, "We hear and we obey. Your forgiveness, our Lord. To you is the destiny."

286. God does not burden any soul beyond its capacity. To its credit is what it earns, and against it is what it commits. "Our Lord, do not condemn us if we forget or make a mistake. Our Lord, do not burden us as You have burdened those before us. Our Lord, do not burden us with more than we have strength to bear; and pardon us, and forgive us, and have mercy on us. You are our Lord and Master, so help us against the disbelieving people."

3. FAMILY OF IMRAN
(Ali 'Imran)

In the name of God,
the Gracious, the Merciful.

1. Alif, Lam, Meem.

2. God, there is no god but He, the Living, the Eternal.

3. He sent down to you the Book with the Truth, confirming what came before it; and He sent down the Torah and the Gospel.

4. Aforetime, as guidance for mankind; and He sent down the Criterion. Those who have rejected God's signs will have a severe punishment. God is Mighty, Able to take revenge.

5. Nothing is hidden from God, on earth or in the heaven.

6. It is He who forms you in the wombs as He wills. There is no god except He, the Almighty, the Wise.

7. It is He who revealed to you the Book. Some of its verses are definitive; they are the foundation of the Book, and others are unspecific. As for those in whose hearts is deviation, they follow the unspecific part, seeking descent, and seeking to derive an interpretation. But none knows its interpretation except God and those firmly rooted in knowledge say, "We believe in it; all is from our Lord." But none recollects except those with understanding.

8. "Our Lord, do not cause our hearts to swerve after You have guided us, and bestow on us mercy from Your presence; You are the Giver."

9. "Our Lord, You will gather the people for a Day in which there is no doubt." God will never break His promise.

10. As for those who disbelieve, neither their wealth nor their children will avail them anything against God. These will be fuel for the Fire.

11. Like the behavior of Pharaoh's people and those before them. They rejected Our signs, so God seized them for their sins. God is Strict in retribution.

12. Say to those who disbelieve, "You will be defeated, and rounded up into Hell—an awful resting-place."

13. There was a sign for you in the two parties that met. One party fighting in the way of God, and the other was disbelieving. They saw them with their own eyes twice their number. But God supports with His help whomever He wills. In that is a lesson for those with insight.

14. Adorned for the people is the love of desires, such as women, and children, and piles upon piles of gold and silver, and branded horses, and livestock, and fields. These are the conveniences of the worldly life, but with God lies the finest resort.

15. Say, "Shall I inform you of something better than that? For those who are righteous, with their Lord are Gardens beneath which rivers flow, where they will remain forever, and purified spouses, and acceptance from God." God is Observant of the servants.

16. Those who say, "Our Lord, we have believed, so forgive us our sins, and save us from the suffering of the Fire."

17. The patient, and the truthful, and the reverent, and the charitable, and the seekers of forgiveness at dawn.

18. God bears witness that there is no god but He, as do the angels, and those endowed with knowledge—upholding justice. There is no god but He, the Mighty, the Wise.

19. Religion with God is Islam. Those to whom the Scripture was given differed only after knowledge came to them, out of envy among themselves. Whoever rejects the signs of God—God is quick to take account.

20. If they argue with you, say, "I have surrendered myself to God, and those who follow me." And say to those who were given the Scripture, and to the unlearned, "Have you surrendered?" If they have surrendered, then they are guided, but if they turn away, then your duty is to convey. God is Seeing of the servants.

21. As for those who defy God's revelations, and kill the prophets unjustly, and kill those who advocate justice among the people, promise them a painful retribution.

22. They are those whose deeds will come to nothing, in this world and in the Hereafter, and they will have no saviors.

23. Have you not considered those who were given a share of the Scripture, as they were called to the Scripture of God to arbitrate between them; then some of them turned back, and declined?

24. That is because they said, "The Fire will not touch us except for a limited number of days." They have been misled in their religion by the lies they fabricated.

25. How about when We gather them for a Day in which there is no doubt, and each soul will be paid in full for what it has earned, and they will not be wronged?

26. Say, "O God, Owner of Sovereignty. You grant sovereignty to whom You will, and You strip sovereignty from whom you will. You honor whom you will, and You humiliate whom you will. In Your hand is all goodness. You are Capable of all things."

27. "You merge the night into the day, and You merge the day into the night; and you bring the living out of the dead, and You bring the dead out of the living; and you provide for whom you will without measure."

28. Believers are not to take disbelievers for friends instead of believers. Whoever does that has nothing to do with God, unless it is to protect your own selves against them. God warns you to beware of Him. To God is the destiny.

29. Say, "Whether you conceal what is in your hearts, or disclose it, God knows it."

He knows everything in the heavens and the earth. God is Powerful over everything.

30. On the Day when every soul finds all the good it has done presented. And as for the evil it has done, it will wish there were a great distance between them. God cautions you of Himself. God is Kind towards the servants.

31. Say, "If you love God, then follow me, and God will love you, and will forgive you your sins." God is Forgiving and Merciful.

32. Say, "Obey God and the Messenger." But if they turn away—God does not love the faithless.

33. God chose Adam, and Noah, and the family of Abraham, and the family of Imran, over all mankind.

34. Offspring one of the other. God is Hearer and Knower.

35. The wife of Imran said, "My Lord, I have vowed to You what is in my womb, dedicated, so accept from me; You are the Hearer and Knower."

36. And when she delivered her, she said, "My Lord, I have delivered a female," and God was well aware of what she has delivered, "and the male is not like the female, and I have named her Mary, and have commended her and her descendants to Your protection, from Satan the outcast."

37. Her Lord accepted her with a gracious reception, and brought her a beautiful upbringing, and entrusted her to the care of Zechariah. Whenever Zechariah entered upon her in the sanctuary, he found her with provision. He said, "O Mary, where did you get this from?" She said, "It is from God; God provides to whom He wills without reckoning."

38. Thereupon Zechariah prayed to his Lord; he said, "My Lord, bestow on me

good offspring from Your presence; You are the Hearer of Prayers."

39. Then the angels called out to him, as he stood praying in the sanctuary: "God gives you good news of John; confirming a Word from God, and honorable, and moral, and a prophet; one of the upright."

40. He said, "My Lord, how will I have a son, when old age has overtaken me, and my wife is barren?" He said, "Even so, God does whatever He wills."

41. He said, "My Lord, give me a sign." He said, "Your sign is that you shall not speak to the people for three days, except by gestures. And remember your Lord much, and praise in the evening and the morning."

42. The angels said, "O Mary, God has chosen you, and has purified you. He has chosen you over all the women of the world.

43. "O Mary, be devoted to your Lord, and bow down, and kneel with those who kneel."

44. These are accounts from the Unseen, which We reveal to you. You were not with them when they cast their lots as to which of them would take charge of Mary; nor were you with them as they quarreled.

45. The Angels said, "O Mary, God gives you good news of a Word from Him. His name is the Messiah, Jesus, son of Mary, well-esteemed in this world and the next, and one of the nearest.

46. He will speak to the people from the crib, and in adulthood, and will be one of the righteous."

47. She said, "My Lord, how can I have a child, when no man has touched me?" He said, "It will be so. God creates whatever He wills. To have anything done, He only says to it, 'Be,' and it is."

48. And He will teach him the Scripture and wisdom, and the Torah and the Gospel.

49. A messenger to the Children of Israel: "I have come to you with a sign from your Lord. I make for you out of clay the figure of a bird, then I breathe into it, and it becomes a bird by God's leave. And I heal the blind and the leprous, and I revive the dead, by God's leave. And I inform you concerning what you eat, and what you store in your homes. In that is a sign for you, if you are believers."

50. "And verifying what lies before me of the Torah, and to make lawful for you some of what was forbidden to you. I have come to you with a sign from your Lord; so fear God, and obey me."

51. "God is my Lord and your Lord, so worship Him. That is a straight path."

52. When Jesus sensed disbelief on their part, he said, "Who are my allies towards God?" The disciples said, "We are God's allies; we have believed in God, and bear witness that we submit."

53. "Our Lord, we have believed in what You have revealed, and we have followed the Messenger, so count us among the witnesses."

54. They planned, and God planned; but God is the Best of planners.

55. God said, "O Jesus, I am terminating your life, and raising you to Me, and clearing you of those who disbelieve. And I will make those who follow you superior to those who disbelieve, until the Day of Resurrection. Then to Me is your return; then I will judge between you regarding what you were disputing.

56. As for those who disbelieve, I will punish them with a severe punishment, in this

world and the next, and they will have no helpers.

57. And as for those who believe and do good works, He will give them their rewards in full. God does not love the unjust."

58. This is what We recite to you of the Verses and the Wise Reminder.

59. The likeness of Jesus in God's sight is that of Adam: He created him from dust, then said to him, "Be," and he was.

60. The truth is from your Lord, so do not be of those who doubt.

61. And if anyone disputes with you about him, after the knowledge that has come to you, say, "Come, let us call our children and your children, and our women and your women, and ourselves and yourselves, and let us invoke God's curse on the liars."

62. This is the narrative of truth: there is no god but God. God is the Mighty, the Wise.

63. But if they turn away—God knows the corrupt.

64. Say, "O People of the Book, come to terms common between us and you: that we worship none but God, and that we associate nothing with Him, and that none of us takes others as lords besides God." And if they turn away, say, "Bear witness that we have submitted."

65. O People of the Book! Why do you argue about Abraham, when the Torah and the Gospel were not revealed until after him? Will you not reason?

66. Here you are—you argue about things you know, but why do you argue about things you do not know? God knows, and you do not know.

67. Abraham was neither a Jew nor a Christian, but he was a Monotheist, a Muslim. And he was not of the Polytheists.

68. The people most deserving of Abraham are those who followed him, and this prophet, and those who believe. God is the Guardian of the believers.

69. A party of the People of the Book would love to lead you astray, but they only lead themselves astray, and they do not realize it.

70. O People of the Book! Why do you reject the revelations of God, even as you witness?

71. O People of the Book! Why do you confound the truth with falsehood, and knowingly conceal the truth?

72. Some of the People of the Book say, "Believe in what was revealed to the believers at the beginning of the day, and reject it at its end, so that they may return."

73. And trust none except those who follow your religion." Say, "Guidance is God's guidance. If someone is given the like of what you were given, or they argue with you before your Lord, say, "All grace is in God's hand; He gives it to whomever He wills." God is Bounteous and Knowing.

74. He specifies His mercy for whomever He wills. God is Possessor of Sublime Grace.

75. Among the People of the Book is he, who, if you entrust him with a heap of gold, he will give it back to you. And among them is he, who, if you entrust him with a single coin, he will not give it back to you, unless you keep after him. That is because they say, "We are under no obligation towards the gentiles." They tell lies about God, and they know it.

76. Indeed, whoever fulfills his commitments and maintains piety—God loves the pious.

77. Those who exchange the covenant of God, and their vows, for a small price, will have no share in the Hereafter; and God will not speak to them, nor will He look at them on the Day of Resurrection, nor will He purify them. They will have a painful punishment.

78. And among them are those who twist the Scripture with their tongues, that you may think it from the Scripture, when it is not from the Scripture. And they say, "It is from God," when it is not from God. They tell lies and attribute them to God, knowingly.

79. No person to whom God has given the Scripture, and wisdom, and prophethood would ever say to the people, "Be my worshipers rather than God's." Rather, "Be people of the Lord, according to the Scripture you teach, and the teachings you learn."

80. Nor would he command you to take the angels and the prophets as lords. Would he command you to infidelity after you have submitted?

81. God received the covenant of the prophets, "Inasmuch as I have given you of Scripture and wisdom, should a messenger come to you verifying what you have; you shall believe in him, and support him." He said, "Do you affirm My covenant and take it upon yourselves?" They said, "We affirm it." He said, "Then bear witness, and I am with you among the witnesses."

82. Whoever turns away after that—these are the deceitful.

83. Do they desire other than the religion of God, when to Him has submitted everything in the heavens and the earth, willingly or unwillingly, and to Him they will be returned?

84. Say, "We believe in God, and in what was revealed to us, and in what was revealed to Abraham, and Ishmael, and Isaac, and Jacob, and the Patriarchs; and in what was given to Moses, and Jesus, and the prophets from their Lord. We make no distinction between any of them, and to Him we submit."

85. Whoever seeks other than Islam as a religion, it will not be accepted from him, and in the Hereafter he will be among the losers.

86. How will God guide a people who disbelieved after having believed, and had witnessed that the Messenger is true, and the clear proofs had come to them? God does not guide the unjust people.

87. Those—their penalty is that upon them falls the curse of God, and of the angels, and of all mankind.

88. Remaining in it eternally, without their punishment being eased from them, and without being reprieved.

89. Except those who repent afterwards, and reform; for God is Forgiving and Merciful.

90. As for those who disbelieve after having believed, then plunge deeper into disbelief, their repentance will not be accepted; these are the lost.

91. As for those who disbelieve and die disbelievers, even the earth full of gold would not be accepted from any of them, were he to offer it for ransom. These will have a painful torment, and will have no saviors.

92. You will not attain virtuous conduct until you give of what you cherish. Whatever you give away, God is aware of it.

93. All food was permissible to the Children of Israel, except what Israel forbade for itself before the Torah was revealed. Say, "Bring the Torah, and read it, if you are truthful."

94. Whoever forges lies about God after that—these are the unjust.

95. Say, "God has spoken the truth, so follow the religion of Abraham, the monotheist; he was not a Pagan."

96. The first house established for mankind is the one at Bekka, blessed, and guidance for all people.

97. In it are evident signs; the Station of Abraham. Whoever enters it attains security. Pilgrimage to the House is a duty to God for all who can make the journey. But as for those who refuse—God is Independent of the worlds.

98. Say, "O People of the Scripture, why do you reject the Revelations of God, when God witnesses what you do?"

99. Say, "O People of the Scripture, why do you hinder from God's path those who believe, seeking to distort it, even though you are witnesses? God is not unaware of what you do."

100. O you who believe! If you obey a party of those who were given the Scripture, they will turn you, after your belief, into disbelievers.

101. And how could you disbelieve, when God's revelations are being recited to you, and among you is His Messenger? Whoever cleaves to God has been guided to a straight path.

102. O you who believe! Revere God with due reverence, and do not die except as Muslims.

103. And hold fast to the rope of God, altogether, and do not become divided. And remember God's blessings upon you; how you were enemies, and He reconciled your hearts, and by His grace you became brethren. And you were on the brink of a pit of fire, and He saved you from it. God thus clarifies His revelations for you, so that you may be guided.

104. And let there be among you a community calling to virtue, and advocating righteousness, and deterring from evil. These are the successful.

105. And do not be like those who separated and disputed after the clear proofs came to them; for them is a great punishment.

106. On the Day when some faces will be whitened, and some faces will be blackened. As for those whose faces are blackened: "Did you disbelieve after your belief?" Then taste the punishment for having disbelieved.

107. But as for those whose faces are whitened, they are in God's mercy, remaining in it forever.

108. These are the revelations of God. We recite them to you in truth. God desires no injustice for mankind.

109. To God belongs everything in the heavens and everything on earth, and to God all events are referred.

110. You are the best community that ever emerged for humanity: you advocate what is moral, and forbid what is immoral, and believe in God. Had the People of the Scripture believed, it would have been better for them. Among them are the believers, but most of them are sinners.

111. They will do you no harm, beyond insulting you. And if they fight you, they will turn around and flee, then they will not be helped.

112. They shall be humiliated wherever they are encountered, except through a rope from God, and a rope from the people; and

they incurred wrath from God, and were stricken with misery. That is because they rejected God's revelations, and killed the prophets unjustly. That is because they rebelled and committed aggression.

113. They are not alike. Among the People of the Scripture is a community that is upright; they recite God's revelations throughout the night, and they prostrate themselves.

114. They believe in God and the Last Day, and advocate righteousness and forbid evil, and are quick to do good deeds. These are among the righteous.

115. Whatever good they do, they will not be denied it. God knows the righteous.

116. As for those who disbelieve, neither their possessions nor their children will avail them anything against God. These are the inhabitants of the Fire, abiding therein forever.

117. The parable of what they spend in this worldly life is that of a frosty wind that strikes the harvest of a people who have wronged their souls, and destroys it. God did not wrong them, but they wronged their own selves.

118. O you who believe! Do not befriend outsiders who never cease to wish you harm. They love to see you suffer. Hatred has already appeared from their mouths, but what their hearts conceal is worse. We have made the messages clear for you, if you understand.

119. There you are, you love them, but they do not love you, and you believe in the entire Scripture. And when they meet you, they say, "We believe," but when they are alone, they bite their fingers in rage at you. Say, "Die in your rage; God knows what is within the hearts."

120. If something good happens to you, it upsets them; but if something bad befalls you, they rejoice at it. But if you persevere and maintain righteousness, their schemes will not harm you at all. God comprehends what they do.

121. Remember when you left your home in the morning, to assign battle-positions for the believers. God is Hearing and Knowing.

122. When two groups among you almost faltered, but God was their Protector. So in God let the believers put their trust.

123. God had given you victory at Badr, when you were weak. So fear God, that you may be thankful.

124. When you said to the believers, "Is it not enough for you that your Lord has reinforced you with three thousand angels, sent down?"

125. It is, but if you persevere and remain cautious, and they attack you suddenly, your Lord will reinforce you with five thousand angels, well trained.

126. God made it but a message of hope for you, and to reassure your hearts thereby. Victory comes only from God the Almighty, the Wise.

127. He thus cuts off a section of those who disbelieved, or subdues them, so they retreat disappointed.

128. It is no concern of yours whether He redeems them or punishes them. They are wrongdoers.

129. To God belongs everything in the heavens and the earth. He forgives whom He wills, and He punishes whom He wills. God is Most Forgiving, Most Merciful.

130. O you who believe! Do not feed on usury, compounded over and over, and fear God, so that you may prosper.

131. And guard yourselves against the Fire that is prepared for the disbelievers.

132. And obey God and the Messenger, that you may obtain mercy.

133. And race towards forgiveness from your Lord, and a Garden as wide as the heavens and the earth, prepared for the righteous.

134. Those who give in prosperity and adversity, and those who restrain anger, and those who forgive people. God loves the doers of good.

135. And those who, when they commit an indecency or wrong themselves, remember God and ask forgiveness for their sins— and who forgives sins except God? And they do not persist in their wrongdoing while they know.

136. Those—their reward is forgiveness from their Lord, and gardens beneath which rivers flow, abiding therein forever. How excellent is the reward of the workers.

137. Many societies have passed away before you. So travel the earth and note the fate of the deniers.

138. This is a proclamation to humanity, and guidance, and advice for the righteous.

139. And do not waver, nor feel remorse. You are the superior ones, if you are believers.

140. If a wound afflicts you, a similar wound has afflicted the others. Such days We alternate between the people, that God may know those who believe, and take martyrs from among you. God does not love the evildoers.

141. So that God may prove those who believe, and eliminate the disbelievers.

142. Or do you expect to enter Paradise, before God has distinguished those among you who strive, and before He has distinguished the steadfast?

143. You used to wish for death before you have faced it. Now you have seen it before your own eyes.

144. Muhammad is no more than a messenger. Messengers have passed on before him. If he dies or gets killed, will you turn on your heels? He who turns on his heels will not harm God in any way. And God will reward the appreciative.

145. No soul can die except by God's leave, at a predetermined time. Whoever desires the reward of the world, We will give him some of it; and whoever desires the reward of the Hereafter, We will give him some of it; and We will reward the appreciative.

146. How many a prophet fought alongside him numerous godly people? They did not waver for what afflicted them in the cause of God, nor did they weaken, nor did they give in. God loves those who endure.

147. Their only words were, "Our Lord, forgive us our offences, and our excesses in our conduct, and strengthen our foothold, and help us against the disbelieving people."

148. So God gave them the reward of this world, and the excellent reward of the Hereafter. God loves the doers of good.

149. O you who believe! If you obey those who disbelieve, they will turn you back on your heels, and you end up losers.

150. God is your Master, and He is the Best of Helpers.

151. We will throw terror into the hearts of those who disbelieve, because they attribute to God partners for which He revealed no sanction. Their lodging is the Fire. Miserable is the lodging of the evildoers.

152. God has fulfilled His promise to you, and you defeated them by His leave; until

when you faltered, and disputed the command, and disobeyed after He had shown you what you like. Some of you want this world, and some of you want the next. Then He turned you away from them, to test you, but He pardoned you. God is Gracious towards the believers.

153. Remember when you fled, not caring for anyone, even though the Messenger was calling you from your rear. Then He repaid you with sorrow upon sorrow, so that you would not grieve over what you missed, or for what afflicted you. God is Informed of what you do.

154. Then after the setback, He sent down security upon you. Slumber overcame some of you, while others cared only for themselves, thinking of God thoughts that were untrue—thoughts of ignorance— saying, "Is anything up to us?" Say, "Everything is up to God." They conceal within themselves what they do not reveal to you. They say, "If it was up to us, none of us would have been killed here." Say, "Even if you Had stayed in your homes, those destined to be killed would have marched into their death beds." God thus tests what is in your minds, and purifies what is in your hearts. God knows what the hearts contain.

155. Those of you who turned back on the day when the two armies clashed—it was Satan who caused them to backslide, on account of some of what they have earned. But God has forgiven them. God is Forgiving and Prudent.

156. O you who believe! Do not be like those who disbelieved, and said of their brethren who marched in the land, or went on the offensive, "Had they stayed with us, they would not have died or been killed." So that God may make it a cause of regret in their hearts. God gives life and causes death. God is Seeing of what you do.

157. If you are killed in the cause of God, or die—forgiveness and mercy from God are better than what they hoard.

158. If you die, or are killed—to God you will be gathered up.

159. It is by of grace from God that you were gentle with them. Had you been harsh, hardhearted, they would have dispersed from around you. So pardon them, and ask forgiveness for them, and consult them in the conduct of affairs. And when you make a decision, put your trust in God; God loves the trusting.

160. If God supports you, there is none who can overcome you. But if He fails you, who is there to help you after Him? So in God let the believers put their trust.

161. It is not for a prophet to act dishonestly. Whoever acts dishonestly will bring his dishonesty on the Day of Resurrection. Then every soul will be paid in full for what it has earned, and they will not be wronged.

162. Is someone who pursues God's approval the same as someone who incurs God's wrath, and his refuge is Hell—the miserable destination?

163. They have different ranks with God, and God is Seeing of what they do.

164. God has blessed the believers, as He raised up among them a messenger from among themselves, who recites to them His revelations, and purifies them, and teaches them the Scripture and wisdom; although before that they were in evident error.

165. And when a calamity befell you, even after you had inflicted twice as much, you said, "How is this?" Say, "It is from your own selves." God is Able to do all things.

166. What befell you on the day the two armies clashed was with God's permission; that He may know the believers.

167. And that He may know the hypocrites. And it was said to them, "Come, fight in the cause of God, or contribute." They said, "If we knew how to fight, we would have followed you." On that day they were closer to infidelity than they were to faith. They say with their mouths what is not in their hearts; but God knows what they hide.

168. Those who said of their brethren, as they stayed behind, "Had they obeyed us, they would not have been killed." Say, "Then avert death from yourselves, if you are truthful."

169. Do not consider those killed in the cause of God as dead. In fact, they are alive, at their Lord, well provided for.

170. Delighting in what God has given them out of His grace, and happy for those who have not yet joined them; that they have nothing to fear, nor will they grieve.

171. They rejoice in grace from God, and bounty, and that God will not waste the reward of the faithful.

172. Those who responded to God and the Messenger, despite the persecution they had suffered. For the virtuous and the pious among them is a great reward.

173. Those to whom the people have said, "The people have mobilized against you, so fear them." But this only increased them in faith, and they said, "God is enough for us; He is the Excellent Protector."

174. So they came back with grace from God, and bounty, and no harm having touched them. They pursued what pleases God. God possesses immense grace.

175. That is only Satan frightening his partisans; so do not fear them, but fear Me, if you are believers.

176. And do not be saddened by those who rush into disbelief. They will not harm God in the least. God desires to give them no share in the Hereafter. A terrible torment awaits them.

177. Those who exchange blasphemy for faith will not harm God in the least. A painful torment awaits them.

178. Those who disbelieve should not assume that We respite them for their own good. We only respite them so that they may increase in sinfulness. A humiliating torment awaits them.

179. God will not leave the believers as you are, without distinguishing the wicked from the sincere. Nor will God inform you of the future, but God elects from among His messengers whom He wills. So believe in God and His messengers. If you believe and practice piety, you will have a splendid reward.

180. Those who withhold what God has given them of his bounty should not assume that is good for them. In fact, it is bad for them. They will be encircled by their hoardings on the Day of Resurrection. To God belongs the inheritance of the heavens and the earth, and God is well acquainted with what you do.

181. God has heard the statement of those who said, "God is poor, and we are rich." We will write down what they said, and their wrongful killing of the prophets; and We will say, "Taste the torment of the burning."

182. "This is on account of what your hands have forwarded, and because God is not unjust towards the creatures."

183. Those who said, "God has made a covenant with us, that we shall not believe in any messenger unless he brings us an offering to be consumed by fire." Say, "Messengers have come to you before me with proofs, and with what you asked for; so why did you assassinate them, if you are truthful?"

184. If they accuse you of lying, messengers before you were accused of lying. They came with the proofs, and the Psalms, and the Illuminating Scripture.

185. Every soul will have a taste of death, and you will receive your recompense on the Day of Resurrection. Whoever is swayed from the Fire, and admitted to Paradise, has won. The life of this world is merely enjoyment of delusion.

186. You will be tested through your possessions and your persons, and you will hear from those who received the Scripture before you, and from the idol worshipers, much abuse. But if you persevere and lead a righteous life—that indeed is a mark of great determination.

187. God received a pledge from those who were given the Scripture: "You shall proclaim it to the people, and not conceal it." But they disregarded it behind their backs, and exchanged it for a small price. What a miserable exchange they made.

188. Do not think that those who rejoice in what they have done, and love to be praised for what they have not done—do not think they can evade the punishment. They will have a painful punishment.

189. To God belongs the sovereignty of the heavens and the earth. God has power over all things.

190. In the creation of the heavens and the earth, and in the alternation of night and day, are signs for people of understanding.

191. Those who remember God while standing, and sitting, and on their sides, and they reflect upon the creation of the heavens and the earth: "Our Lord, You did not create this in vain. Glory to You! So protect us from the punishment of the Fire."

192. "Our Lord, whomever You commit to the Fire, You have disgraced. The wrongdoers will have no helpers."

193. "Our Lord, we have heard a caller calling to the faith: `Believe in your Lord,' and we believed. Our Lord! Forgive us our sins, and remit our misdeeds, and make us die in the company of the virtuous."

194. "Our Lord, and give us what You have promised us through Your messengers, and do not disgrace us on the Day of Resurrection. Surely You never break a promise."

195. And so their Lord answered them: "I will not waste the work of any worker among you, whether male or female. You are one of another. For those who emigrated, and were expelled from their homes, and were persecuted because of Me, and fought and were killed—I will remit for them their sins, and will admit them into gardens beneath which rivers flow—a reward from God. With God is the ultimate reward."

196. Do not be impressed by the disbelievers' movements in the land.

197. A brief enjoyment, then their abode is Hell. What a miserable resort.

198. As for those who feared their Lord, for them will be gardens beneath which rivers flow, wherein they will abide forever—hospitality from God. What God possesses is best for the just.

199. Among the People of the Scripture are those who believe in God, and in what was

revealed to you, and in what was revealed to them. They are humble before God, and they do not sell God's revelations for a cheap price. These will have their reward with their Lord. God is swift in reckoning.

200. O you who believe! Be patient, and advocate patience, and be united, and revere God, so that you may thrive.

4. WOMEN
(an-Nisa')

In the name of God,
the Gracious, the Merciful.

1. O people! Fear your Lord, who created you from a single soul, and created from it its mate, and propagated from them many men and women. And revere God whom you ask about, and the parents. Surely, God is Watchful over you.

2. And give orphans their properties, and do not substitute the bad for the good. And do not consume their properties by combining them with yours, for that would be a serious sin.

3. If you fear you cannot act fairly towards the orphans—then marry the women you like—two, or three, or four. But if you fear you will not be fair, then one, or what you already have. That makes it more likely that you avoid bias.

4. Give women their dowries graciously. But if they willingly forego some of it, then consume it with enjoyment and pleasure.

5. Do not give the immature your money which God has assigned to you for support. But provide for them from it, and clothe them, and speak to them with kind words.

6. Test the orphans until they reach the age of marriage. If you find them to be mature enough, hand over their properties to them. And do not consume it extravagantly or hastily before they grow up. The rich shall not charge any wage, but the poor may charge fairly. When you hand over their properties to them, have it witnessed for them. God suffices as a Reckoner.

7. Men receive a share of what their parents and relatives leave, and women receive a share of what their parents and relatives leave, be it little or much—a legal share.

8. If the distribution is attended by the relatives, and the orphans, and the needy, give them something out of it, and speak to them kindly.

9. Those who are concerned about the fate of their weak children, in case they leave them behind, should fear God, and speak appropriate words.

10. Those who consume the wealth of orphans illicitly consume only fire into their bellies; and they will roast in a Blaze.

11. God instructs you regarding your children: The male receives the equivalent of the share of two females. If they are daughters, more than two, they get two-thirds of what he leaves. If there is only one, she gets one-half. As for the parents, each gets one-sixth of what he leaves, if he had children. If he had no children, and his parents inherit from him, his mother gets one-third. If he has siblings, his mother gets one-sixth. After fulfilling any bequest and paying off debts. Your parents and your children—you do not know which are closer to you in welfare. This is God's Law. God is Knowing and Judicious.

12. You get one-half of what your wives leave behind, if they had no children. If they had children, you get one-fourth of what they leave. After fulfilling any bequest and paying off debts. They get one-fourth of what you leave behind, if you

have no children. If you have children, they get one-eighth of what you leave. After fulfilling any bequest and paying off debts. If a man or woman leaves neither parents nor children, but has a brother or sister, each of them gets one-sixth. If there are more siblings, they share one-third. After fulfilling any bequest and paying off debts, without any prejudice. This is a will from God. God is Knowing and Clement.

13. These are the bounds set by God. Whoever obeys God and His Messenger, He will admit him into Gardens beneath which rivers flow, to abide therein forever. That is the great attainment.

14. But whoever disobeys God and His Messenger, and oversteps His bounds, He will admit him into a Fire, wherein he abides forever, and he will have a shameful punishment.

15. Those of your women who commit lewdness, you must have four witnesses against them, from among you. If they testify, confine them to the homes until death claims them, or God makes a way for them.

16. If two men among you commit it, punish them both. But if they repent and reform, leave them alone. God is Redeemer, Full of Mercy.

17. Repentance is available from God for those who commit evil out of ignorance, and then repent soon after. These—God will relent towards them. God is Knowing and Wise.

18. But repentance is not available for those who commit evils, until when death approaches one of them, he says, "Now I repent," nor for those who die as disbelievers. These—We have prepared for them a painful torment.

19. O you who believe! It is not permitted for you to inherit women against their will. And do not coerce them in order to take away some of what you had given them, unless they commit a proven adultery. And live with them in kindness. If you dislike them, it may be that you dislike something in which God has placed much good.

20. If you wish to replace one wife with another, and you have given one of them a fortune, take nothing back from it. Would you take it back fraudulently and sinfully?

21. And how can you take it back, when you have been intimate with one another, and they have received from you a solid commitment?

22. Do not marry women whom your fathers married, except what is already past. That is improper, indecent, and a bad custom.

23. Forbidden for you are your mothers, your daughters, your sisters, your paternal aunts, your maternal aunts, your brother's daughters, your sister's daughters, your foster-mothers who nursed you, your sisters through nursing, your wives' mothers, and your stepdaughters in your guardianship—born of wives you have gone into—but if you have not gone into them, there is no blame on you. And the wives of your genetic sons; and marrying two sisters simultaneously, except what is past. God is Oft-Forgiving, Most Merciful.

24. And all married women, except those you rightfully possess. This is God's decree, binding upon you. Permitted for you are those that lie outside these limits, provided you seek them in legal marriage, with gifts from your property, seeking wedlock, not prostitution. If you wish to enjoy them, then give them their dowry—a legal obligation. You commit no error by agreeing to any change to the dowry. God is All-Knowing, Most Wise.

25. If any of you lack the means to marry free believing women, he may marry one of the believing maids under your control. God is well aware of your faith. You are from one another. Marry them with the permission of their guardians, and give them their recompense fairly—to be protected—neither committing adultery, nor taking secret lovers. When they are married, if they commit adultery, their punishment shall be half that of free women. That is for those among you who fear falling into decadence. But to practice self-restraint is better for you. God is Most Forgiving, Most Merciful.

26. God intends to make things clear to you, and to guide you in the ways of those before you, and to redeem you. God is Most Knowing, Most Wise.

27. God intends to redeem you, but those who follow their desires want you to turn away utterly.

28. God intends to lighten your burden, for the human being was created weak.

29. O you who believe! Do not consume each other's wealth illicitly, but trade by mutual consent. And do not kill yourselves, for God is Merciful towards you.

30. Whoever does that, out of hostility and wrongdoing, We will cast him into a Fire. And that would be easy for God.

31. If you avoid the worst of what you are forbidden, We will remit your sins, and admit you by a Gate of Honor.

32. Do not covet what God has given to some of you in preference to others. For men is a share of what they have earned, and for women is a share of what they have earned. And ask God of his bounty. God has knowledge of everything.

33. To everyone We have assigned beneficiaries in what is left by parents and relatives. Those with whom you have made an agreement, give them their share. God is Witness over all things.

34. Men are the protectors and maintainers of women, as God has given some of them an advantage over others, and because they spend out of their wealth. The good women are obedient, guarding what God would have them guard. As for those from whom you fear disloyalty, admonish them, and abandon them in their beds, then strike them. But if they obey you, do not transgress against them. God is Sublime, Great.

35. If you fear a breach between the two, appoint an arbiter from his family and an arbiter from her family. If they wish to reconcile, God will bring them together. God is Knowledgeable, Expert.

36. Worship God, and ascribe no partners to Him, and be good to the parents, and the relatives, and the orphans, and the poor, and the neighbor next door, and the distant neighbor, and the close associate, and the traveler, and your servants. God does not love the arrogant showoff.

37. Those who are stingy, and exhort people to stinginess, and conceal what God has given them from His bounty. We have prepared for the disbelievers a disgraceful punishment.

38. And those who spend their money to be seen by people, and believe neither in God nor in the Last Day. Whoever has Satan as a companion—what an evil companion.

39. What would they have lost, had they believed in God and the Last Day, and gave out of what God has provided for them? God knows them very well.

40. God does not commit an atom's weight of injustice; and if there is a good deed, He doubles it, and gives from His Presence a sublime compensation.

41. Then how will it be, when We bring a witness from every community, and We bring you as a witness against these?

42. On that Day, those who disbelieved and disobeyed the Messenger will wish that the earth were leveled over them. They will conceal nothing from God.

43. O you who believe! Do not approach the prayer while you are drunk, so that you know what you say; nor after sexual orgasm—unless you are travelling—until you have bathed. If you are sick, or traveling, or one of you comes from the toilet, or you have had intercourse with women, and cannot find water, find clean sand and wipe your faces and your hands with it. God is Pardoning and Forgiving.

44. Have you not considered those who were given a share of the Book? They buy error, and wish you would lose the way.

45. But God knows your enemies best. God is sufficient as a Protector, and God is sufficient as a Supporter.

46. Among the Jews are some who take words out of context, and say, "We hear and we disobey", and "Hear without listening", and "Observe us," twisting with their tongues and slandering the religion. Had they said, "We hear and we obey", and "Listen", and "Give us your attention," it would have been better for them, and more upright. But God has cursed them for their disbelief; they do not believe except a little.

47. O you who were given the Book! Believe in what We sent down, confirming what you have, before We obliterate faces and turn them inside out, or curse them as We cursed the Sabbath-breakers. The command of God is always done.

48. God does not forgive association with Him, but He forgives anything less than that to whomever He wills. Whoever associates anything with God has devised a monstrous sin.

49. Have you not considered those who claim purity for themselves? Rather, God purifies whom He wills, and they will not be wronged a whit.

50. See how they devise lies against God. That alone is an outright sin.

51. Have you not considered those who were given a share of the Book? They believe in superstition and evil powers, and say of those who disbelieve, "These are better guided on the way than the believers."

52. Those are they whom God has cursed. Whomever God curses, you will find no savior for him.

53. Or do they own a share of the kingdom? Then they would not give people a speck.

54. Or do they envy the people for what God has given them of His grace? We have given the family of Abraham the Book and wisdom, and We have given them a great kingdom.

55. Among them are those who believed in it, and among them are those who held back from it. Hell is a sufficient Inferno.

56. Those who reject Our revelations—We will scorch them in a Fire. Every time their skins are cooked, We will replace them with other skins, so they will experience the suffering. God is Most Powerful, Most Wise.

57. As for those who believe and do good deeds, We will admit them into Gardens beneath which rivers flow, abiding therein forever. They will have purified spouses therein, and We will admit them into a shady shade.

58. God instructs you to give back things entrusted to you to their owners. And

when you judge between people, judge with justice. God's instructions to you are excellent. God is All-Hearing, All-Seeing.

59. O you who believe! Obey God and obey the Messenger and those in authority among you. And if you dispute over anything, refer it to God and the Messenger, if you believe in God and the Last Day. That is best, and a most excellent determination.

60. Have you not observed those who claim that they believe in what was revealed to you, and in what was revealed before you, yet they seek Satanic sources for legislation, in spite of being commanded to reject them? Satan means to mislead them far away.

61. And when it is said to them, "Come to what God has revealed, and to the Messenger," you see the hypocrites shunning you completely.

62. How about when a disaster strikes them because what their hands have put forward, and then they come to you swearing by God: "We only intended goodwill and reconciliation"?

63. They are those whom God knows what is in their hearts. So ignore them, and admonish them, and say to them concerning themselves penetrating words.

64. We did not send any messenger except to be obeyed by God's leave. Had they, when they wronged themselves, come to you, and prayed for God's forgiveness, and the Messenger had prayed for their forgiveness, they would have found God Relenting and Merciful.

65. But no, by your Lord, they will not believe until they call you to arbitrate in their disputes, and then find within themselves no resentment regarding your decisions, and submit themselves completely.

66. Had We decreed for them: "Kill yourselves," or "Leave your homes," they would not have done it, except for a few of them. But had they done what they were instructed to do, it would have been better for them, and a firmer confirmation.

67. And We would have given them from Our presence a rich compensation.

68. And We would have guided them on a straight path.

69. Whoever obeys God and the Messenger—these are among those whom God has blessed—among the prophets, and the sincere, and the martyrs, and the upright. Excellent are those as companions.

70. That is the grace from God. God suffices as Knower.

71. O you who believe! Take your precautions, and mobilize in groups, or mobilize altogether.

72. Among you is he who lags behind. Then, when a calamity befalls you, he says, "God has favored me, that I was not martyred with them."

73. But when some bounty from God comes to you, he says—as if no affection existed between you and him—"If only I had been with them, I would have achieved a great victory."

74. Let those who sell the life of this world for the Hereafter fight in the cause of God. Whoever fights in the cause of God, and then is killed, or achieves victory, We will grant him a great compensation.

75. And why would you not fight in the cause of God, and the helpless men, and women, and children, cry out, "Our Lord, deliver us from this town whose people are oppressive, and appoint for us from Your Presence a Protector, and appoint for us from Your Presence a Victor."

76. Those who believe fight in the cause of God, while those who disbelieve fight in the cause of Evil. So fight the allies of the Devil. Surely the strategy of the Devil is weak.

77. Have you not seen those who were told, "Restrain your hands, and perform your prayers, and spend in regular charity"? But when fighting was ordained for them, a faction of them feared the people as God is ought to be feared, or even more. And they said, "Our Lord, why did You ordain fighting for us? If only You would postpone it for us for a while." Say, "The enjoyments of this life are brief, but the Hereafter is better for the righteous, and you will not be wronged one bit."

78. Wherever you may be, death will catch up with you, even if you were in fortified towers. When a good fortune comes their way, they say, "This is from God." But when a misfortune befalls them, they say, "This is from you." Say, "All is from God." So what is the matter with these people, that they hardly understand a thing?

79. Whatever good happens to you is from God, and whatever bad happens to you is from your own self. We sent you to humanity as a messenger, and God is Witness enough.

80. Whoever obeys the Messenger is obeying God. And whoever turns away—We did not send you as a watcher over them.

81. They profess obedience, but when they leave your presence, some of them conspire something contrary to what you said. But God writes down what they conspire. So avoid them, and put your trust in God. God is Guardian enough.

82. Do they not ponder the Quran? Had it been from any other than God, they would have found in it much discrepancy.

83. When some news of security or alarm comes their way, they broadcast it. But had they referred it to the Messenger, and to those in authority among them, those who can draw conclusions from it would have comprehended it. Were it not for God's blessing and mercy upon you, you would have followed the Devil, except for a few.

84. So fight in the cause of God; you are responsible only for yourself. And rouse the believers. Perhaps God will restrain the might of those who disbelieve. God is Stronger in Might, and More Punishing.

85. Whoever intercedes for a good cause has a share in it, and whoever intercedes for an evil cause shares in its burdens. God keeps watch over everything.

86. When you are greeted with a greeting, respond with a better greeting, or return it. God keeps count of everything.

87. God—there is no god except He. He will gather you to the Day of Resurrection, in which there is no doubt. And who speaks more truly than God?

88. What is the matter with you, divided into two factions regarding the hypocrites, when God Himself has overwhelmed them on account of what they did? Do you want to guide those whom God has led astray? Whomever God leads astray—you will never find for him a way.

89. They would love to see you disbelieve, just as they disbelieve, so you would become equal. So do not befriend any of them, unless they emigrate in the way of God. If they turn away, seize them and execute them wherever you may find them; and do not take from among them allies or supporters.

90. Except those who join people with whom you have a treaty, or those who come to you reluctant to fight you or fight their own people. Had God willed, He

would have given them power over you, and they would have fought you. If they withdraw from you, and do not fight you, and offer you peace, then God assigns no excuse for you against them.

91. You will find others who want security from you, and security from their own people. But whenever they are tempted into civil discord, they plunge into it. So if they do not withdraw from you, nor offer you peace, nor restrain their hands, seize them and execute them wherever you find them. Against these, We have given you clear authorization.

92. Never should a believer kill another believer, unless by error. Anyone who kills a believer by error must set free a believing slave, and pay compensation to the victim's family, unless they remit it as charity. If the victim belonged to a people who are hostile to you, but is a believer, then the compensation is to free a believing slave. If he belonged to a people with whom you have a treaty, then compensation should be handed over to his family, and a believing slave set free. Anyone who lacks the means must fast for two consecutive months, by way of repentance to God. God is All-Knowing, Most Wise.

93. Whoever kills a believer deliberately, the penalty for him is Hell, where he will remain forever. And God will be angry with him, and will curse him, and will prepare for him a terrible punishment.

94. O you who believe! When you journey in the way of God, investigate, and do not say to him who offers you peace, "You are not a believer," aspiring for the goods of this world. With God are abundant riches. You yourselves were like this before, and God bestowed favor on you; so investigate. God is well aware of what you do.

95. Not equal are the inactive among the believers—except the disabled—and the strivers in the cause of God with their possessions and their persons. God prefers the strivers with their possessions and their persons above the inactive, by a degree. But God has promised goodness to both. Yet God favors the strivers, over the inactive, with a great reward.

96. Degrees from Him, and forgiveness, and mercy. God is Forgiving and Merciful.

97. While the angels are removing the souls of those who have wronged themselves, they will say, "What was the matter with you?" They will say, "We were oppressed in the land." They will say, "Was God's earth not vast enough for you to emigrate in it?" These—their refuge is Hell. What a wretched retreat!

98. Except for the weak among men, and women, and children who have no means to act, and no means to find a way out.

99. These—God may well pardon them. God is Pardoning and Forgiving.

100. Anyone who emigrates for the sake of God will find on earth many places of refuge, and plentitude. Anyone who leaves his home, emigrating to God and His Messenger, and then is overtaken by death, his compensation falls on God. God is Forgiver, Most Merciful.

101. When you travel in the land, there is no blame on you for shortening the prayers, if you fear that the disbelievers may harm you. The disbelievers are your manifest enemies.

102. When you are among them, and you stand to lead them in prayer, let a group of them stand with you, and let them hold their weapons. Then, when they have done their prostrations, let them withdraw to the rear, and let another group, that have not prayed yet, come forward and pray

with you; and let them take their precautions and their weapons. Those who disbelieve would like you to neglect your weapons and your equipment, so they can attack you in a single assault. You commit no error, if you are hampered by rain or are sick, by putting down your weapons; but take precautions. Indeed, God has prepared for the disbelievers a demeaning punishment.

103. When you have completed the prayer, remember God, standing, or sitting, or on your sides. And when you feel secure, perform the prayer. The prayer is obligatory for believers at specific times.

104. And do not falter in the pursuit of the enemy. If you are aching, they are aching as you are aching, but you expect from God what they cannot expect. God is Knowledgeable and Wise.

105. We have revealed to you the Scripture, with the truth, so that you judge between people in accordance with what God has shown you. And do not be an advocate for the traitors.

106. And ask God for forgiveness. God is Forgiver and Merciful.

107. And do not argue on behalf of those who deceive themselves. God does not love any treacherous and immoral.

108. They hide from the people, but they cannot hide from God. He is with them, as they plot by night with words He does not approve. God comprehends what they do.

109. There you are, arguing on their behalf in the present life, but who will argue with God on their behalf on the Day of Resurrection? Or who will be their representative?

110. Whoever commits evil, or wrongs his soul, then implores God for forgiveness, will find God Forgiving and Merciful.

111. And Whoever earns a sin, earns it against himself. God is Aware and Wise.

112. And whoever commits a mistake, or a sin, and then blames it on an innocent person, has taken a slander and a clear sin.

113. Were it not for God's grace towards you, and His mercy, a faction of them would have managed to mislead you. But they only mislead themselves, and they cannot harm you in any way. God has revealed to you the Scripture and wisdom, and has taught you what you did not know. God's goodness towards you is great.

114. There is no good in much of their private counsels, except for him who advocates charity, or kindness, or reconciliation between people. Whoever does that, seeking God's approval, We will give him a great compensation.

115. Whoever makes a breach with the Messenger, after the guidance has become clear to him, and follows other than the path of the believers, We will direct him in the direction he has chosen, and commit him to Hell—what a terrible destination!

116. God will not forgive that partners be associated with Him, but will forgive anything less than that, to whomever He wills. Anyone who ascribes partners to God has strayed into far error.

117. They invoke in His stead only females. In fact, they invoke none but a rebellious devil.

118. God has cursed him. And he said, "I will take to myself my due share of Your servants."

119. "And I will mislead them, and I will entice them, and I will prompt them to slit the ears of cattle, and I will prompt them to alter the creation of God." Whoever

takes Satan as a lord, instead of God, has surely suffered a profound loss.

120. He promises them, and raises their expectations, but Satan promises them nothing but delusions.

121. These—their place is Hell, and they will find no escape from it.

122. But as for those who believe and do righteous deeds, We will admit them into gardens beneath which rivers flow, where they will abide forever. The promise of God is true—and who is more truthful in speech than God?

123. It is not in accordance with your wishes, nor in accordance with the wishes of the People of the Scripture. Whoever works evil will pay for it, and will not find for himself, besides God, any protector or savior.

124. But whoever works righteousness, whether male or female, and is a believer—those will enter Paradise, and will not be wronged a whit.

125. And who is better in religion than he who submits himself wholly to God, and is a doer of good, and follows the faith of Abraham the Monotheist? God has chosen Abraham for a friend.

126. To God belongs what is in the heavens and what is on earth, and God encompasses everything.

127. They ask you for a ruling about women. Say, "God gives you a ruling about them, and so does what is stated to you in the Book about widowed women from whom you withhold what is decreed for them, yet you desire to marry them, and about helpless children: that you should treat them fairly." Whatever good you do, God knows it.

128. If a woman fears maltreatment or desertion from her husband, there is no fault in them if they reconcile their differences, for reconciliation is best. Souls are prone to avarice, yet if you do what is good, and practice piety—God is Cognizant of what you do.

129. You will not be able to treat women with equal fairness, no matter how much you desire it. But do not be so biased as to leave another suspended. If you make amends, and act righteously—God is Forgiving and Merciful.

130. And if they separate, God will enrich each from His abundance. God is Bounteous and Wise.

131. To God belongs everything in the heavens and everything on earth. We have instructed those who were given the Book before you, and you, to be conscious of God. But if you refuse—to God belongs everything in the heavens and everything on earth. God is in no need, Praiseworthy.

132. To God belongs everything in the heavens and everything on earth. God suffices as Manager.

133. If He wills, He can do away with you, O people, and bring others. God is Able to do that.

134. Whoever desires the reward of this world—with God is the reward of this world and the next. God is All-Hearing, All-Seeing.

135. O you who believe! Stand firmly for justice, as witnesses to God, even if against yourselves, or your parents, or your relatives. Whether one is rich or poor, God takes care of both. So do not follow your desires, lest you swerve. If you deviate, or turn away—then God is Aware of what you do.

136. O you who believe! Believe in God and His messenger, and the Book He sent down to His messenger, and the Book He

sent down before. Whoever rejects God, His angels, His Books, His messengers, and the Last Day, has strayed far in error.

137. Those who believe, then disbelieve, then believe, then disbelieve, then increase in disbelief, God will not forgive them, nor will He guide them to a way.

138. Inform the hypocrites that they will have a painful punishment.

139. Those who ally themselves with the disbelievers instead of the believers. Do they seek glory in them? All glory belongs to God.

140. He has revealed to you in the Book that when you hear God's revelations being rejected, or ridiculed, do not sit with them until they engage in some other subject. Otherwise, you would be like them. God will gather the hypocrites and the disbelievers, into Hell, altogether.

141. Those who lie in wait for you: if you attain victory from God, they say, "Were we not with you?" But if the disbelievers get a turn, they say, "Did we not side with you, and defend you from the believers?" God will judge between you on the Day of Resurrection; and God will give the disbelievers no means of overcoming the believers.

142. The hypocrites try to deceive God, but He is deceiving them. And when they stand for prayer, they stand lazily, showing off in front of people, and remembering God only a little.

143. Wavering in between, neither with these, nor with those. Whomever God sends astray, you will never find for him a way.

144. O you who believe! Do not befriend disbelievers rather than believers. Do you want to give God a clear case against you?

145. The hypocrites will be in the lowest level of the Fire, and you will find no helper for them.

146. Except those who repent, and reform, and hold fast to God, and dedicate their religion to God alone. These are with the believers; and God will give the believers a great reward.

147. What would God accomplish by your punishment, if you have given thanks, and have believed? God is Appreciative and Cognizant.

148. God does not like the public uttering of bad language, unless someone was wronged. God is Hearing and Knowing.

149. If you let a good deed be shown, or conceal it, or pardon an offense—God is Pardoning and Capable.

150. Those who disbelieve in God and His messengers, and want to separate between God and His messengers, and say, "We believe in some, and reject some," and wish to take a path in between.

151. These are the unbelievers, truly. We have prepared for the unbelievers a shameful punishment.

152. As for those who believe in God and His messengers, and make no distinction between any of them, He will give them their reward. God is Forgiver and Merciful.

153. The People of the Scripture challenge you to bring down to them a book from the sky. They had asked Moses for something even greater. They said, "Show us God plainly." The thunderbolt struck them for their wickedness. Then they took the calf for worship, even after the clear proofs had come to them. Yet We pardoned that, and We gave Moses a clear authority.

154. And We raised the Mount above them in accordance with their covenant, and We

said to them, "Enter the gate humbly", and We said to them, "Do not violate the Sabbath", and We received from them a solemn pledge.

155. But for their violation of their covenant, and their denial of God's revelations, and their killing of the prophets unjustly, and their saying, "Our minds are closed." In fact, God has sealed them for their disbelief, so they do not believe, except for a few.

156. And for their faithlessness, and their saying against Mary a monstrous slander.

157. And for their saying, "We have killed the Messiah, Jesus, the son of Mary, the Messenger of God." In fact, they did not kill him, nor did they crucify him, but it appeared to them as if they did. Indeed, those who differ about him are in doubt about it. They have no knowledge of it, except the following of assumptions. Certainly, they did not kill him.

158. Rather, God raised him up to Himself. God is Mighty and Wise.

159. There is none from the People of the Scripture but will believe in him before his death, and on the Day of Resurrection he will be a witness against them.

160. Due to wrongdoing on the part of the Jews, We forbade them good things that used to be lawful for them; and for deterring many from God's path.

161. And for their taking usury, although they were forbidden it, and for their consuming people's wealth dishonestly. We have prepared for the faithless among them a painful torment.

162. But those among them firmly rooted in knowledge, and the believers, believe in what was revealed to you, and in what was revealed before you; and the observers of prayers, and the givers of charity, and the

believers in God and the Last Day—upon these We will bestow an immense reward.

163. We have inspired you, as We had inspired Noah and the prophets after him. And We inspired Abraham, and Ishmael, and Isaac, and Jacob, and the Patriarchs, and Jesus, and Job, and Jonah, and Aaron, and Solomon. And We gave David the Psalms.

164. Some Messengers We have already told you about, while some messengers We have not told you about. And God spoke to Moses directly.

165. Messengers delivering good news, and bringing warnings, so that people may have no excuse before God after the coming of the messengers. God is Powerful and Wise.

166. But God bears witness to what He revealed to you. He revealed it with His knowledge. And the angels bear witness. Though God is a sufficient witness.

167. Those who disbelieve and repel from God's path have gone far astray.

168. Those who disbelieve and transgress, God is not about to forgive them, nor guide them to any path.

169. Except to the path of Hell, where they will dwell forever. And that is easy for God.

170. O people! The Messenger has come to you with the truth from your Lord, so believe—that is best for you. But if you disbelieve, to God belongs everything in the heavens and the earth. God is Omniscient and Wise.

171. O People of the Scripture! Do not exaggerate in your religion, and do not say about God except the truth. The Messiah, Jesus, the son of Mary, is the Messenger of God, and His Word that He conveyed to Mary, and a Spirit from Him. So believe in

God and His messengers, and do not say, "Three." Refrain—it is better for you. God is only one God. Glory be to Him—that He should have a son. To Him belongs everything in the heavens and the earth, and God is a sufficient Protector.

172. The Messiah does not disdain to be a servant of God, nor do the favored angels. Whoever disdains His worship, and is too arrogant—He will round them up to Himself altogether.

173. But as for those who believe and do good works, He will pay them their wages in full, and will increase His grace for them. But as for those who disdain and are too proud, He will punish them with an agonizing punishment. And they will find for themselves, apart from God, no lord and no savior.

174. O people! a proof has come to you from your Lord, and We sent down to you a clear light.

175. As for those who believe in God, and hold fast to Him, He will admit them into mercy from Him, and grace, and He will guide them to Himself in a straight path.

176. They ask you for a ruling. Say, "God gives you a ruling concerning the person who has neither parents nor children." If a man dies, and leaves no children, and he had a sister, she receives one-half of what he leaves. And he inherits from her if she leaves no children. But if there are two sisters, they receive two-thirds of what he leaves. If the siblings are men and women, the male receives the share of two females." God makes things clear for you, lest you err. God is Aware of everything.

5. THE TABLE
(al-Ma'idah)

In the name of God,

the Gracious, the Merciful.

1. O you who believe! Fulfill your commitments. Livestock animals are permitted for you, except those specified to you; but not wild game while you are in pilgrim sanctity. God decrees whatever He wills.

2. O you who believe! Do not violate God's sacraments, nor the Sacred Month, nor the offerings, nor the garlanded, nor those heading for the Sacred House seeking blessings from their Lord and approval. When you have left the pilgrim sanctity, you may hunt. And let not the hatred of people who barred you from the Sacred Mosque incite you to aggression. And cooperate with one another in virtuous conduct and conscience, and do not cooperate with one another in sin and hostility. And fear God. God is severe in punishment.

3. Prohibited for you are carrion, blood, the flesh of swine, and animals dedicated to other than God; also the flesh of animals strangled, killed violently, killed by a fall, gored to death, mangled by wild animals—except what you rescue, and animals sacrificed on altars; and the practice of drawing lots. For it is immoral. Today, those who disbelieve have despaired of your religion, so do not fear them, but fear Me. Today I have perfected your religion for you, and have completed My favor upon you, and have approved Islam as a religion for you. But whoever is compelled by hunger, with no intent of wrongdoing—God is Forgiving and Merciful.

4. They ask you what is permitted for them. Say, "Permitted for you are all good things, including what trained dogs and falcons catch for you." You train them according to what God has taught you. So eat from what they catch for you, and pronounce God's name over it. And fear God. God is Swift in reckoning.

5. Today all good things are made lawful for you. And the food of those given the Scripture is lawful for you, and your food is lawful for them. So are chaste believing women, and chaste women from the people who were given the Scripture before you, provided you give them their dowries, and take them in marriage, not in adultery, nor as mistresses. But whoever rejects faith, his work will be in vain, and in the Hereafter he will be among the losers.

6. O you who believe! When you rise to pray, wash your faces, and your hands and arms to the elbows, and wipe your heads, and your feet to the ankles. If you had intercourse, then purify yourselves. If you are ill, or travelling, or one of you returns from the toilet, or you had contact with women, and could not find water, then use some clean sand and wipe your faces and hands with it. God does not intend to burden you, but He intends to purify you, and to complete His blessing upon you, that you may be thankful.

7. And Remember God's blessings upon you, and His covenant which He covenanted with you, when you said, "We hear and we obey." And remain conscious of God, for God knows what the hearts contain.

8. O you who believe! Be upright to God, witnessing with justice, and let not the hatred of a certain people prevent you from acting justly. Adhere to justice, for that is nearer to piety, and fear God. God is informed of what you do.

9. God has promised those who believe and work righteousness: they will have forgiveness and a great reward.

10. As for those who disbelieve and reject Our revelations—these are the inmates of Hell.

11. O you who believe! Remember God's blessings upon you; when certain people intended to extend their hands against you, and He restrained their hands from you. So reverence God, and in God let the believers put their trust.

12. God received a pledge from the Children of Israel, and We raised among them twelve chiefs. God said, "I am with you; if you perform the prayer, and pay the alms, and believe in My messengers and support them, and lend God a loan of righteousness, I will remit your sins, and admit you into Gardens beneath which rivers flow. But whoever among you disbelieves afterwards—he has strayed from the right way."

13. Because of their breaking their pledge, We cursed them, and made their hearts hard. They twist the words out of their context, and they disregarded some of what they were reminded of. You will always witness deceit from them, except for a few of them. But pardon them, and overlook. God loves the doers of good.

14. And from those who say, "We are Christians," We received their pledge, but they neglected some of what they were reminded of. So We provoked enmity and hatred among them until the Day of Resurrection; God will then inform them of what they used to craft.

15. O People of the Book! Our Messenger has come to you, clarifying for you much of what you kept hidden of the Book, and overlooking much. A light from God has come to you, and a clear Book.

16. God guides with it whoever follows His approval to the ways of peace, and He brings them out of darkness into light, by His permission, and He guides them in a straight path.

17. They disbelieve those who say, "God is the Christ, the son of Mary." Say, "Who can prevent God, if He willed, from annihilating the Christ son of Mary, and his mother, and everyone on earth?" To God belongs the sovereignty of the heavens and the earth and what is between them. He creates whatever He wills, and God has power over everything.

18. The Jews and the Christians say, "We are the children of God, and His beloved." Say, "Why then does He punish you for your sins?" In fact, you are humans from among those He created. He forgives whom He wills, and He punishes whom He wills. To God belongs the dominion of the heavens and the earth and what lies between them, and to Him is the return.

19. O People of the Book! Our Messenger has come to you, making things clear to you—after a cessation of messengers—so that you cannot say, "No preacher has come to us, and no warner." In fact, a preacher has come to you, and a warner, and God is Capable of everything.

20. When Moses said to his people, "O my people, remember God's blessings upon you, when He placed prophets among you, and made you kings, and gave you what He never gave any other people."

21. "O my people, enter the Holy Land which God has assigned for you, and do not turn back, lest you return as losers."

22. They said, "O Moses, there are tyrannical people in it; we will not enter it until they leave it. If they leave it, we will be entering."

23. Two men of those who feared, but whom God had blessed, said, "Go at them by the gate; and when you have entered it, you will prevail. But put your trust in God, if you are believers."

24. They said, "O Moses, we will not enter it, ever, as long as they are in it. So go ahead, you and your Lord, and fight. We are staying right here."

25. He said, "My Lord, I have control only over myself and my brother, so separate between us and between the wicked people."

26. He said, "It is forbidden for them for forty years. They will wander aimlessly in the land. So do not grieve over the defiant people."

27. And relate to them the true story of Adam's two sons, when they offered an offering, and it was accepted from one of them, but it was not accepted from the other. He Said, "I will kill you." He Said, "God accepts only from the righteous."

28. "If you extend your hand to kill me, I will not extend my hand to kill you; for I fear God, Lord of the Worlds.

29. "I would rather you bear my sin and your sin, and you become among the inmates of the Fire. Such is the reward for the evildoers."

30. Then His soul prompted him to kill his brother, so he killed him, and became one of the losers.

31. Then God sent a raven digging the ground, to show him how to cover his brother's corpse. He said, "Woe to me, I am unable to be like this raven, and bury my brother's corpse." So he became full of regrets.

32. Because of that We ordained for the Children of Israel—that whoever kills a person—unless it is for murder or corruption on earth—it is as if he killed the whole of mankind; and whoever saves a person, it is as if he saved the whole of mankind. Our messengers came to them with clarifica-

tions, but even after that, many of them continue to commit excesses in the land.

33. The punishment for those who fight God and His messenger, and strive to spread corruption on earth, is that they be killed, or crucified, or have their hands and feet cut off on opposite sides, or be banished from the land. That is to disgrace them in this life; and in the Hereafter they will have a terrible punishment.

34. Except for those who repent before you apprehend them. So know that God is Forgiving and Merciful.

35. O you who believe! Be conscious of God, and seek the means of approach to Him, and strive in His cause, so that you may succeed.

36. As for those who disbelieve, even if they owned everything on earth, and the like of it with it, and they offered it to ransom themselves from the torment of the Day of Resurrection, it will not be accepted from them. For them is a painful punishment.

37. They will want to leave the Fire, but they will not leave it. For them is a lasting punishment.

38. As for the thief, whether male or female, cut their hands as a penalty for what they reaped—a deterrent from God. God is Mighty and Wise.

39. But whoever repents after his crime, and reforms, God will accept his repentance. God is Forgiving and Merciful.

40. Do you not know that to God belongs the kingdom of the heavens and the earth? He punishes whom He wills, and He forgives whom He wills. And God is Capable of everything.

41. O Messenger! Do not let those who are quick to disbelief grieve you—from among those who say with their mouths, "We believe," but their hearts do not believe; and from among the Jews—listeners to lies, listeners to other people who did not come to you. They distort words from their places, and say, "If you are given this, accept it; but if you are not given it, beware." Whomever God has willed to divert, you have nothing for him from God. Those are they whose hearts God does not intend to purify. For them is disgrace in this world, and for them is a great punishment in the Hereafter.

42. Listeners to falsehoods, eaters of illicit earnings. If they come to you, judge between them, or turn away from them. If you turn away from them, they will not harm you in the least. But if you judge, judge between them equitably. God loves the equitable.

43. But why do they come to you for judgment, when they have the Torah, in which is God's Law? Yet they turn away after that. These are not believers.

44. We have revealed the Torah, wherein is guidance and light. The submissive prophets ruled the Jews according to it, so did the rabbis and the scholars, as they were required to protect God's Book, and were witnesses to it. So do not fear people, but fear Me. And do not sell My revelations for a cheap price. Those who do not rule according to what God revealed are the unbelievers.

45. And We wrote for them in it: a life for a life, an eye for an eye, a nose for a nose, an ear for an ear, a tooth for a tooth, and an equal wound for a wound. But whoever forgoes it in charity, it will serve as atonement for him. Those who do not rule according to what God revealed are the evildoers.

46. In their footsteps, We sent Jesus son of Mary, fulfilling the Torah that preceded

him; and We gave him the Gospel, wherein is guidance and light, and confirming the Torah that preceded him, and guidance and counsel for the righteous.

47. So let the people of the Gospel rule according to what God revealed in it. Those who do not rule according to what God revealed are the sinners.

48. And We revealed to you the Book, with truth, confirming the Scripture that preceded it, and superseding it. So judge between them according to what God revealed, and do not follow their desires if they differ from the truth that has come to you. For each of you, We have assigned a law, and a method. Had God willed, He could have made you a single nation, but He tests you through what He has given you. So compete in righteousness. To God is your return, all of you. Then He will inform you of what you had disputed.

49. And judge between them according to what God revealed, and do not follow their desires. And beware of them, lest they lure you away from some of what God has revealed to you. But if they turn away, know that God intends to strike them with some of their sins. In fact, a great many people are corrupt.

50. Is it the laws of the time of ignorance that they desire? Who is better than God in judgment for a people who are certain?

51. O you who believe! Do not take the Jews and the Christians as allies; some of them are allies of one another. Whoever of you allies himself with them is one of them. God does not guide the wrongdoing people.

52. You will see those in whose hearts is sickness racing towards them. They say, "We fear the wheel of fate may turn against us." But perhaps God will bring about victory, or some event of His making; thereupon they will regret what they concealed within themselves.

53. Those who believe will say, "Are these the ones who swore by God with their strongest oaths that they are with you?" Their works have failed, so they became losers.

54. O you who believe! Whoever of you goes back on his religion—God will bring a people whom He loves and who love Him, kind towards the believers, stern with the disbelievers. They strive in the way of God, and do not fear the blame of the critic. That is the grace of God. He bestows it upon whomever He wills. God is Embracing and Knowing.

55. Your allies are God, and His Messenger, and those who believe—those who pray regularly, and give charity, and bow down.

56. Whoever allies himself with God, and His Messenger, and those who believe—surely the Party of God is the victorious.

57. O you who believe! Do not befriend those who take your religion in mockery and as a sport, be they from among those who were given the Scripture before you, or the disbelievers. And obey God, if you are believers.

58. When you call to the prayer, they take it as a joke and a trifle. That is because they are people who do not reason.

59. Say, "O People of the Scripture, do you resent us only because we believe in God, and in what was revealed to us, and in what was revealed previously; and most of you are sinners?"

60. Say, "Shall I inform you of worse than that for retribution from God? He whom God has cursed, and with whom He became angry. And He turned some of them into apes, and swine, and idol worshipers.

These are in a worse position, and further away from the right way."

61. When they come to you, they say, "We believe," though they have entered with disbelief, and they have departed with it. But God is well aware of what they hide.

62. You see many of them competing with one another in sin and hostility, and their consuming of what is illicit. What they have been doing is truly evil.

63. Why do the rabbis and the priests not prevent them from speaking sinfully and from consuming forbidden wealth? Evil is what they have been doing.

64. The Jews say, "God's hand is tied." It is their hands that are tied, and they are cursed for what they say. In fact, His hands are outstretched; He gives as He wills. Certainly, what was revealed to your from your Lord will increase many of them in defiance and blasphemy. And We have placed between them enmity and hatred, until the Day of Resurrection. Whenever they kindle the fire of war, God extinguishes it. And they strive to spread corruption on earth. God does not love the corrupters.

65. Had the People of the Book believed and been righteous, We would have remitted their sins, and admitted them into the Gardens of Bliss.

66. Had they observed the Torah, and the Gospel, and what was revealed to them from their Lord, they would have consumed amply from above them, and from beneath their feet. Among them is a moderate community, but evil is what many of them are doing.

67. O Messenger, convey what was revealed to you from your Lord. But if you do not, then you would not have delivered His message. And God will protect you from the people. God does not guide the disbelieving people.

68. Say, "O People of the Scripture, you have no basis until you uphold the Torah, and the Gospel, and what is revealed to you from your Lord." But what is revealed to you from your Lord will increase many of them in rebellion and disbelief, so do not be sorry for the disbelieving people.

69. Those who believe, and the Jews, and the Sabians, and the Christians—whoever believes in God and the Last Day, and does what is right—they have nothing to fear, nor shall they grieve.

70. We made a covenant with the Children of Israel, and We sent to them messengers. Whenever a messenger came to them with what their souls did not desire, some of them they accused of lying, and others they put to death.

71. They assumed there would be no punishment, so they turned blind and deaf. Then God redeemed them, but then again many of them turned blind and deaf. But God is Seeing of what they do.

72. They disbelieve those who say, "God is the Messiah the son of Mary." But the Messiah himself said, "O Children of Israel, worship God, my Lord and your Lord. Whoever associates others with God, God has forbidden him Paradise, and his dwelling is the Fire. The wrongdoers have no saviors."

73. They disbelieve those who say, "God is the third of three." But there is no deity except the One God. If they do not refrain from what they say, a painful torment will befall those among them who disbelieve.

74. Will they not repent to God and ask His forgiveness? God is Forgiving and Merciful.

75. The Messiah son of Mary was only a Messenger, before whom other Messengers had passed away, and his mother was a woman of truth. They both used to eat food. Note how We make clear the revelations to them; then note how deluded they are.

76. Say, "Do you worship, besides God, what has no power to harm or benefit you?" But God—He is the Hearer, the Knower.

77. Say, "O People of the Scripture, do not exaggerate in your religion beyond the truth, and do not follow the opinions of people who went astray before, and misled many, and themselves strayed off the balanced way."

78. Cursed were those who disbelieved from among the Children of Israel by the tongue of David and Jesus son of Mary. That is because they rebelled and used to transgress.

79. They used not to prevent one another from the wrongs they used to commit. Evil is what they used to do.

80. You will see many of them befriending those who disbelieve. Terrible is what their souls prompts them to do. The wrath of God fell upon them, and in the torment they will remain.

81. Had they believed in God and the Prophet, and in what was revealed to him, they would not have befriended them. But many of them are immoral.

82. You will find that the people most hostile towards the believers are the Jews and the polytheists. And you will find that the nearest in affection towards the believers are those who say, "We are Christians." That is because among them are priests and monks, and they are not arrogant.

83. And when they hear what was revealed to the Messenger, you see their eyes overflowing with tears, as they recognize the truth in it. They say, "Our Lord, we have believed, so count us among the witnesses."

84. "And why should we not believe in God, and in the truth that has come to us, and hope that our Lord will include us among the righteous people?"

85. God will reward them for what they say—Gardens beneath which rivers flow, where they will stay forever. Such is the reward of the righteous.

86. But as for those who disbelieve and deny Our signs—these are the inmates of the Fire.

87. O you who believe! Do not prohibit the good things God has permitted for you, and do not commit aggression. God does not love the aggressors.

88. And eat of the lawful and good things God has provided for you, and be conscious of God, in whom you are believers.

89. God does not hold you accountable for your unintended oaths, but He holds you accountable for your binding oaths. The atonement for it is by feeding ten needy people from the average of what you feed your families, or by clothing them, or by freeing a slave. Anyone who lacks the means shall fast for three days. That is the atonement for breaking your oaths when you have sworn them. So keep your oaths. Thus God makes clear His Revelations to you, that you may be grateful.

90. O you who believe! Intoxicants, gambling, idolatry, and divination are abominations of Satan's doing. Avoid them, so that you may prosper.

91. Satan wants to provoke strife and hatred among you through intoxicants and

gambling, and to prevent you from the remembrance of God, and from prayer. Will you not desist?

92. Obey God and obey the Messenger, and be cautious. If you turn away—know that the duty of Our Messenger is clear communication.

93. Those who believe and do righteous deeds will not be blamed for what they may have eaten, provided they obey, and believe, and do good deeds, then maintain piety and faith, then remain righteous and charitable. God loves the charitable.

94. O you who believe! God will test you with something of the game your hands and spears obtain, that God may know who fears Him at heart. Whoever commits aggression after that will have a painful punishment.

95. O you who believe! do not kill game while you are in pilgrim sanctity. Whoever of you kills any intentionally, its penalty shall be a domestic animal comparable to what he killed, as determined by two honest persons among you—an offering delivered to the Kaabah. Or he may atone by feeding the needy, or its equivalent in fasting, so that he may taste the consequences of his conduct. God forgives what is past. But whoever repeats, God will take revenge on him. God is Almighty, Avenger.

96. Permitted for you is the catch of sea, and its food—as sustenance for you and for travelers. But forbidden for you is the game of land while you are in pilgrim sanctity. And fear God, to whom you will be gathered.

97. God has appointed the Kaabah, the Sacred House, a sanctuary for the people, and the Sacred Month, and the offerings, and the garlanded. That you may know that God knows everything in the heavens and the earth, and that God is Cognizant of all things.

98. Know that God is severe in retribution, and that God is Forgiving and Merciful.

99. The Messenger's sole duty is to convey. God knows what you reveal and what you conceal.

100. Say: "The bad and the good are not equal, even though the abundance of the bad may impress you. So be conscious of God, O you who possess intelligence, that you may succeed."

101. O you who believe! Do not ask about things that would trouble you if disclosed to you. But if you were to ask about them while the Quran is being revealed, they will become obvious to you. God forgives that. God is Forgiving and Clement.

102. A people before you asked about them, but then came to reject them.

103. God did not institute the superstitions of Bahirah, Saibah, Wasilah, or of Hami; but the disbelievers fabricate lies about God—most of them do not understand.

104. And when it is said to them, "Come to what God has revealed, and to the Messenger," they say, "Sufficient for us is what we found our forefathers upon." Even if their forefathers knew nothing, and were not guided?

105. O you who believe! You are responsible for your own souls. He who has strayed cannot harm you if you are guided. To God is you return, all of you, and He will inform you of what you used to do.

106. O you who believe! When death approaches one of you, let two reliable persons from among you act as witnesses to the making of a bequest, or two persons from another people if you are travelling in the land and the event of death approaches you. Engage them after the pray-

er; and if you have doubts, let them swear by God, "We will not sell our testimony for any price, even if it was a near relative; nor will we hide the testimony of God, for then we would be sinners."

107. If it is discovered that they are guilty of perjury: let two others take their place, two from among those responsible for the claim, and have them swear by God, "Our testimony is more truthful than their testimony, and we will not be biased, for then we would be wrongdoers."

108. That makes it more likely that they will give true testimony, fearing that their oaths might be contradicted by subsequent oaths. So fear God, and listen. God does not guide the disobedient people.

109. On the Day when God will gather the messengers, then say, "What response were you given?" They will say, "We have no knowledge, it is you who are the Knower of the unseen."

110. When God will say, "O Jesus son of Mary, recall My favor upon you and upon your mother, how I supported you with the Holy Spirit. You spoke to the people from the crib, and in maturity. How I taught you the Scripture and wisdom, and the Torah and the Gospel. And recall that you molded from clay the shape of a bird, by My leave, and then you breathed into it, and it became a bird, by My leave. And you healed the blind and the leprous, by My leave; and you revived the dead, by My leave. And recall that I restrained the Children of Israel from you when you brought them the clear miracles. But those who disbelieved among them said, 'This is nothing but obvious sorcery.'"

111. "And when I inspired the disciples: 'Believe in Me and in My Messenger.' They said, 'We have believed, so bear witness that We have submitted.'"

112. "And when the disciples said, 'O Jesus son of Mary, is your Lord able to bring down for us a feast from heaven?' He said, 'Fear God, if you are believers.'"

113. They said, "We wish to eat from it, so that our hearts may be reassured, and know that you have told us the truth, and be among those who witness it."

114. Jesus son of Mary said, "O God, our Lord, send down for us a table from heaven, to be a festival for us, for the first of us, and the last of us, and a sign from You; and provide for us, You are the Best of providers."

115. God said, "I will send it down to you. But whoever among you disbelieves thereafter, I will punish him with a punishment the like of which I never punish any other being."

116. And God will say, "O Jesus son of Mary, did you say to the people, 'Take me and my mother as gods rather than God?'" He will say, "Glory be to You! It is not for me to say what I have no right to. Had I said it, You would have known it. You know what is in my soul, and I do not know what is in your soul. You are the Knower of the hidden.

117. I only told them what You commanded me: that you shall worship God, my Lord and your Lord. And I was a witness over them while I was among them, but when You took me to Yourself, you became the Watcher over them; for You are Witness over everything.

118. If You punish them, they are Your servants; but if You forgive them, You are the Mighty and Wise."

119. God will say, "This is a Day when the truthful will benefit from their truthfulness." They will have Gardens beneath which rivers flow, wherein they will remain forever. God is pleased with them,

and they are pleased with Him. That is the great attainment.

120. To God belongs the sovereignty of the heavens and the earth and what lies in them, and He has power over everything.

6. LIVESTOCK
(al-An'am)

In the name of God,
the Gracious, the Merciful.

1. Praise be to God, Who created the heavens and the earth, and made the darkness and the light; yet those who disbelieve ascribe equals to their Lord.

2. It is He who created you from clay, then decided a term—a term determined by him. Yet you doubt.

3. He is God in the heavens and the earth. He knows what you keep secret and what you make public; and He knows what you earn.

4. Not one of their Lord's signs comes to them, but they turn away from it.

5. They denied the truth when it has come to them; but soon will reach them the news of what they used to ridicule.

6. Have they not considered how many generations We destroyed before them? We had established them on earth more firmly than We established you, and We sent the clouds pouring down abundant rain on them, and We made rivers flow beneath them. But We destroyed them for their sins, and established other civilizations after them.

7. Had We sent down upon you a book on paper, and they had touched it with their hands, those who disbelieve would have said, "This is nothing but plain magic."

8. And they say, "Why was an angel not sent down to him." Had We sent down an angel, the matter would have been settled, and they would not have been reprieved.

9. Had We made him an angel, We would have made him a man, and confused them when they are already confused.

10. Messengers before you were ridiculed, but those who mocked them became besieged by what they ridiculed.

11. Say, "Travel the earth and observe the final fate of the deniers."

12. Say, "To whom belongs what is in the heavens and the earth?" Say, "To God." He has inscribed for Himself mercy. He will gather you to the Day of Resurrection, in which there is no doubt. Those who lost their souls do not believe.

13. To Him belongs whatever rests in the night and the day. He is the Hearing, the Knowing.

14. Say, "Shall I take for myself a protector other than God, Originator of the heavens and the earth, and it is He who feeds and is not fed?" Say, "I am instructed to be the first of those who submit." And do not be among the idolaters.

15. Say, "I fear, should I defy my Lord, the punishment of a tremendous Day."

16. Whoever is spared on that Day—He had mercy on him. That is the clear victory.

17. If God touches you with adversity, none can remove it except He. And if He touches you with good—He is Capable of everything.

18. He is the Supreme over His servants. He is the Wise, the Expert.

19. Say, "What thing is more solemn in testimony?" Say, "God is Witness between you and between me. This Quran was revealed to me, that I may warn you with it, and whomever it may reach. Do you in-

deed testify that there are other gods with God?" Say, "I myself do not testify." Say, "He is but One god, and I am innocent of your idolatry."

20. Those to whom We have given the Book recognize it as they recognize their own children; but those who have lost their souls do not believe.

21. Who does greater wrong than someone who fabricates lies against God, or denies His revelations? The wrongdoers will not succeed.

22. On the Day when We gather them all together, then say to the idolaters, "Where are your idols, those you used to claim?"

23. Then their only argument will be to say, "By God, our Lord, we were not idolaters."

24. Look how they lied to themselves. And what they invented deserted them.

25. Among them are those who listen to you, but We place covers over their hearts, to prevent them from understanding it, and heaviness in their ears. Even if they see every sign, they will not believe in it. Until, when they come to you, to argue with you, those who disbelieve will say, "These are nothing but myths of the ancients."

26. They keep others from it, and avoid it themselves; but they ruin only their own souls, and they do not realize.

27. If only you could see, when they are made to stand before the Fire; they will say, "If only we could be sent back, and not reject the revelations of our Lord, and be among the faithful."

28. What they used to conceal before will become clear to them. And even if they were sent back, they would revert to what they were forbidden. They are liars.

29. And they say, "There is nothing but our life in this world, and we will not be resurrected."

30. If only you could see, when they are stationed before their Lord. He will say, "Is this not real?" They will say, "Yes indeed, by our Lord." He will say, "Then taste the torment for having disbelieved."

31. Losers are those who deny the encounter with God. Then, when the Hour comes upon them suddenly, they will say, "Alas for us, how we have neglected it." And they will carry their burdens on their backs—evil is what they carry.

32. The life of this world is nothing but game and distraction, but the Home of the Hereafter is better for those who are righteous. Do you not understand?

33. We know that what they say grieves you. It is not you they reject, but it is God's revelations that the wicked deny.

34. Other messengers before you were rejected, but they endured rejection and persecution until Our help came to them. There can be no change to God's words. News of the Messengers has already reached you.

35. If you find their rejection hard to bear, then if you can, seek a tunnel into the earth, or a stairway into the heaven, and bring them a sign. Had God willed, He could have gathered them to guidance. So do not be of the ignorant.

36. Only those who listen will respond. As for the dead, God will resurrect them; then to Him they will be returned.

37. And they say, "If only a sign could come down to him from his Lord." Say, "God is Able to send down a sign, but most of them do not know."

38. There is no animal on land, nor a bird flying with its wings, but are communities like you. We neglected nothing in the Book. Then to their Lord they will be gathered.

39. Those who reject Our revelations are deaf and dumb, in total darkness. Whomever God wills, He leaves astray; and whomever He wills, He sets on a straight path.

40. Say, "Have you considered? if God's punishment came upon you, or the Hour overtook you, would you call upon any other than God, if you are sincere?"

41. In fact, it is Him you will call upon; and if He wills, he will remove what you called Him for, and you will forget what you idolized.

42. We sent messengers to communities before you, and We afflicted them with suffering and hardship, that they may humble themselves.

43. If only, when Our calamity came upon them, they humbled themselves. But their hearts hardened, and Satan made their deeds appear good to them.

44. Then, when they disregarded what they were reminded of, We opened for them the gates of all things. Until, when they delighted in what they were given, We seized them suddenly; and at once, they were in despair.

45. Thus the last remnant of the people who did wrong was cut off. And praise be to God, Lord of the Worlds.

46. Say, "Have you considered? If God took away your hearing and your sight, and set a seal on your hearts, what god other than God would restore them to you?" Note how We explain the revelations in various ways, yet they still turn away.

47. Say, "Have you considered? if God's punishment descended on you suddenly or gradually, would any be destroyed except the wrongdoing people?"

48. We sent the messengers only as bearers of good news and as warners. Those who believe and reform have nothing to fear, nor shall they grieve.

49. But as for those who reject Our revelations, torment will afflict them because of their defiance.

50. Say, "I do not say to you that I possess the treasuries of God, nor do I know the future, nor do I say to you that I am an angel. I only follow what is inspired to me." Say, "Are the blind and the seeing alike? Do you not think?"

51. And warn with it those who fear to be gathered before their Lord—they have no protector or intercessor apart from him—perhaps they will grow in piety.

52. And do not drive away those who call upon their Lord, morning and evening, seeking His attention. You are not accountable for them in any way, nor are they accountable for you in any way. If you drive them away, you would be one of the unjust.

53. Thus We try some of them by means of others, that they may say, "Are these the ones whom God has favored from among us?" Is God not aware of the appreciative?

54. When those who believe in Our revelations come to you, say, "Peace be upon you, your Lord has prescribed mercy for Himself. Whoever among you does wrong out of ignorance, and then repents afterwards and reforms—He is Forgiving and Merciful."

55. Thus We explain the revelations, and expose the path of the unrighteous.

56. Say, "I am forbidden from worshiping those you pray to besides God." Say, "I will not follow your desires; else I would be lost and not be of those guided."

57. Say, "I stand on clear evidence from my Lord, and you have rejected Him. I do not possess what you seek me to hasten; the

decision belongs solely to God. He states the truth, and He is the Best of Judges."

58. Say, "If I possessed what you seek me to hasten, the matter between you and me would have been settled. God is well aware of the unjust."

59. With Him are the keys of the unseen. None knows them except He. And He knows everything on land and in the sea. Not a leaf falls without His knowledge, nor is there a grain in the darkness of the earth, nor is there anything wet or dry, but it is in a clear record.

60. It is He Who takes you by night, and He knows what you earn by day. Then He raises you up in it, until a fixed term is fulfilled. Then to Him is your return, then He will inform you of what you used to do.

61. He is the Conqueror over His servants, and He sends guardians over you, until, when death overtakes one of you, Our envoys take him away, and they never fail.

62. Then they are brought back to God, their true Master. Unquestionably, His is the judgment, and He is the Swiftest of reckoners.

63. Say, "Who delivers you from the darkness of land and sea?" You call upon Him humbly and inwardly: "If He delivers us from this, We will surely be among the thankful."

64. Say, "It is God who delivers you from it, and from every disaster. Yet then you associate others with Him."

65. Say, "He is Able to send upon you an affliction, from above you, or from under your feet. Or He can divide you into factions, and make you taste the violence of one another. Note how We explain the revelations, so that they may understand."

66. But your people rejected it, though it is the truth. Say, "I am not responsible for you."

67. For every happening is a finality, and you will surely know.

68. When you encounter those who gossip about Our revelations, turn away from them, until they engage in another topic. But should Satan make you forget, do not sit after the recollection with the wicked people.

69. The righteous are in no way accountable for them; it is only a reminder, that they may be careful.

70. So leave alone those who take their religion for play and pastime, and whom the worldly life has deceived. But remind with it, lest a soul becomes damned on account of what it has earned. It has no helper or intercessor besides God. Even if it offers every equivalent, none will be accepted from it. These are the ones who are delivered to perdition by their actions. They will have a drink of scalding water, and a painful punishment, because they used to disbelieve.

71. Say, "Shall we invoke besides God something that can neither benefit us nor harm us, and turn back on our heels after God has guided us, like someone seduced by the devils and confused on earth, who has friends calling him to guidance: 'Come to us'?" Say, "The guidance of God is the guidance, and we are commanded to surrender to the Lord of the Universe."

72. "And to perform the prayers, and to revere Him; it is to Him that you will be gathered."

73. It is He who created the heavens and the earth in truth. On the Day when He says: "Be," it will be. His saying is the truth, and His is the sovereignty on the Day when the trumpet is blown. The

Knower of secrets and declarations. He is the Wise, the Expert.

74. Abraham said to his father Azar, "Do you take idols for gods? I see that you and your people are in evident error."

75. Thus We showed Abraham the empire of the heavens and the earth, that he might be one of those with certainty.

76. When the night fell over him, he saw a planet. He said, "This is my lord." But when it set, he said, "I do not love those that set."

77. Then, when he saw the moon rising, he said, "This is my lord." But when it set, he said, "If my Lord does not guide me, I will be one of the erring people."

78. Then, when he saw the sun rising, he said, "This is my lord, this is bigger." But when it set, he said, "O my people, I am innocent of your idolatry.

79. I have directed my attention towards Him Who created the heavens and the earth—a monotheist—and I am not of the idolaters."

80. And his people argued with him. He said, "Do you argue with me about God, when He has guided me? I do not fear what you associate with Him, unless my Lord wills it. My Lord comprehends all things in knowledge. Will you not reconsider?

81. And why should I fear those you associate with Him, and you do not fear associating others with God for which He sent down to you no authority? Which side is more entitled to security, if you are aware?"

82. Those who believe, and do not obscure their faith with wrongdoing—those will have security, and they are guided.

83. That was Our argument which We gave to Abraham against his people. We elevate

by degrees whomever We will. Your Lord is Wise and Informed.

84. And We gave him Isaac and Jacob—each of them We guided. And We guided Noah previously; and from his descendants David, and Solomon, and Job, and Joseph, and Moses, and Aaron. Thus We reward the righteous.

85. And Zechariah, and John, and Jesus, and Elias—every one of them was of the upright.

86. And Ishmael, and Elijah, and Jonah, and Lot—We favored each one of them over all other people.

87. And of their ancestors, and their descendants, and their siblings—We chose them, and guided them to a straight path.

88. Such is God's guidance. He guides with it whomever He wills of His servants. Had they associated, their deeds would have gone in vain.

89. Those are they to whom We gave the Book, and wisdom, and prophethood. If these reject them, We have entrusted them to others who do not reject them.

90. Those are they whom God has guided, so follow their guidance. Say, "I ask of you no compensation for it. It is just a reminder for all mankind."

91. They do not value God as He should be valued, when they say, "God did not reveal anything to any human being." Say, "Who revealed the Scripture which Moses brought—a light and guidance for humanity? You put it on scrolls, displaying them, yet concealing much. And you were taught what you did not know—neither you, nor your ancestors. Say, "God," then leave them toying away in their speculation.

92. This too is a Scripture that We revealed—blessed—verifying what preceded

it, that you may warn the Mother of Cities and all around it. Those who believe in the Hereafter believe in it, and are dedicated to their prayers.

93. Who does greater wrong than someone who invents falsehood against God, or says, "It was revealed to me," when nothing was revealed to him, or says, "I will reveal the like of what God revealed"? If only you could see the wrongdoers in the floods of death, as the angels with arms outstretched: "Give up your souls. Today you are being repaid with the torment of shame for having said about God other than the truth, and for being too proud to accept His revelations."

94. "You have come to Us individually, just as We created you the first time, leaving behind you everything We gave you. And We do not see with you your intercessors—those you claimed were your partners. The link between you is cut, and what you had asserted has failed you."

95. It is God Who splits the grain and the seed. He brings the living from the dead, and He brings the dead from the living. Such is God. So how could you deviate?

96. It is He Who breaks the dawn. And He made the night for rest, and the sun and the moon for calculation. Such is the disposition of the Almighty, the All-Knowing.

97. And it is He Who created the stars for you, that you may be guided by them in the darkness of land and sea. We thus explain the revelations for people who know.

98. And it is He who produced you from a single person, then a repository, then a depository. We have detailed the revelations for people who understand.

99. And it is He who sends down water from the sky. With it We produce vegetation of all kinds, from which We bring greenery, from which We produce grains in clusters. And palm-trees with hanging clusters, and vineyards, and olives, and pomegranates—similar and dissimilar. Watch their fruits as they grow and ripen. Surely in this are signs for people who believe.

100. Yet they attributed to God partners—the sprites—although He created them. And they invented for Him sons and daughters, without any knowledge. Glory be to Him. He is exalted, beyond what they describe.

101. Originator of the heavens and the earth—how can He have a son when He never had a companion? He created all things, and He has knowledge of all things.

102. Such is God, your Lord. There is no god except He, the Creator of all things, so worship Him. He is responsible for everything.

103. No vision can grasp Him, but His grasp is over all vision. He is the Subtle, the Expert.

104. "Insights have come to you from your Lord. Whoever sees, it is to the benefit of his soul, and whoever remains blind, it is to its detriment. I am not a guardian over you."

105. We thus diversify the revelations, lest they say, "You have studied," and to clarify them for people who know.

106. Follow what was revealed to you from your Lord. There is no god but He. And turn away from the polytheists.

107. Had God willed, they would not have practiced idolatry. We did not appoint you as a guardian over them, and you are not a manager over them.

108. Do not insult those they call upon besides God, lest they insult God out of hostility and ignorance. We made attractive to

every community their deeds. Then to their Lord is their return; and He will inform them of what they used to do.

109. They swear by God, with their most solemn oaths, that if a miracle were to come to them, they would believe in it. Say, "The miracles are only with God." But how do you know? Even if it did come, they still would not believe.

110. And We turn away their hearts and their visions, as they refused to believe in it the first time, and We leave them blundering in their rebellion.

111. Even if We sent down the angels to them, and the dead spoke to them, and We gathered all things before them, they still would not believe, unless God wills; but most of them are ignorant.

112. Likewise, We have assigned for every prophet an enemy—human and jinn devils—inspiring one another with fancy words in order to deceive. But had your Lord willed, they would not have done it. So leave them to their fabrications.

113. So that the hearts of those who do not believe in the Hereafter may incline to it, and be content with it, and that they may perpetrate whatever they perpetrate.

114. "Shall I seek a judge other than God, when He is the One who revealed to you the Book, explained in detail?" Those to whom We gave the Book know that it is the truth revealed from your Lord. So do not be of those who doubt.

115. The Word of your Lord has been completed, in truth and justice. There is no changing to His words. He is the Hearer, the Knower.

116. If you were to obey most of those on earth, they would divert you from God's path. They follow nothing but assumption, and they only conjecture.

117. Your Lord knows best who strays from His path, and He knows best the guided ones.

118. So eat of that over which the Name of God was pronounced, if you indeed believe in His revelations.

119. And why should you not eat of that over which the Name of God is pronounced, when He has detailed for you what is prohibited for you, unless you are compelled by necessity? Many lead astray with their opinions, through lack of knowledge. Your Lord knows best the transgressors.

120. So abandon sin, outward and inward. Those who commit sins will be repaid for what they used to perpetrate.

121. And do not eat from that over which the Name of God was not pronounced, for it is abomination. The devils inspire their followers to argue with you; but if you obey them, you would be polytheists.

122. Is he who was dead, then We gave him life, and made for him a light by which he walks among the people, like he who is in total darkness, and cannot get out of it? Thus the doings of disbelievers are made to appear good to them.

123. And thus We set up in every city its leading wicked sinners, to conspire in it, but they conspire only against themselves, and they do not realize it.

124. When a sign comes to them, they say, "We will not believe unless we are given the like of what was given to God's messengers." God knows best where to place His message. Humiliation from God and severe torment will afflict the criminals for their scheming.

125. Whomever God desires to guide, He spreads open his heart to Islam; and whomever He desires to misguide, He

makes his heart narrow, constricted, as though he were climbing up the sky. God thus lays defilement upon those who do not believe.

126. This is the straight path of your Lord. We have explained the revelations in detail for people who recollect.

127. For them is the Home of Peace with their Lord, and He is their Master— because of what they used to do.

128. On the Day when He gathers them all together: "O assembly of jinn, you have exploited multitudes of humans." Their adherents among mankind will say, "Our Lord, we have profited from one another, but we have reached the term that you have assigned for us." He will say, "The Fire is your dwelling, wherein you will remain, except as God wills. Your Lord is Wise and Informed.

129. Thus We make some of the wrongdoers befriend one another, because of what they used to do.

130. "O assembly of jinn and humans, did there not come to you messengers from among you, relating to you My revelations, and warning you of the meeting of this Day of yours?" They will say, "We testify against ourselves." The life of the world seduced them. They will testify against themselves that they were disbelievers.

131. That is because your Lord would not destroy towns for injustice while their inhabitants are unaware.

132. They all have ranks according to what they did; and your Lord is not unaware of what they do.

133. Your Lord is the Rich Beyond Need, the Possessor of Mercy. If He wills, he can do away with you, and substitute whomever He wills in your place, just as He produced you from the descendants of another people.

134. What you are promised is coming, and you cannot thwart it.

135. Say, "O my people! Work according to your ability, and so will I." You will come to know to whom will belong the sequel of the abode." The wrongdoers will not prevail.

136. And they set aside for God a share of the crops and the livestock He created, and say, "This is for God," according to their claim, "and this is for our idols." But the share of their idols does not reach God, yet the share of God reaches their idols. Evil is their judgment.

137. Likewise, their idols entice many idolaters to kill their children, in order to lead them to their ruin, and confuse them in their religion. Had God willed, they would not have done it; so leave them to their fraud.

138. And they say, "These animals and crops are restricted; none may eat them except those we permit," by their claims, and animals whose backs are forbidden, and animals over which they do not pronounce the name of God—fabricating lies against Him. He will repay them for what they used to invent.

139. And they say, "What lies in the wombs of these animals is exclusively for our males, and prohibited to our wives." But if it is stillborn, they can share in it. He will surely punish them for their allegations. He is Wise and Knowing.

140. Lost are those who kill their children foolishly, with no basis in knowledge, and forbid what God has provided for them— innovations about God. They have gone astray. They are not guided.

141. It is He who produces gardens, both cultivated and wild, and date-palms, and crops of diverse tastes, and olives and pomegranates, similar and dissimilar. Eat of its fruit when it yields, and give its due on the day of its harvest, and do not waste. He does not love the wasteful.

142. Among the livestock are some for transportation, and some for clothing. Eat of what God has provided for you, and do not follow the footsteps of Satan. He is to you an open enemy.

143. Eight pairs: two of the sheep, and two of the goats. Say, "Did He forbid the two males, or the two females, or what the wombs of the two females contain? Inform me with knowledge, if you are truthful."

144. And two of the camels, and two of the cattle. Say, "Did He forbid the two males, or the two females, or what the wombs of the two females contain? Were you present when God enjoined this upon you?" Who does greater wrong than he who invents lies and attributes them to God, in order to mislead people without knowledge? God does not guide the wicked people.

145. Say, "In what was revealed to me, I find nothing forbidden to a consumer who eats it, except carrion, or spilled blood, or the flesh of swine—because it is impure—or a sinful offering dedicated to other than God. But if someone is compelled by necessity, without being deliberate or malicious—your Lord is Forgiving and Merciful.

146. For the Jews We forbade everything with claws. As of cattle and sheep, We forbade them their fat, except what adheres to their backs, or the entrails, or what is mixed with bone. This is how We penalized them for their inequity. We are indeed truthful.

147. If they accuse you of lying, say, "Your Lord is Possessor of infinite mercy, but His wrath cannot be averted from the guilty people."

148. The polytheists will say, "Had God willed, we would not have practiced idolatry, nor would have our forefathers, nor would we have prohibited anything." Likewise those before them lied, until they tasted Our might. Say, "Do you have any knowledge that you can produce for us? You follow nothing but conjecture, and you only guess."

149. Say, "To God belongs the conclusive argument. Had He willed, He would have guided you all."

150. Say, "Produce your witnesses who would testify that God has prohibited this." If they testify, do not testify with them. And do not follow the whims of those who deny Our revelation, and those who do not believe in the Hereafter, and those who equate others with their Lord.

151. Say, "Come, let me tell you what your Lord has forbidden you: that you associate nothing with Him; that you honor your parents; that you do not kill your children because of poverty—We provide for you and for them; that you do not come near indecencies, whether outward or inward; and that you do not kill the soul which God has sanctified—except in the course of justice. All this He has enjoined upon you, so that you may understand."

152. And do not come near the property of the orphan, except with the best intentions, until he reaches maturity. And give full weight and full measure, equitably. We do not burden any soul beyond its capacity. And when you speak, be fair, even if it concerns a close relative. And fulfill your covenant with God. All this He has en-

joined upon you, so that you may take heed.

153. This is My path, straight, so follow it. And do not follow the other paths, lest they divert you from His path. All this He has enjoined upon you, that you may refrain from wrongdoing.

154. Then We gave Moses the Scripture, perfect for the righteous, and explaining everything clearly, and a beacon, and mercy, that they may believe in the encounter with their Lord.

155. This too is a blessed Scripture that We revealed; so follow it, and be righteous, that you may receive mercy.

156. Lest you say, "The Scripture was revealed only to two parties before us, and we were unaware of their teachings."

157. Or lest you say, "Had the Scripture been revealed to us, we would have been better guided than they." Clarification has come to you from your Lord, and guidance, and mercy. Who, then, does greater wrong than he who gives the lie to God's messages, and turns away from them? We will repay those who turn away from Our messages with the worst kind of punishment, because of their turning away.

158. Are they waiting for anything but for the angels to come to them, or for your Lord to arrive, or for some of your Lord's signs to come? On the Day when some of your Lord's signs come, no soul will benefit from its faith unless it had believed previously, or had earned goodness through its faith. Say, "Wait, we too are waiting."

159. As for those who divided their religion, and became sects—you have nothing to do with them. Their case rests with God; then He will inform them of what they used to do.

160. Whoever comes up with a good deed will have ten times its like; and whoever comes up with an evil deed will be repaid only with its equivalent—they will not be wronged.

161. Say, "My Lord has guided me to a straight path, an upright religion, the creed of Abraham, the monotheist, and he was no polytheist."

162. Say, "My prayer and my worship, and my life and my death, are devoted to God, the Lord of the Worlds.

163. No associate has He. Thus I am commanded, and I am the first of those who submit.

164. Say, "Am I to seek a Lord other than God, when He is the Lord of all things?" No soul gets except what it is due, and no soul bears the burdens of another. Then to your Lord is your return, then He will inform you regarding your disputes.

165. It is He who made you successors on the earth, and raised some of you in ranks over others, in order to test you throug' what He has given you. Your Lor Quick in retribution, and He is Fr and Merciful.

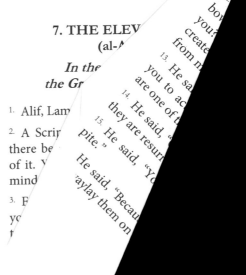

7. THE ELEV
(al-A

In the
the Gr

1. Alif, Lam

2. A Scri'
there be
of it. Y
mind

3. B
y'
t

4. How many cities have We destroyed? Our might came upon them by night, or while they were napping.

5. When Our might came upon them, their only cry was, "We were indeed wrongdoers."

6. We will question those to whom messengers were sent, and We will question the messengers.

7. We will narrate to them with knowledge, for We were never absent.

8. The scales on that Day will be just. Those whose weights are heavy—it is they who are the winners.

9. But as for those whose weights are light—it is they who have lost their souls, because they used to mistreat Our revelations.

10. We have established you firmly on earth, and made for you in it livelihood—but rarely do you give thanks.

11. We created you, then We shaped you, then We said to the angels, "Bow down before Adam;" so they bowed down, except for Satan; he was not of those who bowed down.

He said, "What prevented you from ing down when I have commanded " He said, "I am better than he; You d me from fire, and You created him ud."

d, "Get down from it! it is not for arrogantly in it. Get out! You he lowly!"

Give me respite, until the Day ected."

u are of those given res-

e you have lured me, I Your straight path.

17. Then I will come at them from before them, and from behind them, and from their right, and from their left; and you will not find most of them appreciative."

18. He said, "Get out of it, despised and vanquished. Whoever among them follows you—I will fill up Hell with you all.

19. And you, Adam, inhabit the Garden, you and your wife, and eat whatever you wish, but do not approach this tree, lest you become sinners."

20. But Satan whispered to them, to reveal to them their nakedness, which was invisible to them. He said, "Your Lord has only forbidden you this tree, lest you become angels, or become immortals."

21. And he swore to them, "I am a sincere advisor to you."

22. So he lured them with deceit. And when they tasted the tree, their nakedness became evident to them, and they began covering themselves with the leaves of the Garden. And their Lord called out to them, "Did I not forbid you from this tree, and say to you that Satan is a sworn enemy to you?"

23. They said, "Our Lord, we have done wrong to ourselves. Unless You forgive us, and have mercy on us, we will be among the losers."

24. He said, "Fall, some of you enemies to one another. On earth you will have residence and livelihood for a while."

25. He said, "Therein you will live, and therein you will die, and from it you will be brought out."

26. O children of Adam! We have provided you with clothing to cover your bodies, and for luxury. But the clothing of piety—that is best. These are some of God's revelations, so that they may take heed.

27. O Children of Adam! Do not let Satan seduce you, as he drove your parents out of the Garden, stripping them of their garments, to show them their nakedness. He sees you, him and his clan, from where you cannot see them. We have made the devils friends of those who do not believe.

28. And when they commit an indecency, they say, "We found our parents doing this, and God has commanded us to do it." Say, "God does not command indecencies. Are you attributing to God what you do not know?"

29. Say, "My Lord commands justice, and to stand devoted at every place of worship. So call upon Him, and dedicate your faith to Him alone. Just as He originated you, so you will return."

30. Some He has guided; and some have deserved misguidance. They have adopted the devils for patrons rather than God, and they assume that they are guided.

31. O Children of Adam! Dress properly at every place of worship, and eat and drink, but do not be excessive. He does not love the excessive.

32. Say, "Who forbade God's finery which He produced for His servants, and the delights of livelihood?" Say, "They are for those who believe, in this present world, but exclusively theirs on the Day of Resurrection." We thus detail the revelations for people who know.

33. Say, "My Lord has forbidden immoralities—both open and secret—and sin, and unjustified aggression, and that you associate with God anything for which He revealed no sanction, and that you say about God what you do not know."

34. For every nation is an appointed time. And when their time has come, they cannot delay it by one hour, nor can they advance it.

35. O Children of Adam! When messengers from among you come to you, relating to you My revelations—whoever practices piety and reforms—upon them shall be no fear, nor shall they grieve.

36. But as for those who reject Our revelations, and are too proud to accept them—these are the inmates of the Fire, where they will remain forever.

37. Who does greater wrong than he who invents lies about God, or denies His revelations? These—their share of the decree will reach them. Until, when Our envoys come to them, to take their souls away, they will say, "Where are they whom you used to pray to besides God?" They will say, "They have abandoned us," and they will testify against themselves that they were faithless.

38. He will say, "Join the crowds of jinn and humans who have gone into the Fire before you." Every time a crowd enters, it will curse its sister-crowd. Until, when they are all in it, the last of them will say to the first of them, "Our Lord, these are the ones who misled us, so inflict on them a double punishment in the Fire." He will say, "Each will have a double, but you do not know."

39. The first of them will say to the last of them, "You have no advantage over us, so taste the torment for what you used to earn."

40. Those who reject Our revelations and are too arrogant to uphold them—the doors of Heaven will not be opened for them, nor will they enter Paradise, until the camel passes through the eye of the needle. Thus We repay the guilty.

41. For them is a couch of hell, and above them are sheets of fire. Thus We repay the wrongdoers.

42. As for those who believe and do righteous works—We never burden any soul beyond its capacity—these are the inhabitants of the Garden; abiding therein eternally.

43. We will remove whatever rancor is in their hearts. Rivers will flow beneath them. And they will say, "Praise be to God, who has guided us to this. Had God not guided us, we would never be guided. The messengers of our Lord did come with the truth." And it will be proclaimed to them, "This is the Garden you are made to inherit, on account of what you used to do."

44. And the inhabitants of the Garden will call out to the inmates of the Fire, "We have found what our Lord promised us to be true; did you find what your Lord promised you to be true?" They will say, "Yes." Thereupon a caller will announce in their midst, "The curse of God is upon the wrongdoers."

45. "Those who hinder from the path of God, and seek to distort it, and who deny the Hereafter."

46. And between them is a partition, and on the Elevations are men who recognize everyone by their features. And they will call to the inhabitants of the Garden, "Peace be upon you." They have not entered it, but they are hoping.

47. And when their eyes are directed towards the inmates of the Fire, they will say, "Our Lord, do not place us among the wrongdoing people."

48. And the dwellers of the Elevations will call to men they recognize by their features, saying, "Your hoardings did not avail you, nor did your arrogance."

49. "Are these the ones you swore God will not touch with mercy?" "Enter the Garden; you have nothing to fear, and you will not grieve."

50. The inmates of the Fire will call on the inhabitants of the Garden, "Pour some water over us, or some of what God has provided for you." They will say, "God has forbidden them for the disbelievers."

51. Those who took their religion lightly, and in jest, and whom the worldly life deceived. Today We will ignore them, as they ignored the meeting on this Day of theirs, and they used to deny Our revelations.

52. We have given them a Scripture, which We detailed with knowledge—guidance and mercy for people who believe.

53. Are they waiting for anything but its fulfillment? The Day its fulfillment comes true, those who disregarded it before will say, "The messengers of our Lord did come with the truth. Have we any intercessors to intercede for us? Or, could we be sent back, to behave differently from the way we behaved before?" They ruined their souls, and what they used to invent has failed them.

54. Your Lord is God, He who created the heavens and the earth in six days, then established Himself on the Throne. The night overtakes the day, as it pursues it persistently; and the sun, and the moon, and the stars are subservient by His command. His is the creation, and His is the command. Blessed is God, Lord of all beings.

55. Call upon your Lord humbly and privately. He does not love the aggressors.

56. And do not corrupt on earth after its reformation, and pray to Him with fear and hope. God's mercy is close to the doers of good.

57. It is He who sends the wind ahead of His mercy. Then, when they have gathered up heavy clouds, We drive them to a dead land, where We make water come down, and with it We bring out all kinds of fruits.

Thus We bring out the dead—perhaps you will reflect.

58. As for the good land, it yields its produce by the leave of its Lord. But as for the bad, it produces nothing but hardship and misery. Thus We explain the revelations in various ways—for people who are thankful.

59. We sent Noah to his people. He said, "O my people, worship God; you have no god other than Him. I fear for you the punishment of a tremendous Day."

60. The dignitaries among his people said, "We see that you are in obvious error."

61. He said, "O my people, I am not in error, but I am a messenger from the Lord of the Worlds."

62. "I deliver to you the messages of my Lord, and I advise you, and I know from God what you do not know."

63. "Do you wonder that a reminder has come to you from your Lord, through a man from among you, to warn you, and to lead you to righteousness, so that you may attain mercy?"

64. But they called him a liar. So We saved him and those with him in the Ark, and We drowned those who rejected Our revelations. They were blind people.

65. And to Aad, their brother Hud. He said, "O my people, worship God; you have no god other than Him. Will you not take heed?"

66. The elite of his people who disbelieved said, "We see foolishness in you, and we think that you are a liar."

67. He said, "O my people, there is no foolishness in me, but I am a messenger from the Lord of the Worlds.

68. "I convey to you the messages of my Lord, and I am a trustworthy adviser to you."

69. "Are you surprised that a reminder has come to you from your Lord, through a man from among you, to warn you? Remember how He made you successors after the people of Noah, and increased you greatly in stature. And remember God's blessings, so that you may prosper."

70. They said, "Did you come to us to make us worship God alone, and abandon what our ancestors used to worship? Then bring us what you threaten us with, if you are truthful."

71. He said, "Condemnation and wrath have befallen you from your Lord. Are you arguing with me over names, which you and your ancestors invented, for which God sent down no authority? Just wait; I am waiting with you."

72. So We saved him and those with him, by mercy from Us, and We cut off the roots of those who rejected Our revelations and were not believers.

73. And to Thamood, their brother Saleh. He said, "O my people, worship God; you have no god other than Him. Clarification has come to you from your Lord. This she-camel of God is a sign for you. So leave her to graze on God's earth, and do her no harm, lest a painful penalty seizes you."

74. And remember how He made you successors after Aad, and settled you in the land. You make for yourselves mansions on its plains, and carve out dwellings in the mountains. So remember God's benefits, and do not roam the earth corruptingly."

75. The elite of his people, who were arrogant, said to the common people who had believed, "Do you know that Saleh is sent

from his Lord?" They said, "We are believers in what he was sent with."

76. Those who were arrogant said, "We reject what you believe in."

77. So they hamstrung the she-camel, and defied the command of their Lord, and said, "O Saleh, bring upon us what you threaten us with, if you are one of the messengers."

78. Whereupon the quake overtook them, and they became lifeless bodies in their homes.

79. Then he turned away from them, and said, "O my people, I have delivered to you the message of my Lord, and I have advised you, but you do not like those who give advice."

80. And Lot, when he said to his people, "Do you commit lewdness no people anywhere have ever committed before you?"

81. "You lust after men rather than women. You are an excessive people."

82. And his people's only answer was to say, "Expel them from your town. They are purist people."

83. But We saved him and his family, except for his wife; she was of those who lagged behind.

84. And We rained down on them a rain; note the consequences for the sinners.

85. And to Median, their brother Shuaib. He said, "O my people, worship God; you have no god other than Him. A clear proof has come to you from your Lord. Give full measure and weight, and do not cheat people out of their rights, and do not corrupt the land once it has been set right. This is better for you, if you are believers."

86. "And do not lurk on every path, making threats and turning away from the path of God those who believe in Him,

seeking to distort it. And remember how you were few, and how He made you numerous. So note the consequences for the corrupters."

87. "Since some of you believed in what I was sent with, and some did not believe, be patient until God judges between us; for He is the Best of Judges."

88. The arrogant elite among his people said, "O Shuaib, We will evict you from our town, along with those who believe with you, unless you return to our religion." He said, "Even if we are unwilling?"

89. "We would be fabricating falsehood against God, if we were to return to your religion, after God has saved us from it. It is not for us to return to it, unless God, our Lord, wills. Our Lord embraces all things in knowledge. In God we place our trust. Our Lord, decide between us and our people in truth, for You are the Best of Deciders."

90. The elite of his people who disbelieved said, "If you follow Shuaib, you will be losers."

91. Thereupon, the quake struck them; and they became lifeless bodies in their homes.

92. Those who rejected Shuaib—as if they never prospered therein. Those who rejected Shuaib—it was they who were the losers.

93. So he turned away from them, and said, "O my people, I have delivered to you the messages of my Lord, and I have advised you, so why should I grieve over a disbelieving people?"

94. We did not send any prophet to any town but We afflicted its people with misery and adversity, so that they may humble themselves.

95. Then We substituted prosperity in place of hardship. Until they increased in

number, and said, "Adversity and prosperity has touched our ancestors." Then We seized them suddenly, while they were unaware.

96. Had the people of the towns believed and turned righteous, We would have opened for them the blessings of the heaven and the earth; but they rejected the truth, so We seized them by what they were doing.

97. Do the people of the towns feel secure that Our might will not come upon them by night, while they sleep?

98. Do the people of the towns feel secure that Our might will not come upon them by day, while they play?

99. Do they feel safe from God's plan? None feels safe from God's plan except the losing people.

100. Is it not guidance for those who inherit the land after its inhabitants, that if We willed, We could strike them for their sins? And seal up their hearts, so that they would not hear?

101. These towns—We narrate to you some of their tales. Their messengers came to them with the clear signs, but they would not believe in what they had rejected previously. Thus God seals the hearts of the disbelievers.

102. We found most of them untrue to their covenants; We found most of them corrupt.

103. Then, after them, We sent Moses with Our miracles to Pharaoh and his establishment, but they denounced them. So consider the end of the evildoers.

104. Moses said, "O Pharaoh, I am a messenger from the Lord of the Worlds."

105. "It is only proper that I should not say about God anything other than the truth. I have come to you with clear evidence from your Lord, so let the Children of Israel go with me."

106. He said, "If you brought a miracle, then present it, if you are truthful."

107. So he threw his staff, and it was an apparent serpent.

108. And He pulled out his hand, and it was white to the onlookers.

109. The notables among Pharaoh's people said, "This is really a skilled magician."

110. "He wants to evict you from your land, so what do you recommend?"

111. They said, "Put him off, and his brother, and send heralds to the cities."

112. "And let them bring every skillful magician."

113. The magicians came to Pharaoh, and said, "Surely there is a reward for us, if we are the victors."

114. He said, "Yes, and you will be among my favorites."

115. They said, "O Moses, either you throw, or we are the ones to throw."

116. He said, "You throw." And when they threw, they beguiled the eyes of the people, and intimidated them, and produced a mighty magic.

117. And We inspired Moses, "Throw your staff," and at once, it swallowed what they were faking.

118. So the truth came to pass, and what they were producing came to nothing.

119. There they were defeated, and utterly reduced.

120. And the magicians fell to their knees.

121. They said, "We have believed in the Lord of the Worlds."

122. "The Lord of Moses and Aaron."

123. Pharaoh said, "Did you believe in Him before I have given you permission? This is surely a conspiracy you schemed in the city, in order to expel its people from it. You will surely know."

124. "I will cut off your hands and your feet on opposite sides, then I will crucify you all."

125. They said, "It is to our Lord that we will return."

126. "You are taking vengeance on us only because we have believed in the signs of our Lord when they have come to us." "Our Lord, pour out patience upon us, and receive our souls in submission."

127. The chiefs of Pharaoh's people said, "Will you let Moses and his people cause trouble in the land, and forsake you and your gods?" He said, "We will kill their sons, and spare their women. We have absolute power over them."

128. Moses said to his people, "Seek help in God, and be patient. The earth belongs to God. He gives it in inheritance to whomever He wills of His servants, and the future belongs to the righteous."

129. They said, "We were persecuted before you came to us, and after you came to us." He said, "Perhaps your Lord will destroy your enemy, and make you successors in the land; then He will see how you behave."

130. And We afflicted the people of Pharaoh with barren years, and shortage of crops, that they may take heed.

131. When something good came their way, they said, "This is ours," and when something bad happened to them, they ascribed the evil omen to Moses and those with him. In fact, their omen is with God, but most of them do not know.

132. And they said, "No matter what sign you bring us, to bewitch us with, we will not believe in you."

133. So We let loose upon them the flood, and the locusts, and the lice, and the frogs, and blood—all explicit signs—but they were too arrogant. They were a sinful people.

134. Whenever a plague befell them, they would say, "O Moses, pray to your Lord for us, according to the covenant He made with you. If you lift the plague from us, we will believe in you, and let the Children of Israel go with you."

135. But when We lifted the plague from them, for a term they were to fulfill, they broke their promise.

136. So We took vengeance on them, and drowned them in the sea—because they rejected Our signs, and paid no heed to them.

137. And We made the oppressed people inherit the eastern and western parts of the land, which We had blessed. Thus the fair promise of your Lord to the Children of Israel was fulfilled, because of their endurance. And We destroyed what Pharaoh and his people had built, and what they had harvested.

138. And We delivered the Children of Israel across the sea. And when they came upon a people who were devoted to some statues of theirs, they said, "O Moses, make for us a god, as they have gods." He said, "You are truly an ignorant people."

139. "What these people are concerned with is perdition, and their deeds are based on falsehoods."

140. He said, "Shall I seek for you a god other than God, when He has favored you over all other people?"

141. Remember how We saved you from Pharaoh's people, who subjected you to the worst of sufferings—killing your sons and sparing your women. In that was a tremendous trial from your Lord.

142. And We appointed to Moses thirty nights, and completed them with ten; and thus the time appointed by his Lord was forty nights. And Moses said to his brother Aaron: "Take my place among my people, and be upright, and do not follow the way of the mischief-makers."

143. And when Moses came to Our appointment, and his Lord spoke to him, he said, "My Lord, allow me to look and see You." He said, "You will not see Me, but look at the mountain; if it stays in its place, you will see Me." But when his Lord manifested Himself to the mountain, He turned it into dust, and Moses fell down unconscious. Then, when he recovered, he said, "Glory be to you, I repent to you, and I am the first of the believers."

144. He said, "O Moses, I have chosen you above all people for My messages and for My words. So take what I have given you, and be one of the thankful."

145. And We inscribed for him in the Tablets all kinds of enlightenments, and decisive explanation of all things. "Hold fast to them, and exhort your people to adopt the best of them. I will show you the fate of the sinners."

146. I will turn away from My revelations those who behave proudly on earth without justification. Even if they see every sign, they will not believe in it; and if they see the path of rectitude, they will not adopt it for a path; and if they see the path of error, they will adopt it for a path. That is because they denied Our revelations, and paid no attention to them.

147. Those who deny Our revelations and the meeting of the Hereafter—their deeds will come to nothing. Will they be repaid except according to what they used to do?

148. In his absence, the people of Moses adopted a calf made from their ornaments—a body which lowed. Did they not see that it could not speak to them, nor guide them in any way? They took it for worship. They were in the wrong.

149. Then, when they regretted, and realized that they had erred, they said, "Unless our Lord extends His mercy to us, and forgives us, we will be among the losers."

150. And when Moses returned to his people, angry and disappointed, he said, "What an awful thing you did in my absence. Did you forsake the commandments of your Lord so hastily?" And he threw down the tablets, and took hold of his brother's head, dragging him towards himself. He said, "Son of my mother, the people have overpowered me, and were about to kill me; so do not allow the enemies to gloat over me, and do not count me among the unjust people."

151. He said, "My Lord, forgive me and my brother, and admit us into Your mercy; for you are the Most Merciful of the merciful."

152. Those who idolized the calf have incurred wrath from their Lord, and humiliation in this life. We thus requite the innovators.

153. As for those who commit sins, and then repent afterwards and believe—your Lord, thereafter, is Forgiving and Merciful.

154. When the anger abated in Moses, he took up the tablets. In their transcript is guidance and mercy for those in awe of their Lord.

155. And Moses chose from his people seventy men for Our appointment. When the

tremor shook them, he said, "My Lord, had You willed, You could have destroyed them before, and me too. Will you destroy us for what the fools among us have done? This is but Your test—with it You misguide whomever You will, and You guide whomever You will. You are our Protector, so forgive us, and have mercy on us. You are the Best of Forgivers."

156. "And inscribe for us goodness in this world, and in the Hereafter. We have turned to You." He said, "My punishment—I inflict it upon whomever I will, but My mercy encompasses all things. I will specify it for those who act righteously and practice regular charity, and those who believe in Our signs."

157. Those who follow the Messenger, the Unlettered Prophet, whom they find mentioned in the Torah and the Gospel in their possession. He directs them to righteousness, and deters them from evil, and allows for them all good things, and prohibits for them wickedness, and unloads the burdens and the shackles that are upon them. Those who believe in him, and respect him, and support him, and follow the light that came down with him—these are the successful.

158. Say, "O people, I am the Messenger of God to you all—He to whom belongs the kingdom of the heavens and the earth. There is no god but He. He gives life and causes death." So believe in God and His Messenger, the Unlettered Prophet, who believes in God and His words. And follow him, that you may be guided.

159. Among the people of Moses is a community that guides by truth, and thereby does justice.

160. We divided them into twelve tribal communities. And We inspired Moses, when his people asked him for something

to drink, "Strike the rock with your staff." Whereupon twelve springs gushed from it. Each group recognized its drinking-place. And We shaded them with clouds, and sent down upon them manna and quails, "Eat of the good things We have provided for you." They did not wrong Us, but they used to wrong their own selves.

161. And it was said to them, "Settle this town, and eat therein whatever you wish, and speak modestly, and enter the gate in humility—We will forgive your sins, and will promote the righteous."

162. But the wicked among them substituted other words for the words given to them, so We sent down upon them a plague from the sky, because of their wrongdoing.

163. Ask them about the town by the sea, when they violated the Sabbath. When they observed the Sabbath, their fish would come to them abundantly. But when they violated the Sabbath, their fish would not come. Thus We tried them because they disobeyed.

164. And when a group of them said, "Why do you counsel a people whom God will annihilate, or punish with a severe punishment?" They said, "As an excuse to your Lord, and so that they may become righteous."

165. Then, when they neglected what they were reminded of, We saved those who prohibited evil, and We seized those who did wrong with a terrible punishment, because of their sinfulness.

166. Then, when they rebelled against the commands to refrain, We said to them, "Be despicable apes."

167. Your Lord has announced that, He would send against them, until the Day of Resurrection, those who would inflict terrible suffering upon them. Your Lord is

swift in retribution, yet He is Forgiving and Merciful.

168. And We scattered them into communities on earth. Some of them righteous, and some of them short of that. And We tested them with fortunes and misfortunes, so that they may return.

169. They were succeeded by generations who inherited the Scripture and chose the materials of this world, saying, "We will be forgiven." And should similar materials come their way, they would again seize them. Did they not make a covenant to uphold the Scripture, and to not say about God except the truth? Did they not study its contents? But the Home of the Hereafter is better for the cautious; will you not understand?

170. Those who adhere to the Scripture, and practice prayer—We will not waste the reward of the reformers.

171. And when We suspended the mountain over them, as if it was an umbrella, and they thought it would fall on them: "Hold fast to what We have given you, and remember what it contains, so that you may be saved."

172. And when Your Lord summoned the descendants of Adam, and made them testify about themselves. "Am I not your Lord?" They said, "Yes, we testify." Thus you cannot say on the Day of Resurrection, "We were unaware of this."

173. Nor can you Say, "Our ancestors practiced idolatry before; and we are their descendants who came after them; will you destroy us for what the falsifiers did?"

174. We thus elaborate the revelations, so that they may return.

175. And relate to them the story of him to whom We delivered Our signs, but he detached himself from them, so Satan went after him, and he became one of the perverts.

176. Had We willed, We could have elevated him through them, but he clung to the ground, and followed his desires. His metaphor is that of a dog: if you chase it, it pants, and if you leave it alone, it pants. Such is the metaphor of the people who deny Our signs. So tell the tale, so that they may ponder.

177. Evil is the metaphor of the people who reject Our signs and wrong themselves.

178. Whomever God guides is the guided one. And whomever He sends astray—these are the losers.

179. We have destined for Hell multitudes of jinn and humans. They have hearts with which they do not understand. They have eyes with which they do not see. They have ears with which they do not hear. These are like cattle. In fact, they are further astray. These are the heedless.

180. To God belong the Most Beautiful Names, so call Him by them, and disregard those who blaspheme His names. They will be repaid for what they used to do.

181. Among those We created is a community—they guide by truth, and do justice thereby.

182. As for those who reject Our messages, We will gradually lead them from where they do not know.

183. And I will encourage them. My plan is firm.

184. Do they not think? There is no madness in their friend. He is but a plain warner.

185. Have they not observed the government of the heavens and the earth, and all the things that God created, and that their

time may have drawn near? Which message, besides this, will they believe in?

186. Whomever God misguides has no guide. And He leaves them blundering in their transgression.

187. They ask you about the Hour, "When will it come?" Say, "Knowledge of it rests with my Lord. None can reveal its coming except He. It weighs heavily on the heavens and the earth. It will not come upon you except suddenly." They ask you as if you are responsible for it. Say, "Knowledge of it rests with God," but most people do not know.

188. Say, "I have no control over any benefit or harm to myself, except as God wills. Had I known the future, I would have acquired much good, and no harm would have touched me. I am only a warner, and a herald of good news to a people who believe."

189. It is He who created you from a single person, and made from it its mate, that he may find comfort with her. Then, when he has covered her, she conceives a light load, and she carries it around. But when she has grown heavy, they pray to God their Lord, "if You give us a good child, we will be among the thankful."

190. But when He has given them a good child, they attribute partners to Him in what He has given them. God is exalted above what they associate.

191. Do they idolize those who create nothing, and are themselves created?

192. And can neither help them, nor help their own selves?

193. And if you invite them to guidance, they will not follow you. It is the same for you, whether you invite them, or remain silent.

194. Those you call upon besides God are servants like you. So call upon them, and let them answer you, if you are truthful.

195. Do they have feet with which they walk? Or do they have hands with which they strike? Or do they have eyes with which they see? Or do they have ears with which they hear? Say, "Call upon your partners, then plot against me, and do not wait."

196. "My Master is God, He Who sent down the Book, and He takes care of the righteous."

197. Those you call upon besides Him cannot help you, nor can they help themselves.

198. And if you call them to guidance, they will not hear. And you see them looking at you, yet they do not see.

199. Be tolerant, and command decency, and avoid the ignorant.

200. And when a suggestion from Satan assails you, take refuge with God. He is Hearing and Knowing.

201. Those who are righteous, when an impulse from Satan strikes them, they remind themselves, and immediately see clearly.

202. But their brethren lead them relentlessly into error, and they never stop short.

203. If you do not produce a miracle for them, they say, "Why don't you improvise one." Say, "I only follow what is inspired to me from my Lord." These are insights from your Lord, and guidance, and mercy, for a people who believe.

204. When the Quran is recited, listen to it, and pay attention, so that you may experience mercy.

205. And remember your Lord within yourself, humbly and fearfully, and quietly, in

the morning and the evening, and do not be of the neglectful.

206. Those who are in the presence of your Lord are not too proud to worship Him. They recite His praises, and to Him they bow down.

8. THE SPOILS
(al-Anfal)

In the name of God,
the Gracious, the Merciful.

1. They ask you about the bounties. Say, "The bounties are for God and the Messenger." So be mindful of God, and settle your differences, and obey God and His Messenger, if you are believers.

2. The believers are those whose hearts tremble when God is mentioned, and when His revelations are recited to them, they strengthen them in faith, and upon their Lord they rely.

3. Those who perform the prayer, and from Our provisions to them, they spend.

4. These are the true believers. They have high standing with their Lord, and forgiveness, and a generous provision.

5. Even as your Lord brought you out of your home with the truth, some believers were reluctant.

6. Arguing with you about the truth after it was made clear, as if they were being driven to death as they looked on.

7. God has promised you one of the two groups—that it would be yours—but you wanted the unarmed group to be yours. God intends to prove the truth with His words, and to uproot the disbelievers.

8. In order to confirm the truth and nullify falsehood, even though the guilty dislike it.

9. When you appealed to your Lord for help, He answered you, "I am reinforcing you with one thousand angels in succession."

10. God only made it a message of hope, to set your hearts at rest. Victory comes only from God. God is Mighty and Wise.

11. He made drowsiness overcome you, as a security from Him. And He sent down upon you water from the sky, to cleanse you with it, and to rid you of Satan's pollution, and to fortify your hearts, and to strengthen your foothold.

12. Your Lord inspired the angels: "I am with you, so support those who believe. I will cast terror into the hearts of those who disbelieve. So strike above the necks, and strike off every fingertip of theirs."

13. That is because they opposed God and His Messenger. Whoever opposes God and His Messenger—God is severe in retribution.

14. "Here it is; so taste it." For the disbelievers there is the suffering of the Fire.

15. O you who believe! When you meet those who disbelieve on the march, never turn your backs on them.

16. Anyone who turns his back on them on that Day, except while maneuvering for battle, or to join another group, has incurred wrath from God, and his abode is Hell—what a miserable destination!

17. It was not you who killed them, but it was God who killed them. And it was not you who launched when you launched, but it was God who launched. That He may bestow upon the believers an excellent reward. God is Hearing and Knowing.

18. Such is the case. God will undermine the strategy of the disbelievers.

19. If you desire a verdict, the verdict has come to you. If you desist, it would be best

for you. If you return, We will return; and your troops, however numerous, will not benefit you. God is with the believers.

20. O you who believe! Obey God and His Messenger, and do not turn away from him when you hear.

21. And be not like those who say, "We hear," when they do not hear.

22. The worst of animals to God are the deaf and dumb—those who do not reason.

23. Had God recognized any good in them, He would have made them hear; and had He made them hear, they would have turned away defiantly.

24. O you who believe! Respond to God and to the Messenger when He calls you to what will revive you. And know that God stands between a man and his heart, and that to Him you will be gathered.

25. And beware of discord which does not afflict the wrongdoers among you exclusively; and know that God is severe in retribution.

26. And remember when you were few, oppressed in the land, fearing that people may capture you; but He sheltered you, and supported you with His victory, and provided you with good things—so that you may be thankful.

27. O you who believe! Do not betray God and the Messenger, nor betray your trusts, while you know.

28. And know that your possessions and your children are a test; and that God possesses an immense reward.

29. O you who believe! If you remain conscious of God, He will give you a criterion, and remit from you your sins, and forgive you. God is possessor of infinite grace.

30. When the disbelievers plotted against you, to imprison you, or kill you, or expel you. They planned, and God planned, but God is the Best of planners.

31. And when Our revelations are recited to them, they say, "We have heard. Had we wanted, we could have said the like of this; these are nothing but myths of the ancients."

32. And they said, "Our God, if this is the truth from You, then rain down on us stones from the sky, or visit us with a painful affliction."

33. But God would not punish them while you are amongst them. And God would not punish them as long as they seek forgiveness.

34. Yet why should God not punish them, when they are turning others away from the Sacred Mosque, although they are not its custodians? Its rightful custodians are the pious; but most of them do not know.

35. Their prayer at the House was nothing but whistling and clapping—so taste the punishment for your blasphemy.

36. Those who disbelieve spend their wealth to repel from God's path. They will spend it, then it will become a source of sorrow for them, and then they will be defeated. Those who disbelieve will be herded into Hell.

37. That God may distinguish the bad from the good, and heap the bad on top of one another, and pile them together, and throw them in Hell. These are the losers.

38. Say to those who disbelieve: if they desist, their past will be forgiven. But if they persist—the practice of the ancients has passed away.

39. Fight them until there is no more persecution, and religion becomes exclusively for God. But if they desist—God is Seeing of what they do.

40. And if they turn away, know that God is your Protector. The Best Protector, and the Best Supporter.

41. And know that whatever spoils you gain, to God belongs its fifth, and to the Messenger, and the relatives, and the orphans, and the poor, and to the wayfarer, provided you believe in God and in what We revealed to Our servant on the Day of Distinction, the day when the two armies met. God is Capable of everything.

42. Recall when you were on the nearer bank, and they were on the further bank, and the caravan was below you. Had you planned for this meeting, you would have disagreed on the timing, but God was to carry out a predetermined matter, so that those who perish would perish by clear evidence, and those who survive would survive by clear evidence. God is Hearing and Knowing.

43. God made them appear in your dream as few. Had He made them appear as many, you would have lost heart, and disputed in the matter. But God saved the situation. He knows what the hearts contain.

44. When you met, He made them appear as few in your eyes, and made you appear fewer in their eyes, so that God may conclude a predetermined matter. To God all matters revert.

45. O you who believe! When you meet a force, stand firm, and remember God much, so that you may prevail.

46. And obey God and His Messenger, and do not dispute, lest you falter and lose your courage. And be steadfast. God is with the steadfast.

47. And do not be like those who left their homes boastfully, showing off before the people, and barring others from the path of God. God comprehends what they do.

48. Satan made their deeds appear good to them, and said, "You cannot be defeated by any people today, and I am at your side." But when the two armies came in sight of one another, he turned on his heels, and said, "I am innocent of you; I see what you do not see; I fear God; God is severe in punishment."

49. The hypocrites and those in whose hearts is sickness said, "Their religion has deluded these people." But whoever puts his trust in God—God is Mighty and Wise.

50. If only you could see, as the angels take away those who disbelieve, striking their faces and their backs: "Taste the agony of the Burning."

51. "That is because of what your hands have committed, and because God is not unjust to the servants."

52. Like the behavior of the people of Pharaoh, and those before them. They rejected the signs of God, so God seized them for their sins. God is Powerful, Severe in punishment.

53. That is because God would never change a blessing He has bestowed on a people unless they change what is within themselves, and because God is Hearing and Knowing.

54. Such was the case with the people of Pharaoh, and those before them. They denied the signs of their Lord, so We annihilated them for their wrongs, and We drowned the people of Pharaoh—they were all evildoers.

55. The worst of creatures in God's view are those who disbelieve. They have no faith.

56. Those of them with whom you made a treaty, but they violate their agreement every time. They are not righteous.

57. If you confront them in battle, make of them a fearsome example for those who follow them, that they may take heed.

58. If you fear treachery on the part of a people, break off with them in a like manner. God does not like the treacherous.

59. Let not the disbelievers assume that they are ahead. They will not escape.

60. And prepare against them all the power you can muster, and all the cavalry you can mobilize, to terrify thereby God's enemies and your enemies, and others besides them whom you do not know, but God knows them. Whatever you spend in God's way will be repaid to you in full, and you will not be wronged.

61. But if they incline towards peace, then incline towards it, and put your trust in God. He is the Hearer, the Knower.

62. If they intend to deceive you—God is sufficient for you. It is He who supported you with His aid, and with the believers.

63. And He united their hearts. Had you spent everything on earth, you would not have united their hearts, but God united them together. He is Mighty and Wise.

64. O prophet! Count on God, and on the believers who have followed you.

65. O prophet! Rouse the believers to battle. If there are twenty steadfast among you, they will defeat two hundred; and if there are a hundred of you, they will defeat a thousand of those who disbelieve; because they are a people who do not understand.

66. God has now lightened your burden, knowing that there is weakness in you. If there are a hundred steadfast among you, they will defeat two hundred; and if there are a thousand, they will defeat two thousand by God's leave. God is with the steadfast.

67. It is not for a prophet to take prisoners before he has subdued the land. You desire the materials of this world, but God desires the Hereafter. God is Strong and Wise.

68. Were it not for a predetermined decree from God, an awful punishment would have afflicted you for what you have taken.

69. So consume what you have gained, legitimate and wholesome, and remain conscious of God. God is Forgiving and Merciful.

70. O prophet! Say to those you hold prisoners, "If God finds any good in your hearts, He will give you better than what was taken from you, and He will forgive you. God is Forgiving and Merciful."

71. But if they intend to betray you, they have already betrayed God, and He has overpowered them. God is Knowing and Wise.

72. Those who believed, and emigrated, and struggled in God's cause with their possessions and their persons, and those who provided shelter and support—these are allies of one another. As for those who believed, but did not emigrate, you owe them no protection, until they have emigrated. But if they ask you for help in religion, you must come to their aid, except against a people with whom you have a treaty. God is Seeing of what you do.

73. As for those who disbelieve, they are allies of one another. Unless you do this, there will be turmoil in the land, and much corruption.

74. Those who believed, and emigrated, and struggled for God's cause, and those who gave shelter and support—these are the true believers. They will have forgiveness, and a bountiful provision.

75. As for those who believed afterwards, and emigrated and struggled with you—

these belong with you. But family members are nearer to one another in the Book of God. God is Cognizant of everything.

9. REPENTANCE
(at-Tawbah)

1. A declaration of immunity from God and His Messenger to the polytheists with whom you had made a treaty.

2. So travel the land for four months, and know that you cannot escape God, and that God will disgrace the disbelievers.

3. And a proclamation from God and His Messenger to the people on the day of the Greater Pilgrimage, that God has disowned the polytheists, and so did His Messenger. If you repent, it will be better for you. But if you turn away, know that you cannot escape God. And announce to those who disbelieve a painful punishment.

4. Except for those among the polytheists with whom you had made a treaty, and did not violate any of its terms, nor aided anyone against you. So fulfill the treaty with them to the end of its term. God loves the righteous.

5. When the Sacred Months have passed, kill the polytheists wherever you find them. And capture them, and besiege them, and lie in wait for them at every ambush. But if they repent, and perform the prayers, and pay the alms, then let them go their way. God is Most Forgiving, Most Merciful.

6. And if anyone of the polytheists asks you for protection, give him protection so that he may hear the Word of God; then escort him to his place of safety. That is because they are a people who do not know.

7. How can there be a treaty with the polytheists on the part of God and His Messenger, except for those with whom you made a treaty at the Sacred Mosque? As long as they are upright with you, be upright with them. God loves the pious.

8. How? Whenever they overcome you, they respect neither kinship nor treaty with you. They satisfy you with lip service, but their hearts refuse, and most of them are immoral.

9. They traded away God's revelations for a cheap price, and barred others from His path. How evil is what they did.

10. Towards a believer they respect neither kinship nor treaty. These are the transgressors.

11. But if they repent, and perform the prayers, and give the obligatory charity, then they are your brethren in faith. We detail the revelations for a people who know.

12. But if they violate their oaths after their pledge, and attack your religion, then fight the leaders of disbelief—they have no faith—so that they may desist.

13. Will you not fight a people who violated their oaths, and planned to exile the Messenger, and initiated hostilities against you? Do you fear them? It is God you should fear, if you are believers.

14. Fight them. God will punish them at your hands, and humiliate them, and help you against them, and heal the hearts of a believing people.

15. And He will remove the anger of their hearts. God redeems whomever He wills. God is Knowledgeable and Wise.

16. Or do you think that you will be left alone, without God identifying which of you will strive, and take no supporters apart from God, His Messenger, and the

believers? God is well Aware of what you do.

17. It is not for the polytheists to attend God's places of worship, while professing their disbelief. These—their works are in vain, and in the Fire they will abide.

18. The only people to attend God's places of worship are those who believe in God and the Last Day, and pray regularly, and practice regular charity, and fear none but God. These are most likely to be guided.

19. Do you consider giving water to pilgrims and maintaining the Sacred Mosque the same as believing in God and the Last Day and striving in God's path? They are not equal in God's sight. God does not guide the unjust people.

20. Those who believe, and emigrate, and strive in God's path with their possessions and their persons, are of a higher rank with God. These are the winners.

21. Their Lord announces to them good news of mercy from Him, and acceptance, and gardens wherein they will have lasting bliss.

22. Abiding therein forever. With God is a great reward.

23. O you who believe! Do not ally yourselves with your parents and your siblings if they prefer disbelief to belief. Whoever of you allies himself with them—these are the wrongdoers.

24. Say, "If your parents, and your children, and your siblings, and your spouses, and your relatives, and the wealth you have acquired, and a business you worry about, and homes you love, are more dear to you than God, and His Messenger, and the struggle in His cause, then wait until God executes His judgment." God does not guide the sinful people.

25. God has given you victory in numerous regions, but on the day of Hunayn, your great number impressed you, but it availed you nothing; and the land, as spacious as it was, narrowed for you, and you turned your backs in retreat.

26. Then God sent down His serenity upon His Messenger, and upon the believers, and He sent down troops you did not see, and He punished those who disbelieved. Such is the recompense of the disbelievers.

27. Then, after that, God will relent towards whomever He wills. God is Forgiving and Merciful.

28. O you who believe! The polytheists are polluted, so let them not approach the Sacred Mosque after this year of theirs. And if you fear poverty, God will enrich you from His grace, if He wills. God is Aware and Wise.

29. Fight those who do not believe in God, nor in the Last Day, nor forbid what God and His Messenger have forbidden, nor abide by the religion of truth—from among those who received the Scripture—until they pay the due tax, willingly or unwillingly.

30. The Jews said, "Ezra is the son of God," and the Christians said, "The Messiah is the son of God." These are their statements, out of their mouths. They emulate the statements of those who blasphemed before. May God assail them! How deceived they are!

31. They have taken their rabbis and their priests as lords instead of God, as well as the Messiah son of Mary. Although they were commanded to worship none but The One God. There is no god except He. Glory be to Him, high above what they associate with Him.

32. They want to extinguish God's light with their mouths, but God refuses except

to complete His light, even though the disbelievers dislike it.

33. It is He who sent His Messenger with the guidance and the religion of truth, in order to make it prevail over all religions, even though the idolaters dislike it.

34. O you who believe! Many of the rabbis and priests consume people's wealth illicitly, and hinder from God's path. Those who hoard gold and silver, and do not spend them in God's cause, inform them of a painful punishment.

35. On the Day when they will be heated in the Fire of Hell, then their foreheads, and their sides, and their backs will be branded with them: "This is what you hoarded for yourselves; so taste what you used to hoard."

36. The number of months, according to God, is twelve months—in the decree of God—since the Day He created the heavens and the earth, of which four are sacred. This is the correct religion. So do not wrong yourselves during them. And fight the polytheists collectively, as they fight you collectively, and know that God is with the righteous.

37. Postponement is an increase in disbelief—by which those who disbelieve are led astray. They allow it one year, and forbid it another year, in order to conform to the number made sacred by God, thus permitting what God has forbidden. The evil of their deeds seems good to them. God does not guide the disbelieving people.

38. O you who believe! What is the matter with you, when it is said to you, "Mobilize in the cause of God," you cling heavily to the earth? Do you prefer the present life to the Hereafter? The enjoyment of the present life, compared to the Hereafter, is only a little.

39. Unless you mobilize, He will punish you most painfully, and will replace you with another people, and you will not harm Him at all. God has power over all things.

40. If you do not help him, God has already helped him, when those who disbelieved expelled him, and he was the second of two in the cave. He said to his friend, "Do not worry, God is with us." And God made His tranquility descend upon him, and supported him with forces you did not see, and made the word of those who disbelieved the lowest, while the Word of God is the Highest. God is Mighty and Wise.

41. Mobilize, light or heavy, and strive with your possessions and your lives in the cause of God. That is better for you, if you only knew.

42. Had the gain been immediate, and the journey shorter, they would have followed you; but the distance seemed too long for them. Still they swear by God: "Had we been able, we would have marched out with you." They damn their own souls, and God knows that they are lying.

43. May God pardon you! Why did you give them permission before it became clear to you who are the truthful ones, and who are the liars?

44. Those who believe in God and the Last Day do not ask you for exemption from striving with their possessions and their lives. God is fully aware of the righteous.

45. Only those who do not believe in God and the Last Day ask you for exemption. Their hearts are full of doubts, so they waver in their doubts.

46. Had they wanted to mobilize, they would have made preparations for it; but God disliked their participation, so he held them back, and it was said, "Stay behind with those who stay behind."

47. Had they mobilized with you, they would have added only to your difficulties, and they would have spread rumors in your midst, trying to sow discord among you. Some of you are avid listeners to them. God is Aware of the wrongdoers.

48. They tried to cause conflict before, and they hatched plots against you, until the truth prevailed, and the command of God became evident—in spite of their dislike.

49. Among them is he who says, "Excuse me, and do not trouble me." In fact, they sunk into trouble. In fact, Hell will engulf the disbelievers.

50. If something good happens to you, it upsets them, and if a calamity befalls you, they say, "We took our precautions in advance," and they depart, happy.

51. Say, "Nothing will happen to us except what God has ordained for us; He is our Protector." In God let the faithful put their trust.

52. Say, "Are you expecting for us anything other than one of the two excellences? As for us, we are expecting that God will afflict you with a punishment from Himself, or at our hands. So wait, we are waiting with you."

53. Say, "Whether you spend willingly or unwillingly, it will not be accepted from you. You are evil people."

54. What prevents the acceptance of their contributions is nothing but the fact that they disbelieved in God and His Messenger, and that they do not approach the prayer except lazily, and that they do not spend except grudgingly.

55. Let neither their possessions nor their children impress you. God intends to torment them through them in this worldly life, and that their souls depart while they are disbelievers.

56. They swear by God that they are of you. But they are not of you. They are divisive people.

57. Were they to find a shelter, or a cave, or a hideout, they would go to it, rushing.

58. And among them are those who criticize you in regard to charities. If they are given some of it, they become pleased, but if they are not given any, they grow resentful.

59. If only they were content with what God and His Messenger have given them, and said, "God is sufficient for us; God will give us of His bounty, and so will His Messenger; to God we eagerly turn."

60. Charities are for the poor, and the destitute, and those who administer them, and for reconciling hearts, and for freeing slaves, and for those in debt, and in the path of God, and for the traveler in need—an obligation from God. God is All-Knowing, Most Wise.

61. And among them are those who insult the Prophet, and say, "He is all ears." Say, "He listens for your own good. He believes in God, and trusts the believers, and is mercy for those of you who believe." Those who insult the Messenger of God will have a painful penalty.

62. They swear to you by God to please you. But it is more proper for them to please God and His Messenger, if they are believers.

63. Do they not know that whoever opposes God and His Messenger, will have the Fire of Hell, abiding in it forever? That is the supreme disgrace.

64. The hypocrites worry lest a chapter may be revealed about them, informing them of what is in their hearts. Say, "Go on mocking; God will bring out what you fear."

65. If you ask them, they will say, "We were just joking and playing." Say, "Were you making jokes about God, His messenger, and His revelations?"

66. Do not apologize. You have disbelieved after your belief. If We pardon some of you, We will punish others, because they are guilty.

67. The hypocrite men and hypocrite women are of one another. They advocate evil, and prohibit righteousness, and withhold their hands. They forgot God, so He forgot them. The hypocrites are the sinners.

68. God has promised the hypocrite men and hypocrite women, and the disbelievers, the Fire of Hell, abiding therein forever. It is their due. And God has cursed them. They will have a lasting punishment.

69. Like those before you. They were more powerful than you, and had more wealth and children. They enjoyed their share, and you enjoyed your share, as those before you enjoyed their share. And you indulged, as they indulged. It is they whose works will fail in this world and in the Hereafter. It is they who are the losers.

70. Have they not heard the stories of those before them? The people of Noah, and Aad, and Thamood; and the people of Abraham, and the inhabitants of Median, and the overturned cities? Their messengers came to them with the clear proofs. God never wronged them, but they used to wrong their own selves.

71. The believing men and believing women are friends of one another. They advocate virtue, and forbid evil. They perform regular prayers, and practice regular charity, and obey God and His Messenger. These—God will have mercy on them. God is Noble and Wise.

72. God promises the believers, men and women, gardens beneath which rivers flow, abiding therein forever, and fine homes in the Gardens of Eden. But approval from God is even greater. That is the supreme achievement.

73. O Prophet! Strive against the disbelievers and the hypocrites, and be stern with them. Their abode is Hell—what a miserable destination!

74. They swear by God that they said nothing, but they did utter the word of blasphemy, and they renounced faith after their submission. And they plotted what they could not attain. They were resentful only because God and His Messenger have enriched them out of His grace. If they repent, it would be best for them; but if they turn away, God will afflict them with a painful punishment—in this life and in the Hereafter, and they will have on earth no protector and no savior.

75. Among them are those who promised God: "If He gives us of His bounty, we will donate, and be among the upright."

76. But when He has given them of His bounty, they became stingy with it, and turned away in aversion.

77. So He penalized them with hypocrisy in their hearts, until the Day they face Him—because they broke their promise to God, and because they used to lie.

78. Do they not know that God knows their secrets and their conspiracies? And that God is the Knower of the unseen?

79. Those who criticize the believers who give charity voluntarily, and ridicule those who find nothing to give except their own efforts—God ridicules them. They will have a painful punishment.

80. Whether you ask forgiveness for them, or do not ask forgiveness for them—even

if you ask forgiveness for them seventy times, God will not forgive them. That is because they disbelieved in God and His messenger. God does not guide the immoral people.

81. Those who stayed behind rejoiced at their staying behind the Messenger of God. And they hated to strive with their wealth and their lives in God's way. And they said, "Do not venture out in the heat." Say, "The Fire of Hell is much hotter, if they only understood."

82. Let them laugh a little, and weep much; in recompense for what they used to earn.

83. If God brings you back to a party of them, and they ask your permission to go out, say, "You will not go out with me, ever, nor will you ever fight an enemy with me. You were content to sit back the first time, so sit back with those who stay behind."

84. You are never to pray over anyone of them who dies, nor are you to stand at his graveside. They rejected God and His Messenger, and died while they were sinners.

85. Do not let their possessions and their children impress you. God desires to torment them through them in this world, and their souls expire while they are disbelievers.

86. When a chapter is revealed, stating: "Believe in God and strive with His Messenger," the prominent among them ask you for exemption. They say, "Allow us to stay with those who stay behind."

87. They prefer to be with those who stay behind. Their hearts were sealed, so they do not understand.

88. But the Messenger and those who believe with him struggle with their possessions and their lives. These have deserved the good things. These are the successful.

89. God has prepared for them gardens beneath which rivers flow, wherein they will abide forever. That is the great victory.

90. Some of the Desert-Arabs came to make excuses, asking to be granted exemption, while those who were untrue to God and His Messenger stayed behind. A painful punishment will afflict those among them who disbelieved.

91. There is no blame on the weak, nor on the sick, nor on those who have nothing to give, provided they are true to God and His Messenger. In no way can the righteous be blamed. God is Forgiving and Merciful.

92. Nor on those who approach you, wishing to ride with you, and you said, "I have nothing to carry you on." So they went away, with their eyes overflowing with tears, sorrowing for not finding the means to spend.

93. But blame is on those who ask you for exemption, although they are rich. They are content to be with those who stay behind. God has sealed their hearts, so they do not know.

94. They present excuses to you when you return to them. Say, "Do not offer excuses; we do not trust you; God has informed us of you. And God will watch your actions, and so will the Messenger; then you will be returned to the Knower of the Invisible and the Visible, and He will inform you of what you used to do."

95. They will swear to you by God, when you return to them, that you may leave them alone. So leave them alone. They are a disgrace, and their destiny is Hell; a reward for what they used to earn.

96. They will swear to you that you may accept them. But even if you accept them, God does not accept the wicked people.

97. The Desert-Arabs are the most steeped in disbelief and hypocrisy, and the most likely to ignore the limits that God revealed to His Messenger. God is Knowing and Wise.

98. And among the Desert-Arabs are those who consider their contribution to be a fine. And they wait for a reversal of your fortunes. Upon them will fall the cycle of misfortune. God is Hearing and Knowing.

99. Yet among the Desert-Arabs are those who believe in God and the Last Day, and consider their contribution to be a means towards God, and the prayers of the Messenger. Surely it will draw them closer, and God will admit them into His mercy. God is Forgiving and Compassionate.

100. The Pioneers—The first of the Migrants and the Supporters, and those who followed them in righteousness. God is pleased with them, and they are pleased with Him. He has prepared for them Gardens beneath which rivers flow, where they will abide forever. That is the sublime triumph.

101. Among the Desert-Arabs around you there are some hypocrites, and among the inhabitants of Medina too. They have become adamant in hypocrisy. You do not know them, but We know them. We will punish them twice; then they will be returned to a severe torment.

102. Others have confessed their sins, having mixed good deeds with bad deeds. Perhaps God will redeem them. God is Forgiving and Merciful.

103. Receive contributions from their wealth, to purify them and sanctify them with it; and pray for them. Your prayer is comfort for them. God is Hearing and Knowing.

104. Do they not know that God accepts the repentance of His servants, and that He receives the contributions, and that God is the Acceptor of Repentance, the Merciful?

105. Say, "Work. God will see your work, and so will His Messenger, and the believers. Then you will be returned to the Knower of secrets and declarations, and He will inform you of what you used to do."

106. Others are held in suspense, awaiting God's decree, as to whether He will punish them, or accept their repentance. God is Aware and Wise.

107. Then there are those who establish a mosque to cause harm, and disbelief, and disunity among the believers, and as an outpost for those who fight God and His Messenger. They will swear: "Our intentions are nothing but good," but God bears witness that they are liars.

108. Do not stand in it, ever. A mosque founded upon piety from the first day is worthier of your standing in it. In it are men who love to be purified. God loves those who purify themselves.

109. Is he who founds his structure upon piety and acceptance from God better, or he who founds his structure on the brink of a cliff that is about to tumble, so it tumbles with him into the Fire of Hell? God does not guide the unjust people.

110. The structure which they built will remain questionable in their hearts, until their hearts are stopped. God is Knowing and Wise.

111. God has purchased from the believers their lives and their properties in exchange for Paradise. They fight in God's way, and they kill and get killed. It is a promise

binding on Him in the Torah, and the Gospel, and the Quran. And who is more true to his promise than God? So rejoice in making such an exchange—that is the supreme triumph.

112. Those who repent, those who worship, those who praise, those who journey, those who kneel, those who bow down, those who advocate righteousness and forbid evil, those who keep the limits of God—give good news to the believers.

113. It is not for the Prophet and those who believe to ask forgiveness for the polytheists, even if they are near relatives, after it has become clear to them that they are people of Hellfire.

114. Abraham asked forgiveness for his father only because of a promise he had made to him. But when it became clear to him that he was an enemy of God, he disowned him. Abraham was kind and clement.

115. God would never lead a people astray, after He had guided them, until He makes clear to them what they should guard against. God has knowledge of all things.

116. To God belongs the dominion of the heavens and the earth. He gives life, and He causes death. And besides God, you have neither protector, nor supporter.

117. God has redeemed the Prophet, and the Emigrants, and the Supporters—those who followed him in the hour of difficulty—after the hearts of some of them almost swerved. Then He pardoned them. He is Kind towards them, Compassionate.

118. Also towards the three who were left behind. Then, when the earth, as vast as it is, closed in on them, and their very souls closed in on them, and they realized that there was no refuge from God, except in Him, He redeemed them, so that they may repent. God is the Redeemer, the Merciful.

119. O you who believe! Be conscious of God, and be with the sincere.

120. It is not for the inhabitants of Medina and the Desert-Arabs around them to stay behind the Messenger of God, nor to prefer themselves to him. That is because they never suffer any thirst, nor fatigue, nor hunger in the cause of God, nor do they take one step that enrages the disbelievers, nor do they gain anything from an enemy but it is recorded to their credit as a righteous deed. God does not waste the reward of the righteous.

121. Nor do they spend any expenditure, small or large, nor do they cross any valley, but it is recorded to their credit. That God may reward them in accordance with the best of their deeds.

122. It is not advisable for the believers to march out altogether. Of every division that marches out, let a group remain behind, to gain understanding of the religion, and to notify their people when they have returned to them, that they may beware.

123. O you who believe! Fight those of the disbelievers who attack you, and let them find severity in you, and know that God is with the righteous.

124. Whenever a chapter is revealed, some of them say, "Which of you has this increased in faith?" As for those who believe, it increases them in faith, and they rejoice.

125. But as for those in whose hearts is sickness, it adds disgrace to their disgrace, and they die as unbelievers.

126. Do they not see that they are tested once or twice every year? Yet they do not repent, and they do not learn.

127. And whenever a chapter is revealed, they look at one another, "Does anyone see you?" Then they slip away. God has di-

verted their hearts, because they are a people who do not understand.

128. There has come to you a messenger from among yourselves, concerned over your suffering, anxious over you. Towards the believers, he is compassionate and merciful.

129. If they turn away, say, "God is enough for me; there is no god except He; in Him I have put my trust; He is the Lord of the Sublime Throne."

10. JONAH
(Yunus)

In the name of God,
the Gracious, the Merciful.

1. Alif, Lam, Ra. These are the Verses of the Wise Book.

2. Is it a wonder to the people that We have inspired a man from among them: "Warn mankind, and give good news to those who believe that they are on a sound footing with their Lord"? The disbelievers said, "This is a manifest sorcerer."

3. Your Lord is God, who created the heavens and the earth in six days, then settled over the Throne, governing all things. There is no intercessor except after His permission. Such is God, your Lord—so serve Him. Will you not reflect?

4. To Him is your return, altogether. The promise of God is true. He originates creation, and then He repeats it, to reward those who believe and do good deeds with equity. As for those who disbelieve, for them is a drink of boiling water, and agonizing torment, on account of their disbelief.

5. It is He who made the sun radiant, and the moon a light, and determined phases for it—that you may know the number of years and the calculation. God did not create all this except with truth. He details the revelations for a people who know.

6. In the alternation of night and day, and in what God created in the heavens and the earth, are signs for people who are aware.

7. Those who do not hope to meet Us, and are content with the worldly life, and are at ease in it, and those who pay no heed to Our signs.

8. These—their dwelling is the Fire—on account of what they used to do.

9. As for those who believe and do good deeds, their Lord guides them in their faith. Rivers will flow beneath them in the Gardens of Bliss.

10. Their call therein is, "Glory be to You, our God." And their greeting therein is, "Peace." And the last of their call is, "Praise be to God, Lord of the Worlds."

11. If God were to accelerate the ill for the people, as they wish to accelerate the good, their term would have been fulfilled. But We leave those who do not expect Our encounter to blunder in their excesses.

12. Whenever adversity touches the human being, he prays to Us—reclining on his side, or sitting, or standing. But when We have relieved his adversity from him, he goes away, as though he had never called on Us for trouble that had afflicted him. Thus the deeds of the transgressors appear good to them.

13. We have destroyed generations before you, when they did wrong. Their messengers came to them with clear signs, but they would not believe. Thus We requite the sinful people.

14. Then We made you successors on earth after them, to see how you would behave.

15. And when Our clear revelations are recited to them, those who do not hope to meet Us say, "Bring a Quran other than this, or change it." Say, "It is not for me to change it of my own accord. I only follow what is revealed to me. I fear, if I disobeyed my Lord, the torment of a terrible Day."

16. Say, "Had God willed, I would not have recited it to you, and He would not have made it known to you. I have lived among you for a lifetime before it. Do you not understand?"

17. Who does greater wrong than someone who fabricates lies about God, or denies His revelations? The guilty will never prosper.

18. And they worship, besides God, what neither harms them nor benefits them. And they say, "These are our intercessors with God." Say, "Are you informing God about what He does not know in the heavens or on earth?" Glorified be He, high above the associations they make.

19. Mankind was a single community; then they differed. Were it not for a prior decree from your Lord, the matters over which they had disputed would have been settled.

20. And they say, "If only a miracle was sent down to him from his Lord." Say, "The realm of the unseen belongs to God; so wait, I am waiting with you."

21. When We make the people taste mercy after some adversity has touched them, they begin to scheme against Our revelations. Say, "God is swifter in scheming." Our envoys are writing down what you scheme.

22. It is He who transports you across land and sea. Until, when you are on ships, sailing in a favorable wind, and rejoicing in it, a raging wind arrives. The waves surge over them from every side, and they realize that they are besieged. Thereupon they pray to God, professing sincere devotion to Him: "If You save us from this, we will be among the appreciative."

23. But then, when He has saved them, they commit violations on earth, and oppose justice. O people! Your violations are against your own souls. It is the enjoyment of the present life. Then to Us is your return, and We will inform you of what you used to do.

24. The likeness of the present life is this: water that We send down from the sky is absorbed by the plants of the earth, from which the people and the animals eat. Until, when the earth puts on its fine appearance, and is beautified, and its inhabitants think that they have mastered it, Our command descends upon it by night or by day, and We turn it into stubble, as if it had not flourished the day before. We thus clarify the revelations for people who reflect.

25. God invites to the Home of Peace, and guides whomever He wills to a straight path.

26. For those who have done good is goodness, and more. Neither gloom nor shame will come over their faces. These are the inhabitants of Paradise, abiding therein forever.

27. As for those who have earned evil deeds: a reward of similar evil, and shame will cover them. They will have no defense against God—as if their faces are covered with dark patches of night. These are the inmates of the Fire, abiding therein forever.

28. On the Day when We will gather them altogether, then say to those who ascribed partners, "To your place, you and your partners." Then We will separate between

them, and their partners will say, "It was not us you were worshiping."

29. "God is sufficient witness between us and you. We were unaware of your worshiping us."

30. There, every soul will experience what it had done previously; and they will be returned to God, their true Master; and what they used to invent will fail them.

31. Say, "Who provides for you from the heaven and the earth? And who controls the hearing and the sight? And who produces the living from the dead, and produces the dead from the living? And who governs the Order?" They will say, "God." Say, "Will you not be careful?"

32. Such is God, your Lord—the True. What is there, beyond the truth, except falsehood? How are you turned away?

33. Thus your Lord's Word proved true against those who disobeyed, for they do not believe.

34. Say, "Can any of your partners initiate creation, and then repeat it?" Say, "God initiates creation, and then repeats it. How are you so deluded?"

35. Say, "Can any of your partners guide to the truth?" Say, "God guides to the truth. Is He who guides to the truth more worthy of being followed, or he who does not guide, unless he himself is guided? What is the matter with you? How do you judge?"

36. Most of them follow nothing but assumptions; and assumptions avail nothing against the truth. God is fully aware of what they do.

37. This Quran could not have been produced by anyone other than God. In fact, it is a confirmation of what preceded it, and an elaboration of the Book. There is no doubt about it—it is from the Lord of the Universe.

38. Or do they say, "He has forged it"? Say, "Then produce a single chapter like it, and call upon whomever you can, apart from God, if you are truthful."

39. In fact, they deny what is beyond the limits of their knowledge, and whose explanation has not yet reached them. Thus those before them refused to believe. So note the consequences for the wrongdoers.

40. Among them are those who believe in it, and among them are those who do not believe in it. Your Lord is fully aware of the mischief-makers.

41. If they accuse you of lying, say, "I have my deeds, and you have your deeds. You are quit of what I do, and I am quit of what you do."

42. And among them are those who listen to you. But can you make the deaf hear, even though they do not understand?

43. And among them are those who look at you. But can you guide the blind, even though they do not see?

44. God does not wrong the people in the least, but the people wrong their own selves.

45. On the Day when He rounds them up—as if they had tarried only one hour of a day—they will recognize one another. Those who denied the meeting with God will be the losers. They were not guided.

46. Whether We show you some of what We promise them, or take you, to Us is their return. God is witness to everything they do.

47. Every community has a messenger. When their messenger has come, judgment will be passed between them with fairness, and they will not be wronged.

48. And they say, "When will this promise be fulfilled, if you are truthful?"

49. Say, "I have no power to harm or benefit myself, except as God wills. To every nation is an appointed time. Then, when their time arrives, they can neither postpone it by one hour, nor advance it.

50. Say, "Have you considered? If His punishment overtakes you by night or by day, what part of it will the guilty seek to hasten?"

51. "Then, when it falls, will you believe in it? Now? When before you tried to hasten it?"

52. Then it will be said to those who did wrong, "Taste the torment of eternity. Will you be rewarded except for what you used to do?"

53. And they inquire of you, "Is it true?" Say, "Yes, by my Lord, it is true, and you cannot evade it."

54. Had every soul which had done wrong possessed everything on earth, it would offer it as a ransom. They will hide the remorse when they witness the suffering, and it will be judged between them equitably, and they will not be wronged.

55. Assuredly, to God belongs everything in the heavens and the earth. Assuredly, the promise of God is true, but most of them do not know.

56. He gives life and causes death, and to Him you will be returned.

57. O people! There has come to you advice from your Lord, and healing for what is in the hearts, and guidance and mercy for the believers.

58. Say, "In God's grace and mercy let them rejoice. That is better than what they hoard."

59. Say, "Have you considered the sustenance God has sent down for you, some of which you made unlawful, and some lawful?" Say, "Did God give you permission, or do you fabricate lies and attribute them to God?"

60. What will they think—those who fabricate lies and attribute them to God—on the Day of Resurrection? God is bountiful towards the people, but most of them do not give thanks.

61. You do not get into any situation, nor do you recite any Quran, nor do you do anything, but We are watching over you as you undertake it. Not even the weight of an atom, on earth or in the sky, escapes your Lord, nor is there anything smaller or larger, but is in a clear record.

62. Unquestionably, God's friends have nothing to fear, nor shall they grieve.

63. Those who believe and are aware.

64. For them is good news in this life, and in the Hereafter. There is no alteration to the words of God. That is the supreme triumph.

65. And let not their sayings dishearten you. All power is God's. He is the Hearer, the Knower.

66. Certainly, to God belongs everyone in the heavens and everyone on earth. Those who invoke other than God do not follow partners; they follow only assumptions, and they only guess.

67. It is He who made the night for your rest, and the daylight for visibility. Surely in that are signs for people who listen.

68. And they said, "God has taken a son." Be He glorified. He is the Self-Sufficient. His is everything in the heavens and everything on earth. Do you have any proof for this? Or are you saying about God what you do not know?

69. Say, "Those who fabricate lies about God will not succeed."

70. Some enjoyment in this world; then to Us is their return; then We will make them taste the severe punishment on account of their disbelief.

71. And relate to them the story of Noah, when he said to his people, "O my people, if my presence among you and my reminding you of God's signs is too much for you, in God I have put my trust. So come to a decision, you and your partners, and do not let the matter perplex you; then carry out your decision on me, and do not hold back."

72. "But if you turn away, I have not asked you for any wage. My wage falls only on God, and I was commanded to be of those who submit."

73. But they denounced him, so We saved him and those with him in the Ark, and We made them successors, and We drowned those who rejected Our signs. So consider the fate of those who were warned.

74. Then, after him, We sent messengers to their people. They came to them with the clear proofs, but they would not believe in anything they had already rejected. Thus We set a seal on the hearts of the hostile.

75. Then, after them, We sent Moses and Aaron with Our proofs to Pharaoh and his dignitaries. But they acted arrogantly. They were sinful people.

76. And when the truth came to them from Us, they said, "This is clearly sorcery."

77. Moses said, "Is this what you say of the truth when it has come to you? Is this sorcery? Sorcerers do not succeed."

78. They said, "Did you come to us to divert us from what we found our ancestors following, and so that you become prominent in the land? We will never believe in you."

79. Pharaoh said, "Bring me every experienced sorcerer."

80. And when the sorcerers came, Moses said to them, "Throw whatever you have to throw."

81. And when they threw, Moses said, "What you produced is sorcery, and God will make it fail. God does not foster the efforts of the corrupt."

82. "And God upholds the truth with His words, even though the sinners detest it."

83. But none believed in Moses except some children of his people, for fear that Pharaoh and his chiefs would persecute them. Pharaoh was high and mighty in the land. He was a tyrant.

84. Moses said, "O my people, if you have believed in God, then put your trust in Him, if you have submitted."

85. They said, "In God we have put our trust. Our Lord, do not make us victims of the oppressive people."

86. "And deliver us, by Your mercy, from the disbelieving people."

87. And We inspired Moses and his brother, "Settle your people in Egypt, and make your homes places of worship, and perform the prayer, and give good news to the believers."

88. Moses said, "Our Lord, you have given Pharaoh and his chiefs splendor and wealth in the worldly life. Our Lord, for them to lead away from Your path. Our Lord, obliterate their wealth, and harden their hearts; they will not believe until they see the painful torment."

89. He said, "Your prayer has been answered, so go straight, and do not follow the path of those who do not know."

90. And We delivered the Children of Israel across the sea. Pharaoh and his troops

pursued them, defiantly and aggressively. Until, when he was about to drown, he said, "I believe that there is no god except the One the Children of Israel believe in, and I am of those who submit."

91. Now? When you have rebelled before, and been of the mischief-makers?

92. Today We will preserve your body, so that you become a sign for those after you. But most people are heedless of Our signs.

93. And We settled the Children of Israel in a position of honor, and provided them with good things. They did not differ until knowledge came to them. Your Lord will judge between them on the Day of Resurrection regarding their differences.

94. If you are in doubt about what We have revealed to you, ask those who read the Scripture before you. Indeed, the truth has come to you from your Lord, so do not be of those who doubt.

95. And do not be of those who deny God's revelations, lest you become one of the losers.

96. Those against whom your Lord's word is justified will not believe.

97. Even if every sign comes to them—until they see the painful punishment.

98. If only there was one town that believed and benefited by its belief. Except for the people of Jonah. When they believed, We removed from them the suffering of disgrace in the worldly life, and We gave them comfort for a while.

99. Had your Lord willed, everyone on earth would have believed. Will you compel people to become believers?

100. No soul can believe except by God's leave; and He lays disgrace upon those who refuse to understand.

101. Say, "Look at what is in the heavens and the earth." But signs and warnings are of no avail for people who do not believe.

102. Do they expect anything but the likes of the days of those who passed away before them? Say, "Then wait, I will be waiting with you."

103. Then We save Our messengers and those who believe. It is binding on Us to save the believers.

104. Say, "O people, if you are in doubt about my religion—I do not serve those you serve apart from God. But I serve God, the one who will terminate your lives. And I was commanded to be of the believers."

105. And dedicate yourself to the true religion—a monotheist—and never be of the polytheists.

106. And do not call, apart from God, on what neither benefits you nor harms you. If you do, you are then one of the wrongdoers.

107. If God afflicts you with harm, none can remove it except He. And if He wants good for you, none can repel His grace. He makes it reach whomever He wills of His servants. He is the Forgiver, the Merciful.

108. Say, "O people, the truth has come to you from your Lord. Whoever accepts guidance is guided for his own soul; and whoever strays only strays to its detriment. I am not a guardian over you."

109. And follow what is revealed to you, and be patient until God issues His judgment, for He is the Best of judges.

11. HUD
(Hud)

In the name of God,
the Gracious, the Merciful.

1. Alif, Lam, Ra. A Scripture whose Verses were perfected, then elaborated, from One who is Wise and Informed.

2. That you shall worship none but God. "I am a warner to you from Him, and a bearer of good news."

3. "And ask your Lord for forgiveness, and repent to Him. He will provide you with good sustenance until a stated term, and will bestow His grace on every possessor of virtue. But if you turn away, then I fear for you the punishment of a grievous Day."

4. "To God is your return, and He is Capable of all things."

5. They wrap their chests to hide from Him. But even as they cover themselves with their clothes, He knows what they conceal and what they reveal. He knows what lies within the hearts.

6. There is no moving creature on earth but its sustenance depends on God. And He knows where it lives and where it rests. Everything is in a Clear Book.

7. It is He who created the heavens and the earth in six days—and His Throne was upon the waters—in order to test you—which of you is best in conduct. And if you were to say, "You will be resurrected after death," those who disbelieve would say, "This is nothing but plain witchcraft."

8. And if We postponed their punishment until a stated time, they would say, "What holds it back?" On the Day when it reaches them, it will not be averted from them, and what they used to ridicule will besiege them.

9. If We give the human being a taste of mercy from Us, and then withdraw it from him, he becomes despairing and ungrateful.

10. And if We give him a taste of prosperity, after some adversity has afflicted him, he will say, "Troubles have gone away from me." He becomes excited and proud.

11. Except those who are patient and do good deeds—these will have forgiveness and a great reward.

12. Perhaps you wish to disregard some of what is revealed to you, and you may be stressed because of it, since they say, "If only a treasure was sent down to him, or an angel came with him." You are only a warner, and God is Responsible for all things.

13. Or do they say, "He invented it?" Say, "Then produce ten chapters like it, invented, and call upon whomever you can, besides God, if you are truthful."

14. But if they fail to answer you, know that it was revealed with God's knowledge, and that there is no god but He. Will you then submit?

15. As for those who desire the worldly life and its glitter, We will fully recompense them for their deeds therein, and they will not be defrauded therein.

16. These—they will have nothing but the Fire in the Hereafter. Their deeds are in vain, and their works are null.

17. Is he who possesses a clear proof from his Lord, recited by a witness from Him, and before it the Book of Moses, a guide and a mercy? These believe in it. But whoever defies it from among the various factions, the Fire is his promise. So have no doubt about it. It is the truth from your Lord, but most people do not believe.

18. Who does greater wrong than he who fabricates lies about God? These will be presented before their Lord, and the witnesses will say, "These are they who lied about their Lord." Indeed, the curse of God is upon the wrongdoers.

19. Those who hinder others from the path of God, and seek to make it crooked; and regarding the Hereafter, they are in denial.

20. These will not escape on earth, and they have no protectors besides God. The punishment will be doubled for them. They have failed to hear, and they have failed to see.

21. Those are the ones who ruined their souls, and what they had invented has strayed away from them.

22. Without a doubt, in the Hereafter, they will be the biggest losers.

23. As for those who believe and do good deeds, and humble themselves before their Lord—these are the inhabitants of Paradise, where they will abide forever.

24. The parable of the two groups is that of the blind and the deaf, and the seeing and the hearing. Are they equal in comparison? Will you not reflect?

25. We sent Noah to his people, "I am to you a clear warner."

26. "That you shall worship none but God. I fear for you the agony of a painful Day."

27. The notables who disbelieved among his people said, "We see in you nothing but a man like us, and we see that only the worst among us have followed you, those of immature judgment. And we see that you have no advantage over us. In fact, we think you are liars."

28. He said, "O my people, Have you considered? If I stand on clear evidence from my Lord, and He has given me a mercy from Himself, but you were blind to it, can we compel you to accept it, even though you dislike it?"

29. "O my people! I ask of you no money for it. My reward lies only with God. And I am not about to dismiss those who believed; they will surely meet their Lord. And I see that you are ignorant people."

30. "O my people, who will support me against God if I dismiss them? Will you not give a thought?"

31. "I do not say to you that I possess the treasures of God, nor do I know the future, nor do I say that I am an angel. Nor do I say of those who are despicable in your eyes that God will never give them any good. God is Aware of what lies in their souls. If I did, I would be one of the wrongdoers."

32. They said, "O Noah, you have argued with us, and argued a great deal. Now bring upon us what you threaten us with, if you are truthful."

33. He said, "It is God who will bring it upon you, if He wills, and you will not be able to escape."

34. "My advice will not benefit you, much as I may want to advise you, if God desires to confound you. He is your Lord, and to Him you will be returned."

35. Or do they say, "He made it up?" Say, "If I made it up, upon me falls my crime, and I am innocent of the crimes you commit."

36. And it was revealed to Noah: "None of your people will believe, except those who have already believed, so do not grieve over what they do."

37. "And build the Ark, under Our eyes, and with Our inspiration, and do not address Me regarding those who did wrong; they are to be drowned."

38. As he was building the ark, whenever some of his people passed by him, they ridiculed him. He said, "If you ridicule us, we will ridicule you, just as you ridicule."

39. "You will surely know upon whom will come a torment that will abase him, and upon whom will fall a lasting torment."

40. Until, when Our command came, and the volcano erupted, We said, "Board into it a pair of every kind, and your family—except those against whom the sentence has already been passed—and those who have believed." But those who believed with him were only a few.

41. He said, "Embark in it. In the name of God shall be its sailing and its anchorage. My Lord is indeed Forgiving and Merciful."

42. And so it sailed with them amidst waves like hills. And Noah called to his son, who had kept away, "On my son! Embark with us, and do not be with the disbelievers."

43. He said, "I will take refuge on a mountain—it will protect me from the water." He said, "There is no protection from God's decree today, except for him on whom He has mercy." And the waves surged between them, and he was among the drowned.

44. And it was said, "O earth, swallow your waters," and "O heaven, clear up." And the waters receded, and the event was concluded, and it settled on Judi, and it was proclaimed: "Away with the wicked people."

45. And Noah called to his Lord. He said, "O My Lord, my son is of my family, and Your promise is true, and You are the Wisest of the wise."

46. He said, "O Noah, he is not of your family. It is an unrighteous deed. So do not ask Me about something you know nothing about. I admonish you, lest you be one of the ignorant."

47. He said, "O My Lord, I seek refuge with You, from asking You about what I have no knowledge of. Unless You forgive me, and have mercy on me, I will be one of the losers."

48. It was said, "O Noah, disembark with peace from Us; and with blessings upon you, and upon communities from those with you. And other communities We will grant prosperity, and then a painful torment from Us will befall them."

49. These are some stories from the past that we reveal to you. Neither you, nor your people knew them before this. So be patient. The future belongs to the pious.

50. And to Aad, their brother Hud. He said, "O my people, worship God, you have no other god besides Him. You do nothing but invent lies."

51. "O my people, I ask you no wage for it; my wage lies with Him who originated me. Do you not understand?"

52. "O my people, ask forgiveness from your Lord, and repent to Him. He will release the sky pouring down upon you, and will add strength to your strength. And do not turn away and be wicked."

53. They said, "O Hud, you did not bring us any evidence, and we are not about to abandon our gods at your word, and we are not believers in you."

54. "We only say that some of our gods have possessed you with evil." He said, "I call God to witness, and you to witness, that I am innocent of what you associate.

55. Besides Him. So scheme against me, all of you, and do not hesitate.

56. I have placed my trust in God, my Lord and your Lord. There is not a creature but He holds it by the forelock. My Lord is on a straight path.

57. If you turn away, I have conveyed to you what I was sent to you with; and my Lord will replace you with another people, and you will not cause Him any harm. My Lord is Guardian over all things."

58. And when Our decree came, We saved Hud and those who believed with him, by a mercy from Us, and We delivered them from a harsh punishment.

59. That was Aad; they denied the signs of their Lord, and defied His messengers, and followed the lead of every stubborn tyrant.

60. They were pursued by a curse in this world, and on the Day of Resurrection. Indeed, Aad blasphemed against their Lord—so away with Aad, the people of Hud.

61. And to Thamood, their brother Saleh. He said, "O my people, worship God, you have no god other than Him. He initiated you from the earth, and settled you in it. So seek His forgiveness, and repent to Him. My Lord is Near and Responsive."

62. They said, "O Saleh, we had hopes in you before this. Are you trying to prevent us from worshiping what our fathers worshiped? We are in serious doubt regarding what you are calling us to."

63. He said, "O my people, have you considered? If I stand upon clear evidence from my Lord, and He has given me mercy from Him, who would protect me from God, if I disobeyed Him? You add nothing for me except loss."

64. "O my people, this is the she-camel of God, a sign for you. Let her graze on God's land, and do not harm her, lest an imminent punishment overtakes you."

65. But they hamstrung her, and so He said, "Enjoy yourselves in your homes for three days. This is a prophecy that is infallible."

66. Then, when Our command came, We saved Saleh and those who believed with him, by a mercy from Us, from the disgrace of that day. Your Lord is the Strong, the Mighty.

67. And the Scream struck those who transgressed, and they became motionless bodies in their homes.

68. As if they had never prospered therein. Indeed, Thamood rejected their Lord, so away with Thamood.

69. Our messengers came to Abraham with good news. They said, "Peace." He said, "Peace." Soon after, he came with a roasted calf.

70. But when he saw their hands not reaching towards it, he became suspicious of them, and conceived a fear of them. They said, "Do not fear, we were sent to the people of Lot."

71. His wife was standing by, so she laughed. And We gave her good news of Isaac, and after Isaac, Jacob.

72. She said, "Alas for me. Shall I give birth, when I am an old woman, and this, my husband, is an old man? This is truly a strange thing."

73. They said, "Do you marvel at the decree of God? The mercy and blessings of God are upon you, O people of the house. He is Praiseworthy and Glorious."

74. When Abraham's fear subsided, and the good news had reached him, he started pleading with Us concerning the people of Lot.

75. Abraham was gentle, kind, penitent.

76. "O Abraham, refrain from this. The command of your Lord has come; they have incurred an irreversible punishment."

77. And when Our envoys came to Lot, he was anxious for them, and concerned for them. He said, "This is a dreadful day."

78. And his people came rushing towards him—they were in the habit of committing sins. He said, "O my people, these are my daughters; they are purer for you. So fear God, and do not embarrass me before my guests. Is there not one reasonable man among you?"

79. They said, "You know well that we have no right to your daughters, and you know well what we want."

80. He said, "If only I had the strength to stop you, or could rely on some strong support."

81. They said, "O Lot, we are the envoys of your Lord; they will not reach you. So set out with your family during the cover of the night, and let none of you look back, except for your wife. She will be struck by what will strike them. Their appointed time is the morning. Is not the morning near?"

82. And when Our command came about, We turned it upside down, and We rained down on it stones of baked clay.

83. Marked from your Lord, and never far from the wrongdoers.

84. And to Median, their brother Shuaib. He said, "O my people, worship God; you have no god other than Him. Do not short measure or short weight. I see you in good circumstances, but I fear for you the agony of an encompassing Day."

85. "O my people! Give full measure and full weight, in all fairness, and do not cheat the people out of their rights, and do not spread corruption in the land.

86. What is left by God is best for you, if you are believers. And I am not a guardian over you."

87. They said, "O Shuaib, does your prayer command you that we abandon what our ancestors worshiped, or doing with our wealth what we want? You are the one who is intelligent and wise."

88. He said, "O my people, have you considered? What if I have clear evidence from my Lord, and He has given me good livelihood from Himself? I have no desire to do what I forbid you from doing. I desire nothing but reform, as far as I can. My success lies only with God. In Him I trust, and to Him I turn."

89. "O my people, let not your hostility towards me cause you to suffer what was suffered by the people of Noah, or the people of Hud, or the people of Saleh. The people of Lot are not far away from you."

90. "And ask your Lord for forgiveness, and repent to Him. My Lord is Merciful and Loving."

91. They said, "O Shuaib, we do not understand much of what you say, and we see that you are weak among us. Were it not for your tribe, we would have stoned you. You are of no value to us."

92. He said, "O my people, is my tribe more important to you than God? And you have turned your backs on Him? My Lord comprehends everything you do."

93. "O my people, do as you may, and so will I. You will know to whom will come a punishment that will shame him, and who is a liar. So look out; I am on the lookout with you."

94. And when Our command came, We saved Shuaib and those who believed with him, by mercy from Us, and the Blast struck the wrongdoers, and they became motionless bodies in their homes.

95. As though they never flourished therein. Away with Median, as was done away with Thamood.

96. And We sent Moses with Our signs and a clear mandate.

97. To Pharaoh and his nobles, but they followed the command of Pharaoh, and the command of Pharaoh was not wise.

98. He will precede his people on the Day of Resurrection, and will lead them into the Fire. Miserable is the place he placed them in.

99. They were followed by a curse in this, and on the Day of Resurrection. Miserable is the path they followed.

100. These are of the reports of the towns— We relate them to you. Some are still standing, and some have withered away.

101. We did not wrong them, but they wronged themselves. Their gods, whom they invoked besides God, availed them nothing when the command of your Lord arrived. In fact, they added only to their ruin.

102. Such is the grip of your Lord when He seizes the towns in the midst of their sins. His grip is most painful, most severe.

103. In that is a sign for whoever fears the punishment of the Hereafter. That is a Day for which humanity will be gathered together—that is a Day to be witnessed.

104. We only postpone it until a predetermined time.

105. On the Day when it arrives, no soul will speak without His permission. Some will be miserable, and some will be happy.

106. As for those who are miserable, they will be in the Fire. They will have therein sighing and wailing.

107. Remaining therein for as long as the heavens and the earth endure, except as your Lord wills. Your Lord is Doer of whatever He wills.

108. And as for those who are happy, they will be in Paradise, remaining therein for as long as the heavens and the earth endure, except as your Lord wills—a reward without end.

109. So be not in doubt regarding what these people worship. They worship only as their ancestors worshiped before. We will pay them their due in full, without any reduction.

110. We gave Moses the Scripture, but it was disputed. Were it not for a prior word from your Lord, it would have been settled between them. They are in serious doubt concerning it.

111. Your Lord will repay each one of them in full for their deeds. He is Aware of everything they do.

112. So be upright, as you are commanded, along with those who repented with you, and do not transgress. He is Seeing of everything you do.

113. And do not incline towards those who do wrong, or the Fire may touch you; and you will have no protectors besides God, and you will not be saved.

114. Perform the prayer at the borders of the day, and during the approaches of the night. The good deeds take away the bad deeds. This is a reminder, for those who remember.

115. And be patient. God will not waste the reward of the virtuous.

116. If only there were, among the generations before you, people with wisdom, who spoke against corruption on earth—except for the few whom We saved. But the wrongdoers pursued the luxuries they were indulged in, and thus became guilty.

117. Your Lord would never destroy the towns wrongfully, while their inhabitants are righteous.

118. Had your Lord willed, He could have made humanity one community, but they continue to differ.

119. Except those on whom your Lord has mercy—for that reason He created them. The Word of your Lord is final: "I will fill Hell with jinn and humans, altogether."

120. Everything We narrate to you of the history of the messengers is to strengthen your heart therewith. The truth has come to you in this, and a lesson, and a reminder for the believers.

121. And say to those who do not believe, "Act according to your ability; and so will we."

122. "And wait; we too are waiting."

123. To God belongs the future of the heavens and the earth, and to Him all authority goes back. So worship Him, and rely on Him. Your Lord is never unaware of what you do.

12. JOSEPH
(Yusuf)

In the name of God,
the Gracious, the Merciful.

1. Alif, Lam, Ra. These are the Verses of the Clear Book.

2. We have revealed it an Arabic Quran, so that you may understand.

3. We narrate to you the most accurate history, by revealing to you this Quran. Although, prior to it, you were of the unaware.

4. When Joseph said to his father, "O my father, I saw eleven planets, and the sun, and the moon; I saw them bowing down to me."

5. He said, "O my son, do not relate your vision to your brothers, lest they plot and scheme against you. Satan is man's sworn enemy.

6. And thus your Lord will choose you, and will teach you the interpretation of events, and will complete His blessing upon you and upon the family of Jacob, as He has completed it before upon your forefathers Abraham and Isaac. Your Lord is Knowing and Wise.

7. In Joseph and his brothers are lessons for the seekers.

8. When they said, "Joseph and his brother are dearer to our father than we are, although we are a whole group. Our father is obviously in the wrong.

9. "Kill Joseph, or throw him somewhere in the land, and your father's attention will be yours. Afterwards, you will be decent people."

10. One of them said, "Do not kill Joseph, but throw him into the bottom of the well; some caravan may pick him up—if you must do something."

11. They said, "Father, why do you not trust us with Joseph, although we care for him?"

12. "Send him with us tomorrow, that he may roam and play; we will take care of him."

13. He said, "It worries me that you would take him away. And I fear the wolf may eat him while you are careless of him."

14. They said, "If the wolf ate him, and we are many, we would be good for nothing."

15. So they went away with him, and agreed to put him at the bottom of the well. And We inspired him, "You will in-

form them of this deed of theirs when they are unaware."

16. And they came to their father in the evening weeping.

17. They said, "O father, we went off racing one another, and left Joseph by our belongings; and the wolf ate him. But you will not believe us, even though we are being truthful."

18. And they brought his shirt, with fake blood on it. He said, "Your souls enticed you to do something. But patience is beautiful, and God is my Help against what you describe."

19. A caravan passed by, and they sent their water-carrier. He lowered his bucket, and said, "Good news. Here is a boy." And they hid him as merchandise. But God was aware of what they did.

20. And they sold him for a cheap price—a few coins—they considered him to be of little value.

21. The Egyptian who bought him said to his wife, "Take good care of him; he may be useful to us, or we may adopt him as a son." We thus established Joseph in the land, to teach him the interpretation of events. God has control over His affairs, but most people do not know.

22. When he reached his maturity, We gave him wisdom and knowledge. We thus reward the righteous.

23. She in whose house he was living tried to seduce him. She shut the doors, and said, "I am yours." He said, "God forbid! He is my Lord. He has given me a good home. Sinners never succeed."

24. She desired him, and he desired her, had he not seen the proof of his Lord. It was thus that We diverted evil and indecency away from him. He was one of Our loyal servants.

25. As they raced towards the door, she tore his shirt from behind. At the door, they ran into her husband. She said, "What is the penalty for him who desired to dishonor your wife, except imprisonment or a painful punishment?"

26. He said, "It was she who tried to seduce me." A witness from her household suggested: "If his shirt is torn from the front, then she has told the truth, and he is the liar.

27. But if his shirt is torn from the back, then she has lied, and he is the truthful."

28. And when he saw that his shirt was torn from the back, he said, "This is a woman's scheme. Your scheming is serious indeed."

29. "Joseph, turn away from this. And you, woman, ask forgiveness for your sin; you are indeed in the wrong."

30. Some ladies in the city said, "The governor's wife is trying to seduce her servant. She is deeply in love with him. We see she has gone astray."

31. And when she heard of their gossip, she invited them, and prepared for them a banquet, and she gave each one of them a knife. She said, "Come out before them." And when they saw him, they marveled at him, and cut their hands. They said, "Good God, this is not a human, this must be a precious angel."

32. She said, "Here he is, the one you blamed me for. I did try to seduce him, but he resisted. But if he does not do what I tell him to do, he will be imprisoned, and will be one of the despised."

33. He said, "My Lord, prison is more desirable to me than what they call me to. Unless You turn their scheming away from me, I may yield to them, and become one of the ignorant."

34. Thereupon his Lord answered him, and diverted their scheming away from him. He is the Hearer, the Knower.

35. Then it occurred to them, after they had seen the signs, to imprison him for a while.

36. Two youth entered the prison with him. One of them said, "I see myself pressing wine." The other said, "I see myself carrying bread on my head, from which the birds are eating. Tell us their interpretation—we see that you are one of the righteous."

37. He said, "No food is served to you, but I have informed you about it before you have received it. That is some of what my Lord has taught me. I have forsaken the tradition of people who do not believe in God; and regarding the Hereafter, they are deniers."

38. "And I have followed the faith of my forefathers, Abraham, and Isaac, and Jacob. It is not for us to associate anything with God. This is by virtue of God's grace upon us and upon the people, but most people do not give thanks.

39. "O My fellow inmates, are diverse lords better, or God, the One, the Supreme?"

40. "You do not worship, besides Him, except names you have named, you and your ancestors, for which God has sent down no authority. Judgment belongs to none but God. He has commanded that you worship none but Him. That is the right religion, but most people do not know.

41. "O my fellow inmates, one of you will serve his master wine; while the other will be crucified, and the birds will eat from his head. Thus the matter you are inquiring about is settled."

42. And he said to the one he thought would be released, "Mention me to your master." But Satan caused him to forget mentioning him to his master, so he remained in prison for several years.

43. The king said, "I see seven fat cows being eaten by seven lean ones, and seven green spikes, and others dried up. O elders, explain to me my vision, if you are able to interpret visions."

44. They said, "Jumbles of dreams, and we know nothing of the interpretation of dreams."

45. The one who was released said, having remembered after a time, "I will inform you of its interpretation, so send me out."

46. "Joseph, O man of truth, inform us concerning seven fat cows being eaten by seven lean ones, and seven green spikes, and others dried up, so that I may return to the people, so that they may know."

47. He said, "You will farm for seven consecutive years. But whatever you harvest, leave it in its spikes, except for the little that you eat."

48. Then after that will come seven difficult ones, which will consume what you have stored for them, except for the little that you have preserved.

49. Then after that will come a year that brings relief to the people, and during which they will press.

50. The king said, "Bring him to me." And when the envoy came to him, he said, "Go back to your master, and ask him about the intentions of the women who cut their hands; my Lord is well aware of their schemes."

51. He said, "What was the matter with you, women, when you tried to seduce Joseph?" They said, "God forbid! We knew of no evil committed by him." The governor's wife then said, "Now the truth is out.

It was I who tried to seduce him, and he is telling the truth."

52. "This is that he may know that I did not betray him in secret, and that God does not guide the scheming of the betrayers."

53. "Yet I do not claim to be innocent. The soul commands evil, except those on whom my Lord has mercy. Truly my Lord is Forgiving and Merciful."

54. The king said, "Bring him to me, and I will reserve him for myself." And when he spoke to him, he said, "This day you are with us established and secure."

55. He said, "Put me in charge of the storehouses of the land; I am honest and knowledgeable."

56. And thus We established Joseph in the land, to live therein wherever he wished. We touch with Our mercy whomever We will, and We never waste the reward of the righteous.

57. But the reward of the Hereafter is better for those who believe and are pious.

58. And Joseph's brothers came, and entered into his presence. He recognized them, but they did not recognize him.

59. When he provided them with their provisions, he said, "Bring me a brother of yours from your father. Do you not see that I fill up the measure, and I am the best of hosts?"

60. "But if you do not bring him to me, you will have no measure from me, and you will not come near me."

61. They said, "We will solicit him from his father. We will surely do."

62. He said to his servants, "Put their goods in their saddlebags. Perhaps they will recognize them when they return to their families, and maybe they will come back."

63. When they returned to their father, they said, "O father, we were denied measure, but send our brother with us, and we will obtain measure. We will take care of him."

64. He said, "Shall I trust you with him, as I trusted you with his brother before? God is the Best Guardian, and He is the Most Merciful of the merciful."

65. And when they opened their baggage, they found that their goods were returned to them. They said, "Father, what more do we want? Here are our goods, returned to us. We will provide for our family, and protect our brother, and have an additional camel-load. This is easy commerce."

66. He said, "I will not send him with you, unless you give me a pledge before God that you will bring him back to me, unless you get trapped." And when they gave him their pledge, he said, "God is witness to what we say."

67. And he said, "O my sons, do not enter by one gate, but enter by different gates. I cannot avail you anything against God. The decision rests only with God. On Him I rely, and on Him let the reliant rely."

68. And when they entered as their father had instructed them, it did not avail them anything against God; it was just a need in the soul of Jacob, which he carried out. He was a person of knowledge inasmuch as We had taught him, but most people do not know.

69. And when they entered into the presence of Joseph, he embraced his brother, and said, "I am your brother; do not be saddened by what they used to do."

70. Then, when he provided them with their provisions, he placed the drinking-cup in his brother's saddlebag. Then an announcer called out, "O people of the caravan, you are thieves."

71. They said, as they came towards them, "What are you missing?"

72. They said, "We are missing the king's goblet. Whoever brings it will have a camel-load; and I personally guarantee it."

73. They said, "By God, you know we did not come to cause trouble in the land, and we are not thieves."

74. They said, "What shall be his punishment, if you are lying?"

75. They said, "His punishment, if it is found in his bag: he will belong to you. Thus we penalize the guilty."

76. So he began with their bags, before his brother's bag. Then he pulled it out of his brother's bag. Thus We devised a plan for Joseph; he could not have detained his brother under the king's law, unless God so willed. We elevate by degrees whomever We will; and above every person of knowledge, there is one more learned.

77. They said, "If he has stolen, a brother of his has stolen before." But Joseph kept it to himself, and did not reveal it to them. He said, "You are in a worse situation, and God is Aware of what you allege."

78. They said, "O noble prince, he has a father, a very old man, so take one of us in his place. We see that you are a good person."

79. He said, "God forbid that we should arrest anyone except him in whose possession we found our property; for then we would be unjust."

80. And when they despaired of him, they conferred privately. Their eldest said, "Don't you know that your father received a pledge from you before God, and in the past you failed with regard to Joseph? I will not leave this land until my father permits me, or God decides for me; for He is the Best of Deciders."

81. "Go back to your father, and say, 'Our father, your son has stolen. We testify only to what we know, and we could not have prevented the unforeseen.'"

82. "Ask the town where we were, and the caravan in which we came. We are being truthful."

83. He said, "Rather, your souls have contrived something for you. Patience is a virtue. Perhaps God will bring them all back to me. He is the Knowing, the Wise."

84. Then he turned away from them, and said, "O my bitterness for Joseph." And his eyes turned white from sorrow, and he became depressed.

85. They said, "By God, you will not stop remembering Joseph, until you have ruined your health, or you have passed away."

86. He said, "I only complain of my grief and sorrow to God, and I know from God what you do not know."

87. "O my sons, go and inquire about Joseph and his brother, and do not despair of God's comfort. None despairs of God's comfort except the disbelieving people."

88. Then, when they entered into his presence, they said, "Mighty governor, adversity has befallen us, and our family. We have brought scant merchandise. But give us full measure, and be charitable towards us—God rewards the charitable."

89. He said, "Do you realize what you did with Joseph and his brother, in your ignorance?"

90. They said, "Is that you, Joseph?" He said, "I am Joseph, and this is my brother. God has been gracious to us. He who practices piety and patience—God never fails to reward the righteous."

91. They said, "By God, God has preferred you over us. We were definitely in the wrong."

92. He said, "There is no blame upon you today. God will forgive you. He is the Most Merciful of the merciful."

93. "Take this shirt of mine, and lay it over my father's face, and he will recover his sight. And bring your whole family to me."

94. As the caravan set out, their father said, "I sense the presence of Joseph, though you may think I am senile."

95. They said, "By God, you are still in your old confusion."

96. Then, when the bearer of good news arrived, he laid it over his face, and he regained his sight. He said, "Did I not say to you that I know from God what you do not know?"

97. They said, "Father, pray for the forgiveness of our sins; we were indeed at fault."

98. He said, "I will ask my Lord to forgive you. He is the Forgiver, the Most Merciful."

99. Then, when they entered into the presence of Joseph, he embraced his parents, and said, "Enter Egypt, God willing, safe and secure."

100. And he elevated his parents on the throne, and they fell prostrate before him. He said, "Father, this is the fulfillment of my vision of long ago. My Lord has made it come true. He has blessed me, when he released me from prison, and brought you out of the wilderness, after the devil had sown conflict between me and my brothers. My Lord is Most Kind towards whomever He wills. He is the All-knowing, the Most Wise."

101. "My Lord, You have given me some authority, and taught me some interpretation of events. Initiator of the heavens and the earth; You are my Protector in this life and in the Hereafter. Receive my soul in submission, and unite me with the righteous."

102. This is news from the past that We reveal to you. You were not present with them when they plotted and agreed on a plan.

103. But most people, for all your eagerness, are not believers.

104. You ask them no wage for it. It is only a reminder for all mankind.

105. How many a sign in the heavens and the earth do they pass by, paying no attention to them?

106. And most of them do not believe in God unless they associate others.

107. Do they feel secure that a covering of God's punishment will not come upon them, or that the Hour will not come upon them suddenly, while they are unaware?

108. Say, "This is my way; I invite to God, based on clear knowledge—I and whoever follows me. Glory be to God; and I am not of the polytheists."

109. We did not send before you except men, whom We inspired, from the people of the towns. Have they not roamed the earth and seen the consequences for those before them? The Home of the Hereafter is better for those who are righteous. Do you not understand?

110. Until, when the messengers have despaired, and thought that they were rejected, Our help came to them. We save whomever We will, and Our severity is not averted from the guilty people.

111. In their stories is a lesson for those who possess intelligence. This is not a fabricated tale, but a confirmation of what came before it; and a detailed explanation

of all things, and guidance, and mercy for people who believe.

13. THUNDER
(ar-Ra'd)

In the name of God,
the Gracious, the Merciful.

1. Alif, Lam, Meem, Ra. These are the signs of the Scripture. What is revealed to you from your Lord is the truth, but most people do not believe.

2. God is He who raised the heavens without pillars that you can see, and then settled on the Throne. And He regulated the sun and the moon, each running for a specified period. He manages all affairs, and He explains the signs, that you may be certain of the meeting with your Lord.

3. And it is He who spread the earth, and placed on it mountains and rivers. Of every kind of fruit He made a pair of two. He causes the night to overlap the day. In that are signs for people who reflect.

4. On earth are adjacent terrains, and gardens of vines, and crops, and date-palms, from the same root or from distinct roots, irrigated with the same water. We make some taste better than others. In that are proofs for people who reason.

5. Should you wonder—the real wonder is their saying: "When we have become dust, will we be in a new creation?" Those are they who defied their Lord. Those are they who will have yokes around their necks. Those are the inhabitants of the Fire, where they will remain forever.

6. And they urge you to hasten evil before good, though examples have passed away before them. Your Lord is full of forgiveness towards the people for their wrongdoings, yet your Lord is severe in retribution.

7. Those who disbelieve say, "Why was a miracle not sent down to him from his Lord?" You are only a warner, and to every community is a guide.

8. God knows what every female bears, and every increase and decrease of the wombs. With Him, everything is by measure.

9. The Knower of the Invisible and the Visible, the Grand, the Supreme.

10. It is the same; whether one of you conceals his speech, or declares it; whether he goes into hiding by night, or goes out by day.

11. He has a succession, before him and behind him, protecting him by God's command. God does not change the condition of a people until they change what is within themselves. And if God wills any hardship for a people, there is no turning it back, and apart from Him they have no protector.

12. It is He who shows you the lightening, causing fear and hope. And He produces the heavy clouds.

13. The thunder praises His glory, and so do the angels, in awe of Him. And He sends the thunderbolts, striking with them whomever He wills. Yet they argue about God, while He is Tremendous in might.

14. To Him belongs the call to truth. Those they call upon besides Him do not respond to them with anything—except as someone who stretches his hands towards water, so that it may reach his mouth, but it does not reach it. The prayers of the unbelievers are only in vain.

15. To God prostrates everyone in the heavens and the earth, willingly or unwillingly, as do their shadows, in the morning and in the evening.

16. Say, "Who is the Lord of the heavens and the earth?" Say, "God." Say, "Have you

taken besides Him protectors, who have no power to profit or harm even themselves?" Say, "Are the blind and the seeing equal? Or are darkness and light equal? Or have they assigned to God associates, who created the likes of His creation, so that the creations seemed to them alike? Say, "God is the Creator of all things, and He is The One, the Irresistible."

17. He sends down water from the sky, and riverbeds flow according to their capacity. The current carries swelling froth. And from what they heat in fire of ornaments or utensils comes a similar froth. Thus God exemplifies truth and falsehood. As for the froth, it is swept away, but what benefits the people remains in the ground. Thus God presents the analogies.

18. For those who respond to their Lord is the best. But as for those who do not respond to Him, even if they possessed everything on earth, and twice as much, they could not redeem themselves with it. Those will have the worst reckoning; and their home is Hell—a miserable destination.

19. Is he who knows that what was revealed to your from your Lord is the truth, like he who is blind? Only those who reason will remember.

20. Those who fulfill the promise to God, and do not violate the agreement.

21. And those who join what God has commanded to be joined, and fear their Lord, and dread the dire reckoning.

22. And those who patiently seek the presence of their Lord, and pray regularly, and spend from Our provisions to them, secretly and openly, and repel evil with good. These will have the Ultimate Home.

23. Everlasting Gardens, which they will enter, along with the righteous among their parents, and their spouses, and their descendants. And the angels will enter upon them from every gate.

24. "Peace be upon you, because you endured patiently. How excellent is the Final Home."

25. As for those who violate the promise to God, after pledging to keep it, and sever what God has commanded to be joined, and spread corruption on earth—these, the curse will be upon them, and they will have the Worst Home.

26. God dispenses the provisions to whomever He wills, and restricts. And they delight in the worldly life; yet the worldly life, compared to the Hereafter, is only enjoyment.

27. Those who disbelieve say, "If only a miracle was sent down to him from his Lord." Say, "God leads astray whomever He wills, and He guides to Himself whoever repents."

28. Those who believe, and whose hearts find comfort in the remembrance of God. Surely, it is in the remembrance of God that hearts find comfort."

29. For those who believe and do righteous deeds—for them is happiness and a beautiful return.

30. Thus We have sent you among a community before which other communities have passed away, that you may recite to them what We revealed to you. Yet they deny the Benevolent One. Say, "He is my Lord; there is no god but He; in Him I trust, and to Him is my repentance."

31. Even if there were a Quran, by which mountains could be set in motion, by which the earth could be shattered, or by which the dead could be made to speak. In fact, every decision rests with God. Did the believers not give up and realize that had God willed, He would have guided all hu-

manity? Disasters will continue to strike those who disbelieve, because of their deeds, or they fall near their homes, until God's promise comes true. God never breaks a promise.

32. Messengers before you were ridiculed, but I granted the disbelievers respite, and then I seized them. What a punishment it was.

33. Is He who is watchful over the deeds of every soul? Yet they ascribe associates to God. Say, "Name them. Or are you informing Him of something on earth He does not know, or is it a show of words?" In fact, the scheming of those who disbelieve is made to appear good to them, and they are averted from the path. Whomever God misguides has no guide.

34. There is for them torment in the worldly life, but the torment of the Hereafter is harsher. And they have no defender against God.

35. The likeness of the Garden promised to the righteous: rivers flowing beneath it; its food is perpetual, and so is its shade. Such is the sequel for those who guard against evil, but the sequel of the disbelievers is the Fire.

36. Those to whom We gave the Scripture rejoice in what was revealed to you, while some factions reject parts of it. Say, "I am commanded to worship God, and to never associate anything with Him. To Him I invite, and to Him is my return."

37. Thus We revealed it an Arabic code of law. Were you to follow their desires, after the knowledge that has come to you, you would have neither ally nor defender against God.

38. We sent messengers before you, and We assigned for them wives and offspring. No messenger could bring a sign except with the permission of God. For every era is a scripture.

39. God abolishes whatever He wills, and He affirms. With Him is the source of the Scripture.

40. Whether We show you some of what We have promised them, or We cause you to die—your duty is to inform, and Ours is the reckoning.

41. Do they not see how We deal with the earth, diminishing it at its edges? God judges; and nothing can hold back His judgment. And He is quick to settle accounts.

42. Those before them planned, but the entire plan is up to God. He knows what every soul earns. Those who disbelieve will know to whom the Ultimate Home is.

43. Those who disbelieve say, "You are not a messenger." Say, "God is a sufficient witness between me and you, and whoever has knowledge of the Scripture."

14. ABRAHAM
(Ibrahim)

In the name of God,
the Gracious, the Merciful.

1. Alif, Lam, Ra. A Scripture that We revealed to you, that you may bring humanity from darkness to light—with the permission of their Lord—to the path of the Almighty, the Praiseworthy.

2. God—to whom belongs what is in the heavens and the earth. And woe to the disbelievers from a severe torment.

3. Those who prefer the present life to the Hereafter, and repel from the path of God, and seek to make it crooked—these are far astray.

4. We never sent any messenger except in the language of his people, to make things

clear for them. God leads astray whom He wills, and guides whom He wills. He is the Mighty, the Wise.

5. We sent Moses with Our signs: "Bring your people out of darkness into light, and remind them of the Days of God." In that are signs for every patient and thankful person."

6. Moses said to his people, "Remember God's blessings upon you, as He delivered you from the people of Pharaoh, who inflicted on you terrible suffering, slaughtering your sons while sparing your daughters. In that there was a serious trial from your Lord."

7. And when your Lord proclaimed: "If you give thanks, I will grant you increase; but if you are ungrateful, My punishment is severe."

8. And Moses said, "Even if you are ungrateful, together with everyone on earth—God is in no need, Worthy of Praise."

9. Has not the story reached you, of those before you, the people of Noah, and Aad, and Thamood—and those after them? None knows them except God. Their messengers came to them with the clear proofs, but they tried to silence them, and said, "We reject what you are sent with, and we are in serious doubt regarding what you are calling us to."

10. Their messengers said, "Is there any doubt about God, Maker of the heavens and the earth? He calls you to forgive you your sins, and to defer you until a stated term." They said, "You are only humans like us; you want to turn us away from what our ancestors worshiped; so bring us a clear proof."

11. Their messengers said to them, "We are only humans like you, but God favors whomever He wills from among His serv-

ants. We cannot possibly show you any proof, except by leave of God. In God let the faithful put their trust."

12. "And why should we not trust in God, when He has guided us in our ways? We will persevere in the face of your persecution. And upon God the reliant should rely."

13. Those who disbelieved said to their messengers, "We will expel you from our land, unless you return to our religion." And their Lord inspired them: "We will destroy the wrongdoers.

14. And We will settle you in the land after them. That is for him who fears My Majesty, and fears My threats."

15. And they prayed for victory, and every stubborn tyrant came to disappointment.

16. Beyond him lies Hell. He will be given to drink putrid water.

17. He will guzzle it, but he will not swallow it. Death will come at him from every direction, but he will not die. And beyond this is relentless suffering.

18. The likeness of those who disbelieve in their Lord: their works are like ashes, in a fierce wind, on a stormy day. They have no control over anything they have earned. That is the utmost misguidance.

19. Do you not see that God created the heavens and the earth with truth? If He wills, He can do away with you, and bring a new creation.

20. And that is not difficult for God.

21. They will emerge before God, altogether. The weak will say to those who were proud, "We were your followers, can you protect us at all against God's punishment?" They will say, "Had God guided us, we would have guided you. It is the same for us, whether we mourn, or are patient; there is no asylum for us."

22. And Satan will say, when the issue is settled, "God has promised you the promise of truth, and I promised you, but I failed you. I had no authority over you, except that I called you, and you answered me. So do not blame me, but blame yourselves. I cannot come to your aid, nor can you come to my aid. I reject your associating with me in the past. The wrongdoers will have a torment most painful."

23. But those who believed and did good deeds will be admitted into gardens beneath which rivers flow, to remain therein forever, by leave of their Lord. Their greeting therein will be: "Peace."

24. Do you not see how God presents a parable? A good word is like a good tree—its root is firm, and its branches are in the sky.

25. It yields its fruits every season by the will of its Lord. God presents the parables to the people, so that they may reflect.

26. And the parable of a bad word is that of a bad tree—it is uprooted from the ground; it has no stability.

27. God gives firmness to those who believe, with the firm word, in this life, and in the Hereafter. And God leads the wicked astray. God does whatever He wills.

28. Have you not seen those who exchanged the blessing of God with blasphemy, and landed their people into the house of perdition?

29. Hell—they will roast in it. What a miserable settlement.

30. And they set up rivals to God, in order to lead away from His path. Say, "Enjoy yourselves; your destination is the Fire."

31. Tell My servants who have believed to perform the prayers, and to give from what We have given them, secretly and publicly, before a Day comes in which there is neither trading nor friendship.

32. God is He Who created the heavens and the earth, and sends down water from the sky, and with it produces fruits for your sustenance. And He committed the ships to your service, sailing through the sea by His command, and He committed the rivers to your service.

33. And He committed the sun and the moon to your service, both continuously pursuing their courses, and He committed the night and the day to your service.

34. And He has given you something of all what you asked. And if you were to count God's blessings, you would not be able to enumerate them. The human being is unfair and ungrateful.

35. Recall that Abraham said, "O my Lord, make this land peaceful, and keep me and my sons from worshiping idols."

36. "My Lord, they have led many people astray. Whoever follows me belongs with me; and whoever disobeys me—You are Forgiving and Merciful.

37. "Our Lord, I have settled some of my offspring in a valley of no vegetation, by Your Sacred House, our Lord, so that they may perform the prayers. So make the hearts of some people incline towards them, and provide them with fruits, that they may be thankful."

38. "Our Lord, You know what we conceal and what we reveal. And nothing is hidden from God, on earth, or in the heaven."

39. "Praise be to God, Who has given me, in my old age, Ishmael and Isaac. My Lord is the Hearer of Prayers."

40. "My Lord, make me one who performs the prayer, and from my offspring. Our Lord, accept my supplication."

41. "Our Lord, forgive me, and my parents, and the believers, on the Day the Reckoning takes place."

42. Do not ever think that God is unaware of what the wrongdoers do. He only defers them until a Day when the sights stare.

43. Their necks outstretched, their heads upraised, their gaze unblinking, their hearts void.

44. And warn mankind of the Day when the punishment will come upon them, and the wicked will say, "Our Lord, defer us for a little while, and we will answer Your call and follow the messengers." Did you not swear before that there will be no passing away for you?

45. And you inhabited the homes of those who wronged themselves, and it became clear to you how We dealt with them, and We cited for you the examples.

46. They planned their plans, but their plans are known to God, even if their plans can eliminate mountains.

47. Do not ever think that God will break His promise to His messengers. God is Strong, Able to Avenge.

48. On the Day when the earth is changed into another earth, and the heavens, and they will emerge before God, the One, the Irresistible.

49. On that Day, you will see the sinners bound together in chains.

50. Their garments made of tar, and the Fire covering their faces.

51. That God may repay each soul according to what it has earned. God is Quick in reckoning.

52. This is a proclamation for mankind, that they may be warned thereby, and know that He is One God, and that people of understanding may remember.

15. THE ROCK
(al-Hijr)

In the name of God,
the Gracious, the Merciful.

1. Alif, Lam, Ra. These are the Verses of the Book, a Quran that makes things clear.

2. Perhaps those who disbelieve would like to become Muslims.

3. Leave them to eat, and enjoy, and be lulled by hope. They will find out.

4. We have never destroyed a town unless it had a set time.

5. No nation can bring its time forward, nor can they delay it.

6. And they said, "O you who received the message, you are insane."

7. Why do you not bring us the angels, if you are truthful?"

8. We do not send the angels down except with reason, and they will not be held back.

9. Surely We revealed the message, and We will surely preserve it.

10. We sent others before you, to the former communities.

11. But no messenger came to them, but they ridiculed him.

12. Thus We slip it into the hearts of the guilty.

13. They do not believe in it, though the ways of the ancients have passed away.

14. Even if We opened for them a gateway into the sky, and they began to ascend through it.

15. They would still say, "Our eyes are hallucinating; in fact, we are people bewitched."

16. We placed constellations in the sky, and made them beautiful to the beholders.

17. And We guarded them from every outcast devil.

18. Except one who steals a hearing, and is followed by a visible projectile.

19. We spread the earth, and placed stabilizers in it, and in it We grew all things in proper measure.

20. And in it We created livelihoods for you, and for those for whom you are not the providers.

21. There is not a thing but with Us are its stores, and We send it down only in precise measure.

22. And We send the fertilizing winds; and send down water from the sky, and give it to you to drink; and you are not the ones who store it.

23. It is We who give life and cause death, and We are the Inheritors.

24. And We know those of you who go forward, and We know those who lag behind.

25. It is your Lord who will gather them together. He is the Wise, the Knowing.

26. We created the human being from clay, from molded mud.

27. And the jinn We created before, from piercing fire.

28. Your Lord said to the angels, "I am creating a human being, from clay, from molded mud."

29. "When I have formed him, and breathed into him of My spirit, fall down prostrating before him."

30. So the angels prostrated themselves, all together.

31. Except for Satan. He refused to be among those who prostrated themselves.

32. He said, "O Satan, what kept you from being among those who prostrated themselves?"

33. He said, "I am not about to prostrate myself before a human being, whom You created from clay, from molded mud."

34. He said, "Then get out of here, for you are an outcast".

35. "And the curse will be upon you until the Day of Judgment."

36. He said, "My Lord, reprieve me until the Day they are resurrected."

37. He said, "You are of those reprieved."

38. "Until the Day of the time appointed."

39. He said, "My Lord, since You have lured me away, I will glamorize for them on earth, and I will lure them all away."

40. "Except for Your sincere servants among them."

41. He said, "This is a right way with Me."

42. "Over My servants you have no authority, except for the sinners who follow you."

43. And Hell is the meeting-place for them all.

44. "It has seven doors; for each door is an assigned class."

45. But the righteous will be in gardens with springs.

46. "Enter it in peace and security."

47. And We will remove all ill-feelings from their hearts—brothers and sisters, on couches facing one another.

48. No fatigue will ever touch them therein, nor will they be asked to leave it.

49. Inform My servants that I am the Forgiver, the Merciful.

50. And that My punishment is the painful punishment.

51. And inform them of the guests of Abraham.

52. When they entered upon him, and said, "Peace." He said, "We are wary of you."

53. They said, "Do not fear; we bring you good news of a boy endowed with knowledge."

54. He said, "Do you bring me good news, when old age has overtaken me? What good news do you bring?"

55. They said, "We bring you good news in truth, so do not despair."

56. He said, "And who despairs of his Lord's mercy but the lost?"

57. He said, "So what is your business, O envoys?"

58. They said, "We were sent to a sinful people."

59. "Except for the family of Lot; we will save them all."

60. "Except for his wife." We have determined that she will be of those who lag behind.

61. And when the envoys came to the family of Lot.

62. He said, "You are a people unknown to me."

63. They said, "We bring you what they have doubts about."

64. "We bring you the truth, and we are truthful."

65. "Travel with your family at the dead of the night, and follow up behind them, and let none of you look back, and proceed as commanded."

66. And We informed him of Our decree: the last remnant of these will be uprooted by early morning.

67. And the people of the town came joyfully.

68. He said, "These are my guests, so do not embarrass me."

69. "And fear God, and do not disgrace me."

70. They said, "Did we not forbid you from strangers?"

71. He said, "These are my daughters, if you must."

72. By your life, they were blundering in their drunkenness.

73. So the Blast struck them at sunrise.

74. And We turned it upside down, and rained down upon them stones of baked clay.

75. Surely in that is a lesson for those who read signs.

76. And it is on an existing road.

77. Surely in that is a sign for the believers.

78. The people of the Woods were also wrongdoers.

79. So We took revenge upon them. Both are clearly documented.

80. And the people of the Rock also rejected the messengers.

81. We gave them Our revelations, but they turned away from them.

82. They used to carve homes in the mountains, feeling secure.

83. But the Blast struck them in the morning.

84. All they had acquired was of no avail to them.

85. We did not create the heavens and the earth, and what lies between them, except with truth. The Hour is coming, so forgive with gracious forgiveness.

86. Your Lord is the All-Knowing Creator.

87. We have given you seven of the pairs, and the Grand Quran.

88. Do not extend your eyes towards what We have bestowed on some couples of them to enjoy, and do not grieve over them, and lower your wing to the believers.

89. And say, "I am the clear warner."

90. Just as We sent down to the separatists.

91. Those who made the Quran obsolete.

92. By your Lord, we will question them all.

93. About what they used to do.

94. So proclaim openly what you are commanded, and turn away from the polytheists.

95. We are enough for you against the mockers.

96. Those who set up another god with God. They will come to know.

97. We are aware that your heart is strained by what they say.

98. So glorify the praise of your Lord, and be among those who bow down.

99. And worship your Lord, in order to attain certainty.

16. THE BEE
(an-Nahl)

In the name of God,
the Gracious, the Merciful.

1. The command of God has come, so do not rush it. Glory be to Him, exalted above what they associate.

2. He sends down the angels with the Spirit by His command, upon whom He wills of His servants: "Give warning that there is no god but Me, and fear Me."

3. He created the heavens and the earth with justice. He is exalted above the associations they attribute.

4. He created the human being from a drop of fluid, yet he becomes an open adversary.

5. And the livestock—He created them for you. In them are warmth and benefits for you, and of them you eat.

6. And there is beauty in them for you, when you bring them home, and when you drive them to pasture.

7. And they carry your loads to territory you could not have reached without great hardship. Your Lord is Clement and Merciful.

8. And the horses, and the mules, and the donkeys—for you to ride, and for luxury. And He creates what you do not know.

9. It is for God to point out the paths, but some of them are flawed. Had He willed, He could have guided you all.

10. It is He Who sends down for you from the sky water. From it is drink, and with it grows vegetation for grazing.

11. And He produces for you grains with it, and olives, and date-palms, and grapes, and all kinds of fruits. Surely in that is a sign for people who think.

12. And He regulated for you the night and the day; and the sun, and the moon, and the stars are disposed by His command. Surely in that are signs for people who ponder.

13. And whatsoever He created for you on earth is of diverse colors. Surely in that is a sign for people who are mindful.

14. And it is He who made the sea to serve you, that you may eat from it tender meat, and extract from it ornaments that you wear. And you see the ships plowing through it, as you seek His bounties, so that you may give thanks.

15. And he cast mountains on the earth, lest it shifts with you; and rivers, and roads, so that you may be guided.

16. And landmarks. And by the stars they guide themselves.

17. Is He who creates like him who does not create? Will you not take a lesson?

18. And if you tried to enumerate the favors of God, you will not be able to count them. God is Forgiving and Merciful.

19. And God knows what you hide and what you disclose.

20. Those they invoke besides God create nothing, but are themselves created.

21. They are dead, not alive; and they do not know when they will be resurrected.

22. Your God is one God. As for those who do not believe in the Hereafter, their hearts are in denial, and they are arrogant.

23. Without a doubt, God knows what they conceal and what they reveal. He does not like the arrogant.

24. And when it is said to them, "What has your Lord sent down?" They say, "Legends of the ancients."

25. So let them carry their loads complete on the Day of Resurrection, and some of the loads of those they misguided without knowledge. Evil is what they carry.

26. Those before them also schemed, but God took their structures from the foundations, and the roof caved in on them. The punishment came at them from where they did not perceive.

27. Then, on the Day of Resurrection, He will disgrace them, and say, "Where are My associates for whose sake you used to dispute?" Those who were given knowledge will say, "Today shame and misery are upon the disbelievers."

28. Those wronging their souls while the angels are taking them away—they will propose peace: "We did no wrong." Yes you did. God is aware of what you used to do."

29. Enter the gates of Hell, to dwell therein forever. Miserable is the residence of the arrogant.

30. And it will be said to those who maintained piety, "What has your Lord revealed?" They will say, "Goodness." To those who do good in this world is goodness, and the Home of the Hereafter is even better. How wonderful is the residence of the pious.

31. The Gardens of Perpetuity, which they will enter, beneath which rivers flow, where they will have whatever they desire. Thus God rewards the pious.

32. Those who are in a wholesome state when the angels take them—will say, "Peace be upon you; enter Paradise, for what you used to do."

33. Are they waiting for anything but the angels to come to them, or the decree of your Lord to come? Those before them did likewise. God did not wrong them, but they used to wrong their own souls.

34. So the evils of their deeds assailed them, and what they used to ridicule engulfed them.

35. The idolaters say, "Had God willed, we would not have worshiped anything besides Him, neither us, nor our ancestors; nor would we have prohibited anything besides His prohibitions." Those before them did likewise. Are the messengers responsible for anything but clear communication?

36. To every community We sent a messenger: "Worship God, and avoid idolatry." Some of them God guided, while oth-

ers deserved misguidance. So travel through the earth, and see what the fate of the deniers was.

37. Even though you may be concerned about their guidance, God does not guide those who misguide. And they will have no saviors.

38. And they swear by God with their most solemn oaths, "God will not resurrect anyone who dies." Yes indeed, it is a promise binding on Him, but most people do not know.

39. To clarify for them what they differed about, and for the faithless to know that they were liars.

40. When We intend for something to happen, We say to it, "Be," and it becomes.

41. Those who emigrate for God's sake after being persecuted, We will settle them in a good place in this world; but the reward of the Hereafter is greater, if they only knew.

42. Those who endure patiently, and in their Lord they put their trust.

43. We did not send before you except men whom We inspired. So ask the people of knowledge, if you do not know.

44. With the clarifications and the Scriptures. And We revealed to you the Reminder, that you may clarify to the people what was revealed to them, and that they may reflect.

45. Do those who scheme evils feel secure that God will not cause the earth to cave in with them, or that the punishment will not come upon them from where they do not perceive?

46. Or that He will not seize them during their activities? And they will not be able to prevent it.

47. Or that He will not seize them while in dread? Your Lord is Gentle and Merciful.

48. Have they not observed what God has created? Their shadows revolve from the right and the left, bowing to God as they shrink away.

49. To God bows down everything in the heavens and everything on earth—every living creature, and the angels, and without being proud.

50. They fear their Lord above them, and they do what they are commanded.

51. God has said: "Do not take two gods; He is only One God; so fear only Me."

52. To Him belongs everything in the heavens and the earth; and to Him obedience is due always. Do you, then, fear anyone other than God?

53. Whatever blessing you have is from God. And when harm touches you, it is to Him that you groan.

54. But when He lifts the harm from you, some of you associate others with their Lord.

55. To show ingratitude for what We have given them. Enjoy yourselves. You will soon know.

56. And they allocate, to something they do not know, a share of what We have provided for them. By God, you will be questioned about what you have been inventing.

57. And they attribute to God daughters—exalted is He—and for themselves what they desire.

58. And when one of them is given news of a female infant, his face darkens, and he chokes with grief.

59. He hides from the people because of the bad news given to him. Shall he keep it in

humiliation, or bury it in the dust? Evil is the decision they make.

60. Those who do not believe in the Hereafter set a bad example, while God sets the Highest Example. He is the Mighty, the Wise.

61. If God were to hold mankind for their injustices, He would not leave upon it a single creature, but He postpones them until an appointed time. Then, when their time arrives, they will not delay it by one hour, nor will they advance it.

62. And they attribute to God what they themselves dislike, while their tongues utter the lie that theirs is the goodness. Without a doubt, for them is the Fire, and they will be neglected.

63. By God, We sent messengers to communities before you, but Satan made their deeds appear alluring to them. He is their master today, and they will have a painful punishment.

64. We revealed to you the Scripture only to clarify for them what they differ about, and guidance and mercy for people who believe.

65. God sends down water from the sky, with which He revives the earth after its death. In this is a sign for people who listen.

66. And there is a lesson for you in cattle: We give you a drink from their bellies, from between waste and blood, pure milk, refreshing to the drinkers.

67. And from the fruits of date-palms and grapevines, you derive sugar and wholesome food. In this is a sign for people who understand.

68. And your Lord inspired the bee: "Set up hives in the mountains, and in the trees, and in what they construct."

69. Then eat of all the fruits, and go along the pathways of your Lord, with precision. From their bellies emerges a fluid of diverse colors, containing healing for the people. Surely in this is a sign for people who reflect.

70. God created you; then He takes you away. Some of you will be brought back to the worst age, so that he will no longer know anything, after having acquired knowledge. God is Omniscient and Omnipotent.

71. God has favored some of you over others in livelihood. Those who are favored would not give their properties to their servants, to the extent of making them partners in it. Will they then renounce God's blessings?

72. God has given you mates from among yourselves; and has produced for you, from your mates, children and grandchildren; and has provided you with good things. Will they then believe in falsehood, and refuse God's favors?

73. And yet they serve besides God what possesses no provisions for them in the heavens, nor on earth, nor are they capable.

74. So do not cite the examples for God. God knows, and you do not know.

75. God cites the example of a bonded slave, who has no power over anything; and someone to whom We have given plentiful provision, from which he gives secretly and openly. Are they equal in comparison? All praise belongs to God, but most of them do not know.

76. And God cites the example of two men: one of them dumb, unable to do anything, and is a burden on his master; whichever way he directs him, he achieves nothing good. Is he equal to him who commands justice, and is on a straight path?

77. To God belongs the unseen of the heavens and the earth. The coming of the Hour is only as the twinkling of the eye, or even nearer. God has power over everything.

78. God brought you out of your mothers' wombs, not knowing anything; and He gave you the hearing, and the eyesight, and the brains; that you may give thanks.

79. Have they not seen the birds, flying in the midst of the sky? None sustains them except God. In this are signs for people who believe.

80. And God has given you in your homes habitats for you, and has provided for you out of the hides of livestock portable homes for you, so you can use them when you travel, and when you camp; and from their wool, and fur, and hair, furnishings and comfort for a while.

81. And God has made for you shade out of what He has created, and has given you resorts in the mountains, and has given you garments to protect you from the heat, and garments to protect you from your violence. Thus He completes His blessings upon you, so that you may submit.

82. But if they turn away, your only duty is clear communication.

83. They recognize God's blessing, but then deny it, as most of them are ungrateful.

84. On the Day when We raise up a witness from every community—those who disbelieved will not be permitted, nor will they be excused.

85. When those who did wrong see the punishment, it will not be lightened for them, nor will they be reprieved.

86. And when the idolaters see their associates, they will say, "Our Lord, these are our associates whom we used to invoke besides You." They will strike back at them with the saying, "Surely you are liars."

87. On that Day they will offer their submission to God, and what they had invented will abandon them.

88. Those who disbelieve and obstruct from God's path—We will add punishment to their punishment, on account of the mischief they used to make.

89. On the Day when We raise in every community a witness against them, from among them, and bring you as a witness against these. We have revealed to you the Book, as an explanation of all things, and guidance, and mercy and good news for those who submit.

90. God commands justice, and goodness, and generosity towards relatives. And He forbids immorality, and injustice, and oppression. He advises you, so that you may take heed.

91. Fulfill God's covenant when you make a covenant, and do not break your oaths after ratifying them. You have made God your guarantor, and God knows what you do.

92. And do not be like her who unravels her yarn, breaking it into pieces, after she has spun it strongly. Nor use your oaths as means of deception among you, because one community is more prosperous than another. God is testing you thereby. On the Day of Resurrection, He will make clear to you everything you had disputed about.

93. Had God willed, He would have made you one congregation, but He leaves astray whom He wills, and He guides whom He wills. And you will surely be questioned about what you used to do.

94. And do not use your oaths to deceive one another, so that a foot may not slip after being firm, and you taste misery because you hindered from God's path, and incur a terrible torment.

95. And do not exchange God's covenant for a small price. What is with God is better for you, if you only knew.

96. What you have runs out, but what is with God remains. We will reward those who are patient according to the best of their deeds.

97. Whoever works righteousness, whether male or female, while being a believer, We will grant him a good life—and We will reward them according to the best of what they used to do.

98. When you read the Quran, seek refuge with God from Satan the outcast.

99. He has no authority over those who believe and trust in their Lord.

100. His authority is only over those who follow him, and those who associate others with Him.

101. When We substitute a verse in place of another verse—and God knows best what He reveals—they say, "You are an impostor." But most of them do not know.

102. Say, "The Holy Spirit has brought it down from your Lord, truthfully, in order to stabilize those who believe, and as guidance and good news for those who submit."

103. We are well aware that they say, "It is a human being who is teaching him." But the tongue of him they allude to is foreign, while this is a clear Arabic tongue.

104. Those who do not believe in God's revelations—God will not guide them, and for them is a painful punishment.

105. It is those who do not believe in God's revelations who fabricate falsehood. These are the liars.

106. Whoever renounces faith in God after having believed—except for someone who is compelled, while his heart rests securely in faith—but whoever willingly opens up his heart to disbelief—upon them falls wrath from God, and for them is a tremendous torment.

107. That is because they have preferred the worldly life to the Hereafter, and because God does not guide the people who refuse.

108. It is they whom God has sealed their hearts, and their hearing, and their sight. It is they who are the heedless.

109. There is no doubt that in the Hereafter they will be the losers.

110. But then your Lord—for those who emigrated after being persecuted, then struggled and persevered—your Lord thereafter is Forgiving and Merciful.

111. On the Day when every soul will come pleading for itself, and every soul will be paid in full for what it has done, and they will not be wronged.

112. And God cites the example of a town that was secure and peaceful, with its livelihood coming to it abundantly from every direction. But then it turned unappreciative of God's blessings, so God made it taste the robe of hunger and fear, because of what they used to craft.

113. A messenger from among them had come to them, but they denounced him, so the punishment seized them in the midst of their wrongdoing.

114. Eat of the lawful and good things God has provided for you, and be thankful for God's blessings, if it is Him that you serve.

115. He has forbidden you carrion, and blood, and the flesh of swine, and anything consecrated to other than God. But if anyone is compelled by necessity, without being deliberate or malicious, then God is Forgiving and Merciful.

116. And do not say of falsehood asserted by your tongues, "This is lawful, and this is

unlawful," in order to invent lies and attribute them to God. Those who invent lies and attribute them to God will not succeed.

117. A brief enjoyment—then they will have a painful punishment.

118. For those who are Jews, We have prohibited what We related to you before. We did not wrong them, but they used to wrong their own selves.

119. But towards those who do wrongs in ignorance, and then repent afterwards and reform, your Lord thereafter is Forgiving and Merciful.

120. Abraham was an exemplary leader, devoted to God, a monotheist, and was not of the polytheists.

121. Thankful for His blessings. He chose him, and guided him to a straight path.

122. And We gave him goodness in this world, and in the Hereafter he will be among the righteous.

123. Then We inspired you: "Follow the religion of Abraham, the Monotheist. He was not an idol-worshiper."

124. The Sabbath was decreed only for those who differed about it. Your Lord will judge between them on the Day of Resurrection regarding their differences.

125. Invite to the way of your Lord with wisdom and good advice, and debate with them in the most dignified manner. Your Lord is aware of those who stray from His path, and He is aware of those who are guided.

126. If you were to retaliate, retaliate to the same degree as the injury done to you. But if you resort to patience—it is better for the patient.

127. So be patient. Your patience is solely from God. And do not grieve over them, and do not be stressed by their schemes.

128. God is with those who are righteous and those who are virtuous.

17. THE NIGHT JOURNEY
(al-Isra')

In the name of God,
the Gracious, the Merciful.

1. Glory to Him who journeyed His servant by night, from the Sacred Mosque to the Farthest Mosque, whose precincts We have blessed, in order to show him of Our wonders. He is the Listener, the Beholder.

2. And We gave Moses the Scripture, and made it a guide for the Children of Israel: Take none for protector other than Me.

3. The descendants of those We carried with Noah. He was an appreciative servant.

4. And We conveyed to the Children of Israel in the Scripture: You will commit evil on earth twice, and you will rise to a great height.

5. When the first of the two promises came true, We sent against you servants of Ours, possessing great might, and they ransacked your homes. It was a promise fulfilled.

6. Then We gave you back your turn against them, and supplied you with wealth and children, and made you more numerous.

7. If you work righteousness, you work righteousness for yourselves, and if you commit evil, you do so against yourselves. Then, when the second promise comes true, they will make your faces filled with sorrow, and enter the Temple as they en-

tered it the first time, and utterly destroy all that falls into their power.

8. Perhaps your Lord will have mercy on you. But if you revert, We will revert. We have made Hell a prison for the disbelievers.

9. This Quran guides to what is most upright; and it gives good news to the believers who do good deeds, that they will have a great reward.

10. And those who do not believe in the Hereafter—We have prepared for them a painful punishment.

11. The human being prays for evil as he prays for good. The human being is very hasty.

12. We have made the night and the day two wonders. We erased the wonder of the night, and made the wonder of the day revealing, that you may seek bounty from your Lord, and know the number of years, and the calculation. We have explained all things in detail.

13. For every person We have attached his fate to his neck. And on the Day of Resurrection, We will bring out for him a book which he will find spread open.

14. "Read your book; today there will be none but yourself to call you to account."

15. Whoever is guided—is guided for his own good. And whoever goes astray—goes astray to his detriment. No burdened soul carries the burdens of another, nor do We ever punish until We have sent a messenger.

16. When We decide to destroy a town, We command its affluent ones, they transgress in it, so the word becomes justified against it, and We destroy it completely.

17. How many generations have We destroyed after Noah? Your Lord is sufficient as Knower and Beholder of the sins of his servants.

18. Whoever desires the fleeting life, We expedite for him what We decide to give him, to whomever We desire. Then We consign him to Hell, where he will roast, condemned and defeated.

19. But whoever desires the Hereafter, and pursues it as it should be pursued, while he is a believer—their effort will be appreciated.

20. To all—these and those—We extend from the gifts of your Lord. The gifts of your Lord are not restricted.

21. See how We have favored some of them over others; yet the Hereafter is greater in ranks, and greater in favors.

22. Do not set up another god with God, lest you become condemned and damned.

23. Your Lord has commanded that you worship none but Him, and that you be good to your parents. If either of them or both of them reach old age with you, do not say to them a word of disrespect, nor scold them, but say to them kind words.

24. And lower to them the wing of humility, out of mercy, and say, "My Lord, have mercy on them, as they raised me when I was a child."

25. Your Lord knows best what is in your minds. If you are righteous—He is Forgiving to the obedient.

26. And give the relative his rights, and the poor, and the wayfarer, and do not squander wastefully.

27. The extravagant are brethren of the devils, and the devil is ever ungrateful to his Lord.

28. But if you turn away from them, seeking mercy from your Lord which you hope for, then say to them words of comfort.

29. And do not keep your hand tied to your neck, nor spread it out fully, lest you end up liable and regretful.

30. Your Lord expands the provision for whomever He wills, and restricts it. He is fully Informed, Observant of His servants.

31. And do not kill your children for fear of poverty. We provide for them, and for you. Killing them is a grave sin.

32. And do not come near adultery. It is immoral, and an evil way.

33. And do not kill the soul which God has made sacred, except in the course of justice. If someone is killed unjustly, We have given his next of kin certain authority. But he should not be excessive in killing, for he will be supported.

34. And do not go near the orphan's property, except with the best of intentions, until he has reached his maturity. And honor your pledge, because the pledge involves responsibility.

35. And give full measure when you measure, and weigh with accurate scales. That is fair, and the best determination.

36. And do not occupy yourself with what you have no knowledge of. The hearing, and the sight, and the brains—all these will be questioned.

37. And do not walk proudly on earth. You can neither pierce the earth, nor can you match the mountains in height.

38. The evil of all these is disliked by your Lord.

39. That is some of the wisdom your Lord has revealed to you. Do not set up with God another god, or else you will be thrown in Hell, rebuked and banished.

40. Has your Lord favored you with sons, while choosing for Himself daughters from among the angels? You are indeed saying a terrible thing.

41. We have explained in this Quran in various ways, that they may remember, but it only adds to their rebellion.

42. Say, "If there were other gods with Him, as they say, they would have sought a way to the Lord of the Throne."

43. Be He glorified. He is exalted, far above what they say.

44. Praising Him are the seven heavens, and the earth, and everyone in them. There is not a thing that does not glorify Him with praise, but you do not understand their praises. He is indeed Forbearing and Forgiving.

45. When you read the Quran, We place between you and those who do not believe in the Hereafter an invisible barrier.

46. And We drape veils over their hearts, preventing them from understanding it, and heaviness in their ears. And when you mention your Lord alone in the Quran, they turn their backs in aversion.

47. We know well what they listen to, when they listen to you, as they conspire, when the wrongdoers say, "You only follow a man bewitched."

48. Note what they compared you to. They are lost, and unable to find a way.

49. And they say, "When we have become bones and fragments, shall we really be resurrected as a new creation?"

50. Say, "Even if you become rocks or iron.

51. Or some substance, which, in your minds, is even harder." Then they will say, "Who will restore us?" Say, "The One who originated you the first time." Then they will nod their heads at you, and say, "When will it be?" Say, "Perhaps it will be soon."

52. On the Day when He calls you, you will respond with His praise; and you will realize that you stayed only a little.

53. Tell My servants to say what is best. Satan sows discord among them. Satan is to man an open enemy.

54. Your Lord knows you best. If He wills, He will have mercy on you; and if He wills, He will punish you. We did not send you as their advocate.

55. Your Lord knows well everyone in the heavens and the earth. We have given some prophets advantage over others, and to David We gave the Psalms.

56. Say, "Call upon those you claim besides Him. They have no power to relieve your adversity, nor can they change it."

57. Those they call upon are themselves seeking means of access to their Lord, vying to be nearer, and hoping for His mercy, and fearing His punishment. The punishment of your Lord is to be dreaded.

58. There is no city but We will destroy before the Day of Resurrection, or punish it with a severe punishment. This is inscribed in the Book.

59. Nothing prevents Us from sending miraculous signs, except that the ancients called them lies. We gave Thamood the she-camel, a visible sign, but they mistreated her. We do not send the signs except to instill reverence.

60. We said to you that your Lord encompasses humanity. We did not make the vision We showed you, except as a test for the people, and the tree cursed in the Quran. We frighten them, but that only increases their defiance.

61. When We said to the angels, "Bow down before Adam," they bowed down, except for Satan. He said, "Shall I bow down before someone You created from mud?"

62. He said, "Do You see this one whom You have honored more than me? If You reprieve me until the Day of Resurrection, I will bring his descendants under my sway, except for a few."

63. He said, "Begone! Whoever of them follows you—Hell is your reward, an ample reward."

64. "And entice whomever of them you can with your voice, and rally against them your cavalry and your infantry, and share with them in wealth and children, and make promises to them." But Satan promises them nothing but delusion.

65. "As for My devotees, you have no authority over them." Your Lord is an adequate Guardian.

66. Your Lord is He who propels for you the ships at sea, that you may seek of His bounty. He is towards you Most Merciful.

67. When harm afflicts you at sea, those you pray to vanish, except for Him. But when He saves you to land, you turn away. The human being is ever thankless.

68. Are you confident that He will not cause a track of land to cave in beneath you, or unleash a tornado against you, and then you find no protector?

69. Or are you confident that He will not return you to it once again, and unleash a hurricane against you, and drown you for your ingratitude? Then you will find no helper against Us.

70. We have honored the Children of Adam, and carried them on land and sea, and provided them with good things, and greatly favored them over many of those We created.

71. On the Day when We call every people with their leader. Whoever is given his

record in his right hand—these will read their record, and they will not be wronged one bit.

72. But whoever is blind in this, he will be blind in the Hereafter, and further astray from the way.

73. They almost lured you away from what We have revealed to you, so that you would invent something else in Our name. In that case, they would have taken you for a friend.

74. Had We not given you stability, you might have inclined towards them a little.

75. Then We would have made you taste double in life, and double at death; then you would have found for yourself no helper against Us.

76. They almost provoked you, to expel you from the land. In that case, they would not have lasted after you, except briefly.

77. The tradition of the messengers We sent before you—you will find no change in Our rules.

78. Perform the prayer at the decline of the sun, until the darkness of the night; and the Quran at dawn. The Quran at dawn is witnessed.

79. And keep vigil with it during parts of the night, as an extra prayer. Perhaps your Lord will raise you to a laudable position.

80. And say, "My Lord, lead me in through an entry of truth, and lead me out through an exit of truth, and grant me from You a supporting power."

81. And say, "The truth has come, and falsehood has withered away; for falsehood is bound to wither away."

82. We send down in the Quran healing and mercy for the believers, but it increases the wrongdoers only in loss.

83. When We bless the human being, he turns away and distances himself. But when adversity touches him, he is in despair.

84. Say, "Each does according to his disposition. Your Lord knows best who is better guided in the way."

85. And they ask you about the Spirit. Say, "The Spirit belongs to the domain of my Lord; and you were not given except little knowledge."

86. If We willed, We could take away what We revealed to you. Then you will find for yourself no protecting guardian against Us.

87. Except through a mercy from your Lord. His favors upon you have been great.

88. Say, "If mankind and jinn came together to produce the like of this Quran, they could never produce the like of it, even if they backed up one another."

89. We have displayed for mankind in this Quran every kind of similitude, but most people insist on denying the truth.

90. And they said, "We will not believe in you unless you make a spring burst from the ground for us.

91. Or you have a garden of palms and vines; then cause rivers to gush pouring through them.

92. Or make the sky fall on us in pieces, as you claim, or bring God and the angels before us.

93. Or you possess a house of gold. Or you ascend into the sky. Even then, we will not believe in your ascension, unless you bring down for us a book that we can read." Say, "Glory be to my Lord. Am I anything but a human messenger?"

94. Nothing prevented the people from believing, when guidance has come to

them, except that they said, "Did God send a human messenger?"

95. Say, "If there were angels on earth, walking around in peace, We would have sent down to them from heaven an angel messenger."

96. Say, "God is enough witness between you and me. He is fully aware of His servants, and He sees them well."

97. Whomever God guides is the guided one. And whomever He leaves astray—for them you will find no protectors apart from Him. And We will gather them on the Day of Resurrection, on their faces, blind, dumb, and deaf. Their abode is Hell; whenever it abates, We intensify the blaze for them.

98. This is their repayment for having blasphemed against Our revelations, and having said, "Shall we, when we have become bones and fragments, be resurrected as a new creation?"

99. Do they not consider that God, Who created the heavens and the earth, is Able to create the likes of them? He has assigned for them a term, in which there is no doubt. But the wrongdoers persist in denying the truth.

100. Say, "If you possessed the treasuries of my Lord's mercy, you would have withheld them, for fear of spending." The human being has always been stingy.

101. We gave Moses nine clear signs—ask the Children of Israel. When he went to them, Pharaoh said to him, "I think that you, Moses, are bewitched."

102. He said, "You know that none sent these down except the Lord of the heavens and the earth—eye openers; and I think that you, Pharaoh, are doomed."

103. He resolved to scare them off the land, but We drowned him, and those with him, altogether.

104. After him, We said to the Children of Israel, "Inhabit the land, and when the promise of the Hereafter arrives, We will bring you all together."

105. With the truth We sent it down, and with the truth it descended. And We sent you only as a bearer of good news and a warner.

106. A Quran which We unfolded gradually, that you may recite to the people over time. And We revealed it in stages.

107. Say, "Believe in it, or do not believe." Those who were given knowledge before it, when it is recited to them, they fall to their chins, prostrating.

108. And they say, "Glory to our Lord. The promise of our Lord is fulfilled."

109. And they fall to their chins, weeping, and it adds to their humility.

110. Say, "Call Him God, or call Him the Most Merciful. Whichever name you use, to Him belong the Best Names." And be neither loud in your prayer, nor silent in it, but follow a course in between.

111. And say, "Praise be to God, who has not begotten a son, nor has He a partner in sovereignty, nor has He an ally out of weakness, and glorify Him constantly."

18. THE CAVE
(al-Kahf)

In the name of God,
the Gracious, the Merciful.

1. Praise be to God, who revealed the Book to His servant, and allowed in it no distortion.

2. Valuable—to warn of severe punishment from Himself; and to deliver good news to the believers who do righteous deeds, that they will have an excellent reward.

3. In which they will abide forever.

4. And to warn those who say, "God has begotten a son."

5. They have no knowledge of this, nor did their forefathers. Grave is the word that comes out of their mouths. They say nothing but a lie.

6. Perhaps you may destroy yourself with grief, chasing after them, if they do not believe in this information.

7. We made what is upon the earth an ornament for it, to test them as to which of them is best in conduct.

8. And We will turn what is on it into barren waste.

9. Did you know that the People of the Cave and the Inscription were of Our wondrous signs?

10. When the youths took shelter in the cave, they said, "Our Lord, give us mercy from Yourself, and bless our affair with guidance."

11. Then We sealed their ears in the cave for a number of years.

12. Then We awakened them to know which of the two groups could better calculate the length of their stay.

13. We relate to you their story in truth. They were youths who believed in their Lord, and We increased them in guidance.

14. And We strengthened their hearts, when they stood up and said, "Our Lord is the Lord of the heavens and the earth; we will not call on any god besides Him, for then we would have spoken an outrage."

15. "These people, our people, have taken to themselves gods other than Him. Why do they not bring a clear proof concerning them? Who, then, does greater wrong than he who invents lies and attributes them to God?"

16. "Now that you have withdrawn from them, and from what they worship besides God, take shelter in the cave. And your Lord will unfold His mercy for you, and will set your affair towards ease."

17. You would have seen the sun, when it rose, veering away from their cave towards the right, and when it sets, moving away from them to the left, as they lay in the midst of the cave. That was one of God's wonders. He whom God guides is truly guided; but He whom God misguides, for him you will find no directing friend.

18. You would think them awake, although they were asleep. And We turned them over to the right, and to the left, with their dog stretching its paws across the threshold. Had you looked at them, you would have turned away from them in flight, and been filled with fear of them.

19. Even so, We awakened them, so that they may ask one another. A speaker among them said, "How long have you stayed?" They said, "We have stayed a day, or part of a day." They said, "Your Lord knows best how long you have stayed." "Send one of you to the city, with this money of yours, and let him see which food is most suitable, and let him bring you some provision thereof. And let him be gentle, and let no one become aware of you."

20. "If they discover you, they will stone you, or force you back into their religion; then you will never be saved."

21. So it was, that We caused them to be discovered, that they would know that the

promise of God is true, and that of the Hour there is no doubt. As they were disputing their case among themselves, they said, "Build over them a building." Their Lord knows best about them. Those who prevailed over their case said, "We will set up over them a place of worship."

22. They will say, "Three, and their fourth being their dog." And they will say, "Five, and their sixth being their dog," guessing at the unknown. And they will say, "Seven, and their eighth being their dog." Say, "My Lord knows best their number." None knows them except a few. So do not argue concerning them except with an obvious argument, and do not consult any of them about them.

23. And never say about anything, "I will do that tomorrow."

24. Without saying, "If God wills." And remember your Lord if you forget, and say, "Perhaps my Lord will guide me to nearer than this in integrity."

25. And they stayed in their cave for three hundred years, adding nine.

26. Say, "God knows best how long they stayed." His is the mystery of the heavens and the earth. By Him you see and hear. They have no Guardian apart from Him, and He shares His Sovereignty with no one.

27. And recite what was revealed to you from the Book of your Lord. There is no changing His words, and you will find no refuge except in Him.

28. And content yourself with those who pray to their Lord morning and evening, desiring His Presence. And do not turn your eyes away from them, desiring the glitter of this world. And do not obey him whose heart We have made heedless of Our remembrance—so he follows his own desires—and his priorities are confused.

29. And say, "The truth is from your Lord. Whoever wills—let him believe. And whoever wills—let him disbelieve. We have prepared for the unjust a Fire, whose curtains will hem them in. And when they cry for relief, they will be relieved with water like molten brass, which scalds the faces. What a miserable drink, and what a terrible place.

30. As for those who believe and lead a righteous life—We will not waste the reward of those who work righteousness.

31. These will have the Gardens of Eden, beneath which rivers flow. Reclining on comfortable furnishings, they will be adorned with bracelets of gold, and will wear green garments of silk and brocade. What a wonderful reward, and what an excellent resting-place.

32. And cite for them the parable of two men. To one of them We gave two gardens of vine, and We surrounded them with palms-trees, and We placed between them crops.

33. Both gardens produced their harvest in full, and suffered no loss. And We made a river flow through them.

34. And thus he had abundant fruits. He said to his friend, as he conversed with him, "I am wealthier than you, and greater in manpower."

35. And he entered his garden, wronging himself. He said, "I do not think this will ever perish."

36. "And I do not think the Hour is coming. And even if I am returned to my Lord, I will find something better than this in return."

37. His friend said to him, as he conversed with him, "Are you being ungrateful to Him who created you from dust, then

from a sperm-drop, then evolved you into a man?

38. But as for me, He is God, my Lord, and I never associate with my Lord anyone.

39. When you entered your garden, why did you not say, "As God wills; there is no power except through God"? Although you see me inferior to you in wealth and children.

40. Perhaps my Lord will give me something better than your garden, and release upon it thunderbolts from the sky, so it becomes barren waste.

41. Or its water will sink into the ground, and you will be unable to draw it."

42. And ruin closed in on his crops, and so he began wringing his hands over what he had invested in it, as it lays fallen upon its trellises. And he was saying, "I wish I never associated anyone with my Lord."

43. He had no faction to help him besides God, and he was helpless.

44. That is because authority belongs to God, the True. He is Best in rewarding, and Best in requiting.

45. And cite for them the parable of the present life: it is like water that We send down from the sky; the plants of the earth absorb it; but then it becomes debris, scattered by the wind. God has absolute power over everything.

46. Wealth and children are the adornments of the present life; but the things that last, the virtuous deeds, are better with your Lord for reward, and better for hope.

47. On the Day when We set the mountains in motion; and you see the earth emerging; and We gather them together, and leave none of them behind.

48. They will be presented before your Lord in a row. "You have come to Us as

We created you the first time. Although you claimed We would not set a meeting for you."

49. And the book will be placed, and you will see the sinners fearful of its contents. And they will say, "Woe to us! What is with this book that leaves nothing, small or big, but it has enumerated it?" They will find everything they had done present. Your Lord does not wrong anyone.

50. We said to the angels, "Bow down to Adam." So they bowed down, except for Satan. He was of the jinn, and he defied the command of his Lord. Will you take him and his offspring as lords instead of Me, when they are an enemy to you? Evil is the exchange for the wrongdoers.

51. I did not call them to witness the creation of the heavens and the earth, nor their own creation; and I do not take the misleaders for assistants.

52. On the Day when He will say, "Call on My partners whom you have claimed." They will call on them, but they will not answer them. And We will place between them a barrier.

53. And the sinners will see the Fire, and will realize that they will tumble into it. They will find no deliverance from it.

54. We have elaborated in this Quran for the people every kind of example, but the human being is a most argumentative being.

55. What prevented people from accepting faith, when guidance has come to them, and from seeking their Lord's forgiveness? Unless they are waiting for the precedent of the ancients to befall them, or to have the punishment come upon them face to face.

56. We send the messengers only as deliverers of good news and warners. Those

who disbelieve argue with false argument, in order to defeat the truth thereby. They take My Verses, and the warnings, for a joke.

57. Who does greater wrong than he, who, when reminded of his Lord's revelations, turns away from them, and forgets what his hands have put forward? We have placed coverings over their hearts, lest they understand it, and heaviness in their ears. And if you call them to guidance, they will not be guided, ever.

58. Your Lord is the Forgiver, Possessor of Mercy. Were He to call them to account for what they have earned, He would have hastened the punishment for them. But they have an appointment from which they will find no escape.

59. And these towns—We destroyed them when they committed injustices, and We set for their destruction an appointed time.

60. Recall when Moses said to his servant, "I will not give up until I reach the junction of the two rivers, even if it takes me years."

61. Then, when they reached the junction between them, they forgot about their fish. It found its way into the river, slipping away.

62. When they went further, he said to his servant, "Bring us our lunch; we were exposed in our travel to much fatigue."

63. He said, "Do you remember when we rested by the rock? I forgot about the fish. It was only the devil who made me forget it. And so it found its way to the river, amazingly."

64. He said, "This is what we were seeking." And so they turned back retracing their steps.

65. Then they came upon a servant of Ours, whom We had blessed with mercy from Us, and had taught him knowledge from Our own.

66. Moses said to him, "May I follow you, so that you may teach me some of the guidance you were taught?"

67. He said, "You will not be able to endure with me.

68. And how will you endure what you have no knowledge of?"

69. He said, "You will find me, God willing, patient; and I will not disobey you in any order of yours."

70. He said, "If you follow me, do not ask me about anything, until I myself make mention of it to you."

71. So they set out. Until, when they had boarded the boat, he holed it. He said, "Did you hole it, to drown its passengers? You have done something awful."

72. He said, "Did I not tell you that you will not be able to endure with me?"

73. He said, "Do not rebuke me for forgetting, and do not make my course difficult for me."

74. Then they set out. Until, when they encountered a boy, he killed him. He said, "Did you kill a pure soul, who killed no one? You have done something terrible."

75. He said, "Did I not tell you that you will not be able to endure with me?"

76. He said, "If I ask you about anything after this, then do not keep company with me. You have received excuses from me."

77. So they set out. Until, when they reached the people of a town, they asked them for food, but they refused to offer them hospitality. There they found a wall about to collapse, and he repaired it. He said, "If you wanted, you could have obtained a payment for it."

78. He said, "This is the parting between you and me. I will tell you the interpretation of what you were unable to endure.

79. As for the boat, it belonged to paupers working at sea. I wanted to damage it because there was a king coming after them seizing every boat by force.

80. As for the boy, his parents were believers, and we feared he would overwhelm them with oppression and disbelief.

81. So we wanted their Lord to replace him with someone better in purity, and closer to mercy.

82. And as for the wall, it belonged to two orphaned boys in the town. Beneath it was a treasure that belonged to them. Their father was a righteous man. Your Lord wanted them to reach their maturity, and then extract their treasure—as a mercy from your Lord. I did not do it of my own accord. This is the interpretation of what you were unable to endure."

83. And they ask you about Zul-Qarnain. Say, "I will tell you something about him."

84. We established him on earth, and gave him all kinds of means.

85. He pursued a certain course.

86. Until, when he reached the setting of the sun, he found it setting in a murky spring, and found a people in its vicinity. We said, "O Zul-Qarnain, you may either inflict a penalty, or else treat them kindly."

87. He said, "As for him who does wrong, we will penalize him; then he will be returned to his Lord, and He will punish him with an unheard-of torment.

88. "But as for him who believes and acts righteously, he will have the finest reward, and We will speak to him of Our command with ease."

89. Then he pursued a course.

90. Until, when he reached the rising of the sun, he found it rising on a people for whom We had provided no shelter from it.

91. And so it was. We had full knowledge of what he had.

92. Then he pursued a course.

93. Until, when he reached the point separating the two barriers, he found beside them a people who could barely understand what is said.

94. They said, "O Zul-Qarnain, the Gog and Magog are spreading chaos in the land. Can we pay you, to build between us and them a wall?"

95. He said, "What my Lord has empowered me with is better. But assist me with strength, and I will build between you and them a dam."

96. "Bring me blocks of iron." So that, when he had leveled up between the two cliffs, he said, "Blow." And having turned it into a fire, he said, "Bring me tar to pour over it."

97. So they were unable to climb it, and they could not penetrate it.

98. He said, "This is a mercy from my Lord. But when the promise of my Lord comes true, He will turn it into rubble, and the promise of my Lord is always true."

99. On that Day, We will leave them surging upon one another. And the Trumpet will be blown, and We will gather them together.

100. On that Day, We will present the disbelievers to Hell, all displayed.

101. Those whose eyes were screened to My message, and were unable to hear.

102. Do those who disbelieve think that they can take My servants for masters instead of Me? We have prepared Hell for the hospitality of the faithless.

103. Say, "Shall We inform you of the greatest losers in their works?"

104. "Those whose efforts in this world are misguided, while they assume that they are doing well."

105. It is they who rejected the communications of their Lord, and the encounter with Him. So their works are in vain. And on the Day of Resurrection, We will consider them of no weight.

106. That is their requital—Hell—on account of their disbelief, and their taking My revelations and My messengers in mockery.

107. As for those who believe and do righteous deeds, they will have the Gardens of Paradise for hospitality.

108. Abiding therein forever, without desiring any change therefrom.

109. Say, "If the ocean were ink for the words of my Lord, the ocean would run out, before the words of my Lord run out," even if We were to bring the like of it in addition to it.

110. Say, "I am only a human being like you, being inspired that your god is One God. Whoever hopes to meet his Lord, let him work righteousness, and never associate anyone with the service of his Lord."

19. MARY
(Maryam)

In the name of God,
the Gracious, the Merciful.

1. Kaf, Ha, Ya, Ayn, Saad.

2. A mention of the mercy of your Lord towards His servant Zechariah.

3. When he called on his Lord, a call in seclusion.

4. He said, "My Lord, my bones have become feeble, and my hair is aflame with gray, and never, Lord, have I been disappointed in my prayer to you.

5. "And I fear for my dependents after me, and my wife is barren. So grant me, from Yourself, an heir.

6. To inherit me, and inherit from the House of Jacob, and make him, my Lord, pleasing."

7. "O Zechariah, We give you good news of a son, whose name is John, a name We have never given before.

8. He said, "My Lord, how can I have a son, when my wife is barren, and I have become decrepit with old age?"

9. He said, "It will be so, your Lord says, 'it is easy for me, and I created you before, when you were nothing.'"

10. He said, "My Lord, give me a sign." He said, "Your sign is that you will not speak to the people for three nights straight."

11. And he came out to his people, from the sanctuary, and signaled to them to praise Him morning and evening.

12. "O John, hold on to the Scripture firmly," and We gave him wisdom in his youth.

13. And tenderness from Us, and innocence. He was devout.

14. And kind to his parents; and he was not a disobedient tyrant.

15. And peace be upon him the day he was born, and the day he dies, and the Day he is raised alive.

16. And mention in the Scripture Mary, when she withdrew from her people to an eastern location.

17. She screened herself away from them, and We sent to her Our spirit, and He appeared to her as an immaculate human.

18. She said, "I take refuge from you in the Most Merciful, should you be righteous."

19. He said, "I am only the messenger of your Lord, to give you the gift of a pure son."

20. She said, "How can I have a son, when no man has touched me, and I was never unchaste?"

21. He said, "Thus said your Lord, 'It is easy for Me, and We will make him a sign for humanity, and a mercy from Us. It is a matter already decided.'"

22. So she carried him, and secluded herself with him in a remote place.

23. The labor-pains came upon her, by the trunk of a palm-tree. She said, "I wish I had died before this, and been completely forgotten."

24. Whereupon he called her from beneath her: "Do not worry; your Lord has placed a stream beneath you.

25. And shake the trunk of the palm-tree towards you, and it will drop ripe dates by you."

26. "So eat, and drink, and be consoled. And if you see any human, say, 'I have vowed a fast to the Most Gracious, so I will not speak to any human today.'"

27. Then she came to her people, carrying him. They said, "O Mary, you have done something terrible.

28. O sister of Aaron, your father was not an evil man, and your mother was not a whore."

29. So she pointed to him. They said, "How can we speak to an infant in the crib?"

30. He said, "I am the servant of God. He has given me the Scripture, and made me a prophet.

31. And has made me blessed wherever I may be; and has enjoined on me prayer and charity, so long as I live.

32. And kind to my mother, and He did not make me a disobedient rebel.

33. So Peace is upon me the day I was born, and the day I die, and the Day I get resurrected alive."

34. That is Jesus son of Mary—the Word of truth about which they doubt.

35. It is not for God to have a child—glory be to Him. To have anything done, He says to it, "Be," and it becomes.

36. "God is my Lord and your Lord, so worship Him. That is a straight path."

37. But the various factions differed among themselves. So woe to those who disbelieve from the scene of a tremendous Day.

38. Listen to them and watch for them the Day they come to Us. But the wrongdoers today are completely lost.

39. And warn them of the Day of Regret, when the matter will be concluded. Yet they are heedless, and they do not believe.

40. It is We who will inherit the earth and everyone on it, and to Us they will be returned.

41. And mention in the Scripture Abraham. He was a man of truth, a prophet.

42. He said to his father, "O my father, why do you worship what can neither hear, nor see, nor benefit you in any way?

43. O my father, there has come to me knowledge that never came to you. So follow me, and I will guide you along a straight way.

44. O my father, do not worship the devil. The devil is disobedient to the Most Gracious.

45. O my father, I fear that a punishment from the Most Gracious will afflict you, and you become an ally of the devil."

46. He said, "Are you renouncing my gods, O Abraham? If you do not desist, I will stone you. So leave me alone for a while."

47. He said, "Peace be upon you. I will ask my Lord to forgive you; He has been Kind to me.

48. And I will withdraw from you, and from what you pray to instead of God. And I will pray to my Lord, and I hope I will not be disappointed in my prayer to my Lord."

49. When he withdrew from them, and from what they worship besides God, We granted him Isaac and Jacob. And each We made a prophet.

50. And We gave them freely of Our mercy, and gave them a noble reputation of truth.

51. And mention in the Scripture Moses. He was dedicated. He was a messenger and a prophet.

52. And We called him from the right side of the Mount, and brought him near in communion.

53. And We granted him, out of Our mercy, his brother Aaron, a prophet.

54. And mention in the Scripture Ishmael. He was true to his promise, and was a messenger, a prophet.

55. And he used to enjoin on his people prayer and charity, and he was pleasing to his Lord.

56. And mention in the Scripture Enoch. He was a man of truth, a prophet.

57. And We raised him to a high position.

58. These are some of the prophets God has blessed, from the descendants of Adam, and from those We carried with Noah, and from the descendants of Abraham and Israel, and from those We guided and selected. Whenever the revelations of the Most Gracious are recited to them, they would fall down, prostrating and weeping.

59. But they were succeeded by generations who lost the prayers and followed their appetites. They will meet perdition.

60. Except for those who repent, and believe, and act righteously. These will enter Paradise, and will not be wronged in the least.

61. The Gardens of Eden, promised by the Most Merciful to His servants in the Unseen. His promise will certainly come true.

62. They will hear no nonsense therein, but only peace. And they will have their provision therein, morning and evening.

63. Such is Paradise which We will give as inheritance to those of Our servants who are devout.

64. "We do not descend except by the command of your Lord. His is what is before us, and what is behind us, and what is between them. Your Lord is never forgetful."

65. Lord of the heavens and the earth and what is between them. So worship Him, and persevere in His service. Do you know of anyone equal to Him?

66. And the human being says, "When I am dead, will I be brought back alive?"

67. Does the human being not remember that We created him before, when he was nothing?

68. By your Lord, We will round them up, and the devils, then We will bring them around Hell, on their knees.

69. Then, out of every sect, We will snatch those most defiant to the Most Merciful.

70. We are fully aware of those most deserving to scorch in it.

71. There is not one of you but will go down to it. This has been an unavoidable decree of your Lord.

72. Then We will rescue those who were devout, and leave the wrongdoers in it, on their knees.

73. When Our clear revelations are recited to them, those who disbelieve say to those who believe, "Which of the two parties is better in position, and superior in influence?"

74. How many a generation have We destroyed before them, who surpassed them in riches and splendor?

75. Say, "Whoever is in error, the Most Merciful will lead him on." Until, when they see what they were promised—either the punishment, or the Hour. Then they will know who was in worse position and weaker in forces.

76. God increases in guidance those who accept guidance. And the things that endure—the righteous deeds—have the best reward with your Lord, and the best outcome.

77. Have you seen him who denied Our revelations, and said, "I will be given wealth and children"?

78. Did he look into the future, or did he receive a promise from the Most Merciful?

79. No indeed! We will write what he says, and will keep extending the agony for him.

80. Then We will inherit from him what he speaks of, and he will come to Us alone.

81. And they took, besides God, other gods, to be for them a source of strength.

82. By no means! They will reject their worship of them, and become opponents to them.

83. Have you not considered how We dispatch the devils against the disbelievers, exciting them with incitement?

84. So do not hurry against them. We are counting for them a countdown.

85. On the Day when We will gather the righteous to the Most Merciful, as guests.

86. And herd the sinners into hell, like animals to water.

87. They will have no power of intercession, except for someone who has an agreement with the Most Merciful.

88. And they say, "The Most Merciful has begotten a son."

89. You have come up with something monstrous.

90. At which the heavens almost rupture, and the earth splits, and the mountains fall and crumble.

91. Because they attribute a son to the Most Merciful.

92. It is not fitting for the Most Merciful to have a son.

93. There is none in the heavens and the earth but will come to the Most Merciful as a servant.

94. He has enumerated them, and counted them one by one.

95. And each one of them will come to Him on the Day of Resurrection alone.

96. Those who believe and do righteous deeds, the Most Merciful will give them love.

97. We made it easy in your tongue, in order to deliver good news to the righteous, and to warn with it a hostile people.

98. How many a generation have We destroyed before them? Can you feel a single one of them, or hear from them the slightest whisper?

20. TA-HA
(Ta-Ha)

*In the name of God,
the Gracious, the Merciful.*

1. Ta, Ha.

2. We did not reveal the Quran to you to make you suffer.

3. But only as a reminder for him who fears.

4. A revelation from He who created the earth and the high heavens.

5. The Most Merciful; on the Throne He settled.

6. To Him belongs everything in the heavens and the earth, and everything between them, and everything beneath the soil.

7. If you speak aloud—He knows the secret, and the most hidden.

8. God, there is no god but He, His are the Most Beautiful Names.

9. Has the story of Moses reached you?

10. When he saw a fire, he said to his family, "Stay; I have noticed a fire; Perhaps I can bring you a torch therefrom, or find some guidance by the fire."

11. Then, when he reached it, he was called, "O Moses.

12. I—I am your Lord. Take off your shoes. You are in the sacred valley of Tuwa.

13. I have chosen you, so listen to what is revealed.

14. I—I am God. There is no God but I. So serve Me, and practice the prayer for My remembrance.

15. The Hour is coming—but I keep it almost hidden—so that each soul will be paid for what it endeavors.

16. And do not let him who denies it and follows his desire turn you away from it, lest you fall.

17. And what is that in your right-hand, O Moses?"

18. He said, "This is my staff. I lean on it, and herd my sheep with it, and I have other uses for it."

19. He said, "Throw it, O Moses."

20. So he threw it—thereupon it became a moving serpent.

21. He said, "Take hold of it, and do not fear. We will restore it to its original condition.

22. And press your hand to your side; it will come out white, without a blemish—another sign.

23. That We may show you some of Our greatest signs.

24. Go to Pharaoh; He has transgressed."

25. He said, "My Lord, put my heart at peace for me.

26. And ease my task for me.

27. And untie the knot from my tongue.

28. So they can understand my speech.

29. And appoint an assistant for me, from my family.

30. Aaron, my brother.

31. Strengthen me with him.

32. And have him share in my mission.

33. That we may glorify You much.

34. And remember You much.

35. You are always watching over us."

36. He said, "You are granted your request, O Moses.

37. We had favored you another time.

38. When We inspired your mother with the inspiration.

39. `Put him in the chest; then cast him into the river. The river will wash him to shore, where an enemy of Mine and an enemy of his will pick him up. And I have bestowed upon you love from Me, so that you may be reared before My eye.

40. When your sister walked along, and said, 'Shall I tell you about someone who will take care of him?' So We returned you to your mother, that she may be comforted, and not sorrow. And you killed a person, but We saved you from stress; and We tested you thoroughly. And you stayed years among the people of Median. Then you came back, as ordained, O Moses.

41. And I made you for Myself.

42. Go, you and your brother, with My signs, and do not neglect My remembrance.

43. Go to Pharaoh. He has tyrannized.

44. But speak to him nicely. Perhaps he will remember, or have some fear."

45. They said, "Lord, we fear he may persecute us, or become violent."

46. He said, "Do not fear, I am with you, I hear and I see.

47. Approach him and say, 'We are the messengers of your Lord; so let the Children of Israel go with us, and do not torment them. We bring you a sign from your Lord, and peace be upon him who follows guidance.

48. It was revealed to us that the punishment falls upon him who disbelieves and turns away.'"

49. He said, "Who is your Lord, O Moses."

50. He said, "Our Lord is He who gave everything its existence, then guided it."

51. He said, "What about the first generations?"

52. He said, "Knowledge thereof is with my Lord, in a Book. My Lord never errs, nor does He forget."

53. He who made the earth a habitat for you; and traced in it routes for you; and sent down water from the sky, with which We produce pairs of diverse plants.

54. Eat and pasture your livestock. In that are signs for those with understanding.

55. From it We created you, and into it We will return you, and from it We will bring you out another time.

56. We showed him Our signs, all of them, but he denied and refused.

57. He said, "Did you come to us to drive us out of our land with your magic, O Moses?

58. We will produce for you magic like it; so make an appointment between us and you, which we will not miss—neither us, nor you—in a central place."

59. He said, "Your appointment is the day of the festival, so let the people be gathered together at mid-morning."

60. Pharaoh turned away, put together his plan, and then came back.

61. Moses said to them, "Woe to you. Do not fabricate lies against God, or He will destroy you with a punishment. He who invents lies will fail."

62. They disagreed among themselves over their affair, and conferred secretly.

63. They said, "These two are magicians who want to drive you out of your land with their magic, and to abolish your exemplary way of life.

64. So settle your plan, and come as one front. Today, whoever gains the upper hand will succeed."

65. They said, "O Moses, either you throw, or we will be the first to throw."

66. He said, "You throw." And suddenly, their ropes and sticks appeared to him, because of their magic, to be crawling swiftly.

67. So Moses felt apprehensive within himself.

68. We said, "Do not be afraid, you are the uppermost.

69. Now throw down what is in your right hand—it will swallow what they have crafted. What they have crafted is only a magician's trickery. But the magician will not succeed, no matter what he does."

70. And the magicians fell down prostrate. They said, "We have believed in the Lord of Aaron and Moses."

71. He said, "Did you believe in him before I have given you permission? He must be your chief, who has taught you magic. I will cut off your hands and your feet on alternate sides, and I will crucify you on the trunks of the palm-trees. Then you will know which of us is more severe in punishment, and more lasting."

72. They said, "We will not prefer you to the proofs that have come to us, and Him who created us. So issue whatever judgment you wish to issue. You can only rule in this lowly life.

73. We have believed in our Lord, so that He may forgive us our sins, and the magic you have compelled us to practice. God is Better, and more Lasting."

74. Whoever comes to his Lord guilty, for him is Hell, where he neither dies nor lives.

75. But whoever comes to Him a believer, having worked righteousness—these will have the highest ranks.

76. The Gardens of Perpetuity, beneath which rivers flow, dwelling therein forever.

That is the reward for him who purifies himself.

77. And We inspired Moses: "Travel by night with My servants, and strike for them a dry path across the sea, not fearing being overtaken, nor worrying."

78. Pharaoh pursued them with his troops, but the sea overwhelmed them, and completely engulfed them.

79. Pharaoh misled his people, and did not guide them.

80. O Children of Israel! We have delivered you from your enemy, and promised you by the right side of the Mount, and sent down to you manna and quails.

81. Eat of the good things We have provided for you, but do not be excessive therein, lest My wrath descends upon you. He, upon whom My wrath descends, has fallen.

82. And I am Forgiving towards him who repents, believes, acts righteously, and then remains guided.

83. "And what made you rush ahead of your people, O Moses?"

84. He said, "They are following in my footsteps; and I hurried on to You, my Lord, that you may be pleased."

85. He said, "We have tested your people in your absence, and the Samarian misled them."

86. So Moses returned to his people, angry and disappointed. He said, "O my people, did your Lord not promise you a good promise? Was the time too long for you? Or did you want wrath from your Lord to descend upon you, so you broke your promise to me?"

87. They said, "We did not break our promise to you by our choice, but we were made to carry loads of the people's orna-

ments, and we cast them in. That was what the Samarian suggested."

88. So he produced for them a calf—a mere body which lowed. And they said, "This is your god, and the god of Moses, but he has forgotten."

89. Did they not see that it cannot return a word to them, and has no power to harm them or benefit them?

90. Aaron had said to them before, "O my people, you are being tested by this. And your Lord is the Merciful, so follow me, and obey my command."

91. They said, "We will not give up our devotion to it, until Moses returns to us."

92. He said, "O Aaron, what prevented you, when you saw them going astray.

93. From following me? Did you disobey my command?"

94. He said, "Son of my mother, do not seize me by my beard or my head. I feared you would say, 'You have caused division among the Children of Israel, and did not regard my word.'"

95. He said, "What do you have to say, O Samarian?"

96. He said, "I saw what they did not see, so I grasped a handful from the Messenger's traces, and I flung it away. Thus my soul prompted me."

97. He said, "Begone! Your lot in this life is to say, 'No contact.' And you have an appointment that you will not miss. Now look at your god that you remained devoted to—we will burn it up, and then blow it away into the sea, as powder."

98. Surely your god is God, the One besides whom there is no other god. He comprehends everything in knowledge.

99. Thus We narrate to you reports of times gone by; and We have given you a message from Our Presence.

100. Whoever turns away from it will carry on the Day of Resurrection a burden.

101. Abiding therein forever. And wretched is their burden on the Day of Resurrection.

102. On the Day when the Trumpet is blown—We will gather the sinners on that Day, blue.

103. Murmuring among themselves: "You have lingered only for ten."

104. We are fully aware of what they say, when the most exemplary of them in conduct will say, "You have lingered only a day."

105. And they ask you about the mountains. Say, "My Lord will crumble them utterly."

106. And leave them desolate waste.

107. You will see in them neither crookedness, nor deviation."

108. On that Day, they will follow the caller, without any deviation. Voices will be hushed before the Merciful, and you will hear nothing but murmur.

109. On that Day, intercession will not avail, except for him permitted by the Merciful, and whose words He has approved.

110. He knows what is before them and what is behind them, and they cannot comprehend Him in their knowledge.

111. Faces will be humbled before the Living, the Eternal. Whoever carries injustice will despair.

112. But whoever has done righteous deeds, while being a believer—will fear neither injustice, nor grievance.

113. Thus We have revealed it an Arabic Quran, and We have diversified the warnings in it, that perhaps they would become righteous, or it may produce a lesson for them.

114. Exalted is God, the True King. Do not be hasty with the Quran before its inspiration to you is concluded, and say, "My Lord, increase me in knowledge."

115. And We covenanted with Adam before, but he forgot, and We found in him no resolve.

116. And when We said to the angels, "Bow down to Adam." They bowed down, except for Satan. He refused.

117. We said, "O Adam, this is an enemy to you and to your wife. So do not let him make you leave the Garden, for then you will suffer.

118. In it you will never go hungry, nor be naked.

119. Nor will you be thirsty in it, nor will you swelter."

120. But Satan whispered to him. He said, "O Adam, shall I show you the Tree of Immortality, and a kingdom that never decays?"

121. And so they ate from it; whereupon their bodies became visible to them, and they started covering themselves with the leaves of the Garden. Thus Adam disobeyed his Lord, and fell.

122. But then his Lord recalled him, and pardoned him, and guided him.

123. He said, "Go down from it, altogether; some of you enemies of some others. But whenever guidance comes to you from Me, whoever follows My guidance, will not go astray, nor suffer.

124. But whoever turns away from My Reminder, for him is a confined life. And We

will raise him on the Day of Resurrection blind."

125. He will say, "My Lord, why did You raise me blind, though I was seeing?"

126. He will say, "Just as Our revelations came to you, and you forgot them, today you will be forgotten."

127. Thus We recompense him who transgresses and does not believe in the revelations of his Lord. The punishment of the Hereafter is more severe, and more lasting.

128. Is it not instructive to them, how many generations before them We destroyed, in whose settlements they walk? Surely in that are signs for people of understanding.

129. Were it not for a word that issued from your Lord, the inevitable would have happened, but there is an appointed term.

130. So bear patiently what they say, and celebrate the praises of your Lord before the rising of the sun, and before its setting. And during the hours of the night glorify Him, and at the borders of the day, that you may be satisfied.

131. And do not extend your glance towards what We have given some classes of them to enjoy—the splendor of the life of this world—that We may test them thereby. Your Lord's provision is better and more lasting.

132. And exhort your people to pray, and patiently adhere to it. We ask of you no sustenance, but it is We who sustain you. The good ending is that for righteousness.

133. And they say, "Why does he not bring us a miracle from his Lord?" Were they not given enough miracles in the former scriptures?

134. Had We destroyed them with a punishment before him, they would have said, "Our Lord, if only You had sent us a messenger, we would have followed Your reve-

lations before we were humiliated and disgraced."

135. Say, "Everybody is waiting, so wait. You will know who the people of the straight path are, and who is rightly-guided.

21. THE PROPHETS
(al-Anbiya)

In the name of God,
the Gracious, the Merciful.

1. Mankind's reckoning has drawn near, but they turn away heedlessly.

2. No fresh reminder comes to them from their Lord, but they listen to it playfully.

3. Their hearts distracted, the wrongdoers confer secretly, "Is this anything but a mortal like you? Will you take to sorcery, with open-eyes?"

4. He said, "My Lord knows what is said in the heaven and the earth; and He is the Hearer, the Knower."

5. And they said, "A jumble of dreams," and, "He made it up," and, "He is a poet," "let him bring us a sign, like those sent to the ancients."

6. None of the towns We destroyed before them had believed. Will they, then, believe?

7. We did not send before you except men, whom We inspired. Ask the people of knowledge, if you do not know.

8. And We did not make them mere bodies that ate no food, nor were they immortal.

9. Then We fulfilled Our promise to them, and We saved them together with whomever We willed, and We destroyed the extravagant.

10. We have sent down to you a Book, containing your message. Do you not understand?

11. How many a guilty town have We crushed, and established thereafter another people?

12. Then, when they sensed Our might, they started running away from it.

13. Do not run, but come back to your luxuries, and to your homes, that you may be questioned.

14. They said, "Woe to us. We were unfair."

15. This continued to be their cry, until We made them silent ashes.

16. We did not create the sky and the earth and what is between them for amusement.

17. If We wanted amusement, We could have found it within Us, were We to do so.

18. In fact, We hurl the truth against falsehood, and it crushes it, so it vanishes. Woe unto you, for what you describe.

19. To Him belongs everyone in the heavens and the earth. Those near Him are not too proud to worship Him, nor do they waver.

20. They praise night and day, without ever tiring.

21. Or have they taken to themselves gods from the earth who resurrect?

22. If there were in them gods other than God, they would have gone to ruin. So glory be to God, Lord of the Throne, beyond what they allege.

23. He will not be questioned about what He does, but they will be questioned.

24. Or have they taken, besides Him, other gods? Say, "Bring your proof. This is a message for those with me, and a message

of those before me." But most of them do not know the truth, so they turn away.

25. We never sent a messenger before you without inspiring him that: "There is no god but I, so worship Me."

26. And they say, "The Most Merciful has taken to himself a son." Be He glorified; they are but honored servants.

27. They never speak before He has spoken, and they only act on His command.

28. He knows what is before them, and what is behind them; and they do not intercede except for him whom He approves; and they tremble in awe of Him.

29. And whoever of them says, "I am a god besides Him," We will reward him with Hell. Thus We reward the wrongdoers.

30. Do the disbelievers not see that the heavens and the earth were one mass, and We tore them apart? And We made from water every living thing. Will they not believe?

31. And We placed on earth stabilizers, lest it sways with them, and We placed therein signposts and passages, that they may be guided.

32. And We made the sky a protected ceiling; yet they turn away from its wonders.

33. It is He who created the night and the day, and the sun and the moon; each floating in an orbit.

34. We did not grant immortality to any human being before you. Should you die, are they then the immortal?

35. Every soul will taste death. We burden you with adversity and prosperity—a test. And to Us you will be returned.

36. When those who disbelieve see you, they treat you only with ridicule, "Is this the one who mentions your gods?" And they reject the mention of the Merciful.

37. The human being was created of haste. I will show you My signs, so do not seek to rush Me.

38. And they say, "When will this promise come true, if you are truthful?"

39. If those who disbelieve only knew, when they cannot keep the fire off their faces and off their backs, and they will not be helped.

40. In fact, it will come upon them suddenly, and bewilder them. They will not be able to repel it, and they will not be reprieved.

41. Messengers before you were also ridiculed, but those who jeered were surrounded by what they had ridiculed.

42. Say, "Who guards you against the Merciful by night and by day?" But they turn away from the mention of their Lord.

43. Or do they have gods who can defend them against Us? They cannot help themselves, nor will they be protected from Us.

44. We have given these enjoyments, and their ancestors, until time grew long upon them. Do they not see how We gradually reduce the land from its extremities? Are they then the victors?

45. Say, "I am warning you through inspiration." But the deaf cannot hear the call when they are being warned.

46. And when a breath of your Lord's punishment touches them, they say, "Woe to us, we were truly wicked."

47. We will set up the scales of justice for the Day of Resurrection, so that no soul will suffer the least injustice. And even if it be the weight of a mustard-seed, We will bring it up. Sufficient are We as Reckoners.

48. We gave Moses and Aaron the Criterion, and illumination, and a reminder for the righteous.

49. Those who fear their Lord in private, and are apprehensive of the Hour.

50. This too is a blessed message that We have revealed. Are you going to deny it?

51. We gave Abraham his integrity formerly, and We knew him well.

52. When he said to his father and his people, "What are these statues to which you are devoted?"

53. They said, "We found our parents worshiping them."

54. He said, "You and your parents are in evident error."

55. They said, "Are you telling us the truth, or are you just playing?"

56. He said, "Your Lord is the Lord of the heavens and the earth, the One who created them, and I bear witness to that."

57. "By God, I will have a plan for your statues after you have gone away."

58. So he reduced them into pieces, except for their biggest, that they may return to it.

59. They said, "Who did this to our gods? He is certainly one of the wrongdoers."

60. They said, "We heard a youth mentioning them. He is called Abraham."

61. They said, "Bring him before the eyes of the people, so that they may witness."

62. They said, "Are you the one who did this to our gods, O Abraham?"

63. He said, "No. It was this biggest of them that did it. Ask them, if they can speak."

64. Then they turned to one another, and said, "You yourselves are the wrongdoers."

65. But they reverted to their old ideas: "You certainly know that these do not speak."

66. He said, "Do you worship, instead of God, what can neither benefit you in anything, nor harm you?

67. Fie on you, and on what you worship instead of God. Do you not understand?"

68. They said, "Burn him and support your gods, if you are going to act."

69. We said, "O fire, be coolness and safety upon Abraham."

70. They planned to harm him, but We made them the worst losers.

71. And We delivered him, and Lot, to the land that We blessed for all people.

72. And We granted him Isaac and Jacob as a gift; and each We made righteous.

73. And We made them leaders, guiding by Our command; and We inspired them to do good works, and to observe the prayer, and to give out charity. They were devoted servants to Us.

74. And Lot—We gave him judgment and knowledge, and We delivered him from the town that practiced the abominations. They were wicked and perverted people.

75. And We admitted him into Our mercy; for He was one of the righteous.

76. And Noah, when he called before. So We answered him, and delivered him and his family from the great disaster.

77. And We supported him against the people who rejected Our signs. They were an evil people, so We drowned them all.

78. And David and Solomon, when they gave judgment in the case of the field, when some people's sheep wandered therein by night; and We were witnesses to their judgment.

79. And so We made Solomon understand it, and to each We gave wisdom and knowledge. And We subjected the mountains along with David to sing Our praises, and the birds as well—surely We did.

80. And We taught him the making of shields for you, to protect you from your violence. Are you, then, appreciative?

81. And to Solomon the stormy wind, blowing at His command towards the land that We have blessed. We are aware of everything.

82. And of the devils were some that dived for him, and performed other, lesser tasks. But We kept them restrained.

83. And Job, when he cried out to his Lord, "Great harm has afflicted me, and you are the Most Merciful of the merciful."

84. So We answered him, lifted his suffering, and restored his family to him, and their like with them—a mercy from Us, and a reminder for the worshipers.

85. And Ishmael, and Enoch, and Ezekiel; each was one of the steadfast.

86. And We admitted them into Our mercy. They were among the righteous.

87. And Jonah, when he stormed out in fury, thinking We had no power over him. But then He cried out in the darkness, "There is no god but You! Glory to You! I was one of the wrongdoers!"

88. So We answered him, and saved him from the affliction. Thus We save the faithful.

89. And Zechariah, when he called out to his Lord, "My Lord, do not leave me alone, even though you are the Best of heirs."

90. So We answered him, and gave him John. And We cured his wife for him. They used to vie in doing righteous deeds, and used to call on Us in love and awe, and they used to humble themselves to us.

91. And she who guarded her virginity. We breathed into her of Our spirit, and made her and her son a sign to the world.

92. This community of yours is one community, and I am your Lord, so worship Me.

93. But they splintered themselves into factions. They will all return to Us.

94. Whoever does righteous deeds, and is a believer, his effort will not be denied. We are writing it down for him.

95. There is a ban on the town that We had destroyed—that they will not return.

96. Until, when Gog and Magog are let loose, and they swarm down from every mound.

97. The promise of truth has drawn near. The eyes of those who disbelieved will stare in horror: "Woe to us. We were oblivious to this. In fact, we were wrongdoers."

98. You and what you worship besides God are fuel for Hell. You will descend into it.

99. Had these been gods, they would not have descended into it. All will abide in it.

100. In it they will wail. In it they will not hear.

101. As for those who deserved goodness from Us, they will be kept away from it.

102. They will not hear its hissing, and they will forever abide in what their hearts desire.

103. The Supreme Fear will not worry them, and the angels will receive them: "This is your Day which you were promised."

104. On the Day when We fold the heaven, like the folding of a book. Just as We began

the first creation, We will repeat it—a promise binding on Us. We will act.

105. We have written in the Psalms, after the Reminder, that the earth will be inherited by My righteous servants.

106. Indeed, in this is a message for people who worship.

107. We have not sent you except as mercy to mankind.

108. Say, "It is revealed to me that your God is One God. Are you going to submit?"

109. But if they turn away, say, "I have informed you sufficiently. Although I do not know whether what you are promised is near or far."

110. He knows what is said openly, and He knows what you conceal.

111. "And I do not know whether it is perhaps a trial for you, and an enjoyment for a while."

112. He said, "My Lord, judge with justice." And, "Our Lord is the Gracious, Whose help is sought against what you allege."

22. THE PILGRIMAGE
(al-Hajj)

In the name of God,
the Gracious, the Merciful.

1. O people, be conscious of your Lord. The quaking of the Hour is a tremendous thing.

2. On the Day when you will see it, every nursing mother will discard her infant, and every pregnant woman will abort her load, and you will see the people drunk, even though they are not drunk—but the punishment of God is severe.

3. Among the people is he who argues about God without knowledge, and follows every defiant devil.

4. It was decreed for him, that whoever follows him—he will misguide him, and lead him to the torment of the Blaze.

5. O people! If you are in doubt about the Resurrection—We created you from dust, then from a small drop, then from a clinging clot, then from a lump of flesh, partly developed and partly undeveloped. In order to clarify things for you. And We settle in the wombs whatever We will for a designated term, and then We bring you out as infants, until you reach your full strength. And some of you will pass away, and some of you will be returned to the vilest age, so that he may not know, after having known. And you see the earth still, but when We send down water on it, it vibrates, and swells, and grows all kinds of lovely pairs.

6. That is because God is the truth, and because He gives life to the dead, and because He is Capable of everything.

7. And because the Hour is coming—there is no doubt about it—and because God will resurrect those in the graves.

8. Among the people is he who argues about God without knowledge, or guidance, or an enlightening scripture.

9. Turning aside in contempt, to lead away from the path of God. He will have humiliation in this world, and on the Day of Resurrection We will make him taste the agony of burning.

10. That is for what your hands have advanced, and because God is not unjust to the servants.

11. And among the people is he who worships God on edge. When something good comes his way, he is content with it. But when an ordeal strikes him, he makes a turnaround. He loses this world and the next. That is the obvious loss.

12. He invokes, instead of God, what can neither harm him nor benefit him. That is the far straying.

13. He invokes one whose harm is closer than his benefit. What a miserable master. What a miserable companion.

14. God will admit those who believe and do righteous deeds into Gardens beneath which rivers flow. God does whatever He wills.

15. Whoever thinks that God will not help him in this life and in the Hereafter—let him turn to heaven, then sever, and see if his cunning eliminates what enrages him.

16. Thus We revealed it as clarifying signs, and God guides whomever He wills.

17. Those who believe, and those who are Jewish, and the Sabeans, and the Christians, and the Zoroastrians, and the Polytheists—God will judge between them on the Day of Resurrection. God is witness to all things.

18. Do you not realize that to God prostrates everyone in the heavens and everyone on earth, and the sun, and the moon, and the stars, and the mountains, and the trees, and the animals, and many of the people? But many are justly deserving of punishment. Whomever God shames, there is none to honor him. God does whatever He wills.

19. Here are two adversaries feuding regarding their Lord. As for those who disbelieve, garments of fire will be tailored for them, and scalding water will be poured over their heads.

20. Melting their insides and their skins.

21. And they will have maces of iron.

22. Whenever they try to escape the gloom, they will be driven back to it: "Taste the suffering of burning."

23. But God will admit those who believe and do good deeds into Gardens beneath which rivers flow. They will be decorated therein with bracelets of gold and pearls, and their garments therein will be of silk.

24. They were guided to purity of speech. They were guided to the path of the Most Praised.

25. As for those who disbelieve and repel from God's path and from the Sacred Mosque—which We have designated for all mankind equally, whether residing therein or passing through—and seek to commit sacrilege therein—We will make him taste of a painful punishment.

26. We showed Abraham the location of the House, "Do not associate anything with Me; and purify My House for those who circle around, and those who stand to pray, and those who kneel and prostrate."

27. And announce the pilgrimage to humanity. They will come to you on foot, and on every transport. They will come from every distant point.

28. That they may witness the benefits for themselves, and celebrate the name of God during the appointed days, for providing them with the animal livestock. So eat from it, and feed the unfortunate poor.

29. Then let them perform their acts of cleansing, and fulfill their vows, and circle around the Ancient House.

30. All that. Whoever venerates the sanctities of God—it is good for him with his Lord. All Livestock are permitted to you, except what is recited to you. So stay away from the abomination of idols, and stay away from perjury.

31. Being true to God, without associating anything with Him. Whoever associates anything with God—it is as though he has fallen from the sky, and is snatched by the

birds, or is swept away by the wind to a distant abyss.

32. So it is. Whoever venerates the sacraments of God—it is from the piety of the hearts.

33. In them are benefits for you until a certain time. Then their place is by the Ancient House.

34. We have appointed a rite for every nation, that they may commemorate God's name over the livestock He has provided for them. Your God is One God, so to Him submit, and announce good news to the humble.

35. Those whose hearts tremble when God is mentioned, and those who endure what has befallen them, and those who perform the prayer and spend from what We have provided for them.

36. We have made the animal offerings emblems of God for you. In them is goodness for you. So pronounce God's name upon them as they line up. Then, when they have fallen on their sides, eat of them and feed the contented and the beggar. Thus We have subjected them to you, that you may be thankful.

37. Neither their flesh, nor their blood, ever reaches God. What reaches Him is the righteousness from you. Thus He subdued them to you, that you may glorify God for guiding you. And give good news to the charitable.

38. God defends those who believe. God does not love any ungrateful traitor.

39. Permission is given to those who were wronged, and God is Able to give them victory.

40. Those who were unjustly evicted from their homes, merely for saying, "Our Lord is God." Were it not that God repels people by means of others: monasteries, churches, synagogues, and mosques—where the name of God is mentioned much—would have been demolished. God supports whoever supports Him. God is Strong and Mighty.

41. Those who, when We empower them in the land, observe the prayer, and give regular charity, and command what is right, and forbid what is wrong. To God belongs the outcome of events.

42. If they deny you—before them the people of Noah, and Aad, and Thamood also denied.

43. And the people of Abraham, and the people of Lot.

44. And the inhabitants of Median. And Moses was denied. Then I reprieved those who disbelieved, but then I seized them. So how was My rejection?

45. How many a town have We destroyed while it was doing wrong? They lie in ruins, with stilled wells, and lofty mansions.

46. Have they not journeyed in the land, and had minds to reason with, or ears to listen with? It is not the eyes that go blind, but it is the hearts, within the chests, that go blind.

47. And they ask you to hasten the punishment. But God never breaks His promise. A day with your Lord is like a thousand years of your count.

48. How many a town have I reprieved, although it was unjust? Then I seized it. To Me is the destination.

49. Say, "O people, I am only a plain warner to you."

50. Those who believe and work righteousness—for them is forgiveness and a generous provision.

51. But those who strive against Our revelations—these are the inmates of Hell.

52. We never sent a messenger before you, or a prophet, but Satan interfered in his wishes. But God nullifies what Satan interjects, and God affirms His revelations. God is Omniscient and Wise.

53. In order to make Satan's suggestions a trial for those whose hearts are diseased, and those whose hearts are hardened. The wrongdoers are in profound discord.

54. And so that those endowed with knowledge may know that it is the truth from your Lord, and so believe in it, and their hearts soften to it. God guides those who believe to a straight path.

55. Those who disbelieve will continue to be hesitant about it, until the Hour comes upon them suddenly, or there comes to them the torment of a desolate Day.

56. Sovereignty on that Day belongs to God; He will judge between them. Those who believe and do good deeds will be in the Gardens of Bliss.

57. But those who disbelieve and reject Our revelations—these will have a humiliating punishment.

58. Those who emigrate in God's cause, then get killed, or die, God will provide them with fine provisions. God is the Best of Providers.

59. He will admit them an admittance that will please them. God is Knowing and Clement.

60. That is so! Whoever retaliates similarly to the affliction he was made to suffer, and then he is wronged again, God will definitely assist him. God is Pardoning and Forgiving.

61. That is because God merges the night into the day, and He merges the day into the night, and because God is Hearing and Seeing.

62. That is because God is the Reality, and what they invoke besides Him is vanity, and because God is the Sublime, the Grand.

63. Do you not see that God sends down water from the sky, and the land becomes green? God is Kind and Aware.

64. To Him belongs everything in the heavens and everything on earth. God is the Rich, the Praised.

65. Do you not see that God made everything on earth subservient to you? How the ships sail at sea by His command? That He holds up the sky lest it falls on earth—except by His permission? God is Gracious towards the people, Most Merciful.

66. It is He who gives you life, then makes you die, then revives you. The human being is unappreciative.

67. For every congregation We have appointed acts of devotion, which they observe. So do not let them dispute with you in this matter. And invite to your Lord; you are upon a straight guidance.

68. But if they dispute with you, say, "God is fully aware of what you do."

69. God will judge between you on the Day of Resurrection regarding what you disagree about.

70. Do you not know that God knows everything in the heavens and the earth? This is in a book. That is easy for God.

71. Yet they worship, besides God, things for which He sent down no warrant, and what they have no knowledge of. There is no savior for the transgressors.

72. And when Our Clear Verses are recited to them, you will recognize disgust on the faces of those who disbelieve. They nearly assault those who recite to them Our Verses. Say, "Shall I inform you of something worse than that? The Fire! God has prom-

ised it to those who disbelieve. And what a wretched outcome!"

73. O people! A parable is presented, so listen to it: Those you invoke besides God will never create a fly, even if they banded together for that purpose. And if the fly steals anything from them, they cannot recover it from it. Weak are the pursuer and the pursued.

74. They do not value God as He should be valued. God is Strong and Powerful.

75. God chooses messengers from among the angels, and from among the people. God is Hearing and Seeing.

76. He knows what is before them, and what is behind them. To God all matters are referred.

77. O you who believe! Kneel, and prostrate, and worship your Lord, and do good deeds, so that you may succeed.

78. And strive for God, with the striving due to Him. He has chosen you, and has not burdened you in religion—the faith of your father Abraham. It is he who named you Muslims before, and in this. So that the Messenger may be a witness over you, and you may be witnesses over the people. So pray regularly, and give regular charity, and cleave to God. He is your Protector. What an excellent Protector, and what an excellent Helper.

23. THE BELIEVERS
(al-Mu'minun)

In the name of God,
the Gracious, the Merciful.

1. Successful are the believers.

2. Those who are humble in their prayers.

3. Those who avoid nonsense.

4. Those who work for charity.

5. Those who safeguard their chastity.

6. Except from their spouses, or their dependents—for then they are free from blame.

7. But whoever seeks anything beyond that—these are the transgressors.

8. Those who are faithful to their trusts and pledges.

9. Those who safeguard their prayers.

10. These are the inheritors.

11. Who will inherit Paradise, wherein they will dwell forever.

12. We created man from an extract of clay.

13. Then We made him a seed, in a secure repository.

14. Then We developed the seed into a clot. Then We developed the clot into a lump. Then We developed the lump into bones. Then We clothed the bones with flesh. Then We produced it into another creature. Most Blessed is God, the Best of Creators.

15. Then, after that, you will die.

16. Then, on the Day of Resurrection, you will be resurrected.

17. We created above you seven pathways, and We are never heedless of the creation.

18. And We sent down water from the sky in proper quantity, and settled it in the ground, and We are Able to take it away.

19. With it We produce for you gardens of palms and vines, yielding abundant fruit for you to eat.

20. And a tree springing out of Mount Sinai, producing oil, and seasoning for those who eat.

21. And there is a lesson for you in livestock: We give you to drink from what is in their bellies, and you have many benefits in them, and from them you eat.

22. And on them, and on the ships, you are transported.

23. We sent Noah to his people. He said, "O my people, worship God, you have no deity other than Him. Will you not take heed?"

24. But the notables of his people, who disbelieved, said, "This is nothing but a human like you, who wants to gain superiority over you. Had God willed, He would have sent down angels. We never heard of this from our forefathers of old.

25. He is nothing but a man possessed. Just ignore him for a while."

26. He said, "My Lord, help me, for they have rejected me."

27. So We inspired him: "Build the Ark under Our observation and by Our inspiration. And when Our decree comes to pass, and the oven boils over, load into it two pairs of every kind, together with your family, except those of them against whom the word has already been pronounced. And do not speak to me concerning those who did wrong; for they are to be drowned."

28. Then, when you and those with you are settled in the Ark, say, "Praise be to God, who has saved us from the wrongdoing people."

29. And say, "My Lord, land me with a blessed landing, as you are the best of transporters."

30. Surely in that are signs. We are always testing.

31. Then, after them, We established another generation.

32. And We sent among them a messenger from themselves: "Serve God. You have no god other than Him. Will you not be cautious?"

33. But the dignitaries of his people, those who disbelieved and denied the meeting of the Hereafter, and We had indulged them in the present life, said, "This is nothing but a human like you; he eats what you eat, and he drinks what you drink.

34. If you obey a human being like yourselves, you will be losers.

35. Does he promise you that when you have died and become dust and bones, you will be brought out?

36. Farfetched, farfetched is what you are promised.

37. There is nothing but our life in this world. We die, and we live, and we are not resurrected.

38. He is nothing but a man, making up lies about God. We have no faith in him."

39. He said, "My Lord, help me, for they have rejected me."

40. He said, "Soon they will be filled with regret."

41. Then the Blast struck them, justifiably, and so We turned them into scum. So away with the wicked people.

42. Then, after them, We raised other generations.

43. No nation can advance its time, nor can they postpone it.

44. Then We sent Our messengers in succession. Every time a messenger came to his community, they called him a liar. So We made them follow one another, and made them history. So away with a people who do not believe.

45. Then We sent Moses and his brother Aaron, with Our signs and a clear authority.

46. To Pharaoh and his nobles, but they turned arrogant. They were oppressive people.

47. They said, "Are we to believe in two mortals like us, and their people are our slaves?"

48. So they called them liars, and thus were among those destroyed.

49. And We gave Moses the Scripture, that they may be guided.

50. And We made Mary's son and his mother a sign, and We sheltered them on high ground with security and flowing springs.

51. O messengers, eat of the good things, and act with integrity. I am aware of what you do.

52. This nation of yours is one nation, and I am your Lord, so fear Me.

53. But they tore themselves into sects; each party happy with what they have.

54. So leave them in their bewilderment until a time.

55. Do they assume that, in furnishing them with wealth and children.

56. We race to give them the good things? In fact, they have no idea.

57. Those who, from awe of their Lord, are fearful.

58. And those who believe in their Lord's Verses.

59. And those who associate no partners with their Lord.

60. And those who give what they give, while their hearts quake, knowing that to their Lord they will return.

61. It is they who race towards goodness. It is they who will reach it first.

62. We never burden any soul beyond its capacity. And with Us is a record that tells the truth, and they will not be wronged.

63. But their hearts are puzzled because of this, and they have deeds that do not con-form to this, which they continue to perpetrate.

64. Until, when We seize the decadent among them with torment, they begin to groan.

65. Do not groan today. You will receive no help from Us.

66. My Verses were recited to you, but you turned back on your heels.

67. Arrogant towards it—talked nonsense about it—disregarded it.

68. Have they not pondered the Word? Or has there come to them what came not to their forefathers of old?

69. Or is it that they did not recognize their messenger, so they are denying him?

70. Or do they say, "He is possessed?" In fact, he brought them the truth, but most of them hate the truth.

71. If the truth conformed to their desires, the heavens, the earth, and everyone in them would have gone to ruin. In fact, We have given them their message, but they keep avoiding their message.

72. Or are you asking them for a payment? The revenue from your Lord is better, and He is the Best of providers.

73. You are inviting them to a straight path.

74. But those who do not believe in the Hereafter are swerving from the path.

75. Even if We had mercy on them, and relieved their problems, they would still blindly persist in their defiance.

76. We have already gripped them with suffering, but they did not surrender to their Lord, nor did they humble themselves.

77. Until, when We have opened before them a gate of intense agony, at once they will despair.

78. It is He who produced for you the hearing, and the eyesight, and the feelings. But little gratitude you show.

79. And it is He who multiplied you on earth, and to Him you will be gathered.

80. And it is He who gives life and brings death, and to Him is the alternation of night and day. Do you not understand?

81. But they say the like of what the ancients said.

82. They say, "After we have died, and become dust and bones, will we be resurrected?

83. We were promised this before—we and our ancestors—these are nothing but legends of the ancients."

84. Say, "To whom does the earth belong, and everyone in it, if you happen to know?"

85. They will say, "To God." Say, "Will you not reflect?"

86. Say, "Who is the Lord of the seven heavens, and Lord of the Splendid Throne?"

87. They will say, "To God." Say, "Will you not become righteous?"

88. Say, "In whose hand is the dominion of all things, and He protects and cannot be protected from, if you happen to know?"

89. They will say, "To God." Say, "Then are you bewitched?"

90. In fact, We have given them the truth, and they are liars.

91. God has never begotten a son, nor is there any god besides Him. Otherwise, each god would have taken away what it has created, and some of them would have gained supremacy over others. Glory be to God, far beyond what they describe.

92. The Knower of the hidden and the manifest. He is exalted, far above what they associate.

93. Say, "My Lord, if You would show me what they are promised.

94. My Lord, do not place me among the wicked people."

95. We are surely Able to show you what We promise them.

96. Repel evil by what is better. We are aware of what they describe.

97. And say, "My Lord, I seek refuge with You from the urgings of the devils.

98. And I seek refuge with You, my Lord, lest they become present."

99. Until, when death comes to one of them, he says, "My Lord, send me back.

100. That I may do right in what I have neglected." By no means! It is just a word that he utters. And behind them is a barrier, until the Day they are resurrected.

101. When the Horn is blown, no relations between them will exist on that Day, and they will not ask after one another.

102. Those whose scales are heavy—those are the successful.

103. But those whose scales are light—those are they who have lost their souls; in Hell they will dwell forever.

104. The Fire lashes their faces, and therein they grimace.

105. "Were not My revelations recited to you, and you kept on rejecting them?"

106. They will say, "Our Lord, our wretchedness prevailed over us, and we were a people astray.

107. Our Lord! Bring us out of this. If we ever returned, we would truly be evil."

108. He will say, "Be despised therein, and do not speak to Me.

109. There was a group of My servants who would say, 'Our Lord, we have believed, so forgive us, and have mercy on us; You are the Best of the merciful.'

110. But you made then a target of ridicule, until they made you forget My remembrance; and you used to laugh at them.

111. Today, I have rewarded them for their endurance. They are the ones who are the triumphant."

112. He will say, "How many years did you remain on earth?"

113. They will say, "We remained a day, or part of a day; but ask those who keep count."

114. He will say, "You remained only for a little while, if you only knew.

115. Did you think that We created you in vain, and that to Us you will not be returned?"

116. So Exalted is God, the Ruler, the Real. There is no god except He, the Lord of the Noble Throne.

117. Whoever invokes another god besides God—he has no proof thereof—his reckoning rests with his Lord. The disbelievers will not succeed.

118. And say, "My Lord, forgive and have mercy, for You are the Best of the merciful."

24. THE LIGHT
(an-Nur)

*In the name of God,
the Gracious, the Merciful.*

1. A chapter that We have revealed, and made obligatory, and revealed in it clear Verses, that you may take heed.

2. The adulteress and the adulterer—whip each one of them a hundred lashes, and let no pity towards them overcome you regarding God's Law, if you believe in God and the Last Day. And let a group of believers witness their punishment.

3. The adulterer shall marry none but an adulteress or an idolatress; and the adulteress shall marry none but an adulterer or an idolater. That has been prohibited for the believers.

4. Those who accuse chaste women, then cannot bring four witnesses, whip them eighty lashes, and do not ever accept their testimony. For these are the immoral.

5. Except for those who repent afterwards, and reform; for God is Forgiving and Merciful.

6. As for those who accuse their own spouses, but have no witnesses except themselves, the testimony of one of them is equivalent to four testimonies, if he swears by God that he is truthful.

7. And the fifth time, that God's curse be upon him, if he is a liar.

8. But punishment shall be averted from her, if she swears four times by God, that he is a liar.

9. And the fifth time, that God's wrath be upon her, if he is truthful.

10. Were it not for God's grace upon you, and His mercy, and that God is Conciliatory and Wise.

11. Those who perpetrated the slander are a band of you. Do not consider it bad for you, but it is good for you. Each person among them bears his share in the sin. As for him who played the major role—for him is a terrible punishment.

12. Why, when you heard about it, the believing men and women did not think well

of one another, and say, "This is an obvious lie"?

13. Why did they not bring four witnesses to testify to it? If they fail to bring the witnesses, then in God's sight, they are liars.

14. Were it not for God's favor upon you, and His mercy, in this world and the Hereafter, you would have suffered a great punishment for what you have ventured into.

15. When you rumored it with your tongues, and spoke with your mouths what you had no knowledge of, and you considered it trivial; but according to God, it is serious.

16. When you heard it, you should have said, "It is not for us to repeat this. By Your glory, this is a serious slander."

17. God cautions you never to return to the like of it, if you are believers.

18. God explains the Verses to you. God is Knowing and Wise.

19. Those who love to see immorality spread among the believers—for them is a painful punishment, in this life and in the Hereafter. God knows, and you do not know.

20. Were it not for God's grace upon you, and His mercy, and that God is Clement and Merciful.

21. O you who believe! Do not follow Satan's footsteps. Whoever follows Satan's footsteps—he advocates obscenity and immorality. Were it not for God's grace towards you, and His mercy, not one of you would have been pure, ever. But God purifies whomever He wills. God is All-Hearing, All-Knowing.

22. Those of you who have affluence and means should not refuse to give to the relatives, and the needy, and the emigrants for the sake of God. And let them pardon, and let them overlook. Do you not love for God to pardon you? God is All-Forgiving, Most Merciful.

23. Those who slander honorable, innocent, believing women are cursed in this life and in the Hereafter. They will have a terrible punishment.

24. On the Day when their tongues, and their hands, and their feet will testify against them regarding what they used to do.

25. On that Day, God will pay them their account in full, and they will know that God is the Evident Reality.

26. Bad women are for bad men, and bad men are for bad women, and good women are for good men, and good men are for good women. Those are acquitted of what they say. There is forgiveness for them, and a generous provision.

27. O you who believe! Do not enter homes other than your own, until you have asked permission and greeted their occupants. That is better for you, that you may be aware.

28. And if you find no one in them, do not enter them until you are given permission. And if it is said to you, "Turn back," then turn back. That is more proper for you. God is aware of what you do.

29. There is no blame on you for entering uninhabited houses, in which are belongings of yours. God knows what you reveal, and what you conceal.

30. Tell the believing men to restrain their looks, and to guard their privates. That is purer for them. God is cognizant of what they do.

31. And tell the believing women to restrain their looks, and to guard their privates, and not display their beauty except what is apparent thereof, and to draw their

coverings over their breasts, and not expose their beauty except to their husbands, their fathers, their husbands' fathers, their sons, their husbands' sons, their brothers, their brothers' sons, their sisters' sons, their women, what their right hands possess, their male attendants who have no sexual desires, or children who are not yet aware of the nakedness of women. And they should not strike their feet to draw attention to their hidden beauty. And repent to God, all of you believers, so that you may succeed.

32. And wed the singles among you, and those who are fit among your servants and maids. If they are poor, God will enrich them from His bounty. God is All-Encompassing, All Knowing.

33. And let those who do not find the means to marry abstain, until God enriches them from His bounty. If any of your servants wish to be freed, grant them their wish, if you recognize some good in them. And give them of God's wealth which he has given you. And do not compel your girls to prostitution, seeking the materials of this life, if they desire to remain chaste. Should anyone compel them—after their compulsion, God is Forgiving and Merciful.

34. We have sent down to you clarifying revelations, and examples of those who passed on before you, and advice for the righteous.

35. God is the Light of the heavens and the earth. The allegory of His light is that of a pillar on which is a lamp. The lamp is within a glass. The glass is like a brilliant planet, fueled by a blessed tree, an olive tree, neither eastern nor western. Its oil would almost illuminate, even if no fire has touched it. Light upon Light. God guides to His light whomever He wills.

God thus cites the parables for the people. God is cognizant of everything.

36. In houses which God has permitted to be raised, and His name is celebrated therein. He is glorified therein, morning and evening.

37. By men who neither trading nor commerce distracts them from God's remembrance, and from performing the prayers, and from giving alms. They fear a Day when hearts and sights are overturned.

38. God will reward them according to the best of what they did, and He will increase them from His bounty. God provides for whomever He wills without reckoning.

39. As for those who disbelieve, their works are like a mirage in a desert. The thirsty assumes it is to be water. Until, when he has reached it, he finds it to be nothing, but there he finds God, Who settles his account in full. God is swift in reckoning.

40. Or like utter darkness in a vast ocean, covered by waves, above which are waves, above which is fog. Darkness upon darkness. If he brings out his hand, he will hardly see it. He to whom God has not granted a light has no light.

41. Do you not realize that God is glorified by whatever is in the heavens and the earth, and even by the birds in formation? Each knows its prayer and its manner of praise. God knows well what they do.

42. To God belongs the dominion of the heavens and the earth, and to God is the ultimate return.

43. Have you not seen how God propels the clouds, then brings them together, then piles them into a heap, and you see the rain drops emerging from its midst? How He brings down loads of hail from the sky, striking with it whomever He wills, and diverting it from whomever He wills? The

flash of its lightening almost snatches the sight away.

44. God alternates the night and the day. In that is a lesson for those who have insight.

45. God created every living creature from water. Some of them crawl on their bellies, and some walk on two feet, and others walk on four. God creates whatever He wills. God is Capable of everything.

46. We sent down enlightening revelations, and God guides whomever He wills to a straight path.

47. And they say, "We have believed in God and the Messenger, and we obey," but some of them turn away afterwards. These are not believers.

48. And when they are called to God and His Messenger, in order to judge between them, some of them refuse.

49. But if justice is on their side, they accept it willingly.

50. Is there sickness in their hearts? Or are they suspicious? Or do they fear that God may do them injustice? Or His Messenger? In fact, they themselves are the unjust.

51. The response of the believers, when they are called to God and His Messenger in order to judge between them, is to say, "We hear and we obey." These are the successful.

52. Whoever obeys God and His Messenger, and fears God, and is conscious of Him—these are the winners.

53. And they swear by God with their solemn oaths, that if you commanded them, they would mobilize. Say, "Do not swear. Obedience will be recognized. God is experienced with what you do."

54. Say, "Obey God and obey the Messenger." But if they turn away, then he is responsible for his obligations, and you are responsible for your obligations. And if you obey him, you will be guided. It is only incumbent on the Messenger to deliver the clarifying message.

55. God has promised those of you who believe and do righteous deeds, that He will make them successors on earth, as He made those before them successors, and He will establish for them their religion—which He has approved for them—and will substitute security in place of their fear. They worship Me, never associating anything with Me. But whoever disbelieves after that—these are the sinners.

56. Pray regularly, and give regular charity, and obey the Messenger, so that you may receive mercy.

57. Never think that those who disbelieve can escape on earth. Their place is the Fire, a miserable destination.

58. O you who believe! Permission must be requested by your servants and those of you who have not reached puberty. On three occasions: before the Dawn Prayer, and at noon when you change your clothes, and after the Evening Prayer. These are three occasions of privacy for you. At other times, it is not wrong for you or them to intermingle with one another. God thus clarifies the revelations for you. God is Knowledgeable and Wise.

59. When the children among you reach puberty, they must ask permission, as those before them asked permission. God thus clarifies His revelations for you. God is Knowledgeable and Wise.

60. Women past the age of childbearing, who have no desire for marriage, commit no wrong by taking off their outer clothing, provided they do not flaunt their finery. But to maintain modesty is better for them. God is Hearing and Knowing.

61. There is no blame on the blind, nor any blame on the lame, nor any blame on the sick, nor on yourselves for eating at your homes, or your fathers' homes, or your mothers' homes, or your brothers' homes, or your sisters' homes, or the homes of your paternal uncles, or the homes of your paternal aunts, or the homes of your maternal uncles, or the homes of your maternal aunts, or those whose keys you own, or the homes of your friends. You commit no wrong by eating together or separately. But when you enter any home, greet one another with a greeting from God, blessed and good. God thus explains the revelations for you, so that you may understand.

62. The believers are those who believe in God and His Messenger, and when they are with him for a matter of common interest, they do not leave until they have asked him for permission. Those who ask your permission are those who believe in God and His Messenger. So when they ask your permission to attend to some affair of theirs, give permission to any of them you wish, and ask God's forgiveness for them. God is Forgiving and Merciful.

63. Do not address the Messenger in the same manner you address one another. God knows those of you who slip away using flimsy excuses. So let those who oppose his orders beware, lest an ordeal strikes them, or a painful punishment befalls them.

64. Surely, to God belongs everything in the heavens and the earth. He knows what you are about. And on the Day they are returned to Him, He will inform them of what they did. God has full knowledge of all things.

25. THE CRITERION
(al-Furqan)

In the name of God,
the Gracious, the Merciful.

1. Blessed is He who sent down the Criterion upon His servant, to be a warning to humanity.

2. He to whom belongs the kingdom of the heavens and the earth, who took to Himself no son, who never had a partner in His kingship; who created everything, and determined its measure.

3. And yet, instead of Him, they produce for themselves gods that create nothing, but are themselves created; that have no power to harm or benefit themselves; and no power over life, death, or resurrection.

4. Those who disbelieve say, "This is nothing but a lie that he made up, and others have helped him at it." They have committed an injustice and a perjury.

5. And they say, "Tales of the ancients; he wrote them down; they are dictated to him morning and evening."

6. Say, "It was revealed by He who knows the Secret in the heavens and the earth. He is always Forgiving and Merciful."

7. And they say, "What sort of messenger is this, who eats food, and walks in the marketplaces? If only an angel was sent down with him, to be alongside him a warner."

8. Or, "If only a treasure was dropped on him." Or, "If only he had a garden from which he eats." The evildoers also say, "You are following but a man under spell."

9. Look how they invent examples for you. They have gone astray, and cannot find a way.

10. Blessed is He who, if He wills, can provide you with better than that—gardens

beneath which rivers flow—and He will give you palaces.

11. In fact, they have denied the Hour, and We have prepared for those who deny the Hour a Blaze.

12. When it sees them from a distant place, they will hear it raging and roaring.

13. And when they are thrown into it, into a tight place, shackled, they will plead for death.

14. "Do not plead for one death today, but plead for a great many deaths."

15. Say, "Is this better, or the Garden of Eternity promised to the righteous? It is for them a reward and a destination.

16. They will have therein whatever they desire, forever. That is upon your Lord a binding promise.

17. On the Day when He gathers them, and what they worshiped besides God, He will say, "Was it you who misled these servants of Mine, or was it they who lost the way?"

18. They will say, "Glory be to You. It was not for us to take any lords besides You. But you gave them enjoyments, and their ancestors, until they forgot the Message, and became ruined people."

19. They have denied you because of what you say; so you can neither avert, nor help. Whoever among you commits injustice, We will make him taste a grievous punishment.

20. We never sent any messengers before you, but they ate food and walked in the marketplaces. And We made some of you tempters for one another—will you be patient? Your Lord is always Observing.

21. Those who do not expect to meet Us say, "If only the angels were sent down to us, or we could see our Lord." They have grown arrogant within themselves, and have become excessively defiant.

22. On the Day when they see the angels—there will be no good news for sinners on that Day; and they will say, "A protective refuge."

23. We will proceed to the works they did, and will turn them into scattered dust.

24. The companions of Paradise on that Day will be better lodged, and more fairly accommodated.

25. The Day when the sky is cleft with clouds, and the angels are sent down in streams.

26. On that Day, true sovereignty will belong to the Merciful, and it will be a difficult Day for the disbelievers.

27. On that Day, the wrongdoer will bite his hands, and say, "If only I had followed the way with the Messenger.

28. Oh, woe to me; I wish I never took so-and-so for a friend.

29. He led me away from the Message after it had come to me; for Satan has always been a betrayer of man."

30. And the Messenger will say, "My Lord, my people have abandoned this Quran."

31. Likewise, to every prophet We assign enemies from among the wicked. But your Lord suffices as a guide and savior.

32. Those who disbelieve say, "Why was the Quran not revealed to him at once?" Thus in order to strengthen your heart thereby, and We revealed it in stages.

33. Whatever argument they come to you with, We provide you with the truth, and a better exposition.

34. Those who are herded into Hell on their faces—those are in a worse position, and further astray from the way.

35. We gave Moses the Scripture, and appointed his brother Aaron as his assistant.

36. We said, "Go to the people who rejected Our signs," and We destroyed them completely.

37. And the people of Noah—when they rejected the messengers, We drowned them, and made them a lesson for mankind. We have prepared for the wrongdoers a painful retribution.

38. And Aad, and Thamood, and the inhabitants of Arras, and many generations in between.

39. To each We presented the parables; and each We devastated utterly.

40. And they came upon the city that was drenched by the terrible rain. Did they not see it? But they do not expect resurrection.

41. And when they see you, they take you for nothing but mockery: "Is this the one God sent as a messenger?"

42. "He nearly led us away from our gods, had we not patiently adhered to them." But they will know, when they witness the torment, who is further away from the way.

43. Have you seen him who chose his desire as his god? Would you be an agent for him?

44. Or do you assume that most of them hear or understand? They are just like cattle, but even more errant in their way.

45. Do you not see how your Lord extends the shadow? Had He willed, He could have made it still. And We made the sun a pointer to it.

46. Then We withdraw it towards Us gradually.

47. And it is He who made the night a covering for you, and sleep for rest; and He made the day a revival.

48. And it is He who sends the winds, bringing advance news of His mercy, and We send down from the sky pure water.

49. To revive dead lands thereby, and to provide drink for the multitude of animals and humans We created.

50. We have circulated it among them, that they may reflect, but most people persist in thanklessness.

51. Had We willed, We could have sent to every town a warner.

52. So do not obey the disbelievers, but strive against them with it, a mighty struggle.

53. And it is He who merged the two seas; this one fresh and sweet, and that one salty and bitter; and He placed between them a barrier, and an impassable boundary.

54. And it is He who, from fluid, created the human being. Then He made relationships through marriage and mating. Your Lord is Omnipotent.

55. And yet, instead of God, they serve what neither profits them nor harms them. The disbeliever has always turned his back on his Lord.

56. We sent you only as a herald of good news and a warner.

57. Say, "I ask of you no payment for this— only that whoever wills may take a path to his Lord."

58. And put your trust in the Living, the One who never dies; and celebrate His praise. He suffices as the All-Informed Knower of the faults of His creatures.

59. He who created the heavens and the earth and everything between them in six days, then settled on the Throne. The Most Merciful. Ask about Him a well-informed.

60. And when it is said to them, "Bow down to the Merciful," they say, "And

what is the Merciful? Are we to bow down to whatever you command us?" And it increases their aversion.

61. Blessed is He who placed constellations in the sky, and placed in it a lamp, and an illuminating moon.

62. And it is He who made the night and the day alternate—for whoever desires to reflect, or desires to show gratitude.

63. The servants of the Merciful are those who walk the earth in humility, and when the ignorant address them, they say, "Peace."

64. And those who pass the night prostrating themselves to their Lord and standing up.

65. And those who say, "Our Lord, avert from us the suffering of Hell, for its suffering is continuous.

66. It is indeed a miserable residence and destination."

67. And those who, when they spend, are neither wasteful nor stingy, but choose a middle course between that.

68. And those who do not implore besides God any other god, and do not kill the soul which God has made sacred—except in the pursuit of justice—and do not commit adultery. Whoever does that will face penalties.

69. The punishment will be doubled for him on the Day of Resurrection, and he will dwell therein in humiliation forever.

70. Except for those who repent, and believe, and do good deeds. These—God will replace their bad deeds with good deeds. God is ever Forgiving and Merciful.

71. Whoever repents and acts righteously—has inclined towards God with repentance.

72. And those who do not bear false witness; and when they come across indecencies, they pass by with dignity.

73. And those who, when reminded of the revelations of their Lord, do not fall before them deaf and blind.

74. And those who say, "Our Lord, grant us delight in our spouses and our children, and make us a good example for the righteous."

75. Those will be awarded the Chamber for their patience, and will be greeted therein with greetings and peace.

76. Abiding therein forever—it is an excellent residence and destination.

77. Say, "What are you to my Lord without your prayers? You have denied the truth, and the inevitable will happen."

26. THE POETS
(ash-Shu'ara')

In the name of God,
the Gracious, the Merciful.

1. Ta, Seen, Meem.

2. These are the Verses of the Clarifying Book.

3. Perhaps you will destroy yourself with grief, because they do not become believers.

4. If We will, We can send down upon them a sign from heaven, at which their necks will stay bent in humility.

5. No fresh reminder comes to them from the Most Merciful, but they turn their backs at it.

6. They have denied the truth, but soon will come to them the news of what they ridiculed.

7. Have they not seen the earth, and how many beautiful pairs We produced therein?

8. Surely in this is a sign, but most of them are not believers.

9. Most surely, your Lord is the Almighty, the Merciful.

10. Your Lord called to Moses, "Go to the tyrannical people.

11. The people of Pharaoh. Will they not fear?"

12. He said, "My Lord, I fear they will reject me.

13. And I become stressed, and my tongue is not fluent, so send Aaron too.

14. And they have a charge against me, so I fear they will kill me."

15. He said, "No. Go, both of you, with Our proofs. We will be with you, listening.

16. Go to Pharaoh, and say, 'We are the Messengers of the Lord of the Worlds.'

17. Let the Children of Israel go with us.'"

18. He said, "Did we not raise you among us as a child, and you stayed among us for many of your years?

19. And you committed that deed you committed, and you were ungrateful."

20. He said, "I did it then, when I was of those astray.

21. And I fled from you when I feared you; but my Lord gave me wisdom, and made me one of the messengers.

22. Is that the favor you taunt me with, although you have enslaved the Children of Israel?"

23. Pharaoh said, "And what is the Lord of the Worlds?"

24. He said, "The Lord of the heavens and the earth, and everything between them, if you are aware."

25. He said to those around him, "Do you not hear?"

26. He said, "Your Lord and the Lord of your ancestors of old."

27. He said, "This messenger of yours, who is sent to you, is crazy."

28. He said, "Lord of the East and the West, and everything between them, if you understand."

29. He said, "If you accept any god other than me, I will make you a prisoner."

30. He said, "What if I bring you something convincing?"

31. He said, "Bring it, if you are being truthful."

32. So he cast his staff, and it was a serpent, plain to see.

33. And he pulled his hand, and it was white, for all to see.

34. He said to the dignitaries around him, "This is a skilled magician.

35. He intends to drive you out of your land with his magic, so what do you recommend?"

36. They said, "Delay him and his brother, and send recruiters to the cities.

37. To bring you every experienced magician."

38. So the magicians were gathered for the appointment on a specified day.

39. And it was said to the people, "Are you all gathered?

40. That we may follow the magicians, if they are the winners."

41. When the magicians arrived, they said to Pharaoh, "Is there a reward for us, if we are the winners?"

42. He said, "Yes, and you will be among those favored."

43. Moses said to them, "Present what you intend to present."

44. So they threw their ropes and their sticks, and said, "By the majesty of Pharaoh, we will be the winners."

45. Then Moses threw his staff, and behold, it began swallowing their trickery.

46. And the magicians fell down prostrating.

47. They said, "We have believed in the Lord of the Worlds.

48. The Lord of Moses and Aaron."

49. He said, "Did you believe in Him before I have given you permission? He must be your chief, who taught you magic. You will soon know. I will cut off your hands and feet on opposite sides, and I will crucify you all."

50. They said, "No problem. To our Lord we will return.

51. We are eager for our Lord to forgive us our sins, since we are the first of the believers."

52. And We inspired Moses: "Travel with My servants by night. You will be followed."

53. Pharaoh sent heralds to the cities.

54. "These are a small gang.

55. And they are enraging us.

56. But we are a vigilant multitude."

57. So We drove them out of gardens and springs.

58. And treasures and noble dwellings.

59. So it was. And We made the Children of Israel inherit them.

60. And they pursued them at sunrise.

61. When the two groups sighted each other, the followers of Moses said, "We are being overtaken."

62. He said, "No; my Lord is with me, He will guide me."

63. We inspired Moses: "Strike the sea with your staff." Whereupon it parted, and each part was like a huge hill.

64. And there We brought the others near.

65. And We saved Moses and those with him, all together.

66. Then We drowned the others.

67. In that there is a sign, but most of them are not believers.

68. Surely, your Lord is the Almighty, the Merciful.

69. And relate to them the story of Abraham.

70. When he said to his father and his people, "What do you worship?"

71. They said, "We worship idols, and we remain devoted to them."

72. He said, "Do they hear you when you pray?

73. Or do they benefit you, or harm you?"

74. They said, "But we found our ancestors doing so."

75. He said, "Have you considered what you worship.

76. You and your ancient ancestors?

77. They are enemies to me, but not so the Lord of the Worlds.

78. He who created me, and guides me.

79. He who feeds me, and waters me.

80. And when I get sick, He heals me.

81. He who makes me die, and then revives me.

82. He, who will, I hope, will forgive my sins on the Day of the Reckoning."

83. "My Lord! Grant me wisdom, and include me with the righteous.

84. And give me a reputation of truth among the others.

85. And make me of the inheritors of the Garden of Bliss.

86. And forgive my father—he was one of the misguided.

87. And do not disgrace me on the Day they are resurrected.

88. The Day when neither wealth nor children will help.

89. Except for him who comes to God with a sound heart."

90. And Paradise will be brought near for the righteous.

91. And the Blaze will be displayed to the deviators.

92. And it will be said to them, "Where are those you used to worship?"

93. Besides God? Can they help you, or help themselves?"

94. Then they will be toppled into it, together with the seducers.

95. And the soldiers of Satan, all of them.

96. They will say, as they feud in it.

97. "By God, We were in evident error.

98. For equating you with the Lord of the Worlds.

99. No one misled us except the sinners.

100. Now we have no intercessors.

101. And no sincere friend.

102. If only we could have another chance, we would be among the faithful."

103. Surely in this is a sign, but most of them are not believers.

104. Your Lord is the Almighty, the Merciful.

105. The people of Noah disbelieved the messengers.

106. Their brother Noah said to them, "Do you not fear?

107. I am to you a faithful messenger.

108. So fear God, and obey me.

109. I ask of you no payment for this. My payment is only from the Lord of the Worlds.

110. So fear God, and obey me."

111. They said, "Shall we believe in you, when it is the lowliest who follow you?"

112. He said, "What do I know about what they do?

113. Their account rests only with my Lord, if you have sense.

114. And I am not about to drive away the believers.

115. I am only a clear warner."

116. They said, "If you do not refrain, O Noah, you will be stoned."

117. He said, "My Lord, my people have denied me.

118. So judge between me and them decisively, and deliver me and the believers who are with me.

119. So We delivered him and those with him in the laden Ark.

120. Then We drowned the rest.

121. In that is a sign, but most of them are not believers.

122. Your Lord is the Almighty, the Merciful.

123. Aad disbelieved the messengers.

124. When their brother Hud said to them, "Do you not fear?

125. I am to you a faithful messenger.

126. So fear God, and obey me.

127. I ask of you no payment for this. My payment is only from the Lord of the Worlds.

128. Do you build a monument on every height for vanity's sake?

129. And you set up fortresses, hoping to live forever?

130. And when you strike, you strike mercilessly?

131. So fear God, and obey me.

132. And fear Him, who supplied you with everything you know.

133. He supplied you with livestock and children.

134. And gardens and springs.

135. I fear for you the punishment of an awesome Day."

136. They said, "It is the same for us, whether you lecture us, or do not lecture.

137. This is nothing but morals of the ancients.

138. And we will not be punished."

139. So they denied him, and We destroyed them. Surely in this is a sign, but most of them are not believers.

140. Your Lord is the Almighty, the Merciful.

141. Thamood disbelieved the messengers.

142. When their brother Saleh said to them, "Do you not fear?

143. I am to you a faithful messenger.

144. So fear God, and obey me.

145. I ask of you no payment for it. My payment is only from the Lord of the Worlds.

146. Will you be left secure in what is here?

147. In gardens and springs?

148. And fields, and palm-trees whose fruits are delicious?

149. And you skillfully carve houses in the mountains?

150. So fear God, and obey me.

151. And do not obey the command of the extravagant.

152. Who spread turmoil on earth, and do not reform."

153. They said, "You are surely one of the bewitched.

154. You are nothing but a man like us. So bring us a sign, if you are truthful.

155. He said, "This is a she-camel; she has her turn of drinking, and you have your turn of drinking—on a specified day.

156. And do not touch her with harm, lest the punishment of a great day seizes you."

157. But they slaughtered her, and became full of remorse.

158. So the punishment overtook them. Surely in this is a sign, but most of them are not believers.

159. Your Lord is the Almighty, the Merciful.

160. The people of Lot disbelieved the messengers.

161. When their brother Lot said to them, "Do you not fear?

162. I am to you a faithful messenger.

163. So fear God, and obey me.

164. I ask of you no payment for it. My payment is only from the Lord of the Worlds.

165. Do you approach the males of the world?

166. And forsake the wives that your Lord has created for you? Indeed, you are intrusive people."

167. They said, "Unless you refrain, O Lot, you will be expelled."

168. He said, "I certainly deplore your conduct."

169. "My Lord, save me and my family from what they do."

170. So We saved him and his family, altogether.

171. Except for an old woman among those who tarried.

172. Then We destroyed the others.

173. And We rained down on them a rain. Dreadful is the rain of those forewarned.

174. Surely in this is a sign, but most of them are not believers.

175. Your Lord is the Almighty, the Merciful.

176. The People of the Woods disbelieved the messengers.

177. When Shuaib said to them, "Do you not fear?

178. I am to you a trustworthy messenger.

179. So fear God, and obey me.

180. I ask of you no payment for it. My payment is only from the Lord of the Worlds.

181. Give full measure, and do not cheat.

182. And weigh with the accurate scales.

183. And do not defraud people of their belongings, and do not work corruption in the land.

184. And fear Him who created you and the masses of old."

185. They said, "You are one of those bewitched.

186. And you are nothing but a man like us; and we think that you are a liar.

187. So bring down on us pieces from the sky, if you are truthful."

188. He said, "My Lord is Well Aware of what you do."

189. But they denied him. So the punishment of the day of gloom gripped them. It was the punishment of a great day.

190. Surely in this is a sign, but most of them are not believers.

191. Your Lord is the Almighty, the Merciful.

192. It is a revelation from the Lord of the Worlds.

193. The Honest Spirit came down with it.

194. Upon your heart, that you may be one of the warners.

195. In a clear Arabic tongue.

196. And it is in the Scriptures of the ancients.

197. Is it not a sign for them that the scholars of the Children of Israel recognized it?

198. Had We revealed it to one of the foreigners.

199. And he had recited it to them, they still would not have believed in it.

200. Thus We make it pass through the hearts of the guilty.

201. They will not believe in it until they witness the painful punishment.

202. It will come to them suddenly, while they are unaware.

203. Then they will say, "Are we given any respite?"

204. Do they seek to hasten Our punishment?

205. Have you considered: if We let them enjoy themselves for some years.

206. Then there comes to them what they were promised.

207. Of what avail to them will be their past enjoyments?

208. Never did We destroy a town, but it had warners.

209. As a reminder—We are never unjust.

210. It was not the devils that revealed it.

211. It is not in their interests, nor in their power.

212. They are barred from hearing.

213. So do not pray to another god with God, else you will be of those tormented.

214. And warn your close relatives.

215. And lower your wing to those of the believers who follow you.

216. And if they disobey you, say, "I am innocent of what you do."

217. And put your trust in the Almighty, the Merciful.

218. He Who sees you when you rise.

219. And your devotions amidst the worshipers.

220. He is indeed the Hearer, the Aware.

221. Shall I inform you upon whom the devils descend?

222. They descend upon every sinful liar.

223. They give ear, and most of them are liars.

224. And as for the poets—the deviators follow them.

225. Do you not see how they ramble in every style?

226. And how they say what they do not do?

227. Except for those who believe, do good deeds, remember God frequently, and defend themselves after they are wronged. As for those who do wrong, they will know by what overturning they will be overturned.

27. THE ANT
(an-Naml)

In the name of God,
the Gracious, the Merciful.

1. Ta, Seen. These are the Signs of the Quran—a book that makes things clear.

2. Guidance and good news for the believers.

3. Those who observe the prayers, and give charity regularly, and are certain of the Hereafter.

4. As for those who do not believe in the Hereafter: We made their deeds appear good to them, so they wander aimlessly.

5. It is they who will receive the grievous punishment, and in the Hereafter, will be the greatest losers.

6. You are receiving the Quran from an All-Wise, All-Knowing.

7. When Moses said to his family, "I have glimpsed a fire. I will bring you some news from it; or bring you a firebrand, that you may warm yourselves."

8. Then, when he reached it, he was called: "Blessed is He who is within the fire, and He who is around it, and glorified be God, Lord of the Worlds.

9. O Moses, it is I, God, the Almighty, the Wise.

10. Throw down your staff." But when he saw it quivering, as though it were a demon, he turned around not looking back. "O Moses, do not fear; the messengers do not fear in My presence.

11. But whoever has done wrong, and then substituted goodness in place of evil. I am Forgiving and Merciful.

12. Put your hand inside your pocket, and it will come out white, without blemish—among nine miracles to Pharaoh and his people, for they are immoral people."

13. Yet when Our enlightening signs came to them, they said, "This is obvious witchcraft."

14. And they rejected them, although their souls were certain of them, out of wickedness and pride. So see how the outcome was for the mischief-makers.

15. And We gave David and Solomon knowledge. They said, "Praise God, who has favored us over many of His believing servants."

16. And Solomon succeeded David. He said, "O people, we were taught the language of birds, and we were given from everything. This is indeed a real blessing."

17. To the service of Solomon were mobilized his troops of sprites, and men, and birds—all held in strict order.

18. Until, when they came upon the Valley of Ants, an ant said, "O ants! Go into your nests, lest Solomon and his troops crush you, without noticing."

19. He smiled and laughed at her words, and said, "My Lord, direct me to be thankful for the blessings you have bestowed upon me and upon my parents, and to do good works that please You. And admit me, by Your grace, into the company of Your virtuous servants."

20. Then he inspected the birds, and said, "Why do I not see the hoopoe? Or is he among the absentees?

21. I will punish him most severely, or slay him, unless he gives me a valid excuse."

22. But he did not stay for long. He said, "I have learnt something you did not know. I have come to you from Sheba, with reliable information.

23. I found a woman ruling over them, and she was given of everything, and she has a magnificent throne.

24. I found her and her people worshiping the sun, instead of God. Satan made their conduct appear good to them, and diverted them from the path, so they are not guided.

25. If only they would worship God, who brings to light the mysteries of the heavens and the earth, and knows what you conceal and what you reveal.

26. God—There is no god but He, the Lord of the Sublime Throne."

27. He said, "We will see, whether you have spoken the truth, or whether you are a liar.

28. Go with this letter of mine, and deliver it to them; then withdraw from them, and see how they respond."

29. She said, "O Counselors, a gracious letter was delivered to me.

30. It is from Solomon, and it is, 'In the Name of God, the Gracious, the Merciful.

31. Do not defy me, and come to me submissively.'"

32. She said, "O Counselors, advise me in this matter of mine. I never make a decision unless you are present."

33. They said, "We are people of might and great courage, but the decision is yours, so consider what you wish to command."

34. She said, "When kings enter a city, they devastate it, and subjugate its dignified people. Thus they always do.

35. I am sending them a gift, and will see what the envoys bring back."

36. When he came to Solomon, he said, "Are you supplying me with money? What God has given me is better than what He has given you. It is you who delight in your gift.

37. Go back to them. We will come upon them with troops they cannot resist, and we will expel them from there, disgraced and humiliated."

38. He said, "O notables, which one of you will bring me her throne before they come to me in submission?"

39. An imp of the sprites said, "I will bring it to you before you rise from your seat. I am strong and reliable enough to do it."

40. He who had knowledge from the Book said, "I will bring it to you before your glance returns to you." And when he saw it settled before him, he said, "This is from the grace of my Lord, to test me, whether I am grateful or ungrateful. He who is grateful, his gratitude is to his own credit; but he who is ungrateful—my Lord is Independent and Generous."

41. He said, "Disguise her throne for her, and we shall see whether she will be guided, or remains one of the misguided."

42. When she arrived, it was said, "Is your throne like this?" She said, "As if this is it." "We were given knowledge before her, and we were submissive."

43. But she was prevented by what she worshiped besides God; she belonged to a disbelieving people.

44. It was said to her, "Go inside the palace." And when she saw it, she thought it was a deep pond, and she bared her legs. He said, "It is a palace paved with glass." She said, "My Lord, I have done wrong to myself, and I have submitted with Solomon, to God, Lord of the Worlds."

45. And We sent to Thamood their brother Saleh: "Worship God." But they became two disputing factions.

46. He said, "O my people, why are you quick to do evil rather than good? If only you would seek God's forgiveness, so that you may be shown mercy."

47. They said, "We consider you an ill omen, and those with you." He said, "Your omen is with God. In fact, you are a people being tested."

48. In the city was a gang of nine who made mischief in the land and did no good.

49. They said, "Swear by God to one another that we will attack him and his family by night, and then tell his guardian, 'We did not witness the murder of his family, and we are being truthful.'"

50. They planned a plan, and We planned a plan, but they did not notice.

51. So note the outcome of their planning; We destroyed them and their people, altogether.

52. Here are their homes, in ruins, on account of their iniquities. Surely in this is a sign for people who know.

53. And We saved those who believed and were pious.

54. And Lot, when he said to his people, "Do you commit lewdness with open eyes?

55. Do you lust after men instead of women? You are truly ignorant people."

56. But the only response of his people was to say, "Expel the family of Lot from your town. They are purist people."

57. So We saved him and his family, except for his wife, whom We destined to be among the laggards.

58. And We rained upon them a rain. Miserable was the rain of those forewarned.

59. Say, "Praise God, and peace be upon His servants whom He has selected. Is God better, or what they associate?"

60. Or, who created the heavens and the earth, and rains down water from the sky for you? With it We produce gardens full of beauty, whose trees you could not have produced. Is there another god with God? But they are a people who equate.

61. Or, who made the earth habitable, and made rivers flow through it, and set mountains on it, and placed a partition between the two seas? Is there another god with God? But most of them do not know.

62. Or, who answers the one in need when he prays to Him, and relieves adversity, and makes you successors on earth? Is there another god with God? How hardly you pay attention.

63. Or, who guides you through the darkness of land and sea, and who sends the winds as heralds of His mercy? Is there another god with God? Most exalted is God, above what they associate.

64. Or, who originates the creation and then repeats it, and who gives you livelihood from the sky and the earth? Is there another god with God? Say, "Produce your evidence, if you are truthful."

65. Say, "No one in the heavens or on earth knows the future except God; and they do not perceive when they will be resurrected."

66. In fact, their knowledge of the Hereafter is confused. In fact, they are in doubt about it. In fact, they are blind to it.

67. Those who disbelieve say, "When we have become dust, and our ancestors, shall we be brought out?

68. We were promised that before, we and our ancestors—these are nothing but legends of the ancients."

69. Say, travel through the earth, and observe the fate of the guilty."

70. But do not grieve over them, and do not be troubled by what they plot.

71. And they say, "When is this promise, if you are truthful?"

72. Say, "Perhaps some of what you are impatient for has drawn near."

73. Your Lord is gracious towards humanity, but most of them are not thankful.

74. And your Lord knows what their hearts conceal, and what they reveal.

75. There is no mystery in the heaven and the earth, but it is in a Clear Book.

76. This Quran relates to the Children of Israel most of what they differ about.

77. And it is guidance and mercy for the believers.

78. Your Lord will judge between them by His wisdom. He is the Almighty, the All-Knowing.

79. So rely on God. You are upon the clear truth.

80. You cannot make the dead hear, nor can you make the deaf hear the call if they turn their backs and flee.

81. Nor can you guide the blind out of their straying. You can make no one listen, except those who believe in Our verses; for they are Muslims.

82. And when the Word has fallen on them, We will bring out for them from the earth a creature which will say to them that the people are uncertain of Our revelations.

83. On the Day when We gather from every community a group of those who rejected Our revelations; and they will be restrained.

84. Until, when they arrive, He will say, "Did you reject My revelations without comprehending them? Or what is it you were doing?"

85. The Word will come down upon them for their wrongdoing, and they will not speak.

86. Do they not see that We made the night for them to rest therein, and the day for visibility? Surely in that are signs for people who believe.

87. On the Day when the Trumpet is blown, everyone in the heavens and the earth will be horrified, except whomever God wills; and everyone will come before Him in humility.

88. And you see the mountains, and imagine them fixed, yet they pass, as the passing of the clouds—the making of God, who has perfected everything. He is fully Informed of what you do.

89. Whoever brings a virtue will receive better than it—and they will be safe from the horrors of that Day.

90. But whoever brings evil—their faces will be tumbled into the Fire. Will you be rewarded except for what you used to do?

91. "I was commanded to worship the Lord of this town, who has sanctified it, and to Whom everything belongs; and I was commanded to be of those who submit.

92. And to recite the Quran." Whoever is guided—is guided to his own advantage. And whoever goes astray, then say, "I am one of the warners."

93. And say, "Praise belongs to God; He will show you His signs, and you will recognize them. Your Lord is not heedless of what you do."

28. HISTORY
(al-Qasas)

In the name of God,
the Gracious, the Merciful.

1. Ta, Seen, Meem.

2. These are the Verses of the Clear Book.

3. We narrate to you from the history of Moses and Pharaoh—in truth—for people who believe.

4. Pharaoh exalted himself in the land, and divided its people into factions. He persecuted a group of them, slaughtering their sons, while sparing their daughters. He was truly a corrupter.

5. But We desired to favor those who were oppressed in the land, and to make them leaders, and to make them the inheritors.

6. And to establish them in the land; and to show Pharaoh, Hamaan, and their troops, the very thing they feared.

7. We inspired the mother of Moses: "Nurse him; then, when you fear for him, cast him into the river, and do not fear, nor grieve; We will return him to you, and make him one of the messengers."

8. Pharaoh's household picked him up, to be an opponent and a sorrow for them. Pharaoh, Hamaan, and their troops were sinners.

9. Pharaoh's wife said, "An eye's delight for me and for you. Do not kill him; perhaps he will be useful to us, or we may adopt him as a son." But they did not foresee.

10. The heart of Moses' mother became vacant. She was about to disclose him, had We not steadied her heart, that she may remain a believer.

11. She said to his sister, "Trail him." So she watched him from afar, and they were unaware.

12. We forbade him breastfeeding at first. So she said, "Shall I tell you about a family that can raise him for you, and will look after him?"

13. Thus We returned him to his mother, that she may be comforted, and not grieve, and know that God's promise is true. But most of them do not know.

14. And when he reached his maturity, and became established, We gave him wisdom and knowledge. Thus do We reward the virtuous.

15. Once he entered the city, unnoticed by its people. He found in it two men fighting—one of his own sect, and one from his enemies. The one of his sect solicited his assistance against the one from his enemies; so Moses punched him, and put an end to him. He said, "This is of Satan's doing; he is an enemy that openly misleads."

16. He said, "My Lord, I have wronged myself, so forgive me." He forgave him. He is the Forgiver, the Merciful.

17. He said, "My Lord, in as much as you have favored me, I will never be a supporter of the criminals."

18. The next morning, he went about in the city, fearful and vigilant, when the man who had sought his assistance the day before was shouting out to him. Moses said to him, "You are clearly a troublemaker."

19. As he was about to strike the one who was their enemy, he said, "O Moses, do you intend to kill me, as you killed someone yesterday? You only want to be a bully in the land, and do not want to be a peacemaker."

20. A man came from the farthest part of the city running. He said, "O Moses, the authorities are considering killing you, so leave; I am giving you good advice."

21. So he left, fearful and vigilant. He said, "My Lord, deliver me from the wrongdoing people."

22. As he headed towards Median, he said, "Perhaps my Lord will guide me to the right way."

23. And when he arrived at the waters of Median, he found there a crowd of people drawing water, and he noticed two women waiting on the side. He said, "What is the matter with you?" They said, "We cannot draw water until the shepherds depart, and our father is a very old man."

24. So he drew water for them, and then withdrew to the shade, and said, "My Lord, I am in dire need of whatever good you might send down to me."

25. Then, one of the two women approached him, walking bashfully. She said, "My father is calling you, to reward you for drawing water for us." And when he came to him, and told him the story, he said, "Do not fear, you have escaped from the wrongdoing people."

26. One of the two women said, "Father, hire him; the best employee for you is the strong and trustworthy."

27. He said, "I want to marry you to one of these two daughters of mine, provided you work for me for eight years. But if you complete ten, that is up to you. I do not intend to impose any hardship on you. You will find me, God willing, one of the righteous."

28. He said, "Let this be an agreement between you and me. Whichever of the two terms I fulfill, there shall be no reprisal against me; and God is witness over what we say."

29. When Moses had completed the term, and departed with his family, he noticed a fire by the side of the mount. He said to his

family, "Stay here, I have glimpsed a fire. Perhaps I can bring you some information from there, or an ember from the fire, that you may warm yourselves."

30. When he reached it, he was called from the right side of the valley, at the blessed spot, from the bush: "O Moses, it is I, God, the Lord of the Worlds.

31. Throw down your staff." And when he saw it wiggling, as if it were possessed, he turned his back to flee, and did not look back. "O Moses, come forward, and do not fear, you are perfectly safe.

32. Put your hand inside your pocket, and it will come out white, without blemish. And press your arm to your side, against fear. These are two proofs from your Lord, to Pharaoh and his dignitaries. They are truly sinful people."

33. He said, "My Lord, I have killed one of them, and I fear they will kill me.

34. And my brother Aaron, he is more eloquent than me, so send him with me, to help me, and to confirm my words, for I fear they will reject me."

35. He said, "We will strengthen your arm with your brother, and We will give you authority, so they will not touch you. By virtue of Our signs, you and those who follow you will be the triumphant."

36. But when Moses came to them with Our signs, clear and manifest, they said, "This is nothing but fabricated magic, and We never heard of this from our ancestors of old."

37. Moses said, "My Lord is well aware of him who brings guidance from Him, and him who will have the sequel of the abode. The wrongdoers will not succeed."

38. Pharaoh said, "O nobles, I know of no god for you other than me. So fire-up the bricks for me O Hamaan, and build me a tower, that I may ascend to the God of Moses, though I think he is a liar."

39. He and his troops acted arrogantly in the land, with no justification. They thought they would not be returned to Us.

40. So We seized him, and his troops, and We threw them into the sea. Observe, therefore, what was the end of the oppressors.

41. And We made them leaders calling to the Fire. And on Resurrection Day, they will not be saved.

42. And We pursued them in this world with a curse. And on Resurrection Day, they will be among the despised.

43. We gave Moses the Scripture after We had annihilated the previous generations; as an illumination for mankind, and guidance, and mercy, so that they may remember.

44. You were not on the Western Side when We decreed the command to Moses, nor were you among the witnesses.

45. But We established many generations, and time took its toll on them. Nor were you among the people of Median, reciting Our revelations to them. But We kept sending messengers.

46. Nor were you by the side of the Mount when We proclaimed. Rather, it was a mercy from your Lord, that you may warn people who received no warner before you, so that they may take heed.

47. Otherwise, if a calamity befell them as a result of what their hands have perpetrated, they would say, "Our Lord, if only You had sent us a messenger, we would have followed Your revelations, and been among the believers."

48. But when the truth came to them from Us, they said, "If only he was given the like of what was given to Moses." Did they not

disbelieve in what was given to Moses in the past? They said, "Two works of magic backing one another." And they said, "We are disbelieving in both."

49. Say, "Then bring a scripture from God, more conductive to guidance than both, and I will follow it, if you are truthful."

50. But if they fail to respond to you, know that they follow their fancies. And who is more lost than him who follows his fancy without guidance from God? God does not guide the unjust people.

51. We have delivered the Word to them, that they may remember.

52. Those to whom We gave the Scripture before it believe in it.

53. When it is recited to them, they say, "We have believed in it; it is the truth from our Lord; we were Muslims prior to it."

54. These will be given their reward twice, because they persevered; and they counter evil with good; and from Our provisions to them, they give.

55. And when they hear vain talk, they avoid it, and say, "We have our deeds, and you have your deeds; peace be upon you; we do not desire the ignorant."

56. You cannot guide whom you love, but God guides whom He wills, and He knows best those who are guided.

57. And they say, "If we follow the guidance with you, we will be snatched from our land." Did We not establish for them a Safe Sanctuary, to which are brought all kinds of fruits, as provision from Ourselves? But most of them do not know.

58. And how many a city did We destroy for turning unappreciative of its livelihood? Here are their homes, uninhabited after them, except for a few. And We became the inheritors.

59. Your Lord never destroys cities without first sending a messenger in their midst, reciting to them Our revelations. And We never destroy the cities, unless their people are wrongdoers.

60. Whatever thing you are given is but the material of this world, and its glitter. But what is with God is better, and longer lasting. Do you not comprehend?

61. Can someone to whom We have made a fine promise—which he will attain—be equal to someone to whom We have given enjoyments in this world, but who will be, on Resurrection Day, among the arraigned?

62. On the Day when He will call to them, and say, "Where are My associates whom you used to claim?"

63. Those against whom the sentence is justified will say, "Our Lord, these are they whom we misled. We misled them, as we were misled. We beg Your forgiveness; it was not us they used to worship."

64. And it will be said, "Call on your partners." And they will call on them, but they will not respond to them. And they will see the suffering. If only they were guided.

65. On the Day when He will call to them, and say, "What did you answer the Messengers?"

66. They will be blinded by the facts on that Day, and they will not question each other.

67. But he who repents, and believes, and does righteous deeds, may well be among the winners.

68. Your Lord creates whatever He wills, and He chooses. The choice is not theirs. Glory be to God, and exalted be He above the associations they make.

69. And your Lord knows what their hearts conceal, and what they reveal.

70. And He is God. There is no god but He. To Him belongs all praise in this life, and in the next. And His is the decision, and to Him you will be returned.

71. Say, "Have you considered? Had God made the night perpetual over you until the Day of Resurrection, which god other than God will bring you illumination? Do you not hear?"

72. Say, "Have you considered? Had God made the day perpetual over you until the Day of Resurrection, which god other than God will bring you night to rest in? Do you not see?"

73. It is out of His mercy that He made for you the night and the day, that you may rest in it, and seek some of His bounty; and that you may give thanks.

74. On the Day when He will call to them, and say, "Where are My associates which you used to claim?"

75. And We will draw out from every community a witness, and say, "Produce your evidence." Then they will realize that the truth is God's, and those they used to invent have forsaken them.

76. Quaroon belonged to the clan of Moses, but he oppressed them. We had given him treasures, the keys of which would weigh down a group of strong men. His people said to him, "Do not exult; God does not love the exultant.

77. But seek, with what God has given you, the Home of the Hereafter, and do not neglect your share of this world. And be charitable, as God has been charitable to you. And do not seek corruption in the land. God does not like the seekers of corruption."

78. He said, "I was given all this on account of knowledge I possess." Did he not know that God destroyed many generations be-fore him, who were stronger than he, and possessed greater riches? But the guilty will not be asked about their sins.

79. And he went out before his people in his splendor. Those who desired the worldly life said, "If only we possessed the likes of what Quaroon was given. He is indeed very fortunate."

80. But those who were given knowledge said, "Woe to you! The reward of God is better for those who believe and do right-eous deeds." Yet none attains it except the steadfast.

81. So We caused the earth to cave in on him and his mansion. He had no company to save him from God, and he could not defend himself.

82. Those who had wished they were in his position the day before were saying, "In-deed, it is God who spreads the bounty to whomever He wills of His servants, and restricts it. Had God not been gracious to us, He would have caved in on us. No wonder the ungrateful never prosper."

83. That Home of the Hereafter—We as-sign it for those who seek no superiority on earth, nor corruption. And the out-come is for the cautious.

84. Whoever brings a virtue will receive better than it. But whoever brings evil— the evildoers will be rewarded only accord-ing to what they used to do.

85. He Who ordained the Quran for you will return you Home. Say, "My Lord knows best who comes with guidance, and who is in manifest error."

86. You did not expect the Book to be transmitted to you, except as mercy from your Lord. Therefore, do not be a support-er of the disbelievers.

87. And do not let them divert you from God's revelations after they have been re-

vealed to you. And pray to your Lord, and never be of the polytheists.

88. And do not invoke with God any other god. There is no god but He. All things perish, except His presence. His is the judgment, and to Him you will be returned.

29. THE SPIDER
(al-'Ankabut)

In the name of God,
the Gracious, the Merciful.

1. Alif, Lam, Meem.

2. Have the people supposed that they will be left alone to say, "We believe," without being put to the test?

3. We have tested those before them. God will surely know the truthful, and He will surely know the liars.

4. Or do those who commit sins think they can fool Us? Terrible is their opinion!

5. Whoever looks forward to the meeting with God—the appointed time of God is coming. He is the All-Hearing, the All-Knowing.

6. Whoever strives, strives only for himself. God is Independent of the beings.

7. Those who believe and do righteous deeds—We will remit their sins, and We will reward them according to the best of what they used to do.

8. We have advised the human being to be good to his parents. But if they urge you to associate with Me something you have no knowledge of, do not obey them. To Me is your return; and I will inform you of what you used to do.

9. Those who believe and do good works—We will admit them into the company of the righteous.

10. Among the people is he who says, "We have believed in God." Yet when he is harmed on God's account, he equates the people's persecution with God's retribution. And if help comes from your Lord, he says, "We were actually with you." Is not God aware of what is inside the hearts of the people?

11. God certainly knows those who believe, and He certainly knows the hypocrites.

12. Those who disbelieve say to those who believe, "Follow our way, and we will carry your sins." In no way can they carry any of their sins. They are liars.

13. They will carry their own loads, and other loads with their own. And they will be questioned on the Day of Resurrection concerning what they used to fabricate.

14. We sent Noah to his people, and He stayed among them for a thousand years minus fifty years. Then the Deluge swept them; for they were wrongdoers.

15. But We saved him, together with the company of the Ark, and We made it a sign for all peoples.

16. And Abraham, when he said to his people, "Worship God, and fear Him. That is better for you, if you only knew.

17. You worship idols besides God, and you fabricate falsehoods. Those you worship, instead of God, cannot provide you with livelihood. So seek your livelihood from God, and worship Him, and thank Him. To Him you will be returned."

18. If you disbelieve, communities before you have also disbelieved. The Messenger is only responsible for clear transmission.

19. Have they not seen how God originates the creation, and then reproduces it? This is easy for God.

20. Say, "Roam the earth, and observe how He originated the creation." Then God will

bring about the next existence. God has power over all things."

21. He punishes whom He wills, and He grants mercy to whom He wills, and to Him you will be restored.

22. You cannot escape, on earth or in the heaven; and you have no protector and no savior besides God.

23. Those who disbelieved in God's signs and His encounter—these have despaired of My mercy. For them is a painful torment.

24. But the only response from his people was their saying, "Kill him, or burn him." But God saved him from the fire. Surely in that are signs for people who believe.

25. And he said, "You have chosen idols instead of God, out of affection for one another in the worldly life. But then, on the Day of Resurrection, you will disown one another, and curse one another. Your destiny is Hell, and you will have no saviors."

26. Then Lot believed in him, and said, "I am emigrating to my Lord. He is the Noble, the Wise."

27. And We granted him Isaac and Jacob, and conferred on his progeny the Prophethood and the Book, and gave him his reward in this life; and in the Hereafter he will be among the upright.

28. And Lot, when he said to his people, "You are committing an obscenity not perpetrated before you by anyone in the whole world.

29. You approach men, and cut off the way, and commit lewdness in your gatherings." But the only response from his people was to say, "Bring upon us God's punishment, if you are truthful."

30. He said, "My Lord, help me against the people of corruption."

31. And when Our envoys brought Abraham the good news, they said, "We are going to destroy the people of this town; its people are wrongdoers."

32. He said, "Yet Lot is in it." They said, "We are well aware of who is in it. We will save him, and his family, except for his wife, who will remain behind."

33. Then, when Our envoys came to Lot, they were mistreated, and he was troubled and distressed on their account. They said, "Do not fear, nor grieve. We will save you and your family, except for your wife, who will remain behind.

34. "We will bring down upon the people of this town a scourge from heaven, because of their wickedness."

35. And We left behind a clear trace of it, for people who understand.

36. And to Median, their brother Shuaib. He said, "O my people, worship God and anticipate the Last Day, and do not spread corruption in the land."

37. But they rejected him, so the tremor overtook them, and they were left motionless in their homes.

38. And Aad and Thamood. It has become clear to you from their dwellings. Satan embellished for them their deeds, barring them from the path, even though they could see.

39. And Quaroon, and Pharaoh, and Hamaan—Moses went to them with clear arguments, but they acted arrogantly in the land. And they could not get ahead.

40. Each We seized by his sin. Against some We sent a sandstorm. Some were struck by the Blast. Some We caused the ground to cave in beneath them. And some We drowned. It was not God who wronged them, but it was they who wronged their own selves.

41. The likeness of those who take to themselves protectors other than God is that of the spider. It builds a house. But the most fragile of houses is the spider's house. If they only knew.

42. God knows what they invoke besides Him. He is the Almighty, the Wise.

43. These examples—We put them forward to the people; but none grasps them except the learned.

44. God created the heavens and the earth with truth. Surely in that is a sign for the believers.

45. Recite what is revealed to you of the Scripture, and perform the prayer. The prayer prevents indecencies and evils. And the remembrance of God is greater. And God knows what you do.

46. And do not argue with the People of the Scripture except in the best manner possible, except those who do wrong among them. And say, "We believe in what was revealed to us, and in what was revealed to you; and our God and your God is One; and to Him we are submissive."

47. Likewise, We revealed to you the Scripture. Those to whom We gave the Scripture believe in it, and some of these believe in it. But none renounce Our communications except the disbelievers.

48. You did not read any scripture before this, nor did you write it down with your right hand; otherwise the falsifiers would have doubted.

49. In fact, it is clear signs in the hearts of those given knowledge. No one renounce Our signs except the unjust.

50. And they said, "If only a miracle from his Lord was sent down to him." Say, "Miracles are only with God, and I am only a clear warner."

51. Does it not suffice them that We revealed to you the Scripture, which is recited to them? In that is mercy and a reminder for people who believe.

52. Say, "God suffices as witness between you and me. He knows everything in the heavens and the Earth. Those who believe in vanity and reject God—it is they who are the losers."

53. And they urge you to hasten the punishment. Were it not for a specified time, the punishment would have come to them. But it will come upon them suddenly, while they are unaware.

54. They urge you to hasten the punishment. But Hell will engulf the disbelievers.

55. On the Day when the punishment will envelop them, from above them, and from beneath their feet, He will say, "Taste what you used to do!"

56. O My servants who have believed, My earth is vast, so worship Me alone.

57. Every soul will taste death. Then to Us you will be returned.

58. Those who believe and work righteousness—We will settle them in Paradise, in mansions under which rivers flow, dwelling therein forever. Excellent is the compensation for the workers.

59. Those who endure patiently, and in their Lord they trust.

60. How many a creature there is that does not carry its provision? God provides for them, and for you. He is the Hearer, the Knowledgeable.

61. And if you asked them, "Who created the heavens and the earth and regulated the sun and the moon?" They would say, "God." Why then do they deviate?

62. God expands the provision for whomever He wills of His servants, and restricts it. God is Cognizant of all things.

63. And if you asked them, "Who sends water down from the sky, with which He revives the earth after it had died?" They would say, "God." Say, "Praise be to God." But most of them do not understand.

64. The life of this world is nothing but diversion and play, and the Home of the Hereafter is the Life, if they only knew.

65. When they embark on a vessel, they pray to God, devoting their faith to Him; but once He has delivered them safely to land, they attribute partners to Him.

66. To be ungrateful for what We have given them, and to enjoy themselves. They will surely come to know.

67. Do they not see that We established a Secure Sanctuary, while all around them the people are being carried away? Do they believe in falsehood, and reject the blessings of God?

68. And who does greater wrong than he who fabricates lies and attributes them to God, or calls the truth a lie when it has come to him? Is there not in Hell a dwelling for the blasphemers?

69. As for those who strive for Us—We will guide them in Our ways. God is with the doers of good.

30. THE ROMANS
(ar-Rum)

In the name of God,
the Gracious, the Merciful.

1. Alif, Lam, Meem.

2. The Romans have been defeated.

3. In a nearby territory. But following their defeat, they will be victorious.

4. In a few years. The matter is up to God, in the past, and in the future. On that day, the believers will rejoice.

5. In God's support. He supports whomever He wills. He is the Almighty, the Merciful.

6. The promise of God—God never breaks His promise, but most people do not know.

7. They know an outer aspect of the worldly life, but they are heedless of the Hereafter.

8. Do they not reflect within themselves? God did not create the heavens and the earth, and what is between them, except with reason, and for a specific duration. But most people, regarding meeting their Lord, are disbelievers.

9. Have they not travelled the earth and seen how those before them ended up? They were more powerful than them, and they cultivated the land and developed it more than they developed it, and their messengers came to them with clear signs. God would never wrong them, but they used to wrong themselves.

10. Then, evil was the end of those who committed evil. That is because they rejected God's revelations, and used to ridicule them.

11. God originates creation, and then repeats it. Then to Him you will be returned.

12. On the Day when the Hour takes place, the guilty will despair.

13. They will have no intercessors from among their idols, and they will disown their partners.

14. On the Day when the Hour takes place—on that Day they will separate.

15. As for those who believed and did good deeds—they will be delighted in meadows.

16. But as for those who disbelieved, and rejected Our signs and the encounter of the Hereafter—those will be hauled into the torment.

17. So glorify God when you retire at night, and when you rise in the morning.

18. His is the praise in the heavens and on earth, and in the evening, and when you reach midday.

19. He brings the living out of the dead, and He brings the dead out of the living, and He revives the land after it had died. Likewise you will be resurrected.

20. And of His signs is that He created you from dust; and behold, you become humans spreading out.

21. And of His signs is that He created for you mates from among yourselves, so that you may find tranquility in them; and He planted love and compassion between you. In this are signs for people who reflect.

22. And of His signs is the creation of the heavens and the earth, and the diversity of your languages and colors. In this are signs for those who know.

23. And of His signs are your sleep by night and day, and your pursuit of His bounty. In this are signs for people who listen.

24. And of His signs is that He shows you the lightning, causing fear and hope. And He brings down water from the sky, and with it He revives the earth after it was dead. In this are signs for people who understand.

25. And of His signs is that the heaven and the earth stand at His disposal. And then, when He calls you out of the earth, you will emerge at once.

26. To Him belongs everyone in the heavens and the earth. All are submissive to Him.

27. It is He who initiates creation, and then repeats it, something easy for Him. His is the highest attribute, in the heavens and the earth. He is the Almighty, the Wise.

28. He illustrates an example for you, from your own selves. Do you make your servants full partners in the wealth We have given you? Do you revere them as you revere one another? We thus explain the revelations for a people who understand.

29. Yet the wrongdoers follow their desires without knowledge. But who can guide whom God leaves astray? They will have no helpers.

30. So devote yourself to the religion of monotheism—the natural instinct God instilled in mankind. There is no altering God's creation. This is the true religion, but most people do not know.

31. Turning towards Him—and be conscious of Him, and perform the prayer, and do not be of the idolaters.

32. Of those who divided their religion, and became sects; each faction pleased with what they have.

33. When affliction touches the people, they call on their Lord, turning to Him in repentance. But then, when He gives them a taste of His mercy, some of them attribute partners to their Lord.

34. To show ingratitude for what We have given them. Indulge yourselves—you will surely know.

35. Have We sent down to them any authority, which speaks in support of their idols?

36. When We give people a taste of mercy, they rejoice in it. But when adversity befalls them, because of what their hands have perpetrated, they begin to despair.

37. Do they not see that God expands the provision for whomever He wills, or re-

stricts it? Surely in this are signs for people who believe.

38. So give the relative his rights, and the destitute, and the wayfarer. That is best for those who seek God's presence. Those are the prosperous.

39. The usury you practice, seeking thereby to multiply people's wealth, will not multiply with God. But what you give in charity, desiring God's approval—these are the multipliers.

40. God is He who created you, then provides for you, then makes you die, then brings you back to life. Can any of your idols do any of that? Glorified is He, and Exalted above what they associate.

41. Corruption has appeared on land and sea, because of what people's hands have earned, in order to make them taste some of what they have done, so that they might return.

42. Say, "Roam the earth, and observe the fate of those who came before. Most of them were idolaters."

43. So devote yourself to the upright religion, before there comes from God a Day that cannot be averted. On that Day, they will be shocked.

44. Whoever disbelieves, upon him falls his disbelief. And whoever acts righteously—they are preparing for themselves.

45. So that He may reward those who have believed and done the righteous deeds out of His bounty. Indeed, He does not love the ungrateful.

46. And of His signs is that He sends the winds bearing good news, to give you a taste of His mercy, and so that the ships may sail by His command, and so that you may seek of His bounty, and so that you may give thanks.

47. Before you, We sent messengers to their people. They came to them with clear proofs. Then We took revenge on those who sinned. It is incumbent on Us to help the believers.

48. God is He who sends the winds. They stir up clouds. Then He spreads them in the sky as He wills. And He breaks them apart. Then you see rain drops issuing from their midst. Then, when He makes it fall upon whom He wills of His servants, behold, they rejoice.

49. Although they were before this—before it was sent down upon them—in despair.

50. So observe the effects of God's mercy—how He revives the earth after it was dead. Indeed, He is the Reviver of the dead. He is Capable of everything.

51. But if We send a wind, and they see it turning things yellow, they would continue thereafter to disbelieve.

52. You cannot make the dead hear, nor can you make the deaf hear the call when they turn away.

53. Nor can you guide the blind out of their error. You can make hear only those who believe in Our signs, and so have submitted.

54. God is He Who created you weak, then after weakness gave you strength, then after strength gave you weakness and gray hair. He creates whatever He wills. He is the Omniscient, the Omnipotent.

55. On the Day when the Hour takes place, the sinners will swear they had stayed but an hour. Thus they were deluded.

56. But those endowed with knowledge and faith will say, "You remained in God's Book until the Day of Resurrection. This is the Day of Resurrection, but you did not know."

57. On that Day, the sinners' excuses will not benefit them, nor will they be excused.

58. We have cited in this Quran for the people every sort of parable. But even if you bring them a miracle, those who disbelieve will say, "You are nothing but fakers."

59. God thus seals the hearts of those who do not know.

60. So be patient. The promise of God is true. And do not let those who lack certainty belittle you.

31. LUQMAN
(Luqman)

In the name of God,
the Gracious, the Merciful.

1. Alif, Lam, Meem.

2. These are the Verses of the Wise Book.

3. A guide and a mercy for the righteous.

4. Those who observe the prayer, and pay the obligatory charity, and are certain of the Hereafter.

5. These are upon guidance from their Lord. These are the successful.

6. Among the people is he who trades in distracting tales; intending, without knowledge, to lead away from God's way, and to make a mockery of it. These will have a humiliating punishment.

7. And when Our Verses are recited to him, he turns away in pride, as though he did not hear them, as though there is deafness in his ears. So inform him of a painful punishment.

8. As for those who believe and do good deeds—for them are the Gardens of Bliss.

9. Dwelling therein forever. The promise of God is true. He is the Mighty, the Wise.

10. He created the heavens without pillars that you can see, and placed stabilizers on earth lest it shifts with you, and scattered throughout it all kinds of creatures. And from the sky We sent down water, and caused to grow therein of every noble pair.

11. Such is God's creation. Now show me what those besides Him have created. In fact, the wicked are in obvious error.

12. We endowed Luqman with wisdom, "Give thanks to God." Whoever is appreciative—is appreciative for the benefit of his own soul. And whoever is unappreciative—God is Sufficient and Praiseworthy.

13. When Luqman said to his son, as he advised him, "O my son, do not associate anything with God, for idolatry is a terrible wrong."

14. We have entrusted the human being with the care of his parents. His mother carried him through hardship upon hardship, weaning him in two years. So give thanks to Me, and to your parents. To Me is the destination.

15. But if they strive to have you associate with Me something of which you have no knowledge, do not obey them. But keep them company in this life, in kindness, and follow the path of him who turns to Me. Then to Me is your return; and I will inform you of what you used to do.

16. "O my son, even if it were the weight of a mustard-seed, in a rock, or in the heavens, or on earth, God will bring it to light. God is Kind and Expert.

17. O my son, observe the prayer, advocate righteousness, forbid evil, and be patient over what has befallen you. These are of the most honorable traits.

18. And do not treat people with arrogance, nor walk proudly on earth. God does not love the arrogant showoffs.

19. And moderate your stride, and lower your voice. The most repulsive of voices is the donkey's voice."

20. Do you not see how God placed at your service everything in the heavens and the earth? How He showered you with His blessings, both outward and inward? Yet among the people is he who argues about God without knowledge, without guidance, and without an enlightening Scripture.

21. And when it is said to them, "Follow what God has revealed," they say, "Rather, we follow what we found our parents devoted to." Even if Satan is calling them to the suffering of the Blaze?

22. Whoever submits himself wholly to God, and is a doer of good, has grasped the most trustworthy handle. With God rests the outcome of all events.

23. Whoever disbelieves—let not his disbelief sadden you. To Us is their return. Then We will inform them of what they did. God knows what lies within the hearts.

24. We give them a little comfort; then We compel them to a harsh torment.

25. And if you ask them, "Who created the heavens and the earth?" They will say, "God." Say, "Praise be to God." But most of them do not know.

26. To God belongs everything in the heavens and the earth. God is the Rich, the Praised.

27. If all the trees on earth were pens, filled by the ocean, with seven more oceans besides, the Words of God would not run out. God is Majestic and Wise.

28. Your creation and your resurrection are only as a single soul. God is Hearing and Seeing.

29. Have you not seen how God merges the night into the day, and merges the day into the night? That He subjected the sun and the moon, each running for a stated term? And that God is Cognizant of everything you do?

30. That is because God is the Reality, and what they worship besides Him is falsehood, and because God is the Exalted, the Supreme.

31. Have you not seen how the ships sail through the sea, by the grace of God, to show you of His wonders? In that are signs for every persevering, thankful person.

32. When waves, like canopies, cover them, they call upon God, devoting their religion to Him. But when He has delivered them to dry land, some of them waver. No one renounces Our revelations except the treacherous blasphemer.

33. O people! Be conscious of your Lord, and dread a Day when no parent can avail his child, nor can a child avail his parent, in anything. The promise of God is true. Therefore, do not let this life deceive you, nor let illusions deceive you regarding God.

34. With God rests the knowledge of the Hour. He sends down the rain, and He knows what the wombs contain. No soul knows what it will reap tomorrow, and no soul knows in what land it will die. God is All-Knowing, Well-Informed.

32. PROSTRATION
(as-Sajdah)

In the name of God,
the Gracious, the Merciful.

1. Alif, Lam, Meem.

2. The revelation of the Book, without a doubt, is from the Lord of the Universe.

3. Yet they say, "He made it up." In fact, it is the Truth from your Lord, to warn a people who received no warner before you, that they may be guided.

4. God is He who created the heavens and the earth and everything between them in six days, and then established Himself on the Throne. Apart from Him, you have no master and no intercessor. Will you not reflect?

5. He regulates all affairs, from the heavens, to the earth. Then it ascends to Him on a Day the length of which is a thousand years by your count.

6. That is the Knower of the Invisible and the Visible, the Powerful, the Merciful.

7. He who perfected everything He created, and originated the creation of man from clay.

8. Then made his reproduction from an extract of an insignificant fluid.

9. Then He proportioned him, and breathed into him of His Spirit. Then He gave you the hearing, the eyesight, and the brains—but rarely do you give thanks.

10. And they say, "When we are lost into the earth, shall we be in a new creation?" In fact, they deny the meeting with their Lord.

11. Say, "The angel of death put in charge of you will reclaim you. Then to your Lord you will be returned."

12. If only you could see the guilty, bowing their heads before their Lord: "Our Lord, we have seen and we have heard, so send us back, and we will act righteously; we are now convinced."

13. Had We willed, We could have given every soul its guidance, but the declaration from Me will come true, "I will fill Hell with jinn and humans, altogether."

14. So taste, because you forgot the meeting of this Day of yours; We have forgotten you; so taste the eternal torment for what you used to do.

15. They believe in Our communications, those who, when reminded of them, fall down prostrate, and glorify their Lord with praise, and are not proud.

16. Their sides shun their beds, as they pray to their Lord, out of reverence and hope, and from Our provisions to them, they give.

17. No soul knows what eye's delight awaits them—a reward for what they used to do.

18. Is someone who is faithful like someone who is a sinner? They are not equal.

19. As for those who believe and do righteous deeds, for them are the Gardens of Shelter—hospitality for what they used to do.

20. But as for those who transgressed, their shelter is the Fire. Every time they try to get out of it, they are brought back into it, and it will be said to them, "Taste the suffering of the Fire which you used to deny."

21. We will make them taste the lesser torment, prior to the greater torment, so that they may return.

22. Who is more wrong than he, who, when reminded of his Lord's revelations, turns away from them? We will certainly wreak vengeance upon the criminals.

23. We gave Moses the Book; so do not be in doubt regarding His encounter; and We made it a guidance for the Children of Israel.

24. And We appointed leaders from among them, guiding by Our command, as long as they persevered and were certain of Our communications.

25. Your Lord will judge between them on the Day of Resurrection regarding everything they had disputed.

26. Is it not a lesson for them, how many generations We have destroyed before them, in whose habitations they walk? Surely in that are signs. Do they not hear?

27. Do they not see how We conduct the water to a dry land, and with it We produce vegetation, from which their livestock eat, and themselves? Do they not see?

28. And they say, "When is this victory, if you are truthful?"

29. Say, "On the day of victory, the faith of those who disbelieved will be of no avail to them, and they will not be given respite."

30. So turn away from them and wait. They too are waiting.

33. THE CONFEDERATES
(al-Ahzab)

In the name of God,
the Gracious, the Merciful.

1. O Prophet! Fear God, and do not obey the unbelievers and the hypocrites. God is Knowledgeable and Wise.

2. And follow what is revealed to you from your Lord. God is fully aware of what you do.

3. And put your trust in God. God is enough as a trustee.

4. God did not place two hearts inside any man's body. Nor did He make your wives whom you equate with your mothers, your actual mothers. Nor did He make your adopted sons, your actual sons. These are your words coming out of your mouths. God speaks the truth and guides to the path.

5. Call them after their fathers; that is more equitable with God. But if you do not know their fathers, then your brethren in faith and your friends. There is no blame on you if you err therein, barring what your hearts premeditates. God is Forgiving and Merciful.

6. The Prophet is more caring of the believers than they are of themselves, and his wives are mothers to them. And blood-relatives are closer to one another in God's Book than the believers or the emigrants, though you should do good to your friends. That is inscribed in the Book.

7. Recall that We received a pledge from the prophets, and from you, and from Noah, and Abraham, and Moses, and Jesus son of Mary. We received from them a solemn pledge.

8. That He may ask the sincere about their sincerity. He has prepared for the disbelievers a painful punishment.

9. O you who believe! Remember God's blessings upon you, when forces came against you, and We sent against them a wind, and forces you did not see. God is Observant of what you do.

10. When they came upon you, from above you, and from beneath you; and the eyes became dazed, and the hearts reached the throats, and you harbored doubts about God.

11. There and then the believers were tested, and were shaken most severely.

12. When the hypocrites and those in whose hearts is sickness said, "God and His Messenger promised us nothing but illusion."

13. And when a group of them said, "O people of Yathrib, you cannot make a stand, so retreat." And a faction of them asked the Prophet to excuse them, saying,

"Our homes are exposed," although they were not exposed. They only wanted to flee.

14. Had it been invaded from its sides, and they were asked to dissent, they would have done so with little hesitation.

15. Although they had made a pledged to God, in the past, that they will not turn their backs. A pledge to God is a responsibility.

16. Say, "Flight will not benefit you, if you flee from death or killing, even then you will be given only brief enjoyment."

17. Say, "Who is it who will shield you from God, if He intends adversity for you, or intends mercy for you?" Besides God, they will find for themselves neither friend nor helper.

18. God already knows the hinderers among you, and those who say to their brethren, "Come and join us." Rarely do they mobilize for battle.

19. Being stingy towards you. And when fear approaches, you see them staring at you—their eyes rolling—like someone fainting at death. Then, when panic is over, they whip you with sharp tongues. They resent you any good. These have never believed, so God has nullified their works; a matter easy for God.

20. They assumed that the confederates had not withdrawn. But were the confederates to advance, they would wish they were in the desert with the Bedouins, inquiring about your news. And if they were among you, they would have done little fighting.

21. You have an excellent example in the Messenger of God; for anyone who seeks God and the Last Day, and remembers God frequently.

22. And when the believers saw the confederates, they said, "This is what God and His messenger have promised us; and God and His messenger have told the truth." And it only increased them in faith and submission.

23. Of the believers are men who are true to what they pledged to God. Some of them have fulfilled their vows; and some are still waiting, and never wavering.

24. That God may reward the truthful for their truthfulness; and punish the hypocrites, if He wills, or pardon them. God is Forgiving and Merciful.

25. God repelled the disbelievers in their rage; they gained no advantage. God thus spared the believers combat. God is Strong and Mighty.

26. And He brought down from their strongholds those of the People of the Book who backed them, and He threw terror into their hearts. Some of them you killed, and others you took captive.

27. And He made you inherit their land, and their homes, and their possessions, and a region you have never stepped on. God has power over all things.

28. O Prophet! Say to your wives, "If you desire the life of this world and its finery, then let me compensate you, and release you kindly.

29. But if you desire God, His Messenger, and the Home of the Hereafter, then God has prepared for the righteous among you a magnificent compensation."

30. O wives of the Prophet! Whoever of you commits a proven indecency, the punishment for her will be doubled. And that would be easy for God.

31. But whoever of you remains obedient to God and His Messenger, and acts righteously, We will give her a double reward;

and We have prepared for her a generous provision.

32. O wives of the Prophet! You are not like any other women, if you observe piety. So do not speak too softly, lest the sick at heart lusts after you, but speak in an appropriate manner.

33. And settle in your homes; and do not display yourselves, as in the former days of ignorance. And perform the prayer, and give regular charity, and obey God and His Messenger. God desires to remove all impurity from you, O People of the Household, and to purify you thoroughly.

34. And remember what is recited in your homes of God's revelations and wisdom. God is Kind and Informed.

35. Muslim men and Muslim women, believing men and believing women, obedient men and obedient women, truthful men and truthful women, patient men and patient women, humble men and humble women, charitable men and charitable women, fasting men and fasting women, men who guard their chastity and women who guard, men who remember God frequently and women who remember—God has prepared for them a pardon, and an immense reward.

36. It is not for any believer, man or woman, when God and His Messenger have decided a matter, to have liberty of choice in their decision. Whoever disobeys God and His Messenger has gone far astray.

37. When you said to him whom God had blessed, and you had favored, "Keep your wife to yourself, and fear God." But you hid within yourself what God was to reveal. And you feared the people, but it was God you were supposed to fear. Then, when Zaid ended his relationship with her, We gave her to you in marriage, that there may be no restriction for believers regarding the wives of their adopted sons, when their relationship has ended. The command of God was fulfilled.

38. There is no blame on the Prophet regarding what God has ordained for him. Such is the pattern of God among those who passed before. The command of God is an absolute decree.

39. Those who deliver the messages of God, and fear Him, and never fear anyone except God. God is sufficient as a reckoner.

40. Muhammad is not the father of any of your men; but he is the Messenger of God, and the seal of the prophets. God is Cognizant of everything.

41. O you who believe, remember God with frequent remembrance.

42. And glorify Him morning and evening.

43. It is He who reaches out to you, and His angels, to bring you out of darkness into the light. And He is Ever-Merciful towards the believers.

44. Their greeting on the Day they meet Him is, "Peace," and He has prepared for them a generous reward.

45. O prophet! We have sent you as a witness, and a bearer of good news, and a warner.

46. And a caller towards God by His leave, and an illuminating beacon.

47. And give the believers the good news that for them is a great reward.

48. And do not obey the blasphemers and the hypocrites, and ignore their insults, and rely on God. God is a sufficient protector.

49. O you who believe! When you marry believing women, but then divorce them before you have touched them, there is no waiting period for you to observe in re-

spect to them; but compensate them, and release them in a graceful manner.

50. O Prophet! We have permitted to you your wives to whom you have given their dowries, and those you already have, as granted to you by God, and the daughters of your paternal uncles, and the daughters of your paternal aunts, and the daughters of your maternal uncles, and the daughters of your maternal aunts who emigrated with you, and a believing woman who has offered herself to the Prophet, if the Prophet desires to marry her, exclusively for you, and not for the believers. We know what We have ordained for them regarding their wives and those their right-hands possess. This is to spare you any difficulty. God is Forgiving and Merciful.

51. You may defer any of them you wish, and receive any of them you wish. Should you desire any of those you had deferred, there is no blame on you. This is more proper, so that they will be comforted, and not be grieved, and be content with what you have given each one of them. God knows what is within your hearts. God is Omniscient and Clement.

52. Beyond that, no other women are permissible for you, nor can you exchange them for other wives, even if you admire their beauty, except those you already have. God is Watchful over all things.

53. O you who believe! Do not enter the homes of the Prophet, unless you are given permission to come for a meal; and do not wait for its preparation. And when you are invited, go in. And when you have eaten, disperse, without lingering for conversation. This irritates the Prophet, and he shies away from you, but God does not shy away from the truth. And when you ask his wives for something, ask them from behind a screen; that is purer for your hearts and their hearts. You must never offend the Messenger of God, nor must you ever marry his wives after him, for that would be an enormity with God.

54. Whether you declare a thing, or hide it, God is Aware of all things.

55. There is no blame on them concerning their fathers, or their sons, or their brothers, or their brothers' sons, or their sisters' sons, or their women, or their female servants. But they should remain conscious of God. God is Witness over all things.

56. God and His angels give blessings to the Prophet. O you who believe, call for blessings on him, and greet him with a prayer of peace.

57. Those who insult God and His Messenger, God has cursed them in this life and in the Hereafter, and has prepared for them a demeaning punishment.

58. Those who harm believing men and believing women, for acts they did not commit, bear the burden of perjury and a flagrant sin.

59. O Prophet! Tell your wives, and your daughters, and the women of the believers, to lengthen their garments. That is more proper, so they will be recognized and not harassed. God is Forgiving and Merciful.

60. If the hypocrites, and those with sickness in their hearts, and the rumor-mongers in the City, do not desist, We will incite you against them; then they will not be your neighbors there except for a short while.

61. They are cursed; wherever they are found, they should be captured and killed outright.

62. Such has been God's precedent with those who passed away before. You will find no change in God's system.

63. The people ask you about the Hour. Say, "The knowledge thereof rests with

God. But what do you know? Perhaps the hour is near."

64. God has cursed the disbelievers, and has prepared for them a Blaze.

65. Dwelling therein forever, not finding a protector or a savior.

66. The Day when their faces are flipped into the Fire, they will say, "If only we had obeyed God and obeyed the Messenger."

67. And they will say, "Lord, we have obeyed our superiors and our dignitaries, but they led us away from the way.

68. Lord, give them double the punishment, and curse them with a great curse."

69. O you who believe! Do not be like those who abused Moses; but God cleared him of what they said. He was distinguished with God.

70. O you who believe! Be conscious of God, and speak in a straightforward manner.

71. He will rectify your conduct for you, and will forgive you your sins. Whoever obeys God and His Messenger has won a great victory.

72. We offered the Trust to the heavens, and the earth, and the mountains; but they refused to bear it, and were apprehensive of it; but the human being accepted it. He was unfair and ignorant.

73. God will punish the hypocrites, men and women, and the idolaters, men and women; and God will redeem the believers, men and women. God is Ever-Forgiving, Most Merciful.

34. SHEBA
(Saba')

In the name of God,
the Gracious, the Merciful.

1. Praise be to God, to Whom belongs everything in the heavens and the earth; and praise be to Him in the Hereafter. He is the Wise, the Expert.

2. He knows what penetrates into the earth, and what comes out of it, and what descends from the sky, and what ascends to it. He is the Merciful, the Forgiving.

3. Those who disbelieve say, "The Hour will not come upon us." Say, "Yes indeed, by my Lord, it will come upon you. He is the Knower of the unseen." Not an atom's weight in the heavens and the earth, or anything smaller or larger, escapes His knowledge. All are in a Clear Record.

4. That He may recompense those who believe and do good works. Those will have forgiveness, and a generous provision.

5. As for those who strive against Our revelations, seeking to undermine them—for them is a punishment of a painful plague.

6. Those who received knowledge know that what is revealed to you from your Lord is the truth; and it guides to the path of the Majestic, the Praiseworthy.

7. Those who disbelieved said, "Shall we point out to you a man, who will tell you that, once torn into shreds, you will be in a new creation?

8. Has he invented a lie about God, or is there madness in him?" Indeed, those who do not believe in the Hereafter are in torment, and far astray.

9. Do they not reflect upon what lies before them and behind them, of the heaven and the earth? If We will, We can make the earth cave in beneath them, or make pieces of the sky fall down on them. In that is a sign for every devout servant.

10. We bestowed on David favor from Us: "O mountains, and birds; echo with him." And We softened iron for him.

11. Make coats of armor, and measure the links well; and work righteousness. I am Observant of everything you do.

12. And for Solomon the wind—its outward journey was one month, and its return journey was one month. And We made a spring of tar flow for him. And there were sprites that worked under him, by the leave of his Lord. But whoever of them swerved from Our command, We make him taste of the punishment of the Inferno.

13. They made for him whatever he wished: sanctuaries, statues, bowls like pools, and heavy cauldrons. "O House of David, work with appreciation," but a few of My servants are appreciative.

14. Then, when We decreed death for him, nothing indicated his death to them except an earthworm eating at his staff. Then, when he fell down, it became clear to the sprites that, had they known the unseen, they would not have remained in the demeaning torment.

15. In Sheba's homeland there used to be a wonder: two gardens, on the right, and on the left. "Eat of your Lord's provision, and give thanks to Him." A good land and a forgiving Lord.

16. But they turned away, so We unleashed against them the flood of the dam; and We substituted their two gardens with two gardens of bitter fruits, thorny shrubs, and meager harvest.

17. We thus penalized them for their ingratitude. Would We penalize any but the ungrateful?

18. Between them and the towns We had blessed, We placed prominent towns, and We made the travel between them easy. "Travel between them by night and day, in safety."

19. But they said, "Our Lord, lengthen the distances of our journeys." They wronged themselves; so We made them history, and We scattered them in every direction. In this are lessons for every steadfast and appreciative person.

20. Satan was correct in his assessment of them. They followed him, except for a group of believers.

21. He had no authority over them; except that We willed to distinguish him who believes in the Hereafter, from him who is doubtful about it. Your Lord is Guardian over all things.

22. Say, "Call upon those whom you claim besides God. They possess not an atom's weight in the heavens or the earth, and they possess no share of either, and He has no backers from among them."

23. Intercession with Him is of no value, except for someone He has permitted. Until, when fear has subsided from their hearts, they will say, "What did your Lord say?" They will say, "The truth, and He is the High, the Great."

24. Say, "Who provides for you from the heavens and the earth?" Say, "God. And Either you or we are rightly guided, or in evident error."

25. Say, "You will not be asked about our misdeeds, nor will we be asked about what you do."

26. Say, "Our Lord will bring us together; then He will judge between us equitably. He is the All-Knowing Judge."

27. Say, "Show me those you have attached to Him as associates. No indeed; but He is God, the Powerful, the Wise."

28. We have only sent you universally to all people, as a herald and a warner; but most people do not know.

29. And they say, "When is this promise due, if you are truthful?"

30. Say, "You are promised a Day, which you cannot postpone by one hour, nor bring forward."

31. Those who disbelieve say, "We will never believe in this Quran, nor in what came before it." If you could only see the wrongdoers, captive before their Lord, throwing back allegations at one another. Those who were oppressed will say to those who were arrogant, "Were it not for you, we would have been believers."

32. Those who were arrogant will say to those who were oppressed, "Was it us who turned you away from guidance when it came to you? No indeed, you yourselves were sinful."

33. And those who were oppressed will say to those who were arrogant, "It was your scheming by night and day; as you instructed us to reject God, and to set up rivals to Him." They will hide their remorse when they see the retribution. We will put yokes around the necks of those who disbelieved. Will they be repaid for anything other than what they used to do?

34. We sent no warner to any town, without its affluent saying, "We reject what you are sent with."

35. And they say, "We have more wealth and more children, and we will not be punished."

36. Say, "My Lord spreads out His bounty to whomever He wills, or restricts it; but most people do not know."

37. It is neither your wealth nor your children that bring you closer to Us, but it is he who believes and does good deeds. These will have a double reward for what they did; and they will reside in the Chambers, in peace and security.

38. But those who work against Our revelations, seeking to undermine them—those will be summoned to the punishment.

39. Say, "My Lord extends the provision to whomever He wills of His servants, or withholds it. Anything you spend, He will replace it. He is the Best of providers."

40. On the Day when He gathers them all together, then say to the angels, "Was it you these used to worship?"

41. They will say, "Be You glorified; You are our Master, not them. In fact, they used to worship the jinn, and most of them had faith in them."

42. "Today, none of you has the power to profit or harm the other." And We will say to those who did wrong, "Taste the agony of the Fire which you used to deny."

43. When Our enlightening Verses are recited to them, they say, "This is nothing but a man who wants to divert you from what your ancestors used to worship." And they say, "This is nothing but a fabricated lie." And when the Truth comes to them, the blasphemers say of the Truth, "This is nothing but plain magic."

44. But We gave them no book to study, and We did not send them any warner before you.

45. Those before them also denied the Truth, yet they have not attained one-tenth of what We had given them. They rejected My messengers, so how was My disapproval?

46. Say, "I offer you a single advice: devote yourselves to God, in pairs, or individually; and reflect. There is no madness in your friend. He is just a warner to you, before the advent of a severe punishment."

47. Say, "Whatever wage I asked you for is yours. My wage comes only from God, and He is Witness over all things."

48. Say, "My Lord projects the truth. He is the Knower of the Unseen."

49. Say, "The truth has come; while falsehood can neither originate, nor regenerate."

50. Say, "If I err, I err only to my own loss; but if I am guided, it is by what my Lord inspires me. He is Hearing and Near."

51. If you could only see when they are terrified, and there is no escape, and they are seized from a nearby place.

52. And they say, "We have believed in it." But how can they attain it from a distant place?

53. They have rejected it in the past, and made allegations from a far-off place.

54. And they were barred from what they desire, as was done with their likes before. They were in disturbing doubt.

35. ORIGINATOR
(Fatir)

In the name of God,
the Gracious, the Merciful.

1. Praise be to God, Originator of the heavens and the earth, Maker of the angels messengers with wings—double, triple, and quadruple. He adds to creation as He wills. God is Able to do all things.

2. Whatever mercy God unfolds for the people, none can withhold it. And if He withholds it, none can release it thereafter. He is the Exalted in Power, Full of Wisdom.

3. O people! Remember God's blessings upon you. Is there a creator other than God who provides for you from the heaven and the earth? There is no god but He. So how are you misled?

4. If they reject you, messengers before you were also rejected. To God all matters are returned.

5. O people! The promise of God is true, so let not the lowly life seduce you, and let not the Tempter tempt you away from God.

6. Satan is an enemy to you, so treat him as an enemy. He only invites his gang to be among the inmates of the Inferno.

7. Those who disbelieve will suffer a harsh punishment, but those who believe and do righteous deeds will have forgiveness and a great reward.

8. What of him whose evil deed was made attractive to him, and so he regards it as good? God leads astray whomever He wills, and He guides whomever He wills. Therefore, do not waste yourself sorrowing over them. God knows exactly what they do.

9. God is He who sends the winds, which agitate clouds, which We drive to a dead land, and thereby revive the ground after it had died. Likewise is the Resurrection.

10. Whoever desires honor—all honor belongs to God. To Him ascends speech that is pure, and He elevates righteous conduct. As for those who plot evil, a terrible punishment awaits them, and the planning of these will fail.

11. God created you from dust, then from a small drop; then He made you pairs. No female conceives, or delivers, except with His knowledge. No living thing advances in years, or its life is shortened, except it be in a Record. That is surely easy for God.

12. The two seas are not the same. One is fresh, sweet, good to drink, while the other is salty and bitter. Yet from each you eat

tender meat, and extract jewelry which you wear. And you see the ships plowing through them, so that you may seek of His bounty, so that you may give thanks.

13. He merges the night into the day, and He merges the day into the night; and He regulates the sun and the moon, each running for a stated term. Such is God, your Lord; His is the sovereignty. As for those you call upon besides Him, they do not possess a speck.

14. If you pray to them, they cannot hear your prayer. And even if they heard, they would not answer you. And on the Day of Resurrection, they will reject your partnership. None informs you like an Expert.

15. O people! It is you who are the poor, in need of God; while God is the Rich, the Praiseworthy.

16. If He wills, He can do away with you, and produce a new creation.

17. And that would not be difficult for God.

18. No burdened soul can carry the burden of another. Even if one weighted down calls for help with its burden, nothing can be lifted from it, even if they were related. You are to warn those who fear their Lord inwardly, and perform the prayer. He who purifies himself purifies himself for his own good. To God is the ultimate return.

19. Not equal are the blind and the seeing.

20. Nor are the darkness and the light.

21. Nor are the shade and the torrid heat.

22. Nor are equal the living and the dead. God causes whomever He wills to hear, but you cannot make those in the graves hear.

23. You are only a warner.

24. We sent you with the truth; a bearer of good news, and a warner. There is no community but a warner has passed through it.

25. If they disbelieve you, those before them also disbelieved. Their messengers came to them with the clear proofs, with the Psalms, and with the Enlightening Scripture.

26. Then I seized those who disbelieved— so how was My rejection?

27. Have you not seen that God sends down water from the sky? With it We produce fruits of various colors. And in the mountains are streaks of white and red, varying in their hue, and pitch-black.

28. Likewise, human beings, animals, and livestock come in various colors. From among His servants, the learned fear God. God is Almighty, Oft-Forgiving.

29. Those who recite the Book of God, and perform the prayer, and spend of what We have provided for them, secretly and publicly, expect a trade that will not fail.

30. He will pay them their dues in full, and will increase them from His bounty. He is Forgiving and Appreciative.

31. What We inspired in you, of the Book, is the truth, confirming what preceded it. God is Well-Informed of His servants, All-Seeing.

32. Then We passed the Book to those of Our servants whom We chose. Some of them wrong their souls, some follow a middle course, and some are in the foremost in good deeds by God's leave; that is the greatest blessing.

33. The Gardens of Eden, which they will enter. They will be adorned therein with gold bracelets and pearls, and their garments therein will be of silk.

34. And they will say, "Praise God, who has lifted all sorrow from us. Our Lord is Most Forgiving, Most Appreciative.

35. He Who settled us in the Home of Permanence, by His grace, where boredom will not touch us, and fatigue will not afflict us."

36. As for those who disbelieve, for them is the Fire of Hell, wherein they will never be finished off and die, nor will its punishment be lightened for them. Thus We will repay every ingrate.

37. And they will scream therein, "Our Lord, let us out, and we will act righteously, differently from the way we used to act." Did We not give you a life long enough, in which anyone who wanted to understand would have understood? And the warner did come to you. So taste. The evildoers will have no helper.

38. God is the Knower of the future of the heavens and the earth. He knows what the hearts contain.

39. It is He who made you successors on earth. Whoever disbelieves, his disbelief will recoil upon him. The disbelief of the disbelievers adds only to their Lord's disfavor of them. The disbelief of the disbelievers adds only to their perdition.

40. Say, "Have you considered those partners of yours that you worship instead of God? Show me what they have created on earth. Or do they have any share in the heavens?" Or have We given them a book whose clear teachings they follow? In fact, the wrongdoers promise one another nothing but delusions.

41. God holds the heavens and the earth, lest they fall apart. And were they to fall apart, there is none to hold them together except He. He is Most Clement, Most Forgiving.

42. And they swore by God with their solemn oaths, that if a warner came to them, they would be more guided than any other people. Yet when a warner came to them, it only increased them in aversion.

43. Priding themselves on earth, and scheming evil. But evil scheming overwhelms none but its authors. Do they expect anything but the precedent of the ancients? You will not find any change in God's practice, and you will not find any substitute to God's practice.

44. Have they not journeyed in the land and observed the fate of those who preceded them? They were superior to them in strength. But nothing can defeat God in the heavens or on Earth. He is indeed Omniscient and Omnipotent.

45. If God were to punish the people for what they have earned, He would not leave a single living creature on its surface. But He defers them until a stated time. Then, when their time has arrived—God is Observant of His creatures.

36. YA-SEEN
(Ya-Seen)

In the name of God,
the Gracious, the Merciful.

1. Ya, Seen.

2. By the Wise Quran.

3. You are one of the messengers.

4. On a straight path.

5. The revelation of the Almighty, the Merciful.

6. To warn a people whose ancestors were not warned, and so they are unaware.

7. The Word was realized against most of them, for they do not believe.

8. We placed shackles around their necks, up to their chins, so they are stiff-necked.

9. And We placed a barrier in front of them, and a barrier behind them, and We have enshrouded them, so they cannot see.

10. It is the same for them, whether you warn them, or do not warn them—they will not believe.

11. You warn only him who follows the Message, and fears the Most Gracious inwardly. So give him good news of forgiveness, and a generous reward.

12. It is We who revive the dead; and We write down what they have forwarded, and their traces. We have tallied all things in a Clear Record.

13. And cite for them the parable of the landlords of the town—when the messengers came to it.

14. We sent them two messengers, but they denied them both, so We reinforced them with a third. They said, "We are messengers to you."

15. They said, "You are nothing but humans like us, and the Gracious did not send down anything; you are only lying."

16. They said, "Our Lord knows that we are messengers to you.

17. And our only duty is clear communication."

18. They said, "We see an evil omen in you; if you do not give up, we will stone you, and a painful punishment from us will befall you."

19. They said, "Your evil omen is upon you. Is it because you were reminded? But you are an extravagant people."

20. Then a man came running from the remotest part of the city. He said, "O my people, follow the messengers.

21. Follow those who ask you of no wage, and are themselves guided.

22. "And why should I not worship Him Who created me, and to Whom you will be returned?

23. Shall I take other gods instead of Him? If the Merciful desires harm for me, their intercession will not avail me at all, nor will they save me.

24. In that case, I would be completely lost.

25. I have believed in your Lord, so listen to me."

26. It was said, "Enter Paradise." He said, "If only my people knew.

27. How my Lord has forgiven me, and made me one of the honored."

28. After him, We sent down no hosts from heaven to his people; nor would We ever send any down.

29. It was just one Cry, and they were stilled.

30. Alas for the servants. No messenger ever came to them, but they ridiculed him.

31. Have they not considered how many generations We destroyed before them; and that unto them they will not return?

32. All of them, every single one of them, will be arraigned before Us.

33. And there is a sign for them in the dead land: We give it life, and produce from it grains from which they eat.

34. And We place in it gardens of palm-trees and vines, and cause springs to gush out of it.

35. That they may eat from its fruits, although their hands did not make it. Will they not be appreciative?

36. Glory be to Him who created all the pairs; of what the earth produces, and of their own selves, and of what they do not know.

37. Another sign for them is the night: We strip the day out of it—and they are in darkness.

38. And the sun runs towards its destination. Such is the design of the Almighty, the All-Knowing.

39. And the moon: We have disposed it in phases, until it returns like the old twig.

40. The sun is not to overtake the moon, nor is the night to outpace the day. Each floats in an orbit.

41. Another sign for them is that We carried their offspring in the laden Ark.

42. And We created for them the like of it, in which they ride.

43. If We will, We can drown them—with no screaming to be heard from them, nor will they be saved.

44. Except by a mercy from Us, and enjoyment for a while.

45. Yet when it is said to them, "Beware of what lies before you, and what lies behind you, that you may receive mercy."

46. Yet never came to them a sign of their Lord's signs, but they turned away from it.

47. And when it is said to them, "Spend of what God has provided for you," those who disbelieve say to those who believe, "Shall we feed someone whom God could feed, if He so willed? You must be deeply misguided."

48. And they say, "When will this promise be, if you are truthful?"

49. All they can expect is a single blast, which will seize them while they feud.

50. They will not be able to make a will, nor will they return to their families.

51. The Trumpet will be blown, then behold, they will rush from the tombs to their Lord.

52. They will say, "Woe to us. Who resurrected us from our resting-place?" This is what the Most Gracious had promised, and the messengers have spoken the truth."

53. It will be but a single scream, and behold, they will all be brought before Us.

54. On that Day, no soul will be wronged in the least, and you will be recompensed only for what you used to do.

55. The inhabitants of Paradise, on that Day, will be happily busy.

56. They and their spouses, in shades, reclining on couches.

57. They will have therein fruits. They will have whatever they call for.

58. Peace—a saying from a Most Merciful Lord.

59. But step aside today, you criminals.

60. Did I not covenant with you, O Children of Adam, that you shall not serve the devil? That he is your sworn enemy?

61. And that you shall serve Me? This is a straight path.

62. He has misled a great multitude of you. Did you not understand?

63. This is Hellfire, which you were promised.

64. Roast in it today, because you persistently disbelieved.

65. On this Day, We will seal their mouths, and their hands will speak to Us, and their feet will testify to everything they had done.

66. If We will, We can blind their eyes as they rush towards the path—but how will they see?

67. And if We will, We can cripple them in their place; so they can neither move forward, nor go back.

68. Whomever We grant old age, We reverse his development. Do they not understand?

69. We did not teach him poetry, nor is it proper for him. It is only a reminder, and a Clear Quran.

70. That he may warn whoever is alive, and prove the Word against the faithless.

71. Have they not seen that We created for them, of Our Handiwork, livestock that they own?

72. And We subdued them for them. Some they ride, and some they eat.

73. And they have in them other benefits, and drinks. Will they not give thanks?

74. Yet they have taken to themselves gods other than God, that perhaps they may be helped.

75. They cannot help them, although they are arrayed as troops for them.

76. So let their words not sadden you. We know what they conceal, and what they reveal.

77. Does the human being not consider that We created him from a seed? Yet he becomes a fierce adversary.

78. And he produces arguments against Us, and he forgets his own creation. He says, "Who will revive the bones when they have decayed?"

79. Say, "He who initiated them in the first instance will revive them. He has knowledge of every creation."

80. He who produced fuel for you from the green trees, with which you kindle a fire.

81. Is not He who created the heavens and the earth able to create the like of them? Certainly. He is the Supreme All-Knowing Creator.

82. His command, when He wills a thing, is to say to it, "Be," and it comes to be.

83. So glory be to Him in whose hand is the dominion of everything, and to Him you will be returned.

37. THE ALIGNERS
(as-Saffat)

In the name of God,
the Gracious, the Merciful.

1. By the aligners aligning.

2. And the drivers driving.

3. And the reciters of the Reminder.

4. Your God is indeed One.

5. Lord of the heavens and the earth, and everything between them; and Lord of the Easts.

6. We have adorned the lower heaven with the beauty of the planets.

7. And guarded it against every defiant devil.

8. They cannot eavesdrop on the Supernal Elite, for they get bombarded from every side.

9. Repelled—they will have a lingering torment.

10. Except for him who snatches a fragment—he gets pursued by a piercing projectile.

11. Inquire of them, "Are they more difficult to create, or the others We created?" We created them from sticky clay.

12. But you wonder, and they ridicule.

13. And when reminded, they pay no attention.

14. And when they see a sign, they ridicule.

15. And they say, "This is nothing but plain magic.

16. When we have died and become dust and bones, shall we be resurrected?

17. And our ancestors of old?"

18. Say, "Yes indeed, and you will be totally subdued."

19. It will be a single nudge, and they will be staring.

20. They will say, "Woe to us. This is the Day of Judgment."

21. "This is the Day of Separation, which you used to deny.

22. Gather those who did wrong, and their mates, and what they used to worship.

23. Besides God, and lead them to the way to Hell.

24. And stop them. They are to be questioned."

25. What is the matter with you? Why do you not help one another?

26. In fact, on that Day, they will be submissive.

27. They will come to one another, questioning one another.

28. They will say, "You used to come at us from the right."

29. They will say, "You yourselves were not believers.

30. We had no authority over you. You yourselves were rebellious people.

31. The Word of our Lord has been realized against us. We are tasting it.

32. We seduced you. We were seducers."

33. On that Day, they will share in the punishment.

34. Thus We deal with the sinners.

35. When it was said to them, "There is no god except God," they grew arrogant.

36. And said, "Are we to abandon our gods for a mad poet?"

37. In fact, he came with the truth, and he confirmed the messengers.

38. Most assuredly, you will taste the painful punishment.

39. And you will be repaid only for what you used to do.

40. Except for God's sincere servants.

41. For them is a known provision.

42. Fruits; and they will be honored.

43. In the Gardens of Bliss.

44. On furnishings, facing one another.

45. They will be offered a cup of pure drink.

46. White; a delight to those who drink.

47. Never polluted, and never intoxicating.

48. With them will be bashful women with lovely eyes.

49. As if they were closely guarded pearls.

50. Then they will approach one another, questioning.

51. One of them will say, "I used to have a friend.

52. Who used to say, "Are you of those who believe?

53. That after we die and become dust and bones, we will be called to account?"

54. He will say, "Will you have a look?"

55. He will look, and will see him in the pit of Hell.

56. He will say, "By God, you almost ruined me.

57. Were it not for the grace of my Lord, I would have been among the arraigned."

58. "We will not die.

59. Except for our first death, and we will not be punished."

60. This is the supreme triumph.

61. For the like of this let the workers work.

62. Is this a better hospitality, or the tree of Bitterness?

63. We made it an ordeal for the unjust.

64. It is a tree that grows from the bottom of Hell.

65. Its fruits are like the devils' heads.

66. They will eat from it, and fill their bellies with it.

67. Then, on top of it, they will have a brew of boiling liquid.

68. Then their return will be to the Blaze.

69. They had found their parents astray.

70. And rushed along in their footsteps.

71. And most of the ancients before them went astray.

72. Even though We sent messengers to warn them.

73. So observe the end of those who were warned.

74. Except for the sincere servants of God.

75. And Noah called out to Us, and We are the Best of responders.

76. And We saved him and his family from the great calamity.

77. And We made his descendants the survivors.

78. And We left mention of him among those who succeeded.

79. Peace be upon Noah among all people.

80. We thus reward the righteous.

81. He was one of Our believing servants.

82. Then We drowned the others.

83. Of his kind was Abraham.

84. When he came to his Lord with a sound heart.

85. He said to his father and his people, "What are you worshiping?

86. Is it falsified gods, instead of God, that you want?

87. So what is your opinion about the Lord of the Worlds?"

88. Then he took a glance at the stars.

89. And said, "I am sick."

90. But they turned their backs on him, and went away.

91. Then he turned to their gods, and said, "will you not eat?

92. What is it with you, that you do not speak?"

93. Then he turned on them, striking with his right hand.

94. And they came running towards him.

95. He said, "Do you worship what you carve?

96. When God created you, and what you manufacture?"

97. They said, "Build a pyre for him, and throw him into the furnace."

98. They wished him ill, but We made them the losers.

99. He said, "I am going towards my Lord, and He will guide me."

100. "My Lord, give me one of the righteous."

101. So We gave him good news of a clement boy.

102. Then, when he was old enough to accompany him, he said, "O My son, I see in a dream that I am sacrificing you; see what you think." He said, "O my Father, do as you are commanded; you will find me, God willing, one of the steadfast."

103. Then, when they had submitted, and he put his forehead down.

104. We called out to him, "O Abraham!

105. You have fulfilled the vision." Thus We reward the doers of good.

106. This was certainly an evident test.

107. And We redeemed him with a great sacrifice.

108. And We left with him for later generations.

109. Peace be upon Abraham.

110. Thus We reward the doers of good.

111. He was one of Our believing servants.

112. And We gave him good news of Isaac, a prophet, one of the righteous.

113. And We blessed him, and Isaac. But among their descendants are some who are righteous, and some who are clearly unjust to themselves.

114. And We blessed Moses and Aaron.

115. And We delivered them and their people from the terrible disaster.

116. And We supported them, and so they were the victors.

117. And We gave them the clarifying Scripture.

118. And We guided them upon the straight path.

119. And We left with them for later generations.

120. Peace be upon Moses and Aaron.

121. Thus We reward the righteous.

122. They were of Our believing servants.

123. Also Elijah was one of the messengers.

124. He said to his people, "Do you not fear?

125. Do you call on Baal, and forsake the Best of Creators?

126. God is your Lord, and the Lord of your ancestors."

127. But they called him a liar, and thus they will be brought forward.

128. Except for God's sincere servants.

129. And We left with him for later generations.

130. Peace be upon the House of Elijah.

131. Thus We reward the virtuous.

132. He was one of Our believing servants.

133. And Lot was one of the messengers.

134. We saved him and his family, all of them.

135. Except for an old woman who lagged behind.

136. Then We annihilated the others.

137. You pass by them in the morning.

138. And at night. Do you not understand?

139. And Jonah was one of the messengers.

140. When he fled to the laden boat.

141. He gambled and lost.

142. Then the fish swallowed him, and he was to blame.

143. Had he not been one of those who praised.

144. He would have stayed in its belly until the Day they are raised.

145. Then We threw him into the wilderness, and he was sick.

146. And We made a gourd tree grow over him.

147. Then We sent him to a hundred thousand, or more.

148. And they believed, so We gave them enjoyment for a while.

149. Ask them, "Are the daughters for your Lord, while for them the sons?"

150. Or did We create the angels females, as they witnessed?"

151. No indeed! It is one of their lies when they say,

152. "God has begotten." They are indeed lying.

153. So He preferred girls over boys?

154. What is the matter with you? How do you judge?

155. Will you not reflect?

156. Or do you have some clear proof?

157. Then bring your book, if you are telling the truth.

158. And they invented a relationship between Him and the jinn. But the jinn know that they will be arraigned.

159. God be glorified, far above what they allege.

160. Except for God's sincere servants.

161. Surely, you and what you serve.

162. Cannot seduce away from Him.

163. Except for he who will be roasting in Hell.

164. "There is not one of us but has an assigned position.

165. And we are the arrangers.

166. And we are the glorifiers."

167. Even though they used to say.

168. "Had we received advice from the ancients,

169. We would have been God's faithful servants."

170. But they rejected it, so they will find out.

171. Our Word has already gone out to our servant messengers.

172. It is they who will be supported.

173. And Our troops will be the victors.

174. So disregard them for a while.

175. And watch them—they will soon see.

176. Are they seeking to hasten Our punishment?

177. When it descends into their yard, miserable will be the morning of those forewarned.

178. So avoid them for a while.

179. And watch—they will soon see.

180. Exalted be your Lord, the Lord of Glory, beyond their allegations.

181. And peace be upon the messengers.

182. And praise be to God, the Lord of the Worlds.

38. SAAD
(Saad)

**In the name of God,
the Gracious, the Merciful.**

1. Saad. By the renowned Quran.

2. Those who disbelieve are steeped in arrogance and defiance.

3. How many generations have We destroyed before them? They cried out when it was too late to escape.

4. And they marveled that a warner has come to them from among them. The disbelievers said, "This is a lying magician."

5. "Did he turn all the gods into one God? This is something strange."

6. The notables among them announced: "Go on, and hold fast to your gods. This is something planned.

7. We never heard of this in the former faith. This is nothing but a fabrication.

8. Was the message sent down to him, out of all of us?" In fact, they are doubtful of

My warning. In fact, they have not yet tasted My punishment.

9. Or do they possess the treasuries of the mercy of your Lord—the Majestic, the Giver?

10. Or do they possess the sovereignty of the heavens and the earth and what is between them? Then let them ascend the ropes.

11. An army of confederates with be defeated there.

12. Before them the people of Noah denied the truth, as did Aad, and Pharaoh of the Stakes.

13. And Thamood, and the people of Lot, and the dwellers of the Woods—these were the confederates.

14. None of them but denied the messengers, so My retribution was deserved.

15. These can expect only a single scream, from which there is no recovery.

16. And they say, "Our Lord, hasten Your writ upon us, before the Day of Account."

17. Be patient in the face of what they say, and mention Our servant David, the resourceful. He was obedient.

18. We committed the mountains to glorify with him, in the evening and at daybreak.

19. And the birds, gathered together. All obedient to him.

20. And We strengthened his kingdom, and gave him wisdom and decisive speech.

21. Has the story of the two disputants reached you? When they scaled the sanctuary?

22. When they entered upon David, and he was startled by them. They said, "Do not fear. Two disputants; one of us has wronged the other; so judge between us

fairly, and do not be biased, and guide us to the straight way."

23. "This brother of mine has ninety nine ewes, and I have one ewe, and he said, 'Entrust it to me,' and he pressured me with words."

24. He said, "He has done you wrong by asking your ewe in addition to his ewes. Many partners take advantage of one another, except those who believe and do good deeds, but these are so few." David realized that We were testing him, so he sought forgiveness from his Lord, and fell down to his knees, and repented.

25. So We forgave him that. And for him is nearness to Us, and a good place of return.

26. "O David, We made you a ruler in the land, so judge between the people with justice, and do not follow desire, lest it diverts you from God's path. Those who stray from God's path will have a painful punishment, for having ignored the Day of Account."

27. We did not create the heaven and the earth and everything between them in vain. That is the assumption of those who disbelieve—so woe to those who disbelieve because of the Fire.

28. Or are We to treat those who believe and do righteous deeds like those who make trouble on earth? Or are We to treat the pious like the shameless?

29. A blessed Book that We sent down to you, that they may ponder its Verses, and for those with intelligence to take heed.

30. And We granted David, Solomon, an excellent servant. He was penitent.

31. When the beautiful horses were paraded before him in the evening.

32. He said, "I have preferred the love of niceties to the remembrance of my Lord—until it disappeared behind the veil.

33. Bring them back to me." And he began caressing their legs and necks.

34. We tested Solomon, and placed a body on his throne; then he repented.

35. He said, "My Lord, forgive me, and grant me a kingdom never to be attained by anyone after me. You are the Giver."

36. So We placed the wind at his service, blowing gently by his command, wherever he directed.

37. And the demons—every builder and diver.

38. And others fettered in chains.

39. "This is Our gift; so give generously, or withhold; without account."

40. For him is nearness to Us, and a beautiful resort.

41. And mention Our servant Job, when he called out to his Lord, "Satan has afflicted me with hardship and pain."

42. "Stamp with your foot—here is cool water to wash with, and to drink."

43. And We restored his family for him, and their like with them; as a mercy from Us, and a lesson for those who possess insight.

44. "Take with your hand a bundle, and strike with it, and do not break your oath." We found him patient. What an excellent servant! He was obedient.

45. And mention Our servants Abraham, Isaac, and Jacob—endowed with ability and vision.

46. We distinguished them with a distinct quality: the remembrance of the Home.

47. To Us they are among the chosen, the outstanding.

48. And mention Ishmael, Elisha, and Ezekiel; all are among the outstanding.

49. This is a reminder. The devout will have a good place of return.

50. The Gardens of Eden, with their doors wide-open for them.

51. Relaxing therein, and calling for abundant fruit and beverage.

52. With them will be attendants with modest gaze, of same age.

53. This is what you are promised for the Day of Account.

54. Such is Our bounty, inexhaustible.

55. All This. But the transgressors will have a miserable return.

56. Hell; in which they will roast; what a miserable abode!

57. All this. Let them taste it—boiling and bitter cold.

58. And similar torments of diverse kinds.

59. "This is a crowd rushing headlong with you." There is no welcome for them. They will be scorched by the Fire.

60. They will say, "But it is you! There is no welcome for you! It is you who brought it upon us! What a miserable end!"

61. They will say, "Our Lord, whoever brought this upon us, give him double torment in the Fire."

62. And they will say, "What is it with us that we do not see men we used to count among the wicked?

63. Did we take them for mockery, or have our eyes swerved from them?

64. This is certainly true—the feuding of the people of the Fire.

65. Say, "I am only a warner, and there is no god except God—the One, the Conqueror.

66. The Lord of the heavens and the earth, and everything between them; the Mighty, the Forgiver."

67. Say, "It is a message of great importance.

68. From which you are turning away.

69. I have no knowledge of the Highest Assembly as they dispute.

70. It is only revealed to me that I am a clear warner."

71. Your Lord said to the angels, "I am creating a human being from clay.

72. When I have formed him, and breathed into him of My spirit, fall prostrate before him.

73. So the angels fell prostrate, all of them.

74. Except for Satan. He was too proud, and one of the faithless.

75. He said, "O Satan, what prevented you from prostrating before what I created with My Own hands? Are you too proud, or were you one of the exalted?"

76. He said, "I am better than he; You created me from fire, and You created him from clay."

77. He said, "Then get out of here! You are an outcast!

78. And My curse will be upon you until the Day of Judgment."

79. He said, "Lord, defer me until the Day they are resurrected."

80. He said, "You are one of those deferred.

81. Until the Day of the Time Appointed."

82. He said, "By Your majesty, I will seduce them all.

83. Except for your loyal servants among them."

84. He said, "The truth is, and I say the truth.

85. I will fill Hell with you, and with every one of them who follows you."

86. Say, "I ask of you no wage for this, and I am not a pretender.

87. It is but a reminder to mankind.

88. And you will know its message after a while."

39. THRONGS
(az-Zumar)

In the name of God,
the Gracious, the Merciful.

1. The revelation of the Book is from God, the Mighty and Wise.

2. We sent down to you the Book with the truth, so serve God, devoting your religion to Him.

3. Is not to God that sincere faith is due? As for those who take guardians besides Him, "We only worship them that they may bring us nearer to God." God will judge between them regarding their differences. God does not guide the lying blasphemer.

4. If God wanted to have a son, He could have selected from His creation at will. Glory be to Him. He is God, the One, the Prevailing.

5. He created the heavens and the earth with reason. He wraps the night around the day, and He wraps the day around the night. And He regulates the sun and the moon, each running along a specific course. He is indeed the Almighty, the Forgiver.

6. He created you from one person, then made from it its mate, and brought down livestock for you—eight kinds in pairs. He creates you in the wombs of your mothers, in successive formations, in a triple darkness. Such is God, your Lord. His is the

kingdom. There is no god but He. So what made you deviate?

7. If you disbelieve, God is independent of you, yet He does not approve ingratitude on the part of His servants. And if you are thankful, He will approve that in you. No bearer of burden can bear the burden of another. Then to your Lord is your return; and He will inform you of what you used to do. He is aware of what the hearts contain.

8. When some adversity touches the human being, he prays to his Lord, repenting to Him. But then, when He confers on him a grace of His, he forgets what he was praying for before, and he attributes rivals to God, in order to lead astray from His way. Say, "Enjoy your disbelief for a little while; you will be among the inmates of the Fire."

9. Is he who worships devoutly during the watches of the night, prostrating himself and standing up, mindful of the Hereafter, and placing his hope in the mercy of his Lord? Say, "Are those who know and those who do not know equal?" Only those possessed of reason will remember.

10. Say, "O My devotees who have believed, keep your duty to your Lord. For those who do good in this world, is goodness. And God's earth is vast. The steadfast will be paid their wages in full, without reckoning."

11. Say, "I was commanded to serve God, devoting my religion exclusively to Him.

12. And I was commanded to be the first of those who submit."

13. Say, "I fear, if I disobeyed my Lord, the punishment of a horrendous Day."

14. Say, "It is God I worship, sincere in my faith in Him."

15. "But you can worship whatever you wish besides Him." Say, "The losers are those who lose their souls and their people on the Day of Resurrection." That is indeed the obvious loss.

16. They will have layers of Fire above them, and layers beneath them. That is how God strikes fear into His servants— "O My servants! Beware of Me!"

17. As for those who avoid the worship of idols, and devote themselves to God— theirs is the good news. So give good news to My servants.

18. Those who listen to the Word, and follow the best of it. These are they whom God has guided. These are they who possess intellect.

19. What about someone who has deserved the sentence of punishment? Is it you who can save those in the Fire?

20. But those who fear their Lord will have mansions upon mansions, built high, with streams flowing beneath them. The promise of God; and God never breaks a promise.

21. Have you not considered how God sends down water from the sky, then He makes it flow into underground wells, then He produces with it plants of various colors, then they wither and you see them yellowing, then He turns them into debris? Surely in this is a reminder for those with understanding.

22. What about someone whose heart God has opened to Islam, so that he follows a light from His Lord? Woe to those whose hearts are hardened against the mention of God. Those are in manifest error.

23. God has sent down the best of narrations; a Scripture consistent and paired. The skins of those who reverence their Lord shiver from it, then their skins and

their hearts soften up to the remembrance of God. Such is God's guidance; He guides with it whomever He wills. But whomever God leaves astray, for him there is no guide.

24. What about someone who covers his face against the terrible misery of the Day of Resurrection? To the evildoers it will be said, "Taste what you used to earn."

25. Those before them also denied the truth, so the penalty came upon them from where they did not perceive.

26. God made them taste disgrace in the present life, but the punishment of the Hereafter is worse, if they only knew.

27. We have cited in this Quran for mankind every ideal, that they may take heed.

28. An Arabic Quran, without any defect, so they may become righteous.

29. God cites the example of a man shared by partners at odds, and a man belonging exclusively to one man. Are they equal in status? Praise be to God, but most of them do not know.

30. You will die, and they will die.

31. Then, on the Day of Resurrection, you will be quarrelling before your Lord.

32. Who is more evil than he who lies about God, and denies the truth when it has come to him? Is there not in Hell room for the ungrateful?

33. But he who promotes the truth, and testifies to it—these are the righteous.

34. They will have whatever they please with their Lord. Such is the reward for the virtuous.

35. God will acquit them of the worst of their deeds, and will reward them according to the best of what they used to do.

36. Is God not enough for His servant? And they frighten you with those besides Him. Whomever God sends astray, for him there is no guide.

37. And whomever God guides, for him there is no misleader. Is God not Powerful and Vengeful?

38. And if you asked them, "Who created the heavens and the earth?" they would say, "God." Say, "Have you seen those you pray to instead of God? If God willed any harm for me, can they lift His harm? And if He willed a blessing for me, can they hold back His mercy?" Say, "God suffices for me. On Him the reliant rely."

39. Say: "O my people, work according to your ability; and so will I. Then you will know.

40. Who will receive a humiliating punishment, and on whom will fall a lasting torment."

41. We sent down upon you the Book for mankind in truth. He who follows guidance does so for the good of his soul. And he who strays in error does so to its detriment. You are not their overseer.

42. God takes the souls at the time of their death, and those that have not died during their sleep. He retains those for which He has decreed death, and He releases the others until a predetermined time. In that are signs for people who reflect.

43. Or have they chosen intercessors other than God? Say, "Even though they have no power over anything, and are devoid of reason?"

44. Say, "All intercession is up to God. To Him belongs the kingdom of the heavens and the earth. Then to Him you will be returned."

45. When God alone is mentioned, the hearts of those who do not believe in the Hereafter shrink with resentment. But

when those other than Him are mentioned, they become filled with joy.

46. Say, "Our God, Initiator of the heavens and the earth, Knower of all secrets and declarations. You will judge between your servants regarding what they had differed about."

47. If those who did wrong owned everything on earth, and the like of it with it, they would redeem themselves with it from the terrible suffering on the Day of Resurrection. But there will appear to them from God what they never anticipated.

48. There will appear to them the evils of their deeds, and they will be surrounded by what they used to ridicule.

49. When adversity touches the human being, he calls on Us. But then, when We favor him with a blessing from Us, he says, "I have attained this by virtue of my knowledge." However, it is a test, but most of them do not know.

50. Those before them said it, but what they had earned did not avail them.

51. The evils of their deeds caught up with them. And the wrongdoers among these will also be afflicted by the evils of what they earned, and they cannot prevent it.

52. Do they not know that God extends the provision to whomever He wills, and constricts it? In that are signs for a people who believe.

53. Say, "O My servants who have transgressed against themselves: do not despair of God's mercy, for God forgives all sins. He is indeed the Forgiver, the Clement."

54. And turn to your Lord, and submit to Him, before the retribution comes upon you. Then you will not be helped.

55. And follow the best of what was revealed to you from your Lord, before the punishment comes upon you suddenly, while you are unaware.

56. So that a soul may not say, "How sorry I am, for having neglected my duty to God, and for having been of the scoffers."

57. Or say, "Had God guided me; I would have been of the pious."

58. Or say, when it sees the penalty, "If only I had another chance, I would be of the virtuous."

59. Yes indeed! My Verses did come to you, but you called them lies, turned arrogant, and were of the faithless.

60. On the Day of Resurrection, you will see those who told lies about God with their faces blackened. Is there not a place in Hell for the arrogant?

61. And God will save those who maintained righteousness to their place of salvation. No harm will touch them, nor will they grieve.

62. God is the Creator of all things, and He is in Charge of all things.

63. To Him belong the reins of the heavens and the earth. But those who blaspheme against the revelations of God—it is they who are the losers.

64. Say, "Is it other than God you instruct me to worship, you ignorant ones?"

65. It was revealed to you, and to those before you, that if you idolize, your works will be in vain, and you will be of the losers.

66. Rather, worship God, and be of the appreciative.

67. They have not esteemed God as He ought to be esteemed. The entire earth will be in His grip on the Day of Resurrection, and the heavens will be folded in His righ. Immaculate is He, and transcendent He is beyond the associations they make.

68. And the Trumpet will be sounded, whereupon everyone in the heavens and the earth will be stunned, except whomever God wills. Then it will be sounded another time, whereupon they will rise up, looking on.

69. And the earth will shine with the Light of its Lord; and the Book will be put in place; and the prophets and the witnesses will be brought in; and Judgment will be passed among them equitably, and they will not be wronged.

70. And every soul will be fully compensated for what it had done. He is well aware of what they do.

71. Those who disbelieved will be driven to Hell in throngs. Until, when they have reached it, and its gates are opened, its keepers will say to them, "Did not messengers from among you come to you, reciting to you the revelations of your Lord, and warning you of the meeting of this Day of yours?" They will say, "Yes, but the verdict of punishment is justified against the disbelievers."

72. It will be said, "Enter the gates of Hell, to abide therein eternally." How wretched is the destination of the arrogant.

73. And those who feared their Lord will be led to Paradise in throngs. Until, when they have reached it, and its gates are opened, its keepers will say to them, "Peace be upon you, you have been good, so enter it, to abide therein eternally."

74. And they will say, "Praise be to God, who has fulfilled His promise to us, and made us inherit the land, enjoying Paradise as we please." How excellent is the reward of the workers.

75. And you will see the angels hovering around the Throne, glorifying their Lord with praise. And it will be judged between them equitably, and it will be said, "Praise be to God, Lord of the Worlds."

40. FORGIVER
(Ghafir)

In the name of God,
the Gracious, the Merciful.

1. Ha, Meem.

2. The sending down of the Scripture is from God the Almighty, the Omniscient.

3. Forgiver of sins, Accepter of repentance, Severe in punishment, Bountiful in bounty. There is no god but He. To Him is the ultimate return.

4. None argues against God's revelations except those who disbelieve. So do not be impressed by their activities in the land.

5. Before them the people of Noah rejected the truth, as did the confederates after them. Every community plotted against their messenger, to capture him. And they argued with falsehood, to defeat with it the truth. But I seized them. What a punishment it was!

6. Thus the sentence of your Lord became realized against those who disbelieve, that they are to be inmates of the Fire.

7. Those who carry the Throne, and those around it, glorify their Lord with praise, and believe in Him, and ask for forgiveness for those who believe: "Our Lord, You have encompassed everything in mercy and knowledge; so forgive those who repent and follow Your path, and protect them from the agony of the Blaze.

8. And admit them, Our Lord, into the Gardens of Eternity, which You have promised them, and the righteous among their parents, and their spouses, and their offspring. You are indeed the Almighty, the Most Wise.

9. And shield them from the evil deeds. Whomever You shield from the evil deeds, on that Day, You have had mercy on him. That is the supreme achievement."

10. Those who disbelieved will be addressed, "The loathing of God is greater than your loathing of yourselves—for you were invited to the faith, but you refused."

11. They will say, "Our Lord, you made us die twice, and twice you gave us life. Now we acknowledge our sins. Is there any way out?"

12. That is because when God alone was called upon, you disbelieved; but when others were associated with Him, you believed. Judgment rests with God the Sublime, the Majestic.

13. It is He who shows you His wonders, and sends down sustenance from the sky for you. But none pays heed except the repentant.

14. So call upon God, with sincere devotion to Him, even though the disbelievers resent it.

15. Exalted in rank, Owner of the Throne. He conveys the Spirit, by His command, upon whomever He wills of His servants, to warn of the Day of Encounter.

16. The Day when they will emerge, nothing about them will be concealed from God. "To whom does the sovereignty belong today?" "To God, the One, the Irresistible."

17. On that Day, every soul will be recompensed for what it had earned. There will be no injustice on that Day. God is quick to settle accounts.

18. And warn them of the Day of Imminence, when the hearts are at the throats, choking them. The evildoers will have no intimate friend, and no intercessor to be obeyed.

19. He knows the deceptions of the eyes, and what the hearts conceal.

20. God judges with justice, while those whom they invoke besides Him cannot judge with anything. It is God who is the Hearing, the Seeing.

21. Have they not travelled through the earth, and seen the consequences for those before them? They were stronger than them, and they left more impact on earth. But God seized them for their sins, and they had no defender against God.

22. That is because their messengers used to come to them with clear proofs, but they disbelieved, so God seized them. He is Strong, Severe in retribution.

23. We sent Moses with Our signs, and a clear authority.

24. To Pharaoh, Hamaan, and Quaroon. But they said, "A lying sorcerer."

25. Then, when he came to them with the truth from Us, they said, "Kill the sons of those who have believed with him, and spare their daughters." But the scheming of the unbelievers can only go astray.

26. Pharaoh said, "Leave me to kill Moses, and let him appeal to his Lord. I fear he may change your religion, or spread disorder in the land."

27. Moses said, "I have sought the protection of my Lord and your Lord, from every tyrant who does not believe in the Day of Account."

28. A believing man from Pharaoh's family, who had concealed his faith, said, "Are you going to kill a man for saying, `My Lord is God,' and he has brought you clear proofs from your Lord? If he is a liar, his lying will rebound upon him; but if he is truthful, then some of what he promises you will befall you. God does not guide the extravagant imposter.

29. O my people! Yours is the dominion today, supreme in the land; but who will help us against God's might, should it fall upon us?" Pharaoh said, "I do not show you except what I see, and I do not guide you except to the path of prudence."

30. The one who had believed said, "O my people, I fear for you the like of the day of the confederates.

31. Like the fate of the people of Noah, and Aad, and Thamood, and those after them. God wants no injustice for the servants.

32. O my people, I fear for you the Day of Calling Out.

33. The Day when you will turn and flee, having no defender against God. Whomever God misguides has no guide."

34. Joseph had come to you with clear revelations, but you continued to doubt what he came to you with. Until, when he perished, you said, "God will never send a messenger after him." Thus God leads astray the outrageous skeptic.

35. Those who argue against God's revelations, without any proof having come to them—a heinous sin in the sight of God, and of those who believe. Thus God seals the heart of every proud bully.

36. And Pharaoh said, "O Hamaan, build me a tower, that I may reach the pathways.

37. The pathways of the heavens, so that I may glance at the God of Moses; though I think he is lying." Thus Pharaoh's evil deeds were made to appear good to him, and he was averted from the path. Pharaoh's guile was only in defeat.

38. The one who had believed said, "O my people, follow me, and I will guide you to the path of rectitude."

39. "O my people, the life of this world is nothing but fleeting enjoyment, but the Hereafter is the Home of Permanence.

40. Whoever commits a sin will be repaid only with its like. But whoever works righteousness, whether male or female, and is a believer—these will enter paradise, where they will be provided for without account.

41. O my people, how is it that I call you to salvation, and you call me to the Fire?

42. You call me to reject God, and to associate with Him what I have no knowledge of, while I call you to the Mighty Forgiver.

43. Without a doubt, what you call me to has no say in this world, or in the Hereafter; and our turning back is to God; and the transgressors are the inmates of the Fire.

44. You will remember what I am telling you, so I commit my case to God. God is Observant of the servants."

45. So God protected him from the evils of their scheming, while a terrible torment besieged Pharaoh's clan.

46. The Fire. They will be exposed to it morning and evening. And on the Day the Hour takes place: "Admit the clan of Pharaoh to the most intense agony."

47. As they quarrel in the Fire, the weak will say to those who were arrogant, "We were followers of yours; will you then spare us a portion of the Fire?"

48. Those who were arrogant will say, "We are all in it; God has judged between the servants."

49. And those in the Fire will say to the keepers of Hell, "Call to your Lord to lessen our suffering for one day."

50. They will say, "Did not your messengers come to you with clear signs?" They will say, "Yes." They will say, "Then pray, but the prayers of the disbelievers will always be in vain."

51. Most surely We will support Our messengers and those who believe, in this life, and on the Day the witnesses arise.

52. The Day when their excuses will not profit the wrongdoers, and the curse will be upon them, and they will have the Home of Misery.

53. We gave Moses guidance, and made the Children of Israel inherit the Scripture.

54. A guide and a reminder for those endowed with reason.

55. So be patient. The promise of God is true. And ask forgiveness for your sin, and proclaim the praise of your Lord evening and morning.

56. Those who dispute regarding God's revelations without any authority having come to them—there is nothing in their hearts but the feeling of greatness, which they will never attain. So seek refuge in God; for He is the All-Hearing, the All-Seeing.

57. Certainly the creation of the heavens and the earth is greater than the creation of humanity, but most people do not know.

58. Not equal are the blind and the seeing. Nor are those who believe and work righteousness equal to the sinners. How little you reflect.

59. Indeed, the Hour is coming; there is no doubt about it; but most people do not believe.

60. Your Lord has said, "Pray to Me, and I will respond to you. But those who are too proud to worship Me will enter Hell forcibly."

61. It is God Who made the night for you, that you may rest therein; and the day allowing sight. God is gracious towards the people, but most people do not give thanks.

62. Such is God, your Lord, Creator of all things. There is no god except Him; so how could you turn away?

63. Thus are turned away those who dispute the signs of God.

64. It is God who made the earth a habitat for you, and the sky a structure. And He designed you, and designed you well; and He provided you with the good things. Such is God, your Lord; so Blessed is God, Lord of the Worlds.

65. He is the Living One. There is no god except He. So pray to Him, devoting your religion to Him. Praise be to God, the Lord of the Worlds.

66. Say, "I was prohibited from worshiping those you invoke besides God, now that clear revelations have come to me from my Lord; and I was commanded to submit to the Lord of the Worlds."

67. It is He who created you from dust, then from a seed, then from an embryo, then He brings you out as an infant, then He lets you reach your maturity, then you become elderly—although some of you die sooner—so that you may reach a predetermined age, so that you may understand.

68. It is He who gives life and death; and when He decides on a thing, He just says to it, "Be," and it comes to be.

69. Have you not observed those who dispute regarding God's revelations, how they have deviated?

70. Those who call the Book a lie, and what We sent Our messengers with—they will surely know.

71. When the yokes are around their necks, and they will be dragged by the chains.

72. Into the boiling water, then in the Fire they will be consumed.

73. Then it will be said to them, "Where are those you used to deify?

74. Instead of God?" They will say, "They have abandoned us. In fact, we were praying to nothing before." Thus God sends the disbelievers astray.

75. That is because you used to rejoice on earth in other than the truth, and because you used to behave with vanity.

76. Enter the gates of Hell, to remain therein forever. What a terrible dwelling for the arrogant.

77. So be patient. The promise of God is true. Whether We show you some of what We have promised them, or take you to Us, to Us they will be returned.

78. We sent messengers before you. Some of them We told you about, and some We did not tell you about. No messenger can bring a miracle except by leave of God. Then, when the command of God is issued, fair judgment will be passed, and there and then the seekers of vanity will lose.

79. God is He who created the domestic animals for you—some for you to ride, and some you eat.

80. And in them you have other benefits as well, and through them you satisfy your needs. And on them, and on the ships, you are transported.

81. And He shows you His signs. So which of God's signs will you deny?

82. Have they not journeyed through the land, and seen the outcome for those before them? They were more numerous than they, and had greater power and influence in the land. But what they had achieved availed them nothing.

83. When their messengers came to them with clear proofs, they rejoiced in the knowledge they had, and the very things they used to ridicule besieged them.

84. Then, when they witnessed Our might, they said, "We believe in God alone, and we reject what we used to associate with Him."

85. But their faith could not help them once they witnessed Our might. This has been God's way of dealing with His servants. And there and then the disbelievers lost.

41. DETAILED
(Fussilat)

In the name of God,
the Gracious, the Merciful.

1. Ha, Meem.

2. A revelation from the Most Gracious, the Most Merciful.

3. A Scripture whose Verses are detailed, a Quran in Arabic for people who know.

4. Bringing good news and giving warnings. But most of them turn away, so they do not listen.

5. And they say, "Our hearts are screened from what you call us to, and in our ears is deafness, and between us and you is a barrier. So do what you want, and so will we."

6. Say, "I am only a human like you; it is inspired in me that your God is One God. So be upright towards Him, and seek forgiveness from Him." And woe to the idolaters.

7. Those who do not pay the alms; and regarding the Hereafter, they are disbelievers.

8. As for those who believe and do righteous deeds—for them is a reward uninterrupted.

9. Say, "Do you reject the One who created the earth in two days? And you attribute equals to Him? That is the Lord of the Universe."

10. He placed stabilizers over it; and blessed it; and planned its provisions in four days, equally to the seekers.

11. Then He turned to the sky, and it was smoke, and said to it and to the earth, "Come, willingly or unwillingly." They said, "We come willingly."

12. So He completed them as seven universes in two days, and He assigned to each universe its laws. And We decorated the lower universe with lamps, and for protection. That is the design of the Almighty, the All-Knowing.

13. But if they turn away, say, "I have warned you of a thunderbolt, like the thunderbolt of Aad and Thamood."

14. Their messengers came to them, from before them and from behind them, saying, "Do not worship anyone but God." They said, "Had our Lord willed, He would have sent down angels; Therefore, we reject what you are sent with."

15. As for Aad, they turned arrogant on earth, and opposed justice, and said, "Who is more powerful than us?" Have they not considered that God, who created them, is more powerful than they? And they went on denying Our revelations.

16. So We unleashed upon them a screaming wind, for a few miserable days, to make them taste the punishment of shame in this life; but the punishment of the Hereafter is more shameful; and they will not be saved.

17. And as for Thamood, We guided them, but they preferred blindness over guidance. So the thunderbolt of the humiliating punishment seized them, because of what they used to earn.

18. And We saved those who believed and were righteous.

19. The Day when God's enemies are herded into the Fire, forcibly.

20. Until, when they have reached it, their hearing, and their sight, and their skins will testify against them regarding what they used to do.

21. And they will say to their skins, "Why did you testify against us?" They will say, "God, Who made all things speak, made us speak. It is He who created you the first time, and to Him you are returned."

22. You were unable to hide yourselves from your hearing, and your sight, and your skins, to prevent them from testifying against you, and you imagined that God was unaware of much of what you do.

23. It is that thought of yours about your Lord that led you to ruin—so you became of the losers.

24. If they endure patiently, the Fire will be their residence; and if they make up excuses, they will not be pardoned.

25. We had assigned companions for them, who glamorized to them what was in front of them, and what was behind them. And the Word proved true against them in communities of jinn and humans that have passed away before them. They were losers.

26. Those who disbelieve say, "Do not listen to this Quran, and talk over it, so that you may prevail."

27. We will make those who disbelieve taste an intense agony, and We will recompense them according to the worst of what they used to do.

28. Such is the recompense of God's enemies—the Fire—where they will have their permanent home, in recompense for having disregarded Our revelations.

29. Those who disbelieved will say, "Our Lord, show us those who led us astray—among jinn and humans—and we will trample them under our feet, so they become among of the lowest."

30. Surely, those who say: "Our Lord is God," and then go straight, the angels will descend upon them: "Do not fear, and do not grieve, but rejoice in the news of the Garden which you were promised.

31. We are your allies in this life and in the Hereafter, wherein you will have whatever your souls desire, and you will have therein whatever you call for.

32. As Hospitality from an All-Forgiving, Merciful One."

33. And who is better in speech than someone who calls to God, and acts with integrity, and says, "I am of those who submit"?

34. Good and evil are not equal. Repel evil with good, and the person who was your enemy becomes like an intimate friend.

35. But none will attain it except those who persevere, and none will attain it except the very fortunate.

36. When a temptation from the Devil provokes you, seek refuge in God; He is the Hearer, the Knower.

37. And of His signs are the night and the day, and the sun and the moon. Do not bow down to the sun, nor to the moon, but bow down to God, Who created them both, if it is Him that you serve.

38. But if they are too proud—those in the presence of your Lord praise Him night and day, and without ever tiring.

39. And of His signs is that you see the land still. But when We send down water upon it, it stirs and grows. Surely, He Who revived it will revive the dead. He is Able to do all things.

40. Those who despise Our revelations are not hidden from Us. Is he who is hurled into the Fire better? Or he who arrives safely on the Day of Resurrection? Do as you please; He is Seeing of everything you do.

41. Those who reject the Reminder when it has come to them—it is an invincible Book.

42. Falsehood cannot approach it, from before it or behind it. It is a revelation from One Wise and Praiseworthy.

43. Nothing is said to you but was said to the Messengers before you: your Lord is Possessor of Forgiveness, and Possessor of Painful Repayment.

44. Had We made it a Quran in a foreign language, they would have said, "If only its verses were made clear." Non-Arabic and an Arab? Say, "For those who believe, it is guidance and healing. But as for those who do not believe: there is heaviness in their ears, and it is blindness for them. These are being called from a distant place."

45. We gave Moses the Book, but disputes arose concerning it. Were it not for a prior decree from your Lord, judgment would have been pronounced between them. But they are in perplexing doubt concerning it.

46. Whoever acts righteously does so for himself; and whoever works evil does so against himself. Your Lord is not unjust to the servants.

47. To Him is referred the knowledge of the Hour. No fruit emerges from its sheath, and no female conceives or delivers, except with His knowledge. And on

the Day when He calls out to them, "Where are My associates?" They will say, "We admit to you, none of us is a witness."

48. What they used to pray to before will forsake them, and they will realize that they have no escape.

49. The human being never tires of praying for good things, but when adversity afflicts him, he despairs and loses hope.

50. And when We let him taste a mercy from Us, after the adversity that had afflicted him, he will say, "This is mine, and I do not think that the Hour is coming; and even if I am returned to my Lord, I will have the very best with Him." But We will inform those who disbelieve of what they did, and We will make them taste an awful punishment.

51. When We provide comfort for the human being, he withdraws and distances himself; but when adversity befalls him, he starts lengthy prayers.

52. Say, "Have you considered? If it is from God and you reject it—who is further astray than he who is cutoff and alienated?"

53. We will show them Our proofs on the horizons, and in their very souls, until it becomes clear to them that it is the truth. Is it not sufficient that your Lord is witness over everything?

54. Surely they are in doubt about the encounter with their Lord. Surely He comprehends everything.

42. CONSULTATION
(ash-Shura)

In the name of God,
the Gracious, the Merciful.

1. Ha, Meem.

2. Ayn, Seen, Qaf.

3. Thus He inspires you, and those before you—God the Almighty, the Wise.

4. To him belongs everything in the heavens and everything on earth. He is the Sublime, the Magnificent.

5. The heavens above them almost burst apart, while the angels glorify the praises of their Lord, and ask forgiveness for those on earth. God is indeed the Forgiver, the Merciful.

6. As for those who take masters other than Him, God is in charge of them, and you are not responsible for them.

7. Thus We inspired you with an Arabic Quran, that you may warn the Central City and whoever is around it, and to warn of the Day of Assembly, of which there is no doubt; a group in the Garden, and a group in the Furnace.

8. Had God willed, He could have made them one community, but He admits into His mercy whomever He wills. As for the wrongdoers, they will have no protector and no savior.

9. Or have they adopted protectors besides him? But God is the Protector, and He gives life to the dead, and He has power over all things.

10. Whatever matter you differ about, its judgment rests with God. "Such is God, my Lord, in Whom I trust, and unto Him I repent."

11. Originator of the heavens and the earth. He made for you mates from among yourselves, and pairs of animals, by means of which He multiplies you. There is nothing like Him. He is the Hearing, the Seeing.

12. To Him belongs absolute control of the heavens and the earth. He spreads the bounties to whomever He wills, or reduces it. He is aware of all things.

13. He prescribed for you the same religion He enjoined upon Noah, and what We inspired to you, and what We enjoined upon Abraham, and Moses, and Jesus: "You shall uphold the religion, and be not divided therein." As for the idolaters, what you call them to is outrageous to them. God chooses to Himself whom He wills, and He guides to Himself whoever repents.

14. They became divided only after knowledge came to them, out of resentment among themselves. Were it not for a predetermined decision from your Lord, judgment would have been pronounced between them. Indeed, those who were made to inherit the Book after them are in grave doubt about it.

15. To this go on inviting, and be upright as you were commanded, and do not follow their inclinations, and say, "I believe in whatever Book God has sent down, and I was commanded to judge between you equitably. God is our Lord and your Lord. We have our deeds, and you have your deeds. Let there be no quarrel between us and you. God will bring us together, and to Him is the ultimate return."

16. As for those who dispute about God after having answered His call, their argument is invalid with their Lord; and upon them falls wrath; and a grievous torment awaits them.

17. It is God who revealed the Book with the truth, and the Balance. And what will make you realize that perhaps the Hour is near?

18. Those who do not believe in it seek to hasten it, but those who believe are apprehensive of it, and they know it to be the truth. Absolutely, those who question the Hour are in distant error.

19. God is kind towards His worshipers. He provides for whomever He wills. He is the Powerful, the Honorable.

20. Whoever desires the harvest of the Hereafter, We increase for him his harvest; and whoever desires the harvest of this world, We give him thereof, and he has no share of the Hereafter.

21. Or is it that they have partners who litigate for them religious laws never authorized by God? Were it not for the conclusive decision, it would have been settled between them. The wicked will have a painful punishment.

22. You will see the unjust terrified of what they have earned, and it will befall them. As for those who believe and do good deeds, they will be in the Meadows of the Gardens; they will have whatever they please in the presence of their Lord; that is the supreme blessing.

23. That is the good news God gives to His servants who believe and do good deeds. Say, "I ask of you no wage for it, except affection among the near of kin." Whoever does a good deed, We will increase its goodness for him. God is Forgiving and Appreciative.

24. Or do they say, "He forged a lie about God." If God so willed, He could have sealed your heart. But God obliterates the false, and confirm the true by His Words. He knows what is in the hearts.

25. It is He who accepts the repentance of His worshipers, and remits the sins, And knows what you do.

26. And He answers those who believe and do good deeds, and He increases them of His grace. But the disbelievers will suffer a terrible punishment.

27. If God were to increase the provision to His servants, they would transgress on

earth; but He sends down in precise measure whatever He wills. Surely, regarding His servants, He is Expert and Observant.

28. It is He who brings down the rain after they have despaired, and unfolds His mercy. He is the Guardian, the Praised.

29. And of His signs are the creation of the heavens and the earth, and the creatures He has spread throughout them; and He is Able to gather them at will.

30. Whatever misfortune befalls you, it is because of what your hands have earned; and yet He pardons much.

31. You are not the ones to interfere on earth; and besides God, you have no ally, and no helper.

32. And of His signs are the ships sailing the sea like flags.

33. If He willed, He could have stilled the winds, leaving them motionless on its surface. Surely in that are signs for every disciplined, grateful person.

34. Or He could wreck them, because of what they have earned. And yet He pardons much.

35. Those who dispute Our signs know that there is no asylum for them.

36. Whatever thing you are given is only the provision of this life. But what God possesses is better and more lasting for those who believe and rely on their Lord.

37. And those who avoid major sins and indecencies; and if they become angry, they forgive.

38. And those who respond to their Lord, and pray regularly, and conduct their affairs by mutual consultation, and give of what We have provided them.

39. And those who, when wronged, defend themselves.

40. The repayment of a bad action is one equivalent to it. But whoever pardons and makes reconciliation, his reward lies with God. He does not love the unjust.

41. As for those who retaliate after being wronged, there is no blame on them.

42. Blame lies on those who wrong people, and commit aggression in the land without right. These will have a painful punishment.

43. But whoever endures patiently and forgives—that is a sign of real resolve.

44. Whoever God leaves astray has no protector apart from Him. And you will see the transgressors, when they see the torment, saying, "Is there a way of going back?"

45. And you will see them exposed to it, cowering from disgrace, looking with concealed eyes. Those who believed will say, "The losers are those who lost themselves and their families on the Day of Resurrection." Indeed, the evildoers are in a lasting torment.

46. They will have no allies to support them against God. Whomever God leaves astray has no way out.

47. Respond to your Lord before there comes from God a Day that cannot be turned back. You will have no refuge on that Day, and no possibility of denial.

48. But if they turn away—We did not send you as a guardian over them. Your only duty is communication. Whenever We let man taste mercy from Us, he rejoices in it; but when misfortune befalls them, as a consequence of what their hands have perpetrated, man turns blasphemous.

49. To God belongs the dominion of the heavens and the earth. He creates whatever He wills. He grants daughters to whomev-

er He wills, and He grants sons to whomever He wills.

50. Or He combines them together, males and females; and He renders whomever He wills sterile. He is Knowledgeable and Capable.

51. It is not for any human that God should speak to him, except by inspiration, or from behind a veil, or by sending a messenger to reveal by His permission whatever He wills. He is All-High, All-Wise.

52. We thus inspired you spiritually, by Our command. You did not know what the Scripture is, nor what faith is, but We made it a light, with which We guide whomever We will of Our servants. You surely guide to a straight path.

53. The path of God, to whom belongs everything in the heavens and everything on earth. Indeed, to God all matters revert.

43. DECORATIONS
(az-Zukhruf)

In the name of God,
the Gracious, the Merciful.

1. Ha, Meem.

2. By the Book that makes things clear.

3. We made it an Arabic Quran, so that you may understand.

4. And it is with Us, in the Source Book, sublime and wise.

5. Shall We hold back the Reminder from you, since you are a transgressing people?

6. How many a prophet did We send to the ancients?

7. No messenger came to them, but they ridiculed him.

8. We destroyed people more powerful than they, and so the example of the ancients has passed away.

9. And if you asked them, "Who created the heavens and the earth?" They would say, "The Mighty, the Knower created them."

10. He who made the earth a habitat for you, and traced pathways for you on it, that you may be guided.

11. He who sends down water from the sky in due proportion; and so We revive thereby a dead land. Thus you will be brought out.

12. He Who created all the pairs; and provided you with ships, and animals on which you ride.

13. That you may mount their backs, and remember the favor of your Lord as you sit firmly upon them, and say, "Glory be to Him Who placed these at our service; surely we could not have done it by ourselves.

14. And surely, to our Lord we will return."

15. Yet they turn one of His servants into a part of Him. Man is clearly ungrateful.

16. Or has He chosen for Himself daughters from what He creates, and favored you with sons?

17. Yet when one of them is given news of what he attributes to the Most Gracious, his face darkens, and he suppresses grief.

18. "Someone brought up to be beautiful, and unable to help in a fight?"

19. And they appoint the angels, who are servants to the Most Gracious, as females. Have they witnessed their creation? Their claim will be recorded, and they will be questioned.

20. And they say, "Had the Most Gracious willed, we would not have worshiped them." But they have no knowledge of that; they are merely guessing.

21. Or have We given them a book prior to this one, to which they adhere?

22. But they say, "We found our parents on a course, and we are guided in their footsteps."

23. Likewise, We sent no warner before you to any town, but the wealthy among them said, "We found our parents on a course, and we are following in their footsteps."

24. He would say, "Even if I bring you better guidance than what you found your parents following?" They would say, "We reject what you are sent with."

25. So We wreaked vengeance upon them. Behold, then, what was the fate of those who deny.

26. When Abraham said to his father and his people, "I am innocent of what you worship.

27. Except for He who created me, for He will guide me."

28. And he made it an enduring word in his progeny, so that they may return.

29. I gave these and their forefathers some enjoyment, until the truth and a manifest messenger came to them.

30. But when the truth came to them, they said, "This is sorcery, and we refuse to believe in it."

31. They also said, "If only this Quran was sent down to a man of importance from the two cities."

32. Is it they who allocate the mercy of your Lord? It is We who have allocated their livelihood in this life, and We elevated some of them in rank above others, that some of them would take others in service. But your Lord's mercy is better than what they amass.

33. Were it not that humanity would become a single community, We would have provided those who disbelieve in the Most Gracious with roofs of silver to their houses, and stairways by which they ascend.

34. And doors to their houses, and furnishings on which they recline.

35. And decorations. Yet all that is nothing but the stuff of this life. Yet the Hereafter, with your Lord, is for the righteous.

36. Whoever shuns the remembrance of the Most Gracious, We assign for him a devil, to be his companion.

37. They hinder them from the path, though they think they are guided.

38. Until, when He comes to Us, he will say, "If only there were between me and you the distance of the two Easts." What an evil companion!

39. It will not benefit you on that Day, since you did wrong. You are partners in the suffering.

40. Can you make the deaf hear, or guide the blind, and him who is in evident error?

41. Even if We take you away, We will wreak vengeance upon them.

42. Or show you what We have promised them; for We have absolute power over them.

43. So adhere to what is revealed to you. You are upon a straight path.

44. It is a message for you, and for your people, and you will be questioned.

45. Ask those of Our messengers We sent before you: "Did We appoint gods besides the Most Gracious to be worshiped?"

46. We sent Moses with Our revelations to Pharaoh and his dignitaries. He said, "I am the Messenger of the Lord of the Worlds."

47. But when he showed them Our signs, they started laughing at them.

48. Each sign We showed them was more marvelous than its counterpart. And We afflicted them with the plagues, so that they may repent.

49. They said, "O sorcerer, pray to your Lord for us, according to His pledge to you, and then we will be guided."

50. But when We lifted the torment from them, they immediately broke their promise.

51. Pharaoh proclaimed among his people, saying, "O my people, do I not own the Kingdom of Egypt, and these rivers flow beneath me? Do you not see?

52. Am I not better than this miserable wretch, who can barely express himself?

53. Why are bracelets of gold not dropped on him, or angels came with him in procession?"

54. Thus he fooled his people, and they obeyed him. They were wicked people.

55. And when they provoked Our wrath, We took retribution from them, and We drowned them all.

56. Thus We made them a precedent and an example for the others.

57. And when the son of Mary was cited as an example, your people opposed.

58. They said, "Are our gods better, or he?" They cited him only for argument. In fact, they are a quarrelsome people.

59. He was just a servant whom We blessed, and We made him an example for the Children of Israel.

60. Had We willed, We would have made of you angels to be successors on earth.

61. He is a portent of the Hour, so have no doubt about it, and follow Me. This is a straight way.

62. And let not Satan divert you. He is an open enemy to you.

63. When Jesus came with the clarifications, he said, "I have come to you with wisdom, and to clarify for you some of what you differ about. So fear God, and obey me.

64. God is my Lord and your Lord, so worship Him—this is a straight path."

65. But the factions differed among themselves. So woe to the wrongdoers from the suffering of a painful Day.

66. Are they only waiting for the Hour to come upon them suddenly, while they are unaware?

67. On that Day, friends will be enemies of one another, except for the righteous.

68. O My servants, you have nothing to fear on that Day, nor will you grieve.

69. Those who believed in Our revelations, and were submissive.

70. Enter the Garden, you and your spouses, Joyfully.

71. They will be served around with trays of gold, and cups. Therein is whatever the souls desire and delights the eyes. Therein you will stay forever.

72. Such is the Garden you are made to inherit, because of what you used to do.

73. Therein you will have abundant fruit, from which you eat.

74. As for the sinners, they will be in the torment of Hell forever.

75. It will never be eased for them. In it, they will be devastated.

76. We did them no injustice, but it was they who were the unjust.

77. And they will cry, "O Malek, Let your Lord finish us off." He will say, "You are staying."

78. We have given you the truth, but most of you hate the truth.

79. Have they contrived some scheme? We too are contriving.

80. Or do they think that We cannot hear their secrets and their conspiracies? Yes indeed, Our messengers are by them, writing down.

81. Say: "If the Most Gracious had a son, I would be the first to worship."

82. Glorified be the Lord of the heavens and the earth, the Lord of the Throne, beyond what they describe.

83. So leave them to blunder and play, until they encounter their Day which they are promised.

84. It is He who is God in heaven, and God on earth. He is the Wise, the Knower.

85. And blessed is He Who has sovereignty over the heavens and the earth and what is between them. He alone has knowledge of the Hour, and to Him you will be returned.

86. Those they invoke besides Him are incapable of intercession; only those who testify to the truth and have knowledge.

87. And if you asked them, who created them, they would say, "God." Why then do they deviate?

88. As for his statement: "My Lord, these are a people who do not believe."

89. Pardon them, and say, "Peace." They will come to know.

44. SMOKE
(ad-Dukhan)

In the name of God,
the Gracious, the Merciful.

1. Ha, Meem.

2. By the Enlightening Scripture.

3. We have revealed it on a Blessed Night—We have warned.

4. In it is distinguished every wise command.

5. A decree from Us. We have been sending messages.

6. As mercy from your Lord. He is the Hearer, the Knower.

7. Lord of the heavens and the earth and what is between them, if you know for sure.

8. There is no god but He. He gives life and causes death—your Lord and Lord of your ancestors.

9. Yet they play around in doubt.

10. So watch out for the Day when the sky produces a visible smoke.

11. Enveloping mankind; this is a painful punishment.

12. "Our Lord, lift the torment from us, we are believers."

13. But how can they be reminded? An enlightening messenger has already come to them.

14. But they turned away from him, and said, "Educated, but crazy!"

15. We will ease the punishment a little, but you will revert.

16. The Day when We launch the Great Assault—We will avenge.

17. Before them We tested the people of Pharaoh; a noble messenger came to them.

18. Saying, "Hand over God's servants to me. I am an honest messenger to you."

19. And, "Do not exalt yourselves above God. I come to you with clear authority.

20. I have taken refuge in my Lord and your Lord, lest you stone me.

21. But if you do not believe in me, keep away from me."

22. He appealed to his Lord: "These are a sinful people."

23. "Set out with My servants by night—you will be followed.

24. And cross the sea quickly; they are an army to be drowned."

25. How many gardens and fountains did they leave behind?

26. And plantations, and splendid buildings.

27. And comforts they used to enjoy.

28. So it was; and We passed it on to another people.

29. Neither heaven nor earth wept over them, nor were they reprieved.

30. And We delivered the Children of Israel from the humiliating persecution.

31. From Pharaoh. He was a transgressing tyrant.

32. And We chose them knowingly over all other people.

33. And We gave them many signs, in which was an obvious test.

34. These people say.

35. "There is nothing but our first death, and we will not be resurrected.

36. Bring back our ancestors, if you are truthful."

37. Are they better, or the people of Tubba and those before them? We annihilated them. They were evildoers.

38. We did not create the heavens and the earth and what is between them to play.

39. We created them only for a specific purpose, but most of them do not know.

40. The Day of Sorting Out is the appointed time for them all.

41. The Day when no friend will avail a friend in any way, and they will not be helped.

42. Except for him upon whom God has mercy. He is the Mighty, the Merciful.

43. The Tree of Bitterness.

44. The food of the sinner.

45. Like molten lead; boiling inside the bellies.

46. Like the boiling of seething water.

47. Seize him and drag him into the midst of Hell!

48. Then pour over his head the suffering of the Inferno!

49. Taste! You who were powerful and noble.

50. This is what you used to doubt.

51. As for the righteous, they will be in a secure place.

52. Amidst gardens and springs.

53. Dressed in silk and brocade, facing one another.

54. So it is, and We will wed them to lovely companions.

55. They will call therein for every kind of fruit, in peace and security.

56. Therein they will not taste death, beyond the first death; and He will protect them from the torment of Hell.

57. A favor from your Lord. That is the supreme salvation.

58. We have made it easy in your language, so that they may remember.

59. So wait and watch. They too are waiting and watching.

45. KNEELING
(al-Jathiyah)

In the name of God,
the Gracious, the Merciful.

1. Ha, Meem.

2. The revelation of the Book is from God, the Exalted in Might, the Wise.

3. In the heavens and the earth are proofs for the believers.

4. And in your own creation, and in the creatures He scattered, are signs for people of firm faith.

5. And in the alternation of night and day, and in the sustenance God sends down from the sky, with which He revives the earth after its death, and in the circulation of the winds, are marvels for people who reason.

6. These are God's Verses which We recite to you in truth. In which message, after God and His revelations, will they believe?

7. Woe to every sinful liar.

8. Who hears God's revelations being recited to him, yet he persists arrogantly, as though he did not hear them. Announce to him a painful punishment.

9. And when he learns something of Our revelations, he takes them in mockery. For such there is a shameful punishment.

10. Beyond them lies Hell. What they have earned will not benefit them at all, nor will those they adopted as lords instead of God. They will have a terrible punishment.

11. This is guidance. Those who blaspheme their Lord's revelations will have a punishment of agonizing pain.

12. It is God who placed the sea at your service, so that ships may run through it by His command, and that you may seek of His bounty, and that you may give thanks.

13. And He placed at your service whatever is in the heavens and whatever is on earth—all is from Him. In that are signs for a people who think.

14. Tell those who believe to forgive those who do not hope for the Days of God. He will fully recompense people for whatever they have earned.

15. Whoever does a good deed, it is for his soul; and whoever commits evil, it is against it; then to your Lord you will be returned.

16. We gave the Children of Israel the Book, and wisdom, and prophecy; and We provided them with the good things; and We gave them advantage over all other people.

17. And We gave them precise rulings. They fell into dispute only after knowledge came to them, out of mutual rivalry. Your Lord will judge between them on the Day of Resurrection regarding the things they differed about.

18. Then We set you upon a pathway of faith, so follow it, and do not follow the inclinations of those who do not know.

19. They will not help you against God in any way. The wrongdoers are allies of one another, while God is the Protector of the righteous.

20. This is an illumination for mankind, and guidance, and mercy for people who believe with certainty.

21. Do those who perpetrate the evil deeds assume that We will regard them as equal to those who believe and do righteous deeds, whether in their life or their death? Evil is their judgment!

22. God created the heavens and the earth with justice, so that every soul will be re-

paid for what it has earned. And they will not be wronged.

23. Have you considered him who has taken his desire for his god? God has knowingly led him astray, and has sealed his hearing and his heart, and has placed a veil over his vision. Who will guide him after God? Will you not reflect?

24. And they say, "There is nothing but this our present life; we die and we live, and nothing destroys us except time." But they have no knowledge of that; they are only guessing.

25. When Our clarifying Verses are recited to them, their only argument is to say, "Bring back our ancestors, if you are truthful."

26. Say, "God gives you life, then He makes you die; then He gathers you for the Day of Resurrection, about which there is no doubt. But most people do not know."

27. To God belongs the kingship of the heavens and the earth. On the Day when the Hour takes place, on that Day the falsifiers will lose.

28. You will see every community on its knees; every community will be called to its Book: "Today you are being repaid for what you used to do.

29. This Book of Ours speaks about you in truth. We have been transcribing what you have been doing."

30. As for those who believed and did righteous deeds, their Lord will admit them into His mercy. That is the clear triumph.

31. But as for those who disbelieved: "Were My revelations not recited to you? But you turned arrogant, and were guilty people."

32. And when it was said, "The promise of God is true, and of the Hour there is no doubt," you said, "We do not know what the Hour is; we think it is only speculation; we are not convinced."

33. The evils of what they did will become evident to them, and the very thing they ridiculed will haunt them.

34. And it will be said, "Today We forget you, as you forgot the encounter of this Day of yours. Your abode is the Fire, and there are no saviors for you.

35. That is because you took God's revelations for a joke, and the worldly life lured you." So today they will not be brought out of it, and they will not be allowed to repent.

36. Praise belongs to God; Lord of the heavens, Lord of the earth, Lord of humanity.

37. To Him belongs all supremacy in the heavens and the earth. He is the Majestic, the Wise.

46. THE DUNES
(al-Ahqaf)

In the name of God,
the Gracious, the Merciful.

1. Ha, Meem.

2. The sending down of the Scripture is from God, the Honorable, the Wise.

3. We did not create the heavens and the earth and what lies between them except with reason, and for a finite period. But the blasphemers continue to ignore the warnings they receive.

4. Say, "Have you considered those you worship instead of God? Show me which portion of the earth they have created. Or do they own a share of the heavens? Bring me a scripture prior to this one, or some trace of knowledge, if you are truthful."

5. Who is more wrong than him who invokes, besides God, those who will not answer him until the Day of Resurrection, and are heedless of their prayers?

6. And when humanity is gathered, they will be enemies to them, and will renounce their worship of them.

7. When Our revelations are recited to them, plain and clear, those who disbelieve say of the truth when it has come to them, "This is obviously magic."

8. Or do they say, "He invented it himself"? Say, "If I have invented it, there is nothing you can do to protect me from God. He knows well what you are engaged in. He is sufficient witness between me and you. He is the Forgiver, the Merciful."

9. Say, "I am not different from the other messengers; and I do not know what will be done with me, or with you. I only follow what is inspired in me, and I am only a clear warner."

10. Say, "Have you considered? What if it is from God and you disbelieve in it? A witness from the Children of Israel testified to its like, and has believed, while you turned arrogant. God does not guide the unjust people."

11. Those who disbelieve say to those who believe, "If it were anything good, they would not have preceded us to it." And since they were not guided by it, they will say, "This is an ancient lie."

12. And before it was the Book of Moses, a model and a mercy. And this is a confirming Book, in the Arabic language, to warn those who do wrong—and good news for the doers of good.

13. Those who say, "Our Lord is God," then lead a righteous life—they have nothing to fear, nor shall they grieve.

14. These are the inhabitants of Paradise, where they will dwell forever—a reward for what they used to do.

15. We have enjoined upon man kindness to his parents. His mother carried him with difficulty, and delivered him with difficulty. His bearing and weaning takes thirty months. Until, when he has attained his maturity, and has reached forty years, he says, "Lord, enable me to appreciate the blessings You have bestowed upon me and upon my parents, and to act with righteousness, pleasing You. And improve my children for me. I have sincerely repented to You, and I am of those who have surrendered."

16. Those are they from whom We accept the best of their deeds, and We overlook their misdeeds, among the dwellers of Paradise—the promise of truth which they are promised.

17. As for him who says to his parents, "Enough of you! Are you promising me that I will be raised up, when generations have passed away before me?" While they cry for God's help, "Woe to you! Believe! The promise of God is true!" But he says, "These are nothing but tales of the ancients."

18. Those are they upon whom the sentence is justified, among the communities that have passed away before them, of jinn and humans. They are truly losers.

19. There are degrees for everyone, according to what they have done, and He will repay them for their works in full, and they will not be wronged.

20. On the Day when the faithless will be paraded before the Fire: "You have squandered your good in your worldly life, and you took pleasure in them. So today you are being repaid with the torment of

shame, because of your unjust arrogance on earth, and because you used to sin."

21. And mention the brother of Aad, as he warned his people at the dunes. Warnings have passed away before him, and after him: "Worship none but God; I fear for you the punishment of a tremendous Day."

22. They said, "Did you come to us to divert us from our gods? Then bring us what you threaten us with, if you are being truthful."

23. He said, "The knowledge is only with God, and I inform you of what I was sent with; but I see you are an ignorant people."

24. Then, when they saw a cloud approaching their valley, they said, "This is a cloud that will bring us rain." "In fact, it is what you were impatient for: a wind in which is grievous suffering."

25. It will destroy everything by the command of its Lord. And when the morning came upon them, there was nothing to be seen except their dwellings. Thus We requite the guilty people.

26. We had empowered them in the same way as We empowered you; and We gave them the hearing, and the sight, and the minds. But neither their hearing, nor their sight, nor their minds availed them in any way. That is because they disregarded the revelations of God; and so they became surrounded by what they used to ridicule.

27. We have destroyed many townships around you, and diversified the signs, so that they may return.

28. Why then did the idols, whom they worshiped as means of nearness to God, not help them? In fact, they abandoned them. It was their lie, a fabrication of their own making.

29. Recall when We dispatched towards you a number of jinn, to listen to the Quran. When they came in its presence, they said, "Pay attention!" Then, when it was concluded, they rushed to their people, warning them.

30. They said, "O our people, we have heard a Scripture, sent down after Moses, confirming what came before it. It guides to the truth, and to a straight path.

31. O our people! Answer the caller to God, and believe in Him; and He will forgive you your sins, and will save you from a painful punishment."

32. He who does not answer the caller to God will not escape on earth, and has no protectors besides Him. Those are in obvious error.

33. Do they not realize that God, who created the heavens and the earth, and was never tired by creating them, is Able to revive the dead? Yes indeed; He is Capable of everything.

34. On the Day when those who disbelieved are presented to the Fire: "Is this not real?" They will say, "Yes, indeed, by our Lord." He will say, "Then taste the suffering for having disbelieved."

35. So be patient, as the messengers with resolve were patient, and do not be hasty regarding them. On the Day when they witness what they are promised, it will seem as if they had lasted only for an hour of a day. A proclamation: Will any be destroyed except the sinful people?

47. MUHAMMAD
(Muhammad)

*In the name of God,
the Gracious, the Merciful.*

1. Those who disbelieve and repel from the path of God—He nullifies their works.

2. While those who believe, and work righteousness, and believe in what was sent down to Muhammad—and it is the truth from their Lord—He remits their sins, and relieves their concerns.

3. That is because those who disbelieve follow falsehoods, while those who believe follow the truth from their Lord. God thus cites for the people their examples.

4. When you encounter those who disbelieve, strike at their necks. Then, when you have routed them, bind them firmly. Then, either release them by grace, or by ransom, until war lays down its burdens. Had God willed, He could have defeated them Himself, but He thus tests some of you by means of others. As for those who are killed in the way of God, He will not let their deeds go to waste.

5. He will guide them, and will improve their state of mind.

6. And will admit them into Paradise, which He has identified for them.

7. O you who believe! If you support God, He will support you, and will strengthen your foothold.

8. But as for those who disbelieve, for them is perdition, and He will waste their deeds.

9. That is because they hated what God revealed, so He nullified their deeds.

10. Have they not journeyed through the earth and seen the consequences for those before them? God poured destruction upon them, and for the unbelievers is something comparable.

11. That is because God is the Master of those who believe, while the disbelievers have no master.

12. God will admit those who believe and do good deeds into gardens beneath which rivers flow. As for those who disbelieve, they enjoy themselves, and eat as cattle eat, and the Fire will be their dwelling.

13. How many a town was more powerful than your town which evicted you? We destroyed them, and there was no helper for them.

14. Is he who stands upon evidence from his Lord, like someone whose evil deed is made to appear good to him? And they follow their own desires?

15. The likeness of the Garden promised to the righteous: in it are rivers of pure water, and rivers of milk forever fresh, and rivers of wine delightful to the drinkers, and rivers of strained honey. And therein they will have of every fruit, and forgiveness from their Lord. Like one abiding in the Fire forever, and are given to drink boiling water, that cuts-up their bowels?

16. Among them are those who listen to you, but when they leave your presence, they say to those given knowledge, "What did he say just now?" Those are they whose hearts God has sealed, and they follow their own desires.

17. As for those who are guided, He increases them in guidance, and He has granted them their righteousness.

18. Are they just waiting until the Hour comes to them suddenly? Its tokens have already come. But how will they be reminded when it has come to them?

19. Know that there is no god but God, and ask forgiveness for your sin, and for the believing men and believing women. God knows your movements, and your resting-place.

20. Those who believe say, "If only a chapter is sent down." Yet when a decisive

chapter is sent down, and fighting is mentioned in it, you see those in whose hearts is sickness looking at you with the look of someone fainting at death. So woe to them!

21. Obedience and upright speech. Then, when the matter is settled, being true to God would have been better for them.

22. If you turn away, you are likely to make mischief on earth, and sever your family ties.

23. Those are they whom God has cursed. He made them deaf, and blinded their sight.

24. Will they not ponder the Quran? Or are there locks upon their hearts?

25. Those who reverted after the guidance became clear to them—Satan has enticed them and has given them latitude.

26. That is because they said to those who hated what God has revealed, "We will obey you in certain matters." But God knows their secret thoughts.

27. How about when the angels take them at death, beating their faces and their backs?

28. That is because they pursued what displeases God, and they disliked His approval, so He nullified their works.

29. Do those in whose hearts is sickness think that God will not expose their malice?

30. Had We willed, We could have shown them to you, and you would have recognized them by their marks. Yet you will recognize them by their tone of speech. And God knows your actions.

31. We will certainly test you, until We know those among you who strive, and those who are steadfast, and We will test your reactions.

32. Those who disbelieve, and hinder from the path of God, and oppose the Messenger after guidance has become clear to them—they will not hurt God in the least, but He will nullify their deeds.

33. O you who believe! obey God, and obey the Messenger, and do not let your deeds go to waste.

34. Those who disbelieve, and hinder from God's path, and then die as disbelievers—God will not forgive them.

35. So do not waver and call for peace while you have the upper hand. God is with you, and He will not waste your efforts.

36. The life of this word is nothing but play and pastime. But if you have faith and lead a righteous life, He will grant you your rewards, and He will not ask you for your possessions.

37. Were He to ask you for it, and press you, you would become tightfisted, and He would expose your unwillingness.

38. Here you are, being called to spend in the cause of God. Among you are those who withhold; but whoever withholds is withholding against his own soul. God is the Rich, while you are the needy. And if you turn away, He will replace you with another people, and they will not be like you.

48. VICTORY
(al-Fath)

In the name of God,
the Gracious, the Merciful.

1. We have granted you a conspicuous victory.

2. That God may forgive you your sin, past and to come, and complete His favors upon you, and guide you in a straight path.

3. And help you with an unwavering support.

4. It is He who sent down tranquility into the hearts of the believers, to add faith to their faith. To God belong the forces of the heavens and the earth. God is Knowing and Wise.

5. He will admit the believers, male and female, into Gardens beneath which rivers flow, to abide therein forever, and He will remit their sins. That, with God, is a great triumph.

6. And He will punish the hypocrites, male and female, and the idolaters, male and female, those who harbor evil thoughts about God. They are surrounded by evil; and God is angry with them, and has cursed them, and has prepared for them Hell— a miserable destination.

7. To God belong the troops of the heavens and the earth. God is Mighty and Wise.

8. We sent you as a witness, and a bearer of good news, and a warner.

9. That you may believe in God and His Messenger, and support Him, and honor Him, and praise Him morning and evening.

10. Those who pledge allegiance to you are pledging allegiance to God. The hand of God is over their hands. Whoever breaks his pledge breaks it to his own loss. And whoever fulfills his covenant with God, He will grant him a great reward.

11. The Desert-Arabs who remained behind will say to you, "Our belongings and our families have preoccupied us, so ask forgiveness for us." They say with their tongues what is not in their hearts. Say, "Who can avail you anything against God, if He desires loss for you, or desires gain for you?" In fact, God is Informed of what you do.

12. But you thought that the Messenger and the believers will never return to their families, and this seemed fine to your hearts; and you harbored evil thoughts, and were uncivilized people.

13. He who does not believe in God and His Messenger—We have prepared for the disbelievers a Blazing Fire.

14. To God belongs the kingdom of the heavens and the earth. He forgives whomever He wills, and He punishes whomever He wills. God is Forgiving and Merciful.

15. Those who lagged behind will say when you depart to collect the gains, "Let us follow you." They want to change the Word of God. Say, "You will not follow us; God has said so before." Then they will say, "But you are jealous of us." In fact, they understand only a little.

16. Say to the Desert-Arabs who lagged behind, "You will be called against a people of great might; you will fight them, unless they submit. If you obey, God will give you a fine reward. But if you turn away, as you turned away before, He will punish you with a painful punishment."

17. There is no blame on the blind, nor any blame on the lame, nor any blame on the sick. Whoever obeys God and His messenger—He will admit him into gardens beneath which rivers flow; but whoever turns away—He will punish him with a painful punishment.

18. God was pleased with the believers, when they pledged allegiance to you under the tree. He knew what was in their hearts, and He sent down serenity upon them, and He rewarded them with an imminent conquest.

19. And abundant gains for them to capture. God is Mighty and Wise.

20. God has promised you abundant gains, which you will capture. He has expedited this for you, and has restrained people's hands from you; that it may be a sign to the believers, and that He may guide you on a straight path.

21. And other things, of which you were incapable, but God has encompassed them. God is Capable of everything.

22. If those who disbelieve had fought you, they would have turned back and fled, then found neither protector nor helper.

23. It is God's pattern, ongoing since the past. You will never find any change in God's pattern.

24. It is He who withheld their hands from you, and your hands from them, in the valley of Mecca, after giving you advantage over them. God is Observer of what you do.

25. It is they who disbelieved, and barred you from the Sacred Mosque, and prevented the offering from reaching its destination. Were it not for faithful men and faithful women, whom you did not know, you were about to hurt them, and became guilty of an unintentional crime. Thus God admits into His mercy whomever He wills. Had they dispersed, We would have punished those who disbelieved among them with a painful penalty.

26. Those who disbelieved filled their hearts with rage—the rage of the days of ignorance. But God sent His serenity down upon His Messenger, and upon the believers, and imposed on them the words of righteousness—of which they were most worthy and deserving. God is aware of everything.

27. God has fulfilled His Messenger's vision in truth: "You will enter the Sacred Mosque, God willing, in security, heads shaven, or hair cut short, not fearing. He knew what you did not know, has and granted besides that an imminent victory."

28. It is He who sent His Messenger with the guidance and the religion of truth, to make it prevail over all religions. God suffices as Witness.

29. Muhammad is the Messenger of God. Those with him are stern against the disbelievers, yet compassionate amongst themselves. You see them kneeling, prostrating, seeking blessings from God and approval. Their marks are on their faces from the effects of prostration. Such is their description in the Torah, and their description in the Gospel: like a plant that sprouts, becomes strong, grows thick, and rests on its stem, impressing the farmers. Through them He enrages the disbelievers. God has promised those among them who believe and do good deeds forgiveness and a great reward.

49. THE CHAMBERS
(al-Hujurat)

In the name of God,
the Gracious, the Merciful.

1. O you who believe! Do not place your opinions above that of God and His Messenger, and fear God. God is Hearing and Knowing.

2. O you who believe! Do not raise your voices above the voice of the Prophet, and do not speak loudly to him, as you speak loudly to one another, lest your works be in vain without you realizing.

3. Those who lower their voices before God's Messenger—those are they whose hearts God has tested for piety. They will have forgiveness and a great reward.

4. Those who call you from behind the chambers—most of them do not understand.

5. Had they remained patient until you came out to them, it would have been better for them. But God is Forgiving and Merciful.

6. O you who believe! If a troublemaker brings you any news, investigate, lest you harm people out of ignorance, and you become regretful for what you have done.

7. And know that among you is the Messenger of God. Had he obeyed you in many things, you would have suffered hardship. But God has given you the love of faith, and adorned it in your hearts, and made disbelief, mischief, and rebellion hateful to you. These are the rightly guided.

8. A Grace and Favor from God. God is Knowing and Wise.

9. If two groups of believers fight each other, reconcile between them. But if one group aggresses against the other, fight the aggressing group until it complies with God's command. Once it has complied, reconcile between them with justice, and be equitable. God loves the equitable.

10. The believers are brothers, so reconcile between your brothers, and remain conscious of God, so that you may receive mercy.

11. O you who believe! No people shall ridicule other people, for they may be better than they. Nor shall any women ridicule other women, for they may be better than they. Nor shall you slander one another, or insult one another with names. Evil is the return to wickedness after having attained faith. Whoever does not repent—these are the wrongdoers.

12. O you who believe! Avoid most suspicion—some suspicion is sinful. And do not spy on one another, nor backbite one another. Would any of you like to eat the flesh of his dead brother? You would detest it. So remain mindful of God. God is Most Relenting, Most Merciful.

13. O people! We created you from a male and a female, and made you races and tribes, that you may know one another. The best among you in the sight of God is the most righteous. God is All-Knowing, Well-Experienced.

14. The Desert-Arabs say, "We have believed." Say, "You have not believed; but say, 'We have submitted,' for faith has not yet entered into your hearts. But if you obey God and His Messenger, He will not diminish any of your deeds. God is Forgiving and Merciful."

15. The believers are those who believe in God and His Messenger, and then have not doubted, and strive for God's cause with their wealth and their persons. These are the sincere.

16. Say, "Are you going to teach God about your religion, when God knows everything in the heavens and the earth, and God is aware of all things?"

17. They regarded it a favor to you that they have submitted. Say, "Do not consider your submission a favor to me; it is God who has done you a favor by guiding you to the faith, if you are sincere."

18. God knows the secrets of the heavens and the earth, and God is seeing of everything you do.

50. QAF
(Qaf)

In the name of God,
the Gracious, the Merciful.

1. Qaf. By the Glorious Quran.

2. They marveled that a warner has come to them from among them. The disbelievers say, "This is something strange.

3. When we have died and become dust? This is a farfetched return."

4. We know what the earth consumes of them, and with Us is a comprehensive book.

5. But they denied the truth when it has come to them, so they are in a confused state.

6. Have they not observed the sky above them, how We constructed it, and decorated it, and it has no cracks?

7. And the earth, how We spread it out, and set on it mountains, and grew in it all kinds of delightful pairs?

8. A lesson and a reminder for every penitent worshiper.

9. And We brought down from the sky blessed water, and produced with it gardens and grain to harvest.

10. And the soaring palm trees, with clustered dates.

11. As sustenance for the servants. And We revive thereby a dead town. Likewise is the resurrection.

12. Before them the people of Noah denied the truth, and so did the dwellers of Russ, and Thamood.

13. And Aad, and Pharaoh, and the brethren of Lot.

14. And the Dwellers of the Woods, and the people of Tubba. They all rejected the messengers, so My threat came true.

15. Were We fatigued by the first creation? But they are in doubt of a new creation.

16. We created the human being, and We know what his soul whispers to him. We are nearer to him than his jugular vein.

17. As the two receivers receive, seated to the right and to the left.

18. Not a word does he utter, but there is a watcher by him, ready.

19. The daze of death has come in truth: "This is what you tried to evade."

20. And the Trumpet is blown: "This is the Promised Day."

21. And every soul will come forward, accompanied by a driver and a witness.

22. "You were in neglect of this, so We lifted your screen from you, and your vision today is keen."

23. And His escort will say, "This is what I have ready with me."

24. "Throw into Hell every stubborn disbeliever.

25. Preventer of good, aggressor, doubter.

26. Who fabricated another god with God; toss him into the intense agony."

27. His escort will say, "Our Lord, I did not make him rebel, but he was far astray."

28. He will say, "Do not feud in My presence—I had warned you in advance.

29. The decree from Me will not be changed, and I am not unjust to the servants."

30. On the Day when We will say to Hell, "Are you full?" And it will say, "Are there any more?"

31. And Paradise will be brought closer to the pious, not far away.

32. "This is what you were promised—for every careful penitent.

33. Who inwardly feared the Most Gracious, and came with a repentant heart.

34. Enter it in peace. This is the Day of Eternity."

35. Therein they will have whatever they desire—and We have even more.

36. How many generations before them, who were more powerful than they, did We destroy? They explored the lands—was there any escape?

37. In that is a reminder for whoever possesses a heart, or cares to listen and witness.

38. We created the heavens, and the earth, and what is between them, in six days, and no fatigue touched Us.

39. So endure what they say, and proclaim the praises of your Lord before the rising of the sun, and before sunset.

40. And glorify Him during the night, and at the end of devotions.

41. And listen for the Day when the caller calls from a nearby place.

42. The Day when they will hear the Shout in all truth. That is the Day of Emergence.

43. It is We who control life and death, and to Us is the destination.

44. The Day when the earth will crack for them at once. That is an easy gathering for Us.

45. We are fully aware of what they say, and you are not a dictator over them. So remind by the Quran whoever fears My warning.

51. THE SPREADERS
(adh-Dhariyat)

In the name of God,
the Gracious, the Merciful.

1. By the spreaders spreading.

2. And those carrying loads.

3. And those moving gently.

4. And those distributing as commanded.

5. What you are promised is true.

6. Judgment will take place.

7. By the sky that is woven.

8. You differ in what you say.

9. Averted from it is he who is averted.

10. Perish the imposters.

11. Those who are dazed in ignorance.

12. They ask, "When is the Day of Judgment?"

13. The Day they are presented to the Fire.

14. "Taste your ordeal. This is what you used to challenge."

15. But the pious are amidst gardens and springs.

16. Receiving what their Lord has given them. They were virtuous before that.

17. They used to sleep a little at night.

18. And at dawn, they would pray for pardon.

19. And in their wealth, there was a share for the beggar and the deprived.

20. And on earth are signs for the convinced.

21. And within yourselves. Do you not see?

22. And in the heaven is your livelihood, and what you are promised.

23. By the Lord of the heaven and the earth, it is as true as the fact that you speak.

24. Has the story of Abraham's honorable guests reached you?

25. When they entered upon him, they said, "Peace." He said, "Peace, strangers."

26. Then he slipped away to his family, and brought a fatted calf.

27. He set it before them. He said, "Will you not eat?"

28. And he harbored fear of them. They said, "Do not fear," and they announced to

him the good news of a knowledgeable boy.

29. His wife came forward crying. She clasped her face, and said, "A barren old woman?"

30. They said, "Thus spoke your Lord. He is the Wise, the Knowing."

31. He said, "What is your business, O envoys?"

32. They said, "We are sent to a people guilty of sin."

33. "To unleash upon them rocks of clay."

34. "Marked by your Lord for the excessive."

35. We evacuated all the believers who were in it.

36. But found in it only one household of Muslims.

37. And We left a sign therein for those who fear the painful punishment.

38. And in Moses. We sent him to Pharaoh with a clear authority.

39. But he turned away with his warlords, and said, "A sorcerer or a madman."

40. So We seized him and his troops, and threw them into the sea, and He was to blame.

41. And in Aad. We unleashed against them the devastating wind.

42. It spared nothing it came upon, but rendered it like decayed ruins.

43. And in Thamood. They were told, "Enjoy yourselves for a while."

44. But they defied the command of their Lord, so the lightning struck them as they looked on.

45. They could not rise up, nor could they find help.

46. And before that, the people of Noah. They were immoral people.

47. We constructed the universe with power, and We are expanding it.

48. And the earth—We spread it out—How well We prepared it!

49. We created all things in pairs, so that you may reflect and ponder.

50. "So flee towards God. I am to you from Him a clear warner."

51. "And do not set up any other god with God. I am to you from Him a clear warner."

52. Likewise, no messenger came to those before them, but they said, "A sorcerer or a madman."

53. Did they recommend it to one another? In fact, they are rebellious people.

54. So turn away from them; you are not to blame.

55. And remind, for the reminder benefits the believers.

56. I did not create the jinn and the humans except to worship Me.

57. I need no livelihood from them, nor do I need them to feed Me.

58. God is the Provider, the One with Power, the Strong.

59. Those who do wrong will have their turn, like the turn of their counterparts, so let them not rush Me.

60. So woe to those who disbelieve because of that Day of theirs which they are promised.

52. THE MOUNT
(at-Tur)

In the name of God,
the Gracious, the Merciful.

1. By the Mount.

2. And a Book inscribed.

3. In a published scroll.

4. And the frequented House.

5. And the elevated roof.

6. And the seething sea.

7. The punishment of your Lord is coming.

8. There is nothing to avert it.

9. On the Day when the heaven sways in agitation.

10. And the mountains go into motion.

11. Woe on that Day to the deniers.

12. Those who play with speculation.

13. The Day when they are shoved into the Fire of Hell forcefully.

14. "This is the Fire which you used to deny.

15. Is this magic, or do you not see?

16. Burn in it. Whether you are patient, or impatient, it is the same for you. You are only being repaid for what you used to do."

17. But the righteous will be amid gardens and bliss.

18. Enjoying what their Lord has given them, and their Lord has spared them the suffering of Hell.

19. Eat and drink happily, for what you used to do.

20. Relaxing on luxurious furnishings; and We will couple them with gorgeous spouses.

21. Those who believed and their offspring followed them in faith—We will unite them with their offspring, and We will not deprive them of any of their works. Every person is hostage to what he has earned.

22. And We will supply them with fruit, and meat; such as they desire.

23. They will exchange therein a cup; wherein is neither harm, nor sin.

24. Serving them will be youths like hidden pearls.

25. And they will approach one another, inquiring.

26. They will say, "Before this, we were fearful for our families.

27. But God blessed us, and spared us the agony of the Fiery Winds.

28. Before this, we used to pray to Him. He is the Good, the Compassionate."

29. So remind. By the grace of your Lord, you are neither a soothsayer, nor a madman.

30. Or do they say, "A poet—we await for him a calamity of time"?

31. Say, "Go on waiting; I will be waiting with you."

32. Or is it that their dreams compel them to this? Or are they aggressive people?

33. Or do they say, "He made it up"? Rather, they do not believe.

34. So let them produce a discourse like it, if they are truthful.

35. Or were they created out of nothing? Or are they the creators?

36. Or did they create the heavens and the earth? In fact, they are not certain.

37. Or do they possess the treasuries of your Lord? Or are they the controllers?

38. Or do they have a stairway by means of which they listen? Then let their listener produce a clear proof.

39. Or for Him the daughters, and for you the sons?

40. Or do you demand a payment from them, and they are burdened by debt?

41. Or do they know the future, and they are writing it down?

42. Or are they planning a conspiracy? The conspiracy will befall the disbelievers.

43. Or do they have a god besides God? God transcends what they associate.

44. Even if they were to see lumps of the sky falling down, they would say, "A mass of clouds."

45. So leave them until they meet their Day in which they will be stunned.

46. The Day when their ploys will avail them nothing; and they will not be helped.

47. For those who do wrong, there is a punishment besides that; but most of them do not know.

48. So patiently await the decision of your Lord, for you are before Our Eyes; and proclaim the praises of your Lord when you arise.

49. And glorify Him during the night, and at the receding of the stars.

53. THE STAR
(an-Najm)

In the name of God,
the Gracious, the Merciful.

1. By the star as it goes down.

2. Your friend has not gone astray, nor has he erred.

3. Nor does he speak out of desire.

4. It is but a revelation revealed.

5. Taught to him by the Extremely Powerful.

6. The one of vigor. He settled.

7. While he was at the highest horizon.

8. Then he came near, and hovered around.

9. He was within two bows' length, or closer.

10. Then He revealed to His servant what He revealed.

11. The heart did not lie about what it saw.

12. Will you dispute with him concerning what he saw?

13. He saw him on another descent.

14. At the Lotus Tree of the Extremity.

15. Near which is the Garden of Repose.

16. As there covered the Lotus Tree what covered it.

17. The sight did not waver, nor did it exceed.

18. He saw some of the Great Signs of His Lord.

19. Have you considered al-Lat and al-Uzza?

20. And Manat, the third one, the other?

21. Are you to have the males, and He the females?

22. What a bizarre distribution.

23. These are nothing but names, which you have devised, you and your ancestors, for which God sent down no authority. They follow nothing but assumptions, and what the ego desires, even though guidance has come to them from their Lord.

24. Or is the human being to have whatever he desires?

25. To God belong the Last and the First.

26. How many an angel is there in the heavens whose intercession avails nothing, except after God gives permission to whomever He wills, and approves?

27. Those who do not believe in the Hereafter give the angels the names of females.

28. They have no knowledge of that. They only follow assumptions, and assumptions are no substitute for the truth.

29. So avoid him who has turned away from Our remembrance, and desires nothing but the present life.

30. That is the extent of their knowledge. Your Lord knows best who has strayed from His path, and He knows best who has accepted guidance.

31. To God belongs whatever is in the heavens and whatever is on earth. He will repay those who do evil according to their deeds, and recompense those who do good with the best.

32. Those who avoid gross sins and indecencies—except for minor lapses—your Lord is of Vast Forgiveness. He knows you well, ever since He created you from the earth, and ever since you were embryos in your mothers' wombs. So do not acclaim your own virtue; He is fully aware of the righteous.

33. Have you considered him who turned away?

34. And gave a little, and held back?

35. Does he possess knowledge of the unseen, and can therefore foresee?

36. Was he not informed of what is in the Scrolls of Moses?

37. And of Abraham, who fulfilled?

38. That no soul bears the burdens of another soul.

39. And that the human being attains only what he strives for.

40. And that his efforts will be witnessed.

41. Then he will be rewarded for it the fullest reward.

42. And that to your Lord is the finality.

43. And that it is He who causes laughter and weeping.

44. And that it is He who gives death and life.

45. And that it is He who created the two kinds—the male and the female.

46. From a sperm drop, when emitted.

47. And that upon Him is the next existence.

48. And that it is He who enriches and impoverishes.

49. And that it is He who is the Lord of Sirius.

50. And that it is He who destroyed the first Aad.

51. And Thamood, sparing no one.

52. And the people of Noah before that; for they were most unjust and most oppressive.

53. And He toppled the ruined cities.

54. And covered them with whatever covered them.

55. So which of your Lord's marvels can you deny?

56. This is a warning, just like the first warnings.

57. The inevitable is imminent.

58. None besides God can unveil it.

59. Do you marvel at this discourse?

60. And laugh, and do not weep?

61. Lost in your frivolity?

62. So bow down to God, and worship!

54. THE MOON
(al-Qamar)

In the name of God,
the Gracious, the Merciful.

1. The Hour has drawn near, and the moon has split.

2. Yet whenever they see a miracle, they turn away, and say, "Continuous magic."

3. They lied, and followed their opinions, but everything has its time.

4. And there came to them news containing a deterrent.

5. Profound wisdom—but warnings are of no avail.

6. So turn away from them. On the Day when the Caller calls to something terrible.

7. Their eyes humiliated, they will emerge from the graves, as if they were swarming locusts.

8. Scrambling towards the Caller, the disbelievers will say, "This is a difficult Day."

9. Before them the people of Noah disbelieved. They rejected Our servant, and said, "Crazy," and he was rebuked.

10. So he appealed to his Lord, "I am overwhelmed, so help me."

11. So We opened the floodgates of heaven with water pouring down.

12. And We made the earth burst with springs, and the waters met for a purpose already destined.

13. And We carried him on a craft of planks and nails.

14. Sailing before Our eyes; a reward for him who was rejected.

15. And We left it as a sign. Is there anyone who would take heed?

16. So how were My punishment and My warnings?

17. We made the Quran easy to learn. Is there anyone who would learn?

18. Aad denied the truth. So how were My punishment and My warnings?

19. We unleashed upon them a screaming wind, on a day of unrelenting misery.

20. Plucking the people away, as though they were trunks of uprooted palm-trees.

21. So how were My punishment and My warnings?

22. We made the Quran easy to remember. Is there anyone who would remember?

23. Thamood rejected the warnings.

24. They said, "Are we to follow one of us, a human being? We would go astray, and end up in Hell.

25. Was the message given to him, out of all of us? In fact, He is a wicked liar."

26. They will know tomorrow who the wicked liar is.

27. We are sending the she-camel as a test for them; so watch them and be patient.

28. And inform them that the water is to be shared between them; each share of drink made available.

29. But they called their friend, and he dared, and he slaughtered.

30. So how were My punishment and My warnings?

31. We sent against them a single Cry, and they became like crushed hay.

32. We made the Quran easy to understand. Is there anyone who would understand?

33. The people of Lot rejected the warnings.

34. We unleashed upon them a shower of stones, except for the family of Lot; We rescued them at dawn.

35. A blessing from Us. Thus We reward the thankful.

36. He had warned them of Our onslaught, but they dismissed the warnings.

37. They even lusted for his guest, so We obliterated their eyes. "So taste My punishment and My warnings."

38. Early morning brought upon them enduring punishment.

39. So taste My punishment and My warnings.

40. We made the Quran easy to memorize. Is there anyone who would memorize?

41. The warnings also came to the people of Pharaoh.

42. They rejected Our signs, all of them, so We seized them—the seizure of an Almighty Omnipotent.

43. Are your unbelievers better than all those? Or do you have immunity in the scriptures?

44. Or do they say, "We are united, and we will be victorious"?

45. The multitude will be defeated, and they will turn their backs.

46. The Hour is their appointed time—the Hour is more disastrous, and most bitter.

47. The wicked are in confusion and madness.

48. The Day when they are dragged upon their faces into the Fire: "Taste the touch of Saqar."

49. Everything We created is precisely measured.

50. And Our command is but once, like the twinkling of an eye.

51. We have destroyed your likes. Is there anyone who would ponder?

52. Everything they have done is in the Books.

53. Everything, small or large, is written down.

54. The righteous will be amidst gardens and rivers.

55. In an assembly of virtue, in the presence of an Omnipotent King.

55. THE COMPASSIONATE
(ar-Rahman)

In the name of God,
the Gracious, the Merciful.

1. The Compassionate.

2. Has taught the Quran.

3. He created man.

4. And taught him clear expression.

5. The sun and the moon move according to plan.

6. And the stars and the trees prostrate themselves.

7. And the sky, He raised; and He set up the balance.

8. So do not transgress in the balance.

9. But maintain the weights with justice, and do not violate the balance.

10. And the earth, he set up for the creatures.

11. In it are fruits, and palms in clusters.

12. And grains in the blades, and fragrant plants.

13. So which of your Lord's marvels will you deny?

14. He created man from hard clay, like bricks.

15. And created the jinn from a fusion of fire.

16. So which of your Lord's marvels will you deny?

17. Lord of the two Easts and Lord of the two Wests.

18. So which of your Lord's marvels will you deny?

19. He merged the two seas, converging together.

20. Between them is a barrier, which they do not overrun.

21. So which of your Lord's marvels will you deny?

22. From them emerge pearls and coral.

23. So which of your Lord's marvels will you deny?

24. His are the ships, raised above the sea like landmarks.

25. So which of your Lord's marvels will you deny?

26. Everyone upon it is perishing.

27. But will remain the Presence of your Lord, Full of Majesty and Splendor.

28. So which of your Lord's marvels will you deny?

29. Everyone in the heavens and the earth asks Him. Every day He is managing.

30. So which of your Lord's marvels will you deny?

31. We will attend to you, O prominent two.

32. So which of your Lord's marvels will you deny?

33. O society of jinn and humans! If you can pass through the bounds of the heavens and the earth, go ahead and pass. But you will not pass except with authorization.

34. So which of your Lord's marvels will you deny?

35. You will be bombarded with flares of fire and brass, and you will not succeed.

36. So which of your Lord's marvels will you deny?

37. When the sky splits apart, and becomes rose, like paint.

38. So which of your Lord's marvels will you deny?

39. On that Day, no human and no jinn will be asked about his sins.

40. So which of your Lord's marvels will you deny?

41. The guilty will be recognized by their marks; they will be taken by the forelocks and the feet.

42. So which of your Lord's marvels will you deny?

43. This is Hell that the guilty denied.

44. They circulate between it and between a seething bath.

45. So which of your Lord's marvels will you deny?

46. But for him who feared the standing of his Lord are two gardens.

47. So which of your Lord's marvels will you deny?

48. Full of varieties.

49. So which of your Lord's marvels will you deny?

50. In them are two flowing springs.

51. So which of your Lord's marvels will you deny?

52. In them are fruits of every kind, in pairs.

53. So which of your Lord's marvels will you deny?

54. Reclining on furnishings lined with brocade, and the fruits of the two gardens are near at hand.

55. So which of your Lord's marvels will you deny?

56. In them are maidens restraining their glances, untouched before by any man or jinn.

57. So which of your Lord's marvels will you deny?

58. As though they were rubies and corals.

59. So which of your Lord's marvels will you deny?

60. Is the reward of goodness anything but goodness?

61. So which of your Lord's marvels will you deny?

62. And beneath them are two gardens.

63. So which of your Lord's marvels will you deny?

64. Deep green.

65. So which of your Lord's marvels will you deny?

66. In them are two gushing springs.

67. So which of your Lord's marvels will you deny?

68. In them are fruits, and date-palms, and pomegranates.

69. So which of your Lord's marvels will you deny?

70. In them are good and beautiful ones.

71. So which of your Lord's marvels will you deny?

72. Companions, secluded in the tents.

73. So which of your Lord's marvels will you deny?

74. Whom no human has touched before, nor jinn.

75. So which of your Lord's marvels will you deny?

76. Reclining on green cushions, and exquisite carpets.

77. So which of your Lord's marvels will you deny?

78. Blessed be the name of your Lord, Full of Majesty and Splendor.

56. THE INEVITABLE
(al-Waqi'ah)

In the name of God,
the Gracious, the Merciful.

1. When the inevitable occurs.

2. Of its occurrence, there is no denial.

3. Bringing low, raising high.

4. When the earth is shaken with a shock.

5. And the mountains are crushed and crumbled.

6. And they become scattered dust.

7. And you become three classes.

8. Those on the Right—what of those on the Right?

9. And those on the Left—what of those on the Left?

10. And the forerunners, the forerunners.

11. Those are the nearest.

12. In the Gardens of Bliss.

13. A throng from the ancients.

14. And a small band from the latecomers.

15. On luxurious furnishings.

16. Reclining on them, facing one another.

17. Serving them will be immortalized youth.

18. With cups, pitchers, and sparkling drinks.

19. Causing them neither headache, nor intoxication.

20. And fruits of their choice.

21. And meat of birds that they may desire.

22. And lovely companions.

23. The likenesses of treasured pearls.

24. As a reward for what they used to do.

25. Therein they will hear no nonsense, and no accusations.

26. But only the greeting: "Peace, peace."

27. And those on the Right—what of those on the Right?

28. In lush orchards.

29. And sweet-smelling plants.

30. And extended shade.

31. And outpouring water.

32. And abundant fruit.

33. Neither withheld nor forbidden.

34. And uplifted mattresses.

35. We have created them of special creation.

36. And made them virgins.

37. Tender and un-aging.

38. For those on the Right.

39. A throng from the ancients.

40. And a throng from the latecomers.

41. And those on the Left—what of those on the Left?

42. Amid searing wind and boiling water.

43. And a shadow of thick smoke.

44. Neither cool, nor refreshing.

45. They had lived before that in luxury.

46. And they used to persist in immense wrongdoing.

47. And they used to say, "When we are dead and turned into dust and bones, are we to be resurrected?

48. And our ancient ancestors too?"

49. Say, "The first and the last.

50. Will be gathered for the appointment of a familiar Day."

51. Then you, you misguided, who deny the truth.

52. Will be eating from the Tree of Bitterness.

53. Will be filling your bellies with it.

54. Will be drinking on top of it boiling water.

55. Drinking like thirsty camels drink.

56. That is their hospitality on the Day of Retribution.

57. We created you—if only you would believe!

58. Have you seen what you ejaculate?

59. Is it you who create it, or are We the Creator?

60. We have decreed death among you, and We will not be outstripped.

61. In replacing you with your likes, and transforming you into what you do not know.

62. You have known the first formation; if only you would remember.

63. Have you seen what you cultivate?

64. Is it you who make it grow, or are We the Grower?

65. If We will, We can turn it into rubble; then you will lament.

66. "We are penalized.

67. No, we are being deprived."

68. Have you seen the water you drink?

69. Is it you who sent it down from the clouds, or are We the Sender?

70. If We will, We can make it salty. Will you not be thankful?

71. Have you seen the fire you kindle?

72. Is it you who produce its tree, or are We the Producer?

73. We have made it a reminder, and a comfort for the users.

74. So glorify the Name of your Great Lord.

75. I swear by the locations of the stars.

76. It is an oath, if you only knew, that is tremendous.

77. It is a noble Quran.

78. In a well-protected Book.

79. None can grasp it except the purified.

80. A revelation from the Lord of the Worlds.

81. Is it this discourse that you take so lightly?

82. And you make it your livelihood to deny it?

83. So when it has reached the throat.

84. As you are looking on.

85. We are nearer to it than you are, but you do not see.

86. If you are not held to account.

87. Then bring it back, if you are truthful.

88. But if he is one of those brought near.

89. Then happiness, and flowers, and Garden of Delights.

90. And if he is one of those on the Right.

91. Then, "Peace upon you," from those on the Right.

92. But if he is one of the deniers, the mistaken.

93. Then a welcome of Inferno.

94. And burning in Hell.

95. This is the certain truth.

96. So glorify the Name of your Lord, the Magnificent

57. IRON
(al-Hadid`)

In the name of God,
the Gracious, the Merciful.

1. Glorifying God is everything in the heavens and the earth. He is the Almighty, the Wise.

2. To Him belongs the kingdom of the heavens and the earth. He gives life and causes death, and He has power over all things.

3. He is the First and the Last, and the Outer and the Inner, and He has knowledge of all things.

4. It is He who created the heavens and the earth in six days, then settled over the Throne. He knows what penetrates into the earth, and what comes out of it, and what descends from the sky, and what ascends to it. And He is with you wherever you may be. God is Seeing of everything you do.

5. To Him belongs the kingship of the heavens and the earth, and to God all matters are referred.

6. He merges the night into the day, and He merges the day into the night; and He knows what the hearts contains.

7. Believe in God and His Messenger, and spend from what He made you inherit. Those among you who believe and give will have a great reward.

8. What is the matter with you that you do not believe in God, when the Messenger calls you to believe in your Lord, and He has received a pledge from you, if you are believers?

9. It is He who sends down upon His servant clear revelations, to bring you out of darkness into the light. God is Gentle towards you, Most Compassionate.

10. And why is it that you do not spend in the cause of God, when to God belongs the inheritance of the heavens and the earth? Not equal among you are those who contributed before the conquest, and fought. Those are higher in rank than those who contributed afterwards, and fought. But God promises both a good reward. God is Well Experienced in what you do.

11. Who is he who will lend God a loan of goodness, that He may double it for him, and will have a generous reward?

12. On the Day when you see the believing men and believing women—their light radiating ahead of them, and to their right: "Good news for you today: gardens beneath which rivers flow, dwelling therein forever. That is the great triumph."

13. On the Day when the hypocritical men and hypocritical women will say to those who believed, "Wait for us; let us absorb some of your light." It will be said, "Go back behind you, and seek light." A wall will be raised between them, in which is a door; within it is mercy, and outside it is agony.

14. They will call to them, "Were we not with you?" They will say, "Yes, but you cheated your souls, and waited, and doubted, and became deluded by wishful thinking, until the command of God arrived; and arrogance deceived you regarding God.

15. "Therefore, today no ransom will be accepted from you, nor from those who disbelieved. The Fire is your refuge. It is your companion—what an evil fate!"

16. Is it not time for those who believe to surrender their hearts to the remembrance of God, and to the truth that has come down, and not be like those who were given the Book previously, but time became prolonged for them, so their hearts hardened, and many of them are sinners?

17. Know that God revives the earth after its death. We thus explain the revelations for you, so that you may understand.

18. The charitable men and charitable women, who have loaned God a loan of righteousness—it will be multiplied for them, and for them is a generous reward.

19. Those who believe in God and His messengers—these are the sincere and the witnesses with their Lord; they will have their reward and their light. But as for those who disbelieve and deny Our revelations—these are the inmates of the Blaze.

20. Know that the worldly life is only play, and distraction, and glitter, and boasting among you, and rivalry in wealth and children. It is like a rainfall that produces plants, and delights the disbelievers. But then it withers, and you see it yellowing, and then it becomes debris. While in the Hereafter there is severe agony, and forgiveness from God, and acceptance. The life of this world is nothing but enjoyment of vanity.

21. Race towards forgiveness from your Lord; and a Garden as vast as the heavens and the earth, prepared for those who believe in God and His messengers. That is the grace of God; He bestows it on whomever He wills. God is the Possessor of Immense Grace.

22. No calamity occurs on earth, or in your souls, but it is in a Book, even before We make it happen. This is easy for God.

23. That you may not sorrow over what eludes you, nor exult over what He has given you. God does not love the proud snob.

24. Those who are stingy, and induce people to be stingy. Whoever turns away—God is the Independent, the Praiseworthy.

25. We sent Our messengers with the clear proofs, and We sent down with them the Book and the Balance, that humanity may uphold justice. And We sent down iron, in which is violent force, and benefits for humanity. That God may know who supports Him and His Messengers invisibly. God is Strong and Powerful.

26. We sent Noah and Abraham, and established in their line Prophethood and the Scripture. Some of them are guided, but many of them are sinners.

27. Then We sent in their wake Our messengers, and followed up with Jesus son of Mary, and We gave him the Gospel, and instilled in the hearts of those who followed him compassion and mercy. But as for the monasticism which they invented—We did not ordain it for them—only to seek God's approval. But they did not observe it with its due observance. So We gave those of them who believed their reward, but many of them are sinful.

28. O you who believe! Fear God, and believe in His Messenger: He will give you a double portion of His mercy, and will give you a light by which you walk, and will forgive you. God is Forgiving and Merciful.

29. That the People of the Book may know that they have no power whatsoever over God's grace, and that all grace is in God's hand; He gives it to whomever He wills. God is Possessor of Great Grace.

58. THE ARGUMENT
(al-Mujadilah)

In the name of God,
the Gracious, the Merciful.

1. God has heard the statement of she who argued with you concerning her husband, as she complained to God. God heard your conversation. God is Hearing and Seeing.

2. Those of you who estrange their wives by equating them with their mothers—they are not their mothers. Their mothers are none else but those who gave birth to them. What they say is evil, and a blatant lie. But God is Pardoning and Forgiving.

3. Those who estrange their wives by equating them with their mothers, then go back on what they said, must set free a slave before they may touch one another. To this you are exhorted, and God is well aware of what you do.

4. But whoever cannot find the means must fast for two consecutive months before they may touch one another. And if he is unable, then the feeding of sixty needy people. This, in order that you affirm your faith in God and His Messenger. These are the ordinances of God. The unbelievers will have a painful punishment.

5. Those who oppose God and His Messenger will be subdued, as those before them were subdued. We have revealed clear messages. The unbelievers will have a demeaning punishment.

6. On the Day when God resurrects them all, and informs them of what they did. God has kept count of it, but they have forgotten it. God is Witness over everything.

7. Do you not realize that God knows everything in the heavens and everything on earth? There is no secret counsel between three, but He is their fourth; nor between five, but He is their sixth; nor less than that, nor more, but He is with them wherever they may be. Then, on the Day of Resurrection, He will inform them of what they did. God has knowledge of everything.

8. Have you noted those who were prohibited from conspiring secretly, but then reverted to what they were prohibited from? They conspire to commit sin, and aggression, and defiance of the Messenger. And when they come to you, they greet you with a greeting that God never greeted you with. And they say within themselves, "Why does God not punish us for what we say?" Hell is enough for them. They will roast in it. What a miserable destiny!

9. O you who believe! When you converse secretly, do not converse in sin, and aggression, and disobedience of the Messenger; but converse in virtue and piety; And fear God, to Whom you will be gathered.

10. Conspiracies are from Satan, that he may dishearten those who believe; but he will not harm them in the least, except by leave of God. So let the believers put their trust in God.

11. O you who believe! When you are told to make room in your gatherings, make room; God will make room for you. And when you are told to disperse, disperse. God elevates those among you who believe, and those given knowledge, many steps. God is Aware of what you do.

12. O you who believe! When you converse privately with the Messenger, offer something in charity before your conversation. That is better for you, and purer. But if you do not find the means—God is Forgiving and Merciful.

13. Are you reluctant to offer charity before your conversation? If you do not do so, and God pardons you, then perform the prayer, and give alms, and obey God and His Messenger. God is Aware of what you do.

14. Have you considered those who befriended a people with whom God has become angry? They are not of you, nor of them. And they swear to a lie while they know.

15. God has prepared for them a terrible punishment. Evil is what they used to do.

16. They took their oaths as a screen, and prevented others from God's path. They will have a shameful punishment.

17. Neither their possessions nor their children will avail them anything against God. These are the inhabitants of the Fire, dwelling therein forever.

18. On the Day when God will resurrect them altogether—they will swear to Him, as they swear to you, thinking that they are upon something. Indeed, they themselves are the liars.

19. Satan has taken hold of them, and so caused them to forget the remembrance of God. These are the partisans of Satan. Indeed, it is Satan's partisans who are the losers.

20. Those who oppose God and His Messenger are among the lowliest.

21. God has written: "I will certainly prevail, I and My messengers." God is Strong and Mighty.

22. You will not find a people who believe in God and the Last Day, loving those who oppose God and His Messenger, even if they were their parents, or their children, or their siblings, or their close relatives. These—He has inscribed faith in their hearts, and has supported them with a spirit from Him. And He will admit them into Gardens beneath which rivers flow, wherein they will dwell forever. God is pleased with them, and they are pleased with Him. These are the partisans of God. Indeed, it is God's partisans who are the successful.

59. THE MOBILIZATION
(al-Hashr)

In the name of God,
the Gracious, the Merciful.

1. Glorifying God is all that exists in the heavens and the earth. He is the Almighty, the Most Wise.

2. It is He who evicted those who disbelieved among the People of the Book from their homes at the first mobilization. You did not think they would leave, and they thought their fortresses would protect them from God. But God came at them from where they never expected, and threw terror into their hearts. They wrecked their homes with their own hands, and by the hands of the believers. Therefore, take a lesson, O you who have insight.

3. Had God not decreed exile for them, He would have punished them in this life. But in the Hereafter they will have the punishment of the Fire.

4. That is because they opposed God and His Messenger. Whoever opposes God—God is stern in retribution.

5. Whether you cut down a tree, or leave it standing on its trunk, it is by God's will. He will surely disgrace the sinners.

6. Whatever God has bestowed upon His Messenger from them; you spurred neither horse nor camel for them, but God gives authority to His messengers over whomever He will. God is Able to do all things.

7. Whatever God restored to His Messenger from the inhabitants of the villages belongs to God, and to the Messenger, and to the relatives, and to the orphans, and to the poor, and to the wayfarer; so that it may not circulate solely between the wealthy among you. Whatever the Messenger gives you, accept it; and whatever he forbids you, abstain from it. And fear God. God is severe in punishment.

8. To the poor refugees who were driven out of their homes and their possessions, as they sought the favor of God and His approval, and came to the aid of God and His Messenger. These are the sincere.

9. And those who, before them, had settled in the homeland, and had accepted faith. They love those who emigrated to them, and find no hesitation in their hearts in helping them. They give them priority over themselves, even if they themselves are needy. Whoever is protected from his natural greed—it is they who are the successful.

10. And those who came after them, saying, "Our Lord, forgive us, and our brethren who preceded us in faith, and leave no malice in our hearts towards those who believe. Our Lord, You are Clement and Merciful."

11. Have you not considered those who act hypocritically? They say to their brethren who disbelieved among the People of the Book, "If you are evicted, we will leave with you, and will not obey anyone against

you; and should anyone fight you, we will certainly support you." But God bears witness that they are liars.

12. If they are evicted, they will not leave with them; and if anyone fights them, they will not support them; and if they go to their aid, they will turn their backs and flee; then they will receive no support.

13. Fear of you is more intense in their hearts than fear of God. That is because they are a people who do not understand.

14. They will not fight you all together except from fortified strongholds, or from behind walls. Their hostility towards each other is severe. You would think they are united, but their hearts are diverse. That is because they are a people who do not understand.

15. Like those shortly before them. They experienced the consequences of their decisions. For them is a painful punishment.

16. Like the devil, when he says to the human being, "Disbelieve." But when he has disbelieved, he says, "I am innocent of you; I fear God, the Lord of the Worlds."

17. The ultimate end for both of them is the Fire, where they will dwell forever. Such is the requital for the wrongdoers.

18. O you who believe! Fear God, and let every soul consider what it has forwarded for the morrow, and fear God. God is Aware of what you do.

19. And do not be like those who forgot God, so He made them forget themselves. These are the sinners.

20. Not equal are the inhabitants of the Fire and the inhabitants of Paradise. It is the inhabitants of Paradise who are the winners.

21. Had We sent this Quran down on a mountain, you would have seen it trembling, crumbling in awe of God. These parables We cite for the people, so that they may reflect.

22. He is God. There is no god but He, the Knower of secrets and declarations. He is the Compassionate, the Merciful.

23. He is God; besides Whom there is no god; the Sovereign, the Holy, the Peace-Giver, the Faith-Giver, the Overseer, the Almighty, the Omnipotent, the Overwhelming. Glory be to God, beyond what they associate.

24. He is God; the Creator, the Maker, the Designer. His are the Most Beautiful Names. Whatever is in the heavens and the earth glorifies Him. He is the Majestic, the Wise.

60. THE WOMAN TESTED
(al-Mumtahina)

In the name of God,
the Gracious, the Merciful.

1. O you who believe! Do not take My enemies and your enemies for supporters, offering them affection, when they have disbelieved in what has come to you of the Truth. They have expelled the Messenger, and you, because you believed in God, your Lord. If you have mobilized to strive for My cause, seeking My approval, how can you secretly love them? I know what you conceal and what you reveal. Whoever among you does that has strayed from the right way.

2. Whenever they encounter you, they treat you as enemies, and they stretch their hands and tongues against you with malice. They wish that you would disbelieve.

3. Neither your relatives nor your children will benefit you on the Day of Resurrection. He will separate between you. God is Observant of what you do.

4. You have had an excellent example in Abraham and those with him; when they said to their people, "We are quit of you, and what you worship apart from God. We denounce you. Enmity and hatred has surfaced between us and you, forever, until you believe in God alone." Except for the words of Abraham to his father, "I will ask forgiveness for you, though I have no power from God to do anything for you." "Our Lord, in You we trust, and to You we repent, and to You is the ultimate resort.

5. Our Lord, do not make us a target for those who disbelieve, and forgive us, our Lord. You are indeed the Mighty and Wise."

6. There is an excellent example in them for you—for anyone who seeks God and the Last Day. But whoever turns away—God is the Self-Sufficient, the Most Praised.

7. Perhaps God will plant affection between you and those of them you consider enemies. God is Capable. God is Forgiving and Merciful.

8. As for those who have not fought against you for your religion, nor expelled you from your homes, God does not prohibit you from dealing with them kindly and equitably. God loves the equitable.

9. But God prohibits you from befriending those who fought against you over your religion, and expelled you from your homes, and aided in your expulsion. Whoever takes them for friends—these are the wrongdoers.

10. O you who believe! When believing women come to you emigrating, test them. God is Aware of their faith. And if you find them to be faithful, do not send them back to the unbelievers. They are not lawful for them, nor are they lawful for them. But give them what they have spent. You are not at fault if you marry them, provided you give them their compensation. And do not hold on to ties with unbelieving women, but demand what you have spent, and let them demand what they have spent. This is the rule of God; He rules among you. God is Knowing and Wise.

11. If any of your wives desert you to the unbelievers, and you decide to penalize them, give those whose wives have gone away the equivalent of what they had spent. And fear God, in whom you are believers.

12. O prophet! If believing women come to you, pledging allegiance to you, on condition that they will not associate anything with God, nor steal, nor commit adultery, nor kill their children, nor commit perjury as to parenthood, nor disobey you in anything righteous, accept their allegiance and ask God's forgiveness for them. God is Forgiving and Merciful.

13. O you who believe! Do not befriend people with whom God has become angry, and have despaired of the Hereafter, as the faithless have despaired of the occupants of the graves.

61. COLUMN
(as-Saff)

In the name of God,
the Gracious, the Merciful.

1. Everything in the heavens and the earth praises God. He is the Almighty, the Wise.

2. O you who believe! Why do you say what you do not do?

3. It is most hateful to God that you say what you do not do.

4. God loves those who fight in His cause, in ranks, as though they were a compact structure.

5. When Moses said to his people, "O my people, why do you hurt me, although you know that I am God's Messenger to you?" And when they swerved, God swerved their hearts. God does not guide the sinful people.

6. And when Jesus son of Mary said, "O Children of Israel, I am God's Messenger to you, confirming what preceded me of the Torah, and announcing good news of a messenger who will come after me, whose name is Ahmad." But when he showed them the miracles, they said, "This is obvious sorcery."

7. And who is a greater wrongdoer than he who attributes falsehoods to God, when he is being invited to Islam? God does not guide the wrongdoing people.

8. They want to extinguish God's Light with their mouths; but God will complete His Light, even though the disbelievers dislike it.

9. It is He who sent His Messenger with the guidance and the true religion, to make it prevail over all religions, even though the idolaters dislike it.

10. O you who believe! Shall I inform you of a trade that will save you from a painful torment?

11. That you believe in God and His Messenger, and strive in the cause of God with your possessions and yourselves. That is best for you, if you only knew.

12. He will forgive you your sins; and will admit you into gardens beneath which rivers flow, and into beautiful mansions in the Gardens of Eden. That is the supreme success.

13. And something else you love: support from God, and imminent victory. So give good news to the believers.

14. O you who believe! Be supporters of God, as Jesus son of Mary said to the disciples, "Who are my supporters towards God?" The disciples said, "We are God's supporters." So a group of the Children of Israel believed, while another group disbelieved. We supported those who believed against their foe, so they became dominant.

62. FRIDAY
(al-Jumu'ah)

In the name of God,
the Gracious, the Merciful.

1. Everything in the heavens and the earth glorifies God the Sovereign, the Holy, the Almighty, the Wise.

2. It is He who sent among the unlettered a messenger from themselves; reciting His revelations to them, and purifying them, and teaching them the Scripture and wisdom; although they were in obvious error before that.

3. And others from them, who have not yet joined them. He is the Glorious, the Wise.

4. That is God's grace, which He grants to whomever He wills. God is Possessor of limitless grace.

5. The example of those who were entrusted with the Torah, but then failed to uphold it, is like the donkey carrying works of literature. Miserable is the example of the people who denounce God's revelations. God does not guide the wrongdoing people.

6. Say, "O you who follow Judaism; if you claim to be the chosen of God, to the exclusion of the rest of mankind, then wish for death if you are sincere."

7. But they will not wish for it, ever, due to what their hands have advanced. God knows well the wrongdoers.

8. Say, "The death from which you flee will catch up with you; then you will be returned to the Knower of the Invisible and the Visible, and He will inform you of what you used to do."

9. O you who believe! When the call is made for prayer on Congregation Day, hasten to the remembrance of God, and drop all business. That is better for you, if you only knew.

10. Then, when the prayer is concluded, disperse through the land, and seek God's bounty, and remember God much, so that you may prosper.

11. Yet whenever they come across some business, or some entertainment, they scramble towards it, and leave you standing. Say, "What is with God is better than entertainment and business; and God is the Best of providers."

63. THE HYPOCRITES
(al-Munafiqun)

In the name of God,
the Gracious, the Merciful.

1. When the hypocrites come to you, they say, "We bear witness that you are God's Messenger." God knows that you are His Messenger, and God bears witness that the hypocrites are liars.

2. They treat their oaths as a cover, and so they repel others from God's path. Evil is what they do.

3. That is because they believed, and then disbelieved; so their hearts were sealed, and they cannot understand.

4. When you see them, their appearance impresses you. And when they speak, you listen to what they say. They are like propped-up timber. They think every shout is aimed at them. They are the enemy, so beware of them. God condemns them; how deluded they are!

5. And when it is said to them, "Come, the Messenger of God will ask forgiveness for you," they bend their heads, and you see them turning away arrogantly.

6. It is the same for them, whether you ask forgiveness for them, or do not ask forgiveness for them; God will not forgive them. God does not guide the sinful people.

7. It is they who say: "Do not spend anything on those who side with God's Messenger, unless they have dispersed." To God belong the treasures of the heavens and the earth, but the hypocrites do not understand.

8. They say, "If we return to the City, the more powerful therein will evict the weak." But power belongs to God, and His Messenger, and the believers; but the hypocrites do not know.

9. O you who believe! Let neither your possessions nor your children distract you from the remembrance of God. Whoever does that—those are the losers.

10. And give from what We have provided for you, before death approaches one of you, and he says, "My Lord, if only You would delay me for a short while, so that I may be charitable, and be one of the righteous."

11. But God will not delay a soul when its time has come. God is Informed of what you do.

64. GATHERING
(at-Taghabun)

In the name of God,

the Gracious, the Merciful.

1. Everything in the heavens and the earth praises God. To Him belongs the Kingdom, and to Him all praise is due, and He is Able to do all things.

2. It is He who created you. Some of you are unbelievers, and some of you are believers. And God perceives what you do.

3. He created the heavens and the earth with truth, and He designed you, and designed you well, and to Him is the final return.

4. He knows everything in the heavens and the earth, and He knows what you conceal and what you reveal. And God knows what is within the hearts.

5. Has the news not reached you, of those who disbelieved before? They tasted the ill consequences of their conduct, and a painful torment awaits them.

6. That is because their messengers came to them with clear explanations, but they said, "Are human beings going to guide us?" So they disbelieved and turned away. But God is in no need. God is Independent and Praiseworthy.

7. Those who disbelieve claim that they will not be resurrected. Say, "Yes indeed, by my Lord, you will be resurrected; then you will be informed of everything you did; and that is easy for God."

8. So believe in God and His Messenger, and the Light which We sent down. God is Aware of everything you do.

9. The Day when He gathers you for the Day of Gathering—that is the Day of Mutual Exchange. Whoever believes in God and acts with integrity, He will remit his misdeeds, and will admit him into gardens beneath which rivers flow, to dwell therein forever. That is the supreme achievement.

10. But as for those who disbelieve and denounce Our revelations—these are the inmates of the Fire, dwelling therein forever; and what a miserable fate!

11. No disaster occurs except by God's leave. Whoever believes in God, He guides his heart. God is Aware of everything.

12. So obey God, and obey the Messenger. But if you turn away—it is only incumbent on Our Messenger to deliver the clear message.

13. God, there is no god but He; and in God let the believers put their trust.

14. O you who believe! Among your wives and your children are enemies to you, so beware of them. But if you pardon, and overlook, and forgive—God is Forgiver and Merciful.

15. Your possessions and your children are a test, but with God is a splendid reward.

16. So be conscious of God as much as you can, and listen, and obey, and give for your own good. He who is protected from his stinginess—these are the prosperous.

17. If you lend God a good loan, He will multiply it for you, and will forgive you. God is Appreciative and Forbearing.

18. The Knower of the Unseen and the Seen, the Almighty, the Wise.

65. DIVORCE
(at-Talaq)

In the name of God,
the Gracious, the Merciful.

1. O Prophet! If any of you divorce women, divorce them during their period of purity, and calculate their term. And be pious before God, your Lord. And do not evict them from their homes, nor shall they leave, unless they have committed a proven adultery. These are the limits of

God—whoever oversteps God's limits has wronged his own soul. You never know; God may afterwards bring about a new situation.

2. Once they have reached their term, either retain them honorably, or separate from them honorably. And call to witness two just people from among you, and give upright testimony for God. By that is exhorted whoever believes in God and the Last Day. And whoever fears God—He will make a way out for him.

3. And will provide for him from where he never expected. Whoever relies on God—He will suffice him. God will accomplish His purpose. God has set a measure to all things.

4. As for those of your women who have reached menopause, if you have any doubts, their term shall be three months—and also for those who have not yet menstruated. As for those who are pregnant, their term shall be until they have delivered. Whoever fears God—He will make things easy for him.

5. This is the ordinance of God, which He sent down to you. Whoever fears God—He will remit his sins, and will amplify his reward.

6. Allow them to reside where you reside, according to your means, and do not harass them in order to make things difficult for them. If they are pregnant, spend on them until they give birth. And if they nurse your infant, give them their payment, and conduct your relation in amity. But if you disagree, then let another woman nurse him.

7. The wealthy shall spend according to his means; and he whose resources are restricted shall spend according to what God has given him. God never burdens a soul beyond what He has given it. God will bring ease after hardship.

8. How many a town defied the command of its Lord and His messengers? So We held it strictly accountable, and We punished it with a dreadful punishment.

9. It tasted the result of its decisions, and the outcome of its decisions was perdition.

10. God has prepared for them a severe retribution. So beware of God, O you who possess intellect and have faith. God has sent down to you a Reminder.

11. A messenger who recites to you God's Verses, clear and distinct, that he may bring those who believe and work righteousness from darkness into light. Whoever believes in God and acts with integrity, He will admit him into gardens beneath which rivers flow, therein to abide forever. God has given him an excellent provision.

12. God is He Who created seven heavens, and their like of earth. The command descends through them, so that you may know that God is Capable of everything, and that God Encompasses everything in knowledge.

66. PROHIBITION
(at-Tahrim)

In the name of God,
the Gracious, the Merciful.

1. O prophet! Why do you prohibit what God has permitted for you, seeking to please your wives? God is Forgiving and Merciful.

2. God has decreed for you the dissolution of your oaths. God is your Master. He is the All-Knowing, the Most Wise.

3. The Prophet told something in confidence to one of his wives. But when she disclosed it, and God made it known to

him; he communicated part of it, and he avoided another part. Then, when he informed her of it, she said, "Who informed you of this?" He said, "The All-Knowing, the All-Informed, informed me."

4. If you repent to God, then your hearts have listened. But if you band together against him, then God is his Ally, as is Gabriel, and the righteous believers. In addition, the angels will assist him.

5. Perhaps, if he divorces you, his Lord will give him in exchange wives better than you: submissive, believing, obedient, penitent, devout, fasting—previously married, or virgins.

6. O you who believe! Protect yourselves and your families from a Fire, whose fuel is people and stones. Over it are angels, fierce and powerful. They never disobey God in anything He commands them, and they carry out whatever they are commanded.

7. O you who disbelieved! Make no excuses today. You are being repaid for what you used to do.

8. O you who believe! Repent to God with sincere repentance. Perhaps your Lord will remit your sins, and admit you into gardens beneath which rivers flow, on the Day when God will not disappoint the Prophet and those who believed with him. Their light streaming before them and to their right, they will say, "Our Lord, complete our light for us, and forgive us; You are capable of all things."

9. O prophet! Strive hard against the disbelievers and the hypocrites, and be stern with them. Their abode is Hell. What a miserable destination!

10. God illustrates an example of those who disbelieve: the wife of Noah and the wife of Lot. They were under two of Our righteous servants, but they betrayed them.

They availed them nothing against God, and it was said, "Enter the Fire with those who are entering."

11. And God illustrates an example of those who believe: the wife of Pharaoh, when she said, "My Lord, build for me, with you, a house in Paradise, and save me from Pharaoh and his works, and save me from the wrongdoing people."

12. And Mary, the daughter of Imran, who guarded her womb, and so We breathed into her of Our Spirit; and she believed in the truth of her Lord's Words and His Books, and was one of the devout.

67. SOVEREIGNTY
(al-Mulk)

In the name of God,
the Gracious, the Merciful.

1. Blessed is He in whose hand is the sovereignty, and Who has power over everything.

2. He who created death and life—to test you—as to which of you is better in conduct. He is the Almighty, the Forgiving.

3. He who created seven heavens in layers. You see no discrepancy in the creation of the Compassionate. Look again. Can you see any cracks?

4. Then look again, and again, and your sight will return to you dazzled and exhausted.

5. We have adorned the lower heaven with lanterns, and made them missiles against the devils; and We have prepared for them the punishment of the Blaze.

6. For those who reject their Lord, there is the torment of Hell. What an evil destination!

7. When they are thrown into it, they will hear it roaring, as it seethes.

8. It almost bursts with fury. Every time a batch is thrown into it, its keepers will ask them, "Has no warner come to you?"

9. They will say, "Yes, a warner did come to us, but we disbelieved, and said, 'God did not send down anything; you are very much mistaken.'"

10. And they will say, "Had we listened or reasoned, we would not have been among the inmates of the Blaze."

11. So they will acknowledge their sins. So away with the inmates of the Blaze.

12. As for those who fear their Lord in secret—for them is forgiveness and a great reward.

13. Whether you keep your words secret, or declare them—He is Aware of the inner thoughts.

14. Would He not know, He Who created? He is the Refined, the Expert.

15. It is He who made the earth manageable for you, so travel its regions, and eat of His provisions. To Him is the Resurgence.

16. Are you confident that the One in heaven will not cause the earth to collapse beneath you as it spins?

17. Or are you confident that the One in Heaven will not unleash against you a violent storm? Then you will know what My warning is like.

18. Those before them also denied the truth; and how was My disapproval?

19. Have they not seen the birds above them, spreading their wings, and folding them? None holds them except the Compassionate. He is Perceiver of everything.

20. Or who is this who is a force for you to protect you against the Compassionate? The disbelievers are in nothing but delusion.

21. Or who is this that will provide for you, if He withholds His provision? Yet they persist in defiance and aversion.

22. Is he who walks bent on his own design better guided, or he who walks upright on a straight path?

23. Say, "It is He who produced you; and made for you the hearing, and the vision, and the organs. But rarely do you give thanks."

24. Say, "It is He who scattered you on earth, and to Him you will be rounded up."

25. And they say, "When will this promise be fulfilled, if you are truthful?"

26. Say, "Knowledge is with God, and I am only a clear warner."

27. But when they see it approaching, the faces of those who disbelieved will turn gloomy, and it will be said, "This is what you used to call for."

28. Say, "Have you considered? Should God make me perish, and those with me; or else He bestows His mercy on us; who will protect the disbelievers from an agonizing torment?"

29. Say, "He is the Compassionate. We have faith in Him, and in Him we trust. Soon you will know who is in evident error."

30. Say, "Have you considered? If your water drains away, who will bring you pure running water?"

68. THE PEN
(al-Qalam)

In the name of God,
the Gracious, the Merciful.

1. Noon. By the pen, and by what they inscribe.

2. By the grace of your Lord, you are not insane.

3. In fact, you will have a reward that will never end.

4. And you are of a great moral character.

5. You will see, and they will see.

6. Which of you is the afflicted.

7. Your Lord knows best who has strayed from His path, and He knows best the well-guided.

8. So do not obey the deniers.

9. They would like you to compromise, so they would compromise.

10. And do not obey any vile swearer.

11. Backbiter, spreader of slander.

12. Preventer of good, transgressor, sinner.

13. Rude and fake besides.

14. Just because he has money and children.

15. When Our Verses are recited to him, he says, "Myths of the ancients!"

16. We will brand him on the muzzle.

17. We tested them, as We tested the owners of the garden; when they vowed to harvest it in the morning.

18. Without any reservation.

19. But a calamity from your Lord went around it while they slept.

20. And in the morning it was as if picked.

21. In the morning, they called to one another.

22. "Go early to your plantation, if you are going to harvest."

23. So off they went, murmuring to one another.

24. "No poor person is to enter it upon you today."

25. And early they went, resolved in intent.

26. But when they saw it, they said, "We were wrong.

27. We are now deprived."

28. The most reasonable of them said, "Did I not say to you, 'if only you would glorify?'"

29. They said, "Glory to our Lord—We were indeed in the wrong."

30. Then they turned to one another, blaming one another.

31. They said, "Woe to us—we were indeed domineering.

32. Perhaps our Lord will give us a better substitute for it. We are truly turning to our Lord."

33. Such is the punishment; but the punishment of the Hereafter is greater, if they only knew.

34. For the righteous are Gardens of Delight with their Lord.

35. Shall We treat the Muslims like the villains?

36. What is the matter with you? How do you judge?

37. Or do you have a scripture in which you study.

38. Wherein there is whatever you choose?

39. Or do you have oaths from Us, binding until the Day of Resurrection, that you will have whatever you demand?

40. Ask them, which of them will guarantee that.

41. Or do they have partners? Then let them produce their partners, if they are truthful.

42. On the Day when the Shin will be exposed, and they will be called to bow down, but they will be unable.

43. Their eyes subdued, shame will cover them. They were invited to bow down when they were sound.

44. So leave Me to those who reject this discourse; We will proceed against them gradually, from where they do not know.

45. And I will give them respite. My plan is firm.

46. Or do you ask them for a fee, so they are burdened with debt?

47. Or do they know the future, and so they write it down?

48. So wait patiently for the Decision of your Lord, and do not be like the Fellow of the Fish who cried out in despair.

49. Were it not for his Lord's favor that reached him, he would have been thrown into the wilderness, fully despised.

50. But his Lord chose him, and made him one of the righteous.

51. Those who disbelieve almost stab you with their glances when they hear the message, and say, "He is crazy!"

52. But it is no less than a reminder to all the Worlds.

69. THE REALITY
(al-Haqqah)

In the name of God,
the Gracious, the Merciful.

1. The Reality.

2. What is the Reality?

3. What will make you understand what the Reality is?

4. Thamood and Aad denied the Catastrophe.

5. As for Thamood, they were annihilated by the Overwhelming.

6. And as for Aad; they were annihilated by a furious, roaring wind.

7. He unleashed it upon them for seven nights and eight days, in succession. You could see the people tossed around, as though they were stumps of hollow palm-trees.

8. Can you see any remnant of them?

9. Then Pharaoh came, and those before him, and the Overturned Cities steeped in sin.

10. But they disobeyed the messenger of their Lord, so He seized them with an overpowering grip.

11. When the waters overflowed, We carried you in the cruising ship.

12. To make it a lesson for you—so that retaining ears may retain it.

13. Then, when the Trumpet is sounded a single time.

14. And the earth and the mountains are lifted up, and crushed, with a single crush.

15. On that Day, the Event will come to pass.

16. And the heaven will crack; so on that Day it will be frail.

17. And the angels will be ranged around its borders, while eight will be carrying the Throne of your Lord above them that Day.

18. On that Day you will be exposed, and no secret of yours will remain hidden.

19. As for him who is given his book in his right hand, he will say, "Here, take my book and read it.

20. I knew I would be held accountable."

21. So he will be in pleasant living.

22. In a lofty Garden.

23. Its pickings are within reach.

24. "Eat and drink merrily for what you did in the days gone by."

25. But as for him who is given his book in his left hand, he will say, "I wish I was never given my book.

26. And never knew what my account was.

27. If only it was the end.

28. My money cannot avail me.

29. My power has vanished from me."

30. "Take him and shackle him.

31. Then scorch him in the Blaze.

32. Then in a chain which length is seventy cubits tie him up.

33. For he would not believe in God the Great.

34. Nor would he advocate the feeding of the destitute.

35. So he has no friend here today.

36. And no food except scum.

37. Which only the sinners eat."

38. Indeed, I swear by what you see.

39. And by what you do not see.

40. It is the speech of a noble messenger.

41. And it is not the speech of a poet—little do you believe.

42. Nor is it the speech of a soothsayer—little do you take heed.

43. It is a revelation from the Lord of the Worlds.

44. Had he falsely attributed some statements to Us.

45. We would have seized him by the right arm.

46. Then slashed his lifeline.

47. And none of you could have restrained Us from him.

48. Surely, it is a message for the righteous.

49. And We know that some of you will reject it.

50. And it is surely a source of grief for the unbelievers.

51. Yet it is the absolute truth.

52. So glorify the name of your Lord, the Magnificent.

70. WAYS OF ASCENT
(al-Ma'arij)

*In the name of God,
the Gracious, the Merciful.*

1. A questioner questioned the imminent torment.

2. For the disbelievers; none can repel it.

3. From God, Lord of the Ways of Ascent.

4. Unto Him the angels and the Spirit ascend on a Day the duration of which is fifty thousand years.

5. So be patient, with sweet patience.

6. They see it distant.

7. But We see it near.

8. On the Day when the sky will be like molten brass.

9. And the mountains will be like tufted wool.

10. No friend will care about his friend.

11. They will be shown each other. The criminal wishes he would be redeemed from the punishment of that Day by his children.

12. And his spouse, and his brother.

13. And his family that sheltered him.

14. And everyone on earth, in order to save him.

15. By no means! It is a Raging Fire.

16. It strips away the scalps.

17. It invites him who once turned his back and fled.

18. And accumulated and hoarded.

19. Man was created restless.

20. Touched by adversity, he is fretful.

21. Touched by good, he is ungenerous.

22. Except the prayerful.

23. Those who are constant at their prayers.

24. And those in whose wealth is a rightful share.

25. For the beggar and the deprived.

26. And those who affirm the Day of Judgment.

27. And those who fear the punishment of their Lord.

28. Their Lord's punishment is not to be taken for granted.

29. And those who guard their chastity.

30. Except from their spouses or those living under their control, for then they are free of blame.

31. But whoever seeks to go beyond that— these are the transgressors.

32. And those who honor their trusts and their pledges.

33. And those who stand by their testimonies.

34. And those who are dedicated to their prayers.

35. These will be honored in Gardens.

36. What is with those who disbelieve, stretching their necks towards you.

37. From the right, and from the left, banding together?

38. Is every one of them aspiring to be admitted into a Garden of Bliss?

39. No indeed! We created them from what they know.

40. I swear by the Lord of the Easts and the Wests, that We are Able.

41. To replace them with better than they, and We are not to be outdone.

42. So leave them to blunder and play, until they meet their Day which they are promised.

43. The Day when they will emerge from the tombs in a rush, as though they were hurrying towards a target.

44. Their eyes cast down; overwhelmed by humiliation. This is the Day which they were promised.

71. NOAH
(Nuh)

In the name of God,
the Gracious, the Merciful.

1. We sent Noah to his people: "Warn your people before there comes upon them a painful punishment."

2. He said, "O my people, I am to you a clear warner.

3. Worship God and reverence Him, and obey me.

4. And He will forgive you of your sins, and reprieve you until a stated term. God's term cannot be deferred once it has arrived, if you only knew."

5. He said, "My Lord, I have called my people night and day.

6. But my call added only to their flight.

7. Whenever I called them to Your forgiveness, they thrust their fingers into their ears, and wrapped themselves in their garments, and insisted, and became more and more arrogant.

8. Then I called them openly.

9. Then I appealed to them publicly, and I spoke to them privately.

10. I said, 'Ask your Lord for forgiveness; He is Forgiving.

11. He will let loose the sky upon you in torrents.

12. And provide you with wealth and children, and allot for you gardens, and allot for you rivers.

13. What is the matter with you, that you do not appreciate God's Greatness?

14. Although He created you in stages.

15. Do you not realize that God created seven heavens in layers?

16. And He set the moon in their midst for light, and He made the sun a lamp.

17. And God germinated you from the earth like plants.

18. Then He will return you into it, and will bring you out again.

19. And God made the earth a spread for you.

20. That you may travel its diverse roads.'"

21. Noah said, "My Lord, they have defied me, and followed him whose wealth and children increase him only in perdition."

22. And they schemed outrageous schemes.

23. And they said, "Do not give up your gods; do not give up Wadd, nor Souwa, nor Yaghoos, and Yaooq, and Nassr.

24. They have misled many, so do not increase the wrongdoers except in confusion."

25. Because of their wrongs, they were drowned, and were hurled into a Fire. They did not find apart from God any helpers.

26. Noah said, "My Lord, do not leave of the unbelievers a single dweller on earth.

27. If You leave them, they will mislead your servants, and will breed only wicked unbelievers.

28. My Lord! Forgive me and my parents, and anyone who enters my home in faith, and all the believing men and believing women; and do not increase the wrongdoers except in perdition."

72. THE JINN
(al-Jinn)

In the name of God,
the Gracious, the Merciful.

1. Say, "It was revealed to me that a band of jinn listened in, and said, 'We have heard a wondrous Quran.

2. It guides to rectitude, so we have believed in it; and we will never associate anyone with our Lord.

3. And Exalted is the Grandeur of our Lord—He never had a mate, nor a child.

4. But the fools among us used to say nonsense about God.

5. And we thought that humans and jinn would never utter lies about God.

6. Some individual humans used to seek power through some individual jinn, but they only increased them in confusion.

7. They thought, as you thought, that God would never resurrect anyone.

8. We probed the heaven, and found it filled with stern guards and projectiles.

9. We used to take up positions to listen in; but whoever listens now finds a projectile in wait for him.

10. We do not know whether ill is intended for those on earth, or if their Lord intends goodness for them.

11. Some of us are righteous, but some of us are less than that; we follow divergent paths.

12. We realized that we cannot defeat God on earth, and that we cannot escape Him by fleeing.

13. And when we heard the guidance, we believed in it. Whoever believes in his Lord fears neither loss, nor burden.

14. Among us are those who are submitting, and among us are the compromisers. As for those who have submitted—it is they who pursue rectitude.

15. But as for the compromisers—they will be firewood for Hell.'"

16. Had they kept true to the Path, We would have given them plenty water to drink.

17. To test them with it. Whoever turns away from the remembrance of his Lord, He will direct him to torment ever mounting.

18. The places of worship are for God. So do not call, besides God, upon anyone else.

19. And when the servant of God got up calling on Him, they almost fell on him in a mass.

20. Say, "I pray only to my Lord, and I never associate anyone with Him."

21. Say, "It is not in my power to harm you, nor to bring you to right conduct."

22. Say, "No one can protect me from God, and I will not find any refuge except with Him.

23. Except for a proclamation from God and His messages. He who defies God and His Messenger—for him is the Fire of Hell, in which they will dwell forever."

24. Until, when they see what they were promised, they will know who is weaker in helpers, and fewer in numbers.

25. Say, "I do not know whether what you are promised is near, or whether my Lord will extend it for a period."

26. The Knower of the Invisible; He does not disclose His Invisible to anyone.

27. Except to a Messenger of His choosing. He then dispatches guards before him and behind him.

28. That He may know that they have conveyed the messages of their Lord. He encompasses what they have, and has tallied everything by number.

73. THE ENWRAPPED
(al-Muzzammil)

In the name of God,
the Gracious, the Merciful.

1. O you Enwrapped one.

2. Stay up during the night, except a little.

3. For half of it, or reduce it a little.

4. Or add to it; and chant the Quran rhythmically.

5. We are about to give you a heavy message.

6. The vigil of night is more effective, and better suited for recitation.

7. In the daytime, you have lengthy work to do.

8. So remember the Name of your Lord, and devote yourself to Him wholeheartedly.

9. Lord of the East and the West. There is no god but He, so take Him as a Trustee.

10. And endure patiently what they say, and withdraw from them politely.

11. And leave Me to those who deny the truth, those of luxury, and give them a brief respite.

12. With Us are shackles, and a Fierce Fire.

13. And food that chokes, and a painful punishment.

14. On the Day when the earth and the mountains tremble, and the mountains become heaps of sand.

15. We have sent to you a messenger, a witness over you, as We sent to Pharaoh a messenger.

16. But Pharaoh defied the Messenger, so We seized him with a terrible seizing.

17. So how will you, if you persist in unbelief, save yourself from a Day which will turn the children gray-haired?

18. The heaven will shatter thereby. His promise is always fulfilled.

19. This is a reminder. So whoever wills, let him take a path to his Lord.

20. Your Lord knows that you stay up nearly two-thirds of the night, or half of it, or one-third of it, along with a group of those with you. God designed the night and the day. He knows that you are unable to sustain it, so He has pardoned you. So read of the Quran what is possible for you. He knows that some of you may be ill; and others travelling through the land, seeking God's bounty; and others fighting in God's cause. So read of it what is possible for you, and observe the prayers, and give regular charity, and lend God a generous loan. Whatever good you advance for yourselves, you will find it with God, better and generously rewarded. And seek God's forgiveness, for God is Forgiving and Merciful.

74. THE ENROBED
(al-Muddathir)

In the name of God,
the Gracious, the Merciful.

1. O you Enrobed one.

2. Arise and warn.

3. And magnify your Lord.

4. And purify your clothes.

5. And abandon abominations.

6. And show no favor seeking gain.

7. And be constant for your Lord.

8. When the Trumpet is blown.

9. That Day will be a difficult day.

10. For the disbelievers—not easy.

11. Leave Me to him whom I created alone.

12. And gave him vast wealth.

13. And children as witnesses.

14. And smoothed things for him.

15. Then he wants Me to add yet more!

16. By no means! He was stubborn towards Our revelations.

17. I will exhaust him increasingly.

18. He thought and analyzed.

19. May he perish, how he analyzed.

20. Again: may he perish, how he analyzed.

21. Then he looked.

22. Then he frowned and whined.

23. Then he turned back and was proud.

24. And said, "This is nothing but magic from the past.

25. This is nothing but the word of a mortal."

26. I will roast him in Saqar.

27. But what will explain to you what Saqar is?

28. It neither leaves, nor spares.

29. It scorches the flesh.

30. Over it are Nineteen.

31. We have appointed only angels to be wardens of the Fire, and caused their

number to be a stumbling block for those who disbelieve; so that those given the Scripture may attain certainty; and those who believe may increase in faith; and those given the Scripture and the believers may not doubt; and those in whose hearts is sickness and the unbelievers may say, "What did God intend by this parable?" Thus God leads astray whom He wills, and guides whom He wills. None knows the soldiers of your Lord except He. This is nothing but a reminder for the mortals.

32. Nay! By the moon.

33. And the night as it retreats.

34. And the morning as it lights up.

35. It is one of the greatest.

36. A warning to the mortals.

37. To whomever among you wishes to advance, or regress.

38. Every soul is hostage to what it has earned.

39. Except for those on the Right.

40. In Gardens, inquiring.

41. About the guilty.

42. "What drove you into Saqar?"

43. They will say, "We were not of those who prayed.

44. Nor did we feed the destitute.

45. And we used to indulge with those who indulge.

46. And we used to deny the Day of Judgment.

47. Until the Inevitable came upon us."

48. But the intercession of intercessors will not help them.

49. Why are they turning away from the Reminder?

50. As though they were panicked donkeys,

51. Fleeing from a lion?

52. Yet every one of them desires to be given scrolls unrolled.

53. No indeed! But they do not fear the Hereafter.

54. Nevertheless, it is a reminder.

55. So whoever wills, shall remember it.

56. But they will not remember, unless God wills. He is the Source of Righteousness, and the Source of Forgiveness.

75. RESURRECTION
(al-Qiyamah)

In the name of God,
the Gracious, the Merciful.

1. I swear by the Day of Resurrection.

2. And I swear by the blaming soul.

3. Does man think that We will not reassemble his bones?

4. Yes indeed; We are Able to reconstruct his fingertips.

5. But man wants to deny what is ahead of him.

6. He asks, "When is the Day of Resurrection?"

7. When vision is dazzled.

8. And the moon is eclipsed.

9. And the sun and the moon are joined together.

10. On that Day, man will say, "Where is the escape?"

11. No indeed! There is no refuge.

12. To your Lord on that Day is the settlement.

13. On that Day man will be informed of everything he put forward, and everything he left behind.

14. And man will be evidence against himself.

15. Even as he presents his excuses.

16. Do not wag your tongue with it, to hurry on with it.

17. Upon Us is its collection and its recitation.

18. Then, when We have recited it, follow its recitation.

19. Then upon Us is its explanation.

20. Alas, you love the fleeting life.

21. And you disregard the Hereafter.

22. Faces on that Day will be radiant.

23. Looking towards their Lord.

24. And faces on that Day will be gloomy.

25. Realizing that a back-breaker has befallen them.

26. Indeed, when it has reached the breastbones.

27. And it is said, "Who is the healer?"

28. And He realizes that it is the parting.

29. And leg is entwined with leg.

30. To your Lord on that Day is the drive.

31. He neither believed nor prayed.

32. But he denied and turned away.

33. Then he went to his family, full of pride.

34. Woe to you; and woe.

35. Then again: Woe to you; and woe.

36. Does man think that he will be left without purpose?

37. Was he not a drop of ejaculated semen?

38. Then he became a clot. And He created and proportioned?

39. And made of him the two sexes, the male and the female?

40. Is He not Able to revive the dead?

76. MAN
(al-Insan)

*In the name of God,
the Gracious, the Merciful.*

1. Has there come upon man a period of time when he was nothing to be mentioned?

2. We created man from a liquid mixture, to test him; and We made him hearing and seeing.

3. We guided him on the way, be he appreciative or unappreciative.

4. We have prepared for the faithless chains, and yokes, and a Searing Fire.

5. But the righteous will drink from a cup whose mixture is aroma.

6. A spring from which the servants of God will drink, making it gush abundantly.

7. They fulfill their vows, and dread a Day whose ill is widespread.

8. And they feed, for the love of Him, the poor, and the orphan, and the captive.

9. "We only feed you for the sake of God. We want from you neither compensation, nor gratitude.

10. We dread from our Lord a frowning grim Day."

11. So God will protect them from the ills of that Day, and will grant them radiance and joy.

12. And will reward them for their patience with a Garden and silk.

13. Reclining therein on the thrones; experiencing therein neither sun, nor frost.

14. Its shade hovering over them, and its fruit brought low within reach.

15. Passing around them are vessels of silver, and cups of crystal.

16. Crystal of silver—they measured them exactly.

17. They will be served with a cup whose flavor is Zanjabeel.

18. A spring therein named Salsabeel.

19. Passing among them are eternalized youths. If you see them, you would think them sprinkled pearls.

20. Wherever you look, you see bliss, and a vast kingdom.

21. Upon them are garments of green silk, and satin. And they will be adorned with bracelets of silver. And their Lord will offer them a pure drink.

22. "This is a reward for you. Your efforts are well appreciated."

23. It is We who sent down the Quran upon you—a gradual revelation.

24. So be patient for the decision of your Lord, and do not obey the sinner or the blasphemer among them.

25. And mention the Name of your Lord, morning and evening.

26. And for part of the night, prostrate yourself to Him, and glorify Him long into the night.

27. As for these: they love the fleeting life, and leave behind a Heavy Day.

28. We created them, and strengthened their frame; and whenever We will, We can replace them with others like them.

29. This is a reminder; so whoever wills, let him take a path to his Lord.

30. Yet you cannot will, unless God wills. God is Knowing and Wise.

31. He admits into His mercy whomever He wills. But as for the wrongdoers, He has prepared for them a painful punishment.

77. THE UNLEASHED
(al-Mursalat)

In the name of God,
the Gracious, the Merciful.

1. By those unleashed in succession.

2. Storming turbulently.

3. Scattering far and wide.

4. Separating decisively.

5. Delivering a message.

6. Excusing or warning.

7. Surely what you are promised will happen.

8. When the stars are obliterated.

9. And the sky is fractured.

10. And the mountains are blown away.

11. And the messengers are alerted.

12. Until which day is it deferred?

13. Until the Day of Decision.

14. And what will teach you what the Day of Decision is?

15. Woe on that Day to the deniers.

16. Did We not destroy the ancients?

17. Then succeeded them with the others?

18. This is how We deal with the guilty.

19. Woe on that Day to the liars.

20. Did We not create you from an insignificant fluid?

21. Then lodged it in a secure place?

22. For a known term?

23. We measured precisely. We are the best to measure.

24. Woe on that Day to the rejecters.

25. Did We not make the earth a homestead?

26. For the living and the dead?

27. And set on it lofty mountains, and given you pure water to drink?

28. Woe on that Day to the deniers.

29. "Proceed to what you used to deny."

30. "Proceed to a shadow of three different masses."

31. Offering no shade, and unavailing against the flames.

32. It shoots sparks as castles.

33. As if they were yellow camels.

34. Woe on that Day to the falsifiers.

35. This is a Day when they will not speak.

36. And they will not be allowed to apologize.

37. Woe on that Day to the rejecters.

38. This is the Day of Separation; We have gathered you, together with the ancients.

39. So if you have a strategy, use it against Me.

40. Woe on that Day to the liars.

41. The righteous will be amidst shades and fountains.

42. And fruits as they desire.

43. "Eat and drink pleasantly, for what you used to do."

44. This is how We reward the doers of good.

45. Woe on that Day to the rejecters.

46. "Eat and enjoy yourselves a little; you are indeed criminals."

47. Woe on that Day to the falsifiers.

48. And when it is said to them, "Kneel", they do not kneel.

49. Woe on that Day to the deniers.

50. In what message, beyond this, will they believe?

78. THE EVENT
(an-Naba')

In the name of God,
the Gracious, the Merciful.

1. What are they asking one another about?

2. About the Great Event.

3. About which they disagree.

4. Surely, they will find out.

5. Most certainly, they will find out.

6. Did We not make the earth a cradle?

7. And the mountains pegs?

8. And created you in pairs?

9. And made your sleep for rest?

10. And made the night a cover?

11. And made the day for livelihood?

12. And built above you seven strong ones?

13. And placed a blazing lamp?

14. And brought down from the clouds pouring water?

15. To produce with it grains and vegetation?

16. And luxuriant gardens?

17. The Day of Sorting has been appointed.

18. The Day when the Trumpet is blown, and you will come in droves.

19. And the sky is opened up, and becomes gateways.

20. And the mountains are set in motion, and become a mirage.

21. Hell is lying in ambush.

22. For the oppressors, a destination.

23. Where they will remain for eons.

24. They will taste therein neither coolness, nor drink.

25. Except boiling water and freezing hail.

26. A fitting requital.

27. For they were not anticipating any reckoning.

28. And they denied Our signs utterly.

29. But We have enumerated everything in writing.

30. So taste! We will increase you in nothing but suffering.

31. But for the righteous there is triumph.

32. Gardens and vineyards.

33. And splendid spouses, well matched.

34. And delicious drinks.

35. They will hear therein neither gossip, nor lies.

36. A reward from your Lord, a fitting gift.

37. Lord of the heavens and the earth, and everything between them—The Most Merciful—none can argue with Him.

38. On the Day when the Spirit and the angels stand in row. They will not speak, unless it be one permitted by the Most Merciful, and he will say what is right.

39. That is the Day of Reality. So whoever wills, let him take a way back to his Lord.

40. We have warned you of a near punishment—the Day when a person will observe what his hands have produced, and the faithless will say, "O, I wish I were dust."

79. THE SNATCHERS (an-Nazi'at)

In the name of God,
the Gracious, the Merciful.

1. By those who snatch violently.

2. And those who remove gently.

3. And those who glide smoothly.

4. And those who race swiftly.

5. And those who regulate events.

6. On the Day when the Quake quakes.

7. And is followed by the Successor.

8. Hearts on that Day will be pounding.

9. Their sights downcast.

10. They say, "Are we to be restored to the original condition?

11. When we have become hollow bones?"

12. They say, "This is a losing proposition."

13. But it will be only a single nudge.

14. And they will be awake.

15. Has the story of Moses reached you?

16. When His Lord called out to him in the sacred valley of Tuwa.

17. "Go to Pharaoh—he has transgressed."

18. And say, "Do you care to be cleansed?

19. And I will guide you to your Lord, and you will turn reverent."

20. He showed him the Greatest Miracle.

21. But he denied and defied.

22. Then turned his back, and tried.

23. And gathered and proclaimed.

24. He said, "I am your Lord, the most high."

25. So God seized him with an exemplary punishment, in the last and in the first.

26. In this is a lesson for whoever fears.

27. Are you more difficult to create, or the heaven? He constructed it.

28. He raised its masses, and proportioned it.

29. And He dimmed its night, and brought out its daylight.

30. And the earth after that He spread.

31. And from it, He produced its water and its pasture.

32. And the mountains, He anchored.

33. A source of enjoyment for you and for your animals.

34. But when the Great Cataclysm arrives.

35. A Day when man will remember what he has endeavored.

36. And Hell will be displayed to whoever sees.

37. As for him who was defiant.

38. And preferred the life of this world.

39. Then Hell is the shelter.

40. But as for him who feared the Standing of his Lord, and restrained the self from desires.

41. Then Paradise is the shelter.

42. They ask you about the Hour, "When will it take place?"

43. You have no knowledge of it.

44. To your Lord is its finality.

45. You are just a warner for whoever dreads it.

46. On the Day when they witness it—as though they only stayed an evening, or its morning.

80. HE FROWNED
('Abasa)

In the name of God,
the Gracious, the Merciful.

1. He frowned and turned away.

2. When the blind man approached him.

3. But how do you know? Perhaps he was seeking to purify himself.

4. Or be reminded, and the message would benefit him.

5. But as for him who was indifferent.

6. You gave him your attention.

7. Though you are not liable if he does not purify himself.

8. But as for him who came to you seeking.

9. In awe.

10. To him you were inattentive.

11. Do not. This is a Lesson.

12. Whoever wills, shall remember it.

13. On honorable pages.

14. Exalted and purified.

15. By the hands of scribes.

16. Noble and devoted.

17. Perish man! How thankless he is!

18. From what did He create him?

19. From a sperm drop He created him, and enabled him.

20. Then He eased the way for him.

21. Then He puts him to death, and buries him.

22. Then, when He wills, He will resurrect him.

23. But no, he did not fulfill what He has commanded him.

24. Let man consider his food.

25. We pour down water in abundance.

26. Then crack the soil open.

27. And grow in it grains.

28. And grapes and herbs.

29. And olives and dates.

30. And luscious gardens.

31. And fruits and vegetables.

32. Enjoyment for you, and for your livestock.

33. But when the Deafening Noise comes to pass.

34. The Day when a person will flee from his brother.

35. And his mother and his father.

36. And his consort and his children.

37. Every one of them, on that Day, will have enough to preoccupy him.

38. Faces on that Day will be radiant.

39. Laughing and rejoicing.

40. And Faces on that Day will be covered with misery.

41. Overwhelmed by remorse.

42. These are the faithless, the vicious.

81. THE ROLLING
(at-Takwir)

*In the name of God,
the Gracious, the Merciful.*

1. When the sun is rolled up.

2. When the stars are dimmed.

3. When the mountains are set in motion.

4. When relationships are suspended.

5. When the beasts are gathered.

6. When the oceans are set aflame.

7. When the souls are paired.

8. When the girl, buried alive, is asked:

9. For what crime was she killed?

10. When the records are made public.

11. When the sky is peeled away.

12. When the Fire is set ablaze.

13. When Paradise is brought near.

14. Each soul will know what it has readied.

15. I swear by the galaxies.

16. Precisely running their courses.

17. And by the night as it recedes.

18. And by the morn as it breathes.

19. This is the speech of a noble messenger.

20. Endowed with power, eminent with the Lord of the Throne.

21. Obeyed and honest.

22. Your friend is not possessed.

23. He saw him on the luminous horizon.

24. And He does not withhold knowledge of the Unseen.

25. And it is not the word of an accursed devil.

26. So where are you heading?

27. It is only a Reminder to all mankind.

28. To whoever of you wills to go straight.

29. But you cannot will, unless God wills— The Lord of the Worlds.

82. THE SHATTERING
(al-Infitar)

*In the name of God,
the Gracious, the Merciful.*

1. When the sky breaks apart.

2. When the planets are scattered.

3. When the oceans are exploded.

4. When the tombs are strewn around.

5. Each soul will know what it has advanced, and what it has deferred.

6. O man! What deluded you concerning your Lord, the Most Generous?

7. He Who created you, and formed you, and proportioned you?

8. In whatever shape He willed, He assembled you.

9. But you reject the religion.

10. Though over you are watchers.

11. Honest recorders.

12. They know everything you do.

13. The virtuous will be in bliss.

14. While the wicked will be in Hell.

15. They will enter it on the Day of Justice.

16. And they will not be absent from it.

17. But what will convey to you what the Day of Justice is?

18. Then again, what will convey to you what the Day of Justice is?

19. The Day when no soul will avail another soul anything; and the decision on that Day is God's.

83. THE DEFRAUDERS
(al-Mutaffifin)

In the name of God,
the Gracious, the Merciful.

1. Woe to the defrauders.

2. Those who, when they take a measure from people, they take in full.

3. But when they measure or weigh to others, they cheat.

4. Do these not know that they will be resurrected?

5. For a Great Day?

6. The Day when mankind will stand before the Lord of the Worlds?

7. Not at all. The record of the wicked is in Sijjeen.

8. But how can you know what Sijjeen is?

9. A numerical book.

10. Woe on that Day to the deniers.

11. Those who deny the Day of Reckoning.

12. But none denies it except the sinful aggressor.

13. When Our revelations are recited to him, he says, "Legends of the ancients."

14. Not at all. Their hearts have become corroded by what they used to earn.

15. Not at all. On that Day, they will be screened from their Lord.

16. Then they will roast in Hell.

17. Then it will be said, "This is what you used to deny."

18. No indeed; the record of the righteous is in Elliyyeen.

19. But how can you know what Elliyyoon is?

20. A numerical book.

21. Witnessed by those brought near.

22. Indeed, the righteous will be amid bliss.

23. On thrones, looking on.

24. You will recognize on their faces the radiance of bliss.

25. They will be given to drink a sealed wine.

26. Whose seal is musk—this is what competitors should compete for.

27. Its mixture is of Tasneem.

28. A spring from which those brought near drink.

29. Those who committed crimes used to laugh at those who believed.

30. And when they passed by them, they would wink at one another.

31. And when they went back to their families, they would go back exulting.

32. And if they saw them, they would say, "These people are lost."

33. Yet they were not sent as guardians over them.

34. But on that Day, those who believed will laugh at the unbelievers.

35. On luxurious furnishings, looking on.

36. Have the unbelievers been repaid for what they used to do?

84. THE RUPTURE
(al-Inshiqaq)

In the name of God,
the Gracious, the Merciful.

1. When the sky is ruptured.

2. And hearkens to its Lord, as it must.

3. And when the earth is leveled out.

4. And casts out what is in it, and becomes empty.

5. And hearkens to its Lord, as it must.

6. O man! You are laboring towards your Lord, and you will meet Him.

7. As for him who is given his book in his right hand.

8. He will have an easy settlement.

9. And will return to his family delighted.

10. But as for him who is given his book behind his back.

11. He will call for death.

12. And will enter the Blaze.

13. He used to be happy among his family.

14. He thought he would never return.

15. In fact, his Lord was watching him.

16. I swear by the twilight.

17. And by the night, and what it covers.

18. And by the moon, as it grows full.

19. You will mount stage by stage.

20. What is the matter with them that they do not believe?

21. And when the Quran is read to them, they do not bow down?

22. In fact, those who disbelieve are in denial.

23. But God knows what they hide inside.

24. So inform them of a painful punishment.

25. Except for those who believe and do good deeds; they will have an undiminished reward.

85. THE CONSTELLATIONS
(al-Buruj)

In the name of God,
the Gracious, the Merciful.

1. By the sky with the constellations.

2. And by the Promised Day.

3. And by the witness and the witnessed.

4. Destroyed were the People of the Trench.

5. The fire supplied with fuel.

6. While they sat around it.

7. And were witnessing what they did to the believers.

8. They begrudged them only because they believed in God the Almighty, the Praiseworthy.

9. To Whom belongs the sovereignty of the heavens and the earth. God is witness over everything.

10. Those who tempt the believers, men and women, then do not repent; for them is the punishment of Hell; for them is the punishment of Burning.

11. Those who believe and do righteous deeds will have Gardens beneath which rivers flow. That is the great triumph.

12. The onslaught of your Lord is severe.

13. It is He who begins and repeats.

14. And He is the Forgiving, the Loving.

15. Possessor of the Glorious Throne.

16. Doer of whatever He wills.

17. Has there come to you the story of the legions?

18. Of Pharaoh and Thamood?

19. In fact, those who disbelieve are in denial.

20. And God encloses them from beyond.

21. In fact, it is a Glorious Quran.

22. In a Preserved Tablet.

86. THE NIGHTLY VISITOR
(at-Tariq)

In the name of God,
the Gracious, the Merciful.

1. By the sky and Al-Taareq.

2. But what will let you know what Al-Taareq is?

3. The Piercing Star.

4. There is no soul without a Protector over it.

5. Let man consider what he was created from.

6. He was created from gushing liquid.

7. Issuing from between the backbone and the breastbones.

8. He is certainly able to return him.

9. On the Day when the secrets are disclosed.

10. He will have no strength, and no supporter.

11. By the sky that returns.

12. And the earth that cracks open.

13. It is a Decisive Word.

14. It is no joke.

15. They plot and scheme.

16. But I plot and scheme.

17. Therefore, give the blasphemers respite, a brief respite.

87. THE MOST HIGH
(al-A'la)

In the name of God,
the Gracious, the Merciful.

1. Praise the name of your Lord, the Most High.

2. He who creates and regulates.

1. He who measures and guides.

2. He who produces the pasture.

3. And then turns it into light debris.

4. We will make you recite, so do not forget.

5. Except what God wills. He knows what is declared, and what is hidden.

6. We will ease you into the Easy Way.

7. So remind, if reminding helps.

8. The reverent will remember.

9. But the wretched will avoid it.

10. He who will enter the Gigantic Fire.

11. Where he will neither die, nor live.

12. Successful is he who purifies himself.

13. And mentions the name of his Lord, and prays.

14. But you prefer the present life.

15. Though the Hereafter is better, and more lasting.

16. This is in the former Scriptures.

17. The Scriptures of Abraham and Moses.

88. THE OVERWHELMING
(al-Ghashiyah)

In the name of God,
the Gracious, the Merciful.

1. Has there come to you the news of the overwhelming?

2. Faces on that Day will be shamed.

3. Laboring and exhausted.

4. Roasting in a scorching Fire.

5. Given to drink from a flaming spring.

6. They will have no food except thorns.

7. That neither nourishes, nor satisfies hunger.

8. Faces on that Day will be joyful.

9. Satisfied with their endeavor.

10. In a lofty Garden.

11. In it you will hear no nonsense.

12. In it is a flowing spring.

13. In it are raised beds.

14. And cups set in place.

15. And cushions set in rows.

16. And carpets spread around.

17. Do they not look at the camels—how they are created?

18. And at the sky—how it is raised?

19. And at the mountains—how they are installed?

20. And at the earth—how it is spread out?

21. So remind. You are only a reminder.

22. You have no control over them.

23. But whoever turns away and disbelieves.

24. God will punish him with the greatest punishment.

25. To Us is their return.

26. Then upon Us rests their reckoning.

89. THE DAWN
(al-Fajr)

In the name of God,
the Gracious, the Merciful.

1. By the daybreak.

2. And ten nights.

3. And the even and the odd.

4. And the night as it recedes.

5. Is there in this an oath for a rational person?

6. Have you not seen how your Lord dealt with Aad?

7. Erum of the pillars.

8. The like of which was never created in the land.

9. And Thamood; those who carved the rocks in the valley.

10. And Pharaoh of the Stakes.

11. Those who committed excesses in the lands.

12. And spread much corruption therein.

13. So your Lord poured down upon them a scourge of punishment.

14. Your Lord is on the lookout.

15. As for man, whenever his Lord tests him, and honors him, and prospers him, he says, "My Lord has honored me."

16. But whenever He tests him, and restricts his livelihood for him, he says, "My Lord has insulted me."

17. Not at all. But you do not honor the orphan.

18. And you do not urge the feeding of the poor.

19. And you devour inheritance with all greed.

20. And you love wealth with immense love.

21. No—when the earth is leveled, pounded, and crushed.

22. And your Lord comes, with the angels, row after row.

23. And on that Day, Hell is brought forward. On that Day, man will remember, but how will remembrance avail him?

24. He will say, "If only I had forwarded for my life."

25. On that Day, none will punish as He punishes.

26. And none will shackle as He shackles.

27. But as for you, O tranquil soul.

28. Return to your Lord, pleased and accepted.

29. Enter among My servants.

30. Enter My Paradise.

90. THE LAND
(al-Balad)

In the name of God,
the Gracious, the Merciful.

1. I swear by this land.

2. And you are a resident of this land.

3. And by a father and what he fathered.

4. We created man in distress.

5. Does he think that no one has power over him?

6. He says, "I have used up so much money."

7. Does he think that no one sees him?

8. Did We not give him two eyes?

9. And a tongue, and two lips?

10. And We showed him the two ways?

11. But he did not brave the ascent.

12. And what will explain to you what the ascent is?

13. The freeing of a slave.

14. Or the feeding on a day of hunger.

15. An orphan near of kin.

16. Or a destitute in the dust.

17. Then he becomes of those who believe, and advise one another to patience, and advise one another to kindness.

18. These are the people of happiness.

19. But as for those who defy Our revelations—these are the people of misery.

20. Upon them is a padlocked Fire.

91. THE SUN
(ash-Shams)

In the name of God,
the Gracious, the Merciful.

1. By the sun and its radiance.

2. And the moon as it follows it.

3. And the day as it reveals it.

4. And the night as it conceals it.

5. And the sky and He who built it.

6. And the earth and He who spread it.

7. And the soul and He who proportioned it.

8. And inspired it with its wickedness and its righteousness.

9. Successful is he who purifies it.

10. Failing is he who corrupts it.

11. Thamood denied in their pride.

12. When it followed its most wicked.

13. The messenger of God said to them, "This is the she-camel of God, so let her drink."

14. But they called him a liar, and hamstrung her. So their Lord crushed them for their sin, and leveled it.

15. And He does not fear its sequel.

92. THE NIGHT
(al-Layl)

*In the name of God,
the Gracious, the Merciful.*

1. By the night as it covers.

2. And the day as it reveals.

3. And He who created the male and the female.

4. Your endeavors are indeed diverse.

5. As for him who gives and is righteous.

6. And confirms goodness.

7. We will ease his way towards ease.

8. But as for him who is stingy and complacent.

9. And denies goodness.

10. We will ease his way towards difficulty.

11. And his money will not avail him when he plummets.

12. It is upon Us to guide.

13. And to Us belong the Last and the First.

14. I have warned you of a Fierce Blaze.

15. None will burn in it except the very wicked.

16. He who denies and turns away.

17. But the devout will avoid it.

18. He who gives his money to become pure.

19. Seeking no favor in return.

20. Only seeking the acceptance of his Lord, the Most High.

21. And he will be satisfied.

93. MORNING LIGHT
(adh-Duha)

*In the name of God,
the Gracious, the Merciful.*

1. By the morning light.

2. And the night as it settles.

3. Your Lord did not abandon you, nor did He forget.

4. The Hereafter is better for you than the First.

5. And your Lord will give you, and you will be satisfied.

6. Did He not find you orphaned, and sheltered you?

7. And found you wandering, and guided you.

8. And found you in need, and enriched you?

9. Therefore, do not mistreat the orphan.

10. Nor rebuff the seeker.

11. But proclaim the blessings of your Lord.

94. THE SOOTHING
(ash-Sharh)

In the name of God,

the Gracious, the Merciful.

1. Did We not soothe your heart?

2. And lift from you your burden.

3. Which weighed down your back?

4. And raised for you your reputation?

5. With hardship comes ease.

6. With hardship comes ease.

7. When your work is done, turn to devotion.

8. And to your Lord turn for everything.

95. THE FIG
(at-Tin)

In the name of God,
the Gracious, the Merciful.

1. By the fig and the olive.

2. And Mount Sinai.

3. And this safe land.

4. We created man in the best design.

5. Then reduced him to the lowest of the low.

6. Except those who believe and do righteous deeds; for them is a reward without end.

7. So why do you still reject the religion?

8. Is God not the Wisest of the wise?

96. CLOT
(al-'Alaq)

In the name of God,
the Gracious, the Merciful.

1. Read: In the Name of your Lord who created.

2. Created man from a clot.

3. Read: And your Lord is the Most Generous.

4. He who taught by the pen.

5. Taught man what he never knew.

6. In fact, man oversteps all bounds.

7. When he considers himself exempt.

8. But to your Lord is the return.

9. Have you seen him who prevents?

10. A servant when he prays?

11. Do you think he is upon guidance?

12. Or advocates righteousness?

13. Do you see how he disbelieved and turned away?

14. Does he not know that God sees?

15. No. If he does not desist, We will drag him by the forelock.

16. A deceitful, sinful forelock.

17. Let him call on his gang.

18. We will call the Guards.

19. No, do not obey him; but kneel down, and come near.

97. DECREE
(al-Qadr)

In the name of God,
the Gracious, the Merciful.

1. We sent it down on the Night of Decree.

2. But what will convey to you what the Night of Decree is?

3. The Night of Decree is better than a thousand months.

4. In it descend the angels and the Spirit, by the leave of their Lord, with every command.

5. Peace it is; until the rise of dawn.

98. CLEAR EVIDENCE
(al-Bayyinah)

In the name of God,
the Gracious, the Merciful.

1. Those who disbelieved among the People of the Scripture, and the Polytheists, were not apart, until the Clear Evidence came to them.

2. A messenger from God reciting purified scripts.

3. In them are valuable writings.

4. Those who were given the Scripture did not splinter, except after the Clear Evidence came to them.

5. They were commanded only to worship God, devoting their faith to Him alone, and to practice regular prayer, and to give alms. That is the upright religion.

6. Those who disbelieve among the People of the Scripture, and the Polytheists, will be in the Fire of Hell, where they will abide forever. These are the worst of creatures.

7. As for those who believe and lead a righteous life—these are the best of creatures.

8. Their reward is with their Lord: Gardens of Eternity beneath which rivers flow, where they will abide forever. God is pleased with them, and they are pleased with Him. That is for whoever fears His Lord.

99. THE QUAKE
(az-Zalzalah)

In the name of God,
the Gracious, the Merciful.

1. When the earth is shaken with its quake.

2. And the earth brings out its loads.

3. And man says, "What is the matter with it?"

4. On that Day, it will tell its tales.

5. For your Lord will have inspired it.

6. On that Day, the people will emerge in droves, to be shown their works.

7. Whoever has done an atom's weight of good will see it.

8. And whoever has done an atom's weight of evil will see it.

100. THE RACERS
(al-'Adiyat)

In the name of God,
the Gracious, the Merciful.

1. By the racers panting.

2. Igniting sparks.

3. Raiding at dawn.

4. Raising clouds of dust.

5. Storming into the midst.

6. Indeed, the human being is ungrateful to his Lord.

7. And he bears witness to that.

8. And he is fierce in his love of wealth.

9. Does he not know? When the contents of the graves are scattered around.

10. And the contents of the hearts are obtained.

11. Their Lord, on that Day, is fully informed of them.

101. THE SHOCKER
(al-Qari'ah)

In the name of God,
the Gracious, the Merciful.

1. The Shocker.

2. What is the Shocker?

3. What will explain to you what the Shocker is?

4. The Day when the people will be like scattered moths.

5. And the mountains will be like tufted wool.

6. As for he whose scales are heavy.

7. He will be in a pleasant life.

8. But as for he whose scales are light.

9. His home is the Abyss.

10. Do you know what it is?

11. A Raging Fire.

102. ABUNDANCE
(at-Takathur)

In the name of God,
the Gracious, the Merciful.

1. Abundance distracts you.

2. Until you visit the graveyards.

3. Indeed, you will know.

4. Certainly, you will know.

5. If you knew with knowledge of certainty.

6. You would see the Inferno.

7. Then you will see it with the eye of certainty.

8. Then, on that Day, you will be questioned about the Bliss.

103. TIME
(al-'Asr)

In the name of God,
the Gracious, the Merciful.

1. By time.

2. The human being is in loss.

3. Except those who believe, and do good works, and encourage truth, and recommend patience.

104. THE BACKBITER
(al-Humazah)

In the name of God,
the Gracious, the Merciful.

1. Woe to every slanderer backbiter.

2. Who gathers wealth and counts it over.

3. Thinking that his wealth has made him immortal.

4. By no means. He will be thrown into the Crusher.

5. And what will make you realize what the Crusher is?

6. God's kindled Fire.

7. That laps to the hearts.

8. It closes in on them.

9. In extended columns.

105. THE ELEPHANT
(al-Fil)

In the name of God,
the Gracious, the Merciful.

1. Have you not considered how your Lord dealt with the People of the Elephant?

2. Did He not make their plan go wrong?

3. He sent against them swarms of birds.

4. Throwing at them rocks of baked clay.

5. Leaving them like chewed-up leaves.

106. QURAISH
(Quraysh)

In the name of God,
the Gracious, the Merciful.

1. For the security of Quraish.

2. Their security during winter and summer journeys.

3. Let them worship the Lord of this House.

4. Who has fed them against hunger, and has secured them against fear.

107. ASSISTANCE
(al-Ma'un)

In the name of God,
the Gracious, the Merciful.

1. Have you considered him who denies the religion?

2. It is he who mistreats the orphan.

3. And does not encourage the feeding of the poor.

4. So woe to those who pray.

5. Those who are heedless of their prayers.

6. Those who put on the appearance.

7. And withhold the assistance.

108. PLENTY
(al-Kawthar)

In the name of God,
the Gracious, the Merciful.

1. We have given you plenty.

2. So pray to your Lord and sacrifice.

3. He who hates you is the loser.

109. THE DISBELIEVERS
(al-Kafirun)

In the name of God,
the Gracious, the Merciful.

1. Say, "O disbelievers.

2. I do not worship what you worship.

3. Nor do you worship what I worship.

4. Nor do I serve what you serve.

5. Nor do you serve what I serve.

6. You have your way, and I have my way."

110. VICTORY
(an-Nasr)

In the name of God,
the Gracious, the Merciful.

1. When there comes God's victory, and conquest.

2. And you see the people entering God's religion in multitudes.

3. Then celebrate the praise of your Lord, and seek His forgiveness. He is the Accepter of Repentance.

111. THORNS
(al-Masad)

In the name of God,
the Gracious, the Merciful.

1. Condemned are the hands of Abee Lahab, and he is condemned.

2. His wealth did not avail him, nor did what he acquired.

3. He will burn in a Flaming Fire.

4. And his wife—the firewood carrier.

5. Around her neck is a rope of thorns.

112. MONOTHEISM
(al-Ikhlas)

In the name of God,
the Gracious, the Merciful.

1. Say, "He is God, the One.

2. God, the Absolute.

3. He begets not, nor was He begotten.

4. And there is nothing comparable to Him."

113. DAYBREAK
(al-Falaq)

In the name of God,
the Gracious, the Merciful.

1. Say, "I take refuge with the Lord of Daybreak.

2. From the evil of what He created.

3. And from the evil of the darkness as it gathers.

4. And from the evil of those who practice sorcery.

5. And from the evil of an envious when he envies."

114. MANKIND
(an-Nas)

In the name of God,
the Gracious, the Merciful.

1. Say, "I seek refuge in the Lord of mankind.

2. The King of mankind.

3. The God of mankind.

4. From the evil of the sneaky whisperer.

5. Who whispers into the hearts of people.

6. From among jinn and among people."

Made in the USA
Middletown, DE
22 January 2023

CADOGAN GUIDES

GREEK ISLANDS

Cadogan Books Ltd
M ercury House, 195 Knightsbridge, London SW7 1RE

The Globe Pequot Press
6 Business Park Drive, PO Box 833, Old Saybrook, Connecticut
06475–0833

Copyright © Dana Facaros 1979, 1981, 1986, 1988, 1993
Updated with the help of Michael Davidson and Brian Walsh
Illustrations © Pauline Pears 1986, Suzan Kentli 1993

Book design by Animage
Cover design by Ralph King
Cover illustration by Povl Webb
Maps © Cadogan Guides, drawn by Thames Cartographic Ltd
Typesetting: Book Production Services

Editing: Rachel Fielding and Brenda Eisenberg
Managing Editor: Vicki Ingle
Series Editor: Rachel Fielding

First published as *Greek Island Hopping* in 1979, revised 1981.
Third revised edition published as a Cadogan Guide in 1986.
Fourth revised edition 1988.
This fully revised and updated edition, published 1993.

A catalogue record for this book is available from the British Library

ISBN 0–947754–40 7

Library of Congress Cataloging-in-Publication-Data

Facaros, Dana

  Greek Islands/ Dana Facaros; illustrations by Pauline Pears and Suzan Kentli -- 5th ed.
  p. cm. -- (Cadogan guides)
  Rev. ed. of: Greek island hopping   1979
  Includes index.
  ISBN 1–56440–071–9
  1. Aegean Islands (Greece and Turkey)--Guidebooks   2. Ionian
  Islands (Greece) -- Guidebooks. I. Facaros, Dana.   Greek island
  hopping. II. Title. III. Series.
  DR896.F3 1993
  914.95'50478--dc20   92-28242 CIP

Typeset in Weidemann and entirely produced on Apple Macintosh with Quark XPress, Photoshop, Freehand and Word software.
Printed and bound in Great Britain by Redwood Press Limited, Melksham, Wiltshire.

About the Authors

Dana Facaros is a professional travel writer. Over the past ten years she has lived in several countries concentrating on the Mediterranean area. In collaboration with her husband, Michael Pauls, she has written numerous travel guides mainly covering Italy, Spain, France, and Turkey. Her roots, however, are in the Greek Islands; her father comes from Ikaria. Now in its fifth edition, Dana's first guide to the Greek Islands was published in 1979.

Michael Davidson and **Brian Walsh**, who updated the practical information in this book, are inveterate travellers, teachers and former residents of Skiathos. After time out in Italy and Spain, they returned to Greece, spent several months island hopping, and have now settled in Athens.

Acknowledgements

From the **author**: I would like to thank the many members of the National Tourist Organization of Greece for their kind assistance in writing this guide, and the following people without whose moral, physical and financial assistance it would not have been possible: my parents and my grandmother, Mrs Despina Facaros, Joseph Coniaris, Sotiros S. Kouvaras of Ithaki, Filia and Kosta Pattakos, Carolyn Steiner and Julie Wegner. In this fifth edition, a special thanks goes to my better half, Michael, who added the bull; to my aunt, and Ikariote informant, Toula Cavaligos; and to Michael and Brian for months of gruelling work in the sun.

The **updaters** would like to thank Wendy and Fanis Meletis, Pat, George, John and Robert Shepherd, Sofia Sampsaki, Romy Most, Jack Stauf, Martin Wellbury, Bill Alexander, Jeffrey Brown, Michael Lumley, Angelo Seitis, Andreas Makris, Yiannis Garofalakis, Bent Windahl, Andreas Meletis, Harris Sarakais, Jenny Dewar, Eduard, Hoekstra, Linda, Nikos and Tanya Theodorou, Andreas Fiorentinos, Helen Morgan and last but by no means least the headmaster, secretary and staff and pupils of St. Lawrence college, Athens.

Ο Μιχάλης και Μπράϊαν αφιερώνουν το δικό τους κομμάτι σε αυτό το βιβλίο, στόν Σπυρο και την Κούλα Μελετη των οποιων η αγάπη, η καλωσύνη και η ζεστή φιλοξενια, εκαναν την Ελλάδα ακόμη πιό ξεχωριστή.

The **publishers** extend their warmest thanks to Horatio and Kicca at Animage; Colin, Chris, Mike and Maureen at TCS; Rupert Wheeler, Cheryl Zimmerman, Brenda Eisenberg and Jenny Linford.

Contents

The Cyclades   139

The Dodecanese   227

The Ionian Islands   289

The Northeastern Aegean Islands   339

The Saronic Islands   385

List of Maps

Introduction

What weighs the bosom of Abraham and the immaterial spectres of Christian paradise against this Greek eternity made of water, rock and cooling winds?

—*Kazantzakis*

There's nothing like the Greek islands to make the rest of the world seem blurred, hesitant and grey. Their frontiers are clearly defined by a sea that varies from emerald and turquoise to indigo blue, with none of the sloppiness of a changing tide; the clear sky and dry air cut their mountainous contours into sharp outline; the whiteness and simplicity of their architecture is both abstract and organic. Even the smells, be they fragrant (lemon blossoms, incense, wild thyme, grilling fish) or whiffy (donkey flops, caique diesel engines, plastic melted cheese sandwiches) are pure and unforgettable. In such an environment, the islanders themselves have developed strong, open characters; they have bright eyes and are quick to laugh or cry or scream in fury, or inquire into the most intimate details of your personal life and offer unsolicited lectures on politics, how to properly brush your teeth or find a good husband.

Since the 1970s this clarity has been a magnet to tourists from the blurred, hesitant, grey world beyond. After shipping, tourism is Greece's most important source of income, to the extent that swallows from the north have become a regular fixture in the seasonal calendar: first comes Lent and Greek Easter, then the tourists, followed by the grape harvest, and in

December, the olives. From June to September, ferries and flights are packed with holiday makers, both Greek and foreign. Popular sites and beaches are crowded by day, and often by night as well, by visitors unable to find a room, anywhere—they've been booked for months in advance.

Yet as each island has its own character, each has responded to the tourism cash cow in a slightly different way. On some, resort hotels have toadstooled up willy-nilly in search of the fast package-tour buck; some islands have sacrificed many charming old customs, environmental health, and even sanity itself in their desire to please all comers. And then there are other islands and villages, more self-reliant, clinging stubbornly to their traditions and doing all they can to keep outside interests from exploiting their coasts. Others, including some of the most visited islands, are enjoying a renaissance of traditional arts and customs, often led by the young who are pained to see their centuries-old heritage eroding into Euro-blandness.

If this book has any real purpose, it's to help you find the island of your dreams, whether you want all the mod-cons of home, sports facilities and disco dancing until dawn, or want to visit the ancient sites, study Byzantine frescoes and hone up on your Greek, or perhaps just escape to a secluded shore, where there's the luxury of doing nothing at all. Or perhaps you want a bit of each. For, in spite of all the rush to join the 20th century, the Greek islands have retained the enchantment that inspired Homer and Byron—the wine-dark sea, the scent of jasmine at twilight and nights alive with shooting stars. The ancient Greeks dedicated the islands to the gods, and they have yet to surrender them entirely to us mortals. They have kept something pure and true and alive. Or as the poet Palamas wrote, 'Here reigns nakedness. Here shadow is a dream.'

Symbols used on maps

Monastery

Church

Fortress

Beaches

Ferries

Caves

Ancient Sites

Mountains

The 3000 islands of Greece (of which a mere 170 or so are inhabited) are divided into seven major groupings: the Cyclades in the Aegean, surrounding the holy island of Delos; the Dodecanese, lying off the southwest coast of Asia Minor; the Northeastern Aegean islands, stretching from Thassos to Ikaria; the Ionian islands, sprinkled between Greece and Italy; the Saronic islands, in the Saronic Gulf; the Sporades, spread off the coast of Thessaly and Evia; and Crete, the largest island in Greece.

The Islands at a Glance

An overall picture of the islands may help you pinpoint likely destinations. You may want to head for a lively cosmopolitan place, followed by a few days of absolute peace and quiet (say, Mykonos and then Amorgos). Or you may decide to follow the Greeks to Evia and Tinos. Below are thumbnail sketches, starting with the liveliest, trendiest and most touristy.

Mykonos still manages to retain an air of class, despite the hordes that it attracts. This is as jet-setty as you can get. Great beaches and the best nightlife, and a short boat ride from the holy Delos, now an outdoor archaeological museum. Cosmopolitan **Skiathos**, lusher, greener, with some of the best beaches in the Mediterranean, matches Mykonos in prices, if not in spirit. In **Ios** you'll feel old at 25; the emphasis here is definitely on pubbing and beach-life. The lovely islands of **Kos** and **Zakynthos** have lost much of their original character under the strain of mass package tourism, but there's plenty going on to keep you amused, as in **Paros**, which paradoxically has retained its island charm, despite being one of the top destinations for backpackers of all ages. Volcanic **Santorini** has a lot to live up to as almost everyone's favourite, and is the number one spot for backpackers from both hemispheres, visiting cruise boats and practically every first-timer to Greece. If you tire of the breathtaking views and chi-chi bars in Fira, the main town, you can escape to smaller villages. The two queens of Greek tourism, **Corfu** and **Rhodes** are both large enough to absorb huge numbers of tourists, but both suffer from pockets of mass package tourism of the least attractive type. Stay clear of those spots and there's plenty left. Both have stunning capitals and charming mountain villages. **Crete** has everything for everyone: the glories of Minoan civilization, the dubious delight of overexposed Ag. Nikolaos, the mighty mountain ranges, the Venetian charm of Chania and the laid-back ex-hippy colony of Matala.

3

Arguably the best type of island holiday can be found on islands where there are enough tourists to ensure more than basic facilities—places with a choice of decent tavernas, a bar or two for an evening drink, and most of all, a place to sit out and watch life idle by. **Serifos, Sifnos, Kalymnos, Kefalonia, Lefkas, Naxos, Skopelos, Skyros** and **Syros** fall happily into this category; all have a mixture of rugged island scenery, typical villages, good restaurants and swimming. There are special gems like little **Patmos**, undeveloped but sophisticated, and known only for its monastery; **Tinos**, mecca for pilgrims and popular with Greeks and families; **Paxos**, with its sheltered bays, harbours and coves, a haven for sailors; **Karpathos**, with dramatic scenery and strong folklore tradition. Stand-offish **Andros** is still largely tourist free, and the islands of **Kea** and **Kythnos**, while close to Athens, are seldom visited except for passing yachtsmen and Greek tourists. The large, lush and lovely islands of **Samos, Chios, Lesbos** and **Thassos** provide everything required for the perfect island holiday, as well as plenty of places to explore by car or scooter if the beach/taverna life palls. Greek tourists have always preferred them to the barren Cyclades.

There remain a few islands that come under the heading of 'almost away from it all'—not quite your desert island in that they have several places to stay, eat and explore, but beyond that not a lot to do after a couple of days, unless you are resourceful—**Folegandros, Milos, Astypalaia, Amorgos, Alonissos, Limnos, Samothraki, Ikaria, Leros, Nissyros, Halki, Symi, Kastellorizo** and **Kythera**.

If, however, you genuinely want to get away from it all and don't mind eating in the same little taverna every night, then head for **Tilos, Lipsi, Ithaca**, or the cluster of islands east and south of Naxos: **Koufonissia, Keros, Shinoussa** and **Iraklia**. On any of these islands you can treat yourself to some serious introspection and brush up on your modern Greek with the locals.

Evia and **Salamis** hardly feel like islands at all, though this is part of their charm. The former has stunning scenery and an endless number of beaches, with a high percentage of Greek tourists to ensure you are experiencing the Real Thing. Salamis is little more than an Athenian suburb—not too glamorous but very Greek in every way, from its nondescript houses to its excellent, cheap little tavernas.

The Argosaronic islands come as a pleasant surprise, from well ordered, green and pleasant **Spetses** and **Poros**, to friendly little **Aegina**, very much an island despite its proximity to Athens. **Hydra**, now past its heyday as an art colony, is a bit frayed around the edges, and battered by daily one-day excursion visitors.

When choosing your island/s, the time of the year is of paramount importance, and from mid-July to 20 August you can expect nothing but frustration on the more popular islands, or the smaller ones with a limited number of beds. Don't assume that the more isolated the island the cheaper the accommodation, as supply and demand dictate the prices. You could well pay more for a room in Folegandros, for example, than in the old town of Rhodes, where rooms are far more plentiful. Out of season you can pick and choose, and places with a high percentage of Greek tourists (Kythnos, Kea and Evia) who tend to go for a 6-week burst in the height of summer, are a bargain.

Travel

By Air

Charter Flights

Charter flights to Athens and occasionally to the islands are frequent in the summer from European and North American capitals. Check the travel sections in newspapers, or get advice from travel agencies. In London peruse the so-called 'bucket shops', which have made spare charter tickets their speciality, and look through publications such as *Time Out*, the *Evening Standard* or the Sunday papers. Americans and Canadians with more time than money may well find their cheapest way of getting to Greece is to take a trans-Atlantic economy flight to London and from there to buy a bucket shop ticket to Greece. This may be difficult in July or August, however. Trans-Atlantic bargains can still be found, but bear in mind that the peak season runs from late May to mid-September. Many charters go direct to the islands—Rhodes, Crete, Corfu, Kos, Skiathos, Zakynthos, Lesbos, Samos, Mykonos, Kefalonia, Santorini and Ios—as well as to Athens and Thessaloniki, whereas scheduled flights rarely go from London to the islands.

There are several rules about charters to Greece. One is that a charter ticket is valid for a minimum of 2 nights and a maximum of 6 weeks. Visitors to Greece using a charter flight may visit Turkey or any other neighbouring country for the day, but must not stay overnight. To be on the safe side, make sure you don't get a Turkish stamp on your passport. The Turkish officials will happily stamp a removable piece of paper. Even if you intend to stay longer than 4 weeks or travel to other countries, using just half a charter ticket may still come out less than a scheduled flight, so shop around.

Scheduled Flights

Scheduled flights direct to Athens are daily from London and New York and less frequently from Toronto and Montreal. There are also direct flights from London to Thessaloniki. While the basic carriers from the United States are Olympic Airways and TWA, from London there's a vast and everchanging number of airlines, so again it's advisable to shop around and see which offers the best deal. Superpex flights offer substantially reduced fares, with flights from London to Athens ranging from £250 low season to £300 high season. They must, however, be paid for instantly and are not refundable or flexible. American economy fares range from $700 New York–Athens in low season to $1400 high season.

OA: ✆ (071) 493 3965 (London); ✆ (212) 838 3600 (New York)

TWA: ✆ (071) 439 0707; ✆ (212) 290 2141

Students under 26 are eligible for discounts; Trailfinders, 42–50 Earls Court Road, W8 6EJ, ✆ (071) 937 5400, the Student Travel Centre, 37 Store Street, London WC1, ✆ (071) 434 1306 and STA Travel, 86 Old Brompton Road, London SW7 3LQ, ✆ (071) 937 9921 can get you some of the best current deals. Returning from Greece, it is advisable to confirm your return flight a few days prior to departure.

Flights from Athens to the islands are available on Olympic Airways, Commonwealth House, 2 Chalkhill Road, London, W6 8SB, © (081) 846 9080. To be assured of a seat, especially in the summer, you should book your ticket as far in advance as possible. Infants up to 2 years old receive a 90% discount, and children of 2–12 years a 50% discount. Americans who do not have an Olympic Airways office in their town can call a toll-free no. 800 223 1226 for information.

In the past few years Olympic Airways have been offering island-to-island flights in season, a pleasant innovation that precludes the need to go to Athens. Although these have a habit of changing from year to year, routes between Crete and Rhodes, Crete and Santorini, Crete and Mykonos, Rhodes and Kos, Rhodes and Santorini, and Rhodes and Mykonos seem fairly well-established.

At the time of writing the prices of the following flights in drachmas are:

Athens to	Frequency	dr.
Alexandroupolis (for Samothraki)	daily	13,700
Chania (Crete)	daily	12,100
Chios	daily	9200
Corfu	daily	15,900
Herakleon (Crete)	daily	14,400
Kavala (for Thassos)	daily	13,600
Kefalonia	daily	11,600
Kos	daily	13,700
Kythera	daily	8500
Leros	daily	15,100
Limnos	daily	9900
Karpathos	daily	19,200
Milos	daily	7800
Mykonos	daily	9900
Mytilini (Lesbos)	daily	11,600
Paros	daily	10,300
Rhodes	daily	17,800
Samos	daily	11,300
Santorini	daily	12,300
Skiathos	daily	9500
Skyros	daily	11,000
Thessaloniki (for N. Aegean Is.)	daily	13,700
Zakynthos	daily	11,300

Aeroflot: 14 Xenofondos; © 322 0986

Air Canada: 10 Othonos; © 322 3206

Air France: 4 Karageorgi Servias; © 323 8507. Airport © 969 9334

Air Zimbabwe: 39 Panepistimiou; © 323 9101

Alitalia: 10 Nikis; © 322 9414. Airport © 961 3512

Austrian Airlines: 8 Othonos; © 323 0844. Airport © 961 0335

British Airways: 10 Othonos; © 325 0601. Airport © 961 0402

Canadian Pacific: 4 Karageorgi Servias; © 323 0344

Cyprus Airways: 10 Filellinon; © 324 6965. Airport © 961 0325

Iberia: 8 Xenofondos; © 323 4523. Airport © 969 9813

Japan Airlines: 4 Amalias; © 324 8211. Airport © 961 3615

KLM: 22 Voulis; © 325 1311. Airport © 962 4303

Lufthansa: 11 Vass. Sofias; © 771 6002 Airport © 961 3628

Olympic: 6 Othonos; © 929 2555 (Int.), 929 2444. (Dom.) Also 96 Leoforos
Syngrou; © 929 2333. East Airport © 969 9317. West Airport © 989 2111

Qantas: 11 Vass. Sofias; © 360 9411.

Sabena: 8 Othonos; © 323 6821. Airport © 961 3903

SAS: 6 Sina & Vissarionos; © 363 4444. Airport © 961 4201

South African Airways: 11 Vass. Sofias; © 361 6305. Airport © 969 9720

Swissair: 4 Othonos; © 323 1871. Airport © 961 0203

TWA: 8 Xenofondos; © 322 6451. Airport © 961 0012

Getting to and from Ellinikon Airport, Athens

Ellinikon Airport is divided into two: East (international airlines) and West (Olympic Airlines, both international and domestic flights). Double decker blue-and-yellow express buses leave for either terminal (but not both, so be sure you are getting on the right one) from Amalias Avenue, at the top of Syntagma Square, every 20 minutes between 6 am and 9 pm, every ½-hour between 9 pm and 2 am, and every hour from 2 am to 6 am. The fare is 160 dr. from 6 am to midnight, 200 dr. otherwise. Alternatively, public bus no. 133 from Othonos St, Syntagma Square (5.40 am–midnight, every 15 minutes), or no. 122 from Vass. Olgas (5.30 am–11.30 pm, every 15 minutes) both go to the West terminal. The fare is 75 dr. The East terminal may be reached by public bus no. 121 from Vass. Olgas Avenue (6.50 am–10.50 pm, every 40 minutes; 75 dr.). From Piraeus, express bus no. 19 goes to both the East and West terminals (160 dr.). Note that the bus stops are along the road in front of the terminals, not on the airport grounds themselves. A taxi between Athens and the airport will cost you about 1500 dr. (more at night).

By Train

There are 3 daily trains from London to Athens, the *Athenai Express*, the *Acropolis Express* and the *Hellas Express*, all of which take about 3 days. And a hot, crowded, stuffy 3 days too. Given the current situation in the former Yugoslavia it is advisable to double check on trains from Britain to Greece with British Rail International © (071) 834 2345. The alternative and pleasant, though slightly costlier route, is to go through Italy, either to Ancona or further south to Brindisi and take the ferry over to Corfu and Patras. British people under age 26 can travel by **Interail** passes, good for a month's rail travel in Europe—which gets you there and back, at a reasonable price. Interail passes are also available to British residents over 26 for either 15 days or a month. Americans and Canadians can buy 2-month **Eurail** and **Youth Eurail** passes before leaving home. However, the Eurail Pass is a bad bargain if you're only going to Greece, which has a limited rail service. For men over 65 and women over 60, the **Rail Europ** senior card saves up to 50% on rail fares in Greece and several other European countries, 30% in Germany, and 30% on most sea crossings. It costs £5 and can be purchased at any British Rail Travel Centre by holders of a British Rail card.

Hardy souls who deny themselves even one night in a couchette or cabin are advised to bring with them 3 days' provisions, including water, and some toilet paper. Those who intend to sleep in a prone position, beneath seats and feet, should also bring something to lie on. Wear the oldest and most comfortable clothes you own (and save yourself the trouble of washing them before you go).

Routes

Domestic train routes of possible interest to island-hoppers are as follows:

Athens–Thessaloniki (for NE. Aegean Is.)	10 a day
Athens–Alexandroupolis (for Samothraki)	2 a day
Thessaloniki–Alexandroupolis	2 a day
Athens–Chalki (Evia)	17 a day
Athens–Patras (for Ionian Is).	7 a day
Athens–Kalamata (for Kythera)	8 a day
Athens–Volos (for Sporades)	7 a day

Groups of more than 10 people can obtain a 30% discount on domestic fares; foreign students receive no special reductions.

In Athens, the railway station for northern Greece is Larissa Station, Delighianni St, © 524 0601. The station for the Peloponnese is across the tracks, © 513 1601. In Piraeus, the station for the Peloponnese is near the Piraeus–Athens metro on Akti Kalimassioti. The station for northern Greece lies further down the road on Akti Kondili. For further information telephone the OSE (Hellenic Railways Organization): 522 2491 or 362 4402/6. Recorded timetables can be obtained by dialling 145 (for Greece) or 147 (for the rest of Europe).

By Bus

Taking a bus from London to Athens is always a possible alternative for those who decide that a train trip is too expensive or too easy a route to travel. With 3½ days (or more) on the road and Adriatic ferry, adventures are practically included in the ticket price but it probably isn't worthwhile unless you intend to spend some time in Greece. Eurolines, 52 Grosvenor Gardens, Victoria, London SW1, ✆ (071) 730 0202 offer 3-day journeys from London to Athens and Olympic Bus Ltd, 70 Brunswick Centre, London WC1 1AE, ✆ (071) 837 9141 offer 4-day journeys from London to Athens via Brussels or 5-day journeys from London to Athens via Paris. In Greece, you'll find agencies selling bus tickets on the most obscure islands, as well as in Athens; Filellinon St near Syntagma Square is Athens' budget travellers' boulevard, so check there for other possibilities.

Domestic

The domestic bus service in Greece is efficient and regular, if not always a bargain. Each bus is decorated at the whim of its driver, with pin-ups, saints, wallpaper, tinsel, tassels, and plastic hands which wave violently when the bus falls into a pothole. Bus services from Athens relevant to this book are as follows:

Athens to	No. per day	Terminal	✆	Duration
Chalki (Evia)	33	Liossion	831 7153	1.30 hrs
Edipsos (Evia)	3–4	Liossion	831 7253	3.15 hrs
Gythion	4	Kifissou	512 4913	5.30 hrs
Igoumenitsa (for Corfu)	3	Kifissou	512 5954	8.30 hrs
Kefalonia	4	Kifissou	512 9498	8 hrs
Kerkyra (Corfu)	3	Kifissou	512 9443	11 hrs
Lefkas	4	Kifissou	513 3583	5.30 hrs
Patras (for Ionian Is.)	16	Kifissou	513 6185	3 hrs
Rafina (for Cyclades and Evia)	18	Mavromateon	821 0872	1 hr
Thessaloniki (for N.E. Aegean Is.)	9	Kifissou	514 8856	7.30 hrs
Volos (for Sporades)	9	Liossion	831 7186	5.15 hrs
Zakynthos	3	Kifissou	512 9432	7 hrs

To get to the terminal at 100 Kifissou St, take bus no. 51 from Omonia Square (Zinonos and Menadrou Sts). For the terminal at 260 Liossion St take bus no. 24 from Leoforos Amalias, by the National Garden. Take a bus or tram north, towards Areos Park on 28th Octovriou St for the Mavromateon terminal.

During the summer it is advisable to reserve seats in advance on the long-distance buses. Tickets for these journeys must normally be bought before one boards the bus. Note that two islands, Lefkas and Evia, are joined to the mainland by bridge, which is good to remember if no ferries are running to the islands due to either strikes or bad weather.

There are never enough buses on the islands in the summer nor is it customary to queue.

However, you will not be left behind if it is humanly possible for you to squeeze on. If you can wake up in time, you will find that buses are rarely crowded early in the morning.

Within the Athens area the bus fare is 75 dr. Stamp your ticket on the bus to validate it—if you can fight your way to the machine, that is.

By Sea

The most common sea route to Greece is from Italy, with daily ferry services from Ancona, Bari, Brindisi, Otranto, and Venice. The most popular of these is the daily service from Brindisi, which leaves at 10 pm (connecting with the train from Rome) and arrives in Corfu the next morning. Passengers are allowed a free infinite stopover in Corfu if that island is not their ultimate destination, before continuing to Igoumenitsa or Patras, but make sure it is noted on your ticket. If you plan to sail in the summer, it's advisable to make reservations in advance, especially if you bring a car (most travel agents can do this for you). Students and young people can get a discount of up to 20%. Discounts of up to 20% are also offered when buying a return ticket. The quality of service among the different lines varies, of course; some ships are spanking clean and are plushly furnished—one at least even has a laser disco—while others have been in service so long that they creak. However, the sullen demeanour of the crews seems to be uniform.

Steamer and ferry services of varying regularity also connect Piraeus to the ports listed on the next three pages.

New **catamaran** and **hydrofoil** services now link Brindisi with Corfu in under 4 hours but neither take cars.

Ferries

Ports	Frequency	Company
Ancona–Patras	Twice weekly	Karageorgis Lines 119 Kalirois St Athens, ✆ 923 4201
Ancona–Corfu–Patras	2/4 times a week	Strinzis Lines 26 Akti Possidonos Piraeus, ✆ 412 9815
Ancona–Corfu–Igoumenitsa–Patras	2/4 times a week	ANEK Lines 54 Amalias Avenue Athens, ✆ 323 3481
Ancona–Igoumenitsa–Corfu–Patras	5 times a week	Minoan Lines 2 Vass. Konstantinou Athens, ✆ 751 2356
Ancona–Igoumenitsa–Patras	2 times a week	Marlines 38 Akti Possidonos Piraeus, ✆ 411 0777

Ortona–Corfu–Igoumenitsa–Patras	3 times a week	Hellenic Mediterranean Lines 28 Amalias Avenue Athens, ✆ 323 6333
Bari–Corfu–Igoumenitsa–Patras	Daily	Ventouris Ferries 26 Amalias Avenue Athens, ✆ 324 0276
Brindisi–Corfu–Igoumenitsa–Patras	Daily	Fragline 5a Rethymnou St Athens, ✆ 822 1285
	Daily	Adriatica 4 Filellinon St Athens, ✆ 324 6000
	Daily	Hellenic Mediterranean Lines (see above)
Brindisi–Patras	Daily	Mediterranean Lines 274 Alkiviadou St Piraeus, ✆ 453 1882
	4 times a week	European Seaways 9 Filellinon St Piraeus, ✆ 429 4303
Brindisi–Kefalonia–Patras	Daily in summer	Hellenic Mediterranean Lines (see above)
Brindisi–Corfu	Daily in summer	Marlines (see above)
Venice–Bari–Piraeus–Herakleon– Alexandria	Once a week March–Jan	Adriatica (see above)
Ancona–Corfu–Kefalonia– Piraeus–Paros–Samos– Kuşadassi	Daily in summer	Minoan Lines (see above)

Boats to the Islands

The daily newspaper *I Nay Temporiki* lists all the activities of the port at Piraeus and publishes weekly ship schedules. The National Tourist Office also publishes a monthly list of ship departures, both abroad and to the islands.

A little travelling through the islands will soon show you that each boat is an individual. The many new ones are clean and comfortable and often air conditioned. The older boats may lack some modern refinements but nevertheless they can be pleasant if you remain out on deck. The drinking water is never very good on the boats, but all sell beer, Coca Cola and lemon or orange soda. Biscuits and cigarettes complete the fare on the smaller boats, while the larger ones offer sandwiches, cheese pies or even full meals.

All the boats are privately owned and although the Greek government controls the prices some will charge more for the same journey, depending on the facilities offered, speed, etc. If caiques relay you from shore to ship, you will pay more. In most cases children under the age of 4 travel free, and between 4 and 10 for half-fare. Over 10 they are charged the full fare. In the summer it is wise to buy tickets in advance, to guarantee a place and because they often cost 20% more when bought on board. Refunds are rarely given unless the boat itself never arrives, stuck in Piraeus for tax delinquencies. Boats will arrive late or divert their course for innumerable reasons, so if you have to catch a flight home allow for the eccentricities of the system and leave a day early to be safe.

When purchasing a ticket, either in Piraeus or on the islands, it's always best to do so from your ship's central agency. Other agencies may tell you that the boat is full, when in truth they've merely sold all the tickets allotted them by the central agency. On many islands, agents moonlight as bartenders or grocers and may only have a handwritten sign next to the door advertising their ship's departures.

Because Piraeus is so busy there's a new trend to use smaller mainland ports, especially Rafina and Lavrion. Neither of these is far from Athens, and bus connections are frequent. They are a bit of a bother for most tourists, though, which means that islands mainly served by these outlying ports are often quieter, if you take the trouble to go.

Most inter-island ferries have three or four classes: the first class, with an airconditioned lounge and cabins (and often as expensive as flying); the second class, often with its own lounge as well, but smaller cabins; tourist class, for which you can reserve a cabin, segregated by sex, and deck class, which usually gives you access to the typically large, stuffy rooms full of 'airline seats' and the snack bar area. As a rule the Greeks go inside and the tourists stay out—on summer nights in particular this is perhaps the most pleasant alternative if you have a sleeping bag.

You'd do well to always keep your ticket with you on a Greek ship, at least until the crew enacts its 'ticket control', a comedy routine necessitated by the fact that Greeks don't always check tickets when passengers board. Instead, after one or two pleas on the ship's loud-speaker system for passengers without tickets to purchase them forthwith, you suddenly find all the doors on the boat locked or guarded by a bored but obdurate sailor, while bands of officers rove about the boat checking tickets. Invariably mix-ups occur: children are separated from their parents, others have gone to the wc, someone has left a ticket with someone on the other side of the immovable sailor, crowds pile up at the doors, and stowaways are marched to the purser's office. In the worst cases, this goes on for an hour; on smaller ships it's usually over in 15 minutes.

Prices, though no longer cheap, are still fairly reasonable for passengers, rather dear for cars.

The following is a list of some of the more popular scheduled mainland and inter-island connections. Duration of each boat trip and approximate prices are given in drachmas but are subject to change without notice.

Piraeus to	2nd Class (dr.)	Tourist Class (dr.)	3rd Class (dr.)	Duration (hours)
Ag. Nikolaos, Crete	6900	5200	3900	13
Amorgos	3100	2400	2300	11
Anafi	5500	4200	3300	18
Astypalaia	5200	3900	3000	13
Chania, Crete	5100	3800	2800	11
Chios	4400	3200	2400	9
Donoussa	3100	2400	2300	10
Elafonissos	3800	3100	2500	10
Folegandros	4400	3400	2600	12
Halki	8600	6300	4700	17
Herakleon, Crete	5400	4000	3000	12
Heraklia	3100	2400	2300	15
Ikaria	3800	2800	2100	12
Ios	4000	3200	2600	10
Kalymnos	5200	3900	3000	13
Karlovassi, Samos	4600	3500	2700	12
Karpathos	6300	4800	3700	18
Kassos	6300	4800	3700	18
Kimolos	3200	2600	2100	8
Kos	6400	4800	3700	15
Koufonissia–Shinoussa	3100	2400	2300	14
Kythera	4300	3400	2700	10
Kythnos	2400	1800	1400	4
Leros	5200	3900	3000	11
Lesbos (Mytilini)	5000	3700	3000	15
Limnos	5200	4100	3300	18
Milos	3200	2600	2100	8
Mykonos	3200	2500	2100	6
Naxos	3200	2500	2100	8
Nissyros	6400	4800	3700	22
Paros	2800	2200	1900	6
Patmos	5200	3900	3000	10
Rhodes	7000	5300	4100	18
Samos	5100	3700	2800	12
Santorini	4000	3200	2600	10
Serifos	2700	2000	1600	5
Sifnos	2900	2300	1900	6
Sikinos	5200	4000	3100	10
Sitia, Crete	7700	5800	4400	13
Symi	6400	4800	3700	22
Syros	2700	2100	1900	5
Tilos	6400	4800	3700	24
Tinos	3000	2400	2100	5

Not included in the above prices are embarkation taxes and contributions to the seamen's union, but these are minimal.

Argosaronic Line ✆ 411 5801, 451 1311

Piraeus to	1st Class (dr.)	3rd Class (dr.)	Duration (hours)
Aegina	700	600	2.00
Hydra	1300	1000	4.00
Poros	1100	900	3.30
Spetses	1700	1300	5.00

Sporades Line ✆ 417 8084, 417 2415

Ag. Konstantinos to	Tourist Class (dr.)	Duration (hours)
Alonissos	2700	5.30
Glossa	2400	4.25
Limnos	2800	10.30
Skiathos	2200	3.15
Skopelos	2500	5.30

Kymis, Evia to		
Ag. Efstratios	1500	6.00
Alonissos	2300	3.00
Glossa	2600	5.00
Skiathos	2800	5.30
Skopelos	2500	3.30
Skyros	1200	2.00

Volos to		
Alonissos	2300	5.00
Glossa	1900	3.45
Skiathos	1700	3.00
Skopelos	2100	4.30

Evia and Cyclades Line ✆ (0294) 26166

Rafina to		
Andros	1200	2.30
Karystos, Evia	1300	4.00
Marmari, Evia	700	5.00
Mykonos	2300	5.00
Naxos	2200	6.30
Paros	2100	5.00
Syros	2000	3.30
Tinos	2000	4.00

Kea—Kythnos Line ✆ (0292) 25249

Lavrion to		
Kea	900	2.30
Kythnos	1600	4.00

There are several fleets of hydrofoils thumping over the Greek seas. The Flying Dolphins leave Piraeus Zea Marina for three of the Saronic islands—Poros, Hydra and Spetses, and links them with neighbouring mainland ports at Porto Heli and Nafplion; one goes as far as Kythera. For Aegina, hydrofoils leave from the main harbour in Piraeus. Two services ply the Dodecanese, from Rhodes all the way north to Samos, calling at Kalymnos, Kos, Leros and Patmos in between. Others connect Kilini to Zakynthos, the mainland with Evia, the Sporades, Kea and Kythnos. All the hydrofoils run throughout the year but are less frequent in winter.

Hydrofoils as a rule travel twice as fast as ships and are twice as expensive (in some cases as much as a plane). In the peak season they are often fully booked, so buy tickets as early as you can. In a choppy sea a trip may leave you saddle-sore, and if the weather is very bad, they don't leave port.

Tourist Excursion Boats

These are generally slick and clean, and have become quite numerous in recent years. They are more expensive than the regular ferries or steamers, but often have schedules that allow visitors to make day excursions to nearby islands (though you can also take them one way), and are very convenient, having largely taken the place of the little caique operators, many of whom now specialize in excursions to remote beaches instead of island-hopping on request. They may well be the only transport available to the most remote islands, but do inquire about scheduled ferries. Friendly yachtsmen may give you a lift—it never hurts to ask.

Boats to Turkey

Whatever axes are currently being ground between Greece and Turkey, a kind of *pax tourista* has fallen over the mutually profitable exchange of visitors from the Greek islands to the Turkish mainland. Connections run daily year-round between Rhodes and Marmaris (3½ hrs); between Kos and Bodrum daily in summer, less frequently in winter (1½ hrs); from Chios to Cêsme daily from spring to autumn (1 hr); from Samos to Kuşadasi (near Ephesus) at least twice a day, April–October (1½ hrs); and from Lesbos to Ayvalik daily in summer (2 hrs). While there isn't much difference in crossing times, prices can vary enormously according to when you go and whose boat you take (both Greek and Turkish boats make the crossings). There is a mysterious array of taxes, everywhere different (sometimes less if you only make a day excursion); generally speaking, the return fare is 8000 dr. On the whole, Turkish shops around the ports will take drachma, but the Greeks will not take Turkish lira—and the exchange rate between the two is pretty dreadful. Also, beware the charter restriction: things as they are, if you have spent a night in Turkey the Greek airport authorities might invoke the law and refuse you passage home on your flight.

For the most recent information on Greek sea connections, get a copy of the National Tourist Organisation's *Greek Travel Pages* or *Key Travel Guide*, which is updated every week. Travel agents in Great Britain often have a copy, and it is easy to find in Greece itself.

By Car

Driving from **London to Athens** (and taking the ferry from Italy to Greece) at a normal pace takes around 3½ days, which is why one sees so few British cars in Greece. Unless you are planning to spend a few weeks on one or two islands, a car is not really worth the expense and trouble of bringing it to Greece. If you do decide to bring one, the smaller the better, both for squeezing it onto the ferry, and for negotiating the sometimes very narrow village roads.

One of the best bets for **North Americans and Australians** who want to drive in Greece is to buy a car for the duration of your trip, with an agreement to sell it back to the company when you leave. Several companies in Paris can arrange this, though it is not possible in Greece itself. Alternatively, there are many rent-a-car companies on the mainland and the islands.

An **International Driving Licence** is not required by British, Austrian, Belgian or German citizens. Other nationals can obtain an international licence at home, or at one of the Automobile Club offices in Greece (ELPA), by presenting a national driving licence, passport and photograph. The minimum age is 18 years.

The Motor Insurance Bureau at 10 Xenofontos St, Athens, ✆ (01) 323 6733, can tell you which Greek insurance company represents your own, or provide you with additional cover for Greece.

Customs formalities are very easy and usually take very little time. One is allowed a year of free use of the car in Greece, and after that can apply for a 4-month extension. North Americans and Australians are allowed 2 years. If you leave Greece without your car, you must have it withdrawn from circulation by a customs authority. ELPA has a list of lawyers who can offer free legal advice on motorcars. They also have a 24-hour recording of information useful to foreign motorists, ✆ 174.

Parking in the centre of Athens, or the **Green Zone**, is forbidden outside designated parking areas. The following streets form the borders of the Green Zone: Sekeri, Botassi, Stournara, Marni, Menandrou, Pireos, Likourgou, Athias, Mitropoleos, Filellinon, Amalias and Vassilissis Sophias.

While driving in the centre of Athens may be a hair-raising experience, the rest of Greece is easy and pleasant. There are few cars on most roads, even in summer, and all signs have their Latin equivalents. Traffic regulations and signalling comply with standard practice on the European Continent (i.e. driving on the right). Crossroads and low visibility in the mountains are probably the greatest hazards. Where there are no right of way signs at a crossroads, give priority to traffic coming from the right, and always beep your horn on blind corners. Take special care when approaching an unguarded railway level crossing. It is also advisable to take a spare container of petrol along with you, as petrol stations are inconsistent in their frequency. There is a speed limit of 50 km per hour (30 mph) in inhabited areas: other speed limits are indicated by signposts in kilometres. Horn blowing is prohibited in Athens and other big cities, though you'd never guess it from the cacophony that starts when the red light changes to green. The Greek Automobile Club (ELPA) operates a breakdown service within 60 km (40 miles) of Athens, Salonika, Larissa, Patras and Herakleon: dial 104.

Athens: 2–4 Messogion St, Tower of Athens, ℂ (01) 779 1615. Telex: 215763

Chania (Crete): 1 Apokoronou & Skoula, ℂ (0821) 26059 & 57177

Corfu: Pat. Athinagora, ℂ (0661) 39504

Herakleon (Crete): Knossos Ave & G. Papandreou, ℂ (081) 289440

Kavala: 8 Cristostomou Smyrnis, ℂ (051) 229778

Larissa: At the 3rd km on the national road Athens/Larissa, ℂ (041) 239660

Patras: Astingos & 127 Korinthou, ℂ (061) 425411 & 426416

Rhodes: 38 Akti Miaouli, ℂ (0241) 25066

Thessaloniki: 230 Vass. Olgas & Egeou, ℂ (031) 426319 & 426320

Tripolis: 47 Nafplio, ℂ (071) 224101

Volos: 89 Iolkou, ℂ (0421) 47404

By Bike

By Motorbike, Scooter or Moped

Scooters, and even more popular, mopeds are ideal for the islands in the summer. It almost never rains and what could be more pleasant than a gentle thyme-scented breeze freshening your journey over the mountains? Scooters are both more economical and more practical than cars. They can fit into almost any boat and travel paths where cars fear to tread. Many islands have scooter rentals which are not expensive, and include third party coverage in most cases. For larger motorbikes you may be asked to show a driver's licence. However, be warned that not a few hospital beds in Greece are occupied every summer by tourists who have been careless about moped safety rules.

By Bicycle

Cycling has not caught on in Greece, either as a sport or as a means of transport, though you can usually hire an old bike in most major resorts. Trains and planes carry bicycles for a small fee, and Greek boats generally take them along, for nothing. Crete and Evia are the best islands for cycling enthusiasts, Crete being the more rugged by far. On both islands you will find fresh water, places to camp, and a warm and surprised welcome in the villages.

Hitch-hiking

With the rarest of exceptions, hitch-hiking, or 'autostop' as it is known in Greece, is perfectly safe. However, the lack of cars makes it a not particularly speedy mode of transport. The Greek double standard produces the following percentages for hopeful hitch-hikers:

Single woman: 99% of cars will stop. You hardly have to stick out your thumb.
Two women: 75% of cars will find room for you.

Woman and man: 50%; more if the woman is pretty.

Single man: 25% if you are well dressed with little luggage; less otherwise.

Two men: start walking.

The best time for soliciting a ride is when you disembark from a ship. Ask your fellow passengers, or better still write your destination on a piece of paper (in Greek if possible) and pin it to your shirt with a naïve and friendly smile. What you lose in dignity you will generally gain in a lift.

Specialist Holidays

A list of tour operators including specialist ones is available from the:

National Tourist Organization of Greece ✆ (071) 734 5997 (London), (212) 421 5777 (New York), (312) 782 1084 (Chicago), (213) 626696 (Los Angeles).

British Museum Tours, 46 Bloomsbury Street, London, WC1B 3QQ. ✆ (071) 323 8895
   Archaeological guided tours, such as the 'Palaces and Tombs of the Mycenaean Kings'.

Cox & Kings Travel Ltd, St James Court, Buckingham Gate, London SW1E 6AF.
   Botanic and natural history holidays. ✆ (071) 834 7472

Exodus, 9 Weir Road, London, SW12 0LT. ✆ (081) 675 5550
   Trekking holidays including a 'Cretan Odyssey'.

Greek Islands Sailing Club, 66 High Street, Walton-on-Thames, Surrey, KT12 1BU.
   Activity holidays including painting, weaving, birdwatching , photography, mountain biking, dinghy sailing and windsurfing.. ✆ (0932) 220416

Laskarina Holidays, St Mary's Gate, Wirksworth, Derbyshire, DE4 4DQ.
   Painting holidays. ✆ (062 982) 481

Pure Crete, 90–92 Southbridge Road, Croydon, Surrey, CR0 1AF. ✆ (081) 760 0879
   Wildflower and painting holidays.

Ramblers Holidays, Box 43, Welwyn Garden City, Hertfordshire, AL8 6PQ.
   Walking holidays with emphasis on archaeology and wildflowers ✆ (0707) 331133

Skyros Centre, 92 Prince of Wales Rd, London NWS 3NE. ✆ (071) 267 4424
   Two-week writers' workshops, Tai Chi, snorkelling, drama, dance and aromatherapy for singles and families on Skyros.

Swan Hellenic Ltd, 77 New Oxford Street, London, WC1A 1PP. ✆ (071) 831 1515
   Cultural, archaeological and art history tours and cruises.

Wine Dark Seas, Ardross, Comrie, Perthshire PH6 2JU. ✆ (0764) 70107
   Cretan specialists offering cultural, natural history and painting holidays.

Zoe Holidays, 34 Thornhill Road, Surbiton, KT6 7TL. ✆ (081) 390 7623
   Rural holidays through the Women's Agricultural Tourist Cooperatives on Chios and Lesbos.

Self-catering Holidays

Airtours, Wavell House, Helmshore, Rossendale, Lancashire, BB4 4NB. © (0706) 260000
Self-catering on Corfu, Lesbos, Rhodes, Kos, Zakynthos, Kalymnos, Kefalonia and Crete.

Corfu à la Carte, 8 Deanwood House, Stockcross, Newbury, Berkshire, RG16 8JP.
Villas and cottages on Corfu, Paxos and Skiathos. © (0635) 30621

CV Travel, 43 Cadogan Street, London, SW3 2PR. © (071) 581 0851
Villas and apartments on Corfu and Paxos.

Greek Islands Club, 66 High Street, Walton-on-Thames, Surrey, KT12 1BU.
Apartments and villas on Paxos, Ithaca, Kefalonia and Kythera © (0932) 220477

Greek Sun Holidays, 1 Bank Street, Sevenoaks, Kent, TN13 1UW. © (0732) 740317
Apartments and studios on Alonissos, Kos, Kythera, Lesbos, Lipsi, Milos, Mykonos, Maxos, Paxos, Patmos, Samos, Skiathos, Skopelos and Skyros.

Ilios Island Holidays, 18 Market Square, Horsham, West Sussex, RH12 1E.© (0403) 59788
Villas and apartments on Skiathos, Skopelos, Zakynthos, Lefkada, Meganissi, Kefalonia, Tinos and Naxos, plus the opportunity to rent the island of Argironisos.

Laskarina Holidays, St Mary's Gate, Wirksworth, Derbyshire, DE4 4DQ.. © (062982) 4881
Studios and apartments on Symi, Kalymnos, Halki, Tilos, Karpathos, Astypalaia, Spetses,Skiathos, Skopelos, Alonissos and Skyros (*see* Specialist Holidays).

Meon Travel, Meon House, College Street, Petersfield, Hampshire, GU32 3JN.
Villas on Corfu and Paxos. © (0730) 268411

Pure Crete, 90-92 Southbridge Road, Croydon, Surrey, CRO 1AF. © (081) 760 0879
Houses and farms on Crete (see also Specialist Holidays).

Something Special, 10 Bull Plain, Hertford, Hertfordshire, SG14 1DT. © (0992) 552231
Villas and apartments on Corfu.

Customs and Immigration

The formalities for foreign tourists entering Greece are very simple. American, Australian, British and Canadian citizens can stay for up to 3 months in Greece simply on presentation of a valid passport. However, unless you are entering with a car, immigration officials no longer stamp EC passports. South Africans are permitted 2 months.

If you want to extend your stay in Greece, you must report to the police 10 days before your visa runs out. (If you are staying in Athens, register at the Athens Alien Dept, 173 Alexandras Ave, 115 22 Athens, © 646 8103). Take your passport, four photographs, and if possible, the name of a reference in Greece. You will receive a slip of paper authorizing you to stay for a period of up to 6 months. This has to be stamped at the end of every 3 successive months that you remain in Greece.

By Yacht

One of the great thrills of sailing the Greek waters is the variety of places to visit in a relatively short time, with the bonus that nowhere in Greece is far from safe shelter or harbours with good facilities for yachtsmen. There is little shallow water, except close to the shoreline, few currents and no tides or fog. The 100,000 miles of coastline, and a collection of islands and islets numbering three thousand, provide a virtually inexhaustible supply of secluded coves and empty beaches, even at the height of the tourist season. Equally, there are berthing facilities in the most popular of international hotspots—it's all there beneath the blue skies and bright sunshine. The Greek National Tourist Organization has initiated a programme of rapid expansion in the face of mounting competition from Turkey and Spain; facilities are being improved and new marinas are being constructed throughout the country.

The **colour map** on the inside front cover shows the marinas, yacht supply stations, ports of entry and exit, shipping and weather forecast areas in Greece and the islands.

Greek weather guarantees near-perfect sailing conditions, the only real problem being the strong winds in parts of the country at certain times of the year, notably April to October, when most yachtsmen are at sea.

The Ionian Sea and the west coast of the Peloponnese are affected by the *maistros*, a light-to-moderate northwest wind which presents itself in the afternoon only. Less frequently there are westerly winds, from moderate to strong, to the west and south of the Peloponnese. To the south of Attica, and east of the Peloponnese, the sea is to a great extent sheltered by land masses and it is not until summer that the menacing *meltemi* blows. The Aegean Sea is affected by a northwest wind in the south, and a northeasterly in the north, and when the *meltemi* blows in August and September, it can reach force eight, testing all your skills at the helm. The Turkish coast has light, variable breezes, which are rudely interrupted by the forceful *meltemi*.

This chart shows average wind speeds (in knots) during the months April to October.

Area	Apr	May	Jun	Jul	Aug	Sep	Oct
N.E.Aegean	NE	NE	NE	NE	NE	NE	NE
(Limnos)	10.2	8.2	8.2	10.2	10.2	10.2	11.4
Thrakiko	NE	NE	NE	NE	NE	NE	NE
(Thassos)	1.4	1.4	1.4	1.4	1.4	1.6	2.3
Kos–Rhodes	WNW	WNW	NW	NW	NW	NW	WNW
(Kos)	13.6	13.0	13.0	13.6	13.6	13.0	11.4
S.W. Aegean	N	SW	N	N	N	N	N
(Milos)	9.0	6.6	6.6	8.6	8.6	8.6	9.8
W. Cretan	SW	NNW	NWN	NNW	N	N	N
(Chania)	5.0	4.4	4.4	4.4	4.1	4.1	3.8
E. Cretan	NW	NW	NW	NW	NW	NW	NW
(Herakleon)	6.6	4.4	6.2	8.2	7.4	6.6	5.8
E. Cretan	NW	NW	NW	NW	NW	NW	NW
(Sitia)	6.6	5.0	7.0	8.6	8.2	6.6	5.0
Kythera	NE	W	W	NE	NE	NE	NE
(Kythera)	9.8	8.2	7.8	7.4	8.2	9.0	10.6
Samos Sea	NW	NW	NW	NW	NW	NW	NW
(Samos)	9.4	7.8	9.4	11.0	10.2	8.6	7.0
W. Karpathion	W	W	W	W	W	W	W
(Karpathos)	6.6	6.2	8.6	10.6	9.4	8.2	6.2
N. Ionian	SE	WSE	W	NWW	NW	SE	SE
(Corfu)	2.9	2.6	2.9	2.6	2.6	2.3	2.6
N.Ionian	NW	NW	NW	NW	NW	NWN	NWNE
(Argostoli)	5.8	5.0	5.4	5.8	5.4	4.4	5.0
S. Ionian	N	NEN	NE	N	NNE	N	NE
(Zakynthos)	9.8	9.4	9.8	10.2	9.8	9.0	10.2
S.Ionian	W	W	W	W	W	W	NE
(Methoni)	11.8	11.0	11.4	11.8	11.0	10.2	9.8

If you wish to skipper a yacht anywhere within the Greek seas, you must consult the *Compile Index Chart of Greek Seas*, otherwise known as *XEE*, published by the Hellenic Navy Hydrographic Service. Basically it is a map of Greece divided into red squares, each with an index number, from which you can select the appropriate charts and order them accordingly (cost approx. 1500 dr.). For non-Greeks, 2500 dr. will buy you what is known as *XEE 64*, a booklet of abbreviations explaining the signs on the charts, with texts in English and Greek.

You also need one of the *Pilot* series books, which cost 2500 dr. each and cover the following areas in great detail:

Pilot A: South Albania to Kythera; Ionian Sea, Corinthian Gulf and North Peloponnese shores.
Pilot B: Southeastern Greek shores; Crete, Eastern Peloponnese, Saronic Gulf and Cyclades.
Pilot C: Northeastern Greek shores; Evoikos, Pagassitikos, Sporades, Thermaikos, Chalkidiki.
Pilot D: North and Eastern Aegean shores; Eastern Macedonia, Thrace, Limnos, Lesbos, Chios, Samos, the Dodecanese and Asia Minor.

These describe geographical data, possible dangers, and the present state of transportation and communication. All ports and marinas are mentioned, including where to obtain fresh water and fuel, and there are descriptions of visible inland features. The Hydrographic Service constantly updates the books and sends additional booklets to authorized sellers and to all port authorities, where you may consult them. The nautical charts are updated using the latest most sophisticated methods, and follow standardized dimensions. They are on a 1:100,000 scale for bigger areas and 1:750,000 for ports. Heights and depths are given in metres with functional conversion tables for feet and fathoms.

Further information is provided in booklets called *Notes to Mariners*, published monthly and available for consultation at port authorities. These give information on any alterations to naval charts you have purchased for your voyage. Besides all this there is the Navtex service. A special department of the Hydrographic Service keeps you informed about the weather or any special warnings for the day, through telex, or Navtex. The text is in Greek and English, and there are four retransmission coastal stations covering the Greek seas. Weather forecasts for yachtsmen are broadcast at intervals throughout the day on VHF Channel 16 (in Greek and English); security warnings are also broadcast on this channel, e.g. dangerous wrecks, lights not in operation, etc.

Bunkering Ports and Supply Stations

The following is a list of ports where fuelling facilities and other provisions may be obtained:

Adamas (Milos)*, Aegina, Ag. Nikolaos (Kea), Ag. Nikolaos (Crete)*, Alexandroupolis*, Alimos Marina, Argostoli (Kefalonia)*, Chios*, Corfu Port*, Ermoupolis (Syros)*, Flisvos Marina, Gouvia Marina*, Gythion*, Chalkida*, Chania (Crete)*, Hydra, Itea*, Kalamata*, Kalymnos, Kamares (Sifnos), Kapsali (Kythera), Kastellorizo, Kastro (Andros), Katakolo*, Katapola (Amorgos), Kavala*, Kimi (Evia), Korinthos*, Kos*, Lakki (Leros), Lavrion*, Lefkas, Limeni (Mani), Limaria (Skyros), Mirina (Limnos)*, Mytilini*, Monemvasia, Mykonos*, Nafpaktos, Nafplion*, Naxos, Nea Roda, Palea Epidavros, Paleokastritsa, Parga, Parikia (Paros), Pigadia (Karpathos), Pilos*, Poros, Porto Koufo, Porto Rafti, Preveza*, Rhodes (Mandraki)*, Skala (Patmos)*, Skiathos*, Skopelos, Spetses, Thessaloniki Marina*, Thessaloniki Port*, Tinos, Vathi (Ithaca)*, Volos*, Vouliagmeni Marina, Zakynthos*, Zea Marina.

* indicates official ports of entry and exit, where there are port, customs and health authorities, as well as immigration and currency control services. Others are: Egion, Gerakini (Chalkidiki), Glyfada, Igoumenitsa, Herakleon, Kimissi (Evia), Patras, Perama, Pithagorion and Vathi (Samos), Dafni (Agion Oros), Elefsina, Fira (Santorini), Ivira (Agion Oros), Kali Limenes (Crete), Drepanon (Ahaia) and Stili (Lamia).

Main Port Authorities' telephone numbers are as follows:

Piraeus: (01) 451 1311

Elefsina: (01) 554 3504

Thessaloniki: (031) 531504

Corfu: (0661) 39918

Herakleon: (081) 244912

Chios: (0271) 23097

Kavala: (051) 224472

Patras: (061) 341024

Rhodes: (0241) 22220

Volos: (0421) 38888

Yachts entering Greek waters must fly the code flag 'Q' until cleared by entry port authorities. Upon arrival the **port authority** (*Limenarkion*) issues all yachts with a transit log, which entitles the yacht and crew to unlimited travel in Greek waters. It also allows crew members to buy fuel, alcohol and cigarettes duty free. It must be kept on board and produced when required, and returned to the customs authorities on leaving Greece at one of the exit ports. Permission is normally given for a stay of 6 months, but this can be extended. Small motor, sail or rowing boats do not require a 'carnet de passage', and are allowed into Greece duty free for 4 months. They are entered in your passport and deleted on exit. For more information, apply to the Greek National Tourist Organisation, 4 Conduit Street, London, W1R 0DJ, ✆ (071) 734 5997 who produce a useful leaflet *Sailing the Greek Seas*.

Anyone taking a yacht by road is strongly advised to obtain boat registration documentation from the DVLA, Swansea, SA99 1BX, ✆ (0792) 783355. The **Royal Yachting Association**, R.Y.A. House, Romsey Road, Eastleigh, Hampshire, SO5 4YA, ✆ (0703) 629962 is a useful source of yachting information.

A brief guide to monthly mooring rates, in dr.:

In Alimos Marina (Athens)	summer	winter
Up to 7 m 3	300 per m	2800 per m
8–17 m	3600 " "	2900 " "
18 m and above	3700 " "	3000 " "
In Gouvia Marina (Corfu)		
Up to 7 m	2000 " "	1700 " "
8–17 m	2200 " "	1800 " "
18 m and above	2400 " "	1900 " "

Chartering yachts is very popular these days, and as the promotional literature says, can be cheaper than staying in a hotel (if you have enough friends or family to share expenses). Between the various firms (the National Tourist Organisation has a list) there are over a thousand vessels currently available in all sizes, with or without a crew (though without a crew—bareboat charter—both the charterer and another member of the party must show proof of seamanship: a sailing certificate or letter of recommendation from a recognized yacht or sailing club). There are various options: motor yachts (without sails), motor sailors (primarily powered by motor, auxiliary sail power) and sailing yachts (with auxiliary motor power). Charters can be arranged through licensed firms of yacht brokers, or by contacting yacht owners directly. The **Yacht Charter Association**, 60 Silverdale, New Milton, Hampshire, BH25 7DE, ✆ (0425) 619004 supplies a list of its recognized yacht charter operators and offers advice on chartering overseas. For more information on chartering in Greece, write to:

The Hellenic Professional Yacht Owners Association, 43 Freatidos St, Zea Marina, 18536 Piraeus.
✆ 452 6335

Greek Yacht Brokers and Consultants Association, 7 Filellinon St, 105 57 Athens.
✆ 323 0330

Greek Yacht Owners Association, 10 Lekka St, 185 37 Piraeus.
✆ 452 6335

One of the largest and most reputable firms is **Valef**, located at 22 Akti Themistokleous, Piraeus, ✆ 428 1920, fax 413780 (in the USA: 7254 Fir Rd, PO Box 391, Ambler, Pa 19002). They have more than 300 craft, accommodating 4–50 people in comfort.

Yacht Charter Operators Based in England

Bareboat yacht charter prices start from around £350–£400 per week for a 31-ft boat in low season and £2,500 for a 48-ft boat in high season. Prices peak during July and August and are lower during the spring and autumn months.

BUOYS Cruising Club, 8 Chase Side, Enfield, Middlesex, EN2 6NF. ✆ (081) 367 8462
Offers charters from Athens.

Carefree Sailing Ltd, 122 Pavilion Gardens, Laleham, Middlesex, TW18 1HW.
Offers charters from Corfu, Lesbos and Rhodes. ✆ (0784) 462796

Creative Holdays & Cruises, 36 Charlton Street, London, NW1. ✆ (071) 383 4243
Offers charters from Piraeus.

Marinair, 188 Northdown Road, Cliftonville, Kent, CT9 2QN. ✆ (0843) 227140
Offers charters from Corfu, Rhodes, Kos and Athens.

McCulloch Marine, 60 Fordwych Road, London, NW2 3TH. ✆ (081) 452 7509
Offers charters from Athens.

Tenrag Yacht Charters, Bramling House, Bramling, Canterbury, Kent, CT3 1NB.
Offers charters from Poros and Skiathos. ✆ (0227) 721874

World Expeditions Ltd, 8 College Rise, Maidenhead, Berkshire, SL6 6BP.
Embarkation points are from Athens and a number of Greek islands. ✆ (0628) 74174

A number of English-based flotilla companies offer one- or two-week sailing holidays, the air-fare being included in the total cost. High season prices for a fortnight's holiday range from £550 per person to £1000 per person, depending on the number of people per yacht, expensive enough, but much cheaper than a yacht charter. The yachts have 4–6 berths, are supervised by a lead boat, with experienced skipper, engineer and hostess. Flotilla companies based in England include:

Falcon Sailing, Groundstar House, 390 London Road, Crawley, West Sussex, RH10 2TB.
℃ (0293) 599944

Odysseus Yachting Holidays, 33 Grand Parade, Brighton, BN2 2QA.   ℃ (0273) 695094

Practical A-Z

If you have children, they won't be alone if you bring them to the islands—more and more come to Greece all the time. Depending on their age, they go free or receive discounts on ships and buses. You can also save on hotel bills by bringing sleeping bags for the children. However, if they're babies, don't count on island pharmacies stocking your baby's brand of milk powder or baby foods—they may have some, but it's safest to bring your own supply. Disposable nappies or diapers are widely available except in the smaller villages. Pushchairs or prams are convenient on the larger islands with big towns and pavements, but are less useful in hilly villages, where there tend to be more steps than smooth stretches. A back carrier, however, can come in handy.

Greeks adore children and, with the aid of a long afternoon nap, keep theirs up till all hours. They will probably give yours all kinds of sticky sweets and chocolate on the hottest of days, and offer you an endless supply of advice on their upbringing. Refrain, however, from commenting on a Greek child's intelligence, beauty, or whatever may call down the jealous interest of the old gods; a superstitious grandmother will respond by spitting in the child's face, for its own protection.

Climate and Conversion Tables

Average Daily Temperatures

	ATHENS		CRETE (HERAKLEON)		CYCLADES (MYKONOS)		DODECANESE (RHODES)		IONIAN (CORFU)		N.E. AEGEAN (MYTILINI)		SARONIC (HYDRA)		SPORADES (SKYROS)	
	F°	C°	F°	C°	F°	C°	F°	C°	F°	C°	F°	C°	F°	C°	F°	C°
JAN	48	11	54	12	54	12	54	12	50	10	50	10	53	12	51	10
FEB	49	11	54	12	54	12	54	13	51	10	48	10	53	12	51	10
MAR	54	12	58	14	56	13	58	14	52	12	52	12	56	13	52	11
APR	60	16	62	17	60	17	60	17	60	15	60	16	61	16	58	15
MAY	68	20	68	20	68	20	66	20	66	19	68	20	68	20	66	19
JUN	76	25	74	24	74	23	73	21	71	21	74	24	76	25	74	23
JUL	82	28	78	26	76	25	78	27	78	27	80	27	82	28	77	25
AUG	82	28	78	26	76	25	79	27	78	26	80	27	81	28	78	25
SEP	76	25	76	24	74	23	78	25	74	23	74	23	76	25	71	22
OCT	66	19	70	21	68	20	72	21	66	19	66	19	71	21	65	19
NOV	58	15	64	18	62	17	66	17	58	15	58	15	62	17	58	15
DEC	52	12	58	14	58	14	58	14	54	12	52	12	58	15	51	12

Two Greek measurements you may come across are the *stremma*, a Greek land measurement (1 stremma = ¼ acre), and the *oka*, an old-fashioned weight standard, divided into 400 *drams* (1 *oka* = 3 lb; 35 *drams* = ¼ lb, 140 *drams* = 1 lb).

The **electric current** in Greece is mainly 220 volts, 50 Hz. In more out-of-the-way places you may find 110 volts. US 60-cycle appliances equipped for dual voltage will function on 50 Hz but will work more slowly than normal.

Greek time is Eastern European, or two hours ahead of Greenwich Mean Time.

Embassies and Consulates in Greece

Australia: 37 D. Soutsou St, 115 21 Athens, ✆ 644 7303

Austria: 26 Leof. Alexandras, 106 83 Athens, ✆ 821 1036

Canada: 4 I. Gennadiou St, 115 21 Athens, ✆ 723 9511

France: 7 Vass. Sofias, 106 71 Athens, ✆ 361 1665

Germany: 10 Vass. Sofias, 151 24 Athens, ✆ 369 4111

Ireland: 7 Vass. Konstantinou, 106 74 Athens, ✆ 723 2771

Japan: Athens Tower, 2–4 Messogion St, 115 27 Athens, ✆ 775 8101

New Zealand: apply to British Embassy

South Africa: 124 Kifissias & Iatridou, 115 10 Athens, ✆ 692 2125

United Kingdom: 1 Ploutarchou St, 106 75 Athens, ✆ 723 6211

USA: 91 Vass. Sofias, 115 21 Athens, ✆ 721 2951

United Nations Office: 36 Amalias Ave, Athens, ✆ 322 9624

Food and Drink

Eating Out

Eating establishments in Greece are categorized into Luxury, A, B, and C classes. Prices are controlled by the Tourist Police, who also enforce sanitary and health regulations.

The menu in Luxury restaurants is often international; in others you will rarely find more than the basic Greek cuisine. This is steeped in rich golden olive oil and the ingredients are fresh and often produced locally. You may go back into the kitchens to examine the offerings before making a choice. There is usually a menu posted on the door with an English translation, listing the prices. The availability and variety of fish depends on the catch. Sadly, seafood has become one of the most expensive meals you can order. A combination of increased demand, marketing to Athens, and greedy, unsound fishing practices (such as illegal dynamiting) has decreased the fish population in the Mediterranean, so that what was once common and cheap is now costly and in some places quite rare. Each type of fish has its own price, and your choice is usually weighed for you before it's cooked. Remember, the redder the gills the fresher the fish.

Pork has taken the place of lamb as the most common meat in Greek tavernas since the country joined the Common Market. Almost all *souvlaki* (the ubiquitous chunks of meat grilled on a stick) you get these days is pork, though lamb, roasted or stewed, is still widely available. Beef and chicken are often stewed in a sauce of tomatoes and olive oil, or roasted, accompanied by potatoes, spaghetti or rice. Village feasts, or *paneyéri* often feature wild goat meat with rice or potatoes. A Greek salad can be just tomatoes or just cucumbers, or village-style with tomatoes, cucumbers, black olives, peppers, onions and feta cheese—a small one for one person and a big one for two or three. You eat this during the meal, dipping your bread in the olive oil. In the summer dinner is generally followed by melon or watermelon.

Restaurants (*estiatórion*) serve baked dishes (*etimo fagito*) and often grills (*tis oras*) as well. Those serving just a grill and roasts are called *psistariá*. A taverna may serve baked dishes or a grill or both, and is less formal than a restaurant. A sweet shop, or *zacharoplasteíon*, sells honey pastries, cakes, puddings and drinks and sometimes home-made ice cream. Many also serve breakfast, along with the less common dairy shops, or *galaktopoleíon* which sell milk, coffee, bread, yoghurt, rice pudding and custard pies. Cheese pies and 'tost' can appear almost anywhere. Lager beer is now common in most restaurants, Amstel and Heineken being the most popular, and wine is considered essential to most meals.

Prices on Greek menus are written first without, then with, service and tax charges. If you are served by a young boy (*mikró*), give him something or leave it on the table—tips are generally all he earns. If you've been given special service, you may leave a tip for your waiter on the plate.

Wine

The national favourite wine, *retsina*, is the very essence of Greece, with its particularly resinated taste, dating from the time when Greeks stored their wine in untreated wooden casks. It is an acquired taste, and many people can be put off by the pungent odour and sharp taste of some bottled varieties. Draught retsina (*retsina apo to vareli*) can be found only on some islands, but in Athens it is the accepted, delicious accompaniment to the meal. Any taverna worth its salt will serve it, and if it's not available you're in the wrong place, unless you've chosen a foreign or fairly exclusive Greek restaurant. In cases of desperation, where no barrelled retsina is on offer, the wine house Kourtaki produce a very acceptable bottled version at a low price. Retsina is admirably suited to Greek food, and after a while a visitor may find non-resinated wines a rather bland alternative. Traditionally it is served in small stemless tumbler glasses, and etiquette requires that they are never filled to the brim or drained in one mouthful. There is a great deal of toasting throughout the meal (*stin yamas*— to our health, *stin yassas*—to your health), and by all means clink glasses with someone else, but on no account bring your glass down on another person's (unless your intentions for the evening are entirely dishonourable).

Other than retsina, Greece has an ample selection of red and white wines. All the principal wine companies—Boutari, Achaia Clauss, Carras, Tsantali, Kourtaki—produce some acceptable table wines at very affordable prices—*Lac des Roches* (white), *Kava Boutari* (red), for example, or, only if there's nothing else available, *Demestika* (affectionately referred to as Domestos).

If your palate is more discerning and won't be satisfied with those, then look out for the nobler labels; some classic reds from Achaia Clauss—the aromatic, fruity *Château Clauss*; the Boutari *Naoussa*, a savoury taste of spice, herb and fruit reserved for special red meat dishes; the smoky Tsantali *Naoussa*, that goes well with game; the gentle, medium-bodied *Ktima Papaioannou* and *Kouros Nemea* for subtler white meat dishes; Boutari's deliciously rich and velvety *Paros*; and from Carras *Château Carras-Côtes de Meliton*, a Bordeaux-type wine made from the Cabernet Sauvignon and Merlot grape. Rosé wines can be fairly nondescript, exceptions being *Palatino* and *Erodios*, both fragrant and fruity, and ideal also as an aperitif, or well-chilled with *meze* on a hot summer's day. Boutari's *Santorini* is one of many fine whites with that label. The island itself produces the aromatic grape *asyrtico*, and Santorini's most famous wines are its whites, including a *Visanto*, a popular sweet white similar to its Italian cousin *Vin Santo*. Samos has the name for the best dessert wines, whilst Rhodes supplies Greece with its champagne, *Cair*. Cretan wine, like its sons, are robust and full-blooded. For wine bars in Athens, see the 'Eating Out' section under 'Athens'.

Cafés

Cafés or *kafeneíons* (in small towns these are frequented mostly by men, who discuss the latest news, and play cards or backgammon) serve Turkish coffee—now known more often as Greek coffee (*café hellinikó*). There are 40 different ways to make this, although *glykó* (sweet), *métrio* (medium) and *skéto* (no sugar) are the basic orders. It is always served with a glass of water. Nescafé with milk has by popular tourist demand become available everywhere, though Greeks prefer it iced, with or without sugar and milk, which they call *frappé*. Soft drinks and *ouzo* round out the average café fare. Ouzo—like its Cretan cousin *raki*—is a clear anise-flavoured aperitif which many dilute (and cloud) with water. It can be served with a little plate of snacks called *mezédes* which can range from grilled octopus through nuts to cheese and tomatoes, though often these days you must request *mezédes* specially. Brandy, or Metaxa (the Greeks know it by the most popular brand name), is usually a late-night treat. The more stars on the label (from three to seven) the smoother the drink. In the tourist haunts, milkshakes, fruit juices, cocktails and even capuccino are readily available; in the backwaters you can usually get ice cream and good Greek yoghurt.

In the last few years the influx of tourists has resulted in the birth of a new type of bar on the Greek scene—the British-style pub, usually playing the latest hit records and serving fancy cocktails as well as standard drinks. These establishments usually come to life later in the evening, when everyone has spent the day on the beach and the earlier part of the evening in a taverna. They close at 3 or 4 am. In general they're not cheap, and it can be disconcerting to realise that you have paid the same for your Harvey Wallbanger as you paid for the entire meal of chicken and chips, salad and a bottle of wine, half an hour before in the taverna next door. Cocktails have now risen to beyond the 1000 dr. mark in many bars, but before you complain remember that the measures are triples by British standards. If in doubt stick to beer, ouzo, wine and Metaxa (Metaxa and coke is generally about half the price of the better-known Bacardi and coke). You may have difficulty in finding beer, as the profit margin is so small that many bars stop serving it in the peak season, thus obliging you to plump for the higher-priced drinks. One unfortunate practice on the islands is the doctoring of bottles, whereby some bar owners buy cheaper versions of spirits and use them to refill brand name bottles (Tequila made in Piraeus?). The only way to be sure is to see the new bottle being opened in front of you.

A list of items which appear frequently on Greek menus is included in the language section at the end of the guide *(see* pp. 443–452).

Health

In theory there is at least one doctor (*iatrós*) on every island, whose office is open from 9 am to 1 pm and from 5 pm to 7 pm. On many islands too there are hospitals which are open all day, and usually have an outpatient clinic, open in the mornings. British travellers qualify for treatment here, and need to have Form EI11, available at all DHSS offices. Otherwise you'll have to pay, unless it is for emergency treatment, and you can legally prove that you are uninsured and unable to pay. Doctors' fees are, however, usually reasonable. Private doctors and hospital stays can be very expensive, and you should seriously consider taking out a traveller's insurance policy.

Most doctors pride themselves on their English, as do their friends the pharmacists, whose advice on minor ailments is good, although their medicine is not particularly cheap.

A few hints: Coca Cola or retsina cuts down the oil in Greek foods. Lemon juice or fresh parsley can also help stomach upsets. The sea quickly cures cuts and abrasions. If anything else goes wrong, the Greek villagers will advise you to pee on it.

Money

The word for bank in Greek is *trápeza*, derived from the word *trapezi*, or table, used back in the days of money changers. On all the islands with more than goats and a few shepherds there is some sort of banking establishment. If you plan to spend time on one of the more remote islands, however, such as Antikythera or Kastellorizo, it is safest to bring enough drachma with you. On the other hand, the small but popular islands often have only one bank, where exchanging money can take a long time. Waiting can be avoided if you go at 8 am, when the banks open (normal banking hours are 8–2, 8–1 on Fri). Most island banks are closed on Saturdays and Sundays.

Traveller's cheques are always useful, not only in case of theft, but also because they command a better exchange rate than currency. The major brands of traveller's cheques and international banking cards are accepted in all banks (travel agents and hotels can also give you drachma for most of these when the banks are closed), but note that there are no cash dispensers for 'Eurocheque' cards. Athens and Piraeus, with offices of many British and American banks, are the easiest places to have money sent if you run out, though even if you're a customer it may take a few days—it's easiest if you have someone at home who can send it to you.

The **Greek drachma** is circulated in coins of 100, 50, 20, 10, 5, 2 and 1 drachma and in notes of 100, 500, 1000 and 5000 drachma.

Museums

All significant archaeological sites and museums have regular admission hours. Nearly all are closed on Mondays, and open other weekdays from 8 or 9 am to around 2 pm, though outdoor sites tend to stay open later, until 4 or 5 pm. As a rule, plan to visit cultural sites in the mornings to avoid disappointment, or unless the local tourist office can provide you with current opening times. Hours tend to be shorter in the winter. Students with a valid identification card get a discount on admission fees; on Sundays admission is generally free.

If you're currently studying archaeology, the history of art or the Classics and intend to visit many museums and sites in Greece, it may be worth your while to obtain a free pass by writing several weeks in advance of your trip to the Museum Section, Ministry of Science and Culture, Aristidou 14, Athens, enclosing verification of your studies from your college or university. Entrance fees for sites or museums are not listed in this book. Count on 400–600 dr. in most cases; exceptions are Knossos (Crete) at 1000 dr. and the Acropolis and National Archaeology Museum in Athens at 1500 dr. Recent EC rulings mean that Greek nationals no longer have the privilege of free admission to places of cultural interest.

Music and Dancing

Greek music is either city music or village music. The music of the city includes the popular tunes, *rebetiko* (derived from the hashish dens of Asia Minor) and most bazouki music, whereas village music means traditional tunes played on the bagpipes (*tsamboúna*), the clarinet (*klaríno*), the violin and sometimes the dulcimer (*sandoúri*). Cretan music specializes in the lyre and is in a category of its own.

On the islands you can hear both city and village music, the former at the *baóukia*, or Greek nightclubs, which usually feature certain singers. Many play records or washed-out musak until midnight as the customers slowly arrive. One generally buys a bottle of white wine and fruit and dances until 4 in the morning, though expect to pay a pretty drachma for the privilege. To hear traditional music, you must go into the villages, to the festivals or weddings. In many places Sunday evening is an occasion for song and dance. Village music is generally modest and unpretentious, while city music is the domain of the professional singers, although any bold member of the audience with a good voice will often get up to sing a few songs. After a few hours of drinking, a particular favourite or a good dancer is liable to make the enthusiasts forget the law against *spásimo*, or plate breaking, and supporters may end up paying for missing place settings. If the mood really heats up, men will dance with wine glasses or bottles on their heads, or even sink their teeth into a fully-set table and dance without spilling a drop. When the matrons begin to belly-dance on the table, you know it's time to go.

In the tavernas you're liable to hear either city or village music. Some put on permanent shows, and others have music only occasionally. Athens is awash with tourist shows and discotheques during the summer but starts pulsating to all kinds of Greek music in November, when Plaka is returned to the Athenians. Most musicians on the islands go to Athens in the winter.

The lyrics to most Greek songs deal with the ups and downs of love. Serious composers (Mikis Theodorakis is the best known) often put poetry to music, providing splendid renderings of the lyrics of George Seferis and Yannis Ritsos. The guerrillas (*partizanis*) and the Communists have a monopoly on the best political songs, many by Theodorakis. Cretan songs are often very patriotic (for Crete) and many are drawn from the 17th-century epic poem, the *Erotókritos*, written in the Cretan dialect by Vincento Kornaro.

Every island in Greece has its special dance, although today it is often only the young people's folkdance societies that keep them alive, along with the island's traditional costumes. The best time to find them dancing is on each island's Day of Liberation from the Turks or any other anniversary of local significance. Here are details of the two best-known professional folkdance companies:

Athens
Dora Stratou Greek Folk Dances, Dora Stratou Theatre, Philopappou Hill, © 324 4395 or © 921 4650. From beginning of May to end of September. Shows begin at 10 pm every day, with an additional show at 8 pm on Wednesdays and Sundays.

Rhodes
Nelly Dimoglou Greek Dances, The Rodini Theatre, © (0241) 20157. From May to October. Performances at 9.15 pm daily except Saturdays.

Tickets for both average 1200 dr.; 700 dr. for students.

Although these shows are beautiful and interesting, there's nothing like getting up to dance yourself—a splendid way to work off the big dinner just consumed at a *paneyeri*. For a brief overview of the most popular dances, *see* p. 59.

National Holidays

Note that most businesses and shops close down for the afternoon before and the morning after a religious holiday. If a national holiday falls on a Sunday, the following Monday is observed. The Orthodox Easter is generally a week or so after the Roman Easter.

1 January	New Year's Day	*Protochroniza*
6 January	Epiphany	*Ton Theofanzion*
	'Clean Monday'	*Kathari Theftéra*
	(precedes Shrove Tuesday, and	
	follows a three-week carnival)	
25 March	Greek Independence Day	*Ikosi pémpti Martíou*
	Good Friday	*Megáli Paraskevi*
	Easter	*Páscha*
	Easter Monday	*Theftéra tou Páscha*
1 May	May Day	*Protomayíou*
15 August	Assumption of the Virgin	*Koímisis tis Theotókou*
28 October	'Ochi' Day (in celebration of	
	Metaxas' 'no' to Mussolini)	
25 December	Christmas	*Kristoúyena*
26 December	St Stephen's Day	*Théfteri i mera ton Kristoúyena*

Packing

Even in the height of summer, evenings can be chilly in Greece, especially when the *meltemi* wind is blowing. Always bring at least one warm sweater and a pair of long trousers. Those who venture off the beaten track into the thorns and rocks should bring sturdy and comfortable shoes—tennis shoes are very good. They should cover the ankles if you really like wilderness, where scorpions and harmful snakes can be a problem. Plastic swim shoes are recommended for rocky beaches, where there are often sea urchins.

Summer travellers following whim rather than a pre-determined programme should certainly bring a sleeping bag, as lodgings of any sort are often full to capacity. Serious sleeping-baggers should also bring an air-mattress to cushion them from the gravelly Greek ground. Torches are very handy for moonless nights, caves and rural villages.

On the pharmaceutical side, seasickness pills, insect bite remedies, tablets for stomach upsets and aspirin will deal with most difficulties encountered. Soap, washing powder, a clothesline and especially a towel are necessary for those staying in class C hotels or less. Bring a sink plug if you like sinks full of water. A knife is a good idea for *paneyeria*, where you are often given a slab of goat meat with only a spoon or fork to eat it with. A photo of the family and home is always appreciated by new Greek friends.

On all the Greek islands except for the most remote of the remote you can buy whatever you forgot to bring. Toilet paper and mosquito coils are the two most popular purchases on arrival. However, special needs such as artificial sweeteners, contact lens products and so on can generally be found only in Athens and the more popular islands.

Let common sense and the maxim 'bring as little as possible and never more than you can carry' dictate your packing; work on the theory that however much money and clothing you think you need, halve the clothing and double the money.

Photography

Greece lends herself freely to beautiful photography, but a fee is charged at archaeological sites and museums. For an 8- to 16-mm still camera, without tripod, one buys a ticket for the camera; with a tripod one pays per photograph at sites, but tripod-mounted cameras are not allowed in museums.

A large variety of film, both instamatic and 35-mm, can be found in many island shops, though it tends to be expensive. Large islands even have 24-hour developing services, though again this costs more than at home.

The light in the summer is often stronger than it seems and is the most common cause of ruined photographs. Greeks invariably love to have their pictures taken, and although it's more polite to ask first, you should just go ahead and take the photo if you don't want them to rush off to beautify themselves and strike a pose. You should avoid taking pictures of the communications systems on the mountain tops.

If you bring an expensive camera to Greece, it never hurts to insure it. Above all, never leave it alone 'for just a few minutes'. Although Greeks themselves very rarely steal anything, other tourists are not so honest.

Post Offices

Signs for post offices (*tachidromío*) as well as postboxes are bright yellow and easy to find. Many post office employees speak English. Stamps can also be bought at kiosks and in some tourist shops, although they charge a small tax. A stamp is a *grammatósima*.

If you do not have an address, mail can be sent to you *Poste Restante* to any post office in Greece, and can be picked up with proof of identity. After 3 months all unretrieved letters are returned to sender. If someone has sent you a parcel, you will receive a notice of its arrival, and you must go to the post office to collect it. You will often have to pay a handling fee, and customs charges and duties should the parcel contain dutiable articles. 'Fragile' stickers attract scant attention. In small villages, particularly on the islands, mail is not delivered to the house but to the village centre, either a café or bakery. Its arrival coincides with that of a ship from Athens.

If you want to mail a package, any shop selling paper items will wrap it sturdily for you for a small fee.

Watersports

Naturally they predominate in the islands. All popular beaches these days hire out pedal boats and windsurf boards; some have paragliding and jet skis. Waterskiing prevails on most islands and large hotel complexes. Several islands offer sailing and windsurfing instruction. For more details contact:

Hellenic Yachting Federation, 7 Akti Navarchou Kountourioti, Piraeus, ✆ 413 7351.
Greek Windsurfing Association, 7 Filellinon St, Piraeus, ✆ 323 3696.

Nudism by law is forbidden in Greece, except in designated areas. In practice, however, many people shed all in isolated coves, ideally on beaches accessible only by private boat. On the other hand, topless sunbathing has become the norm on a majority of popular beaches. Elsewhere, do exercise discretion. It isn't worth wounding local sensibilities, no matter how prudish other people's attitudes may seem to you.

Underwater activities with any kind of breathing apparatus are strictly forbidden to keep divers from snatching any antiquities and to protect marine life. However, three islands have diving schools—Rhodes, Evia (Halkida) and Corfu (Paleokastritsa)—where, even if you already know how to dive, you have to go out with their boats.

Average Sea Temperatures

Jan	Feb	Mar	Apr	May	Jun	Jul	Aug	Sep	Oct	Nov	Dec
59°F	59°F	59°F	61°F	64°F	72°F	75°F	77°F	75°F	72°F	64°F	63°F
15°C	15°C	15°C	16°C	18°C	22°C	24°C	25°C	24°C	22°C	18°C	17°C

Land Sports

Tennis is slowly catching on among the Greek elite. Islands with courts and their addresses are:

> **Corfu:** 4 Romanou St, ✆ 37021, and a second club at Kefalomandouko.
> **Crete:** in Herakleon, 17 Beaufort Av., ✆ (081) 283015.
> in Chania, Dimokratias Av., in the stadium, ✆ (0821) 21293.
> **Rhodes:** Rhodes Tennis Club, ✆ (0241) 2230.
> **Evia:** Halkida Tennis Club, ✆ (0221) 25230.

Otherwise there are courts at all major resort hotels, where, if you are not a resident, you may be allowed to play in the off season.

There are **golf** courses on Corfu and Rhodes, and both admit non-members.

The **Corfu Golf Club**, Ropa Valley, P.O. Box 71, ✆ 94220/1. The course has 18 holes, par 72, practice range, equipment hire and shop, changing rooms, and restaurant. Green fees are 7000 dr. daily in May, Sept and Oct, less in other months. Lessons can be had for 4000 dr. per half hour.

The **Afandou Golf Club**, 19 km (12 miles) from Rhodes town, ☏ 51257, has 18 holes, par 70. The club has equipment hire and shop, lounges, changing rooms, and a restaurant. Fees are 3000 dr. per round, or 16,000 dr. for 7 rounds in one week, lessons 4000 dr. per half hour.

Organised **horse riding** is offered only on Corfu at the Corfu Riding Club, Korkira Beach, Gouvia, ☏ 91325. Open Apr–Oct, 7–10 am and 5–9 pm.

Mountain Climbing and Skiing

Crete is the island queen of Greek mountain sport, with three mountain refuges. A fourth is on the island of Evia.

Lefka Ori (White Mountain), Crete
Kallergi, alt. 1680 m (5510 ft); 40 beds, ☏ Chania (0821) 24 647.
Volikas, alt. 1480 m (4860 ft); 30 beds, ☏ as above.

Psiloritis (Mt Ida), Crete
Prinias, alt. 1100 m (3610 ft); 16 beds, ☏ Herakleon (081) 287 110.

Mount Dirfys, Evia
Liri, alt. 1100 m (3610 ft); 36 beds, ☏ Chalki (0221) 25 230.

There is skiing from December to March at both Kallergi and Liri.

Three important addresses in Athens for mountaineers and skiers are:

The Hellenic Alpine Club, 7 Karageorgi Servias, ☏ 323 4555.

The Hellenic Touring Club, 12 Polytechniou St, ☏ 524 8600/1.

The Hellenic Federation of Excursion Clubs, 4 Dragatsaniou, ☏ 323 4107.

Telephones

The *Organismos Telephikinonion Ellathos*, better known as *OTE*, has offices in the larger towns and at least one on every island that has a telephone service. One can call both direct and collect (reverse charges), although the latter usually takes at least half an hour to put through. On the larger islands one may dial abroad direct (for Great Britain dial 0044 and for the USA 001 before the area code). A 3-minute call to the UK will cost about 500 dr., to the US 1300 dr. You should also use OTE for calling other places in Greece. Telegrams can be sent from either OTE or the post office.

Payphones take 5, 10 and 20 dr. coins dated 1976 or later. Calls can also be made from kiosks (more expensive), kafeneíons, and shops (always ask first).

It is often impossible to call Athens from the islands in mid-morning; chances improve in the evening. To defeat the beeps, whirrs, and buzzes you often get instead of a connection, try dialling slowly.

Toilets

Greek plumbing has improved remarkably in the past few years, especially in the hotels. However, public toilets and those in cheaper hotels and pensions often have their quirks. Tavernas, *kafeneíons*, and sweet shops almost always have facilities (it's good manners to buy something before you excuse yourself). Popular beaches usually have public toilets nearby, though you may have to pay a small fee.

Often the plumbing makes up in inventiveness for what it lacks in efficiency. Do not tempt fate by disobeying the little notices 'the papers they please to throw in the basket'—or it's bound to lead to trouble. Also, a second flush in immediate succession will gurgle and burp instead of swallow. Many places in Greece have only a ceramic hole. Women who confront this for the first time should take care not to wet their feet: squat about halfway and lean back as far as you can. Always have paper of some sort handy.

If you stay in a private room or pension you may have to have the water heater turned on for about 20 minutes before you take a shower, so if you were promised hot water but it fails to appear, ask the proprietor about it. In larger hotels there is often hot water in the mornings and evenings, but not in the afternoons. Actually 'cold' showers in the summer aren't all that bad, because the tap water itself is generally lukewarm, especially after noon. A good many showers are of the hand-held variety, but if a black cat has recently crossed your path you may get the Special Greek Squirt, where a quarter of the water trickles on your head and the rest ricochets off the ceiling and onto your towel. If the water stops, try jiggling the sink or toilet. Sinks in Greece rarely have rubber plugs.

Greek tap water is perfectly safe to drink, though big plastic bottles of spring water are widely available, even on ships. On dry islands, remember to ask what time the water is turned off.

Tourist Information

If the Greek National Tourist Organisation (in Greek the initials come out: EOT) can't answer your questions about Greece, at least they can refer you to someone who can.

In Athens:
Head Office: 2 Amerikis St, Athens 10564, © (01) 322 3111; telex 5832.
EOT Information Desk: National Bank of Greece, Syntagma Square, 2 Karageorgi Servias St, © (01) 322 2545, 323 4130.
EOT, East Airport: © (01) 969 9500, 961 2722.
EOT, West Airport: © (01) 979 9264.

In Australia: 51–57 Pitt St, Sidney, NSW 2000, © 2411 663/4; fax 235 2174.

In Canada:
1300 Bay St, Toronto, Ontario, © 968 2220, fax 968 6533.
1233 De La Montagne, Montreal, Quebec, © 871 1535, fax 871 1535.

In Great Britain: 4 Conduit St, London W1R ODJ, © (071) 734 5997, fax 287 1369.

In USA:
Head Office: Olympic Tower, 645 Fifth Ave, 5th Floor, New York, NY 10022,
✆ (212) 421 5777; fax 826 6940.
168 N. Michigan Ave, Chicago, Ill. 60601, ✆ (312) 782 1084; fax 782 1091.
611 West Sixth St, Suite 2198, Los Angeles, Calif. 90017, ✆ (213) 626 6696; fax 489 9744.

Islands without a branch of the EOT often have some form of local tourist office; if not, most have **Tourist Police** (often located in an office in the town's police station). You can always tell a Tourist Policeman from other policemen by the little flags he wears on his pocket, showing which language he speaks. They have information about the island, and can often help you find a room. In Athens there are three Tourist Police stations, and a magic telephone number—171. The voice on 171 not only speaks good English, but can tell you everything from ship departures to where to spend the night.

Tourist Police stations in **Athens** are at:

> 7 Syngrou St (the home of 171).
> Larissa Train Station, ✆ 821 3574.
> East Airport, ✆ 981 9730 and 981 4093.
> At Piraeus the Tourist Police are on Akti Miaouli, ✆ 452 3670.

Where to Stay

Hotels

All hotels in Greece are divided into six categories: Luxury, A, B, C, D and E. Prices are set and strictly controlled by the Tourist Police. Off season you can generally get a discount, sometimes as much as 40%. In the summer season prices can be increased by up to 20%. Other charges include an 8% government tax, a 4.5% community bed tax, a 12% stamp tax, an optional 10% surcharge for stays of only one or two days, an air conditioning surcharge, as well as a 20% surcharge for an extra bed. All of these prices are listed on the door of every room and authorized and checked at regular intervals. If your hotelier fails to abide by the posted prices, or if you have any other reason to believe all is not on the level, take your complaint to the Tourist Police.

1993 rate guideline in drachma (thousands)*

	L	A	B	C	D
Single room with bath	12–30	8–15	6–10	4–8	2–5
Double room with bath	12–35	9–17	8–14	5–10	3–6
Breakfast	1.5–3	1–2	8–12	6–1	
Lunch or dinner	3–6	3–4	2–3		

*The above prices are thousands of dr., except for breakfast prices, i.e. 1.5=1500, 8=800, 12=1200, 6=600.

Prices for E hotels are not quoted officially, but should be about 20% less than D rates.

During the summer, hotels with restaurants may require guests to take their meals in the hotel, either full pension or half pension, and there is no refund for an uneaten dinner. Twelve noon is the official check-out time, although on the islands it is usually geared to the arrival of the next boat. Most Luxury and class A, if not B, hotels situated far from the town or port supply buses or cars to pick up guests.

Hotels down to class B all have private bathrooms. In C some do and some don't. In D you will be lucky to find a hot shower, and in E forget it. In these hotels neither towel nor soap is supplied, although the bedding is clean.

The importance of reserving a room in advance, especially during July and August, cannot be over-emphasized. Reservations can be made through the individual hotel or:

The Hellenic Chamber of Hotels, 24 Stadiou St, 105 61 Athens, © (01) 323 6962 (from Athens: between 8 am and 2 pm); fax 322 5449, telex 214269 XEPE GR, cable EXENEPEL

In the 'Where to Stay' sections of this book, accommodation is listed according to the following price categories:

> **luxury**: 15,000 dr. and above
> **expensive**: 8–15,000 dr.
> **moderate**: 4–8000 dr.
> **cheap**: 4000 dr. and below

Please note that prices quoted are for **double** rooms.

Rooms in Private Homes

These are for the most part cheaper than hotels and are sometimes more pleasant. On the whole, Greek houses aren't much in comparison to other European homes mainly because the Greeks spend so little time inside them; but they are clean, and the owner will often go out of his or her way to assure maximum comfort for the guest. In most houses you can also get an idea of Greek taste, which is sometimes simple and good, but at other times incredibly corny, from plastic cat pictures that squeak to lamps in the shape of ships made out of macaroni. Increasingly, however, rooms to rent to tourists are built in a separate annexe and tend to be rather characterless.

While room prices are generally fixed in the summer—the going rate in high season is now 4000 dr.—out of season they are always negotiable (with a little finesse), even in June. Speaking some Greek is the biggest asset in bargaining, although not strictly necessary. Claiming to be a poor student is generally effective. Always remember, however, that you are staying in someone's home, and do not waste more water or electricity than you need. The owner will generally give you a bowl to wash your clothes in, and there is always a clothes line.

The Tourist Police on each island have all the information on rooms and will be able to find you one, if you do not meet a chorus of Greeks chanting 'Rooms? Rooms?' as you leave the boat. Many houses also have signs.

Some of these are official and require a membership card from the Association of Youth Hostels, or alternatively an International Membership Card (about 2500 dr.) from the Greek Association of Youth Hostels, 4 Dragatsaniou St, Athens, © 323 4107; other hostels are informal, have no irksome regulations, and admit anyone. There are official youth hostels on the islands of Corfu, Santorini and Crete, which has several. Most charge extra for a shower, sometimes for sheets. Expect to pay 600–1200 dr. a night, depending on the quality of facilities and services offered.

Camping Out

The climate of summertime Greece is perfect for sleeping out of doors. Unauthorized camping is illegal in Greece, although each village on each island enforces the ban as it sees fit. Some couldn't care less if you put up a tent at the edge of their beach; in others the police may pull up your tent pegs and fine you. All you can do is ask around to see what other tourists or friendly locals advise. In July and August you only need a sleeping bag to spend a pleasant night on a remote beach, cooled by the sea breezes that also keep hopeful mosquitoes at bay. Naturally, the more remote the beach, the less likely you are to be disturbed. If a policeman does come by and asks you to move, though, you had best do so; be diplomatic. Many islands have privately-operated camping grounds—each seems to have at least one. These are reasonably priced, though some have only minimal facilities. The National Tourist Office controls other, 'official', campsites which are rather plush and costly.

There are two main reasons behind the camping law: one is that the beaches have no sanitation facilities for crowds of campers, and secondly, forest fires are a real hazard in summer. Every year they rage through the dry timberlands on the islands and mainland. If the police are in some places lackadaisical about enforcing the camping regulations, they come down hard on anyone lighting any kind of fire in a forest, and may very well put you in jail for 2 months.

National Tourist Office of Greece **camping rates** per day during high season, in drachma:

Adult : 600–800
Child (4–12) : 300–500
Caravan : 1000–1300
Small tent : 500–650
Large tent : 900–1200
Car : 150–200

Renting a House or Villa

On most islands it is possible to rent houses or villas, generally for a month or more at a time. Villas can often be reserved from abroad: contact a travel agent or the National Tourist Organisation (NTOG) for names and addresses of rental agents. In the off season houses may be found on the spot with a little inquiry; with luck you can find a house sleeping 6, 8 or 10 people, and depending on the facilities it can work out quite reasonably per person. Islands with sophisticated villa rentals (i.e. with a large number of purpose-built properties with all the amenities, handled by agents in Athens, Great Britain and North America) are Rhodes, Skiathos, Corfu, Mykonos, Crete, Paros and Symi. The NTOG has a list of agents offering villas and apartments. Facilities normally include a refrigerator, hot water, plates and utensils, etc. Generally, the longer you stay the more economical it becomes. Things to check for are leaking roofs, water supply (the house may have a well) and a supply of lamps if there is no electricity.

Traditional Settlements in Greece

This is a programme sponsored by the National Tourist Organisation of Greece to preserve old villages and certain buildings while converting their interiors into tourist accommodation with modern amenities. Often these are furnished with handmade furniture and weaving typical of the locale. The aim is to offer visitors a taste of rural life while improving the economy in these areas. So far guesthouses are available on Santorini, Chios, Psara and Kefalonia, and in several villages on the mainland; others are planned for the future. Prices are quite reasonable (especially when compared with the going rate for villas) and reservations and information may be had by writing to the Greek National Tourist Organisation/EOT dieftynsi Ekmetalefseos, 2 Amerikis St, 105 64 Athens.

Art Centres of the School of Fine Arts

Four of the five annexes of the Athenian School of Fine Arts are located on the islands, namely, Hydra, Mykonos, Rhodes and Lesbos (Mythimna). These provide inexpensive accommodation for foreign artists (for up to 20 days in the summer and 30 in the winter) as well as studios, etc. One requirement is a recommendation from the Greek embassy in the artist's home country. Contact its Press and Information Office for further information.

Women

Greece is a perfect destination for women travelling on their own. Not only is it safe, but out of respect Greeks refrain from annoying women as other Mediterranean men are known to do. Yet, on the plus side, they remain friendly and easy to meet. While some Greek men can't fathom what sexual equality might mean—they are usually the same who hold the fantasy that for a woman a night without company is unbearable mortification of the flesh—they are ever courteous and will rarely allow even the most liberated female (or male) guest to pay for anything. Any Greek who tries to take advantage of a woman or chases tourists earns himself a bad reputation.

Many young Greek women are beginning to travel alone—that leggy blonde with the rucksack could just as well be Greek as Swedish nowadays—but this is no indication that traditional values are fast disappearing. Although many women in the larger towns now have jobs, old marriage customs still exert a strong influence, even in Athens. Weddings are sometimes less a union of love than the closing of a lengthily negotiated business deal. In the evenings, especially at weekends, you'll see many girls of marriageable age join the family for a seaside promenade, or *volta*, sometimes called 'the bride market'. A young man, generally in his late twenties or early thirties, will spot a likely girl on the promenade or will hear about her through the grapevine. He will then approach the father to discover the girl's dowry— low wages and high housing costs demand that it contains some sort of living quarters from the woman's father, often added on top of the family house. The suitor must have a steady job. If both parties are satisfied, the young man is officially introduced to the daughter, who can be as young as 13 or 14 in the villages. If they get along well together, the marriage date is set. The woman who never marries and has no children is sincerely pitied in Greece. The inordinate number of Greek widows (and not all wear the traditional black) is due to the 10- to 20-year age difference which often occurs between husband and wife.

Because foreign men don't observe the Greek customs, their interest in a Greek woman will often be regarded with suspicion by her family. Although the brother probably won't knife a man for glancing at his sister, he is likely to tell him to look elsewhere.

Working

If you run out of money in Greece, it usually isn't too difficult to find a temporary job on the islands, ranging from polishing cucumbers to laying cement. The local *kafeneíon* is a good place to inquire. Work on yachts can sometimes be found by asking around at the Athenian marinas. The theatre agents, for work as extras in films, are off Academias Ave, by Kanigos Square. Teachers may apply to one of the seven English/American schools in Athens, or apply to a *frontistirion*, a poorly-paid private school, which concentrates mainly on the teaching of English. The *Athens News*, the country's English daily, and *The Athenian*, a monthly publication, often have classified advertisements for domestic, tutorial, and secretarial jobs.

Modern History, Art and Architecture

Aphrodite

Unless you're one of those dullards who unplug themselves from their earphones and novels only to take photographs of donkeys, then you'll want to meet the Greeks. Although the massive influx of foreign visitors in recent years has had an inevitable numbing effect on the traditional hospitality offered to strangers, you will find that almost everyone you meet is friendly and gracious, and the older islanders—especially in the small villages—full of wonderful stories.

And rare indeed is the Greek who avoids talking about politics. It was Aristotle, after all, who declared man to be a political animal and if Greeks today have any link with their Classical past it is in their enthusiasm for all things political. An enthusiasm especially evident during an election, when all means of transport to the Greek islands are swamped with Athenians returning to their native villages to vote. Some knowledge of modern history is essential in understanding current Greek views and attitudes, and for that reason the following outline is included. Ancient and Byzantine history, which touches Greece less closely today, is dealt with under Athens and the individual islands.

The Spirit of Independence

From ancient times to the end of the Byzantine Empire, Greek people lived not only within the boundaries of modern-day Greece but throughout Asia Minor, in particular that part of Asia Minor now governed by Turkey. Constantinople was their capital, and although founded as a new Rome by Constantine, it was Greek. Not even during the 400-year Turkish occupation did these people and their brethren in Europe stop considering themselves Greeks—and the Turks, for the most part, were content to let them be Greek as long as they paid their taxes.

The revolutionary spirit that swept through Europe at the end of the 18th and beginning of the 19th centuries did not fail to catch hold in Greece, by now more than weary of the lethargic inactivity and sporadic cruelties of the Ottomans. The Greek War of Independence was begun in the Peloponnese in 1821, and it continued for more than six years in a series of bloody atrocities and political intrigues and divisions. In the end the Great Powers, namely Britain, Russia and France, came to assist the Greek cause, especially in the decisive battle of Navarino (20 October 1827) which in effect gave the newly formed Greek government the Peloponnese and the peninsula up to a line between the cities of Arta and Volos. Count John Capodistria of Corfu, ex-secretary to the Tsar of Russia, became the first President of Greece. While a king was sought for the new state, Capodistria followed an independent policy which succeeded in offending the pro-British and pro-French factions in Greece—and also the powerful Mavromikhalis family who assassinated him in 1831. Before the subsequent anarchy spread too far, the Great Powers appointed Otho, son of King Ludwig I of Bavaria, as King of the Greeks.

The Great Idea

Under Otho began what was called The Great Idea of uniting all the lands of the Greek peoples with the motherland, although Athens lacked the muscle to do anything about it at the time. Otho was peaceably ousted in 1862 and the Greeks elected William George, son of the King of Denmark, as 'King of the Hellenes'. By this they meant all the Greek people, and not merely those within the borders of Greece. The National Assembly drew up a constitution in 1864 which made the nation officially a democracy under a king, a system that began to work practically under Prime Minister Kharilaos Trikoupis in 1875. With the long reign of George I, Greece began to develop with an economy based on sea trade. The Great Idea had to wait for an opportune moment to ripen into reality.

In 1910 the great statesman from Crete, Eleftherios Venizelos, became Prime Minister of Greece for the first time. Under his direction the opportune moment came in the form of the two Balkan Wars of 1912–13, as a result of which Crete, Samos, Macedonia and southern Epirus were annexed to Greece. In the meantime King George was assassinated by a madman, and Constantine I ascended to the throne of Greece. Constantine had married the sister of Kaiser Wilhelm and had a close relationship with Germany, and when the First World War broke out, so did a dispute as to whose side Greece was on. Venizelos supported the Allies and Constantine the Central Powers, although he officially remained neutral until the Allies forced him to mobilize the Greek army. Meanwhile, in the north of Greece, Venizelos had set up his own government with volunteers in support of the Allied cause.

After the war to end all wars The Great Idea still smouldered, and Venizelos made the blunder of his career by sending Greek forces to occupy Smyrna (present-day Izmir) and advance on Ankara, the new Turkish capital. It was a disaster. The Turks, under Mustapha Kemal (later Ataturk) had grown far more formidable after their defeat in the Balkan War than the Greeks had imagined. In August 1922 the Greek army was completely routed at Smyrna, and many Greek residents who could not escape were slaughtered. Constantine immediately abdicated in favour of his son George II, and died soon afterwards. The government fell and Colonel Plastiras with his officers took over, ignobly executing the ministers of the previous government. Massive population exchanges were made between Greece and Turkey to destroy the rationale behind Greek expansionist claims, and the Greeks were confronted with the difficulties of a million Anatolian refugees.

In 1929 a republic was proclaimed which lasted for ten shaky years, during which the Greek communist party, or KKE, was formed and gained strength. After the brief Panglos dictatorship, the Greeks elected Venizelos back as President. He set the present borders of Greece (except for the Dodecanese Islands, which belonged to Italy until 1945). During his term of office there was also an unsuccessful uprising by the Greek Cypriots, four-fifths of the population of what was then a British Crown Colony, who desired union with Greece.

World War–Civil War

The republic, beset with economic difficulties, collapsed in 1935, and King George II returned to Greece, with General Metaxas as his Prime Minister. Metaxas took dictatorial control under the regime of 4 August, which crushed the trade unions and all leftist activities, exiling the leaders. Having prepared the Greek army long in advance for the coming war, Metaxas died in 1941 after his historic 'No!' to Mussolini. Indeed, in 1940, with Italian troops on the Albanian border, Greece was the first Allied country voluntarily to join Britain against the Axis. The Greek army stopped the Italians and then pushed them back into Albania.

But by May 1941 all of Greece was in the hands of the Nazis, and George II was in exile in Egypt. The miseries of Occupation were compounded by political strife, fired by the uncertain constitutionality of a monarch who had been acting for so many years without parliamentary support. The Communist-organised EAM, the National Liberation Front, attacked all the competing resistance groups so rigorously that they came to support the monarchy as a lesser evil than the Communists. These Monarchists were supported in turn by the British. Nothing could be done, however, to prevent Civil War from breaking out three months after the liberation of Greece. The army of the EAM almost took Athens before the King finally agreed not to return to Greece without a plebiscite.

After the World War and the Civil War the country was in a shambles, economically and politically. Americans began to supersede the British in Greek affairs, and acted as observers in the elections of March 1946. A few months later the King was officially welcomed back to Greece, although he died a year later to be succeeded by his brother Paul.

Recovery and the Issue of Cyprus

Recovery was very slow, despite American assistance. Stalin also became very interested in the strategic location of Greece. In a roundabout way this caused the second Civil War in 1947 between the Communists and the government. The Americans became deeply involved defending the recent Truman Doctrine (on containing Communism, especially in Greece) and government forces finally won in October 1949, allowing the country to return to the problems of reconstruction.

With the Korean War in 1951 Greece and Turkey became full members of NATO, although the Cyprus issue again divided the two countries. In 1954, the Greek Cypriots, led by Archbishop Makarios, clamoured and rioted for union with Greece. Either for military reasons (so believe the Greeks) or to prevent a new conflict between Greece and Turkey, the Americans and British were hardly sympathetic to Cyprus' claims. Meanwhile Prime Minister Papagos died, and Konstantinos Karamanlis replaced him, staying in office for eight years. The stability and prosperity begun under Papagos increased, and agriculture and tourism began to replace Greece's traditional reliance on the sea. The opposition to Karamanlis criticized him for his pro-Western policy, basically because of the Cyprus bugbear, which grew worse all the time. Because of the island's one-fifth Turkish population and its strategic location, the Turks would not agree on union for Cyprus—the independence or partitioning of the island was as far as they would go. Finally in 1960, after much discussion on all sides, Cyprus became an independent republic and elected Makarios its first President. The British and Americans were considered to be good friends again.

Then once more the economy began to plague the government. The royal family became unpopular, there were strikes, and in 1963 came the assassination of Deputy Lambrakis in Thessaloniki, (see the film Z) for which police officers were tried and convicted. Anti-Greek government feelings rose in London, just when the King and Queen were about to visit. Karamanlis advised them not to go, and their insistence sparked off his resignation. George Papandreau of the opposition was eventually elected Prime Minister. King Paul died and Constantine II became King of Greece.

In 1964 violence broke out in Cyprus again, owing to the disproportional representation in government of the Turkish minority. A quarrel with the King led to Papandreau's resignation resulting in much bitterness. The party system deteriorated and on 21 April 1967 a group of colonels established a military dictatorship. George Papandreau and his son Andreas were imprisoned, the latter charged with treason. Col. George Papadopoulos became dictator, imprisoning thousands without trial. In 1967 another grave incident occurred in Cyprus, almost leading to war. King Constantine II fled to Rome.

Moral Cleansing

The proclaimed aim of the colonels' junta was a moral cleansing of 'Christian Greece'. Human rights were suppressed, and the secret police tortured dissidents—or their children. Yet the British and American governments tolerated the regime, the latter very actively because of NATO. The internal situation went from bad to worse, and in 1973 students of the Polytechnic school in Athens struck. Tanks were brought in and many were killed. After this incident popular feeling rose to such a pitch that Papadopoulos was arrested, only to be replaced by his arrester, the head of the military police and an even worse dictator, Ioannides. The nation was in turmoil. Attempting to save his position by resorting to The Great Idea, Ioannides tried to launch a coup in Cyprus by assassinating Makarios, intending to replace him with a president who would declare the long-desired union of Cyprus with Greece. It was a fiasco. Makarios fled, and the Turkish army invaded Cyprus. The dictatorship resigned and Karamanlis returned to Athens from Paris where he had been living in exile. He immediately formed a new government, released the political prisoners and legalized the Communist party. He then turned his attention to Cyprus, where Turkish forces had occupied 40% of the island. But the Greek army was not strong enough to take on the Turks, nor did the position taken by the British and the American governments help.

Today's Republic

On 17 November 1974 an election was held, which Karamanlis easily won. The monarchy did less well and Greece became the republic it is today. In 1977 Archbishop Makarios died leaving the Cyprus issue unresolved in the minds of the Greeks, although the Turks seem to consider it well nigh settled. This remains one of the major debating points in Greek politics. The desire for social reform and an independent foreign policy were to be the ticket to

Andreas Papandreau's Socialist victories in the 1980s. The arrogant Papandreau succeeded in alienating nearly all of Greece's allies while overseeing a remarkable economic boom, thanks to the growth of tourism and EC loan money. In the end, scandals and corruption among Papandreau's cronies brought Mitsotakis and the conservatives to power in 1990 to grapple with Greece's latest problems: the pan-European recession and the re-igniting of the flammable Balkan powder keg in ex-Yugoslavia. The world visits Greece for its holidays but no one has yet been able to give Greece the holiday it needs—from history.

A Brief Outline of Greek Art and Architecture

Neolithic to 3000 BC

The oldest known settlements on the islands date back to approximately 6000 BC—Knossos, Phaistos and the cave settlements of **Crete**, obsidian-exporting Phylokope on **Milos**, sophisticated Paleochoe on **Limnos** and Ag. Irene on **Kea**. Artistic finds are typical of the era elsewhere—dark burnished pottery, decorated with spirals and wavy lines and statuettes of the fertility goddess in stone or terra cotta.

Bronze Age: Cycladic and Minoan styles (3000–1100 BC)

Contacts with Anatolia and the Near East brought Crete and the Cyclades to the cutting edge of not only Greek, but European civilization. Around 2600 BC Cycladic dead were buried with extraordinary white marble figurines, or idols that border on the modern abstract (in the museums in **Naxos** and **Athens**). In the same period the first Minoans in Crete were demonstrating an uncanny artistic talent in their polychrome pottery— Kamares ware—and their stone vases (carved to resemble ceramic) and gold jewellery. They buried their dead in round *tholos* tombs up to 18 m in diametre. Hieroglyphs, learned from the Egyptians, were used to keep track of the magazines of oil, wine and grain stored in huge *pithoi* which characterize Minoan palaces and villas.

By the Middle Minoan period (2000–1700 BC) Crete ruled the Aegean with its mighty fleet. The Minoan priest-kings were secure enough from external and internal threats to build themselves unfortified palaces and cities, inevitably centred around a large rectangular courtyard. They installed a system of canals and drains which suggests that the Romans were hardly the first to take regular baths. Hieroglyphic writing was replaced by the still undeciphered script Linear A. Cretan civilization reached its apogee in the Late Minoan period (1700–1450 BC), when the Minoans had colonies across the Aegean and their elegant ambassadors figured in the tomb paintings of the Pharaohs; their own palaces at **Knossos, Phaistos, Zakros, Mallia** and at their outpost of Akrotiri on the island of **Santorini** were adorned with elegant frescoes of flowers, animals, human figures and bull dancers and other treasures now in the archaeology museums of **Herakleon** and **Athens**.

Built mostly of wood and unbaked brick, the Minoan palaces collapsed like card castles in a great natural disaster *c.* 1450 BC. The Achaeans of Mycenae rushed in to fill the vacuum of power and trade in the Aegean, taking over the Minoan colonies; their influence extended to the language of Linear B, which has been deciphered as a form of early Greek. The Achaeans adopted the Minoans' artistic techniques, especially in goldwork and ceramics. Little of this ever reached the islands, although many have vestiges of the Achaeans' stone walls, known as *cyclopean* after their gigantic blocks. As impressive as they are, they failed to keep out the northern invaders known as the Dorians, who destroyed Aegean unity and ushered in one of history's perennial Dark Ages.

Geometric (1000–700 BC) and Archaic (700–500 BC)

The break-up of the Minoan and Mycenaean world saw a return to agriculture and the development of the *polis* or city-state. In art the Geometric period refers to the simple, abstract decoration of the pottery; traces of Geometric temples of brick and wood are much rarer. The temple of Apollo at **Dreros** on Crete and the first Temple of Hera on **Samos** were built around the 8th century, although both pale before the discovery in 1981 of the huge sanctuary at **Lefkandi** on Evia, believed to date from *c.* 900 BC. The most complete Geometric town discovered so far is Zagora on **Andros**.

The Archaic Period is marked by the change to stone, especially limestone, for the building of temples and a return to representational art in decoration. The first known stone temple— and a prototype of the Classical temple with its columns, pediments and metopes—was **Corfu**'s stout-columned Doric Temple of Artemis (580 BC), its pediment decorated with a formidable 10-ft Medusa (now in Corfu's museum). The beautiful Doric Temple of Aphaia on **Aegina** was begun in the same period and decorated with a magnificent 6th-century pediment sculpted with scenes from the Trojan war (now in Munich). The excavations at Emborio, on **Chios** are among the best extant records we have of an Archaic town; the 6th-century Efplinion tunnel at Pythagorio, **Samos** was the engineering feat of the age.

This era also saw the beginning of life size—and larger—figure sculpture, inspired by the Egyptians: poses are stiff, formal, and rigid, one foot carefully placed before the other. The favourite masculine figure was the *kouros*, or young man, originally one of the dancers at fertility ritual (see the marble quarries of **Naxos** and the *Kriophoros* of **Thassos**); the favourite feminine figure was the *kore*, or maiden, dressed in graceful drapery, representing Persephone and the return of spring. The Archaeology Museum in **Athens** has the best examples of both. The 7th century also saw the development of regional schools of pottery, influenced by the black-figured techniques of Corinth: **Rhodes** and the Cycladic islands produced some of the best.

Classic (500–380 BC)

As Athens became the dominant power in the Aegean, it attracted much of the artistic talent of the Greek world and concentrated its most refined skills on its showpiece Acropolis, culminating with the extraordinary mathematical precision and perfect proportions of the Parthenon, the greatest of all Doric temples, yet built without a single straight line in the entire building. Nothing on the islands approaches it, although there are a few classical-era sites to visit: **Limen** on Thassos and **Eretria** on Evia, **Lindos, Kamiros** and **Ialysos** on Rhodes.

Hellenistic (380–30 BC)

This era brought new stylistic influences from the eastern lands, conquered and hellenized by Alexander the Great and his lieutenants. Compared to the cool, aloof perfection of the Classical era, Hellenistic sculpture is characterized by a more emotional, Mannerist approach, of windswept drapery, violence, and passion. Much of what remains of **Samothrace**'s Sanctuary of the Great Gods, and the Louvre's dramatic *Victory of Samothrace* are from the Hellenistic period. Ancient Rhodes was at the height of its powers, and produced its long-gone Colossus, as well as the writhing *Laocoon* (now in the Vatican museum) and Aphrodite statues in the **Rhodes** museum. Houses became decidedly more plush, many decorated with mosaics and frescoes as in the commercial town of **Delos** and in the suburbs of **Kos**.

Roman (30 BC–529 AD)

The Pax Romana ended the rivalries between the Greek city-states and pretty much ended the source of their artistic inspiration, although sculptors, architects, and other talents found a ready market for their skills in Rome, cranking out copies of Classic and Hellenistic masterpieces. The Romans themselves built little in Greece: the stoa and theatre of Heroditus Atticus (160 AD) were the last large monuments erected in ancient Athens. On the islands, the largest site is **Gortyna** the Roman capital of Crete.

Byzantine (527–1460)

The art and architecture of Byzantine Empire began to show its stylistic distinction under the reign of Justinian (527–565) and the immediate post-Justinian period saw a first golden age in the splendour of the Ag. Sofia in Istanbul and the churches of Ravenna, Italy. On the islands you'll find only the remains of simple three-naved basilicas—with two important exceptions: the 6th-century Ekatontapyliani of **Paros** and 7th-century Ag. Titos at **Gortyna**, Crete.

After the austere anti-art puritanism of the Iconoclasm (726–843) the Macedonian style (named for the Macedonian emperors) slowly infiltrated the Greek provinces. The old Roman basilica plan was jettisoned in favour of what became the classic Byzantine style: a central Greek-cross plan crowned by a dome, elongated in front by a vestibule (narthex) and outer porch (exonarthex) and in the back by a choir and three apses. **Dafni** just outside Athens and Nea Moni on **Chios** with its massive cupola, are superb examples; both are decorated with extraordinary mosaics from the second golden age of Byzantine art, under the dynasty of the

Comnenes (12th–14th centuries). As in Italy, this period marked a renewed interest in antique models: the stiff, elongated hieratic figures with staring eyes have more naturalistic proportions in graceful, rhythmic compositions; good examples are at **Dafni**. The age of the Comnenes also produced some fine painting: the 12th-century frescoes and manuscripts at the Monastery of St John on **Patmos**; the beautifully-frescoed early 13th-century Kera Panayia at **Kritsa**, near Ag. Nikolaos on Crete. Crete's occupation by Venice after 1204 marked the beginning of an artistic cross-fertilization that developed into the highly-esteemed Cretan school of icon painting, most conveniently seen in the Byzantine museums in Ag. Katerina in **Herakleon** and in **Athens**.

What never changed was the intent of Byzantine art, which is worth a small digression because in the 14th century Western sacred art went off in an entirely different direction—so much so that everything before is disparagingly labelled 'primitive' in most art books. One of the most obvious differences is the strict iconography in Byzantine painting: if you know the code you can instantly identify each saint by the cut of beard or his or her attribute. Their appeal to the viewer, even in the 11th century when the figures were given more naturalistic proportions, is equally purely symbolic; a Byzantine Christ on the Cross, the Virgin *Panayia*, the 'all-holy', angels, saints and martyrs never make a play for the heartstrings, but reside on a purely spiritual and intellectual plane. As Patrick Leigh Fermor wrote: 'Post-primitive religious painting in the West is based on horror, physical charm, infant-worship and easy weeping.' Icons and Byzantine frescoes never ask the viewer to relive vicariously the passion of Christ or coo over Baby Jesus; Byzantine angels never lift their draperies to reveal a little leg; the remote, wide-eyed Panayia has none of the luscious charms of the Madonna. They never stray from their remote otherworldliness.

And yet, in the last gasp of Byzantine art under the Paleologos emperors (14th–early 15th centuries), humanist and naturalistic influences combined to produce the Byzantine equivalent of the Late Gothic/early Renaissance painting in Italy, in Mistras in the Peloponnese. It is the great might-have-been of Byzantine art: after the Turkish conquest the best painters took refuge on Mount Athos, or on the islands ruled by Venice, but none of their work radiates the same charm or confidence in the temporal world.

Turkish Occupation to the Present

The Turks left few important monuments in Greece, and much of what they did build was wrecked by the Greeks after independence. **Rhodes** town has the best surviving mosques, hammams, houses and public buildings, not only because the Turks loved it well, but because it only became Greek in 1945. **Crete** and **Corfu** have a number of fine Venetian relics: impressive fortifications and gates, fountains, public buildings and town houses. Elsewhere, islands with their own fleets, especially **Hydra**, **Spetses** and **Symi** have impressive captain's mansions, while other islands continued traditional architectural styles: the whitewashed asymmetry of the Cyclades, the patterned sgraffito in the mastic villages of Chios, the Macedonian wooden upper floors and balconies of the northernmost islands.

In the 19th century, public buildings in both Athens and **Syros** (briefly Greece's chief port) are fairly bland neo-Classical works; a host of neo-Byzantine churches went up, while many older ones were unfortunately tarted up with tired bastard painting, Byzantine in iconography but most of it no better than the contents of a third rate provincial museum in Italy.

On the whole, the less said about 20th century architecture on the islands the better: the Fascist architecture left by the Italians on the Dodecanese islands has a sense of style, which is more than can be said of the cheap concrete slabs that have gone up elsewhere. Prosperity in the 1980s has brought an increased interest in local architecture and historic preservation: following the lead of the National Tourist Organization's traditional settlement programme (*see* p. 43), private individuals have began to restore old monasteries, abandoned villages, and captains' mansions, while many of the newest resort developments are less brash and more in harmony with local styles.

Topics

The 'Toreador Fresco', Knossos

> *...there too is Knossos, a mighty city, where Minos was king for nine years, a familiar of mighty Zeus.*

—Odyssey, book XIX

The so-called 'Toreador Fresco', found in the palace at Knossos, has become one of the most compelling icons of the lost world of ancient Crete (*see* p. 55). The slender, sensual bare-breasted maidens who seem to be controlling the action are painted in white, the moon's colour, as in all Cretan frescoes, while the athlete vaulting through the bull's horns appears like all males in red, the colour of the sun. Mythology and archaeology begin to agree, and the roots of the story of Theseus, Ariadne and the Minotaur seem tantalizingly close at hand.

When you see this fresco in Herakleon's Archaeology Museum, take time to look at the decorative border—four striped bands and a row of multicoloured lunettes. Neither Arthur Evans nor any archaeologist since noticed anything unusual about it. A professor of English in Maine named Charles F. Herberger (*The Thread of Ariadne*; Philosophical Library, New York, 1972) was the first to discover that this border is in fact a complex ritual calendar, the key to the myth of Theseus in the Labyrinth and to much else. The pairs of stripes on the tracks, alternately dark and light, for day and night, count on average 29 through each cycle of the five-coloured lunettes, representing the phases of the moon—this is the number of days in a lunar month. By counting all the stripes on the four tracks, Herberger found that each track gives roughly the number of days in a year; the whole, when doubled, totals exactly the number of days in an eight-year cycle of 99 lunar months, a period in which the solar and lunar years coincide—the marriage of the sun and moon.

To decipher the calendar, you can't simply count in circuits around the border; there are regular diagonal jumps to a new row, giving the course of the eight-year cycle the form of a rectangle with an 'x' in it. The box with the x is intriguing, a motif in the art of the Cretans and other ancient peoples as far afield as the Urartians of eastern Anatolia. A Cretan seal shows a bull apparently diving into a crossed rectangle of this sort, while a human figure vaults through his horns. Similar in form is the most common and most enigmatical of all Cretan symbols, the double axe or *labrys*. The form is echoed further in a number of Cretan signet-rings that show the x-shaped cross between the horns of a bull, or between what appear to be a pair of crescent moons.

The home of the labrys, the axe that cuts two ways, is the *labyrinth*. Arthur Evans believed the enormous, rambling palace of Knossos itself to be the labyrinth, a pile so confusing that even a Greek hero would have needed Ariadne's golden thread to find his way through it. In the childhood of archaeology, men could read myths so literally as to think there was a tangible labyrinth, and perhaps even a minotaur. Now, it seems more likely that the labyrinth was the calendar itself, the twisting path that a Minos, a generic name for Cretan priest-kings, representing the sun, followed in his eight-year reign before his inevitable rendezvous with the great goddess. This meeting may originally have meant his death (in a bull mask perhaps) and replacement by another Theseus. Later it would have been simply a ceremony of re-marriage to the priestess that stood in the transcendent goddess' place, celebrated by the bull-vaulting ritual. It has been claimed that the occasion was also accompanied by popular dancing, following the shape of the labyrinth, where the dancers proceeded in a line holding a cord—Ariadne's thread.

Homer said 'nine years', and other sources give nine years as the period after which the Athenians had to send their captives to Crete to be devoured by the minotaur—it's a common ancient confusion, really meaning 'until the ninth', in the way the French still call the interval of a week *huit jours*. Whatever this climax of the Cretan cycle was, it occurred with astronomical precision according to the calendar, and followed a rich, many-layered symbolism difficult for us scoffing moderns ever to comprehend.

That the Cretans had such a complex calendar should be no surprise—for a people that managed modern plumbing and three-storey apartment blocks, and still found time to rule the seas of the eastern Mediterranean. The real attraction lies not simply in the intricacies of the calendar (the nasty Mesopotamians and many other peoples had equally interesting calendars) but more particularly in the scene in the middle, where the diagonals cross and where the ancient science translates into celebration, into dance. Cretan art speaks to everyone, with a colour, beauty and immediacy never before seen in art, and all too lacking in our own time. No other art of antiquity displays such an irresistible grace and joy, qualities which must have come from a profound appreciation of the beauties and rhythms of nature—the rhythms captured and framed in the ancient calendar.

Endangered Animals and Some Plain Old Pests

For years Greek environmentalists have pushed for legislation to protect rare species of wildlife in the Aegean and Ionian Seas. National parks, wildlife sanctuaries and hunting laws are well regulated on the mainland, but it is the fragile ecologies of the dying seas that cry out most desperately for protection. In the early 1980s, efforts to save the Mediterranean green loggerhead turtle centred on Zakynthos; information kiosks sprouted on the island, representing not only a conscious effort to protect marine life, but also the first public information outlets directly in conflict with the mighty gods of tourism. Because the turtles lay their eggs on the sandy beaches, sometimes immediately in front of resort hotels, the noise, lights, and innocent trampling of buried turtle eggs was decimating a turtle population already struggling against a hundred natural predators. Controls and schedules were imposed on the use of beaches by tourists, infuriating local proprietors who saw their incomes theatened, while to environmentalists, who considered tourists little better than 'terrorists' the regulations hardly went far enough. Gradually both sides have moderated their stance to reach a compromise: tourists must respect the turtles, an attitude that has proved profitable in drawing eco-tourists.

What Greece has long needed was a National Marine Park to protect the entire eco-system. Although it has yet to pass at the presidential level, the crystalline seas around the Northern Sporades have been chosen as the country's first, and only, Marine Park. It encompasses some of the most beautiful and untouched islands and a diversity of marine life, including the most endangered species in Europe, the monk seal. Biologists believe the seal to be our closest relative in the sea, and use the animal as a yardstick to measure the sea's health, habitability and biological balance. It doesn't bode well; only 300 monk seals remain in Greek waters, and a mere 500 in the entire world.

But there is room for hope. Since international attention has been focused on the monk seals and their dwindling numbers, a research station and rehabilitation centre have been established on the island central to the park, Alonissos. The Hellenic Society for the Study and Protection of Monk Seals (HSSPMS) has managed to rehabilitate 5 orphaned seals in the past three years—a 20% increase in the park's population of 30, and the best population stabilizer ever, as seals will not breed in captivity. Combined with the orphan programme and their public awareness drive, the HSSPMS is beginning to bring the species back from the brink of extinction. Tourists have helped by observing the park laws, such as not entering caves where seals are born and suckled, and not disturbing islands known to be inhabited by seals. However, dangers still remain. Mass tourism and over-fishing are the greatest threats. Although legislation controls tourist and fishing activities in the park, the logistics problem of patrolling so many islands remains staggering. Laws limiting industrial fishing are constantly flouted—demand for fish has drained the Aegean's key resource by nearly 60%. Some islanders have responded enthusiastically, acting as voluntary, part-time rangers, reporting orphaned or injured seals to the HSSPMS. Another endangered species in the park is Eleanora's Falcon, a small migratory falcon which nests almost exclusively in the Sporades in spring and summer. Many other birds use the Northern Sporades as a stepping stone on their migratory paths—swallows, storks, herons and egrets all pass at one time of the year or another, and take advantage of sanctuary. If you see a dolphin, consider yourself lucky. Not for superstitious reasons (although local fishermen paint dolphins on their boats), but because there are so few. As for turtles in the Aegean, well, if you see one, put it down to the effects of *ouzo*.

The biggest hurdle faced by Greek environmentalists is the lack of local support. Businesss people fear that even the slightest restrictions on tourist activity will make tourists and their money stay away. The facts prove the contrary. Island councils, restaurants, hotels and tour boat operators are gradually becoming aware that people long to go to places where the environment is healthy and clean. They are happy to see wildlife in its natural habitat, even if only a glimpse. Tourists tend to return to places which are naturally beautiful with few gimmicks, enticed by harmony with nature, and locals are slowly beginning to realize that that place is Greece.

As for creatures unfortunately *not* on the endangered list, the wily mosquito tops the list for pure incivility. Most shops stock the usual defenses: lotions, sprays and insect coils; or pick up one of those inexpensive electric mosquito repellents that fit right in the wall plug and don't stink as badly as the smouldering coils. Public insect enemy Number Two is the wasp, either taking bites out of that honey baklava you've just ordered, or spoiling your picnic on the beach (a special hazard on the lush Ionian islands). Dangers lurk in the sea as well: harmless pale brown jellyfish (*médusas*) may drift in anywhere depending on winds and currents, but the oval transparent model (*tsouitres*) are stinging devils that can leave scars on tender parts of your anatomy if you brush against them. Pincushiony sea urchins live by rocky beaches, and if you're too cool to wear rubber swimming shoes and step on one, it hurts like hell. The spines may break and embed themselves even deeper if you try to force them out; the Greeks recommend olive oil and a lot of patience to get the spine to slip out.

Much less common are Greece's shy scorpions, who hide out in between the rocks in rural areas; unless you're especially sensitive, their sting is no more or less painful than a bee's. Always avoid the back legs of mules, unless you've been properly introduced. The really lethal creatures are rare: the small, grey-brown viper that lives in the nooks and crannies of stone walls, where it is well camouflaged, only comes out occasionally to sun itself. Although seldom seen (it prefers abandoned villages and quiet archaeological sites), the Greeks are terrified of it; the mere word *fithi* (snake) will turn the most stout-hearted villager to jelly. Mountain sheepdogs are a more immediate danger in outer rural areas; by stooping as if to pick up a stone to throw, you might keep a dog at bay.

Sharks seldom prowl near the coastal regions of Greece. Blood attracts them, so if you are wounded, swim for shore without delay. Divers should ask their Greek confrères about other dangerous fish in the area, such as the dracula, an unlikely delicacy whose razor-sharp fins can kill.

On *Kefi* and Dancing

In the homogenized European Community of the 1990s, only the Spaniards and Greeks still dance to their own music with any kind of spontaneity, and it's no coincidence that both have untranslatable words to describe the 'spirit' or 'mood' that separates going through the steps and true dancing. In Spain, the word is *duende*, which, with the hard driving rhythms of flamenco, has an ecstatic quality; in Greek, the word is *kefi*, which comes closer to 'soul'. For a Greek to give his all, he must have *kefi*; to dance without it could be considered dishonest. The smart young men in black trousers and red sashes who dance for you at dinner probably don't have it; two craggy old fishermen, in a smoky café in Crete, who crank up an old gramophone and dance for their own pleasure, do. You can feel the *kefi* at Easter when the village elders join hands and dance an elegant *kalamatiano*, or when a group of children celebrate the local saint's day in North Karpathos. Any sensitive person can't help but be moved by the atmosphere, especially in constrast with the stark, technically perfect stage performances of the dance troupes under the Acropolis or in the old fort of Corfu. If the *kefi* moves you to leap up and dance, your Greek friends will see you in a new light, your bond with Greece established, and you may find it just that bit harder to book your ticket home.

Nearly every island has its own dance, some of which are extremely difficult. Then there are the dances everyone knows, from the elementary 'one two three kick kick', or *Stae Tria*, footed in a circle with hands on shoulders. The circle is never complete, however: even in this simple dance a man or woman will lead, handkerchief in hand, setting the pace and supplying the special effects with leaps, foot slaps, kicks, little skips or whatever he or she likes. Cretans are among the most energetic leaders—some are almost contortionists.

Stae Tria often begins slowly and picks up to a furious pace towards the end. The *sýrto*, on the other hand, retains its slow graceful pace throughout. It has only six easy steps which are repeated until the end, but watch the leader for variations. This is considered the oldest Greek dance of all, dating back to Hellenistic, if not Homeric times. The *kalamatíano*, a 12-step dance, takes some practice. If a Greek invites you to dance the *bállo*, the most common couple's dance, follow your partner's lead and hope for the best. While there are certain set steps to the *tsíphte téli*, or belly dance, it has become a free-spirited dance for the loose limbed.

The *zeybetiko* is normally but not exclusively performed by men, a serious, deliberate solo dance with outstretched arms, evoking the swooping flight of the eagle; a companion will go down on one knee to encourage the dancer and clap out the rhythm. The *hasápiko*, better known as the Zorba dance in the West, and traditionally performed by two men, will require some practice but is well worth learning—like Alan Bates who finally began to fathom *kefi* from Anthony Quinn at the end of the film *Zorba*. Plenty of practice and energy are the rules for joining in most Cretan dances, where the music demands furious, machine-gun fire steps

and hops that go on until your adrenalin has pumped its last. But toss back another *raki*, and before you know it you'll be up dancing another *pentozale* or *pedekto*.

You can get off on the right foot with *Greek Dances* by Ted Petrides (published by Lycabettus Press in Athens), supplemented by some private coaching from the Greeks—or their children, who usually have more patience.

Musicians from the Tomb of the Leopards 480–470 BC Fresco

Orthodoxy

With the exception of a handful of Catholics in the Cyclades, nearly all Greeks belong to the Orthodox, or Eastern church; indeed, being Orthodox and speaking Greek are the two most important criteria in defining a Greek, whether born in Athens, Alexandria or Australia. Orthodoxy is so fundamental that even the greatest sceptics can hardly conceive of marrying outside the church, or neglecting to have their children baptized.

One reason for this deep national feeling is that unlike everything else in Greece, Orthodoxy has scarcely changed since the founding of the church by Constantine in the 4th century. As Constantinople took the place of Rome as the political and religious capital, the Greeks believe their church to be the only true successor to the original church of Rome. Therefore, a true Greek is called a *Romiós* or Roman, and the Greek language of today is called *Romaíka*. It is considered perfect and eternal and beyond all worldly change; if it weren't, its adherents could not expect to be saved. Hence, the Greeks have been spared the changes that have rocked the West, from Vatican II to discussions over women in the clergy to political questions of abortion, birth control and so on—matters on which Orthodoxy has always remained aloof. Much emphasis is put on ceremony and ritual, the spiritual and aesthetic, with very little appeal to the emotions.

This explains the violence of Iconoclasm, the one movement to change the rules. Back in the early 8th century Byzantine Emperor Leo III the Isaurian, shamed by what his Moslem neighbours labelled idolatry, deemed the images of divine beings to be sacreligious. Iconoclasm began the rift with Rome, that worsened in 800 when the Pope crowned Charlemagne as emperor, usurping the position of the Emperor of Constantinople. Further divisions arose over the celibacy of the clergy (Orthodox may marry before they are ordained) and the use of the phrase 'and the son' in the Holy Creed, the issue which caused the final, fatal schism in 1054 when the Pope's representative Cardinal Humbert excommunicated the Patriarch of Constantinople.

After the fall of the Byzantine Empire (that 'thousand-year-long mass for the dead' as one recent Greek writer put it), the Turks not only tolerated the Orthodox church, but they had the political astuteness to impart considerable powers to the patriarch. The church was thus able to preserve many Greek traditions and Greek education through the dark age of Ottoman rule; on the other hand it often abused this power against its own flock, especially on a local scale. According to an old saying, priests, headmen and Turks were the three curses of Greece and the poor priests (who in truth are usually quite amiable fellows) have not yet exonerated themselves from the list they now share with the king and the cuckold.

The extraordinary quantity of churches and chapels on some islands has little to do with the priests, however. Nearly all were built by families or individuals, especially by sailors, seeking the protection of a patron saint. Some were built to keep a promise, others in simple thanksgiving. Architecturally they come in an endless variety of styles depending on the region, period and terrain, as well as the wealth and whim of the builder. All but the tiniest have an *iconostasis*, or altar screen, made of wood or stone to separate the *heiron* or sanctuary, where only the ordained are allowed, from the rest of the church. Most of the chapels are now locked up; some light-fingered tourists have decided that icons make lovely souvenirs; if you track down the caretaker, do dress discreetly (no shorts!) and leave a few drachmas for upkeep.

Almost all these chapels have only one service a year, on the name day of the patron saint (name days are celebrated in Greece more widely than birthdays: 'Many years!' *(Chrónia pollá!)* is the proper way to greet someone on their name day). This annual celebration is called a *yiortí* or more frequently *paneyéri*, and is the cause for feasts and dancing before or after the church service. If feasible, *paneyeria* take place directly in the churchyard, if not, in neighbouring wooded areas or in tavernas. The food can be superb but is more often basic and plentiful; for a set price you receive more than your share and a doggy bag full, generally of goat. *Paneyeria* (festivals) are also the best places to hear traditional island music and learn the dances, and it's sad that they're only a fond memory in most major tourist centres (although alive and well in less frequented areas). The Assumption of the Virgin, 15 August, is the largest *paneyeri* in Greece apart from Easter, the biggest holiday. The faithful sail to Tinos, the Lourdes of Greece, and to a dozen centres connected with Mary, making mid-August a very uncomfortable time to travel among the islands, especially the Cyclades. Not only are the ships packed to the brim, but the meltemi wind also blows with vigour, and Greek matrons, the most ardent pilgrims of all, are the worst of all sailors.

Orthodox weddings are another lovely if long-winded ritual. The bride and groom stand solemnly before the chanting priest, while family and friends in attendance seem to do everything but follow the proceedings. White crowns, bound together by a white ribbon, are placed on the heads of bride and groom, and the *koumbáros*, or best man, exchanges them back and forth. The newlyweds are then led around the altar three times, which spurs the guests into action as they bombard the happy couple with fertility-bringing rice and flower petals. After congratulating the bride and groom guests are given a small *boboniéra* of candied almonds. This is followed by the marriage feast and dancing, which in the past could last up to five days. If you are in the vicinity of a village wedding you may be offered a sweet cake; you may even be invited to come along to the feasting as a special guest.

Baptisms are cause for similar celebration. The priest completely immerses the baby in the Holy Water three times (unlike Achilles, there are no vulnerable spots on modern Greeks) and almost always gives the little one the name of a grandparent. For extra protection from the forces of evil, babies often wear a *filaktó*, or amulet, the omnipresent blue glass eye bead. If you visit a baby at home you may well be sprinkled first with Holy Water, and chances are there's a bit of beneficial garlic squeezed somewhere under the cradle. Compliments to the little one's parents should be kept to a minimum; the gods do get jealous.

Funerals in Greece, for reasons of climate, are carried out as soon as possible, and are announced by the tolling of the village church bells. The dead are buried for three to five years (longer if the family can pay) after which time the bones are exhumed and placed in the family box to make room for the next resident. *Aforismós*, or Orthodox excommunication, is believed to prevent the body decaying after death—the main source of Greek vampire stories. Memorials for the dead take place three, nine and forty days after death, and on the first anniversary. They are sometimes repeated annually. Sweet buns and sugared wheat and raisin *koúliva* are given out after the ceremony; children wouldn't miss them for the world.

The *Periptero* and the Plane Tree

In Greece you'll see it everywhere, the greatest of modern Greek inventions, the indispensable *periptero*. It is the best-equipped kiosk in the world, where people gather to chat, make local or international calls, or grab a few minutes' shade under the little projecting roof. The *periptero* is a substitute bar, selling everything from water to ice cream to ice cold beer; an emergency pharmacy stocked with aspirin, mosquito killers, condoms and band aids; a convenient newsagent for Greek and international publications, from *Ta Nea* to *Die Zeit*; a tourist shop offering travel guides, postcards and stamps; a toy shop for balloons, plastic swords and Teenage Mutant Ninja Turtles; a general store for shoelaces, batteries and rolls of film. In Athens they're at most traffic lights. On the islands they are a more common sight than a donkey. You'll wonder how you ever survived before *peripteros* and the treasures they contain.

The other great meeting centre of Greek life is the mighty plane tree, or *platanos*, for centuries the focal point of village life, where politics and philosophy have been argued since time immemorial. Since Hippocrates the Greeks have believed that plane shade is wholesome and beneficial (unlike the ennervating shadow cast by the fig) and one of the most extraordinary sights in the islands is 'Hippocrates' plane tree' on Kos, propped up on scaffolding and as protected as any national monument would be. In Greek the expression *herete mou ton platano* loosely translates as 'go tell it to the marines', presumably because the tree has heard all that nonsense before. For a Greek village the *platanos* represents that village's identity; the tree is a source of life, for it only grows near abundant fresh water; its deep roots a symbol of stability, continuity and protection—a huge majestic umbrella, even the rain cannot penetrate its sturdy leaves. Sit under its spreading branches and sip a coffee as the morning unfolds before you; the temptation to linger there for the day is irresistible.

Shirley Valentines

> *Know thyself*
>
> *—the inscription over the gate of the oracle at Delphi*

There isn't an island without at least one Shirley Valentine, drawn years ago by something special, a holiday romance perhaps that turned into a love affair with a place rather than a person, an enjoyment of living in a country where eccentrics are welcomed rather than scorned. Shirley Valentines come in all shapes and sizes, male or female, young or old, cynical or innocent, birdwatchers or bartenders, pensioners from New York, English gym teachers and marine insurance agents, lost souls from Hamburg, Dutch advertizing execs, an occasional black sheep or social misfit; all characters who have found their Atlantis, and can now only live as strange birds in foreign nests.

These people have become part of island daily life and, as far as many locals are concerned, add a missing ingredient. They know their island well, and are usually a good source of information, whether it be tracking down the friendliest watering hole, or blackmailing the builder who promised to turn up weeks ago. Bjorn from Stockholm has been there for years, married a local girl and can outswear the locals. Penny from Bath can drink the village boys under the table. She has her reasons for doing so; her heart is broken with regularity, and every day brings tears and laughter, but turning Ipanemian brown under the Greek sun, far from the monochrome office blocks, and watching the sun set at the most beautiful time of the day brings a serenity and happiness previously unknown.

'Greece' once remarked President Karamanlis, 'reminds me of an enormous madhouse'. True or not, whether the Shirley Valentines have a streak of madness in them, Greece has allowed them to invent for themselves a way of living their fantasies, of finding or building a new personality that was just under the surface anyway.

As the days shorten and the cafés close, the last forlorn tourists sit on the deserted waterfront, and the empty echoes of summer fade away. There's now a chill to the wind as the waiters collect up the tables and chairs, no longer needed for the rest of the year, and the island returns to normality. The discotheques, not long ago throbbing to Michael Jackson, close down; the bouzouki replaces the electric guitar, boogie gives way to the *zembekiko* and the overall tempo of life changes. The real Greece re-emerges, the islanders claim back their island. Plastic cafés are re-transformed into lively little *ouzeri*, and it is time to sit and reflect on the summer, count the precious drachmas and lick wounds. The evening stroll, or *volta* returns with full intensity, and the greeting is *Kalo chimona*, or 'Have a good winter'. Wild seas reclaim the beaches; the last Coca Cola bottle is washed away as the pebbles are rinsed of suntan lotion. Even the swallows decamp, and head south to warmer climes. As the wind kicks up, bare-bones ferry schedules go haywire; fresh vegetables, meat and milk become scarce on many islands, and many a meal consists of beans or lentils, sardines and pasta.

Cold, wet and windy, the Greek winter takes hold of the summer paradise, and people huddle around wood stoves discussing the spoils and adventures, the highs and lows of the summer. The sun's warmth is replaced by the warmth of the family, and grandma can now take repossession of her little room rented out on the black to backpackers. The only voices in the main street are those of the blue-smocked children wandering in a ragged line to the village school, clutching their schoolbags and midday snacks of bread and spam. The few hardy perennial foreign residents make a reappearance in the cafés, and the lingua franca once again returns to demotic Greek.

The summer spirit flickers briefly in winter's depths, and the gentle sun sometimes provides enough warmth to sit out by the still, sparkling blue sea, watching the caiques come in with their haul. Spring, the loveliest of all seasons in Greece, sees the trees blossom and the islands transformed into carpets of flowers, as Easter approaches. Even the noisiest, most boisterous Greeks are subdued in the week preceding the Easter weekend, which erupts into a frenzy of dancing, rejoicing, eating and drinking, as fireworks light up the midnight sky. *Christos anesti!* is the greeting, 'Christ has risen!' and millions of candles are lit around the country.

Like magic any harsh memories of the previous summer are forgotten, vendettas are forgiven, and a rejuvenated population prepares itself for a new season, painting café chairs, mending shopfronts, whitewashing walls. There's a feeling of expectancy in the air as, first the swallows, then the tourists arrive, and the whole show winds up again.

Athens and Piraeus

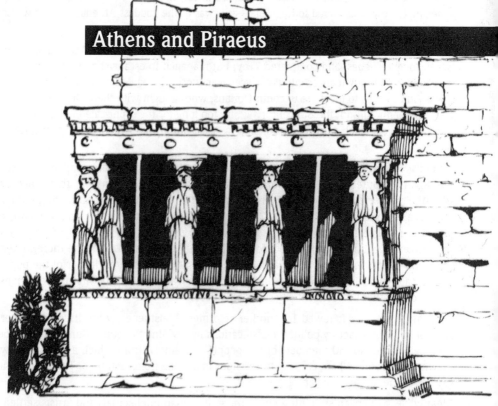

The Caryatid Porch of the Erechtheion

Many travellers to the Greek islands eventually find themselves in Athens and Piraeus, and anyone making their first journey to Greece will particularly want to spend two or three days in the capital. It's rarely love at first sight; Athens, with its ramshackle architecture and grubby, dusty exterior, wins no beauty prizes. Look closely, however, and you may be won over by this urban crazy quilt of villages—small oases of green parks hidden amidst the hustle and bustle; tiny family-run tavernas tucked away in the most unexpected places; the feverish pace of its nightlife and summer festivals devoted to wine and song; and best all, the Athenians themselves, whose friendliness belies the reputation of most inhabitants of capital cities.

Historical Outline of Athens

Inhabited by pre-Hellenic tribes in the Neolithic Age (*c.* 3500 BC) Athens made its proper debut on the stage of history in the second millennium, when Ionians from Asia Minor invaded Attica and established several small city-states. Their main centre was Kekropia, named for the serpent god Kekrops, (he later became connected with King Erechtheus, who was himself a snake from the waist down and is considered to be the original founder of Athens). The owl was sacred to Kekropia—as it was to the goddess Athena, and her worship and name gradually came to preside in the city.

In the 14th century BC Athens, as part of the Mycenaean empire of the Achaeans, invaded Crete, fought Thebes, and conquered Troy, but managed to escape the subsequent Dorian invasion which brought chaos into the Mycenaean world. Two hundred years later, however, it was Attica's turn to meet the uncouth Dorians, who brought with them Greece's first Dark Age. This endured until the 8th century BC, far too long for the sophisticated Ionians and Aeolians, who went back to their homelands in Asia Minor and settled many of the Aegean islands.

Sometime during the 8th century all the towns of Attica were peaceably united, an accomplishment attributed to the mythical King Theseus (1300 BC). Athens was then ruled by a king (the chief priest), a *polemarch* (or general), and an *archon* (or civil authority), positions that became annually elective by the 6th century. The conflict between the landed aristocracy and rising commercial classes gradually brought about the solution of democratic government, beginning under the reforms of Solon. Yet under every stone there lurked a would-be tyrant; Solon was still warm in the grave when Pisistratos, leader of the popular party, made himself boss (545 BC) and began the naval build-up that first made Athens a threat to the other independent city-states of Greece.

Pisistratos' son was followed by another reformer, Kleisthenes, who discarded Athens' ancient but unsatisfactory political classifications by dividing the population into ten tribes. Each selected by lot 50 members of the people's assembly, from which a further lot was drawn to select an archon, creating ten archons in all, one from each tribe. The head archon gave his name to the Athenian year.

Meanwhile, as Persian strength grew in the east, Ionian intellectuals and artists settled in

Athens, bringing with them the roots of Attic tragedy. They encouraged Athens to aid the Ionians against the Persians, an unsuccessful adventure that landed the city in the soup when Darius, the King of Kings, turned to subdue Greece, and in particular Athens, which posed the only threat to the Persian fleet. In 490 BC Darius' vast army landed at Marathon only to be defeated by a much smaller Athenian force under Miltiades. Powerful Sparta and the other Greek states then recognized the eastern threat, but continued to leave 'national' defence primarily in the hands of the Athenians and their fleet, which grew ever mightier under Themistokles. However, it failed to keep the Persians from having another go at Greece, and in 480 BC the new king Xerxes showed up with the greatest fleet and army the ancient world had ever seen. Athens was destroyed, but the Persian navy was neatly outmanoeuvred by the Athenian ships at Salamis (*see* p. 400) and the invasion was finally repelled by the Athenians and Spartans at the battle of Plataea.

Having proved her naval might, Athens set about creating a maritime empire, not only to increase her power but also to stabilize her combustible internal politics. She ruled the confederacy at Delos (*see* p. 153) demanding contributions from the islands in return for protection from the Persians. Sea trade became necessary to support the city's growing population, while the founding of new colonies around the Mediterranean ensured a continual food supply to Athens. The democracy became truly imperialistic under Perikles, who brought the treasure of Delos to Athens to skim off funds to rebuild and beautify the city and build the Parthenon. It was the golden age of Athens, the age of the sculptures of Phidias, the histories of Herodotos, the plays of Sophocles and Aristophanes, the philosophy of Socrates.

The main cause of the Peloponnesian War (431–404 BC) was concern over Athenian expansion in the west. Back and forth the struggle went, Sparta with superiority on land, Athens on the seas, until both city-states were near exhaustion. Finally Lysander captured Athens, razed the walls, and set up the brief rule of the Thirty Tyrants.

Although democracy and imperialism made quick recoveries (by 378 the city had set up its second Maritime League), the Peloponnesian War had struck a blow from which Athens could not totally recover. The population grew dissatisfied with public life, and refused to tolerate innovators and critics to the extent that Socrates was put to death. Economically, Athens had trouble maintaining the trade she so desperately needed. Yet her intellectual tradition held true in the 4th century, bringing forth the likes of Demosthenes, Praxiteles, Menander, Plato and Aristotle.

Philip II of Macedon took advantage of the general discontent and turmoil to bully the city-states into joining Macedon for an expedition against Persia. Athenian patriotism and independence were kept alive by the orator Demosthenes until Philip subdued the city (338). He was assassinated shortly before beginning the Persian campaign, leaving his son Alexander to conquer the East. When Alexander died, Athens had to defend herself against his striving generals, beginning with Dimitrios Poliorketes (the Besieger) who captured the city in 294. Alexandria and Pergamon became Athens' intellectual rivals, although Athens continued to be honoured by them.

In 168 BC Rome captured Athens, but gave her many privileges including the island of Delos. Eighty years later Athens betrayed Roman favour by siding with Mithridates of Pontos, for which Sulla destroyed Piraeus and the walls of the city. But Rome always remembered her cultural debt; leading Romans attended Athens' schools and gave the city great gifts. Conversely many Greek treasures ended up in Rome. St Paul came to preach to the Athenians in AD 44. In the 3rd century Goths and barbarians sacked Athens, and when they were driven away the city joined the growing Byzantine Empire.

Justinian closed the philosophy schools in AD 529 and changed the temples to churches and the Parthenon into a cathedral. By now Athens had lost almost all of her former importance. She became the plaything of the Franks after they pillaged Constantinople in 1204. St Louis appointed Guy de la Roche as Duke of Athens, a dukedom which passed through many outstretched hands; the Catalans, Neapolitans and Venetians all controlled it at various times. In 1456 the Turks took Athens, turning the Parthenon into a mosque and the Erechtheion into a harem. While attacking the Turks in 1687 Morosini and the Venetians blew up part of the Parthenon, where the Turks had stored their gunpowder. A year later the Venetians left, unsuccessful, and the citizens who had fled returned to Athens. In 1800 Lord Elgin began the large-scale removal of monuments from Athens to the British and other museums.

In 1834, after the War of Independence, Athens—then a few hundred war-scarred houses deteriorating under the Acropolis—was declared the capital of the new Greek state. Otho of Bavaria, the first King of the Greeks, brought his own architects with him and laid out a new city on the lines of Stadiou and El. Venezelou streets, which still boast most of Otho's neo-Classical public buildings. The rest of the city's architecture was abandoned to unimaginative concrete blocks, spared monotony only by the hilly Attic terrain. More and more of these hills are being pounded into villas and flats by the ubiquitous cement mixer; greater Athens squeezes in over three million lively, opiniated inhabitants (a third of the entire Greek population) who thanks to native ingenuity and EC membership are now more prosperous than they have been since the age of Perikles. Unfortunately this means a million cars now crawl the ancient streets, creating the worst smog problem east of Los Angeles, and one that threatens to choke this unique city.

Orientation

Syntagma (or **Constitution**) **Square** is to all intents and purposes the centre of the action, and it's here that the **Parliament Building** is to be found, backing on to the **National Gardens** and **Zappeion Park**, a haven of green and shade to escape the summer heat, with ducks to feed and a hundred benches useful for grabbing a few winks. The square itself is the perfect place to sit and let the afternoon or evening slip by, although the best place to do this has now been taken over by a certain ubiquitous burger chain. From here it's a short walk down to the **Plaka**, the medieval centre of Athens at the foot of the Acropolis, where many of the older houses have been converted into intimate tavernas or bars, each tinkling away with its own electric bazouki. During the day meander through its market district, **Monastiraki**, where bulging shops sell everything from decorated ceramic tiles and leather bags to garden hoes and second hand fridges. From Monastiraki stroll along Athinas St, the very essence of this most mercantile city, until you reach **Omonia Square**, once a vortex of traffic and sleaze, but currently undergoing a facelift with new pedestrian shopping walkways; Omonia's restaurants are known for their delicious suckling pig.

A 10-minute walk from Syntagma will take you to **Kolonaki Square**, Athens' Knightsbridge in miniature, complete with fancypants shops and restaurants (all of course expensive) and plenty of well heeled Athenians to patronize them. Up from the square (it's a long haul on foot, but there's a funicular) is the hill of **Lycavitos**, illuminated like a fairytale tower at night. On the top sits the chapel of **St George**, a restaurant/bar and a cannon fired on national holidays. It offers the best panoramic views of Athens, including a sweeping vista down to the sea at Piraeus, *nefos* (Athens' special brand of smog) permitting.

A 20-minute walk from Syntagma, along Vass. Sofias, brings you to the Hilton Hotel, a useful landmark. Behind it are the essential Athenian neighbourhoods of **Ilissia** and **Pangrati**, the best place to get a feel for everyday life in the city. Lose yourself in their backstreets and you may find your own little taverna, of which there are plenty, rather than restrict yourself to the tourist haunts in the centre.

From Zappeion Park buses run frequently down to the coast and suburbs of **Glyfada**, **Voula** and **Vouliagmenis**. Glyfada, close to the airport, is a green and pleasant suburb, and the town itself has grown into a busy resort and a rival Kolonaki. Many smart city dwellers shop at the ritzy boutiques, and there are even a couple of well-designed (but small, fortunately) indoor shopping centres. Here and further down the coast at Voula are pay beaches run by EOT, the National Tourist Organisation. The water is generally clean, but nothing like the more remote islands. There's also good swimming beyond Voula in the rocky coves at Vouliagmenis. Beyond Vouliagmenis, the road continues along the coast to **Sounion** and its **Temple of Poseidon** (440 BC), famous for its magnificent position and sunsets and where there's always at least one Japanese tourist searching for the column where Byron carved his name.

Museums and Sites in Athens

Agora Museum (the Theseum and Ancient Agora)

Open 8.30–3, closed Mon, adm. The Agora was not only the market but the centre of Athenian civic and social life where citizens spent much of their day; here Socrates questioned their basic conceptions of life and law. In 480 BC the Persians destroyed all the buildings of the Agora, which were rebuilt in a much grander style; many suffered the wrath of the Romans and fires set by the barbarians. Only the foundations remain of the **Bouleuterion** or council house, and the neighbouring Temple of the Mother of the Gods, the **Metroon**, built by the Athenians in reparation for their slaying of a priest from the cult. The round **Tholos** or administration centre is where the administrators or *prytanes* worked, and as some had to be on call day and night, kitchens and sleeping quarters were included. Its final reconstruction took place after Sulla's rampage in 88 BC. Only a wall remains of the **Sanctuary of the Eponymous Heroes of Athens**, the ten who gave their names to Kleisthenes' ten tribes. The **altar of Zeus Agoraios** received the oaths of the new archons, a practice initiated by Solon.

The 4th-century **Temple of Apollo** was dedicated to the mythical father of the Ionians, who believed themselves descended from Ion, son of Apollo. The huge statue of Apollo in the Agora museum once stood inside the temple. Almost nothing remains of the **Stoa Basileios**, or of Zeus Eleutherios, which played a major role in Athenian history as the court of the annual archon, where trials concerning the security of the state took place. By the Stoa of Zeus stood the **Altar of the Twelve Gods**, from which all distances in Attica were measured. Alongside it ran the **Panathenaic Way**; some signs of its Roman rebuilding may be seen by the Church of the Holy Apostles. After crossing the Agora, this ceremonial path ascended to the Acropolis, where devotees celebrated the union of Attica. South of the Altar of Twelve Gods is the site of the Doric **Temple to Ares** (5th century BC). The **Three Giants** nearby were originally part the **Odeon of Agrippa** (15 BC); parts of the orchestra remain intact after the roof collapsed in AD 190. Confusingly, the site and the giants were reused in the façade of a 5th-century AD gymnasium, that served for a century as the site of the University of Athens until Justinian closed it down. Near the **Middle Stoa** (2nd century BC) are ruins of a **Roman temple** and the ancient shops and booths. On the other side of the Middle Stoa is the people's court, or **Heliaia**, organized by Solon in the 6th century BC to hear political questions; it remained active well into Roman times.

Between the **South and East Stoas** (2nd century BC) is the 11th-century **Church of the Holy Apostles** (Ag. Apostoli), built on the site where St Paul addressed the Athenians and restored, along with its fine paintings, in 1952. Across the Panathenaic Way run the remains of **Valerian's Wall** thrown up in AD 257 against the barbarian, its stone cannibalized from Agora buildings wrecked by the Romans. Between Valerian's Wall and the Stoa of Attalos are higgledy-piggledy ruins of the **Library of Pantainos**, built by Flavius Pantainos in AD 100 and destroyed 167 years later. Finds from the entire Agora are in the museum in the **Stoa of Attalos**, the 2nd-century BC portico built by King Attalos II of Pergamon, reconstructed by John D. Rockefeller.

The same ticket gets you into the mid-5th-century BC **Theseum**, nothing less than the best-preserved Greek temple in existence. Doric in order and dedicated to Hephaistos, the god of metals and smiths, it may well have been designed by the architect of the temple at Sounion. It is constructed almost entirely of Pentelic marble and decorated with metopes depicting the lives of Heracles and Theseus (for whom the temple was named). Converted into a church in the 5th century, it was the burial place for English Protestants until 1834, when the government declared it a national monument.

Acropolis

*Mon–Fri 8–4.30, Sat and Sun 8.30–2.30, adm. Two nights before and two nights after a full moon the Acropolis is open from 9 pm–11.45 pm. On nights without a full moon there is a **sound and light show**, 1 Apr–31 Oct presented daily in English 9 pm–9.45 pm. Tickets are 500 dr., or 200 dr. for students. They can be obtained at the Athens Festival Box Office, 4 Stadiou St (in the arcade), © 322 1459 or 322 3111 extension 240; or at the entrance gate at Ag. Dimitriou, Loumbardis Hill before the performance, © 922 6210.*

The naturally-fortified **Acropolis** was inhabited from the end of the Neolithic Age. The Mycenaeans added a Cyclopean wall and the palace of their king. This was later replaced by a temple to the god of the spring, Poseidon, and to Athena. In mythology, these two divinities took part in a contest to decide who would be the patron of the new city. With his trident Poseidon struck the spring Klepsydra out of the rock of the Acropolis, while Athena invented the olive tree, which the Athenians judged the better trick.

The tyrant Pisistratos ordered a great gate constructed in the wall, but Delphi cursed it and the Athenians dismantled it. In 480 BC the temple's cult statue of Athena was hurried to the protection of Salamis, just before the Persians burnt the Acropolis. Themistokles built a new rampart out of the old Parthenon, and under Perikles the present plan of the Acropolis buildings was laid out.

The path to the Acropolis follows the Panathenaic Way, laid out at the consecration of the Panathenaic Festival in 566 BC. The Acropolis entrance is defended by the **Beulé Gate** (named after Ernest Beulé, the archaeologist who found it); the monumental stairways were built by the Romans and the two lions are from Venice. The reconstructed Panathenaic ramp leads to the equally reconstructed **Propylaia**, the massive gateway replacing Pisistratos' cursed gate, built by Perikles' architect Mnesikles. The ancient Greeks considered the Proplyaia the architectural equal of the Parthenon itself, although it was never completed because of the Peloponnesian War. On either side of the Propylaia's entrance are two wings; the north held a picture gallery (Pinakotheke) while the smaller one to the south consisted of only one room of an unusual shape, because the priests of the neighbouring Nike temple didn't want the wing in their precinct. The original entrance had five doors, the central one pierced by the Panathenaic Way.

Temple of Athena Nike

The Ionic Temple of Athena Nike, or *Wingless Victory*, was built by the architect Kallikrates in 478 BC of Pentelic marble. Inside was kept the cult statue of Athena, a copy of a much older wooden statue. Its lack of wings, unlike later victory statues, gave it its second name. In 1687 the Turks destroyed the temple to build a tower. It was rebuilt in 1835 and again in 1936, when the bastion beneath it threatened to crumble away. The north and western friezes were taken to England by Lord Elgin and have been replaced by cement casts. From the temple of Athena Nike the whole Saronic Gulf could be seen in the pre-smog days, and it was here that Aegeus watched for the return of his son Theseus from his Cretan adventure with the Minotaur. Theseus was to have signalled his victory with a white sail but forgot; at the sight of the black sail of death, Aegeus threw himself off the precipice in despair.

The Parthenon

The Parthenon, the glory of the Acropolis and probably the most famous building in the world, if not the most imitated, is a Doric temple constructed between 447 and 432 BC under the direction of Phidias, the greatest artist and sculptor of the Periclean age. Originally called the Great Temple, it took the name Parthenon (Chamber of Virgins) a hundred years after its completion. Constructed entirely of Pentelic marble, it originally held Phidias' famous statue of Athena Parthenos, more than 36 ft high and made of ivory and gold. Look closely, and you'll see that the Parthenon's foundation is curved slightly to prevent an illusion of drooping caused by straight horizontals. To make the columns appear straight the architect bent them a few centimetres inward. Corner columns were made wider to complete the illusion of perfect form.

The outer colonnade consists of 46 columns and above them are the remnants of the Doric frieze left behind by the beaverish Lord Elgin: the east side portrayed the battle of giants and gods, the south the Lapiths and Centaurs (mostly in the British Museum today), on the west the Greeks and the Amazons, and on the north the battle of Troy. Little remains of the pediment sculptures of the gods. Above the interior colonnade, the masterful Ionic frieze designed by Phidias himself shows the quadrennial Panathenaic Procession in which Athena was brought a golden crown and a new sacred garment, or *peplos*.

The Parthenon's roof was blown sky high in 1687 when a Venetian bomb hit the Turks' powder stores inside; the destruction was continued in 1894 by an earthquake and today the nefarious *nefos* smog threatens to give the kiss of death to this graceful prototype of a thousand bank buildings. Entrance within the Parthenon itself is forbidden, to save on wear and tear. What is intriguing—and sometimes you can see the work in progress—is that after all these years the Greek government has decided to pick up all the pieces lying scattered since Morosini's day, and reconstruct as much of the temple as possible.

The Erechtheion

The last great monument on the Acropolis is the Erechtheion, a peculiar Ionic temple that owes its idiosyncrasies to the various cult items and the much older sanctuary it was built to encompass. Beneath the temple stood the Mycenaean House of Erechtheus, mentioned by Homer, and the primitive cult sanctuary of Athena; on one side of this grew the Sacred Olive Tree created by Athena, while under the north porch was the mark left by Poseidon's trident when he brought forth the divine spring. The tomb of Kekrops, the legendary founder of Athens, is in the Porch of the Maidens or Caryatids, where Erechtheus died at the hand of either Zeus or Poseidon. Within the temple stood the ancient cult statue of Athena Polias, endowed with the biggest juju of them all, solemnly dressed in the sacred *peplos* and crown.

After the Persian fires, the sanctuary was quickly restored, but the marble temple planned by Perikles was not begun until 421 BC. Used as a church in the 7th century, it became a harem under the Turks, who used the sacred place of the trident marks as a toilet. Lord Elgin nicked parts of this temple as well, including one of the caryatids; acidic air pollution has forced the Greek government to replace the other girls with casts.

Basically the Erechtheion is a rectangular building with three porches. Inside were two cellas, or chambers: the East Cella dedicated to Athena Polias, the smaller to Poseidon–Erechtheus. Six tall Ionic columns mark the north porch where the floor and roof were cut away to reveal Poseidon's trident marks, for it was sacrilegious to hide something so sacred from the view of the gods. The six famous maidens gracefully supporting the roof on their heads are another Ionian motif.

The Acropolis Museum

The museum (*open Tues–Fri 8–4.30, Mon 10–4.30, Sat and Sun 8.30–2.30*) houses sculptures and reliefs from the temples, in particular the Erechtheion's maidens, or Kores. At the moment a fervent and long-standing debate rages over the construction of a new museum, especially equipped to house the long-desired Elgin marbles; it could be ready by 1996.

Below the Acropolis is the **Areopagos**, or hill of Ares, the god of war. There sat the High Council, who figured so predominantly in Aeschylos' play *The Eumenides* where mercy defeated vengeance for the first time in history during the trial of the matricide Orestes. Although Perikles removed much of the original power of the High Council, under the control of the ex-archons it continued to advise on the Athenian constitution for hundreds of years.

The Theatres

On the south side of the Acropolis are two theatres. The older, the **Theatre of Dionysos**, was used from the 6th century BC when Thespis created the first true drama, and was continually modified up to the time of Nero. In this theatre the annual Greater Dionysia was held, in honour of the god of wine and patron divinity of the theatre, Dionysos. The dramatic competitions led to the premiers of some of the world's greatest tragedies. The stage that remains is from the 4th century BC, while the area before the stage, the **proskenion**, is decorated with 1st century AD scenes based on the life of Dionysos. Beside the theatre stood two temples to Dionysos Eleutherios.

Above the theatre is an **Asklepieion**, a sanctuary to the god of healing. The stoa which remains is from the second rebuilding, while the first and oldest sanctuary to the west first belonged to a water goddess, but very little of it remains. Both the old and new Asklepieions were connected with the parent cult at Epidauros.

The **Theatre of Herodes Atticus** was built and named for the Rockefeller of his day in AD 161 and originally partially covered. Now it hosts the annual mid-May and September **Festival of Athens**, where the cultures of modern Europe and ancient Greece are combined in theatre, ballet, and classical music concerts performed by companies from all over the world.

> *Prices vary greatly but there are always student tickets. Children under 10 are not admitted. Advance booking begins 10 to 15 days before each programme and further information and tickets may be obtained from: The Athens Festival Box Office, 4 Stadiou St (in the arcade), © 322 1459 or 322 3111 ext 240, daily 8.30–1.30 and 6–8.30; Sun 9–12 noon; or the Herod Atticus Theatre, © 323 2771 or 322 3111 ext 137, 6.30 pm–9 pm before each performance (performances begin at 9 pm).*

Other Museums

Benaki Museum: On the corner of Vassilis Sofias and Koumbari St, *8.30–2, closed Tues.* This museum holds the collection of Antonios Benaki, who spent 35 years amassing objects from Europe and Asia, Byzantine and Islamic. The Byzantine artworks (6th–14th centuries) are fascinating examples of early Christian art: icons, jewellery, ceramics, silver and embroidery, while the post-Byzantine exhibits (15th–17th century) show the influences of Islamic and Italian art. There are two icons by the Cretan-born El Greco, painted before his departure to Venice and Spain—the *Adoration of the Magi* (1560–65) and the *Evangelist Luke* (1560). The section on folk art, dating from the Ottoman occupation, contains a superb collection of costumes and artefacts from the Ionian islands to Cyprus.

National Archaeology Museum: Patission and Tossitsa Sts, *8–5, Sat and Sun 8.30–3, Mon 11–5, free Thurs and Sun.* The National Museum con-tains some of the most spectacular ancient Greek art anywhere—the Minoan-style frescoes from Santorini, gold from Mycenae (including the famous mask of Agamemnon), statues, reliefs, tomb stelai, and ceramics and vases from every period. The Cycladic collection includes one of the first known musicians of the Greek world, the sculpture of the little harpist that has become the virtual symbol of the Cyclades. The star of the sculpture rooms is a virile bronze of Poseidon (5th-century BC) about to launch his trident, found off the coast of Evia in 1928; around him are some outstanding archaic Kouros statues and the Stele of Hegeso, an Athenian beauty, enveloped by the delicate folds of her robe, seated

on a throne. The museum has a shop on the lower level, with reproductions of exhibits by expert craftsmen, so accurate that each piece is issued with a certificate declaring it an authentic fake so you can take it out of the country.

National Gallery: 50 Vass. Konstantinou, across from the Athens Hilton, *open 9–3, Sun 10–2, closed Mon.* Also known as the Alexander Soustou Museum, the National Gallery con-centrates on art by modern Greek artists. Works by the leading contemporary painter, Nikos Hadzikyriakos-Ghikas, are permanently displayed on the ground floor, while the lower level is used for rotating exhibitions. The museum shop has posters, cards, catalogues and jew-ellery, and there's a pleasant outdoor café, for when you've done the rounds.

Historical and Ethnological Museum: At the Palea Vouli (Old Parliament), Stadiou St, *9–1, closed Mon.* This imposing neo-Classical edifice is the guardian of Greek history, from the fall of Constantinople to the present day. The bronze warrior on horseback is Theodoros Kolokotronis, hero of the War of Independence, while exhibits within trace the history of modern Greece in paintings, sculptures, armaments (including Byron's sword and helmet), maps, folk costumes, jewellery and more covering every period, from Ottoman rule to resis-tance against the Nazis in 1940.

Popular Art Museum: 17 Kydathinaion St, *10–2, closed Mon.* The museum has a collec-tion of Greek folk art, both religious and secular, along with paintings by naïve artists.

The Pnyx: On the hill west of the Acropolis. Nowadays the setting for the Acropolis Sound and Light Show, the Pnyx once hosted the General Assembly of Athens and the great speeches of Perikles and Demosthenes. On assembly days citizens were literally rounded up to fill the minimum attendance quota of 5000, but they were paid for their services to the state. Later the assembly was transferred to the theatre of Dionysos. On the summit of the nearby Hill of the Muses is the **Philopappos Monument**, the tomb of Caius Julius Antiochos Philopappos, a Syrian Prince and citizen of Athens. The monument was built for him by the Athenians in AD 114 in gratitude for his beneficence to the city.

Roman Agora: Located between the Agora and the Acropolis, *8.30–3 pm closed Mon.* Dating from the end of the Hellenistic age, the Roman Agora contains the celebrated **Tower of the Winds**, or Clock of Andronikos, built in the 1st century BC. Run by a hydraulic mechanism, it stayed open day and night so that the citizens could know the time. Its name comes from the frieze of the eight winds that decorate its eight sides, although it has lost its ancient bronze Triton weathervane. The Roman Agora also contains the **Gate of Athena Archegetis**, built by money sent over from Julius and Augustus Caesar; there is also a court and the ruins of stoas. Beside the Agora is the Fehiye Camii, the Victory or Corn Market Mosque.

Byzantine Museum: 22 Vassilis Sofias, *8.30–3, closed Mon.* This monumental collection of religious treasures and paintings dates from the Early Byzantine period to the 19th century—not only icons but marble sculptures, mosaics, woodcarvings, frescoes, manuscripts and ecclesiastical robes. There are three rooms on the ground floor arranged as chapels, one Early Christian, another Middle Byzantine, and the third post-Byzantine.

Museum of Cycladic Art: 4 Neoforos Douka St (between Byzantine and Benaki museums), *10–3.30, Sat 10–2.30, closed Tues and Sun.* This museum houses a vast collection of Cycladic figurines and objects dating back to 3200–2000 BC, illustrating everyday life. The female figurines with folded arms are unique. The newest addition is the 'Treasure of Keros', a small island near Naxos where excavations in the 1950s and 60s unearthed a wealth of figurines.

Keramikos and Museum: 148 Ermou St, *open 8.30–3, closed Mon.* The ancient cemetery or Keramikos was used for burials from the 12th century BC into Roman times, but the most impressive and beautiful finds are in the rich private tombs built by the Athenians in the 4th century BC. Large stone vases mark the graves of the unmarried dead, while others are in the form of miniature temples and stelai; the best are in the National Museum.

Temple of Olympian Zeus: Olgas and Amalias Avenues, *8.30–3, closed Mon.* Fifteen columns recall what Livy called 'the only temple on earth of a size adequate to the greatness of the god'. The foundations were laid by the tyrant Pisistratos, but work ground to a halt with the fall of his dynasty, only to be continued in 175 BC by a Roman architect, Cossutius. It was half finished when Cossutius' patron, Antiochos IV of Syria kicked the bucket, leaving the Emperor Hadrian to complete it in AD 131. Nearby are the ruins of ancient houses and a bath and at the far end stands **Hadrian's Arch**, neatly dividing the city of Theseus from the city of Hadrian. The Athenians traditionally come here to celebrate the Easter Resurrection.

Museum of the City of Athens: Plateia Klafthmonos, *open Mon, Wed, Fri, Sat 9–1.30; free Wed.* Located in the re-sited neo-Classical palace of King Otho, this new museum contains photos, memorabilia and a model showing Athens as it was soon after it became the capital of modern Greece.

Agii Theodori: This 11th-century church in Klafthmonos Square at the end of Dragatsaniou St is most notable for its beautiful door; the bell tower and some of the decorations inside are more recent additions.

Kapnikarea: A few blocks from Agii Theodori, on Ermou St. Tiny Kapnikarea (the chapel of the University of Athens) was built in the late 11th century in the shape of a Greek cross, its central cupola sustained by four columns with Roman capitals.

Panayia Gorgoepikoos (or Ag. Eleftherios): Situated in Mitropoleos Square, known as the little Metropolitan to distinguish it from the nearby cathedral, this is the loveliest church in Athens. Built in the 12th century almost entirely of ancient marbles the builders found lying around; note the ancient calendar of state festivals embedded over the door. Curiously, the **Cathedral** (just to the north) was built in 1840–55 with the same collage technique, using bits and pieces from 72 destroyed churches.

Dafni and its Wine Festival: 10 km from Athens; take bus 282 from Eleftherias Square. The name Dafni derives from the temple of Apollo Dafneios (of the laurel), built near the Sacred Way. The site became a walled monastery in the 6th century and in 1080, a new church was built, decorated with the best Byzantine mosaics in southern Greece. These are dominated in the vault of the dome by the tremendous figure of Christ Pantokrator 'the all powerful' his eyes spellbinding and tragic, 'as though He were in flight from an appalling doom' as Patrick Leigh Fermor has written. From 9 July–11 September, daily 7pm–1am, the monastery park holds a festival with over 60 different Greek wines (free once you've paid the admission at the gate) accompanied by food, singing and dancing, an event well-attended by Athenians and visitors alike.

Where to Stay in Athens

Athens is a big noisy city, especially so at night when you want to sleep—unless you do as the Greeks do and take a long afternoon siesta. Piraeus (*see* below) may be a better bet, no less noisy but much more convenient for catching those up-at-the-crack-of-dawn ships to the islands, although women on their own may find too many sailors about to feel at ease. All accommodation fills up quickly in the summer and if you don't have a reservation, or erratic boat schedules have mangled your booking, it's best to head straight for the EOT office on Syntagma Square (in the National Bank building) and use their hotel finding service.

luxury

New luxury chain hotels are mushrooming up everywhere just outside the city centre—there's the **Ledra Marriott** at 113–115 Syngrou, © 934 7711, featuring a Polynesian–Japanese restaurant, and a hydrotherapy pool you can soak in with a view of the Parthenon. Another addition to the scene (and one on a human scale) is the 76-room **Astir Palace Athens Hotel** on Syntagma Square, © 364 3112, owned by the National Bank of Greece. While it was under construction, ancient foundations and waterpipes were uncovered and these are incorporated into the décor of the hotel's restaurant, the **Apokalypsis**, located below street level (Greek and international cuisine). Despite its location, specially insulated glass windows keep out the hubbub below. There's a sauna, and each room features a mini bar and colour TV (with an in-house movie channel). Directly across the square from the Astir is the **Grande Bretagne**, © 323 0251, originally built in 1862 to house members of the Greek royal family who couldn't squeeze into the main palace (the current Parliament building) up the square. The Grande Bretagne is the only 'grand' hotel in Greece worthy of the description, with a vast marble lobby, elegant rooms (now air conditioned and appointed with such modern conveniences as direct dial phones and colour TV), a formal dining room, perfect service, and a grandeur and style that the newer hotels, with all their plushness, may never achieve. Even if you can't afford to stay there, you may want to poke your head in to see where the crowned heads of Europe lodge in Athens—and where the Nazis set up their headquarters during the Second World War. Winston Churchill spent Christmas 1944 at the Grande Bretagne and was lucky to escape a bomb meant for him, planted in the hotel's complex sewer system.

On a less exalted level, but with a far more fetching view is the **Royal Olympic Hotel** at 28 Diakou, © 922 6411, facing the Temple of Olympian Zeus and Mt Lykavitos. Rooms here are American in spirit, with a number of family-sized suites, and if you have the misfortune to get a room without a view, there's the wonderful panorama from the rooftop bar.

expensive

The **Electra Palace** at 18 Nikodimou St, © 324 1401, has views of the Acropolis and a wonderful rooftop swimming pool in a garden setting—something you don't find every day in Athens. Rooms are air conditioned and there's a garage adjacent to the hotel. Half-board is obligatory—unfortunately, because the hotel is quite close to the good tavernas of Plaka. More reasonable, and centrally located just off Syntagma Square, the **Astor**, 16 Karagiorgi Servias, © 325 5555, also has fully air conditioned rooms and a rooftop garden restaurant.

moderate

The best value in this category (and a big favourite with Americans) has long been the **Hotel Alkistis** at 18 Plateia Theatrou, © 321 9811, all rooms with private baths and phones, all very modern and perfectly clean. If the Alkistis is full, a good second bet is the **Hotel Museum** at 16 Bouboulinas St, © 360 5611, right at the back of the Archaeology Museum. The rooms are about the same, but the prices are a bit higher. **Hotel Tempi**, 29 Eolou St, © 321 3175, near Monastraki, is more downgrade, but is cheaper and has washing facilities.

cheap

Most of the inexpensive hotels are around Plaka. For better or worse, the government has shut down many of the old dormitory houses that grew up in the 1960s to contain the vanguard of mass tourism in Greece—every hippie in Europe, or at least so it seemed to the amazed Greeks. Survivors of the government purge have upgraded themselves but are still a bargain—and many still let you sleep on the roof for a thousand drachmas (not an unpleasant option in the thick heat of August). Best bets in the cheaper category include:

Hotel Phaedra, 16 Herefondos St, ✆ 323 8461, just off Filellinon St, with free hot showers.

John's Place, 5 Patroou St, ✆ 322 9719.

Hotel Cleo, 3 Patroou St, ✆ 322 9053, small and near Plaka.

Student Inn, 16 Kidathineon, ✆ 324 4808, very conveniently placed in the Plaka, and ideal for the younger crowd.

Joseph's House, 13 Markou Botsari, ✆ 923 1204, in a quieter area on the south side of the Acropolis; washing facilities available (take advantage of it—if you're travelling in the islands for any length of time, washing clothes will be your biggest headache).

Less savoury, but less expensive is the city's **IYHF Youth Hostel**, inconveniently located far from the centre at 57 Kypselis St, Kypseli, ✆ 822 5860. A better option, though not a member of the YHA, is the **Student's Hostel** at 75 Damareos St, Pangrati, ✆ 751 9530. The nearest **campsites** to Athens are at Dafni Monastery (*see* p. 76), and down on the coast at Voula.

Eating Out in Athens

Athenians rarely dine out before 10 or 11 pm, and they want to be entertained afterwards. If it's warm, chances are they'll drive out to the suburbs or the sea shore. **Glyfada**, near the airport, is a popular destination and on a summer evening the cool sea breeze can be a life saver after the oppressive heat of Athens. The obvious meal to choose is something from the sea, and most of the tavernas specialize in fish (especially red mullet, or *barbounia*) lobster, squid and shrimp, although, as everywhere in Greece, it's the most expensive food you can order. Remember that prices marked for fish usually indicate how much per kilo, not per portion.

Glyfada

Leading off the main square in Glyfada is a street almost entirely devoted to excellent restaurants and friendly, inexpensive bars. At reasonably priced **George's**, the steak will be cooked according to your specifications and the meatballs (*keftedes*) are a speciality. To feed the large foreign community in Glyfada, a plethora of fast food joints has grown up in the area; and now expensive Arab restaurants (complete with imported Middle Eastern singers and belly dancers) have made an appearance on the scene.

Central Athens

Back in central Athens, **Gerofinikas** at 10 Pindarou St, off Kolonaki Square, is the most popular restaurant with tourists and Greek businessmen alike. Whatever the origin of the specialities here (the management and staff hail from Istanbul) many Greeks will tell you this is what true Greek cuisine should be, and indeed the standard of the food and service is high. One superb speciality is lamb with artichokes and aubergine (eggplant) purée. By Greek standards the place is expensive—a typical meal will cost about 4–5000 dr. upwards. Fewer tourists know about **Costayiannis**, 37 Zaimi, near the National Archaeology Museum, with a succulent display of food in the glass cabinets near the entrance preparing you for a memorable culinary evening. Apart from the superb seafood, the 'ready food' is unbeatable—try the quail with roast potatoes, the roast pork in wine and herb sauce or the rabbit *stifado*, accompanied by barrelled retsina, if you've developed a taste for it. Prices here are very reasonable—3500 dr. for a full meal. As near to a traditional taverna that you'll find, the **Taverna Karavitis** is a few streets up from the old Olympic stadium, on the corner of Arkitinou and Pafsaniou and housed in a long, low white building, with barrels lining the walls. Athenians come here for a good time; the food, served by friendly young lads in jeans, is better than average, and it's open till late (1500 dr.). Just off Mikalakopoulou St, and not far from the Hilton Hotel is **John's Village (To Chorio tou Yianni)**, a cut above the ordinary taverna and warmly decorated with hand-woven rugs and island pottery. The accompanying music, played by a strolling minstrel, makes this a favourite spot to spend an evening without breaking the bank. There's a good variety of well-prepared dishes and a meal will cost about 3000 dr. Behind the Hilton, on Mikalakopoulou, is the Cypriot restaurant **Othello's**, with delicious, authentic cuisine at around 2500 dr. for a meal.

The Plaka

The Plaka is, of course, the perennial favourite with both Greeks and tourists; the atmosphere at night is exciting with its crowded tavernas perched precariously on uneven steps, Greek dancers whirling and leaping on stages the size of postage stamps, light bulbs flashing and *bouzouki* music filling the air. A typical charming Plaka taverna is the rooftop **Thespes**, 100 m along from the Plaka Square, where a selection of starters, such as *tzatziki, taramasalata* and fried aubergine (eggplant) followed by lamb chops and several flagons of wine won't cost you much more than 2000 dr. In some of the other tavernas you may not be as lucky and will have to pay well over the odds, particularly if there's live music, for food that rarely rises above the mediocre. One other outstanding exception is **Platanos**, the oldest taverna in the Plaka, near the Tower of the Four Winds. The same people have been eating there for donkey's years, and if George is still around accept with good grace the carafe of wine he may send over, but none of his other suggestions. The food here is good and wholesome, but forget about perusing the menu—it's definitely an 'in the kitchen and point' joint, and inexpensive at 1500–2000 dr. for a meal. In the heart of Plaka, in Filomoson Square, where every visitor lands up sooner or later, you can eat well at **O Costas** or **Xynou Taverna**, 4 Geronda St, which serves excellent food in a garden setting, with strolling musician playing traditional Greek music. It's very popular (closed on Sat and Sun), and reservations are a must (© 322 1065; 2500 dr.).

Off touristy Adrianou St, with all its souvenirs, the family-run taverna **Tsegouras**, 2 Epicharmou, is in a walled garden in the shade of an enormous gum tree, with good Greek food for around 2000 dr.

Around the Plaka

Just outside the Plaka, two blocks south of Hadrian's arch at 5 Lembessi St, **O Kouvelos** is another typical, reliable Athenian taverna, serving excellent *meze* and barrelled retsina. They'll save you the bother of ordering the meze by planting it on the table in front of you; don't be shy to change it if you want something different (2000 dr.) In the same area (cross Makriyianni St), don't miss **Socrates Prison**, 20 Mitseon St, a real favourite with locals and expats. Greek food with a real flair in friendly, attractive surroundings. Delicious pork roll with celery and carrots in lemon sauce, lamb with mushrooms and potatoes from the oven, beef roll with special rice and green peppers, and a host of others. Bottled or barrelled wine (2000 dr., evenings only, closed Sun). A few blocks west of here, at 7 Garivaldi St, the **Greek House** has dining on a rooftop terrace with a most beautiful view of the Acropolis. Don't be put off by the name; this restaurant serves superb and reasonably priced specialities—try the 'Virginia', slices of *filet mignon* with mushrooms, or the shrimp salad. They also make wonderful spinach and cheese pies (2500 dr.). Near the Monastiraki *eletriko* (underground) station, search out **Taverna Sigalas**, a bustling place where you can soak up the least pretentious side of Athenian life; usual Greek food served at unpredictable temperatures, and Greek folk music to make you feel you never want to go home (1500–2000 dr.).

Around Omonia Square

Near Omonia Square are a number of cheap restaurants displaying cuts of roast lamb, pork and the occasional grinning sheep's head. They're really worth a try if you are watching your drachma, but feel like a 'proper' meal—a portion of chicken with rubber fried spuds and a small bottle of retsina will set you back about 1000 dr. Of the half-a-dozen or so places, try **Platanos** on Satombriandou.

Ethnic

Athens is well supplied with ethnic eating places—French, Italian, Spanish, Chinese, Japanese, Mexican, American and restaurants of other nationalities are scattered around the capital. Of particular note for lovers of German food is the **Rittenburg** at 11 Formionos in Pangrati, where the boiled and grilled sausages, and pork with sauerkraut are tops. North German dishes are on the menu in the small, intimate and aptly named **Delicious** in Kolonaki at 6 Zalokosta—marinated fish, *bratkartoffeln*, lovely goulash and home-made black bread (2500 dr.). Chinese restaurants are all relatively expensive. The **Rosa Sayang**, in the seaside suburb of Glyfada, on Palea Leoforos Vouliagmenis and 2 Kiou, serves great Peking Duck and beef with mango slices, among many other items (3000 dr.). A little further down the coast at Voula, **Loon Fung Tien** does fixed-price Dim Sum (buffet) lunchtimes on Sunday. Italian restaurants are established in every major European city, and Athens is no exception. **Boschetto**, in the Evangelismos Gardens opposite the Hilton, is one of the city's best. Exquisite spaghetti with *frutti di mare*, inventive main courses (guinea hen with bacon and pomegranate sauce) and fine desserts (4000 dr.). In Kolonaki the trendy **Pane e Vino**, 8 Spefsipou, is popular for its antipasta (eggplant and Gorgonzola rolls) and pasta (tagliolini with smoked salmon), together with main dishes such as sole with mussels, *filetto afrodisiaco* or scaloppine with prosciutto (4–5000 dr.) A collection of top class, expensive French restaurants have graced the Athens culinary scene for years. In Kolonaki **Je Reviens**, 49 Xenokratous, is an old favourite, with live music and outdoor seating (5000 dr.). Near the American Embassy **Balthazar**, 27 Tsoha and Vournazou, is a renovated mansion with an attractive bar and a comprehensive selection of international dishes, but it's best to book ✆ 644 1215; 3500 dr.

Hotel Restaurants

Some of the luxury hotels in Athens have some swish theme restaurants (with swish prices of course). The Ledra Marriott (76) has the Polynesian **Kona Kai** in an exotic tropical setting, with all the delicacies from that other paradise archipelago; a few blocks down, the **Atheneum Intercontinental** also has Asian cuisine in its **Kublai Khan** restaurant.

Bars

Watering holes abound in Athens, many of them serving bar food, and most of the English-speaking community do the rounds of the **Red Lion**, the **Underground** and the **Ploughman's**, all within a stone's throw of the Hilton.

Wine bars are a fairly recent addition to Athens' nightlife. If you want to try some finer wines from Greece and Europe, the following places will oblige: **Kelari**, in the Hilton, serving Greek dishes as an accompaniment, in a friendly, warm décor; **Loutro**, 18 Feron, way north near Victoria Square, decorated in sophisticated Roman bath style, serving imaginative dishes to accompany the French, Italian and lesser known Greek wines; **Le Sommelier d'Athènes**, Leof. Kifissias in Kifissia, in a beautiful old suburban villa, with an emphasis on French and Italian; **Strofilia**, 7 Karitsi (behind the Historical Museum), with mainly Greek labels, and an extensive salad bar.

Piraeus

The port of Athens, Piraeus—pronounced 'Pirefs'—was the greatest port of the ancient world and remains today one of the busiest in the Mediterranean. In Greece, a country that derives most of its livelihood from the sea in one way or another, Piraeus is the true capital, while Athens is a mere sprawling suburb where the bureaucrats live. Still, it takes a special visitor to find much charm in the tall grey buildings and dusty hurly-burly in the streets, although

Marina Zea and Mikrolimani with their yachts, brightly-lit tavernas and bars are a handsome sight, as are the neon signs flashing kinetically as you sail to or from Piraeus in the evening. The tall, half-finished building on the waterfront was built and abandoned by the junta when they found that the foundations were mixed with sea water. Somehow its useless silhouette makes a fitting monument to that ignorant and often cruel government.

Historical Outline of Piraeus

Themistokles founded the port of Piraeus in the 5th century BC when Phaliron, Athens' ancient port, could no longer meet the growing needs of the city. From the beginning Piraeus was cosmopolitan and up-to-date: the Miletian geometrician Hippodamos laid it out in a straight grid of streets that have changed little today. The centre of action was always the huge agora in the middle of the city. Under its stoas the world's first commercial fairs and trade expositions were held, some on an international scale. All religions were tolerated, and women were allowed for the first time to work outside the home.

As Piraeus was so crucial to Athens' power, the conquering Spartan Lysander destroyed the famous Long Walls that linked city and port in 404, at the end of the Peloponnesian War. Piraeus made a brief comeback under Konon and Lykurgos, who rebuilt its arsenals. After the 100-year Macedonian occupation and a period of peace, Sulla decimated the city to prevent any anti-Roman resistance, and for 1900 years Piraeus dwindled away into an insignificant village with a population as low as 20, even losing its name to become Porto Leone (for an ancient lion statue, carved from runes by Harald Hadraada and his Vikings in 1040 and carted off by Morosini as a trophy to embellish Venice's Arsenal). Since the selection of Athens as the capital of independent Greece, Piraeus has regained its former glory as the reigning port of a sea-going nation.

Getting Around

In Piraeus this usually means getting out of town as quickly as possible. **Ships** are grouped according to their destination and almost anyone you ask will be able to tell you the precise location of any vessel. The cluster of ticket agents around the port are very noisy and competitive, but prices to the islands are fixed, so the only reason to shop around is to see if there is an earlier or faster ship to the island of your choice. Beware that ticket agents often don't know or won't tell you information on lines other than the ones they carry. Only the Tourist Police on Akti Miaouli have complete information on boat schedules.

There are three **railway stations.** The half-underground Elektriko serves Athens as far north as the posh suburb of Kifissia, setting off every 10 minutes from 6 am to 1.30 am from the terminal opposite the quay. Stations for northern Greece and for the Peloponnese are a bit further down the road.

Buses to Athens run day and night, the main 'Green' line (no. 040) taking you directly to Syntagma Square. The express line no. 19 bus service to East and West Airport leaves from Karaiskaki Square.

Akti Miaouli, © 452 3670.

Irron Politechniou, © 412 0325.

The Sights

If you find yourself in Piraeus on a Sunday morning, take a prowl through the flea market parallel to the underground (Elektriko) line, where you may well happen across some oddity brought back by a Greek Sinbad. If culture beckons, there's an **Archaeology Museum** at 31 Har. Trikoupi St, with an above average collection of antiquities (*8.30–3, closed Mon*), or perhaps the **Maritime Museum** on Akti Themistocles by Freatidos St, with intriguing plans of Greece's greatest naval battles, ship models and mementoes from the War of Independence (*8.30–1, closed Sun and Mon*). The **Hellenistic Theatre** at Zea occasionally has performances in the summer.

Beaches are not far away, although the sea isn't exactly sparkling and on most you must pay. Kastella is the closest, followed by New Phaliron which is free. Buses go to Ag. Kosmos by the airport, where you can play tennis or volleyball; at Glyfada, further down the road, there's more wholesome swimming and a golf course for duffers.

Zea, Glyfada and Vouliagmeni are the three **marinas** organized by the National Tourist Organization. Piraeus is also the place to charter yachts or sail boats, from 12-foot dinghies to deluxe twin-screw yachts, if you've missed your island connection (*see* sailing pp. 21–26).

Where to Stay

Hotel accommodation in Piraeus is geared towards businessmen, and unfortunately less so towards people who have arrived on a late-night ship or plan to depart on an early morning one. Brave souls sleep out in the squares, particularly in Karaiskaki, but they have to put up with lights, noise, the neighbouring discotheques and sailors of every nationality who hang around hoping for something to happen.

expensive

If you're with the kids, try the quiet and very clean **Hotel Anemoni**, at Karaoli Demetriou and Evripidou 65–67, © 413 6881; since it's not directly on the port you miss the sailors and some of the racket. All rooms are air conditioned, and there's a free transfer service to the port.

moderate

If you want to be within walking distance of the docks, the **Hotel Triton**, © 417 3457, is one of the best of the many in the area; its B class doubles start at 5500 dr., but go shooting up in high summer. All rooms have private bath and breakfast is available. A mediocre alternative is the **Ideal**, 142 Notara St, © 451 1727, 50 m from the customs house, with air conditioning and private bath.

On the lower end of the scale there are many D & E class hotels, some of which are not as appetizing as they might be, but their rates range from 3000 dr. to around 5000 dr. Typical of these is **Achillion**, 63 Notara St, © 412 4029.

Eating Out

Around the port the fare is generally fast food and giro spinners, while the tavernas are so greasy it's a wonder they don't slide off the street. For seafood (especially if you're on an expense account), the bijou little harbour of Mikrolimano (or Turkolimano) is the traditional place to go, although too many tourists with too much money have inflated the price to a nasty pitch. A far better idea is to forego fish and eat up at the excellent **Kaliva** in Vass. Pavlou, Kastella, with a splendid view down over the harbour (excellent meat dinners for 2500 dr.) followed by a stroll through Mikrolimano for a coffee and Metaxa on the harbour front. But if it's fish you must have, head over to Frates, around from the Zea Marina yacht harbour, where several moderately-priced places offer fresh fish and sea views. There's really not all that much to distinguish one from another; just stroll around until you find a fish that winks at you. Zea Marina itself is a vast necklace of neon, where the locals haunt the inexpensive **American Pizza**, but there are places with Greek pizza and other fare, both on the harbour and on the streets giving into it.

If you've got time between boats or flights, the stretch of coast between Piraeus and the airport has a few possibilities. Chefs from the eastern Mediterranean are undoubtedly the kings of kebab; try the **Adep Kebab**, 20 Leof. Possidonos in Paleo Phaliron, where the meat is delicately flavoured with the spices of the Levant. Specialities are the *adana* kebab, *domatesli* kebab (cooked with tomatoes on charcoal) and the succulent shish-kebab, marinated in milk, lemon juice, oil and spices. Alternatively, in Nea Smyrni, the **Tria Asteria**, 7 Melitos and 77 Plastira, is run by Armenians from Istanbul. The choice of appetizers is endless, including delicious *cli kofte*, a meatball of veal and lamb, bulgur and pine nuts. This is also the only place in Athens to find *tandir* kebab, lamb which has been smoked and then baked in a red wine sauce. At either of these restaurants count on around 3000 dr.

Crete (Kriti)

Storage Jars at Knossos, Crete

Crete, the largest island in Greece (roughly 260 by 50 km) is in a hundred ways the most extraordinary. Endowed with every earthly delight—a warm climate, fresh springs, fertile soil, spectacular scenery—it was the cradle of Europe's very first civilization, the Minoan, so elegant, sophisticated and peaceful (the only weapons found on Minoan sites date from the later Mycenaean period) that you begin to wonder if the first civilization wasn't also the best. Crete is the source of the most ancient Greek myths, and in the island's remote villages old customs survive that have been long abandoned in the rest of Greece. And yet, in the past few years, no island has undergone such a striking metamorphosis. In the 1960s guidebooks warned foreign men not to cast an admiring eye on a Cretan woman, for fear that her father and brothers would draw their famous daggers. These days the danger is suffocation under wave after wave of package tours. There are even rumours that Crete's main attraction, Knossos, may eventually be closed owing to the wear and tear inflicted on the soft gypsum by half a million visitors a year. Hotels have sprung up along the beaches like giant concrete weeds, and the northeast coast is rapidly becoming one unplanned, ecologically disastrous, unaesthetic mess. The Cretan national character has never done anything by halves, and the island's headlong rush to realise its tourist potential is only its most recent manifestation.

But for most people Crete's many natural charms and the monuments left by its layers upon layers of history more than compensate for an occasional lack of elbow room in the summer months. No fewer than four mighty mountain ranges lend Crete a dramatic grandeur disproportionate to its size. The White Mountains in the west are threaded by Europe's longest gorge, Samaria. Sandy beaches soften the often savage coastline; 1500 species of wild flowers, including a few hundred unique to Crete, brighten the landscape with a technicolour intensity in the springtime. Vineyards, olive and citrus groves and plastic-covered greenhouses filled with vegetables cover the plains and terraces; on the south coast, a mere 320 kilometres from Egypt, you can pick fresh bananas. The two largest cities, Chania and Rethymnon, rival one another in the charm of their Venetian buildings, while many small mountain villages are masterpieces of folk architecture, their churches often adorned with Byzantine frescoes and icons of a quality seldom seen on the other islands. Then of course there are the Minoan sites and the archaeology museum in Herakleon, which along with the National Museum in Athens is the finest in Greece.

Crete also has its own distinct culture, dialect, music and dances, and it is an encouraging sign that many young Cretans are taking an active role in preserving the island's traditions. These tend to be even more predominately masculine than other islands: men don baggy trousers, high boots and black headbands, and take up the *lyra*, a three-stringed instrument held upright on the lap that plays the quarter-tone lead in Cretan melodies, accompanied by the *lauto* (similar to a large mandolin) and often a violin and whining clarinet. On feast days you can still hear men singing *Mantinadhes*, the improvised couplets, or *rizitika*, 'songs from the roots' with themes of Cretan patriotism. Then there is the *Erotokritos*, a 10,000-line romance, written in the Cretan dialect, composed in the 17th century by Vincenzo Kornaros and still memorized and recited today. Internationally famous Cretans include El Greco, Nikos Kazantzakis, Mikis Theodorakis, and Greece's best-known statesman, Eleftherios Venizelos.

Best time to go

The ideal time to visit Crete is towards the end of April. That way not only will you avoid the worst crowds, but the Libyan Sea is usually warm enough for bathing, the flowers are glorious and the higher mountains are still capped with snow. Note, however, that the Gorge of Samaria doesn't officially open until 1 May, when its torrent recedes sufficiently for safe passage.

Mythology

As Cronus, the ruler of the world, had been warned that he would be usurped by his own child, he swallowed every baby his wife Rhea, daughter of the Earth, presented to him. After this had happened five times, Rhea determined a different fate for her sixth child, Zeus. When he was born she smuggled him to Crete and gave Cronus a stone instead, which the old fellow duly swallowed. Mother Earth hid the baby in the Diktean cave and set the Kouretes to guard him; they were ordered to shout and beat their shields to drown out the baby's cries so that Cronus' suspicions would not be aroused.

After Zeus grew up and had indeed taken his father's place by castrating him, a girl named Europa caught his fancy. To avoid making his wife Hera jealous, Zeus disguised himself as a beautiful bull and carried Europa off to Crete, where she bore him three sons: Minos, Rhadamanthys and Sarpedon. When Minos became the King of Crete at Knossos, he was asked to prove that his claim to the throne was sanctioned by the gods. Minos remembered the form his father had taken and asked Poseidon to send him a bull from the sea to sacrifice. However, the bull was so magnificent that instead of killing it, Minos sent it to service his herds.

The kingdom of Minos prospered, ruling the seas and exacting tributes from across the Mediterranean. But Poseidon never forgave Minos' lack of piety in not sacrificing the sea bull. In revenge he made Minos' wife Pasiphaë (daughter of the sun and the nymph Crete, who gave the island its name) fall passionately in love with the bull. The unfortunate Pasiphaë confided her problem to the famous inventor Daedalus, who had been banished from Athens for murder and was now living at Minos' court. Daedalus responded by making her a hollow wooden cow, which she entered and with which the bull mated. This resulted in the birth of a monster with the head of a bull and the body of a man, the Minotaur.

Revolted by this new member of his household, Minos asked Daedalus to hide it. Obediently, Daedalus built the Labyrinth, an impossible maze of corridors, and in the centre he set the Minotaur. As this strange beast also showed a liking for human flesh, Minos took advantage of an Athenian insult and ordered that city to pay a tribute every nine years of seven maidens and seven youths, whom he would feed to the Minotaur.

Two tributes had been paid when Theseus, the son of Aegeus, King of Athens, demanded to be sent as one of the victims. With great reluctance his father agreed, and Theseus sailed to Crete with the other youths and maidens. But Ariadne, daughter of Minos, fell in love with him at first sight and demanded that the ever-resourceful Daedalus should help her save his life. Daedalus gave Ariadne a ball of thread. Theseus made his way into the labyrinth, slew the Minotaur with his bare hands, retraced his way out with the ball of thread and escaped, taking the Cretan princess and the other Athenians along with him. Although he left Ariadne on Naxos (*see* p. 184) he later married her younger sister Phaedra.

Minos was furious when he discovered the part Daedalus had played in the business and threw the inventor and his young son Ikaros into the Labyrinth. Although they managed to find their way out, escape from Crete was impossible, since Minos controlled the seas. But Daedalus was never at a loss, and decided that what they couldn't accomplish by sea they would do by air. He made wings of feathers and wax for himself and Ikaros, and on the first fine day they flew towards Asia Minor. All went well until an exhilarated Ikaros disobeyed his father's command not to fly too close to the sun. The wax in his little wings melted, and he plunged and drowned in what is now the Ikarian Sea. The island on which Daedalus buried him took the name Ikaria.

When Minos heard of Daedalus' escape he was furious and pursued him all over the Mediterranean. Knowing how clever Daedalus was he brought along a nautilus shell and a piece of thread, hoping to trap him by offering a great reward to whoever could figure out a way to thread the shell. Finally, in Sicily, Minos met a king who took the shell away and brought it back threaded. At once Minos demanded that the king turn Daedalus over to him. The king hedged, and instead invited Minos to stay at his palace. While Minos was in his bath, Daedalus and the king's daughters put a pipe through the ceiling and poured boiling water through it, scalding him to death. Zeus took him down to Hades to judge the dead alongside his brother Rhadamanthys and his enemy Aeacus.

History

Midget hippopotamus *Pentlandi* bones discovered on Crete suggest that not so very long ago, (in geological time) Crete was part of the mainland. When it broke away, the hippopotami were stranded, and, faced with diminished food supply slowly diminished themselves until, sadly, they disappeared altogether. The first humans arrived c. 6000 BC, a people probably from Asia Minor, who built small houses in Knossos and other future Minoan sites. At the end of the Neolithic period, or the Early Minoan (3000 BC) they began to create new forms in pottery and moved from stone tools to copper. The Middle Minoan (1900 BC) saw the advent of palaces, towns and a system of writing in pictographs, but in 1700 BC an earthquake (probably) devasted the buildings, forcing the people to start afresh.

From 1700 to 1450 BC was the height of the Minoan civilization. The palaces were rebuilt and decorated with frescoes, and equipped with water and drainage systems. Colonies were founded on the islands, and the Minoans (who ruled the seas) made contact with cities in Africa, Asia Minor and on the Greek mainland, inspiring the myths of the great King Minos, which may have been the dynastic name of the Knossos kings. The writing system known as Linear A was developed, linked to Indo-European and Semitic languages. But in 1450 BC, disaster struck again. A volcanic eruption, tidal waves and earthquakes from Santorini left the magnificent Minoan kingdom in ruins.

At this time Mycenaeans from the mainland invaded Crete, taking advantage of its disarray. In this, the late Minoan period (1550–1050 BC) only the Knossos palace was rebuilt, and Linear B writing, a very ancient form of Greek, predominated (similar Linear B tablets were also found at Mycenae and Thebes). Other towns began to be repopulated and Chania prospered in particular, although Crete no longer exerted external influence. By 1100 BC, the beginning of the Iron Age, Minoan civilization ground to a halt, and the Cretans took to the hills.

The Dorians invaded Crete, but by the Geometric period (8th century BC) Crete was on its feet again. The invaders apparently co-existed peacefully with the natives, who adopted their alphabet, using Greek letters to spell Minoan, non-Greek words. As on the mainland, by the 5th century BC, small city-states had formed which fought among themselves and minted their own coins, ruled by a powerful aristocracy. Romans under Q. Metellus Creticus conquered Crete in 67 BC, and Gortyna, inhabited since Minoan times, became the capital of the province of Crete and Cyrenaica in West Africa.

Rich churches were constructed in Crete in the early Byzantine period, but in AD 823 Saracen Arabs conquered the island and stayed until its liberation in 961 by the Emperor Nikephoros Phokas. In the 13th century the Genoese ruled Crete, but later sold it to the Venetians, who occupied the island from 1210 to 1669. On the whole Crete prospered under the Venetians, in particular after the fall of Constantinople, when the island became a refuge for scholars and painters. The Cretan school of art flourished in the 15th and 16th centuries, its painters working both at home and throughout Greece, including a certain Domeniko Theotokopoulos, who moved to Venice and later Spain, where he became known as El Greco. There was a Cretan-Venetian school of romantic poetry that culminated in the epic *Erotokritos* by Kornaros. The Venetians built tremendous fortifications and lavish public buildings.

For all the benefits of Venetian rule, the fiercely independent Cretans attempted to revolt, and many actually welcomed the arrival of the Turks. But not for long. When the Ottomans finally took Herakleon from Venice in 1669 after a 21-year siege Crete descended into a new dark age, spiritually and economically. The Cretans rose up against the Turks more than 400 times, notably in 1821, but were inevitably the losers to the superior Moslem forces. In 1898 the Great Powers appointed Prince George as High Commissioner of an independent Crete, and with the work of Venizelos the island became part of Greece in 1913. During the Second World War, Nazi paratroopers launched the world's first successful invasion by air on Crete, routing the Allied troops who had fled there from the mainland. Once again the Cretan guerrillas took to the mountains and along with British agents waged a heroic resistance, despite brutal reprisals by the Germans.

Note: The mountain ranges of Crete neatly divide the island into four sections. These have become modern Crete's political divisions and are used for reference in this book. West of the White Mountains is the *nomos* (county) of Chania; between the White Mountains and Psiloritis (Mt Ida) is the *nomos* of Rethymnon; between Psiloritis and the Lassithi Mountains lies the *nomos* of Herakleon; and east of the Lassithi Mountains is the *nomos* of Lassithi, of which Ag. Nikolaos is the capital.

Connections

By Air

To Herakleon, direct charter flights from London and other European cities, less frequently to Chania. Seven daily flights from Athens to Herakleon, four daily to Chania. Daily connection to Rhodes, twice a week to Thessaloniki, and regular services to Karpathos, Santorini, Mykonos and Kassos in high season.

CRETE

The people of Crete own the large clean and comfortable ships—among the finest in Greece—that daily link Herakleon and Chania to Piraeus. The 12-hour journey through the night, in a cabin, or on a warm night out on deck in a sleeping bag, can be quite pleasant and the restaurant prices on board are astonishingly low. Ships from Alexandria, Haifa, Turkey, Cyprus, Ancona and Venice call at Herakleon once a week.

There are daily ships in the summer to Santorini, Ios and Paros, and frequent connections to Mykonos, Naxos, Rhodes and Thessaloniki. In summer there is a hydrofoil connection with Santorini, together with a new fast catamaran service.

Other inter-island connections are now made via Crete's smaller ports. From Kastelli you can sail twice a week to Kythera, as well as to Gythion, Neapolis and Monemvassia in the Peloponnese. Ag. Nikolaos has a twice-weekly connection with Kassos, Karpathos, Rhodes, Milos and Piraeus, and at least once-weekly with Santorini, Sikinos, Folegandros, Sifnos, Symi and Chalki. From Sitia there are boats three times a week to Piraeus, twice a week to Kassos, Karpathos, Rhodes and Milos, and once a week to Folegandros, Santorini, Chalki, Sifnos and Sikinos.

By Bus

There is now a bus which you can board in Crete which combines with the ferries to Piraeus/Athens and takes you all the way to Thessaloniki, leaving four times a week.

Chania

Crete's former capital, **Chania**, is a pleasant, relaxed city of modern, stately neo-Classical buildings, where palm trees sway against a background of snow-capped mountains. Most visitors never get much further than the old port (the new one is a few kilometres away in Souda, and buses connect with ferries) and its charming, dilapidated, and increasingly trendy ensemble of half-restored Venetian buildings. Two of the city's traditional industries, hand-carved wooden chairs and leather goods, are still very much in evidence; Chania is the cheapest place in Crete to have a pair of shoes made to order.

History

Known in ancient times as Kydonia, Chania was one of the Minoans' most westerly outposts on Crete, although most of their buildings lie buried inaccessibly underneath the modern city (in 1984 a new site was opened up along Kanevarou St in Kastelli where parts of the ancient walls can still be seen). After the disaster of 1450 BC Chania became the third most important city on Crete.

In 1252 the Venetians set about refortifying La Canea, as they called it. On the site of the ancient acropolis they constructed their fortress, Kastelli, and in its walls the Venetian nobles built their handsome palazzi. In the late 15th century, alarmed after Barbarossa had struck in

NOMOS CHANIA, CRETE

20 km

miles

To Piraeus

RETHYMNON

Ag. Triada

Gouvernetoy Monastery

AKROTIRI

Stavros

Kourakies

Aroni

Profitis Elias

Souda

Nea Souda

Aptera

CHANIA

Kalyves
Kokkino Chora
Almirida
Vamos
Kefalos

Georgioupolis

Lake Kournas

Alikampos

Askyfou

Asigonia

Asfendos

Frangokastello

Vryses

Neo Chorio

Fre

Malaxa

Mournies

Ag. Theodoro

Platanias

Galatas

Ag. Marina

Fournes

Meskla

Therisson

Sourva

Lakki

Omalos

Prassa

White Mountains

Mt. Pachnes
(2451m / 8045ft)

Samara Gorge

Ag. Roumeli

Ag. Ioannis

Loutro

Anapolis

Chora Sfakion

Maleme

Kolimbari

Afrata

Radopou

Menias (Diktyna)

Ag. Ioannis Gionas

SPATHA RODOPOU

Agriagramousa

Gramvousa

Kastelli

Kissamos

Phalassarna

Topolia

Polyrenia

Sfanari

Kambos

Kouneni

Elos

Chyrsoskalitissa Monastery

Kakodiki

Kandanos

Temenia

Elyros

Lissos

Sougia

Paliochora

Elafonision ∞

To Gavdos

Libyan Sea

Alikianou

92

neighbouring Rethymnon, the Venetians created a wall around the entire town and surrounded it with a moat more than 45 m wide and 9 m deep. A long jetty divided the harbour in two. As it turned out, these precautions were to no avail; in 1645, less than 60 years after the completion of the walls, the Turks besieged and took Chania, installing pashas and beys at Kastelli and raising further fortifications. In 1850 they transferred the capital of Crete from Herakleon to Chania, where it remained until the island's annexation to Greece.

On 20 May 1941, while General Student's parachutists invaded Crete, the Nazis bombed Chania, demolishing a large section of the old walls and houses. While the Battle of Crete was a victory for the Nazis, their specially trained parachutists were almost all slaughtered as they landed. Chania commemorates the anniversary of the battle during the **Chania Festival**, which runs from the middle to the end of May, and includes folkdancing on the waterfront.

Tourist Information

NTOG Turkish Mosque, very helpful and open year-round ✆ (0821) 43300.
Tourist Police: 44 Karaiskaki St. ✆ (0821) 24477.

Topanas, or the Venetian Quarter

The centre of daily life in Chania is the cruciform **covered market** (*mornings only*), from where it's a short walk down to the old port and handsome **Venetian Quarter** around the old port. The whole neighbourhood is a National Historical Landmark, and while the façades of the buildings may not be altered, the interiors are rapidly being restored to house pensions, restaurants and jazz clubs. The landmark at the east end of the harbour is the **Mosque of the Janissaries** (1645), with its funny little domes, where the crack Christian-born troops of the Ottoman Empire once worshipped.

On the west end of the harbour, among sections of the Inner Venetian wall (quarried from the stones of ancient Kydonia), are the ship's models from ancient and modern times in the **Naval Museum of Crete** (*10–4, closed Mon*). The west end of Topana is still defended by the **Outer Venetian Walls**—dated 1590 on the Koum Kapissi Gate on Minos St. Wandering through the nearby maze of tiny streets, look for the ruined synagogue and the Venetian church of **San Salvatore**, used by the Turks as a mosque. On nearby Theofanous St a gate bears the Venieri coat-of-arms, dated 1608. Seek out Theotokopoulou street, one of the most picturesque in the quarter.

On Khalidon St, the handsome Venetian basilica of San Francesco has been converted into an **Archaeology Museum** (*8–3, closed Mon*), containing an intriguing collection of Chania's Minoan finds, ceramics imported from Cyprus by ancient Kydonia, Classical artefacts, Roman mosaics and glass. Opposite is the old Jewish quarter, Evraiki, where the ancient synagogue seems to be on the point of total collapse.

Kastelli and Chiones

The Kastelli quarter is on a low hill at the east end of the harbour, encompassed by the first Venetian walls; it took the worst of the German bombs, but today is one of the most charming parts of Chania. Walk along Kanevarou and Lythinon streets to pick out Venetian architectural details. There are remains of a loggia facing the port and the vaults (1600) of the **Venetian Arsenal**, or shipbuilding yard. South, on Vourdouba street and near an enormous plane tree is Venetian-built **Ag. Nikolaos** (note the coffered ceiling), converted by the Turks into an Imperial mosque to shelter a magical healing sword. Since 1918 it has been Orthodox. In the same vicinity is San Rocco (1630) and **Ag. Anargyrii**, built in the 16th century and the only church in Chania to hold Orthodox services throughout the Venetian and Turkish occupations.

To the southeast, Tzanakaki St leads into the 19th-century **Chalepa** quarter with its many 19th-century mansions, and the house and statue of statesman Eleftherios Venizelos. Opposite from Venizelos' house stands a Russian Orthodox church donated by the mother of a former governor. Near the pleasant, shady public garden in Tzanakaki St (with a small zoo and outdoor cinema, often showing films in English) is the excellent **Historical Museum and Archives** (*open weekdays 9–1, closed weekends*). Situated in a villa at 20 Sfakianaki St, it has Greece's second largest collection of historical material, dating back from the Venetian occupation to the liberation of Crete in 1944.

The nearest beach, **Neo Chora**, is a 15-minute walk from the harbour. Although sandy, shallow, and safe for children, it's not especially clean. The beaches tend to improve the further west you go, towards Platanias, where developers are gradually moving in. The town bus goes as far as Kalamaki and **Oasis beach**, a popular place with good swimming and windsurfing, cafés and tavernas. Other, less crowded beaches along the way can be reached by road, but prepare for a long walk. One kilometre west of Chania stands the **monument of the diving eagle**, a German memorial to the 2nd Parachute Regiment, economically adopted by the Cretans as a monument to their own couragous resistance in the bitter Battle of Crete.

Festivals

On 15 August Chania hosts the Pan Cretan Festival. The Chania festival runs from the middle to the end of May. In the neighbouring village of Chryssopigi there is a festival on Good Friday at Zoodochos Pigi.

Where To Stay

luxury

In Kato Galatsas, 5 km from Chania, the **Panorama**, ☎ 31 700, provides the most comfort. Built in the modern Mediterranean style, all rooms have air conditioning and balconies with sea views. There are 2 swimming pools, for those who find the 50 m walk to the sea too strenuous.

In Chania, on the waterfront at Akti Enosseos is the B class **Porto Veneziano**, © 29 311, a modern but comfortable hotel with 63 rooms. **Pandora**, 29 Lithinon, © 43 588, has comfortable, traditionally furnished apartments available by the day.

There are a number of small hotels located in refurbished Venetian houses. **Pension Thereza**, 8 Angelou, © 40 118, has been lovingly restored and has magnificent views from the rooftop terrace and rooms. Another, the **Contessa Hotel** on Theofanous Street, © 23 966, has the intimate air of an old fashioned guesthouse, with only 6 rooms, furnished in traditional Cretan style. The Contessa's owners speak little English, but make up for it by being extremely helpful in any way they can. Because it's so small, reserve well in advance. If that's full, above the Remezzo Café in the harbour is the **Plaza**, 1 Tombazi, © 22 540; it's small, too, but ask for one of the 4 rooms with a balcony.

Chania is blessed with a large number of pleasant pensions, most with rates below the Cretan norm. One with character, the **Hotel Piraeus**, has clean rooms, is marvellously situated overlooking the bustling harbour front and the friendly Greek-American owner encourages a relaxed family atmosphere. There are cooking and washing facilities, © 54 154. A little more done up is the **Pension Kastelli**, 39 Kanevarou St, © 57 057, on the quieter east end of the harbour.

There's also a **youth hostel**, which is very decent and very quiet because it's almost out of the city limits, at 33 Drakonianou, © 53 565. To get there, take the Ag. Ioannes bus from in front of the market. You don't need a card to stay. There are two campsites near Chania, though again you'll need a bus to reach them: **Camping Ag. Marina**, © 68 555, is 8 km west of the town and open throughout the season; **Camping Chania** is 5 km west of town, © 51 090. The former is the nicer of the two. Buses leave every hour from the station.

Eating Out

It's hard not to find a restaurant in Chania—the harbour is one great crescent of tavernas, almost all specializing in fish. It's worth your while to check over their prices: some have succumbed to tourism mark-ups, while others have remained true to Greek prices. Around the corner from the mosque at the end of the waterfront you'll find a number of fish restaurants straggling along the water's edge, any of which you can safely choose for an excellent seafood dinner in a lovely setting. The favourite here is **Dino's**, with dinner for 3–4000 dr. For inexpensive Cretan food you'll have to look hard to find **El Greco**, in the back streets of the old town. It's next door to **Les Vagabonds**, which makes a valiant effort to recreate a taste of France, serving Salade Niçoise and Boeuf Bourgignon for about 2500 dr. A good local place is directly across from the Kydonia Pension on Isodon Street, called **Taverna Apovrado**. For around 1500 dr. you can try a number of Chaniote specialities, including the local wine and sausages, of which the natives are quite proud. Just off the harbour in Halidon St, the **Lukulos** offers a fairly wide selection, from pizza to pepper steak, at reasonable prices. The **Kavouria**, near the mosque also serves typical Greek dishes for standard prices and has a good selection of wines. A pleasant surprise is **Emerald Bistro**, a friendly Irish restaurant just off the harbour front at 17 Kondilaki serving all the comfort foods you may have developed a longing for—steaks, baked potatoes and, naturally, Irish coffee (2000 dr.).

Bars

Of the many bars on the waterfront, **Remezzo**, at the mosque end, is the best place to sit and watch the activity. For an inexpensive after-dinner drink, accompanied by *meze*, head to the hole-in-the-wall **Lyraki**, near the customs sheds. The atmosphere is fun and the music impromptu. If you stay long enough you're guaranteed to see some equally impromptu Cretan dancing. For the best fish in town head for **Agroyialli**, on the beach at Nea Chora, where for 3000 dr. you'll have a memorable meal. At Korakies, east of town in the direction of Akrotiri, **Nikteritha Taverna** is worth visiting at weekends, when there's music and dancing in its very pretty garden (2500 dr.).

Nomos Chania

The city of Chania is the best point of departure for the rest of the county, or *nomos* (buses leave from 7 Kydonia St, near the Samaria Hotel). This is the land of the White Mountains, the west end of Crete that over the centuries has been slowly rising inch by inch out of the sea, while eastern Crete is subject to a gradual sinking. Nomos Chania is the home of the Gorge of Samaria, the last place in the world where the Cretan wild goat, the *kri kri*, lives in its natural habitat. The Chaniotes are known in Crete as the best musicians and warriors, especially those from Chora Sfakion. The *nomos* produces excellent oranges, honey and olive oil, and western Chania is Crete's big chestnut producer. Kastelli and Kissamos wines are well known throughout Greece.

East of Chania: Akrotiri and Souda

Akrotiri is one of the three peninsulas, or 'heads' as the Greeks call them, along the north coast of Crete. Eleftherios Venizelos and his son are buried there, by **Profitis Elias** church. It was here that the Cretans raised the Greek flag in 1897 in the midst of a bombardment by international navies, who had come to help the Turks put down a revolt. The story runs that the admirals were so impressed by the courage of the Cretans, who at the risk of their lives held up the flag with their hands when it was shot off its pole, they stopped fighting and applauded. A Russian shell destroyed the church, but it is said that Prophet Elijah got his revenge by blowing up part of the Russian ship the next day, killing many sailors.

Akrotiri has Chania's airport, a fact that hasn't stopped the wealthier Chaniotes from dotting it with new villas. There are two monasteries on the headland. **Ag. Triada**, near Kabani, was founded by a Venetian at the beginning of the 17th century and has a lovely Renaissance church. It still functions as a monastery and has a small museum containing old manuscripts, relics and icons. The second monastery, **Ag. Ioannes Gouvernetou** is near the stalactite cave Kimisios (or Katholikon), where St John the Hermit lived and died. Although cave enthusiasts may not mind, it's a good hour's walk to Gouvernetou, but there are no longer monks at the end of the trek to ply you with refreshments—unless you join the pilgrimage and *paneyeri* on 8 October. At Spiliani another cave, **Anemospilia** (Cave of the Wind), has a pond and stalactites, and **Arkoudia** (Bear) cave has a rock bear inside and also an ancient church. There's a pretty beach at the small village of **Stavros**, with a lovely circular bay providing good swimming, and a couple of tavernas for lunch.

Souda, at the head of the bay of Akrotiri, is Chania's port and wins no prizes for charm, but it has restaurants, snack bars and hotels. Frequent buses connect it with the capital. On the outskirts of the town is the Allied War Cemetery. A major NATO base is located at Souda and its airforce exercises can be rather obnoxious. But NATO is not the first to appreciate the superb harbour of Souda Bay, one of the finest in the Mediterranean. The Venetians fortified the bay's islet **Nea Souda**, and it was the last place on Crete to hold out against the Turks, despite their repeated attempts to capture it. At one point they even tried psychological warfare by piling 5000 Christian heads around the walls. The fort, however, remained in the hands of the Venetians and Greek rebels, who took shelter there until 1715.

The Turks built their own fort, **Idzeddin**, at the south end of the bay, using the ruins of the ancient city Aptera as a convenient quarry. **Aptera** was important into the Christian era, although little remains except the story of its name: the Muses defeated the Sirens in a musical contest here, but the Sirens were sore losers, tore out their feathers (hence *aptera* or 'featherless') and plunged into the sea, where they turned into offshore rocks. Among the ruins you can pick out Cyclopean walls, two temples, a theatre and underground, an impressive vaulted cistern built by the Romans. Further along the coast, **Kalyves** and **Almirida** are small budding, low-key resort towns—the latter more attractive with a sheltered bay and pleasant beach with good windsurfing.

From Almirida on round to the coast to Georgopoulis (see below), the coast is rocky and access to the sea is difficult. Inland, south from Aptera, **Stilos** is the site of the Anzac troops' final encounter in the battle of Crete (to this day there remain strong ties between Chania and New Zealand, and many of the bilingual young Greeks you will meet in the city were born and brought up on the other side of the world). From Stilos it's worth making your way down to the village of **Samonas**, where the Byzantine church of Ag. Nikolaos contains some beautiful frescoes. Southwest of Idzeddin is the village **Malaxa**, an ancient mining centre. Ruins of two Byzantine churches, Ag. Saranta and Ag. Eleousa remain, but most spectacular is the ravine to the south, 400 m deep, riddled with caves. Venizelos was born in the neighbouring village of **Mournies**.

South of Chania

In the heart of the nomos of Chania grow some of the best oranges in Crete—and as the locals will tell you, Cretan oranges are the best in the world. **Fournes** claims to have more than 120,000 orange trees; it also boasts the Cave of the Pig, and has a large *paneyeri* to Ag. Panteleimon on 27 July. At **Alikianou** the wedding massacre of Kantanoleo's Cretans took place, at the Venetian tower of Da Molin. Besides more bright green orange groves, Alikianou has a church of Ag. Georgiou (1243) with exceptional frescoes. From Alikianou a passable road continues south to **Prassa**, where a small ravine has unusual rock formations and caves.

Southeast of Fournes, **Meskla** is a lovely little village, set in lush green countryside, where one glossy orange grove succeeds another. One church has mosaics from a temple of Aphrodite, left by the ancient city of Rizinia; another, the Transfiguration of the Saviour, has frescoes from 1303. Byzantine frescoes can also be seen in the church of Christ the Saviour. Above Meskla, **Sourva** is a whitewashed village with amazing views. **Lakki**, to the west, is yet another picturesque village, set like a horseshoe into mountain terraces over the Plain of Omalos. East of these villages runs the majestic **Therisson gorge**, pierced by a road from Mournies (*see* above). It is known in Cretan history for the 1905 Revolution of Therisso, when the Cretans rose for union with Greece.

West of Chania: Spatha, or Rodopou Peninsula

En route towards the middle 'head' of Chania province, Rodopou (more commonly known by its cape, **Spatha**), the village of **Ag. Marina** has old Venetian and Turkish houses, and a long beach lined with hotels, tavernas, and watersport facilities. The islet facing Ag. Marina is **Ag. Theodoro**, and it, too, attracted Venice's fortification experts. The vast gaping mouth of its cave originally belonged to a hungry sea monster, with an appetite as big as Crete; Zeus, however, couldn't bear to see his home island devoured, and petrified the monster with a thunderbolt. Ag. Theodoro today is a refuge for the wild Cretan goat, the *kri kri*.

Just west of Ag. Marina, **Platanias** has a sandy beach and bamboo forest, yet this stretch of coast is pretty much taken over by tourism. The Battle of Crete began at **Maleme**, further west, and has a large German war cemetery as a grim reminder. At the foot of the rugged Spatha pensinsula, **Kolimbari** is the point of departure for excursions; its pebbly beach is itself a lovely little spot for a swim and a meal. Its wealthy 17th-century monastery **Gionas**, also known as the Hodegetria, has many fine icons dating from its foundation; its monks were brave fighters and to this day Turkish cannon balls are embedded in the monastery walls. Its *paneyeri* takes place on 15 August; on 29 August pilgrims make the 2-hour trek to the chapel of **St John the Hermit Gionas**, north of Rodopou. **Afrata**, the last village on the 'head' accessible by car, is the site of the cave **Hellenospilios**, its 90-m long corridors lined with stalactites and stalagmites. Out of Afrata you can pick your way down to rocky coves for a swim in crystal clear water. From Afrata it is a few hours on foot (or 1½ hours by caique from Kolimbari, or by excursion boat from Chania) to **Menias**, the port of ancient **Diktyna**, the most famous shrine to Artemis in Greece. Menias has a rocky beach (but good for swimming) and shady caves, and there are some ruins of the ancient port. Diktean Artemis had a popular following up to the end of the Roman Empire. The Diktean mountains in Lassithi were named after her, and Agamemnon stopped by to offer a sacrifice at her shrine in Polyrenia (*see* below) on his return home from Troy.

To Crete's West Coast: Kastelli Kissamou and Phalassarna

Further west, the road descends dramatically through the hills to a beautiful plain densely planted with olives and vineyards and surrounded by knobbly hills. The chief town and port (with ferries to Neapolis and Gytheion, in the Peloponnese) here is **Kastelli Kissamou**, recalling its ancient predecessor Kissamos, the port of Polyrenia. Kissamos' temple and theatre were dismantled by the Venetians and refashioned as a castle in 1550. This castle has a melodramatic history: when the Cretan Kantanoleo captured it from the Venetians, the Venetians pretended to recognise Kantanoleo's authority and offered a highborn Venetian girl as his son's bride. At the wedding feast the Cretans were given drugged wine, the Venetians slit their throats, and recaptured the fort. Kastelli also has a small **museum** with a few finds from ancient Kissamos, a rocky beach with a taverna. Wine is the major product of the town, and there are paneyeria on 30 May, 27 June (Ag. Pandeliemenon) and 29 August (Ag. Ioannes).

Two buses a day from Kastelli will take you to **Phalassarna**—the beach is vast and sandy, one of the finest in Crete, and dotted with a handful of tavernas and inns. Only a stone throne, a marker and a few walls by Koutri pinpoint the site of the ancient city of Phalassarna among a sea of plastic tomato tunnels. You can measure how much this western end of Crete has risen—Phalassarna's port is now 200 m from the sea. Further north, on the islet **Agria** off the westernmost peninsula, **Gramvousa** is the famous Venetian fort occupied during the War of Independence by Greek refugees, especially from the devastated islands of Psara and Kassos. Forced to make a living in troubled times, these refugees took to pirating so successfully that Capodistria had to intervene personally to stop them, and Gramvousa fort became Turkish once more. You can hire a caique in Phalassarna to visit the fortress.

Polyrenia, south of Kastelli, was founded by the Achaeans and Dorians. Polyrenia ('many flocks') supported a large population, supplied by a still visible aqueduct. Parts of the ancient walls remain, added to by the Romans and perhaps the Turks. The church of the 99 Holy Fathers was built from the stone of an ancient temple, and the cemetery occupies another temple's foundations. There are also ruins of roads and houses. The road leading to Polyrenia from Kastelli is also a ruin; buses attempt it twice a day from Kastelli, although it's a charming 8-km walk.

Heading south from Kastelli, the coastal road provides some spectacular scenery down through Platanos to **Sfanari**, which has a pebble beach nearby, some tavernas and simple places to stay. Further south, a paved corniche road continues to Kambos, a small village which won't detain you long, but it has a wild beach for healthy hikers.

The rough road winds south to the Libyan Sea and the **Monastery Chrysoskalitissa**, 'Our Lady of the Golden Stair' (although only the faithful, or according to some, non-liars can see the steps of gold). Remote though it is, many people come to its paneyeri on 14–15 August. Wonderfully isolated, amid many fine beaches, is the islet **Elafonision**, increasingly popular with Chaniotes who want to escape from the cares of the world, or at least from those of Crete. The water is a glorious blue, and the pinkish sand gives it a tropical aura; awkward to get to by road, it can be reached by boat or a magnificent coastal path from Paliochora (*see* below) or by bus from Chania.

Where to Stay

expensive

On Maleme Beach the **Crete Chandris Hotel** provides the luxury. Once a week the hotel has a Cretan dance evening, ℂ (0821) 62 221.

moderate

In Ag. Marina there are a number of C class hotels in the 5000–8000 dr. range. **Santa Marina**, on the beach, ℂ (0821) 68 570, is typical, and more likely to have a room when the season is in full swing. In Kastelli, right in the centre of town is the **Castle Hotel**, Plateia Kastelliou, ℂ (0822) 22 140, a decent fairly modern place, and rooms have private bath.

cheap

There are also a number of pensions and rooms, both in the towns and on the beaches. In Phalassarna you have the option of renting a room or simply camping out—that's about it.

Eating Out

In Kastelli there are several seaside fish restaurants; try **Makedonas** near Teloniou Square, where prices are fairly moderate (about 1200 dr. for a full dinner). Others may be found by the pretty caique harbour (where you can also swim before eating) just west of town. On the road to Chania there are small tavernas here and there, only open in the summer; to the east there's precious little. At Phalassarna there are a couple of tavernas on the beach (expect to pay a bit more because of transport costs). There's also a restaurant up at Polyrenia—the village is small and you can't miss it. The food is average, but the view is quite wonderful.

South of Kastelli to the Libyan Sea

Once a day a bus leaves Kastelli for **Topolia**, with its pretty stalactite cave of **Ag. Sophia**, used since Neolithic times and still the shelter for a little church. At the nearby church of

Ag. Kyryianni (960) is the tomb of Bishop Psaromilingos, who was martyred in the cave. South of Topolia is Chania's chestnut country, an area of dramatic, mountainous beauty reminiscent of Corsica. The main village, **Elos**, hosts a chestnut harvest festival (Yiorti tou Kastanas) the second Sunday of October. Eight other villages in the area live off the chestnut; in July they have some of the best weddings in Crete. One, **Kouneni**, on the road to Chrysoskalitissa Monastery, has three Byzantine chapels, in particular Ag. Georgios, constructed in 1284, and Michail Archangelos (14th century), both with frescoes.

A secondary road south of Topolia leads to **Kandanos**, a village inhabited from ancient times; the population resisted the Nazis so strongly that in reprisal the Germans destroyed the village, and Kandanos today is all new. Ruins of the ancient walls remain on the hill, and there are many frescoed Byzantine churches in the area, especially the Panayia. **Kakodiki** to the southwest has a hundred springs with soft mineral waters known for curing kidney stones; Michail Archangelos church (1387) contains frescoes. Other curative springs are at **Temenia,** a muscat-producing village built on the site of ancient Yrtakina. Nearby was far grander **Elyros**, one of the largest Doric settlements on Crete. According to legend, two sons of Apollo, Philakides and Philandros, founded the pugnacious town, which exported bows, arrows and bronze and prospered until the Saracens destroyed it in the 9th century. Walls and the acropolis still exist.

Paliochora, Sougia and Gavdos

In 1279 the Venetians built **Castel Selino** on a narrow peninsula in the Libyan Sea, more with the aim of subduing the rebellious Greeks than of protecting their new territory. When tested in 1539 by Khair Eddin Barbarossa, Castel Selino failed to do its job, and was demolished by the pillaging Turks. The small town of Selino, now known as **Paliochora** (bus from Chania) was once known as the Bride of the Libyan Sea, a sobriquet that must have been due to its location rather than to any architectural splendour, although the parish church, Panayias, has a pretty campanile. The town is an incongruous mixture of charter flight tourists and hippies left over from the stone age, who consider it home. The supermarkets are well-stocked with yoghurt and muesli, and the video shop does a brisk trade with the year-round residents who are attracted by the warm temperatures and relaxed atmosphere. The town separates the two beaches—one sandy, the other stony. The locals will tell you that when one beach is windy, the other is not, so be prepared to pick up your towel and move according to the weather, unless you want to enjoy the superb windsurfing the sandy beach provides.

From Paliochora it is an hour's caique trip to ancient **Lissos**, the port of Yrtakina and a properous Doric-Roman-Byzantine town in its own right until it fell victim to the Saracens. Currently undergoing restoration, a theatre, baths, houses and an Asklipieion or healing sanctuary, dating from the 3rd century BC, can still be seen of this once prosperous Doric–Roman–Byzantine town. Very close to Lissos was ancient Syia, modern **Sougia**, the port of Doric Elyros. Many signs of ancient times remain, including walls, an aqueduct and a bath. On the floor of the 6th-century church are lovely mosaics, both geometrical and scenic. Ag. Antonios (1382) is painted with frescoes. A cave near Sougia, Spyliara, is one of a multitude believed to have housed the Cyclops Polythemos. The modern town has little charm, but the long, pebbly beach never gets too crowded (paneyeri 8 September).

Over frequently rough seas to the south, the triangular islet **Gavdos** (ancient Clauda, pop. 100—down from 20,000), vies with the tiny Italian island of Lampedusa for the title of the southernmost point in Europe. It also claims (as do many islands) to have been the home of the fair Calypso. Boats leave four times a week in summer from Paliochora for this rustic end of the world, with charming beaches, a Venetian castle, Gozzo, and shepherds but little tourist accommodation—there are a few rooms but camping is your best option. Gavdos is also a paradise for fishing, which is just as well for there's little choice in the way of food, save what's imported from Crete; it's very much the Greek island of decades ago, with no mains electricity and few telephones.

Gorge of Samaria

The gorge is open officially from 1 May–31 Oct from 6am–4pm, when the water is low enough to ensure safe fording of the streams, and when the the staff of the National Forest Service patrols the area (it's for their services that you're asked to pay admission).

The most dramatic way to reach Crete's southern coast is by walking through the **Gorge of Samaria**, among the most spectacular 18 km in Crete. Once considered a rather adventurous excursion, the hike has become a 'must' for nearly everyone, and unless you can manage to go very early or very late in the year you may as well forget any private communion with Mother Nature (especially at weekends, when as many as 2000 other people will be down with you). If the water's low enough, you can go through the gorge in May, but it's at your own risk. To walk all the way through takes most people between five and six hours going down, and about twice that going up towards **Omalos**, the small village at the head of the gorge. You must be in the gorge by 3 pm, although almost everyone starts much earlier, to avoid the midday heat, and to make the excursion a single day's outing. The first bus (or buses, depending on demand) departs from Chania for Omalos at around 5 in the morning; organized tour buses leave almost as early, some even setting out from Herakleon and Rethymnon (you can, however, get a jump on the crowds by staying overnight at Omalos). Alternatively, in the high season, consider paying the extra drachmas for a tour bus, for once you reach the end of the gorge at Ag. Roumeli there is often a mad rush to catch a caique either to Chora Sfakion, Sougia or Paliochora, and another dash once you're at one of these villages to buy a bus ticket home. Everyone seems to want to catch the last bus of the after-noon, to allow time beforehand for lunch and a swim on the coast. The tour buses do allow for this, and also assure you of a seat going back. However you go, wear good walking shoes and bring something to eat (it is safe to drink water from any of the streams in Samaria).

If you haven't the time or energy to make the whole trek, you can at least sample Samaria (the bus trip from Chania, twisting around the steep slopes of the White Mountains, is itself an experience) by descending only a mile or so into the gorge down the **Xyloskalo**, the great wooden stair from Omalos, or alternatively, if you're based in the south, by going a mile up from Ag. Roumeli to the famous **Sideropontes** ('the iron gates'), the oft-photographed section of the gorge where the sheer rock walls rise almost 300 m on either side of a passage only 3 m wide. The Forest Service will admit visitors until nearly dusk for either of these short excursions.

The name Samaria derives from Ossa Maria, a chapel (1379) and ruined village in the centre of the gorge, which over the years was corrupted to Samaria. There are several other abandoned chapels along the way, about 20 fords in the stream, and if you're very, very lucky, you'll catch a glimpse of the *kri kri*, the rare long-horned Cretan goat. The White Mountains National Park, of which Samaria is a part, is the only place on Crete itself where they may be found; others live on offshore islets where they are also carefully protected.

Ag. Roumeli, Loutro and Around

Ag. Roumeli, at the southern mouth of the gorge, was built on the site of ancient Tarra and its sanctuary of Tarranean Apollo. In Roman times Tarra was famed for its fine glassware. The Venetians built a frescoed church, **Panayias**, on the foundation of a temple to Artemis. Since it has no roads, Ag. Roumeli was all but abandoned until the 1960s, when people began to come in through the gorge. Now it has numerous places to stay and eat, and a pebble beach.From Ag. Roumeli the caiques take 1½ hours either to Paliochora or to Chora Sfakion, less to Sougia which is less tourist-oriented but also less frequently served by bus. Between Ag. Roumeli and Sfakion, the coast around **Loutro** has many quiet beaches, including the isolated strand of Sweetwater Beach, cut off on one side by sheer cliffs and on the other by deep blue sea. There are small springs which surface on the beach, providing fresh drinking water. Despite daily boat services from Loutro and Chora Sfakion, the beach is still a pleasant, remote spot for swimming and sunbathing and, except in high summer, is a pleasant hour's walk from Loutro.

Ag. Ioannis is a 3-hour mule ride east of Ag. Roumeli. A few vestiges remain of the autonomous ancient city, Aradin, some of which were cannibalized for the church of Archistratigos Michail (Archangel Michael as Generalissimo). The environs are pitted with caves. **Drakolakki** cave is noteworthy—an underground labyrinth with a bottomless lake that requires both a torch and Ariadne's ball of string to explore.

Gorge of Aradena

If the Gorge of Samaria is too crowded, make the hour's walk from Loutro (or catch a bus from Chora Sfakion) to **Anapolis**, a pleasant village with a handful of inns and restaurants, and a statue of Daskaloyannis, hero of the revolt of 1770. From here follow the road and path to Ardena, a ghost village, where a mule track descends into the beautiful **Gorge of Aradena**—smaller than Samaria but count on a good 6 hours (so start early, and bring your own water). Anyone with vertigo should beware that there is a sheer 50-ft rockface along the track. It's been fitted with a fixed ladder and pair of ropes, so you don't need to bring any climbing gear, but neither is there a park service patrol to pick you up if you fall. The path brings you back to Loutro.

Chora Sfakion and the Ghosts of Frangokastello

Legendary in Crete for the ferocity and courage of its inhabitants, **Chora Sfakion** today is hardly distinguishable from the island's other coastal villages, with its seaside tavernas, hotels, souvenir shops and pebble beach. At one time, however, it was the capital of its own province—a province that Crete's various occupiers never quite subdued. Remote, it still supplied innumerable Cretan revolutions, and often turned to smuggling and piracy. At one time Chora Sfakion was said to have a hundred churches, enabling the townfolk to gather at seemingly harmless paneyeria every two or three days to plot the next moves of a revolt.

Villages in the ex-province of Sfakia are often fortified on small hills, as the Sfakiots, when not united against a common enemy, fought bloody feuds among themselves. The Venetians constructed a castle on the hill over Chora after the revolt of 1570, to supplement their 1317 fortress Ag. Nikitas, or **Frangokastello** ('Frankish castle'), 14 km down the coast, unhappily set among a straggle of concrete buildings. Both fortresses were used mainly to keep the wild Sfakiots under control. During the War of Independence, an Epirot insurgent, Khatzimichalis Dalianis, held Frangokastello with 650 Cretans until 8000 Turkish troops arrived to force them out. The Turks took the fort, and all of the Greeks inside were slain, including Dalianis. The Turks' victory was short-lived: bands of Cretans who had remained outside the fort quickly recaptured Frangokastello, while other Cretan chieftains captured the mountain passes and caused havoc when the remainder of the Turkish army turned to the north, seizing guns and much needed supplies.

This event, the Massacre of Frangokastello, has given rise to the most authenticated of the million or so Greek ghost stories that exist. On 17 May, the anniversary of the massacre, the phantoms of the Cretan dead rise up at dawn, fully armed, and march silently towards the fortress to disappear into the sea. These are the famous Drosoulites, the 'dew shades', still ready to fight the enemy Turk. They have been seen so often that scientific explanations have been attempted, although as yet none has proved satisfactory. A less spooky *paneyeri* of the Virgin takes place at Frangokastello on 15 August. Otherwise Frangokastello is a sleepy seaside settlement with a long, fine beach that offers some of the best swimming waters in Crete. North of Frangokastello, half hidden among the trees is **Asfendos**, with a brook of roaring water and **Askyfou**, a village with the ravine that spelt doom to Turkish armies chased out of Frangokastello. Pretty little **Asigonia**, with a large *paneyeri* on 23 August at the church of Ag. Georgios, is surrounded by plane trees and springs. Mountain villages such as these are rarely visited by foreign tourists, and are ideal for those who want to experience Cretan rural life. Closer to civilization is **Alikampos**, whose frescoed church of the Virgin (1315) celebrates on 15 August.

Where to Stay

There are quite a few places to stay in the main centres here, especially in Ag. Roumeli, Chora Sfakion and Paliochora. Unfortunately, in the first two places the word 'rip-off' is all too often heard, especially since the gorge has become so popular.

Primitive Pictographs from Crete

White Cornelian. Eastern Crete.

Green Jasper. Province of Siteia.

Brown Steatite. Uncertain Locality

Illustrations from:

Cretan Pictographs and Prae-Phoenician Script

by Arthur J. Evans, M.A., F.S.A.

In Paliochora there are a large number of rooms for tourists, and at the end of the beach the pleasant B class **Elman**, © (0823) 41 412, is open all year.

In Ag. Roumeli there are several restaurant-pension combos, like **Aghia Roumeli**, © (0821) 25 657, or the **Cri-Cri** (no tel) in the medium price range. You may do better in Chora Sfakion, where there's more choice; some average Class C hotels, and the long-established **Xenia**, a class B pension, © (0825) 91 202, located on the dour quay. In Paliochora the well-designed and comfortable **Aris Pension**, © (0823) 41 502, near the beach has lovely views. The **Polydoros**, © (0823) 41 068, is an old favourite and serves good breakfasts.

Paliochora has a fair selection of pensions, with rooms for around or under 4000 dr.: **Pension Lissos**, © (0823) 41 266; **Paliochora**, © 41 023 and **Oassis**, © 41 328. If the above towns are crowded—and they do get crowded—consider hopping in one of the many little ferry boats that ply the southern coast to Loutro (connections from Chora Sfakion and Ag. Roumeli) where there's a little clump of inexpensive pensions, or to Sougia (boat from Paliochora), where the rooms are even cheaper and quieter. There are a number of simple rooms for rent at Frangokastello.

Eating Out

In Paliochora superb souvlaki, among other simple dishes, can be found at **Stavros**, and especially good fish at **Kima**. Round the bay on the sandy beach side, the **Galaxy** is a local favourite, with good fish at normal prices. Ag. Roumeli has a number of tavernas, none of which stand out in any way, and Chora Sfakion has a line of reliable little tavernas along the waterfront. In Frangokastello you can get meals on the beach at one of the four or five simple tavernas.

East of Chania: Zorba and a Lake

The inland route, beyond Souda bay (*see* p. 97) passes through **Neo Chorio** with vast citrus orchards and a few remains of ancient habitations. There's a wonder-working icon in the Evangelistria church at **Fre**, where a large *paneyeri* is held on 25 March. The coastal route takes in **Kalyves** with its long beach, near the fortress Apokorona, built by the Genoese before they turned Crete over to the Venetians. Most, however, will find a detour to **Kokkino Chora**, on Cape Drapanon, more rewarding for its scenery and beaches. This is the village that was selected as the location for the film *Zorba the Greek* although it seems too bright in summer; for the brooding, overcast atmosphere portrayed on celluloid you must come to Kokkino Chora in the winter.

Georgioupolis was named in honour of Prince George and has a long sandy beach, part of the stretch which extends intermittently all the way to Rethymnon. Although a favourite area for hotel builders, you can still find cheap rooms to rent around the village. Many people who stay there return year after year, which speaks well for the place. Hundreds of eucalyptus trees provide a welcome respite from the sun, and a fresh stream flows into the sea in the centre of the village. In the nearby village of **Mathe** is the church of Ag. Antonios with a carob tree for its roof.

Inland, **Vryses** is on the main road, but has retained much of its shady charm, interspersed with busts of heroic, grandly moustachioed Cretans. Locals come here to picnic and swim in its creek. Crete's only lake, **Lake Kournas**, is near here as well, deep and eerie and full of eels. If you're looking for a place to stay, there's a taverna with a few rooms on the lake shore, which is a better bet than staying in the dull village.

Rethymnon

Rethymnon, Crete's third city, and according to many, its most charming, has long bemoaned its lack of a proper harbour. The Venetians dug one, but even now it keeps silting up. But in several ways this has proved a blessing, for much of what passes for progress has passed Rethymnon by. Like Chania, its Venetian architecture has earned it National Historical Landmark status, but Rethymnon suffered far less from Nazi bombing. Two minarets lend the skyline an exotic touch; wooden balconies left over from the Turkish occupation project overhead, darkening the already narrow streets. This medieval atmosphere and the long stretch of sandy beach in front of the town are Rethymnon's major attractions.

Rethymnon was built over ancient Rithymna, a Classical-era city, although the discovery of Late Minoan tombs indicate even earlier inhabitants. A fortress was built over the ancient acropolis, and the Venetians reinforced it with a further wall. Below, by the sea, the town began to expand unprotected. All the same, its relative isolation attracted scholars who fled Constantinople, giving Rethymnon a reputation as an intellectual centre which it retains to this day. It was raided by pirates three times, beginning with the wily Barbarossa in 1538, and followed by Uluch Ali in 1562 and 1571, when Rethymnon was burnt. The Venetians finally decided something should be done, and walled in the entire city. They also built the Fortezza, one of the best-preserved Venetian castles in Greece, although it was captured by the Turks in 1645. For a vivid account of Rethymnon as it existed under the Turks at Independence and during the exchange of populations read *The Tale of a Town* by Pandelis Prevelakis, a native son. (The English translation is available in Rethymnon.)

Tourist Information

NTOG, L. Venizelou, ✆ (0831) 29 148.
Tourist Police: Platia Heroon, ✆ (0831) 28 156.

The Old Town

Rethymnon's compact old town has yet to be given over to the tourists and is still home to a number of nearly medieval little shops—herbalists, cobblers, lacemakers, barbers, plastic bucket and broom shops and so on. All that remains of the city wall is the picturesque **Goora**, the grand gate that leads into the old city in the Plateia of the Four Martyrs, honouring four young men beheaded by the Turks. In Thessalonikis street, note the 17th-century lion-headed **Rimondi Fountain**, built by the Venetians in 1629 at the junction of several streets. The nearby **Loggia**, where Venice's soldiers would gather, is from 1600. For a good view over Rethymnon, climb the minaret of the **Neradzes Mosque** (a former Venetian church) on Manouli Vernadou St. Built in the 18th century, the mosque is now used for musical programmes.

The Waterfront and New Town

Rethymnon's waterfront has inevitably been given over to the tourist trade. Restaurants line the beach and especially the utterly bijou little Venetian port, where fish is the speciality. From here it's a short walk to the **Fortezza**, built in 1574, with its fine view of the town and sea. Built by forced labour, then surrendered by the Venetians, it has never really been loved. The best preserved building within the powerful walls is the mosque; the rest has been left in dishevelled, poetic abandon. The **Archaeology Museum** is housed in the eastern side of the fortress, in the former prison. Inside are Neolithic items from Amari cave, Late Minoan pottery, Roman artefacts and ornate Turkish headstones (*8.30–3, closed Mon*). Nearby, on Mesolongiou, the **Historical and Folk Art Museum** (*9–1 and 7–9*), offers a collection of costumes, embroidery, farming implements, and pottery from more recent times.

In the new part of town, a city park has been made over the old Turkish cemetery. A bit dishevelled, it contains a small zoo, where one unhappy *kri kri*, forced to share quarters with the peacocks, hides in his den; it may well be the only one you'll see.

Festivals

The Cretan Wine Festival and Handicrafts Exhibition takes place in the park for two weeks in mid-July, and a Handicrafts Exhibition every second year. Also in July–August there's an annual Renaissance Festival for 20 days, with concerts and theatre in the Venetian fortress.

Where to Stay

luxury

Just outside Rethymnon in Adele (6.5 km) is the very popular (especially with American families) class A **Rithymna Beach Hotel** and **Bungalows** on a lovely beach, © 29 491. It fills up early in the spring and stays that way, so book early. Rates are 30,000 dr. upwards a night in season for a double, and the bungalows much more.

expensive

Well-priced for its facilities, the **Hotel Fortezza**, Melissinou 16, © 21 551, has a courtyard and swimming pool. Less expensive, **Garden House**, on 82 N. Fokas (near the Fortezza), © 28 586, is a small but delightful historical residence, with a fountain and beautiful rooms.

The **Hotel Ideon**, ✆ 28 667, is well placed by the ferry dock, and also has a small pool. Within the city itself the **Hotel Brascos**, at Ch. Daskalaki and Th. Moatsou, ✆ 23 721, is slick and clean, but on a more reasonable level, with former elegance and a view of the harbour from the balcony, the **Hotel Achillion**, at 151 Arkadiou, ✆ 22 581, offers more in the way of atmosphere—and noise at night. For peace and quiet, **Zorba's** is reasonably priced and located at the east end of the beach; rooms come with private shower and WC, ✆ 28 540. Before trekking out there, give them a ring to see if there's a vacancy.

The **youth hostel** is exceptionally nice and convenient, only a few blocks from the tourist office at Tombazi 41, ✆ 22 848. You don't need a card to stay there; breakfast and cooking facilities are available.

A few kilometres east of Rethymnon there are two neighbouring campsites, **Elizabeth**, ✆ 28 694 and **Arkadia Campings**, ✆ 22 361.

Eating Out

The trendy place to eat, with its tiny fish restaurants is the Venetian harbour, but expect to pay at least 3500 dr. for the privilege (although the quality and variety are excellent). On the west side of the Fortezza, all by itself, is the **Sunset Taverna**, with good solid Greek food (about 1300 dr. a person for kalamari, salad, chips and retsina) and a view of you know what, as well as of the numerous cranes that frequent the shore. For something different, try **Famagusta** on Nikalou Plastira, a moderately-priced eatery specializing in Cypriot dishes. In Platia Petihaki there are two popular tavernas, **Vangeli** and **Agrimi**, serving all the old favourites, usually well-prepared and fairly priced. But as is so often the case, to find the genuine article you have to head out of town; in this case 5 km in the direction of Chania, the **Faros** is an enormous restaurant serving up excellent grilled food, good barrelled wine and live Cretan music. A further 12 km on there's **Kaklis**, which is equally popular, with a more limited but still excellent menu, wonderful local wine and live music. At either of these places there's a good chance that a wild Cretan wedding will be in full swing—complete with sozzled mustachioed warriors firing rifles into the air, but not to worry, even after a few *karafaki* of raki they're still pretty good shots and seldom hit tourists. To hear traditional music in Rethymnon itself, seek out the little place on Koronaiou Street near the church of the Mikri Panayias; if it has a name, no one remembers it.

Nomos Rethymnon

The *nomos* of Rethymnon is rugged, dominated in the east by Mt Ida, or Psiloritis (2456 m); several paths lead to its summit and to its sacred cave, one of two on Crete dedicated to Zeus.

The nomos also has Crete's two famous fortress-monasteries, Preveli and Arkadi. In the south are several undeveloped beaches, as well as the popular resort of Ag. Galini. Good swimming places are also to be found along the coast from Rethymnon west towards Chania.

To the Libyan Coast

Southwest of Rethymnon, the road towards Episkopi forks left for the ancient city of **Lappa**, also called Phoenix, and Lambe during the Byzantine period. The oldest monument here is the well-preserved Classical wall. The road continues to **Selia**, although to reach the tiny mountain village of **Rodakinon** ('the peach') the only public transport is from Frangokastello (*see* p. 104). Below Rodakinon is a lovely beach of soft sand and caves where you can shelter from the hot sun.

Further east along the coast, a corniche road leads to the village and resort of **Plakias**, near another lovely beach. Plakias is a little more ready for tourists than Rodakinon, with more accommodation of every type added each year. It's a great centre for long walks and serious swimming on some splendid beaches under the tamarisks, here and 2 km away at **Damnoni**. Late in the afternoon, head up to Mirthios, where the taverna terrace offers a superb sunset view of the coves below.

From Plakias it's 12 km to **Preveli Monastery**. Beautifully situated between the coast and Kourtaliotiko ravine, this 17th-century monastery was a great resistance centre during the Turkish and German occupations. In 1941 it sheltered Allied troops from the Nazis until they could be picked up by submarine and taken to Egypt. In gratitude for its assistance the British gave Preveli two silver candlesticks and a marble plaque. There are some fine icons as well (decent dress required), and a kilometre down the mule track, yet another superb beach, with palm trees and a huge rock in the sand. Preveli's *paneyeri* takes place on 8 May.

Central Rethymnon, Ag. Galini and Mt Ida

The road straight south of Rethymnon leads to **Armeni**, where a Late Minoan cemetery has been discovered. There's a sign just before you enter the village: future excavations depend on availability of government funds. Almost the entire Armeni population between the ages of 20 and 40 works in Germany now. **Spili** is a large mountain village on the way south. It is known for its greenery and has a long fountain of 17 Venetian lion heads. The town celebrates paneyeria on 29 June and 27 May. **Kissos**, a much smaller village to the south, has a 14th-century chapel covered with frescoes.

On these western slopes of snow-capped Mt Ida, a group of small villages are well known for their resistance to invaders, but are now accessible to all from Rethymnon. Beautiful **Gerakari** was conquered under Venetian, Turkish and German occupations, and has many houses from the Middle Ages, along with a tower. In **Amari**, the former capital of the province, the church Asomatos has the oldest dated frescoes in Crete, from 1225. A tranquil little village, it offers enchanting views. A nearby monastery has more frescoes to see, and, pride of the village, there's an agricultural college.

Two ancient towns lie near the sleepy village of **Thronos: Vene,** founded by Ptolemy and **Sivritos,** up a steep track, destroyed by the Saracens in the 9th century. A remarkable amount of their walls remains and Sivritos has a gateway and a monumental stair. **Vizari** to the south was built beside a later Roman settlement, **Ellinika,** and among the ruins are a mosaic floor and part of an Early Christian basilica. From **Fourfouras** village a shale path leads up to one of the peaks of Mt Ida, a 5-hour trek in good walking shoes. There is a little chapel and well on top, as well as an unforgettable view of Crete. Another ascent can be made from **Platania** to the Cave of Pan (2 hours).

The roads to the south end up at **Ag. Galini,** its jumble of houses spilling prettily down the hill, with an impressive backdrop of mountains, although here too the concrete culture has taken over, with every available square metre devoted to new building. Once a picturesque fishing village, it now does most of its fishing for the tourists. The beach isn't all that good, but some of the best cooks in Crete work in the numerous restaurants here. The islets to the southwest are called **Paximathia** for their resemblance to the crunchy twice-baked bread sold in Greek bakeries.

Arkadi, the North Coast and Mt Ida

A good road from Rethymnon leads to **Arkadi Monastery,** founded in the 11th century, although the present building dates from the 17th century and the façade (pictured on the 100-drachma note) was conserved from 1587. Even so, Arkadi resembles a small fort rather than a religious building, which is perhaps why the rebel Koroneos used it to hide his powder magazine, and why surrounding villagers took refuge there. On 7 November 1866, the Turks under Mustafa Kyrtil Pasha attacked Arkadi. After a 2-day siege they had begun to enter the monastery. Rather than surrender, the Abbot Gaberiel turned his gun onto the powder magazines, blowing up 829 people, both Cretan and Turkish. The event caused a furore in Europe, and many influential writers, Swinburne and Hugo among them, took up the cause of Cretan independence. At the monastery you can visit the Gunpowder Room, where Giambudakis fired the fatal shot that exploded the powder, and three rooms of relics, including the stacked skulls of the martyrs in an old windmill. The event is celebrated every year on 8 and 9 November at the monastery. There is also a tourist pavilion at Arkadi and a small hotel.

Viranepiskopi, a popular camping area on the north coast, possesses two churches of interest: a 10th-century basilica near a sanctuary of Artemis, and a 16th-century Venetian church. Further east, **Panormos** is at the mouth of the Milopotamos river, guarded by the fortress of Milopotamos, built by the Genoese in 1206, but taken by their arch-rivals, the Venetians only six years later. Panormos also has the ruins of a 5th-century basilica. Further east along the coastal expressway, **Bali** has been transformed from a quiet steep-stepped fishing village to a crowded resort in summer. However, if you're passing, the delicious cove behind its port is well worth a swim and lunch.

Just north of Perama, **Melidoni cave** is one of Crete's famous grottoes, this one so large that mythographers have made it the residence of Talos, a bronze giant with a bull's head, given

NOMOS RETHYMNON, CRETE

by Zeus to Minos to guard the coasts of Crete. Talos' job was to run around the island three times each day, flinging boulders at foreign ships. It was also his duty to visit all the towns of Crete with tablets bearing Minos' laws, until Medea slew him by removing a pin from his heel, draining away all his blood. Melidoni was to see much worse in 1824, when 270 women and children took refuge here during the War of Independence. When the Turk Houssein discovered their hideaway, he built a fire at the entrance and suffocated them all.

From Perama another road leads to **Margarite** with a thriving pottery industry and Maranthospilios cave. Nearby, high on a plateau, ancient **Eleftherna** was founded in the Classical period and survived into the Byzantine age. Ruins of the walls, acropolis, a bridge, a Byzantine tower, and huge Roman cisterns remain, the latter handy in times of siege. Higher and more precipitous is ancient **Axos**, of which nothing remains but its 8th-century BC acropolis walls.

Near Axos is **Anogia**, another stalwart resistance centre, burned by both the Turks and the Germans, the latter in reprisal for the daring kidnapping of General Kriepe, who was hidden in the village by the Resistance. Today it produces some of Crete's finest woven cloth, with 700 traditional patterns in all, and also Crete's best *raki*, *ouzo's* stronger cousin, also known as *tsikoutha*. Recently Anogia has taken advantage of its weaving traditions to become a 'typical' village for package tour excursions. From Anogia a path leads to the **Idean cave**, where Zeus lived as a young man before dethroning his father Cronus (although some say he was born there). Ancient even to the ancient, the Idean cave was the centre of a cult that preserved remnants of Minoan religion into Classical times. Pythagoras was initiated into its mysteries; Robert Graves, for one, believed the cult was the source of Pythagoras' mystical theories on numbers. The ascent to the summit of **Mt Ida** from Anogia takes more than 12 hours. Other approaches begin from *nomos* Herakleon to the east.

Where to Stay

moderate

Ag. Galini is packed with all sorts of accommodation but if you arrive in the summer without a reservation, you'll very likely find them packed with people, especially package tourists. In town the best value is the **Aktaeon**, with private baths and good views over the town, located at Kountouriotou, © 91 208. Also with good views and facilities is the **Galini Mare**, © 91 358. There are a number of pensions on the roads leading into Ag. Galini and the **Hotel Minos**, class D, © 91 218, with a good view. In Plakias there are two good hotel options, the **Livikon**, next to the bus station, © 31 216, and **Lamon**, © 31 318; both have good rates for private rooms with bath. In Spili, that verdant oasis in the centre of the province, there's the wonderful **Green Hotel**, © 22 225—a class C—bedecked with flowers and plants.

cheap

In Ag. Galini, the budget place is **Rent Rooms Acropol**; the rooms aren't much but the situation, on the top of the cliff, is superb. There is a **youth hostel** in Plakias, © 31 202, which doesn't even demand a card.

In Ag. Galini the **Ariston** restaurant serves good *stifado*, moussaka, and an excellent aubergine (eggplant) salad—2000 dr. for a full meal. Next door, the **Akropol** is open all day for breakfast snacks or full meals fom the grill. Opposite, **Eleni's** has a few alternative choices—a perfect shrimp curry with almonds, together with some Italian dishes. One of Ag. Galini's favourites is **Onar**, where excellent Cretan food, cooked by mother, can be enjoyed while gazing out over the deep blue sea. The little bar next to the petrol pump serves good souvlaki and *giro*.

In Plakias, plump for a swordfish steak on the terrace at **Kolamios** or the excellent spread at **Gorgons** before resorting to the local nightspots: **Pub House**, or the trendier high-tech **Swing**.

Herakleon

Herakleon (also Iraklion among other spelling variations) is Crete's capital and Greece's fifth largest city, with a population nearing 120,000. It holds little charm for most visitors, all very urban and new—which in Greece translates as lots of concrete—and the centre overflows with all the noisy hustle and bustle that most people come to the Greek islands to escape. However, nearly everyone visiting Crete ends up here at least once, for not only is Herakleon the transport hub of Crete, with its busy international port and airport, but it has the world's greatest collection of Minoan artefacts and the grand palace of Knossos in its suburbs. The Venetians have also left their mark in Herakleon, endowing it with some of Crete's finest public buildings and churches.

History

Herakleon began modestly enough as one of Knossos' two ports and as such survived until the Dark Ages. The Saracens built a new town over its ruins, and called it Kandak ('moat') for the trench they dug around its walls. Used as a base for piracy, Kandak also became the leading slave market in the Mediterranean. When Nikephoros Phokas liberated Crete in 961, the Byzantines called Kandak 'Kandax', a name further garbled into Candia or Candy when the Venetians made it the seat of their duke of Crete in 1210. The Greeks simply called it Megalo Kastro, after the huge fortifications constructed under the Venetians. Michele Sammicheli, the greatest defence architect of the 16th century, designed Candia's walls.

In a tribute to Sammicheli's genius, the Turkish siege of Candia lasted for 21 years, from 1648 to 1669. Louis XIV sent the French to assist the Venetians towards the end of the struggle although the venture ended in disaster for his forces. By the time Francesco Morosini (uncle of the Francesco Morosini who blew the top off the Parthenon) surrendered the city to the Turks on 5 September, 30,000 Christian defenders and 117,000 Turks had perished. Candia remained the capital of Crete under the Turks until 1850 when they transferred it to Chania. After independence the Greeks revived the city's ancient name, Herakleon, and it was made the island's administrative capital when Crete was united with Greece.

NTOG: 1 Xanthoudidou St, across from the archaeology museum, ℂ (081) 22 24 87.

Tourist Police: Dikeosinis St, ℂ (081) 28 31 90.

The Archaeology Museum

To avoid the endless busloads of tourists, arrive early—the doors open at 8 am in the summer and at 8.30 from Nov–May and close at 7 pm (also closed Mon morning).

In the heart of Herakleon is **Plateia Eleftheria**, dotted with monuments to great Cretans with equally great moustaches, where evening strollers meet in the many cafés, sweet shops and pizzerias. It is also the address of the one sight on the top of everyone's list of things to see in Herakleon: the **Archaeology Museum**. By law every important antiquity found on Crete belongs to the museum, resulting in a collection as vast as it is unique.

The museum is laid out in chronological order from the Neolithic Age to the last of the Romans, although it's the famous Minoan collection in between that bewitches and intrigues with its delicate beauty and intricate craftsmanship: the polychromatic Kamares ware vases, the snake goddess, and the mysterious Phaistos disc (1700 BC) believed to be the world's first example of moveable type, although as yet no one has been able to translate the language. There are examples of Linear A and Linear B scripts, a chessboard in ivory and rock crystal (1600 BC) and magnificent bull's head rhyton, or libation cup in serpentine and precious gems, both found at Knossos, models of towns and palaces, bronze statuettes, exquisite seal stones and gold jewellery. The sarcophagi and graceful frescoes of acrobats, dancers, the *Parisienne* and *Prince of the Lilies* are

Faience Snake Goddess

upstairs; almost as fascinating as the paintings themselves is the amount of work that went into their reconstruction by the Gillierons, a Swiss father-and-son team. Note in particular the border surrounding the well-known fresco of the bull leapers, or Toreadors: it is a ritual Minoan calendar.

Venetian Herakleon

Daedalou St leads from the Plateia Eleftheria to Herakleon's other main square, Venizelou. In the centre water dribbles (usually) from the mouths of the lions of the **Morosini Fountain**, commissioned in 1626 by the then Venetian governor. Just below, on 25 Augoustou St, is **San Marco** (Ag. Markos), the first church built by the Venetians in Herakleon and now used as a concert hall and permanent exhibition centre, with reproductions of Crete's best Byzantine frescoes (so if you can't get into any of the churches, you can at least get an idea of what you're missing). Also here, at the top of 25 Augoustou St, is the lovely **Venetian Loggia** (1620s), completely reconstructed after it was bombed in the war. On one side of the Loggia you can see what remains of the Sagredo Fountain, with its figure of a woman representing Crete, while on the other side, the former Venetian Armeria now bristles with local politicians instead of weapons in its role as Herakleon's city hall.

Adjacent, set back in its own square, the handsome Byzantine church of **Ag. Titos**, reconstructed after various earthquakes, used by the Turks as a mosque and by the Cretans to house the island's most precious relic, the head of their patron saint, Titus, who converted the island to Christianity and received an Epistle from St Paul. When forced to give up Crete, the Venetians made off with Titus' skull and only returned it in 1966.

Around the Port

After Ag. Titos, 25 Augustou Street is lined with ticket agencies, car rental shops, and banks as it descends to the port. The great arches of the restored **Venetian Arsenali** are just to the right, where one of Crete's most revered heroes met a cruel end. Called Daskaloyiannis, or 'Teacher John', he led a major revolt against the Turks in 1770, believing a Russian promise to support the uprising. The Russians never appeared, and in order to save the rest of his men, Daskaloyiannis surrendered to the Turks and was publicly flayed to death. The event inspired one of the island's best known popular poems, 'The Song of Daskaloyiannis'.

Out on the harbour mole is the Venetian fortress **Rocco al Mare** (16th century), recently restored and guarded by the winged Lion of St Mark. *For a small fee you can explore the interior, open 8–3.* Alternatively, take a stroll west along the coast past the Xenia Hotel to the **Historical Museum of Crete**, in a mansion once belonging to the Kalakairinou family. The collection picks up where the archaeology museum leaves off, with artefacts from Roman times to the present, featuring fine Venetian and traditional arts, and the reconstructed library of modern Herakleon's most famous son, Nikos Kazantzakis *(weekdays 9–5, Sat 9–2)*.

Plateia Kornarou, Ag. Minas and Around

South of Plateia Venizelou, the city's busy outdoor market runs along 1866 Street, while the narrow alleys branching off are crowded with inexpensive restaurants. At one end of the market, **Plateia Kornarou** has the Venetian **Bembo Fountain** (1588) made from ancient fragments, and a Turkish fountain, converted into a kiosk. From here Karterou St leads to the elephantine 19th-century cathedral dedicated to Herakleon's patron saint, **Ag. Minas**. Just below the cathedral is its older, smaller predecessor with a more interesting interior. Even better is **Ag. Katerina** (1555), in the same square. Used today to display an impressive collection of Cretan–Byzantine art, Ag. Katerina once housed a famous school of icon-painting, and some believe El Greco studied there before leaving for Venice. The pride of the museum are six icons by Mikalis Damaskinos, the 16th-century contemporary of El Greco who also went to Venice but returned to Crete to adorn his motherland with Renaissance-inspired icons.

The Walls

Brilliantly restored, Sammicheli's massive walls surrounding the historic centre are nearly as vexing to get on top of today as they were for the besieging Turks—4000 m in their total length, in places 14 m thick, with 12 fort-like bastions. Tunnels have been pierced through the old gates, although the **Chania Gate** at the end of Leoforos Kalokairnou preserves much of its original appearance. The only place with access to the top of the walls is Bastion St Antonio, from where you can walk south to the Martinengo Bastion and the tomb of Nikos Kazantzakis. This great Cretan writer, who died in 1957, had inscribed on his tombstone: 'I believe in nothing, I hope for nothing, I am free.' Perhaps some of his ancestors shared his sentiments, for from his tomb you can make out Mt Iouktas in the distance—the burial place of the great Zeus himself. See if you can make out the god's profile in the shape of the mountain.

Knossos

Knossos is linked by Herakleon city bus (no. 2) every 10 minutes, starting at the harbour and stopping in Plateia Venizelou. The site is open daily except for important holidays, 8–7 (8–5 in winter). Again, to avoid the crowds, arrive as the gate opens. There are rooms to rent near the site, as well as restaurants and cafés.

The chronology of Knossos is quickly told: remains indicate that the first inhabitants came during the 7th millennium BC. Circa 1950 BC they built a palace, which collapsed in the earthquake of 1700. Construction of a new palace followed, and it is the remains of this that one sees today. In 1400 BC most of it was destroyed by a great fire. The inhabitants at the time were probably Mycenaean, as shown by the primitive Greek of Linear B tablets. The lack of later construction on the immediate palace site and the discovery of coins depicting the Minotaur suggest the spot was considered sacred as the site of the ancient Labyrinth.

In the Geometric era, a community flourished near Knossos that became one of the leading cities of Crete in the 3rd century BC, although following a war with Lyttos it lost its supremacy to Gortyna. The Romans built a large city in the area that survived until the early Byzantine period, when the annals of the church refer to a bishop of Knossos. Afterwards Knossos lay abandoned, but not forgotten, although interest in the rediscovery and excavation of its Minoan past had to wait until Heinrich Schliemann electrified the world with his excavations of Troy and Mycenae. In 1878 a merchant from Herakleon named Minos Kalokairinos dug the first trenches, at once striking part of the palace and uncovering the first known Linear B tablet, which he showed to Sir Arthur Evans in 1894. Evans, thrilled by the discovery, negotiated for the property (something Schliemann himself attempted to do unsuccessfully) and began excavations in March 1900.

At first Evans believed that he was excavating a Mycenaean site, then to his astonishment realised he had found something far older—a whole civilization right out of the myths of the ancient Cretans. It was one of history's great archaeological finds, and Evans took it upon himself to try to reconstruct what he could of Minos' palace. In recent years scholars have bitterly disagreed on the accuracy of these reconstructions and even more on the various names

The Dolphin Fresco at Knossos

Evans gave the different chambers and courts of Knossos, but to the casual visitor they are quite extraordinary, and give a sense of a Middle Minoan palace circa 1700 BC that none of the unreconstructed sites can match.

Space doesn't permit a detailed description of Knossos, although there are several guides for sale at the excavations (especially Pendlebury's). Roughly, the excavations at Knossos are entered by the west court of the palace. If you continue directly to the left, you'll find the oldest road in Europe, the **Royal Road**, which leads to the so-called Little Palace. At the head of it stands the **Theatre**—perhaps used to view religious processions (it looks more like a large stairway). To the right of the west court is a porch leading to the **Corridor of the Procession** and the **Propylaeum**, or south entrance, of the palace with reproductions of the original frescoes on the wall.

A staircase from the Propylaeum leads to an upper floor, apparently used in part for storage. Another staircase descends to the **Throne Room** and **Lustral Basin** believed to have held water used in rituals; this, and other wells were also apparently used to reflect light into the rooms. Unfortunately wear and tear by so many visitors has made it necessary to rope off the stone throne so that you can no longer sit where Minos sat 3800 years ago (although if you're elected judge of the Court of International Justice in The Hague you may sit on its reproduction). Evans found evidence in the Throne Room of a last-ditch effort, perhaps by the King himself, to placate the gods as disaster swept through Knossos. From the large central court back up the stairs is a series of rooms containing huge storage pithois and rooms with their frescoes recopied on the walls. On the north side of the palace is a brightly painted charging bull. Note the columns that thicken near the top, unique to Minoan architecture but distinctly similar to the trunks of a certain cyprus native to the Gorge of Samaria.

On the east side of the palace are huge pithoi dating from the first palace. The excellent water and sewer system that supplied Knossos is visible under the floor in the **Queen's Megaron** and its bathroom, complete with a flush toilet—an amenity that Versailles could scarcely manage. Also in this area are the upper and main **Halls of the Double Axes**, the **Grand Stairway**, the **Corridor of the Draught-board**, the separate **House of the Chancel Screen** and others, most labelled in English. A path to the south leads to the **House of the High Priest** and the **Royal Temple Tomb**, although these can only be visited with special authorization. The same is true of the **Little Palace** across the road, although not of the **Caravanserai**, where travelling caravans could spend the night. This lies up the main road, across the ravine.

It is intriguing to speculate on exactly how the Minoans lived at Knossos, and how the myths of Minos, Ariadne, the Minotaur and the Labyrinth grew up (*see* p. 56). The myths may well describe Minoan religious rituals: how Ariadne was the Great Goddess, the Moon Goddess of the snakes, and that Minos (a title like that of Pharaoh) was her consort, a sacred sun king, who ruled a prescribed number of years before his sacrifice. The word labyrinth comes from the ancient word *labrys*, or 'Double Axe', and means 'House of the Double Axe'. The double axe, a symbol seen throughout Knossos, would kill both the victim and slayer; among other things, the Labyrinth was the descent into the underworld, from which only an exceptional hero (like Theseus) could emerge alive, 'reborn'. The maze story may also have been suggested by the complicated spiral dance, described by Homer in the *Iliad*, 'a dancing floor like that which Daedalus once fashioned in spacious Knossos for Ariadne of the lovely hair', a fertility dance that culminated in the acrobatic bull leaping. The Minotaur, or 'Bull of Minos', may have been the form the king would take in his ritual matings with the Moon Goddess, since Pasiphaë, 'the shining one', or moon, was herself disguised as a cow.

South of Knossos: Arkane

Most of Crete's table grapes are produced in the two villages of **Arkane**, Kato Arkanes and larger, Epano Arkanes. Its Asomatos church (1315) has good frescoes of the same period as those in Ag. Triada. But it's especially interesting for the many Minoan remains in the region, including the walls in the village, a well, tombs and other buildings. However, two of the sites—the large necropolis at Phouri and the temple at Anemopilia—are closed (although the Herakleon tourist office may be able to refer you to the caretaker who can let you in). The necropolis contained many wealthy burials in a wide variety of tomb styles, the earliest dating back to 2500 BC. Above Arkane's town dump, on a windswept promontory called Anemopilia, a Minoan temple was discovered in 1979, containing four skeletons, apparently of people caught in the temple as the great earthquake struck and toppled it over them. The archaeologists who excavated the site concluded that one of the skeletons, a young man, was in the act of being sacrificed to appease the furious god. Their findings have poured oil on the flaming controversy among scholars as to whether or not the Minoans practised human sacrifice.

In nearby **Vathypetro** a Minoan villa has been found. **Kanli Kastelli**, or the Bloody Fortress, also near Arkane, is believed to have been built by Nikephoros Phokas when he liberated Crete from the Saracens in 961. It later sheltered a harried Duke of Crete, much tried by the Duke of Naxos, Marcos Sanudo, who captured towns in Crete in defiance of Venice.

Amnisos

Amnisos (take bus no. 1 from Plateia Eleftheria) was the port of Minoan Knossos, and ruins remain from that period as well as from the Archaic (the sanctuary of Zeus Thenatas). From here Idomeneus and his 90 ships set sail for Troy. More recently, it was in Amnisos that archaeologist Spyridon Marinatos discovered pumice flung from Santorini's volcano, evidence that led him to formulate his theory on Knossos' untimely demise (*see* p. 198). Within walking distance, up the Episkopi road, is the *Cave of Eileithia*, the protectress of childbirth.

Sacred even among the early Minoans, this cave yielded many Minoan ritual objects; for the modern visitor its main attraction is a fair crop of stalactites. Amnisos is the closest beach to Herakleon, although the sand is on the grubby side, and charter flights swoop overhead with alarming frequency. For a tidier, quieter strand try **Hani Kokkini**. Large hotels dot sandy beaches along the coast east to Malia.

Festivals

Herakleon flower festival 2–6 June; grape festival 11–19 September; and a huge *paneyeri* for the patron saint Ag. Minas on 11 November.

Where to Stay

expensive

Near the museum is the imposing **Atlantis Hotel**, an A class with imposing prices to match, ✆ 22 91 03.

moderate

Also convenient for the archaeological museum and other sights in the central city, yet located on the quiet (well, traffic-free) pedestrians-only Daedalou Street, **Hotel Daedalos**, ✆ 22 43 91, is a spacious C class establishment with 115 beds, and paintings by local artists in the lobby. Otherwise it's plain and modern.

cheap

The quiet **Hotel Rea** near the sea at Kalimeraki St, ✆ 22 36 38, is much lower on the price scale. There's also a large number of pensions scattered all over the city and a **youth hostel** at Vironos 5, ✆ 286 281. There's now a pension in the old youth hostel building, called **Yours Hostel**, Chandakos 24, ✆ 280 858, with all sorts of accommodation available at low prices. For good value, try the pleasant, friendly **Hotel Hellas** with a courtyard, at Kandanoleontos 11, ✆ 225 121. Near the Venetian Loggia, the **Idaeon Andron**, Perdikari 1, ✆ 281 795, has pleasant small rooms for slightly less. Five km west of town is an A class campsite with all modern facilities, ✆ 25 09 86.

Eating Out

The **Glasshouse** on the quay near the Xenia hotel has long been a fashionable place to eat among the locals and prices are accordingly expensive, as are the restaurants near the fountain, one of which is Italian and quite good, but pricey. Increasingly popular are the ten or so tavernas along Fotiou ('Dirty') Lane between Odos 1866 and Evans Street, all jammed together in the narrow confines, and all offering your basic Greek cuisine and grilled meats at moderate prices (2000–2500 dr. for a dinner). If you've a hankering for fish, **Ta Psaria** at the foot of 25 Augustou Street has fish at reasonable prices and there's seating outside, if you don't mind the constant hum of traffic. Herakleon is awash with pizzerias, especially around Plateia Eleftherias and

Daedalou Street. In the latter the taverna **Minos** has a delicious selection of 'ready food', excellent grilled meats and fresh fish daily. Try the lamb with yoghurt, a Cretan speciality (2500 dr.). In the same street, **Victoria Pizzeria** certainly has the widest variety of pies—22 kinds, no less, averaging out at 1000 dr. Less expensive, and a real oasis if you can no longer stand the sight of moussaka is the **Curry House** near Daedalou Street off Perdikari Street, featuring several curry specialities daily at around 900 dr. a dish. There are also two respectable Chinese restaurants in the same area.

Nomos Herakleon

The *nomos* of Herakleon has plenty to see: not only most of Crete's Minoan sites, but also its ancient Roman capital Gortyna and once notorious Matala Beach, on the south coast. If you're relying on public transport, your first problem is getting out of Herakleon, with its complex system of **bus stations**. From the harbour station just below the city walls buses depart for destinations along the north coast as far as Vai, and to Ierapetra and the Lassithi Plateau; from outside the Chania Gate the buses cover all other destinations in the nomos; from the Evans Gate buses head to Ano Vianos, Myrtos and Thrapsano; from the west side of the harbour near the Xenia Hotel you'll find buses go to Rethymnon and Chania.

West of Herakleon

Along the coastal road to Rethymnon are a pair of possible detours: **Rogdia** with a seaside Venetian fort, or **Fodele** considered the birthplace of El Greco, although there isn't much to see beyond a monument erected in his honour by the University of Valladolid. The inland road to Rethymnon passes **Minoan Tylissos** by a pretty village of the same name, where three large country villas from the Late Minoan period were discovered. Destroyed *c.* 1450 BC, they stood two or three storeys high and had extensive storage facilities; you can get a fair notion of their plans from the surviving stairs, pavements, walls, and pillars (*open daily for a small fee*). A similar, although less intact Minoan villa was found up the road at **Skla-vokambos**.

The southwest route towards Ag. Varvara passes **Ag. Myron** , a large village with a 13th-century Venetian church and a paneyeri on 8 August. Ancient **Rafkos** with scanty ruins is to the north. Off the main road, **Krousonas**, a small village in the afternoon shadow of Mt Ida, celebrates St Charalambos' Day with a big fete on 10 February. **Prinias**, just off the road, has the ruins of ancient Ryzenia on its acropolis with two Archaic temples and a later Hellenistic fort. Straggling **Ag. Varvara** has a large rock on one end, said to mark the 'omphalos', or navel of Crete.

From Ag. Varvara, a road leads west to **Vrondisi Monastery** , where the church Ag. Antonios has good 14th-century frescoes; even better, the partly Venetian church of **Valsamonero** (just below the road, or by path from Vorizia village) has some of the most beautiful frescoes in Crete, by 14th-century master Konstantinos Rikos. The road continues to **Kamares** from whence you can climb to **Kamares cave** on the flank of Mt Ida. The cave gave its name to the fine, colourful Minoan pottery discovered there. By mule the trip takes 4 hours and you can travel all the way to the top of Mt Ida from Kamares in another 6 hours (for information on the Hellenic Alpine Club shelter, *see* p. 38).

Mesara Plain, and Gortyna

South of Ag. Varvara lies Crete's largest and most fertile plain, the Mesara. Since Minoan times it has been one of the most densely populated corners of the island. For centuries the most important city was **Gortyna** (or Gortyns). Although inhabited from Neolithic times, its big moment came after the fall of Knossos, when it became one of the ruling cities of Crete under the Dorians, with ports at Matala and Lebena. In 189 BC Hannibal passed through Gortyna, and later the Romans made it the capital of their provinces of Crete and Cyrenaica (Libya). Although in the *Iliad* Homer describes Gortyna as walled, the walls you see today are Hellenistic, begun by Ptolemy Philopator. St Paul sent St Titus to convert Gortyna and become its first bishop. In 828 the Saracens destroyed the city.

The single most remarkable find in the vast ruins of Gortyna is the civil **Law Code of Gortyna**, discovered in a mill stream in the 19th century AD and now displayed in the **Roman Odeon**. Written in a Dorian dialect in 500 BC, in *boustrophedon*, 'as the ox plows' from left to right, then right to left, the laws cover marriage, sex offences and property law. The **theatre** is under the **acropolis**, with an 8th-century BC temple and long sacrificial altar. There is also the 2nd-century AD residence of the Roman governor (**Praetorium**), the oft-rebuilt Archaic **Temple of Pythian Apollo**, and a **Temple of Isis and Serapis**, the Egyptian gods who became popular in the late Empire. To the south is the massive brick Roman Great Gate, and ruins of an amphitheatre and stadium. Near the entrance, the apse ruins of the great **Basilica of Ag. Titos** date from the 6th century and have traces of early frescoes.

Phaistos and Ag. Triada

Superbly situated on a high hill overlooking the lush Mesara plain and Idean mountains, **Phaistos** was one of the oldest cities in Crete, mentioned in Homer, and in Minoan times second only to Knossos on the island. It was destroyed in Hellenistic–Roman times by its powerful rival across the plain, Gortyna. Its first palace was constructed in the Middle Minoan period, 2100 BC, and destroyed in 1700 BC; the second palace was built on top of the first and destroyed in 1400 BC. Below the palace, 50,000 people lived and worked for the king; ruins of their villages are scattered across the Mesara.

Archaeological purists dismayed by Evans' reconstructions at Knossos will breathe a sigh of relief at Phaistos, where only your imagination will restore the palace to its original three storeys. It was reached by a grand stairway, where traces of sacred snakes carved in the steps are still visible. In the palace are the chambers of the king and queen, with bathrooms and gypsum-paved lustral basins, and below the West Court, a **theatre**, with tiers of seats believed to have been used for watching ritual ceremonies. In the palace are impressive storage rooms and cisterns for collecting rain water, and one of the oldest metal forges in the world. Near the excavations, a tourist pavilion has a café and food.

Just to the north, **Vori** is worth a short stop for its **Museum of Ethnology** (*10–6*), illustrating traditional country life in Crete with exhibits of pottery, musical instruments, furniture, tools and utensils.

Ag. Triada (connected to Phaistos by a dirt road) supplied much of the gypsum and alabaster for the building of Phaistos. It was a Late Minoan settlement in its own right, where many people lived after the great destruction of 1400 BC. A small palace or villa remains at Ag. Triada that yielded some of the Minoans' finest art—all now in Herakleon's museum. No one knows why it was built so close to Phaistos (the walk takes less than an hour); it may well have been a royal summer villa or perhaps a wealthy Minoan simply fell in love with the splendid site. The name Ag. Triada is derived from a small Venetian church near the site; a second church at the excavations, Ag. Georgios Galatas (1302), contains some frescoes.

Matala and the Coast

A road west of Myres leads to **Matala**, the lovely and very popular beach enclosed by sandstone cliffs. The cliffs are riddled with ancient tombs, which over the years Cretans have enlarged into cosy little rooms. In the 1960s and 70s these were inhabited by a sizeable international colony of young troglodytes. Now the local authorities prefer people to sleep on the beach if they must sleep out. The nightlife is pretty lively, and the inexpensive bars and tavernas do a brisk trade. The beach here is safe for children, as at nearby **Limenes**. During Easter it's nearly impossible to find a room in or around Matala, as many Greeks come here annually for their first official swim of the year. On the road between Matala and Pitsidia a track leads to **Kommo**, where archaeologists in the last few years have uncovered sizeable Minoan remains of Phaistos' port.

Eastwards along the coast (no road; you'll have to backtrack to Myres) is **Kali Limenes**, the 'fair havens' where St Paul is thought to have landed. East of this was the port of ancient Gortyna, near the quiet fishing village of **Lebena**. In late Classical times an Asklepieion to the god of healing was built here. Both it and the Hellenistic treasury have mosaic floors and there are also two large bath tubs.

East of Gortyna

Pyrgos is the largest village along the road, just before **Philippi**, where a Byzantine fortress was renovated by the Genoese and called **Castel Belvedere** for its remarkable view. To the east, a clutch of small hamlets including the monastery Foundadon is called the **Kastelliana** region. East of this is **Ano Viannos**, or ancient Vienna, which is credited with founding Vienne on the Rhône, the chief route up to the tin mines of the British Isles. On the acropolis of Ano Viannos are the ruins of a Venetian castle and Turkish tower. Ag. Pelagia (1360) has frescoes. On the coast, there is a castle near **Kastri** (of Mt Kairatos), and an excellently-preserved Venetian fort at **Vigla** called Vigla of Kairatokambos. It was here that the Saracens entered Crete in 823. Down the coast is the **Monastery Arvi**, and a pretty beach.

North of Ano Viannos is a region called the Pethiada. The main road passes **Arkalohori** with a large paneyeri on 21 May. Minoan tombs and a sacred cave have been found there. In nearby **Voni**, a folk festival takes place from 17 to 20 July. **Kastelli** is the largest village of the region, topped by a ruined Venetian castle; its 15th-century church Eisodia Theotokon has very interesting frescoes. To the east is the ancient city of **Lyttos**, or Lyktos, the enemy of Knossos in Doric times. High up on the foothills of Mt Dikti, Lyttos was wealthy and minted its own coins in Classical times, but in 220 BC Knossos destroyed it to put an end to the rivalry. Hellenistic walls remain, as does a later Christian basilica with mosaics. Another ancient city, **Chersonisou**, to the north of Kastelli, had a famous temple to Artemis; down on the waterfront, **Limin Chersonisou** was the port of Lyttos and is now the trendiest and snootiest resort in Crete, with a strip of big hotels, restaurants and discotheques. There is a later fort on the islet across from it (the larger, more distant islet, **Dia** is now a sanctuary for Crete's wild *kri kri*). **Nirou Hani** has a Minoan villa; **Gournes** is the home of an American Air Force Base.

Malia is also well supplied with all possible tourist amenities and a comfortable youth hostel. The history of the **Minoan Malia** (closed Sun) follows the same pattern as that of the other sites: built in 1900 BC it was devastated by the earthquake 200 years later, and the second palace, built over the first, was ruined in the mysterious catastrophe of 1450 BC. From the west court is the entrance to a long rectangular central court with a pit in the middle. In the Pillar Crypt to the left you can discern symbols carved in the pillars. Another little room further north is set at an oblique angle to the others, and might have been used for moon study or worship. On the same side are the Megaron, Lustral Basin and archives. Outside the palace a paved Minoan road still exists, the sunken Hypostyle Crypt and, the famous great court full of gargantuan pithoi. By the sea is the cemetery, and to the west are the remains of a 6th-century basilica.

Where to Stay

expensive

Outside the capital most people opt for hotels down in Matala or along the crowded coast to the east around Malia. In Malia, the centre of the over-developed coast, you can ensconce yourself in the **Ikaros Village**, class A, © (0897) 31 267, intriguingly designed as a traditional Cretan village (most of the big hotels lack any design whatsoever), or the **Malia Park**, © (0897) 31 461, with bungalows, watersports and mountain bike centre. In Hersonisou there are untold pensions and hotels covering every price range, the most luxurious being the **Creta Maris Hotel** and **Bungalow** complex, © (0897) 22 115.

moderate

As you enter Matala, the **Zafira Hotel**, © (0892) 42 112, is the first thing you see, handy for town and beach, and reasonably priced. The **Valley Village**,

NOMOS HERAKLEON, CRETE

© (0892) 42 776, on the edge of the village has a swimming pool, Greek dancing shows and barbecue nights. One advantage of its location is that it's out of earshot of the town's other nocturnal activities. If you have to stay in Malia, there are a large number of small, cheaper hotels. Typical (and favoured by British tour operators, however) is **Elen**, © (0897) 31 545, a km from the beach.

cheap

Just outside Matala, opposite the petrol station, is the **Corali** pension, © (0892) 42 785, with an area for children to play, and in town, near the church and 150 m from the beach the pension **Xenios Dias**, © (0892) 42 116, popular because of its friendly, family atmosphere. In Matala, the police are tough cookies if you disobey the notices about no sleeping in the caves or on the beach. If you've a sleeping bag, though, head straight for **Matala Camping** near the beach, a good cool place to stay with ridiculously low prices. There are also cheap beds in the neighbouring villages of Kalamaki and Pitsidia. One of the cheapest hotels you'll find in Malia is the E class **Ermioni**, © (0897) 31 093. A pleasant economy alternative is the charming **youth hostel** just east of town, © (0897) 31 555. There are two **campsites** near Limen Chersonisou.

Eating Out

Both coasts can be hard on the wallet, and the food tends to be Greek-international-bland to please all tastes. In Matala people tend to drink more than eat. However, in the row of tavernas overlooking the beach, the **Syrtaki** has the centre spot and serves all the Greek favourites (with barrelled wine) at reasonable prices. At the end of the bay, **Neosilos** has the most idyllic setting of all, and the speciality is fish (3000 dr.). Near the Corali pension, **Antonio's** serves inexpensive, reliable Greek food (2000 dr.) and the **Blue Restaurant** has fish, meat and pizza in the same price range.

The best place to eat in Malia is in the old village, where the tavernas are authentic and the atmosphere pleasant. Locate the churches and then take your pick of the bunch, all serving good wine and local food at fair prices—**Kipouli, Zorba's** or **Maria's House**—none will disappoint.

Ag. Nikolaos

When Ag. Nikolaos became capital of *nomos* Lassithi only 95 people lived there.Today its summertime population reaches 10,000. Of all the Cretan capitals, Ag. Nikolaos caters most obviously to the cosmopolitan crowd, and has made tourism its sugar daddy. For that reason it tends to be rather expensive, its oft-extolled smallness, charm and quaintness is its business. However, because of ever increasing displays of drunkenness and rowdiness, and surly service in most cafés and restaurants, it's not the place to find Crete at its best.

Tourist Office: 20 Akti Koundourou, ✆ (0841) 22 357.

Tourist Police: in town, ✆ (0841) 26 900.

Around Town

In ancient times, Ag. Nikolaos was the port of Lato and the town still concentrates much of its rather mercenary soul around the port and picturesque little **Lake Voulismeni**, more than 60 m deep. In 1907 Voulismeni was connected to the sea. A sad bird or two is pent up in an attempt at an aviary at its far end. Restaurants and cafés line every available space on the waterfront. Akti Koundourou follows the sea shore, past rocky places where you can swim. There is a beach at the very end and the church that gave the town its name **Ag. Nikolaos**, with 9th- and 14th-century frescoes (ask at the police station for the key). A second old church, the 12th-century church **Panayia** is off Plateia Venizelou. The modest **Archaeology Museum** up the hill on Kon. Palaiologo (*closed Mon*) displays Minoan and later artefacts discovered in Eastern Crete.

Ag. Nikolaos bus station is near a rocky beach at the end of Sof. Venizelou St. **Beaches** within easy bus range are Elounda (*see* below) Kalo Chorio (on the road to Sitia), Ammoudi and, a couple of kilometres to the east is Almyros, the local nudist beach, lined with bamboo. There are also daily boat excursions from the port to other beaches, as well as to Spinalonga and to the so-called sunken city, Olous.

Festivals

6 December, Ag. Nikolaos; 29 May, Ag. Triada. Nautical week 27 June–3 July, with fireworks on the last day.

Where to Stay

Sometimes it seems as if all of Europe has descended on Ag. Nikolaos, and if you come unprepared, sleeping on the beach is a wretched alternative.

luxury

Ag. Nikolaos' reputation as a posey tourist hotspot owes much to the very luxurious hotels in the area, of which the most famous is the **Astir Palace** in Elounda, 10 km outside the town, ✆ 41 580, with 200 plush rooms and 96 bungalows. Half pension is obligatory in midsummer. Equally sumptuous is the **Minos Beach** with 132 bungalows on the secluded promontory of Akti Elia Sotirchou, ✆ 22 345—all spanking new and modern, the grounds decorated with modern sculpture. The complex includes three good restaurants, but the beach is crummy—however Elounda Beach is only a 10-minute drive away.

Panorama on Akti Koundourou, ℂ 28 890, has a good view over the harbour, and all rooms come with bath. On a more modest level, **Hotel New York** at 21a Kontogiani St, ℂ 28 577, is known for having rooms when the other hotels are all booked up with package tours. It's very near the bus station. Even nearer is the **Possidonas**, which has rooms for the same price, ℂ 24 086.

The delightful **Green House** pension at 15 Modatsou, ℂ 22 025, will charm you with its little wooden rooms leading out to a small courtyard, filled to overflowing with shrubs and trees, and patrolled by a small army of cats. Shared facilities and friendly owners. If you plan to stay for several days, immediately next to the youth hostel on Strat. Koraka 7 is a small family-run pension (it has no name, but ℂ is 22 525) with cooking facilities and immaculately clean modern rooms at a very reasonable 4000 dr. Otherwise, your best bet may well be taking pot luck at the bus station, where anyone with an available room to let will offer it as you arrive.

Eating Out

A favourite with tourists and locals alike is the **Trata** near Kitroplateia, with standard Greek food, lovely roof garden, reasonable prices, and it's sparkling clean (1500–2000 dr.). Just up from the bus station, in the direction of the central square, are two small tavernas, the **Posidon** and opposite, the **Roumeli** serving, unexpectedly, specialities from central Greece. They are popular places, especially with Greek visitors, for the *kokoretsi, kondasouvli* and souvlaki, all grilled over coals. At both expect to pay 1500 dr. for dinner. The **Pine** serves charcoal-grilled meat and fish by the lake, where you can sit outside and, if your luck is in, have a front seat for a free show of Cretan music and dance (2000 dr.). Just up the hill from the lake you can enjoy dinner in a pleasant garden setting at **Aouas**, with good grilled food, standard dishes and barrelled Cretan wine (1500–2000 dr.).

On Kitroplateia beach the romantic **Myrto** has lovely views across the water to the province of Sitia. Excellent grilled food, especially chicken (2000 dr). The last taverna on the stretch, the **Oriental**, serves delicious Egyptian specialities (2000 dr.). At Ammoudi beach the **Dirina**, opposite the Minos Beach Hotel, has become very popular not only for its food but also for its lively, fun atmosphere, and you may have no choice but to get up and dance—if not to the Greek music then to an old-fashioned ballroom number (2000 dr.). Down by the bus station are a couple of places where you can eat your fill of souvlaki, chicken or hamburgers with chips, salad and retsina for around 1000 dr., while savouring murals of Canadian mountains and pots of plastic ivy on the walls.

Nomos Lassithi

Nomos Lassithi (the name comes from a corruption of the Venetian La Sitia) is the most varied county in Crete: its famous mountain plain covered with windmills is too cold for olives, but produces apples, wheat and potatoes, while down at the eastern end there is Vai, a luxuriant palm-lined tropical beach. Lassithians claim to be the best lovers in Crete, although this is not by any means unanimously agreed by other Cretans; they do, however, give credit to Lassithi for its potatoes and pigs. The *Erotokritos* poet Kornaros was from *nomos*, as well as a pope and Zeus himself, and a church near Ag. Nikolaos, Panayia Kera, has the best fresco paintings in Crete.

Mirambelou Bay

The beautiful bay that lends Ag. Nikolaos its panache got its name from Genoese fortress of Mirabello, demolished by the Turks. It is dotted with islets: opposite Ag. Nikolaos is the islet **Ag. Pandes**, a refuge for the *kri kri*. The chapel of the same name draws pilgrims on 20 June, but to visit at other times you need special permission. Other islets in Mirambelou Bay are to the east: **Psira** and **Mohlos**, both with Minoan ruins. You can hire caiques from Ag. Nikolaos or the village of Mohlos to visit them, although Mohlos islet is a stone's throw from the mainland, and if you can't find a caique, you can always swim out to it.

Elounda and Westward

Twelve kilometres northwest of Ag. Nikolaos is **Elounda**, on the site of **Olous**, the unexcavated port of Dreros. Inscriptions from the 2nd century BC prove a treaty between Rhodes and Olous, and the walls of the port are submerged in the sea. The moon goddess Artemis Britomartis, inventor of the fishing net, was worshipped at the city; the city was reported to have a wooden cult statue (made by Daedalus) of the goddess with a fish tail because she escaped the amorous pursuit of Minos by turning into a fish. Curiously enough, a basilica with fish mosaics has been excavated to the northwest of the village. Almost overnight Elounda has become a resort town and makes an attractive alternative to Ag. Nikolaos. The central *plateia* is a particularly pleasant place to sit and relax, and take in the sea view. There are plenty of places to swim here, and if you've brought your snorkelling gear, so much the better.

Spinalonga, a half-hour caique trip from Elounda (the journey can also be made from Ag. Nikolaos) is a small islet created by Venetian engineers when they dug a canal separating it from the Kolokytha ('squash' or 'marrow') peninsula. In 1579 they built a huge fortress on Spinalonga, on the ruins of the ancient fort of Olous. During the Turkish occupation Spinalonga held out like the other small island forts of Nea Souda and Grambousa, until the Venetians handed it over by treaty to the Ottomans in 1715. The Turks settled it with soldiers and civilians. When they were evacuated in 1904, Spinalonga became a leper colony—the last in Europe—that survived until 1957, when it was realized that leprosy wasn't contagious. Today the poignant little streets, houses and the lepers' church are

NOMOS LASSITHI, CRETE

Cape Sideros

Cape Plaka

Dragonan

Gianysada

Koufonisi

Vai

Itanós **Ⅱ**

Toplou **Ⅱ**

Petsofas **Ⅱ**

Palaikastro

Kato Zakro

Zakro

Xiro

Kambos

Ziros

Praisos **Ⅱ**

Handras

Etia

Goudouros

Sitia

Piskokephelo **Ⅱ**

Zou **Ⅱ**

Lithine

Maronia

Makri Yalos

Chamezi **Ⅱ**

Mouliana

Mesa **Ⅱ**
Mouliana

Mochlos

Myrsini

Kavousi

Psira

Marimbelou Bay

Spinalonga

AG. NIKOLAOS

Ag. Pandes

Pahia Ammos

Koutsouras

Gournia **Ⅱ**

Vrokastro Vasiliki **Ⅱ**

Faneromenos Monastery

Episkopi

Ierapetra

Plaka

Elounda

Olous **Ⅱ**

Kalo Chorio

Lato **Ⅱ**

Kritsa

Kroustas

Kalamafka

Dreros **Ⅱ**

Zenia

Males

Myrtos **Ⅱ**

Pyrgos **Ⅱ**

Gaidouronisi

Milatos **Ⅱ**

Ag. Georgios Selinaris

Neapolis

Ag. Georgios

Karphi **Ⅱ**

Tzermiadon

Psychro

Plain of Lassithi

Plati

Diktean Cave

Mt. Dikti
(2142m / 7045ft) ▲

▲ Mt. Afendis

Krasi

Kera

Malia

To Ano Viannos

N

km

miles

0   5   10

0   5   10   15   20

abandoned. **Plaka**, opposite the islet, was the supply centre for the lepers and is popular today with those seeking rest and relaxation.

West of Elounda a road leads up to a saddle between two hills and ancient **Dreros**, discovered at the beginning of this century. Its remains include walls, a cistern, an Archaic agora and a Geometric temple to Apollo Delphinios built in the 7th century BC, which yielded the oldest hammered bronze statues ever found in Greece. **Milatos** to the north of Dreros was considered an enemy. Tradition has it that when Sarpedon, one of Minos' brothers, won the affections of a certain boy the brothers had quarrelled over, he left Crete for Asia Minor, taking not only the boy but the inhabitants of Milatos, and they founded the great city of Miletus. In the 3rd century BC the Lyttians destroyed Milatos. During the War of Independece, the **Cave of Milatos** served as a refuge for 2700 people. Upon their discovery the Turks besieged them, and after two battles the refugees surrendered, as the Turks had previously promised them safe conduct—a promise they betrayed when they massacred all the old men and children, and enslaved the women. The cave is 3 km out of the village on an unpaved road.

Neapolis is the largest village on the road to Herakleon; in its former incarnation as a village named Kares, it witnessed the birth of Petros Filagros in 1340. Raised by Catholics, he became a professor of theology and was elected Pope Alexander V in 1409, one of several popes-for-a-year during the Great Schism. His native village Kares predeceased him, however, when the Venetians thoroughly destroyed it in 1347 after a revolt. The rebuilt town became the 'new town', Neapolis. It has a small museum with items from Elounda and Dreros, and on 14–15 August a large paneyeri celebrates the Assumption. West of Milatos, on the highway from Herakleon, many Greek buses and cars stop at the shrine of **Ag. Georgios Selinaris** with its miraculous icon.

South of Neapolis, the small village of **Zenia** has the following tale: during the Turkish occupation there lived a lovely young girl in Zenia who had hair down to her knees. Her beauty caught the eye of the Turkish captain, who threatened to destroy the village if she would not marry him. On those terms, she reluctantly agreed. During the wedding feast she poured him more wine than he could hold, and during the night she decapitated him. Running to the church, she cut off her famous hair and took the clothes of a soldier and the name of Captain Manolis, performing many heroic deeds before she was killed. Her hair and the murder weapon are still on display in the Zenia church.

The Plain of Lassithi and the Birthplace of Zeus

The spectacular high **Plain of Lassithi** is connected by regular public bus with both Herakleon and Ag. Nikolaos; many tour buses make the ascent too, and you may want to spend a night or two in one of the 18 villages on the plain—Tzermiadon, the largest, Psychro and Ag. Georgios all have rooms—to get an idea of what the place is really like. For it is unique: a green carpet hemmed in on all sides by the Lassithi Mountains, irrigated by white-sailed windmills, 10,000 in all. This scenic way of supplying water was designed by Venetian engineers in 1464, to re-establish the orchards that had been destroyed to punish rebellious locals. Although fewer than 6000 of the windmills are in use today, they still make a splendid sight against the mountains—snowcapped into April—and patchwork fields and orchards of the plain.

Of all the villages encircling the plain, **Tzermiadon** (pop. 1500) is the largest and has the most tourist facilities and a *paneyeri* on 6 November. Its **Trapeza cave** was inhabited in Neolithic times, but today you can only see the entrance, as its mouth has been boarded up to prevent accidents. Tzermiadon's **Kroustalenia Monastery** was built in 1541, and housed the local revolutionary council during the war. From Tzermiadon you can walk to the ancient city of **Karphi** ('the nail'), excavated by John Pendlebury from 1937 to 1939. Karphi served as a city of Minoan refuge from the Doric invaders in 1100 BC, but its difficult situation caused it to be abandoned later. Still visible are the temple, chieftain's house, tower and barracks, and there is an especially lovely view of Lassithi. The walk up takes about 1½ hours.

Psychro, on the west end of the plain, is the base for visiting the **Diktean cave**, the birthplace of Zeus. Ascent can be made easily by foot or by donkeys which are available at the site along with local guides. Descent into the often-slippery cave is rather more difficult, and it is advisable to wear old trousers and rubber-soled shoes and to bring a torch, although candles are available at the site. The cave, only rediscovered in the 1880s, contained relics from Middle Minoan up to Archaic times. According to the Homeric *Hymn of the Kouretes*, Zeus was hidden in this cave by his mother Rhea (*see* p. 87). A niche in the cave wall is known as his cradle while a curtain of large stalactites has been dubbed 'Zeus' mantle'. Other stories claim that Europa conceived Minos in the cave, and that when he became king he went there every nine years for paternal advice from Zeus. While the cult objects found suggest a continuity of worship at Dikti before and after the Doric invasion, in a later period the worship of Zeus was transferred to the Idean cave.

In Psychro a tourist pavilion caters to cave visitors, and there are other restaurants and small hotels and rooms. On 29–31 August there is a 3-day *paneyeri* in the village. Nearby **Ag. Georgios**, site of a new folklore museum, celebrates its eponymous on 23 April. **Plati**, west of Psychro, has the remains of a Minoan settlement, inhabited before and after the Doric invasion.

If you descend from the Lassithi Plain by the Herakleon road, there are two tempting stops: the hilltop village of **Kera**, where the 12th-century **Monastery Kardiotissa** has good frescoes, and further down, **Krasi**, built around the largest plane tree on Crete, some 80 ft in circumference.

Kritsa and Kroustas

Lovely **Kritsa** west of Ag. Nikolaos is the 'authentic' Cretan village swamped by tourists from the capital. Its architecture is delightful (although destroyed by the Saracens, it was reconstructed after the liberation of Crete by Nikephoros Phokas) and there are fine views of the bay below; it's convenient for excursions to ancient Lato, and particularly to the magnificent church of **Kera Panayia** (*9–12 noon and 2–5*). Built in the early 13th century, the entire wall surface is covered with magnificent frescoes, depicting the life of Mary's mother,

St Anne, of Mary herself, and other scenes from the New Testament. On 15 August a *paneyeri* is held at the church, and around this time traditional Cretan weddings are enacted with food and dancing, in which you can participate for a fee.

The extensive remains of Archaic **Lato** (or Goulas) are an hour's walk above Kritsa, or a rough drive, but are splendidly situated in a depression between two hills that formed twin acropolises. Built in the 7th century BC, Minoan influences have been noted in the architecture of its agora and stairway. Lato's streets are paved with flagstones, and the walls have a double gateway. There are remains of temples, houses, a cistern and a Hellenic *prytaneion*, or meeting place of the elders.

A few buses from Kritsa continue up to **Kroustas** which is just as pretty but has been spared the tourist hordes. It has some Byzantine frescoed churches and a huge festival on 25 June, the feast of St John, celebrated with bonfires and dances. A rough road continues through the village to flower-bedecked **Prina**, affording magnificent views over Kalo Chorio and the sea below.

The Coast East of Ag. Nikolaos

Frequent buses from Ag. Nikolaos go to the popular beach at **Kalo Chorio;** from Kalo Chorio's model farm a path leads to **Vrokastro**, inhabited from 1000 BC and used as a refuge settlement during the Doric invasion. A Geometric-era fort stands on the hill. Another site nearby, **Gournia**, was excavated by Harriet Boyd Hawes between 1901 and 1904, the first woman to lead a major archaeological dig. It is the best-preserved Minoan town on Crete, having reached its peak in 1600 BC; along its narrow lanes, workshops, storerooms, houses and a small palace were uncovered, as well as signs of a mine near the shore. From Gournia, it's a short walk or drive to **Pahia Ammos**, a growing resort with a good beach.

To the south (the road turns near Gournia) is the late Byzantine monastery **Faneromenos**, high on the hill and the site of many resistance activities during the Turkish occupation. Another road south of Pahia Ammos runs to **Vasiliki**, where an Early Minoan settlement was discovered at the beginning of this century by two Americans, Boyd and Seager. Mottled red and black Minoan pottery was first found on the site, giving it the name Vasiliki ware. Red-plastered rooms, corridors and a courtyard of the palace remain among other ruins from Mycenaean and Roman times. If you're aiming for Sitia from Pahia Ammos, the new road is perhaps the island's most scenic, a long winding serpent slithering along a jagged and often precipitous coast.

South to Ierapetra

If you're heading south, the road from Pahia Ammos bisects the narrowest part of Crete (12 km) to **Ierapetra** (pop. 7000), the southernmost town in Europe—a mere 370 km from Egypt. In mythology Ierapetra was founded by the Telchines, those ugliest of nymphs, with their dog heads and seal flippers. The name they gave Ierapetra was Kamiros, like that of another city they had founded on Rhodes, but when their presence on Crete continued to foul up the weather, Zeus sent them elsewhere. The Dorians renamed the town Ierapytna. It prospered in the Hellenistic period, becoming the most powerful city in eastern Crete, but was destroyed by the Romans, as punishment for being the last Cretan city to hold out against them. However, the Romans rebuilt it in such grand style that Ierapetra soon recovered. Under the Byzantines it was the seat of a bishop, but it was sacked by the Saracens and toppled by an earthquake in 1508.

In the 13th century the Venetians built their **Kastelli**, a well-preserved fort which overlooks a port bobbing with fishing and pleasure craft. Nearby is the house where tradition claims that Napoleon spent the night of 26 June 1798, before sailing off to campaign in Egypt. There's an interesting mosque and minaret nearby, and to the west, a few Roman remains including a theatre. The most beautiful thing in this rather dull town is in its one-room museum, in the Town Library: a Late-Minoan painted sarcophagus found in Episkopi. While in summer it can be very hot, Ierapetra is very pleasant in the winter, when it draws a large contingent of heat-seeking retirees and gadabouts. There is a youth hostel and some hotels, but the best of its long beaches are to the east towards Makriyialos. On 3 October every year a big festival celebrates the 1821 revolution.

Along the coast west of Ierapetra is **Myrtos**, where in 1968 the British School excavated an early Minoan town which had been a weaving centre, dating from 2500 to 2100 BC. Some of the finds are in the Myrtos schoolhouse, while the more important ones are in the Ag. Nikolaos museum. Further west in **Pyrgos** a Minoan villa has been found with large rooms and a stairway. One popular way of going to Myrtos other than by the new road, is to walk through the river bed from **Males**, after taking in Males' frescoed church, Panayia Messochoritissa (1431). On route, there's another Byzantine church, Ag. Georgios, further south in a ruined village.

East of Ierapetra

Along the coastal road east of Ierapetra, old houses at **Koutsouras** have been restored and are rented out to visitors; in **Makri Yialos**, an excellent sandy beach has its complement of pensions and a campsite. To the north, the village **Etia** was one of the major towns in the Byzantine and Venetian periods, noted for its lovely setting. The region was ruled by the De Mezzo family, who in the 15th century built a fortified *palazzo*, considered the most beautiful Venetian building on Crete. It was three storeys high, with vaulted ceilings and sculptured decorations. The Turks were besieged in the palace, however, and a later fire and earthquake finished the destruction, although today it has been partially restored. Of the many outlying buildings, the wall, gate and fountain house have inscriptions.

Ag. Sofia monastery is close by, towards the village of **Handras**. During the Turkish occupation it served as a fortress and secret Greek school, and was often besieged and destroyed. **Praisos**, the ancient city north of Handras, has three acropolises. Habitation dates from Late Minoan to Hellenistic times, and walls and houses remain. Praisos was the stronghold of the Eteocretans—the 'true Cretans' or descendants of the Minoans—but was destroyed by Ierapetra in 155 BC.

Kato Zakro and the East Coast

East of Praisos is **Zakro**, a market village at the head of a huge, grandly scenic gorge that leads down to the Minoan palace of **Kato Zakro**. Minoan tombs from 2600 BC found along the way have given rise to the name 'Gorge of Death'. By foot it's a good 8-km walk, but softies can take the road along the top of the ravine.

The Minoan town of Zakro was excavated by the English archaeologist Hogarth in 1901, but the palace itself was only found in 1961 by N. Platon, and because the east coast of Crete is sinking, part of the excavations are under water. Built around 1600 BC, the palace suddenly collapsed in the general catastrophe of 1450 BC, followed by fire. Among its remains are a central court, a west wing with inscriptions, magazines, a Lustral Basin, archives, and a banquet hall with fragments of its original decoration. After the disaster, the surrounding town of narrow cobblestoned streets was rebuilt, but the palace lay untouched. The evidence of such a large settlement in Zakro, which could hardly have been supported by agriculture, demonstrates how extensively the Minoans traded by sea. There are rooms to let and tavernas in Kato Zakro and a delightful beach. Back up in Zakro itself (there's nowhere else to go) a Minoan villa has been uncovered with wall paintings and wine presses, and on a summit is a round, Hellenistic beacon tower.

The road north of Zakro leads to **Petsofas**, where a peak sanctuary dedicated to the fertility goddess yielded a trove of votive offerings. Further north is **Palaikastro**, the last bus stop for **Vai**, a beautiful beach of silver sand lined with Europe's only wild date palms (some say they were planted by the Saracens). Unfortunately, it has become a stop on the package tour itinerary, so on any given day expect to share this little tropical paradise with hundreds of peeling bodies—unless everyone's been chased off for the filming of another Bounty Bar ad. The ancient Cretans appreciated Vai as well: at **Roussolakos** there's a late Minoan settlement with streets and houses by the sea, and on the hill at **Kastri**, the ruins date from Geometric to Hellenistic times. A Classical temple to Diktean Zeus existed there, and a hymn to Zeus from the 4th century was found engraved on a stone. Palaikastro has a fine beach lined with restaurants and tavernas, and, 2 km out on the road to Vai a small road leads down to hidden Kouremenos beach.

To the north, near Cape Sideros, lies ancient **Itanos**, accessible by the road from Palaikastro or Toplou. Also known as Erimoupolis, this was inhabited from Early Minoan times, although the stones there today are Geometric to Hellenistic. Ptolemy used Itanos as a naval station, and the city thrived on the trade of dyes and glass. Ruins of an Early Christian settlement are below, but this and the small 15th-century village were deserted because of pirate raids. Itanos also has quiet, sandy beaches, a much more pleasant alternative to suffering the coachloads at Vai.

Toplou

Southwest of Itanos is the famous **monastery of Toplou**. Its real name is Panayia Akroteriani, but the name *toplou* ('cannon' in Turkish, named for the monks' mighty piece of ordnance) is more popular. Believed to have been founded in the late 15th-century by the Kornaros family, Toplou was repaired after the earthquake of 1612: it stands three storeys high, a veritable castle with a tall Italian campanile dated 1558. Above the monastery gate is a hole, the *fonias*, through which the besieged monks used to pour hot oil onto their attackers.

The monastery has a venerable history as a place of refuge and resistance. At the beginning of the War of Independence in 1821, the Turks captured it and hung twelve monks over the gate as a warning. At the end of the war, the Turks found themselves in turn attacked by Cretans and surrendered the monastery when the Cretans offered to spare the lives of other Turkish prisoners. Cretan occupation of Toplou ended when the Great Powers decided the island should remain Turkish. There is a very beautiful icon in the monastery painted by Ioannis Kornaros in 1770 entitled 'Great is the Lord', one of the masterpieces of Cretan art. There are other icons, manuscripts and a Hellenistic inscription recounting the arbitration of Magnesia in an argument between Itanos and Ierapytna. One of the aisles in the church is part of a chapel to Ag. Isidoros, built when Nikephoros Phokas liberated Crete; it gave its name to Cape Sideros.

Sitia

West of Toplou is the sleepy town of **Sitia** (Sithia in the softer Cretan pronunciation). The site was once occupied by ancient Eteia, the birthplace of Myson, one of the Seven Sages of Greece. In the 17th century, Sitia gave the world Vincenzo Kornaros, author of the *Erotokritos*, the Cretan national epic of a love found, lost, and found again between Erotokritos and Aretousa, daughter of the King of Athens. Once surrounded by Byzantine, Genoese and Venetian walls, as well as a Venetian fortress, little now remains of these defences in Sitia, thanks to earthquakes and the bombardment of Barbarossa. The **Archaeology Museum** on the road out of town to the south has interesting exhibits from the Neolithic to the late Roman period, most locally excavated. There's also a small **Folklore museum** on G. Arkadion St with colourful examples of local arts and crafts. Today Sitia exports raisins and is known for its wine. In the middle of August, a 3-day wine festival is held here. There is a lovely youth hostel run by a slightly mad Englishman, and there are many tavernas and restaurants along the shady waterfront.

The region around Sitia has a plethora of minor archaeological sites. South of Sitia is **Piskokephelo**, another peak sanctuary, near which an ancient farm has been excavated. On 24 June a large festival is held in the village. **Zou**, to the south, has a Minoan village, while a cave in **Maronia** contained Early Minoan finds. **Lithine**, even further south, is a charming village with the remains of a once important Venetian tower. On the handsome 'Cretan Riviera'—the corniche road west to Ag. Nikolaos, **Chamezi** has an oval, prehistoric house or sanctuary. Two beehive tombs in **Mesa Mouliana** date from the end of the Bronze Age; and in **Exo Mouliana**, famous for its red wine, is a frescoed church, Ag. Georgios (1426). **Myrsini** is a Venetian village with important Minoan tombs in the vicinity; and **Kavousi** had a small Sub-Minoan settlement and a peak sanctuary, although little now remains of them.

luxury

The **Lyktos Beach Hotel**, ✆ (0842) 61 480, is the queen of the luxury resort hotels on the coast near Ierapetra. Seven km from town, it sits on a lovely beach, and offers 7 floodlit tennis courts, watersports, gymnasium, sauna, jacuzzi, basketball and volleyball courts, children's pool, 3 restaurants, nightclub and piano bar. 'Let yourself be pampered' is their slogan, and pampered you will be. All rooms are air conditioned and have their own balcony or terrace. In a similar vein, but on a smaller scale is **Sunwing** at Makri Yialos, ✆ (0843) 51 002.

expensive

Eight km east of Ierapetra you can stay in one of the **Traditional Cottages** at Koutsounari, ✆ (0842) 61 291, each decorated in Cretan style, and with full cooking facilities. The beach is an 800-m walk. In town itself, and on the so-so town beach, the brand new, pristine **Astron**, 56 M. Kothri, ✆ (0842) 25 114, is a pleasant, friendly hotel, and all rooms are air conditioned, with sea view balconies.

moderate

In Sitia there are many places to choose from. **Hotel Itanos** on Plateia Venizelou, ✆ (0843) 22 146, is a classy C class near the park. Good value are the modern **Alice**, 34 Papanastassiou, ✆ (0843) 28 450, in a good position and offering Cretan evenings once a week; the **Crystal**, 17 Kapetan Sifi, ✆ (0843) 22 284, 50 m from the water, with modern, comfortable rooms; and in the centre of the action, above Zorba's restaurant, the **Denis**, 60 El. Venizelou, ✆ (0843) 28 356. In Ierapetra there are also many mid-range hotels and pensions; the **Hotel Iris**, 36 M. Kothri, ✆ (0842) 23 136, by the water, with 12 pleasant rooms, is typical for price and comfort, as is **El Greco**, 42 M. Kothri, ✆ (0842) 28 471. If you don't fancy staying in town, you may do better to go west along the coast to Myrtos and the **Myrtos Hotel**, ✆ (0842) 51 215. The best hotel in Tzermiadon up on the Plain of Lassithi, is the **Kourites**, ✆ (0844) 22 194.

cheap

Things up on the plain are cheaper in Ag. Georgios; try the **Rhea Hotel**, ✆ (0844) 31 209. In Psychro, where many people stay, there are quite a few rooms to supplement the class D **Zeus**, ✆ (0844) 31 284, and the class E **Dikteon Andron**, ✆ (0844) 31 504. In Sitia the **Hotel Stars**, at 37 M. Kolyvaki, ✆ (0843) 22 917 offers some peace and quiet, and convenience for ferry boats. The **youth hostel** at 4 Therissou St, ✆ (0843) 22 693 is just east of town and again, quite pleasant and friendly, with kitchen facilities and a garden. In Ierapetra the nicest cheap hotel is the **Ierapytna** on Plateia Ag. Ioannou Kale, ✆ (0842) 28 530. There are campsites at Pahia Ammos, ✆ (0842) 93 243, and Ierapetra, ✆ (0842) 61 351.

There are plenty of little tavernas on the Lassithi, some catering to the local trade, some to the tourists. **Kronias Restaurant** in Tzermiadon is somewhere in between; the food is good and the price is surprisingly low. If you're going to eat fish in Crete, Sitia is the place to do it. The prices are reasonable and, it's said, the fish tastes the best. **Zorba's** has a wonderful location on the water, and although the ready food can look a bit tired, the seafood and grilled meats are fresh and delicious (2500 dr.). Two other good choices are **Paragadi**, serving very reasonably priced Greek specialities, and the more expensive **Kolios**. Two km out on the road to Ierapetra, look out for **Klimateria**, a country taverna serving wonderful *meze* and grilled foods. If you feel like steak and chips at 4 am, while you're waiting for the ferry to Karpathos or Rhodes, the **Faros Taverna** is open 24 hours a day. It's by the second harbour where the big ferries dock. Two km out in the other direction **Karavopetka** is next to the sea and also serves good *meze*; try their sausages *omaties*, a local speciality. Near Palaikastro look out for the tiny fishing village of **Chionas**, which has some very good fish tavernas, at least one open 24 hours.

In Ierapetra, the great favourite is **Napoleon**, on the waterfront, with authentic Greek and Cretan food. Fresh fish (the owner has his own caique) and varieties of snails are specialities. Don't turn up on Sunday, though—the owner takes the sabbath seriously. Good local dishes can also be had at the **Gorgora** and **Konakei**. There are two British restaurants here also, if you're missing mum's cooking. Out at Vai there's a mediocre taverna overlooking the crowded beach—and if you wonder why people are hopping about in the water, it's because the fish there actually bite!

The Cyclades

The Harbourside at Mykonos

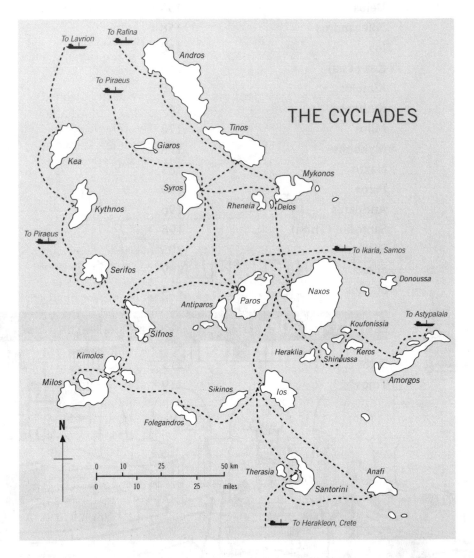

THE CYCLADES

To Lavrion
To Rafina
Andros
To Piraeus
Tinos
Giaros
Kea
Mykonos
Syros
Kythnos
Rheneia
Delos
To Piraeus
To Ikaria, Samos
Serifos
Donoussa
Naxos
Antiparos
Paros
To Astypalaia
Sifnos
Koufonissia
Kimolos
Heraklia
Keros
Shinoussa
Amorgos
Milos
Sikinos
Ios
Folegandros

N

0   10   25   50 km
0   10   25   miles

Therasia
Anafi
Santorini
To Herakleon, Crete

Say Greek island, and many people picture one of the Cyclades: barren, rock rising from a crystal sea, little villages with asymmetrical white houses and labyrinthine streets fit only for dwarfs, a pocket-sized church squeezed in at every corner. As the Cyclades are close together, one can visit a variety of the islands without losing much of the holiday in transit; in the summer there are daily communications between them. Within the Cyclades (the 'circling' islands, around sacred Delos) you'll find such constant favourites as Mykonos, Santorini and Paros, but also Heraklia and Anafi, among the least spoiled islands in Greece.

Archaeological evidence suggests that the Cyclades have been inhabited since at least 6000 BC, the first settlers arriving from what is now Karia in Asia Minor and speaking a non-Greek language. At the beginning of the Bronze Age (3000–2000 BC) the islanders developed a culture known as Early Cycladic, which if nothing else had a staggeringly modern sense of design, at least in their elegant, almost abstract marble figurines.

In myth, King Minos of Crete conquered the Aegean Islands in order to rid himself of his overly-just brother Rhadamanthys, whom he sent to administer the new Cretan colonies. This corresponds to the Minoan influence that marks the prosperous Middle Cycladic period, when artists adopted a more natural style. The Late Cycladic period coincides with the fall of Crete and the rise of the Mycenaeans. When the Mycenaeans in turn fell to the uncouth Dorians, the islands dropped out of history for hundreds of years. The luckier islands fell under sway of the Ionians and at the end of the 8th century BC, were part of the Ionian cultural rebirth called the Archaic period.

The rise of the Persians forced the Ionians to flee westwards to Attica, leaving the islands in Persian hands; several islands sided with the Persians at Marathon and Salamis, and were subsequently punished by Athens. To prevent future breakaways, Athens obliged the islands to enter into the new maritime league at Delos in 478 BC, replacing an older Ionian council, or Amphictyony. But what began as a league of allies gradually turned into vassals paying tribute to the Athenians, whose fleet was the only one capable of protecting the islands from the Persian menace. Cycladic resentment often flared into open revolt, and the Athenians had to work ever harder to extort the islands' annual contribution of money and ships.

During the Peloponnesian War the islands tended to side with the front-runner at any given time, and many jumped at the chance to support Sparta against their Athenian oppressors. But when Athens recovered from the war in 378 BC, it was only to form a second Delian league, again subjugating the Cyclades. Most of the islands turned to Philip of Macedon as a saviour from the Athenian bullies, only to be fought over a generation later by the generals of Alexander the Great. Only the 2nd-century BC

Roman conquest brought the Cyclades peace, except for the islands given to Rhodes, a less kindly ruler than distant Rome. The fall of Rome spelt centuries of hardship; although the Cyclades were officially part of the Byzantine Empire, Constantinople could not protect them from marauders prowling the high seas, and the islanders were left to fend for themselves, building villages in the most inaccessible places possible.

When Constantinople fell in 1204, the Frankish conquerors allotted the Aegean to the Venetians, and the Archipelago, as the Venetians called it, became a free for all between grasping young noblemen and pirates (often one and the same). The Cyclades became the special territory of Marco Sanudo, nephew of the leader of the Fourth Crusade, Doge Enrico Dandolo. Marco Sanudo declared himself Duke of Naxos and ruled that island and Paros, and gave his faithful thugs the smaller islands as fiefs. The Sanudos gave way to the Crispi dynasty in 1383, but threatened by pirates and the growing Ottoman Empire Venice herself stepped in to police the Cyclades at the end of the 15th century. There was little even Venice could do against the fierce renegade admiral Khair-ed-din-Barbarossa, who systematically decimated the islands. By the mid-16th century they were under Turkish domination, ruled by a puppet Duke of Naxos.

Venetian priests had converted many of the Greeks on the Cyclades to Catholicism, in particular on Syros, and despite the Ottoman occupation both Orthodox and Catholic monasteries thrived. Turkish rule in the Archipelago was harsh only in economic terms and most of the islands were spared the cruelties inflicted on Crete. From 1771–74, one of the more outlandish episodes in Greek history brought a brief interlude from the Ottomans: Russia and Turkey were at each other's throats over Poland, so Catherine the Great decided to open a second front in the war by capitalizing on Greek discontent. Her fleet in the Aegean led an insurrection against the Sultan and occupied some of the Cyclades. By the time the Russians gave it up and went home, they had made themselves unpopular with all concerned.

When the Greek War of Independence broke out, the Cyclades offered naval support and provided a safe harbour for refugees; the islands with Catholic populations were brought under the protection of the French and remained neutral in the conflict. Nevertheless, the Cyclades were soon incorporated in the new Greek state, and Syros became the country's leading port until Piraeus took over with the advent of the steamship. Today Syros' capital, Ermoupolis, is still the largest town and administrative centre of the Cyclades.

Before the advent of tourism, the population of the Cyclades dropped to an all time low; it was simply too hard to make a living from the dry, rocky soil. Even now, the winter months can be lonely as many islanders retreat to flats in Athens. The climate, more than anywhere else in Greece, is influenced by the winds. Winter is plagued by the *voreas*, the north wind that turns ship schedules into a fictional romance. After March the sirocco blows from the south, warming islands still green from the winter rains. By July many of the Cyclades look brown and parched, except where there are sources of underground water. From July to September the notorious *meltemi* from the Russian steppes huffs and puffs like the big bad wolf, quadrupling sales of dramamine in the ports. If you're really a landlubber you can fly: Paros, Mykonos, Milos, Santorini, Naxos and Syros have airports.

Water continues to be a problem on some islands, and it may be turned off for part of the day. However, since these islands are so popular with visitors (and thus important to the national economy) efforts have been made to ensure that they and their new hotels have ample water supplies, even in August.

Amorgos

Easternmost of the Cyclades, Amorgos is also one of the most dramatically rugged islands. On the south coast cliffs plunge vertically into the sea, and trying to cross the island from north to south by road is so rocky a journey that most people prefer to get about by caique. For many years Amorgos was a destination for the adventurous, then all of a sudden travellers arrived en masse seeking the quiet Cycladic life of their dreams, swooping down on Amorgos by surprise until there were people literally camping out in the streets. There still aren't enough rooms to accommodate everyone who would like to stay on the island, so if you come in the height of summer without a reservation be prepared to sleep under the stars.

History

Both Amorgos and its neighbouring islet Keros were inhabited as far back as 3300 BC. In 1885 the German archaeologist Dummler uncovered 11 ancient cemeteries, producing many fine ceramics and marbles now to be seen in the museums of Oxford and Copenhagen; artefacts pointed to early trade with Milos and Egypt. Three ancient independent cities occupied Amorgos, each minting its own coins and worshipping Dionysos and Athena: Kastri (modern Arkesini) was settled by Naxians, Minoa by Samians, and Aegiali by Milians.

After Alexander the Great, Amorgos came under the Hellenistic rule of Ptolemy of Egypt who made it a centre of worship of the Alexandrian gods, Serapis and Isis. The Romans used the island as a place of exile, beginning a downhill trend which continued as the island was ravaged by Goths, Vandals and Slavs during the Byzantine period. One bright moment in this dark history came during the War of the Iconoclasts, when a miraculous icon sailed to Amorgos, set adrift, according to tradition, by a religious lady from Constantinople. As the icon showed a distinct preference for staying by the cliffs on Amorgos' south coast, Emperor Alexis Comnenus founded the Chozoviotissa monastery there in 1088. In 1209 the Duke of

Naxos, Marco Sanudo, seized the island, and gave it to the Gizzi, who built the town castle. In spite of the Turkish occupation, Amorgos prospered in the 17th century, mostly from the export of exquisite embroideries made by the women, some of which are now in the Victoria and Albert Museum in London. Between the 17th and 19th centuries so many of these extraordinary pieces were sold, that a hero of the War of Independence, General Makriyiannis, threatened to declare war on Amorgos should the island send any more abroad. Rather than battle Makriyiannis, the island simply ran out of embroideries, and no one today remembers how to make them. The highlight of the island's more recent history occurred when Brigitte Bardot paid a visit in 1973.

Connections

Six times a week with Naxos and Paros, five times a week with Syros and Piraeus, four times a week with Heraklia, Koufonissia and Shinoussa, three times a week with Mykonos and Tinos, once a week with Astypalaia, Ios, Santorini and Anafi. Several times a week to these islands and Rafina by hydrofoil or catamaran.

Tourist Information

Information office on the quay in Katapola, © (0285) 71 278; also regular police, © 71 210.

Because of the condition of the road linking the two halves of Amorgos, ships tend to call at both island ports, **Katapola** in the south and **Aegiali** in the north. Katapola isn't much: a yacht supply station, a place to swim, a couple of hotels and a few pensions, and a bus up to the capital Chora. From Katapola you can walk up the hill to the ancient city of **Minoa** where walls, part of the acropolis, a gymnasium and a few remains of a temple to Apollo can still be seen. The name Minoa comes from Minos, the King of the Mountain, or Minos, the King of Crete, although the great city states of Amorgos were closely linked to the Ionians, geographically closer to Asia Minor than the other Cyclades. Also near Katapola is **Rahidi** where the church Ag. Georgios occupies the site of an ancient oracle.

The capital of **Amorgos**, also known as Chora, is a typical white Cycladic town, perched more than 300 m above sea level. A neat column of windmills (each family had its own) once laboured with the winds that rose up the dizzying precipices from the sea. In the middle of town, steps lead up the rocky mount to the well-preserved castle built by Geremia Gizzi in 1290. The locals call it **Apano Kastro**, and it affords a panoramic view of the island.

Chozoviotissa

A road has been built to the island's main sight, the grand **Monastery of Chozoviotissa** ('life saving') and cars have replaced mules as the easiest form of transport. Most people, however, prefer to make the 20-minute walk down the dramatic, serpentine path from the bus stop. Below, at the foot of a steep 180-m orange cliff stands the monastery—a huge white fortress, resembling one great wall built into the living rocks. The monastery is open mornings and after 5 pm; be sure to dress modestly to be allowed inside.

Within are some 50 rooms, two churches and exactly three monks. The miraculous icon of the Madonna from Constantinople is still in place, and the library contains 98 hand-written manuscripts. For many years a mysterious spear, thrown by an unknown hand, was stuck in the living rock of the cliff over the monastery, and although it finally fell, worn away by time, there are still many stories about it. In 1976 a less mysterious rock fell on the monastery and went crashing through three floors; repairs were carried out by the government.

Arkesini

The other ancient city in the southern half of Amorgos is **Arkesini**, which has extensive tombs, walls and houses, near the modern hamlet of **Kastri**, accessible on foot. A well-preserved Hellenistic tower may be seen near here at **Ag. Trias**. There are several quiet beaches (like **Kolofana**) in the south. Most people who stay in Chora swim off white **Ag. Anna** beach, the closest to town and the monastery; the water is deep blue and crystal clear.

Aegiali

Although it's easiest to reach the north side of Amorgos by boat, a rough road braves the wild terrain, guarded on either side by an occasional tower (the walk takes about 5 hours).

Aegiali, small and charming, is Amorgos' northern port and main resort, boasting the island's one genuine sandy beach. In some shops here, and in Chora, you can find embroidered scarves made locally, but they are nothing like the original embroideries of Amorgos. Near Aegiali you can take in the scant remains of ancient Aegiali; at **Tholaria** are Greek vaulted tholos tombs which date from the Roman period. A pleasant walk from Aegiali along the mule paths leads to **Potamos,** where the terrace of a tiny café has a commanding view of the port below, with its amphitheatre of hills, and the sunset.

Festivals

The good people of Amorgos have yet to become bored by tourism, and they go out of their way to invite guests to their celebrations: 26 July, Ag. Paraskevi at Arkesini; 15 August at Langada and 21 November at the Chozoviotissa Monastery.

Where to Stay

expensive

Set back from the waterfront on the other side of the bay in Katapola, is the attractive **St. George Balsamitis,** © 71 147, with breakfast included in its rates. In Aegiali, the **Aegialis,** © 73 244, is a smart hotel complex with pool and taverna, and a great view from the verandah.

moderate–cheap

In the port Katapola, there's the traditional-style **Hotel Minoa,** © 71 480, with reasonable rates, and several pensions, most prominently the **Pension Amorgos,** © 71 214. Most people prefer to stay elsewhere—in one of the numerous rooms in Chora (there are no official pensions or hotels here) or Aegiali, where you can choose between the ageing **Mike Hotel,** © 71 252, (open only in the summer) or the **Pension Lakki,** with a garden. Both are on the beach, where those who can't get rooms (or don't care to) can sleep out without too many hassles. Ag. Anna beach serves the same function on the south half of the island.

Eating Out

Amorgos has good, inexpensive, and very Greek tavernas in its main centres. In Chora you can sit in a whitewashed alley and eat at **Kastanis,** on the roof garden at **Zygos,** or take in the view from **Tsampoukas;** all serve similar Greek dishes. The deservedly most popular taverna by the sea in Katapola is **Vinzenzos,** where arriving late could mean missing the day's speciality; try the kid and potato casserole, stuffed aubergines with tomatoes, mushroom, parsley and onion (2000 dr.). Aegiali boasts a whole range of good tavernas and restaurants. In Tholaria the **Panorama** is good, with a wonderful view, while the **Corali** on the beach specializes in fish.

Islands between Amorgos and Naxos

Between Amorgos and Naxos lie a bevy of tiny islands, three of which—Heraklia (or Iraklia), Shinoussa and Koufonissia—are served by the daily boat *Scopelitis*, which rolls and buckets its way between Naxos and Amorgos, and the occasional steamer from Piraeus. These three all have rooms to rent; they are certainly quiet places, and not prepared to take many visitors. If you plan to stay any length of time, you should bring some food along, and be prepared to be sparing with the water.

Heraklia, the most westerly and the largest, has rooms in its port, Ag. Georgios; from here it's a 20-minute walk to the large sandy beach at **Livadi**. The one excursion, other than to the beach, is to walk along the mule path from Ag. Georgios to the tiny hamlet of **Iraklia**, and from there to the large cave overlooking Vourkaria Bay, then back along the west coast to Ag. Georgios. **Shinoussa**, a short hop from Heraklia, has a hotel in its 'capital' of the same name, and two beaches, one at the charming, miniature port, and the other across the island at **Psili Ammos**. Shinoussa is blessed with fresh springs, and supports a species of mastic bush on its relatively flat surface.

Koufonissia is actually two islands; lower, or Kato Koufonisi, is just barely inhabited, while **Koufonisi** itself has two restaurants and two beaches, at **Harakopou** and **Pori**. From here you may be able to take a caique to **Keros**, which has the ruins of a Neolithic settlement at **Daskalio** on the west coast, and those of an abandoned medieval settlement in the north. To reach **Donoussa**, east of Naxos, you have to take the steamer from Piraeus or the small boat from Naxos or Amorgos. A Geometric-era settlement was excavated on the island, but most of its visitors come for its fine sandy beaches near the south coast villages of Donoussa, the port, and **Mersini**.

Anafi

Anafi, most southerly of the Cyclades, is a primitive island, difficult of access, its one village lacking many amenities, its coasts unblessed with accessible beaches. Food is not easy to find, and visitors should bring along provisions to supplement the little fish and macaroni available locally. But if the crowds and noise seem too thick elsewhere, Anafi may be the antidote of peace and quiet you seek; here the inhabitants continue to go about their lives as they always have. Little contact with the outside world has meant that several old customs have been preserved, and some scholars have found in the Anafiotes' songs and festivals traces of the ancient worship of Apollo.

History

Apollo had a particularly strong following on Anafi; myth has it that the island rose at the god's command to shelter Jason and the Argonauts when they were besieged by a tempest, and ever since then it has kept its 28 km²-head out of the water. In the 15th century BC, however, a great deal of volcanic rock, 5 m thick in some places, was added to Anafi from the explosion of Santorini, carried to the island by wind and tidal wave. The twelfth Duke of

Naxos, Giacamo Crispi, gave Anafi to his brother who built a castle, but his fortification had little effect when the terror of the Aegean, Barbarossa, turned up, and enslaved the entire population. For a long time after that Anafi remained deserted, people trickling back only when it was safer.

Connections

Twice a week with Piraeus, Santorini, Ios, Naxos and Paros, once a week with Amorgos and Syros; occasional catamaran from other Cyclades and Piraeus.

Around the Island

The island's one village, **Chora**, with some 300 people, is a short walk up from the landing, **Ag. Nikolaos**. A path east of Chora leads to **Katalimatsa**, with a few ruins of ancient houses, and to the island's main attraction, the **Monastery of Panayia Kalmiotissa**, built near the remains of the ancient temple to Apollo, dedicated by the grateful Jason. The **Kastro** built by Guglielmo Crispi is to the north of the village and half ruined; a path leads up to its rocky height.

Festivals

15 August, Panayia at the monastery, known for its authentic folkdances.

Where to Stay

Needless to say, there are no hotels nor pensions here. There are a few primitive rooms to rent in Chora, and 6 beds in the community guest house. Ask around if you're not offered a room when you get off the ship.

Eating Out

Food, as mentioned above, is another problem, but such is the price of solitude these days. People seem to like **Roussos** in Ag. Nikolaos, while up in Chora **Kyriakos** is the gathering spot for dinner.

Andros

One of the largest and most populated of the Cyclades, Andros is much more visited by Greeks with summer villas than by foreigners. In the south only the narrowest of straits separates Andros from Tinos, while in the north the blustery Doro Channel, long dreaded by sailors, lies between the island and Evia. However, the same irksome wind also makes Andros, and especially its capital, one of the coolest spots in the Aegean in July and August. Lush vegetation, orchards and forests, covers the land between the rocks, and fresh water is abundant, especially commercially-exploited mineral water. It is a prosperous island, neat, well ordered, adorned with white dovecots first built by the Venetians and famed for its captains and shipowners; many from elsewhere come here to retire.

History

The name Andros is thought to be derived from the Phoenician Arados, or from Andrea, the general sent by Rhadamanthys of Crete to govern the island. In 1000 BC Ionians colonized Andros, leading to its early cultural bloom in the Archaic period. Dionysos was the most popular god worshipped at the pantheon of Palaiopolis, the leading city at the time, and a certain temple of his had the remarkable talent of turning water into wine during the Dionysia.

For most of the rest of its history, Andros has been the square peg in a round archipelago. After the Athenian victory at Salamis, Themistokles fined Andros for supporting Xerxes. The Andrians refused to pay up, and Themistokles besieged the island, but was unsuccessful and had to return home empty-handed. Although the islanders later assisted the Greeks at Plataea, Athens continued to hold a grudge against Andros, and in 448 BC Perikles divided the island between Athenian colonists, who taxed the inhabitants heavily. In response, the Andrians supported Athens' enemies whenever they could: when the Peloponnesian War broke out, they withdrew from the Delian league and sided with Sparta, supporting the neurotic reactionaries throughout the war, in spite of another Athenian siege led by Alcibiades and Konon. Spartan oppression, however, proved just as awful as Athenian oppression, and things were no better during the succession of Hellenistic rulers, although a magnificent statue of Hermes, the Conductor of the Dead, dating from the 1st or 2nd century BC and found at Palaiopolis, suggests that at least art survived the constant change of bosses.

For resisting their inevitable conquest, the Romans banished the entire population of Andros to Boetia, and gave the island to Attalos I, King of Pergamon. When permitted to return, the inhabitants found their homes sacked and pillaged. Byzantium proved a blessing compared with the past, despite Saracen pirate raids. In the subsequent Venetian free-for-all, another nephew of Doge Enrico Dandolo, Marino Dandolo, took Andros, and allied himself with his cousin Marco Sanudo, the Duke of Naxos. Most of the surviving fortifications were constructed under the Dandoli.

In 1566 the Turks took the island. Apart from collecting taxes, they left it more or less to its own devices, and many Albanians from nearby Karystos (Evia) settled on Andros. In 1821 Andros' famous son, the philosopher Theophilos Kairis, declared the revolution at the cathedral of Andros, and the island contributed large sums of money and weapons to the struggle. In 1943 the Germans bombed the island for two days when the Italians stationed there refused to surrender.

Connections

Daily with Rafina, Tinos and Mykonos, less often with Syros, three times a week with Paros, Naxos, Kos and Rhodes, once a week with Astypalaia, Kalymnos, Heraklia, Shinoussa, Koufonissia and Amorgos.

Tourist Police

See regular police, Gavrion, ✆ (0282) 71 220 or Chora, ✆ 22 300.

The capital, alternatively known as Chora or **Andros**, is built on a long, narrow tongue of land, decorated with the grand neo-Classical mansions of the island's ship-owners. At the edge of the town a bridge leads to the Venetian castle, **Kato Kastro**, built by Marino Dandolo and damaged in the 1943 bombardment, now watched over by a statue of the Unknown Sailor. **Plateia Riva**, the square before the arch, has a small **museum** dedicated to Andros' seafaring history, but you may have to ask around for the key. Below, at a spot called **Kamara** the locals dive into the sea—there are sandy beaches on either side of town, but they're often windswept.

The pedestrian-only main street, paved with marble slabs and scented with cheese and custard pies made at the local bakery is lined with old mansions converted into public offices; post and telephone offices and banks are in the centre of town, and the bus station is just a few steps away. Chora's inadequate port, **Emborios** has given up sheltering large boats (the ferry calls at Gavrion) to become a popular beach; a small church, **Ag. Thalassini** guards one end of the harbour from a throne of rock. The cathedral **Ag. Georgios**, is built on the ruins of a 17th-century church.

The following legend is told about a third church, **Theoskepasti**, built in 1555. When the wood for the church's roof arrived in Andros from Piraeus, the priest found that he couldn't afford the price demanded by the captain of the ship. Angrily, the captain set sail again only to run into a fierce, boiling tempest. The sailors prayed to the Virgin, promising to bring the wood back to Andros should she save their lives. Instantly the sea grew calm again, and Theoskepasti, or Roof of God, was completed without further difficulty. It was dedicated to the Virgin Mary, who apparently is on a hotline to the miracle-working icon inside the church.

Two other museums in Chora are gifts from the Goulandris shipping family: the 1981 **Archaeology Museum**, where the 'Hermes of Andros'—the real McCoy—is on display, along with material found on the island, architectural illustrations and pottery collections; and the **Museum of Modern Art**, in Plateia Kairis, which houses exhibitions of international modern artists, together with sculptures by Michael Tombros.

The Villages Outside Chora

From Chora frequent buses leave for the island's many villages, with extra journeys to Gavrion when a ship is coming in (check the timetable at the bus station). Nearby attractions include **Stenies** with its lovely beach, Yialya. **Apikia** bottles Sariza mineral water and owns the 16th-century monastery Ag. Nikolaos to the north. The main road to the west coast passes through the fertile Mesaria Valley with its numerous farming villages, winding stone walls and dovecots. One old custom may still be seen: in the evening after a hard day's work, the patriarch will pipe the family home from the fields.

Up in the mountains **Menites** is a well-watered village and its church **Panayias tis Koumulous** may have been the site of Dionysos' miraculous temple. Nearby **Mesaria** has a Byzantine church of the Taxiarchos built in 1158 by the Emperor Manuel Comnenos. Mesaria was the home of an 18th-century nun named Rose, a faith healer who made an icon of Ag. Nikolaos from her own hair, which you can still see in the church of eponymous saint (1732). From Mesaria an hour's walk takes you to the most important monastery on Andros, **Panahranto**, founded shortly after Nikephoros Phokas' liberation of Crete in 961, and supposedly visited by the emperor himself. South of Mesaria, at **Aladino**, a stalactite cave called Chaos may be visited—bring a light—the villagers know its location as Lasthinou.

Other buses go to the Bay of Korthion in the southeast, with a beach, hotel and rooms. The fishing here is excellent, but if they're not biting you can always eat in one of the seafood tavernas along the waterfront. To the north of the bay is the ruined **Castle of the Old Woman,** named after a gritty old lady who abhorred the Venetians. She tricked them into letting her inside the fort, and later secretly opened the door to the Turks. Appalled at the subsequent slaughter of the Venetians, the old woman leapt from the castle and landed on a rock now known as 'Tis Grias to Pidema' or Old Lady's Leap.

Just to the north of Korthion is **Palaiokastro**, another fortification built by Dandolo and now in ruins. Ruined **Zagora** on the west coast, was inhabited until the 8th century BC, when it boasted a population of 4000. Heavily defended, sheer cliffs surrounded it on three sides, while the fourth was a solid wall. Within, inhabitants lived in small, flat-roofed houses (some remains still exist) and cultivated the fields outside the wall. Excavated by Australians in the 1960s, finds from Zagora are now in the island's museum.

Palaiopolis, further up the coast, was the original capital of Andros, inhabited until around AD 1000 when the people moved to Mesaria. An earthquake in the 4th century AD destroyed part of it, and over the years pirates finished the job. Walls and part of the acropolis are preserved, along with the ruins of buildings and temples, although the site has yet to be thoroughly explored. **Vatsi**, to the north, is Andros' most popular tourist resort. Occasionally the steamer calls here, as well as at Gavrion. From Vatsi you can visit the convent **Zoodochos Pigi**, built in the 14th century and containing icons from that century onwards. The nuns run a weaving factory. Shady well-watered **Arnas**, on the northern slopes of Andros' highest peak, Mt Petalo, is the garden of Andros, and it doesn't take long for a visitor to the Cyclades to appreciate how important fresh water and greenery are to the inhabitants.

The main port, **Gavrion**, lies further up the coast, with many facilities and a beach, although with little charm to distinguish itself. From here it's a 40-minute or so walk up to **Ag. Petros**, the best-preserved ancient monument on Andros. Dating from the Hellenistic era, the tower stands some 20 m high—the upper storeys were reached by ladder—and its inner hall is still crowned by a corbelled dome. The landscape around here squirms with stone walls that resemble humped caterpillars.

Further north, **Amolohos** is an isolated mountain village locally famous for its beauty. Another ancient tower is located further north at Zorkos Bay.

Festivals

15 August, at Korthinon; Theoskepasti, 15 days before Easter, and 19 June, Analapsis, both at Andros; 23 August, at Menites.

Where to Stay

Like Kea, Andros is an island whose tourism infrastructure is geared to long-term stays. The Athenians who don't own villas fill up the hotels and it may well be difficult, especially in the capital, to find a hotel or pension that will let you stay for only a few nights.

expensive

The most elegant place in the capital is the **Paradissos Hotel**, © 22 187 in a graceful, neo-Classical confection near the centre of town. The **Xenia** has rooms at about the same price, © 22 270. In Gavrion, on the beach, the mini-complex **Andros Holiday** has a pool, tennis, sauna and gym, © 71 443.

Most visitors end up staying in Gavrion or Vatsi, both of which have small hotels and numerous rooms to rent. The latter is much nicer and of its pensions the **Chryssi Akti**, © 41 236, with 60 rooms, is pleasant and just on the beach. The smaller **Skouna**, © 41 240, is also by the water, and costs about the same.

In Vatsi **Avra**, © 41 216, is the cheapest pension; facilities are shared. Otherwise there are simple rooms (except at the peak period) to be had in Vatsi, Gavrion and Chora. Apikia, just north of the capital, also has rooms.

Waves of foreign tourists always hike up prices, but this hasn't happened yet in Andros. The best restaurants are in Andros town, **Platanos** and **Delfinia**, where a full meal runs to around 2000 dr. In Gavrion you can get standard Greek fare at **Petros** for the same price. There are two tavernas in Vatsi.

Delos

Delos, holy island of the ancient Greeks, centre of the great maritime alliance of the Athenian golden age, a major free port in Hellenistic and Roman times that controlled much of the east–west trade in the Mediterranean, is today completely deserted except for the lonely guardian of the ruins. Even though the ancients allowed no burials on Delos, the islet is haunted by memories of the 'splendour that was Greece'; the Delians themselves have been reincarnated as little lizards, darting among the poppies and broken marble.

Mythology

The most ancient name of Delos was Ortygia, derived from one of Zeus' love affairs, this time with a maiden named Asteria. Asteria fled the lusty king of the gods in the form of a quail, and Zeus turned himself into an eagle the better to pursue her. The pursuit proved so hot that Asteria turned into a rock and fell into the sea. This rock was known as Ortygia ('quail') or Adelos, the invisible one, as it floated all over Greece like a submarine just below the surface of the sea. Some time later Zeus fell in love with Asteria's sister Leto, and despite the previous failure of the bird motif, succeeded in making love to her in the form of a swan— the subject of some of the most erotic fancies produced by Michelangelo and other artists in the Renaissance.

But Zeus' humourless, jealous, Thurberesque wife Hera, soon got wind of the affair and begged Mother Earth not to allow Leto to give birth anywhere under the sun. All over the world wandered poor, suffering, overripe Leto, unable to find a rock to stand on, as all feared the wrath of Hera. Finally in pity Zeus turned to his brother Poseidon and asked him to lend a hand. Poseidon thereupon ordered Ortygia to halt, and anchored the islet with four columns of solid diamond. Thus Adelos the Invisible, not under the sun but under the sea, became Delos, the Visible. Delos, however, was still reluctant to have Leto, fearing her divine offspring would give her a resounding kick back into the sea. But Leto promised the islet that no such thing would happen; indeed her son would make Delos the richest sanctuary in Greece. The island conceded, and Leto gave birth first to Artemis, goddess of the hunt and virginity, and then nine days later to Apollo, the god of truth and light.

History

In the 3rd millennium BC Delos was settled by people from Karia. By 1000 BC the Ionians had made it their religious capital, centred around the cult of Apollo whom they believed to be the father of the founder of their race, Ion—a cult first mentioned in a Homeric hymn of the 7th century BC. Games and pilgrimages took place, and Delos was probably the centre of the Amphictyonic maritime league of the Ionians. In 550 BC Polycrates, the Tyrant of Samos, conquered the Cyclades but respected the sanctity of Delos, putting the islet Rheneia under its control, and symbolically binding it to Delos with a chain.

With the rise of Athens, notably under Pisistratos, began the greatest glory and greatest difficulties of Delos. What was once sacred began to take on a political significance, and the Athenians invented stories to connect themselves to the islet—did not Erechtheus, the King of Athens, lead the first delegation to Delos? After slaying the Minotaur on Crete did not Theseus stop at Delos and dance around the altar of Apollo? In 543 BC the Athenians even managed to trick the oracle at Delphi into ordering the purification of the island, which meant removing the old tombs, a manoeuvre designed to alienate the Delians from their past and diminish the island's importance in comparison to Athens' rising status.

In 490 BC the population of Delos fled to Tinos before the Persian king of kings Darius, who, according to Herodotos, not only respected the sacred site and sacrificed 300 talents' worth of incense to Apollo but allowed the Delians to return home in safety. The Persians lost the war, and after the Battle of Salamis the Athenians, to prevent further invasions, organized a new Amphictyonic league, centred at Delos. Only the Athenian fleet could guarantee protection to the island allies, who in return were required to contribute a yearly sum and ships to support the navy. Athenian archons administered the funds.

The Delian alliance was effective, despite resentment among islanders who disliked being lorded over by the Athenians. No one was fooled in 454 BC when Perikles, in order better to 'protect' the league's treasury, removed it to Athens' acropolis; some of the money went to repair damage incurred during the previous Persian invasion, and some to beautify Athens generally. Shortly afterwards, divine retribution hit Athens in the form of a terrible plague, and as it was determined to have been caused by the wrath of Apollo, a second purification of Delos (not Athens, mind) was called for in 426 BC. This time not only did the Athenians remove all the old tombs, but they forbade both births and death on Delos, forcing the pregnant and the dying to go to Rheneia. Thus the alienation of the Delians was complete. When the people turned to Sparta for aid during the Peloponnesian War, the Spartans remained unmoved: since the inhabitants couldn't be born or die on the island, they reasoned that Delos wasn't really their homeland, and why should they help a group of foreigners? In 422 BC Athens punished Delos for courting Sparta by exiling the entire population (for being 'unpure') to Asia Minor, where all the leaders were slain by cunning. Athenian settlers moved in to take the Delians' place, but Athens herself was punished by the gods for her greed and suffered many setbacks against Sparta. After a year, hoping to regain divine favour, Athens allowed the Delians to return home. From 403 to 394 BC Delos had a breath of freedom when the Spartans defeated Athens. Then Athens formed its second Delian alliance, although it was far less forceful, and 50 years later the Delians had plucked up the courage to ask the league to oust the bossy Athenians altogether. But the head of the league at the time, Philip II of Macedon, refused the request, wishing to stay in the good graces of the city that hated him most.

In the confusion following the death of Philip's son, Alexander the Great, Delos became free and prosperous, supported by the pious Macedonian general-kings. New buildings and shrines were constructed and by 250 BC Delos was a flourishing cosmopolitan, commercial port, inhabited by merchants from all over the Mediterranean. When the Romans defeated the Macedonians in 166 BC they returned the island to Athens, which once again exiled the Delians. But by 146 BC and the fall of Corinth, Delos was the centre of all east–west trade, and declared a free port by the Romans in order to undermine the competition at Rhodes. People from all over the world settled on Delos and set up their own cults in complete tolerance. Roman trade guilds, each with its own *lares*, centred on the Italian Agora. New quays and piers were constructed to deal with the heavy flow of vessels. Markets thrived.

In the battle of the Romans against Mithradates of Pontus in 88 BC, Delos was robbed of many of her treasures; 20,000 people were killed, and the women and children carried off as slaves. This was the beginning of the end of Delos. Sulla regained the island, but 19 years later Delos was again destroyed by pirates allied to Mithradates, and the population was again dragged off to the slave markets. General Triarius retook the island and fortified it with walls, and Hadrian attempted in vain to revive the waning cult of Apollo with new festivities. Wretched Delos went into such a decline that when Athens tried to sell the islet, no one offered to buy it. In AD 363, Roman Emperor Julian the Apostate tried to renew paganism on Delos until the oracles solemnly warned: 'Delos shall become Adelos'. Later Theodosius the Great banned heathen ceremonies altogether. A small Christian community survived on Delos until the 6th century, when it was given over to the rule of pirates. House builders on Tinos and Mykonos used Delos for a marble quarry, and its once busy markets became a pasture.

After the war of independence, Delos and Rheneia were placed in the municipality of Mykonos. Major archaeological excavations were begun in 1872 by the French School of Archaeology in Athens under Dr Lebeque, and work continues to this day.

Connections

Tourist boat from Mykonos daily (except Mon) at 9 am, returning at 12.30 pm, or at 10.15 am, returning at 1.30 pm, with a guide (cost 4000 dr.), or hire a private boat at

Stadium

Synagogue

Gymnasium

Archighession

House of
the Comedians

Palaestras

Terrace
of the
Lions

Sacred Lake

Wall of Triarius

Temple
Of Leto

Italian Agora

Stoa of Antigonos

Dodekatheon

Temples of Apollo

Sanctuary of
Dionysos

Museum
Building

Stoa of
Poseidon

Agora of
Theophrastos

House of
the Naxians

Propylaea

Bull's Shrine

Prytaneion of
the Rectors

Philip's Stoa

Sacred
Way

Delians'
Agora

Sacred Harbour

Agora of the
Competalists

South Stoa

DELOS

Theatre Quarter

House of
Hermes

Sanctuary
of the
Syrian Gods

House of
Dionysos

Shrine of the
Samothracian
Great Gods

Serapeions

House of
Cleopatra and
Dioscourides

House of the Trident

Temple of
Hera

Maritime
Quarter

Reservoir

Theatre

House of Dolphins

House of
the Masks

Shrine of
Good Luck

Sacred Cave
(Grotto of Herakles)

Mt. Kynthos

the main harbour. There's an admission fee (1000 dr.) to the island, which is a 3.5 km² outdoor archaeology museum.

The Excavations

*A trip to **Delos** begins as one clambers out of the caique and pays the entrance fee. After this the rest is easy. All the major sites are labelled, and at a normal walking pace everything of interest can be seen in hours. The site is now illuminated at night, fed by underwater cable from Mykonos.*

To your left from the landing stage is the **Agora of the Competalists**. *Compita* were Roman citizens or freed slaves who worshipped the Lares Competales, or crossroad gods. These Lares gods were the patrons of Roman trade guilds, while others came under the protection of Hermes, Apollo or Zeus. Many of the remains in the Agora are votive offerings to these gods. A road, once lined with statues, leads from here to the sanctuary of Apollo. To the left of the road stood a tall and splendid Doric colonnade called **Philip's Stoa**, built by Philip V of Macedon in 210 BC, and now marked only by its foundations; it once held a votive statue dedicated by Sulla for his victory over Mithradates. The kings of Pergamon built the **Southern Stoa** in the 3rd century BC, and you can also make out the remains of the **Delians' Agora**, the local marketplace in the area.

The **Sanctuary of Apollo** is announced by the **Propylaea**, a gateway built in the 2nd century BC of white marble. Little remains of the sanctuary itself, once crowded with temples, votive offerings and statues. Next door to it is the **House of the Naxians**, built in the 6th century BC. A huge kouros, or statue of Apollo as a young man originally stood there, of which only the pedestal remains. According to Plutarch the kouros was crushed when a nearby bronze palm donated by Athens (symbolic of the tree clutched by Leto in giving birth) toppled over in the wind.

Next are the **three temples of Apollo**. The first and largest was begun by the Delians in 476 BC. The second was an Athenian construction of Pentelic marble, built during the Second Purification, and the third, of porous stone, was made by the 6th-century Athenian tyrant Pisistratos. Dimitrios the Besieger contributed the **Bull's Shrine**. This originally held a trireme in honour of the sacred delegation ship of Athens—the very one Theseus sailed in on his return to Athens after slaying the Minotaur, the ship whose departure put off executions (most famously that of Socrates) until its return to Athens. Other buildings in the area were of an official nature—the **Prytaneion of the Rectors** and the **Councillor's house**. Towards the museum is the **sanctuary of Dionysos** of the 4th century BC, flanked by its lucky marble phalli. The **Stoa of Antigonos** was built by a Macedonian king of that name in the 3rd century BC. Outside the stoa is the **Tomb of the Hyperborean Virgins**, who came from Ireland to help Leto give birth to Apollo and Artemis, a sacred tomb and thus the only one to stay put during the two purifications.

On the opposite side of the Stoa stood the **Abaton**, the holy of holies, where only the priests could enter. The **Minoan fountain** nearby is from the 6th century BC. Through the **Italian Agora** one comes to the **Temple of Leto** (6th century) and the **Dodekatheon**, dedicated to the twelve gods of Olympos in the 3rd century BC. Beyond, where the **Sacred Lake** has dried up, is the famous **Terrace of the Lions**, ex-votos made from Naxian marble in the 7th century BC. The lake, called sacred for having witnessed the birth of Apollo, was surrounded by a small wall which still exists. When Delos' torrent Inopos stopped flowing, the water evaporated. Along the shore are two **Palaestras** (for exercises and lessons) along with the foundation of the **Archighession**, or temple to the first mythical settler on Delos, worshipped only on that

The Terrace of Lions, Delos

island. Besides the **Gymnasium** and **Stadium** are remains of a few houses and a **synagogue** built by the Phoenician Jews in the 2nd century BC.

A dirt path leads from the tourist pavilion to Mt Kynthos (110 m). Along the way stand the ruins of the **Sanctuary of the Syrian Gods** of 100 BC with a small religious theatre within. The first of **three Serapeions** follows, dedicated to the Egyptian god Serapis and all built in the 2nd century BC. Between the first and second Serapeions is the **shrine to the Samothracian Great Gods**, the Cabiri or underworld deities. Next is the third Serapeion, perhaps the main sanctuary, with temples to both Serapis and Isis, with half a statue remaining. In the region are houses with mosaic floors, and a **temple to Hera** from 500 BC. The **Sacred Cave** is on the way to the top of Mt Kynthos, where Apollo ran one of his many oracles. Later it was dedicated to Herakles. On the mountain itself is the **Shrine of Good Luck**, built by Arsinoe Philadelphos, wife of her brother, the King of Egypt. On the summit of Kynthos signs of a settlement dating back to 3000 BC have been discovered, but better yet is the view, encompassing nearly all the Cyclades.

The **Theatre Quarter** consists of private houses surrounding the 2nd-century BC **Theatre of Delos**, with a capacity for 5500; beside it is a lovely eight-arched **reservoir**. The houses of this quarter date from the Hellenistic and Roman ages and many have mosaics, some beautifully preserved, such as in the **House of the Dolphins** and the **House of the Masks**. All of these residences have a cistern beneath the floor, spaces for oil lamps and sewage systems. Some are built in the peristyle 'style of Rhodes' with a high-ceilinged guest room; colonnades surround the central courts which are open to the sun. Seek out the **House of the Trident** and the **House of Dionysos**, both with mosaics, and the **House of Cleopatra and Dioscourides**, where the statues stand a headless guard over the once-great town.

Surrounding Delos are the islets **Ag. Georgios** (named after its monastery), **Karavonissi, Mikro** and **Megalo Rematiaris**, the last consecrated to Hecate, the Queen of the Night. **Rheneia**, also known as Greater Delos, lies just west of Delos and is just as uninhabited. Here came the pregnant or dying Delians—a large number of little rooms were excavated in the rock to receive them, before they moved into the realm of tombs and sepulchral altars. A necropolis near the shore was the repository of the coffins which the Athenians exhumed in the second purification. On the other side of Rheneia are the ruins of a lazaretto, once used by Syros-bound ships sent into quarantine.

Where to Stay

It is illegal to stay the night on Delos. Permission may be granted to archaeologists by the relevant authorities in Athens or Mykonos.

Folegandros

Folegandros is a small dry island of 650 inhabitants, one of the smallest in Greece with a permanent population. It has become a popular place for escapists, whose peace and quiet is only interrupted by an occasional load of day-trippers from Ios. Its name Folegandros comes from the Phoenician 'Phlegundum' meaning 'rocky island', which fits it to a tee.

Connections

Daily excursion boats from Ios, ferry 4-5 times a week with Piraeus, Ios, Santorini, less frequently with Sikinos, Milos, Paros, Naxos, Sifnos, Serifos and Kythnos, once a week with Kimolos, Crete, Kassos, Karpathos, Halki, Symi and Rhodes. Catamaran once a week to Ios, Naxos, Paros, Mykonos, Tinos, Syros and Piraeus.

Around Folegandros

Boats to Folegandros land at **Karavostassis**, the tiny harbour, where you'll find restaurants and rooms to rent. It lies within walking distance of shady **Livadi** beach, from where a rough path continues inland to remote **Evangelistra monastery** dominating the rocky southern shores of the island. An easier path leads back to Chora from here, although if you're considering any long walks in the summer, a sun hat and a bottle of water are essential.

A bus runs from the port to medieval **Chora**, the capital, perched on the pirate-proof cliffs some 300 m above the sea. It is a pretty village with shady, sleepy squares. The sparse remains of an ancient city are located on a high plateau above Chora, where in the 13th century Marco Sanudo built his fortress, or **Kastro**; the walls are formed by the solid square of tall, inward-looking houses themselves.

The church **Panayia** stands high up on a commanding headland; beyond it, a large grotto, **Chrisispilio** (the Golden Cave) has stalactites and stalagmites, but access is difficult; ask in Chora for someone to guide you.

Ano Mera, 5 km west, is the only other village on Folegandros, and has two tavernas and a limited number of rooms to rent; from here on a clear day you can see Crete. Tracks weave down to seldom-visited beaches at **Vigla**, **Livadaki** and **Vathi**. From the road between Ano Mera and Chora a path descends to the beach of **Agali**, as away from it as you can get, with two simple tavernas and 15 rooms for rent, but no electricity. Next door is the quiet Ag. Nikolaos beach with a basic canteen. Both of these beaches can be reached by the boat which leaves Karavostassis at 11.15 am, returning at 5 pm.

Festivals

15 August at Panayia; and Easter, when an icon is paraded and trips are made in boats around the island.

Where to Stay

moderate

Folegandros only has 4 small hotels, 3 of them in Chora: the largest (with 17 rooms) and most comfortable B class **Fani-Venis**, © 41 237; the friendly E class **Odysseus**, © 41 239, with private bath; and the cheaper **Danassis**, another class E with shared showers, © 41 230. Down in Karavostassis the pleasant **Aeolos**, © 41 205, with 12 rooms, is on the beach.

cheap

There are rooms to let in private homes in Chora. The beach at Livadi has a **campsite**, with taverna, bar and laundry facilities. However, there are always more visitors than available space in the summer, so be prepared to sleep out, and, if it comes to that, be sure to find shelter from the strong, nagging winds.

Eating Out

In Chora the taverna **O Kritikos** (the owner is Cretan) has delicious chicken on the spit, and with wine a meal will run to an exorbitant 1000 dr., more if you opt for the freshly-caught lobster sizzling on the grill. Also in Chora **Nicos Taverna** serves standard chops and salads for 1500 dr. a person in an unpretentious garden setting. On Livadi beach **To Kati Allo** ('the something else') has a small army of ladies in the kitchen producing an excellent selection of ready-cooked dishes, which you can demolish while gazing out across the serene bay.

Ios

Although desperately trying to change its image as the Torremolinos or Benidorm of the Aegean, Ios remains the Mecca for throngs of young people who spend their days lounging on the best beach in the Cyclades and their evenings sauntering from one watering hole to another. To discourage raucous parties and late-night revellers sleeping out on the beach, four lovely campgrounds have been provided. The seasonal Irish invasion is so great that the island's name has been re-interpreted as the acronym for 'Irish Over Seas'. If it's the easy life you're seeking, Ios is the place. Otherwise, despite the loveliness of Ios and its beach, you may well feel disenchanted by the crowds and the rock 'n roll. There are people who go back to Ios every summer, and people you couldn't pay to ever return there again.

In a backlash against rowdy youth, island authorities are attempting to promote alternatives while taking up the ecological banner. Efforts are finally being made to protect the turtles which come ashore to lay their eggs on the south side of Ios, and the Islanders are lobbying to keep tankers out of the Cyclades to safeguard their 31 km of beach.

Connections

Ios is very well connected. There are daily ferries to all the major Cyclades and Piraeus, five times a week to Crete, once a week to Thessaloniki; daily excursion boats to Santorini, Mykonos, Paros, Naxos, Sikinos and Folegandros; catamaran to Santorini, Sikinos, Folegandros and Piraeus.

Tourist Information

Information office in the port of Gialos, ✆ (0286) 91 028. Also see regular police in Chora, ✆ (0286) 91 222.

Gialos and Ios Town

The island's name comes from the Ionians who built cities on the sites of Gialos and Ios town, when the island was famous for its luxuriant oak forests. Over the century, the oaks became ships and Ios became the arid rockpile it is today; after the earthquake of 1951, when all the water was sucked out of Ios Bay and rushed back to flood and damage Gialos, the island may well have been abandoned had not the first tourists begun to trickle in.

Gialos, the port, has the island's best fish tavernas and quietest lodgings; it has a beach in the bay, but it tends to be very windy. From the port beach a rough track leads to **Koumbara** beach, a pretty sandy cove that is usually less crowded, and offers a couple of convenient tavernas for lunch. From Gialos frequent buses go up to Ios town and Milopotas Beach, or you can brave the 15-minute climb up the steps.

Ios town, one of the finest in the Cyclades, is increasingly hard to find behind the discos, bars and tourist shops. Traces of the ancient walls are preserved, and only bits more survive of the fortress built in 1400 by the Venetian Lord of Ios, Marco I Crispi. A local story shows how remote the inhabitants of small islands were to the big political events in Greek history: when Otho of Bavaria, the first modern King of Greece, paid a visit to Ios, he greeted the villagers in the café, treated them to a round of drinks and promised he would pay to have the village cleaned up for them. The grateful Niotes, scarcely knowing what majesty Otho pretended to, toasted him warmly: 'To the health of the King, Ios' new rubbish collector!'

Of the 18 original windmills behind the town, 12 remain, along with three olive oil presses. Two very old churches, out of the 400 or so chapels on the island, stand half-ruined on the hill above the town, where supposedly an underground tunnel leads to Plakotos, used as a hiding place during pirate raids. All the main facilities—police, telephone, post office, the bus stop—are at one end of the town, by a square; once there was a swing on this square, where Niotes courted their fair ladies and where ghosts now dance when no one's looking.

Beaches Around Ios

Milopotas with its superb sandy beach has several tavernas and two campsites, although most people just bed down where they can find room. Don't count on getting much shut-eye wherever you end up: Ios' all night beach parties are infamous, and have unfortunately ended in several deaths caused by overdoses of drugs and alcohol. Excursion boats leave Gialos every day for **Manganari Bay**, where there is a smart German-built bungalow resort, and **Psathis Bay**, where a church dedicated to the Virgin fell into the sea; at **Ag. Ioannis Kalamos**, a huge *paneyeri* takes place on 29 August.

More remote (but now accessible by bus) is the fine beach at **Ag. Theodotis Bay**, near the ancient Ionian city of Aegina and overlooked by the ruined **Paliokastro**, a fortress built in the Middle

Monastery on Ios

Ages. On one occasion attacking pirates managed to bore a hole in the fortress gate, big enough to allow one man in at a time—only to be scalded to death one by one in burning oil poured on them by the besieged men and women. In Ag. Theodotis monastery the door the pirates broke through on the way to their doom is on display, and on 8 September a big celebration there commemorates the event with food and dance. In **Perivolia**, a small settlement in the middle of the island, are clustered Ios' fresh water and trees; its valley church **Ag. Barbara**, has a *paneyeri* on 26 July. **Apano Kambos**, once inhabited by a hundred families but today reduced to three or four, is another pretty place. Nearby, at a place called **Hellinika**, are huge monoliths of mysterious origin.

Plakotos and Homer

Tradition has it that the mother of Homer came from Ios, and it was here that the great poet returned at the end of his life. Some say it was a riddle told by the fishermen of Ios that killed Homer in a fit of perplexity: to wit, 'What we catch we throw away; what we don't catch, we keep' (not wanting any readers to meet a similar fate, the answer's just below). Homer's supposed tomb is at **Plakotos** on the mountain, although earthquakes have left only the rock on which it was built. On 15 May each year, the *Omiria*, or Homer festival, takes place in town, with much merriment and many sporting events, and a flame is carried from the port to his grave. Plakotos itself was an ancient Ionian town which once had a temple to Apollo as well, but it slid down the cliff. You can look down and see the ruined houses; only one tower, Psarapyrgos, remains intact to mark the town.

Local Speciality

Ios' speciality, megithra—a hard white cheese similar to Parmesan, mixed with perfume and fermented in a goatskin—is hard to find these days (all the better, some might add). But megithra cheese is not the answer to Homer's riddle: what the fishermen caught was lice.

Where to Stay

Ios, the paradise of the footloose and fancy free, is surprisingly reasonable. You would get more peace and quiet staying in the port, but it's not much fun, and there are hundreds of rooms to let and several small hotels up in Chora.

luxury

Down at Manganari Bay, the **Manganari Bungalow complex** offers luxury rooms and suites, with a restaurant and nightclub for those who like their entertainment sane and close to home, © 91 200/215. Accessible only by boat from Gialos.

expensive

On Milopotas beach the **Ios Palace** is designed and decorated in the old island style, and has good views of the bay, © 91 224. A few minutes from the beach at Milopotas the **Far Out** is named for its tranquil geographical location rather than any existential experience you are likely to have there; rooms are extremely comfortable and all have a balcony with superb views.

moderate

The **Afroditi Hotel**, © 91 546, a bit outside of the tumultuous town centre is one of the best values you'll find. **Homer's Inn** in the town is also good value, but in high season you must book ahead, © 91 365. On Milopotas Beach, **Markos Beach**, © 91 571 has standard rooms at lower rates in this category, and rooms come with private shower. In town, or just on the fringe of town near the 'Dubliner Disco', **Markos Pension**, © 91 059, is for the younger crowd. It has a friendly little bar, and doesn't suffer from its proximity to the nightclub.

cheap

The cheapest pension in Ios is **Violetta**, © 91 044, with basic, simple rooms. There are hundreds of rooms for rent in private homes, and 3 **campsites** on Milopotas beach. If you want to sleep out, remember that the police are cracking down, but in high season you may well have no other choice.

Eating Out

The **Ios Club**, on the footpath up from the harbour, has long been renowned for views of the sunset, good drinks and Classical music (programme posted daily). At night it turns into a discotheque; it now has a restaurant as well with good food, some Greek and some more exotic dishes (3000 dr. a meal). The **Pithari**, near the church, is one of the best places on the island, serving excellent Greek food and barrelled wine (2500–3000 dr.). In the heart of Ios town **Saini** has inexpensive Greek dishes; try the *dolmades* and stuffed squid (1500 dr.). The **Calypso** maintains its high reputation; the good music and civilized atmosphere is matched by the food (2500 dr). **The Nest** continues to be good and popular, especially for its prices—you can eat well for 1200 dr. One thing you wouldn't expect on Ios is an excellent *ouzeri*; **Ouzeri Manolis** has a fine spread of meze, and good wine if you're not up to tippling anis fire water. Opposite the Dubliner Disco there's English grub on offer at the **Captain's Table**, with 'Fair dinkum Aussie Hamburgers' for the more discerning palate. Down in Gialos the **Afroditi** is worth a look-in; choose well and a fine Greek meal is yours for 2000 dr. On Koumbara beach, a 15-minute walk from the port, try the **Polydoros** for good homemade dishes, seafood and vegetarian dishes (you can also ask here about rooms).

Fish 'n chips and hot dogs can be found everywhere, but drinking takes priority over eating, and many of the little houses in the charming town have been turned into bars. Draught Guinness is on sale all over. One of the best places to sit and have a drink and gawk is **Frankie's**. The big discotheques, **The Dubliner**, **Sweet Irish Dream** and the **Red Lion** are all a short stagger apart.

Kea (Tsia)

Closest of all the Cyclades to Athens, Kea has for many years been a favourite place to build a summer villa—timed correctly, the island can be reached from the metropolis in less than 4 hours. It feels very different from the other Cyclades: well watered, Kea has been famed since antiquity for its fertility, its delicious red wine, lemons, honey and almonds. Its traditional architecture, while interesting, lacks the pristine white cubism of its sister isles. Its beaches are lovely, but hardly empty in the summer. Most weekends it is brimming with Athenians, so if you are planning a short stay, try and time it for mid-week. If you want to enjoy Kea's unhurried pace and atmosphere, do it now, before the entrepreneurs and tour operators develop her unexploited charms; regrettably, more and more hotels materialize each year, with people to fill them.

History

Traces of a Neolithic fishing settlement dating back to 3000 BC were discovered at Kefala on Kea's north coast. These first settlers were certainly no pushovers; when the mighty Minoan thalassocrats founded a colony *c.* 1650 BC at modern-day Ag. Irene, they were forced to build defences to protect themselves from attacks, not by sea but by land. The discovery (1960) of the colony by John L. Caskey of the University of Cincinnati, is one of the more intriguing in recent years. Built on a small peninsula, it coincides nicely with the myth that Minos himself visited Kea and begot the Kean race of a native lady named Dexithea; it also reveals a fascinating chronicle of trade and diplomacy between the Minoans and the older Cycladic culture, and later, after the fall of Crete, with the Mycenaeans.

In the Classical era, Kea was divided into four towns: Ioulis, near modern Chora, Karthaea, Poiessa and Korissia. The 5th-century BC Lyric poets, Simonides and Bacchylides, the philosopher Ariston and the physician Erasistratos were all sons of Kea. During the Middle Ages, the Venetian Domenico Michelli used Ioulis' temple of Apollo to build a castle; in the 1860s the Greek government dismantled the cannibalized Classical bits to put in a museum.

Kea's name cropped up again in 1916, when the hospital ship *Britannic*, sister-ship to the *Titanic*, sank 3 miles off shore after an explosion. Of the more than a thousand people aboard, only 21 lost their lives when their lifeboat capsized. Speculation at the time produced two theories; one, that the ship had secretly been carrying munitions, which had accidentally exploded in the hold, or that the British had scuttled the ship themselves, hoping to pressure Athens to forbid enemy craft from navigating freely in Greek waters.

Connections

Daily with Lavrion, weekly with Kythnos. Daily hydrofoil in summer from Piraeus and Anavissos on the southwest Attica coast, a 2-hour drive from central Athens.

Tourist Police

On the quay, © (0288) 31 300.

Tourist police, © 21 100.

Korissia and Ag. Irene

Kea's port **Korissia** has recently expanded beyond its purely functional role, anxious to become a resort like Kea's other coastal villages. Korissia, of course, recalls the ancient town that once stood on the site; most locals, however, still call it Livadi, as they continue to call their island Tsia instead of the official Kea. Just north is the small sandy beach of **Yialisari** with a taverna, and a kilometre further north, on attractive Ag. Nikolaou Bay, **Vourkari** is a pretty fishing village and resort. North of Vourkari, on the peninsula of Ag. Irene (named after a small church) are the excavations of the **Bronze Age–Minoan–Mycenaean settlement**. It's not hard to make out the temple, originally constructed in the Bronze Age, a late Minoan palace-type hall, walls and a street. Among the artefacts found at Ag. Irene are inscriptions in the Minoan script Linear A.

From here the coastal road continues to the delightful but popular beach resort at **Otzias**, its bay ringed with a lacey mass of almond blossom in early spring, and to **Kastrianis**, with an 18th-century monastery dedicated to the Virgin and panoramic views down the coast.

Buses connect Korissia port with **Chora**, the island capital, hidden inland like so many Cycladic towns from the view of sea-going predators. The **Kastro** quarter of town occupies the site of ancient Ioulis' acropolis and medieval walls; all that remains are the stone blocks from the original temple of Apollo. A small museum in town contains other pieces of it, as well as artefacts from ancient Kea's four cities. A few Venetian mansions remain intact around Kastro, and several churches date back to the Byzantine era: one, **Panayia Kastrianni**, is noted for a miracle-working icon. A 10-minute walk east of Chora leads to the town's most curious attraction—a powerful **petrified Lion**, an ancient guardian some 3 m high and 6 m long, gazing bemusedly out of the chiselled rock.

Equally majestic is the restored, square Hellenistic tower at the ruined monastery of **Ag. Marina**, southwest of Chora. One of the finest of such towers in Greece, its excellent masonry has stood up to time better than the monastery built around it. From Ag. Marina the road cuts across to the west coast beaches and resort communities at **Pisses** (which perhaps should consider reviving the ancient spelling of its name, Poiessa, of which a few traces remain) and **Koundouros**. On the southeast shore at Poles Bay is **ancient Karthaea**, where Simonides had his school of poetry. Inside its walls you can see the remains of a Doric temple dedicated to Apollo and several other buildings.

Festivals

1 July, Ag. Marna; 10 February, Ag. Charalambos, patron of Kea, at Chora; 15 August, Panayia, at Chora; 7 September, Ag. Soustas, at Otzias.

Where to Stay

expensive

Nearly all the places to stay are along the coast. In Korissia you can sleep in something you don't find every day on a Greek island—a motel, the **I Tzia Mas**, © 31 303, a clean and friendly place, but book well in advance for the summer. The same warning holds for the **Kea Beach**, © 31 230, a hotel and bungalow complex at Koundouros, with restaurant, nightclub, pool, tennis and watersports; bungalows here accommodate up to 4 persons.

moderate

There are only two places that fall into this category, the C class **Carthea**, © 21 204, and **Filoxenia**, © 22 057, both in Korissia.

cheap

There's not a wealth of places to stay on the cheap. Rooms are to be found in private homes in Korissia, some in Chora, Koundouros and Pisses, where there's a **campsite**.

Although foreign visitors have begun trickling in, Kea is still very Greek and the tavernas serve up unadultered Greek fare at fairly reasonable prices. On the front in Korissia, as you get off the ferry, are a line of eating places, where you can spend a pleasant evening over a grilled fish at **Faros** or **Kostas** (3000 dr.), or have lunch on traditional Greek food further along at **Nostimies**, although in the evening the emphasis switches to continental and Cypriot specialities (2500 dr.) Good fish dinners await at any of the beachside tavernas, particularly at **Aristos** in Vourkari, popular with yachtsmen who can moor their boats a few feet from where they eat. Good Greek cooking and, if the wind has been blowing the right way and there's been a good haul of fish, a delicious Greek *bouillabaisse* will be on the menu (2500 dr.). At Pisses, two respected fish tavernas are **O Simitis** and **Kabi**.

Kimolos

Once known as Echinousa, or sea urchin, the island's modern name is thought to be derived from its first inhabitant. But Kimolia also means chalk in Greek, and whether the name comes from the producer (chalk was once a main export of Kimolos) or vice versa, no one is quite sure. Another ancient export was fuller's earth, used in the dying of cloth. At one time Kimolos was attached to Milos, but the isthmus linking the two islands sank into the sea, leaving a channel only a kilometre wide. An ancient town went under the waves as well, but its necropolis survives on Kimolos at a site called Elliniko.

Kimolos is a quiet island, a perfect place to relax and do absolutely nothing. Most of it is rocky and barren (the Venetians chopped down the once-plentiful olive groves and nothing has grown there since). The largest building on the island is a retirement home built by a local philanthropist, where Kimolos' elderly live free of charge. Apart from the one town, there are several shady beaches, but the only chalk you'll find these days is in the local school.

Connections

Three times a week with Piraeus, Milos, Kythnos, Serifos and Sifnos, once a week with Folegandros, Sikinos, Ios and Santorini, water taxi three times a day to Milos.

Chora and Around

At the little port, **Psathi**, caiques relay passengers to shore, and from here it's a 15-minute walk up to the typically white capital village **Chora**. On the way up you'll pass the retirement home, where a small museum in the basement takes in whatever potsherds and ancient bric-à-brac the locals happen to dig up. Chora has a few small cafés and tavernas, and a main church, **Evangelistra**, built in 1614. From here you can walk up to the ruined Venetian castle built by Marco Sanudo at **Paliokastro**, at Kimolos' highest point (355 m). Within its forbidding walls is the island's oldest church, Christos. Another walk, taking in the Elliniko cemetery and its graves from the Mycenaean period (2500 BC) to the early centuries AD, follows the mule path to the west coast, near **Ag. Andreas**. You can finish up with a swim at the beach at **Kambana**.

A small hamlet near Psathi has the odd nickname of **Oupa**; Oupa has the most abundant fish in the Aegean these days, and here, supposedly, people used to scoop them out by the basketful. It's a very pretty little place, with a good beach untouched by tavernas or snack bars. **Prassa**, 6 km to the north, has another good beach and an undeveloped radioactive spring. Goats are the only inhabitants of **Poliegos**, the large islet facing Psathi.

Festivals

27 August, Ag. Fanouris; 27 July, Ag. Panteleimonos; 21 November, Panayias; 20 July, Profitis Elias; 4 August, Ag. Theothoso.

Where to Stay

Not many people stay overnight on Kimolos, and if you want to you'll have to ask around in the bars and tavernas to see who has a vacant room. Camping is usually 'no problem' as the Greeks say—try Klima and Aliki beaches.

Eating Out

Up in Chora are three tavernas, all serving standard Greek fare at low prices: **Ramfos, Panorama** and **Boxoris**, which also has rooms. If Kimolos' charms are wearing thin, you can sit under the umbrellas at the port snack bar and ogle the new arrivals off the ferry.

Kythnos

Time your visit right and you can have this island to yourself, avoiding the Athenian invasion of July and August. Like its neighbours, Kea and Serifos, Kythnos receives relatively few foreigners, and even the majority of Greek arrivals are not tourists, but folks full of aches and pains who come to soak in the thermal spa. But it does its best by them; since the closure of Kythnos' iron ore mines in 1940, islanders who closed their ears to the siren song of emigration have had to get by as best they can by fishing, farming (mostly figs and vines) and basket weaving. Perhaps because of their frugal, hard lives Kythniotes tend to celebrate *paneyeria* and special days with great gusto, donning their traditional costumes; carnival is a big event here. Best of all, it's the kind of island where the old men still offer to take you fishing—and the fishing off Kythnos is good indeed.

History

In Classical times the tale was told that Kythnos was uninhabited because of its wild beasts and snakes and Ofiouso ('snake') was one of the island's ancient names. Recently, however, archaeologists have uncovered a Mesolithic settlement (7500–6000 BC) just north of the port of Loutra that not only spits in the eye of tradition, but currently holds the honour of being the oldest settlement yet discovered in the Cyclades.

Much later the Minoans held the island, followed by the Driopes, a semi-mythical tribe who were chased out of their home on the slopes of Mt Parnassos by Heracles and scattered to Evia, Cyprus and Kythnos; their king Kythnos gave his name to the island and their capital to this day is known as Dryopis. During the Hellenistic period Kythnos was dominated by Rhodes. Two great painters came from the island, Kydian and Timatheus (416–376 BC), the latter famous in antiquity for his portrait of Iphegenia. In 198 BC all Kythnos was pillaged, except for Vyrokastro, which proved impregnable. Marco Sanudo took the island for Venice, and for 200 years it was under the rule of the Cozzadini family who still live in Bologna today. In order to maintain their authority the Cozzadini paid taxes both to the Venetians and to the Turks.

Connections

Daily with Piraeus, Serifos, Sifnos and Milos, 2–3 times a week with Lavrion, Kimolos, Folegandros, Sikinos, Ios and Santorini. Kythnos has two ports; all ships these days put in at **Merihas** on the west coast, though when the winds are strong they'll come in to **Loutra** in the northeast.

Tourist Police

Chora, ✆ (0281) 31 201.

Merihas is a typical Greek fishing harbour, with a small beach, Martinakia. Just to the north are the meagre Hellenistic ruins of the once impregnable **Vyrokastro**, and another beach.

Buses make the 7-km trip from Merihas to the capital **Chora**, also known as Messaria. Although as Cycladic towns go it's on the dull side, it does have a pretty church, **Ag. Saba**, founded in 1613 by the island's Venetian masters, the Cozzadini, who decorated it with their coat-of-arms. Other churches in Chora claim to have icons by the Cretan-Venetian master Skordilis. The buses continue to **Loutra**, the most important thermal spa in the Cyclades. The iron once mined on Kythnos impregnates the water, leaving a characteristic reddish deposit. Since ancient times Loutra's two springs have been used for bathing and as a cure for gout, rheumatism, eczema and other complaints. Loutra has a beach as well, and the afore-mentioned Mesolithic settlement was found on the promontory just to the north. On the northernmost tip of Kythnos, Cape Kefalos, stands the **medieval citadel** (known variously as Paliokastro or Kastro tou katakefalou). About an hour's walk from Loutra, you can poke around its derelict towers, houses and churches (one, **Our Lady of Compassion**, still has some frescoes), all abandoned around the middle of the 17th century.

A paved road leads from Merihas up to **Dryopis**, the only other inland village and departure point for **Katafiki cave**, the most accessible of several Kythnos' grottos, where the people of Dryopis hid during pirate raids. From Dryopis you can also walk down to the beaches at **Ag. Stefanos** and **Ag. Dimitri** or take a four-wheel drive down to the one at **Kanala**. Over-looking the bay, the monastery **Panayia tin Kanala** houses the island's most venerated icon, supposedly painted by St Luke himself. Other beaches on the island, attainable only by foot or boat, include Fikiado, Lefkas and Episkopi.

Festivals

15 August and 8 September, at Kanala; 2 November, Ag. Akindinos, at Merihas. On Sundays you can often hear the island's music at Dryopis.

Where to Stay

expensive

Merihas is the most convenient place to stay on Kythnos and there are quite a few rooms to rent as well as the large, modern class C **Possidonion Hotel**, © 32 100, due to re-open in 1993 after refurbishment. The most luxurious place to stay on the island is the hotel **Kythnos**, © 31 218 in Loutra.

moderate–cheap

In Loutra the **Xenia Anagenissis** overlooks the beach, © 31 217. There are also rooms to rent in Loutra, and pensions catering primarily to spa customers. You can also find rooms in Chora, and in Merihas there are many pensions near to where the ferry docks.

There's an average restaurant in Chora and several good tavernas in Merihas and Loutra. In Merihas **Kissos** has a good name, and **Yalos**, with tables right by the water, whips up a few facsimiles of international specialities (Stroganoff, schnitzel) to complement the Greek staples and fish. When you eat out, ask for the locally made cheese, which is excellent.

Milos

Like Santorini, Milos is a volcanic island, but where the former is a glamorous beauty associated with misty tales of Atlantis, Milos is a sturdy fellow who has made his fiery origins work for a living. Although the island lacks drama, it certainly has a catalogue of geological eccentricities: hot springs bubble up here and there amid its low rolling hills, the rocks startle with their Fauvist colours, and the landscape is gashed with obsidian, sulphur, kaolin, barium, alum, bensonite and perlite quarries begun in the Mesolithic era and exploited to this day. Walks through the gently undulating countryside will bring you down to tiny whitewashed chapels at the water's edge, or unique little settlements that sit on the water, with boat garages beneath their balconies. Milos also has one of the finest natural harbours in the whole of the Mediterranean. It seems an odd trick of Mother Nature to so endow such an out-of-the-way island. In spite of all its strange and wonderful rocks, Milos still mourns for the one which it lost—the renowned Venus, now in the Louvre.

History

Milos has a history as dramatic as its geology. At the dawn of the Neolithic era people braved the Aegean to mine its uniquely rich sources of obsidian, that hard black, volcanic glass, prized for the manufacture of tools before the discovery of copper. Until the recent discovery of the Mesolithic settlement in Kythnos, Milos laid claim to the oldest town in the Cyclades, at Phylokope, settled by either Phoenicians or Cypriots. Obsidian tools from Milos have been found in the earliest Minoan and even pre-Minoan settlements on Crete, dating from before 3000 BC; under Minoan and later Mycenaean rule the island became rich from trading obsidian all over the Mediterranean.

As the inhabitants of Milos in later years were predominately Dorian, they sided with their fellow Dorians from Sparta in the Peloponnesian War. When the Athenians made war in the east, the Milians again refused to fight with them. Athens sent envoys to Milos to change their minds. Their discussion, 'The Milian dialogue', included in the fifth chapter of Thucydides, is one of the most moving passages in Classical history. When Milos still refused to cooperate, the Athenians besieged the island, and when the Milians unconditionally surrendered, they massacred all men of fighting age, enslaved all the women and children, and resettled the island with colonists from Athens.

After the fall of Athens, the island prospered until the inhabitants asked the Romans to come to protect them from the pirates. Pompey put an end to the pirates, but in return the Romans

MILOS

N

moved in for good at Klema, the Dorian town which the Athenians had previously destroyed, and took over the island. Christianity came early to Milos in the 1st century and the faithful built a great series of catacombs—the only ones in Greece. Marco and his brother Angelo Sanudo captured Milos, and later placed it under the Crispi dynasty. The Turks laid claim to the island in 1580, even though Milos was infested with pirates. One of them, John Kapsis, declared himself King of Milos, a claim which Venice recognised for three years, until the Turks tricked Kapsis into coming to Istanbul, where he was slain. In 1680 a party of colonists from Milos emigrated to London, where James, Duke of York, granted them land to build a Greek church—the origin of Greek Street in Soho.

In 1820, farmer George Kentrotis (or Betonis) found a cave while planting his corn and discovered within a sensuous statue of the goddess Aphrodite. What happened next is uncertain; either the Turkish authorities seized it, or George's friends warned him that they would do so, and advised him to sell it to (or give it into the safekeeping of) the French consul in Istanbul. Whatever happened, the statue lost her arms and pedestal in transit. It was presented to Louis XVIII, who put it on display in the Louvre, where it remains to this day.

In 1836 Cretan war refugees from Sfakia fled to Milos and founded the village Adamas, the present port. During the Crimean War the French navy docked at the great harbour of Milos and left many monuments, as they did during the First World War; at Korfos you can see the bases of the anti-aircraft batteries installed during the German occupation in the Second World War.

Connections

Daily by air from Athens; ferry six times a week from Piraeus, five times a week to Sifnos, Serifos and Kythnos, four times a week with Crete. Three times a week with Folegandros and Santorini, twice a week with the Dodecanese. Daily taxi boat from Kimolos to Pollonia.

Tourist Information

Tourist information booth, on the quay, ✆ (0287) 22 290.

Tourist police, see regular police, Plaka, ✆ (0287) 21 204.

Adamas, Plaka and its Plaster Venus

Even before you reach the port Adamas, you can see a sample of Milos' eccentric rocks: a formation called the **Arkoudes**, or bears, who guard the vast Bay of Milos (to the left as you sail into the harbour). The Cretans who founded **Adamas** brought their holy icons, now displayed in the churches of **Ag. Triada** and **Ag. Charalambos:** in the latter, one ex-voto, dating from 1576, portrays a boat attacked by a raging fish; the captain prayed to the Virgin, who resolved the struggle by snipping off the fish's nose. West of town a monument commemorates the French who died here during the Crimean War.

Adamas has most of Milos's available rooms and hotels; several shops hire out bicycles, and it's the main departure point for the island's buses. Above the village a site known locally as 'the Volcano' is actually a steaming fissure in the ground.

Buses leaves frequently for **Plaka**, the pleasant but modern capital. Next to the bus stop is the **Archaeology Museum** (*9–3, closed Mon*), its entrance marked by a queue of broken statues. Inside are finds dating back to the Neolithic era; in a back room is a plaster cast of the Venus which Milos lost, a thoughtful consolation prize from Paris. Signs point the way to the **Folklore and Laographic Museum** (*10–1 and 6–8, closed Mon*), especially fun if you can find someone to tell you the stories behind the exhibits, which include everything—and a kitchen sink to boot. The Frankish castle on top of **Plaka Kastro** affords good views of the island. Within its ruined walls is the 13th-century church **Thalassitras**, its unusual name evoking Milos' seafaring past.

Ancient Melos and its Catacombs

Archaeologists believe that Plaka is built over the acropolis of ancient **Melos**, the town destroyed by the Athenians and resettled by the Romans. In the 1890s the British school excavated the site at **Klima**, a short walk below Plaka (if you take the bus, ask to be let off at Tripiti). Here you can see the **Catacombs** (*daily except Wed and Sun, 8.45–3*), dating from the 1st century and one of the best-preserved Early Christian monuments in Greece: carved into the rock are long corridors of arched tomb niches, each with a little light before it that you can move about in order to examine a tomb more closely. When first discovered, the catacombs were full of bones, but contact with the fresh air turned them to dust. Some niches held five or six bodies; others were buried in the floor. On some, inscriptions in red still remain (writing in black is later graffiti).

The habit of building underground necropoli (besides the many at Rome, there are catacombs in Naples, Syracuse and Malta) coincides with the presence of soft, easily worked volcanic tufa more than with romantic notions of Christian persecution and secret underground rites; burying the dead underground saved valuable space and answered to the desire of early Christians to stick as close as possible to the holiest members of their congregations, as if hoping to grab onto their bootstraps when their souls ascended on Judgement Day. Curiously, the modern cemetery of Milos near Plaka resembles a row of catacombs above ground.

A path from the Catacombs leads to the place where the Venus of Milos was discovered (there is a marker by the fig tree) and past the ancient walls to the well-preserved **Roman Theatre**, where spectators looked out over the sea. Part of the stage remains, although three tiers of seats have been left unexcavated, they say, as evidence of the Milians' indifference to tourism. However a theatre company from Athens sometimes performs in the theatre in August. Remains of a **temple** are on the path back to the main road.

Most of the population of Milos is concentrated in the villages around Plaka. On the north coast, paths lead down to a wide selection of beaches, some adorned with wonderfully-coloured rocks. Two of most popular swimming holes are **Platina** near the Arkoudes and the best place on Milos to watch the sun set, and **Mandrakia** on the opposite side of the peninsula, where you can drink the purgative **waters of Tsillorneri** if too much ouzo hasn't already done the trick.

Pollonia and Phylokope

From Adamas or Plaka buses depart for **Pollonia**, with its many trees, tavernas, rooms and places to camp out, as well as the caiques to Kimolos. Pollonia is within walking distance of **Phylokope** (or Filokopi) one of the great centres of Cycladic civilization, excavated by the British in the 1890s. The dig yielded three successive levels of habitation: the early Cycladic (3500 BC), the Middle Cycladic (to around 1600 BC) and Late Cycladic/Mycenaean.

Even in Early Cycladic days Milos traded obsidian far and wide—pottery found in the lowest levels at Phylokope shows an Early Minoan influence. Great urban improvements were made in Phylokope during the Middle Cycladic period: a wall was built around the more spacious and elegant houses, some with frescoes—one depicts a flying fish, that in the absence of Venus has become the artistic symbol of Milos. A Minoan-style palace was built; fine vases and Minoan ware were imported from Knossos; the obsidian trade reached the coasts of Asia Minor. Late in this period Phylokope, like the rest of the Cyclades, may have come under the direct rule of the Minoans, suggested by a tablet found on the site written in a script similar to Linear A. The top, or Late Cycladic level revealed a Mycenaean wall around the palace, a shrine, and Mycenaean pottery and figurines. Phylokope survived to see the decline of Milos' importance, as the use of metals began to replace the need for obsidian. Unfortunately, for all that, there's not very much to see at the site itself, and what can be seen—walls, mostly—are quite overgrown and inexplicable to the layman.

A Geological Mystery Tour of Milos

From Adamas excursion boats putter across the bay to the beach at **Embourios**, which also has rooms to rent and a taverna, or to visit the curious **Glaronisia**, four cave-pocked basalt islets north of Milos, the largest of which is shaped like a massive pipe organ. Near **Ag. Konstantinos**, off the road to Pollonia, steps lead down to **Papafragas**, where a pool of brilliant azure water is enclosed by a circular rock formation, once used by trading boats as a hiding place from pirates. More remote, on the southwest coast, is **Kleftiko**, another set of fantastic rock formations, accessible only from the sea. You can also sail near **Andimilos** to the northwest, home to a rare variety of chamois goat.

No buses—and therefore few tourists—visit the rest of Milos, but there are many rewards for anyone willing to don their walking shoes. South of Pollonia, at **Komia** are ruined Byzantine churches and nearby at **Demenayaki** are some of Milos' obsidian mines. **Zefyria** further inland is also called Chora, for it served as the capital of Milos from the Middle Ages to the 18th century. Panayia Portiani was the principal church of the village; a story recounts that its priest was accused of fornication by the inhabitants, and although he steadfastly denied it, the villagers refused to believe him. With that the priest angrily cursed the people, a plague fell on the town, and everyone moved down to Plaka. Today Zefyria is a very quiet village of old crumbling houses, surrounded by olive trees. Alyki on the bay is a good beach near the **Mavra Gremna**, or the black cliffs, with more fantastical rock formations. At several places out in the bay the sea bubbles from the hot springs released below.

At **Loutra Provata** you can examine remains of Roman mosaics, followed by a natural sauna. The waters are famous for relieving rheumatism; Hippocrates wrote of the healing properties of Milos' waters. Local legend has it that the generous **Alikis** spring near the airport is a sure bet against sterility in women.

South and West Milos

Kipos, towards the south coast, has two churches: one, the 5th-century Panayia tou Kipou, is the oldest in Milos. The old monastery Chalaka is at **Ag. Marina**, and from here you can climb to the top of **Profitis Ilias**, with a gods' eye view over Milos and neighbouring islands. There are beaches at **Patrikia** and further north at **Ag. Dimitriou**, although the latter is often battered by winds. If you hire a boat, the small coves carved in the south coast make ideal stopovers for a skinny dip.

Ag. Ioannis Theologos, in the southwestern corner of Milos, has a celebrated *paneyeri* on 7 May. Ag. Ioannis is known here as the Iron Saint—during one festival the party-goers were attacked by pirates, and in response to the people's prayers, the saint saved them by turning the door of the church into iron (one can still see a scrap of a dress caught in the door as the last woman entered). The pirates could not break in, and when one of them tried to shoot someone through a hole in the church dome, Ag. Ioannis made his hand fall off.

Festivals

17 July, Ag. Marina; 19 July, Profitis Elias on the mountain; 20 June and 31 October, Ag. Anargyroi (Byzantine church); 7 May and 25 September, Ag. Ioannes Theologos at Chalaka; 14 August at Zefyria; 28 August, Ag. Ioannes Prodromou; 5 August, Sotiris at Paraskopou; 26 July, Ag. Panteleimonos at Zefyria; and 25 July, Ag. Paraskevi at Pollonia.

Where to Stay

Except for a few scattered rooms to let in Plaka and near the more popular beaches, the only accommodation is at Adamas.

expensive

New in Adamas is **Venus Village**, a large hotel and bungalow complex on the beach, © 22 030, that dwarfs the local competition.

Prettiest among the less expensive hotels is the D class **Semiramis**, ℂ 22 118, each room with private bath. The large, casual and slightly tatty hotel **Corali** is a little walk up the hill from the waterfront, but fairly convenient all the same, ℂ 22 204. In Klima the **Panorama** , ℂ 21 623, has rooms with private bath.

cheap

Rooms in private houses on the island go for around 3500–4000 dr. If you want to sleep out, do so with caution—the local police can be sticky and do levy big fines.

Eating Out

Again, nearly everything is in Adamas, and if you come in an off-season month, look for oysters from Ahivadolimni. On Adamas' waterfront the friendly **Flisvos** has the usual fish and ready food offerings, and you can eat well for 2000 dr. Next door **O Kynigos** serves similar fare in unpretentious but pleasant surroundings (2000 dr.). After contemplating the bay in Adamas over an evening ouzo, a short stroll (past the taxi and bus stop) will take you to an excellent pair of tavernas, where the food is of the highest quality, the wine good and the prices low: **Trapatselis** and **Navyio**. In town head for **O Kiniyos**, where they take extra care in the preparation of seafood and standard Greek dishes (2–3000 dr.). Local favourites in Pollonia and Plaka are the **Petrakis** and **Karamitsos**, respectively.

Mykonos

This dry, barren island frequently plagued by high winds, but graced with excellent beaches and a beautiful, colourful, cosmopolitan town has the most exciting and sophisticated nightlife in Greece. This, and its proximity to Delos, has earned it the reputation as the most popular island in the Cyclades. If the surge in tourism in recent years caught the other islands unawares, Mykonos, at least, didn't bat an eyelid, having made the transformation long ago—relatively speaking—from a traditional economy to one dedicated to the whims of the international set. If you seek the simple, the unadorned, the distinctly Greek—avoid Mykonos, but the party will go on without you; Mykonos' streets are jammed with some of the zaniest, wildest, raunchiest and most beautiful people in Greece. It also has the distinction of being one of the most expensive islands, and the first officially to sanction nudism on some of its beaches.

History

The Ionians built three cities on Mykonos: one on the isthmus south of Chora, the second at Dimastos, dating back to 2000 BC, and the third at Panormos near Paliokastro. During the war between the Romans and Mithridates of Pontos, all three were destroyed. Chora was rebuilt during the Byzantine period, and the Venetians surrounded it with a wall that no longer exists; however, at Paliokastro a fort built by the Gizzi rulers still remains.

MYKONOS

To Tinos

To Syros

To Ikaria, Samos

To Naxos, Paros

N

Dragonisi

Merdias Bay

Profitis Ilias
(392m / 1294ft)

Kalafati

Dimastos

Cape Mavros

Paliokastro

Ano Mera

Ag. Anna

Panormos Bay

Ftelia

Super Paradise (nudist beach)

Marathi

Paradise (nudist beach)

Platis Yialos

Ag. Sostis

Ag. Stephanos

Tourlos

Tourlos Bay

MYKONOS CHORA

Ornos

Psarou (nudist beach)

Korfos Bay

Ag. Giannis

Prasonisi

Kounelonisi

Megalo Rematiariso

Delos

Rheneia

5 km

3 miles

Mythology

In myth Mykonos is best known as a graveyard, site of the rock tombs of the last giant slain by the hero Heracles and that of Ajax of Oileus, one of the Achaean heroes of the Trojan War. This Ajax was known as Little Ajax to differentiate him from Big Ajax, who committed suicide when the weapons of the dead Achilles were not given to him but to Odysseus. After the capture of Troy, Little Ajax proved himself just as pathetic a hero when he raped Priam's daughter Cassandra who had sought protection in a temple of Athena. Athena avenged this blasphemy by wrecking Ajax's ship off the coast of Mykonos. Poseidon saved him in a sea storm but, as horrid as ever, Ajax declared that he would have been perfectly able to save himself without the god's assistance. Poseidon's avenging trident finished Ajax then and there, and his Mycenaean tomb can still be seen at Linos.

Connections

By air: frequent daily connections with Athens, several times a week with Santorini, Rhodes and Herakleon, Crete. Less frequently with Chios, Mytilini and Samos.

By ship: daily with Piraeus, Rafina, Andros, Tinos, Syros, Paros, Naxos, Ios and Santorini; several times a week with Samos, Herakleon (Crete), Amorgos, Astypalaia, Kos, Rhodes, Koufonissia, Shinoussa and Heraklia. Twice a week with Sikinos, Folegandros, Skiathos and Thessaloniki, once a week with Kalymnos, Sifnos, Serifos, Nissyros, Tilos and Ikaria; hydrofoil daily to Rafina and other Cyclades; catamaran and hydrofoil daily to Piraeus, Tinos, Paros, Naxos, Andros and Syros. Daily to Delos at 9 am, or at 10.15 am with a guide (4500 dr.), returning at 1.30 pm.

Tourist Police

On the quay, ✆ (0289) 22 482.

Chora

Prosperity has kept the homes of **Chora**, the island's picture-postcard capital and port well maintained, gleaming and whitewashed, with brightly painted wooden trims. In the main square a bust of Manto Mavroyenous (the heroine from Mykonos who fought in the War of Independence) once served as the island's guardian of left luggage; now dire little notices keep the backpacks away. The square also maintains the taxi stand and several inexpensive snack bars here. Further up the waterfront is the departure quay for the boats to Delos (*see* p. 153). The pelican mascot of Mykonos, the successor of the original Petros, may often be found preening himself in the shadow of the small church here. This side of the harbour also has the Tourist Police office, and on the hill overlooking the harbour are several windmills. Until recently one of them still ground wheat; another has been converted into a cottage. They are a favourite subject for the many local artists, as is 'the little Venice of

Mykonos', the houses of Alefkandra, tall and picturesque and built directly beside the sea, just below the windmills.

Mykonos claims to have 400 churches, and the most famous of these is the unusual **Panayia Paraportiani**, an asymmetrical masterpiece of folk architecture. Next to it is the island's **Folklore Museum**, a collection of bric-à-brac salvaged from Mykonos' past. Upstairs you can visit a re-created bedroom and kitchen, and a gallery of 19th-century prints of sensuous Greek odalisques gazing dreamily into space; downstairs is an exhibition, 'Mykonos and the Sea' (*7–9 pm*).

The **Archaeology Museum**, on the far side of the harbour near the Leto Hotel, highlights artefacts from the islet of Rheneia, excavated by the Greek archaeologist Stavropoulos; after the Athenian purifications, Rheneia served as the necropolis of Delos. Other exhibits include a pithois carved with scenes from the Trojan War, discovered on Mykonos itself (*8.45–3, Sun 9.30–2.30, closed Tues*). The **Nautical Museum**, at the end of the main street Matogianni, consists of four rooms containing ships' models from ancient times and a collection of paintings, prints and old coins. The attractive garden has become the last resting place of old anchors, ships' wheels, cannons, compasses and huge fans from a lighthouse operated by an oil lamp (*11–1 and 6–9*).

Around Mykonos

In ancient times Mykonos had the dubious distinction of being famous for the baldness of its men and even today the old fishermen of the island never take off their distinctive caps. Despite all the changes they've seen, they have kept their sense of humour, and if you speak a little Greek they'll regale you with stories of the good old days—before all the tourist girls began chasing them around! The only other town on Mykonos is **Ano Mera**, where the **Tourliani Monastery** with its 15th-century carved steeple is the main attraction (open mornings only). Sandy **Panormos Bay** to the north was the site of one of Mykonos' three ancient cities. The second ancient city, **Dimastos**, is believed to have been on top of Mt Ayios, Mykonos' highest point. At Linos are the remains of a Hellenistic tower and walls; at **Portes** you can spit on the tomb of Ajax the troublemaker. The greenest spot on the island is the **Garden of Rapaki**, east of Chora (a good half-hour walk).

Dragonisi, the islet off the east coast of Mykonos, has lost its dragon but has numerous caves, and if you're very lucky you may see a rare monk seal in one of them. Boats for the excursion or a private trip to Delos may be hired at **Platis Yialos**. **Paradise** and gay **Super Paradise** are the main nudist beaches on the island; there are so many others scattered along the island's coasts that you could spend an entire holiday visiting them all. Particularly popular are **Psarou**, just before Platis Yialos, and **Ornos**. Both have a selection of tavernas serving fresh fish.

Where to Stay

There's certainly no lack of places to stay on Mykonos, although not too surprisingly prices tend to be higher than almost anywhere else in Greece. Sleek new hotels, many incorporating elements of the local architecture, occupy every feasible spot on the coast, especially along the road to Platis Yialos.

luxury

On the beach, within walking distance of town is the cubist beauty **Cavo Tagoo**, © 23 692, with a sea water pool, beautiful view of Mykonos, and the chance to rub shoulders with the occasional Greek celebrity or politician. Smaller and in an equally pretty location is **Petinos Beach** at Platis Yialos, © 24 310, again with its own pool, and watersports.

expensive

If you want to be in the centre of the action (extremely difficult to do without reservations from June onwards), **Carbonaki**, 27 Panahrantou, © 22 461, is a good choice, with rooms arranged in cubist blocks, and it has a pool. **Leto**, © 22 207, has a wonderful view over the harbour and town, and has for many years been the classiest place to stay on the island, but again the high season price reflects this. Off season, prices drop by around 20% or more. Adjacent to the apron of sand that forms the town beach is the small, 7-roomed **Delos**, © 22 312. **Manto**, 1 Evangelistrias, © 22 330, is convenient for connoisseurs of the night scene, while **Apollon** is a comfortable, friendly hotel, perfectly situated in the middle of the windy seafront, © 22 223. Two km outside town, **Rhenia** offers tranquil bungalows overlooking Chora and Delos, © 22 300.

moderate

Even if you arrive in the middle of summer without a reservation, you may well be greeted by a convoy of hotel vans and people with rooms to let in town or along Ag. Stefanos beach, where the C class **Artemis**, © 22 345, or the smaller D class **Mina**, © 23 024, both have perfectly acceptable rooms with bath. For a little more you can make reservations at the delightful **Hotel Philippi**, located in the heart of Chora at 32 Kalogera St, © 22 295. The rooms are spotless and scented by the hotel's lovely garden. Just out of town at Vrissi, the **Sourmeli**, © 22 905, has a pleasant garden, and equally pleasant rates.

cheap

It would be naïve optimism to expect any hotels or pensions in this category on Mykonos. Rooms in private houses are at least 4000 dr. All campers are referred to the large campground at Paradise Beach and next door Paranga Beach (continuous boat service from Platis Yialos).

Eating Out

Again, no lack of opportunities here, especially if you have deep pockets. Within a few blocks you can sample a genuine American doughnut, top that off with a seafood pizza, and wash it down with a pint from the Irish Bar. There are numerous snack bars and bakeries with cheese pies, etc. if you're counting pennies. You can eat swordfish kebabs and squid and not pay an arm and a leg for it at the large restaurant connected to the motel on Platis Yialos Beach (dinner for 2000 dr.); **Philippi's** restaurant (connected to the Hotel Philippi) has the best reputation in town for international and Greek cuisine, served in the lovely garden—count on 6000 dr. Close by and in the same price range (the wine is more expensive) is the **Edem**, also offering a varied international menu in a garden setting. Centrally placed **Katrin's**, again fairly expensive, has many French specialities. If, in the wave of international food and music, you need to be reminded that you're in Greece, head for **Niko's** taverna, in the centre of town or **Maky's**, just around the corner, with good dinners in the 2000 dr. range. Eat at least once at **Spiro's**, below the windmills, with a view of waves rolling up to the foot of the houses of 'little Venice'; seafood specialities in the medium price bracket. A notable exception to the rule that the backstreets hide the best, secret tavernas is **Antonini's**, slap in the middle of the activity on taxi square; genuine Greek food at fair prices: varied and excellent meze, shrimp salad and very tasty veal or lamb casserole (2000 dr.). For fish, dine out at **Kounelas**, at the end of the waterfront, where the owner, a colourful character, promises consistently fresh seafood (4000 dr.). At Tourlos Bay, north of town before Ag. Stefanos, **Mathew** is well patronized, and at Ag. Anna, at the end of the road that crosses the island, **Nikolas** is the place to eat.

Nightlife

The international and gay set still bop the night away in a number of spots ranging from the cosy to the crazy. The **Veranda Bar** has a pleasant view of the windmills; **Bolero**, in the centre of town, has good music and cocktails; **Kastro's** in Little Venice will be forever famous for its sunset views; live music and snazzy cocktails can be had at the **Piano Bar** above taxi square, but get there early for a seat; **Thalami**, below the city hall, has Greek music and dancing, as does the perennial favourite, the **Mykonos Dancing Bar**; **Pierro's** remains the most frenzied of the lot, where hordes of people, from the young to the not-so-young, dance to the loud, lively music and spill out into the square.

Naxos

Naxos, 448 km^2 in area, is the largest of the Cyclades and the most mountainous, its highest point, Mt Zas (or Zeus), crowning the archipelago at 1004 m. It can also claim to be the most fertile, its cultivated valleys a refreshing green even in the height of the dry, sun-browned Cycladic summer. Lemons, and kitro, a liqueur distilled from them, are Naxian specialities, as is emery, found nowhere else in Greece. Souvenirs of the island's ancient, Byzantine and Venetian past abound, and the entire west coast is almost one uninterrupted beach. It's not surprising, then, that this once little-known island attracts more visitors each year. The new airport will accelerate the island's tourist industry; until now it has served mostly as a retreat for people overwhelmed by the summer hordes on Mykonos and Paros.

Mythology

After slaying the Minotaur, the Athenian hero Theseus and the Cretan princess Ariadne stopped to rest at Naxos on their way to Athens. Yet the next morning, while Ariadne slept, Theseus set sail and abandoned her. This, even in the eyes of the Athenians, was dishonourable, especially since Theseus had promised to marry Ariadne in return for the vital assistance she had rendered him in negotiating the Labyrinth. Various explanations for Theseus' ungallant behaviour have sprung up over the centuries. Did he simply forget about her, did he find a new mistress, or did the god Dionysos, who later found her and married her, desire her from the moment she set foot on Naxos, and warn Theseus away? Historically, some believe the myth demonstrates the rise of a late Cycladic civilization after the fall of Crete; some say that Ariadne, as a priestess of Crete, would have forfeited her rights and authority if she had gone to Athens. Common, however, are the accounts that it was the jilted bride's curse on Theseus that made him forget to change his black sails to white, inadvertently causing his father's death. In all events, Ariadne lived happily ever after with Dionysos, who taught the Naxians how to make their excellent wine and set Ariadne's crown, the Corona Borealis, amongst the stars; the Celts called it Ariansrod, where their heroes went after death. The story of Theseus and Ariadne inspired many later artists, including Richard Strauss, who composed the opera *Ariadne auf Naxos*.

History

Naxos was one of the major centres of the distinct Cycladic culture. Around 3000 BC, as now, the main settlements appear to have been near Chora, on the hill of the Kastro, and at Grotta, where the sea-eroded remains of the Cycladic town can still be seen in the clear water. Tradition has it that the island was later colonized by a party from Karia, led by a son of Apollo named Naxos.

Although these Naxians were Ionians, their most troublesome enemy was Miletus in Ionia proper, where some Naxian refugees, eager to take back the island for themselves, helped stir up trouble. According to Plutarch, many battles were fought between the two rivals at the fort called Delion, of which a few vestiges remain near Naxos town. The Naxian heroine Polykrite sought refuge here when her island was besieged by Miletus, only to find the gate of the fortress closed against her. One of the Miletian leaders found her there and fell so much in love with her that he agreed to help and informed Polykrite of all the movements of his armies. His information enabled the Naxians to make a sudden and vicious attack on the Miletians. However, in the confusion of the battle, Polykrite's lover, turned traitor for her sake, also perished, and the girl died in sorrow the next day, despite being acclaimed as the saviour of Naxos.

Naxos was one of the first islands to work in marble, and in the Archaic period produced the lions of Delos and kouroi statues of incredible size. Indeed, for a period, huge was beautiful on Naxos; in 523 BC the tyrant Lugdamis declared he would make the buildings on the island the highest and most glorious in all Greece. All that remains today of Lugdamis' ambition is the massive lintel from the gate of the Temple of Apollo on the islet of Palatia. An ancient mole still links Palatia to the mainland, attesting to the glory of Naxos when the island was the leader of the Ionic Amphictyonic league. As with most of the islands, Naxos declined in importance in the Classical age. In Hellenistic times it was governed by Ptolemy of Egypt who fortified Apano Kastro and Chimaru. The Byzantines continued to build defences on this rich and strategic island: and at their Castle T'apaliru, Marco Sanudo besieged them for two months in 1207.

With the taking of T'apaliru, Marco Sanudo became the self-proclaimed Duke of Naxos and held sway over all the Venetians who had grabbed Aegean Islands after the conquest of Constantinople in 1204. When Venice refused to grant Sanudo the independent status he desired, he broke away in 1210 and went over to the Latin Emperor, becoming the Duke of the

NAXOS

Archipelago. The word archipelago, 'the chief sea', was the Byzantine name for the Aegean; under Sanudo and his successors, it took on its modern meaning, 'a group of islands', in this case the Cyclades, which the Venetians ruled as a fief for 300 years. They built a palace and a Catholic cathedral on the top of Chora, and a second residence at Apano Kastro, used in defence against both outsiders and rebellious islanders. Even after the Turkish conquest in 1564 the Dukes of Naxos remained in nominal control of the Cyclades, although answerable to the Sultan.

A latter-day Naxian, Petros Protopapadakis, planned the Corinth canal and gave many public works to the island. He was the Minister of Economics in 1922 during the misadventure in Asia Minor, and was executed with other members of that sad government by the subsequent regime. His statue now stands by the port.

Connections

Daily ferry to Paros, Syros, Ios, Santorini, Mykonos, Tinos, Andros and Piraeus; daily boat to Amorgos via Koufonissia, Heraklia and Shinoussa, connections three times a week with Herakleon (Crete), Sifnos, Serifos, Samos, Ikaria and Rafina, twice a week with Sikinos and Folegandros; catamaran or hydrofoil daily to other Cyclades and Piraeus. The new airport is ready and should be fully operational in 1993, capable of handling charters and large planes from Athens.

Tourist Police

See regular police, Naxos town, © (0285) 22 100.

Naxos Town and its Venetian Citadel

Naxos, or Chora, the island's port and capital, is a fine Cycladic town, although some people find its twisting streets so narrow as to be almost claustrophobic and bewildering, which is just as the natives intended them to be, to confuse invading marauders. The old town, up on the hill, is divided into two neighbourhoods: **Bourgos** where the Greeks lived, and **Kastro** above, residence of the Venetian–Catholic nobility. In the former, the Orthodox cathedral, the **Metropolis of Zoodochos Pigi**, was created in the 18th century out of an old temple and older churches; its iconostasis was painted by Dimitrios Valvis of the Cretan school. Archaeologists have made some interesting discoveries near the Metropolis and would gladly knock it down for a slam bang dig if only the bishop would let them.

Although the city walls have all but disappeared, the inner walls of the Kastro remain. Inside, some 19 Venetian houses still bear their coats-of-arms—something you'll almost never see in Venice proper, where displays of pride were frowned upon, if not forbidden. Most of the Kastro's current residents claim descent from the Venetians, and many of their grandparents' tombstones in the 13th-century **Catholic Cathedral** boast grand titles. The cathedral was founded by Marco Sanudo, whose own palace, or what remains of it, can be seen directly across the square. Only one of the seven original towers of Kastro survives, locally known as **Pirgos,** guarding one of the three entrances to the enceinte. During the Turkish occupation

Naxos had a reputation for its schools. In the Kastro there was the School of Commerce, and a school run by Catholic friars, attended for two years by the young Nikos Kazantzakis. One of the school's buildings, not far from the cathedral, is now an **Archaeology Museum** (*8.45–3, Sun and holidays 9.30–2.30, closed Tues*), with improved lighting to display its collection of Cycladic figurines, Mycenaean pottery, a Roman mosaic of Europa, pieces of Archaic kouroi and a statuette of a pig about to be sick in a sack.

North of the port, the ancient causeway stretches out to the islet of Palatia and the unfinished **Temple of Apollo**, begun in 522 BC. The massive lintel on the temple platform, a lone gateway to nowhere, is now used as a dramatic frame for sunset photos. A small sandy beach curves around the causeway, protected by the ancient **harbour mole**, rebuilt by Marco Sanudo. **Grotta**, so named for its numerous caves, occupies the north shore of Chora, and it is here that you can see remains of the Cycladic buildings underwater. In one place a few steps are discernible; the locals claim that in ancient times a tunnel went from Grotta to Palatia. It is near the site of the ancient **Fort Delion**.

The busy waterfront has filled up with tourist establishments; in early August the main square, near the ferry port and bus station, is the site of the Dionysia, a festival of folk music and dance, wine and souvlaki. To the south, above the Agrarian Bank, is the 11th-century **Church of Panayia Pantansassa**, once part of a Byzantine monastery and famous for its very early icon of the Virgin. Further south numerous hotels and a whole new suburb of Chora, Nea Chora, has sprung up around popular **Ag. Georgios beach**.

Naxian Beaches

The busiest beach on the sandstrewn west coast of Naxos is **Ag. Anna**, linked by public bus and caique from Chora; well sheltered from the notorious meltemi, this beach and the neighbouring ones of **Ag. Prokopios** to the north, and **Plaka** to the south, offer a variety of watersports for experts and beginners alike; Ag. Prokopios even has jet skis to rent. Plaka has a camping site and beach, considered the best in Naxos, and a favourite of a new crop of young hippies.

Further south stretch the vast strands of **Mikri Vigla** and **Kastraki**. The sea here is brilliantly clear, the beaches are of pure white sand. Mikri Vigla is in fact a cape; to the north, **Parthena** beach is excellent for surfing and swimming, and to the south, **Sahara** is well equipped for sea sports. Further south, Sahara extends into **Kastraki**, again with sparkling clean sea and white sands, ideal for swimming, sunbathing and letting the kids run wild. Kastraki derives its name from the ruined Mycenaean fortress, built over the remains of a Cycladic acropolis. From here you can walk up to **T'apaliru**, the Byzantine castle high on its rock that defied Marco Sanudo and his mercenaries for two months. If the above beaches are too busy for your taste, there's a more remote strip of sand beyond Kastraki at **Pirgaki**.

Marble Quarries, Venetian Towers and Olive Groves

The main asphalted road south of Chora leads up to the fertile **Livadi Valley**. After a couple of kilometres the road splits, the left branch leading towards **Melanes** and the ancient marble quarries in the heart of Naxos; at the one called Flerio, 3 km east, lie two 7th-century BC *kouroi*, each 18-ft high. *Kouros* means 'young man', and in the Archaic period such statues—highly stylized, stiff figures, their arms hugging their sides, one foot stepping forward—were probably inspired by Egyptian art; the young men they portray are believed to have been Zeus' ancient guardians (the Cretan Curetes) or perhaps the Ionian god Apollo. At **Kourounochori** near Melanes stand ruins of a Venetian castle; **Ag. Thaleleos** in the same area has a monastery with a fine 13th-century church.

Back at the crossroads, the right branch of the main road from Naxos town leads to **Galanado**, site of the ruined Venetian tower called **Belonia** and the twin Venetian church of St John, with a Catholic chapel on one side and an Orthodox church on the other. The recently restored **Ag. Mamas**, dating from the 8th century and Naxos' original cathedral, is a short walk from the road on route to **Sangri**. Sangri's name is the Hellenized version of Sainte Croix, in turn the French name for the 16th-century Monastery Timious Stavrou. Sangri actually consists of three small villages spread out over the plateau, with many Byzantine and medieval towers and churches in the area; one of these, **Ag. Ioannis Gyroulas** in Ano Sangri, is built over a temple of Demeter.

The Valley of Tragea and Slopes of Mt Zas

From Sangri the road descends into the beautiful Valley of Tragea, flanked on either side by Naxos' highest mountains. Olives are the main product of the numerous small villages in the valley, including **Chalki**, where both the Byzantines and Venetians built towers: the Byzantine **Francopoulo**, in the centre, and up a steep path the **Apano Kastro**, last repaired by the Venetians and used, it is believed, as Marco Sanudo's summer home. He was not, however, the first to enjoy the splendid panorama of forests, olive groves and mountains from the summit; the fortress sits on Cyclopean foundations, and Mycenaean tombs have been discovered in the immediate area. In Chalki itself there are two fine churches with frescoes: 12th-century **Panayia Protothronis** and 9th-century **Ag. Diasoritis**.

From Chalki a paved road leads up to **Moni**, home of the most unusual church on Naxos, **Panayia Drossiani**, crowned with ancient corbelled domes of field stones. The main road through the Tragea valley continues on to **Filoti**, on the slopes of Mt Zas, the largest village in the region, with splendid views, and the chance to eavesdrop on everyday life in a traditional Naxian village. There are many good walking paths in the region, one leading up the slopes of **Mt Zas**. Dedicated to the goddess Za or to Zeus, the father of the gods, there's a cave near the summit once used as a religious sanctuary. A 3-hour path from Filoti follows the west flanks of the mountain to the excellently preserved Hellenistic **Tower of Chimarou**, built by Ptolemy, its isolation the main reason for its survival over the centuries. In Filoti itself there's the Venetian stronghold of the De Lasti family, and the church **Koimisis tis Theotokou** with a fine carved marble iconostasis, and another church, **Panayia Filotissa** with a marble steeple.

From Filoti the road skirts the slopes of Mt Zas on its way to **Apiranthos**, where the Venetian families Crispi and Sommaripa built towers. Many contemporary families, however, claim Cretan blood, descended from migrants who came during the Turkish occupation to work in the emery mines. Apiranthos is one of Naxos' more traditional villages, where some women still weave on looms; it's also the site of a small **museum**, devoted to mostly Neolithic finds. A road from here descends to the port of **Mutsuna**, where the emery used to be brought down from the mountains near Koronos by a rope funicular (more successful than the disastrous one used in *Zorba the Greek*) and loaded onto ships. Mutsuna has a fine beach; from here a dirt road follows the east coast south to the remote beach of **Psili Ammos**. Another beach, **Lionas**, is linked by paved road to **Koronos**.

Beyond Koronos the road turns into a winding, hairpin serpent leading to pretty **Komiaki**, highest of the island's villages, and **Apollon**, a popular summertime destination with its beach and pensions. Ancient marble quarries are carved out of the slopes of the mountain, and steps lead up to a colossal unfinished **kouros**, abandoned in the 7th century BC. Because Apollon was sacred to Apollo, the kouros is believed to represent the god; even more intriguingly, the long-vanished temple that stood here is part of the equilateral triangle formed by the temples of Apollo on Delos and Paros (*see* p.194). Apollon is as far as the bus goes; by car you can chance the unpaved road along the north coast back to Naxos town, passing the isolated beaches of **Ormos Abram** and **Pachia Ammos**, near the 1606 **monastery of Faneromeni**. There are lovely beaches in this northwest corner of the island, although when the *meltemi* roars they are far from pleasant. **Galini**, where the road improves, has the Byzantine fortified monastery **Ipsiloteras**. From here it's 6 km back to Chora.

Festivals

Like the Cretans, the Naxians sometimes improvise verses at their *paneyeria*, a custom dating back to ancient times. Some of the many celebrations are: 20 May, Ag. Thaleleos; 17 July, at Koronos; 15 August, Panayia at Filoti; 1 July, Ag. Anargyroi at Sangri; 23 August, at Tripodes; 14 July, Ag. Nikodimos at Naxos; 29 August, Ag. Ioannis at Apollon and Apiranthos; 23 April, Ag. Georgios at Kinidaros. The first week of August sees the Dionysia festival in Naxos town, with folkdancing in local costume; free food in the central square.

Where to Stay

Naxos is still one of the less expensive of the popular islands in this group, and even in August there still seem to be plenty of private rooms available, especially in the suburb of Nea Chora. If you take one, however, make sure you can find it again. This new addition to the capital is as bewildering as the old with its anonymous streets and countless skeletons of future buildings.

expensive

One of the most genteel places to stay is in the capital, at the traditionally-styled **Château Zevgoli**, in the backstreets up towards Kastro, © 22 993, with 10 rooms in rustic antique decor. At Mikri Vigla, the new **Mikri Vigla** is a low rise mini-resort hotel in the Cyclades style, on the beach with a pool, surfing centre and restaurant, © 75 240.

Five minutes from the Chora centre, **Hotel Anatoli**, ℂ 24 426, has a pool and views of the town and sea. Of the small hotels in Bourgos, just outside Kastro's walls, **Panorama** on Amphitris Street is the loveliest, with a marvellous sea view, ℂ 22 330. Outside the capital in Ag. Anna is a C class hotel of the same name (no tel). In Ag. Georgios there's a fairly wide selection of moderately priced hotels, including the family-run **Aeolis Hotel**, ℂ 22 321, and the smaller **St. George Pension** on the beach, ℂ 23 162.

cheap

Rooms in Nea Chora are cheap—around 3000 dr. Cheapest of all is the dormitory at the **Dionysos**, up near the Kastro, ℂ 22 331, where beds go for 1000 dr. a night. You can find rooms in most of the seaside villages, but the pickings are on the slim side, and rooms at Chalki, Filoti and Apollon. There are campgrounds at Ag. Georgios, Ag. Anna and Plaka.

Eating Out

There's a restaurant or taverna to suit all tastes and wallets in Naxos, and you don't have to depend on the numerous fast food joints if you're on a budget. Just behind the National Bank try **Thomas' Grill**, with good food (excellent souvlaki) but slow service (about 1500 dr.). The **Meltemi** is another old favourite by the water's edge, where a good Greek meal will set you back around 2500 dr. Two worthy *ouzeri* on the front serve all the usual *meze*. For rather more special Greek food in a lovely setting, **Niko's**, above the Commercial Bank, specializes in swordfish kebabs (3000 dr.). A beautiful spot for cocktails and 'alternative' dishes such as chef's salad and liver in cream sauce, the rooftop **Flamingo** looks over the harbour (3000 dr.). Quality grills are prepared at **Christo's Grill**, and if you want a change from the Greek diet, **Pharos**, next to the tourist information centre, offers pepper steaks and schnitzels (3000 dr.). For inexpensive, good Greek homecooking, try **Free Time** (walk up to square past the post office, 20 m from the little church on the left), where the food is just what you should expect from a little taverna. On Prokopios Beach there are a batch of excellent fish tavernas.

Paros

Despite the thousands of tourists who descend on Paros each summer, the peculiar Cycladic style of houses, the narrow alleys, little bridges and balconies overflowing with potted plants seem to dilute their presence, and the Parians have approached the inevitable increase in tourism with less fervour than their neighbours on Mykonos, managing, against overwhelming odds, to maintain a Greek island atmosphere. The inhabitants have, for the most part, remained fun-loving and hospitable and, if you can find a place to stay, it's a fine spot to while away a few days on golden beaches and charming villages, whose main building material comes from the underbelly of Paros' gentle mountain, Profitis Ilias (771 m)—some of the finest, most translucent marble in the world, prized by Classical sculptors and architects. Paros is one of the larger and more fertile Cyclades, with vineyards, wheat and barley fields, citrus and olive groves, and—an unusual sight in the archipelago—pastures of grazing cattle and sheep. Apart from its beaches, the island has several other attractions, including a famous Byzantine cathedral and a valley filled with butterflies in the summer.

History

With the trade of Parian marble, the island of Paros prospered early on. Its thriving Early Cycladic town was connected with Knossos and later with the Mycenaeans in the Late Cycladic period (1100 BC). In the 8th century BC Ionians moved in and brought about a second wave of prosperity. The 7th-century BC poet Archilochos, inventor of Iambic verse, and the sculptor Ariston were famous sons of ancient Paros. During the Persian Wars, Paros supported the Persians at both Marathon and Salamis; when Athens' proud General Miltiades came to punish them after Marathon, they withstood his month-long siege, leaving Miltiades to retire with a broken leg that developed into the gangrene that killed him. During the Peloponnesian Wars Paros remained neutral until forced to join the second Delian league in 378 BC. The island produced the great sculptor Skopas in the Hellenistic period and did well until Roman times, exporting marble to make the Temple of Solomon, the Venus of Milo, the temples on Delos and, much later, part of Napoleon's tomb. When the Romans took over Paros, their main concern was to take over the marble business.

Later invasions and destructions left the island practically deserted, and after 1207 the Venetian Sanudos ruled Paros from Naxos. Barbarossa captured the island in 1536, and from then on the Turks ruled by way of their proxy Duke of Naxos, although his control was often shaky, especially in the 1670s, when Paros was the base of Hugues Chevaliers, the original of Byron's *Corsair*. In 1770, the Parians had to put up with more unlikely visitors when the Russian fleet wintered on the island. During the War of Independence Manto Mavroyenous, whose parents were from Paros and Mykonos, led guerrilla attacks against the Turks throughout Greece; after the war the heroine returned to Paros and died there.

Connections

By air: three flights daily (six in the summer) from Athens; in the summer daily flights from Rhodes and three times a week from Herakleon, Crete.

By sea: daily ferry connections to Syros and Piraeus, Naxos, Mykonos, Ios, Santorini, Herakleon (Crete), Antiparos and Sifnos, three–four times a week with Rafina, Samos, Ikaria, Karpathos, Rhodes, Koufonissia and Amorgos, less frequently with the lesser Cyclades, Tinos, Skiathos and Thessaloniki; once a week in summer to Corfu and Ancona in Italy, once a week to Kuşadasi in Turkey; frequent boats to Antiparos from Paroikia and Pounta; summer hydrofoil and catamaran connections with Naxos, Mykonos, Ios, Santorini, Tinos, Syros, Amorgos and Piraeus.

Tourist Information

Plateia Manto Mavroyenous, ✆ (0284) 21 673. There is also an information centre in the Windmill on the quay.

Paroikia

Paroikia, the island's chief town and main port, offers at first glance a tatty vision of neglect: its municipal gardens are untended, its sidewalks left to crumble, as if to ward off prospective visitors who may be eyeing it from sea. But this initial impression is belied by the immaculate streets, white houses and tidy blue domes within Paroikia itself: a Cycladic beauty traversed by a long, winding main street that invites leisurely exploration, without having to trudge up hundreds of stairs.

It is the home of the **Aegean School of Fine Arts**, founded by Brett Taylor in 1966 and attended chiefly by American art students. The most striking monument in the heart of town is a narrow **13th-century wall**, a survivor of the Venetian castle, built out of the temples of Apollo and Demeter, forming an attractive collage of columns and pediments that now serve as the walls of neighbouring houses.

The Church of a Hundred Doors

On the west side of town, beyond a pine grove, stands Paros' chief monument, the cathedral **Ekatontapyliani** or 'church of a hundred doors'. According to tradition, it was founded by St Helen, mother of the Emperor Constantine, whose ship put into port at Paros during a storm, although actual construction of the church wasn't begun until the 6th century by Justinian. He hired an architect named Ignatius, an apprentice of the master builder of Ag. Sofia in Constantinople, and the story goes that when the master builder came to view his pupil's work, he was consumed by jealousy and pushed Ignatius off the roof of the church—but not before Ignatius had seized his foot and dragged him down to his death as well—a story told by the frieze in the north corner of the walled courtyard in front of the church. Another story accounts for its name: in reality only 99 doors have ever been found but when the 100th is discovered, it is a sign that Constantinople will return to the Greeks. To be honest, it's hard to find more than ten, and the Turks in Istanbul don't seem to be losing any sleep over it.

Since the 6th century, earthquakes have forced several alterations and rebuildings, and in the 1960s an attempt was made—although not entirely successfully—to remove the Venetian Baroque trappings from the façade to restore its early Byzantine appearance. Yet in the interior, reshaped in the 10th century to form a Greek cross with a dome on pendentives, the atmosphere is shadowy, jewel-like and Byzantine. Many stones are recycled from earlier Byzantine and pagan structures. Roman tombs and a well lie beneath the church floor.

On the carved wooden iconostasis is an icon of the Virgin, worshipped for its healing virtues; the church also contains the mortal remains of the Parian saint, Ag. Theoktisti. After being captured by pirates, she managed to flee into the forests of Paros. For 30 years Theoktisti lived a pious existence alone in the wilderness. A hunter finally found her, and when he brought her the communion bread she requested, she lay down and died. Unable to resist a free saintly relic, the hunter cut off her hand (now on display in a box) and made to sail away, but he was unable to depart until he had returned it to the saint's body. Beneath a wooden pallet is Theoktisti's footprint: the Greeks take off their shoes and fit their feet into it for good luck. Behind the iconostasis are frescoes and a carved marble Holy Table. The Baptistry to the right of the church has a sunken font.

Archaeology Museum

Near the church, a new building houses the **Archaeology Museum** (*closed Tues*), containing a section of the renowned 'Parian Chronicles'—a history of Greece, emphasizing the arts, from Kerkops (*c.* 1500 BC) to Diognetos (264 BC). The chronicle, carved in marble tablets, was discovered in the 17th century and to read the rest of it you'll have to visit the Ashmolean Museum in Oxford. The Paros museum also has finds from the local temple of Apollo, a 5th-century BC Winged Victory, and a short biography and frieze about Antilochos, a Parian who took part in the colonization of Thassos before he turned to lyric poetry.

Nearby is the small church of **Ag. Nikolaos**, built at the same time as the Ekatontapyliani. Just outside Paroikia, by a spring, are the ruins of a Classical-era **Asklepieion** (dedicated to the god of healing). Originally a temple to Pythian Apollo stood nearby.

Naoussa

Frequent buses connect Paroikia with the island's second port, the lovely **Naoussa**. Near the harbour stand the half-submerged ruins of the Venetian castle, as colourful fishing boats bob below. On the night of 23 August a hundred of these craft don torches and 'storm' the harbour in memory of the islanders' battle against Barbarossa, and all ends in merriment, music and dance. Naoussa has a **Byzantine Museum** with good icons, and there are others in the church Ag. Nikolaos Mostratos. Beaches are within walking distance of the port, or you can make sea excursions to others, notably **Kolimbithres**, with its bizarre, wind-sculpted rocks; other strands nearby are at Langeri, Santa Maria, and the fishing village of **Ambelas**, with a taverna and a quiet hotel.

Between Naoussa and Paroikia, men only may visit the **Monastery of Longovardes**, founded in 1683 by Christophoros Paleologos. The walls are covered with 17th-century frescoes, while other icons pre-date the monastery, which runs a monkish icon painting school. Nearby, the 7th-century basilica **Tris Ekklisies** was built over the site of a 4th-century BC heröon, or tomb-shrine of a hero or notable, in this case of the poet Archilochos. Northeast of Paroikia the marble foundation and altar of the **temple of Delian Apollo** still remain. Curiously, together with temples to Apollo on Delos and Naxos, it forms part of a perfect equilateral triangle. One of the triangle's altitudes extends to Mycenae and Rhodes town, site of the Colossus—the biggest of all the statues of Apollo. Another heads up to Mt Athos, for what it's worth.

Into the Land of Marble

From Paroikia, the main road east leads to Paros' ancient marble quarries at **Marathi**, not far from the fortified but abandoned monastery of Ag. Minas. The quarries too are abandoned, for economic reasons (they were last used for Napoleon's tomb), but it's fun to poke around, especially if you bring a light—the longest tunnel stretches 90 m underground. It produced an almost translucent stone called 'Lychnites' by the ancients, or 'candlelit marble', for its wonderful ability to absorb light. One of the quarries still has an ancient inscription.

The road continues to Paros' attractive medieval capital **Lefkas**, where farming, textiles and ceramics are the major industries. East of Lefkas **Prodromos** is an old farming village; **Marmara**, another village, lives up to its name ('marble')—even some of the streets are paved with it. Prettiest of the three, though, is **Marpissa**. Above its windmills are the ruins of a 15th-century Venetian fortress and the 16th-century **monastery of Ag. Antonios**, constructed out of Classical materials and containing lovely marbles and paintings (note the 17th-century fresco of the Second Coming). The ancient city of Paros is believed to have been in this area.

Down on the east coast **Piso Livadi** historically served as the port for these villages and the marble quarries, Now it's the centre of Paros' beach colonies: **Molos, Dryos**, and the island's best beach, the golden **Chrysi Akti**, stretching 700 m, and a favourite with surfers. Luxurious villas line the bay at Dryos where the Turkish fleet used to put in on its annual tax-collecting tour of the Aegean.

Beyond the ruins of the Asklepieion, the road south of Paroikia continues to **Petaloudes** (or Psychopiani), where swarms of butterflies set up housekeeping in July and August and fly up in clouds as you walk by. Petaloudes/Psychopiani has the ruins of a Venetian tower, while just outside the village stands the convent of Paros' second patron saint, **Ag. Arsenios**, the schoolteacher, abbot and prophet who was canonized in 1967. The saint is buried in the convent, but this time men are not allowed in. At **Pounta** there is a beach, and from here the small boat crosses to Antiparos (*see* p. 196). There's another beach at **Alyki** which has some facilities—and Paros' airport.

Festivals

15 August, Ekatontapyliani at Paroikia; 23 April, Ag. Georgios at Agkairia; 21 May, Ag. Konstantinos at Paroikia; 40 days after Orthodox Easter, Analypsis at Piso Livadi; in July, Fish and Wine Festival, Paroikia; 29 August, Ag. Ioannis at Lefkas; 18 August, Petaloudes.

Where to Stay

Paros is packed in the summer, and it's very hard to find a place if you just drop in. Nearly everyone stays in Paroikia, Naoussa or Piso Livadi.

expensive

Paros' best hotel is on the beach in Pounta, the **Holiday Sun**, ✆ 91 284, with all mod cons. The B class **Xenia** above Paroikia has a lovely view out over the village in its green amphitheatre, and there's a bar and restaurant, ✆ 21 394.

moderate

In the town of Paroikia, **Dina**, ✆ 21 325, with its garden is the most charming, with prices (6000 dr.) typical of Paros. The **Argonauta**, just back from the waterfront, is a pleasant family-run place, ✆ 21 440. An alternative in the interior, the stone-walled **Xenia Hotel** up in Lefkas, is a mere 10-minute bus ride from the beaches at Piso Livadi, ✆ 41 646. In Naoussa prices tend to be about the same: try the **Pension Naoussa**, right on the sea, ✆ 51 207. In Piso Livadi the class B pension **Marpissa**, ✆ 41 288, has slightly lower prices and an attractive view, although rooms are without bath.

cheap

Private rooms exist in Paroikia, Naoussa, Piso Livadi, and some principal beaches, and go for 3–4000 dr. There are several campsites on the island—**Camping Koula** and **Parasporos** near Paroikia, **Capt. Kafkis Camping** near Piso Livadi, **Surfing Beach Paros** at Alyki (the biggest, and best organized) and **Krios** at Krios, the beach opposite the port.

The best food in Paroikia, or on all of Paros for that matter, is at **To Tamarisko**, where you can dine delectably in a garden for around 3000–4000 dr. **Levantis**, back from the harbour to the right of the Venetian castle walls, has Greek, Lebanese and French dishes (3500 dr.). Near Ekatontapyliani church, is the **Lobster House** with the obvious speciality. Take a full wallet. For a simple, inexpensive taverna try **Nissiotissa**, behind the hospital; everything's good, especially the fresh fish. If you're fond of Vietnamese cuisine, **May Tey**, tucked away in the backstreets and a bit hard to find, has a limited but high quality choice (3000 dr.). For sunset views over a cocktail, the popular **Pebbles Bar** along from the port will provide, with classical music till sunset, thereafter jazz, occasionally live.

Naoussa is one of the most picturesque places to eat in all Greece; tavernas huddle by the water's edge in the little port, and cars can neither be seen nor heard. The **Limani** is where the local fishermen go for seafood (surely the highest recommendation), and the *ouzeri* **Trata** has all types of seafood *meze*, grilled octopus, shrimp, etc.

Antiparos

Little Antiparos ('before' Paros) was anciently known as Oliaros, and was connected to its larger neighbour by a causeway. In the time of Alexander the Great a large, deep cave full of stalactites was discovered on Antiparos, and for the past 2000 years it has been a must stop for every traveller in the region. Many who find Paros too tourist-ridden end up on a quiet Antiparian beach (there are good ones at Kastro, at Sifnaikos Yialos in the north, and Ag. Georgios in the south). Fish is plentiful, even in the restaurants, and there are many rooms to rent and three hotels.

Connections

Hourly every day by caique from Paroikia, Paros and hourly car ferry from Pounta, Paros.

Tourist Police

See regular police in town, © (0284) 61 202.

Kastro and the Cave

Lacking any defenses, Antiparos was uninhabited after the fall of Rome until the Venetians, under Leonardo Lorentani, built a small castle. The remains of it can still be seen in the harbour of Antiparos' one town, **Kastro**. There are also two 17th-century churches, the cathedral **Ag. Nikolaos** and **Evangelismos**.

The **cave** remains Antiparos' star attraction, despite centuries of tourists whacking off free souvenir stalactites. In the summer excursion boats run not only from Kastro, but also from

Paroikia and Pounta. From the boat landing stage it's a half-hour walk up by foot and less by donkey, and then a 70-m descent by steps into the fantastic, spooky chamber. The cave is really about twice as deep, but the rest has been closed as too dangerous for visits. Perhaps to make up for breaking off the stalactites, famous visitors of the past have smoked and carved their names on the walls, including Lord Byron and King Otho of Greece (1840). One stalagmite attests in Latin to a Christmas mass celebrated in the cavern by Count Nouantelle in 1673, attended by 500 (paid) locals. Unfortunately, a famous older inscription has been lost; its several authors declared that they were hiding in the cave from Alexander the Great, who had accused them of plotting an assassination attempt. The church by the entrance of the cave, **Ag. Ioannis**, was built in 1774. If you come in the winter, you'll have to pick up the key to the cave's entrance in Kastro.

Of the islets off Antiparos, **Strogilonisi** and **Despotiko** are rabbit-hunting reserves. On **Saliagos**, a fishing village from the 5th millennium has been excavated by John Evans and Colin Renfrew, the first Neolithic site discovered in the Cyclades.

Festivals

23 April, Ag. Georgios; 21 May, Ag. Konstantinos at Glyfa; and 8 May, Ag. Ioannis Theologos, by the cave.

Where to Stay

moderate–cheap

Many people who can't find a place to stay in Paros come to Antiparos, though prices are only a tiny bit lower here. Little **Chryssi Akti** on the beach is an elegant class C hotel, © 61 220. Slightly less expensive, the 36-room **Mantalena** on the waterfront offers nice views of the harbour and Paros, © 61 206. There are also quite a few pensions (**Korali** seems to be about the cheapest, © 61 236), and rooms to let, and although there's an organized **campsite**, © 61 221, freelancers are winked at if they distance themselves from town.

Eating Out

Unfortunately, demand has also jacked up the price of food here, and eating out is no cheaper than Paros. In the port a number of self-service and fast food places have sprouted up, among them **Anargiros**, with a decent selection of ready food. In town the locals head for **Klimataria** for good food at (reasonably) low prices, or the slightly more expensive **Makis. Giorgios Taverna**, open at night, is known for well-prepared fish dinners.

Santorini (Thira)

As most people's favourite Greek island, the pressure is on Santorini to come up with the goods; it does, though the awesome mixture of towering, sinister multi-coloured volcanic cliffs, dappled with the 'chic'-est, most brilliant-white, trendiest bars and restaurants in the country, gives the island a peculiar split personality. Usually bathed in glorious sunshine, but occasionally lashed by high winds and rain, everything seems more intense here, especially daily life. Some call it Devil's Island, and find a stay here both exhilirating and disturbing—with such a concentration of visitors, something out of the ordinary is guaranteed to happen every day.

As your fragile ship sails into the volcano's rim, the black islands on your right indeed look demonic. Volcanically fertile Santorini has, literally, had its ups and downs: throughout history parts of the island and its circular archipelago have seismatically appeared and disappeared under the waves. Human endeavours on the island have fared similarly: you can visit no less than three former 'capitals'—the Minoan centre of Akrotiri, a favourite candidate for Metropolis, the capital of the legendary Atlantis; the Classical capital Thira at Mesa Vouna; and the medieval Skaros, as well as the picturesque modern town of Fira, perched on the edge of Santorini's cliffs. But this, too, was flattened by an earthquake in 1956 (though lovingly rebuilt). Alhough now one of the most popular destinations in the Aegean and a must on the itinerary of most cruise ships, older inhabitants can remember when Santorini hosted more political prisoners than tourists, and nights were filled with the rumour of vampires rather than the chatter of café society sipping Bloody Marys, watching the sun go down in one of the world's most enchanting settings.

History

The history of Santorini, or Thira, is closely related to its geology. In the long distant past the island was created from volcanic debris, circular in shape, with a crater called Strogyle in the centre. Its regular eruptions created a rich, volcanic soil, which attracted inhabitants early on—from Karia originally, until they were chased away by the Cretans. They built their colony at Akrotiri at the height of the Minoan civilization and in approximately 1450 BC, the volcano erupted again, destroying not only Akrotiri, but causing irreparable damage to the mighty Minoan civilization in Crete as well.

This relatively recent theory was proposed by the Greek archaeologist Spirydon Marinatos. In 1939 he decided that the destruction of Amnisos, the port of Knossos on Crete, could only have been caused by a massive natural disaster, such as a tidal wave from the north. What, he wondered, could have caused such a catastrophe? Marinatos put together the following clues: southeast of Santorini oceanographers had discovered volcanic ash from Strogyle on the sea bed, covering an area of 900 by 300 km^2; on nearby Anafi and Eastern Crete itself there's a layer of volcanic tephra 3–20 mm thick. This would be sufficient to destroy plant growth and ruin farming for a generation.

A Classical clue came from the Athenian reformer Solon, who in 600 BC wrote of his journey to Egypt, where the scribes told him of the disappearance of Kreftia (Crete?) 9000 years before, a figure Solon might have mistaken for a more correct 900. The Egyptians, who had maintained steady trade links with Crete and Santorini, supposedly described to Solon the lost land of Atlantis, made of red, white and black volcanic rock (like Santorini today) and spoke of a city vanishing in 24 hours. In his *Critias*, Plato described Atlantis as being composed of one round island and one long island, connected by one culture and rule (Santorini and Crete, under Minos?); a sweet land of art, flowers and fruit—as portrayed on the frescoes discovered at Akrotiri. In the 19th century French archaeologists had discovered Minoan pots at Akrotiri, and it was there that Marinatos began to dig in 1967, bringing to light from under its deep tephra tomb a well-preserved Minoan town.

Whether or not Santorini was in fact the Atlantis of the ancients, the theory of the ruin of Minoan life by a series of earthquakes, volcanic explosions and subsequent tidal wave has support in the similar explosion of Krakatoa in 1883, of such force that it could be heard 3000 miles away in Western Australia. When the island blew up, it created a caldera (a crater left by an explosion) of 8.3 km^2. As the sea rushed in to fill the caldera, it created a tidal wave more than 200 m high that destroyed everything in a 150-km path. Consider that the caldera left by Strogyle, that is the present bay of Santorini, is 22 km^2. The fact that no bodies were found at Akrotiri lead archaeologists to suppose that earthquakes and other omens warned the inhabitants to flee in time. The islets of Therasia and Aspronisi mark the edges of the caldera.

In the 8th century BC the Dorians moved into Santorini, building their capital at Mesa Vouna, which survived until the early decades after Christ. Thira was the island's Doric name, and legends have it that the Thirians founded the city of Cyrene in Libya. In Hellenistic times, Ptolemy of Egypt fortified the island and dedicated temples to Dionysos and to his own family.

Church and Cliffs on Thira, Cyclades

Like the Ptolemies, the Byzantines also considered the island to be of strategic importance and fortified it, but most of their citadels have been toppled by earthquakes. Skaros near Imerovigli became the Venetian capital, when it was ruled by the Crispi, who preferred to call their fief after its patron saint Saint Irene, elided over the years into Santorini. Throughout its history Santorini has enjoyed a considerable reputation for its high octane wine.

Connections

By air: daily flights from Athens; frequent air connections with Mykonos, Herakleon (Crete) and Rhodes.

By sea: daily ferry connections with Piraeus, Ios, Paros, Naxos, Mykonos and Herakleon (Crete). Frequently with other Cyclades, two–three times a week with the Dodecanese, Skiathos and Thessaloniki. Ferries call at Athinios, from where there is a road up to the capital; there are also frequent hydrofoil and catamaran services to other Cyclades islands and Piraeus.

SANTORINI
(THIRA)

See regular police, 25 tou Martiou St, © (0286) 22 649.

Fira

Most passengers disembark at **Athinios**; those who disembark beneath the towering cliffs at Fira (cruise ships, mostly), can take a motor launch to the tiny port of Skala Fira, and from there hire a donkey to travel the winding path to the town 270 m above. Those in more of a hurry can pop up on the Austrian-built cable car in two minutes. Donated to the island by ship-owner Evangelos Nomikos, profits from the cable car go to Santorini's communities—and to the donkey drivers, who receive a percentage of each ticket. It operates every 15 minutes from 6.45 am to 8.15 pm.

Those who remember **Fira** (also spelt Thira or Thera), the capital, before 1956 say that the present town bears no comparison architecturally to its original, although it's pleasant enough—Cycladically white, built on several terraces, adorned with pretty churches. The cliff is hung with cafés and restaurants, all boasting one of the world's most magnificent views.

Santorini's **museum** (*8.45–3, Sun 9.30–2.30, closed Tues*) is near the cable car on the north side of town. It houses finds from Akrotiri, Mesa Vouna and Early Cycladic figurines found in the local pumice mines. The famous Santorini frescoes are still in the National Museum in Athens, although there are rumours that a new museum will be built in Fira to house them on the island. As well as the museum one can also visit the handicraft workshop founded by Queen Frederika, where women weave large carpets on looms. The **Megaron Gyzi museum**, located in a beautiful 17th-century mansion, houses exhibits on the island's history—manuscripts from the 16th–19th centuries, costumes, old maps of the Cyclades, and some photographs of Santorini before the 1956 earthquake (*10.30–1.30 and 5–8*).

Akrotiri

Buses from Fira make several trips daily to **Akrotiri** (*daily, 8–7*), the Minoan town discovered in 1967 by Marinatos. Excavations here are infinitely laborious due to the thick layer of tephra, or volcanic glass that buried Akrotiri; fittingly, tephra is quarried to make cement for tombstones. The ancient city revealed beneath it is wonderful and strange, made even more unreal by the huge modern roof that protects the excavations from the elements. A carpet of volcanic dust silences all footsteps as you walk amid houses up to three storeys high, many still containing their huge pithoi, or storage pots. In one of the houses is the controversial grave of Marinatos, who died recently after a fall on the site and asked to be buried by his life's work. The huge filing cabinets hold pottery sherds yet to be pieced together. For more details, pick up the locally available *Art and Religion in Thira: Reconstructing a Bronze Age Society*, by Dr Nanno Marinatos, son of the archaeologist. Below the excavation site is a black rock beach and taverna; there are also some coffee shops and rooms in the vineyard-surrounded villages above.

East of Akrotiri, **Exomitis** has one of the best-preserved Byzantine fortresses of the Cyclades; submerged nearby are the ruins of the ancient town of Eleusis. The island's best beach, **Perissa**, is around to the east, linked by road to the attractive old village of **Embourion**; like the other beaches of Santorini, the sand here is volcanic and black and warms quickly in the sun. Perissa has good restaurants, tavernas and a campsite. A modern church stands on the site of the Byzantine Saint Irene, for whom the island is named.

Up on the rocky headland of Mesa Vouna (a track leads up from Perissa) is **Ancient Thira**, its extensive ruins built on great terraces. Excavated by the German archaeologist Hiller von Gortringen in the late 19th century, the site produced the fine 'Santorini vases' in the museum. Most of what you see today dates from the Ptolemies, who used the city as a base for their enterprises further north and adorned it with temples to the Egyptian gods, Dionysos, Apollo, to their semi-divine selves and to the mythical founding father Thira. There are impressive remains of the agora and theatre, with a dizzying view down to the sea; also several cemeteries and a gymnasium. Numerous houses still have mosaics; graffiti dating from 800 BC may be seen on the Terrace of Celebrations, recording the names of competitors and dancers of the gymnopedies. Note the unusual Cyclopean walls nearby.

North of Ancient Thira stretches another black beach, **Kamari**, with tavernas, while inland, up the slope from Mesa Vouna, is the 1712 **Monastery Profitis Ilias** on Santorini's highest point (566 m). On a clear day you can see Crete from here, and on an exceptionally clear day, it is said, even Rhodes hovers faintly on the horizon. The locals, never forgetting the terrifying earthquake of 1956, say the monastery is the only place that will protrude above sea level when the rest of Santorini sinks into the sea to join its other half. Profitis Ilias has a museum of valuable church objects, diamond gospels, the mitre of Gregory V, a crusader's cross and local folk items (*8–1 and 2.30–sunset, closed Sun; but check at Fira's tourist office to see if it has re-opened*). At the foot of Profitis Ilias, by the village of Mesa Gonia, is the 11th-century **Panayia Episkopi** or Kimisis Theotokou, converted by the Venetians to the Catholic rite when they conquered Santorini, but under the Turks the Orthodox recovered their own. Inside are Byzantine icons, and on 15 August it holds the biggest *paneyeri* on the island.

Pirgos, near the centre of Santorini, shares with Embourion the title of the oldest surviving village on the island, with interesting old houses, Byzantine walls, and a Venetian fort. **Athinios**, the port below, has a small beach, bars and restaurants.

North of Fira

Skaros, on the road to Oia, was the medieval capital of Santorini, but it has been much damaged by earthquakes. Its Ag. Stephanos is the oldest church on the island, and you can also see the crumbling ruins of a Catholic convent of Santa Katerina, built after a young girl's vision in 1596. The nuns lived a life of extreme hardship until 1818 when they moved to Fira, and now the desolate convent is about to tumble down. In **Imerovigli** stands a convent, built in 1674 and still inhabited, dedicated to Ag. Nikolaos.

At the end of the road that mouthful of vowels called **Oia**, or Ia, is the third port of Santorini, and at least one ship still calls here regularly. Half-ruined by the earthquake, its white houses are piled on top of one another up the steep slope. Although it's a long hard walk up from the beach, you can fill your pockets with pumice-stone souvenirs for friends at home.

Around the Caldera

Santorini's caldera is 10 km wide and 380 m deep. Curving around the northwestern rim, the islet **Therasia** was part of Santorini until another eruption-earthquake in 236 BC blasted them apart. Pumice mined here went into the building of the Suez Canal. In one of the quarries a Middle Cycladic settlement was discovered, pre-dating Akrotiri, though there are no traces of it now. There are three villages on Therasia; the largest, **Manolas**, has tavernas and rooms to rent. Excursion boats also make trips out to the 'burnt isles', **Palia and Nea Kameni**, both still volcanically active, especially the Metaxa crater on Nea Kameni. However, even though a local brochure refers to Nea Kameni as 'the strange volcano which cause you greatness', be forewarned that half the people who visit it come away disappointed.

Festivals

19 and 20 July, at Profitis Ilias; 20 October, Ag. Artemiou in Fira; 26 October, Ag. Dimitriou in Karterthos; 15 August, at Mesa Gonia and Fira.

Where to Stay

There's nothing like staying in Fira with a view over the great caldera, but do book in advance.

luxury

Still at the top of the list for luxury and the view is the **Hotel Atlantis**, © 22 232, a class A establishment near the heart of town. In Oia, the **Katikies** are a set of beautifully decorated apartments with views of the sea and neighbouring islands, © 71 401.

expensive

With the classic view, facing the volcano, the **Porto Carra**, © 22 979, is typical of the many C class hotels in Fira. In the central square, the **Pelican**, © 23 113, is another. Should either of these be full, try the larger **Kallisti Thira**, another pleasant option, with 33 rooms, © 22 317. If you are travelling in company, consider staying at **Dana Villas**, with self-contained apartments for 2–6 people, fully furnished in traditional island style, with fabulous views and sunsets, © 22 566.

moderate

When Fira is full, you can almost always find a room elsewhere on the island, and as bus connections are good it's not all that hard getting about. Kamari has many modest-sized hotels and pensions, although the prices tend to be rather bold—the C class **Matina** has doubles starting at 6500 dr., © 31 491. Another place in Kamari which (just) fits into this category is **Hotel Sunshine**, next to the sea, 31 394. In Oia there are a number of moderately-priced rooms and pensions. Better yet, the NTOG has restored 30 traditional homes to let out to visitors at reasonable prices, furnished with native embroideries and handcarved furniture. Each house accommodates 2–7 people; for reservations and current prices, contact the NTOG or Paradosiakos at Ikismos Oias, Oia, © 71 234.

cheap

There are **youth hostels** in Fira, © 22 722, and Oia, © 71 465, open April–Oct, card not required. In town the **Kamares Hostel** is near the cable car. The island's campsites are at Fira, Kamari and Perissa. If you land in Athinios, the owners of rooms (mostly in Messaria, Embourion and Karterados) will meet you in their vans and whisk you away. Expect to pay at least 4000 dr. in season.

Eating Out

Be prepared for above average prices. Some places serve local wines by the glass. The most famous labels are Atlantis, Santina, Nikteri, Kaldera, Vulcan and Vissanto.

For international cuisine and reputedly the best food on Santorini, **Castro** near the cable car will set you back a good 5000 dr. or more for one of its lavish spreads. **Nikolaos Taverna**, situated right in the heart of Fira, is a reassuring real Greek taverna in this island of excess; you'll recognize it by the people waiting at the door to get in (so get there early). On the main street near the port police, try and squeeze in at **The Roosters**, a fun little restaurant with tasty Greek dishes, where the owner will know all about you within 5 minutes of your arrival. It would be worth the price to eat at **Meridiana** for the view alone, but the food is good, too, and the atmosphere elegant, with a piano bar; dinner here costs around 4000 dr., with good Santorini wine.

In Oia there are two excellent choices—**Kyklos**, built into the caves and romantically atmospheric, with main courses starting at 1500 dr., and **Mama Africa** with an exotic menu that includes Thai and Indian dishes. In Kamari, **Kamari** has good, inexpensive dining in a family-run taverna, serving the island speciality *fava* (a purée of yellow peas, oil, lemon and onion). Next to the sea, **Irinis** is another local favourite. More expensive, and offering some international dishes, **Camille Stefan** is at the end of the main road on Kamari beach. Perissa has the **Retsina**, a simple, popular taverna.

Cafés and Nightlife

Café and bar life takes up as much time as eating in Santorini. Many people like to be seen at **Bonjour** in the main square, while **Bebis** is the watering hole for a pleasantly loony young crowd. **Kirathira** appeals to all types and age groups, while **Alexandria** is more sedate and attracts an older set (by Santorini's standards, anyway). **Franco's** is still *the* place to go for sunset, even if the price of a coffee there is sky high. In Kamari the **Sail Inn** has loud music, fun evenings and glamorous bar girls,

Senfa:

sign to Beach in (our) town
Shows to the left.

also me to right in Shore

and **Valentino's** always has a large crowd. Drop in at the **Yellow Donkey** discotheque in the early hours and dance till dawn—there's very little point in trying to get an early night on this fun-loving island anyway.

For those who prefer a bouquet to a bop, there are two wineries which offer wine tasting; **Boutari**, at Megalochori, towards Akrotiri, and **Kutsoyanopoulos**, on the road to Kamari. While connoisseurs are most welcome, they still insist you have a good time.

Serifos

Where its neighbour Sifnos welcomes the visitor with green terraces and dovecots, Serifos, 'the barren one' tends to intimidate with its stark rocks. The island owed much of its prosperity in antiquity to its iron and copper mines, among the richest in Greece. However, when other sources were discovered in Africa that could be exploited more economically, the mines on Serifos were abandoned, and the population drastically decreased. Historically, the fate of Serifos follows that of the other Cyclades; Chora, high above the sea, was once fortified with a Byzantine-Venetian castle and walls, and here and there on the island are odd remains left by other conquerors.

The appealing, if dishevelled port, Livadi, with a little line of friendly tavernas and bars straggling along an unpaved dirt road, provides an informal foreground to the imposing view of Chora behind, seemingly inaccessible as it climbs impressively up the steep slopes. After the gleaming, spotless artificial waterfronts of some more popular islands, Serifos' unkempt air is a refreshing reminder that you are in Greece after all, where the *kafeneíons* buzz with village

SERIFOS

gossip, and walking about means side-stepping fishing boats being repainted in the back-streets. If you can put up with water shortages in August, Serifos offers not only island authenticity but also some of the most serene beaches in the Cyclades.

Mythology

What Serifos may lack in history is more than compensated for by its mythology, for it was here that Danaë, set adrift in a box with her infant son Perseus, washed up on shore. This cruel deed was done by Danaë's own father, Acrisius, King of Argos, for it had been prophesied that a son of Danaë would slay him. In order to foil the oracle Acrisius had locked his daughter in a tower, but even there her beauty did not fail to attract the amorous attentions of Zeus, who came to her in a shower of golden rain and fathered Perseus.

Enraged but unable to put his daughter or grandson to death, Acrisius decided to leave the issue to fate and set them adrift in the box. Zeus guided them to Serifos, where a fisherman discovered them and brought them to Polydectes, the king of the island. Struck by her beauty, Polydectes wanted to marry Danaë but she refused him, and as Perseus grew older he defended his mother's decision. Polydectes pretended to lose interest in Danaë, while he plotted to remove Perseus from the scene by asking him to do a favour: fetch the head of the gorgon Medusa, the only mortal of the three horrible Gorgon sisters, who had hair made of living snakes, whose eyes bulged and whose teeth were fangs. The sisters were so ugly that a mere glance at one of them turned a human to stone.

Despite Danaë's horror at this treachery of Polydectes, Perseus accepted and accomplished the task, assisted by the goddess Athena, who helped him procure a mirror-like shield, winged shoes, a cloak of invisibility and other essential tools. With Medusa's awful head in his pouch Perseus returned to Serifos (saving Andromeda from a sea monster on the way), to find his mother hiding from the forceful Polydectes in the hut of the fisherman who had saved them so long ago. Angrily Perseus went up to the palace, where he found a very surprised Polydectes at a great banquet. Perseus told him that he had succeeded in his quest and held up the prize as proof, instantly turning everyone in the room into stone.

The kind fisherman was declared King of Serifos by Perseus, and the hero and his mother went home to Argos. Still fearing the old prophecy, Danaë's father fled before them. But fate caught up with the old King in another town, where Perseus was competing in an athletic contest and accidentally killed his grandfather with a javelin in the foot.

Connections

Daily with Piraeus, Sifnos, Milos and Kythnos, four times a week with Kimolos, three times a week with Santorini and Folegandros, twice a week with Sikinos and Ios, once a week to Syros.

NTOG, Livadi, ✆ (0281) 51 300.

Livadi and Chora

Most people who visit Serifos stay in **Livadi**, the port, where there's a beach and many rooms to rent. There are two other beaches within easy walking distance from Livadi, towards the south; the second has become the unofficial campsite on the island.

Serifos, or **Chora**, the main town, is linked to the port by an hourly bus service—it's also the end of the line; and to see the rest of the island you'll have to rely on your own steam. Chora is a pretty town, with houses here and there made from pieces salvaged from the old fortress while others date back to the Middle Ages; its old windmills still stand, and in the spring you may find a rare carnation that grows only on Serifos. From Chora a 20-minute walk leads down to **Psili Ammos**, an excellent beach on the east coast.

Around Serifos

The road continues beyond Chora past the 6th-century Byzantine **Aspropirgos** (White Castle) to **Megalo Chorio**, believed to occupy the site of the ancient capital of Serifos; below, **Megalo Livadi**, now visited for its beach, once served as the loading dock for the iron and copper mined near Megalo Chorio. From Megalo Livadi you can walk around **Mesa Akrotiri** where there are two caves: the cave of the Cyclops Polythemus with stalactites and another at **Koutala**, where signs of prehistoric settlement were found. Both caves are now off limits but Koutala offers a beach by way of compensation, and a mule path from here follows the south coast back to Livadi.

Sikamia Bay in the north is a good place to get away from it all, not only for its beach but also for the rare bit of shade and fresh water. The village of **Galani** is half an hour on foot from Sikamia, and from here you can visit **Taxiarchos Monastery**, built in 1500 and containing a precious old table, 18th-century frescoes by Skordilis, and Byzantine manuscripts in the library. The oldest church on Serifos is from the 10th century, at **Panayia**. **Kalitsos**, not far from Galani, is another pleasantly green place, with two restaurants.

Other beaches on Serifos are Karavi, Lia, Ag. Sostis, Platys Yialos, Halara and Ganima. Most of these are remote but can be reached by motorcycle. Karavi, south of Livadi, is one of the most popular.

Festivals

Fava beans are the big speciality at these celebrations: 5 May, Ag. Irene at Koutala; 27 July, Ag. Panteleimonos at Mt Oros; 7 September, Ag. Sosoudos at Livadi; 6 August, Sotiros at Kalobelli; 15–17 August, Panayia near the Monastery and at a different village each day.

Serifos is well-known enough for its hotels and rooms to fill up in the summer. These are all near the sea, most of them in Livadi.

moderate

All the hotels are in Livadi, and all are on the beach. The **Serifos Beach Hotel** is the island's biggest, © 51 209, with a nice taverna downstairs, or for the same price you can stay at the **Areti**, a B class pension with a garden and view over the water, © 51 479. More expensive is the **Maistrali**, © 51 381, while the smaller **Pension Perseus**, © 51 273, is an old standby. Not far from the Serifos Beach there are excellent rooms with balcony for 5500 dr. above the Cavo d'Oro supermarket.

cheap

If you can put up with no lock on the communal bathroom door, erratic showers even by Greek standards, and the odd pane of glass missing, **Corali's** dilapidated charms may suit your budget—it's well situated a few metres from the harbour above the bakery. Otherwise there are rooms in Livadi and 20 or so up in Chora. There's a campsite in Livadakia, with good facilities.

Eating Out

The sea is clean and the fish is especially good in Serifos' seaside tavernas. Popular with locals and tourists alike, **Teli's**, on the waterfront in Livadi, offers excellent and inexpensive food and friendly service. For a pleasantly zany atmosphere, with good, wholesome food (spaghetti, chicken curries) apart from the usual Greek fare, try **Benny's Tavern-Mokkas** at the end of the port where the locals, yachties, tourists, various children and an assortment of cats and dogs mingle happily together. Whenever you come across that endangered species, the *ouzeri*, treasure it; the **Meltemi** will give you a *carafaki* (enough for three or four good drinks) and plenty of tasty nibbles (hot cheese pies, etc) for less than 800 dr. Round the bay, wiggle your toes in the sand at **Stamatis Taverna**, and enjoy his excellent ready food or grilled meats (2000 dr.). A few metres away, in the restaurant of the hotel Cyclades, you can savour spaghetti with shrimps, mussels and clams, or an excellent shrimp casserole with feta cheese and tomatoes (2500 dr.). Up in Chora, **Maroulis** is in the lovely piazza by the town hall (climb up the steps where the bus stops), and serves *meze* with a difference, a definite relief if your relationship with Greek salads is wearing thin; try the sun-dried tomatoes, sautéed in butter, fennel done the same way, Serifot specialities such as *keftedes*, *spetsofai* and chick-peas from the wood oven, all washed down with the family's own wine (2500 dr.). Also in Serifos, open in mid-summer only, the **Petros** is a long-time favourite with the usual Greek food, but cooked just that bit better.

Sifnos in recent years has become the most popular island in the western Cyclades, with good reason—it's the prettiest, with its peaceful green hills and terraces, charming villages, friendly people and one long sandy beach. Here and there the landscape is dotted with Venetian dovecots, windmills, some 40 ruined Classical towers and over 300 miniature chapels. It is an exceptionally pleasant island for walks. Among the Greeks Sifnos is famous for its pottery and its cooks, both of which have been in such demand elsewhere that few remain on Sifnos, although the legacy of good cooking remains. The island's olives are said to produce the best oil in the Cyclades, but sadly agriculture on the island is in decline (as is often the case, in direct correlation with the rise in tourism), and once-fertile Sifnos now has to import almost all of its foodstuffs.

History

The Phoenicians, one of the first groups of people to settle on Sifnos, named the island Meropia according to Pliny and began to mine its gold. They were followed by the Cretans, who founded Minoa near Apollonia, who were in turn replaced by Ionians who lived near Ag. Andreas and elsewhere. Meropia, meanwhile, had become famous for its gold; at one time, it is said, there was so much of the precious stuff that the Sifniotes simply divided it among themselves each year, with enough left over in the 6th century to pave their main square with the most costly Parian marble. In the same century Apollo at Delphi demanded that the wealthy Sifniotes contribute a tithe of gold in the form of a solid egg to his sanctuary every year. In 530 BC they constructed a magnificent treasury at Delphi to house the gold and adorned it with a fine frieze and pediment which can still be seen,

The Chapel on Sifnos

and for many years Sifnos could boast the richest of all the oracle's treasures. But one year the Sifniotes, who began to have a reputation for greed and cunning, decided they needed the gold more than Apollo, and sent the god a gilded rock. Apollo soon discovered he had been duped and cursed the island. This gave Polycrates, the Tyrant of Samos, a good excuse to extract a huge fine from Sifnos; 40 triremes plundered and ransomed most of the island's gold, and the curse supposedly caused the mines to sink and give out. Thus the island became empty, or *sifnos* in Greek. Nowadays most of the ancient mines are underwater, at Ag. Mina, Kapsalos and Ag. Suzon.

After shooting itself in the foot with its twopenny fraud, Sifnos went into decline and the inhabitants moved up to Kastro, where a Roman cemetery has been discovered. In 1307 the Da Koronia family ruled the island for Venice; in 1456 Kozadinos, the Lord of Kythnos, married into the family and his descendants ruled Sifnos until the Turks took the island in 1617. Towards the end of the 17th century the Ottomans made an attempt to re-open the ancient mines, or at least got as far as sending out experts from Istanbul to examine them. Supposedly, when they got wind of these plans, the islanders hired a band of French pirates to sink the Sultan's ship. The experts, in turn, heard of the deal with the pirates, and simply went home. Later the French themselves exploited the local deposits of iron ore and lead; mining ended in 1914.

Sifnos has also made an important contribution to Greek letters. At the end of the 17th century the 'School of the Holy Tomb' was founded on the island to keep alive the ancient Greek language and classics during the Turkish occupation, attracting students from all over Greece. Nikolaos Chrysogelos, the most famous headmaster, led a contingent of Sifniotes in the War of Independence, and went on to become modern Greece's first Minister of Education. Another islander, the 19th-century poet-satirist Cleanthis Triandafilos, who wrote under the name Rabagas, was a thorn in the side of the monarchy until he was imprisoned and committed suicide. Ioannis Gyparis (d. 1942) was another Sifniote of note; along with Cadafy, he was one of the first poets to espouse the use of the demotic language (as opposed to the formal *katharevousa*) in literature.

Connections

Daily with Piraeus, Kythnos, Serifos and Milos; four times a week with Kimolos, two–three times a week with Ios, Santorini, Folegandros and Sikinos, once a week with Paros, Crete, Rhodes, Karpathos, Kassos, Halki and Symi.

Tourist Information

NTOG, Kamares, ✆ (0284) 31 977.

Tourist police, see regular police, Apollonia, ✆ (0284) 31 210.

From Kamares to Apollonia and Artemon

The island's port, shady **Kamares**, has become in recent years a typical waterside jumble of tourist facilities. Situated between two steep, barren rocks that belie the fertility inland, Kamares has some good places to camp, tavernas, etc. Only two of the many pottery workshops that once lined the north side of the harbour still survive. Sifnos' single bus route begins from Kamares: a dramatic climb up to the capital **Apollonia**, then on to Artemon, Chrissopigi, the resort Platys Gialos, Faros and Kastro.

Apollonia is a Cycladic idyll, spread out across the hills, a circle of white from the distance. Its name comes from a 7th-century BC temple of Apollo, superseded in the 18th century by the church **Panayia Ouranoforia** in the highest part of town. Fragments of the temple can still be seen, and there's a marble relief of St George over the door. Another church, **Ag. Athanasios** (next to the pretty square dedicated to Cleanthis Triandafilos), has frescoes and a carved wooden iconostasis. In the bus stop square the **Museum of Popular Arts and Folklore** houses a fine ethnographic collection of Sifniot pottery, embroideries and costumes (*6–10, closed Mon*). There are numerous dovecots in the region with triangular designs which are repeated in the architecture of some of the houses. Local music, played on the violin and *laouto*, can frequently be heard in the cafés on Sundays.

Artemis is Apollo's twin sister; similarly **Artemon** is Apollonia's twin village and the second largest on Sifnos. Beneath its windmills are the island's most ambitious residences and churches. The church of **Kochi**, with its cluster of domes, occupies the site of a temple of Artemis; also in Artemon, little 17th-century **Ag. Georgios tou Afendi** contains several fine icons from the period, and **Panayia ta Gournia**, near the bridge has a beautiful interior (keys next door). Between Apollonia and Platys Yialos the monastery of **Ag. Andreas**, sitting on a hill, has some ruins of the double walls that once encircled the ancient citadel, and a little further north, but not accessible by road, is the monastery of **Profitis Ilias**, with a small network of catacombs and cells. Check that these are open before setting out.

Kastro, Trouble in the Evening, and Panayia Chrissopigi

Kastro, overlooking the east coast, is a 3-km walk from Artemon. This was the Classical and medieval capital of Sifnos, a charming village overlooking the sea, surrounded by Byzantine-style walls made from the backs of the houses; some of the older residences still bear their Venetian coats-of-arms. Ruins of the Classical acropolis and walls remain, and there are many churches with attractive floors, among them the two of the Panayia, Eleoussa (1653) and Koimmissi (1593), and Ag. Aekaterini (1665). The old Catholic church, St Antonio, may soon be converted into a museum of local antiquities. The site of the School of the Holy Tomb, closed in 1834, is now Kastro's cemetery. At Kastro there's plenty of deep blue sea to dive into from the rocks, and many people dispense with costumes. If you prefer sand, paths from Kastro lead down to **Seralia** and **Poulati** and their lovely beaches.

Just south of Artemon the bus passes through **Exambela**, a quiet village in the middle of one of Sifnos' most fertile areas. The village's name derives from the Turkish *aksam bela* ('trouble in the evening'): during the occupation the inhabitants were notorious for their rowdy mischief-making. A monastery near Exambela called **Vrissi** (1612) contains many old manuscripts and objects of religious art.

Further south, by the seaside village and beach at **Faros** is the island's most famous church, **Panayia Chrissopigi**, built in 1650 on a holy rock. Long ago two women fled to the monastery from a band of approaching pirates. Desperately they prayed to the Virgin and she answered their pleas by splitting the cape right in the pirates' path, creating a gap 18 m wide, which in these pirate-free days is spanned by a bridge. The icon of the Virgin in the church was discovered in the sea by fishermen attracted by the light it radiated. To visit the church ask the bus driver to let you off at Chrissopigi and walk down the mule path; there's also a road for cars. Near Faros is the beach of **Fasolou**, popular with nudists.

Platys Gialos and Around

Platys Gialos with its broad sandy beach is the island's busiest resort, though you can escape its worldly concerns by lodging in the serene convent of **Panayia tou Vounou** up on the cliff, affording a gorgeous view over the bay below. The last nuns left nearly a century ago, but the church with its ancient Doric columns is still used for island paneyeria. Two other seaside hamlets, **Vathi** and **Heronissos** are best accessible by boat from Kamares (although they can be reached by jeep, and Vathi is a 1-hour hike from Platys Gialos). **Vathi**, surrounded by high hills, has several tavernas on the beach and rooms—some available in the 16th-century monastery of Taxiarchis. Heronissos is simpler, and has no electricity.

Festivals

1 September, Ag. Simeon near Kamares; 20 July, Profitis Ilias near Kamares; 29 August, Ag. Ioannes in Vathi; 25 March and 21 November, Panayia tou Vounou; 15 August, Panayia ta Gournia; 14 September, Stavros, at Faros; Ascension (Analypsis) at Chrissopigi.

Most of the island's accommodation is in Kamares and Apollonia.

expensive

Platys Gialos offers two places with all the comforts of home, although their rates (around 17,000 dr.) are very high considering the facilities: **Platys Gialos**, on the beach, ℗ 31 324, where all rooms are air conditioned and come with a fridge to raid, and the **Alexandros Sifnos Beach** two minutes from the water, ℗ 32 333, with a rather redundant pool.

moderate

In Kamares **Boulis** is on the beach, and good value, ℗ 32 122. The C class **Hotel Stavros** has rooms with baths, ℗ 31 641, or, for the same price, you can stay at the B class **Kamari**, 300 m from the beach, ℗ 31 710. In Chrissopigi the small, family-run **Flora** pension has rooms with private bath for under 6000 dr., ℗ 31 778.

cheap

Up in Apollonia is one of the real bargains on the island: the charming class B **Pension Apollonia**, ℗ 31 490, with 9 rooms going for under 4000 dr. There are also rooms in Kastro, Artemon, Faros and Vathi, and freelance camping is tolerated, so much so that there are even showers for campers on Kamares beach and elsewhere. If you come in summer without a room reservation, you'll be grateful for them after a night out under the stars.

Eating Out

The local speciality is *rivithia*—oven-baked chick-peas—and on Sunday they are served in many Sifniot homes and at the taverna **Mangana** in Artemon. In general, the restaurant fare on Sifnos is better than on the other islands (undoubtably the influence of its famous chefs); a good place to enjoy it and a view besides is **Zorba's** up in Kastro. Almost next door you can sit on the terrace of the little **Astron** (which humbly advertises itself as a grocery store-cum-snack bar), take in the mountain view and enjoy a simple plate of fried fish or meatballs, a tasty salad and a bottle of wine, all for under 1500 dr. For seafood **Captain Andreas** on the waterfront in Kamares has a good selection of fresh temptations and, as seems to be the trend these days, an Italian restaurant, **Lorenzo's**, has opened to entice the jaded palate. Across the street **Dionysos** serves breakfast on its rooftop, with nice views of the bay (they also provide hot showers for yachties, 200 dr.). A pre-dinner ouzo, watching the sun go down, is a must at the friendly **Café Folie**, at the far end of Kamares beach; very good snacks during the day, too. Out at Platys Gialos there is a good choice of seaside restaurants serving fresh fish. For good Sifniote dishes try the **Cyklades Beach** or **Sofia**. A popular Italian restaurant here is **Mama Mia**. At any of these three 2500 dr. will buy you a full meal. If you get to Vathi, reward yourself with a fish lunch at one of the tavernas in the bay; for 3000 dr. feast on fresh fish, local cheese, salad and wine.

Sikinos

If you find the other Cyclades too cosmopolitan, or you want to try out your Greek, you can always visit Sikinos, which is small and charming, untouched by history, unaffected as yet by organized tours (although its proximity to Ios may soon change all that). The one town on Sikinos is very pretty if sleepy, there's a beach, and a few other things to see if you should begin to tire of the simple pleasures of old-fashioned island life. The main ways of getting around are on foot and by mule. Vines still cover much of the fertile areas. In ancient times it was one of several islands called Oenoe, or 'wine island'.

Connections

Daily tourist boat to Folegandros and Ios; ferry five times a week to Piraeus, four times a week to Santorini, less frequently with Paros, Naxos, Sifnos, Serifos and Syros, once a week with Kythnos, Kimolos, Crete and the Dodecanese; catamaran once a week to other Cyclades and Piraeus.

Walks Around Sikinos

The island's port, **Alopronia**, affords little shelter from the winds or for weary visitors—most facilities are up at the capital, known either as **Sikinos**, Chora or Kastro. This is the island's only real town, and an hour's walk up from the jetty, if the bus hasn't put in an appearance. Looming over the village is the ruined **monastery of Zoodochos Pigi**, fortified against the frequent pirate incursions which the island endured in the past. The 300 inhabitants are most proud, however, of their 'cathedral' with its icons by the 18th-century master Skordilis.

There are two walks to make on Sikinos, each taking about 1½ hours. The path to the northeast leads to the rather scant remains of a Classical fortress at **Paliokastro;** the second, to the southwest, will take you to **Episkopi**, where a Roman heroon of the 3rd century was converted into the Byzantine church Koimisis Theotokou; the church itself was remodelled in the 17th century after an earthquake.

Sikinos' beaches lie along the southeastern coast, from the port Alopronia to Ag. Georgiou Bay; the most popular is **Spilia**, named after the island's many caves.

Where to Stay

expensive

The only proper accommodation is at the brand new **Porto Sikinos**, on the beach, prettily laid out in traditional island design, with 18 rooms, bar and restaurant, © 51 220.

cheap

Only a handful of rooms are available in private houses up in Chora, where you'll also find two small tavernas. In Alopronia there are also a few rooms and simple tavernas.

Syros

Inhabitants of Syros have affectionately nicknamed their island home 'our rock', as dry and barren a piece of real estate as you can find in Greece. But at the beginning of the Greek War of Independence in 1821 it was blessed with three important qualities: a large natural harbour, the protection of the King of France, and a hardworking population. The result was Syros' capital, Ermoupolis, once the major port in Greece, and today the largest city and capital of the Cyclades. It is also the best-preserved 19th-century neo-Classical town in the whole of Greece.

Syros is an island that doesn't need tourism, and looks upon its visitors as guests rather than customers—except when it comes to *loukoumia*, better known as Turkish Delight. These sweet, gummy squares, smothered in icing sugar, are an island speciality, and vendors stream aboard any ship that calls at Syros to peddle it to passengers, who are often eager to buy it.

History

Homer wrote that Syros was a rich, fertile isle, whose inhabitants never suffered any illness, and died only when they were struck by the gentle arrows of Apollo or Artemis after living long, happy lives. The first inhabitants may have been Phoenicians, settled at Dellagracia and at Finikas. Poseidon was the chief god of Syros, and in connection with his cult one of the first observatories in the world, a heliotrope (a kind of sundial), was constructed by the philosopher Ferekides, the teacher of Pythagoras. In Roman times the population emigrated to the site of present-day Ermoupolis, at that time known as 'the Happy' with its splendid natural harbour and two prominent hills. After the collapse of the *pax Romana*, Syros was abandoned until the 13th century, when Venetians founded the hilltop town of Ano Syros.

Because Ano Syros was Catholic, it enjoyed the protection of the French, and remained neutral at the outbreak of the War of Independence in 1821. War refugees from Chios, Psara and Smyrna brought their Orthodox faith with them and founded settlements on the other hill, Vrontatho, and down at Syros' harbour. This new port town boomed from the start, as the premier 'warehouse' of the new Greek state where cotton from Egypt and spices from the East were stored and as the central coaling station for the entire eastern Mediterranean. When the time came to name the new town, Ermoupolis—'the city of Hermes' (the god of commerce)—was the natural choice.

For 50 years Syros ran much of the Greek economy, and great fortunes were made and spent not only on elegant mansions, but also on schools, public buildings and streets; Ermoupolis built the first theatre in modern Greece and the first high school, financed by the citizens and government; and when the Syriani died, they were so pleased with themselves that the most extravagant monuments to be seen in any Greek cemetery were erected in their memory. By the 1870s, however, oil replaced coal and Piraeus replaced Ermoupolis as Greece's major port; Syros declined, but always remained the largest city and capital of the Cyclades, supporting itself with shipyards and various industries, prospering just enough to keep its grand old buildings occupied, but not enough to tear them down to build new concrete blocks. Today Ermoupolis is a National Historical Landmark.

By air: daily flights from Athens.

By sea: daily with Mykonos, Tinos, Piraeus, Paros, Naxos and Amorgos, four–five times a week with Andros, Santorini, Ios and Rafina, three times a week with Sikinos and Folegandros, twice a week to Astypalaia, Koufonissia, Shinoussa and Heraklia, once a week to Ikaria, Samos and Anafi; catamaran daily to Piraeus and other Cyclades.

Tourist Information

NTOG on quay, next to the port authority in Ermoupolis.

Information at Town Hall, ✆ (0281) 22 375.

Tourist police, see regular police, ✆ (0281) 22 610.

The Teamwork travel office in the port offers excellent guided tours of Ermoupolis.

As you sail into the **commercial port**, Ermoupolis presents an imposing sight much commented on by early travellers. Above are the two hills; catholic Ano Syros to your right (or north), and Vrontatho on the left. The rest of the city is built on a 20° angle in a grand amphitheatre. On the other side of the harbour are the revitalized shipyards which declare this to be one of the rare working islands in the archipelago.

Ermoupolis' central square, **Plateia Miaoulis** is paved with marble and lined with cafés and pizzerias, dominated by a grand **town hall**, where you can take in full-length portraits of King George I and Queen Olga painted by Prossalendis. The **Archaeology Museum**, up the steps to the left, contains proto-Cycladic and Roman finds from Syros and other islands. In front of the town hall stands a statue of Miaoulis, revolutionary hero and old sea-dog, as well as a bandstand presided over by the seven muses. Sadly, the local Philharmonic Society, owing to lack of money, not interest, no longer performs there, but the municipality is endeavouring to raise funds for its revival. To the right, behind the square, stands the **Apollon Theatre**, a copy of La Scala and the first built in Greece since ancient times; until 1914 it supported a regular Italian opera season. Undergoing extensive renovation at the time of writing, you may be able to talk the workers into letting you in for a peek. Up the street a little way from here, the central **Union Hall**, formerly a private mansion, is one of the few places you can get into to see the elaborate ceiling and wall murals characteristic of old Ermoupolis.

The next square up holds one of the town's best churches, **Ag. Nikolaos**, boasting a carved marble iconostasis by the 19th-century sculptor Vitalis. In front of the church, a memorial topped by a stone lion, also by Vitalis, is the world's first **monument to an Unknown Warrior**. The Cyclades capitol building is near here as well. On the opposite side of the square in St. Prioiou Street, the bell tower of the church **Koimesis** is one of the landmarks of Syros; its elegant neo-Classical interior contains a rare icon painted by Dominicos Theotokopoulos, known as **El Greco** after he left for Venice and Spain. Another fine church in Ermoupolis is the **Metamorphosis**, the Orthodox cathedral.

Crowning **Vrontatho Hill** (take the main street from behind Plateia Miaoulis) is the church of the **Anastasis** with a few old icons and superb views stretching to Tinos and Mykonos. Even better, if you have the energy, is the hours' climb up Omirou St to the medieval Catholic quarter of **Ano Syros**. On the way up don't miss the **Orthodox cemetery of Ag. Georgios**, with its elaborate marble mausoleums of Syros' wealthy shipowners and merchants. Since the Crusades, most of the families in Ano Syros have been Catholic, and some have lived in the same mansions for generations and attended the **Catholic cathedral of St George** on top of Ano Syros. A large, handsome **Capuchin convent of St Jean** was founded there in 1635 by France's Louis XIII and has archives dating from the 1400s. Another church, the 15th-century **Ag. Nikolaos**, was founded in the 15th century as a house for the poor.

A 45-minute walk from Ermoupolis leads to the pretty seaside church of **Ag. Dimitrious**, founded after the discovery of an icon there in 1936; alternatively, a 15-minute walk will take you to Dili and its **Temple of Isis** built in 200 BC. Across the harbour at **Lazaretta** stood a 5th-century BC temple of Poseidon, although the only traces of it are a few artefacts in the museum. In ancient times this was probably the Poseidonia mentioned in the *Odyssey*. Also near Ermoupolis at Pefkakia, there was a **Roman-era cemetery**, although nothing remains of the actual tombs.

Around Syros

Other ancient sites are in the north of the island. At **Grammaton Bay** (reached only by boat), a prophylactic inscription to keep ships from sinking is carved in the rock, dating back to Hellenistic times. **Kastri**, just north of Chalandriani, was settled in the Bronze Age: its walls, foundations of houses and overgrown necropolis have contributed much to the understanding of this period in the Cyclades. Signs suggest it was re-inhabited for a brief period around 8000 BC. The **cave** where the philosopher Ferekides supposedly lived in the summer is nearby; his winter cave is at Alythini. Another path in the north leads to the quiet beach at **Megas Lakkos**.

Buses from Ermoupolis travel to the other seaside resorts of Syros: **Kini**, a small fishing village with a beach and tavernas, is a popular rendezvous for sunset-watching, while **Galissas** has the best beach on the island. Further south is another beach at **Finikas** (Phoenix), originally settled by the Phoenicians and mentioned in Homer. **Vari** has become a major resort, while **Dellagracia**, better known as **Posidonia**, and **Megas Gialos** have fewer tourists. **Azolimnos** is particularly popular with the Syriani for its ouzeries and cafés, but there are no hotels or rooms. In the middle of the island, **Piskopio** claims the oldest Byzantine church on Syros, Profitis Ilias, situated in the pine-covered hills. The Orthodox convent **Ag. Barbara** has an orphanage for girls and a school of arts and crafts; the walls of the monastery church are decorated with frescoes depicting Barbara's complicated martyrdom that led to her role as the patron saint of bombadiers. Inland, **Hroussa** is a pleasant, pine-shaded village with a number of new villas, while nearby **Faneromeni** ('can be seen from everywhere') itself has panoramic views of the island. **Agathopes** is a fairly quiet, sandy beach with a couple of snack bars.

Festivals

6 December, Ag. Nikolaos in Ermoupolis; the last Sunday in May, the finding of the icon at Ag. Dimitriou; 26 October, also at Ag. Dimitriou; 24 September, an Orthodox and Catholic celebration at Faneromeni.

Every two years, in either the last week of July or the first week of August, the **Apanosyria Festival** is organised by the municipality of Ano Syros, with exhibitions of local handicrafts and performances of popular plays. Another folklore festival is held, usually in June, at **Azolimnos** with three days of dancing, wine and song.

Where to Stay

Syros is one island where you may well be able to book a flat at a moment's notice; the Teamwork Agency by the port has an extensive listing of seaside properties.

Teamwork's owner, Panayiotis Boudouris, also manages the municipally owned **Hotel Europe**, in a building that originally served as Syros' first hospital (early 19th century). Designed like a cloister, with a serene pebble mosaic courtyard, it has much larger rooms than the average hotel, each with a private bath, ℂ 28 771. Alternatively, **Omiros** is a traditional pension, well placed in the middle of the harbour, ℂ 24 910.

The ageing but pleasant **Hermes**, near the ferry boat quay, ℂ 28 011, is a low-priced class B; try to get a room on the top floor facing the square. It has access in the back to a windy and rocky little strand where the locals swim.

In the lower price range, there are several old houses in Ermoupolis with rooms to let—two inexpensive choices are the **Aktaeon**, ℂ 22 675, and the **Mykonos**, ℂ 28 346. There are also quite a few hotels and pensions on Syros' beaches, at Vari, Posidonia and Finikas, all catering for longer stays, and you may be able to get a room without a reservation— rarely the case with beach hotels on the other Cyclades. There is a **campsite** at Galissas.

International dishes including crêpes, filet mignon, shrimp hors d'oeuvres and various soups await at the **Eleanna** restaurant on the main square, but not surprisingly a meal will be in the 3–4000 dr. range. Behind Eleanna is the **Esperides** taverna-cum-snack bar with simple food at low prices. Near the Hermes Hotel, the **Yiannena** has an extensive selection, including roast meats of all types and very good, reasonably priced ready food. In Azolimnos locals flock to the **Balopitas Taverna** right on the waterfront and in Kini one of the favourite spots is the **Bouzouki** restaurant run by the Dakrotsi brothers, well known Syriani musicians. In the off season you can work up an appetite hiking up to one of the tavernas on the hills, both for good food and the view over the town and port. Most beaches have low-cost tavernas. When you've finished dining in Ermoupolis, there's an array of snazzy little bars that play American music.

Tinos

If Delos was the sacred island of the ancient Greeks, Tinos occupies the same place in the hearts of their modern descendants. Chances are in ancient times Delos had much the same atmosphere as Tinos—numerous lodgings and eating places, shaded stoas (in Tinos, awnings over the street) where merchants sell votives and other holy objects, and busy harbours. Delos, however, evolved into a booming free trade port, an unlikely fate for Tinos. Besides its miraculous icon, Tinos is best known for its beautiful Venetian dovecots, of which some 600

TINOS

Skali

Firi Mithi

Ismael
Mamados
Marlas
Pirgos
Platia
Ormos Panormou
Isternia
Aetofolia
Kardiani
Koris Pyrgos
Kolympidra
Kalloni
Komi
Plakiani
Ag. Nikitas
Ormos
Kardianis Bay
Agapi
Smardaki
Tarambados
Kambos
Chatzirados
Ktikades
Gastrion Cave
Kionia
Kehrovouni Convent
Tripotamos
Xinara
Loutra
Xombourgo
Falatados
Steni
Arnados
Thio Choria
Trianthros
Volo
Livada
Keyros
Potamia
Myrsini
Tsiknias
(729m / 2406ft)
TINOS
Ag. Fokas
Vryokastro
Xera
Porto

To other Cyclades

To Piraeus

N

km
0   1   2   3   4   5

3 miles
0   1   2

220

survive, scattered across the island's great sloping terraces like little houses of whitewashed stone embroidery. Tinos may be the centre of Orthodox pilgrimage, but of all the Cyclades it has the highest percentage of Catholics; many of the island's pretty white villages have somewhat atypical campaniles for landmarks—Tinos has 1200 chapels. As the 'Lourdes of Greece', Tinos maintains its relaxed family atmosphere, very much in contrast with neighbouring Mykonos, and anyone disturbing the tranquillity will be politely but firmly placed on the first ferry out.

History

Inhabited by the Ionians in Archaic times, Tinos was occupied by the Persians in 490 BC, but set free after the Battle of Marathon. In the 4th century a sanctuary of the sea god Poseidon was founded on the island (after he chased away all its snakes) and it became a sacred place, where pilgrims would come to be cured by the god and to participate in the December festivals of the Poseidonia. There were two ancient cities on the island, both confusingly named Tinos, one at the site of the present town and the other at Xombourgo. When the war between the Romans and Mithridates of Pontos broke out in 88 BC, the latter destroyed both towns. Not much happened until the Fourth Crusade, when the Venetians built a fortress called Santa Elena at Xombourgo, using the stone of the ancient acropolis and city. It was the strongest fortress of the Cyclades, and stood impregnable to eleven assaults by the Turks. Even the terrible Barbarossa was defeated by Santa Elena and its Venetian and Greek defenders. In revenge, the frustrated Turks often pillaged and destroyed the rest of Tinos.

In 1715, long after the rest of Greece had submitted to Ottoman rule, the Turkish admiral arrived in Tinos with a massive fleet and army. After sustaining a terrible attack, the Venetians decided that this time Santa Elena would not hold out, and, to the surprise of the Greeks, surrendered. The Turks allowed the Venetians to leave in safety, but in Venice, where it was a crime to fail in the course of duty, the officers were put on trial for treason, accused of having been bribed to surrender, and executed. Meanwhile the Turks blew up a good deal of Santa Elena in case the Venetians should change their minds and come back. Tinos was thus the last territorial gain of the Ottoman Empire.

In 1822, during the Greek War of Independence, a nun of the convent Kehrovouni, Sister Pelagia, had a vision of the Virgin directing her to a certain rock where she discovered a miraculous icon of Mary and the Archangel at the Annunciation. The icon was found to have extraordinary healing powers, and a church was soon built for it in Tinos town, called Panayia Evangelistra or Christopiliopsia. It quickly became the most important place of pilgrimage in Greece and because of its timing, a shrine of Greek nationalism; the discovery of the icon at just that moment in history helped to give the fight for independence the morale-boosting aura of a holy war. On 15 August 1940, during the huge annual celebration at the church, an Italian submarine entered the harbour of Tinos and sank the Greek cruise boat *Elli*—one of the major incidents directly before Mussolini involved Greece in World War II. Under the Colonels' regime the entire island was declared a holy place (part of that government's so-called 'moral cleansing') and the women of Tinos were required to behave at all times as if they were in church, by wearing skirts, etc., a rule quickly abolished when the junta itself went out the window.

Daily ferry from Piraeus, Mykonos, Syros, Andros and Rafina. Six times a week with Paros, five times a week with Amorgos, three times a week to the Dodecanese and Santorini, twice a week with Crete, Ios, Skiathos, Thessaloniki, Koufonissia, Shinoussa and Heraklia, once a week with Sikinos, Samos and Ikaria; daily hydrofoil or catamaran to other Cyclades and Piraeus. Note that ships from Tinos to Pireaus are often full, although surplus passengers are let on all the same. Two landing areas operate, often simultaneously, and when it's time to depart, be sure to ask the ticket agent which pier to queue up at in the tourist pens.

Tourist Information

There's no NTOG, but Tinos Mariner travel agency on the front has helpful information and an excellent map of the island. The Tourist Police are at 5 Plateia L. Sohon, © (0283) 22 255.

Panayia Evangelistra

As your ship pulls into **Tinos**, the port and capital, the outline of the yellow church **Panayia Evangelistra** floats above the town. It's actually a short walk up Evangelistra Street, a street closed to traffic that becomes a solid mass of pilgrims on the two principal feast days of the Virgin, 15 August and 25 March. Some ascend the entire distance on their knees. As well as plastic bottles for holy water, candles and incense, Evangelistra Street offers almost anything you could want under its great awnings, from coffee cups with political logos to Monopoly games.

A red carpet covers the grand marble stair leading up to the neo-Classical church, (*open daily 6.30 am–8.30 pm*), hung with hundreds of gold and silver ex-votos and lamps donated by the faithful; note especially the silver ship with a silver fish plugging up the hole in its side—one of the icon's more original miracles. Hundreds of shimmering lamps strung overhead create a magical effect, while on the floor level the church employs men who do nothing all day but remove candles from the stands so that new arrivals will have somewhere to put their own candles—the largest are the size of elephant's tusks. The pilgrims then queue up to kiss the icon itself, another work of the prolific St Luke, although its artistic merits are impossible to judge under the layers of gold, diamonds and pearls. Near the church four hostels have been built for pilgrims waiting to be healed by the icon, but there is still not enough room to house them, and the overflow camp out patiently in the courtyard.

The crypt, where Ag. Pelagia discovered the icon, is now the **Chapel of Evreseos**. Silver lines the spot in the rocks where the icon lay; the spring here, believed to be holy, is said to have curative properties. Parents from all over Greece bring their children here in August to be baptized in the font. Next to the chapel the victims of the *Elli* are interred in a mausoleum, which displays a piece of the fatal fascist torpedo.

Among the church's museums (*all open 8.30 am–8.30 pm*) there are: an **art gallery**, with works from the Ionian school, a reputed Rubens, a dubious Rembrandt partially hidden by the radiator, and many 19th-century works; a museum devoted to the works of the Tiniote sculptor **Antonios Soxos**, and above it the **Sculpture Museum** housing pieces by a variety of Greek sculptors such as Ioannis Boulgaros and Vitalis; old icons in the **Byzantine Museum**; and another museum containing items used in the church service.

Around Tinos Town

Parallel with Evangelistra Street, opposite a shady pine grove, the island **archaeological museum** contains artefacts from the Sanctuary of Poseidon and Amphitrite, including a sundial and a sea monster in various pieces and huge decorated storage vessels from the Archaic period.

From the port it's a short walk west to **Kionia** ('the columns'), with a beach and the **sanctuary of Poseidon and Amphitrite** which was discovered by the Belgian archaeologist Demoulin in 1902. Of the famous sanctuary the temple, the treasuries, entrances, little temple, baths, fountain of Poseidon and inns for pilgrims have been excavated. In many ways the ancient cult of the sea god and his wife Amphitrite parallels the contemporary cult of the icon—both Panayia Evangelistra and Poseidon have impressive records in rescuing sailors from storms. East of town, the closest and busiest beach is **Ag. Fokas**; a few minutes further east, at **Vryokastro**, are the walls of an ancient settlement, and a Hellenistic tower. The beaches further east at **Porto** and **Xera** tend to be less crowded than Ag. Fokas and Kionia.

Around the Island

Buses from the town pier wend their way north to the 12th-century **Kehrovouni Convent**, one of the largest in Greece. It is here that Sister Pelagia, canonized in 1971, had her two visions, in which the Virgin told her where to find the icon. You can visit her old cell and see her embalmed head. **Arnados** to the north is a charming little village, as is **Thio Choria**. From here a rough track leads down to a usually deserted beach.

In the winter Tinos turns lush and green, a colour that lingers until May when it takes on a more typical Cycladic barren brown, its hills corrugated with sun-parched terraces, relieved by the white dovecots and their white residents. Some of the most elaborate dovecots are in **Smardaki**, one of a cluster of small villages above Tinos town. Looming over them on a 564-m hill is the famous Venetian fortress, **Santa Elena** at **Xombourgo**, ruined by the Turks but still affording a superb view over the Tinos' island neighbours.

First inhabited around 1000 BC, this commanding hill has a few ancient walls, although most of the stone was reused by later inhabitants, especially the Gizzi family of Venice, who built Santa Elena. Besides medieval houses, a fountain and three churches remain in the citadel walls. The easiest approach is from **Xinara**, seat of the Catholic arch-diocese. From here, too, you can walk to the site of one of the 8th-century BC towns called Tinos, where a large building and Geometric period temple were discovered. **Loutra**, one of the prettier villages, has a 17th-century Jesuit monastery where a school is still run by the Ursulines. From **Komi**, a long valley runs down to the sea at **Kolympidra**, with a fine sandy beach where many people camp.

A paved road follows the mountainous ridge overlooking the southwest coast of Tinos. One possible detour descends to the valley village of **Tarambados**, with more good dovecots; at **Kardiani** a difficult path winds down to a remote beach; otherwise, from **Isternia**, a pleasant village with plane trees, you can drive down to popular Ormos or **Ag. Nikitas beach**, the latter with rooms and tavernas. This part of Tinos is famous for its green marble, and the island has a long tradition in working the stone. Several well-known Greek artists came from or have worked in **Pyrgos**. Just by the bus stop is a small **museum** and the **residence of sculptor Giannolis Halepas**; the old grammar school, built in the first flush of Greek independence, is now a School of Fine Arts. A shop near the main square exhibits and sells students' works—Byzantine eagles are still popular motifs. Below Pyrgos the public bus continues down to the beach at **Panormos bay**, with more tavernas and rooms. **Marlas**, further north, is in the centre of the old marble quarries. From the tip of Tinos it's only a nautical mile to the island of Andros.

Festivals

15 August and 25 March at the Panayia Evangelistra, the two largest in Greece; 15 June, Ag. Triada at Kardiani; 26 October, Ag. Dimitriou in Tinos town; 21 December, Issodia of Mary at Tripotamos; 20 October, Ag. Artemiou at Falatados; 29 August, Ag. Ioannes at Komi (Catholic); 19 January, Megalomatas at Ktikades.

Where to Stay

expensive

For something modern, **Tinos Beach** is close to the capital on the beach at Kionia, © 22 626; by far the largest of the island's accommodation, it also has bungalows.

moderate

Because Tinos has long been receiving pilgrims, it boasts a fine, old-fashioned hotel infrastructure not found on the other islands. Perhaps the Grande Dame of these hostelries is the **Hotel Tinion** on the left end of the harbour as you sail in, © 22 261, rated class B. A little cheaper, and with none of the frills, **Vyzantion**, 26 Alavanou, © 22 454, is nonetheless a pleasant alternative. Cheapest in this category is the **Meltemi**, 7 D. Filipoli, © 22 881, rooms have private facilities.

cheap

There are quite a few rooms to rent in the town of Tinos, though little elsewhere; as mentioned above, it will be tough getting anything at all during the great feast days, although on 15 August sleeping outside isn't a terrible price to pay if you want to witness the greatest pilgrimage in Greece.

You can find inexpensive food throughout the town, though the restaurants near the ferry docks tend to be hurried and rather mediocre. For a better meal, **Michalis Taverna** on Gavou Street serves good moussaka, lamb dishes and fresh fish for around 2,000 dr. Other recommended places are **Lefteris**, near the pharmacy, and the more expensive **Dionysos** on Megalochori St. Both are popular for Greek specialities and fish. If you're not too picky about quality, a memorable meal can be had in a little taverna off Evangelistra Street, currently called **O Patsos** ('the Madman') run by Greek–American Sotiris Fisas, who is almost as much an institution as the holy icon. The walls are decorated with murals of plump mermaids and photos of the ships Mr Fisas served on in the navy, all of which, he will tell you, were sunk.

Anidron

Arki

Agathonissi

Marathi

TURKEY

Patmos

Lipsi

Farmakonissi

To Piraeus

Fiagos

Ag. Marina

Leros

Lakki

Kalymnos

Bodrum

Pserimos

Kos

Levitha

Mastihari

Kos

TURKEY

Giali

Marmari

Astypalaia

Symi

Astypalaia

Nissyros

Rhodes

To Amorgos

Tilos

Alimia

Rhodes

THE DODECANESE

Halki

N

Saria

Diafani

Karpathos

| 0 | 10 | 25 | 50 km |

| 0 | 10 | 25 | miles |

Karpathos

To Sitia, Crete

Fry

Kassos

The Harbour at Rhodes

The Dodecanese

Furthest from mainland Greece, the Dodecanese, or 'twelve islands' (although there are actually 16 inhabited ones in the *nomos*) only became Greek in 1947—officially, that is, for throughout centuries of occupations, the inhabitants of these islands have stubbornly clung to their Greek language, Orthodox religion and traditions. But their long separation from the mainstream has given them a distinct character and architecture.

Lying just off the coast of precocious Asia Minor, the Dodecanese flourished in early antiquity. Various peoples lumped together as 'Aegeans' were their first inhabitants. They were subjugated by the seafaring Minoans, and when Crete fell in the 15th century BC, the Mycenaeans took over the Dodecanese; many islands sent ships to Troy. In the 12th–11th centuries BC the Dorians invaded the Dodecanese, heralding a dark age that lasted for three centuries.

Ionians eventually regained control of the islands, and by the Archaic period city-states, particularly on Rhodes and Kos, knew so much prosperity that they established colonies abroad. The Persians invaded the islands, and when they were defeated at Salamis, the Dodecanese joined the maritime league at Delos as a hedge against further attacks. Their greater distance from Athens, however, allowed them more autonomy than the Cyclades were permitted, and they produced many great artists and intellectuals, including Hippocrates, the father of medicine.

With the death of Alexander the Great, his general Ptolemy of Egypt controlled most of the Dodecanese. One of the greatest unsuccessful sieges in antiquity took place when one of Ptolemy's rival generals, Antigonos, sent his son Dimitrios to take Rhodes. Emboldened by its victory, in 164 BC Rhodes made an alliance with Rome, enabling her to exert a powerful influence of her own over an empire of Greek islands.

St Paul visited some of the Dodecanese and began their early conversion to Christianity; St John the Theologian was exiled from Asia Minor to Patmos, where he converted the inhabitants and wrote the book of the *Apocalypse*, or *Revelations*. In 1095, the Dodecanese had their first taste of a more aggressive Christianity, when Crusaders on route to the Holy Land made them a port of call. The pillaging and piracy in which the Westerners occasionally indulged along the way climaxed in the capture of Constantinople in 1204.

In 1291, the tables turned when Jerusalem fell to the other side, the rising Ottoman Empire. This disrupted, among other things, the work of the Knights of St John, a wealthy order made up of the second and third sons of the cream of European nobility, who had devoted themselves to running a hospital for pilgrims in Jerusalem. The Knights abandoned Jerusalem for Cyprus, and eighteen years later set up headquarters on Rhodes, purchasing all the Dodecanese outright from Admiral Vinioli, a Genoese pirate. In 1309 they built a hospital and fortified Rhodes and the other islands against the Turks and pirates, the Knights themselves little better than pirates in their swift vessels made on Symi. Ottoman tolerance of their escapades soon wore thin, especially after the Knights took to letting Christian pirates pass through their territory unmolested, but stopped ships carrying Moslem pilgrims.

In 1522 Sultan Suleiman the Magnificent had had enough and attacked Rhodes (the third major Moslem offensive on the Knights) and all the men of the Dodecanese rallied to its defence. Only information from a traitor brought about the defeat of the Knights after a long siege. Always a gentleman, Suleiman permitted them and their followers to depart in safety with their possessions to their new fief, Malta, for which they paid the king of Spain their famous tribute of a golden falcon. Turkish occupation of the Dodecanese lasted until 1912, when the Italians took 'temporary possession' of the islands. This occupation was made 'permanent' after the Greek débâcle in 1922 by the second Treaty of Lausanne. Mussolini poured money into the islands, sponsoring massive public works programmes, reforestation, archaeological excavations and historical reconstructions. While Turkish rule had been depressing, negligent, and sometimes brutal, the fascists, in spite of their lavish expenditures, were even worse, outlawing the islanders' Orthodox religion and Greek language; even today you can find older people on the Dodecanese who are more comfortable speaking Italian. After the Second World War, the islands were united with Greece, the last territory gained by the government; to encourage growth, especially through tourism, the islands were granted duty-free concessions.

Rhodes and Kos have succeeded, perhaps too well, in attracting tourists. Their climate, beaches, and natural beauty make them popular year round; the charter flights and busloads of package tourists are relentless. On a much more intimate scale, Patmos and its magnificent monastery of St John attract a good crowd in the summer. A certain village on Karpathos maintains the dress and customs of 300 years ago; tiny Kastellorizo, tucked under the bulge of Turkey, is haunted with war-ruined mansions; Kalymnos is the sponge capital of Greece; the volcano on Nissyros still smokes; rocky Kassos has a glorious but tragic history; lovely neo-Classical mansions decorate Symi; Astypalaia, Halki and Tilos are small and serene; and Leros, the island of Artemis, may serenade you one evening with the strains of the *santouri*, or hammer dulcimer.

Connections

Nearly every day there is a large ferry from Piraeus to Patmos, Leros, Kalymnos, Kos and Rhodes—a 20- to 24-hour journey all told. Smaller ferries and excursion boats link the smaller islands; two hydrofoil companies also ply the most popular routes, some running daily, others a few times a week. There are flights to Rhodes, Kos and Leros direct from Athens; inter-Dodecanese flights also connect Karpathos, Kassos and Kastellorizo. Kos and Rhodes have connections with Turkey, the Rhodes–Marmaris ferries running all year round.

Lastly, there is an agency based in Romford, Essex, called 'Twelve Islands' which specializes in arranging flights and good accommodation (some out of the ordinary that you would never find on your own) in the Dodecanese. They go out of their way to accommodate children, which is unusual.

Astypalaia

The westernmost island of the Dodecanese, located halfway between Amorgos and Kos, Astypalaia closely resembles its neighbouring Cyclades, particularly in its architecture and austere rocky geography. Unlike many of the Cyclades, however, Astypalaia has a rich fertile valley, Livadia, and equally fertile fishing in the sheltered bays of its wildly indented coast-line—in antiquity the island was called *Ichthyoessa*, the fishy island. Besides the lure of seafood, Astypalaia's relative inaccessibility makes it a good place to escape the summer crowds, although there are times when you may find yourself wishing that the locals had more than a couple of streets on which to exercise their scooters in the evening. The womens' traditional costumes are famous for their elaborate detail and beauty.

History

The name Astypalaia means 'old city', but mythology claims that the name is derived from a sister of Europa, the mother of King Minos. Its early inhabitants may have founded the ancient capital of Kos, also called Astypalaia. In Classical times the island was most famous for a tragically short-tempered boxer named Kleomedes, who, in competing in the Olympics, killed his opponent, which even then was enough to get you disqualified. Kleomedes returned to Astypalaia, seething with rage, and took his disappointment out on the local school building, knocking it down and killing all the children within.

From 1207 to 1522, the Quirini family of Venice occupied the island, styling themselves the Counts of Astypalaia and building a castle in Chora. During the last Italian occupation of the Dodecanese another fortification called Kastellano was built in the east of the island, south of Vathi.

Connections

Three times a week with Kos, Kalymnos, Mykonos, Tinos and Piraeus; twice a week with Rhodes and Syros; once a week in summer with Santorini, Andros and Rafina.

Tourist Police

See regular police, Chora, ✆ (0243) 61 207.

Around Astypalaia

The capital and main port of the island, **Astypalaia** (or Skala) is picturesquely piled beneath the glowering Venetian castle and ruined windmills down to a sandy stretch of beach. Up the narrow streets, lined with pretty, cubist white houses (many fitted with Turkish-style balconies) is **Chora**, the medieval and Venetian capital; the gate of the **fortress** still bears the Quirini coat-of-arms, a display of pride that would have been much frowned-on back in Venice itself. Within the citadel walls, you can roam through the ruins of stone houses on tiny streets, and two churches, **St George** and the **Madonna of the Castle**, one of the most beautiful in the Dodecanese, topped with a white-tiled dome, decorated inside with intricate lace-like designs. All is being slowly restored.

Green, and comparatively lush **Livadia** with Astypalaia's best beach, is a little to the west, while a bit further south is an unofficial nudist beach. Other possible excursions from Astypalaia Skala include a walk to the monastery, **Ag. Libies**, or a taxi trip to the more remote villages of **Analypsis** and **Vathi**, the latter near Mussolini's **Kastellana** and the stalagmite caves of **Drakou** and **Negri**. It is possible to visit them on foot or by boat, but take a flashlight with you.

Festivals

21 May, Ag. Konstantinos; 15 August, Panayia.

Where to Stay

moderate–cheap

Astypalaia is blessed with three class D hotels and one class E, plus a number of rooms in private houses, all in Skala. Prices for the D class hotels are all about the same—3500–4500 dr. for a double. Of the three, the **Paradissos**, © 61 224, may not be paradise, but it's clean and well run. The **Aigaion**, © 61 236, is the better second option. You can also find rooms at Livadia where people camp out without much difficulty. Other possibilities include rooms in remote Analypsis by the taverna, and in Vathi. There's an organized **campsite** at Deftero Marmari beach, © (0242) 61 338, 3 km from the port.

Eating Out

Most of the island's eateries are clustered around the wharf and serve local fare at reasonable prices. Popular with locals are **Babis** and **Vakroyiali**. Food seems to taste better, however, in the tavernas at Livadia, although the menu is the same. There's a taverna at Vathi serving delicious fish: Analypsis has a couple of standard tavernas.

Halki

Little Halki, basically a big arid rock with its small port overlooked by half-derelict neo-Classical houses—mansions, by Greek island standards—reminds many people of a miniature

Symi. Despite its proximity to Rhodes, it is a wonderfully quiet place, with only a few hundred inhabitants and no cars; many of those visitors it does get come back year after year. Its name (also spelled Chalki, among other variations) comes from the Greek word for copper which was mined here long ago.

Although puny, Halki is celebrated for its love songs and has declared itself 'an island of peace and friendship'; UNESCO has allocated several million dollars to promote the local fishing economy and tourism, and plans to designate marine reserves to protect the beleaguered fish. Abandoned houses are being converted to guesthouses, and, if red tape permits, a centre will be built for the study and protection of the endangered Mediterranean monk seal.

Connections

Three times a week with Rhodes, once a week with Karpathos, Kassos, Sitia (Crete), Ag. Nikolaos (Crete), Symi, Santorini, Sikinos, Folegandros, Milos, Sifnos, Piraeus; caique (daily in high season, twice a week at other times) from Kamiros Skala, Rhodes. In summer hydrofoil connection with Rhodes and Tilos.

Skala and Around

The main claim to fame of **Skala**, the one town, is that its Ag. Nikolaos has the tallest campanile in the Dodecanese. Other than that, it's an infectiously charming hamlet, full of rabbits, who seem nearly as relaxed as the human residents.

From Skala a 15-minute walk along 'Boulevard Tarpon Springs' (just wide enough for a single delivery van) will take you to the small sandy beach; the boulevard was paid for by Halkiot immigrants in Florida. Visitors determined to 'see' something else should continue walking along the boulevard's extension another hour for **Chorio**, the ghost-town capital of Halki. Here the Knights of St John built a castle on the earlier acropolis and re-used most of the ancient building stone. Chorio's church has a few Byzantine frescoes and there are good views over rock and sea.

Halki has a few caiques to hire for visiting its quiet swimming coves—Areta, Kania, Yali and Trachia are among the best. The most scenic excursion, however, is to the green isle of **Alimia**, which has a deep harbour where Italian submarines hid during the war. Now it is a beautifully tranquil place to laze about, swim and picnic.

Festivals

2 August, Ag. Ioannis; 15 August, Panayia.

Where to Stay

moderate–cheap

There are no hotels on Halki; accommodation is limited to small guesthouses and private rooms. Although UNESCO officials seem to fill most of accommodation with themselves and friends, there are still enough rooms in private homes to go round. Expect to pay about 3500 dr. Otherwise there's the small but very lovely **Captain's House**, a turn-of-the-century mansion with three lovely rooms remodelled by a returned Greek navy admiral and his British wife. One of Halki's largest trees shades the terrace, overlooking the sea and town. It's located near the church.

Eating Out

Of the restaurants along the waterfront in Skala, head to **Omonia** for good fresh fish, or see if they have the island speciality, lamb stuffed with rice and liver. Meals average 2500 dr., 3–4000 dr. for a full fish dinner.

Kalymnos

Breathe a sigh of relief when you get to Kalymnos—you're in the real Greece. Although the bustling waterfront has all the usual paraphernalia of tourism, the tavernas, cafés and souvenir shops, venture one street back and you'll find yourself in the midst of a fully functioning Greek village, going about its daily life, winter or summer, whether you are there or not. Because of the many Greek visitors, the prices are not sky high, and the food is good and wholesome. Just as it finds an attractive balance between tourism and carrrying on its everyday business, Kalymnos also strikes a harmonious geographical equilibrium, with fertile valleys wedged into its dry, rocky face. Even the most fleeting visitor will notice that this island is preoccupied with sponges: Kalymnos has Greece's last active fleet of sponge divers.

History

The first Kalymniotes lived in a Neolithic settlement at Vothini and worshipped Zeus in a cave shrine which still exists. After the destruction of Crete, Argos sent colonists to the island, naming their capital after their mother city. Homer mentions ships from Kalymnos at Troy, and archaeologists have uncovered Homeric tombs on the island. An ally of Persia, the Queen of Halikarnassos, conquered the island at the beginning of the 5th century BC, but after Persia's defeat Kalymnos joined Athens' maritime league at Delos.

Kalymnos next enters history in the 11th century, when Seljik Turks launched a sudden attack on the island and killed almost everyone. The few survivors fled to fortified positions at Kastelli and the virtually impregnable Kastro, which by necessity became the capital of the island. The Vinioli of Genoa occupied Kalymnos, but later sold it to the Knights of St John, who strengthened the fortress of Kastro. In 1522 they abandoned it to succour Rhodes, leaving the Turks quickly to take their place. During the Italian occupation, Kalymnos rioted when the fascists tried to close the Greek schools, and the islanders painted everything in sight Greek blue and white as a sign of solidarity with the motherland.

A Note on Sponges

When fresh from the sea sponges are foul, smelly and black, and have to be stamped, squeezed and soaked until their skeletons (the part you use in the bathtub) are clean.

Many sponges are then chemically treated to achieve the familiar yellow colour. Diving for these primitive plant-like porifers is a difficult and dangerous art. In ancient times the divers strapped heavy stones to their chests to bear them down to the sea bed, where they speared the sponges with tridents, then at a signal, were raised to the surface by a lifeline. As modern equipment has permitted divers to plunge to new depths, cases of the 'bends' were frequent; old-timers on Kalymnos remember when, not so long ago, it was common to see sponge divers crippled, paralysed, or made deaf. Nowadays divers wear oxygen tanks and attack the sponges with axes, going down to a depth of 90 m. Politics limiting access to Mediterranean sponge beds and the invention of synthetic sponges has undermined Kalymnos' traditional livelihood; in the last century, many divers immigrated to Florida to exploit the sponge beds off Tarpon Springs.

In the past Kalymnos' sponge fleet left home for seven months of the year to work off the coast of North Africa. Today it makes only one four-month trip a year, sticking mostly to Greek and Italian waters. On Kalymnos, the week before the fleet sets out (the week after Orthodox Easter) is called the *Iprogros*, or sponge week, devoted to giving the sponge divers a rousing send-off, with plenty of food, free drinks, traditional costumes and dances—including the Sponge Dance, where the local schoolmaster mimes the part of the sponge fishermen while his pupils play the sponges. The last night of Sponge Week is tenderly known as *To Dipnos tis Agapis*, or the Feast of the Lovers. It ends with the pealing of church bells, calling the divers to their boats for another dangerous four months at sea.

Connections

Daily to Piraeus, Rhodes, Kos, Leros and Patmos; four times a week with Samos, three times a week with Lipsi and Astypalaia, twice a week with Nissyros, Tilos, Symi, and Agathonissi, once a week with Lesbos, Limnos, Ikaria, Mykonos, Santorini, Tinos, Andros, Rafina and Thessaloniki. Summer hydrofoil connection with Kos. Daily boats to Pserimos, daily caique from Myrties to Xirokambos, on Leros; special boat to connect passengers with Kos airport, arriving on that island at Mastihari.

Tourist Information

NTOG, April–Oct, next to Olympic Hotel, ✆ (0243) 29 310.

Tourist police, see regular police on the waterfront, ✆ (0243) 22 100.

Pothia

Pothia, the port, the capital, and second largest city in the Dodecanese, encompasses the harbour and much of Kalymnos' largest valley. More spread out than the typical tightly knotted island town, Pothia has many lovely old mansions along its back streets, walled orchards, and some fine views from the town's upper level. Local sculptors Michail Kokkinos and his daughter Irene have adorned Pothia with statues: *Poseidon* by the Olympic Hotel and, near the waterfront, a monument to Liberty with the history of sponge diving in relief. The police occupy one of Kalymnos' most fanciful confections, pink Italiate villa on the sea. On the far side of it is the sponge diving school.

The **archaeological museum**, in an old mansion, contains a typical miscellany of local antiquities and more recent items, including a barrel organ. Pothia also has one of Greece's rarer institutions—an orphanage, and until recently many Orthodox priests came here to choose a dowryless bride before they were ordained. There is a small beach near the yacht club, and beyond that a radioactive spring at **Thermapiges**, reputed to cure rheumatism, arthritis and digestive and kidney disorders. At night Pothia's hilltop landmark is a huge illuminated cement cross.

From Pothia caiques sail to **Nera** islet, south of Kalymnos, with a monastery and a small taverna, or to **Kephalas Cave**, a half-hour trip and walk of a couple of kilometres. Discovered in 1961, the cave was found to have been a sanctuary of Zeus; it is full of multicoloured stalactites and stalagmites. Another cave never thoroughly explored, is the **Cave of the**

Nymphs or the **Cave of the Seven Virgins**, after the seven maidens who hid themselves there during a pirate raid and were never seen again. A few traces of ancient nymph worship may be seen if you bring a torch. The cave's entrance is at Flakas, by the hospital.

Myli and Chorio

Inland, just behind Pothia, is a suburb called **Myli**, for its three monumental derelict windmills looming over the road. On a hill to the left stands the ruined **Castle of the Knights**, also known as the Chryssocheria (Golden-handed) after the church of the Virgin built within its walls, over an ancient temple of the Dioscuri. A treasure was once supposedly discovered there, and the area has been thoroughly combed on the off-chance of more.

Myli blends imperceptibly into the pretty white town of **Chorio**, the old capital of Kalymnos. It grew up around **Pera Kastro**, the striking though very dilapidated citadel that rises over the village and served as a place of refuge during the perilous Middle Ages. The ruined village within the Kastro's walls was inhabited from the 11th to the 18th centuries, and on a gloomy day looks more Transylvanian than Greek. The only undilapidated buildings are nine chapels kept freshly whitewashed by the faithful in Chorio. In Pigadia, just beyond Chorio, only the apse survives of the church of **Christ of Jerusalem**, built by the Byzantine Emperor Arkadios in gratitude for his shelter at Kalymnos during a terrible storm. It replaced a temple of Apollo, and made use of its stone as well; nearby are many rock-cut Mycenaean tombs. A road branching to the west at Chorio leads to **Argos**, named by the settlers from Argos on the mainland of Greece. Although some ruins have been found there, scholars doubt whether the ancient city stood at precisely the same spot as the present village.

North Kalymnos: Beaches, Monasteries, and Telendos

North of Chorio the road passes Kalymnos' best beaches, most offering shade if you don't want to bake and sizzle: **Kantouni, Panormos** (known locally as **Elies** because it sits in the olive groves), **Myrties** and **Massouri** (bus every half-hour from Pothia). Although as beaches go they're only just adequate, the deep blue coves offer excellent swimming. These villages are the quietly buzzing centre of Kalymnos' tourist industry.

From Myrties frequent caiques make the short trip to the islet of **Telendos**, which broke off from Kalymnos in a 6th century AD earthquake. On Telendos, facing the strait are the derelict monastery of **Ag. Vassilos** and a fort, both from the Middle Ages. There are ruins of **Roman houses** on Telendos and up to a mile offshore, and two small beaches. Most of the islanders are fishermen, who have ringside seats for the best sunsets on Kalymnos. See if in the profile of Telendos' mountain you can trace the form of the sleeping or **marble princess**, and the marble prince who faces her on the Kalymnos side of the strait. There are a couple of tavernas on Telendos, and a few rooms for rent.

North of Massouri, **Kastelli** was the refuge of survivors of the terrible 11th-century Turkish massacre, and overlooks the sea in a wild region of rocky cave mouths full of fangs. The church **Panayia** is below. **Arginonta**, the next village, lends its name to the entire northern peninsula, a perfect place for strenuous, isolated treks in the quiet hills; **Emporios**, the north-ernmost village (bus twice a day from Pothia) is within walking distance of some exceptional countryside, and has **cyclopean walls** and a tower close by. The tower is believed to have been a Neolithic temple; a sacrificial altar was found in the vicinity. Arginonta and Emporios both have quiet beaches.

Vathi

The narrow volcanic valley of Vathi ('the deep') is the beauty spot of Kalymnos: it has three charming, lush villages, Rhina, Platanos and Metoki, superbly situated at the mouth of a magnificent fjord. Fragrant groves of mandarins and lemons provide the valley's income, and houses and white-walled roads fill in the gaps between the trees. The middle village, **Platanos** is named for its enormous plane tree and has Cyclopean walls; Rhina has a mysterious 'throne' carved in the rock. North of Vathi you can walk to the Monastery of **Kyra Psilas**, the Tall Lady. Near Vathi, but accessible only by sea, near the mouth of the fjord, is the **Cave of Daskaleio**, the largest of Kalymnos' grottoes; a trove of Neolithic to Bronze Age items was found in its inner stalactite chamber.

Festivals

15 August, Panayia; 14 September, Stavros on Nera islet; 27 July, Ag. Panteleimonos at Brosta; a week after Easter, the Iprogros (sponge week). Other celebrations are held when the divers return, although each boat arrives at a different time and celebrations are not as general as at the Iprogros.

Where to Stay

moderate

In Pothia, a few strides from the ferry will bring you to the fancy **Olympic Hotel**, ✆ 28 801, with good rates for its C class rooms. The **Thermae Hotel**, ✆ 29 425, is in a pleasant location right on the waterfront, above a restaurant, if you want to be in the thick of it. The **Panorama**, ✆ 23 138, provides furnished apartments with a good view of the town and harbour. In Massouri the **Massouri Beach Hotel**, ✆ 47 555, has comfortable rooms at low rates, and at Myrties the peaceful **Zephyros**, ✆ 47 500 is 100 m from the beach and looks across to the islet of Telendos.

cheap

One of the best in this range, with a certain dilapidated charm, is the nearby **Alma** at 8 Patr. Maximou, ✆ 28 969. Alternatively, try the comfortable, convenient pension by the taxi station, **Aris**. There are also private rooms in Kalymnos town and out at the other popular beaches, although you may have to pound the pavements or mule tracks to find them; best to set forth with a list from the tourist office.

In Pothia most of the restaurants are on the far end of the quay, beyond the Italian villa of the tourist police; the high percentage of Greek clientele ensures that you can't go too wrong. **Uncle Petros** is perhaps the best known. Round by the churches **Vouvaly Fish Restaurant** occupies the original sponge factory and is done out with shells, nets, ship carvings and nautical bric-a-brac; more importantly, it has seawater tanks where you can choose your own lobster or fish—otherwise try their excellent fish casseroles and octopus *keftedes*. On summer nights, there's often Greek music and dancing (3000 dr.). Not far away in the backstreets, search out the friendly, family-run **Xefteris**, near the Metropolis church, where you can sit out in a garden and the fresh fish and roast lamb won't send you running to the bank; try their island versions of *dolmades* and *stifado*. On the other side of the harbour, the little **Flaskos** taverna serves delectable roast chicken flavoured with mountain herbs and excellent salads. Order carefully and you'll get change for your 1500 dr. In the village of Argos, you'll find authentic Kalymnot food at the **Argos** taverna; try the *moori*, lamb cooked overnight in a ceramic pot (2000 dr.). In Massouri, enjoy excellent *meze* in the **Mathaios**, and in Kantouni **Ursula's** serves German food (2000 dr.).

Karpathos

Nearly halfway in between Crete and Rhodes, Karpathos has for decades been an island-hopper's best kept secret: hard to reach, but well worth the long hours of travelling. For one thing, Karpathos is two islands for the price of one: long and thin, austere and ruggedly mountainous in the north and fertile, prosperous, beach-fringed and 'European' in the south, separated by the two peaks rising over 3000 ft. These two distinct geographical personalities extend to the population; it has even been suggested that the northerners and southerners originally belonged to different races and for long generations had little if any contact with one another. The 'road' connecting the two halves was finished in 1979 and is only suitable for four-wheel drives.

The long isolation of the north has made it a goldmine for students of customs lost a century ago in the rest of Greece. In Olympos, the chief village, women still bake their bread in out-door ovens; the men, even the young ones, play the traditional three-stringed lyra, the goatskin bagpipe *tsabouna*, and the *laouto*. Most striking of all, the women wear their traditional costumes every day—costumes considered the most beautiful in Greece, and the chosen dress of Queen Frederika at the ceremony of 1947 that formally joined the Dodecanese to Greece. So far Olympos has not lost its unique charm, even though Karpathos now boasts a large international airport, bringing in more tourists every year. However, Karpathos is by no means overrun, and the north especially has many places offering refuge from the crowds.

History

One of the many ancient names of Karpathos was Porfiris, or 'Red', after a red dye once manufactured on the island and used for the clothes of kings. It was also known as Tetrapolis, describing its four ancient cities of Vrykous, Possidion, Arkessia and Nissyros. Homer referred to the island as Krapathos, although another story claims its name comes from the dark days of piracy, when sheltered Vrontis bay hid pirate ships that darted out to plunder any passing vessel. Disgruntled captains dubbed the island Arpaktos, or 'robbery', and the name was eventually corrupted to Karpathos. The Venetians knew it as Scarpanto, a name you may occasionally see on maps.

Of the four ancient cities of Karpathos, Nissyros, on the northern islet of Saria, is believed to have been colonized by the island of Nissyros, to exploit the iron and silver mines at Assimovorni. Off the coasts, the prized *scarus* (or parrot fish, which as Aristotle noted, ruminates its food) was so abundant that the Roman Emperors hired special fishing fleets to bring them back for the imperial table. Any signs of prosperity, however, had long ended by the time the pirates made the island their headquarters and one of its towns, Arkessia, their chief slave market. Things were so rough that even the Turks didn't really want Karpathos, and sent only a *cadi*, or judge, to the island a few times a year; he never stayed longer than a few days, having to depend entirely on the Greeks to protect him from the pirates. To this day the bays at Vrontis and Arkessia are said to hold a fortune in sunken pirate treasure.

Connections

By air: daily with Rhodes, several times a week with Kassos and Sitia (Crete).

By ship: three times a week with Piraeus, four times a week with Rhodes, three times a week with Santorini, twice a week with Kassos, Sitia (Crete), Ag. Nikolaos

(Crete) and Milos, once a week with Paros, Sikinos, Folegandros and Sifnos. Some ships call at both Diafani and Pigadia (Karpathos). Small boats daily in the summer connect the two ports, and at weekends there's a caique from Pigadia to Kassos.

Tourist Police

See regular police on the waterfront, Pigadia, © (0245) 22 218.

Karpathos Town

The island capital and southern port, Karpathos (or Pigadia) is attractively sheltered in that old pirate cove, mountain-ringed Vrontis Bay; Karpathos was the ancient city of Possidion, dedicated to the sea god. Abandoned in the Byzantine era, all that's left are a clutch of Mycenaean tombs and a few stones of the old acropolis on the rocky outcrop to the east. The modern town is just that—modern, with many new buildings, and it's no accident that the local National Bank branch has such an air of prosperity: Karpathos has the distinction of receiving more money from its emigrants abroad than any other island in Greece.

The most distinctive architecture in town is by the park and playground: an Italian-built administration building that doubles as a small **museum** containing an early Christian baptismal font, coins, ceramics and inscriptions. From here it is a short walk to the 3-km stretch of sand around Vrontis Bay. The beach is lined with trees, dotted with pleasant tavernas specializing in grilled fish, and on the beach, within an enclosure, are the ruins of a 5th-century basilica, **Ag. Fotini**, recently discovered by accident. Several of the columns have been raised in their original places. Across the bay stands the chapel of **Ag. Nikolaos**, the saint who replaced Poseidon as the protector of sailors; a cave nearby called Kamara has sweet water. Another ancient site, on the south side of the Vrontis bay, **Ag. Kiriaki** (the track is signposted from the road) was a Geometric-era sanctuary dedicated to Demeter; a few years back one of the tombs hewn in the rock yielded a golden statuette.

Villages in Southern Karpathos

If you're using public transport, check schedules before setting out; buses are fairly infrequent, and there are villages served only once a day, or even only once or twice a week. South from Karpathos town vegetation is sparse, and the few trees are bent over from the wind. The road passes **Ammopi**, a sandy beach and small resort on route to the airport. This occupies the site of the ancient city of Thaetho, although little now remains.

The road west of Karpathos town passes below the picturesque old mountain village of **Menetes**, with a small ethnographic museum. Towards the west coast, **Arkassa** is prettily immersed in orchards. A track leads up to the ruins of its predecessor, ancient **Arkessia** where a Mycenaean acropolis with Cyclopean walls stands on a rocky headland known as Paleokastro. The surrounding cliffs are riddled with caves that have offered shelter to shepherds for centuries. Here you'll find the ruins of an early Byzantine church, **Ag. Sophia,** with brightly coloured floor mosaics just under the fine layer of weeds and dirt; the best sections of these have been moved to the museum at Rhodes. Another ruined basilica, around the chapel **Ag. Anastasia**, dates from the 5th century. The coast below is jagged and wild, but there is a small beach wedged between the cliffs. Further north, **Finiki** is a bijou little fishing harbour with a good, inexpensive restaurant; the sponge divers of Kalymnos call here, and caiques part for Kassos, if the sea isn't too rough—as is often the case.

From Finiki the road approaches the slopes of Karpathos' tallest mountain, Kalilimni, the highest point in the Dodecanese at 1188 m, where there's a pretty village, whose name in Roman letters unfortunately reads **Piles**. From here a rough road continues up the west coast to remote **Lefkos**, with a white sandy beach, a wealth of pine trees and scattering of antiquities, including a large stone that strikingly resembles a Celtic menhir. A short walk away are the ruins of a small medieval fort; there was another on the offshore islet of **Sokastro**. There are a few small hotels and rooms to rent in Lefkos, which the Karpathiots themselves consider the most beautiful spot on their island.

In the centre of the south, **Othos** is another lovely spot, the highest village of Karpathos, and one of the oldest, its houses decorated with carved wooden balconies. Although you may need a pullover, even in summer, it produces a fine local sweet red wine, *othitiko krasi* and, they say, the island's prettiest girls. A traditional house here has been opened as a small ethnographic museum. Neighbouring **Volada** is a delightful whitewashed village with pretty lanes and well-kept houses, and a ruined castle built by the Cornaros of Venice, who owned the island until 1538.

Circling back towards Karpathos town, **Aperi** with exquisitely tended gardens and houses, was the capital of Karpathos up to 1896. It is reputed to be the richest village in Greece per capita; nearly everyone here has lived in New Jersey. One kafeneíon still proudly displays a picture of Roosevelt; another, the Eleftheria Café run by a PASOK leprechaun, is full of curios and rubber items from the 1960s. In the new cathedral you can pay your respects to Karpathos' most venerated icon, credited with several miracles, among them that of saving the life of a young boy who was pushed off a cliff. He went on to become a rich American lawyer and contributed the funds for many of the island's new buildings. A track leads down to **Ahata**, a quiet pebbly beach, but it is very steep.

Other beaches along the east coast are easiest reached by caique from Karpathos town, especially **Apella**, the most beautiful, with fine sand, turquoise water and dramatic scenery, and **Kyra Panayia**, a lovely wide beach, varying from fine white sand to large pebbles. An alternative way of getting to Kyra Panayia: a 45-minute walk down through the lush greenery and trees from the mountain village of **Mertonas**. Mertonas is the place to be 22 August, when it hosts the best *paneyeri* on the Karpathiot calendar with music and folkdancing that goes on well into the following day, and free food to boot. **Messochorio** in the mountains is another pretty village. From here or Spoa the sturdy of foot can begin the long trek to Olympos, or take the somewhat perilous road by taxi-jeep, a long (and rather expensive) proposition. Unfortunately, a massive forest fire in 1983 has left most of the island between Spoa and Diafani denuded and melancholy.

The easiest and least expensive way to reach Olympos from Karpathos is by caique to **Diafani**, the village's port, from where a minibus makes the connection to Olympos. Diafani has a beach with flat rocks and is within walking distance of several others.

Olympos, one of the most striking villages on the Greek islands, is draped over a stark mountain ridge, with a long line of ruined windmills running like vertebrae down its spine. To the west are magnificent views of mountains plunging headlong into the sea. Decorative painted balconies, many incorporating two-headed Byzantine eagles (one head Rome, one Constantinople), adorn the houses which in many places are literally stacked one on another and opened with wooden locks and keys that Homer himself might have recognized. The village church has smoke-darkened frescoes, perhaps going back to the 18th-century, and an awe-inspiring, sombre ambience, that even the garrulous Greeks speak of in hushed tones.

The origins of Olympos are shrouded in mystery. Some evidence suggests that the original inhabitants of northern Karpathos came from Phrygia in Asia Minor; certainly the village was isolated for so long that linguists were amazed to find people here using ancient Dorian expressions long forgotten elsewhere in the country. Some matrilinear customs have survived, a family's property going to the eldest daughter, the *kanakara*; if you're lucky enough to be in Olympos during a *paneyeri* or wedding, you can recognize a *kanakara* by the weight of gold coins she wears on chains, coins that her forefathers will have earned while working abroad. The women wear their flowing white costumes every day, including fine goatskin boots (it is said that snakes hate the smell of goat). The boots, which last for years, are handmade in the village and are perhaps the one souvenir you can buy at Olympos.

The best time to visit Olympos is during the weekends, when the women bake bread and vegetable pies in their outdoor ovens, the miller grinds the wheat in the last working windmill, out of 40 that turned a generation ago, and when the two *kafeneíons* are filled with Karpathos' music, uncannily similar to Irish music in one of its wilder moods. But you're not quite as far away as you think; in the *kafeneíon* across from the church the owner displays a certificate from the Governor of Alabama, thanking him for his service in the state militia! Otherwise, there is little to do but stroll the quiet streets and absorb what you can of a vanishing way of life.

From Olympos you can drive most of the way to **Avlona**, a village inhabited only during the harvest season by farmers from Olympos, who work the surrounding valley; some of the tools they use are more commonly seen in museums. From Avlona it is a rough walk down to **Vourgounda** (Vrykus), the ancient Phrygian city, remembered today by a stair, a breakwater, burial chambers and walls. In a cavern in Vourgounda the chapel of **Ag. Ioannis** hosts the largest *paneyeria* in north Karpathos, a two-day event where everyone sleeps out, roasts meat over an open fire and dances to the haunting music.

On Sundays boats from Diafani sail to the islet of **Saria**, which dots the 'i' of long, narrow Karpathos. Here was the ancient kingdom of Nissyros, of which little remains. A chapel now stands on the site of the proto-Christian basilica. More interesting to see are *Ta Palatia* (the palaces), actually a post-Byzantine pirate base, the houses built in the dolmus style, with barrel-vaulted roofs. It is a good walk up from the landing place, so wear sturdy shoes.

Festivals

25 March, Evanglismos at Pigadia; 1 July, Ag. Marinas, near Menetes; 15 August, at Aperi and Menetes; 27–29 August, Ag. Ioannis at Vourgounda; 22–23 August, Kyra Panayia and Mertonas; 6 September, Larniotisa at Pigadia; 8 September, Playias at Messochorio.

Where to Stay

expensive

The brand new A class **Possirama Bay** at Pigadia is 400 m from the town centre, on the sandy beach of Affoti, offering hotel apartments for 2–4 people, with fully equipped kitchen facilities, and large balconies overlooking the sea, ✆ 22 916. In the same area **Miramare Bay Hotel** is another new operation, with swimming pool, sea views and good breakfast included, ✆ 22 802.

moderate

If you've the money the most charming place to stay in the capital is the **Pension Romantica**, ✆ 22 460/1. Located in a grove of citrus trees, and a short walk from the beach, it has 32 rooms and serves a delicious breakfast. Equally pleasant is the modern **Blue Bay Hotel** near the beach at Affoti Pigadia, 1½ km from the town, ✆ 22 479. A good bargain in this category is the D class **Karpathos Hotel** in Pigadia; most of its 16 rooms come with private shower and balcony, ✆ 22 347. In northern Karpathos, there are several places to stay in Diafani; the **Chryssi Akti** with 11 rooms near where the ferry boat lands is clean and comfortable, ✆ 51 215.

cheap

On the cheap side, in Pigadia, there are quite a few small pensions and rooms for rent. **Seva'** is a clean, friendly place, a km from the beach, 300 m from the port. There are rooms for rent in Diafani, Olympos and Arkassa.

Eating Out

Food in Karpathos is relatively inexpensive. A favourite with locals is the **Anemoussa** in Pigadia, with a terrace overlooking the sea, with some Italian specialities (dinner only; 2500 dr.). **Kali Kardia** and **Panomanolis** are rated highly, too. The **Land and Sea Taverna** on the waterfront specializes in fresh seafood, but there are some meat dishes (4000 dr.). At Affoti beach, 1 km away, a taverna features live bouzouki music to go with its international dishes and Greek food. In Ammopi, look for the **Nikos Mastrominas**, just 500 m from the beach, with good Greek food and swift service (3000 dr.) In Diafani, **Nik Orphanos** has the best name for fresh fish (3500 dr.).

Kassos

The southernmost Dodecanese island and one of the most remote of all islands, Kassos is a barren rock with steep coasts and sea grottoes, with an odd beach or two wedged in between. The port, Emborio, is small, and if the sea is rough, as it often is, simply landing can be a big headache.

History

Homer mentions Kassos in the *Iliad*, for the ships it sent to Troy to aid the Achaeans. The ancient city stood at the site of the present village of Poli, and at Hellenokamera cave there are Mycenaean walls. During the Turkish occupation, Kassos retained a good deal of its autonomy, especially with regard to its ships, which it quickly put at the disposal of the Greek cause when the War of Independence was declared, in 1821. For the first three years of the war the Greeks generally came out ahead in the struggle, but the Sultan, angered by his set-backs, prepared powerful counter-attacks through Ibrahim Pasha, son of the Ottoman Empire's governor of Egypt. In June 1824 Ibrahim left Egypt with a massive fleet to crush the Greek rebellion. His first stop was Kassos, which he decimated, slaying the men and taking the women and children as slaves. The few who managed to escape went either to Syros or Grambousa, an islet off the northwestern coast of Crete, where they turned to piracy for survival, defiantly flying the Greek flag in Turkish waters. But Capodistria and his allies put a stop to their activities, and their refuge, Grambousa, was returned to Turkish rule. Thousands of Kassiotes later emigrated to Egypt to work on the Suez Canal.

Connections

By air: daily with Rhodes, two–three times a week with Sitia and Karpathos.

By sea: twice a week with Piraeus, Crete, Milos, Rhodes and Karpathos, once a week with Halki, Symi, Santorini, Sikinos, Folegandros and Sifnos; weekend caique from Finiki, Karpathos.

Around Kassos

Small **Fry** is the capital of the little island, where the main occupation, fishing, is much in evidence. Every year on 7 June a ceremony is held there in memory of the massacre of 1824, and many people from Karpathos also attend, coming on the special boats.

There are hardly any trees on Kassos because, it is claimed, Ibrahim Pasha burnt them all down, but many lighthouses stick out above the rocky terrain. A road and the island's one bus link Fry with Kassos' four other dinky villages. There is a lovely cave with stalactites called Hellenokamara near the beach at **Ammoua**. **Poli** is built on the island's ancient acropolis, and you can still see a few surviving walls at Kastro. Beyond the villages a path leads across the island to **Khelathros Harbour**, with the best beach on the island. Another nice beach is on **Armathia**, the only inhabited islet off Kassos; there are frequent excursions from the port.

14 August, at Ag. Marina; 23 April, Ag. Georgios; 7 July, at Fry; late July, Ag. Spyridon.

The place to stay is the **Hotel Anagennissis**, © 41 323, comfortable and run by an engaging former American. You'll pay more for the rooms facing the sea with bath, less for those in the back. There are also several pensions and rooms, and another small hotel, the class C **Hotel Anessis**, © 41 201, where the doubles tend to be a little less. All of the above are in Fry.

There are a handful of tavernas in Fry; at **Milos** or **Zagora**, a typical meal costs 1500 dr. There are also a couple of tavernas in Ag. Marina and Emborio.

Kastellorizo (Megisti)

The easternmost point of Greece, oddball Kastellorizo is 6 hours by ship from Rhodes and in spitting distance of Turkey. It is the smallest island of the Dodecanese, 3 km by 6, yet the mother hen of its own small clutch of islets; hence its official name, Megisti, 'the largest'. The Turks know it as the 'eye-land', for one nautical mile away is their town of Kaş ('eyebrow'), while the most commonly heard name is Kastellorizo, in memory of the days when the Venetians called it the 'Red Castle'. Dry, depopulated, more than half ruined by numerous vicissitudes, its streets are patrolled by turkeys, and its inhabitants noticeably affected by the isolation. The new airport is slowly bringing the island in closer contact with Greece, and its success as a film set—for Philippe de Broca's *King of Hearts* and the recent Italian film *Mediterraneo*, about a group of Italian soldiers stationed there during the war, has given Kastellorizo a psychological boost. At present it remains a quiet if quirky backwater surrounded by a crystal sea brimming with marine life. And while there aren't any sandy strands, the local people will never fail to tell you that there are plenty of rocks to beach on.

History

According to tradition, Kastellorizo's first settler was King Meges of Echinada who gave his name to the island. Neolithic finds suggest an early arrival for Echinada, and Mycenaean graves coincide with the mention in Homer of the island's ships at Troy. Subsequently, the Dorians built two forts on the island, the Kastro by the present town and on the mountain, called Palaeokastro—the acropolis of the ancient capital, where Apollo and the Dioscuri were the chief gods. The little island had a great fleet of ships based in its sheltered harbour and traded with Lycia on the mainland, transporting its timber to ports in Africa and the Middle East. From 350 to 300 BC Kastellorizo was ruled by Rhodes, and in Roman times the pirates of Cassius used it as their hideout. The island was converted to Christianity from the time of St Paul, who preached along the south coast of Asia Minor at Myra.

During the Byzantine period Kastellorizo's fortifications were repaired, and this work was continued by the Knights of St John after the fall of Jerusalem. They named the island after the red rock of the castle which they used to imprison knights who misbehaved on Rhodes. The Sultan of Egypt captured Kastellorizo in 1440, but ten years later the King of Naples, Alfonso I of Aragon, took it back. Although Kastellorizo belonged to the Ottoman Empire by 1523, the Venetians later occupied it twice in their endless struggles against the Turks, in 1570 and in 1659. Despite all the see-sawing to and fro, Kastellorizo was doing all right for itself; at the beginning of the 19th century it had a population of 15,000, who lived either from the sea or their extensive holdings along the coast of Asia Minor. Things began to go wrong with the outbreak of the Greek War of Independence. The islanders were the first in the Dodecanese to join the cause, and taking matters into their own hands, seized the island's two fortresses from the Turks. The Great Powers forced them to give them back to the Turks in 1833. In 1913 Kastellorizo revolted again only to be put down this time by the French, who were trying to get their mitts on Syria. During the First World War the island was bombarded from the Turkish coast. In 1927 an earthquake caused extensive damage but the Italian fascists, then in charge, refused to do any repairs, as Kastellorizo had failed to cooperate with their programme of de-Hellenisation. There was another revolt in 1933, but it was crushed by soldiers from Rhodes. By now Kastellorizo was in sharp decline—in 1941 only 1500 inhabitants remained.

This, however, does not end the tale of misfortunes for the gutsy little island. During the Second World War the Allies shipped the entire population to refugee camps in the Middle East. Although this was done for their safety, the islanders were not allowed to take many of their precious belongings with them, and the occupying Allied troops pillaged the empty houses they left behind. To hide their crime, they burnt the town down, destroying more than 1500 homes. As if this was not enough, the ship carrying the refugees home after the war sank, drowning many. Those who survived to return to Kastellorizo discovered that, although they had finally achieved Greek citizenship they had lost everything else, and that there was nothing to do but emigrate.

Connections

By air: 3 times a week from Rhodes; **boat** twice a week from Rhodes.

Tourist Police

See regular police in the harbour by the post office.

Kastellorizo Town

There is only one town on the island, also called **Kastellorizo**, full of ruined houses and mansions, some burnt, others crumbling from earthquakes or bombardments. One can see how wealthy some of the inhabitants once were from the remaining interiors, with elegant coffered ceilings and lovely carved balustrades. Some are being restored, others are inhabited by cats and chickens. Small tavernas line the waterfront, so close to the edge of the quay that a discreet kick is all it takes to rid yourself of an unwanted guest at your table. A hotel occupies one lip of the harbour mouth, while on the other sits the fort (*kastro*), last repaired by the eighth Grand Master of the Knights of St John, Juan Fernando Heredia, whose red coat-of-arms is another possible explanation for the name of the island. If you climb the ladder to the top, you'll have a fine view of the sea and Turkey. An inscription in Doric Greek discovered at the fort suggests the existence of an ancient castle on the same site. A tomb nearby yielded a golden crown, and in the mosque is a small **museum** (*5–7.30*) containing photographs of the days of past prosperity, a few frescoes, folk costumes and items found in the harbour. Above the fort you can also visit the 'Gobelins of Kastellorizo', part of a government sponsored programme to create employment for women in remote areas; here two women at a loom may take several months to weave one large rug.

Another path leads up to a **Lycian tomb** cut into the living rock and decorated with Doric columns. The whole southwest, or Lycian coast of modern Turkey, is dotted with similar tombs, but this is the only one in modern Greece. The **cathedral of Ag. Konstantinos and Helena** re-uses granite columns from a temple of Apollo in Anatolia. From town a steep path with steps leads up to four white churches and **Palaeokastro**, the Doric fortress and acropolis. On the gate there is a Doric inscription from the 3rd century BC referring to Megiste; walls, a tower and cisterns also remain.

Kastellorizo's Grotto Azzurro

There are no beaches on Kastellorizo, but the sea is clean, and there are a multitude of tiny islets to swim out to. An excursion not be missed is to the **Blue Cave**, or Parastas, an hour by caique from the town. The effects are best in the morning when some light filters in, for the entrance is so low, you'll have to duck down in the boat to enter. As in the famous Blue Grotto of Capri, the reflections of the water inside bathe the cavern walls with an uncanny blue. There are many stalactites, and if you're very lucky, you may meet the monk seal who lives inside.

The fishing around Kastellorizo is excellent, and serves as the main occupation for the island's 200 souls. Almost everyone, however, is ready to leave, and the only reason they stay is to keep the island Greek. The Turks in Kaş deny it, but many Greeks will tell you that if the population of Kastellorizo drops below 200, it will revert to Turkey. Whatever the case, the Greek government pays people to stay there, has built a desalination plant, and has bent over backwards to bring Greek television, radio and an airport to the island.

Festivals

20 July, Profitis Ilias; 21 May, Ag. Konstantinos; 24 April, Ag. Georgios.

The island's most comfortable digs is the class C **Hotel Megisti**, overlooking the excellent natural harbour, © 29 072; for something less expensive, just take up one of the offers you'll receive as you get off the boat. As like as not the room you get will be as quirky as its owner.

Nearly everything's by the harbour; the fish is inexpensive and fresh (and the only thing that doesn't have to be shipped in). Expect to pay between 1500–2000 dr. for a full dinner. At least once a week in the summer, a tour agency in Kaş brings over a boatload of visitors for 'Greek Night' which considerably enlivens the evening.

Kos

Dolphin-shaped Kos with its natural beauty, wealth of fascinating antiquities, beaches and comfortable climate is Rhodes' major Dodecanese rival in the tourist industry, so much so that there's a decidedly un-Greek feeling to the place in high season. Nothing remains of the Greece of thirty years ago—the *kafeneíon* and *ouzeri*, serving octopus sizzling from the grill, have been replaced with cafés, with brightly coloured plastic chairs, serving international snacks; garlanded donkeys no longer carry their patrons home from the fields, while swarms of rent-a-bikes drone around the island. English, German and Swedish are more commonly heard than Greek. Yet, for all this, the island still holds charm for many people, who find everything they need for a summer vacation. Even the architecture isn't particularly Greek: the Italian occupation provided some attractive buildings, and the pair of minarets rising from the Turkish-built mosques complete its aura of *cosmopolitana.*

History

Evidence in Aspri Petra cave dates Kos' first settlement to 3500 BC. A Minoan colony flourished on the site of the modern city of Kos; the Mycenaeans who superseded them traded extensively throughout the Mediterranean. After their decline Kos' history is obscure, except for references to two of the island's early names, Meropis, after its mythical king, and Nymphaeon, for its numerous nymphs. Astypalaia was the ancient capital, although in 366 BC the inhabitants began to rebuild the Mycenaean city of Kos.

Poised between East and West (the ancient city of Halikarnassus, present-day Bodrum in Turkey, is very near), Kos flourished with the trade of precious goods—and revolutionary ideas. Halikarnassus was the birthplace of Herodotos, called the 'father of history' for his attempt to distinguish legend from fact, and in the 5th century Kos produced an innovator of its own, Hippocrates, the father of medicine. Hippocrates realized that diseases were not punishments sent from the gods, but had natural causes, and was the first to suggest that healers should discover as much as possible about each patient and their symptoms before making a

To Piraeus

Lampi
KOS
Psalidi

Tingaki
Marmari Saltpans
Platanos
Zipario Asklepieion II
Linopolis Ag. Fokas
Mastihari Asfendiou II Empros Thermae
Logoudi Ag. Dimitrio
Pyli Zia
Dikaios Christos ▲ (685m / 2250ft)
Castle of Antimacheia Pisotherma
Antimacheia II
Toliri

Limonas
Kardamena
To Rhodes

KOS

Kefalos
Ag. Stefanos Paradise Beach

N

Kamario
Ag. Ioannis Aspri Petra
Ag. Theologos Astypalaia
Beach

0   2   5   10 km
0   2   5   miles

diagnosis. His school on Kos, where he taught pupils a wholesome medicine based on waters, special diets, herbal remedies and relaxation was renowned throughout the ancient world, and he set a standard of medical ethics incorporated in the Hippocratic oath taken by doctors to this day. When Hippocrates died an Asklepieion (a temple to Asklepios, the god of healing) was founded, and people from all over the Mediterranean world came to be healed in its hospital-sanctuary. Besides physicians, Kos produced a school of Bucolic poetry, led by Theocritus (319–250 BC). The Hellenistic ruler of Egypt, Ptolemy II Philadelphos, was born here, and many of the Ptolemies were sent to Kos for their education. The Romans were later to prize Kos for its silk industry, the only one in the Mediterranean, producing a fine, translucent cloth.

The island's wealth and strategic position excited the envy of others, and from the 6th century BC it was invaded by Persians, Romans and Saracens. The gods themselves, it seems, were jealous, and earthquakes in AD 142, 469, 554 and 1933 levelled most of the island's buildings. In 1315 the Knights of St John took control of Kos, and in 1391, began fortifications using material from the ancient city, incorporating even works of art from the Asklepieion as stone for their walls. In 1457 and 1477 the Turks besieged Kos without success, but they gained the fortress after the fall of Rhodes.

By air: direct from London and several other European cities, three times a day with Athens, once a day with Rhodes, twice a week with Leros.

By hydrofoil: daily with Rhodes, several times a week with Patmos and Leros. Once a week with Samos. Also connections with Kalymnos, Nissyros, Tilos and Symi.

By boat: in season, daily boat to Bodrum, Turkey. Ferry every day to Piraeus, Rhodes, Kalymnos, Leros and Patmos; small boats daily in season to Patmos, Nissyros, Pserimos and Kalymnos. Three times a week with Tilos, Mykonos, Andros and Rafina, twice a week with Samos, Symi and Astypalaia, once a week with Chios, Lesbos, Limnos and Thessaloniki.

Tourist Information

NTOG, waterfront, ✆ (0242) 28 724.

Tourist police, with regular police, by the castle, ✆ (0242) 22 222.

Kos Town

Bustling **Kos**, the capital and main port, looks towards the north, roughly in the region of the dolphin's eye. Its garden setting, the multitude of flowers and stately palm trees make up somewhat for its lack of architectural interest; most of Kos town was built after the 1933 earthquake, this time using anti-seismatic construction. From the archaeologist's point of view, the disaster had a good side-effect; when the rubble was cleared away, several ancient sites were revealed, and excavations were carried out throughout the city by the Italians. One block up from the harbour, in Plateia Eleftherias, is the **Museum** (*9–3.30, Sun 10–3, closed Tues*). Fittingly, the prize exhibit is a 4th-century BC statue of Hippocrates; there's also a good collection of Hellenistic and Roman vases, statues and mosaics from the Casa Romana and the Asklepieion.

Dominated by the 18th-century **Defterdar Mosque** (still used by Kos' 50 or so Moslem families, but not open to the public), Plateia Eleftheria also has the city's fruit market and the **Porta tou Forou**, the gate to Kos' **Agora**. Within its walls the Knights built their town and auberges, and when these collapsed in the earthquake, excavations revealed the Roman Agora, the harbour quarter of the city, a temple of Aphrodite, and a 5th-century Christian basilica.

On the northern end of the Agora, the Plateia Platanou is almost entirely filled by **Hippocrates' plane tree**, its trunk 47 ft in diametre, its huge boughs now supported by an intricate metal scaffolding instead of the marble columns that once kept the venerable old tree from disaster. Signs in eight languages warn people not to touch for fear of insecticides. Yet it still seems quite healthy, and at between 500- and 600-years-old may well be the senior plane tree in Europe. Hippocrates may well have taught under its great grandmother, for he believed, as do modern Greeks, that of all the trees the shade of the plane is the most salubrious. The Greeks' first cousins, the Turks, loved the old plane just as much, and built a fountain under it with a sarcophagus for a basin, and overlooking it constructed the lovely **Mosque of the Loggia** (1786). On 1 September the citizens of Kos come to pluck a leaf from the tree to include in their harvest wreaths as a symbol of abundance.

The Castle of the Knights

A stone bridge off Plateia Platanou takes you over the fosse to the entrance of the **Castle of the Knights of St John** (*9–3.30, Sun 10–3, closed Tues*). Together with their fortress across the strait in Bodrum, this castle served as the most important outer defence of Rhodes. After an earthquake in 1495, Grand Master Pierre d'Aubusson rebuilt the walls and added the outer enceinte, and the tower overlooking the harbour bears his name and coat-of-arms. Since d'Aubusson mostly used stones from the Agora, there's a patchwork of ancient inscriptions and reliefs of the knights' coats-of-arms throughout the castle; some have been removed to the castle's **Antiquarium**, along with stacks of defunct columns and marble. The castle's dishevelled weeds and wildflowers and stillness of the noonday sun attracted director Werner Herzog, who set his *Signs of Life* within its walls; however, the elaborate cockroach traps and hypnotized chickens that played such a large role in the film are no longer in evidence.

Roman Kos

From Plateia Eleftheria take Vass. Pavlou to Kos' other main archaeological sites. In the quarter called the Seraglio, Minoan and Mycenaean houses were discovered, as well as later structures. Opposite the Olympic Airways office stands a ramped Hellenistic **Altar of Dionysos**, and across Grigoriou St is the **Casa Romana** (*9–3.30, Sun 10–3, closed Tues*), excavated and reconstructed by the Italians in the 1930s. The house and neighbouring baths fell in the earthquake of AD 554; the house has well-preserved mosaics and offers a fair idea of the spacious elegance a wealthy Roman could afford. To the west along Grigoriou St is the **Roman Odeon**, or concert hall, with its rows of marble seats. Opposite, the so-called **western excavations** were also begun by the Italians in the 1930s. On one side are the great Hellenistic walls built around the acropolis, where a minaret stands today; on the other side runs the finely paved *cardo*, the main artery of Roman Kos, lined with houses (many containing fine mosaics, especially the House of Europa), a gymnasium and well-preserved baths used as a basilica by 5th-century Christians. In the baptistry you can see a well-preserved font. Alongside the baths and basilica runs the colonnade of the covered running track, or *xystos*, used in the winter months. The open **stadium** was at the northern end of the *xystos*, down Tsaldari St. Only a few of the seats have yet been excavated, but on the far side near the church is a well-preserved *aphesis*, or starting gate.

The Asklepieion

Many places in Kos hire out bicycles, the ideal transport to the **Asklepieion** (*8–7, Sun 9–6*) a few easy kilometres inland from the town. The German archaeologist Herzog, following the description in Strabo, discovered it in 1902, and it has been partially restored by the Italians. This was one of the ancient world's most important shrines to the healing god Asklepios, worshipped by the Asklepiada, a secret order of priests who found that calm baths in beautiful settings did much to remedy the ills of body and soul.

The symbol of the cult were snakes for their supposed aptitude in seeking out healing herbs and their semi-divine status as transmitters of dreams—the Asklepiada made good use of drugs and the power of suggestion in their cures. The sanctuary on Kos was built after the death of Hippocrates, himself a member of the Asklepiada, but most of the buildings you see today are Hellenistic in origin, when it was last reconstructed after an earthquake; many of the structures were dismantled by the Knights, who found it a very convenient quarry. Nowadays, the Greeks have big plans to build a 'City of Hippocrates' near the present Hippocrates Foundation, where every five years they would hold an international medical olympiad. It is amusing to speculate on what that might have encompassed.

Set on a hillside, the Asklepieion is built in a series of terraces. On the lowest level are Roman baths, built in the 3rd century AD; on the next up is the main entrance and another large bath, and near the stair are the remains of a temple dedicated by the Kos-born physician G. Stertinius Xenophon, who went on to become the Emperor Claudius' personal doctor and murdered his patient by sticking a poisoned feather down his throat, before retiring on Kos, hailed as a hero, rather in the face of the Hippocratic Oath. On this level there is a spring, where water has flowed for over 2000 years. On the third terrace is the altar of Asklepios, and Ionic temples of Apollo and Asklepios (a few of the columns have been reconstructed by the Italians); on the fourth level stood a Doric temple of Asklepios from the 2nd century BC, the grandest and most sacred of all, and enjoying a view that in itself might shake away the blues. On the way back to the capital, stop for refreshments in **Platanias**, Kos' main Turkish settlement, with some good tavernas and cafés.

Buses to other points on Kos leave from the terminal behind the Olympic Airways office, but the services are infrequent, and you'll inevitably find yourself at the wrong end of a 100-m line-up, waiting for a taxi. The closest beaches to the east are at **Psalidi** (3 km) and **Ag. Fokas**, both along the road to the modern spa, **Empros Thermae**. On the north coast there are beaches at **Lampi** and **Tingaki**; the latter, located near the salt pans, is especially fine and a popular place for a skinny dip.

Just inland, two ruined Byzantine basilicas (Ag. Pavlos and Ag. Ioannis) lie on the outskirts of **Zipario**; from here the road heads up to **Asfendiou**, a pleasant mountain village, although many of its houses have been abandoned as families moved down into town. Up the road, **Zia** has become the official 'traditional village' of package tours on Kos. You can escape them from Zia by following the path up **Mt Oromedon** in an hour, or more ambitiously scale Kos' highest peak, Dikaios Christos. This area is the bucolic Pryioton described by Theocritus, and Mt Dikaios produced much of the marble used by Kos' sculptors.

Another inland road leads to **Pyli**, from where it's a strenuous walk up to **Palaiopili**, a Byzantine ghost town surrounded by concentric walls camouflaged in the rocks. Within its walls is the church of Ypapandi, said to have been built in the 11th century by the Blessed Christodoulos before he went to Patmos. It, and Ag. Nikolaos nearby, have well-preserved 14th-century frescoes. In Pyli itself is the Charmyleion, an ancient hero shrine converted into the church of Stavros.

A sandy beach stretches between the villages of **Tolari** and **Kardamena**, the latter a fishing village famous for its ceramics and now one of Kos' major resorts.

A quieter place to stay (although it is being rapidly developed) is **Mastihari** on the north coast. Frequent boats leave Mastihari for Kalymnos and Pserimos (*see* below), and it is the port for the ungainly village of **Antimacheia**, near the airport. The **Castle of Antimacheia** was built by the Knights as a prison in the mid-14th century. Within its great, battlemented triangular walls are two churches, cisterns and, over the gateway, the arms of Pierre d'Aubusson.

Towards the dolphin's tail, near the beach at **Kamario**, stand the extensive ruins of the twin 5th-century basilicas of **Ag. Stefanos**, with mosaics, Ionian columns and remains of an atrium and baptistries, while out at sea, you can contemplate the dramatic rock of Ag. Nikolaos. A superb beach just to the east called **Paradise** for once deserves its name. Great swimming for children, but you'll have to fight your way through the forest of umbrellas to get to the water.

Kefalos to the west is high up on the headland of the dolphin's tail. When the hotels are full on the rest of Kos, chances are you can find a room here. South of Kefalos are ruins of yet another castle used by the Knights, one that inspired many travellers' tales in the Middle Ages, all involving a dragon; Mandeville claims the serpent was none other than Hippocrates' daughter, enchanted by Artemis and awaiting a knight brave enough to kiss her to transform her back into a maiden. Neolithic remains were found in the **Aspri Petra cave** near Kefalos, which is also near the site of the ancient capital of Kos, **Astypalaia**, the birthplace of Hippocrates; a few bits of the ancient city remain, and on a hill above the town is a fort used by the Knights. Isthmioton, another ancient city on the peninsula, was important enough in the past to send its own delegation to Delos, but not a trace of it remains. The **monastery Ag. Ioannis** is 6 km west of Kefalos, along a track through dramatic scenery. Nearby **Ag. Theologos** beach provides some of the island's most secluded swimming.

Festivals

23 April, Ag. Georgios, with horse races at Pyli; 8 September, Panayias at Kardamena; 29 July, Ag. Apostoli at Antimacheia; 29 August, Ag. Ioannis at Kefalos; 25 March, Evangalismos at Asfendiou; 21 November, Isodia tis Panayias at Zia; 6 December, Ag. Nikolaos at Kos. In August the **Hippocrates Cultural Festival** attracts people from all over Greece, and includes art exhibitions, concerts of classical and modern music, and screenings of Greek and foreign films.

Where to Stay in Kos Town

expensive

In the old days those in need of a cure would stay in the Asklepieion at Kos and sacrifice a chicken to the god. If you want to do the same, there's the new **Hippocrates Palace Hotel**, ✆ 24 401, with its Olympic Health Centre, a medical spa supervised by Dr Christian Barnard. However, it will cost you more than a chicken. The nearby A class **Oceanis** is in the same price range, ✆ 24 641.

moderate

Well located on the harbour is the new **Astron Hotel**, ✆ 23 705, a pretty class B with a rooftop garden, and a charming view of the sea and city. With lower prices, the **Helena Hotel**, at 5 Megalou Alexandrou St, ✆ 22 740, is very pleasant, with pretty balconies.

cheap

There are over a dozen D and E class hotels in the town, but not many have rooms for less than 5000 dr. One good option, however, is **Hara**, 6 Halkonos St, one street back from the waterfront of Vas. Georgiou, ✆ 22 500. For something less expensive, get the list of rooms and pensions at the tourist office, and in the summer have plenty of telephone change handy; these places fill up fast.

Where to Stay out of Town

expensive

If you don't mind the overwhelming package tourism atmosphere, Kardamena has scores of rooms in its pensions and hotels. Dominant here is the **Norida Beach hotel** complex, ✆ 91 231.

Smaller and less expensive in Kardamena, **Stelios**, ℂ 91 210, is on the main square and the sea, though do book well in advance. Even more than in Kos town, accommodation fills up quickly in Kardamena, though if you come early in the day you can probably find a room in a private house. Other accommodation is to be found in Mastihari, Kefalos (always the last to fill up) and Tingaki, which is more pricey than the other places, although the pension **Meni Beach**, ℂ 29 217 has rooms for lower rates in this bracket. Inquire at the NTOG office in Kos about renting a house in Asfendiou; currently they are being refurbished as part of the organization's Traditional Settlements scheme.

cheap

Cheapest, but respectable, in Mastihari is **Zevgas**, ℂ 22 577, and all rooms have private bath. Otherwise consult the tourist office handouts for rooms in villages and seaside resorts. The official **campsite** is by the beach at Psalidi about 3 km from town, ℂ 23 275.

Eating in Kos Town

Because it tries to please all, the typical restaurant food in Kos is notoriously bland and dull, if not downright bad. As on Rhodes, you'd do well to avoid the tacky places that advertise with illuminated photos of meatballs and wurst. In town you can eat reasonably well in the newer quarter, at **Hellas** or **Ageilos** on Psarron Street; in and on the waterfront at Vass. Georgiou the **Miramare** is largely unchanged by tourism and serves good Greek dishes at normal prices. Arguably the most authentic and reasonably priced taverna, hidden way in the backstreets (you'll have to ask half a dozen times to find it, but it's worth it) is **Frangolis**, serving the best *stifado* in town, among many of its other delicious dishes (1800 dr.). The chic **Bristol**, on Vass. Giorgiou, offers some Chinese dishes, and nearby the sparkling **Le Chevalier** has a French menu, with prices to match. The **Kastro**, near the ancient Agora, belongs in the same league, except the setting is much more alluring.

Eating Out of Town

Outside town is Platano, with a handful of tavernas serving Turkish food. The best of the bunch is the **Arap**, offering excellent eggplant with yoghurt, *borek*, grilled shish kebab and chicken (1500 dr.). Out in Psalidi by the campsite the **Nestoras** and **Thessaloniki** both have good Greek fare, and sea views. In Ag. Fokas, on the way to the spa, the beautiful **Villa Café** has an impressive choice of smoked swordfish, barbecue ribs, some Chinese and Japanese dishes, and some delectable homemade pastries, with fine views over to Turkey (2000 dr.).

Kardamena caters very much to the tastes of British package tourists, but it also has an attractive row of tavernas at the water's edge. **Teo's**, by the square where the bus arrives, serves good fish, and standard Greek ready food (2000 dr.). The **Cavo d'Oro**, by the water, also has seafood and pizza. More down to earth is the *ouzeri* **Nikos O Vrahos** in Plateia Konitsis, one block up from the Agora, where a selection of delicious dishes will provide a wholesome, inexpensive meal. The beaches have tavernas as well. One of the best is located above Paradise Beach, serving traditional Greek and Italian dishes for 2000 dr. with Nissyros as a backdrop. If you're from Montreal, you'll get a warm welcome from the owner, who raised his family there.

In Mastihari the long established **Kalia Kardia** (1500–2000 dr.) is the best of several. Up in Zia, **To Vouno** is recommended by locals. It has an outside grill, good food and a beautiful view.

Pserimos

Located between Kos and Kalymnos, Pserimos has a beautiful sandy beach, making it a popular destination for day-trippers from the larger islands and a quiet paradise if you choose to stay longer. Fewer than a hundred people live on Pserimos, although the *paneyeri* at its monastery on 15 August attracts many times that number of visitors from Kos and Kalymnos. Regular boats run between Kos town, Mastihari and Kalymnos.

Where to Stay

cheap

The seaside **Pension Tripolitis** is pleasant, and the **monastery** has simple accommodation for up to 10 people. There are a few rooms to be had in the village; if they are full, you can sleep out on one of the island's more distant beaches, a kilometre from the village.

Eating Out

Besides the Tripolitis there are tavernas on the main beach that fill up with day-trippers at lunchtime, but regain their serenity in the evening.

Leros

With one of the most serrated coastlines of any island, Leros defies easy description. Unlike many of the other Dodecanese, most of the visitors are Greek, and many of those who come to Leros tend to combine their holiday with a visit to a relative in one of the island's three mental hospitals, built during the Italian occupation. Indeed, here more than on the other islands you are aware of the Italians, to the extent that some older residents have a hard time speaking Greek. Although there are several beaches, none is special, and in the hotels you need all your mosquito defences. However, the people are friendly, and you can walk almost everywhere; there are enough incongruities to make a visit interesting, if not occasionally bizarre.

LEROS

Archangelos Islet · Tripiti Islet · Strongili Islet · Partheni · Plefouti · Kryfos · Panatias · Ag. Sideros · Alinda · Alindas Bay · Ag. Marina · PLATANOS · Gournas · Gournas Bay · Panteli · Ag. Kyriaki Islet · Drymon · Panteli Bay · Koulouki · Lakki · Merikia · Temenia · Lakkiou Bay · Lepida · Xirokambos · Piganousa Islet · Diapori Islet

N

0   2   5 km
0 1 2 3 miles

To Kos, Rhodes

History

When the hero Meleager (of Chalydonian boar hunt fame) died, his sisters mourned him so passionately that Artemis turned them into guinea fowl and put them in her temple at Leros, the wooded island dedicated to her. This worship of the goddess of the chase and the guinea fowl might be traced back to Ionian colonists from Miletus; Robert Graves notes that, perhaps because of their religious conservatism, the Greeks called the Leriots 'evil-livers.' Fittingly for an island dedicated to Artemis, property has been passed down through the female line, to the extent that most of Leros is owned by women.

Homer includes Leros with Kalymnos in his catalogue of ships as the Kalydian isles. The island sided with Sparta in the Peloponnesian War, despite its Ionian ancestry. Under the Romans, pirates preyed among the islets that surround Leros; some nabbed a handsome young lawyer named Julius Caesar on his way home from Bithynia, where according to rumour he had a dissolute affair with the governor; released after a month when his ransom was paid, Julius later got his revenge by capturing and crucifying every brigand around Leros. Under the Byzantines, the island was part of the theme of Samos, but in 1316 it was sold to the Knights of St John and governed by the Duke of Naxos as part of the monastic state of Patmos. The town and harbour of Lakki were badly battered by the combined allied air forces in 1943 during a prolonged bombardment; photographs taken by German paratroopers at the time are on display in the Kastis Travel Agency. During the later Cyprus dispute the Greek government dismantled the military installations to show that it had no warlike intentions against Turkey. When the junta took power in 1967, Communist dissidents were exiled on Leros and kept under the strictest surveillance.

Connections

By air: daily from Athens, twice a week from Kos and Rhodes.

By sea: ferry every day from Piraeus, Rhodes, Kos, Kalymnos and Patmos, twice a week with Lipsi and Agathonissi, once a week with Samos, Chios, Lesbos, Limnos, Thessaloniki, Nissyros, Tilos, Symi and Ikaria.

By hydrofoil: four times a week from Ag. Marina to Patmos and Kos, once a week to Pythagorio (Samos); six times a week excursion boat from Ag. Marina to Lipsi. Daily boat from Myrties (Kalymnos) to Xirokambos.

Tourist Information

Information booth on quay.

Tourist police, see regular police, ✆ (0247) 22 222.

Platanos, Alinda and North

Platanos, as near the centre of Leros as possible, is the capital of the island. It is crowned by the **Kastro**, a Byzantine fortress renovated by the Knights of St John and the Venetians, and used even today as a military observation post. Although it seems steep and inaccessible, a fairly easy footpath leads up from the town picturesquely piled below. Once at the top you have a splendid view of Leros' 'four seas': the bays of Panteli, Alindas, Gournas and Lakkiou. Two churches in the fortress walls have been repaired by the Greek Archaeology Service, **Moni Megalochiro** and **Kyras Kastrou**. Of the latter, the following is told: during the Turkish occupation a miraculous icon of the Virgin with a candle set sail from Constantinople and landed at Leros. The inhabitants, led by the bishops, met it and carried it in great procession to the cathedral. The next day, however, the icon had vanished, but before dismay had spread too far the Turkish captain of the Kastro found it with its candle in the powder stores, even though the door had been firmly bolted and locked. The icon was returned to the cathedral, but the next night the very same thing happened. And the next night, and the next. Finally the Turkish captain grew weary of the affair and gave the powder storeroom to the Christians, who turned it into the church Kyras Kastro. Here the wilful icon has decided to remain ever since. In Platanos' main square is a small **museum**, housing local finds, which is usually open in the morning. It is a short walk from Platanos to the beach at **Panteli** in one direction and **Ag. Marina**, Leros' main resort—such as it is—in the other direction. North of Ag. Marina **Alinda**, the old commercial port of Leros, has a long beach, one of the best on the island and recently developed for proper tourist broiling. Near here are the ruins of an Early Christian basilica along with a few vestiges of the ancient city, as well as a British war cemetery from the battle of 1943. Other beaches nearby are at **Gournas**, where the monastery Ag. Sideros was built on a small islet linked to Leros by a long causeway.

Lakki and South Leros

Frequent buses run between Platanos and the island's main port, **Lakki**. If Fellini had been Greek, Lakki would have been one of his favourite sets. The streets are perfectly paved and wide enough to accommodate several lanes of traffic, although usually they're perfectly empty, overlooked by stately if forlorn *fascisti* art deco buildings, genteelly dilapidated in empty, litter-strewn lots. Nightlife here centres around the grandiose cinema. Near the waterfront there's a monument to the many who perished when the Greek ship, the *Queen Olga*, was attacked by German planes and sank in Lakki's harbour. A path leading up from the jetty goes to the nearest beach at **Koulouki**, a favourite place for unofficial camping. At **Lepida**, across the harbour, the Moni Panayia is built on the ruins of an old lighthouse, and further south, overlooking Xirokambos, is the fort **Paliokastro**, built near an older fortification dating back to the 3rd century BC. The church inside has mosaics and Xirokambos itself has a pleasant pebble beach with several tavernas and a campsite.

Partheni on the northern shore had an ancient temple to Artemis, near the present church of Ag. Matrona. This former centre of guinea fowl worship on Leros is now the centre of military activity on the island; it was the base used by the colonels to detain political dissidents. There is a better beach with a taverna nearby at **Plefouti**.

Aghia Marina Harbour, Leros

Carnival at which the children don monks' robes and visit the homes of the newly married, reciting verses made up by their elders; 16–17 July, Ag. Marinas at Ag. Marina; 6 August, Sotiros at Platanos; 15 August, Panayias at the Kastro; 20 August, foreign tourist day at Alinda; 20 October, Ag. Kyras at Partheni; 26 September, Ag. Ioannis Theologos at Lakki. Often at the paneyeria you can hear the Greek hammer dulcimer, the *santouri.*

Starting on 26 September, three days of memorial services are held for those who lost their lives on the *Queen Olga*; Greek naval vessels always attend this annual commemoration.

Where to Stay

moderate

In these days of the cloned concrete beach hotel, you can still stay at the elephantine **Leros Palace Hotel**, © 22 940, in the heart of Lakki, where the corridors seem endless, the ceilings high enough to accommodate a trapeze, and you get free audio from the cinema next door. It's the perfect place to stay in Lakki, and the price (if nothing else) is right. The nearby **Miramare** has rooms in the same price bracket, © 22 043. Other, arguably more comfortable, lodgings may be had at Alinda, in Ag. Marina Bay such as the B class **Xenon Angelou Alinda**, © 22 749, the **Hotel Maleas Beach** class C, © 23 306, and the **Pension Chryssoula**, boasting the best view in town, © 22 460. In Panteli there are a number of pensions, including **To Rodon**, © 22 075.

cheap

There are two E class hotels in Lakki and two in Alinda with rooms around 4000 dr.; for cheaper accommodation, ask around for a room in a private house. There's a **campsite** at Xirokambos, © 22 236.

Eating Out

In Lakki the fare is generally limited to fast food and pizza, a notable exception being **O Sotos** taverna (behind the Leros Palace Hotel), which enjoys an excellent reputation, especially for its fish dishes (3000 dr.). Ag. Marina has most of the island's tavernas, one of the best being **Ta Kamakia**, where again the fish is excellent, and they also serve some Italian specialities. **Finikas** is a dependable favourite in Alinda, while the places to eat in Panteli are **To Limani** and **Kaliro**. Generally speaking, wherever you eat on the island, particularly if you choose fish, you cannot go wrong.

Lipsi (Lipso)

Lipsi is a little gem of an island midway between Leros and Patmos, its lovely beaches a magnet for day excursions from its larger neighbours. However Lipsi is still as quiet a place as one can find with good food and good swimming, near the fine harbour and beach. Other beaches nestling along the jagged coastline are at Katsadia and Lendori; the best, **Plati Yialo**, is a half-hour walk to the south (it is also accessible by taxi). Another pleasant stroll leads to a green cultivated valley beyond the town, where a good wine is produced. One tradition connects the island with Calypso, and there certainly is a similarity, in the name and the quiet magic spells the island casts once the trippers have been herded away.

Connections

Daily excursion boats from Leros and Patmos. Ferry connections three times a week with Samos, Patmos, Leros and Kalymnos, twice a week with Kos and Agathonissi, once a week with Nissyros, Tilos, Symi, Rhodes and Ikaria.

Where to Stay

moderate–cheap

There's only one hotel on Lipsi, the **Kalypso**, © 41 242, which also has an information service. Plenty of other rooms can be found in the village besides. Otherwise you can sleep out at Katsadia or Lendori beach.

Eating Out

The tavernas on the waterfront are good and not very expensive; a fish dinner at **Mangou** or **Kali Kardia** will set you back about 2500 dr. Some of the cafés serve breakfast.

Nissyros

In the great war between gods and giants, one of the casualties was the fiery Titan Polybates, who so incurred Poseidon's wrath that the sea god yanked off a chunk of Kos and hurled it on top of Polybates as he attempted to swim away. This became the island of Nissyros, and the miserable Polybates, pinned underneath, eternally sighs and fumes, unable to escape.

Geologically Nissyros was indeed once part of Kos and Polybates is the Dodecanese's only volcano. Even in its dormant state it dominates the character of Nissyros, where fertile slopes are green with olives, figs, citrus groves and almond trees. The islanders have traditionally worked the pumice fields, both on Nissyros and its little sister islet **Yiali**. The coasts of both islands are a jumble of black volcanic boulders and black sandy beaches, though Yiali also has a fine golden, sandy beach.

Connections

Ferry once a week from Rafina, Andros, Tinos, Mykonos, three times a week with Kos, Rhodes and Tilos, twice a week with Kalymnos and Symi, once a week with Leros, Patmos, Lipsi, Agathonissi and Samos. In summer, daily excursion boat from Kardamena on Kos; also less frequently connections with Rhodes, Symi and Tilos.

Tourist police, see regular police on the quay, ℂ (0242) 31 201.

Tourist office, ℂ (0242) 31 459.

Mandraki and Around

Nissyros, despite the advent of day-trippers, has retained its quiet charm. Even the new houses constructed in bijou **Mandraki**, the capital and port, conform to the old style: tall and narrow with small wooden balconies. Of late it has become fashionable to paint them in deep, almost gaudy colours. One of the houses near the church has opened a small **Historical and Ethnographical Museum**, with household implements and costumes and a tiny library of books about the island.

Fortunately most of the streets of Mandraki are too narrow for traffic, but the town has been kind enough to signpost the way to its major attraction: the stair up to the monastery of **Panayia Spiliani** (1825), in a cave within the walls of the old Venetian **Kastro**. Inside is a finely carved iconostasis and a much-venerated icon of the Virgin, loaded down with a bushel of gold and silver offerings. The Kastro itself isn't much, but the height offers a spectacular view at sunset. Higher up at **Paliokastro** are impressive Cyclopean walls. Nearest swimming to town is at **Hohlaki** beach, covered with small volcanic stones of a light bluish hue. Locals will tell you that the sea is best here, even if the stones can be rather uncomfortable underfoot. A 10-minute walk from Mandraki takes you to **Miramare** beach, just as suitable for swimming and convenient for the nearby fish tavernas.

Just east of Mandraki is the thermal spa of **Loutra** where the hot volcanic springs are used as a cure for arthritis and rheumatism; further east is Nissyros' best sandy beach, **Pali**, where you can top off a swim with a lunch of fresh fish, or try nearby **Yialliskari**, with crystal clear water and a beach of fine, white sand. A modern hotel has been built here.

Into the Volcano

The excursion not to be missed on Nissyros, however, is to **Polybates**, ex-Titan and now plugged-up volcano. Buses for the crater leave the port, coinciding with the arrival of the tourist boats, or there is the regular village bus from Mandraki up to Emborios and Nikia, two villages perched on the crater's rim, from where you can walk down (buses wait about 45 minutes before returning to Mandraki).

The winding road manages to take in most of Nissyros' rustic charms before it begins to twist its way down into an other-worldly landscape of pale greys and yellows, the smell of sulphur so pungent that you can almost see cartoonish stink lines curling up out of the great crater (you may have to hang out your clothes to air when you get back to keep from smelling like a rotten egg.) After passing several geothermal pools, the bus stops near the great fuming heart of Polybates. A zigzag path descends to the floor of the crater, where you can feel the great heat and turmoil of the volcano underfoot. Stout shoes are essential; rubber soles may melt on the surface hot enough to cook an egg. Beware, too, that your foot can go through the floor, so follow the group heavyweight for safety.

Here and there small fumaroles emit steam and stench, and weird and eerie as it is no one can stand to stick around for long. There is talk of harnessing the volcano's energy to provide electricity for the whole Dodecanese. Even hotter is the natural sauna below **Emborios**, in a cave heated by hot springs. The village with its ruined Byzantine fort and ancient walls offers memorable views of the infernal crater 300 m below, as does pretty **Nikia**.

Festivals

29 June, Ag. Apostoli at Pali; 27 July, Ag. Panteleimonos at Nikia; August 15, Panayias at Mandraki.

Where to Stay

moderate

The B class pension **Haritos**, ℭ 31 322, in Mandraki provides the most comfort.

cheap

Another comfortable place to stay in Mandraki is the pension/taverna **Romantzo**, near the ferry dock, ℭ 31 340, with a large shady terrace. Alternatively the small **Tria Adelfia**, ℭ 31 344, has rooms for about the same price, and also has a pleasant taverna. There are also rooms to rent in the village and, if you thread your way through the streets west of town (on the other side from where the ferry docks), you'll find the **Drossia** pension, where the waves crash on the black rocks beneath your balcony.

Eating Out

All of the tavernas in Nissyros are exceptionally friendly and reasonably priced. Not far from the public lavatories are the tavernas **Tsardka** and **Karava**, with excellent ready food and items from the grill, and how good fish tastes when the sea is just a few feet away (2000 dr.). Don't just rely on the waterfront tavernas, though, as there are some pleasant culinary surprises waiting for you in town, where **Sfakianos, Koulakis** and **Magganas** provide good food and Greek music. Just outside the port, **Miramare** has a good name locally. Out at Pali there are some reliable fish tavernas on the beach.

Patmos

Of all the Greek islands, Patmos is the most sacred to Christians, both Orthodox and Western alike, for here St John the Theologian received the vision written in the Apocalypse, or Book of Revelations, and here, in the 11th century, was founded a monastery more wealthy and influential than any in Greece except for Mt Athos. Many find even today a spirituality in Patmos that the other islands lack, a quiet solemnity, a sacred (though hardly apocalyptic) aura that seems especially strong in the evening, after the cruise ships have sailed away. If a hectic nightlife is what you look forward to, you won't want to stay long on Patmos. It is a quiet place, especially up at Chora, and people tend to retire early.

History

Patmos was inhabited from the 14th century BC, with the capital near present-day Skala, its acropolis and fortifications at Kastelli. It was a subject to Asia Minor and not very important. In AD 95, however, the island's destiny was forever altered when St John the Theologian (or the Divine) was exiled here from Ephesus during the Emperor Domitian's persecution of Christians, and while living here in a cave he received his extraordinary Revelations. Most believe he stayed only a year on Patmos before returning to Ephesus, but in that year John provided not only a fairly accurate prophecy of the fall of the Roman Empire, but enough to keep fire-eating preachers and literal-minded crank interpreters in material for the next 1900 years.

Patmos was abandoned from the 7th century, its barren, volcanic rock not worth defending against pirates. Destiny remained on hold until the late 11th century, when in faraway Constantinople, things were going badly for Alexis Comnenus 'born to the purple' as the

Byzantines put it, but to Alexis, battered by fate and politics, the purple seemed impossible to attain. A saintly hermit named Christodulos nevertheless predicted his ascent to the throne, and the miserable Alexis promised him, that were it to come true, he would grant him any wish in his power. Of course it did, and in 1088, Christodulos made his wish of the Emperor: the island of Patmos, to found a monastery on the site of an ancient temple of Artemis. The Emperor provided not only the island but the building funds.

The entire island of Patmos remained under absolute control of the monastery for centuries, against poverty, pirates, and a thousand other afflictions. The Venetian Dukes of Patmos, its nominal rulers, were content to leave it as an autonomous monastic state. In the 13th century the village of Chora was built in the shadow of the powerful walls of the monastery, offering a safe refuge in case of attack. Patmos flourished particularly during the 16th to 19th centuries, and its school of theology and liberal arts, founded in 1713, cast a healthy glow over the long, dark domination of the Turks. Gradually monastic control lessened as the islanders turned to sea trade, and in 1720 the monks and laymen had divided the land between them. Patmos prospered to the extent that in the 18th century it established colonies abroad; a prosperity nipped in the bud, as in the case of other island shipping centres, with the invention of the steamship.

Connections

Hydrofoils on most days in the summer to Kos, Rhodes, Leros and Pythagorio, Samos; daily excursion boats to Lipsi and Pythagorio (Samos); ferry daily to Piraeus, Kalymnos, Leros, Kos and Rhodes, four times a week with Samos, three times a week with Ikaria, twice a week with Agathonissi, once a week with Nissyros, Tilos, Symi, Chios, Lesbos, Limnos and Thessaloniki.

Tourist Police

See regular police, © (0247) 31 303, in the harbour.
Tourist information office, in Skala, © (0247) 31 666.

Skala

All boats to Patmos drop anchor at **Skala**, the main tourist centre of the island. One of the first things you'll see is a statue of Protergatis Xanthos Emmanuel who led an uprising against the Turks in 1821. Skala itself didn't even exist until that year, so fearsome were the pirate raids. Near the beach, marked by a red buoy, is a reminder of another local menace, the evil magician Yenoupas, who at the urging of priests from the temple of Apollo challenged St John to a duel of miracles. Yenoupas' miracle was to dive into the sea and bring back effigies of the dead; John's was to ask God to petrify the submerged magician, which abruptly ended the duel. Behind Skala you can visit what was once one of the world's largest desalination plants, work now performed by a reservoir. The water tastes better without it, but there still isn't enough to meet the island's needs in the summer. You can also hike up to the site of the ancient city, **Kastelli**, in about 20 minutes, a walk rewarded more with stunning views than any archaeological excavations.

From Skala you can see whitewashed **Chora** clinging to the mighty castle walls of the monastery. Buses make the ascent in a few minutes, but if you have the time it isn't too strenuous to walk up from Skala, to leisurely enjoy the ever-widening panorama spread out below. Chora is a lovely, almost Cycladic town, with numerous mansions built during the wealthy days of Patmos' great merchant fleet.

Monastery of St John the Theologian

*If it's your first visit, however, make a beeline for this magnificent monastery (Mon, Wed and Fri 8–2, Tues and Thurs 8–1 and 4–6, Sun 8–12 noon and 4–6); no shorts and women **must** wear skirts). At the entrance, pick up the guide in English by S. A. Papadopoulos, with a good history of the monastery and description of its frescoes and works of art.*

Inside the massive walls (restored after the earthquake of 1956) is a charming entrance court of 1698, incorporating the outer narthex of the church. Just before the narthex itself is the chapel and tomb of its founder, the Blessed Christodulos. The church itself is in the form of a Greek cross set in a square, and still retains its original marble floor; its icon of St John was presented to the monastery by Alexis Comnenus. Beautiful frescoes cover almost all paintable surfaces, although all but those in the 12th-century **Chapel of the Theotokos** are much later than the church. There are more 12th-century frescoes in the Refectory, off the inner courtyard. The **Treasury Museum** contains the priceless 6th-century *Codex Prophyrius*, St Mark's gospel written on purple vellum; the monastery foundation deed—a golden bull, signed and sealed, from the Emperor; remains of the temple of Artemis on which the monastery was built (a temple said to have been founded by Orestes, in gratitude for being rid of the Furies); gold and silver crosses, croziers and stoles; superb icons and ship pendants made of diamonds and emeralds donated by Catherine the Great. The library contains hundreds of rare codices and manuscripts, but may only be visited with permission from the abbot. Lastly, climb up to the roof terrace for a commanding view over the Aegean.

Around Chora

After the monastery, you could spend a day visiting the 40 or so churches wedged in the narrow lanes of Chora: especially good are the **Convent of Zoodochos Pigi** (1607) with fine frescoes and icons (*open mornings and late afternoons*) and 11th-century **Ag. Dimitrios**, contemporary with the monastery, but likely to be locked like many of the others. Nor is hunting out the caretaker particularly easy, as Chora is one of those very old, silent places where the streets always seem to be deserted.

This changes dramatically on Orthodox Maundy Thursday, when Chora is packed with visitors and even TV crews for the Niptiras ceremony, when the abbot of the monastery re-enacts Christ's washing of his disciples' feet—a rite once performed by the proud emperors of Byzantium. It takes place either in Plateia Ag. Levias or Plateia Loza, depending on the weather.

It's a 15-minute walk down from Chora to the **Monastery of the Apocalypse** (*8–12 noon, Thurs 8–12 and 2.30–5.30*), where a stair covered with pots of flowers leads down to the cave where St John lived and dreamed and dictated what he saw to his follower. The cave itself has been converted to a church, where you can see the rock where the good saint rested his head and hand (though one can't help thinking he must have been a contortionist to manage it), and the massive overhanging roof, split in three sections by the voice of God.

Beaches and Villages around Patmos

Caiques from Skala run most days from in front of the Arion Café to the island's many lovely beaches: **Psiliammos**, with fine white sand is the unofficial nudist beach, an hour away by boat; **Lampi**, another port of call (or 30-minute walk), has a lovely, multi-coloured pebble beach. Another beach, **Meloi** is close to town and therefore tends to get crowded; enclosed **Grikou** can be reached by bus or boat (or a 45-minute walk) from Skala, and has windsurfs and water skis for hire. Halfway between Skala and Kambos, look for the sign to **Agriolivadi**, pointing the way to a quiet, clean beach. Other beaches in the region are often completely deserted, such as the one at **Sapsila**.

In fertile **Sykamia** is an old Roman bath said to have been used by St John to baptize his converts. In **Stavros**, a tiny village to the south, the **Kalikatsou rock** has carved rooms in rather unlikely places and may have been the 11th-century hermitage mentioned in the writings of Christodulos. Across the island from here, a grotto on **Cape Yenoupas** was the home of the evil magician (*see* above), and even today it's unpleasantly hot and smelly inside.

Heading north, **Kambos** lies in the centre of Patmos' main agricultural valley and has a popular sandy beach, complete with restaurants and the chance to windsurf and waterski. Just over the hill lies the peaceful beach of **Vagia**. Further along are more wild and windswept shores for daring swimmers at **Levkes**. Even more remote is the 19th-century **Hermitage of Apollon**, near a small mineral spring (ask for directions in Kambos). *Boats leave Skala for all these places between 9 and 11, returning about 4. Excursions to Lipsi (one hour away) are especially popular; boats leave at 10 and return at 5.*

Festivals

Besides the Maundy Thursday Niptiras ceremony, the monastery holds important services for St John on 8 May and 26 September. More popular (feasting and dancing) paneyeria take place 5 August (Sotiris) at Kambos and 15 August, Panayias, also at Kambos; 14 September, Stavros; 27 July, Ag. Panteleimonos, on the islet of Xiliomodi.

moderate

On the edge of Skala, **Hotel Byzance** is designed in the traditional style featuring a roof garden with lovely views over the port and a small restaurant, ✆ 31 052. Two others that deserve a mention down in the port are the **Patmion**, ✆ 31 313, and the **Skala**, ✆ 31 343, with an attractive pool and just two minutes from the ferry. **Kasteli** commands fine views in the upper part of town, ✆ 31 361; the friendly **Aftsralis**, ✆ 31 576, is beautifully decorated and costs slightly less. In Grikou, the **Panorama** offers furnished apartments by the sea, ✆ 31 209, or try the more economical **Flisvos**, ✆ 31 380.

cheap

On the whole the private rooms in Skala are very comfortable and better value than the hotels, and you're sure to be offered one as soon as you get off the boat. There are also rooms up in Chora, and in Kambos, and an excellent campground at Meloi.

Eating Out

There are three good restaurants in Chora: **Vangelis** and **Olympia** in Plateia Ag. Levias (follow the little signs) both with solid Greek fare at around 2000 dr. and the bonus of sitting in the beautiful old square, where Saturday nights sometimes see some inspired dancing. The third place, **The Patmian House** is an old Patmian mansion that has been converted into a luxury restaurant, a wonderful setting for a romantic dinner (3000 dr., open evenings only). Down in Skala the **Old Harbour** has very elegant service, good seafood, and rather higher prices. Much more down to earth is **Grigoris Grill**, opposite the ferry—good charcoal grilled fish and meat (2000 dr.).

Out at Grikou are two popular tavernas: the small, family-run **Flisvos** up on the hill, with Greek staples and fish (1800–2400 dr.) and, in the middle of the beach, **Stamatis**, serving the same at similar prices. There are tavernas on most other beaches. Meloi has **Stefani's**, where the food is simple but tasty (2000 dr.).

Agathonissi, Arki and Marathi

Agathonissi is a remote island off Patmos, connected only two–three times a week with the outside world, as is its even smaller sister **Arki**. These are poor islets, inhabited only by a few fishing families. Agathonissi has two villages, Megalo Chorio and Mikro Chorio, and a few ancient remains. Occasional caiques run from Patmos to Arki, where there are two cafés and a bit of a beach. You can also visit (but you may have to hire your own caique) the even smaller **Marathi**, which has a better, sandy beach, with excellent swimming, and a taverna.

Rhodes (Rodos)

Rhodes, 'more beautiful than the sun' according to the ancient Greeks, is the largest and most fertile of the Dodecanese, ringed by sandy beaches, bedecked with flowers, blessed with some 300 days of sun a year, dotted with handsome towns and villages full of monuments evoking a long, colourful history—in a nutshell, all that it takes to sit securely throned as the reigning queen of tourism in Greece. As a year-round resort for cold northerners and major package tour destination, it's not quite fair to compare it with Greece's other islands. Rhodes is rather a Euro-playground, a modern tourist Babylon, where people shed their inhibitions with their woollens and don't feel stupid walking around with 'No Problem!' and 'Relax' emblazoned on their bosoms. If large crowds of tourists bother you, head for the south of the island or try smoking a smelly cigar and pretend you only speak Albanian. Or Greek.

Mythology

Long ago, when Zeus divided the world's real estate among the gods and goddesses, he forgot to leave a portion for Helios, the god of the sun. Dismayed, Zeus asked Helios what he could do to make up for his omission. The sun god replied that he knew of an island just emerging off the coast of Asia Minor which would suit him admirably. Helios named his new home 'Rhodes' after his wife, the daughter of Poseidon and one of the nine Telchines—those rather unlikely nymphs with seal flippers and dog heads. The Telchines are said to have founded the three ancient cities of Kamiros, Ialysos and Lindos, although other accounts say they were the work of three grandsons of Helios, or perhaps of Tlepolemos, who led the nine ships of Rhodes to Troy.

Kamiros even had a fourth possible founder, Althaemenes, son of the Cretan King Catreus and grandson of Minos. When an oracle predicted that Catreus would be slain by one of his offspring, Althaemenes went to Rhodes, where he founded Kamiros and built an altar of Zeus, surrounding it with magical metal bulls that would bellow if the island were invaded. Oracles, however, are not often wrong, and in later life Catreus sailed to Rhodes to visit his son, whom he missed dearly. He arrived at night, and what with the darkness and the bellowing of the metal bulls, Althaemenes failed to recognize his father and fellow-Cretans and slew them, thinking that they were invaders. When he realized his error in the morning he begged Mother Earth to swallow him up, which she did.

History

Inhabited since the Stone Age, Rhodes was conquered by the Minoans who built shrines to the moon at Philerimos, Lindos and Kamiros. The Achaeans took the island in the 15th century BC, and according to Homer sent nine ships to Troy, led by Tlepolemos, son of Heracles, who met an unhappy end before the Trojan walls. Before settling on Rhodes for its name, the island was often known as *Telchinia* for its dog-headed Telchines or *Ophioussa*, for its numerous vipers; even today villagers wear snake-repelling goatskin boots when working out in the fields.

RHODES

To Kastellorizo

To Symi, Kos

To Piraeus,
Karpathos, Halki

To Marmaris,
Turkey

RHODES

Trianda

Paradissi Ialysos
Kremasti Ixia
Kato Kalamonos Tris
Pastida Asgouru
Damatria Koskinou
Maritsa
Tholos Therme
Soroni Kallithea
Fanes Kalamonas Kallithies Kallithea Bay
Kalavarda Faliraki
Epano Ladiko
Kamiros
Psinthos
Mandriko Dimilia Afandou
Salakos Eleousa Afandou Bay
To Halki Archipolis Kolymbia
Kamiros Nani Plantania
Skala Mt. Profitis Ilias Apollona Epta Pigi
Kritinia (790m / 2600ft)
Archangelos
Embona
Mt. Ataviros Malona Stegena
(1215m / 3986ft)
Massari Faraclos
Chimarasi Haraki
Ag. Isidoros Laerma
Siana Kalathos
Fourni Monolithos Vliha Bay
Bay
Istrios
Profilia Pilona
Lardos Lindos
Apolakia Vati
Arnitha Asklipio Pefki
Gennadi Chiotari
Messanagros

Kattavia Lahania
Ag. Pavlos
Plimiri

Cape Prassonisi

N

0   5   10   20 km

0   5   10   miles

The three cities mentioned by Homer—Lindos, Ialysos and Kamiros—long dominated the island's affairs. Rhodes' position along the main Mediterranean trade routes led to its early importance both in trade and naval power. Around 1000 BC, in response to the first Ionian confederacy, the three cities joined the Doric Hexapolis with Kos, Cnidos and Halikarnassus, a prototype EC that united the six city-states politically, religiously and economically. For four centuries the Doric Hexapolis prospered, establishing trade colonies from Naples to the Costa Brava in Spain.

The Founding of Rhodes City, and its Colossus

Rhodes sided with the Persians in both of their major campaigns against Greece, but upon their defeat switched sides and joined the Delian confederacy. In 480 BC, in order to prevent rivalries and increase their wealth and strength, Lindos, Ialysos, and Kamiros united to found one central capital, Rhodes, in Greek *Rodos*, the rose. Hippodamos of Miletus, the geometrician, designed the new town on a grid plan as he had with Piraeus, and the result was considered one of the most beautiful cities of ancient times, surrounded by walls encompassing a much greater area than that enclosed by the existing medieval walls. Celebrated schools of Philosophy, Philology and Oratory were founded, and the port had facilities far in advance of its time. Although Lindos, Kamiros and Ialysos continued to exist, they lost all their importance and most of their populations to the mighty new city they had created.

During the Peloponnesian War, Rhodes sided with whichever power was on top at any given time, and later supported the rising star of Alexander the Great. He in turn lent his support to Rhodes and its commerce, enabling the island to surpass politically-hostile Athens; thanks to Alexander, Rhodes dominated Mediterranean trade, its navy ruled the waves and policed the seas, and it founded colonies all over the known world. Rhodes' trade and navigation laws were later adopted by the Romans and remain the basis of maritime trade today.

Egypt was one of Rhodes' most lucrative trading partners, and in the struggles between the Macedonian generals after Alexander's death, Rhodes allied itself with Ptolemy, who had taken Egypt as his spoils. When another of Alexander's generals, the powerful Antigonas, ordered Rhodes to join him against Ptolemy, the Rhodians refused. Furious, Antigonas sent his son Dimitrios Poliorketes (the Besieger), the army of Syria and the Phoenician fleet to besiege the uppity islanders.

The ensuing year-long siege by one of the greatest generals of all time against the greatest city of the day has gone down in history, not only as a contest of great strength and endurance, but as a battle of wits. Over and over again Dimitrios would invent some new ingenious machine, such as the ten-storey Helepolis siege tower only to have it ingeniously foiled by the Rhodian defenders (who tripped up the Helepolis with a hidden, shallow ditch). After a year both sides grew weary of fighting and made a truce, Rhodes agreeing to assist Dimitrios' father Antigonas except in battles against Ptolemy.

So Dimitrios departed, leaving the Rhodians all of his vast siege machinery. This they either sold or melted down to construct a great bronze statue of Helios, their patron god of the sun. The famous sculptor from Lindos, Chares, was put in charge of the project, and in 290 BC, after twelve years of work and a cost of 20,000 pounds of silver, Chares completed the Colossus. Standing somewhere between 30 to 40 m tall (at her crown the Statue of Liberty is 34 m), the Colossus did not straddle the entrance of Rhodes harbour, as popularly believed, but probably stood near the present Castle of the Knights, gleaming bright in the sun, one of the Seven Wonders of the Ancient World. But of all the Wonders, the Colossus had the shortest lifespan; in 225 BC, an earthquake brought it crashing to the ground. It lay forlorn until AD 653 when the Saracens, who had captured Rhodes, sold it as scrap metal to a merchant from Edessa. According to legend, it took 900 camels to transport it to the ships.

In 164 BC, when they had repaired their city and walls, the Rhodians signed a peace treaty with Rome. Alexandria was their only rival in wealth, and tiny Delos, with all its trade concessions, their only rival in Mediterranean trade. A famous school of rhetoric on Rhodes attracted Roman students such as Cicero, Cassius, Julius Caesar and Mark Anthony. However, entanglement in Roman politics brought Rhodes trouble as well as privileges. When Rhodes supported Augustus after the death of Caesar, Cassius sacked the island city, destroyed or captured its fleet, and sent many of its treasures to Rome. It was a blow from which Rhodes never recovered; she lost control of her colonies and islands, and other Roman allies muscled in on her booming trade. In the first century St Paul preached on the island and converted many of the inhabitants; by the end of the Roman empire, Rhodes was a sleepy backwater.

Two Hundred Years of Knights

Byzantium brought many invaders and adventurers to Rhodes: Saracens, Genoese, Venetians and the Crusaders all passed through; in 1191 Richard the Lionheart and Philip Augustus of France came to Rhodes in search of mercenaries to fight in the Holy Land. After the fall of Jerusalem in 1291, the Knights Hospitallers of St John took refuge on Cyprus, but by 1306 they had become interested in the wealthier and better positioned Rhodes. They asked the Emperor Andronicus Palaeologus to cede them the island in return for their loyalty, but after 1204 the rulers of Byzantium had learned better than to trust the Franks. The Knights, under Grand Master Foulques de Villaret, then took the matter into their own hands. Although they purchased the Dodecanese from the Genoese pirates who controlled them, it was a prize the Knights had to fight for; they had to spend their first three years subduing the Rhodians themselves.

By 1309, with the help of the Pope, the Knights were secure in their possession and began to build their hospital and inns in Rhodes town. They built eight inns, or auberges in all, one for each of the 'tongues', or nationalities in the Order (England, France, Germany, Italy, Castile, Aragon, Auvergne and Provence). Each tongue had a bailiff, and the eight bailiffs elected the Grand Master, who lived in a special palace. There were never more than 600 men in the Order, sworn to care for and protect pilgrims to the Holy Land. As time went on, they became more and more warlike, and although they built a hospital on Rhodes, defence and raiding were their primary concerns. Already wealthy to begin with, they were given a tremendous boost in 1312, when Pope Clement and Philip the Fair gave them the property of the recently-dissolved Knights Templars.

With their new fortune, the Knights of St John replaced the outdated Byzantine fortifications—and continued to replace them up until the 16th century, hiring the best Italian fortification engineers of the time, who perfected one of the most splendid defences of the day. The knights were besieged without success by the Sultan of Egypt in 1444 and by Mohammed II the Conqueror in 1480. Then in 1522 Suleiman the Magnificent moved in with a 100,000 troops. The siege lasted for six months, and Suleiman was on the point of abandoning it when a traitor informed him that of the original 650 Knights, supplemented by 250 Genoese and Venetians and a thousand Greeks, only 180 survived, and they were on their last legs. The Sultan redoubled his efforts and the Knights at last were forced to surrender. They were permitted to leave in safety, with their Christian retainers and possessions, and set up a new headquarters in Malta. In 1831 they ended up in Rome.

The Turks were very fond of Rhodes, but for the Greeks their rule brought 400 years of darkness. When the inhabitants revolted during the War of Independence, the Turks reacted by slaughtering a quarter of the population. The Italian rulers in 1912 brought material prosperity but spiritual tyranny. They claimed that the island was their inheritance from the Knights of St John, although of course only an eighth of the knights had been Italian. Mussolini even had the Palace of the Grand Masters reconstructed (it and many other of the medieval buildings of the old town had been destroyed in the Great Gunpowder Explosion of 1856, when lightning struck a minaret and exploded a Turkish powder magazine). During the Second World War Rhodes remained in the hands of a German garrison until May 1945. By then most of the island's Jewish community, originally 2000 strong, had been sent off to the concentration camps. Rhodes, with the rest of the Dodecanese, officially joined Greece in 1945, whereupon the government declared it a free port, boosting its already great tourist potential.

Connections

By air: In summer at least five daily flights from Athens, and frequent connections with Thessaloniki, Herakleon (Crete), Karpathos, Kos, Kastellorizo and Kassos. Numerous charter flights.

By sea: daily ferry to Piraeus, Patmos, Leros, Kalymnos, Kos and Symi, four–five times a week with Crete, Santorini and Paros, less frequently with the other Cyclades and Rafina, and Samos, Chios, Lesbos, Limnos, Thessaloniki, Nissiros, Tilos, Halki, Karpathos, Kassos and Astypalaia. Daily excursion boats to Marmaris, Turkey and twice a week to Limassol (Cyprus) and Haifa (Israel).

By hydrofoil: daily with Kos, Patmos and Symi, three times a week with Leros, once a week with Samos, also connections with Kalymnos, Halki, Nissyros, Karpathos and Kastellorizo.

Tourist Information

NTOG, Papagon and Makariou St, ℂ (0241) 23 255.

City of Rhodes Tourist Information Centre, Sound and Light Sq, ℂ (0241) 35 945.

Both have town maps and copies of the English events paper, *The Rhodes Tourist*.

Lindos Information, Lindos, © (0244) 39 227.

Tourist Police, Papagon and Makariou St, © (0241) 27 423.

British Consulate 17, 25th Martiou, © (0241) 27 306.

Rhodes Town

One of the Statues in Bronze overlooking the Harbour at Rhodes

Spread across the northern tip of the island, **Rhodes** (pop. 39,000) is the largest town and capital of the Dodecanese. It presents an opulent face to the sea: the massive walls of the old town and the Castle of the Knights rise out of a lush subtropical garden; graceful minarets and the arcaded waterfront market, bright with strings of lightbulbs at night add an exotic, Eastern touch. Monumental Italian public buildings loom to one side, trying to look serious, while opposite three windmills turn lazily. If your vessel is small, you'll disembark at the smallest of three harbours, **Mandraki**, guarded by a bronze doe and buck and the old fort of **Ag. Nikolaos**, with its small church. On larger ferry and cruise ships you'll enter the **commercial harbour**, nearer the Old Town walls.

These **walls** are a masterpiece of late medieval fortifications, and although you'll often be tempted to climb up for a walk or view, *access is by guided tour only, Tues and Sat at 2.45 pm*. Constructed on the foundation of the old Byzantine walls under four of the most ambitious Grand Masters, d'Aubusson, d'Amboise, del Carretto and Villiers de l'Isle Adam, they stretch 4 km and average 12 m thick. They are curved to better deflect missiles, and the landward sides were safeguarded by a 30 m wide moat. Each national group of Knights was assigned its own bastion and towers to defend. Of the many gates that linked the walled Old Town with the village outside, the most magnificent is the **Gate of Emery d'Amboise** near the Palace of the Grand Masters, built in 1512. The Turks blocked up the two harbour gates; they also made a law that all Greeks had to be outside the inner walls by sundown or forfeit their heads.

Within the Inner Walls

The town within these walls was called the **Collachium**, where the Knights could retreat if the outer wall were taken. Most of their buildings are here, beginning with the **Palace of** the **Grand Masters** (*8.30–3, closed Mon*), or Kastelli, as the Greeks call it. Construction of this citadel, on the site of a sanctuary of Helios, was completed in the 14th century and it survived intact under the Turks, who used it as a prison until it accidentally blew up in the Great Gunpowder Explosion of 1856. Mussolini, fancying himself a Grand Master, ordered it be reconstructed as his summer villa. The Italians filled it with lovely Roman mosaics and Hellenistic sculptures from Kos, a hodgepodge of Renaissance furniture and installed an elevator and modern plumbing, but the war broke out and ended before Il Duce could ever make use of it. In the garden below the palace a Sound and Light show is held most evenings (*in English on Mon and Tues at 8.15 pm, Wed, Fri and Sat at 9.15 pm, Thurs 10.15 pm*).

Quiet, cobblestoned Ippoton Street ('of the Knights') has been carefully spared souvenir claptrap, the better to evoke the medieval city. It leads down from the palace into the centre of the Collachium, passing first the arcaded **Loggia** where the Knights would muster, then several of their inns: the **Inn of Provence** on the left and the two buildings of the **Inn of Spain** on the right, then the French chapel and elaborate **Inn of France** (1509), adorned with escutcheons and crocodile gargoyles; as there were always more French knights than any other 'tongue', their inn was the most spacious. Opposite is the handsome Catalan **House of Villaragut**; further down, the **Inn of Italy** (1519), and at the end of the street, the 13th-century **St Mary**, a Byzantine church used by the Knights as their cathedral until they built their own—destroyed in the Gunpowder debacle. St Mary's is now used as a little **Byzantine Museum**. To the right, at the end of Ippoton Street, **Inn of England** (1483) was abandoned by the English Knights in 1534, when the Pope excommunicated Henry VIII. It was hard hit by an earthquake in 1851, then rebuilt by the British, bombed and rebuilt again in 1947. The British consul of Rhodes (see above for the address) has the key to it.

Across the street stands the Flamboyant Gothic Hospital of the Knights, built between 1440 and 1481 and restored by the Italians in 1918, which now houses the **Archaeology Museum** (*daily except Mon 8–3*). The long ward, where the Knight's surgeons cared for patients in elaborate canopy beds, still has coats-of-arms and other heraldic devices. In the sculpture gallery the star attraction is the kneeling *Aphrodite of Rhodes* (90 BC), combing out her hair after emerging from the sea; it was she who provided the title for Lawrence Durrell's *Reflections on a Marine Venus*. Other rooms contain funerary stele, Mycenaean jewellery, and a mosaic from Karpathos.

Through the arch just to the north, charming Argyrokastro Square has the most beautiful auberge of all, the 15th-century **Inn of Auvergne** (now a cultural centre) with a **fountain** reconstructed from bits found in the Byzantine fort at Arnitha. Here, too, is the 14th-century **Palace of the Armeria**, constructed by Grand Master Roger de Pins as the Knight's first hospital on Rhodes. The **Museum of Decorative Arts** (*8.30–3, closed Mon*), has folk arts and handicrafts from all over the Dodecanese, including costumes, embroideries and a reconstruction of a traditional room. In Plateia Symis, the next square north, are the ruins of a 3rd-century BC **temple of Aphrodite**, discovered by the Italians in 1922. Fragments of another temple of the same epoch, dedicated to **Dionysos**, are in a corner behind the Ionian and Popular Bank.

The Turkish Quarter

South of the Collachium of the Knights is the former Turkish bazaar and Old Town's shopping district, centred around bustling **Sokratous Street**, thick with tourist and duty-free luxury shops (many on the isle of eternal sun sell nothing but umbrellas and fur coats). On the top of Sokratous St stands the slender minaret of the lovely **Mosque of Suleiman**, built in 1523 by Suleiman to celebrate his conquest of Rhodes (now closed). The **Turkish library** (1793) opposite contains rare Persian and Arabian manuscripts and illuminated Korans.

Off Sokratous Street, the Turkish Quarter dissolves into a zigzag of narrow streets, where charming Turkish balconies of latticed wood project beside crumbling stone arches and houses built directly over the street. On the square off Archelaos Street is the hammam, or **Turkish baths**, built in 1765 (*Wed–Sat 7–7, Tues 1–7, closed Sun and Mon, reduced adm on Thurs and Fri*). Although heavily bombed, they have been restored to full working order. Another old mosque, **Ibrahim Pasha** (1531) is off Sophokles St; its minaret was restored by the Italians.

On Hippocrates Square, where Sokratous St turns into Aristotelous St, stands the **Kastellania Palace**, built by d'Amboise in 1507, perhaps as a tribunal or commercial exchange from the Knights. It stands at the head of Pithagora St, the main street of **Evriaki**, the Jewish quarter. Continuing east along Aristotelous St, the **Plateia Evrion Martyron** (the Square of Hebrew Martyrs), recalls the inhabitants of Rhodes sent off to die in the concentration camps. The so-called **Admiral's Palace** is here, with a bronze seahorse fountain; it was more likely the seat of Rhodes' bishop. From here, Pindarou St continues to the ruins of **Our Lady of Victory**, built by the Knights in thanksgiving for their defeat of the Turks in 1480. The Turkish and Jewish Quarters offer many other little cobbled lanes to explore, dotted with old frescoed churches converted into mosques and converted back again.

New Town

Outside the walls, facing the little port of Mandraki is a seafront row of sweet shops, a good bet for a quick snack; behind them, is the **Market** and bus depot for Rhodes' west coast. Beyond them is a fairly austere ensemble of public buildings built by the fascists in the 1920s—post office, theatre, city hall. The Italians also left Rhodes some attractive buildings: the fine Venetian-Gothic **Governor's Palace** and the cathedral **Evangelismos**, designed after the church of St John, the Knights' cathedral (demolished in 1856); the fountain is a copy of Viterbo's Gothic Fontana Grande.

For the Turks, Rhodes was an island paradise, and many Moslem notables in exile (including a Shah of Persia) chose to spend the rest of their lives here. Many lie buried in the cemetery north of the theatre, next to the **Mosque of Murad Reis**, named for the admiral of the Egyptian Sultan, killed during the siege of Rhodes; and buried in a turban-shaped tomb, or *turbeh*. The mosque has a lovely, though crumbling, minaret. Next to it looms the grand, forlorn Art Deco Hotel des Roses, awaiting resurrection of some kind, and a long, crowded stretch of public beach. At the northernmost tip of the island is the **Aquarium** (*daily 9–9*), said to be the only one in the Balkans, with tanks of Mediterranean fish and sea turtles, and a startling horror show collection of stuffed denizens of the deep, their twisted grimaces the result not of any prolonged agony but amateur taxidermy. Another beach stretches from the aquarium down the west coast, but it's often battered by strong winds and frequently deserted.

Many places hire out bicycles, scooters and cars, but any reasonably active visitor can walk south of the New Town to the ancient acropolis of Rhodes, **Mt Smith**, named after Admiral Sydney Smith who kept track of Napoleon's Egyptian escapades from here. On the way (North Epirous St) are the ruins of an **Asklepieion**, dedicated to the god of healing, and a **Cave of the Nymphs**. On the top of Mt Smith, the Italians have partly reconstructed a 2nd-century BC Doric **temple of Pythian Apollo** who was later associated with Rhodian Helios. A few columns also remain of temples of Zeus and Athena, and you can trace the outline of a 3rd-century BC **stadium**. The **ancient theatre**, the only square one on the islands, has been reconstructed, and hosts Classical dramas in July (see the Tourist Office for programme details).

Other Rhodian distractions include the **Casino** at the Grand Hotel on Akti Miaoulis where the guests may win or lose their fortunes at roulette and baccarat. **Folkdances** by the Nelly Dimoglou company are performed in the Old City Theatre (*nightly except Sat, June–Oct; for information © (0241) 20 157 or 27 524*). Two km from the centre, lovely **Rodini Park** is where Aeschines built his School of Rhetoric in 330 BC—there's a rock-cut tomb from the same period, a later tomb of the Ptolemies, and ruins of a Roman aqueduct. The Knights grew their medicinal herbs here, and now in July and August merry drinkers join Rodini's peacocks for a **Wine Festival**; *open from 7 pm to 1 am, buses transport revellers to and from Mandraki harbour*. Try Rhodes' own wines: *Chevaliers de Rhodes*, *Lindos* and *Embonas* as well as other Greek vintages, celebrated with music, dance and food.

Bus connections for points east on the island depart from Papagou St in Rhodes town; for the west they leave from the market. **Excursion boats** to Lindos and Symi and the diving school boat dock near here, in Mandraki, while other caiques leave in the mornings for the beaches at Lardos, Tsambika, Faliraki, Kallithea, Ladiko, Kolymbia and Lindos.

Around Rhodes: Down the East Coast

The sandy shore just southeast of Rhodes town is lined with luxury hotels, from the coves of **Kallithea**, an old, disused thermal spa in a magnificent kitsch Italianate-Moorish building to **Faliraki**, a major resort near a long beach.

Afandou has the ultimate rarity in this part of the world—a golf course with 18 holes as well as tennis courts. There are fine beaches in the bay below and next to **Ladiko**, and a beautiful pebbly beach named after Anthony Quinn, who had his own private stretch here. At **Kolymbia** down the coast, farms are irrigated thanks to the nymph-haunted pool set in the pines in the lush hamlet of **Epta Pigi**, the 'Seven Springs'. Long sandy **Tsambika** beach is very popular, set in a cliff-edged bay. The road then goes down to the charming village of **Stegena**, set by a shingle beach in a pretty bay.

Continuing down the main highway, **Archangelos** (pop. 3500), the largest village on Rhodes, has a North African feel, its little white houses spread under a ruined castle of the

Knights. Its churches, **Archangelos Gabriel** and **Archangelos Michael** are considered two of the prettiest on the island; another nearby, *Ag. Theodoroi*, has 14th-century frescoes. The villagers have a reputation for their musicianship, their carpets, pottery and bootmaking; local cobblers can make footwear to order.

One of the strongest citadels on Rhodes towers on a promontory below Malona called **Faraclos**. Faraclos was occupied by pirates, until the Knights gave them the boot, repaired the walls and used the fort as a prison. Even after the rest of the island fell to Suleiman, Faraclos held, only surrendering after a long determined siege. The nearby fishing hamlet of **Haraki** has a lovely shaded esplanade running along the enclosed bay; there's excellent swimming and postcard views of Lindos.

Lindos

Dramatically situated on a promontory high over the sea, beautiful Lindos is Rhodes' second town and a National Historic Landmark. Of the island's three ancient cities it was the most important, first inhabited around 2000 BC; the first temple on its magnificent acropolis was erected in 1510 BC. It grew rich from its many colonies, especially Parthenope (modern Naples). Lindos owed its precocious importance to its twin natural harbours, the only ones on Rhodes, and to its 6th-century BC ruler Cleobulos, one of the Seven Sages of Greece: his maxim 'Nothing to Excess' was engraved on the oracle at Delphi and his reservoir supplies water to Lindos to this day. The town was important enough to merit a visit from St Paul; the Knights fortified it, and during the Turkish occupation, merchants from Lindos handled most of the island's trade. Their elegant flat-roofed 'Captain's mansions', built between the 15th–17th centuries line the serpentine pebbled lanes and stairs. Below town are two fine beaches, while high overhead is Lindos' **Acropolis**, one of the most stunningly sited in all of Greece—accessible by foot or hired donkey (*daily except Mon 8.30–3*). The route up is lined with billowing blouses, tablecloths and other items put out for sale by the good women of Lindos, who sit by their wares, needles clicking away as if weaving the fates of the thousands of tourists who pass every day.

Near the top, before the Knights' stairway, note the prow of a trireme carved into the living rock. This once served as a podium for a statue of Agesander, priest of Poseidon, sculpted by Pythocretes, best known for his *Victory of Samothrace*. At the top of the stair are two vaulted rooms and to the right, a crumbling 13th-century **church of St John**. Continue straight on for the raised Dorian arcade, or stoa of Lindian Athenas, the patron goddess of the city. From here the 'stairway to Heaven' leads up to the mighty foundations of the **Propylaea** and on the edge of the precipice, the **temple of Athena** itself, of which only seven columns are standing. Both were built in the 4th century BC and reconstructed by the Italians. In ancient times, the temple was celebrated for its golden inscription of Pindar's Seventh Ode, now gone without a trace. The views from the acropolis are extraordinary, especially towards the round azure pool of the small harbour, or **Porto Piccolo** where St Paul landed in AD 58; its small white chapel has a huge *paneyeri* on 28 June. The larger harbour was the home port of Lindos' navy, 500 ships strong.

Many of the houses in the village have collections of Lindian ware, faience painted with highly stylized Oriental motifs first manufactured in Asia Minor; the oldest ones date back to Byzantium. Potters who took refuge in Lindos taught their craft to the islanders. Some of their finest works are displayed in the town's most lavish house, the Papakonstandis mansion (or **Lindos museum**). Lindos' reputation for embroideries dates back to the time of Alexander the Great. A *sperveri*, the fine bridal dress that all Lindian girls once wore, can be seen at **Kashines house**. Among the shady plane trees and restaurants in the Plateia where the bus stops, the **church of the Panayia** (1479) has good 18th-century frescoes. To the northeast of the larger harbour, the cylindrical **tomb of Cleobulos** actually pre-dates Cleobulos, and in the Middle Ages was converted into a church.

Around South Rhodes: Lindos to Monolithos

Lardos, west of Lindos, is a pretty little valley village. The beach below Lardos has sand dunes: indeed the whole southeast coast of Rhodes is a series of beaches, many deserted, although good fish tavernas and rooms to rent may be found at **Pefki**, just south of Lindos, little more than a beach and a few houses spread out along the line of low cliffs; other progressively quieter beaches with tavernas are at **Chiotari** (where you can detour inland to the medieval hill village **Asklipio**, with a frescoed church of 1060), **Gennadi** and **Plimiri**. As you approach the southernmost tip of Rhodes, **Prassonisi Cape**, the desolate landscape may as well be the end of the world. You can spend the night at Skiadi Monastery nearby.

Heading up the west coast from Katavia are yet more beaches and scenic views (often battered by strong winds) on the way to **Mesangagros**, an old fashioned mountain village. In the Kourkourtahi valley below, **Apolakia** is a charming village that produces the best watermelons and marriage feasts on Rhodes. It has a few eating spots and rooms for rent. Further up the west coast, **Monolithos** is the most important village of the region, the monolith in its name a 200 m high rocky spur rising above the sea, capped by a castle built by the Grand Master d'Aubusson. A fairly difficult footpath winds to the top, where you can see the frescoed chapel of **Ag. Panteleimon** (15th century), and at sunset a view across to little Halki. Below, the shady bay of **Fourni** has a beach, and ancient cave dwellings, and not far away is the monastery Ag. Anastasia. The road continues through **Siana**, an attractive old stone village built on a hillside, offering a superb view of the coast and islets.

In the face of all of Rhodes' cosmopolitan urges, **Embona** in the mountains keeps to its traditional ways. The dances of the women are exceptionally beautiful, as are the homespun costumes that a few older people wear every day. Increasingly though, Embona's purity is polluted by tour buses from Rhodes town. The island's highest peak, **Mt Ataviros** (1215 m) is a tough 2-hour climb from Embona. Here Althaemenes is said to have built the temple of Zeus Atavros, although little remains of it now. But there are views of the whole island from the summit, and on a clear day they say you can see Crete from the peak; perhaps poor Althaemenes used to come up here when he longed, like all Cretans, for his mother island. Althaemenes supposedly founded the village below Embona, **Kritinia**, which he named in honour of Crete.

But Althaemenes' most celebrated foundation was **Kamiros**, one of the three Dorian cities of Rhodes, destroyed by an earthquake in the 2nd century BC, abandoned in the Dark Ages and covered with the dust of centuries and forgotten until 1859, when two archaeologists, Biliotti and Salzmann, began excavating where some villagers had uncovered a few graves. The city they eventually brought to light is well preserved; the **cemetery**, in particular, rendered many beautiful items and in archaeological terms was one of the richest ever discovered in Greece. An excellent water and drainage system, supplied by a large reservoir, served the many excavated Hellenistic-era houses. Also to see are the baths, the agora with its rostrum for public speeches, the agora's Great Stoa with its Doric portico, and two temples, one 5th-century BC dedicated to Athena and the other, from the 3rd century, possibly to Apollo Kamiros (*daily except Mon 8.30–3*).

Kamiros Skala, a modern fishing village about 16 km south of Kamiros, was ancient Kamiros' port, although these days it more modestly sends out caiques for Halki. **Fanes**, further north, has a long, narrow stony beach with a few tavernas.

Inland, on a high hill over the village of **Salakos** are the ruins of another medieval fort; Salakos itself is beloved for its shade and fresh water from the Spring of the Nymphs. This region, with its cedar and pine forests and views of the sea, is one of the prettiest in Rhodes for walks. Further up the road leads to **Mt Profitis Ilias** (790 m). The trees here belong to the Prophet Elijah, who according to legend strikes down any sinner who dares to cut one down. The chief settlements on its slopes are **Apollona** with a museum of popular art and **Eleousa** with a pretty Byzantine church.

Another enchanting spot, if you manage to get there before or after the tour buses, is the **Valley of the Butterflies**, or Petaloudes. Sliced by a tiny stream and laughing waterfalls, the long, narrow valley has a roof of fairytale trees, crossed by a winding path and little wooden bridges. From June to September a sooty orange species of butterfly (*Callimorpha quadripuctaria*) flocks here, attracted by the sweet resin of the styrax tree, which is used in the making of frankincense. The butterflies rise in a cloud when you clap your hands (*daily 9–6*). Just up the road the monastery, **Panayia Kalopetra**, claimed to have been built by the hero who began the Greek revolution in 1821, Alexander Ypsilantis. Below Kalamonas is the very popular beach **Paradissi** and the airport.

Kremasti, a village of few tourists, is best known for its wonder-working icon, Panayias Kremasti, occasioning one of biggest *paneyeri* in the Dodecanese, lasting from 15–23 August; at the climax on the 23rd the villagers don traditional costumes and cut a wonderful sousta. On nearby **Mt Philerimos** stood Orychoime, the acropolis of the ancient city of **Ialysos**. Ialysos, the least important of the three Dorian cities, was situated near Trianda village, but its acropolis presents the greatest interest. Built over the foundations of a Phoenician temple are the remains of a 3rd-century BC **temple of Athena** and a way down below, a reconstructed 4th-century **Doric fountain**. An early Christian basilica from around the 5th century still has its cruciform font and frescoes from the 1300s. The **cemetery** yielded finds from Mycenaean to Hellenistic times. At the Byzantine fortress at Orychoime, **Our Lady of Philerimos**, the

Genoese fought John Cantacuzene in 1248. There are a few Byzantine churches nearby; the one used by the Knights had both Catholic and Orthodox altars.

Nearby **Trianda**, a resort area, was settled by Minoans in 1600 BC, and may have been damaged in the explosions and subsequent tidal wave from Santorini. The still functioning mosque at **Asgouru** was originally a church of St John.

Festivals

In August, dance festivals at Kallithies, Maritsa and Embona; 29–30 July, Ag. Soula at Soroni, an occasion for donkey races; 28 June at Lindos; 14 June, Profitis Ammos at Faliraki; 26 July, Ag. Panteleimonos at Siana; 7 September, at Monastery Tsabikas, when barren women go to pray for fertility; 14–22 August at Kremasti; 26 August, Ag. Fanourious in the Old Town; 5 September, Ag. Trias near Rhodes; 13 September, Stavros at Apollona and Kallithies; 26 September, Ag. Ioannis Theologos at Artamiti; 18 October, Ag. Lukos at Afandou; 7 November at Archangelos; carnival at Apokries; Scandinavian midsummer festivities in Rhodes town.

Where to Stay

Rhodes has a plethora of accommodation in every class and price range. Many places are booked solid by package tours 12 months of the year, but there are so many rooms available on the island that you're bound to find something without booking, although it may be inconvenient.

luxury

In Rhodes town, at the top of the list, is the deluxe **Grand Hotel Astir Palace** on Akti Miaouli, © 26 284, with the island's casino, a nightclub, tennis courts and what's reputed to be the largest swimming pool in the country.

expensive

With similar facilities at a lower price, the **Miramare Beach** is directly on the beach in Ixia, just south of Rhodes town, © 24 251/4, and offers bungalows as well as hotel rooms. Also in Ixia the **Rodos Bay**, © 23 661/5, has a pool and bungalows by its private beach, while the rooftop restaurant has one of Rhodes' finest views. One of the nicer places in Faliraki is the **Rodos Beach Hotel**, which also has bungalows, © 85 471. In Lindos, where it's illegal to build hotels, nearly every other house has been converted into a holiday villa, and if you want to stay at one you'll have to book through a holiday company before you arrive. Nearby is the new **Lindos Bay Hotel**, © (0244) 42 212, on the beach and within walking distance of town. Three km from Lindos, in the bay of Vlyha, the **Steps of Lindos** has luxury rooms and facilities, and offers a variety of watersports, © (0244) 42 262. To get away from the sun-and-fun crowds, there are two Swiss chalets that lost their way and ended up in the eastern Mediterranean, near the top of pine-forested Mt Profitis Ilias, to be specific. These are the **Elafos** (the stag) and the **Elafina** (doe), both class A, quiet and comfortable and not as silly as they sound. The telephone is (0246) 21 221 for both.

There are scores of class B, C and D hotels in and around Rhodes town, especially in the new quarter. One of the best value here is the **Ambassadeur**, a class C hotel at 53 Othonos & Amalias, © 24 679. **Marie Rodos**, by Elli Beach, 2 minutes walk from the town centre, at 7 Kos St, © 30 577, has a swimming pool and English-style pub. Other, less expensive (on the whole) beach hotels run down the west coast of the island solidly to Paradissi.

Most of the inexpensive (and to be honest, the most interesting) places to stay are in the old town. Look around Omirou Street, where a clean and friendly spot is **Steve's Pension** at no. 60, © 24 357. Another very informal pension is the **Apollon** at no. 28, with laundry facilities and hot showers. **Athinea**, 45 Pythagora, also has decent rooms and shared facilities. A must for budget travellers, **Pithagora**, 56 Fanouriou, is a friendly little place for the young, or young at heart. It's one of the cheapest places in town; even if it's full, drop into their miniscule bar to swap travelling yarns. Cheap accommodation can be difficult to find in the purpose-built resorts. In the southern half of the island the pickings are sparse—little rooms over tavernas and the like. There are **campsites** at Lardos, 2 km from Lindos, © (0244) 44 203, and at Faliraki, © 85 358.

Eating Out

In Rhodes Town

Getting lost in the old city and finding your own little taverna is the best way to enjoy eating out in Rhodes town. After an aperitif in Ippocratous Square, possibly at **Café Brazil**, take the plunge into the maze of backstreets—in some of the industrious little shops you'll see tailors and cobblers still hard at work—and come across several decent tavernas, the most reasonable and authentic places to eat in town. **Alexis**, on Socratous St, is expensive but good, and specializes in fish. Nearby, **Argo** is a local favourite, with all the Greek standards. If you're down to your last 1000 dr. before your ferry or flight, eat at the **Astra**, underneath the Sydney Hotel in Apellou St,

where you'll get change from 600 dr. for chicken and chips, plus a drink. One of the cheapest places to eat in Rhodes is the market, where numerous greasy spoons offer several varieties of grilled meats and souvlaki. If you have a taste for Scandinavian food there are many possibilities. **The Danish House** on Akti Miaouli is the real thing, serving *smorgasbord* and other specialities; 3500 dr. for dinner, with healthy belts of Danish beer and schnapps. The **Mascot**, on Sofocleos St, is worth a visit for its ultra-kitsch décor alone—artificial tree, plastic waterfall, model of the Colossus—and the food is tops: souvlaki stuffed with garlic and cheese, oven-baked tomatoes with cheese and garlic, and good local Rhodian wines (2000 dr.).

Outside Rhodes, try not to miss **Ta Koupia**, on the road to Trianda (best to take a short taxi ride); wonderfully decorated with antique Greek furniture, the food matches the décor in quality—excellent *meze* and upmarket Greek dishes with an Eastern influence (4000 dr.). On the road to Lindos, near the seven palms, more refined Greek cuisine can be sampled at **The Old Story**, with a zany ex-actor owner and particularly good vegetarian dishes (2500 dr.). Most tavernas in Koskinou are like the village itself, small and typically Greek. **Yiannis** here serves meze, ouzo and a meal for under 2000 dr. Don't be put off by the elegant air of **Le Chef**, also in Koskinou. It looks like a luxury restaurant, and serves international fare (good steaks and schnitzel), but at everyday prices (2–3000 dr.). For good fish tavernas head for Kamiros Skala, where the tavernas on the beach are popular. In lovely Lindos the **Triton** serves fish on the beach, but be warned that in Lindos prices are prettty lofty and service can be abrupt.

Nightlife

After dinner there's plenty to do in Rhodes. If you're not up to participating in the Miss Wet T-shirt competition or the Mister Muscle show (or both) at the lively **La Scala** disco with open garden and swimming pool, then you may care to simply sit and people-watch at the **Trianon Bar** in Academia Square, and try one of their many types of coffee.

Symi

Few other islands have the crisp brightness of Symi, with its amphitheatre of half-restored, half-derelict neo-Classical mansions, stacked one on top of the other like a Cubist lemon meringue. There are few trees to block the sun, for unlike its neighbour Rhodes, Symi is an arid island, unable to support many visitors. Most who do come arrive and depart on the excursion boat from Rhodes, and when they're gone, Symi regains much of its serenity. Although its can get as hot as a cat on a tin roof in the middle of summer, its climate is quite pleasant for the rest of the year.

History

According to legend, Symi was a princess of Ialysos on Rhodes, who was abducted by Glaukos, the builder of the *Argo*, before she ended up on the little island that bears her name. If such was the case, Princess Symi's descendants inherited Glaukos' shipbuilding skills; throughout history Symi was famous for its ships—resulting in the current lack of trees.

Pelasgian walls in Chorio attest to the prehistoric settlement of Symi. In the *Iliad* Homer tells how the island mustered three ships for the Achaeans at Troy, led by King Nireus. After Achilles, Nireus was the most beautiful of all the Greeks, but as in Achilles' case, beauty was no defense against the Trojans. In historic times Symi was part of the Dorian Hexapolis, dominated by Rhodes. The Romans fortified the acropolis at Chorio; the Byzantines converted it into a fort, which was renovated by the first Grand Master of the Knights of Rhodes, Foulques de Villaret. From Symi's Kastro the Knights could signal to Rhodes, and they favoured swift Symiot skiffs for their raiding activities.

Thanks to the Knights, Symi began to know a certain measure of prosperity through ship-building and trade. When Suleiman the Magnificent came to the Dodecanese in 1522, the Symiotes, known as the most daring divers in the Aegean, avoided the inevitable invasion by offering him the most beautiful sponges he had ever seen. A consignment of sponges became Symi's yearly tribute to the Sultan in return for a relative degree of independence. Like the Knights, the Turks made use of the swift Symiot ships, this time for relaying messages. In order to keep Symi thriving, the Sultan declared it a free port and gave the inhabitants the rights to dive freely for sponges in Turkish waters.

Little Symi thus became the third richest island of the Dodecanese, a position it held from the 17th to the 19th centuries. Large mansions were constructed befitting the islanders' new status; many bought forests in Asia Minor. Schools thrived. Even after certain privileges were withdrawn because of its participation in the 1821 revolution, Symi continued to flourish. The Italian occupation and the steamship, however, spelt the end of the little island's for-tunes: the Italians closed the lands of Asia Minor and the steamship killed the demand for wooden sailing vessels altogether; during their tenure the population of Symi dropped from 23,000 to 6000 at the outbreak of World War II. At its end the treaty giving the Dodecanese to Greece was signed on Symi on 1 March 1948.

At least one tourist boat a day from Rhodes; hydrofoils from Rhodes and Kos; two ferries a week with the other Dodecanese.

Clock Tower, Yialos, ✆ (0241) 71 215.

Yialos and Chorio

Symi's capital is divided into two quarters: Yialos around the harbour and Chorio, the older settlement on the hill. In **Yialos** you'll find most of Symi's tourist facilities and what is left of its shipyards. In honour of its shipbuilding tradition, a copy of the stone trireme in Lindos has been erected on the waterfront. Nearby, the restaurant **Les Katerinettes** has a plaque commemorating the signing of the 1948 treaty of the Dodecanese. At the end of the harbour behind the ungainly concrete clock tower and the statue of the fishing boy is small **Charani bay** where ships wait to be finished or repaired. Here especially one can see the result of the bombing during World War II. There are no beaches near Yialos, but **Nos**, at the end of Charani, is where the local people swim. Further on, **Emborio**, the island's other little harbour, is another pleasant place to eat and swim.

Most of the neo-Classical houses in Yialos date from the 19th century, while older architecture dominates at **Chorio**, connected to the port by a dirt road or mansion-lined stairway from Plateia tis Skala. By the derelict windmills, a **stone monument** was erected by the Spartans for their victory over the Athenians off the coast of Symi. Houses in Chorio are similar to Cycladic houses, small and asymmetrical, often with neo-Classical elements incorporated into their doorways and windows. Many houses have very lovely interiors with carved woodwork.

Among the most interesting buildings at Chorio are the **19th-century pharmacy;** the fortress-mansion **Chatziagapitos**; and the churches with their pebble mosaics of evil mermaids sinking hapless ships. The island's **museum** up at Chorio houses objects dating from Hellenistic times to the present. Up at the top, the **Kastro's** Byzantine and medieval walls were built from an ancient temple of Athena; the coat-of-arms belongs to d'Aubusson; the church near the walls, **Megali Panayia**, has good frescoes and post-Byzantine icons.

Around Symi

From Chorio it's a half-hour walk to **Pedhi**, the only fertile area on Symi. On a small bay, it has a beach and is the best place on the island to camp out. A new road from Chorio travels to the extreme southern tip of the island and Symi's main attraction, the 18th-century **monastery of Taxiarchis Michael Panormitis** (in the summer there are also caiques, and the tourist boat from Rhodes often stops there). Archangel Michael of Panormitis bay is Symi's patron saint and a big favourite of all Greek sailors. The carved wooden **iconostasis** in the monastery church is remarkable, while the walls are liberally adorned with frescoes. Gold and silver ship ex-votos dangle from the ceiling, and the **sacristy** contains more rich gifts from faithful sailors, and little bottles which drifted to shore with money for the monastery. Panormitis also has one of the best beaches on Symi, and there are restaurants and cafés and rooms to rent, more in the spirit of a resort than a religious sanctuary.

Sesklia, an islet near Panormitis, also belongs to the monastery. Its ancient name was Teutlousa, and Thucydides writes that it was here that the Athenians took refuge after their defeat by the Spartan navy during the Peloponnesian War. A few Pelasgian walls remain, and there are also a few ruins on the nearby islet **Stroggilos**.

The other sites of Symi are also religious in nature. Of its 77 churches, the most interesting is **Michael Roukoumiotis**, an hour's walk from Yialos. Built in the 18th century, it is a curious combination of Gothic and folk architecture, and holds its feast day beneath an old umbrella-shaped cypress. **Ag. Emilianos** is on an islet in the bay of the same name, connected to the shore by a causeway with a pleasant pebbly beach nearby. Another 18th-century church,
Ag. Noulias is a half-hour walk from Chorio, and nearby **Ag. Marina** had a famous school before the War of Independence broke out. On the east coast, best reached by caique, **Nanos bay** has an excellent beach.

Festivals

5 May, Ag. Athanasios; 21 May, Ag. Konstantinos; 4 June, Analypsis; 24 June, Ag. Ioannis; 17 July, Ag. Marinas; 6 August, Nymborio and Panormitis; 15 August, Panayias; 8 November, Taxiarchis at the monastery.

Where to Stay

Except for rooms at the monastery, all the island's accommodation is in town.

expensive

The two prettiest places to stay are both in old sea captains' mansions, each lovingly restored with fine wood interiors. These are the **Aliki**, ℭ 71 665, where you can almost dive straight out of the front door into the sea, and the **Dorian**, ℭ 71 181.

moderate

The hotel **Grace**, ℭ 71 415, is in another traditional house, with lower rates than the above. Otherwise, Symi Tours by the harbour, ℭ 71 307, has a large listing of houses for rent in town.

cheap

On the less expensive side there are rooms to let here and there, usually on the condition that you stay three nights (to economise on sheet washing—water is scarce). The **Pension Les Katerinettes** on the quay is very pleasant, ℭ 71 676.

The portside tavernas of Symi are known for their fresh seafood. **Les Katerinettes** also has good food with a French flavour, if a bit expensive (3000 dr.), but for a meal with a view (and good food), try **George's** near the top of Chorio, where dinner is around 2000 dr.

Tilos

One of the least-visited islands in Greece, Tilos still tries to do its best for visitors; one village, Livadia, has even gone so far as to build communal bungalows from public funds. It is as fine a place as any to do nothing; a dreaminess surrounds all practical activities and the visitor who neglects to wind his watch is in danger of losing all track of time. While parts of Tilos are arable and there's water (although it's turned off in the evening), much of Tilos is desolate; pockets of sandy beach may be found along the island's indented shoreline. The only really remarkable thing about Tilos is that mastodon bones were discovered in one of its caves. The other remarkable thing is that it has managed to stay just about the same over the years.

Connections

Two–three times a week by ferry to the other Dodecanese islands; once a week with Samos, Mykonos, Tinos, Andros and Rafina; in the summer occasional tourist boat and hydrofoil from Rhodes, Symi and Kos; twice a week from Halki.

Tourist Police

See regular police in Megalo Chorio, © (0241) 53 222.

Livadia and Megalo Chorio

The islanders live in two settlements: the port **Livadia**, with a rocky beach and in the capital **Megalo Chorio,** 8 km up the road. Megalo Chorio stands on the site of ancient Tilos, and near the castle you can see Pelasgian walls built by the earliest known residents (if you discount the mastodons) dating back to 1000 BC. The castle, or Kastro was built by the Venetians, who incorporated a Classical gateway and stone from the ancient acropolis. There is a pleasant beach and taverna near Megalo Chorio at **Nausica**, and paths lead down to other small beaches. In Megalo Chorio a one-room museum awaits a brilliant discovery. Further north is the deserted village of Mikro Chorio and the cave where the mastodon bones were discovered. The best beaches are at **Erestos** and **Plaka**.

Besides no water in the evenings, be warned that transport between Livadia and Megalo Chorio may be hard to find (except when a ship comes in) and there is little fresh food available except around midsummer; even the bread is shipped in from Rhodes. But the people are very kind and help as much they can.

25–27 July, Ag. Panteleimonos; 28 June, Ag. Pavlos; 17 January, Ag. Antonio at Megalo Chorio.

Where to Stay

moderate–cheap

In Livadia you'll find Tilos' two hotels, the **Irini**, a class C with 18 rooms, ✆ 53 293, and the **Livadia**, a slightly down-at-heel class E establishment, ✆ 52 202. When it's full you can start looking for rooms elsewhere in the Livadia (but the rule is, not before). There are also rooms up in Megalo Chorio and at Erestos; the fancy apartments in Livadia are always booked by a holiday company. You can also camp out on any beach without protest.

Eating Out

There are little tavernas in Livadia—try your luck at **Stefanaki** or **Economou**, and in Megalo Chorio, **Milios**. The food is nothing special here or anywhere else on Tilos, but it's reasonably priced and authentic Greek. There's also a taverna at Erestos, the **Tropicana**, but don't expect south sea island exotica at your table.

The Monastery on Corfu

The Ionian Islands

The seven westerly islands scattered randomly in the Ionian Sea, from Corfu in the north to Kythera at the southern tip of the Peloponnese, have been lumped together politically since the Byzantine era and more or less share a common history. Individually, however, the seven are quite distinct, both geologically and in character. Even connections between the Ionians were long scanty at best. Now—at least in the summer—you can with relative ease visit six of them, and there's a ferry to Italy (usually to Brindisi, Otranto or Bari) from Corfu, Paxos, Kefalonia and Ithaca.

In the off season getting around becomes more difficult. Not only do ships sail less frequently, but from late October to March heavy rains are the rule. They give the Ionian islands a lushness the Aegean islands lack; springtime, especially in Corfu, is breathtaking, and the autumn wild flowers are nearly as beautiful as those in spring. Summers, however, tend to be hot, lacking the natural air conditioning provided by the meltemi on Greece's eastern shores.

History

Lying between Greece and Italy, the Ionian islands have spent centuries out of the mainstream of Greek politics, although from the beginning their inhabitants have been Hellene to the core. Not to be confused with Ionia in Asia Minor (named for the Ionians' legendary father Ios, son of Apollo), the Ionian sea and islands are named for Io the priestess, who caught the roving eye of Zeus. When the jealous Hera was about to catch the couple *in flagrante delicto* Zeus changed the girl into a white cow, but Hera was not fooled. She asked Zeus to give her the cow as a present, and ordered the sleepless hundred-eyed Argus to watch over her. With the help of Hermes, who charmed Argus to sleep and killed him, Io escaped, only to be pursued by a terrible stinging gad-fly sent by Hera. The first place through which she fled has ever since been named the Ionian Sea in honour of the tormented girl.

Very little remains of the ancient past on the islands, although they were probably settled in the Stone Age by people from Illyria (present-day Albania) and then by the Eretrians. Homer was the first to mention them, and were he the last they would still be immortal as the homeland of crafty Odysseus. In the 8th century BC, mercantile Corinth colonized the islands. As trade expanded between Greece and the Greek colonies in southern Italy and Sicily, the islands became ever more important; Corfu, the richest, grew so high and mighty that she defeated mother Corinth at sea, and proclaimed herself the ally of Athens. This forced Sparta, Corinth's ally, either to submit to this expansion of the Athenian Empire and control of western trade through the Ionians islands, or to attack. They attacked. The result was the disastrous Peloponnesian War.

The Romans incorporated the Ionian islands into their province Achaia (still the current name of the province). After the fall of the Roman Empire, the Ostrogoths from Italy overran the islands, only to be succeeded by the Byzantines, who fortified them for their strategic importance as a bridge between Constantinople and Rome. In 1084, during the Second Crusade, however, the Normans under Duke Robert Guiscard of Sicily took the islands by surprise and

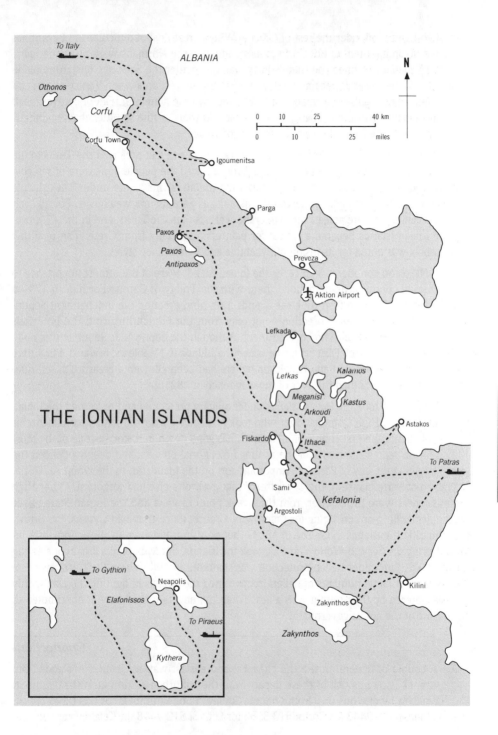

THE IONIAN ISLANDS

established bases to plunder the rest of Greece. With a great deal of difficulty the Byzantines succeeded in forcing them out of Corfu at least, although the Normans were no sooner gone when the Venetians claimed the islands in the land grab after the Sack of Constantinople in 1204. The southern islands became the County Palatine of Kefalonia when Venice put an end to the claims of the Sicilian Norman pirate, Vetrano, by crucifying him. Fate, however, dealt Corfu into the hands of the grasping Angevins for 150 years, a rule so bitter that the inhabitants surrendered their island to the 'protection' of Venice.

Venetian rule was hardly a bed of roses. The average Greek in fact preferred the Turks to the bossy Catholic 'heretics': if nothing else, the Turks allowed the people a measure of self-government and demanded fewer taxes. Some of the Ionian islands came under Turkish rule until 1499, and the Ottomans renewed the assaults as Serenissima weakened. For all their faults, the Venetians were at least more tolerant of artists than the Turks, and in the 17th century the Ionian islands became a refuge for painters, especially from Crete. The resulting Ionian school was noted for its fusion of Byzantine and Renaissance styles.

In 1796, Napoleon conquered Venice; as the Ionian islands were of the utmost importance to his schemes of conquest he demanded them with the Treaty of Campo Formio. In 1799 a combined Russo–Turkish fleet took the islands from him, creating the independent Septinsular Republic under their protection—not only from the French but from the notorious tyrant of Epirus, Ali Pasha, who coveted them. Although the Septinsular Republic was nullified by the 1807 Treaty of Tilsit which returned the islands to Napoleon, it was the first time in almost four centuries that any Greeks anywhere had been allowed a measure of self-rule. Most importantly, it kindled the War of Independence in 1821.

In 1815 the British took the Ionian islands under military protection and re-formed the Ionian State, appointing a High Commissioner who took precedence over the Ionian parliament. Sir Thomas Maitland, the first High Commissioner, has gone down in history as one of the most disliked British representatives ever; he assumed dictatorial powers, and deeply offended the Greeks by giving the city of Parga, an important port on the mainland, to the tyrant Ali Pasha, obeying an obscure clause in the 1815 treaty that everyone else had forgotten. Other High Commissioners were little better from the Greek point of view and the Ionian State never stopped demanding or conspiring for union with Greece. Once they had Cyprus, the British agreed to cede the islands to Greece in 1864—but only after blowing up all the fortresses on Corfu. During the Second World War Italy took the islands, but Mussolini's dream of creating a new Ionian State under Italian protection was shattered in 1943 when the Germans occupied the islands. Large numbers of Italian troops joined the Greeks in fighting the Nazis, only to be slaughtered by their former Axis allies. When the news reached Italy, it contributed to the collapse of the fascist government.

Connections

A couple of general notes: the cheapest and easiest way to reach the islands from Athens is by bus. All of these depart from the suburban station at 100 Kifissou St, reached by city bus 051 from Omonia Square. Phone numbers for bus times are (in Athens) 512 9443 for Corfu; 513 3583 for Lefkas; 512 9498 for Kefalonia and Ithaca;

and 512 9432 for Zakynthos. Secondly, there is a long-established company which specializes in renting villas on Paxos, Ithaca, Kefalonia, Zakynthos and Kythera called **Greek Islands Club**; you can get their brochure by writing to Villa Centre Holidays, 66 High St, Walton-on-Thames, Surrey, KT12 1BU, ✆ (0932) 220477.

Corfu (Kerkyra)

Luxuriantly beautiful Corfu is a Garden of Eden cast up in the northwest corner of Greece, a sweet mockery of the grim grey mountains of Albania, so close and so unenticing. From Shakespeare to Edward Lear, from Gladstone to Lawrence and Gerald Durrell, Corfu has long held a special place in the English heart. Its reputation as a distant paradise began with Homer, who called it Scheria, the happy isle of the Phaeacians, beloved of the gods, where the shipwrecked Odysseus was entertained by the lovely Nausica. Shakespeare made it the magical isle of *The Tempest*, where Prospero offered a different sort of hospitality to his ship-wrecked guests. The unique Venetian city-capital of the island is one of the loveliest and most elegant in Greece; if you squint, perhaps, you won't notice that nearly every building's ground floor has been given over to souvenir shops and tourist bars. For it's a sad and unavoidable fact that no other island (except Rhodes) has been so exploited and developed: every year Paradise descends a little closer to an international package tour Babylon for yahoos and lager louts.

For all that, head into the hinterland (especially in the mountains to the north) and you'll find villages and landscapes blissfully virgin of monster concrete hotels, enclaves of expensive villas, tourist compounds and golf courses. Come in the off season (good times are early spring, when the almonds blossom, around Palm Sunday or the first part of November, coin-ciding with the colourful celebrations of Ag. Spyridon), and seek out the old cobbled donkey paths that in Venetian times provided the main link between villages, and you'll be rewarded with a poignant vision of the old Corfu, strewn with wild flowers, scented with the blossoms of lemons and kumquats, silvery with forests of ancient olives—which still outnumber tourists by three and half million. Just don't go out without your wet-weather clothes.

History

In ancient times Corfu was Corcyra, named after a mistress of the sea god Poseidon. She bore him a son called Phaeax, who became the founder of the Phaeacian race. In 734 BC the Corinthians sent a trading colony to the island and founded a city at Paliapolis; modern Ana-lypsis was the site of the Corinthian citadel-acropolis.

Although Corcyra thrived to become the richest of the Ionian islands, it was cursed with vio-lent political rivalries between its democrats and the oligarchs. Although the Corcyrian fleet defeated the ships of Corinth when the two quarrelled over a colony in Albania (the dispute that set off the Peloponnesian war) internal strife had so weakened Corcyra that at the begin-ning of the 4th century BC it was captured first by Syracuse, and then by King Pyrrhus of Epirus and in 229 BC by the Illyrians. Yet whatever the turmoil, ancient Corcyra never lost its lofty reputation for fertility and beauty; Nero, the ham emperor, paid it a special visit in AD 67 to dance and sing at the temple of Zeus in modern Kassiopi.

CORFU

Ag. Spiridon
Astrakeri
Roda
Sidari
Kassiopi
Perouludes
Ag.
Avliotes
Panteleimonos
Loutses
Karoussades
Lafki
Nimfes
Agnitsini
Ag. Stefanos
Magoulades
Episkepsis
Perithia
Kouloura
Arillas
Mt. Pantokrator
(900m)
Afionas
Valanion
Spartilas
Nissaki
Choreopiskopi
Pirgi
Manatrades
Ag. Markos
Korakiani
Makrades
Mt. Pylide
Ipsos
(619m)
Angelokastro II
Lakones
Dassia
Paliokastritsa
Dassia Bay
Liapades
Dafnila Bay
Gouvia
Vido
Giannades
Kontokali
To Italy, Yugoslavia
Mandouki
KERKYRA (CORFU)
Ermones
Mon
Repos
Pelekas
Analypsis
To Igoumenitsa
Glyfada
Perama
Kanoni
To Paxos, Patras
Sinarades
Achilleion Palace
Gastouri
Ag. Gordios
Benitses
Miramare
Mt. Ag. Deka
Ano Pavliana
(549m / 1800ft)
Moraitika
Ag. Mathias
Messoghi
Mt. Kava Louvouno
Mt. Ag. Mathias
(213m / 700ft)
(427m / 1400ft)
Hlomos
Alikes
Kouspades
Argirades
Limni
Perivolion
Lefkimi
Korission
Ag. Georgios
Kavos
Arkodila
Cape
Asprokav

N

0   2   5   10 km
0   2   5   miles

The remnants of the population that survived the ravages of the Goths founded a new town on the two hills of Cape Sidaro where they would be better protected (*corypho* in Greek means two peaks, hence 'Corfu'). It failed to thwart the Normans in 1081, and in 1148 when their raids menaced the Byzantine Empire itself, Emperor Emmanuel Comnenus sent a special force and fleet to dislodge them. When the siege of the Byzantines made no progress, Emmanuel came to lead the attack in person. By craftily causing subversion among the Normans themselves, he succeeded in winning back the island.

In 1204, when Venice came to claim Corfu, the inhabitants put up a stiff resistance. Although the Venetians succeeded in taking the island's forts, the islanders aligned themselves with the Despotat of Epirus, an Orthodox state. Fifty years later, however, the King of Naples and brother of St Louis of France, Charles I of Anjou, snatched Corfu and the rest of Achaia when his son married the princess of Villehardouin. Angevin rule, already infamous for provoking the Sicilian Vespers, was equally intolerant and hateful on Corfu. After 120 years, the Corfiots swallowed their pride and in 1386 asked Venice to put them under the protection of the Republic.

In 1537 a serious threat, not only to Corfu but to all of Europe, landed at Igoumenitsa in the form of Suleiman the Magnificent. Suleiman, the greatest of the Turkish sultans, already had most of the rest of Greece under his belt and was determined to take Corfu as a base for attacking Italy and Western Europe. Thanks to a peace treaty with Venice, Suleiman was able to plot his attack in the utmost secrecy. When the Corfiots discovered only a few days in advance what was in store for them, they tore down their houses for stone to repair the fortress and to leave nothing behind for the Turks. The terrible Barbarossa was the first to arrive and begin the siege of the city, during which he suffered massive losses. Thousands of Corfiots who had been pitilessly abandoned outside the fortress were caught in the Venetian and Turkish crossfire, and fell prey to Barbarossa's fits of rage at his continual setbacks. Those who managed to survive were carted off to the slave markets of Constantinople when Suleiman, discouraged by his losses and bad weather, ordered the withdrawal of the siege.

Only 21 years later Venice, under pressure from the Corfiots, expanded the island's fortifications to include the town. Many houses were left unprotected, however, and when the Turks reappeared in 1571 under Ouloudj Ali, these and the rest of the villages, trees and vineyards on Corfu were decimated. This time the Turks took no prisoners and massacred whoever they caught. The devastation was given a final touch two years later by another pirate admiral, Sinan Pasha: of the entire Corfiot population, only a tenth remained on the island after 1573.

In 1576 Venice finally began to build the walls required for the safety of all the Corfiots, together with the Fortezza Nuova and other fortifications designed by the expert Sammicheli; few remains of these still exist but they were considered superb in their day. They were given the ultimate test in 1716, when Turks staged furious attacks for one terrible month, before being repulsed by a tempest sent by Ag. Spyridon, Corfu's patron saint.

After the fall of Venice, the French occupied Corfu but quickly lost it again in a fierce battle against the Russo–Turkish fleet. When Napoleon finally got the island back, he personally designed new fortifications for the town. These were so formidable that the British, when allotted the Ionian islands after Waterloo, did not care to attack them when the French commander Donzelot refused to give them up. The French government finally had to order Donzelot home, and in 1815 Corfu came under British protection with the blessing of Count John Capodistria. Capodistria, soon to be the first president of Greece, was a native of Corfu and at that time was working for the Tsar of Russia.

But while Capodistria had requested 'military protection', the British, headquartered on Corfu, took upon themselves all the affairs of the Ionian State. One of the first things they did was demolish part of the Venetian walls to build new, more powerful ones in their place, calling upon the Ionian government to cough up more than a million gold sovereigns to pay for the improvements. But in 1864, when the Brits decided to pull out and let the Ionian islands unite with Greece, it was with the ungracious condition that they first destroy the fortresses of Corfu—not only the walls they themselves had just made the Corfiots build but also the historic Venetian buildings. A wave of protest from all corners of the Greek world failed to move the British, and in 1864 the fortifications were blown up, leaving the few ruined relics standing today. In 1923 Mussolini bombarded and occupied Corfu after the assassination on Greek territory of an Italian delegate to the Greek–Albanian border council; the Italians left only when Greece paid a large indemnity. An even worse bombardment occurred in 1943, when the Germans blasted the city for ten days to force its Italian garrison to surrender; a year later, in turn, the British and Americans bombed the Germans. At the end of the war, a quarter of the old city was destroyed, including 14 of the loveliest churches.

Connections

By air: Frequent charter flights from London, Manchester and Glasgow; also regular flights from many European cities; four flights a day from Athens, two in the winter.

By sea: All year round ferries from Brindisi, Bari and Ancona (the ships stop on route to Patras, most allowing a free stop-over in Corfu, although you must specify this when you purchase your ticket). In the summer there are also connections with Otranto, on the tip of Italy's heel. A new catamaran service links Brindisi to Corfu in a mere 3½ hours (in Corfu contact Charitos Travel, 35 Arseniou, © (0661) 44 611, in Athens, 28 Nikis Syntagma, © 322 0503). Services to Croatia have been suspended. Also in the summer there are ferries from Igoumenitsa, less frequently in the off season. In season connections with Patras, Ithaca, Kefalonia and year round daily ferry to Paxos, including links with the small islands of Ereikoussa, Othoni and Mathraki. Frequent bus service from Athens and Thessaloniki to Igoumenitsa.

By bus: The central city bus depot in Plateia Theotoaki–San Rocco Square has buses to villages just beyond the city (Potamos, Gouvia, Dassia, Benitses), while the bus station in Avramiou St has connections to the more distant villages (Glyfada, Paliokastritsa, Ag. Stefanos, Roda), as well as buses to Athens and Thessaloniki.

Tours: Travel agents in Corfu offer one-day classical tours to the mainland: to Epirus to visit the **Oracle of the Dead**, (consulted by Odysseus after crossing the perilous River Styx) and the ancient cities of **Kassopea** and **Nicopolis**, founded by Augustus after the defeat of Mark Anthony and Cleopatra in 31 BC. A second tour takes in

Dodoni, with its ancient theatre and **Ioannina**, the modern capital of Epirus, with its island of Ali Pasha and museum.

Tourist Information

Note: at time of writing the following were due to be moved for a period of two years, to an unspecified location:

NTOG, Governors House (Palace of St Michael and St George), ✆ (0661) 39 730.

Tourist police, next door to above, ✆ 39 503, and at 31 Arseniou St.

Consulates

Great Britain: 1 Menekratous St, ✆ 30 055 and 37 995

Germany: 57 Guilford St, ✆ 31 453

France: 15 Desillas St, ✆ 26 312

Corfu Town

Corfu town, or Kerkyra, the largest town in the Ionian islands, was laid out by the Venetians in the 14th century, when the medieval town, crowded onto the peninsula of Cape Sidaro (where the old fortress now stands) had no room to expand. They began with the quarter known as Campiello, where narrow three- or four-storey houses loom over the narrow streets, as they do back in the lagoon capital. By the time the new walls were added in the 16th century, the Venetians built at a more leisurely pace in the more open style of the Renaissance, laying out an exquisite series of central streets and small squares. The British knocked down a number of old Venetian walls to allow for further growth, and then built a set of elegant Georgian public buildings.

Besides Campiello, the old city is divided into a number of small quarters. The 19th-century residential district to the south is called Garitsa; if you arrive from Italy, you enter the city through its back door at **Mandouki** or New Port, west of the New Fortress. Mandouki isn't one of the more attractive parts of town, but it's a good place to look for cheap rooms and food. The ferries from the mainland and islands call to the east of the New Port, at the **Old Port**.

The New Fortress

Confusingly, the Old Port is dominated by the **New Fortress**, or Neo Frourio, where many people get their first look at the town; this was built by the Venetians following the third attack on Corfu, although most of the walls were destroyed by the British. The New Fortress bore the brunt of the Turks' siege of 1716. Nowadays it serves as a Greek naval base, and although you can't get inside you can stroll around the walls adorned with the lions of St Mark. One street near the fortress is named for the crafty and heroic Marshal Schulenburg, a soldier of fortune from Saxony, who outwitted the Turkish High Admiral in the Great Siege—

the last major attempt of the Ottoman Empire to expand in the west. Near the bus station stands the 1749 **Catholic Church of Tenedos**, named for an icon brought to Corfu by the Venetians from the Turkish island of Tenedos.

From the Old Port you can reach the centre of town through the 16th-century **Spilia Gate**, incorporated into a later structure, or take the narrow steps next to the Hotel Nea Yorki into the medieval Campiello Quarter (*see* below); the **Jewish Quarter**, equally old and picturesque, lies at the south end of the fortress walls. Although the synagogue remains in the heart of the quarter, few of its congregation survived the concentration camps to return to Corfu after the war.

The Esplanade

A series of long parallel streets—the main residential district of the Venetians—all lead to the town's centre, the great green space called the Spinada or **Esplanade**, one of the largest public squares in Europe. Originally the area was left open for defensive purposes; under Napoleon it began to take its present form as a garden and promenade. The French arcades of the Liston on the west edge are full of cafés, the flowerbeds are immaculately kept, and at night the monuments and trees are floodlit for dramatic effect.

The northern end of the Esplanade is occupied by the Georgian **Palace of St Michael and St George** with its two grand gates. Designed by Sir George Whitmore, the palace was built as the residence of Sir Thomas Maitland, first High Commissioner of the Ionian islands—hence the symbols of the seven islands that adorn the façade. In 1864 it became the residence of the King of Greece, then fell into disuse until it was renovated in 1953 to house a **Museum of Far Eastern Art** (*8.30–3, Sun 9.30–2.30, closed Mon*), the only one of its kind in Greece. The impressive collection, a gift to Corfu from two diplomats, Gregory Manos and Micholos Chadjivasiliou, contains 10,000 works from all the countries of the Far East dating back to 1000 BC. The palace also houses the public library, the tourist and traffic police, and the NTOG office. Note that for 1993–1994, the museum and tourist office will be relocated temporarily, to provide space in the palace for European cultural exhibitions planned in those years.

Just in front of the palace is another oddity left over from British rule—the **cricket ground**, where little boys play football until their older white-clad brothers chase them off the field. In the summer, matches are held, pitting the two local teams against visitors from Britain and Malta.

Numerous monuments embellish the Esplanade. Towards the centre is the **memorial to Sir Thomas Maitland**, another work of Sir George Whitmore, designed in the form of an Ionian rotunda. Near here is the British-built bandstand, where the local brass bands, an *opera buffo* speciality of Corfu (you can often hear them practising in the evening in the old quarters) perform in the summer. There is a heroic marble **statue of Marshal Schulenburg**, and most charmingly, a seated statue of Corfu's favourite Englishman, the Hellenophile Frederick North, Earl of Guilford (better known as Lord North) (1769–1828), who with Capodistria founded the first university in Greece. The **Guilford Memorial** portrays him in ancient robes, a touch which he would probably have appreciated. A statue of his friend,

Count Capodistria, first president of Greece, stands towards the southern end of the Esplanade.

The **Old Fortress** on Cape Sidaro is separated from the Esplanade by the moat, or contra fosse, dug over a 100-year period by the Venetians. The medieval town of Corfu was located on the two little hills of the cape; scholars have identified the site with the Heraion acropolis mentioned by Thucydides. The fortress' walls, built up over the centuries, were mostly blown to smithereens by the Brits; others have fallen into decay. Part of the fortress is still used by the Greek army, but you can wander about and explore the Venetian tunnels, battlements, drawbridge, the Venetian well, cannons dating back to 1684 and **St George's**, the church of the British garrison. Best of all, however, is the view of the city from the hills. In the summer there's a **Sound and Light Show** (*in English on weekdays, French on Sundays, Italian on Mondays, from 1–31 Aug*); evening performances of **folkdancing** (*1 June–30 Sept; combined ticket 600 dr.*).

Ag. Spyridon

The church of Corfu's patron saint Ag. Spyridon is in the old town, not far from the Ionian and Popular Bank of Greece. It's easy to find: the campanile soars above town like the mast of a ship, covered with flags and Christmas lights. Ag. Spyridon was the Bishop of Cyprus in the 4th century; when Constantinople fell to the Turks, his bones were smuggled in a sack of straw to Corfu. The church was built in 1596 to house the precious relics, no longer in straw but contained in a silver Renaissance reliquary which with great pomp is carted though town on the saint's feast days. According to the Corfiots, the good saint has brought them safely through many trials, frightening both cholera and the Turks away from his beloved worshippers. He even gave the Catholics a good scare when they considered placing an altar in his church; the night before its dedication, he blew up a powder magazine in the Old Fortress with a stroke of lightning to show his displeasure. The Orthodox Palm Sunday, Easter Saturday, 11 August and the first Sunday in November are dedicated to huge celebrations for Ag. Spyridon.

The nearby Ionian Bank houses a **Museum of Paper Money**, with a collection of banknotes from around the world, and Greek notes dating from the nation's birth. The second floor is given over to an exhibition demonstrating the various stages in the production of banknotes. Across the square, the 1689 church of the **Holy Virgin Faneromeni** contains some fine icons of the Ionian School.

The square gives on to the main street **Nikiforou Theotoki**, one of the prettiest in the town. From there head up E. Voulgareos St to the elegant square with Corfu's **Town Hall**, a lovely Venetian confection begun in 1691 that later did duty as the municipal opera house. The **Catholic Cathedral of St James** on the square was seriously damaged by the German bombing in 1943; only the bell tower survived intact. The rest has been reconstructed.

Campiello

There are a number of buildings worth seeking out in the Campiello quarter between the Old Port and the Esplanade, begining with the 1577 **Orthodox Cathedral**, dedicated to

Ag. Theodora Augusta, Empress of Byzantium and canonized for her role in restoring icon worship in the Orthodox Church following the Iconoclasm. Her relics were brought to Corfu along with those of Ag. Spyridon. The cathedral façade dates from the 18th century and the interior is richly adorned with 16th- to 18th-century icons. The **Byzantine Museum of Corfu** is near here, up the steps from Arseniou St, with fine exhibits of Byzantine icons (at time of writing closed indefinitely for restoration). On the same street is the **Solomos Museum**, with a collection of old photographs and memorabilia associated with the poet Dionysos Solomos (*6–9 pm weekdays*).

On a narrow stairway off Philharmoniki St, **Ag. Nikolaos** had the distinction of once serving as the parish church for the King of Serbia. After the defeat of the Serbian army by the Austro–Hungarians in 1916, the King, his government, and some 150,000 Serbs took refuge on Corfu. A third of them died shortly thereafter from the flu and are buried on **Vido island**. Boats from the Old Port regularly make the trip to Vido; the Venetians fortified it after the Turks built a gun battery on it to attack the Old Fortress in 1537. The walls were demolished by the British, and today the island is a quiet refuge with footpaths and a little beach, and a memorial to the Serbs.

Garitsa and the Southern Suburbs

South of the Old Fortress, **Garitsa Bay** is believed to have been the harbour of King Alcinoos of the Phaeacians. Amid its neo-Classical buildings, is a **Municipal Art Gallery** on Moustoxidi St (*10–1 and 6–9*), and on Kolokotroni St the **British Cemetery** is set in beautiful, peaceful gardens; the graves, many with intriguing headstones, date from the beginning of British protectorate.

The star attraction in the district of Garitsa is the **Archaeology Museum** (*open 8.30–3, Sun 9.30–2.30, closed Mon*), with an excellent collection of finds from the island and nearby mainland, including the famous wall-sized Gorgon Pediment discovered near the 5th-century BC temple of Artemis Kanoni, housed in a room all to itself. Other items are from the 7th-century BC **Menecrates tomb**, found in the 19th century in an excellent state of preservation, and still standing at the junction of Marassli and Kiprou St.

South of Garitsa is the suburb of **Anemomilos** ('windmills'), where for a small fee you can swim at the beach of **Mon Repos**. Mon Repos palace above was built by Sir Frederick, the second High Commissioner of the Ionian State, for his Corfiot wife. The Greek royal family later adopted it as a summer villa; the Duke of Edinburgh, Phil the Greek was born there. Here, too, is one of the oldest churches on the island, the 11th-century **Ag. Iassonos and Sosipater** (two martyrs instructed by St Paul). The martyrs' tombs and rare icons are inside; the church is one of the island's best examples of Byzantine architecture.

It is a short stroll to **Analypsis**, just south of Mon Repos. Near the Venetian church, along the wall of Mon Repos, a path leads to the **spring of Kardaki**, which flows from the mouth of a lion; the Venetians used it to supply their ships. The cold water is good, but an inscription above warns: 'Every stranger who wets his lips here to his home will not return.' Below the spring are the ruins of a 6th-century BC temple. It is one of the most tranquil spots in Corfu.

Kanoni, at the southern tip of the little peninsula, is named for the old cannon once situated on the bluff, where two cafés now overlook the pretty bay, the harbour of ancient Corcyra. Two islets protected it: that of the picturesque convent **Panayia Vlancharina**, now connected to the shore by a causeway, and **Pontikonissi**, the Isle of the Mouse, with a 13th-century chapel, **Ag. Pnevmatos**. Pontikonissi was the Phoenician ship that brought Odysseus home to Ithaca, but which, on its way home, the angry Poseidon smote 'with his open palm, and made the ship a rock, fast rooted in the bed of the deep sea', according to the *Odyssey*. Bus no. 3 from Corfu town passes all the above suburbs of gardens and trees, its route ending at Kanoni.

Where to Stay

luxury

There's a cache of luxurious high rise palaces in Kanoni, like the **Corfu Hilton**, a hotel and bungalow complex, ✆ 36 540, and one of the few hotels in Greece with a bowling alley, but a room here could cost 30,000 dr. in high season. In the same league, north of Corfu town, at Komeno Bay, is the **Astir Palace**, ✆ 91 481.

expensive

For old-style elegance, no hotel on Corfu can compete with the **Cavalieri Corfu**, located on the Esplanade at 4 Kapodistriou, ✆ 39 336, in a renovated French mansion; comfortable, air conditioned and rated class A. In the old port there's the **Astron Hotel** in a charming neo-Classical structure at 15 Donzelotou, ✆ 39 505.

moderate

A little further along the Esplanade from the Cavalieri Hotel is a class C hotel, the **Arcadion** at 44 Kapodistriou, ✆ 37 671. Next to it, in another old building, is the gallant class D **Hotel New York**, ✆ 39 922. The **Bella Venezia**, 4 Napoleon Zambeli, is a renovated old building in a quiet part of the centre of town, ✆ 46 500. If you'd prefer something newer, there's always the **Europa** at the New Port (Mandouki, ✆ 39 304) which has, along with modern, clean rooms, a self-service laundrette. Much lower on the price scale to the competition in Kanoni, but in an equally commanding position is the **Royal**, a C class hotel that could be luxury class, with its 3 swimming pools on descending levels, roof garden and its fine view over Mouse Island, ✆ 37 512.

cheap

For something less dear, go to the National Tourist office in the palace, ✆ 39 730 or 30 520, and pick up their list of rooms to let in town. Most of these are in the old quarters and cost 4000 dr. upwards for a bed in season.

At some point of your stay in Corfu you'll spend some time relaxing on the Esplanade, at the Liston, watching the crowds go by or cheering on the local cricket team. Eating in that area can be expensive, but one place that serves good, authentic Greek dishes at a reasonable price is the **Acteon**. One street back on Kapodistriou, **Rex** is even better value—try the local speciality *sofrito* (meat stew with garlic) and pay 2000 dr. for a meal. Just as good is **Dionysos**, off N. Theotiki. The **Bella Napoli** serves international cuisine, with a bias on Italian (3000–4000 dr.). In Kremasti Square the **Venetian Well** has a varied menu which changes daily: Greek, international and oriental specialities (2500 dr.). **Pizza Pete**, in Arseniou St, overlooking the old port, prides himself on the best in town—a pizza meal will run to 1000 dr. Down in Mandouki, where the ferries dock, **Xenichtes**, 12 Potamou, serves excellent Greek food with a sprinkling of dishes from other countries (2500 dr.), and the **Averof**, at Alipou and Prosselendou St, is a long-established favourite of tourists and locals alike. In Xen. Stratigou St, the smart **Orestes** has dining inside and in a pleasant little garden opposite; if you order their seafood specialities, you'll pay 3000 dr. There are several other fish restaurants in the same area.

South of the fortress in Garitsa one of the most popular and reliable tavernas is **Koromios**, where it's difficult to run up a bill of more than 2500 dr. A little way out of town to the south at Kynoplastes is **Gloupos**, where you can watch folkdancing from your table. Nearby, on the Achillion road (about 7 km from town) are two tavernas with live music and good, reasonably priced food, the **Barbathomas**, with meat specialities, and **Pontis**, with a big selection of mezedes, spit-roasted lamb, charcoal grills and local dishes; you can eat well at either for 2500 dr. On the road out to Kontokali (take a taxi) the **Mandarin Chinese Restaurant** has an excellent reputation for top class food and swift service, and its splendid view does justice to the Peking Duck (3000 dr.). For a perfectly artificial evening, **Danilia's Village** is a reconstruction of a typical, old Corfiot settlement, with museum, shopping arcade, folklore museum, and displays of traditional Ionian dancing. It's one of Corfu's bigger attractions and a colourful night out, although the food doesn't match the quality of the floor show. Tickets available from most travel agents or hotel reception.

North of Corfu Town

The roads along the east coast of Corfu are quite good and hotel and resort developers have followed them nearly every inch of the way. To the immediate north begins a long series of beach, hotel and restaurant complexes, along with most of Corfu's campsites, at Kontokali, Gouvia, Dassia, Ipsos and Pirgi. **Kontokali**, 8 km from Corfu town, and **Gouvia**, a little further north, overlook a lagoon once used by the Venetians as a harbour, and today as a popular marina for visiting yachts. Both villages offer watersports and reasonable swimming off the pebble beach. A few kilometres further north **Dassia** has a long, narrow sand and shingle beach fringed by olive groves, a favourite for sports from waterskiing to paragliding. From here you can take boat trips to Kassiopi (north), Mouse Island and Benitses (south).

If a good night's sleep is a priority, avoid **Ipsos**, north of Dassia where the plethora of bars and discos reverberate till dawn. Its long scimitar of beach set against cliffs in the background is attractive. Again, there are plenty of watersports along this stretch of sand which extends into the small village of **Pirgi**, now totally given over to tourism. You can escape the frenetic crowds by carrying on just to the north, where the mountains meet the sea to form a series of small coves and tiny beaches. Here, **Kouloura**, a kilometre or so from the rugged Albanian coast, is a lovely seaside hamlet, which (as yet) has not succumbed to the developers, unlike its neighbour **Kalami**. Kouloura was favoured by Venetians: note the 16th-century **Kouartanou Gennata**, part villa and part fortified tower, and two 17th-century mansions, **Vassila** and **Prosalenti**. Near Kouloura, a steep, twisting path descends to the pretty **Kaminaki** beach; the reward is a fine pebbly beach with the clearest of water. There are some watersports here, and a few beach tavernas. The brothers Durrell lived in a seaside villa here in the 1930s. Both have written about the island: Lawrence Durrell in *Prospero's Cell* and Gerald, the naturalist, in *My Family and Other Animals*.

Behind Kouloura looms 900-m **Mt Pantokrator**, Corfu's highest point. Its slopes can be tackled from the village of **Nissaki** (south), a charming fishing hamlet and quiet resort, where goat tracks lead down to little coves. From Nissaki, find your way to the village of **Palio Sinies**, from where the path to the summit of Pantokrator is an arduous one, but rewarded with a wondrous display of flora, and a view of emerald Corfu spread at your feet and white-capped Albanian peaks on the mainland.

Kassiopi

Kassiopi lies at the northern end of the good paved road. An important Hellenistic town founded by Pyrrhus of Epirus, Kassiopi flourished under the Romans who surrounded it with great walls. Its famous shrine of Zeus Cassius was visited by Cicero and Emperor Nero; its Byzantine fortress was the first place in Greece to fall to Robert Guiscard's Normans, who invaded from their fief in Calabria, after first pillaging Rome. As every subsequent marauder from the north passed by Kassiopi to reach Corfu town, the town bore the brunt of their attacks. When after a long struggle the Venetians finally took the fortress, they rendered it useless to avenge themselves. Without their defences the Kassiopians suffered terribly at the hands of the Turks and the town lost all of its former importance.

The ruined fortress still stands above the village, guarding only wild flowers and sheep. Although still a fishing village, Kassiopi has discovered the profits to be made from the tourist trade and has become one of Corfu's busiest resorts, with a more refined atmosphere than Benitses. Most visitors stay in smart apartments or villas. There are four small, well-equipped beaches reached by footpath from the headland, and when you're tired of windsurfing or basting yourself belly up on the beach you can explore the rocky coastline on foot. The more adventurous (and hardy) can go inland towards **Bodholahos**, where a fairly steep climb into the hinterland affords beautiful views of Kassiopi and coastline.

If you take the road from **Spartilas** to **Perithia**, a charming cobblestoned village nestling in the hills, you'll have a rough but memorable ride through some of the island's most beautiful countryside. **Ag. Panteleimonos**, another inland village, has a huge ruined tower mansion called **Polylas**, complete with prisons used during the Venetian occupation. All along the north coast from **Roda** (another small resort, where egg and chips seems to be everyone's special of the day) to Sidari are fine sandy beaches, considered among the best on Corfu; one is **Akaravi**, a half-hour walk east from Roda, with a large sand and shingle beach framed by gorgeous scenery.

Sidari, although almost entirely given over to tourism (like so many Corfu resorts, British tour operators seem to have the monopoly), is one of the most charming spots on the island, a contrast of lush greenery and picturesque sandstone cliffs, eroded by the wind to form strangely shaped caves. In the bay is the **Canal d'Amour**, a peculiar rock formation said to be two lovers—swim between them and you are guaranteed eternal love, which is more than can be said for the local disco. There are less crowded beaches near Sidari at **Peroulades**, whose sandy beach is divided by a cliff; at **Arillas**, a wide, sandy bay with an attractive backdrop of green hills; at **Ag. Stefanos**, a rather characterless bay with villas and served by two hotels, yet nonetheless uncrowded even at the height of summer; and at **Ag. Georgios**, another long, sandy stretch of beach under steep cliffs, just in the budding stages of development. This whole northwest corner of Corfu is covered with forests; be warned that the roads can grind down the best shock absorbers. Between Sidari and Roda, **Karoussades**, with the 16th-century mansion of the famous Theotoki family, is a pretty agricultural centre; there is good swimming at sandy **Astrakeri** beach.

Northwest of Corfu are three islets, **Othonos** (the largest), **Erikoussa** and **Mathraki**, comprising the westernmost territory of Greece. Nowadays the easiest way to visit the islands is on an organized excursion from Sidari or Corfu, or in the summer from Ag. Stefanos. On Othonos a well-preserved medieval fort, **Kastri**, can be seen on a pine-covered hill. Olives and grapes are produced locally, and fresh fish is always available. Many places on the islets are still without electricity, and the population consists mainly of women whose husbands fish or work in America.

Paliokastritsa and the Western Beaches

Paliokastritsa, endowed with beautiful horseshoe bay and sandy coves, olive and almond groves, mountains and forests, has become the major resort area in west Corfu, jam-packed in the summer; in the early spring, however, you can easily believe its claim to have been the fabled home of the princess Nausica. On a promontory above town, **Paliokastritsa monastery** was built in 1228 on the site of a Byzantine fortress, and tarted up by an abbot with rococo taste in the 1700s. Inside, a one-room museum contains some very old icons; outside, a peach of a view of the sapphire sea below. The best view of all however, is on the steep climb (or drive) out of Paliokastritsa through cypress and pine woods towards the village of **Lakones** and its celebrated Bella Vista taverna. Behind Lakones rises the island's third highest peak, with more splendid views over the island.

Lakones itself is the hub of the loveliest walks on Corfu, especially to the formidable **Angelokastro** (you can also walk from Paliokastritsa). Built in the 13th century by the Byzantine despot of Epirus, Michael Angelos, it is mostly ruined, but makes an impressive sight perched on the wild red rocks over a 300 m precipice. Angelokastro played a major role during the various raids on the island, sheltering the surrounding villagers (as well as the Venetian governor, who lived there). However, the Corfiots were rarely content to stay behind the walls of Angelokastro, and often spilled out to attack their attackers. If you have a car, the mountain roads from Lakones north to Roda through the little villages of **Chore-opiskopi**, **Valanion** (3 km on a byroad) and **Nimfes** offer a lovely bucolic journey through the Corfu of yesteryear.

East of Paliokastritsa stretches the fertile, startlingly flat and intensely cultivated **Ropa plain**. To the south are good beaches and resorts at **Ermones** (another candidate for Odysseus' landing point) and **Glyfada**, one of the island's best. Unfortunately it fills up during the day with hotel residents and day-trippers, but early evening is perfect for a swim here, with steep cliffs dropping straight down into the blue bay. **Pelekas**, a 17th-century village up on a mountain ridge, was Kaiser Wilhelm II's favourite spot to watch the sunset; busloads of people come out every evening in the summer to do the same, from a tower known as the **Kaiser's Throne**. During the day, Miriotissa beach at Pelekas is Corfu's unofficial naturist beach. After sunset the village throbs to the sound of disco music.

Southern Corfu

The half of the island south of Corfu town has attracted the worst excesses of tourism on the island, especially the east coast. The more inaccessible west coast is more worthwhile: continuing south of Pelekas is **Ag. Gordios** with a lovely, sheltered 2-mile-long beach that so far has scarcely been developed. A Byzantine castle at **Gardiki**, south of Ag. Gordios, was another work by the despot of Epirus, Michael Angelos II. This is one of the most unspoilt areas of Corfu, and is a good starting point for some excellent walks. A minor road by Gardiki leads in 4 km to Corfu's only lake, **Limni Korission**, which is separated from the sea by a long stretch of dunes; in spring and autumn it fills with migratory birds. Nearby **Ag. Mathias** is a serene place to daydream under the plane tree and write up your diary, disturbed only by the occasional roar of hired scooters and jeeps as they zip through the village on a quest for true peace and quiet in this least discovered corner of the island. The village remains delightfully Greek, where the locals are more concerned about their olive crop than threatened decreases in tourist numbers. There are 24 churches in, or near, the village, and by asking around you can find your way down the steep hill slopes to the really peaceful beaches of **Tria Avlakia, Paramonas** and **Skithi**, with a few rooms and the odd inexpensive taverna. **Lagoudia**, two islets off the southwest coast, are the home of a tribe of donkeys; some of their ancestors were eaten by a boatload of Frenchmen who were wrecked there for three days.

Other fine beaches, deserted for the most part, line the southwest coast to **Ag. Georgios**, recommended for its swimming, although the village has few charms. **Lefkimi**, in the centre of a large fertile plain, is Corfu's second most important village but not terribly interesting if you aren't a farmer; nearby **Kavos**, however, has an important monastery, **Prokopios** at Arkodila and an excellent beach with all variety of watersports; it also has a limited but lively nightlife as does **Asprocavos**, both famous for their white sand.

Heading north up the east coast towards Corfu town, **Moraitika, Miramare** and **Benitses** are tourist babylons. British pubs and rowdy crowds have turned Benitses into Corfu's Costa Brava (at its worst), to the point where many of the resort's former enthusiasts have moved out of earshot. One family diversion in Benitses is the **shell museum**, with a colourful collection of shells, coral, fossils, starfish and other natural treasure from the sea (*daily 10–7*). To escape Benitses on foot, walk through the old, residential quarter of the village, past the local cemetery and head off towards **Stavros** and the Benitses Waterworks, built by Sir Frederick Adam, British High Commissioner from 1824–32, a walk through some delightful rural scenery.

For something completely different, visit Corfu's casino (*summer only*) and museum in the Italianate **Achilleion** near Gastouri, perhaps the best kitsch palace in all of Greece—used as a location for the James Bond film *For Your Eyes Only*. Built in 1890 by the Empress Elisabeth ('Sissi') of Austria, the villa was named for that lady's passion for the hero of Homer's *Iliad*; a large marble statue of the wounded Achilleus stands in the garden. When Sissi was assassinated in 1898 by an Italian anarchist, Kaiser Wilhelm made the Achilleion his summer residence from 1908 to 1914. The small museum (*8.45–3.30*) contains, among its curious collection of imperial mementoes, the Kaiser's riding saddle, from which he dictated some of his plans for the First World War. **Perama** on the coast, claims to be the site of King Alcinoos' wonderful garden, and still offers more luxury and swish villas to rent than any other place on this luxurious island.

Festivals

10 July, Ag. Prokopios at Kavos; 14 August, The Procession of Lights at Mandouki; first Friday after Easter, Paliokastritsa; 5–8 July, at Lefkimi; 15 August, Panayias at Kassiopi; 21 May, Union with Greece; procession of Ag. Spyridon in Corfu town on Palm Sunday, Easter, 11 August and first Sunday in November.

Where to Stay

expensive

In lovely Paliokastritsa everything is overpriced; the **Akrotiri Beach**, 5 minutes uphill from the beach enjoys some of the best views, and there's a swimming pool for those who don't want to commute to the sea, © (0663) 41 275. If you're lucky (or book early) you may get one of the 8 rooms right on the beach at the **Pavillion**

Xenia, © (0663) 41 208, with a good restaurant below, and priceless view and location. Glyfada beach is dominated by the **Grand Glyfada Hotel** and its many watersport activities, © 94 201. The **Three Brothers** hotel in Sidari may be full of package tourists, but if they haven't got a room they'll know where to find one, © 95 342. Lastly, for dramatic modern architecture on the beach, stay at the **Ag. Gordios** on Ag. Gordios, © 96 213. Renting villas is big business on Corfu: pick up details from any travel agency.

moderate

There are plenty of hotels in the moderate price range on the coast north of Corfu town, such as the **Pyrros**, © 91 206, at Kontokali, the **Galaxias** at Gouvia, © 91 223, and the **Doria** at Dassia, © 93 865, all at around 6000–8000 dr. for a room, although it's wise to book or at least ring ahead. Some very presentable D class hotels are **Costas Beach**, © 93 205, at Ipsos, or the **Louvre** at Gouvia, © 91 508, but don't expect any original masterpieces here.

cheap

For rooms and information on accommodation outside Corfu town, contact the Tourist Police near the waterfront on 43 Arseniou St, or at the palace. There's a **campground** 2 km inland from Paliokastritsa; others are at Messoghi, Kontokali (the nearest to Corfu town), Ipsos, Karoussades (these two the best on the island), Pirgi and Dafnila. Nearly every village has rooms to let, some, like Kassiopi, Pelekas and Kavos, with long listings. Corfu's **youth hostel** is in Kontokali (take bus no. 7 from San Rocco Square, © 91 202), and an IYHF card is required.

Eating Out

Nearly all beaches, even the more distant and remote, have at least a couple of tavernas, where the speciality is obviously seafood, fresh and simply served. In Ipsos, **Parrotts** has excellent fare for around 3000 dr., and Gouvia's most popular eating place is **Taverna Filippas** (2500 dr.). Up in Sidari the biggest culinary draw for many is the full works British breakfast, but good Greek food can be found at **Sophocles** and the **Canal D'Amour** for a fair price. Paliokastritsa has a number of seafood restaurants. **Chez George** commands the prime location and the highest prices; residents and long term visitors prefer the **Astakos** for its authentic food and reasonable prices. Drinking rather than eating seems to be the order of the day down in Benitses, but the **Marabou** bravely presents some tasty local dishes (2500 dr.), while **Pat's Place** pulls in the visitors with good British standards like roast beef and two veg—2000 dr.

Ithaca (Ithaki)

Every traveller is a citizen of Ithaca.

—the sign in the port.

Ithaca is one of those places that has become a compelling and universal symbol although many who have heard of it have no idea where it is, and those who do visit it usually have a hard time reconciling the island's reality with their idea of Odysseus' beloved home. And yet re-read your Homer before you come, and you'll find that nearly all of his descriptions of Ithaca fit this small mountainous island—it is indeed 'narrow' and 'rocky' and 'unfit for riding horses'. Some ancient and modern scholars, most famously the archaeologist Dörpfeld, have theorized that Homer's Ithaca was elsewhere—Lefkas and Kefalonia are popular contenders. Don't believe them. Thiaki as the locals call their home, the eternal symbol of all homes and journey's end, is the real thing, and 'even if you find it poor,' as Cavafy wrote, 'Ithaca does not deceive. Without Ithaca your journey would have no beauty'.

Ithaca has a jagged, indented coast (as Homer says), but no exceptional beaches and its roads are in such a state that most islanders prefer to travel to distant villages by caique. Its excellent harbour makes it a big favourite with sailors and best of all, it has changed little over the years. The atmosphere is relaxed and low-key, quiet and pleasant.

History

Inhabited from 2000 BC, Ithaca, the name of the prosperous Mycenaean kingdom of the intrepid Odysseus, is believed to have included not only the island proper but the four cities of Kefalonia. In the last 200 years scholars and archaeologists have sought for signs of Odysseus. Schliemann came after his great discovery of Troy, and since Schliemann inevitably found what he was looking for, he unearthed a large structure he immediately called 'Odysseus' Palace', and although it dates from a far later date (700 BC), the name has stuck. Later finds indicate that at least the ancients considered Ithaca Homer's Ithaca. Inscriptions indicate that Odysseus was worshipped as a divine hero, ancient coins bore Odysseus' picture, and pottery decorated with the cock, the symbol of Odysseus, has been found on the island. Homer describes the palace of Odysseus as above 'three seas' and in Stavros a hillock matches the description (over three bays) and where in 1930 two ancient fortifications were discovered that may have been used for signals and beacons to the palace. Then there's the Fountain of Arethusa, where Odysseus met his faithful swineherd Eumaeus, and the cave where he hid the treasure given him by the Phaeacians.

After the Mycenaeans, Ithaca lost most of its importance and even its name; for a period it was humiliatingly known as 'Little Kefalonia'. By the time of the Venetians, invaders and pirates had so despoiled the island that it was all but abandoned, and the Venetians offered generous incentives to anyone who would settle and farm there. Once again Ithaca prospered, but unlike the other Ionian islands, it never had an aristocracy. Ironically, union with Greece in 1864 initiated the great migration from the island, many Ithakians going to Romania, Australia and South Africa. Like their countryman Odysseus, the islanders are well known as great sailors; even those who call Ithaca home spend much of the year away at sea.

To Vassiliki (Lefkas)

Mt. Marmacas

Aphales Bay

Ag. Ilias

Exogi

Kalamos

Ag. Saranta

Platrithias

Frikes

Pilikata

Kioni

Stavros

Spialouisa

Pilos Bay

To Fiskando

Levki

Anogi

Mt. Neritos
(784m / 2572ft)

Kathara
Monastery

Agros
(The field
of Laerles)

Ag. Ioannis

Skinos

Bay of
Dexia

Aetos

VATHI

Castle of Odysseus

Cave of the Nymphs

Piso Aetos

Paleochora

Perachori

Mt. Stefano
(648m / 2126ft)

Perapigadia
(Ligia)

Taxiarchos
Monastery

Fountain of
Arethusa

Ag. Ioannis

To Sami, Patras

N

ITHACA

0   1   2   5 km
0   1   2   3 miles

Daily ferry with Patras, Kefalonia (Sami, Fiskardo and Ag. Efthimia), Vassiliki (Lefkas) and Astakos, frequent connections to Corfu, Paxos and Igoumenitsa.

Tourist Police

See regular police at Vathi, ℭ (0674) 32 205.

Vathi and the South

Vathi, built around the end of a long sheltered bay, is the capital of the island, although little larger than a village itself. Its beautiful harbour, surrounded by mountains on all sides, holds a wooded islet called **Lazaretto** in its embrace, and attracts many yachts. Although devastated by the 1953 earthquake, Vathi was reconstructed as it was and is considered a 'traditional settlement' of Greece. One building that survived the quake is the mansion of the Drakolis family, who brought the first steamship to Greece, which they named the *Ithaka*. The **Archaeology Museum** is behind the Mentor Hotel, housing a collection of vases, offerings and other objects, many dating from Homeric times. In the **church of the Taxiarchos** an icon of Christ is attributed to the young El Greco. An annual conference on Homer, the International Odessa Congress, has taken place in Vathi since 1981.

West of Vathi it's an hour walk to the **Cave of the Nymphs** or Marmarospilia (signposted) where Odysseus hid the gifts of King Alcinoos. The cave is especially interesting for the hole in the roof—'the entrance of the gods'—which permitted the smoke of the sacrifices to rise to heaven. The cave has a few stalactites—bring a torch. Below is the **Bay of Dexia**, where the Phaeacians put the sleeping Odysseus on shore. South of Vathi above the little beach and islet of **Perapigadia**, flows the **Fountain of Arethusa**. According to the myth, Arethusa wept so much when her son Corax was killed that she turned into a spring and it was here that Odysseus, disguised as a beggar, first met the faithful Eumaeus. The water flows from the rock Corax—also mentioned by Homer—and is good to drink, although beware that it has a reputation for increasing the appetite.

The only other real village in the south of Ithaca is **Perachori**, also within walking distance of Vathi. Perachori lies in the island's most fertile region and dates from the Venetians, although the first houses were built in **Paleochora**, where you can see the ruins of the fortified houses and churches, one minus its roof but still adorned with fading Byzantine frescoes. In Perachori the villagers will show you which path to take. Another road from the village goes up to the 17th-century **Monastery of the Taxiarchos** near the top of Mt Stefano. Although not all that much remains, the views from the monastery and the road are good. In August Perachori hosts a wine festival.

North of Vathi

Ithaca has an hourglass figure, with a waist only 500 m wide. This narrow mountain stretch is called **Aetos**. There is a beach in the bay below and at **Piso Aetos** in the west. Overlooking the bay is Schliemann's **Castle of Odysseus**, actually the citadel of the 8th-century BC town of Alalcomenes. Impressive Cyclopean walls and the foundations of a temple remain.

Just north of Aetos is the so-called **Field of Laertes** or Agros, from where a road ascends the slopes of Mt Neritos (formerly Mt Korifi—Ithaca is slowly reclaiming its Homeric names) to the **Monastery of Kathara**, founded in 1696. From the monastery you can see the Gulf of Patras, and even though the monastery is now abandoned, its church of the **Panayia** is kept open in the summer for visitors to see the frescoes and icon attributed to St Luke. From Kathara the road continues to **Anogi**, passing many large and unusually-shaped boulders. The village retains some Venetian ruins, including a campanile and another church dedicated to the **Panayia** with very old frescoes.

The second and better road from Agros follows the west coast. At Ag. Ioannis, just opposite Kefalonia, is a lovely, seldom-used beach, with many trees. **Levki**, the small village to the north, was an important base and port for the resistance movement during the war, and when it was destroyed by the 1953 earthquake, Britain officially adopted it and helped to rebuild it. Further north is **Stavros**, the most important village in the north, overlooking lovely **Polis Bay** ('city bay'), its name referring to the Byzantine city of Ierosalem, which sank into it during an earthquake in the 10th century. A bust of Odysseus in the centre of Stavros looks out over the bay, which has one of Ithaca's more popular beaches. The **Cave of Louizos** on the bay was an ancient cult sanctuary, where archaeologists found a number of items dating back to the Mycenaean age; one of the gods worshipped here was Odysseus (unfortunately the cave and path to it have collapsed). By common consent Odysseus' palace was located at **Pilikata**, just north of Stavros. Although the ruins you see on the site are of a Venetian fort, excavators have found evidence underneath of buildings and roads dating back to the Neolithic era. Some of the finds from Pilikata and the Cave of Louizos are in the small but interesting **Stavros Archaeological Museum** on the Platrithias road (*open 9–2*). The site also fits the Homeric description almost perfectly, in sight of 'three seas' (the bays of Frikes, Polis and Aphales) and 'three mountains' (Neritos, Marmacas and Exogi).

North of Stavros, **Frikes** is a tiny fishing village and port for Fiskardo in Kefalonia and Vassiliki in Lefkas, as well as for daily caiques to Vathi, and a popular stopping-off point for flotilla yachts. There's a new hotel here and rooms and tavernas, as there are in nearby **Kioni**, one of Ithaca's prettiest villages, which has the better beaches. Kioni means 'column', and an ancient one still stands on the altar in the village church. In **Platrithias**, the centre of a group of small settlements north of Stavros, there's a small **ethnographic museum**, at Kolieri. This fertile area is one of the most pleasant on the island to stroll through; it was here that King Odysseus was ploughing his field when he was dragged off to Troy by the Achaeans, never suspecting he'd be gone for 20 years.

Festivals

15 August, Platrithias; 24 June, Ag. Ioannis, at Kioni; mid-August to mid-September, theatre and cultural festival at Vathi; 5–6 August, Sotiros at Stavros; 8 September, Kathara Monastery; 1 May, Taxiarchos and August wine festival, Perachori.

Ithaca as a whole has very little accommodation—four hotels, two of which are in Vathi. Most modern and most expensive is the **Hotel Mentor**, class B, in Vathi on Georgiou Drakouli Street, ✆ 32 433, a bit out of the centre, on the far side of the bay. A bit less dear and more convenient is the **Odysseus**, also in the B category, ✆ 32 381. Although C class, the **Nostos Hotel**, at Frikes, has high rates—7500 dr., which is on a par with the Mentor, ✆ 31 644. Less expensive, but get there early in the summer to find a room, is the **Pension Enoikiazomena** behind the town hall, on a narrow alley off Odysseus Street. The rooms are old but charming; try to get one looking out over the bay. There are also a few rooms to rent, here and in Perachori, Kioni and around Stavros.

In the centre of Vathi, near the main square, is **Trexandiri**, a restaurant serving good local food and, 800 m from town, **Palio Karavo** is a favourite, especially for fish (2000 dr.). Both the Mentor and Odysseus hotels have good restaurants.

Kalamos and Kastus

Kalamos and Kastus, two islands off Meganisi, near Mitikas on the mainland, are under the jurisdiction of Ithaca. Kalamos, the larger one, is connected once a week to Sami, Ithaca, the port Astakos and Meganisi, as well as Nidri and Vassiliki on Lefkas. There is also a more frequent service from Mitikas. There are three small fishing villages on its rocky coast: Kalamos, Episkopi, and Kefali. Only two or three families live on Kastus, now unable to care for all the vineyards which once produced a fine wine.

Kefalonia

Mountainous and lacking the voluptuous lushness of Zakynthos and Corfu, Kefalonia may be the largest of the Ionian islands but supports only 30,000 people, many of whom live in Athens in the winter. Kefaloniotes are among Greece's most famous emigrants (one, Constantine Yerakis, went on to make a fortune in the British East India Company and become Regent of Siam), and it's not uncommon to meet someone whose entire family lives in Canada, Australia or the United States: if the tourist boom has had a positive social benefit, it's that more people can make a living on their beautiful but untamed island. Kefaloniotes are friendly, easy-going people, and have the reputation of being Greece's worst blasphemers.

Although the earthquake in 1953 destroyed many of Kefalonia's grand old houses it has many charms to woo its visitors: fine beaches (one of which, Myrton, is perhaps the most dramatic in all of Greece), two of the country's loveliest caves, and great pine forests to picnic in and walk through, with many splendid views. Because Kefalonia is so large, it is easy to escape the summertime crowds.

History

Recent finds date the first Kefaloniotes to at least 50,000 BC and perhaps earlier; Fiskardo man, as the archaeologists have dubbed him, has proved to have many similarities with his peers in western Sicily and Epirus. The island is also exceptionally rich in its Mycenaean finds. Although the name Kefalonia does not occur in Homer, it is believed that the 'glittering Samos' of the *Odyssey* refers to Kefalonia's mountains, and that the island may well have been part of the kingdom of Odysseus, and certainly the home of many of Penelope's ill-mannered suitors.

Historically the first reference to Kefalonia describes its four city-states: Sami, the most powerful, Pali, Krani and Pronnoi. Hesiod refers to a renamed sanctuary of Zeus which stood on the top of Mt Ainos. Little else, however, is known of the 'Kefalonian Tetrapolis' until the Roman invasion, when the besieged Sami held out heroically for four months before the inevitable defeat, and the equally inevitable sale of its citizens into slavery.

In 1085, the Norman Duke Robert Guiscard of Sicily unsuccessfully besieged the Byzantine forts of the island and died of fever in the village that has taken his name—Fiskardo. If the Kefaloniotes breathed a sigh of relief then, it was too soon; for the next 800 years the island, like its sisters, was to become the plaything of the Normans, of Venice, the Vatican, and a motley assortment of dukes and counts in need of a tax income. Most famous of its occupiers was the pirate Count Matteo Orsini, who lived at the end of the 12th century. In 1483 the Turks captured the island, but lost it again in the early 1500s when Venice and Spain under the Gran Capitan, Gonzalo Fernández de Córdoba besieged and captured the fort of Ag. Georgios and slaughtered the Turkish garrison.

After this the fortress was repaired and the town nearby became the Venetian capital. A huge earthquake caused heavy damage to Ag. Georgios, and by the 18th century it was abandoned, and Argostoli became the new capital. In 1823 Lord Byron showed up on Kefalonia (along with a retinue including his faithful Venetian gondolier Tita) as an agent of the Greek Committee in London before going to die a pathetic death from fever in Missolongi. During the British occupation of the Ionian islands, the Kefaloniotes demanded Greek union more stridently than anyone else, and many nationalist leaders were imprisoned there. Ioannis Metaxas, prime minister-dictator of Greece from 1936 to 1941, came from Kefalonia; and for all his faults has gone down in history for saying 'No' to Mussolini's ultimatum at the beginning of the Second World War—celebrated nationally in November as *Oxi* ('No') day. In 1943, the Italian occupiers of the island joined forces with the EAM (Greek National Liberation Front) and for seven days fought the invading Germans. Three thousand of the Italians who were forced to surrender died in the subsequent mass executions ordered, it is said, by Hitler himself.

Connections

By air: daily flights from Athens, several a day in summer, and weekly summer flights to Zakynthos; frequent charters from British cities.

By sea: ferry daily from Sami to Ithaca, Lefkas, Patras and Brindisi, twice a week with Piraeus, Corfu and Ancona, once a week with Crete, Samos and Kuşadasi; every half hour from Argostoli to Kilini, on the Peloponnese, daily from Fiskardo to Ithaca and Lefkas, Ag. Efthimia to Ithaca and Astakos, on the mainland, Pessada to Zakynthos, Poros to Kilini.

By bus: From Athens, bus three times a day.

Around Kefalonia: Bus services to the rest of the island have been improved and next to the KTEL station on the waterfront there is a local tourist office to help you plan excursions. Many taxi drivers specialize in trips around the island, and caiques go to the more popular beaches. There is a car ferry across the Gulf of Argostoli six times a day from Argostoli to Lixouri.

NTOG, Argostoli (0671) 22 248.

Tourist police, see regular police, Argostoli (0671) 22 200.

Argostoli

When Kefalonia was so badly damaged by the earthquake in 1953—only Fiskardo, in the extreme north, survived unscathed—the wealthy emigrants of the island donated large sums of money for the reconstruction of its villages. A fair portion of their money has gone to rebuilding the island's capital **Argostoli** (pop. 10,000), situated on a thumb of the great bay in the south. Part of this bay is so shallow that the British built the **Drapanos Bridge** over it, with its many low arches and commemorative obelisk that considerably shortens the journey to the other side of the bay. The port of Argostoli is especially safe and used for winter berthing of yachts and larger ships.

Argostoli has more public buildings than most island capitals, nearly all grouped around the large, central **Plateia Vallanou**. Pre-earthquake Argostoli was famous for its bell towers, some of which have been rebuilt—don't miss the German Expressionist tower of the Catholic church near the square. Two museums are nearby: the **Archaeology Museum** contains a room of Mycenaean finds—bronze swords and gold jewellery, coins from the four ancient cities of Kefalonia, and a bronze bust of a man from the early 3rd century BC that's startlingly modern. The **Koryalenios Historical and Folklore Museum** in the basement of the library on Ilia Zervou St contains the Venetian records of the island, icons, a traditional bedroom and other ethnographic items.

There are two sandy beaches south of Argostoli, the organized **Platis Yialos** and the free **Makri Yialos**. A pleasant walk along **Lassi**, the little peninsula north of Argostoli, leads to one of Kefalonia's more peculiar features—the **Katavothri** or swallow holes, where the sea is sucked into two large tunnels under the ground. No one knew where the water emerged until 1963, when Austrian geologists poured a vast quantity of dye into the water. Fifteen days later the dye appeared in the lake of the Melissani cave and at Karavomylos, near Sami, on the other side of the island. The sea mills that harnessed the rushing water, which were destroyed by the earthquake, have since been reconstructed. On the other side of the peninsula is the lovely **lighthouse of Ag. Theodoros**, reconstructed in its rotunda of columns. On the other side of Argostoli, above the lagoon formed by the Drapanos Bridge and up off the road to Sami are the massive 7th-century BC walls of the acropolis of ancient **Krani**.

Lixouri and Western Kefalonia

Across the bay from Argostoli is the capital's longstanding rival, **Lixouri**, Kefalonia's second city, all new houses on wide streets and in itself not terribly interesting. In the central square near the waterfront stands a **statue of poet Andreas Laskaratos**, a local man of letters of the 19th century, remembered in particular for his dislike of the church. He was a poor man with a large family to support, and he kept heckling the priests so much that they finally excommunicated him—in Greek *aforismos*, meaning that the body will not decompose after death. When Laskaratos found out he hurried home, collected his children's decomposing shoes and returned to the priest, asking him to please excommunicate the footwear, too. You can get a sense of what pre-earthquake Lixouri was like on the west end of town at the **Iakovatos Mansion**, a rare survival and now a library and icon museum.

Lixouri is on the large westerly peninsula of Kefalonia that once formed part of the ancient city of Pali. There are beaches at **Michalitsata** and **Lepeda**, both sandy, and **Ag. Georgios** further south, a long stretch of golden sand most easily reached by caique. Just south of it the famous **Kounopetra** once created the optical illusion of opening and closing; the earthquake, however, fouled up the magic, and likewise destroyed the houses on the pretty, deserted **Vardiana islet** off the coast. The peninsula is shot full of caves: the most interesting, **Drakondi Spilio**, can be reached from the monastery of **Ag. Paraskevi Tafion**. Another monastery, **Kipoureon**, perched on the west cliffs, has spectacular views and overnight rooms. South of Manzavinata there's another fine beach, **Xi**, a long crescent of reddish sand. North of Lixouri there are more beaches: **Ag. Spyridon** near town and safe for children and **Petani**, pretty and quiet and rarely crowded. Even more remote—accessible by a minor road—is another beach called **Ag. Spyridon**, a stretch of sand tucked into the northernmost tip of the Pali peninsula.

Southeast of Argostoli: the Livatho and Mt Ainos

Most of Kefalonia's rural population lives in the fertile region of valleys and rolling hills called the Livatho. At one village, **Metaxata**, Byron rented a house for four months in 1823 and finished his satirical rejection of romanticism, *Don Juan* while dithering over what to do as the representative of the London Committee, while each Greek faction fighting for independence jostled for the poet's attention—and especially his money. Nearby **Kourkomelata** was rebuilt by the wealthy Kefaloniote shipowner Vergotis; everything is as bright, new and pastel-coloured as a suburb of California.

On the road from Metaxata to Travliarata is the convent of **Ag. Andreas**, its bizarre prize possession the sole of St Andrew's foot. The quake of 1953 shook loose the whitewash in the interior of the church, revealing frescoes that date back to 1700 and have now been restored. Above the church looms the **Castle of Ag. Georgios**, and the town that until 1757 was the capital of Kefalonia. Most of the impressive ruins date from the early 16th century, when the citadel was rebuilt by Nikolaos Tsimaras. Held by the Byzantines, Franks, Turks and, after the fierce siege of 1500, the Venetians, it retains most of its walls, a ruined Catholic church, some forgotten coats-of-arms, and a bridge built by the French during their occupation. The castle commands a wonderful view of the surrounding plains and mountains; check opening hours at the tourist office.

To the east lies the green **plain of Omalos** and the **monastery of Ag. Gerasimos**, containing the body of the patron saint of the island. If 50% of Corfiots are named Spiros after St Spyridon, then 50% of the Kefaloniotes are named Gerasimos after their saint, whose speciality is intervening in mental disturbances, especially if the afflicted keeps an all-night vigil at his church on 20 October, his feast day. Architecturally, the monastery is most notable for its grotesque and ungainly bell tower. From the Argostoli–Sami road a branch leads off to Megalos Soros, the highest point of majestic **Mt Ainos**, at 1628 m the loftiest in the Ionian islands. Before the arrival of Venetian shipbuilders the mountain was blanketed with the unique Kefalonian black pine—*Abies cefalonica*—so dense that the Venetians called Ainos the 'Black Mountain'. In 1962 what has survived of the forest was declared a national park, and it's still impressive to stroll among the tall, scented trees seemingly on top of the world; on a clear day the Peloponnese, Zakynthos, Ithaca, Lefkas, the Gulf of Patras and even Corfu are spread out below as if on a great blue platter.

The Southeast Coast: Beaches and the Virgin's Snakes

The south coast of Kefalonia, busting with good sandy beaches, has become the island's tourism magnet. **Afrata, Trapezaki** and **Lourdata** (the longest and most crowded) have good beaches, while **Katelios** is a pretty place with springs, greenery and a beach, and becomes more popular every year, as does **Skala**, boasting another long beach. Near Skala a Roman villa was excavated, with 3rd-century mosaic floors, portraying Envy being devoured by wild beasts and two men making sacrifices to the gods. To the north of Skala a 7th-century BC temple of Apollo has also been discovered, though most of its stones were used to construct the nearby chapel of Ag. Georgios.

Just inland, Kefalonia's most unusual religious event also takes place in the village of **Markopoulo**. On 15 August, small harmless snakes 'inoffensive to the Virgin Mary' with little crosses on their heads, suddenly appear in the village streets. Formerly they slithered to the church, went inside and mysteriously disappeared near the Virgin's icon. Nowadays to keep them from being run over, the villagers collect them in glass jars and bring them to the church, where they are released after the service and immediately disappear as they did in the past. Although sceptics believe that the church is simply along the route of the little snakes' natural migratory trail, the faithful point out that the snakes fail to appear when the island is in distress—as during the German occupation and in the year of the earthquake.

The road north, between Skala and **Poros** has been improved but is still narrow and difficult, although worth the trouble for the scenery and the pretty 'Poros Gap'. Because of its direct connection with Kilini, Poros is rapidly developing as the island's major resort area.

North Kefalonia: Caverns and Castles

Sami, the port for ships to Patras and Italy, is a growing resort in its own right, with beaches and a campsite, although the town itself is not very interesting. On the two hills behind the port are the **walls of ancient Sami**, where the citizens put up a heroic resistance to the Romans in 187 BC. Sami is also the best base for visiting Kefalonia's magnificent grottoes: **Drogarati cave**, near the hamlet of Haliotata, is a fairyland of orange and yellow stalactites and stalagmites; one of its great chambers has such fine acoustics that in the summer concerts are held there. The other, steep-sided **Melissani** ('purple cave') is a half-hour's walk from

Sami; small boats wait to paddle you across its mysterious salt water lake (supplied by the swallow holes near Argostoli), immersing you in a vast shimmering play of blue and violet colours, caught by the sun filtering through a hole in the roof 30 m overhead. *Both caves open 8–7 in summer, but close after October.* There are other, undeveloped caves in the vicinity of Sami, many with lakes and dangerous, precipitous drops, best of which is **Anglaki cave**, near Poulata.

Ag. Efphimia, the port for Ithaca and Astakos, also has a harbour for yachts and a hotel. Continuing up to the northernmost tip of Kefalonia, tiny **Fiskardo** derives its name from a mispronunciation of Robert Guiscard, who died there and was buried in a cairn (by the hotel). Some of Fiskardo's Venetian houses survived the 1953 earthquake, a poignant last reminder of the handsome architecture Kefalonia once had; some have been fixed up for guests (*see* below).

South of Fiskardo on the Argostoli road, is the magnificent castle of **Assos** set on a small peninsula, toy-sized from the lofty mountain road. Built by the ancient Greeks, the Venetians restored it and sent a proveditor to govern it. On one of the harbours formed by the peninsula, is the little fishing village of Assos, once full of sleepy charm, now unfortunately 'discovered' in a big way. Just to the south of it lies the superb beach of **Myrton**, embraced by sheer cliffs, spectacularly snow-white against a sea so blue it hurts.

Festivals

16 August and 20 October, Ag. Gerasimos; 15 August, Panayias at Markopoulo; 23 April, Ag. Georgios; 21 May, Ag. Konstantinos near Argostoli; carnival celebrations on the last Sunday and Monday before Lent; Easter festival in Lixouri; 21 May, Festival of the Radicals (celebrating union with Greece) in Argostoli; 23 June, Ag. Ioannis, at Argostoli; first Saturday after 15 August, Robola Festival of wine in Fragata.

Where to Stay

Expensive

On the beach at Lassi, there's the A class **Mediterranee**, the island's pride and joy, with all mod cons and air conditioned rooms, and offering a variety of land and sea sports, but its high summer rates will have you reaching for your fattest credit card, © (0671) 28 761. On the beach Platis Yialos there's the **White Rocks**, another A class hotel-bungalow complex with air conditioning and other assorted comforts, © (0671) 23 167.

moderate

Hotels in Argostoli can be surprisingly expensive; an example is the class C **Cefalonia Star** at 50 Metaxa St, © (0671) 23 180, at 8000 dr. in season. Alternatively there's the **Regina**, two streets up from the waterfront at 24 Vergoti, for a little less, © 23 557. In Sami there are more rooms to rent and two decent, clean hotels, the

Ionion near the ferry, © (0674) 22 035, and the **Kyma**, © 22 064. On a more real-
istic level in Lassi is the C class **Irilena**, © (0671) 23 172. In bijou Fiskardo, where
everybody likes to stay, four typical houses have been renovated by the NTOG; for
reservations, write to Paradosiakos Ikismos Fiskardou, Kefalonia, © (0674) 51 398.
There are two pensions, renovated and done out in traditional style, the **Filoxenia**,
© 51 487, and the **Fiskardona**, © 51 484, and self-contained apartments for rent—
Stella, © 51348, and **Kaminakia**, © 51 578. Although used by tour operators, the
Summery in Lixouri, © 91 771, is a pleasant place to stay.

cheap

In Argostoli you can get basic rooms at **Hara**, 87 Leof. Vergoti, © 22 427, and
Parthenon, 4 Zakynthou, © 22 246. Simple accommodation may also be found in
Lixouri, Poros, Lassi, Skala, Ag. Efthimia and Fiskardo. There's a **campsite** near Sami
on Karavomilos beach, 1 km from town and near Argostoli at Fanari, 2 km from
town.

Eating Out

In Sami there are two tavernas side by side on the waterfront, **Saoulis** and **Port
Sami**, both serving fish, regular Greek dishes and some local specialities (meat pie
and octopus pie); the latter has a delicious rosé retsina. Count on 1500–2000 dr. for a
meal at either. In Argostoli, the **Kaliva** has an attractive garden to match its pleasant
prices, and is popular with tourists and locals alike. On the waterfront the **Kalafate** is
also good and reasonable. In Lassi the most popular spot is the **Ambassador**, for its
excellent Greek food, garden and prices. Fiskardo, which is used to loads of
yachtsmen dropping in, boasts a fine fish restaurant in the harbour, **Dendrinos**
(3000 dr.), and it's worth searching out **Nicolas' Garden** (if Nicolas doesn't find you
first), hidden up a narrow alley in the middle of the village; excellent food in a
relaxing setting (2500 dr.). In Assos there isn't much choice—most people go to
Kokolis. In Lixouri **Akroyiali** has good fish in season, and it doesn't cost an arm and
a leg. There is a selection of little tavernas in Poros and Skala.

Kythera

The opening of the Corinth canal doomed any commercial importance Kythera once had by
virtue of its position between the Ionian and Aegean seas. Today, unless you take the small
plane from Athens, the island is rather difficult to reach. It has so lost its connections with its
sister Ionian islands far to the northwest that politically it now belongs to Attica and is administered from Piraeus. In this century the population has decreased by more than half, most of
them emigrating to the other side of the world; some 100,000 people of Kytheran origin now
live in Australia ('Big Kythera' according to the locals, when other Greeks call their island the
Kangaroo Colony). All the emigrants who can, come back to Kythera in the summer, consti-
tuting its main tourist rush. With only a few hotels and rooms to let, the island is one of the
quietest in Greece, and the non-Aussies who do visit are usually of the hardy Hellenophile

type anxious to escape their own countrymen, or the wealthy who have scattered their villas all over Kythera. The island is not without its charms, although it hardly matches the shimmering luxuriance of Watteau's *Pélérinage à l'Ile de Cythère*.

History

When Zeus castrated his father, Cronus, then ruler of the world, he cast the bloody member into the sea. This gave birth to Aphrodite, the goddess of love, who rose out of the foam at Kythera, but finding it small she moved to Paphos, Cyprus, and was called either the Cypriot or the Kytherian. An ancient sanctuary dedicated to Aphrodite on Kythera was the most sacred of all such temples in Greece.

Aphrodite was known as Astarte by Kythera's first settlers, the Phoenicians, who came for the murex shells, from which they extracted a purple dye to colour royal garments, and from which the island derived its other early name, Porphyrousa. The Minoans, the first in Greece to worship Aphrodite, made Kythera a central trading station, for its location at the crossroads between Crete and the mainland, and the Aegean and Ionian Seas. The location was also convenient for aggressors: Kythera was invaded 80 times in recorded history. Particularly frightful were the visits of the Saracens from Crete, so ferocious in the 10th century that the island was abandoned altogether until Nikephoros Phokas won Crete back for Byzantium.

The rulers of Kythera in the Middle Ages were the Eudhaemonoyannis family from Monemvassia. The Venetians occupied the island in 1204, but with the help of Emperor Michael Palaeologos, Kythera was regained for the Eudhaemonoyannis, and for long years it served as a refuge for Byzantine nobles, especially after the Turks grabbed the Peloponnese. However, in 1537, Barbarossa stopped at Kythera on his way home from the unsuccessful siege of Corfu and destroyed the island. The Venetians occupied the island again in the 15th century and called it 'Cerigo', the name by which it is known in the old history books. The Turks took over again in the early 18th century; in 1864 it was ceded to Greece by the British with the rest of the Ionian islands.

Connections

At least one flight a day from Athens; hydrofoil five times a week from Gythion, three times a week from Piraeus, Hydra, Spetses and Monemvassia; regular ferry boat from Neapolis daily, five times a week with Gythion, twice a week with Monemvassia, Crete and Piraeus, once a week with Antikythera.

Tourist Police

See regular police, ✆ (0733) 31 206.

Chora

Kythera, or **Chora**, the capital of Kythera, is a pretty blue and white village, 275 m above the port of Kapsali, impressively guarded by a fortress finished by the Venetians in 1503. Chora's location was supposedly selected by pigeons, who took the tools of the builders from a less protected site. Ten old **Venetian mansions** in Chora still retain their coats-of-arms, and a small **museum**, generally open in the mornings, contains artefacts dating back to Minoan times. Below, a 20-minute walk down the hill, **Kapsali** has a large house with rooms to let owned by one Emmanuel Comnenus (probably a descendant of the Byzantine nobles who fled to Kythera from Mystra), a few restaurants and two beaches.

Buses leave Chora about once a day for the major villages of the island. Alternatively there are taxis which charge a set fee for different excursions. **Kalamos**, just east of Chora, is within walking distance. One of its churches, Ag. Nikitis, has a pretty bell tower, and there is a taverna by the square. A dirt road continues across the rugged landscape to **Vroulaia**, a pebble beach and taverna, where many people pitch their tents.

Northwest of Chora

From Chora the paved road heads north to **Livadi**, where once-golden wheatfields have run wild from a lack of labour and there's a pretty bridge of 13 arches. Heading west from Livadi via Drimon is the important **Monastery of the Panayia Mirtidion** with a tall carved bell tower, set on the wild west coast among cypresses, flowers, peacocks. The monastery is named for a golden icon of the Virgin and Child, whose faces are blackened with age—a sign of special holiness that attracts a huge number of pilgrims to the monastery on 15 August. Two small islets just off shore are said to be pirate ships that the Virgin turned to stone for daring to attack the monastery.

North of Drimon, **Milopotamos** is the closest thing to Watteau's vision of Kythera. It is the island's loveliest village, criss-crossed by tiny canals of clear water—so much water, in fact, that the toilet in the valley is in a constant state of flush. The stream valley through the middle of town is called the Neraida, or Nymph, and a good restaurant there has music and dancing at night. An old watermill lies along the path to the waterfall, surrounded by the ancient plane trees, flowers and banana plants; on quiet evenings you can hear the nightingales sing.

The ghost town **Kato Chora** lies just below Milopotamos in the walls of a Venetian fortress built in 1560. Above the gate there's a bas-relief of the lion of St Mark and a Latin inscription, welcoming you to a desolation of empty stone houses. By the sea below is the cave **Ag. Sophia**, at the end of a rugged, descending road. In the past the cave was used as a church, and inside there are frescoes and mosaics, as well as stalactites and stalagmites and small lakes that go on and on...some say it tunnels all the way under Kythera to Ag. Pelagias. And at Ag. Pelagias a sign does indeed point down a rocky hill to a mysterious Ag. Sophia.

The East Coast

Skandeia was the port of the ancient town of Kythera, mentioned by Thucydides, and ruins of the settlement may be seen at the site now known as **Kastri**. The ancient town itself was above Paliopolis up at **Paliokastro**; here worshippers came to the ancient temple of Urania Aphrodite 'Queen of the Mountains' to pay their respects to the goddess. The Christians, however, destroyed the sanctuary to build the church of Ag. Kosmas (with the temple's Doric columns). All that remains at Paliokastro are the acropolis walls.

From Paliopolis the coastal road leads to **Avlemonas**, where the Minoans had a trading settlement dating from 2000 BC until the rise of the Mycenaeans. By the sea is a small octagonal fortress built by the Venetians, who left a coat-of-arms and a few rusting cannon inside. There is also a small beach.

Much further north is **Palio Chora** (or Ag. Dimitriou) the town built by the Eudhaemonoyannis clan in the Monemvassian style. High on the rocks, it was hidden from the sea—Barbarossa found it only by capturing the inhabitants and forcing them to tell him where it was. Beside the ruins of the fort is a terrible abyss down which the mothers threw their children before leaping themselves, to avoid the Turks. Most of the island's ghost stories and legends are centred on this tragic place.

Palio Chora is near **Potamos**, which despite its name, has no river. It is the largest village in the north, all blue and white like Chora. It has a bank and the Olympic Airways office, and the largest building at the edge of town is the island's retirement home. At **Gerakido** to the northwest you can see yet another tower, this time built by the Turks in the early 18th century. From Karaves a by-road continues to the fine beach at **Platia Ammos**. **Ag. Pelagias**, Kythera's northern port and most pleasant resort, also has a long beach.

Elafonissos and Antikythera

From Ag. Pelagias you can see the islet **Elafonissos**, connected by ship once a week (or daily in the summer by caique from Neapolis). Its village is mostly inhabited by fishermen and sailors, although a new village, **Kata Nisso**, is under construction with a hotel, for little Elafonissos is endowed with two gorgeous sandy beaches a kilometre or so long, as yet hardly discovered by tourists.

Another islet, **Antikythera** (or Lious) lies to the south of Kapsali, nearly midway to Crete. Ships call once a week on route between Kythera and Crete. Fewer than 150 people live in Antikythera's two villages, Potamos and Sochoria, and the rest is very rocky with few trees; curiously, like west Crete, the island is slowly rising. By Potamos, ancient **Aigilia** has walls dating back to the 5th century BC.

Festivals

15 August, Panayias Mirtidion; 29–30 May, Ag. Trias at Mitata.

Where to Stay

expensive

When it comes to finding a place to stay on Kythera you may be hard-pressed. For families and longer stays there are furnished apartments in Kapsali, © 31 265, Ag. Pelagias, © 33 466, and at Pitsinades, © 33 570, with daily rates ranging from 8000 dr. to 18,000 dr., depending on the number of people. The **Raikos** pension in Kapsali is the island's biggest (24 rooms) and most expensive hotel accommodation, © 31 629, followed by the **Aphrodite** in Kapsali, © 31 328. There's one B class pension in Livadi, the **Aposperides**, © 31 790.

moderate–cheap

In Kythera town (Chora) there are the small B class pensions **Keti**, © 31 318, and **Margarita** (no phone). Up in Ag. Pelagias the 10-roomed **Kytheria** pension, © 33 321, serves breakfast, and in Manitochori, **Ta Kythera** (again, another small pension) has clean, pleasant double rooms, © 31 563. Potamos has the pretty **Porfyra**, © 33 329, with 8 rooms. Other than that there are a few rooms to be had at Ag. Pelagias, Potamos, Kythera town and Milopotamos.

Kapsali has the most in the way of restaurants, including the American-style **Kapsi Kamales**, where you can dine for around 2500 dr. For about the same price, well-prepared Greek dishes can be had at **Kamares tou Mayeira**, also in Kapsali. There are a number of typical, simple tavernas offering straightforward Greek food at Greek prices up in Chora, notably **Zorba's**, in the main street; there's also the restaurant in Milopotamos and in Ag. Pelagias a limited selection of tavernas.

Lefkas (Lefkada)

Lefkas (more popularly known in Greece by its genitive form Lefkada) was named for its white cliffs. It barely qualifies as an island; in ancient times Corinthian colonists dug what is now the 20-m (66-ft) wide Lefkas ship canal, separating the peninsula from the mainland. This is kept dredged by the Greek government and is easily crossed by a pontoon bridge; beyond the canal a series of causeways surrounds a large, shallow lagoon (salt is one of Lefkada's industries). A series of earthquakes—most recently in 1948—destroyed nearly all of the island's architectural interest. Lefkada is especially well known for the laces and embroideries produced by its women, many of whom keep a loom in the back room of their houses. Lefkada is gradually developing its tourist potential, in part based on the perfect conditions for windsurfing at Vassiliki. There's a fair amount of hotel and villa construction underway, but most of the holiday-makers are Greek.

History

Although inhabited at least as far back as the Early Bronze Age, Lefkada first enters the scene of recorded history in 640 BC, when it was colonized by the Corinthians. After digging the channel that gave Lefkada its island status, the Corinthians built a fort at the northern tip, near the mainland, throughout history the key to Lefkada. During the Peloponnesian War Lefkada sided with Sparta and was devastated twice, by the Corcyraeans and the Athenians. The ancient capital was near Themodern, and at the white cliffs of Cape Doukata stood a temple of Apollo, where Sappho leapt to her death, in despair over an unrequited love. Another great moment in the island's history was the Battle of Aktium, which once and for all settled the claims of Augustus on the Roman Empire over those of Mark Anthony and Cleopatra. The Venetians built the original fortress of Santa Maura, a name they adopted for the whole of the island. When Constantinople fell in 1453, the mother of the last Emperor Constantinos XI, Helene Palaeologos, founded a monastery in the walls of Santa Maura. When the Turks took Lefkas in 1479, they turned the monastery into a mosque.

In 1500 the combined forces of Spain and Venice under the Gran Capitan, Gonzales de Cordova captured Lefkas and Santa Maura in the name of Christianity, but the very next year Venice made a treaty with Turkey and returned the island. In 1684, Venetian nobleman Francesco Morosini, angry at losing his own fortress at Herakleon, Crete, was determined to win Lefkas back for Venice, and he did with the help of a great number of Ionian islanders. With the fall of Venice, the French and then the Russians took Lefkas, the latter establishing it as part of the Septinsular Republic. In 1807 the tyrant Ali Pasha of Epirus moved to take

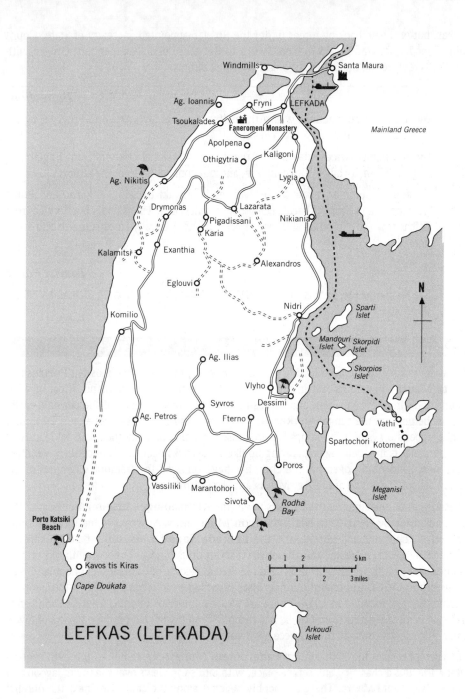

Windmills

Santa Maura

Ag. Ioannis
Fryni
LEFKADA

Tsoukalades
Faneromeni Monastery

Mainland Greece

Apolpena

Othigytria
Kaligoni

Ag. Nikitis

Lygia

Drymonas
Lazarata

Pigadissani
Nikiania
Karia

Kalamitsi
Exanthia

Alexandros

Eglouvi

Komilio

Nidri

Sparti
Islet

Mandouri
Islet
Skorpidi
Islet

Ag. Ilias

Skorpios
Islet

Vlyho
Syvros
Dessimi

Ag. Petros
Fterno

Vathi

Spartochori
Kotomeri

Poros

Meganisi
Islet

Vassiliki
Marantohori

Sivota
Rodha
Bay

Porto Katsiki
Beach

Kavos tis Kiras

Cape Doukata

N

LEFKAS (LEFKADA)

Arkoudi
Islet

0   1   2   5 km

0   1   2   3 miles

Lefkas, but was held back by forces under the Russian-appointed Secretary of State, Count John Capodistria, who is said to have sworn to the cause of an Independent Greece with rebellious refugees on the island, among them Kolokotronis.

Connections

By road: bus connections with Athens (five times a day), Arta and Preveza; by car about six hours' drive.

By air: flights twice a day from Athens and occasional charters from England to Aktion, 26 km away on the mainland, and bus connection from the airport.

By sea: in summer, boats from Nydri and Vassiliki to Sami, Fiskardo and Poros (Kefalonia) and Kioni (Ithaca). Daily boat to Meganisi. The island's bus service from Lefkas town to the other villages is irregular and generally stops running mid-afternoon.

Tourist Police

See regular police, Lefkas town, ☎ (0645) 22 346, Vassiliki, ☎ 31 218 and Vlichos, ☎ 95 207.

Lefkas Town

If you approach Lefkada from land, the first thing you'll first see is the massive **Fortress of Santa Maura**, dipping its feet in the sea near Arkanania on the mainland. Most of what stands dates from the Venetian and Turkish reconstructions. It survived the periodic earthquakes better than the capital, **Lefkas** which collapsed in the last earthquake in 1948; the fragile upper storeys of its buildings are an antiseismic measure. Another unusual feature of the town are its iron bell towers, rearing up like oil derricks near the 18th-century Venetian churches. Solidly built of stone, the churches have survived the tremors; examples of the Ionian school of painting are in **Ag. Minas** and **Ag. Dimitrios**.

There are three small museums in Lefkas town: the **Archaeology Museum**, housing mostly the finds made by Dörpfeld in Nidri; the **Icon Museum**, with works of the Ionian school, housed in the municipal library; and the **Lefkada Sound Museum**, at 29 Kalkani St, founded by a local collector and the only museum of its kind in Greece, with old gramophones sent over by relatives from the United States, records of Cantades and popular Greek songs of the 1920s, and one of the first discs recorded by a Greek company, 'Orpheon' of Constantinople, founded in 1914. There are also a number of antiques from Lefkada (*open daily*). A cemetery dating from 600 BC has recently been discovered on the outskirts of town, and archaeologists from all over Greece are swooping on the site.

Just above Lefkas is the 17th-century **Faneromeni Monastery**, rebuilt in the 19th century after a fire. It is a charming and serene place, with bird's-eye views over the town, lagoon and the walls of Santa Maura. There are pebbly beaches along the causeway, near the derelict windmills. The central bus station is on the waterfront, near the bridge, and buses to the coastal villages are frequent.

The rest of Lefkada still retains much of its rural charm, and it's not unusual to encounter an older woman still dressed in her traditional costume. A short distance from Lefkas town on a hill near the east shore are the ruins of ancient **Leukas**, the Corinthian city, although there's little to see except the walls and traces of a theatre. Further south is **Nidri**, one of Lefkada's small resort towns, looking out over the lovely wooded islets of **Mandouri, Sparti, Skorpidi** and **Skorpios**, the last belonging to the Onassis family. From the sea you can spy Aristotle's tomb and excursion boats now have permission to land on the beaches if no one is in residence. You may notice a little red caique taking over a small army of workers who maintain the island; Onassis stipulated in his will that they must be from Nidri. On the plain behind Nidri, Wilhelm Dörpfeld, who assisted Schliemann in the excavation of Troy, found a number of Bronze Age tombs that he believed proved his theory that Lefkas was the Ithaca of Homer. He died in 1940 and is buried near the house in which he lived, on the peninsula facing the town.

Sit at a café in Nidri at twilight—there's one so near the shore you may sit with your feet in the sea—and, to the sound of croaking frogs, watch Mandouri float above the horizon on a magic carpet of mist. The mansion on Mandouri belongs to the family of the poet Aristelis Valaoritis who, like Angellos Sikelianos, came from Lefkas and was inspired by Lefkada's mix of mainland and island cultures.

Vlyho, the next village south, is a quiet charmer and in walking distance of sandy Dessimi beach. From **Syvros**, one of the larger villages in the interior, you can climb to the cave **Karouha**, the largest on the island. **Poros** and **Sivota** (with several tavernas, rooms and pensions) are popular swimming places with the local people.

Vassiliki, Windsurfing and the Original Lover's Leap

Vassiliki is at once a shady, charming village with beaches and one of the best places in Europe to windsurf. Shops there specialize in all types of boards. A gentle breeze blows up by mid-morning, perfect to teach beginners the fundamentals, and by mid-afternoon it's blowing strong for the experts; by evening, the wind, like a real gent, takes a bow and exits, allowing a pleasant dinner by the water's edge. From Vassiliki you can take a caique (or road from Komilio) to see the 60 m white cliffs of **Cape Doukata**, the original Lover's Leap, where Sappho, rejected by Phaon, hurled herself into the sea below. Evidence suggests, however, that the leap was not always a fatal cure for unrequited love; like the divers of Alcapolco, priests serving at the temple of Apollo Lefkada (of which only the scantiest ruins remain) would make the jump safely as part of their cult, called *katapontismos*. Later, Romans rejected by their sweethearts would make the leap—with the precaution of strapping on feathers or even live birds and employing rescue parties to pull them out of the sea below. The white cliffs are a famous landmark for sailors; Byron's Childe Harold 'saw the evening star above Leucadia's far-projecting rock of woe' as he sailed past. Today, a lighthouse marks the historic spot. Also reachable by caique from Vassiliki is the beautiful and remote beach of **Porto Katsiki**, covered with brilliantly white pebbles.

Up the West Coast

The west coast of Lefkada is rocky and rugged as far as **Ag. Nikitis**, which has blossomed into a sizeable resort with a long beach and clean, if cold, water. Don't let your windsurfer run away with you, though—the odd shark fin has been spotted off the coast. Just south of here a new road allows access to **Kathisma**, a good place to swim with a snack bar on the beach. **Ag. Petros** is the prettiest village on this side of the island. In the interior there are several notable churches with frescoes, among them the Red Church (Kokkino Eklisia) in **Alexandros**, and the 15th-century church at **Othigytria**, its design incorporating Byzantine and Western influences.

Festivals

Carnival festivities, with a parade; in August, the Arts and Letters Festival and large International Folklore Festival, in Lefkas town; two weeks in mid-August, Ag. Spyridon, at Karia, when the people bring out their old costumes (Karia is well known for its handmade lace and woven carpets); 30 May, Faneromeni Monastery; 11 November, Ag. Minas in Lefkas; 26 July, Ag. Paraskevi near Ag. Petros.

Where to Stay

expensive

In Lefkas town, on the waterfront overlooking the canal, is the **Xenia**, ✆ 24 762, with compulsory half board in high season. More comfortable in the same price range is the **Hotel Lefkas**, ✆ 23 916. In Ag. Nikitis the **Odyssia** is one of the island's nicest hotels, ✆ 99 366. At Nikiana, between Lefkas town and Nidri, the **Porto Galini** provides luxurious furnished apartments, and watersports down on the beach, ✆ 92 431. Two km north of Nidri in Perigiali, **Scorpios** has studios and apartments for rent, and there's a pool, ✆ 92 452. Just outside Nidri, the **Athos** is a popular place, with pool, pleasant bar and Chinese food, ✆ 92 384.

moderate

Next door to the Hotel Lefkas is the **Niricos Hotel**, ✆ 24 132, also a class B. Less expensive and on the main drag is the small and ordinary **Byzantium Hotel**, ✆ 22 629. Down in Nidri the **Nidri Beach Hotel I and II** are run by the same family and have good views, ✆ 92 400. Good value in Vassiliki is the **Paradissos**, an E class, but some rooms come with private bath, ✆ 31 256. In Ag. Nikitis smart rooms with private bath and overlooking the sea are around 6000 dr.

cheap

Rooms in private homes on the island start at 2500 dr. In Nidri, Vlyho and especially in Vassiliki you can usually find a room without too much difficulty from 3000 dr. upwards. There are **campsites** at Dessimi Beach near Vlyho, at Poros Beach further south, and at Vassiliki.

Restaurants are numerous and reasonably priced on Lefkas and portions seem to be larger than elsewhere in Greece. In Lefkas town **Pyrofani** taverna has a good variety of Greek dishes and seafood. The **Adriatika**, in a pleasant garden setting, is pricier but has some good Greek specialities and excellent service (2500 dr.). Eat at least once at **Kavos** on the beach at Nidri for the view and consistently good food for 1500–2000 dr. Just outside Nidri, **Haradiatika** is popular with locals for its good quality meat and *meze*. Vassiliki has a fine taverna on the beach, **Alex's**, serving some good English dishes and curries. Sivota has several tavernas on the beach, and you can pick your lobster from the sea cages; try the fish soup here.

Meganisi lies off the southeast coast of Lefkada. Ferries go there daily from Nidri, calling at **Vathi**, its port and largest settlement. It is a rocky islet but not without beauty. The only time when many people go there is for the *paneyeri* of Ag. Konstantinos on 21 May at the hamlet of Kotomeri. **Arkoudi**, another islet south of Lefkas, is uninhabited.

Paxos

Tiniest and yet one of the most charming islands in the Ionian Sea, Paxos and its little sister Antipaxos have long served as a kind of outlet from the mass package tourism and over-development of Corfu. Paxos (or Paxi) is so small and so flat you can easily walk its 8-km length in a day; its one road twists and turns through the immaculate groves of olives that brought the islanders most of their income before tourism. Paxos' olive oil is still considered among the best produced in Greece and has won many international medals. Besides the beauty of the silvery trees (there are some 300,000—each family owns at least 500) and the tidy stone walls, the little island has some of the friendliest people you'll find anywhere in Greece.

History

Paxos was happily shunned by history. What mention it received in antiquity referred to its seven sea caves—Homer mentions one, Ipparandi, describing it as having rooms of gold. In another cave the Greek resistance hero Papanikolaos hid and waylaid passing Italian ships in the Second World War, a trick unfortunately copied by the German U-boats the following year.

Plutarch recounts an incident of great moment that took place off the shore of Paxos, at the beginning of the 1st century AD. Thamus, the Egyptian pilot of a ship sailing near the island, heard a voice call his name and say: 'When the ship comes opposite Palodes, you must announce the death of the Great God Pan.' When Thamus did so at the designated spot, great cries of lamentation arose. So the old gods were replaced with a new, marking the end—and the beginning—of a Great World Age.

Daily with Corfu, Brindisi (Italy), Igoumenitsa and Parga (on the mainland), also infrequent connections with Patras, Kefalonia and Ithaca. Connections are far less frequent in the off season. In the summer you may well be asked to have a room reservation before boarding a ferry to the island which is small, wooded, and fearful of campers and their fires.

Tourist Police

See regular police in Gaios, ✆ (0662) 31 222.

Gaios

Gaios, the pretty little capital of the island, is named after a disciple of St Paul who brought Christianity to Paxos and is buried there. Most of the islanders live here, and it's where you'll find a small sandy beach and all of Paxos' facilities, including a tiny **aquarium** on the harbour-front. The streets of Gaios are fortunately too narrow for cars, although human traffic jams occur during the day in the summer, when day-trippers from Corfu and cruise ships sail into the little port; in the evening, however, the island regains its composure.

On a rocky islet facing the harbour is the well-preserved **Kastro Ag. Nikolaos**, built by the Venetians in 1423, and an old windmill, and beyond it, the islet of **Panayia**, which on 15 August is crowded with pilgrims. In the evening they come back to Gaios and dance all night in the village square. **Mongonissi**, another islet, is connected by caique—belonging to the family which owns a pretty little restaurant there—which brings customers over for dinner in the evening.

Sea Caves and Forests of Olives

Caiques may also be rented for a tour of Paxos' seven sea caves of brilliant blue. Most of these grottoes are located among the sheer cliffs on the western side of Paxos, including the impressive **Kastanitha**, 185 m high. Another distinctive cave, **Ortholithos**, has a sentinel-like monolith at its entrance. It is possible to penetrate about 5 m inside by caique. Homer's **Ipparandi** does not have the golden rooms he mentions, although it often shelters monk seals. **Grammatiko** is the largest cave of them all. When sailing around the island, you can also see the **Mousmouli Cliffs** and their natural bridge **Tripitos**.

The main road from Gaios across the island was donated by Aristotle Onassis, a great fan of Paxos. At its northern end is **Lakka**, a tiny port where the boats from Corfu usually call (connected by minibus with Gaios). Lakka has a small beach, and the Byzantine church in the village has particularly musical Russian bells, which you can ring if you find the villager with the key. The 19th-century **Grammatikou mansion** near Lakka is fortified with a tower. In **Boikatika** village the church Ag. Charalambos contains an old icon of the Virgin and in nearby **Magazia** are two churches of interest, Ag. Spyridon and Ag. Apostoli; the latter's churchyard affords an impressive view of the Eremitis cliffs. At **Apergatika** the Papamarkou mansion dates from the 17th century.

Festivals

Easter Monday procession from Gaios to Velliantitika; 15 August, Panayias; 11 August, Ag. Spyridon; 10 February, Ag. Charalambos.

Where to Stay

expensive

Official accommodation is extremely limited, rather expensive, and block-booked by tour operators in the summer: a case in point the class B **Paxos Beach Bungalows**,

© 31 211, in Gaios, with pleasant, comfortable chalet bungalows near the beach, attainable only in the off season.

moderate

Paxos has two E class hotels, the **Ilios**, © 31 808, and **Lefkothea**, in Lakka, © 31 807; again, they are both small, and fill up in season. Everyone else stays in private rooms, which are invariably pleasant, tidy and double, and average 4000 dr.

Eating Out

Again, be prepared for prices a little above the norm. Restaurants and cafés take full advantage of the day-trippers who come from Corfu, and the yachting set berthed in Gaios. Take the caique to Mongonissi for the excellent restaurant there (2500–3000 dr.) and to while the day away on the beach. There are a handful of tavernas in Gaios such as the **Taka Taka** serving solid Greek fare and fish, the former reasonably priced, the latter about 3500 dr. for a meal. There is not much to choose between the tavernas in Longos and in Lakka you can eat well and reasonably at **Sgarelios** and **Klinis**.

Antipaxos

South of Paxos lies tiny Antipaxos, with only a few permanent residents. From June until September four or five caiques leave Gaios daily for the 40-minute trip to its port **Agrapoia**. Although both Paxos and Antipaxos were created with a resounding blow of Poseidon's trident (the sea god thought that the gap between Corfu and Lefkas was a bit too large), the two islands are very different in nature. Rather than olive oil, Antipaxos produces good white and red wines, and instead of rocky sea caves, its coasts are graced with fine sandy beaches: **Voutoumia** and **Vrika** are 'softer than silk'. There is no accommodation on the islet, but those planning to stay should bring a sleeping bag, and be discreet. This could well be the uncontaminated paradise you've been seeking.

Zakynthos (Zante)

Of all their Ionian possessions the Venetians loved Zakynthos the most for its charm and natural beauty. *Zante, fiore di Levante*—'the flower of the East'—they called it, and built a city even more splendid than Corfu on its great semi-circular bay, all turned to dust and rubble by the earthquake of 1953. Nevertheless, the disaster did nothing to diminish the soft, luxuriant charm of the landscape and its fertile green hills and mountainsides: the valleys with their vineyards and currant vines, olive and almond groves and orchards, the brilliant garland of flowers and beautiful beaches (the flowers are best in spring and autumn, a time when few foreigners visit the island). And if the buildings are gone, the Venetians left a lasting impression—many islanders have Venetian blood, are Catholic and sing lyrical Italianate Cantades. On the other side of the coin, the once-politically-progressive Zakynthos has bellied up to the trough of grab-the-money-fast tourism that doesn't do the island justice, to the extent of sabotaging efforts to preserve the beaches where the loggerhead turtles breed.

History

According to tradition, Zakynthos was named for its first settler, a son of Dardanus from Arcadia. Pliny refers to a cavern on its Mons Nobilis (now Mt Skopos), as the entrance to the underworld. According to Homer, the Zantiots fought under the command of Odysseus at the Trojan War, although their island later became an independent, coin-minting state which set up colonies throughout the Mediterranean, especially Saguntum in Spain, which was besieged and demolished by Hannibal. Levinus took the island for Rome in 214 BC, and when the inhabitants rebelled, he burnt all the buildings on Zakynthos. Uniting with the Aeolians, the Zantiots forced the Romans to leave, although in 150 BC Flavius finally brought the troublesome island under control.

In 844 the Saracens captured the island from their base in Crete, but the Byzantines were strong enough to expel them. The Norman–Sicilian pirate Margaritone took Zakynthos in 1182, and three years later made it part of the County Palatine of Kefalonia, first governed by Margaritone. One of his successors ceded the island to the Venetians in 1209, who kept the island for almost 350 years, although the Turks captured and pillaged it between 1479 and 1484. The aristocratic privileges of the Venetians and wealthy Zantiots caused so much resentment among the commoners that they rose up in 'the Rebellion of the Popolari' and took control of the island for four years. In the 17th century, many Cretan artists took refuge on the Venetian Zakynthos, and the island became the centre of the Ionian school of painting, producing artists like Doxaras, Koutouzis and Kantorinis. The song cult of the Cantades flourished as well and the island saw the birth of several poets: Ugo Foscolo (d. 1827). who wrote in Italian, and the nationalist poets Andreas Kalvos (d. 1867) and Dionysos Solomos (d. 1857); Solomos, 'the poet of the Greek War of Independence', was one of the first to write in Demotic Greek and composed the lyrics to the Greek National Anthem.

The Zantiots responded actively to the ideas of the French Revolution, forming their own Jacobin Club and destroying the hated rank of nobility. The Russians in 1798 forced the French garrison and the inhabitants to surrender, after a siege of months, and when the Septinsular Republic established aristocrats of its own, Zakynthos rebelled again in 1801. During the War of Independence many rebels on the mainland found asylum on the island before it joined Greece with its Ionian sisters in 1864.

Connections

By air: daily flights from Athens, two–three times a week with Kefalonia and Corfu. Several charters from major European cities.

By sea: ferry six or seven times a day from Kilini, twice a day from Kefalonia. Bus two or three times a day from Athens.

Tourist Police

1 Tzoulati, ℂ (0695) 22 200.

ZAKYNTHOS

Kianoun Cave (Blue Grotto)
Korithi
Askos
Sklavou Cave
Ag. Gerasimou Cave
Skinari
Ano Volimes
Orthonies
Alikanes
Tsilivi
Xinthia Cave
Anafonitria
Alikes Salt Pans
Katastari
Pigadakia
Kipseli
Planos
Maries
Tragaki
Megali Cave
Kallithea
Gerakari
Kalipado
Ag. Ioannis
Exo Chora
Yiri
Skoulikado
Ag. Kirikos
Vanato
Bohali
Louha
Ag. Marina
Ag. Pandes
Sarakinado
ZAKYNTHOS
Kampi
Ag. Leon
Fiolitis
Vouyiato
Lagadakia
Argassi
Lagopoda
Macherado
Romiri
Xirokastello
N
Ag. Nikolaos
Mouzaki
Pantokrator
Lithakia
Mt. Skopos
Kalamaki
Ano Vassilikos
Lagana
Vassiliki
Porto Roma
Agalas
Pelouza
Geraki
Pitchsprings
Marathonissi
To Kilini

0   5   10 km
0   5   miles
Keri

Zakynthos Town and the Eastern Peninsula

When the capital of the island, Zakynthos town, was rebuilt after the earthquake, the inhabitants gamely tried to incorporate some of the lost city's charm into the dull lines of modern Greek architecture. The town's setting gives it an added lustre—the graceful curve of the harbour, the ancient acropolis rising above, crowned by a castle, and to the right the unusual form of **Mt Skopos** ('look-out'), the Mons Nobilis of Pliny. A path leads to the top from the edge of the town; in the old days someone would make the 2-hour ascent every day to scan the horizon for pirate ships.

The city itself is long and narrow, and can easily be explored by horse-drawn cab or the cute double-pedal canopied vehicles for hire in the square. The streets are lined by arcades, all full of shops selling the local speciality, *mandolato* (white nougat with almonds). In central **Plateia Solomou** the 15th-century church of **Ag. Nikolaos** was pieced back together after the quake; here, too is the **Neo-Byzantine Museum** (*8.30–3, closed Tues*) with paintings by the Ionian school, icons and other works of art salvaged from shattered churches across the island and a relief by neo-Classical sculptor Thorvaldsen dedicated to High Commissioner Maitland. Another museum, two streets up at Ag. Markou Square, is the **Solomos Museum**, near the mausoleums of Dionysos Solomos and Andreas Kalvos, with mementoes of the poets and other famous Zantiots, as well as photographs of the island before 1953. Little 17th-century **Kyra ton Angelous**, another reconstructed chapel, is near the Xenia Hotel. At the south end of town a huge new basilica housed the relics of the island's patron saint, **Ag. Dionysos**, and is filled with gold and silver ex-votos, and frescoes by Cozzara, a student of Tiepolo.

Looming over the town is the well-preserved **Venetian Kastro**, an hour's walk from Plateia Solomou. It's an easier haul than tramping up Mt Skopos, and rewards with views not only of Zakynthos, but of the Peloponnese and the Bay of Navarino, where on 20 October 1827 the most famous battle of modern Greece was fought between the Turco-Egyptian navy and the Anglo-Franco-Russian fleet, leading directly to Greek independence. On the north edge of town is the old **British cemetery**.

The town beach isn't all that good—better to take a bus to the beaches on the eastern peninsula: **Argassi** under Mt Skopas, with a long line of hotels and tavernas along its waterfront; **Porto Zorro** (pension and taverna); **Vassiliki** (rooms and camping available) and the charming, pine-shaded sandy strand at **Porto Roma**, but bear in mind that because of the infrequent bus service you may well have to get back to town by taxi. **Geraki**, at the tip of the peninsula has another long, lovely stretch of sandy beach.

The Southern Peninsula

On the map, Zakynthos looks like a piranha with gaping jaws, about to devour the crumb-sized islets of **Marathonissi** and **Pelouza**, the latter colonized in 1473 BC by King Zakynthos. Today both are rich fishing grounds. **Kalamaki** has a sandy beach under Mt Skopos, at the beginning of currant country. The next town, **Lagana** is Zakynthos' most developed resort, a favourite both of British and German package tourists and families over for the weekend from the Peloponnese. The fine sandy beach overlooks some curious rock formations by the sea—a beach also popular as an egg-laying ground for loggerhead turtles. It became the centre of an international stir when environmentalists themselves were at logger-heads with government ministries and the island tourist industry to protect the fragile beach areas the turtles have for generations used as hatcheries. Uncompensated for the beaches they owned, some Zantiots even resorted to setting fires on them to keep the turtles away; in 1992 the World Wide Fund for Nature purchased 30 hectares of nesting beach and hired wardens to watch over them.

Behind Lagana extends the **plain of Zakynthos**, a lovely region to cycle through with its old country estates. Further south is **Keri**, with another sandy beach below but it's best known for its nearby **Pissa tou Keriou**: natural pitch wells, used, as in ancient times, to caulk boats. These were well known in antiquity, referred to by both Herodotos and Pliny. There are tavernas by the beach and fine views from the village of Keri.

North, in the central cluster of farming villages, **Macherado** stands out with its lovely church of **Ag. Mavra**, with a beautiful old icon of the saint and church bells noted for their musical quality. In nearby **Lagopoda** there is also the pretty Eleftherias monastery. **Ag. Nikolaos** is a very pretty village overlooking the plain from the west; on the main inland road northwest of Zakynthos town is **Katastari**, the island's second largest town, marking the northern edge of the plain. Below Katastari, **Alikes** marks the beginning of a wonderful long stretch of sand which continues west around the bay to **Alikanes**. From Katastari you can take a taxi up to **Anafonitria** and its monastery, a rare survivor of the earthquake, with frescoes and the cell of Ag. Dionysos (d. 1622) and a medieval tower.

Unlike the low rolling hills and plain of the east, the west coast of Zakynthos plunges steeply and abruptly into the sea. It does, however, have many caves. **Ag. Gerasimou, Xinthia** (track from Anafonitria) with sulphur springs—evidence of the island's volcanic origins—and **Sklavou** are the most interesting, excluding of course **Kianoun Cave**, the local rival for Capri's Blue Grotto, glowing with every imaginable shade of blue. Kianoun can be visited by caique, either from Zakynthos town or Alikes. The largest village on the west coast is **Volimes**; to go swimming there wear swim shoes, so hot are the rocks and sand. **Ano Volimes** just above it is a pretty little mountain village.

A small islet some 50 km south of Zakynthos, called **Strophades**, has a Byzantine monastery which served as a fortress for many years, until the Saracens finally overcame the defence of the monks and plundered it. Today only the building remains, and a lighthouse. The island is a popular resting station for migratory doves. If you have your own boat and have been looking for an out-of-the-way, romantic destination you won't find a better one.

Festivals

A carnival initiated by the Venetians remains strong in Zakynthos and lasts for two weeks prior to Lent, known for its masked singers and dancing. For the *paneyeri* of Ag. Dimitriou on 24 August and 17 December, Zakynthos town is strewn with myrtle and there are fireworks at the church. During Holy Week the inhabitants also give themselves over to an infectious merriment. Slightly more modest is Zoodochos Pigi in the town on 10 November. In July the Zakynthia takes place with cultural activities; at the end of August and beginning of September, the International Meeting of Medieval and Popular Theatre, with performances.

Where to Stay

There are hotels in town and around the island in about equal proportion, although on the whole it's more pleasant to stay outside the centre.

expensive

In Zakynthos town, you can choose between the **Strada Marina** at 14 K. Lombardou St, © 22 761, nicely located on the quay. A little more expensive is the **Reparo** at

Roma and Voultsou St, © 23 578, clean, pleasant and friendly. **Alfa** on Tertseti St, © 26 641, has bungalows for about the same price. Outside the town, most of the accommodation is at Lagana, which has the giant **Zante Beach**, © 51 130, with pool and tennis. In Tragaki the A class **Caravel** (sister to the one in Athens) will lighten your wallet, but it has all the trimmings, © 25 261, as does the new **Plagos Beach** at Tsilivi, © 24 147.

moderate

Zakynthos town has nothing outstanding in this category. Two decently priced places are **Ionion**, 18 A. Roma, © 23 739, and **Dessy**, 73 N. Koliva, © 28 505. There are almost 20 class C hotels in Laganas, scores of rooms to rent and the people to fill them up. Unless you like that sort of thing, head to more serene haunts such as Planos where the C class **Cosmopolite**, © 28 752, has 14 good rooms, Tsilivi (**Orea Heleni**, © 28 788), Vassiliki (**Porto Roma**, © 22 781), or Keri, which is serene and has the cheapest rooms on the island.

cheap

Simple rooms are mostly available in Zakynthos town and Lagana, although you can find simple accommodation elsewhere—Keri, for example, is tranquil, and has some of the cheapest rooms on the island. If you have any difficulty, the tourist police off the Plateia Solomou have a list of rooms to let. There are **campsites** at Tsilivi, Lagana, Gerakari and near Lithakia.

Eating Out

In Zakynthos town, you can eat well at **P. Evangelos** on Alex Roma St for 2500 dr.; the food is freshly prepared and good. There are several expensive places on Ag. Marko square and one that's not, **Boukios**, serving reliable Greek fare for around 2500 dr. Other moderate restaurants can be found near the city hall. The **Panorama** is in a lovely spot up by the castle, and you can listen to live Cantada music while indulging in some traditional Zaniote dishes such as rabbit casserole or *mouskari kokkinisto*, beef in tomato sauce (2500–3000 dr.). On the road to Argassi, near the church of Ag. Dionysos, **Karavomilos** has the name for the best fish on the island (3500 dr.). For more dining with a view, there's **Alla** up on Filikon 38, located in one of the few houses to have survived the earthquake (2000–3000 dr.). Lagana has a host of restaurants, both Greek and international, and many British pubs serving bar food.

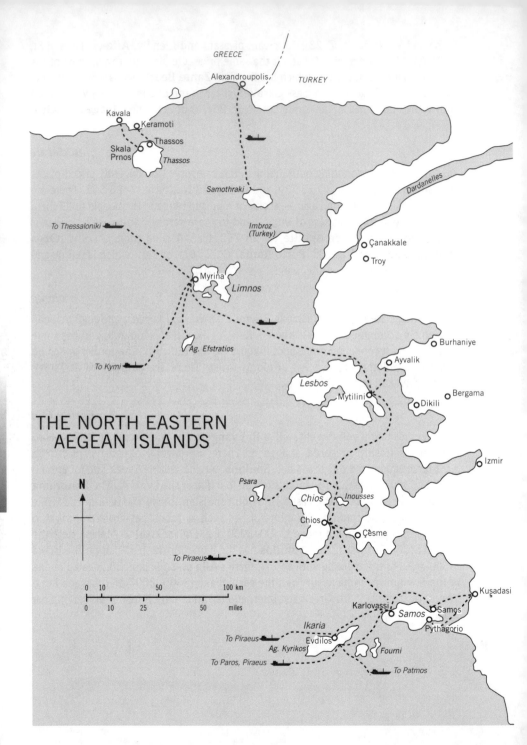

THE NORTH EASTERN
AEGEAN ISLANDS

N

Christos Rachon, Ikaria

The Northeastern Aegean Islands

The grouping of these seven major islands (Chios, Ikaria, Lesbos, Limnos, Samos, Samothrace and Thassos) under one title is done for convenience rather than for any cultural or historical consideration. What they have in common, however, is their location off the coast of Turkey and Northern Greece. Most were colonized during the Dorian invasion of the 12th century BC, when the invaders forced the Ionian settlers of the mainland to seek new homes in the east. The Ionians occupied the coastal regions of Asia Minor and the islands, and between the 7th and 6th centuries BC, seeded much of what we call Western civilization: the islands alone produced talents like Pythagoras, Sappho and probably Homer himself. Their cities were among the most important in Greece in trade, in the production of wine and olive oil, and in religion. Samothrace is practically synonymous with its sanctuary of the gods of the underworld; Limnos was dedicated to the smithy god Hephaestus, and on Samos the temple of the goddess Hera was one of the wonders of the Ancient World.

Once prosperous and independent, the islands slipped into obscurity as they fell prey to the greater powers around them, first the Persians from Asia Minor and then the Athenians from the West, and then from Asia Minor again in the form of the Ottoman Empire. They were annexed to Greece only in 1912, following the Balkan Wars.

Connections

The Northeastern Aegean islands were the last to be discovered by the summer invasions of visitors, partly due to their great distance from Athens—Ikaria, the closest island to Athens, is a 10-hour journey by ship. Almost all the islands, however, now have airports to shorten the trip, although anyone planning to fly there during the summer should reserve a seat as much as two months in advance. Connections between the islands are regular if not exceptionally frequent.

Chios

Chios is a wealthy island, not only because of its numerous shipowning dynasties but also for its agriculture, especially its mastic trees, or lentisks (*pistacia lentiscus*) which grow naturally only on Chios and were long used as a varnish for paintings. In August and early September the sweet sap drips down the stumpy trunks of the trees, glistening like liquid diamonds in the sun, and by September it is ripe for the mastic manufacturer. Chewing gum, sweets and a devilishly sweet sticky liqueur are the major products of Chios.

The geography of the island surprises with its variety. While some parts are so barren that you can walk for miles without seeing a touch of green, other places are thickly forested, and still others are fertile plains yielding citrus fruits, olives, almonds and wine. A large mountain range cuts across the island, giving rise to its Homeric epithet of 'craggy'; the highest peak,

Mt Profitis Ilias, rises to a height of 1297 m. Byzantine and medieval monuments abound, and the International Society of Homeric studies is based on Chios, where a conference is held every summer.

Mythology

Merope, daughter of King Oenopion, was pledged in marriage to the handsome giant Orion, the mighty hunter. Oenopion had little enthusiasm for marrying his daughter to anyone, for he loved her very much himself. However, he promised her to Orion on the condition that he rid Chios of its ferocious beasts, a task the young man easily performed. But rather than give Orion his reward, Oenopion kept putting him off, and finally Orion took the matter into his own hands and raped Merope. For this the king poked out his eyes. Orion then set out blindly, but the goddess of dawn, Eos, fell in love with him and persuaded Helios the sun god to restore his sight. Before he could avenge himself on Oenopion, however, Orion was killed. His foolhardy boast that he could rid the entire world of harmful creatures made Mother Earth send a giant scorpion after him. Orion fled the scorpion, but his friend Artemis, the goddess of the hunt, killed him by mistake. In mourning, she placed his image among the stars.

History

Inhabited from approximately 3000 BC, Chios was colonized by the mysterious sea people called the Pelasgians who left walls near Exo Didyma and Kourounia and a temple of Zeus on top of Mt Pelion. The Achaeans followed, and were in turn usurped by the Ionians. A strong tradition asserts that Homer was born on the island in the 9th or 8th century BC, although this claim is disputed (chiefly by Smyrna). At the time Chios was an independent kingdom with colonies abroad (notably Voroniki in Egypt); in the 7th century BC the island was famed across the Greek world for its sculpture workshop and system of government, studied by Solon and adapted into his Athenian reforms. Around 490, a Chiote named Glaucus invented the art of soldering metals; it also earned the disgrace of becoming the first state in Greece to engage in slave trading. As a member of the famous Ionian confederacy, Chios joined Athens in the Battle of Lade (494 BC) in an unsuccessful attempt to overthrow the Persian yoke. Fifteen years later, however, after the battle of Plateia, Chios regained its independence, and held on to it even after Athens subjugated its other allies as tribute-paying dependencies.

Expediently, Chios allied itself with Rome and fought the enemy of the Empire, Mithridates of Pontus (83 BC), only to be defeated and destroyed, although it was liberated two years later when Mithridates was defeated by Sulla. A few hundred years later Chios made the mistake of siding with Galerius against his brother-in-law Constantine the Great. Constantine conquered the island and carried off to his new city of Constantinople many of Chios' famous ancient sculptures, including the four bronze horses that ended up on the front of St Mark's in Venice in 1204. In 1261 the Emperor Michael Paleologos gave Chios to the Genoese Giustiniani family for their assistance in reconquering Byzantium from Venice and its Frankish allies. Under the Genoese, Chios prospered thanks to the Maona, a company chartered in

1344 to govern and defend the island, which they did successfully until 1566 when Chios was lost to the Turks.

The Sultans were fond of the island, especially its mastic, which they chewed to sweeten their breath, and they granted Chios more benefits and privileges than any other island, including a degree of independence. Despite this, Chios rebelled with the rest of Greece in 1822, and the Sultan, furious at this subversion of his favoured island, ordered his admiral Kara Ali to mercilessly quell the revolt. This led to one of the worst massacres in history. In a few days 30,000 Greeks were slaughtered, and another 45,000 taken into slavery. All who could fled to other islands, especially Syros. News of the massacre deeply moved the rest of Europe; Delacroix painted his stirring canvas of the tragedy and Victor Hugo sent off reams of rhetoric. On 6 June of the same year, the Greek Admiral Kanaris took revenge on Kara Ali by blowing up his flagship, killing Kara Ali and 2000 men. In 1840 Chios attained a certain amount of autonomy under a Christian governor, and it was incorporated into Greece in 1912.

Connections

By air: three flights a day from Athens, twice a week with Lesbos and Thessaloniki.

By ship: daily with Piraeus, Lesbos and Inousses; daily in summer to Cêsme, Turkey, out of season less frequently, three times a week to Limnos and Psara; at least twice a week with Samos, Thessaloniki, Kavala and Rafina, once a week with Patmos, Leros, Kalymnos, Kos, Rhodes, Volos and Ag. Efstratios.

Tourist Information

NTOG, 11 Kanari St, ✆ (0271) 24 217. The Tourist Police ✆ (0271) 23 211, are to be found at the far end of the quay, next to the regular police and the customs house, from where you can take the boat to Turkey.

Chios Town

The town and main port of Chios, also called Chios or **Chora**, still belongs very much to its people and not to the tourists, although the recent extension of the airport's runway to accommodate international charters casts doubts on how long that state of affairs will last. The town—a sister city of Genoa—is mostly new and reflects the island's considerable wealth in its spanking new apartment blocks and high-rise (by island standards) offices. The old town surviving from the Turkish occupation is enclosed within the Byzantine **fortress**, replacing the Macedonia castle destroyed by Mithridates, it walls repaired by the Giustiniani of Genoa. Under the Turks, the Greeks were forced to live outside the walls, and the gate was closed every day at sundown. Within the walls is a ruined **mosque** and in the Turkish cemetery is the **tomb of Kara Ali**, the same who ordered the massacre of Chios. In a closet-sized **prison** by the gate Bishop Plato Fragiadis and 75 leading Chiotes were incarcerated as hostages in crowded, inhumane conditions before they were all hanged by the Turks in 1822.

The **main square**, Plateia Vounaki, with its café and sweet shops, is a few minutes' walk away. On one side stands a statue of Bishop Plato Fragiadis, and in the municipal gardens behind the square, a statue of Kara Ali's avenging angel, 'Incendiary' Kanaris. Also in Plateia Vounaki, a crumbling mosque is marked with the *Tugra*, the swirling 'thumbprint of the Sultan' that denotes royal possession. Tugras, though common in Istanbul, are rarely seen elsewhere, even in Turkey, and this one is a mark of the favour that Chios enjoyed from the Sultan. Today the mosque houses the **Post-Byzantine Museum**, with a collection of Byzantine and post-Byzantine art and an art student copy of Delacroix's *Massacre at Chios* of 1824 (the original is in the Louvre). Near Plateia Vounaki is the **Korais Library**, the fourth largest in Greece with 95,000 volumes, housing the private collection of London scholar Philip Argentis; the same building houses the **Folklore Museum** of the Argentis Society, containing Chiote costumes and handicrafts.

The **archaeology museum**, on Michalon St in the new part of town, contains many lovely finds, some bearing ancient Chios' symbol, the sphinx (the same as Thebes); there's also a letter from the Chiotes addressed to Alexander the Great. **Karfas**, the nearest beach to the capital has sand as fine as flour. The quayside shops sell sticky mastic products; here too is Michalakis Travel, with bikes to hire. Buses depart from the corner of Mylonadi and Vlattarias Sts near the Plateia Vounaki (timetable posted in the window).

Nea Moni

A trip to **Nea Moni** (*open mornings until noon and 5–8; women should wear knee-length skirts*) is perhaps the most beautiful excursion on Chios. Perched high above the town among the pine-wooded mountains, Nea Moni was 'new' in 1042, when Emperor Constantinos Monomarchos VIII had it built to replace an older monastery erected by three monks. The monks had found a miraculous icon of the Virgin in a burning bush on the site, and the Emperor gave them a new home in gratitude for the Virgin's prophecy (relayed by a monk) that he would return from exile and gain the throne of Byzantium. The new, powerful monastery ruled most of the island. The church, built by architects from Constantinople, has a sumptuous double narthex and subtle, complex design of pilastres and niches and pendentives that give it a rare harmony. Its 11th-century mosaics, among the most beautiful examples of Byzantine art anywhere, were badly damaged in the earthquake of 1881, which brought down the great dome—7 m in diametre. Among the other items on display in the monastery is a large water clock which keeps Byzantine time (the sun rises and sets at 12 every day). You can also visit the chapel containing the bones of the victims of Kara Ali's massacre, and there is an ancient refectory, a huge underground vaulted cistern, an old olive press and ruins of a hamlet that once surrounded the monastery. Just south of Nea Moni the forest suffered considerable damage by fire in the summer of 1987.

A rough road leads to the monastery **Ag. Pateras**, built in honour of the three monks who founded Nea Moni. The present Ag. Pateras dates from 1890, and only men are allowed inside. Further up the road is the striking, deserted medieval village of **Anavatos**, the scene of some of the worst Turkish atrocities. Above Anavatos is a medieval castle. If you plan to walk, take provisions and wear good shoes—it's a good 8 km. By **Karyes**, a pretty mountain village on the way back to Chios town, is the church **Ag. Markos** (1835).

North of Chios Town

The beach at **Vrontados** is pebbly, and above it are three windmills. Oldest of all is the **Petra Omirous** (Homer's Stone), or *Daskalopetra* (teacher's stone), a rather uncomfortable natural rock throne where the poet is said to have sung and taught, although killjoy archaeologists say it was part of an ancient altar. A curious legend relates that the most famous Genoese of all, Christopher Columbus, stopped and sat here before going on to America. The headquarters of the International Society of Homeric Studies is in Vrontados; the 19th-century **Monastery of Panayia Myrtidiotissa** nearby has the robes of Gregory V, the Patriarch of Constantinople.

Near **Vrontados** stood the church of **Ag. Isidoros**, built on the site of the first church of Chios founded in the 3rd century. A later church, erected by Emperor Constantinos the Great, fell in an earthquake and was replaced by three successive structures, the last ruined by the Turks in 1822. Saint Isidoros was buried on Chios, but his relics were snatched by the Venetians in the 12th century, where a chapel was constructed in St Mark's to house them. In 1967 Pope Paul ordered the return of one of Isidoros' bones to Chios, and it was placed in the town's cathedral. Seventh-century mosaics from the ruined church can now be seen in the museum.

Kardamila, the largest village of northern Chios, is actually two villages: the picturesque upper town and the seaside **Marmaros**, blessed with many philanthropic gifts from wealthy Chiote shipowners. By **Nagos beach** (pebbly, with good swimming) to the north are the ruins of a **temple of Poseidon**, and nearby **Giossona** was named for Jason of the Golden Fleece, even if the legend fails to make Chios one of the Argonauts' ports of call.

Taxis have a monopoly on transport to the medieval mountain village **Pitios**, which claims to be the birthplace of Homer; you can still see his 'house' and olive grove. A 12th-century Aegean tower dominates the village and you can find food at the local café. The landscape from Pitios towards Chios town is lunar in its burnt emptiness, but just above the village is a lovely pine forest, filled with fire warnings.

Further to the west is the 13th-century **Monimoudon Monastery** near Katavasis. Byzantine nobles were exiled in the medieval fortress at **Volissos**, known as the Castle of Belisarius for Justinian's famous general, although what you see was built by the Genoese. The 16th-century Ag. Markella came from Volissos, which also claims to be the birthplace of Homer, or at least the place where the poet came to bathe; it was the chief town of a clan called the Homeridai, who claimed descent from him. The beach below the town, **Skala Volissou** or Limnia, has a restaurant and a few rooms to let.

Another medieval tower rises above the middle of little **Pirama**, where the lovely church of Ag. Ioannis contains some very old icons. **Parparia** to the north is a medieval hamlet of shepherds, and at **Melanios** many Chiotes were slain before they could flee to Psara in 1822. On the northwest shore stands the Byzantine church **Ag. Gala**, by a cave which drips whitish deposits, or milk (*gala* in Greek), believed by some curious logic to be the milk of the Virgin.

South of Chios Town: Genoese Gentility

The Genoese especially favoured the area south of Chios town towards **Vavili**, where the church **Panayia Krina** (1287) contains contemporary frescoes of the Cretan school. **Sklavia** has many 14th-century Genoese villas and gardens; its name is derived from the Greeks forced to work as slaves for the Genoese nobility. But despite that bitter memory, this part of Chios, encompassing **Thymiana** and **Kampos**, is enchanting and wonderfully evocative to explore (bicycles are the perfect means of transport) full of secret orchards and gardens enclosed by tall stone walls, with the gates bearing some long forgotten coat-of-arms. Many of the large medieval houses have their own slowly turning water wheels; while outside the walls the flowering meadows, wooden bridges and ancient trees create a scene of sophisticated rural serenity unique on the Greek islands. Among the Genoese country mansions that of the **Argenti** in Kambos has been restored, down to its oxen-turned 'Hesiod's water wheel'. Even it seems young compared to the mastodon bones discovered at Thymiana.

South of Karfas on the coast is the **Ag. Minas monastery**, built in 1590. In 1822 it saw one of the worst massacres on Chios, when women and children from the surrounding villages took refuge there, thinking to escape from the blood-maddened Turks. A small, hopeless battle took place before Ag. Minas was overrun and all 3000 of the Greeks were slain, their bodies thrown down the well. Recently their bones have been recovered and set in an ossuary by the church (*closed in the afternoons until 6*).

The Mastic Towns of the South

The southernmost region of Chios is mastic land, where nearly all the villages date from the Middle Ages—or earlier. Along the road from Chios town, ancient walls and wild rock formations, along with a 12th-century **Panayia Sicelia**, can be seen at **Tholopotami. Armolia** is the site of the castle **Oreas tis Kastro**, a Byzantine fort that was the abode of a beautiful but fatal seductress. Armolia is known for its potteries, **Nenita** and **Kalamoti** are mastic-growing medieval villages.

Charming **Pirgi** is the largest mastic village, dating from the 13th century. It was defended by a Byzantine-style fort, whose walls consisted of the thick outer walls of the houses. Pirgi's tiny arched lanes and medieval houses are decorated with what the Italians call *sgraffito*, geometric black and white designs scratched into the surface of the walls. While seen here and there elsewhere in Greece, Pirgi is unique in that nearly every house is decorated with *sgraffito*; in the main square of the village they are particularly lavish. The 12th-century **Ag. Apostoli** is decorated with frescoes from the 16th century. The inhabitants of the village preserve many traditional customs and dress. Near the bus stop is the central mastic cooperative for the region.

Two other medieval villages, **Olympi** and **Mesta**, are on the road from Pirgi. Near the former once stood the Great Temple of Faneo Apollo, which has an oracle that Alexander the Great is said to have consulted. Only the fountain by the temple remains today, other items excavated from the site are now in the Chios museum. Mesta, with its stone houses and narrow, arched streets, is another medieval charmer, where you can almost hear the silence. Two churches in Mesta are worth a stop: the medieval **Ag. Paraskevi** and the 18th-century **Taxiarchis**. To the south, **Fana** has a fine, wild beach.

One of Chios' ancient cities was Levkonion, a rival of Troy that was later mentioned by Thucydides. Near the old mastic exporting port of **Emborio**, archaeologists discovered signs of a settlement that may well fit the bill, dating from 3000 BC. East of the port a 7th-century BC **temple of Athena** was found on the ancient acropolis, surrounded by ancient walls. The wealth of amphorae found under water here hint at the extent of Chios' wine trade (according to Aristophanes, the ancient Chiotes were terrible tipplers). The beach at Emborio is black and pebbly and hauntingly beautiful. Some way from the shore are the ruins of a 6th-century **Christian basilica** with mosaics.

8 August, Ag. Emilianos at Kallimasia; 12 August, Ag. Fotini at Kallimasia; 15 August, Panayia at Pirgi, Nenita, Kambos and Ag. Georgios; 22 July, Ag. Markella at Volissos and Karies; 26 July, Ag. Paraskevi at Kastello and Kalamoti; 27 July, Ag. Pandeleimon at Kalamoti.

Where to Stay

luxury

The **Argentikon** in town is set in a 19th-century mansion built on a Renaissance plan, and has been divided into four luxury suites; food provided by a chef famous for his chocolate pudding.

expensive

In Chios town you can stay where the shipowners hobnob, in the large **Chios Chandris,** on the sea at Prokymaea, ✆ 25 761, class B and wielding a bizarre 1960-ish lobby with cellophane chandeliers. In Karfas there's a new first class hotel on the beach, **Golden Sand**; it also has its own pool, ✆ 32 080. The **Hotel Kardamyla** in Kardamila is also on the beach, and there are watersports available, ✆ (0272) 25 551.

moderate

Next to the Chandris you'll find the more convivial **Hotel Kyma**, ✆ 25 551. The main body of the hotel was built by a local shipowner in the style of an Italian villa, with a fine painted ceiling adorning the lobby. There's a new addition, but try to stay in the older part, for the sea view and atmosphere. All rooms have bathrooms *en suite*, and breakfast is available. Nearby, also looking out over the harbour, **Chios Rooms** is a renovated neo-Classical shipowner's house, ✆ 27 295. In the heart of town the **Anesis**, Aplotarias and Vasilikari 2, ✆ 23 925, is a beautiful, traditional guesthouse. In Kambos there's the B class **Perivoli**, a quiet and serene traditional pension with 9 rooms, ✆ 31 513, though it's best to get directions from the tourist policeman before setting out. In medieval Mesta the NTOG has refurbished some of the traditional buildings as *guesthouses*, each furnished with local handicrafts and giving on to a courtyard. Each house can accommodate up to 5 people—a bargain at under 4000 dr. a night. For reservations, contact Paradosiakos Ikismos, Mesta, ✆ (0272) 76 319.

cheap

Cheapest in Chios town is the **Filoxenia**, near the waterfront towards the centre of town, where most rooms have private bath, ✆ 22 813. In Mesta, Armolia, Pirgi and Olympi the **townswomen's agrotourist cooperative** rent rooms for around 3000–4000 dr. a night. There are also rooms in private houses to be found in Chios town. There's a **campsite** at Ag. Isidoros, Sikiada.

Because of the numbers of Greek tourists who come to Chios, there are several inexpensive tavernas, *psistaria* (grills) and snack bars in Chios town. Open to all is the **Chios Marine Club**, a modern concrete affair behind the Chandris Hotel, with Continental alternatives to Greek cuisine, at a price. A few metres beyond is **Tassos** taverna, with reliable Greek food at normal Greek prices. Try not to miss the oldest taverna, the **Hotzas**, away from the port in town; you'll have to ask directions to get there, but it's worth the visit for its excellent food—aubergine (eggplant) simmered with tomatoes, delicious whitebait, and other standard Greek dishes, topped off with good barrelled retsina, a rare find on any island (1500 dr.) On the port, where the ferries dock, is an excellent *psistaria* **Theodosiou**, with a wide variety of freshly grilled meats, a full dinner costing no more than 1500 dr. Next door is an ouzeri serving very good fresh *mezedes*. In Langada, 14 km north of Chios, a group of little tavernas specialize in fish. Nearly all the beaches have at least one taverna. Karfas has a couple of fine eating places, the **Karatza** and **O Karfas**, where you can sit on pleasant terraces and look out over the sea to Turkey. Both serve all kinds of grilled or ready food for around 1500–2000 dr.

Inousses and Psara

Three times a day caiques leave Chios for **Inousses**, an archipelago of nine islets to the northeast. On the largest is a School of Navigation, along with other buildings donated by the wealthy shipowners who were born here. The new naval museum in the Pandelis Loimos house has a rare collection of ship models and other nautical items dating from before Napoleon; exhibits are French, British and Greek. Near the village is a medieval fort; there are a few small beaches for swimming, and an inexpensive D class hotel, the **Thalassoporos**, © (0272) 51 475.

Psara to the west of Chios is connected only a few times a week with the larger island. Archaeologists have discovered signs of a 13th-century BC Achaean settlement near Paliokastro, a town founded by Chiote refugees during Turkish rule, for the tiny rock of an islet was generally ignored by the Sultan. During the War of Independence the Psariotes contributed many ships to the cause, and they even invented a weapon, the *bourleta*, which the captains of the revolution used to destroy the Turkish fleet. So irksome were the rebel attacks from Psara that the Sultan finally demanded vengeance.

On 20 June 1824, he sent 25,000 troops to destroy Psara. In the subsequent slaughter only 3000 of the 30,000 men, women and children managed to escape to Eretria. The rest were either slain with the Turks in their own suicidal explosions, or were massacred when the Turks finally swarmed into Paliokastro after the heroic battle. Thus Psara was annihilated as the Sultan had ordered. And it never recovered: today 500 people live on Psara, a very quiet place with a couple of pensions, a small taverna and a small beach. As in Mesta, the National Tourist Organisation offers unusual accommodation, in this case in an old church cloister, offering bed and breakfast, © (0272) 61 293, or contact the main office in Mytilini, Lesbos, © (0251) 28 199.

IKARIA

Map labels:
- To Piraeus
- To Samos
- Drakanon
- Faros
- Monokambos
- Katafyio
- Gialiskari
- Karavo Stamo
- Oxea
- Therma
- Armenistis
- Oenoe
- Evdilos
- Keramai
- Christos
- Kountamos
- Chrissomilia
- Kambos
- AG. KYRIKOS
- Mandria
- Atheras
- (1037m / 3422ft)
- Therma Lefkada
- Thymena
- Ag. Minas
- Nas
- Christos
- Xilosirti
- spring
- Kámpos
- Vrakades
- Raches
- Chrissostomos
- Ammondia
- (1033m / 3409ft)
- Playa
- Manganitis
- FOURNI
- To Piraeus
- N
- 0 2 5 km 10
- 0 2 5 miles

Ikaria

More accustomed to Greeks coming for curative soaks in its radioactive waters than to foreign tourists, Ikaria over the past few years has adjusted to its new breed of guests. Each year there are more paved roads, and a few more rooms and villas to let; the breakwater has been extended to ensure safer landings at its gale-ridden port (the Ikarian sea is one of the wildest corners of the Aegean), and the enormous 'Welcome to the Island of Radiation' painted on the breakwater that once greeted visitors and gave many a traveller second thoughts about disembarking has been discreetly whitewashed.

Long, narrow Ikaria is divided by a dorsal spine of rugged mountains, many over 1000 metres high. It presents a forbidding, rocky face to the world, and much of it is inaccessible except on foot; but in the centre both the popular north and more rugged south coast are watered by mountain springs that keep the villages cool and green under oak and plane trees, with added natural air conditioning from the wind. If it's calm on one side, it's bound to be blustery on the other, leaving you with the impression that it was the wind that did in Ikaros and not the sun.

Few islands have so stubbornly clung to their traditional identity, or indeed their very soul. Ikaria means to keep its secrets—symbolized by the statue of a sphinx recently carved in the stone between Ag. Kyrikos and Xilosirtis. But as the place synonymous with the world's first hang glider, it has been deeply involved since 1990 in setting up the Ikariad, the Olympics of airsports, to be held every four years in different parts of the world (beginning in Paris); Ikaria will keep the sacred flame.

History

When fleeing Minos and Crete with his father Daedalus, Ikaros flew too near to the sun with the lovely wings his father had made him. The wax binding the feathers melted and the boy plummeted to his death off the south coast of an island thereafter known as Ikaria; Pausanius mentions that his grave could be seen on the island in the 2nd century BC. Other ancient names of the island include Ichthyoessa, for its fish, or Oenoe, for its wine. So much wine was produced that some said it was the birthplace of Dionysos, the god of wine; an inscription found on Athens' acropolis describes a certain Oenoe as being second only to Athens in sending the yearly contributions to Apollo on Delos. Under the Byzantines the island was a place of exile for officials who had fallen from grace. Kambos was one of their centres, and another large settlement existed by the hot springs at Therma.

In July 1912 during the Balkan War, the local doctor and priest led the inhabitants in forcing the Turks to leave, and for five months Ikaria was an independent state with its own flag and stamps. When it joined Greece, the government promptly forgot about it, and many Ikariotes immigrated to the states. Papadopoulos and the Colonels used Ikaria as a dumping ground for political dissidents and Communists (who at one point numbered 15,000, twice the number of Ikariotes); even today 'Red' Ikaria is one of the most leftwing islands in Greece.

Connections

The airport at Fanari should be finished by 1994; until then, by sea only. Ferries daily to Piraeus and Samos (note that some call at the island's northern port, Evidlos and others at the main port Ag. Kyrikos). Also four–five times a week connections with Paros, Mykonos, Fourni and Samos; twice weekly with Naxos and Patmos (in summer, hydrofoils two days a week to Patmos); once a week connections with Kalymnos, Leros, Lipsi, Mykonos and Syros. Small tourist excursion boats to Fourni daily.

Tourist Police

See regular police, © (0275) 22 222.

Ag. Kyrikos and Therma

Ag. Kyrikos, the capital and largest town, is in fact rather small and easy going, with more trees than buildings or people. The statue at the end of the breakwater honours Ikaros, who doesn't seem very airworthy even here. The little pier on the other side of the town has a constant bezina taxi service to Therma, only 10 minutes away (there is also a road), where most of the older hotels and restaurants are located. Buses from the square leave once a day for the villages. The string of kafeneíons along the waterfront see most of the social life, and shops in 'Agios' sell Ikaria's locally made sweets and honey made from thyme or koumaro bush blossoms.

People come from far and wide to **Therma**, where the natural highly radioactive springs bubbling up from the earth at 33–55°C are used to treat chronic rheumatism, arthritis, gout and spondylitis; one is even reputed to make women fertile. The springs are considered among the most radioactive in Europe; one, Artemidas, is so strong (790 degrees of radiation) that it's closed to the public.

To the east, near the future airport, **Fanari** has a round tower from the 3rd century BC—one of the best preserved Hellenistic towers in Greece. The entire castle survived until the War of

Independence, when Admiral Miaoulis sailed by and used it for target practice. It stood over the ancient town of **Drakanon**, of which only a few 5th-century BC remains can be seen on the acropolis. Another ancient city of Ikaria was at **Katafyio**, where the acropolis that remains is Archaic. The name Katafyio means 'shelter' and refers to an underground passageway beneath the church. One day Turkish raiders came to Katafyio, but as it was Sunday all the villagers were at church. The Turks decided to wait outside and capture the people as they came out. They waited and waited, then impatiently broke into the church—to find it empty. The priest had opened the secret trapdoor in the floor, and everyone escaped in safety.

The second most popular spring on Ikaria is also on the south coast, called **Therma Lefkados**, or Loutra. Situated in the pine trees by the Anyfantis Hotel, some of its water is so hot that villagers on picnics use it to boil their eggs. Athanatos Nero (the fountain of youth) runs between the neo-Byzantine **Evangilistrias** monastery (1775) and **Xilosirti** where they'll show you exactly where Ikaros fell. Xilosirti is spread out among olive and apricot trees; Ikaria is said to produce the tastiest fruit in Greece. On the way up to the mountain village of **Chrissostomos** is the abandoned hamlet of Hartia, with many springs and plane trees. After centuries of isolation, **Manganitis**, the westernmost village on the south shore was, in 1987, finally reached by a new road and tunnel bored through the rock. Built on a steep hillside, its lonely position belies the fact that it is one of the liveliest spots on Ikaria, with parties lasting until dawn.

The North Coast

Ikaria's northern half atttracts far more tourists; it is a gentler place with its pine forests, vineyards, sumptuous sandy beaches and excellent roads and guesthouses. A scenic bus trip links Ag. Kyrikos to **Evdilos**, the largest village, which also serves as a steamer stop several times a week between Piraeus and Samos. Nearby was the site of ancient Oenoe (or Doliche) the capital of Ikaria in antiquity, while the Byzantine princelings in exile installed themselves nearby in **Kambos**, where the columns and arches of their palace remain as well as their churches **Ag. Irene** and **Ag. Panton** (All Saints). The local museum houses finds mostly dating back to the Neolithic era. Above Kambos are the ruins of the 11th-century **Kastro of Koskinou**, near the village of the same name.

Further west along the coast is **Gialiskari**, the unofficial nudist beach, where tall pines grow down the mountainside to a sandy shore. There are a few rooms, but always full in the summer; many people camp here and at Livadi. Further west **Armenistis** is a large, attractive village with Ikaria's best sandy beach and most accommodation. It's also the point of departure for the wooded, mountain village of **Christos Raches**, the 'Little Switzerland of Ikaria'. Further west, a dirt road leads to the beach and ancient city of **Nas**, with remnants of the ancient harbour. In the ruins of the temple of Artemis Tauropolos a marvellous statue of the goddess was discovered in the 19th century, with eyes that followed the viewer from every angle. The local priest decided at once that it was the work of heathen if not of the devil himself and ordered it to be thrown in the lime kiln. Thus perished the *Artemis of Ikaria*, never to hold its place in the Louvre with the *Venus of Milo* or *Victory of Samothrace*.

In the summer *paneyeria* occupy the attention of the whole island, when many Ikariotes who live abroad come home just to make merry. These feasts are run in the old style: guests order a *prothesi*—a kilo of wild goat meat, a bottle of wine, a huge bowl of soup and a loaf of bread—enough to feed four. At one of the larger paneyeria at Christos (above Ag. Kyrikos) 2200 pounds of meat are consumed each year. But the biggest festival of all is on 17 July, in honour of the defeat of the Turks and Ikaria's independence in 1912. Feasts, speeches, music and folkdancing in costume are part of the day's agenda.

Other *paneyeria* are on 26 July, Ag. Paraskevi in Xilosirti; 27 July, at Ag. Panteleimonos; 6 August at Christos; 8 September, at Playa and Manganitis; 17 September, Ag. Sophia at Mesokambos; 15 August at Akamatra and Chrissostomos.

Where to Stay

expensive

There are two new hotels at Armenistis, **Cavos** and **Daidalos**, © 41 410. The latter is built and furnished in a traditonal style, set among the cedars overlooking the sea, with a pool, children's pool and restaurant. In Evdilos, the **Atheras**, © 31 434, offers similar comforts and pool.

moderate–cheap

In the capital there are small pensions and rooms, and in Therma Lefkada (or Loutra) a mile west of Ag. Kyrikos you'll find the B class **Adam's**, © 22 418, and in the same price range is the slightly larger **Marina** pension, © 22 188. In Therma, hotels cater primarily for the arthritic; nicest here is the class C **Apollon**, © 22 477, which includes one of the baths if the doctors okay a dip. On the more popular north coast you'll have to rely primarily on rooms (not always easy to find). In Evdilos, the **Evdoxia** pension has pricey doubles at around 8000 dr., © 31 502. There are many more rooms in Armenistis; the **Armena**, © 41 415, has nice views. The current rate on the island for a double room in a private home is 2500–3000 dr., and no one cares (at least no one official) if you sleep on the beach.

Eating Out

In Ag. Kyrikos, there are a couple of simple tavernas and the island's best pizzas at **Filoti**; the sweet shop next door is a good place for snacks, and the bakery near the main square does good hot cheese pies (*tiropita*). In Evdilos, the ouzeri **Flisvos** is also the place to go for fish; for grilled meats, try **Kolonakia** overlooking the port, where many people end up in the evening for a heavenly plate of warm honey doughnuts or *loukomades*. There are tavernas or snack bars along most of the beaches on the coast: **Kelari** overlooking fishing boats at Gialiskari has good seafood, or **Charlie's** in Armenestis.

Fourni

Connected daily by caique from Ag. Kyrikos and twice weekly from Samos, Fourni are a pair of quiet islets just about midway between two larger sisters, Samos and Ikaria. The larger island encircles a huge harbour that long hid a band of Algerian pirates, from where they would pounce on passing ships. Today the harbour is better known for its fish, especially the much loved *barbounia* (red mullet) and lobster, which although plentiful, isn't cheap; the surprising number of fishing boats in the harbour ship most of their catch to Athens. Many fish by night, using bright lamps that set the sea aglitter.

Kampos, the 'capital' and largest village, is a pleasant little town with many trees, belying the barren rockpile which Fourni resembles from its outer coasts. There is a sandy beach, but unfortunately it's in the harbour, and not as clean as one might wish. Several caiques run trips to the crystal-clear outer beaches, although you're more likely to find pebbles instead of sand. Rooms and tavernas (**Miltos** for lobster and fresh fish) are available near the port, and at the time of writing a road is being built to the island's other village, **Chrissomilia**. Caiques leave from here for **Thymena**, a village on Fourni's smaller islet, where you'll be stared at if you disembark.

Festivals

23 April, Ag. Georgios; 6 December, Ag. Nikolaos.

Lesbos (Mytilini)

Officially Lesbos, but more often called Mytilini after its principal city, the island is the third largest in Greece, but one of the most elusive. Its undulating hills are said to support 11 million olive trees, which glisten silver in the sunlight, while the higher peaks are swathed in deep pine forests. The island has long been a cradle of poetry and art; Sappho ran a marriage school here for young ladies, to whom she dedicated many of her love poems; Alcaeus and Terpander, 'father of Greek music', were born here, as too were Arion, inventor of the dithyramb, Longus, author of *Daphnis and Chloe*, and Theophilos (1873-1934), a poor villager who earned his ouzo in exchange for the finest naïve canvas modern Greece has produced. Even in this century Lesbos produced the last Greek to win a Nobel Prize (1979)—poet Odysseus Elytis. On the other hand, it was also the birthplace of the Barbarossa brothers, red-bearded Greeks turned pirates for the Sultan, and the worst terrors the Aegean has ever known.

For the most part Lesbos is an island of quiet villages, and the tourists tend to stay in just a few areas. Its size makes transport difficult unless you have a car or scooter. Although much of the island is quite lovely, it has little that stands out in particular—an attractive artist's colony, a bit of a petrified forest, a handful of charming villages, a few rather ordinary beaches. Like Evia, it is still very much a place where the people go about their everyday business unconcerned with the great wave of international tourism that has swept over the other islands.

LESBOS

To Limnos

To Chios

MYTILINI

Ag. Marina

Varia

Loutra

Kratigos

Thermi

Pamfilla

Moria

Ag. Ermougenis

Misstegna

Perama

Pappados

Gulf of Yera

Paliokipos

Messagros

Skopelos

Palios

Asapropotamos

Pigi

Agiassos

Ag. Isidoros

Piomari

Plomari

Skala Sikamia

Sikamia

Klio

Pelopi

Kapi

Mantamandos

Ag. Paraskevi

Megalochori

Mt. Olympos
(964m / 3167ft)

Eftalou

Karakas 968m

Stipsi

Kalloni

Kerami

Skala Kalloni

Kalloni Bay

Vassilika

Methymna (Molyvos)

Petra

Skoutaros

Polichnitos

Vatera

Vrissa

Parakila

Vatoussa

Skalochori

Antissa

Ag. Ioannis

Antissa

Agra

Mesotopos

Apothikes

Eressos

Sigri

Skala Eressou

Megalonissi

N

10 km

miles

| 0 | 2 | 5 | 10 km |
| 0 | 2 | 5 | miles |

354

Mythology

Even in myth Lesbos is connected with music and poetry. The mytho-historical musician Arion was a son of the island, accredited with the invention of the dithyramb. His talents brought him great wealth—and headaches. After a musical contest in Italy, where he had won all the prizes, the crew of the ship returning him to Lesbos decided to throw him overboard and keep his treasures for themselves. Arion was allowed to sing one last time, after which he dived into the sea. But his swan song had charmed the dolphins, and they saved his life, carrying him safely to shore. The ship's crew were later executed for their treachery. Another myth deals with the great poet Orpheus, who was torn to pieces by orgiastic maenads and followers of Dionysos and thrown into a river of Thrace. His beautiful head floated to Lesbos, where the inhabitants carried it to a cave. There Orpheus' head sang and prophesied so well that people stopped patronizing Delphi. This loss of business angered Apollo, the god of Delphi, who made a special trip to Lesbos to order Orpheus' head to shut up.

History

Like many of the islands that hug the coast of Asia Minor, Lesbos both enjoyed the benefits and suffered the penalties of its east-west geography as early as the Trojan War. Homer describes the island as an ally of Troy, and it suffered raids by both Odysseus and Achilles. In the 10th century BC Aeolians from Thessaly colonized the island and the coast of Asia Minor. The Aeolians lacked the vital intellectual curiosity of the Ionians, but by the 6th century BC they had managed to make Lesbos a cultural centre, especially under the rule of Pittachos, one of the Seven Sages of ancient Greece. He went far in healing the ancient rivalry between Lesbos' two principal cities, Mytilini and Methymna, and promoted trade with Egypt.

Methymna, having lost the fight for island dominance, got back at Mytilini when that city decided to leave the Delian league and join Sparta in the Peloponnesian War, in 428 BC. Methymna tattle-taled to Athens, and according to Thucydides, an order was sent for a general massacre in Mytilini. However, soon after the ship with the order sailed, the Athenians reconsidered (for once) and sent a second ship countermanding the massacre. It arrived in the nick of time, and the citizens were spared.

In the 4th century BC, Lesbos continued to change hands frequently, its most memorable ruler being Hermeias, who governed both the island and the Troad on the mainland. Hermeias was a eunuch and a student at Plato's Academy, and he attempted to rule his principality on the precepts of the *Republic* and the ideal city-state; Aristotle helped him found a branch of the Academy in ancient Assos and while there married Hermeias' niece. Later the island was occupied by Mithridates of Pontos, who was in turn ousted by the Romans in a battle believed to be Julius Caesar's first.

Like Chios, Lesbos was given by the Byzantine Emperor Michael Palaeologos to the Genoese for their help in restoring the Byzantine Empire (1261). In 1462 Mohammed the Conqueror captured the island, despite the heroic resistance led by Lady Oretta d'Oria, and the island remained in Turkish hands until 1912.

By air: numerous charters from various European cities; at least three daily flights from Athens, daily with Thessaloniki, three times a week with Limnos, twice a week with Chios.

By sea: daily ferry boat from Piraeus and Chios; three times a week with Kavala and Limnos, at least twice a week with Thessaloniki, Rafina and Ag. Efstratios, once a week with Samos, Patmos, Leros, Kalymnos, Kos, Rhodes and Volos. In the summer, daily boat to Ayvalik (near ancient Assos) in Turkey.

Tourist Information

Tourist police, Mytilini harbour, ✆ (0251) 22 776. There is also a Tourist Information Office in Molyvos.

Mytilini

The capital of Lesbos, **Mytilini** is a large town of magnificent old mansions, impressive public buildings, and beautiful gardens. Its two harbours are divided by what was once an islet, but today is a peninsula, with a **Byzantine-Genoese castle** on top. This used to be the acropolis of ancient Mytilini, where a temple of Apollo (600 BC) stood. Where a canal once flowed between Mytilini and the islet, the remains of an ancient trireme were found, stranded in the accumulation of sand and sediment that over the centuries filled in the 'Euripos of the Mytilineans'. The present **kastro** was founded in the 6th century, and in 1373 the Genoese repaired it with any available material including ancient columns hastily crammed in between the stones like a collage. Inside are numerous buildings left by the various occupants of the fortress, and a well-preserved Roman cistern and Turkish *medrese*.

In the **north harbour**, the least picturesque side of town, are many small antique shops selling some very unexpected items. By the pine forest above the town to the northwest, the Hellenistic **Theatre** was one of the largest of ancient Greece; Pompey admired it so much that he used its plans to build his theatre in Rome in 55 BC. Just north of the north harbour is a wooded hill where campers pitch their tents, and there is a small beach at **Tsamakia**.

Heading towards the south harbour, back from the pier on 8 November St, is the **Archaeology Museum** (*8.30–3, closed Mon*); highlights include reliefs found in a Roman house, depicting scenes from the comedies of Menander, as well as mosaics and prehistoric finds from Thermai. Dominating the town, the cathedral **Ag. Athanasios** (16th–17th century) has a finely-carved wooden iconostasis. Near **Ag. Therapon** are Turkish fountains, and in front of the church is the **Byzantine Museum**, stocked with icons. Near **Ag. Kyriaki** are some of the walls of ancient Mytilini. Between the new **Municipal Theatre** (1968) and the post office behind it, the placards advertise films that often include some real classics, a cut above the Kung-Fu/Schwarzenegger shoot 'em ups offered on other islands.

Just South of Mytilini

It's not hard to escape from the city; many shops hire cars, scooters or bicycles to explore the rest of the island. Buses depart from two separate stations: distant villages are served from the far end of the harbour, nearer ones from the centre. Buses from the latter station can take you in a few minutes to **Varia**, the home town of Theophilos. His house is now a **Theophilos museum**—the best on the island, containing some 80 examples of his work, pictures that evoke the island's charm far better than any photograph. Near here is the **Museum of Modern Art**, founded by another native artist Eleftheriades (possibly better known by his adopted French name Theriade) with many of his own works, as well as minor works by Picasso, Gauguin, Matisse and Chagall. Theriade became Theophilos' patron, but not in time to save the artist from dying unknown and penniless. **Neapolis** is just south of Varia and has the ruins of a 5th-century basilica. This whole peninsula is one of the prettiest areas of Lesbos. There are two long beaches, one at **Kratigos** and another at **Ag. Ermougenis**, with a taverna. From Koundouroudia, near Loutra, a ferry crosses the Gulf of Yera for Perama.

North of Mytilini

The road north passes **Moria**, where the arches of Mytilini's Roman aqueduct remain intact. To the north is **Thermi**, a spa with hot saline springs recommended by Galen and the 12th-century Byzantine church of Panayia Troullouti. Thermi was inhabited before 3000 BC; its five successive levels of civilization were excavated by Winifred Lamb between 1923 and 1933. Ancient Thermi had connections with Troy, and during the Trojan War the Achaeans apparently burnt it to the ground; the dates match the traditional dates of the Trojan War (1250 BC). A large Turkish tower stands near the baths, and there are rooms and restaurants and a beach nearby.

Leaving the coast, the road north rises to **Mantamandos**, a large village with the interesting 18th-century church **Taxiarchis Michael**, with a miraculous black icon of Archangel Michael that is said to smell of wildflowers. One modern and rather unpleasant explanation has it that pirates killed all the monks except one, who collected the blood-soaked earth and moulded it into an icon; the truth is surely much older. Mantamandos is one of the last villages in Greece that has preserved the ancient custom of ritually sacrificing bulls for the village Easter feast. From **Klio** to the north a track leads down to pretty **Skala Sikamia**, one of the more remote corners of Lesbos, renowned on the island for its mild winters.

Methymna and the North

Up at the northernmost tip of the island is its second city **Methymna**, pronounced Mithymna although the locals call it Molyvos, its Venetian name. By whatever name it is the most popular and prettiest town on Lesbos, Mytilini's arch rival for a long time, although it has now dropped to third in terms of population. Methymna was the birthplace of the poets Arion and Longus and was the site of the tomb of the Achaean hero Palamedes, buried here by Achilles and Ajax. Achilles besieged the ancient fortress of Mithymna, but with little success until the daughter of the King fell in love with him and opened the city gates, a kindness Achilles rewarded by having her slain for betraying her father. From Roman times onwards Mithymna was frequently attacked. In 1373, when Lesbos belonged to the Genoese, Francesco Gattilusi repaired the old Byzantine fortress on top of the hill, but it fell to Mohammed the Conqueror in 1462.

Modern Molyvos is a symphony of red-tiled roofs, flowers and windows stacked above the lovely harbour and fine long beach, reaching up to the striking **Genoese Castle** perched on top, with views of Turkey. Besides the town beach, there are others nearby at Petra and **Eftalou**, the latter with hot springs. Both have tavernas and are less crowded than Molyvos. In the summer Molyvos hosts a theatre festival.

Charming **Petra**, besides its splendid beach, has for its landmark the church of **Panayia Glykofiloussa** (1747), looming high up on a sheer precipice. **Kalloni**, a large village further south, replaces the ancient city of Arisbe; its acropolis was located where the medieval **Kastro of Kalloni** is today. Arisbe flourished until a few of the local young men abducted some girls from Methymna; the people of Methymna responded in wrath, destroying Arisbe and enslaving all its people. Near Kalloni, you'll find the foundations of a 3rd-century BC temple of Aphrodite and the 16th-century monastery **Ag. Ignatius Limonos**. From Kalloni a road leads up to **Ag. Paraskevi** in the east, where bulls are sacrificed and eaten in the spring-time feast of Ag. Charalambos in conjunction with horseraces (perhaps a relic of the Roman rites of Mithras). To the south is **Skala Kalloni**, where three beach tavernas serve the sardines caught in Kalloni Bay. **Apothikes**, west along the bay, is a ruined village still retaining a long wall and tower.

Northwest Lesbos and the Petrified Forest

The northwest quarter of Lesbos is volcanic, and until modern times was the home of wild horses—some believe they may be the last link with the horse-breeding culture of the Troad in the Late Bronze Age, mentioned in the *Iliad*. The largest village here, **Eressos** was Sappho's birthplace and minted coins bearing her portrait. Ancient Eressos was actually north of the present village, near the castle **Xokastro**, where a few fragments remain. Nearer the sea, looming over **Skala Eressou** is a Byzantine fortress on Vigla hill that stood up to the Genoese siege in 1333. There is a lovely beach near here, although beware that it's also a favourite of tour operators.

The modern village of **Antissa** has inherited the name of Bronze Age Antissa, on the north coast. Once an islet, ancient Antissa was joined to Lesbos in an earthquake; Orpheus' prophetic talking head supposedly ended up here and it was the birthplace of another of Lesbos' great poet musicians, Terpander, inventor of choric poetry. The Romans destroyed the town to punish the inhabitants for their support of the Macedonians, and all that remains is below **Horeokastro**, a Genoese fort facing the sea. Near Antissa, the monastery **Ag. Ioannis Theologos Ipsilos**, set high on a promontory, was founded in the 9th century and rebuilt in the 12th, and contains a collection of antique religious paraphernalia. In the triangle between Antissa, Skala Eressou and **Sigri** is Lesbos' **petrified forest**— petrified after being buried in volcanic ash for hundreds of thousands of years; what remains has slowly become visible as the ash erodes away. Some of the best specimens are near Sigri itself, but they entail a long walk, and inevitable disappointment unless you're a geologist. But Sigri does have a charming beach and by the shore is a Turkish castle (1757) still bristling with cannons.

South Lesbos

Southern Lesbos, between the bays of Kalloni and Yera, is dominated by **Mt Olympos** (967 m). At last count, there are 19 mountains in the Mediterranean named Olympos. Almost all were peaks sacred to the local sky god, who, in this most syncretic corner of the world, became associated with Zeus, and thus the local sky god's mountain would take the name of Zeus' home, or Olympos. In the shadow of Olympos lies the lovely village of **Agiassos**, which despite its discovery by tourists, remains one of the most interesting villages on Lesbos, with its picturesque houses, medieval castle, Kastelli, and **church of the Panayia**, founded in the 1100s by the Archbishop of Mytilini, Valerios Konstantinos, to house an old icon of Mary saved from the iconoclasts. The present church building was constructed in 1812 after a fire destroyed the older structure, and it has one of the most beautiful 19th-century interiors of any Greek church. On 15 August the village is thronged with pilgrims. From the **Kipos Panayias** taverna (up the steps from the bus stop) there's a splendid view of the village and its orchards that produce excellent black plums. Chestnut and pine groves cover the region, one of Lesbos' prettiest, and the road west to Polichnitos is especially lovely.

To the west, **Polichnitos** has a thermal spa and a beach with tavernas, while on the south coast **Vrissa** was the home town of Briseis, the captive princess who caused the rift between Achilles and Agamemnon at Troy. Only a wall remains of the ancient Trojan town destroyed in 1180 BC. A Genoese tower stands west of Vrissa, while to the south the beach of **Vatera** extends for some kilometres, dotted with pensions and tavernas. **Plomari** to the east has an ouzo distillery producing Greece's best aperitif, and is now a burgeoning resort. Further east along the coast, **Ag. Isidoros** is a smaller resort, with an excellent pebble and sandy beach. By **Pappados** is the ruined Paliokastro, of uncertain date, and at **Perama** there is a good sandy beach and ferry across the Gulf of Yera to **Koundouroudia**, near Loutra.

Festivals

26 August, Ag. Ermolaou at Paliokipos; 8 May, Ag. Theologos at Antissa; 26 July, at Ag. Paraskevi; 2nd day of Easter and 15 August, at Agiassos; 15 August, at Petra; Ag. Magdalinis at Skopelos; end of September, at Plomari; 'Week of Prose and Drama' in May.

Where to Stay

expensive

Right where the ferry docks in Mytilini (so be prepared for some noise) and with a view over the harbour, is the B class **Blue Sea**, © (0251) 23 994. In Molyvos, slightly set aside from the town and near the beach is the B class **Delfinia**, with comfortable rooms, © (0253) 71 373. A pleasant alternative is **Adonis**, also near the sea and rates are about the same, © (0253) 71 866.

moderate

In Mytilini, also on the waterfront the **Sappho Hotel** is a picturesque if somewhat noisy place to stay in the city, rated class C, © (0251) 28 415. On the whole you're better off in one of the many pensions; get the list from the tourist police near the ferry quay. On Neapolis Beach near the city, there's the **Lesvos Beach**, © (0251) 61 531/2, with furnished apartments for lengthy stays. In Molyvos there are a collection of hotels and pensions, which tend to be expensive and full. If you book in advance, the **Poseidon**, © (0253) 71 570, is pleasant and intimate, with only 6 rooms. By the harbour you stand a better chance at the **Sea Horse** pension, with 13 rooms, © (0253) 71 320. At Skala Eressou, **Sappho The Eressian** is a medium-sized place with decent rooms at a decent price, © (0253) 53 233. In Petra there are two moderately priced choices, the **Ilion**, © (0253) 41 227 and **Petra**, on the central square, © (0253) 41 257.

cheap

Rooms in private houses start at around 3000 dr.—ask at the tourist information office. The women of Petra have formed an **agrotourist cooperative**, pooling their houses to rent more than a hundred rooms to visitors, and provide excellent food at their restaurant. Rooms start at about 3500 dr. and are immaculately clean and tastefully decorated, © (0253) 41 238. If you are a bona fide artist, you can stay at the lodgings of the Athens School of Fine Arts in Molyvos. There are also numerous rooms to rent in Plomari, Eressos, Sigri, Thermi and Vrissa.

Eating Out

Lesbos is fairly well supplied with restaurants and tavernas; try **Asteria** on the waterfront in Mytilini, where regular, well-cooked Greek meals cost about 2000 dr. Two places popular with the locals are about 5 km out of town towards the airport, **Achivada** and **Asteria**; both serve good Greek dishes and fresh fish at reasonable prices (2000–2500 dr.). Nearly all of the beaches have good tavernas, with prices more reasonable than most other islands. The main 'street' in Molyvos is the most expensive place to eat; there's an attractive selection of good tavernas, all serving freshly prepared oven dishes and a variety of offerings from the grill. Get in early to claim a table on the small terraces that overlook the town and beach. If your tastebuds need a change, try **Melinda's**, with an extensive menu of alternative food, such as vegetarian dishes and curries. In Petra, **Niko's** is recommended for seafood (3000 dr.), and **Marina** serves food with an international flavour in a courtyard by the water; good asparagus *au gratin*, various types of steak, and a pleasing wine list (3500–4000 dr.).

Limnos

Limnos hardly fits any Greek island stereotypes. It lies low and flat, a lush green carpet in the spring that becomes crackling yellow-brown in the summer, when water is in short supply. The landscape is dotted with fields of grain, quirky scarecrows and beehives (the island's thyme honey was favoured by the gods) but the main occupation of Limnos is military: its magnificent natural harbour near the mouth of the Dardenelles has ensured that the island has always been of strategic importance. It was the holy island of the smithy god Hephaistos (Vulcan), who was worshipped on Mount Moschylus, which in ancient times emitted a fiery jet of asphaltic gas; today Limnos' volcanic past is manifest in its astringent hot springs and the highly sulphuric 'Limnian earth', found near Repanidi, used from ancient times until the Turkish occupation for healing wounds and stomach aches.

Mythology

The smithy god Hephaistos was so weakly when he was born that his mother Hera hurled him off Mt Olympos. He survived by falling in the sea, off Limnos, where the sea goddesses Thetis and Eurynome cared for him. Years later, when Hera found Thetis wearing a magnificent brooch made by Hephaistos, she changed her mind about her son, brought him back to Olympos and married him to the lovely Aphrodite. Hephaistos became so reconciled with his mother that when Zeus hung Hera by her wrists from the sky for rebelling against him, Zeus in his fury hurled him again from Mt Olympos. This time he smack fell on Limnos, a fall that left Hephaistos crippled for life, despite all the care lavished on him by the islanders (in the early days of metallurgy, the seemingly magic powers of the smith were so valued that in many cultures he was hobbled, to keep him from running away or joining an enemy).

Hephaistos was so beloved on Limnos that when his wife Aphrodite betrayed him with the war-god Ares, the women of Limnos stopped worshipping her and tossed her cult statue into the sea. Aphrodite retaliated by making their breath and underarms stink (Robert Graves suggests this may have been because they worked with woad, a putrid substance used in the manufacture of tattoo ink). This led the good men of Limnos to prefer the company of captive Thracian women to that of their own wives. This led to further incidents: the women of Limnos doctored their husbands' wine to make them sleep, and then slit their throats, throwing their bodies into the sea. Henceforth the smelly women of Limnos lived as Amazons, warlike and independent. When Jason and the Argonauts appeared on the horizon, the women would have attacked had not one of them realized that a shipload of Greek heroes was just what they needed to continue the Limniote race. So the Argonauts met only the kindest courtesy, and a son born to Jason, Euneus, went on to become King of Limnos during the Trojan War, supplying the Achaeans with wine.

The Achaeans' best archer, Philoctetes the son of Heracles, spent the ten years of the Trojan War on Limnos, suffering from a wounded foot. Philoctetes had inherited his father's famous bow when Heracles was dying in torment caused by Nessus' shirt, for Philoctetes was the only one who would light the pyre to put him out of his misery. When Zeus made Heracles an immortal, Hera in a fit of pique sent a poisoned snake after Philoctetes when the Achaeans landed on Limnos on route to Troy. Throughout the war the poor man lingered in pain, living in an island cave, with only his bow. After the death of Achilles, an oracle declared that Achaeans could only capture Troy with the aid of Philoctetes' bow. Odysseus and Neoptolemos, the son of Achilles, tried to take it from him by trickery (in Sophocles' *Philoctetes*) but in the end, according to most accounts, Philoctetes himself took his bow to Troy, where he slew Paris.

In Classical times the expression 'Limnian deeds' meant especially atrocious acts. The phrase was first used by Herodotos in his account of an event in the Persian War, when some Limniotes brought home some Athenian women they had captured. When the children they bore began putting on airs, the Limniotes supposedly slaughtered them and their mothers.

History

Limnos' highly intriguing past also bucks the stereotypes. Homer wrote that the first islanders hailed from Thrace, but Herodotos says they were Tyrrhenian—related to the mysterious, sophisticated Etruscans of Rome and Tuscany. This remarkable claim has been given substance by pre-6th century BC non-Greek inscriptions found on Limnos that show linguistic similarities to the Etruscans, as do some of the ancient burials. The Etruscans themselves claimed to have originally immigrated to Italy from Asia Minor. Whoever they were, the ancient Limniotes were not Greek.

But Limnos was exceptional from the start. Excavations at Poliochne have uncovered a settlement dating back to 4000 BC—the most advanced Neolithic civilization yet discovered in the Aegean. These precocious ancient Limniotes may have been the first to colonize Troy; the dates coincide and there were certainly close cultural contacts between the two into the Mycenaean era.

In historical times, Hephestia was the island's capital, and for a time the island was the centre of the Cabiri cult until it set up headquarters on Samothrace (*see* p. 376). The Venetians took Limnos in the 13th century, but it was soon regained by the Byzantines. In 1475 Mohammed the Conqueror sent troops to conquer Limnos. They would have captured the island were it not for the leadership of the Limniote heroine Maroula, who seized her dying father's weapons and shouted the battle cry. In 1478, however, Mohammed himself came and took the island and the Turks held it until 1912. In the First World War Moudros Bay was the naval base of the Allies in the Gallipoli campaign.

Connections

By air: twice daily with Athens, once a day with Thessaloniki, three times a week with Lesbos.

By sea: four–five times a week with Lesbos, Chios and Kavala; four times a week with Ag. Efstratios and Rafina, three times a week with Piraeus, twice a week with

Thessaloniki, once a week with Samos, Patmos, Leros, Kalymnos, Kos and Rhodes (also occasional excursion caiques in summer).

Buses around Limnos are few and infrequent. Many villages have only one service a day, so there's no way to get back to Myrina the same day, hence the town's many taxis and moped and car hire firms.

Tourist Police

Regular police in Myrina, ✆ (0254) 22 200.

Myrina

Myrina on the west coast serves as the island's port and capital and is the only town of any size, with a long main shopping street noodling up from the commercial harbour in the south. There's a sprinkling of houses built in the Turkish or Thracian style, and with their gardens they lend Myrina a touch of charm. Myrina is sometimes known as Kastro for its landmark, the romantic **Turkish fort** built over the rocky promontory that divides the shore in two. Although there isn't much inside, the walk up to the castle offers a view over much of the island. Its foundations date back to Classical times, when it was the site of a temple of Artemis. The Kastro divides Myrina's waterfront into two: a 'Turkish beach' on the south side of town, near the commercial port and to the north, the long sandy 'Greek beach', its promenade and Limnos' nightlife (such as it is). The north port is closed by the cape and pretty beach of **Akti Myrina**, where the amazons of Limnos hurled their hapless husbands into the sea after slitting their throats.

On the north edge of town, a villa once belonging to the Turkish pasha has been converted into an **Archaeological Museum**, with ten rooms chronicling the history of Limnos. Upstairs are prehistoric relics from Poliochne, divided into four different periods by colours, beginning with the 'Black' period, from 4000 BC. Downstairs are more recent discoveries from Hephestia, Chloi and Myrina.

North, and East Towards Moudros Bay

North of Myrina 423-m **Mt Skopia** is the highest point on Limnos, and can be climbed from Ag. Nikolaos where the road ends. **Pirgos** on the coast has a small fort, Mikro Kastelli, and ancient tombs have been found in the region. Nearby **Skala** has some pretty sea caves; caiques make the excursion from Myrina's north harbour.

The southern road towards Moudros Bay passes quiet beaches at **Platis** and **Thanos** (a particularly beautiful, golden stretch of sand, but difficult to find from the village), and scattered here and there all the way to **Kontias**, many with shade and good places to camp. South of Kontias at **Vryokastro** are the ruins of a Mycenaean fort.

Other beaches, the locally popular **Tsimantria** and **Nea Koutalis** both with restaurants, are on Limnos' great natural harbour, **Moudros Bay**. In April 1915, the Anglo-French fleet launched its ill-fated attack on the Dardanelles from here, a campaign planned partly on

LIMNOS

N

Cape
Hermaeon

Chryse

Plaka

Panayia

Ag. Alexandros

II Chloi

Aliki
Lake

Cape
Keros

Ag. Ioannis

Hephestia II

Pournias Bay

Repanidiou Kontopouli

Kalliopi

Luxna

Romano

Chortarolimni
Lake

Rosopouli

II Poliochne

Ag. Sozos Monastery

Propouli

Astiki

Karpasi
Kotsinas

Varos

Moudros

Kaminia

Ag. Sofia

Finisi

Skandali

Skala

Sergitsi

Katalakkon

Pirgos

Ag. Nikolaos

Sveria

Sardes

Kornos

Ag. Dimitrios

Leibadoxori

Nea Koutalis

Tsimantria

Agkariones

Tsoutsfia

II Vryokastro

Moudros Bay

Mt. Skopia
(423m / 1390ft)

Kaspakas

MYRINA (KASTRO)

Platis

Kontias

Thanos

Cape
Mourtzeflos

Melouna

Avlonas

To Kavala

To Lesbos, Ag. Efstratos

10 km

miles

5

5

2

2

0

0

364

Limnos by Lord of the Admiralty Winston Churchill; in 1918, after leaving over 30,000 dead at Gallipoli, an armistice with the Turks was signed on board a ship in the Bay where it had all begun. East of Moudros town (even today dependent on the large military presence) is a British Commonwealth war cemetery. Limnos' airport (civil and military), is at the north end of the bay, where the island is only a few kilometres wide.

The North Coast

On Pournias Bay to the north, **Kotsinas** was the walled medieval capital of Limnos. A statue of the heroine Maroula stands here and a spring with good water flows down a long stairway by the church **Zoodochos Pigi**. There is a good beach below and views across Limnos from the top of the village. Another former capital of Limnos was ancient **Hephestia**, to the east, named after the god who crashlanded on the spot. Part of the theatre remains, and you can make out ancient houses and an agora. Nearby, the village of **Kokkino** is defended by a medieval castle. Further east, **Chloi** is the site of the **cave of Philoktetis** and the earliest-known sanctuary of the Underworld deities of fertility, the Cabiri. In the Archaic period women came here to pray for fertility. The most important building discovered by the Italian archaeologists was a 6th–7th century BC temple of initiation, dedicated to Thracian Aphrodite.

Plaka lies on the tip of Cape Hermaeon, where a beacon was lit by order of Agamemnon to signal the end of the Trojan War—a signal relayed over the islands back to Mycenae. About 30 m off the shore of Plaka are the ruins of **Chryse**, a very ancient city submerged by an earthquake. A temple of Apollo was discovered in a reef; on a calm day you can see its marble blocks from a boat.

The Southeast

Limnos has two lakes, both near its east coast: **Aliki**, which has salt water, and **Chortapolimni**, which is dry in the summer and filled by river torrents in the spring. Here too is Limnos' major archaeological site, **Poliochne** (partly signposted from Kaminia), where the Italians discovered four different layers of civilization, one on top of the other. The Neolithic town pre-dates the Egyptian dynasties, the Minoan kingdoms of Crete, and even the earliest level of Troy. Walls and houses remain of the next oldest city (2000 BC) which was probably destroyed by an earthquake. Here the Italians found the oldest baths in the Aegean. The third city dates back to the Copper Age, while the last settlement dates from the Bronze Age and was contemporary with the Mycenaeans—the Limnos of Homer—dating from 1500 to 100 BC. Unfortunately there's little to see other than the walls of the second city and the foundations of houses. The abandoned monstery **Ag. Sozos** to the south looks over the sea from a high cliff. This whole southeastern peninsula is planted with vineyards.

23 April, Ag. Georgios at Kalliopi—horseraces are run by the locals, who wager goats on the outcome; 26 October, Ag. Dimitrios at Ag. Dimitrios; 15 August, at Kaminia and Tsimantria; 6 August, Sotiris at Vlaka; 7 September, Ag. Sozos; 21 May, Ag. Konstantinos at Romano.

Where to Stay

luxury

The locals call it 'Little Switzerland', but otherwise the posh deluxe bungalow complex on the beach in Myrina is known as the **Akti Myrina**, *✆* 22 681. Owned by Swiss interests, it has its own nightclub, four restaurants, private stretch of beach, swimming pool, tennis courts and its own caique. Wooden chalets house 125 rooms. The complex is famous throughout Greece, for its prices alone: a bungalow starts at 25,000 dr., but there are some for double that figure.

moderate

At the Akti Myrina international tourism begins and ends on Limnos. Otherwise you'll be competing for a room with the Greeks in the class C **Lemnos** on Plateia 28 Octovriou, *✆* 22 153, where a double costs around 3800 dr., or the more reasonable **Aktaeon** at 2 Arvanitaki, *✆* 22 258. In Moudros **To Kyma** is a tranquil place to stay, and it has a restaurant and bar.

cheap

There are a limited number of rooms to let in the town, which tend to be overpriced. If you want to camp out, try Platis beach, a little under 2 km from Myrina.

Eating Out

You could throw all caution and good sense to the wind, and have a blow out meal at the Akti Myrina; the dining will be memorable and the bill unforgettable. Otherwise there's a small selection of tavernas and grills along the waterfront, including a couple of fish tavernas in the north harbour; the no-name taverna where the boat docks is undoubtedly the best deal in town, a full dinner costing around 1500 dr. Along the northern waterfront, or Promenade, is a stretch of pizzerias and cafés. Outside the capital it's harder to find food at places other than the beach tavernas at Platis and Thanos.

Ag. Efstratios

The flat, little volcanic triangle of **Ag. Efstratios** (ferry four times a week from Kavala, Limnos and Rafina, once a week from Lesbos and Chios) lies 37 km off its big sister Limnos. Rich in minerals (including petroleum), the islet has been inhabited from Mycenaean times, and on the north coast stand the walls and ruins of the ancient settlement, which lasted into

Byzantine times. In 1967 an earthquake struck Ag. Efstratios, and ruined its port and major village which now stands derelict, although a few of the least damaged structures have been repaired. Everyone else lives next to a wide, sandy beach in a rather dreary village of concrete huts thrown up by the government after the disaster; here there is a small guesthouse with 9 rooms, and several cafés with food. Most of the island's 300 people live off the sea—the surrounding waters are transparent and rich in fish. Besides the village beach, which is really quite pleasant, there are several others scattered about, but you will need to walk or hire a caique to reach them. In times of strife Ag. Efstratios received its share of political prisoners, for it is remote, and even today receives very few visitors.

Samos

Known since antiquity as the 'Island of the Blest', Samos has historically and economically always been one of the most important islands in Greece, and since the 1980s it has become one of the most touristed as well. Only the lovely 2-kilometre-wide Strait of Mycale separates Samos from Turkey, and like that coast, is remarkably fertile (producing a famous wine, and also olives, tobacco and raisins). Pine forests cover much of the rest of Samos; the coast is indented with numerous sandy coves, while two mighty mountains furnish dramatic background scenery: central Mt Ampelos (1140 m) and in the west, Mt Kerkis, a looming 1445 m, both a continuation of the mainland chain. Samos is big enough to absorb large numbers of visitors without seeming too crowded; on the other hand, it is one of the most expensive islands, and to arrive in Pythagorio, the major tourist centre, without a hotel reservation in the summer is paramount to sleeping on the beach.

History

By 3000 BC Samos was inhabited by Pelasgians who worshipped Hera, who was born on the island by the stream Imbrassos; her first temple was built by the Argonaut King Angaios. The Ionians invaded in the 11th century BC, and by the Archaic period Samos was one of the most prosperous states in the Aegean, trading far and wide, most profitably their excellent wine. In 670 BC the island became a democracy, which brought out all manner of talents. The swift ship known as the *Samaina* was designed there, and in 650 BC a Samian captain named Kolaios became the first known man to sail through the Straits of Gibraltar (the Phoenicians most certainly did, but they never told anyone about it). The next century saw the birth of Pythagoras, not only the inventor of the right-angle theorem that put his name on the lips of every schoolchild in the world, but the first to define the mathematics of music, the planets and proportions in beauty which were to give Classical architecture and sculpture their perfect harmony. Aristarchus, a later Samian mathematician, was the first in history to put the sun in the centre of the universe.

In the late 6th century Samos was ruled by the famous tyrant Polycrates, probably the most powerful man in Greece at the time. Under Polycrates, Samos ruled even Delos briefly; he oversaw the building of the great temple of Hera and dug the Efplinion tunnel through a mountain to bring water to his capital, modern Pythagorio.

A constant through all of ancient history is Samos' lifelong feud with its chief rival on the Ionian mainland, Miletus. Whatever Miletus did, Samos did the opposite, siding in turn with the Persians, the Spartans and the Athenians in the great disputes of the age. During their second invasion of Greece, the Persians occupied Samos and kept their fleet at the island. During the battle of Plataea (479 BC) the Greeks attacked the Persian fleet at the Strait of Mycale, soundly defeating them—helped by the defection of the Samians in the Persian navy. The battle of Mycale was one of the most crucial in the war, and once and for all eliminated Persian threats from the sea. After the battle, Samos allied herself with Athens, and under that city's influence became a democracy (again) and even sheltered Athenian democrats during the gangsterish Revolution of the Four Hundred (411 BC).

In 129 BC Rome incorporated Samos into her Asia Province, and Augustus often visited the island in the winter, granting it many privileges, despite the fact that his enemies Antony and Cleopatra had lived there for a short time.

After the sack of Constantinople Samos was captured by the Venetians and Genoese. In 1453, when the Turks came to take their place, the inhabitants took refuge on Chios, leaving their island deserted for 80 years. Gradually the population returned, and many Turks also settled on the fertile island, although life became uncomfortable for them in 1821 when the Samians joined the revolution. A second battle of Mycale was fought in 1824, and again the enemy from Asia Minor was defeated at sea, this time when Kanaris blew up a Turkish frigate. Although the Great Powers excluded Samos from Greece in 1830, it was granted semi-independence under the 'prince of Samos', a Christian governor appointed by the Sultan. In 1912, the Samian National Assembly took advantage of Turkey's defeats in the Balkan Wars to declare unity with Greece, under the leadership of Sophoulis, who later became Prime Minister of the country.

By air: daily flights from Athens, and less frequent connections to Chios, Mykonos, Kos and Lesbos. Rather too many charters from northern Europe, rising to 20 a day in July.

By sea: Samos has four ports, the two principal ones being Vathi and Karlovassi; most ferries call at both. Ferry boats daily to Piraeus and Ikaria, four times a week to Chios (from Karlovassi only) and Paros, twice a week to Naxos, once a week to Mykonos, Syros and Kuşadasi; throughout the year there is an excursion boat between Kuşadasi, Turkey and Samos, as well as the island's third port, Pythagorio. In season hydrofoils run between Pythagorio and Patmos and Kos; there are also frequent tourist boats from Pythagorio to Patmos and Fourni; from the fourth port, Ormos Marathokampos in the west, there are excursions to Fourni, Patmos and the islet Samiopoula.

Tourist Information

NTOG, Samos town, ✆ (0273) 28 530.

Tourist Police, Samos town, ✆ (0273) 27 333.

NTOG, Pythagorio, ✆ (0273) 61 389.

Tourist Police, Pythagorio, ✆ (0273) 61 100.

NTOG, Kokari, ✆ (0273) 92 333.

Police in Karlovassi, ✆ (0273) 31 444.

Samos

Samos, the capital and main port of the island, dates from the 19th century, when it was called Stephanoupolis; more recently it was known as Vathi, although this name now applies only to the 'deep end' of the city's magnificent harbour. By island standards, Samos is a smart town with many new buildings, all harmonized by their red-tiled roofs. Only recently has it begun to recover its deep green setting, devastated in a 1987 fire.

The **public garden**, with its dishevelled flower beds and a small zoo, is near the centre of town; behind it is the new **Archaeology Museum** (*8.30–3, Sun 9–2, closed Mon*) which has a fine collection of griffon heads (the ancient symbol of Samos), funerary stele, and pottery, mainly from the Hereon. Another museum, the **Byzantine Religious Museum**, in the Bishop's office at 28th Oktroviou St (*Mon, Wed and Fri 8.30–1.30*) contains items used in the church liturgy. A favourite spot in town is **Plateia Pythagorio**, where café dawdlers are guarded by a stone lion and shaded by palms. The nearest (but often crowded) beach to Vathi is **Gagou**, to the west.

East of Vathi, with the best views over the beautiful Strait of Mycale and rugged coast of Turkey, is the monastery **Zoodochas Pigi** (1756). The church has many intricate wooden carvings, but they can hardly compete with the views over the turquoise sea. If you want to get closer, there are good sandy beaches at **Possidonion** and **Psili Ammos**, the latter long and shady, with three tavernas.

Buses run frequently from Samos to Pythagorio on the southeast coast, now the island's most popular village. It marks the site of the tyrant Polycrates' capital, renamed in 1955 (when it was Tigani) to honour Samos' most famous son. Many relics remain from the Samian golden age, beginning with the extraordinary **Efplinion tunnel**, a couple of kilometres north of the town. Efplinos, the chief engineer of Polycrates, employed crews of slaves who worked on the project for years, beginning in 524 BC; some started on one side of Mt Kas, some on the other, and Efplinos' calculations were so precise they met exactly in the middle. Over 900 m long, the tunnel was used to bring water to Pythagorio from the springs of Mt Ampelos. Recently the tunnel (open mornings, but check at the tourist office before setting out) has been electrically lit, so it no longer seems as old and mysterious; visitors are allowed in the first 300 m. The middle of the tunnel has collapsed.

The **long walls** that surrounded ancient Pythagorio are also impressive, although they were partly destroyed by Lysander when the Spartans took Samos during the Peloponnesian War. Originally 6500 m long, the walls ran all the way to Cape Fonias, and bristled with towers and gates. The modern village of Pythagorio was built on the **ancient harbour mole**, another masterpiece of Efplinos; some of its foundations may still be seen.

Little remains of the **ancient theatre** (en route to the tunnel), but above Pythagorio is **Spiliani**, the cave where the sybil Feto prophesied a one and true god. Along with her nine sister sybils, Feto would provide an important artistic link between antiquity and Christianity in the Renaissance: see the sybils on the Sistine Chapel ceiling or the floor of Siena cathedral. Inside the cave there's a lake and a church **Panayia Spiliani**, built in 1836. Lycurgos Logothetis, a hero of the 1821 Revolution, built a **fort** by the town; an **archaeological museum** in the Community Hall (*9.30–2*) houses finds from the area. Excavations of the city itself, begun in 1985, occasionally turn Pythagorio into a minefield of trenches. The nearest beaches to town are at **Fonias** and **Iratis Bay**.

To the west of Pythagorio, the **Sacred Way** (now the profane airport road) led the faithful the 8 km from Pythagorio to the **Hereon**, or the Temple of Hera, at 108 m by 52 m the second largest temple ever built in Greece (*open daily 9.30–3*). It appears on many lists as one of the Seven Wonders of the Ancient World, although just like another shortlisted ancient wonder, the Temple of Artemis at Ephesus (just over the Strait of Mycale) only a single column of its original 133 remains intact. The site was sacred as early as the Bronze Age, and two temples had been built when in 800 BC what is considered the first of all Greek temples (i.e. with a colonnaded peristyle) was built here. It was destroyed in 670 BC, and replaced on a much larger scale by the Great Temple begun under Polycrates. Twice a year grand celebrations took place, one in honour of Hera's birth by the nearby Imbrassos stream and the other in honour of her marriage to Zeus. In mythology Zeus had to use cunning to seduce an uninterested Hera (perhaps because he was her brother), and they spent a 300-year-long wedding night on Samos. Other curiosities at the Hereon include the **altar, a Mycenaean wall**, other small temples and buildings, and a **tribute** sent by Cicero. The

damage to Polycrates'
Great Temple and sur-
roundings is attributed mostly
to a latter-day need for building
stone and Christian piety; part of it
went into nearby **Sarakini castle**, built
by a naval officer of the same name in 1560.
The Hereon village is quickly losing its pleasant
backwater atmosphere, as hotels, apartments and
bars have mushroomed on its short stretch of beach.

The Temple of Hera, Samos

Chora, just north of Hereon, was the capital of Samos from 1560 to 1855. Now it's the charming backwater, except when jets pounce on the nearby airport. Ceramics and pottery are made at **Mavratzei**, where you can also visit the **Timios Stavros Monastery** (1592). In **Mytilini** to the north animal fossils dating back 15 million years have been gathered in the **Paleontology Museum** in the City Hall, on the main street (*open weekdays 8.30–3*). Samos had a reputation for fierce monsters in mythology. The museum's prize exhibit, among the bones of ancient hippopotami and rhinoceroses, is a 13-million-year-old fossilized horse brain. Another pretty village in the region is mountainous **Pirgos**, by the lovely stream **Koutsi**; ancient trees, clear waters and cool mountain air make it a popular destination on a hot, lazy afternoon.

Western Samos

From Pirgos, the mountain road shuns the coast until boat-building **Marathokampos** village and its pretty beach and regional port, **Ormos Marathokampos**, both connected by bus from Karlovassi to the north. The Samians' favourite beach is **Votsalakia**, and it and nearby **Psili Ammos** have restaurants and pensions. All three of these beaches are still relatively quiet. To the north is Samos' highest peak, **Mt Kerkis**, where **Kastanea** is surrounded by chestnut groves, as its name implies.

Karlovassi, Samos' second city and port, was planned as an industrial tanning centre, an idea that failed but left its port rather dreary. The city itself, though, is pleasant, and neatly divided into old, middle and new Karlovassi. There are many old houses, some veritable mansions, and an interesting bridge. Near Karlovassi are two monasteries: **Panayia tou Potamou** (Our Lady of the River) dating from the 10th century, and **Profitis Ilias**, founded in 1703. Fewer tourists come to Karlovassi than to Vathi or Pythagorio, although the town does have swimming places nearby (a city bus goes to **Potami**, where there is sand and shade), tavernas, restaurants and a nightclub. Not all the ships calling at Samos also stop at Karlovassi, so always check if you intend to leave from that port.

Buses run along the north coast of the island between Vathi and Karlovassi, passing the pretty seaside village of **Ag. Konstantinos**. Further east a road leads up the slopes of Mt Ampelos to Manolates, one of the beauty spots of Samos, where you can eat under the plane trees and listen to the nightingales sing. There is good swimming at the pebbly beaches of **Avlakia** and **Kokkari**, the latter now a busy resort. In between them you can walk from **Vourliotes** to the island's oldest monastery, **Our Lady of Vrontiani**, founded in 1560.

Festivals

27 July, Ag. Panteleimonos at Kokkari (one of the most popular); 6 August, Celebration of the Revolution, all Samos; 29 August, Ag. Ioannis at Pythagorio; 21 November, Panayia Spiliani by Pythagorio; 26 July, Ag. Paraskevi at Vathi; 8 September at Vrontiani Monastery; 20 July, Profitis Ilias celebrated in many villages throughout the island. Finally, the **Samos Wine Festival** takes place every year in August and dancing groups perform dances from various parts of Greece.

Where to Stay

Finding a place to stay on Samos is very difficult for travellers who just drop in; nearly every available room seems to be booked from June to September.

expensive

Samos' only real pretences to luxury and comfort are to be found at the **Doryssa Bay Hotel** in Pythagorio, © 61 360, offering air conditioned bungalows, pool, tennis and waterskiing.

moderate

Samos has two lovely pensions: the **Athina** at 34 Efplinou St and the **Ionia Pension** at 5 Kalomiri, run by the friendly Evagelia Zavitsanou, © 28 782; both have rooms for 4000–5000 dr. If they're full, get the tourist police (next to the **Hotel Xenia**) to help out. Both the Xenia (class B, © 27 463) and the **Samos** hotels (class C, © 28 377) are modern and clean and face the huge natural harbour; the Samos is particularly good value at under 5000 dr. Pythagorio is packed with small up-scale pensions that are also inevitably full, as well as a typical selection of class C hotels, all costing more than they should. One of the better bargains, if you can get one of its 8 rooms, is the D class **Alexandra** at 11 Metamorfosseos, © (0273) 61 429 with doubles at just under 2000 dr. Many people these days avoid both Samos and Pythagorio and stay in

Kokkari, conveniently linked by frequent buses to Samos town. Prices are more reasonable here; for comfort, stay at the **Kokkari Beach Hotel**, © (0273) 92 263, located, as it's name suggests, right on the shore; doubles here are between 4500 dr. and 6500 dr. a night. Less expensive, and also near the sea, is the **Pension Galina**, © (0273) 92 331 with doubles around 3800 dr. In Karlovassi there's the class B **Merope Hotel**, © 32 650, a favourite of many for its old–world service. Peace and quiet can be found at the **Hotel Kerkis Bay**, © 37 202, in Ormos Marathokampos. In Hereon there are a group of small C and D class hotels with prices ranging from 4000–7000 dr., a typical (and cheap) one being the **Faros**, © 61 193. To the west there are rooms and pensions on the bucolic slopes of Mt Ampelos, at Platanos and above Ag. Konstantinos.

cheap

There are rooms to be had in private homes in Vathi and Pythagorio, and in most seaside villages, although they are more scarce, and sometimes you can pay the same as for a budget pension. If you have any difficulty locating them, the helpful NTOG office in Samos town will help you.

Eating Out

Samos grows much of its own food and produces its own wine, so eating is usually quite good. The waterfront in Vathi has a collection of tavernas which are all reliable but, as ever, pricey if you order fish. There is also a host of snack bars. The most beautiful restaurant in town is the **Kouros**, in an exotic garden setting, enhanced by good music and topnotch Greek and international food in the 4000 dr. range. Less expensive are two excellent and very popular tavernas serving all the Greek favourites, **Gregori** up past the Olympic Airways office on Sinikismos St, and the **Pergola**, behind the bus station; both serve dinner for under 2500 dr. Pythagorio is overpriced not only for accommodation but eating out as well. The waterfront is one solid uninterrupted line of tavernas and cafés. Check out the menus before you sit down, although the **Tria Adelphia** and **Lito** are worth a try. On the water's edge in Kokkari, **Stathis Taverna** has tasty, freshly prepared Greek dishes (1500 dr.) with reasonably-priced lobster on the menu too. Here also is the **Avgo tou Kokkora**, with consistently reliable fare. In Karlovassi the local favourite is the **Kima**. In Hereon the sea laps up to the edge of the few tavernas, and the food is straightforward and not expensive.

Samothrace (Samothraki)

In the far right-hand corner of Greece, Samothraki is one of the least accessible islands for the pleasure tourist; its bleak, rocky shores are uncluttered by day-trippers or people just passing through—in a way, they would seem frivolous. For this is a sombre, dramatically stern, rugged island, rising to a peak in the lofty Mountain of the Moon (Mt Fingari), where the sea god Poseidon sat and watched the tides of the Trojan War. Often whipped by the wind and lacking a natural harbour, with only a small strip of arable land between the mountain and the sea, it nevertheless was one of the best known and most visited islands of antiquity, for here was the cult centre of the great gods of the Underworld; from all over the Mediterranean people came to be initiated into its mysteries.

History

Once the densely populated and forested 'Samos of Thrace' Samothraki owes its importance to its position near that busy thoroughfare, the Dardanelles—the strait named for the legendary Samothrakian Dardanosm the founder of Troy. Inhabited from Neolithic times, the island's first temple (the rock altar beneath the Arsinoeion) was built in the Iron Age by people from the Thracian mainland. In the 8th century BC Aeolians from Mytilini colonized Samothraki and mingled peaceably with the earlier settlers, worshipping Athena and the Great Gods of the Thracians, whose language survived at least in religious rituals, until the 1st century.

By the 5th century BC, Samothraki had reached the height of its importance; it had colonized Alexandroupolis, contributed a ship to the battle of Salamis and joined the Delian alliance. Although her military power, such as it was, declined with the rise of Athens, Samothraki's

The Northeastern Aegean Islands: Samothrace (0551–)

Sanctuary of the Great Gods had become the religious centre of the whole North Aegean, attracting a steady stream of pilgrims and adherents.

The Great Gods of Samothraki were chthonic, mysterious underworld deities, older and more potent than the Olympian upstarts of the patriarchal state religion, at whom even the first poet Homer could have a good laugh. But no one dared to mess around with the Great Gods; no writer dared to reveal what went on at their sanctuary, but it is likely that Samothracian mysteries included rites of initiation similar to those at the cult centre at Eleusis. The focus of worship was the Great Mother Goddess, in this case the Thracian fertility goddess (Axieros Cybele) whom the Greeks indentified with Demeter, with other attributes personified by Aphrodite and the witch Hekate, the Queen of the Night. Of secondary importance was her consort, Kadmilos-Hermes and the demonic twins, the Cabiri (later identified with the Dioscuri, Castor and Pollux), the special protectors of sailors who are thought to have been Phoenician in origin.

The cult had two levels of initiation, and compared to Eleusis, had few restrictions. Anyone male or female, free or slave, could be initiated, and even the uninitiated were permitted to attend the mysteries. The second level of initiation is thought to have demanded an unusually lofty moral standard, confession and baptism. Ambassadors from all over the world were invited to the sanctuary's high feasts in the summer, where ceremonies took place at night, by torchlight. Lysander of Sparta, Herodotos, Philip II of Macedon and nearly all the Ptolemies were initiates, and in mythology even the Argonauts, at Orpheus' suggestion, joined the cult for extra protection before entering the Hellespont.

Hellenistic and Roman rulers continued to patronize the sanctuary. Occasionally they used Samothraki as a naval base, relying on its sacred soil for protection. Nevertheless, under the Romans the island began to suffer its first invasions and earthquakes. St Paul stopped on the island, but failed to convert the locals, who continued to repair their sanctuary until the 4th century AD, when the Byzantines forced paganism out of business, and Samothraki was depopulated and forgotten. Pirate raids forced the remaining inhabitants to the hills, where they settled Chora. The Genoese ruler Gattilusi fortified the castle, and when it fell to the Turks, the Samothracians were sent to resettle Constantinople. The island then vanished from history until the 1820s, when it rose up during the War of Independence, but like the other islands in the northeast, had to wait until 1912 to join Greece.

Connections

By air: flights three times a day from Athens to Alexandroupolis.

By sea: daily ferry from Alexandroupolis, occasionally twice a day in summer; twice a week from Kavala.

Tourist Police

In Chora, near the Kastro, © (0551) 41 203.

Kamariotissa, the port of Samothraki, has a rocky beach and most of the island's tourist facilities, increasingly filled up with Germans and Scandinavians. Samothraki's three bus routes begin in Kamariotissa, and in the summer caiques make excursions to the island's one sandy beach at **Pahia Ammos**, and around the whole of Samothraki—the only way to visit the spectacularly rugged southern coast and the waterfall **Kremasto Nero** ('hanging water').

Buses run frequently from Kamariotissa to **Chora**, the capital, high on the slopes of Mt Fingari. Laid out in a picturesque amphitheatre below the ruins of a Byzantine castle, Chora is a quiet Thracian village crowned with red-tiled roofs but where you'll find amenities like the island bank. From here (or from Therma) you can make the 5-6-hour ascent of **Mt Fingari** (1676 m), locally known as Mt Saos, and on a clear day enjoy the same view as Poseidon, a stunning panorama of the North Aegean from the Troad in the east to Mt Athos in the west. The paths up are not clearly marked, however, and if you don't want to go up with a guide, at least get clear instructions before setting out. Mt Fingari wears a snow cap for nine months of the year and has long been a landmark for seamen; Strabo wrote that it resembled a woman's breast.

Alonia, a pretty agricultural village near Chora, is the island's second largest settlement and has ruins of a Roman bath; the other spots on the map—Xeropotamo, Lakoma and **Profitis Ilias** are little more than hamlets, although the last is pretty and shady and offers views of Turkey. From **Lakoma** a rough track leads to the church Panayia Kremniotissa, from where the energetic can walk down to sandy Pahia Ammos beach.

Palaeopolis and the Great Gods

Buses run frequently to **Palaeopolis**, where the ongoing excavations of the **Sanctuary of the Great Gods** were begun in 1948 by Dr Karl and Phyllis Williams Lehmann, who have written an excellent guide to the site, on sale in the adjacent museum. *Both the site and museum are open daily 8.30–3, closed Mon.*

Begin with the **museum**, with its explanation of the excavations and display of artefacts discovered on the site, or at least those things missed by previous excavators. The French, of course, took the prize, the *Winged Victory of Samothrace*, one of the masterpieces of Hellenistic art, dug up in 1863 by Champoiseau, the French consul at Adrianople and ever since then prominently displayed in the Louvre; the museum displays a plaster copy, a consolation prize from the French.

The sanctuary itself, impressive in its ruined grandeur, begins a short distance from the museum. The first building you come across, the **Anaktorion** (the House of the Lords) dates from the 6th century BC and was rebuilt by the Romans; first-level initiations were held in its inner sanctum. Adjacent, the **Arsinoeion**, at 20 m in diameter, was the largest circular structure ever built by the ancient Greeks. It was dedicated to the Great Gods in 281 BC by Queen Arsinoe II, wife (and sister) of Ptolemy Philadelphos, after the Great Gods had answered her prayers for a child. The ancient altar within its walls is thought to have belonged to the original Thracian cult. The rectangular foundation south of the Arsinoeion belonged to the **Temenos**, where ceremonies may have taken place; adjacent stand the five re-erected Doric columns of the **Hieron**, where the upper level of initiation was held, a structure dating from 300 BC and last restored after an earthquake in the 3rd century AD. Here you can still see the stone seats where the initiates' confessions were heard, as well as the Roman viewing benches.

Only the outline remains of the theatre on the hill; here also is the **Nike Fountain**, named for the *Winged Victory* discovered there. The *Victory*, donated by Dimitrios Poliorketes (the Besieger) in 305 BC, once stood as the figurehead of a great marble ship, a votive offering thanking the gods for Dimitrios' naval victory over Ptolemy II. Ptolemy II himself donated the monumental gateway to the sanctuary, the **Propylae Ptolemaion**. Near here is a small circular **Tholos** of uncertain use and a Doric building, dedicated by Philip and Alexander, Hellenistic rulers of Macedon. It was at a ceremony in the sanctuary that King Philip II of Macedon first met Olympias of Epiros, later to become the mother of Alexander the Great.

The buildings on the site were extensively cannibilized to construct the medieval Genoese castle near the Nike Fountain and the two watchtowers along the road. The road continues briefly west through shady plane groves and along rocky shores, past many good campsites towards Samothraki's little hot spring spa, **Loutra**, and its budding resort, **Therma**, with a typical rocky island beach.

Festivals

6 August, at Sotirou in Chora; 26 July, Ag. Paraskevi, near Palaeopolis; 20 July, Profitis Ilias at Kormbeti; 15 August, Panayias at Loutra; 8 January, Ag. Athanassios at Alonia.

Where to Stay

expensive

The island's most sophisticated accommodation is at the **Aeolos** in Kamariotissa, © 41 595, a B class with 56 rooms.

moderate

In the port of Kamariotissa there's the brand new class C **Niki Beach Hotel**, © 41 561, with 38 rooms by the sea. For archaeology lovers, the little **Xenia Hotel**, © 41 230, is in the grove by the Sanctuary of the Great Gods; in season you may have to take half board. Up in Chora there's a small pension and rooms to rent (expect to pay around 3500 dr. a night). There are also rooms in Therma and Profitis Ilias. When you step off the ferry in Kamariotissa there's a small booth where the Room Renters Association has a list of available rooms.

In the summer you can do fairly well in Samothraki. The waterfront in Kamariotissa is lined with cafés and tavernas, all typical and inexpensive. Particularly good is the **Aigeon Taverna**, which has a wide choice of Greek food, including the local speciality, kid. Others favoured by locals are the **Oasis** and **Voyatzis**. Small tavernas spill over on the premises of neighbouring shops, so you could well find yourself eating *souvlaki* in a hardware store. There is fresh fish in the town's only fish taverna, **Turkovrisso** and the *ouzeri* in the middle of the waterfront grills delicious giant shrimp over the coals. Chora and Therma have a number of simple tavernas. In the winter everything closes down except for one or two places in the port.

Thassos

Northernmost of the islands in Greece, Thassos is also one of the fairest, almost perfectly round and mantled with fragrant, intensely green pinewoods, plane trees, walnuts and chestnuts. Unlike the other Aegean islands, it is almost never afflicted by the meltemi winds, but has a moist climate, much subject to lingering mists; on hot summer days the intense scent of the pines by the calm sapphire sea can make even the most practical soul sink into a sensuous languor. Also unlike many of the other islands, it is well watered with a stream gushing down the slopes of 1070-metre Mt Ipsaron; a necklace of sandy beaches divides the forest from the sea. For many years its relative inaccessibility kept it a virgin in spite of the orgy of package tourism that has deflowered so many of the Greek islands. However, Germans soon discovered how easily and quickly they could reach Thassos by car (the current situation in ex-Yugoslavia has halted that somewhat), and the opening of Kavala airport to international charter flights is beginning to affect the all-Greek character of this beautiful island. At present, the hotels are still small and geared to families, most of whom come from northern Greece. Many people camp out, either on the organized sites or elsewhere, even though it is, as usual, forbidden. Prices are still reasonable, and despite the new oil rigs northwest of the island, the water is sparkling clean.

One problem that afflicts most people (apart from the trouble it takes to get there) is that Thassos must be shared with the mosquitoes, so come prepared, particularly if you intend to sleep out. Thassos is also especially vulnerable to forest fires (a terrible one in 1985 devastated large swathes of woodland), so take extra care.

History

Herodotos wrote that Thassos was first inhabited by the Phoenicians in 1500 BC, but in 710 BC when colonists from Paros came ashore to found a town (at the command of Heracles, they said), they found Thassos inhabited by a Thracian tribe. The likeable Parian poet, Archilochus, was sent to do battle with them, but found himself out-manoeuvred and ran away into the trees, dropping his shield in his haste; his description of the incident was the first known self-deprecating poem in history. The Parians who stayed on as colonists had better luck, extracting some 900 talents of gold a year from the rich mines of Thassos and the lands they soon annexed on the mainland. The 6th century BC saw the height of the island's prosperity and political independence.

In 490 BC Thassos was attacked by the Persians, who razed the walls. When Xerxes and his army turned up ten years later, the defenceless islanders responded by throwing a fabulous feast for the Persians, and with many slaps on the back sent them off to defeat at Salamis. When Thassos later revolted against the Delian league, Athens sent Kimon to teach it a lesson which he did—after a two-year siege. After that Thassos was ruled by Athens or Sparta (whenever it had the upper hand). Philip of Macedon seized its mainland gold mines.

In 197 BC the Romans defeated the Macedonians, and Thassos gladly became part of Rome, sheltering the defeated republican allies of Brutus after their defeat at the battle of Philippi. Among the various marauders who troubled the island after the fall of Rome, the Genoese had it for the longest, from the 14th century until the Turks chased them out in 1460. Russia took over from 1770 to 1774. In 1813 the Ottoman Sultan granted the island to Mohammed Ali, Governor of Egypt, who had been brought up in the village of Theologos, hoping to secure his loyalty with the gift. Thassos continued to be ruled by Egypt until 1902, when the Turks returned briefly before the island's union with Greece during the Balkan Wars, in 1912. In 1916 the allies occupied it, and from 1941 to the end of the war, the Bulgars.

THASSOS

By air: there are daily flights from Athens to Kavala, and buses from Athens and Thessaloniki; Kavala airport is also open to international charter flights.

By sea: ferry from Kavala to Skala Prinos almost every hour, from Peramo (20 km west of Kavala) four times a day, from Keramoti (a 20-minute bus ride from Kavala) to Thassos' capital (Limenas) 12 times a day.

Tourist police in Limenas, on the waterfront, © (0593) 22 500.

Tourist Information booth on quay in Limenas.

Tourist Police in Limenaria, see regular police, © (0593) 51 111.

Limenas (Thassos Town)

The capital and port of the island is officially Thassos, locally called **Limenas**, or sometimes just Limen (even more confusingly, the island's second town is Limenaria). It has nearly as many flags as the United Nations waving along the waterfront, so everyone can feel at home. Although it has 2000 people, it hardly occupies the extent of ancient **Thassos**, the ruins of which are scattered helter-skelter among the new town. The ancients used an amazing amount of marble—the island's highest peak, Mt Ipsarion, is one great white and greenish marble block (ecologically-minded residents worry about the current widespread quarrying that mars the island's soft green contours). The marble is especially beautiful in the **Roman Agora** in the centre of town, entered by way of a gate near the harbour. Here are the foundations of porticoes and stoas, a massive altar, sanctuaries, and from the 7th century BC, predating the rest of the Agora by 500 years, the mysterious paved 'Passage of Theoria' leading to a Temple of Artemis. The adjacent **museum** (*8.30–3, Sun 9–2.30, closed Mon*) has a fine collection of coins, ivories, bronzes, a magnificent 6th-century BC *Kriophoros*—a young man bearing a lamb on his shoulders—a lion's head carved in ivory, fine reliefs, ceramics, coins, a lovely head of Dionysos from the 3rd century, and some exceptional Roman imperial busts. Also near the Agora is part of an ancient street, an exedra, a few tiers of the **Odeon** and the **Sanctuary of Hercules**, with an altar and an Ionic temple.

A path from behind a stately Turkish building on the harbour follows the extensive marble **walls** and gates of the ancient city and acropolis. These were reconstructed after the first Persian invasion and the later Athenian siege, and were last repaired by the Genoese. Many of the gates still bear the bas-reliefs, including the two naval gates, the **Chariot Gate** (with Artemis) and the **Gate of Semel-Thyone** (with Hermes). Near these stood sanctuaries dedicated to Poseidon and Dionysos. From here the walls extend beyond the ancient moles of the commercial harbour and rise to the **Greek Theatre** on the lower slopes of the acropolis, magnificent not so much for its state of preservation, but for the marvellous view it affords of pinewoods and sea and used in the summer for performances of Classical comedies and tragedies by the Northern Greek State Theatre as part of its Philippi and Thassos Festival.

From the theatre a path continues up to the **acropolis**, spread out across three summits which on a clear day afford views from Mt Athos to Samothraki. On the first hill stands a Genoese fortress built out of the temple of Pythian Apollo that once occupied the site. The museum's *Kriophoros* was discovered embedded in its walls, and a fine relief of a funerary feast (4th century BC) can still be seen near the guardroom. The second hill had a **temple of Athena** (5th century BC), but the Genoese treated her no better than Apollo, leaving only the foundations. Just below, a Hellenistic relief of Pan piping to his goats can still be seen at his sanctuary, and from here the path continues to the third and highest summit of the acropolis, where little more than the view remains.

The so-called **Secret Stair**, carved into the rock in the 6th century, descends precipitously from this third summit to the walls and the watchful stone eyes of the **Apotropaion** (to protect Thassos from the Evil Eye), the well-preserved **Gate of Parmenon**, and most interesting of all, a short distance further on, the large **Gate of Silenus**, where the vigorous bas-relief of the phallic god (6th century BC) has lost its most prominent appendage to a 'moral cleansing' of the 20th century. Continuing back towards the modern town are, respectively, the **Gate of Dionysos and Hercules** with an inscription, and the **Gate of Zeus and Hera** with an Archaic relief.

The town beaches are sandy but are also the most crowded on the island, although a half-hour's walk in either direction will bring you to prettier, emptier and cleaner strands. There is a healthy nightlife at Limenas, and the evening *volta* along the waterfront is well worth a look. This becomes a stupendous fashion parade in the summer months, perhaps because most of the tourists who come to Thassos are Greek.

Around the Island

Thassos has one main road encircling the coast of the island. Buses make the circuit several times a day. Of the many beaches, Kalirahi, Pefkari, Pharos, Panayia, Potamia, Rachoni and Aliki are considered the best; **Makryammos** is lovely but has become a hyper chi-chi tourist beach with an entrance fee for use of its facilities; Archangelos and Ag. Ioannis are isolated and forested. Directly south of Limenas, along a picturesque road, lies **Panayia**, the most charming village of Thassos. Its old whitewashed Macedonian houses, decorated with carved wood and slate roofs overlook the sea, and have high walled gardens, watered by a network of mountain streams, some flowing directly under their ground floor. The church **Panayias** has an underground spring. Down by the sea, the town beach **Chrysi Ammoudia** has many tavernas.

To the south of Panayia is another large, pretty mountain village, **Potamia**, which also has a beautiful beach **Skala Potamou** below, lined with tavernas. **Kastro** in the centre of the island, was the refuge of the Limenarians in the days of piracy, but was abandoned in the 19th century. High up on a steep precipice (a good track leads up from Kalives), some of its old houses have recently been restored. **Aliki** on the south coast was an ancient town that thrived on marble exports, and ruins are strewn about its sandy shore—especially an Archaic double sanctuary. Another ancient settlement was at **Thimonia** nearby, where part of a Hellenistic tower still stands.

Further along, the **Monastery Archangelou** under the jurisdiction of Mt Athos, may be visited (proper attire, even long sleeves, is required); paradoxically, the sandy beach nestling in the cliffs below is frequented by naturists. **Astris**, above pretty Cape Sapuni, is still defended by its medieval towers, and is one of several places in the Mediterranean that claims the Sirens, whose sweet singing almost lured Odysseus to his destruction.

Continuing clockwise around the island, **Psili Ammos** and **Potos** are some of the island's best beaches, the latter especially popular with foreigners. From Potos you can take the road up to **Theologos**, one of the Thassos's greenest spots and the capital of the island until the 19th century, where the water from the mountain springs literally flows through the streets. One of the old houses of the village has been done up as a museum of popular crafts, here also are the ruins of the castle **Kourokastro**. The church Ag. Dimitrios has 12th-century icons. **Pefkari** on the coast below is a lovely beach with pine trees along the sand. It can be reached by caique from **Panorama** or Limenaria.

Limenaria, the second largest town on Thassos, draws a fair crowd of tourists in the summer. In 1903 the German Spiedel Company arrived in Limenaria to mine the ores in the vicinity—its plant can still be seen south of town, while the company's grand offices, locally known as the **Palataki**, 'Little Palace', stand alone in a garden on the headland. From Limenaria excursion boats tour the coast of Mt Athos—the closest women can get to the great monastic state—or you can hire a little boat for a swim off the islet of **Panayia**. Limenaria has retained more of a village atmosphere than Limenas. It is surrounded by trees, with a huge stretch of shady beach.

The west coast of Thassos is lined with beaches, usually less frequented than the beaches on the east coast. There are small resorts at the three scenic Skalas—**Marion, Kallirachis** and **Sotiros**. The village of **Maries** proper, 10 km inland, is the least changed of the island's villages, where the old men still wear their old costumes. **Skala Prinos** has the closest connections to Kavala, although there isn't much to the village itself. Inland from here is the village of **Prinos**, beyond which lie the two smaller villages of **Megalo** and **Mikro Kasavati**, worth a visit for their lovely setting and charming old houses, many of which have been bought up and renovated by Germans. **Rachoni** and **Ag. Georgios** are two quiet inland villages. A small islet off the north coast, **Thassopoula**, is pretty and wooded but full of snakes, according to the locals.

Festivals

6 August, Metamorphosis tou Sotirou at Sotiros; end of July–beginning of August, traditional weddings performed at Theologos; first Tuesday after Easter, all over the island; 15 August, Panayia at Panayia; 26 October, Ag. Dimitrios at Theologos; 18 January, Ag. Athanasiou at Kastro; 27 August, at Limenaria with special dances; 6 December, Ag. Nikolaos at Limenas; 28 April at Ag. Georgios. (Thassos festival runs from 10 July to 15 August.)

Where to Stay

expensive

Limenas is well endowed with hotels. One street back from the waterfront is the spacious **Amfipolis**, recently converted from a tobacco warehouse, an A class with a pool, ℂ 23 101. The poshest place to stay on the island is the very modern **Makryammos Bungalows** on the much-lauded soft sandy beach of the same name, near Limenas,ℂ 22 101. Rooms hover around 10,000 dr., bungalows are much more.

moderate

The class B **Timoleon**, ℂ 22 177, in Limenas is a very pleasant option, but it's best to phone ahead in season. The **Akti Hotel** on the waterfront, ℂ 22 326, is less expensive but clean and friendly. In Skala Prinos the C class **Europa** has 12 double rooms for fairly low rates, ℂ 71 212. In Limenaria rooms are very plentiful and relatively cheap, and there's an overpowering class E hotel, the **Papageorgiou**, ℂ 51 205, where you can get a room with private bath.

cheap

Thassos has many **campsites**, the least expensive at Panayia. The **Ioannides Rahoni** campsite, with its excellent facilities, is ideal for families, beautifully situated on a sandy beach under the pine trees between Prinos and Limenas. Others are to be found at Prinos (run by NTOG), Pefkari, Potos, Limenas, Skala Sotiros and Skala Panayias. There are rooms in the pretty village of Panayia, and also the small E class **Hotel Helvetia** , ℂ 61 231. Completely off the beaten track at Kastro, some of the old homes are available to let. For real isolation, permission can be obtained from the Forestry Commission to stay at the hostel on **Mt. Ipsarion**, for a small fee. Details from the tourist police or tourist information office.

Eating Out

Every beach, it seems, has at least one taverna, and the towns are very well supplied with everything from snack bars to fancypants restaurants, all catering to Greek tastes. At the eastern end of the harbour, towards the town beach, the **Platanakia** serves fish at the appropriate price, and just beyond, the **New York Pizza Restaurant** covers all options with traditional Greek food, giant pizza for five (about 2500 dr.), various pasta dishes and occasionally fresh mussels. One street back from the main seafront is the **Asteria** *psistaria* with lots to offer from the spit including revolving goats' heads sporting lascivious grins. A few steps along, and less macabre, is **George's Restaurant** and although the menu outside is extensive, in reality the choice, like the name, is typically Greek. At the nearby **Thessaloniki Taverna**, you can eat the day's special in its shady garden under the trees. 2000 dr. at any of these places will buy you an excellent meal with wine. As you step off the boat at Prinos, **Kyriakos Taverna**, in front of you, has good fresh food and a wider than average selection. Next door, **Zorba's** is just as popular, and an added treat is the traffic policemen assailing your eardrums with their whistles.

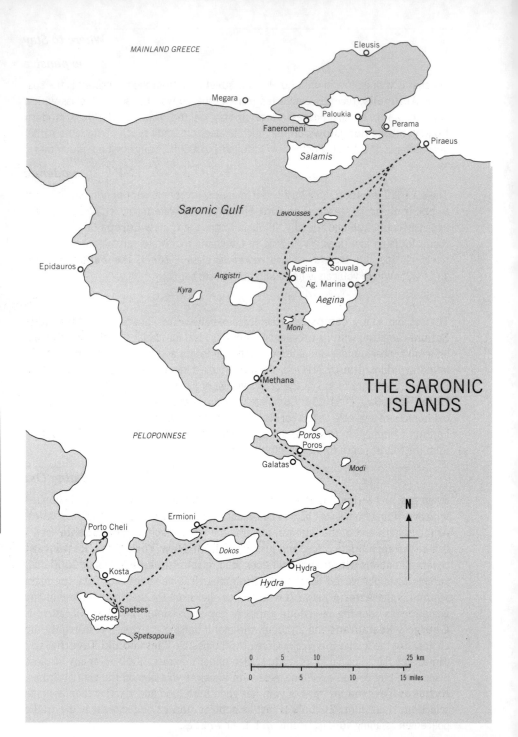

MAINLAND GREECE

Eleusis

Megara

Paloukia

Faneromeni
Perama

Salamis

Piraeus

Saronic Gulf

Lavousses

Epidauros

Angistri

Aegina
Souvala

Kyra

Ag. Marina

Aegina

Moni

Methana

**THE SARONIC
ISLANDS**

PELOPONNESE

Poros
Poros

Galatas

Modi

N

Ermioni

Porto Cheli

Dokos

Kosta

Hydra

Hydra

Spetses

Spetses

Spetsopoula

0   5   10   25 km

0   5   10   15 miles

The Saronic Islands

The history of the five islands in the Saronic Gulf is inextricably bound up with the sea. Aegina was one of the most powerful maritime states in Greece; Poros is the island of Poseidon; Salamis gave its name to one of the world's greatest sea battles, and Hydra and Spetses led the Greek fleets in the battles of the War of Independence. Other than their unique sea-worthiness and their location near Athens, these five small islands have little else in common. This makes them ideal for a quick visit if you have little time at your disposal. Connected by hydrofoil and ferry almost hourly with Athens and with each other, they are by far the most accessible of all the Greek islands.

Not surprisingly, the Saronic group was also the first island group to be regularly visited, from the beginning of this century when Athenian families bought or rented villas for the three summer months while the family breadwinner commuted to and fro at weekends. After the introduction 20 years ago of such conveniences as reservoirs, electricity and telephones, sun and fun seekers from all over the world began to arrive. In 1985, Aegina was the most visited island in all Greece; Hydra has earned itself the nickname 'the St-Tropez of Greece', although the once quiet Spetses is increasingly laying a claim on the title.

Connections

Note that only hydrofoils for Aegina leave from the main port of Piraeus; other hydro-foils for Saronic Gulf ports depart from Zea Marina on the other side of Piraeus. Some are express services directly to Hydra and Spetses; others call at Aegina, Poros, Hydra and Spetses. Regular passenger ships for all Saronic ports, and car ferries to Aegina and Poros leave from Piraeus' central harbour.

Aegina

Connections between Aegina and Piraeus are so frequent that many residents commute to work in the city. But Aegina is no fuddy-duddy bedroom suburb, and the islanders stubbornly maintain their traditional economy of fishing and agriculture. The pistachio is king of the latter; Greeks know them as 'Aegina peanuts' and patriotically claim that they are the best in the world. In late August, the pistachio harvest, the ripe nuts are gently knocked from the bushes with sticks so that they fall onto the canvas spread below. They are then hulled, soaked in salt water and dried in ovens or sundried on flat roofs and terraces. After uprooting orchards of fruit and olive trees to make room for the more profitable pistachio, the farmers realised that the newcomers demanded far more water than the trees they had destroyed. Deeper and deeper went the wells to relieve the pistachios' thirst, until the wells ran dry or turned into salt water. For many years—until the completion of the new reservoir—water had to be shipped in daily from the mainland.

Aegina has recently become extremely popular with the pleasure craft set, who seek to avoid the crowds along some of the island's more inaccessible coasts; even if you haven't brought the yacht, try to steer clear of summer weekends, when half of Athens descends on the island. Aegina has a few beaches (often packed), numerous hotels and good fish tavernas; it also has a clutch of fine Byzantine churches and the best-preserved ancient temple on any Greek island, the lovely temple of Aphaia.

Mythology

The name Aegina comes from one of Zeus' many loves, with whom he fathered Aeacus, the first king of the island. To honour his mother, Aeacus renamed what was then called Oenone 'Aegina'. This was too much for that ever jealous nag Hera. She punished Aeacus for being an illegitimate son of Zeus by plaguing Aegina with poisonous serpents, polluting the water and causing all the people to perish. Aeacus begged his father Zeus for help, wishing for as many inhabitants to repopulate his island as there were ants on a nearby oak, a wish Zeus granted. Thus the new Aeginetans were known as the ant people, or Myrmidons.

Aeacus went on to father three sons—Peleus, Telemon and Phocos. When Telemon and Peleus jealously killed Phocos, their father's favourite, they were forced to flee the island, Telemon going to Salamis, and Peleus to Thessaly. These two brothers, in turn, fathered two of the greatest heroes of the Trojan War, Ajax and Achilles respectively. When Aeacus died, Zeus appointed him one of the three judges of the dead with Minos, his arch enemy, and Rhadamanthys, his other son from Crete.

History

Aegina was inhabited from the 4th millennium BC by people from the Peloponnese, followed by the usual trail of Minoans, Mycenaeans and Dorians. In 950 BC its city joined an amphictyony of seven towns (the Heptapolis), initiating its commercial development. In 650 BC Aegina town was the first place in Europe to mint coins, imprinted with the picture of a turtle, and it became the first to develop a banking system; money from Aegina has been discovered all over the Mediterranean world. Situated between Corinth, Attica and centres in the east, trade made Aegina fat, especially through exports of its fine pottery and perfumes in the holds of its powerful commercial fleet. With the fall of Samos to Persia, Aegina knew no rivals in trade in the Mediterranean Sea.

This prominence lasted less than 50 years, however, with the rise of a very close neighbour and serious rival: Athens. In the first Persian War Aegina favoured Persia, one of its main trading partners, and would have militarily supported Darius had not the Athenians kidnapped several prominent citizens and held them hostage in return for the island's neutrality. In a complete turn-around Aegina sent 30 ships to aid the Greeks at the Battle of Salamis, and won the first choice of spoils for the most heroic conduct. Even so, Perikles could not forgive Aegina for its prosperity and competition with Athens, sneeringly referring to it as 'a speck that blocked the view of Piraeus'. In 458 BC the Athenian fleet defeated the triremes of Aegina, and three years later the city of Aegina was forced to surrender to the bullying Athenians, who made the inhabitants destroy their fortifications and hand over their fleet.

When the Peloponnesian War broke out, the Athenians, knowing they had few friends on the island, deported the entire population, who were welcomed by the Spartans and were later returned to their homes by Lysander. Saracens, Venetians and Turks took the island many times, the last occupation of the Ottomans lasting from 1715 to 1821. Aegina was one of the first places in Greece to be liberated and war refugees flocked to the island from other parts of Greece. In 1828 Aegina became the capital of free Greece under Capodistria. Fittingly, the first modern drachma, bearing a phoenix rising from the ashes was minted on the island; it also saw the new country's first newspaper and, less pleasantly, the first prison. A year later the capital was relocated in Nauplia.

Connections

Every hour by hydrofoil (40 minutes) until late afternoon, or by boat 1½ hours from Piraeus; frequent connections with Methana (the closest port to Epidauros), and other Saronic islands. Ferries go either to Aegina town or to Ag. Marina on the east coast; at weekends some call at Souvala. If you have only one day left in Greece and want to see one last island, it's the obvious choice.

Tourist Police

Vass. Georgiou St, ✆ (0297) 22 391.

Aegina town, the capital and chief port retains a lingering whiff of grandeur from its days as the capital of Greece. Its large crescent-shaped harbour was financed in 1826 by Samuel Greenly Howle, an American philanthropist and Hellenophile; its completion was celebrated with the building of the waterfront chapel Ag. Nikolaos, patron of sailors.

Ancient writers often referred to Aegina's 'secret port' just north of here—secret because only the islanders knew the entrance. Overlooking it, at **Kolona** (a 10-minute walk up from town) stood the ancient city, dating back to the Early Helladic period. Excavations have uncovered a road, a walled settlement and a temple. The name of the hill, however, comes from the one lonely Doric column of an early 5th-century **Temple of Apollo** (once thought to belong to Aphrodite, resulting from a confusion in Pausanias); the rest of its marble went into building the quay. Graves found in the vicinity yielded the British Museum's 'Aegina Treasure' of gold Minoan ornaments from the 16th century BC. The new **Archaeology Museum** at Kolona replaces what was the first archaeology museum in Greece; most of collections soon went to Athens, but still to be seen among others are ceramics from the Neolithic era to the Classical period, sculptural decorations from the temple of Aphaia, a sphinx and a mosaic from an ancient synagogue.

Other sights recall Aegina's fleeting role as the capital of Greece. The first government building was the pink **Tower of Markellos**, near large Ag. Nikolaos church. It is grim and austere, as is the hastily erected **Residence** (now the public library) on Kyverneou St. Capodistria, the first president, slept in his office on the upper floor, while downstairs the mint churned out the drachmas of the new state. When the rest of the government relocated to Nauplia, the once dapper count from Corfu lingered here, estranged from his own government and suspected of intrigues with Russia, until his assassination. On the waterfront many elegant 19th-century buildings are half-hidden behind the tourist clutter, and the numerous horse-drawn carriages are a nice touch.

An evening stroll, or *volta* as the Greek call it, around the waterfront is often rewarded with lovely sunsets (probably due to the *nefos*—smog emanating from Athens) which bathe the town in a gentle light far different to the daytime glare. Colourful fishing boats solidly line the waterfront. They rarely catch for the famous *katsoulas*, once a speciality of Aegina but now almost extinct, and the sponge fleet has been pushed out of business by synthetics. Now the *marida* (whitebait) comprises most of the catch, which go down nicely with Aegina's own retsina in one of the many tavernas at the port. There are two beaches near the capital, one by the secret port, the other, with more shade, to the south of town.

Boats leave the harbour for Moni islet and Angistri; buses to the rest of Aegina depart from the square near the quay. However, it's not far to walk along the sea north of Aegina town to **Livadi**; a plaque here marks the house where Nikos Kazantzakis wrote *Zorba the Greek*.

Further afield, on the north coast, the beach and spa at **Souvala** offers radioactive baths for your rheumatism or arthritis. A road south from Souvala leads up to crumbling, ruined

Paleachora, founded in the 9th century, when the Saracens were terrorizing the coast (visit in the morning, when the caretaker is usually around with the keys to the churches—and be sure to wear your walking shoes). In its history, Paleachora was twice destroyed, first by Barbarossa in 1538 and then by Venice's Morosini in his siege of 1654. A score of 13th-century churches—out of the original 365—still stand in various states of decay, many with contemporary frescoes; among the best are the **Basilica of Ag. Anargyroi**, the **Chapel of Taxiarchis**, and the **Cathedral of the Episkopi**, founded by Ag. Dionysos, the patron saint of Zakynthos. Looming over all is a dilapidated **Venetian castle** of 1654.

Seven km inland, on the road to Ag. Marina, stands the recent **monastery of Ag. Nektarios**, named for the bishop of Aegina (d. 1920) canonized in 1967—the youngest Greek Orthodox saint and protector of the island. Nektarios' tomb is in the church, and on 9 November a large pilgrimage is made to the convent to commemorate the date of the saint's death. An hour's walk leads to the fortified **convent of Chrysoleontissa** (1600) with an especially fine wooden iconostasis and a famous rain-making icon of the Virgin (a job once held by Zeus, *see below*). The nuns are well-known for their hospitality and for the delicious products of their farm. East of Paleachora is the pretty village of **Mesagros**, surrounded by the vineyards and pine groves that combine to make Aegina's excellent retsina.

Temple of Aphaia

On a pine-covered hill above Mesagros is the prize attraction of the island, the beautiful **temple of Aphaia** (a stop on the bus to Ag. Marina). Like Apollo and Artemis, Aphaia was a

child of Leto. She often went hunting with her sister Artemis and followed her cult of virginity. Minos of Crete fell in love with her, but she would have nothing to do with him. He chased her, and she fled him for nine whole months. Unable to bear running away any longer, Aphaia threw herself into the sea, but was rescued by kindly fisherfolk. Artemis later made her a goddess, although she was hardly known outside Aegina.

The Temple of Aphaea, Aegina

The Doric temple of Aphaia (*8–7, Sun 8–3, adm*), the best-preserved temple on any Greek island was built of locally-quarried limestone in the early years of the 5th century BC. It was one of the finest of the period, and like most temples, was originally covered with a coat of brightly painted stucco. Of the original 32 columns, 25 are still standing, partly thanks to reconstruction. The pediment sculptures of Parian marble, depicting scenes of the Trojan war, are masterpieces of Archaic art; purchased by Ludwig of Bavaria in 1812, they're now in

Munich's Glyptothek. The cella, where the cult statue of Aphaia once stood is now decorated with 19th-century graffiti. Outside the temple are the ruins of an ancient wall, altars, a cistern and houses of the temple priests. The café opposite the temple offers a splendid view of the east coast of Aegina, including **Ag. Marina**, the seaside resort of the island with a long sandy beach.

Perdika, Oros and the Wildlife Sanctuary

One of the most popular excursions is to cycle from Aegina town south along the coast to **Perdika**. Perdika ('Partridge') is a pretty fishing village-cum-resort with a small beach and tavernas that offer the best fresh fish on the island. Inland on a sturdy, conical mountain called simply 'Mountain' or **Oros** is the third temple of Aegina, dedicated to Zeus Hellanios, 'the rainmaker'; clouds gathering around its summit have long been observed as a sign of showers. The walk up from Marathon village takes about 3 hours, rewarded by a magnificent view stretching across the Saronic Gulf on a clear day; at the sanctuary of Zeus two terraces, cisterns and a monumental stair remain to be seen.

Finally, you can visit Aegina's **wildlife sanctuary**. Probably the most effective animal protection and rehabilitation centre in Greece, the sanctuary accepts wounded and sick animals from all over the country and releases them after recovery. Phillipos, the founder and director, together with his volunteer staff of specialists, has cared for some 3000 birds, vultures, wolves, jackals, and a range of smaller mammals. This farm has also become the home for numerous stray cats and dogs, many from overcrowded Athens. Funding comes from international donors such as WWF, businesses and public donations. The centre has been running for over five years and has expanded to include a former prison, now used as the infirmary. Once the animal has recovered it is released, either into its original habitat or, if that is deemed unsafe, to one of the wildlife reserves on the mainland. Visitors are welcome at the farm and can see a good cross-section of native Greek wildlife (even if they may not be in their perfect state of health).

Festivals

9 November, Ag. Nektarios; 6 December, Ag. Nikolaos at Aegina; 14 September, Stavros in Paleachora; 6–7 September, Ag. Sostis in Perdika; 23 April, Ag. Georgios at Ag. Georgios.

Where to Stay

expensive

A few kilometres north of Perdika there's the **Moondy Bay Bungalows**, with a well-tended garden, swimming pool and its own jetty, © 61 146; book well in advance.

moderate

In Aegina town most of the accommodation is on the oldish side, and there are many relatively inexpensive places to stay (at least for such a popular island). One of the more comfortable places is the **Pension Xenon Pavlou** at 21 P. Aeginitou, ℂ 23 091, a block from the waterfront. Opposite the beach, the **Hotel Brown** at 4 Toti Hatzi, ℂ 22 271 has a friendly staff; for peace and quiet, ask for a room in the back. Near the temple of Apollo, and within easy access to the beach, the **Plaza**, ℂ 25 600 is pleasant and friendly, and rates low for this category. There are also plenty of hotels (too many) on Ag. Marina beach, and you'll pay from 5000 dr. to 8000 dr. for a C class double room here, and not much less for a D or E class. In Souvala the **Xeni**, ℂ 52 435, with seven rooms, offers relative comfort for 5000 dr., but there are a few cheaper rooms in private houses, and in nearby Vathi. On Angistri island there's no shortage of accommodation, most of it centred around Skala, and it's all much of a muchness. The **Hotel Anagennissis** is right on the beach here, with low rates, ℂ 91 332, and for about the same price there's the **Aktaeon** in the village, ℂ 91 222. You'll also find rooms to let in private homes.

cheap

For B movie atmosphere, try the **Hotel Miranda** in Aegina town, beyond the football field on the far end of the beach, ℂ 22 266; the price for one of its wistful rooms is right at 3500 dr. In Ag. Marina, one place with rooms under 4000 dr. is the **Blue Horizon**, ℂ 32 303, which has 12 to choose from, some with bath. The friendly **Kolona Tours** agency near the boat dock in Aegina can also help you find inexpensive rooms, self-catering apartments, as well as a villa. The tourist police are also helpful and open all year.

Eating Out

Aegina town is packed with eateries all along the waterfront where you can tuck into anything from hamburgers and souvlaki to lobster. For reasonably priced fish try the ouzeri **To Spiti tou Psara** where a typical meal costs around 2000 dr. **Lekkas**, near the first town beach, is a typical taverna, serving reliable fare at fair prices, and **Maridaki**, near the hydrofoil landing point, has a name for excellent fish (3000 dr.). A little more expensive, but serving top quality fish and lamb from the spit is **Taverna Stratigos**, south of town at Faros. Many locals like to hop in a taxi and eat outside of town; especially popular and lively is **Vatzoulia's** en route to the temple of Aphaia. Open only Wednesday and weekend evenings, it serves excellent Greek food often accompanied by music (3000–4000 dr.); generally speaking, because Aegina is so close to Athens, and patronized heavily by that city's inhabitants, the food in all tavernas is good and affordable to all.

Moni and Angistri

The islet of Moni lies just off Perdika on Aegina's west coast, and is linked by boats from Perdika or Aegina town. Once owned by the monastery of Chrysoleontissa, it now belongs to the Touring Club of Greece; an admission fee is included in the price of the boat ticket. It is a pretty island, with trees and a small beach, ruled by brazen, nosey peacocks and wild *kri kri* mountain goats from Crete—exotic creatures with long horns—which are, by contrast, extremely shy. Moni is a popular place for picnics, and you can walk up through the trees to a look-out post built by the Germans during the war for a wonderful view of the Saronic Gulf.

Regular boat service from Aegina and Piraeus plies to **Angistri** ('hook island'), an islet of pine woods, fertile fields and relatively quiet beaches. The inhabitants are descendants from Albanian refugees and still keep up some Albanian customs. There are several landing places on the island: **Milo** the principal village in the north and **Skala** with its excellent beach. A bus connects the two villages with the third, **Limenaria**, in the south. There's nothing luxurious about Angistri—it offers the basics for a restful holiday, and little more.

Hydra

Hydra's role in the War of Independence has earned it a secure place in Greek history books and a picture on the 1000-drachma note; its extraordinary harbour, piled high with the tall, sombrely elegant mansions of its legendary sea captains, once served as the backdrop to Greece's largest fleet of sailing ships. Restored and inhabited by artists and their camp followers, they now serve as backdrops for paintings. The original tourist invasion of the island was sparked off by the film *Boy on a Dolphin*, set on Hydra and starring Sophia Loren. While the film gave the island overnight success, today the glamour is slightly tarnished, and tired Hydra has to put up with hordes of day-trippers, replacing the trendy models and idle rich yachties of yesteryear. Hydra is expensive, and because accommodation is limited, few visitors spend the night.

History

In the 6th century BC the tyrant Polycrates of Samos purchased dry, rocky Hydra with the tribute he captured in Sifnos. However, no permanent settlers lived on the island until the 15th century, when Greeks and Albanians from Epirus took refuge here from the Turks, especially when the tyranny of Ali Pasha made life unbearable in western Greece.

Hydra is a rocky, barren island, and through necessity the new arrivals turned to the sea for their livelihood: in shipbuilding, the island's fleet of 150 merchant ships—and piracy. By the end of the 18th century, Hydra was very much its own little island state. It boasted a wealthy population of 25,000 and sent only a few sailors as an occasional tribute to the Sultan, who prized their prowess in his fleet—especially the Albanians who made fortunes by daring to run the British blockade in the Napoleonic Wars. When Ibrahim Pasha visited the island, he was so impressed by its naval strength that he nicknamed it 'Little England'.

Thanks to its refugee population, Hydra was a centre of insurgency, and in 1821 it sprang into the fight for independence with enthusiasm. Its fleet was fitted out for war with funds given by the wealthy merchants and sea captains, most notably the prominent Koundouriotis family. Under such leaders as Miaoulis, commander-in-chief of the Greeks, Tombazis, Voulgaris and Tsamados, the Hydriot navy terrorized the Turkish fleets, especially with their fire ships: under cover of night, a few intrepid Greeks would row a decrepit vessel full of

HYDRA

To Hydra Beach

To Ermoni

To Poros, Piraeus

To Spetses

HYDRA
Kamini
Mandraki
Alonaki

Dokos
Islet
Dokos
Kastelli
Kastello
Islet
Vlichos

Riva
Ag. Apostolii

Molos
Mt. Eros
Profitis Ilias
Limoniza
Bay

Petassi
Islet
Beesti

Pontikonissi
Islet
Episkopi

Ag. Nikolaos

Tsigri
Bay
Ermonissa
Islet

Alexandros
Islet

N

0 1 2   5 km
0 1   2   3 miles

explosives alongside the Turkish ships, set it alight and swim for their lives. The Turks, should they be lucky enough to notice it in time, could only do the same. After the war, sponge fishing became the islanders' chief occupation, but then that too declined through lack of demand. By the 1950s Hydra was beginning to look like a ghost island, when it began to attract artists, beginning with the Greek Hadjikyriakos Ghikas, and a new page in the island's history was turned.

Connections

Passenger ships connect Hydra with the other Saronic islands and ports several times a day; twelve hydrofoils a day from Zea Marina (Piraeus), some going 'express' to Hydra in about 1½ hours; frequent hydrofoil connections to Poros and Spetses, and Nafplion, Porto Heli and Ermioni, in the Peloponnese; less frequently to other Peloponnese ports and Kythera.

Tourist Police

Navarhan N. Botsi, St, ℂ (0298) 52 205.

For general information, hydrofoil and boat tickets, accommodation, etc., contact **Pan Travel** on the quay, ℂ (0298) 53 135.

Hydra Town

Arriving at Hydra's steep-sided port, capital and only town is a breathtaking experience. The island seems to be a god-forsaken rock as you sail along the coast, then suddenly your vessel makes a sharp turn, and there it is: the scene that launched a thousand cruise ships. The grey and white mansions, built in the late 18th century by Venetian and Genoese architects, are unique on the islands and lend Hydra its special character. The island has no cars, but many narrow streets that peter out into stairs, rewarding the wanderer with many charming scenes and views, and surprising tranquillity. Although many of the artists have fled the cosmopolitan onslaught, a branch of the **School of Fine Arts** survives in the fine old residence of the Tombazi family, and there are several galleries amid the boutiques and jewellery shops. Another school, recalling an older tradition, is the **Skoli Borakis Naftilias**, Greece's oldest school for merchant marine captains, housed in the old Tsamados house. The loveliest mansions—and the largest—belonged to the Koundouriotis family, which produced two important men in Greek history: Georgios, who converted his merchantmen into warships at his own expense, and Pavlos, who was elected president of Greece.

The churches in Hydra also reflect its former wealth and influence with their marble campaniles and gold chandeliers. The 17th-century **Panayia tis Theotokou**, next to the port, has a lovely iconostasis and silver chandelier; the cells of its former convent are now used for town offices. Here, too, is a **statue of Miaoulis,** the famous fighter for independence on the high seas. It is said that Nelson once captured Miaoulis on one of his more piratical adventures, but Miaoulis in turn captured Nelson with his charm. In his honour the **Miaoulia celebrations** are held in the town on 20 June, complete with mock re-enactments of the Hydriot admiral's battles.

A climb up to **Kalo Pigadi** is an easy and worthwhile excursion just above the town (go by Miaoulis St). There are 18th-century mansions on top and two deep wells with fresh water. The one real beach on Hydra is a 20-minute walk away at **Mandraki**, the old shipbuilding docks of the Hydriots. You can also swim at **Kamini** (Italian for 'whitewash', which was once made there) although the beach is mostly rocks. Kamini is packed with Hydriots and visitors who come to watch the moving Good Friday candlelit procession the *epitaphios*, that culminates here by the sea. Another place to swim near to town is the cave **Bariami**, converted into a kind of swimming pool.

Around Hydra

Other swimming holes and inland excursions require more walking but it's a guaranteed way to escape the throngs who stay close to the cafés and shops in the town. At **Kastello** are the ruins of a thick-walled castle down near the shore. Further on, **Vlichos** has a couple of good tavernas. A pine forest and cove for swimming make **Molos** a popular place for outings; according to ancient tradition a nearby cliff was used to dispose of the aged and sick who could no longer contribute anything to the austere island. Wealthy hunters have their lodges at **Episkopi**, in Hydra's pine forest. Another excursion inland is to **Profitis Ilias monastery** and the nearby convent **Ag. Efpraxia**, an hour on foot above the town. The view from the top is lovely and you can buy textiles woven by the nuns on their ancient looms.

Festivals

15 August Panayias in town; 13–14 November Ag. Konstantinos of Hydra the island's patron saint; mid-June the Miaoulia; 20 July Profitis Ilias; Good Friday and Easter. 25 July at Ag. Efpraxia.

Where to Stay

It is absolutely impossible to come to Hydra in the summer and expect to find anywhere to stay without a reservation. Now that you've been warned here are some to choose from:

expensive

Orloff, in beautiful restored 19th-century mansion near the port has only 10 rooms, each individually designed and set around a courtyard; add plus is one of the best breakfasts in Greece. **Pension Miranda**, another charming, traditional Hydriot house, outside town at Mandraki, ✆ 52 230. Equally pleasant and just a bit larger the **Hydra Hotel** is similarly located in a historic mansion once belonging to a sea captain, ✆ 52 597. In the centre of town is the fully air conditioned **Hotel Greco**, ✆ 53 200. Also at Mandraki there's the **Miramare**, class A, with mandatory pension, ✆ 52 300.

moderate

Somewhat larger than the others, the **Hotel Leto** might be able to squeeze you in at short notice, ✆ 52 280. Least expensive and right in the heart of things is the **Hotel Sophia**, class D, ✆ 52 313.

Eating Out

For the privilege of sitting and eating on the lovely quay of Hydra expect to pay through the nose for anything from a cup of coffee upwards. A depressing trend is to throw a fixed menu at the hurried day-trippers, leaving little time to linger over the meal Greek style. The one taverna that keeps humane prices is called **The Three Brothers** (near the cathedral); expect to pay between 2000 and 3000 dr. for their excellent Greek cooking. Just nearby is **Douskas**, with courtyard dining in a similar price range. Also reasonably priced is the **Hydra Corner**, which often has live *bouzouki* music to accompany your meal from the grill. Out at Kamini, the tranquil taverna run by the Mavromatis family seems worlds away from the cosmopolitan port, and 30 m behind it, the **Anastasakis** taverna serves some of the best traditional Greek food on Hydra for a moderate price.

Dokos

From Hydra it is an hour's caique trip to the islet of **Dokos**, best known for a kind of marble called *marmaropita*, grey and red and as hard as steel, used in building. The beach at Dokos is longer than at most ports but there is little accommodation on this islet, almost untouched by tourism. As no regular service goes to Dokos it is best to round up as many people as can fit into a caique, thus making the trip more reasonable.

Poros

Of the four major islands in the Saronic Gulf, Poros, for some unknown reason, receives the most package tours. A mere 370 metres of sea let it be classified as an island at all: sailing through the narrow Strait of Poros on a large ferry boat is a unique experience—you feel as if you could touch the balconies of the waterside buildings (or at least see what their inhabitants are watching on television). Curiously, Poros actually consists of a marriage of two islands from two different geological periods: larger Kalavria is pine-forested and embellished with innumerable quiet sandy coves; little Sferia is a volcanic leftover that popped out of the sea during the eruptions at Methana on the mainland. The two are joined by a sandy belt of land and a bridge.

Although Poros itself has little to offer in the way of excursions, it is close to some of the principal sights in the Peloponnese: the ancient theatre of Epidauros and its festival of ancient Greek drama, ancient Troezen (of Theseus, Phaedra and Hippolytus) and its lush 'Devil's Bridge', and nearer to Galatas, the fragrant Lemonodassos ('lemon forest'), of some 30,000 trees.

History

'Poros' means passage, but in antiquity the entire island was known as Kalavria. It was the headquarters of the Kalavrian league, a 7th-century BC amphictyony, or maritime confederation, that included seven cities: Athens, Aegina, Epidauros, Troezen, Nauplia, Ermioni, Orchomenos and Pasiai. One of the few things known about the Kalavrian league is that it operated under the protection of the sea god Poseidon, to whom Poros was sacred. A famous sanctuary of the god stood in the centre of Kalavria. Little remains of it today beyond the memory of the great Athenian orator, Demosthenes, who roused his city's love for freedom against Alexander the Great. Although years had passed since the Macedonians had defeated the Athenians at Chaeronea (338 BC), Demosthenes still had little, if anything, kind to say about Athens' masters, and in 322 Alexander's general Antipater went after him. Demosthenes sought sanctuary at the temple of Poseidon; cornered there by Antipater's men he took poison (significantly from the tip of his pen) and died.

One of the bays of Poros is called Russian Bay, recalling some of the confusing events that occurred on Poros in 1828, when emissaries of the Great Powers (British, French and Russian) gathered here for a conference on the new Greek kingdom. The Russians were always close friends with the first president, Capodistria—too close, thought many

POROS

independent-minded revolutionaries from Hydra and Poros, who formed their own 'constitutional committee'. On the committee's orders, Admiral Miaoulis seized the national fleet base at Poros in 1831 and when ordered by the Great Powers to hand it over to the Russians, he blew up the flagship instead.

The name of the island's other bay, Askeli, is derived from the princess Skylla of Poros, whose father, the king, had a magic lock of hair that made him immortal. When Minos of Crete besieged her father's castle, Skylla watched the battle and fell in love with the handsome Cretan king. To prove her love for him, she cut off her father's magic lock of hair while he slept and brought it to Minos proclaiming her affection. By killing the king, Minos succeeded in taking Poros the next day. But rather than thank and love Skylla for her help, he was revolted by what she had done and left for Crete without her. Desperately, Skylla swam after him, but she was attacked by her father's spirit in the form of an eagle, and drowned in the bay which still bears her name.

Connections

Car ferry from Piraeus, Aegina and Methana several times a day; car ferries every 20 minutes to Galatas; frequent passenger ships and hydrofoils to other places in the

Saronic Gulf. Galatas is three hours from Athens by land, and water taxis (*benzinas*) make the short trip across the strait on demand.

On the waterfront, © (0298) 22 462.

Poros Town and the Temple of Poseidon

Poros, the capital and port of the island, faces Galatas on the mainland, almost like a reflection. Like Hydra, many of its inhabitants trace their history back to Albanian forebears who fled Turkish depredations in their homeland. These days the town is given over almost completely to the needs of tourists, except for the **Naval Training School**, a kind of public school housed in the buildings of the first arsenal of the Greek State. More visible, however, is Poros' waterski school, which offers lessons in the beautiful port.

A new crop of hotels has sprung up on Kalavria in recent years, some on the often polluted beach of **Neorion** to the west, and **Askeliou** and **Kokkinos**, which are rather cleaner to the east. Although they are hot stuff for Poros, true beach lovers will probably turn up their noses at all of them. From Kokkinos a bus route continues to the 18th-century **monastery of Zoodochos Pigi** which has a lofty gilt iconostasis with impressive icons but no longer any monks. A new road in front of the monastery climbs to the plateau of Palatia and the wonderfully situated if scant remains of the celebrated **temple of Poseidon**, built in the 6th century, although the sanctuary itself is as old as the Mycenaeans. The ancient city was also up at Palatia and Pausanias, who visited it, writes that he saw the tomb of Demosthenes in the precinct. The view from here of the Saronic Gulf is spectacular.

Festivals

15 August; Good Friday at Zoodochos Pigi monastery.

Where to Stay

Hotel prices on Poros tend to be a little on the high side.

expensive

Heading the list are the **Dionyssos** in Poros town, © 23 511 and the **Pavlou**, out at Neorion, © 22 734. Both are B class establishments with rooms around 8–10,000 dr. At Askeli beach is Poros' only real resort hotel, the **Neon Aegli**, where each room has a balcony and sea view, and there are watersports on its private stretch of beach, © 22 372.

moderate–cheap

In the heart of the busy waterfront are **Saron**, © 22 279, where rooms come with private facilities, and the much cheaper **Aktaeon**, © 22 281, where rooms come without. There are also a large number of guesthouse-pensions with more reasonable rates (many open summer only).

There are restaurants all over town, as well as at Neorion, and in the Kokkinos area, as well as near the monastery and temple of Poseidon. Near the waterfront try the **Epta Adelfia** with good food at the best prices in Poros (1500–2000 dr. for a meal). For fish try **Lagoudera**, directly on the waterfront, where red mullet *barbounia*) is the speciality. The waterfront also offers the **Africana**—but don't expect wildebeest or cous-cous—it's a Chinese restaurant with well-prepared dishes for about 900 dr. By the naval academy **Zazzas** has all the Greek favourites, including moussaka and stuffed tomatoes, with occasional Spanish dishes. There's good food and music at **Zorba's** on Askeli Bay.

Salamis (Salamina)

Of all the islands in this book Salamis is the most suburban, but perhaps also the most Greek. The uninspiring suburb of Perama and the shipyards of Piraeus are a mere 3 km across the famous Strait of Salamis, which in 480 BC saw Athens' historic victory over the Persians. With the exception of the frescoes in the Faneromeni convent, neither nature's nor man's creations are particularly inspiring. The southeast coast of Salamis is the prettiest part of the island, with its pine forests and beaches, although they are only accessible by private car and on foot. The villages of Salamis are connected by an efficient bus system. Moulki, also called Eantion, and Selinia are popular seaside villages among families from Athens and Piraeus.

History

When Telemon and his brother Peleus slew their brother Phocos (*see* Aegina), Telemon fled to Salamis, the island of serpents. It acquired this name from the destructive serpent killed by its first king, Cychreus, who nevertheless nurtured one of its offspring to serve as an attendant of Demeter at the Eleusian mysteries. Telemon married Cychreus' daughter to become king of the island; however, his son, Great Ajax, a hero of the Trojan War, was born of his second wife, a princess of Athens. When Megara and Athens quarrelled over the possession of Salamis in 620 BC, it is said that Solon visited the tomb of Cychreus to invoke his aid in the dispute, and when the Spartans, the arbiters of the dispute, decided to give the island to Athens, they did so on the strength of the Salamian serpent at Eleusis and Telemon's marriage to an Athenian. Further proof occurred during the Battle of Salamis, when the Athenians claimed that Cychreus appeared among their ships in the form of a mighty serpent to spur them on to victory.

Solon wanted Salamis as an Athenian colony in order to protect Piraeus. During this time Kamatero was the capital of Salamis, and on Mt Patsi there are remains of fire towers used to communicate with the mainland. The island was also defended to the west against possible Megarian aggression.

In September of 480 BC a massive Persian fleet under Xerxes, the King of Kings, moved into Faliron Bay with the intention of conquering Greece once and for all. Greek commentators pumped the Persian fleet up to an incredible 1200 ships, while the Athenians and their allies could only muster a mere 378. Thanks to their scouts, the Greeks knew the Persians were coming and made preparations, sending their old men to Salamis and the women and children of Athens to Troezen. Numerous accounts of the subsequent battle have been passed down to us, most poetically *The Persians* of Aeschylus, who participated in the battle.

The Greeks won as much by their wits as by the use of their superior, highly manoeuvrable ships. Themistokles, the Athenian commander-in-chief, had a rumour leaked to Xerxes that the Greeks, hearing of a Persian land invasion in the Peloponnese, had split up and were in disarray. Xerxes decided to take advantage of the supposed confusion, and in the night ordered his fleet to block up the Strait of Salamis at Megara and in the east. Confident of victory the next day, Xerxes had his silver throne carried to the summit of Mt Egaleo in Perama, where he sat down to watch the battle unfold.

But Themistokles had been warned of the Persian plan. At dawn he moved his triremes up against the strongest Persian vessels, which initiated the attack. The Greeks pretended to fall back, then quickly spun their swift ships around, driving the bulkier craft of the Persians into the dangerous shallows. Helpless, Xerxes' fleet foundered and his ships in the south fled back to Faliron Bay. The King of Kings watched his incredible defeat in anguish and was eventually forced to create a diversion to escape with his 300 surviving ships. The army he left behind was defeated later by the Greeks at Plataea, thus ending the Persian threat.

The victory at Salamis gave Athens a moral boost that brought about their golden age. It also demonstrated the might of the Athenian navy, emboldening them to form the Delian league and control the fate of so many islands. As for Salamis, it gave birth to the tragedian Euripides and then fell back into obscurity.

Connections

Ferry every 15 minutes from Perama to Paloukia and at least five a day from Piraeus.

Salamis

Salamis, the capital of the island, is nicknamed Koulouri ('crescent') for the way it curls around its harbour. There is a small beach near town and the harbour hosts Japanese pearl oysters—stowaways on the Japanese freighters that have stopped there.

Above Koulouri is **Mt Profitis Ilias**, with views across the whole island. From Koulouri a bus leaves every hour for **Faneromeni**, the convent and ferry-boat landing stage. Set in a large pine wood popular with picnickers and campers, Faneromeni was built in 1661, reusing the foundation of an ancient temple. The church, Metamorphosis, is decorated with extraordinary frescoes of the Last Judgement, containing more than 3000 figures. Recently restored, they were painted in the 18th century by Georgios of Argos and his pupils. The best time to find the monastery open is in mid-morning or around 5 pm. Across the road by the sea is a fine open-air taverna and there are many places to swim all along the shore. To the east is the beach **Psili Ammos** (village and taverna) which unfortunately smells of petrol much of the time.

South Salamis

South of Koulouri is the pleasant village of **Mouliki**, with a beach; it has some accommodation, but no one minds if you sleep out under the pine trees nearby. From Mouliki a bus goes to **Kaki Vigla**, and a rough road from there leads to **Ag. Nikolaos**, a monastery with a 15th-century chapel. Between Ag. Nikolaos and Kaki Vigla you'll find excellent, isolated camping sites and many of the beaches are sandy. On the east coast of Salamis **Paloukia** is a ferry-boat landing stage with a naval festival at the end of August.

South of Paloukia woebegone **Ambelakia** has become a ships' rubbish dump and is very smelly—the oil slick antithesis of everything a Greek island village is supposed to evoke. **Selinia**, a few kilometres south of Ambelakia, is a collection of summerhouses, although the beach is nothing special.

The biggest celebration is the great pilgrimage to the convent of Faneromeni on 4 September. Salamis is also noted for its religious processions during Holy Week; also 5 June at Metamorphosis, and the last Sunday of Carnival at Koulouri.

Most of the hotels on Salamis are very simple and 'ethnic'. The best on the island is the **Gabriel Hotel**, © 466 2275 in Eantion. In Selinia there are several small pensions and hotels, like the **Vorsalakia** at 64 Themistocleous, © 465 3494. In the same street and for about the same price is the **Akroyali**, © 465 3341.

Because Salamis gets very few foreign tourists, its tavernas are pure Greek and the food tasty and inexpensive. In Salamis town the **Antzas** has a good name, and in Kaki Vigla **Kanellos** is known for its fish.

Spetses

Spetses is a charming, pine-scented island, the furthest in the group from Athens, a factor that has long kept it quieter and more relaxed than its more accessible sisters. Sadly, that's no longer the case and it's not unusual to see helicopters hovering in to deposit members of the jet set. The hotels, cafés and even the streets are packed, especially with the British who have practically colonized the island. Spetses is not new to tourism—its first hotel was built in 1914, and since the Second World War, families have come for its safe beaches and excellent climate—but there is a new, trendy atmosphere which seems foreign and strange. As it is, unless you're terribly lonely, you may want to avoid Spetses in July and August.

History

Discoveries at Ag. Marina indicate that Spetses (ancient Pityoussa) has been inhabited since 2500 BC. The modern name of the island may come from the Italian word for spice 'spezie', given it by the Venetians. Like the other Saronic islands, Spetses attracted many refugees from the mainland during the Turkish occupation. Shipbuilding was important from the early 17th century; by the 19th century Spetses was renowned for its seamanship and, like Hydra, the island had grown wealthy thanks to the daring of its merchantmen in blockade-running. Early on Spetses joined the fight for independence, first raising the Greek flag on 2 April 1821. Two days later Spetses won the first naval victory of the war, capturing three Ottoman ships near Milos. Many of the island's subsequent victories were won by the famous capitana of Spetses, Lascarina Bouboulina, the indomitable muse of patriotic Greek writers and artists.

Several hydrofoils daily from Piraeus and other Saronic islands, less frequently with Kythera and ports on the Peloponnese; ferry connections daily with Piraeus, other Saronic islands and Peloponnese ports; frequent excursion boats to Porto Heli, Kosta and other small beaches and ports on the mainland.

Tourist Police

Botassi St, ✆ (0298) 73 100.

Spetses Town

The capital and port of the island is officially Spetses, but it's more often known as **Dapias**, the name of the sloping square you see as you leave the quay. Bristling with cannon, the Dapia was the centre of the town's defense, although now it plays a more peaceful role as the vortex of Spetses' café society. The Dapia's pebble mosaics commemorate the revolt planned here in 1821; there's a bust of Bouboulina, who lived in a house on the Dapia, and behind the bust stands the large yellow mansion of island philanthropist Sotiris Anargyro, founder (in 1927) of a boys' school on the English model, the **Anargyrios and Korgialenios School**, where John Fowles taught and wrote *The Magus* (another book by Fowles, *Islands* is a good read while staying on Spetses, or on any other island for that matter).

Spetses' **Museum** (*open mornings*) is housed in the late-18th-century mansion of Hadziyiannis Mexis. On the ground floor the original furnishings have been preserved, while upstairs there's a box holding Bouboulina's bones (she was so ugly, the Greeks say, that she could only keep lovers by holding them at gunpoint), the flag 'Freedom or Death' of the War of Independence, some ancient coins, paintings and costumes. Of the churches in town, the cathedral **Ag. Nikolaos** by the old harbour is the oldest and was once part of a monastery where Napoleon's brother stayed. On Ag. Nikolaos' tower the Spetsiots raised their defiant flag in 1821 (a bronze cast of it may be seen just opposite), becoming the first to openly revolt against the Turks (although *see* Skiathos, p. 416). The serene old harbour rimmed with white houses now doubles as a town beach and yacht marina. A story is told that when the Turks came to occupy the island, the inhabitants created mannikins, with bright red fezzes and Turkish-appearing uniforms, and set them up along the quay. Seeing them from a distance, the Turkish commander thought that the island had already been taken and sailed on.

Two other fine churches are up at **Kastelli**, the oldest quarter of town, the 17th-century **Koimistis Theotokou**, with frescoes, and **Ag. Triada**, with a superb, carved iconostasis.

Circling Around Spetses

The only cars allowed on Spetses are official vehicles, one taxi and the municipal bus. Horse-drawn fiacres provide the most romantic means of transport and will take you part of the way around the island; *benzinas* or boat taxis (for hire at the new harbour) can take up to four people to other places along the coast; scooters may be hired (but not used in town during siesta time), although they hardly seem necessary—you can walk all the way around the island in a day on the partially asphalted road that encircles Spetses. The buses go as far as Ag. Anargyroi (from the town beach) and to Ligoneri (from the Possidonion Hotel).

The entire jagged coast of Spetses is embellished with beaches whose access depends on the reliability of your shoes. It's an easy walk, however, to the **Faros** (lighthouse) to visit **Panayia Armata**, a church built after the victory on 8 September 1822. Inside, a large painting by Koutzis commemorates the heroic scene. Just beyond is **Ag. Marina**, a beach and summer nightlife centre. Off the south coast hovers a tempting, idyllic islet called **Spetsopoula**, but don't think you can get much closer—it's a private retreat of the shipowning tycoon Niarchos.

Ag. Anargyroi, with its shady beach and good taverna, is the most popular destination on the island. From there it is a short walk to **Bekeiris' cave**. This Turkish name is derived from 1770, when Moslems from Albania came to take revenge on the Spetsiots for siding with Russia in the war. As they burnt and pillaged, the women and children took refuge in the cave. It is said that one mother killed her whimpering baby to prevent discovery, but just as many other stories claim that the refugees were eventually found and slain anyway. You can enter from the sea or there is a low entrance by land (be sure to duck). The best time of day to go is in the afternoon, when the sun shines inside. The tunnel inside is said to have run to Profitis Ilias monastery until it collapsed in an earthquake. There are also a few stalactites. **Zogeria** in the northwest is a pretty, rocky bay, with good swimming, although no sandy beaches. Isolated **Xokeriza** in the south, offers pleasant swimming from its uncrowded, shingle beach.

From **Vrello** in the north one can walk up to Profitis Ilias, although it is far more pleasant just to stay in Vrello, a corner of Spetses called **Paradise** for its beauty, although the beach is not exactly heavenly.

Festivals

The most colourful festival of the year takes place on the nearest weekend to 8 September, when the Spetsiots commemorate their victory over the Turks in the Straits of Spetses, in 1822. The Ottomans, coming to attack the island, were held at bay throughout the day by the island's fleet, and in the end withdrew when confronted with a drifting fireboat. The battle is re-enacted in the harbour, with fireworks and folkdancing and other festivities. Also, first Friday after Easter, at Zoodochos Pigi; 26 July, Ag. Paraskevi at Zogeria; 1 July and 1 November, Anargyroi; 23 April, Ag. Georgios.

Where to Stay

expensive

The classy place to stay on Spetses is the grand old **Possidonion Hotel**, an Edwardian palace and one of the dominant features of the skyline, built by Sotiris Anargyro in 1914 to revitalize the island economy, © 72 208. Also popular is the class C **Hotel Myrtoon**, © 72 555 with a roof garden and bar. For both of the above reserve well in advance.

moderate

There are several pensions on Botassi Street (where you can also find the tourist police). A little way out of town, at Ag. Mamas, there are a few low-key hotels and pensions, such as the D class **Klimis**, © 73 777, with rooms around 6000 dr., and the cheaper **Argo**, © 73 225. In Spetses town the E class **Alexandri** has about the cheapest rates. As you disembark at the port there are two travel bureaus that seem to control the rooms on the island, especially Takis Travel Office, © 72 215. Not a few people get fed up and sleep on the beach.

The best seafood on Spetses is at **Trehandiri** near Ag. Nikolaos; prices are fairly high (expect to pay at least 4000 dr.) but the food is worth it and you have a fine view over the harbour. They serve the island's speciality, *psari Spetsiotiko* (sea bream in spicy sauce). For something in the 2000–2500 dr. range try the excellent dishes at **Lazaros** and **Spyros** tavernas.

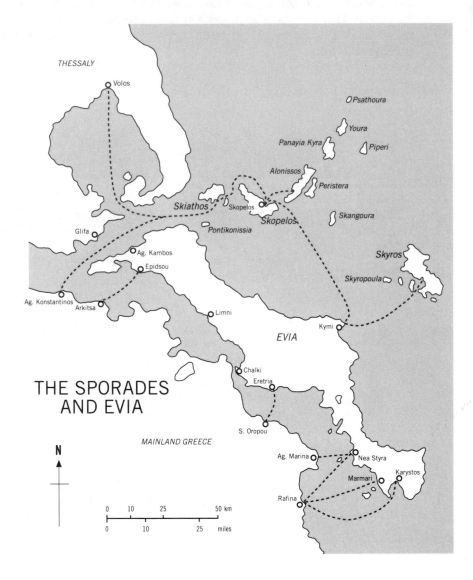

THESSALY

Volos

O Psathoura

Youra

Panayia Kyra

Piperi

Alonissos

Skiathos

Skopelos

Peristera

Pontikonissia

Skopelos

Skangoura

Glifa

Skyros

Ag. Kambos

Epidsou

Skyropoula

Ag. Konstantinos

Arkitsa

Limni

EVIA

Kymi

THE SPORADES
AND EVIA

Chalki

Eretria

MAINLAND GREECE

S. Oropou

N

Ag. Marina

Nea Styra

Karystos

Marmari

Rafina

| 0 | 10 | 25 | 50 km |
| 0 | 10 | 25 | miles |

The Harbour and Capital of Skiathos

The Sporades and Evia

The Sporades ('sporadic' or 'scattered') islands were for donkey's years one of the least visited corners of Greece—not only were they relatively inaccessible but they lacked the historical associations evoked by so many other islands. Then, slowly, Greek vacationers began to make two of the islands—Skiathos and Skopelos—their own, attracted by their exquisite sandy beaches, cool summer breezes and thick pine forests. A vanguard of Germans began to restore the old homes on Alonissos for summer villas. Then an airport was built on Skiathos, linking the island to Athens; in recent years it has been opened to international charters—and the rest is history.

Perhaps it was inevitable. Some immortal hand or eye has framed these islands to fit nearly everyone's idea of a holiday paradise. Each of the four islands has retained its individual character, although that of Skiathos, with the loveliest beaches of all, has increasingly blurred as Euro-tourism casts its homogenizing Euro-dull pall over the island. Skyros, the hardest to get to, remains one of the more original islands in Greece, with tourist facilities mainly of the home-made variety; Skopelos, the greenest and most naturally endowed of the group, remains very Greek and very dignified; and Alonissos is an odd mixture of cosmopolitan tourism and old fashioned ways; women still wear their traditional dress and card wool as they chat. Evia, the second largest island in Greece, historically has been a land of quiet farms, too close to the mainland to have a personality of its own (you can take a bus from Athens to its capital Chalkida in 1¼ hours). Still, its long, scarcely developed coastline is beginning to attract both Greek and foreign visitors escaping the crowds.

The first settlers on the Sporades were of Thracian origin. In the 16th century BC Crete colonized the islands, introducing the cultivation of olives and grapes. With the fall of Minoan civilization, Mycenaeans from Thessaly known as the Dolopians (first cousins of the Achaeans) settled the Sporades, using them as bases for daring naval expeditions. Much of the rich mythology of the islands has its roots during this period: Achilles himself was raised on Skyros.

In the 8th century BC the Chalkidians of Evia captured the Sporades as stepping stones to their colonial ambitions in Macedonia. These new invaders continued the sea traditions of the Dolopians but increasingly came into conflict with Athenian interests until 476 BC, when Athens sent Kimon to crush the Sporades' fleets. The Athenians then colonized the islands, but successfully presented themselves as liberators rather than conquerors; of all the Greek islands, none had closer ties with Athens. The government of the Sporades was run on the model of Athenian democracy, and Athena became a prominent goddess in the local pantheon.

When the Spartans defeated Athens in the Peloponnesian War, the Sporades were part of their spoils, although their reign was short. A greater threat to Athenian influence came in the person of Philip II of Macedon, who claimed the islands as his own, a dispute that attracted the attention of the entire Greek world. Philip took the islands in 322 BC as a prelude to nabbing Athens itself.

During the Roman occupation (beginning in the 2nd century BC), the Sporades retained their traditional links with Athens. Christianity, with a good helping of pagan rites, spread over the islands in the 2nd and 3rd centuries. The Byzantines sent many of their exiles there, who arrogantly made themselves the local aristocracy until 1207, when the Venetian Gizzis took over the Sporades. Philip Gizzi, the most notorious of the dynasty, usurped control from a senior relative and ruled the islands as a pirate king until Likarios, the Admiral of Emperor Michael Palaeologos, took him in chains to Constantinople and only let him go when he agreed to hand the islands over to the restored Byzantine Empire. Afterwards possession continued to see-saw back and forth between Greeks and Franks, until Mohammed the Conqueror took Constantinople in 1453. The islanders quickly invited the Serenissima back as the lesser evil, although the Venetians were forced out when all their crafty agreements with the Ottoman Empire crumbled before the violent attacks of Barbarossa.

Once they had the Sporades, the Turks promptly forgot all about them, although never neglecting to send a cadi over once a year to collect taxes. The islands were so subject to raids that a permanent Turkish population never settled there. In the 1821 revolution, Thessalian insurgents found refuge on the islands and in 1830 the Treaty of London included them in the original kingdom of Greece.

Connections

If you're departing from Athens, Alkyon Tours, at 98 Academias, © (01) 362 2093, has long specialized in travel to the islands, and has all the latest bus and boat timetables. Skyros may only be reached from or via Kymi, in Evia, from where there are weekly sailings (at least) to the other Sporades. The main ferry ports to Skiathos, Skopelos and Alonissos are Volos in Thessaly and Ag. Konstantinos. Hydrofoils also ply these routes daily in summer from Volos and Ag. Konstantinos. The only other connection is the occasional boat from Limnos to Skopelos.

Alonissos

Generally the least known of the four main islands, Alonissos is the queen of its own little archipelago of nine islets. It once produced a large crop of grapefruit, but the trees on the island all perished from disease; a similar fate has recently afflicted many of the grapevines in the area. More significant for the island's current condition was the earthquake of 1965, which devastated the principal town, Chora. The government transferred all the inhabitants to a new village by the sea, and Chora, magnificently situated high up above the sea, was abandoned—until some Germans, enchanted by the serenity and the view, began to buy and repair the old homes, agreeing together to do without such conveniences as running water and electricity. Beyond the one paved carriageway, good roads are scarce and for the time being nine-tenths of Alonissos is accessible only by foot; but this is fine walking country, the heights inhabited only by the rare Eleanora's falcon. Heading in the opposite direction, the beauty of Alonissos' underwater caves and ruins and the chance of seeing a seal make it a favourite for divers.

History

The history of Alonissos is complicated by the fact that the modern Alonissos is not ancient Halonnesos, but actually bore the name Ikos. The confusion resulted from an over-eager restoration of ancient place names after independence, but in Alonissos' case, the mistake was an improvement. As for the real ancient Halonnesos, some scholars say it must have been tiny Psathoura, northernmost of the islets that surround Alonissos, where the extensive ruins of an ancient city lie submerged off shore. Another possibility is Kyra Panayia, a fertile islet with two fine harbours.

Inhabited from Neolithic times, Ikos/Alonissos was part of the Cretan colony of Prince Stapylos, who planted the first of the vines that were to make Ikos famous. In the 14th century BC the Mycenaeans took over the affairs of the island, counting among their settlers Peleus, the father of Achilles. In Classical times the two city-states on Ikos thrived through exporting wine. The Athenians established a naval base there in the 4th century, and later, in Roman times, Ikos was given to Athens (42 BC).

During the Middle Ages Ikos was ruled by Skopelos and slowly lost its identity, and was variously known as Achilliodromia, Liadromia or simply Dromos (road). Barbarossa wreaked havoc on the island in 1538 when it was added to the Ottoman Empire.

As for ancient Halonnesos (wherever it may be), in Classical times it belonged to Athens, although in the 4th century BC it was governed de facto by the pirate Sostratos. Philip of Macedon took it from him, quoting the famous speech of Demosthenes 'Concerning Alonissos', which initiated the troubles between Athens and Macedonia. Skopelos took the island in 341 BC when Philip offered to return it to Athens; Philip, however, crushed these opportunists and the island lost all its importance, until even its identity faded from human memory.

Connections

At least once a day with Volos, Skopelos, Skiathos and Ag. Konstantinos; three times a week with Thessaloniki, once a week with Kimi (Evia). Daily hydrofoils to Skopelos, Skiathos, Thessaloniki, Volos and Ag. Konstantinos, frequent connections with Skyros and Moundania.

Tourist Police

See regular police, ✆ (0424) 65 205.

Patitiri and Chora

The island's port, **Patitiri**, and the relief village built by the government after 1965 and the fishing hamlet of **Votsi** have all merged together in recent years. Most of the buildings are new, but perhaps to make up for their dull design many are ensconced in luxuriant gardens. The limpid waters off Alonissos provide a good income for local fishermen, and the whole port area is lined with almost identical, shady tavernas. There's a small beach at Patitiri, and another at Votsi, but most people opt for one of the many caique excursions to the island's coves. The one really sandy beach is at **Vrisitsa**, although there are many others on the nearby islet of Peristera. Shops have mopeds to hire (even cars go as far as Kalamakia these days) if you feel the need to get somewhere quickly.

South of Patitiri are two beaches, **Vithisma** and **Marpounta**; under the sea, at the latter, you can see the remains of a round temple of the healing god Asklepios. There was a 5th-century BC settlement (almost certainly ancient Ikos) at the beach **Kokkino Kastro**, but it too sank into the sea; you can make out some of its walls from shore. It's a 2-hour walk from Patitiri, and boats often chug there as well.

The old capital of the island, **Chora**, is perched above Patitiri and enjoys superb views and cinemascope sunsets. If you walk up, you have the choice of two delicious routes: the mule path is hedged with raspberry bushes, while the road is lined with pear and nut trees. The walls of Chora were built by the Byzantines and repaired by the Venetians, and ghosts are said to dance around the 17th-century church **Christos**. As well as the summertime Germans, several local families have returned to Chora, and you can occasionally see the older women dressed in their traditional pale blue and white dresses and scarves, their long braids hanging about their shoulders. The two oldest churches on Alonissos are in Chora: **Ag. Athanasios** and **Ag. Georgios**. From Chora it's a 20-minute walk down to Vrisitsa beach.

Steni Vala and **Kalamakia**, both on the east coast, have small pensions, beaches and tavernas. They are well sheltered in the embrace of nearby Peristera islet, and offer the best fishing and watersports on the island; frequent boats connect them with Patitiri. The delicious Mediterranean lobster or *astakos* is plentiful off the remote northern coast, by **Kopelousako** beach and the old shepherd's village of Gerakis. **Ag. Dimitrios** has the ruins of a Byzantine fountain and another ancient settlement in the sea; fossils of prehistoric beasts were found at Megliamos. The beach is also lovely and usually deserted.

Alonissos' Archipelago

Peristera (Dove) islet follows the east coast of Alonissos, its Siamese twin until separated by a natural upheaval. Also known as Xiro, Peristera has many sandy beaches and three tiny shepherds' hamlets, Mnimata, Livadhia and Xilos, the last by a ruined castle. Every ten days a caique goes to **Psathoura**, where one of the most powerful lighthouses in Greece guides passing ships. It is another candidate for the island of the Sirens as well as a possible ancient Halonnesos. A submerged city may be seen by the lighthouse, as well as a sunken volcano.

Lovely, wooded **Kyra Panayia** (Pelagos) is two or three hours by caique from Patitiri. Now uninhabited (except for wild goats and the odd shepherd) the island once supported two monasteries, the original one founded by medieval monks from Mt Athos and the other, on the east coast, established at a later date; although both are now abandoned the islet still belongs to Mt Athos. At the port Ag. Petros you can see the remains of a 12th-century Byzantine ship in the waters; when it was discovered its hold was filled with ceramics. Kyra

Panayia has some pleasant beaches, a pretty cave (believed to have been the home of the Cyclops) and plenty of opportunities for wild bushwalking.

There is another monastery connected to Mt Athos on **Skangoura**, which offers excellent fishing in its many sea coves and caves. **Pappou**, home to a diminishing hare population, has the remnants of a tiny 7th-century church, while on **Youra** (ancient Geronta) a rare breed of goat skips about the rocks. A large empty house there is said to be owned by King Konstantine of Greece, should he ever desire to come to Youra to visit the goats. A few Classical and Roman remains have been discovered there; most spectacular of all is another Cyclops cave with stalactites. Another islet, **Piperi**, on the outskirts of the National Marine Park, is a wildlife sanctuary, and home to a small but stable population of monk seals.

Festivals

All on Alonissos: 1 July, Ag. Anargaroi; 26 July, Ag. Paraskevi; 15 August, Panayias; 17 July, Ag. Marina; 40 days after Easter, Analypsos.

Where to Stay

Most of the island's accommodation is in Patitiri and Votsi, though the spiffier hotels and pensions tend to be booked solid by packagers. To make up for it, there are plenty of rooms to rent in private houses and generally plenty of people to offer them to you when you get off the boat.

expensive

The **Marpounta Bungalows**, if you can get a room, are the most comfortable lodgings on Alonissos, near the sea at Votsi, © 65 219.

moderate

In Alonissos town (Chora) the **Alkyon** (if not fully booked) is a pleasant pension, © 65 450, and good value. Less expensive is the simple pension **Ioulieta** in Patitiri, © 65 463.

cheap

For a room, take pot luck or go to Ikos Travel near the wharf, which has a listing of rooms, © 65 320. There are also a few rooms available in Chora (though harder to find). There's also an official campsite, **Ikoros Camping**, © 65 258, at Steni Vala.

Eating Out

If you've wanted to splurge on a feast of Mediterranean lobster (*astakos*), Alonissos is the place for it; many of the shady, seaside restaurants in Patitiri serve it as well as other marine delectables; one, **Naffilos**, sometimes accompanies its seafood with singers and violins. For good food and a magnificent view, eat at the **Paraport Taverna** up in Chora, where a meal costs about 2500 dr. There are tavernas at all the most popular beaches.

Skiathos

Racy Skiathos is not for the sun-shy teetotaller. It's beach life by day and bar life by night, with few places of historical interest to distract the scholar. Still a peasant island community in the early 1970s, Skiathos has been catapulted faster than most into the frantic world of tourism, with all the pros and cons that this inevitably entails. It is now one of the most popular destinations in Greece, and with good cause. It is a stunningly beautiful island; its magnificent beaches (by most counts there are 62) provide some of the best swimming in Greece, and its lush foliage is a pleasure to the eye. Add to this a host of lively bars and restaurants and you have the ingredients for a potent, heady cocktail.

History

When the great Persian fleet of King Xerxes sailed on its way to its eventual defeat at Salamis in 480 BC, it encountered a fierce storm in the waters off Skiathos. So many of Xerxes' ships were damaged that he put in at Skiathos for repairs, in the bay that now bears his name.

During his stay Xerxes came up with a stunning innovation: the world's first known light-house on the islet of Kyrminx—now a reef known as Lepheteris and to this day a dangerous menace to ships sailing between Skiathos and the mainland; Xerxes lit it up, not as a public service, but to enable his fleet to slip past the Athenian patrol ships at night. A few traces of the lighthouse still exist on Lepheteris.

The rest of Skiathos' history follows that of the other Sporades. The Gizzis ruled the island for Venice and built the fort on Bourtzi islet by the present-day town, which was settled in 1790 by refugees from Limni on Evia. The Skiathiot navy assisted the Russians in the campaign at Cêsme, when they defeated the Ottoman fleet. Feeling their oats, the islanders revolted against the distant Turks in 1805, and sent so many ships to aid the cause of independence that Skiathos itself was left unprotected and prey to marauders. It was one of the first places to be touched by the Orthodox reformist movement, Kollivades, emanating from Mt Athos (although Skiathos means 'shadow of Athos' in Greek, its name comes from a pre-Hellenic source). A local writer, Alexandros Papadiamantis (1851–1911) immortalized Skiathos in his novels there, although the books have yet to be translated into English.

Connections

By air: At least four flights a day from Athens, and numerous charters from European cities.

By sea: Daily from Volos, Ag. Konstantinos, Skopelos and Alonissos, four times a week to Thessaloniki, twice a week to Tinos, Mykonos, Paros, Santorini and Herakleon (Crete), once a week to Skyros and Kimi (Evia).

Hydrofoils daily in summer from Volos and Ag. Konstantinos with connections to Skopelos and Alonissos, less frequently with Skyros, Marmaras and Moundania (Halkidiki). Daily excursion boat to Skopelos and Alonissos.

Tourist Police

See regular police, © (0427) 21 111.

Skiathos Town

The capital and only town, **Skiathos**, is a spread of traditional whitewashed houses, over-hung with bougainvillaea and with freshly washed sheets rippling in the breeze. A walk through the backstreets will help you absorb the feeling of the place, but don't expect to encounter many donkeys; you're more likely to find yourself dodging high speed trial bikes. The town has two harbours, separated by the pretty **Bourtzi** promontory, where a medieval fortress now serves as a primary school. For a sweeping panorama of Skiathos town and the neighbouring island of Skopelos, take the steps at the end of the old harbour past the lazy waterfront cafés and souvenir shops. Late afternoon brings the scene to life and cocktail hour seems to last forever as you sit and watch an extraordinary international selection of the human race go by. If this flagrant hedonism pricks the conscience, you can get your shot of culture by locating the house of Skiathos' illustrious poet and novelist, **Alexander Papadia-mantis**, situated just off the main street, which bears his name.

The boats bobbing up and down in front of the cafés in the old harbour will take you to most beaches and you'll hear the owners calling out their destinations. Some offer round the island trips but be warned that on the north side there is a fairly uninteresting stretch of coast and the water on that side can be rough—many a day-tripper returns green about the gills. If you want to get about the island under your own steam, there are a number of places to rent cars and scooters. Be careful on the roads—traffic is fast-moving and if on a bike keep an eye out for gritty curves and the demon taxi drivers.

Buses to other parts of the islands run hourly in season from the new harbour (in summer your feet may not touch the floor throughout the journey, but you could make some new friends). Taxis also operate from here and are in great demand, so don't be shy to share.

Koukounaries and Other Beaches

Skiathos' main road runs from town along the southern flank of the island ending up at the legendary **Koukounaries**, with a sweeping crescent bay of soft sand fringed with pine trees that somehow escaped from the South Pacific. From town, the most convenient beach is **Megali Ammos**, although it's generally crowded. Moving westward, **Ahladies** beach, dominated by the large Esperides hotel (with tennis court open to the public) is also densely populated for most of the summer season. Beyond that, 5 km from town, there's **Kanapitsa** beach, situated on the **Kalamaki** peninsula, a popular cove for swimming and watersports, and there's a restaurant by the water. Nearby **Vromolimnos**, hard to pronounce and even harder to find, is one of the finest places to swim on the island, and when the rest of Skiathos is bulging at the seams, you'll always find room to toss a frisbee around on the next beach, **Platanias**.

Convenient by bus or boat, **Troulos** has an attractive taverna waiting to welcome the round-the-island trippers, so be sure to get there well before or after them to avoid the busy rush. On the other side of Koukounaries lies **Krassa**, nowadays called **Banana** beach, perhaps because it's where you can peel off everything, although beware: it's cheek-to-cheek in the high season; it's up the hill with the sea on your left when you get off the bus at Koukounaries. Next door is the lovely **Ag. Eleni**, the last beach accessible by road, a somewhat quieter spot with a view across to the Pelion peninsula on the mainland.

On the north coast, **Mandraki**, reached by footpath from the lagoon behind Koukounaries, has lovely sand (and a snack bar). For more isolation, try sandy **Aselinos**, an hour's walk from the 17th-century monastery **Panayia Kounistra**, itself accessible by car or bicycle: it was built where an icon of the Virgin was found dangling in a tree. The beach at **Lalaria** is a marvel of silvery pebbles, accessible only by boat, as are the nearby sea grottoes—**Skotini** ('the dark'—so bring a light if you want to see anything), **Galazia**, 'the blue', and **Chalkini**, 'the copper'.

When charter-set life begins to pall, there are several escape hatches. A little over 2-hour walk across Skiathos will take you to **Kastro**, the medieval ghost village and place of refuge during times of danger; the path is well marked from Ag. Konstantinos near Skiathos town. The ruins within the crumbling walls include Byzantine churches and a Turkish hammam; the view from the top is quite lovely and there's a quiet beach below. (Boats sometimes make the excursion.) A detour on the path could be made to the 15th-century monastery **Panayia Kechis**, the oldest on the island, containing some fine 17th-century icons.

Another walk from town begins just before the turning to the airport road and leads in roughly an hour to the only occupied monastery left on the island, **Evangelistria** (*8–12 noon and 5–7, proper attire required*). The monastery was founded in 1797 by monks from Mt Athos during the Kollivades movement. On its tall blue and white pole, the Skiathiots hoisted the flag of independent Greece in 1827—the first to do so (although Spetses, for one, would dispute this); a small museum has items relating to Skiathos and the monastery.

Hourly excursion boats in the summer wait to whisk you off in half an hour to **Tsougrias Islet**, facing Skiathos town. In the sixties the Beatles wanted to buy it. It's an ideal place to escape the droves of summer visitors, with its fine sand and excellent swimming. The simple snack bar usually provides freshly caught *marides* (white bait) to munch at a table under the trees, but you may have to share your food with the resident wasp population. Tsougrias has two other beaches, accessible by foot, where you really can play Robinson Crusoe for the day. If you find yourself in Skiathos town and simply can't summon the energy to join the queues for bus, boat or taxi, dive off the rocks at the **Bourtzi**, and pretend you're in your own Martini ad.

Festivals

15 August, at Evangelismos; 27 August, Ag. Fanourios; 26 July, Ag. Paraskevi; 27 July, Ag. Panteleimonos.

Where to Stay

Skiathos has accommodation to suit everyone's taste and pocket, but remember that in high season finding a bed without a reservation can be a trial, especially in the torrid month of August, when it seems the island will sink beneath the weight of its visitors.

expensive

To escape the madding crowd you'll find peace out at the **Skiathos Palace Hotel**, which enjoys dubious luxury class status, but it does have a superb view of Koukounaries bay, © 22 242. In one of the best positions, on one of the best beaches, the new **Skiathos Princess Elizabeth** deserves its luxury status, although its rates are not sky high, © 49 369. At Nostos, 5 km from town, the **Nostos Hotel** commands a majestic position and at night glitters like a real palace; an Olympic size pool is handy for those who can't face the long trek down to the sea, and its rustically decorated interior makes a refreshing change, © 22 420. Closer to town is the B class **Esperides** at Ahladies beach. As large hotels go it's one of the best and thus popular with the major tour operators, © 22 245. On the edge of Skiathos town, on the road to Koukounaries, the **Athos** has comfortable rooms with pleasant views, © 22 477.

moderate

In town itself there are many offerings, most notably the **Meltemi**, on the new harbour front, © 22 493, but generally booked solid in summer months. However, have a drink at their pleasant bar and watch the antics of the flotilla yachties as they moor and unmoor with zealous gung-ho. A few steps beyond is the colourful **San Remo Hotel**, whose terraced rooms give you dress circle seats to observe the harbour traffic and wave at the greenhorn passengers on the incoming charter jets, © 22 078. Follow the harbour front around to find the **Alkyon**, a standard B class hotel with a cool marble lobby and comfortable rooms overlooking the hotel's pleasant gardens, © 22 981. Lowest rates in this category, and a good bet, is the centrally placed **Australia Hotel**, just off Papadiamantis St, © 22 488, behind the post office. Rooms are simple, cheap and come with private bath.

cheap

Rooms for rent can be found all over the town, but you'll have to seek them out; it's not common practice in Skiathos to meet incoming boats or planes to hawk cheap rooms. Wander up the hilly streets and ask the ladies sitting on their doorsteps. Prices are rising at a brisk pace, so expect to pay up to 4000 dr. for a double room. Megali Ammos has a number of delightful pensions on the beach. The rooms are basic but the thriving flora on the terraces lend an exotic atmosphere. If you come unstuck in your quest for a room, stroll into any of the tourist offices on the waterfront.

Eating Out

Eating out in Skiathos is a hit and miss affair. Some of the most beautifully located tavernas serve mediocre food, as in the case of the hard to find but spectacular **Tarsanas**. Generally speaking, the tavernas on the steps at the western end of the old harbour tend to be expensive, but look out for the **psistaria** lodged between them where they serve good spit-roasted chicken and *souvlaki* at low prices, and you have the same view as those next door. By common consent the best bargain in town is **Stavros** (in Evangelistrias St, 50 m from the post office); especially good for oven-ready food and steaks, at 3000 dr. for a full meal. **Ilias** taverna (rather more difficult to find, it's two blocks past Stavros on the left) is traditionally everyone's favourite, particularly the South African and British island residents who, jockeying for position on the local social scale, like to be recognized by the owner. Try the shrimp *youvetsi*, rabbit *stifado* and all sorts of other enticing dishes on display (closed lunchtime and all day Sun); prices for a full dinner range from 2000–3500 dr. At **Limenaki**, on the waterfront past the new harbour, you can enjoy such luxuries as avocado, shrimps and pepper steak, as near to the real thing as you'll find in Greece without paying through the nose. While sampling some of the standard but well prepared dishes at **Dionyssos**, just off the main street, the waiters will treat you to a floor show of Greek dancing—dinner with wine around 2500 dr. Up the steps at the end of the harbour, search out **La Piazza**, an excellent Italian restaurant serving pasta et al. that even picky Italians tuck into (3000 dr.) On Megali Ammos, the town beach, the friendly little **Ellas** has simple but tasty salads, fried fish and wine for 2000 dr., and is a lovely spot for refreshments between swims.

Having eaten, you'll be spoilt for choice when it comes to bars, but they're not cheap. An oasis of tranquillity in the Skiathos summer madhouse, **Adagio** opposite Stavros taverna in Evangelistrias St. has a pleasant décor and classical music to soothe the eye and ear, and Sophia, the multilingual owner, will give you a genuinely warm and friendly welcome; a favourite place for an after-dinner drink or coffee. The **Kentavros**, in Papadiamantis Square off the main street, is always popular for its lively but not deafening music. The charming little **Admiral Benbow Inn** (Polytechniou St) provides a corner of old England on Skiathos while in the same street the **Borzoi**, for years the place to go, is still worth a try after midnight if you can afford the drinks. On a warm summer evening the picturesque waterfront bars come into their own, the best being **Jimmy's** and the more upscale **Oasis**.

Skopelos

Where Skiathos has given its all to tourism, Skopelos has kept aloofly to itself; a good many of its hotels and restaurants are operated by outsiders who leave at the end of summer when the flow of tourist money stops. Yet Skopelos is an exceptionally beautiful island, more dramatic than Skiathos, its beaches as lovely (and safe for children), its entire 100 km^2 shaded by pine forests, its two main towns, Skopelos and Glossa, among the finest in the Sporades. There's an accepted if unofficial campsite, many small pensions and a modest amount of nightlife. Skopelos has learned to take the summer invasion in its stride, if not perhaps with any great enthusiasm. Traditionally, at least half of the young men on the island spend most of their lives working abroad or at sea; the easy money to be had catering to the needs of tourists holds no appeal.

History

Known in antiquity as Perparethos, Skopelos formed part of the Cretan colony ruled by Staphylos (who, according to some, was the son of Theseus and Ariadne)—a fact given dramatic confirmation in 1927 when Staphylos' wealthy Minoan tomb was discovered by the cove that has always borne his name. Subsequent tradition–history–mythology recounts that King Pelias, usurper of the Iolkan kingdom in Thessaly, settled Skopelos in the 13th century BC; it was this same Pelias who sent the rightful heir to Thessaly, Jason, on the famous quest for the Golden Fleece. Under Athens, Skopelos retained a certain amount of autonomy and minted its own coins, and worshipped in particular Dionysos and Demeter. Under the

Romans it took its current name, which means 'cliff'. Reginos, first bishop of Skopelos was martyred in 362 and became the island's patron saint.

Venetian renegade Philippo Gizzi used Skopelos as his piratical headquarters, and his capture by the resurgent Byzantines meant a decline in local excitement until Barbarossa decimated the community. Gradually Skopelos regained its population, attracting many refugees from the Turks. Skopeliot sailors fought so bravely with the Russians at Cêsme, that the Russian admiral gave the islanders a new church bell in thanks for their help. After assisting the Thessalian mountaineers in the War of Independence, Skopelos joined Greece in 1830.

Connections

Ferries daily from Volos, Ag. Konstantinos, Skiathos and Alonissos, three times a week with Thessaloniki, once a week with Kimi (Evia). Note that the ferries usually call at both Skopelos town and Loutraki, the port of Glossa. Hydrofoils daily to Skiathos, Alonissos, Volos and Ag. Konstantinos, less frequently to Skyros and Marmaras (Chalkidiki).

Tourist Police

See regular police, Skopelos town, ✆ (0424) 22 235.

Skopelos Town and its Harbour

Skopelos or Chora forms an exceptionally pretty collage of old blue slate and new red-tile roofs, artfully arranged in a steep amphitheatre around the port. There's a touch of Venice in the older buildings (see especially the **Fragomacholas house**), while others are built either in a sturdy Thessalian or Macedonian style. The newer houses fit in harmoniously, incorporating wooden balconies and other traditional features, while in between the Greek obsession for planting a seed wherever it might have half a chance has resulted in a lush growth of flowers and plants. Perched above town, where a temple to Athena once stood, is the **Kastro**, a Venetian castle built by the Gizzi, so formidable that Skopelos was left untouched during the War of Independence. Within the walls you can visit the 9th-century church of **Ag. Athanasios**, with frescoes from the 1500s.

Skopelos town claims 123 churches altogether, of all shapes and sizes, many with charming iconostasis. Two to look out for are **Zoodochos Pigi** which has an icon attributed to St Luke, and **Christo** with its exceptionally handsome gilded interior. At **Ampeliki** the ruins of an Asklepieion lie half-submerged in the sea, while at the other end of town the fortified monastery **Episkopi** encompasses an ancient church believed to mark the site where Bishop Reginos was martyred. Just outside Chora you can also visit the **Fournou Damaskinon**, the gargantuan oven where in August plums are dried to become Skopelos' famous prunes; many of these are later crystallized and served with *raki* to guests, along with a sprig of basil to tuck behind the ear. There's a convenient sandy beach next to the town and under the trees a row of sweet shops that scent the evening air with *loukoumades* (delicate deep-fried pastries served in a warm syrup of cinnamon and honey).

The hills overlooking Skopelos' large but windswept harbour shelter three monasteries. The closest, **Evangelistria**, with a magnificent view over Skopelos town, was founded by monks from Mt Athos, but is now occupied by nuns who offer their weavings for sale in a little shop (open mornings and late afternoons). Further afield the monastery **Ag. Barbara**, a short walk from Skopelos town, is a fortified monastery containing frescoes from the 15th century. **Metamorphosis** has been abandoned, but still hosts one of the island's biggest *paneyeria* (5 June). Over the ridge, looking towards Alonissos, is the third monastery **Prodromos**, also taken over by nuns (same hours as Evangelistria). One path connects them all; a road for vehicles ascends as far as Metamorphosis. On the other side of the bay near the pleasant shingle beach **Ag. Konstantinos** are the ruins of a Hellenistic water tower; if this beach is overcrowded, try **Glysteri**, a 3-km walk to the north. Lastly, caiques from the port make the short excursion to the sea cave of **Tripiti**, the island's chief lobster lodge and fishing hole or to the islet of **Ag. Georgios**, with a 17th-century monastery and herd of wild goats.

Buses run regularly from Skopelos town to Glossa along the island's one main road. Along the route you'll find **Staphylos** where the Minoan tomb was discovered, now a popular family beach, while **Velanio**, on the opposite side of its small headland is the unofficial nudist beach. **Agnondas**, the next stop, serves as a kind of emergency port when rough seas prevent landing at Skopelos town; a special bus then relays passengers to the capital. Inaccessible from land, sandy **Limonari beach** is a popular boat destination from Agnondas.

From Agnondas the road cuts through the pine groves to another popular campsite and beach, **Panormos**. Tucked between Panormos and Milia, are small secluded swimming coves, fringed by pines, accessible only on foot from the road by threading your way down through the trees. **Milia** itself is shady and has a pebbly beach, with a large taverna and campsite (path from the main road). Further along, **Elios** beach is lined with prefab housing—emergency shelters thrown up after the 1965 earthquake.

Glossa

At the end of the road, set in the woods high above the sea is Skopelos' second town, Glossa, a beautiful village constructed mainly during the Turkish occupation. The houses managed to survive the 1965 earthquake; one of their more peculiar architectural features is the toilet on the balcony. Three 4th-century BC towers, at **Mavragani, Helliniko** and **Sendouka** continue to stand watch over Glossa. There's a pebble beach, and a couple of tavernas under the plane trees at **Loutraki**, the town's port, 3 km below. Near Loutraki's church **Ag. Nikolaos** are the 7th-century ruins of an earlier basilica. There are also the remains of a fortress at **Selinus**.

Most of the island's almonds grow in the region of Glossa, especially in three little villages, **Makhalas, Kato Klima** and **Ano Klima**, the latter with rooms to rent. **Kalogiros** on the rugged north coast is a small isolated village, most easily reached by caique; alternatively, a well-marked track from Glossa leads in an hour across the island to the church **Ag. Ioannis**, perched like an eagle's nest over the sea—the last leg of the walk is 100 steps carved in the living rock; take a canteen of water.

Festivals

25 February, Ag. Reginos; 6 August, Megosotiri on Skopelos Bay; 15 August, Panayias in Skopelos; 9 November, Esothia Theotokos at the edge of the town; 25 November, Christos, also in the town.

Where to Stay

Like Skiathos, Skopelos is expensive; unlike Skiathos, there are no huge slabs of hotels. For most people, Skopelos town is the best place to stay.

On the outskirts of Skopelos town, in Livadi, the **Prince Stafylos** is a gem; pool, restaurant, pretty courtyard, well-furnished rooms. There's a courtesy bus from the port, © 22 775. Among the choices in town are the **Xenia Pension**, © 22 232, and the slightly more expensive **Hotel Adonis**, © 22 231, with a fast food restaurant on the ground level. In Panormos the spacious **Panormos Beach Pension** caters mostly to packagers, but is a little pricey (up to 12,000 dr. in season; © 22 711). For about the same price **Rigas House** is the place to stay at Staphylos, © 22 618.

moderate

There are also a fair number of pensions, such as the **Drossia**, © 22 490, and **Archontiko**, © 22 049, but unfortunately these are likely to be full in high summer. Outside town you can find rooms at Loutraki, the port of Glossa, and the **Pension Valentina**, © 33 694.

cheap

You'll have no problem finding a simple room; offers as you step off the boat are plentiful, and honest. Otherwise, near the port at Skopelos an agency specializes in finding rooms in houses (a free service); ask there for possibilities elsewhere on the island as well.

Eating Out

There is no shortage of tavernas in the town, and more or less all cook to a decent standard. Visitors and locals both like **Selini**, a 15-minute stroll around the harbour, a smart restaurant in a sub-tropical garden setting, specializing in seafood; it also has an extensive wine list. Count on 4–5000 dr. for dinner, but it's well spent. **Anatoli**, set in the ruins of the old Venetian castle, serves excellent, inexpensive meze, with a free panoramic view from the terrace. The owner, Giorgos, is a well-known bouzouki player and plays most nights (200 dr.). Down in the town **Alexanders** is a romantic spot to dine beneath the date palms. The menu is a mix of Greek standards, good pizza and so-so pasta (2500 dr.). For spicier, more exotic fare, try **Pirates** (it's well sign-posted), where they concoct such delights as green prawn curries, chicken Madras, a variety of lamb dishes, and excellent vegetarian food (3000 dr.). There are tavernas on most of the beaches, but one not to miss is **Takonis**, on the beautiful beach of Agnondas, with fresh fish and good ready food (2000 dr.).

Skyros

Skyros is an exceptional island in many respects. Geologically it is an odd marriage of two distinct islets: its southern half is wild, rugged and uninhabitable, while the north is fertile and pine-forested. A race of small native ponies called the Pikermies roams the southern part undisturbed, except at harvest time when they are traditionally rounded up to help with the chores. Skyros is also the most difficult to reach from Athens—under ideal conditions it takes about 7 hours by land and sea; for many years connections even from Kymi were so limited that the isolated Skyriotes purchased their own ferry to get about. These long years of inaccessibility account in part for the island's immense charm and the staying power of its customs. The older men, in particular, still don their baggy blue trousers, black caps and flat leather sandals with many straps, and the older women often wear their long skirts and yellow scarves. The interiors of Skyros' sugar-white houses are among the most charming and cluttered in Greece: carved wooden furniture and lofts, a large wooden loom in one room, and tubby round hearths decorated with rows of colourful ceramic plates. Plate collecting has been a Skyriot obsession since the 16th century, when the conquest by the Turks forced the island's wealthy Byzantine exiles into such poverty that they had to sell off even their dinnerware. Ever since, plates have been the enduring Skyriot status symbol; a Skyriot sailor far away at sea never has to think twice about the perfect gift for his wife or mother: some plates come from as far away as China.

The earliest inhabitants of the island are said to have worshipped goats and cattle and some very curious vestiges of this cult remain on modern Skyros. During carnival, three characters dance down the street led by a man in a goatskin costume and sheep bells called the Old Man, followed by the *Frangos* (the Frank, or European) and the *Korela* (a man dressed up as a woman). These perform the *Horos tou Tragoun*, or the Goat Dance, possibly a relic of the ancient rite that gave us the word 'tragedy' (*tragoudia*, or 'goat song'). Every day during carnival the Old Man, the Frangos and the Korela make their rollicking way through town, joining in satires (another goatish word, derived from the mischievous half-goat Satyrs) until they end up at the monastery of Ag. Georgios, the patron saint of Skyros.

Mythology

When it was prophesied that Achilles, son of the sea goddess Thetis and Peleus, would either win great glory at Troy and die young, or live peacefully at home to a ripe old age, his doting mother thought to hide him from the Achaeans by disguising him as a girl and sending him to live among the women at King Lycomedes' palace in Skyros. Achilles didn't mind, and took advantage of his stay in the harem by fathering a son, Neoptolemis. All would have been well had not another oracle declared that the Achaeans would never win the Trojan War without Achilles, and crafty Odysseus was sent in search of the young hero. Suspecting Thetis' ploy, Odysseus brought a chest full of gifts for the women when he called on King Lycomedes—perfumes, jewellery, finery—and a sword, which the young transvestite in the crowd seized joyfully for his own, just as Odysseus had anticipated. Once discovered, Achilles willingly joined the Achaeans. When an arrow in his heel ended his life, Odysseus returned to Skyros to fetch his son Neoptolemis to Troy, and the war was eventually won.

King Lycomedes of Skyros plays a less benign role in another story: when the hero Theseus returned to Athens after spending four years glued to the Chair of Forgetfulness in Hades (his punishment for trying to help a friend abduct Persephone, the queen of Hell), he found Athens corrupt and divided into factions against him. Theseus laid a curse on his native city and sought asylum in Crete, but was blown off course to Skyros, where he was received with such honour by Lycomedes that Theseus announced that he meant to retire on an estate his family owned on Skyros—an estate coveted by Lycomedes himself. After a drinking party he led Theseus to the pinnacle of Skyros' acropolis and gave him a push, hurtling him to his death on the rocks below.

History

Theseus was buried on Skyros and his memory neglected by the Athenians until his spirit was seen at Marathon, rising out of the earth to lead the Athenians to victory over the Persians. The Delphic oracle then charged the Athenians to bring Theseus' bones back to Athens—just the excuse the Athenians needed to capture Skyros for themselves. In 476 BC Kimon captured it, enslaved the inhabitants and, guided by a she-eagle, was led to the grave of a tall skeleton buried with his weapons. Certain that it was Theseus, Kimon exhumed the coffin, carried it back to Athens, and enshrined it in the Theseion.

So many Athenians then came to settle the island that Athens treated Skyros as an equal and demanded no tribute. As in Athens, the Dionysia was the biggest festival on the island. Skyros, like Lesbos, has a Mount Olympos, named by the Athenian settlers, who adopted the island's cult of the sky god into their own state religion of Zeus and the Olympians. The Skyriotes also worshipped Achilles—a bay on the island is still named for him.

Skyros remained part of Athens until 86 BC when Sulla captured the proud capital. Under Byzantine rule, many important people were exiled to Skyros, creating a tyrannical upper class. Barbarossa captured the island in 1538; unlike the other Sporades, Skyros had a small Turkish settlement. In this century, it is best known as the last resting place of the young poet Rupert Brooke.

Connections

Daily flight from Athens; alternatively, if it's all booked up, fly to Skiathos and connect with a hydrofoil on the appropriate day, at present Tues, Wed, Fri, Sat and Sun. Ferry from Kymi (Evia) twice a day, once a week to Tinos, Mykonos, Paros, Santorini and Herakleon (Crete). Hydrofoil four–five times a week to the other Sporades and Volos.

Tourist Information

NTOG, near Brooke Square, © (0222) 91 616.

Tourist police, see regular police, Skyros town, © (0222) 91 274.

Skyros Town

There are basically only two settlements on Skyros: **Linaria**, a colourful if mostly modern fishing village and port with ticket offices and a bus to the capital **Skyros**, or Chora, a striking town that wouldn't look out of place in the Cyclades, its white houses stacked one on top of the other along the steep, narrow pedestrian-only lanes. From the distance it sweeps like a full skirt around the massive rock of the ancient acropolis, looming high over the sea. The ruined Venetian **kastro** complete with a lion of St Mark over the gate, was built by Marco Sanudo, Duke of Naxos, and occupies the site of the Classical fortifications (traces can still be made out) from where Lycomedes gave Theseus his famous shove. Within the Venetian walls, perhaps on the site of the temple of Dionysos, is the **monastery of Ag. Georgios the Arab**, founded in 962 by Emperor Nikephoros Phokas, himself known as 'the Pale Death of the Saracens' after his liberation of Crete. The emperor gave Ag. Georgios to his saintly friend Athanasios, who incorporated it with the Great Lavra monastery of Mt Athos. Although once famed for its miracles, Ag. Georgios has been closed because of earthquake damage. Down the hill from the monastery is a church dedicated to Ag. Athanasios himself.

A bit further down on Brooke Square, a rather gormless **Statue of Immortal Poetry** by sculptor M. Tombros (1931) commemorates poet Rupert Brooke. Here, too, you'll find Skyros' town hall, with an **archaeology museum** (*closed Tues*) with a few odds and ends dating back to Mycenaean times, and the **Faltaits Museum of Folklore** (*10–1 and 6–8*), housing a collection of domestic items and fine embroideries, including traditional Skyriote costumes made to order. If you aren't staying in a typical house, there are furnished rooms to examine; island craftsmen still make wooden furniture, and in early August there's an annual exhibition of local handicrafts. You can buy chairs and tables made in Skyros, but taking them home is about as easy as shipping an elephant to Alaska—although Olympic Airways' world-wide freight service are determined to change things.

From Skyros town a path winds down to a long sandy beach **Magazia**, named after the Venetian powder magazines once stored here. Behind Magazia stretches the island's one fertile plain, and next to it is **Molos beach**, with accommodation and tavernas. If these two beaches seem crowded there are others near at hand, at **Basales, Achilli** and nearby **Papa ta Chomata** ('Priests' Land'), where no one minds if you sunbathe in your altogether. From **Ormos Achilli**, Achilles is said to have embarked for Troy.

Into the Hinterland

Although buses run intermittently between Linaria, Skyros town and Molos, the only way to visit the rest of the island is by foot, taxi or by hired moped. The wooded northern half of Skyros has better roads, and there are many small sandy beaches just off the dirt tracks that follow the coast. One track criss-crosses the island to the beaches and tavernas at **Atsitsa** and **Pefkos**, the latter with ancient quarries of variegated marble. Because of military installa-tions, you are forbidden to take photographs in many areas.

In the south a bus goes as far as **Kalamitsa**, one of the loveliest beaches, also with tavernas and a small pension. Signs of one of ancient Skyros' three rival towns, Chrission, were found near here, as well as an ancient tomb locally said to be Homer's, and traces of an Early Chris-tian basilica. From Linaria, the port, you can visit the grottoes **Pentekali** and **Gerania Spilies**, or take a caique to the islet **Skyropoula** between Skyros and the mainland. Sky-ropoula has two beaches and another cave, **Kavos Spili**, and a herd of the wild ponies, now rarely seen in their native domain in south Skyros.

A taxi, 2-hour walk, or caique (far the most pleasant on a calm day) will take you to **Tris Boukes** and the **grave of Rupert Brooke** at the southernmost point of Skyros. On 23 April 1915, the poet, on his way to fight at Gallipoli, died of blood poisoning aboard a French hos-pital ship and was buried in this olive grove at dawn the next morning. His well-tended grave is maintained by the Anglo-Hellenic society. Fittingly, the ground where Brooke is buried is officially British soil; it was only a year before he died that he wrote his famous lines:

> *If I should die think only this of me:*
> *That there's some corner of a foreign field*
> *That is forever England.*

Festivals

Carnival; 23 April, Ag. Georgios; 2 September, Ag. Mamon near Kalikri (Ag. Mamon is the patron of shepherds, and like Carnival, their festival also includes traces of ancient rites); 12 March, in town; 27 July, Ag. Panteleimon, near Pefkos.

expensive

Skyros Palace at Grismata, ✆ 91 994, 50 m from the beach is the most sophisticated place to stay. A new hotel, built in the traditional Skyros/Cyclades style, it has a sea water pool, restaurant, superior rooms and a very relaxed atmosphere. On the beach at Magazia, another comfortable if older place, the class B **Hotel Xenia**, ✆ 91 209, has 22 rooms.

moderate

There's very little hotel accommodation in this category: the small C class **Nefeli**, ✆ 91 964, and the cheaper E class **Pension Elena**, in Skyros town, ✆ 91 738.

cheap

In Skyros town there are scores of rooms to let, many of them in charming traditional houses (just mind you don't break the plates). Current rates for a stay of more than two days are about 4000 dr. per double room per night. No one cares if you sleep on the beach, although there is a conveniently placed **campsite** in Magazia.

Eating Out

Moraiti restaurant, on the main street, is a great spot to eat, with good food and location (dinners are around 2000 dr.), but certainly not the only place to watch the bustling pedestrian traffic. In fact any of the tavernas here serve excellent Greek food and on the whole prices are lower than on most islands and the atmosphere livelier— perhaps the good retsina of Skyros has something to do with it. Another good place, at the bottom of the main street, is **Sisyphos**, serving good quality Greek dishes, including a selection for vegetarians. If you've been waiting for the right moment to eat lobster, this could be it, as seafood prices are surprisingly low on Skyros. Down in Magazia the **Green Corner**, by the campsite entrance, will provide a lobster dinner for two for under 8000 dr., and the **campsite taverna** itself can be fun, especially at the weekends when there is often spontaneous dancing to live Skyriote music.

Evia (Euboea)

Lovely Evia is the second largest island in Greece after Crete and endowed with some of the finest scenery in the entire country, ranging from rolling meadows, olive groves and vineyards (Evia is one of the country's top food producers) to dense forests and snow-capped mountains. Despite its size and proximity to Athens, Evia is not overrun with tourists, except in a few established resorts, and even there the majority of Greek visitors means reasonable prices and excellent tavernas and restaurants. The whole island is lush and green, especially the north, where you could be forgiven for thinking you were in Austria. Even the bus ride from Chalki to the north via Limni is stunning, and the coast has long stretches of beaches washed by crystal-clear water.

Evia is linked to the mainland with a short bridge over the famous Euripos Strait. The dangerous currents of the strait inexplicably change direction every few hours, a phenomenon that drove Aristotle so crazy that he threw himself in the waters in despair—or so they say. Under the Ottomans, Evia's fertile soil attracted a wave of Turkish peasantry, some of whom still live on the island by a special agreement made during the population exchanges. Although nearly every hill on the island is crowned with a crumbling Frankish or Byzantine fort, there are relatively very few Classical remains; quiet rural farming has been the Eviot's way of life for centuries, and it remains so today.

Mythology

Evia, split from the nearby mainland by a blow of Poseidon's mighty trident, was the sea god's favourite island, and he lived with his wife Amphitrite in a fabulous underwater palace just off shore in the Evian Gulf. South of the gulf stretches the Myrtoan Sea, named for Myrtilus, son of Hermes and the charioteer of a team of divine horses owned by King Oenomaus. Oenomaus had a beautiful daughter, and he declared that only the suitor who defeated his invincible chariot in a race would have her hand. Now the charioteer Myrtilus himself was hopelessly in love with the princess, and when one challenger in the race, the hero Pelops, suggested that if he throw the race by replacing the lynch pins in the axles of the king's chariot with wax (thus enabling Pelops to win the race and the princess), then Pelops would share the girl with him. The charioteer eagerly agreed and events unfolded as predicted: Oenomaus' chariot collapsed in the heat of the race, the king was killed and Pelops was given the princess as his prize. He and Myrtilus took her in the direction of Evia, but Pelops, never intending to keep his bargain with Myrtilus, pushed him into the sea where he drowned. Hermes then named the sea in the honour of his son the dupe.

History

Inhabited in prehistoric times by settlers from Thessaly, and later by Dorians, Aeolians and Ionians, Evia is first mentioned by Homer. Seven city-states ruled the long island, but the most powerful in the 8th–7th centuries BC were the two rivals, Chalki and Eretria, great commercial ports with colonies as far away as Sicily. Between them lay Evia's desirable, fertile Lelantine Plain 'rich in vineyards'; both cities claimed it and extended their disagreement into international affairs, doing neither of them any good. In 506 BC Chalki joined Boeotia in a war against Athens, only to be conquered and divided; the Eretrians joined Athens in supporting the Ionian uprising on Asia Minor, and in retribution were sacked and enslaved when Darius came to punish the Athenians. In the 5th century BC the whole island came under the rule of Athens.

In 338 BC Macedonia took Evia, and the Romans who followed them were the first to use the name of an Eviot tribe, the Graeci, to refer to the entire Hellenic people, hence the Greeks of today. After the Fourth Crusade, the Franks gave the fertile island to the King of Thessalonika, Boniface de Montferrat, who divided the fertile island into three baronies. This initiated the great castle-building period on the island, each lordling the master of his own little fort. Over the next hundred years, Evia came under the direct rule of the Venetians, who called it the kingdom of Negroponte ('black bridge'), a corruption of Euripos. When the Turks took the island in 1470, they did not even allow the usual puppet Frankish governor to hang around and collect the taxes, but settled the prize themselves, treasuring it more than any other island in the Aegean. In 1830 Evia became part of the original Greek kingdom.

Connections

By bus: Bus every half-hour, and train every hour from Athens to Chalki (1½ hours), the main bus terminal of the island. The terminal in Athens is Liossion, from where you can also travel direct to Kymi (and Skyros) and many other points in Evia, but for Rafina (also the main port for the island of Andros), buses leave Athens from the Mavromateon terminal.

By sea: Ferry boats link Evia with the mainland from Rafina to Karystos (three times a day), Rafina to Marmari (three–four times a day), Ag. Marina to Nea Styra (five times a day), Arkitsa to Edipsos (twelve times a day), Oropos to Eretria (every half hour), and Glifa to Agiokambos (every two hours); ferries go to Skyros daily, and twice a week to the other Sporades; **hydrofoil** connections from Loutra Edipsos to the other Sporades.

Tourist Police

2 Eleftheriou Venizelou, Chalki, ✆ (0221) 24 662.

3 Okeanidou St, Edipsos, ✆ (0226) 22 456.

Chalki and Mount Dirfis

Chalki, the bustling industrial rhinoceros-shaped capital of Evia, occupies the narrowest point of the Euripos, only 40 m from the mainland. Its location has been an important source of its prosperity, not least through its potential of seriously blocking trade between Athens and the north. Its name comes either from bronze (*chalkos*), another early source of its wealth, or perhaps from *chalki*, the sea snail prized in antiquity for making murex, the purple dye of kingly cloaks. The city had so many colonies in the north of Greece that it gave its name to the peninsula, Chalkidiki; in Italy it founded the colonies of Messina, Reggio Calabria and Cumae near Naples.

By the 7th century BC Chalki had asserted its position over Eretria as the island's dominant city. The first bridge to the mainland was built in 411 BC (the modern sliding drawbridge dates from 1962). The ruined Turkish **castle of the Karababa** (Turkish for 'black father') was built in 1686, over Chalki's ancient acropolis and affords excellent views over the city and the Euripos.

Facing the mainland, Chalki puts on its most attractive face, and there are many cafés where you can sit and ponder the still unexplained mystery of the Euripos (some days the current may change as many as 14 times). In the new town, on Leof. Venizelou, the **Archaeology Museum** has some of the finest items discovered in Eretria, including the Archaic marble pediment from the temple of Apollo Daphnephoros. Nearby, there's a **Byzantine Museum** in an old mosque with a marble fountain, marking the entrance to the **Kastro**, the old Turkish quarter. Not far from the mosque the city's best-known church, **Ag. Paraskevi** began its life as a basilica and was converted by the Crusaders into a Gothic cathedral in the 13th century, resulting in the curious architectural collage inside. Every year, in late July, a market for the feast of Ag. Paraskevi enlivens Chalki for 10 days, attracting buyers from all over Evia and mainland to hunt for bargains on the stalls. Kastro also has its arcaded **Turkish aqueduct** that brought water to the city from Mount Dirfis.

Dirfis at 1745 m is Evia's highest mountain, wrapped in forests and supporting a surprising quantity of alpine flora. It towers some 25 km east of Chalki, from where you can take a taxi or bus as far as **Steni**, a village of wooden A-frame houses that makes a refreshing change in the summer. From Steni there's a well-marked if rather strenuous path to the summit of Dirfis. Overnight stays are possible in Steni or in the refuge of the Hellenic Alpine Club, © (0221) 25230 for information.

The nearest beach to Chalki, **Asteria** has restaurants and every facility. Boats also leave Chalki daily for the islet of **Tonnoiron**, with a hotel and beach. A good bus service connects Chalki with all the major villages of Evia and nearby towns on the mainland such as Thebes. If you have the time and energy, there is no better way of seeing Evia than by bicycle. The roads are good and not too steep—except for the rugged east coast.

South Evia: Karystos, Around Mt Ochi and North to Dystos

The best way to see all of the island, with a minimum of backtracking, is to take the ferry from Rafina to the extreme southern tip of Evia to **Karystos** (pop. 3500), the largest village and most popular holiday resort in the area. Karystos faces the sea where Myrtilus was drowned, and in antiquity was renowned for its green cipollino marble and asbestos 'the unquenchable' in ancient times confused with quicklime, that smoulders when wet.   The otherwise unremarkable modern town is near a Mycenaean settlement, and is still defended by the 14th-century coastal fort, or **Bourdzi**, although these days most of its invaders prefer to assault its long sandy beach, **Psili Ammos**.

For most of the Middle Ages, however, the safest spot around was the huge citadel above Karystos, called **Castel Rosso** by the Venetians, although built in 1030 by the Byzantines. The road up to it passes the lovely village of **Myli**, set in a ravine, then continues over a handsome stone bridge crossing another ravine at Gravia. When the Turks captured Castel Rosso, they settled 400 families in its walls and were unusually intolerant, giving local Christians the chop if they refused to convert to Islam. Here, too, are the ancient cipollino **marble quarries**. If you've brought your walking shoes, a 3-hour path from Myli continues to the mountain refuge and then the summit of **Mt Ochi**, through some of the most dramatic scenery on Evia.

Asminion

Artemissi

Pefki

Kastri

Ag. Kambos

Pirgos

Istiaia

Lixas

Orepi

Ayios

Monokaria

Basilika

Ag. Georgios

Gialtra

Edipsos

Loutra Edipsou

Boutas

To Ag. Konstantinos

Ilia

Kokkinomilia

Achladi

Robiai

Kourkouloi

Ag. Anna

To Arkitsa

Limni

Strofilia

Mantoudi

Kimassi

Galataki

Prokopi

Pilion

N

Neo Patongas

Mili

Politika

Makpykapi

*Mainland
Greece*

Kastella

Psakna

NORTH EVIA

Nea Artaki

Kadenoi

Steni
Dirfios

CHALKI

| 0 | 5 | 10 | 20 km |
| 0 | 5 | 10 | miles |

If Karystos is too crowded for your taste, there's another long sandy beach, 13 km away at **Bouros**, where no one cares if you sleep out, although you'll have to bring your own water; there's also a large cave, **Ag. Triada** to explore. **Platanistos** to the east is named for its large plane trees and has rooms to rent in private houses. At the southeasternmost tip of Evia, the notorious, tempest-tossed **Cape Kafireus** (the Venetian Cabo Doro), stand a few woebegone ruins of a Byzantine fortress, repaired in the 1260s by Admiral Likarios, the right-hand man of Emperor Michael Paleologos, who restored the Byzantine Empire after the conquest of the Franks—beginning in Greece at this weatherbeaten fort.

The main road north of Karystos follows the spectacular west coast of Evia, its cliffs a favourite nesting place for hawks and eagles. Along the road are two small resorts, the sheltered if charmless, marble quarrying **Marmari**, and **Nea Styra**, connected by ferry from Rafina, with a long sandy beach and excellent swimming. Near Nea Styra are the so-called 'homes of the Dragons', believed to be ruined Homeric watch towers. Ancient **Styra** stood above the modern town, under the Venetian fort. Nearby also are the meagre ruins of Mycenaean **Dryopes**. Further north, by Evia's largest lake, are the well-preserved polygonal walls and towers of 5th-century BC **Dystos** (not to be confused with the modern town of the same name), as well as some very rare houses and streets from the period.

Lepoura to Kymi

At **Lepoura** the main road forks, one branch heading towards Chalki (*see* below) and the other north to **Kymi**. Along the way, a turn-off to the right leads down to **Avlonari**, where a small fortress has a Venetian church inside, and beyond to **Oxdonia**, an attractive east coast resort crammed beneath a Frankish castle. After the Oxdonia turn off, the Lepoura–Kymi road plunges and writhes through the valley of Oxilithos, exceptionally lovely, pastoral and dotted with Frankish towers until it reaches **Kymi**, the main port for Skyros (with occasional connections to the other Sporades). Lush, surrounded by vineyards and fig orchards, Kymi is perched on a shelf high above the sea, surrounded by forests. Many Greeks have summer villas in the hills, including some rather ambitious nouveau riche designs. But while well endowed with restaurants and rooms to rent, Kymi has little nightlife. Daytime explorations may take you to **Cheili** with ruins of a Mycenaean fort, or north along a rough road to a sheer rocky ledge, the probable site of the acropolis of ancient Kyme Phyrkontis, crowned by a ruined Byzantine castle Apokledi and the handsome convent **Sotira** (1634, women only admitted). Four km below the village footpaths or the bus continue to the port **Paralia Kymi**, with a sandy, and generally crowded beach, tufts of grass and other greenery.

Lepoura to Chalki, and Eretria

Back on the main road from Lepoura to Chalki the first major village is **Aliveri**, its old red-roofed houses inhabited by coal miners and men working in the nearby power station. There is a beach just below and restaurants and pensions in town. Near Aliveri stood three ancient towns: Tamynae above Aliveri, Porthmos near the beach, and Amarinthos, by the bay of Aliveri, now marked by a tall Venetian tower with its door suspended 20 ft above ground level, to be entered only by a retractable ladder.

Eretria, connected to the mainland by ferry from Oropou, is also called Nea Psara; the modern town was founded by refugees from the island of Psara near Chios, who rather unfortunately built their new town on top of the ruins of the old. Still, Eretria is the most complete ancient site on Evia, as well as the biggest holiday resort after Edipsos. Ancient Eretria, a maritime state in Homeric times, reached its prime during its rivalry with Chalki over the the lush Lelantine Plain. In the end the two cities decided to sort out their differences by leaving their weapons at home and meeting at a midway point in order to fight it out in a general free-for-all punch-up. Eretria lost the fight and the Plain, but suffered an even worse disaster in 490 BC when the Persians decimated the city. The Eretrians recovered from their misfortunes to rebuild, and soon earned themselves a reputation for their excellent ceramics. They generally stayed allied with Athens until 87 BC, when Mithridates sacked the city. It was the straw that broke the camel's back; Eretria was never rebuilt.

The **museum** (*daily except Mon, 8.30–3*) is at the top of Arcaiou Theatrou St. The museum isn't much—the best of the finds went off to old rival Chalki—but the excavations near the museum (*same hours*) have revealed the excellent trapezoidal masonry of the walls, an elaborate **West Gate**, once topped with a corbelled arch, a 4th-century BC palace (complete with a clay bath tub) and the **theatre**, where you can see a rare survival of the mechanism that boosted the plots of many a play, the **deus ex machina**: an underground passage from the orchestra that leads to the built-up *skene* behind the stage, where gods or goddesses could make sudden appearances. A path west of the theatre leads to a tumulus tomb, built in the Macedonian style with a square chamber, marble beds and thrones. Another path from the theatre leads in 15-minutes up to Eretria's walled **acropolis** affording an excellent view of the fertile Lelantine Plain, subject of so much contention, and, on a clear day, Mt Parnassos on the mainland. Of the temples, the only substantive remains are believed to have belonged to a Sanctary of Athena Olympia. Down in the centre of the modern town itself stand the foundations of a 7th-century BC **temple of Apollo Daphnephoros** 'the laurel-bearer', who enjoyed a popular following throughout Evia. Near Eretria, a holiday centre, **Malakonta beach** has mushroomed up to accommodate package tourists.

One last spot along the Chalki road that may tempt a detour is the mysterious 9th-century BC sanctuary of immense proportions (54 by 10 m) unearthed in 1981 at **Lefkanti** (near Vasilikon). Female (only) skeletons and golden ornaments were buried here, but the biggest connundrum of all is that the style of the building is extremely precocious for the period, with features more in line with known 6th-century structures. It may have been part of Homeric Eretria, listed in the famous *Catalog of Ships*. **Fila** nearby is dominated by a medieval castle perched on an ancient mound.

Northern Evia: Prokopi and Limni

The northern half of Evia has some splendid scenery, pretty little whitewashed houses with rose-filled gardens, lofty mountains as a backdrop and some distinctive villages. Two of the latter are just to the north of Chalki, **Psakna**, a little market town, and **Politika** with a late Byzantine church. Both villages have castles, but the most striking one, on a nearly inaccessible precipice is in **Prokopi**, an enchanting village set near the end of the magnificent narrow, wooded ravines of the Kleisoura valley, where the road offers grand views over the Sporades. Sometimes still called by its Turkish name Ahmet Aga, Prokopi is largely inhabited by Greeks from the fantastical Cappadocian town of Ürgüp, who came over in the 1920s population exchange following the Greek fiasco in Asia Minor. The Cappocians brought along their most holy relics, of St John the Russian, who went from being a soldier in the Tsar's army to a slave in Ürgüp (1730), to a saint of the Russian Orthodox Church (in 1962). In the centre of Prokopi, the handsome estate and tulip and rose gardens of the Turkish pasha is now a model farm and health centre run by the British-owned North Euboean Foundation.

At Strofilia the road west leads to **Limni**, an old fishing village around a charming sleepy bay with beaches and a slowly growing resort community under its pine woods. A track from

Limni leads up in an hour to **Galataki** a Byzantine monastery with frescoes. From Limni a track goes briefly up the coast to the quiet fishing village and beach of **Robiai**.

The North Coast: Artemissi to Loutra Edipsou

The main road at Strofilia continues to the east, avoiding the mountains before cutting back to the northeast coast and Loutra Edipsos. Along the latter, on the north coast facing the Trikeri peninsula, the seaside village of **Artemissi** witnessed the first indecisive naval battle between the Greeks and the Persians in 480 BC. Near the shore are the ruins of the vast Temple of Artemis Proseoa, although the greatest archaeological treasure yielded by the area was a shipwreck of ancient bronzes, discovered offshore in 1928, the source of two star attractions in Athens' National Archaeological Museum: the full length bronze Zeus (or Poseidon) and the Cape Artemision jockey. A few ruins of the temple of Artemis Proseoa remain in intact. Below Artemissi is a pretty beach under the pines known as **Pefki**, with rooms to rent. This entire north coast of the island is dotted with beaches, popular with holidaymakers from Chalki.

Istiaia is the largest village along the northern road, founded by Thessalians who thumbed their noses at Athens so often that Perikles captured the town and booted out the inhabitants, repopulating Istiaia with Athenians. Although few towns are more attractively situated than Istiaia, in its amphitheatre of hills, the Athenians didn't find it to their liking, preferring to found the nearby **Orei** instead; when they in turn were driven out by the Spartans in the Peloponnesian War, the Istianians returned. The whole population of Evia contributed to the building of Istiaia's Venetian Kastro, built over the ancient city. Orei's medieval fortifications are less impressive, but its central square has an expressive marble Hellenistic bull, found offshore in 1962. These days the offshore treat is the islet of **Argironisos**, abandoned at the turn of the century and now the only private island in Greece taking paying guests.

Edipsos owes its initial success to the hot sulphurous waters of **Loutra Edipsos**, noted for treating rheumatism, arthritis, gallstones, and even depression. The waters squirt out of the ground at up to 160° F and have been famed since ancient times, when it was believed that Loutra's source was connected under the sea with the hot springs at Thermopylae. Aristotle praised the waters; Sulla, Augustus and Hadrian called in for lengthy soaks in the now ruined Roman baths, and to this day Loutra Edipsos has the lazy, old fashioned neo-Classical ambience typical of spas all over the world, embellished with matronly hotels, shady avenues and flowery gardens for idling away an afternoon. A long, lovely beach is an added attraction, and Edipsos has frequent ferry connections with Arkitsa on the mainland, along the main highway from Athens to Thessaloniki. A seaside village on the peninsula facing Edipsos, **Lixas**, is connected with Ag. Konstantinos on the mainland. Lixas has rooms and restaurants, and a beach at Ag. Georgios, or there's a thoroughly modern resort complex at **Gregolimano**.

Festivals

15 August, at Kymi, Oxilithos, Haito, Satsaroni and Koupeios; 26 July, Ag. Paraskevi, long celebrations at Chalki, Myli and Rukia; 17 July, Ag. Marinas near Karystos; 21 May, Ag. Konstantinos at Vitalakimis; 27 May, St John the Russian at Prokopi.

Evia's coasts have nearly all the facilities for tourists, most of whom are Greek; major centres are Chalki, Edipsos, Karystos, Limni, Kymi and Eretria (the last especially popular among foreign visitors).

luxury

You and 9–12 of your friends can hire the private isle of Argironisos from May to October; all-inclusive rates include the price of a return flight from London, room and board. Contact the Best of Greece in Kent, ✆ (0622) 692 278.

expensive

If you're stuck in workaday Chalki, there's the class A **Lucy**, directly facing the Euripos strait on 10 L. Voudouri, ✆ (0221) 23 831. Karystos, at the southern tip of Evia, offers a wide selection, from the seaside **Apollon Resort Hotel** on Psili Ammos beach, ✆ (0224) 22 045, to the **Hironia Hotel** in town by the sea, ✆ (0224) 22 238. In Edipsos there's no shortage of accommodation: the **Aegli Hotel**, 18 Paraliakis, ✆ (0226) 22 215, is the best for grand old spa atmosphere.

moderate

In Eretria just south of Chalki there are many new hotels (mainly filled with package tourists) and old favourites like the C class **Delfis**, ✆ (0221) 62 380. Slightly cheaper is the **Xenia**, ✆ 61 202. In Nea Styra further south you'll find no bargains (the **Aktaeon** on the beach, ✆ (0224) 41 261, is typical). The **Venus Beach Hotel** has twin bungalows for around 5500 dr., ✆ 41 226. Karystos has the comfortable **Hotel Als**, ✆ (0224) 22 202, very conveniently placed on the waterfront, near all the cafés and tavernas; you can watch all the action from your balcony. A little quieter, at the end of the seafront, the **Galaxy** is similar and somewhat cheaper, ✆ 22 600. In Kymi, the most pleasant place to stay is **Hotel Krinion**, ✆ (0222) 22 287, in the Plateia G. Papanikolaou; ask for a room with a balcony. Down in Paralia Kymi there are a few rooms to be had along with the **Beis**, an anonymous C class, ✆ 22 604. In Limni the **Limni Hotel**, at the end of the bay, has fine rooms with balconies looking down into the water, and low rates, ✆ (0227) 31 316; even cheaper is the centrally placed **Plaza**, ✆ 31 235. Near the ferry in Edipsos **Hotel Edipsos** has pleasant views and a private bus to the thermal baths, ✆ (0226) 22 035; near the baths **Capri**, ✆ 22 496, has lovely views. Pefki, a cool, busy beach town popular with Greek holidaymakers, has a small number of pleasant hotels, among them **Galini**, ✆ 22 448.

cheap

Unfortunately there's no central clearing house for rooms on Evia; you just have to go to each village and take pot luck. Most are on the coasts, but they are few and far between, while villages in the interior have little or no facilities. In Istiaia most of the accommodation is apartments or rooms. Further along in Orei, a pretty little town, with a so-so beach, the **Corali Hotel** is very reasonable with simple rooms,

© (0226) 71 217, and the pension **Kentrikon**, © 71 525, is small and cheap. Evia is a very popular place for camping, both with tents and trailers; there are official camp-sites at Malakonta beach, near Eretria, Pefki, Ag. Anna and Rovies.

Eating Out

On the whole Evia is not expensive and the food good and authentic, thanks to the numbers of Greek tourists. It is perhaps the best island for appreciating the true eating habits of the country, where such Greek institutions as the *ouzeri*, now extinct on some of the more popular islands, are alive and well. Even today in many parts of Evia you can take your evening ouzo with delicious *meze* for 150 dr. The fish is especially good, especially in Amarinthos, south of popular Eretria; prices in latter, however, have been jacked up to accommodate foreign currencies, but nowhere near the Mykonos level. **O Ligouris** has set menus (in French, to cater to the large numbers who come here from France), or you can pick your own lobster from the tank (3000 dr., more for lobster). **Gorgona** and **Dionysos** offer similar fare for a little less. One of the best places to eat seafood in Limni, whose attractive little waterfront sports some excellent cafés and tavernas, is at the **Avra**, with well-prepared Greek favourites and fresh fish for under 2000 dr.

In Loutra Edipsos there are a number of good places, notably the **Agle** on the water-front and **Kaliva** near the post office. Near the OTE you'll find **O Pappas**, with a few delicious Cypriot specialities to complement the standard Greek fare (2000 dr. with barrelled wine). If you're killing time in Istiaia, the restaurant **Vlachopoulos** near the main square is most favoured by locals. The **Patsas** off the other end of the square has its own distinctive personality, decorated with out-of-date Father Christmas calendars and food is served at the same temperature as the wine (chilled), accompanied by the news on the black and white TV. It's also disarmingly cheap. In Pefki, there's the excellent **Mirtia** and the **Cavo d'Oro** and a good *ouzeri* as well; all three have lovely views across to the Pelion peninsula and, just around the corner, Skiathos. Down in Karystos are more pleasant waterfront tavernas and, if you search out the backstreets for **Kavontoros**, you'll find the most reasonably priced of the lot, with good ready food and barrelled wine for 1500 dr.

BC

7000–2800	Neolithic Era
4000	Precocious civilization at Palaeochoe, Limnos
3000	Milos exports obsidian
3000–2000	Early Cycladic civilization
2800–1000	Bronze Age
2600–2000	Early Minoan civilization in Crete
2000–1700	Middle Minoan: Cretan thalassocracy rules the Aegean
1700–1450	Late Minoan
1600–1150	Mycenaean civilization begins with invasion of the Peloponnese
c.1450	Eruption of Santorini's volcano decimates the Minoans; Mycenaeans occupy ruined Crete and Rhodes
1180	Traditional date of the fall of Troy (4 July)
c.1150	Beginning of the dark ages: Dorian invasion disrupts Mycenaean culture; Ionians settle Asia Minor and islands.
1000	Kos and the three cities of Rhodes join Doric Hexapolis
1100–100	Iron Age
1100–700	Geometric Period
700–500	Archaic Period
650	Aegina is first in Greece to mint coins
Late 600s	Sappho born on Lesbos
570–480	Pythagoros of Samos
500–323	Classical Age
490–479	Persian Wars end with defeat of Persian army and fleet
478	Delos becomes the headquarters of the Athenian-dominated Maritime League
460–377	Hippocrates of Kos
431–404	Peloponnesian War cripples Athens
378	Second Delian League
338	Philip of Macedon conquers Athens and the rest of Greece
334–323	Conquests of Alexander the Great
323–146	Hellenistic Age
146–AD 410	Roman Age

Chronology

AD

88	Mithridates of Pontus, sworn enemy of Rome, devastates many islands
86	Romans under Sulla destroy Athens and other Greek rebels who supported Mithridates

58	St Paul visits Lindos, Rhodes
95	St John the Divine writes the Apocalypse on Patmos
391	Paganism outlawed in Roman Empire
410–1453	Byzantine Era
727–843	Iconoclasm in the Eastern Church
824–861	Saracen/Arab Occupation
961	Emperor Nikephoros Phokas reconquers Crete from the Saracens
1054	Pope ex-communicates Patriarch of Constantinople over differences in the creed
1088	Foundation of the Monastery on Patmos
1204	Venetians lead Fourth Crusade conquest of Contantinople and take the islands as their share of the booty
1261	Greek retake Constantinople from Latins
1309	Knights of St John, chased out of Jerusalem, establish their base on Rhodes
1453	Turks begin conquest of Greece
1522	Ottomans defeat Knights of St John
1541	El Greco born on Crete
1669	Venetians lose Herakleon, Crete to the Turks after a 20-year siege
1771–74	Catherine the Great sends Russian fleet into the Aegean to harry the Sultan
1796	Napoleon captures Venice and her Ionian islands
1815–64	British rule Ionian islands
1821–27	Greek War of Independence begins
1823	Aegina made the capital of free Greece
1827	Annihilation of Turkish fleet by the English, French and Russian allies at the Battle of Navarino
1833	Otho of Bavaria becomes the first king of the Greeks
1883–1957	Cretan writer Nikos Kazantzakis
1912–13	Balkan Wars give Greece Macedonia, Crete and the Northeast Aegean Islands; the Italians pick up the Dodecanese
1922–23	Greece invades Turkey with catastrophic results
1924	Greece becomes a republic
1935	Restoration of the monarchy
1941	Nazi paratroopers complete first ever invasion by air on Crete
1945	Dodecanese islands united with Greece
1949	End of civil wars between communists and the US-backed government
1953	Earthquake shatters the Ionian islands
1967	Colonels' coup establishes a dictatorship
1974	Failure of the Junta's Cyprus adventure leads to the regime's collapse and restoration of democracy
1983	Greece joins the EEC

Although modern Greek, or Romaíka is a minor language spoken by few non-Greeks, it has the distinction of having caused riots and the fall of a government (in 1901). In Greece today there are basically two languages, the purist or katharevóusa and the popular or demotikí. Both are developments of ancient Greek, but although the purist is consciously Classical, the popular is as close to its ancient origins as French is to Latin. While many purist words are common in the speech of the people, the popular dominates, especially in the countryside.

Until the turn of the century all literature appeared in the purist language. What shook Athens with riots in 1901 was the appearance of the Iliad and the New Testament in the demotic. When the fury had died down a bit, more and more writers were found to be turning their pens to the demotic. Cavafy, the first great modern Greek poet, wrote in both the popular and purist. In its "moral cleansing" of Greece the Papadopoulos government tried to revive the purist, but with little success.

Knowing the language of any country makes the stay twice as enjoyable; in Greece, especially, people spend much of the day talking. But modern Greek isn't a particularly easy language to pick by ear, and it is often spoken at great velocity (if you speak slowly someone is sure to interrupt). If you buy a modern Greek grammar, check to see if it has the demotic and not just the purist. Even if you have no desire to learn Greek, it is helpful to know at least the alphabet—so that you can find your way around—and a few basic words and phrases.

The Greek Alphabet

A	α	álfa	(short a as in father)
B	β	víta	(v sound)
Γ	γ	gámma	(slightly gutteral g or y sound)
Δ	δ	thélta	(hard th as in though)
E	ε	épsilon	(short e as in bet)
Z	ζ	zíta	(z sound)
H	η	íta	(long e as in bee)
Θ	θ	thíta	(soft th as in thin)
I	ι	yóta	(long e as in be; sometimes like y)
K	κ	káppa	(k sound)
Λ	λ	lámtha	(l sound)
M	μ	mi	(m sound)
N	ν	ni	(n sound)
Ξ	ξ	ksi	(x as in ox)
O	o	omicron	(o as in open)
Π	π	pi	(p sound)
P	ρ	ro	(r sound)
Σ	σ (ς)	sigma	(s sound)
T	τ	taf	(t sound)

Language

Y	υ	ipsilon	(long e as in bee)
Φ	φ	fi	(f sound)
X	χ	chi	(German ch as in doch)
Ψ	ψ	psi	(ps as in stops)
Ω	ω	omega	(o as in open)

Dipthongs and Consonant Combinations

αι   (short e as in bet)
ει, οι, υι   (i as in machine)
ου   (oo as in too)
αυ   (av or af sound)
ευ   (ev or ef sound)
ηυ   (iv or if sound)
γγ   (ng as in angry)
γκ   (hard g; ng within word)
ντ   (d; nd within word)
μπ   (b; mp within word)

Vocabulary

Yes	ne or ah me (This is accompanied by a short nod or tilt of the head)	Ναί
no	óchi, óxi (This is accompanied by a backwards jerk of the head, with a click of the tongue, smack of the lips or raise of the eyebrows)	Ὄχι
yes	málista (This is the formal yes)	Μάλιστα
I don't know	then xéro (An even greater throwing back of the head, or a display of empty hands)	Δὲν ξέρω
I don't understand (Greek)	then katalavéno (helliniká)	Δὲν καταλαβαίνω (Ἑλληνικά)
Does someone speak English?	Iné kanés poo na milá angliká?	Εἶναι κανείς ποὺ νὰ μιλᾶ ἀγγλικά;
go away	fíyete	Φύγετε
help	voíthia	βοήθεια
my friend	o fílos moo (m) ee fíli moo (f)	ὁ φίλος μου ἡ φήλη μου
please	parakaló	Παρακαλῶ
thank you (very much)	evcharistó (párapolí)	Εὐχαριστῶ (πάραπολύ)
you're welcome	parakaló	Παρακαλῶ
it doesn't matter	then pirázi	Δὲν πειράζει
all right	en táxi	Ἐν τάξει
excuse me	signómi	Συγγνώμη
pardon?	oríste?	Ὁρίστε;
be careful!	proséchte	Προσέξατε!
nothing	típote	Τίποτε

what is your name?	pos sas léne?	Πῶς σᾶς λένε;
how are you?	ti kánete?	Τί κάνετε;
hello	yásou	Γειάσου
goodbye	yásou, andío, hérete	Γειάσου, 'Αντίο, χαίρετε
good morning	kaliméra	Καλημέρα
good evening	kalispéra	Καλησπέρα
good night	kaliníkta	Καληνύκτα
what is that?	ti íne aftó?	Τί εἶναι αὐτό;
what?	ti?	τί;
who?	piós? (m), piá? (f)	ποιός; ποιά;
where?	poo	ποῦ;
when?	póte?	πότε;
why?	yiatí?	γιατί;
how?	pos?	πῶς;
I (am)	egó (íme)	ἐγὼ (εἶμαι)
you (are) (*sing*)	isí (íse)	ἐσὺ (εἶσαι)
he, she, it (is)	aftós, aftí, aftó (íne)	αὐτός, αὐτὴ, αὐτὸ (εἶναι)
we (are)	imés (ímaste)	ἐμεῖς (ἔμαστε)
you (are) (*pl*)	isís (íste)	ἐσεῖς (εἶστε)
they (are)	aftí (*m*), aftés (*f*), aftá (*n*) (íne)	αὐτοὶ, αὐτὲς, αὐτά (εἶναι)
I have	écho	ἔχω
You have (*sing*)	échis	ἔχεις
he, she, it has	échi	ἔχει
we have	échomen	ἔχομεν
you have (*pl*)	échete	ἔχετε
they have	échoon	ἔχουν
I am lost	échasa to thrómo	''Εχασα τό δρόμο
I am hungry	pinó	Πεινῶ
I am thirsty	thipsó	Διψῶ
I am tired	íme kourasménos	Εἶμαι κουρασμένος
I am sleepy	nistázo	Νυστάζω
I am ill	íme árostos	Εἶμαι ἄρρωστος
I am poor	íme ftochós	Εἶμαι πτωχός
I love you	sagapóh	Σ'ἀγαπῶ
good	kalá	καλά
bad	kakó	κακό
so-so	étsi kétsi	ἔτσι κ'ἔτσι
slow	sigá sigá	σιγά σιγά
fast	grígora	γρήγορα
big	megálo	μεγάλο

small	mikró	μικρὸ
hot	zésti	ζέστη
cold	crío	κρύω

Shops, Services, Sightseeing

I would like	tha íthela	Θὰ ἤθελα
where is?	poo íne?	Ποῦ εἶναι;
how much is it?	póso káni?	Πόσο κάνει;

bakery	artopoíon	Ἀρτοποιεῖον
bank	trápeza	Τράπεζα
beach	paralía	παραλία
bed	kreváti	κρεββάτι
bookshop	vivliopolío	Βιβλιοπολεῖο
book	vivlío	βιβλίο
butcher	kreopolíon	Κρεοπωλεῖον
church	eklisía	Ἐκκλησία
cinema	kinimatográfos	Κινηματογράφος
food (see also p 410)	fayitó	φαγητὸ
hospital	nosokomío	Νοσοκομεῖο
hotel	xenodochío	Ξενοδοχεῖο
hot water	neró zestó	νερό ζεστό
house	spíti	σπίτι
kiosk	períptero	Περίπτερο
money	leftá	λεφτά

museum	mooséo	Μουσειο
music	musikí	μουσική
newspaper (foreign)	efimerítha (xéni)	ἐφημερίδα (ξένη)
pharmacy	farmakío	Φαρμακεῖο
police station	astinomía	Αστυνομία
policeman	astifílaka	ἀστυφύλακα
post office	tachithromío	Ταχυδρομεῖο
restaurant	estiatório	Ἑστιατόριο
ruins	archéa	ἄρχαῖα
sea	thálassa	Θάλασσα
shoe store	papootsís	Παπουτσῆς
shower	doush	ντούς
student	fititís	φοιτητής
telephone office	OTE	OTE
theatre	théatro	Θέατρο
toilet	tooaléta	τουαλέττα
tourist policeman	astifílaka tooristikí	ἀστυφύλακα τουριστηκή
a walk	vólta	βόλτα

Time

| what time is it? | ti óra íne? | Τὶ ὥρα εἶναι; |
| month | mína | μήνα |

week	evthomáda	ἑβδομάδα
day	méra	μέρα
morning	proí	πρωί
afternoon	apóyevma	ἀπόγευμα
evening	vráthi	βράδυ
yesterday	chthés	χθές
today	símera	σήμερα
tomorrow	ávrio	αὔριο
now	tóra	τώρα
later	metá	μετά
it is early	íne norís	Εἶναι νωρίς
it is late	íne argá	Εἶναι ἀργά

Travel Directions

| I want to go to . . . | thélo na páo sto (m), sti (f) . . . | Θέλω νὰ πάω στὸ, στή . . . |
| how can I get to . . . ? | póso boró na páo sto (m), sti (f) . . . ? | Πόσο μπορῶ νὰ πάω στὸ, στή . . . ; |

| can you give me a ride to . . . ? | boréte na me páte sto (m), sti (f) . . . ? | Μπορείτε νὰ μὲ πάτε στὸ, στή . . . ; |
| where is . . . ? | poo íne . . . ? | Ποῦ εἶναι . . . ; |

how far is it?	póso makriá íne?	Πόσο μακριὰ εἶναι;
when will the . . . come?	póte tha érthi to (n), ee (f), o (m) . . . ?	Πότε θά ἔρθει τὸ, ἡ, ὁ . . . ;
when will the . . . leave?	póte tha févi to (n), ee (f), o (m) . . . ?	Πότε θά φύγει τὸ, ἡ, ὁ . . . ;
from where do I catch . . . ?	apó poo pérno . . . ?	Ἀπὸ ποῦ παίρνω . . . ;
how long does the trip take?	póso keró tha pári to taxíthi?	Πόσο καιρὸ θὰ πάρη τό ταξίδι;
please show me	parakaló thíkstemoo	Παρακαλῶ δεῖξτέμου
how much is it?	póso káni?	Πόσο κάνει;
the (nearest) town	o horió (o pió kondá)	τὸ χωριὸ (τὸ πιό κοντά)

good trip	kaló taxíthi	Καλὸ ταξίδι
here	ethó	ἐδῶ
there	ekí	ἐκεῖ
close	kondá	κοντά
far	makriá	μακριά
full	yemáto	γεμάτο
left	aristerá	ἀριστερά
right	thexiá	δεξιά
forward	embrós	ἐμπρός
back	píso	πίσω
north	vória	Βόρεια
south	nótia	Νότια

east	anatoliká	Ἀνατολικά
west	thitiká	Δυτικά
corner	gonía	γωνία
square	platía	πλατεῖα

Driving

where can I rent...?	poo boró na enikiáso...?	Ποῦ μπορῶ νά ἐνοικιάσω...;
a car	énan aftokínito	ἕνα αὐτοκίνητο
a motorbike	éna mechanáki	ἕνα μηχανάκι
a bicycle	éna pothílaton	ἕνα ποδήλατον
where may I buy petrol?	poo boró nagorázso venzíni?	Ποῦ μπορῶ ν'ἀγοράζω βενζίνη;
where is a garage?	poo íne éna garáz?	Ποῦ εἶναι ἕνα γκαράζ;
a mechanic	éna mikanikó	ἕνα μηχανικό
a map	ena chárti	ἕνα χάρτη
where is the road	poo íne o thrómos	Ποῦ εἶναι ὁ δρόμος
to...?	yiá...?	γιά...;
where does this road lead?	poo pái aftós o thrómos?	Ποῦ πάει αὐτὸσ ὁ δρόμος;
is the road good?	íne kalós o thrómos?	Εἶναι καλός ὁ δρόμος;
exit	éxothos	ΕΞΟΔΟΣ
entrance	ísothos	ΕΙΣΟΔΟΣ
danger	kínthinos	ΚΙΝΔΥΝΟΣ
slow	argá	ΑΡΓΑ
no parking	apagorévete ee státhmevsis	ΑΠΑΓΟΡΕΥΕΤΑΙ Η ΣΤΑΘΜΕΥΣΙΣ
keep out	apagorévete ee ísothos	ΑΠΑΓΟΡΕΥΕΤΑΙ Η ΕΙΣΟΔΟΣ

Numbers

one	énas (m), mía (f), éna (n)	῎Ενας, μία, ἕνα
two	théo	Δύο
three	tris (m, f), tría (n)	Τρεῖς, τρία
four	téseres (m, f), téssera (n)	Τέσσερεις, τέσσερα
five	pénde	Πέντε
six	éxi	῎Εξι
seven	eptá	Ἑπτά
eight	októ	Ὀκτώ
nine	ennéa	Ἐννέα
ten	théka	Δέκα
eleven	éntheka	῎Ενδεκα
twelve	thótheka	Δώδεκα
thirteen	thekatría	Δεκατρία
fourteen	thekatéssera	Δεκατέσσερα

twenty	íkosi	Εἴκοσι
twenty-one	íkosi énas/mía/éna	Εἴκοσι ἕνας/μία/ἕνα
thirty	triánda	Τριάντα
forty	saránda	Σαράντα
fifty	penínda	Πενήντα
sixty	exínda	Ἑξήντα
seventy	evthomínda	Ἑβδομήντα
eighty	ogthónda	Ὀγδόντα
ninety	enenínda	Ἐνενήντα
one hundred	ekató	Ἑκατό
one thousand	chília	Χίλια

Months/Days

January	Ianooários	Ἰανουάριος
February	Fevrooários	Φεβρουάριος
March	Mártios	Μάρτιος
April	Aprílios	Ἀπρίλιος
May	Máios	Μάϊος
June	Ioónios	Ἰούνιος
July	Ioólios	Ἰούλιος
August	Avgoostos	Αὔγουστος
September	Septémvrios	Σεπτέμβριος
October	Októvrios	Ὀκτώβριος
November	Noémvrios	Νοέμβριος
December	Thekémvrios	Δεκέμβριος

Sunday	Kiriakí	Κυριακή
Monday	Theftéra	Δευτέρα
Tuesday	Tríti	Τρίτη
Wednesday	Tetárti	Τετάρτη
Thursday	Pémpti	Πέμπτη
Friday	Paraskeví	Παρασκευή
Saturday	Sávato	Σάββατο

Transport

the airport	to arothrómio	τὸ ἀεροδρόμιο
the aeroplane	to aropláno	τὸ ἀεροπλάνο
the bus station	ee stási ton leoforíon	ἡ στάση τῶν λεωφορεῖων
the bus	o leoforío	τὸ λεωφορεῖο
the railway station	o stathmós too tréno	ὁ σταθμὸς τοῦ τραῖνου
the train	to tréno	τὸ τραῖνο
the port	to limáni	τὸ λιμάνι
the port authority	to limenarchíon	τὸ λιμεναρχεῖον
the ship	to plíon *or* to karávi	τὸ πλοῖον/τὸ καράβι
the steamship	to vapóri	τὸ βαπόρι
the car	to aftokínito	τὸ αὐτοκίνητον
a ticket	éna isitírio	ἕνα εἰσιτήριο

Hors d'oeuvre	Orektiká	ΟΡΕΚΤΙΚΑ
yoghurt and cucumbers	tsatsíki	Τσατσίκι
olives	eliés	Ἐληὲς
stuffed vine leaves	dolmáthes	Ντολμάδες
mixed hors d'oeuvre	thiáfora orektiká	Διάφορα ὀρεκτικά

Soups	Soupes	ΣΟΥΠΕΣ
egg and lemon soup	ávgolemono	Αὐγολεμονο
vegetable soup	soúpa apó chórta	Σοῦπα ἀπό χόρτα
fish soup	psarósoupa	Ψαρόσουπα
giblets in egg and lemon soup	magirítsa	Μαγειρίτσα

Pasta and Rice	Zimárika	ΖΥΜΑΡΙΚΑ
pilaf	piláfi sáltsa	Πιλάφι σάλτσα
spaghetti	spagéto	Σπαγέττο
macaroni	makarónia	Μακαρόνια

Vegetables	Lathéra	ΛΑΔΕΡΑ
potatoes	patátes	Πατάτες
stuffed tomatoes	tomátes yemistés	Ντομάτες γεμιστές
stuffed aubergines/ eggplants	melitzánes yemistés	Μελιτζάυες γεμιστές
stuffed peppers	piperíes yemistés	Πιπερίες γεμιστές
beans	fasólia	Φασόλια
lentils	fakí	Φακή
greens	chórta	Χόρτα

Fish	Psária	ΨΑΡΙΑ
lobster	astakós	Ἀστακὸς
little squid	kalamarákia	Καλαμαράκια
octopus	oktapóthi	Οκταπόδι
red mullet	barboúnia	Μπαρμπούνια
prawns (shrimps)	garíthes	Γαρίδες
whitebait	maríthes	Μαρίδες
sea bream	sinagrítha	Συναγρίδα
fried cod (with garlic and vinegar sauce)	bakaliáros (skorthaliá)	Μπακαλιάρος (σκορδαλιά)
oysters	stríthia	Στρείδια
bass	lithrínia	Λιθρίνια

Eggs	Avga	ΑΥΓΑ
ham omelette	omeléta zambón	Ὀμελέτα Ζαμπὸν
cheese omelette	omeléta me tirí	Ὀμελέτα μὲ τυρί
fried (scrambled) eggs	avgá tigetá (brouyé)	Αὐγά τηγαιτά (μπρουγὲ)

Entrées	Entráthes	ΕΝΤΡΑΔΕΣ
chicken	kotópulo	Κοτόπουλο

beefsteak	biftéki	Μπιφτέκι
rabbit	kounéli	Κουνέλι
meat and macaroni	pastítsio	Παστίτσιο
meat and aubergine/ eggplant with white sauce	mousaká	Μουσακά
liver	skóti	Σκώτι
veal	moskári	Μοσχάρι
lamb	arnáki	Αρνάκι
pork chops	brizólas chirinés	Μπριζόλας χοιρινὲς
meat balls in tomato sauce	tsoutsoukákia	Σουτσουκάκια
sausage	lukániko	Λουκάνικο

Grills	**Skáras**	**ΣΧΑΡΑΣ**
meat on a skewer	souvlákia	Σουβλάκια
veal chops	kotolétes	Κοτολέτες
roast chicken	kóta psití	Κότα ψητή
meat balls	keftéthes	Κεφτέδες

Salads	**Salátes**	**ΣΑΛΑΤΕΣ**
tomatoes	tomátes	Ντομάτες
cucumbers	angouráki	'Αγγουράκι
Russian salad	rossikí	Ρωσσικὴ
village salad with cheese	choriatikiá	Χοριατικιά
courgettes/zucchini	kolokithákia	Κολοκυθάκια

Cheeses	**Tiriá**	**ΤΥΡΙΑ**
cheese pie	tirópitta	Τυρόπιττα
goat cheese	féta	Φέτα
hard buttery cheese	kaséri	Κασέρι
blue cheese	rokfór	Ροκφὸρ
like Gruyère	graviéra	Γραβιέρα

Sweets	**Glyká**	**ΓΛΥΚΑ**
ice cream	pagotó	Παγωτό
white Greek biscuits	kourabiéthes	Κουραμπιέδες
hot honey fritters	loukomáthes	Λουκομάδες
sesame seed sweet	halvá	Χαλβά
honey pastry	baklavá	Μπακλαβά
custard pastry	galaktoboúrekkon	Γαλακτομπούρεκκον
yoghurt	yiaoúrti	Γιαοῦρτι
rice pudding	rizógalo	Ρυζόγαλο
shredded wheat with nuts and honey	kataifi	Καταϊφι
custard tart	bougátsa	Μπουγάτσα
almond cookies	amigthalotá	'Αμιγδαλωτά

Fruit	Frúta	ΦΡΟΥΤΑ
pear	akláthi	Ἀχλάδι
orange	portokáli	Πορτοκάλι
apple	mílo	Μῆλο
peach	rothákino	Ροδάκινο
melon	pepóni	Πεπόνι
watermelon	karpoúzi	Καρπούζι
plum	thamáskino	Δαμάσκηνο
fig	síka	Σύκα
grapes	stafília	Σταφύλια
banana	banána	Μπανάνα
apricot	veríkoko	Βερύκοκο

Miscellaneous

water (boiled)	neró (vrastó)	Νερό (βραστό)
bread	psomí	Ψωμί
butter	voútiro	Βούτυρο
honey	méli	Μέλι
jam	marmelátha	Μαρμελάδα
salt	aláti	Ἀλάτι
pepper	pipéri	Πιπέρι
sugar	zákari	Ζάχαρη
oil	láthi	Λάδι
vinegar	xíthi	Ξύδι
mustard	mustárda	Μουστάρδα
lemon	lemóni	Λεμόνι
milk	gála	Γάλα
tea	chái	Τσάϊ
chocolate	sokoláta	Σοκολάτα
the bill/check	logariasmó	Λογαριασμὸ
to your health!	stíniyásas	Στὴν ἠγειά σας!

Clogg, Richard and Yannopoulos, George, *Greece Under Military Rule* (London 1972)

Dakin, Douglas, *The Unification of Greece 1770–1923* (London 1972)

Heurtley, W. A., Darby, H. C., Crawley, C. W. and Woodhouse, C. M., *A Short History of Greece from Early Times to 1964* (Cambridge and New York 1966)

Kousoulas, George D., *Revolution and Defeat: The Story of the Greek Communist Party* (Oxford 1965)

Legg, Keith R., *Politics in Modern Greece* (Stanford, Calif., 1969)

Mavrogordato, J., *Modern Greece 1800–1921* (London 1931)

O'Ballance, Edgar, *The Greek Civil War 1944–1949* (London and New York 1966)

Pallis, A. A., *Greece's Anatolian Adventure and After* (London 1937)

Papandreou, Andreas, *Democracy at Gunpoint* (New York 1970, London 1971)

Stephens, Robert, *Cyprus: A Place of Arms* (London and New York 1966)

Sweet-Escott, Bickham, *Greece: A Political and Economic Survey 1939–53* (London and New York 1954)

Ware, Timothy, *The Orthodox Church* (Baltimore, Ma. 1963, London 1964)

Woodhouse, C. M., *The Greek War of Independence* (London 1952, New York 1967)

Woodhouse, C. M., *Modern Greece: A Short History* (London 1977)

In London a likely place to find these books is at the Hellenic Book Service, 122 Charing Cross Road, London WC2, tel. (071) 836 7071. In Athens the best bookstore for English books on Greek subjects can be found on 4 Nikis St, Syntagma Square, and is called Eseftheroudakis.

Further Reading

Islands are indexed both individually and within each group of islands. Alternative spellings or names are shown in brackets.

Index